Proceedings of the
Ninth International Joint Conference
on
Artificial Intelligence

Volume 2

August 18-23, 1985
sponsored by
**International Joint Conferences on
Artificial Intelligence, Inc.**
cosponsored and hosted by
**American Association for Artificial
Intelligence**
in cooperation with
University of California at Los Angeles

Edited by
Aravind Joshi

Distributed by
Morgan Kaufmann Publishers, Inc.
95 First Street
Los Altos, California 94022

ISBN 0-934613-02-8
Printed in the United States of America

Table of Contents

Volume 1

Volume 2

Artificial Intelligence Conference Proceedings
Ordering Information

Below is a listing of all artificial intelligence conference proceedings. For information regarding these volumes and to place orders, please contact:

Morgan Kaufmann Publishers, Inc.
95 First Street, Los Altos, California   94022

United States of America
Phone: 415-941-4960

IJCAI-85 Proceedings
Proceedings of the Ninth International Joint Conference on Artificial Intelligence (IJCAI-85), Los Angeles, California, August 1985. Two volumes.
$40.00 for AAAI members and registrants at IJCAI conferences
$55.00 for nonmembers

AAAI-84 Proceedings
Proceedings of the Fourth National Conference on Artificial Intelligence, Austin, Texas, United States, August 1984. One volume.
$30.00 for AAAI members and registrants at IJCAI conferences
$45.00 for nonmembers

IJCAI-83 Proceedings
Proceedings of the Eighth International Joint Conference on Artificial Intelligence (IJCAI-83), Karlsruhe, West Germany, August 1983. Two volumes.
$35.00 for AAAI members and registrants at IJCAI conferences
$50.00 for nonmembers

AAAI-83 Proceedings
Proceedings of the Third National Conference on Artificial Intelligence (AAAI-83), Washington, D.C., United States, August 1983. One volume.
$30.00 for AAAI members and registrants at IJCAI conferences
$45.00 for nonmembers

AAAI-82 Proceedings
Proceedings of the Second National Conference on Artificial Intelligence, Pittsburgh, Pennsylvania, United States, August 1982. One volume. 456 pages.
$30.00 for AAAI members and registrants at IJCAI conferences
$45.00 for nonmembers

IJCAI-81 Proceedings
Proceedings of the Seventh International Joint Conference on Artificial Intelligence, Vancouver, British Columbia, Canada, August 1981. Two volumes. 1,116 pages.
$25.00 for AAAI members and registrants at IJCAI conferences
$40.00 for nonmembers

AAAI-80 Proceedings
Proceedings of the First National Conference on Artificial Intelligence, Stanford, California, United States, August 1980. One volume. 339 pages.
$25.00 for AAAI members and registrants at IJCAI conferences
$40.00 for nonmembers

IJCAI-79 Proceedings
Proceedings of the Sixth International Joint Conference on Artificial Intelligence, Tokyo, Japan, August 1979. Two volumes. 1,146 pages.
$25.00 for AAAI members and registrants at IJCAI conferences
$40.00 for nonmembers

IJCAI-77 Proceedings
Proceedings of the Fifth International Joint Conference on Artificial Intelligence, Cambridge, Massachusetts, United States, August 1977. Two volumes. 1,005 pages.
$25.00 for AAAI members and registrants at IJCAI conferences
$40.00 for nonmembers

IJCAI-75 Advance Papers
Advance papers from the Fourth International Joint Conference on Artificial Intelligence, Tbilisi, Georgia, USSR, September 1975. Two volumes. 944 pages.
$40.00 for AAAI members and registrants at IJCAI conferences
$65.00 for nonmembers

IJCAI-73 Advance Papers
Advance papers from the Third International Joint Conference on Artificial Intelligence, Stanford, California, United States, August 1973. One volume. 703 pages.
$40.00 for AAAI members and registrants at IJCAI conferences
$65.00 for nonmembers

IJCAI-71 Advance Papers
Advance papers from the Second International Joint Conference on Artificial Intelligence, London, England, United Kingdom, September 1971. One volume. 697 pages.
$50.00 for AAAI members and registrants at IJCAI conferences
$80.00 for nonmembers

IJCAI-69 Proceedings
Proceedings of the International Joint Conference on Artificial Intelligence, Washington, D.C., United States, May 1969. One volume. 715 pages.
$50.00 for AAAI members and registrants at IJCAI conferences
$80.00 for nonmembers

Awards, Speakers, and Panels

Computers and Thought Lecture
Hector Levesque

IJCAI Award for Research Excellence
John McCarthy

MIT Press, Best Paper Award
Joseph Halpern
Ronald Fagin

INVITED SPEAKERS

Alan Bundy, University of Edinburgh
Barbara Grosz, SRI International
Hirochika Inoue, University of Tokyo

Elaine Kant, Schlumberger-Doll Research
Hector Levesque, University of Toronto
John Perry, Stanford University

PANELS

AI and Legal Reasoning
Panel Chair: Edwina L. Rissland, University of Massachusetts at Amherst
Kevin D. Ashley, University of Massachusetts at Amherst
Michael G. Dyer, University of California at Los Angeles
Anne vdL. Gardner, Stanford University
Thorne McCarty, Rutgers University
Don Waterman, The RAND Corporation

Artificial Intelligence in the Personal Computer Environment
Panel Chair: Tom J. Schwartz, Window on Wall Street
Stan Curtis, Gold Hill Computers
Alan Kay, Apple Computer Inc.
Robert Laddaga, Artelligence, Inc.

Artificial Intelligence and Legal Responsibility
Panel Chair: Margaret Boden, University of Sussex
Robert Kowalski, Imperial College
Susan Nycum, Gaston Snow Sly Bartlett
Marshall Willik, The Atrium
Jay BloomBecker, National Center for Computer Crime
Yorick Wilkes, New Mexico State University
Henry Thomphson, University of Edinburgh
Ben Du Boulay, University of Sussex
John Fox, Imperial Cancer Research Fund

Reasoning with Uncertainty for Expert Systems
Panel Chair: Ronald Yager, Iona College
Michael Fehling, Teknowledge, Inc.
Edward Shortliffe, Stanford University
Peter Szolovits, Massachusetts Institute of Technology
Sholom Weiss, Rutgers University
Lotfi Zadeh, University of California at Berkeley

User Modeling
Panel Chair: Derek Sleeman, Stanford University
Doug Appelt, SRI International
Kurt Konolige, SRI International
Elaine Rich, University of Texas at Austin, MCC
N. S. Sridharan, BBN Labs
Bill Swartout, University of Southern California

US and Japan Cooperative AI Research and Development Opportunities
Panel Chair: Howard E. Jacobson, Jacobson Corporation
Woodrow Bledsoe, Microelectronics and Computer Corporation and the University of Texas at Austin
Kazuhiro Fuchi, Institute for New Generation Computer Technology
John C. Williams, U.S. Department of Commerce

Expert Systems: How Far Can They Go?
Panel Chair: Terry Winograd, Stanford University
Randy Davis, Massachusetts Institute of Technology
Stuart Dreyfus, University of California at Berkeley
Brian Smith, Xerox Parc

IJCAI-85 Proceedings Schedule

	Tuesday, August 20	Wednesday, August 21	Thursday, August 22	Friday, August 23
9:00 a.m.	Invited Talk: Alan Bundy *Discovery and Reasoning in Mathematics*	IJCAI Award for Research Excellence: John McCarthy	Invited Talk: Hirochika Inoue *Building a Bridge Between AI and Robotics*	Invited Talk: Elaine Kant *Understanding and Automating Algorithm Design*
10:00 a.m.	BREAK	BREAK	BREAK	BREAK
10:30 a.m.	Theorem Proving 1 Natural Language 1 Perception 1 Knowledge Representation 1 Automated Reasoning 1 Expert Systems 1 Learning and Knowledge Acquisition 1	Theorem Proving 2 Robotics 1 AI Architectures and Languages 2 Automated Programming 1 Natural Language 4 Planning and Search 2 Learning and Knowledge Acquisition 4	Theorem Proving 3 Robotics 3 Knowledge Representation 4 Cognitive Modelling 2 Expert Systems 5 Learning and Knowledge Acquisition 6 Philosophical Foundations 1 Invited Talk: John Perry *Self-Knowledge and Self-Representation*	Theorem Proving 4 Automatic Programming 2 Natural Language 7 Planning and Search 4 Perception 5 Expert Systems 6 Panel 5: User Modelling
12:00 p.m.	Lunch	Lunch	Lunch	Lunch
1:30	Natural Language 2 Learning and Knowledge Acquisition 2 Expert Systems 2 Perception 2 Planning and Search 1 Panel 1: AI and Legal Reasoning Panel 2: Artificial Intelligence in the Personal Computer Environment	Natural Language 5 Knowledge Representation 2 Automated Reasoning 3 Perception 3 Planning and Search 3 Panel 3: Artificial Intelligence and Legal Responsibility Panel 4: Reasoning with Uncertainty for Expert Systems		Panel 6: US and Japan Cooperative AI Research and Development Opportunities
3:00	BREAK	BREAK		BREAK
3:30 p.m.	AI Architectures and Languages 1 AI and Education 1 Natural Language 3 Invited Talk: Barbara Grosz *Discourse Structure and Intention* Expert Systems 3 Automated Reasoning 2 Learning and Knowledge Acquisition 3 Logic Programming 1	Cognitive Modelling 1 Expert Systems 4 Knowledge Representation 3 Automated Reasoning 4 Logic Programming 2 Learning and Knowledge Acquisition 5 Perception 4/Robotics 2 Natural Language 6		Expert Systems: How Far Can They Go?
8:00 p.m.	Computers and Thought Lecture: Hector Levesque			

Proceedings of the Ninth International Joint Conference on Artificial Intelligence IJCAI-85

VOLUME 1

AUTOMATIC PROGRAMMING

COGNITIVE MODELLING

EXPERT SYSTEMS

LOGIC PROGRAMMING

PROLOG-ELF INCORPORATING FUZZY LOGIC

Mitsuru ISHIZUKA   and   Naoki KANAI

Institute of Industrial Science, University of Tokyo
7-22-1, Roppongi, Minato-ku, Tokyo, 106, Japan

ABSTRACT: Prolog-ELF incorporating fuzzy logic and some useful functions into Prolog has been implemented as a basic language for building knowlegde systems with uncertainty or fuzziness. Prolog-ELF inherits all the preferable basic features of Prolog. In addition to assersions with a truth-value between 1.0 and 0.5 (0 for an exceptional case), fuzzy sets can be manipulated very easily to a certain extent. An application to a fuzzy logical database is illustrated.

1. INTRODUCTION

As a basic language for building knowledge systems, Prolog has many preferable features, such as pattern matching (unification), automatic backtracking and relatinal database. It has been chosen as the kernel language of Japanese fifth generation computer. Many Prolog-based knowledge systems have become to appear recently.

Prolog, which is based on first-order predicate logic (more precisely, Horn logic), deals with only a two-valued logic. Knowledge sometimes manifests uncertainty in real-world problems. Uncertain knowledge has played important role in many expert systems, such as Mycin[1], Prospector[2], Casnet[3], Speril[4,5], etc.. When dealing with uncertain knowledge in Prolog, some special programming techniques are required [6], which are annoying for us to build a large system. Therefore, there exists a need for a basic language capable of dealing with uncertain knowledge.

In fuzzy logic, the uncertainty of a fact or a rule is expressed with a truth-value between 1 and 0. There are of course several other methods, such as Mycin's certainty factor[1], subjective Bayesian method[2], and Dempster-Shafer theory[5]. However, unlike these methods, the fuzzy logic has a certain kind of logical feature. This logical feature can be extended to a fist-order predicate logic, which provids us a rich expressive power.

This paper presents a language called Prolog-ELF [7] incorporating fuzzy logic into Prolog. The Prolog-ELF is different from existing fuzzy languages such as described in [8,9], because the Prolog-ELF is a general-purpose language which inherits all the preferable basic features of Prolog. Moreover, several useful predicates are imbedded in the Prolog-ELF. Using these predicates, we can manipulate fuzzy sets very easily to a certain extent.

The Prolog-ELF is implemented on Pascal and completely operational on VAX-11. This paper describes some features and considerations on the Prolog-ELF and its application to a fuzzy logical database.

2. TOWARD FUZZY PROLOG

Although fuzzy sets are considered in general fuzzy logic [10], we will at first consider logical formulae expressed with symbols in ordinaly sense. The certainty of the logical formula is expressed with a truth-value T, where $1 \geqq T \geqq 0$, in the fuzzy logic. (A different kind of fuzzy logic in which linguistic truth-values are used is presented in [11].)

Let $T(P)$ be the truth-value of a logical formula P. The following treatments of the truth-value are foundamental. ($\neg$ denotes NOT.)

If P=A and A is an atomic formula: $T(P)=T(A)$
If $P=\neg Q$: $T(P)=1-T(Q)$
If P=Q AND R : $T(P)=\min(T(Q),T(R))$
If P=Q OR R : $T(P)=\max(T(Q),T(R))$.

For example, if
$T(P)=0.6$, $T(Q)=0.9$, $T(R)=0.8$ and
$S=(P$ OR $Q)$ AND $\neg R$
then,
$T(S)=\min(\max(T(P),T(Q)),1-T(R))$
$=\min(\max(0.6,0.9),1-0.8)$
$=0.2$.

Most of logical laws, such as commutative, associative, distributive and DeMorgan's laws, are hold in fuzzy logic, except excluded-middle law; that is, $T(P$ AND $\neg P)$ and $T(P$ OR $\neg P)$ are not always 0 and 1, respectively.

Lee[12] and Mukaidono[13] considered the resolution principle as a mechanical inference of fuzzy logic. If we interpret P->Q as ($\neg P$ OR Q) in fuzzy logic, the well-known inference rules, i.e., Modus ponens, Modus tollens and syllogism, become the special cases of the resolution principle. By introducing arguments attached to the logical symbol (predicate) and unification, the fuzzy logic can be extended to fuzzy first-order predicate logic.

Lee[12] has proved that, if all the truth-values of parent clauses are greater than 0.5, then a resolvent clause derived by the resolution principle is always meaningful and has a truth-value between the maximum and minimum of those of the parent clauses. Mukaidono[13] showed an interpretation that, even if a truth-value of the parent clause is less than 0.5, a resolvent clause is meaningful in the sense of reducing ambiguity.

Expressions in Prolog are restricted to Horn clauses which have at most one positive literal, so that the efficient linear input resolution can work as a complete resolution. If we define a Horn clause witrh a truth-value less than 0.5 in fuzzy Horn logic, it is equivalent to the negation of the clause which goes beyond the scope of Horn clause. Therefore, in order to realize a fuzzy-Prolog, we basically restrict our logical expression to the Horn clause with a truth-value greater than 0.5. The result of the resolution in this case is guaranteed to be meaningful based on the Lee's paper[12].

It is a problem if the truth-value of a clause including variables changes when the variables are instantiated by the unification. We take however a position that the truth-value of the clause will not change due to the unification.

One major difference in the inference process of fuzzy-Prolog from that of ordinary Prolog is that exhaustive search is often required at an OR-branch, since the maximum truth-value of a literal is looked for at this branch.

3. PROLOG-ELF

Prolog-ELF has been implemented based on the above-mentioned principle and by adding some useful functions for a basic language of knowledge systems.

The clauses in Prolog-ELF are expressed in the following forms.

Definition clause: +P-Q···-R. or +P.
Goal clause   : -Q···-R.

The truth-value of the clause can be assigned as;

0.7:+P-Q. or -assert(0.7:+P-Q.).

When the definition of the truth-value is omitted, then the default truth-value is 1. If all the clauses have the truth-value 1, the behavier of the Prolog-ELF is essentially the same as that of ordinary Prolog.

The reason why we have adopted above notation for a clause, i.e., +P-Q-R., instead of a popular notation such as P:-Q,R., is to avoid a question regarding the interpretation of implication. In fuzzy logic, ¬P∨Q is not only the interpretation of P->Q; there are several other interpretations [10,14]. Using our notation, we can make it clear that our Prolog-ELF works starting from axioms defined in clause forms, some of which can be interpreted, if appropriate, into implication forms.

A variable in Prolog-ELF is denoted as a character string headed by *. (Single * can be also a variale.) The result of the execution of a goal clause, if its truth-value is larger than a predetermined threshold (described later), is displayed in the form of, for example;

0.75:-P(apple).

Some of the system predicates characterizing Prolog-ELF are as follows.

(1)**THRESH** : This predicate sets a value given as its argument to a threshold. The clause with a truth-value less than this threshold is ignored or regarded as false, which initiates the backtracking during the execution process. The default of this threshold is 0.5. A threshold below 0.5 is permitted only for exceptional cases, which suffer a risk of going out of the scope of Horn logic. (See a comment regarding a predicate NOT.)

(2)**Mode setting predicates** : There are three operational modes in Prolog-ELF. The following predicates perform as a switch to change the mode.

(2-1)**NO-QUERY** : The system searches and displays a first-encountered answer regardless of its truth-value. This is the default mode and the behavior is equivalent to that of ordinary Prolog.

(2-2)**QUERY** : All the answers are searched and displayed.

(2-3)**BEST(n)** : The system displays top n answers according to their truth-values. In order to improve search efficiency, a dynamic thresholding strategy is adopted in this mode. The threshold is set dynamically to the value of the n-th truth-value from the top of already obtained answers.

(3)**USEVALUE** : This pridicate assigns a truth-value given as its argument to the associated clause. Using this predicate, we can represent fuzzy sets very easily as exemplified in Fig.1.

(4)**VALUE** : This is a deterministic predicate which returns a truth-value of a clause given as its first argument to its second argument. For example, suppose that

0.8:+P(a).
0.6:+P(b).

have been defined. Then, when

-value(-P(*x)., *val).

is executed, *x and *val are at first unified to a and 0.8, respectively. Once the backtrack occurs, *x and *val are then unified to b and 0.6, respectively. Fig.2 shows an interaction exemplifying a usage of the predicate VALUE.

(5)**CHVALUE** : This predicate updates the truth-value of an associated clause to a new value.

(6)**MAXCL, DMAXCL** : An exhaustive search for the goal clause with the maximum truth-value is essential at OR-branch in fuzzy logic. In general, this is achieved in the BEST(1) mode in Prolog-ELF. The use of predicates MAXCL and DMAXCL is another way to specify this search. They are also used in sub-goal node for the following reason. For example, if

0.9:+R(*x)-P(*x)-Q(*x).
0.9:+P(a).
0.7:+P(b).
0.6:+Q(a).
0.8:+Q(b).

are defined, then

T(R(a))=min(0.9, min(0.9,0.6))=0.6
T(R(b))=min(0.9, min(0.7,0.8))=0.7.

This means that, if we take an instance of R(*x) with the maximum truth-value, i.e., R(b) in this case, this instantiation does not necessarily correspond to that of P(*x) with the maximum truth-value. There exists a case where we want to fix a sub-goal literal to the unification yielding its maximum truth-value. For example, if we add the following clause to the above definition,

0.9:+S(*x)-maxcl(P(*x).)-Q(*x).

then the system operates as follows.

>-maxcl(S(*x).).
0.6:maxcl(S(a).).

MAXCL is a non-deterministic predicate, whereas DMAXCL is a deterministic predicate. That is, if more than one answers with the same maximum truth-value are obtained, an alternative answer is used upon the backtracking in the case of MAXCL, whereas the search fails upon the backtracking in the case of DMAXCEL.

+old(*age)-gt(*age,70)-/-usevalue(1).
+old(*age)-gt(*age,50)-/-minus(*age,50,*x)
  -times(*x,0.015,*y)-plus(*y,0.7,*z)-usevalue(*z).
+old(*age)-gt(*age,30)-/-minus(*age,30,*x)
  -times(*x,0.01,*y)-plus(*y,0.5,*z)-usevalue(*z).

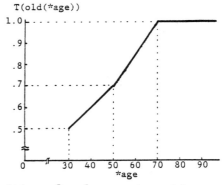

Fig.1 Definition of a fuzzy set — old — using USEVALUE (/ denotes the cut operator) and its graphical representation.

```
>-load(demo_).
>+very(*cl)-value(*cl,*x)-sqr(*x,*y)-usevalue(*y).
success
>-old(60).
 0.8500:-old(60).
>-very(-old(60).).
 0.7225:-very(-old(60).).
```

Fig.2 An example of the usage of VALUE.
(> is a system prompt.)
The definition of Fig.1 is assumed.

(7)**NOT** : As in ordinary Prolog, NOT fails in the normal threshold setting of Prolog-ELF if there exists at least one answer. However, if the threshold setting is less than 0.5, the result of unification during the execution of NOT may remain in Prolog-ELF. For example, suppose that the threshold is 0.2 and the answer of dmaxcl(P(*x).) is 0.7:dmaxcl(P(a).), then not(P(*x).) will succeed with the truth-value of 0.3(=1-0.7) and with the unification that *x is a.

4. APPLICATION TO A FUZZY LOGICAL DATABASE

As an application of Prolog-ELF, a fuzzy logical database including fuzzy rules and fuzzy set concepts is illustrated in Fig.3, where a person who may possibly have a second house is retrieved from stored facts and heuristic rules. Several other applications including a production system have been written by the authors.

5. CONCLUDING REMARKS

Prolog-ELF incorporating fuzzy logic and related some useful functions has been implemented as a basic language of knowledge systems with uncertainty or fuzziness.

One problem of the Prolog-ELF is its slow speed, since the exhaustive search is often required at the OR node. One way to avoide this problem is to set the threshold to an appropriatly high value. Some mechanisms to improve search efficiency are planned to implement in a future version; but it seems that ultimate solution may be a parallel processors like Japanese fifth-generation computer. A knowledge management mechanism using meta-predicates is scheduled to be added to Prolog-ELF.

ACKNOWLEDGMENT: The Prolog-ELF has been implemented with reference to the program of Dr. H.Nakashima at Electrotechnical Lab., who is the author of Prolog/KR. The authors are grateful to him.

This work was supported by Grant-in-aid for Special Project Research, Ministry of Education, Japan.

REFERENCES

[1] E.H.Shortliffe, "Computer-Based Medical Consultation: Mycin," American Elsevier, New York, 1976
[2] R.O.Duda, P.Hart, N.J.Nilson, "Subjective Bayesian Methods for Rule-Based Inference Systems," NCC, 1976
[3] S.M.Weiss, C.A.Kulikowski et al., "A Model-Based Method for Computer-Aided Medical Decision-Making," Artificial Intell., 11, pp.145-172, 1978
[4] M.Ishizuka, K.S.Fu, J.T.P.Yao, "Rule-Based Damage Assessment System for Existing Structures," Solid Mechanics Archives, 8, pp.99-118, 1983
[5] M.Ishizuka, "Inference Methods Based on Extended Dempster & Shafer's Theory for Problems with Uncertainty/Fuzziness," New Generation Computing, 1, pp.159-168, 1983
[6] E.Y.Shapiro, "Logic Programs with Uncertainties: A Tool for Implementing Rule-Based Systems," 8th IJCAI, 1983
[7] N.Kanai, M.Ishizuka, "Prolog-ELF incorporationg Fuzzy Logic," Report of Research Group on KE and AI, Info. Soc. of Japan, 34-4, 1984
[8] L.A.Zadeh, "PRUF--A Meaning Representation Language for Natural Language," Int'l J. Man-Machine Studies, 10, pp.395-460, 1978
[9] M.Umano, M.Mizumoto, K.Tanaka, "FSTDS System: A Fuzzy-Set Manipulation System," Info. Sci., 14, pp.115-159, 1978
[10] D.Dubois, H.Prade, "Fuzzy Set and Systems: Theory and Applications," Academic Press, 1980
[11] L.A.Zadeh, "Fuzzy Logic and Approximate Reasoning," Synthese, 30, pp.407-428, 1978
[12] R.C.T.Lee, "Fuzzy Logic and the Resolution Principle," J.ACM, 19, pp.109-119, 1972
[13] M.Mukaidono, "Fuzzy Inference of Resolution Style," in Fuzzy Set and Possibility Theory (R.R.Yager Ed.), Pergamon Press, 1982
[14] T.Whalen, B.Schott, "Issues in Fuzzy Production Systems," Int'l J. Man-Machine Studies, 19, pp.57-71, 1983

```
; Have a second house ;
+have_a_second_house(Kato).
0.9:+have_a_second_house(*who)-rich(*who).
0.7:+have_a_second_house(*who)-president(*who).

; Rich ;
+rich(*who)-income(*who,*yen)-rich2(*yen).
+rich2(*yen)-gt(*yen,30000000)-/.
+rich2(*yen)-gt(*yen,15000000)-/
     -minus(*yen,1.5e7,*x)-rdiv(*x,1e8,*y)
     -times(3,*y,*z)-plus(0.5,*z,*w)
     -usevalue(*w).

; Income ;
+income(Yamada,20000000).
+income(Sato,25000000).
+income(Nomura,8000000).
+income(Kobayashi,40000000).

; President ;
+president(Suzuki).
+president(Kobayashi).
```

(a) database

```
%elf
Prolog-ELF version 2.1a          6/12/84
    written by N. Kanai, Ishizuka lab.
    type "-help." for help, "-exit." for exit.
>-load(house_).
>-have_a_second_house(*who).
 1.0000:-have_a_second_house(Kato).
>-best(5).
 1.0000:-best(5).
>-have_a_second_house(*who).
 1.0000:-have_a_second_house(Kato).
 0.9000:-have_a_second_house(Kobayashi).
 0.8000:-have_a_second_house(Sato).
 0.7000:-have_a_second_house(Suzuki).
 0.6500:-have_a_second_house(Yamada).
```

(b) execution

Fig.3 An application to a logical database.

TYPE INFERENCE IN PROLOG AND ITS APPLICATION

Tadashi KANAMORI, Kenji HORIUCHI

Central Research Laboratory
Mitsubishi Electric Corporation
Tsukaguchi-Honmachi 8-1-1,Amagasaki,Hyogo,Japan 661

Abstract

In this paper we present a type inference method for Prolog programs. The new idea is to describe a superset of the success set by associating a type substitution (an assignment of sets of ground terms to variables) with each head of definite clause. This approach not only conforms to the style of definition inherent to Prolog but also gives some accuracy to the types infered. We show the basic computation method of the superset by sequential approximation as well as an incremental method to utilize already obtained results. We also show its application to verification of Prolog programs.

1. Introduction

It gives usefull information not only to programmers but also to meta-processing systems to infer characteristics of execution-time behavior from program texts. Especially in Prolog, it is usefull to know of what type a variable in a query is when the query succeeds. We call such a task *type inference* [8]. In this paper we present a type inference method for Prolog programs. After summarizing preliminary materials in section 2, we describe type inference algorithms for Prolog programs in section 3. An application to verification is shown in section 4. See [7] for more details.

2. Preliminaries

In the followings, we assume familiarity with the basic terminologies of first order logic such as term,atom,substitution and most general unifier(mgu). We also assume knowledge about semantics of Prolog such as Herbrand universe H,Herbrand interpretation I,minimum Herbrand Model M_0 and transformation T of Herbrand interpretation associated with Prolog programs (see [1],[4]). We follow the syntax of DEC-10 Prolog [10]. An atom $p(X_1, X_2, \ldots, X_n)$ is said to be *in general form* when $X_1, X_2, \ldots, X_n$ are distinct variables. A substitution σ is called *substitution away from* an atom A when σ instanciates each variable X in A to a term t such that every variable in t is a fresh variable not in A.

2.1. Definition of Data Types

We introduce **type** into Prolog to separate definite clauses for data structures from others for procedures,e.g.,

```
type.
    list([ ]).
    list([X|L]) :- list(L).
end.
```

type defines a unary relation by definite clauses. The head of the definite clause takes a term defining a data structure as the argument, either a constant b called *bottom element* or a term of the form $c(t_1, t_2, \ldots, t_n)$ where c is called *constructor*. The body shows a type condition about the proper subterms of the argument.

Here note the set of ground terms prescribed by type predicates. The set of all ground terms t such that ?-$p(t)$ succeeds is called *type of p* and denoted by $\underline{p}$.

Example 2.1. Let the definition of a data type *number* be
```
type.
    number(0).
    number(s(X)) :- number(X).
end.
```
Then $\underline{number}$ is a set $\{0, s(0), s(s(0)), \ldots\}$.

Suppose there are defined k data types $p_1, p_2, \ldots, p_k$ and $\underline{p_1}, \underline{p_2}, \ldots, \underline{p_k}$ are disjoint. We denote the set of all ground terms contained in no $\underline{p_i}$ by $\underline{others}$ and consider it like one of types. Then the Herbrand universe H is divided into $k + 1$ disjoint sets as follows.

$$H = \underline{p_1} \uplus \underline{p_2} \uplus \ldots \uplus \underline{p_k} \uplus \underline{others}.$$

Procedures are defined following the syntax of DEC-10 Prolog [10],e.g.,

```
append([ ],K,K).
append([X|L],M,[X|N]) :- append(L,M,N).
```

Throughout this paper, we use P as a finite set of definite clauses defining data types and procedures. We assume variables in each definite clause are renamed at each use so that there occurs no variable names conflict.

2.2. A Fundamental Theorem for Type Inference in Prolog

Let I and J be Herbrand interpretations. I is said to *cover success set under a restriction J* when it contains the intersection of the minimum Herbrand model M_0 and J.

An Herbrand interpretation J is said to be *closed with respect to P* when for any ground instance of definite clause in P such that the head is in J, any ground atom in the body is also in J. This means $M_0 \bigcap J$ is computable within it.

Theorem If J is closed with respect to P, $T(I) \subseteq T'(I)$ and $T'(I) \bigcap J \subseteq I$, then I covers success set under J.

Proof. $T(I) \bigcap J \subseteq I$ from $T(I) \subseteq T'(I)$. Let T_J be a monotone transformation of Herbrand interpretations such that $T_J(I)$ is $T(I) \bigcap J$ for any I. T_J has a least fixpoint $\bigcap_{T_J(I) \subseteq I} I$ by the Knaster-Tarski fixpoint theorem ([1] p.843,

Theorem 2.1). Because J is closed, $M_0 \bigcap J$ is a fixpoint of T_J. Moreover it is the least fixpoint, since $M_0 \bigcap J = \bigcup_{i=0}^{\infty} T_J^i(\emptyset)$ ([1] p.843,Theorem 2.2). Therefor $M_0 \bigcap J \subseteq I$ for any I satisfying $T_J(I) \subseteq I$.

Our goal of type inference is to describe an Herbrand interpretation I covering success set under a restriction J in terms of the types. This is performed by defining an appropriate transformation T^I satisfying the theorem above.

3. Type Inference in Prolog

In this section, we show how to describe a class of Herbrand interpretations in terms of the types first. Then we define an appropriate transformation satisfying the condition in the theorem in 2.2. The basic computation method and the incremental version are presented in 3.4 and 3.5.

3.1. Interpretation by Type

(1) Type Set

A set of ground terms represented by a union of types is called *type set*. Type sets are denoted by $\underline{t}, \underline{t_1}, \underline{t_2}, \ldots$ etc.

Example 3.1.1. $\underline{number} \bigcup \underline{list}$ is a type set. $\emptyset$ is a type set,too. $\underline{p_1} \bigcup \underline{p_2} \bigcup \ldots \bigcup \underline{p_k} \bigcup \underline{others}$ is a type set.We denote it by $\underline{any}$. ($\underline{any}$ is not a type but an abbreviation of a type set.)

(2) Type Substitution

An assignment of type sets to variables
$$\Sigma = < X_1 \Leftarrow \underline{t_1}, X_2 \Leftarrow \underline{t_2}, \ldots, X_n \Leftarrow \underline{t_n} >$$
is called *type substitution*. A type assigned to a variable X by Σ is denoted by $\Sigma(X)$. We assume $\Sigma(X) = \underline{any}$ for any variable X not appearng explicitly in the domain of Σ. A type substitution $\Sigma = < X_1 \Leftarrow \underline{t_1}, X_2 \Leftarrow \underline{t_2}, \ldots, X_n \Leftarrow \underline{t_n} >$ is considered the same as a set of substitutions
$$\{< X_1 \Leftarrow t_1, \ldots, X_n \Leftarrow t_n > | t_1 \in \underline{t_1}, \ldots, t_n \in \underline{t_n}\}.$$

Example 3.1.2. $< L \Leftarrow \underline{list} >$ is a type substitution. This is considered the same as a set of substitution $\{< L \Leftarrow t > | t$ is any ground term in $\underline{list}$ $\}$. The empty substitution $<>$ is a type substitution assigning $\underline{any}$ to any variable.

The union of two type substituions Σ_1 and Σ_2 is a type substitution Σ such that $\Sigma(X) = \Sigma_1(X) \bigcup \Sigma_2(X)$ for any X and denoted by $\Sigma_1 \bigcup \Sigma_2$. The intersection of two type substituions Σ_1 and Σ_2 is a type substitution Σ such that $\Sigma(X) = \Sigma_1(X) \bigcap \Sigma_2(X)$ for any X and denoted by $\Sigma_1 \bigcap \Sigma_2$.

(3) Interpretation by Type

Let B_0 be a head of a definite clause "$B_0 :\text{-} B_1, B_2, \ldots, B_m$" in P and Σ be a type substitution. Then $\Sigma(B_0)$ is considered a set of ground atoms $\{\sigma(B_0) | \sigma \in \Sigma\}$. An Herbrand interpretation I represented by a union of all such forms,i.e.
$$\bigcup_{``B_0 :\text{-} B_1, B_2, \ldots, B_m" \in P} \Sigma(B_0)$$
is called *interpretation by type*.

Example 3.1.3. Let I be an Herbrand interpretation
$$<> (append([\,], K, K)) \bigcup$$
$$< L \Leftarrow \emptyset, M \Leftarrow \emptyset, N \Leftarrow \emptyset > (append([X|L], M, [X|N])).$$
Then I is an interpretation by type.This is an Herbrand interpretation $\{$ append($[\,],t,t$) $| t$ is any ground term $\}$.

3.2. Restriction by Type

An Herbrand interpretation J of the form $\bigcup_i \Sigma_i(A_i)$ is called *restriction by type*, where each A_i is not necessarily a head of definite clauses in P.

Example 3.2. $J = <> (append(N, [A], M)) \bigcup <> (reverse (L, M))$ is a restriction by type.

3.3. A Transformation for Type Inference

(1) Computation of Type Set of Superterm and Subterm

When each variable X in a term t is instanciated to a ground term in $\Sigma(X)$, we compute a type set containing all ground instances of t as follows and denote it by t/Σ.

$$t/\Sigma = \begin{cases} \emptyset, & \Sigma(X) = \emptyset \text{ for some } X \text{ in } t; \\ \Sigma(X), & \text{when } t \text{ is a variable } X; \\ \underline{p}, & \text{when } t \text{ is a bottom element } b \text{ of } p \text{ or} \\ & \text{when } t \text{ is of the form } c(t_1, t_2, \ldots, t_n), \\ & c \text{ is a constructor of } p \text{ and} \\ & t_1/\Sigma, t_2/\Sigma, \ldots, t_n/\Sigma \text{ satisfy} \\ & \text{the type conditions;} \\ \underline{any}, & \text{otherwise.} \end{cases}$$

Example 3.3.1. Let t be $[X|L]$ and Σ be $< L \Leftarrow \underline{list} >$. Then t/Σ is $\underline{list}$. Let t be $[X|L]$ and Σ be $<>$. Then t/Σ is $\underline{any}$.

When a term t containing an occurrence of a variable X is instanciated to a ground term in $\underline{t}$, we compute a type set containing all ground instances of the occurrence of X as follows and denote it by $X / < t \Leftarrow \underline{t} >$.

$$X / < t \Leftarrow \underline{t} > = \begin{cases} \underline{t}, & \text{when } t \text{ is a variable } X; \\ X / < t_i \Leftarrow \underline{t_i} >, & \text{when } t \text{ is of the form} \\ & c(t_1, t_2, \ldots, t_n), t \text{ is } \underline{p}, \\ & c \text{ is a constructor of } p, \\ & X \text{ is in } t_i \text{ and} \\ & \underline{t_i} \text{ is a type set assigned} \\ & \text{to the } i\text{-th argument } t_i; \\ \emptyset, & \text{otherwise.} \end{cases}$$

Example 3.3.2. Let t be $[X|L]$ and $\underline{t}$ be $\underline{list}$. Then
$$X / < [X|L] \Leftarrow \underline{list} > = \underline{any},$$
$$L / < [X|L] \Leftarrow \underline{list} > = \underline{list}.$$
Let t be $[X|L]$ and $\underline{t}$ be $\underline{number}$. Then
$$X / < [X|L] \Leftarrow \underline{number} > = \emptyset,$$
$$L / < [X|L] \Leftarrow \underline{number} > = \emptyset.$$

(2) Computation of Covering Type Substitution

Let $B_1, B_2, \ldots, B_m$ be a sequence of atoms and I be an interpretation by type. A type substitution is called *covering type substitution* with respect to $B_1, B_2, \ldots, B_m$ and I when it contains every substitution σ such that all ground instances $\sigma(B_1), \sigma(B_2), \ldots, \sigma(B_m)$ are in I. A transformation T^I is defined using the covering type substitutions.

Let I be an interpretation by type $\bigcup_i \Sigma_i(A_i)$ and $B_1, B_2, \ldots, B_m$ be a sequence of atoms. When $B_1, B_2, \ldots, B_m$ are unifiable with $A_{i_1}, A_{i_2}, \ldots, A_{i_m}$ by an mgu τ, we define a type substitution Σ on variables in $B_1, B_2, \ldots, B_m$ as follows. Note that we can assume without loss of generality that t contains no variable in $B_1, B_2, \ldots, B_m$ when a variable X in $B_1, B_2, \ldots, B_m$ is instanciated to t by τ, because the unifiability shows there is no cycle.

When $m = 0$ then $\Sigma = <>$.

When $m > 0$ then

(a) Let t be a term containing variables in A_{i_j} and X be a variable in B_j. If τ substitutes t for X, then we assign t/Σ_{i_j} to X.

(b) Let t be a term containing an occurrence of X in B_j and Y be a variable in A_{i_j}. If τ substitutes t for Y, then we assign $X/ <t \Leftarrow \Sigma_{i_j}(Y)>$ to the occurrence of X.

Then Σ assigns the intersection $\bigcap_i \underline{t_i}$ to X when $\underline{t_1}, \underline{t_2}, \ldots$ are computed as type sets at different occurrences of X in $B_1, B_2, \ldots, B_m$. (When Σ assigns $\emptyset$ to some variable in $B_1, B_2, \ldots, B_m$, we assume Σ assigns $\emptyset$ to any variables.)

By $\lceil \frac{B_1 B_2 \cdots B_m}{I} \rceil$, we denote the union of Σ for every possible combination of $A_{i_1}, A_{i_2}, \ldots, A_{i_m}$ and its mgu τ.

Example 3.3.3. Let I be a type interpretation
$$<> (append([\,], K, K)) \bigcup$$
$$< L \Leftarrow \emptyset, M \Leftarrow \emptyset, N \Leftarrow \emptyset > (append([X|L], M, [X|N]))$$
and B_1 be a seqence of atoms (though it is only one atom)
$$append(A, B, C).$$
Then There are two possibity of unification. One is $\tau_1 = <A \Leftarrow [\,], B \Leftarrow K, C \Leftarrow K >$ and the corresponding type substitution is $< A \Leftarrow \underline{list} >$. Another is $\tau_2 = < A \Leftarrow [X|L], B \Leftarrow M, C \Leftarrow [X|N] >$ and $< A \Leftarrow \emptyset, B \Leftarrow \emptyset, C \Leftarrow \emptyset >$ is the corresponding type substitution. Hence by taking their union, we have
$$\lceil \tfrac{append(A,B,C)}{I} \rceil = < A \Leftarrow \underline{list} >$$

(3) A Transformation T'

We define T' as folows.

$$T'(I) = \bigcup_{``B_0 :- B_1, B_2, \ldots, B_m" \in P} \lceil \frac{B_1 B_2 \cdots B_m}{I} \rceil (B_0)$$

It is obvious that $T(I) \subseteq T'(I)$ and T' is monotone for interpretations by type.

3.4. Computation of Type Inference

An interpretation by type covering success set under a restriction J is called *type inference under J*. The theorem in 2.2 holds for interpretations by type as well. We already have an appropriate transformation T' so that we can compute a type inference under a closed restriction J. The outlook of the basic algorithm for type inference is similar to the bottom-up computation of minimum Herbrand models.

$i := -1; I_0 := \emptyset;$
repeat $i := i + 1; I_{i+1} := T'(I_i) \bigcap J$ **until** $I_{i+1} \subseteq I_i$
return $I_i;$

Figure 1. Computation of Type Inference

In order to compute type inference under a closed restriction J, we need $T'(I) \bigcap J$, which is obtained by using $\lceil \frac{B_1 B_2 \cdots B_m}{I} \rceil (B_0) \bigcap \lceil \frac{B_0}{J} \rceil (B_0)$. $\lceil \frac{B_0}{J} \rceil (B_0)$ is common to all repetitions of the type inference process and can be computed once and for all before the repetitions.

3.5. Incremental Type Inference

An atom A is said to be *closed with respect to P* when for any ground instance of the definite clause in P such that the head is a ground instance of A, any recursive call in the body is also a ground instance of A. (Hence any

non-recursive definite clause and any definite clause with a head nonunifiable with A are negligible.) This means the set of ground atoms in M_0 of the form of instance of A is computable by some instances of definite clauses. Note that $p(X_1, X_2, \ldots, X_n)$ in general form is always closed.

Example 3.5.1. An atom $append(N, [X], M)$ is closesd. This means $\{append(t_1, [t_2], t_3)|t_1, t_2$ and t_3 are ground terms$\} \bigcap M_0$ is computable by
    append([ ],[Y],[Y]).
    append([X|L],[Y],[X|N]) :- append(L,[Y],N).

The closedness of an atom A can be checked as follows.

(a) Check whether the head B_0 is unifiable with A by a substitution for A away from A (see section 2). If it is, decompose the mgu to $\sigma \circ \tau_0$ where σ is the restriction to variables in B_0 and τ_0 is the restriction to variables in A. If it is not, neglect the definite clause.

(b) Check whether each instance of the recursive call in the body $\sigma(B_i)$ is an instance of A and if it is, compute the instanciation τ_i. If it is not, A is not closed.

The set of all instances of definite clauses by σ is called *instanciated program for A*.

Example 3.5.2. Let the atom A be $append(A, [U], C)$. Then the first head $append([], L, L)$ is unifiable with $append(A, [U], C)$ by $< L \Leftarrow [Y] > \circ < A \Leftarrow [], U \Leftarrow Y, C \Leftarrow [Y] >$. The second head $append([X|L], M, [X|N])$ is unifiable with $append(A, [U], C)$ by $< M \Leftarrow [Y] > \circ < A \Leftarrow [X|L], U \Leftarrow Y, C \Leftarrow [X|N]$ and the instance $append(L, [Y], N)$ in the body is also an instance of $append(A, [U], C)$ by $< A \Leftarrow L, U \Leftarrow Y, C \Leftarrow N >$.
    append([ ],[Y],[Y]).
    append([X|L],[Y],[X|N]) :- append(L,[Y],N).
is the instancated program for $append(A, [U], C)$.

An atom satisfying the following condition is called *closure of A with respect to P* and denoted by $\overline{A}$.

(a) $\overline{A}$ is closed with respect to P,
(b) A is an instance of $\overline{A}$ and
(c) $\overline{A}$ is an instance of any $\overline{A}'$ satisfying (a) and (b).

Example 3.5.3. $reverse(A, B')$ is a closure of $reverse(A, [V|B])$.

The closure is unique up to renaming and A is closed iff $A = \overline{A}$ modulo renaming. (See [7] for the proof of uniqueness and the algorithm to compute the closure.)

Now suppose we would like to compute type inference about p under a restriction by type $<> \overline{p(t_1, t_2, \ldots, t_n)}$ and denote it by $\mathcal{T}(\overline{p(t_1, t_2, \ldots, t_n)})$. Let $A_1, A_2, \ldots, A_l$ be non-recursive calls in the bodies of instanciated program for $\overline{p(t_1, t_2, \ldots, t_n)}$. (If some $B_i = q(s_1, s_2, \ldots, s_m)$ and $B_j = q(s'_1, s'_2, \ldots, s'_m)$, we distinguish the predicate symbols by q_1 and q_2 and assume both of them have the same definite clause program as q.) Then we compute $\mathcal{T}(\overline{p(t_1, t_2, \ldots, t_n)})$ by initializing I_0 to $\mathcal{T}(\overline{A_1}) \uplus \mathcal{T}(\overline{A_2}) \uplus \cdots \uplus \mathcal{T}(\overline{A_l})$, where each $\mathcal{T}(\overline{A_i})$ is computed recursively.

$i := -1; I_0 := \mathcal{T}(\overline{A_1}) \uplus \mathcal{T}(\overline{A_2}) \uplus \cdots \uplus \mathcal{T}(\overline{A_l});$
repeat $i := i + 1; I_{i+1} := T'(I_i)$ **until** $I_{i+1} \subseteq I_i$
return $I_i - I_0;$

Figure 2. Incremental Type Inference

If there is no mutual recursion,this process stops. The base case is the type inference for predicates which call no other predicate,e.g. *append*.

Example 3.5.4. Suppose we compute $T(reverse(L, M))$. The computation proceeds by initializing I_0 to $T(append(N, [X], M))$ as follows.

$$I_0 = <> (append([\,], [Y], [Y]) \cup$$
$$< L \Leftarrow \underline{list}, N \Leftarrow \underline{list} > (append([X|L], [Y], [X|N]))$$
$$I_1 = I_0 \cup <> (reverse([\,], [\,]) \cup$$
$$< X \Leftarrow \emptyset, L \Leftarrow \emptyset, M \Leftarrow \emptyset > (reverse([X|L], M)),$$
$$I_2 = I_0 \cup <> (reverse([\,], [\,]) \cup$$
$$< L \Leftarrow \underline{list}, M \Leftarrow \underline{list} > (reverse([X|L], M))$$

and $I_3 = I_2$. Hence the type inference of *reverse* is
$$<> (reverse([\,], [\,]) \cup$$
$$< L \Leftarrow \underline{list}, M \Leftarrow \underline{list} > (reverse([X|L], M))$$

Recursive computation of $T(\overline{A_i})$ is sometimes unnecessary. For example,when A_i is an atom $q(X_1, X_2, \ldots, X_m)$ in general form and $T(q(X_1, X_2, \ldots, X_m))$ is already computed before, then recomputing it all the way slows down the whole computation. As another example, when some $A_i = q(s_1, s_2, \ldots, s_m)$ and $A_j = q(s'_1, s'_2, \ldots, s'_m)$, we distinguish their predicate symbols by q_1 and q_2. But if $\overline{q(s_1, s_2, \ldots, s_n)} = \overline{q(s'_1, s'_2, \ldots, s'_n)}$ modulo renaming, it turns out to compute the same result twice and the distinction is useless. In order to avoid the defficiency and accerelate the convergence, we store the results computed before for each closed atom, or more precisely for each instanciated program, and utilize them immediately if possible.

4. Verification of Prolog Programs Using Type Information

Type inference is used effectively in our verification system [5],[6],[7]. In verification we sometimes simplify the theorem to be proved by assuming that some atom is true or false. In such a case,some information about variables left in the simplified theorem may be lost and we need to retain it to prove the right theorem. This problem was first noticed by Boyer and Moore [2] in their theorem prover(BMTP) for pure LISP. The same problem arises in verification of Prolog programs.

Example 4. Suppose we prove a theorem
$$\forall U, V, C(\exists B reverse(C, [V|B]) \supset \exists B' reverse([U|C], [V|B'])).$$
Because of the definition of *reverse*, it is transformed to
$$\forall U, A, V, C (\exists B \; reverse(C, [V|B]) \supset$$
$$\exists B', D (reverse(C, D) \wedge append(D, [U], [V|B'])))$$
Now let us decide D to be $[V|B]$. This decision is sound and we have a new subgoal
$$\forall U, V, C, B (reverse(C, [V|B]) \supset$$
$$\exists B' (reverse(C, [V|B]) \wedge append([V|B], [U], [V|B'])))$$
Here we can utilize the antecedant. If $reverse(C, [V|B])$ is false,the theorem is trivially true. Hence we can only need to consider the case $reverse(C, [V|B])$ is true. By replacing $reverse(C, [V|B])$ with true,we have a new subgoal
$$\forall U, V, B \; \exists B' \; append([V|B], [U], [V|B'])$$
which is further transformed to
$$\forall U, B \; \exists B' \; append(B, [U], B')$$
because $append([V|B], [U], [V|B'])$ iff $append(B, [U], B')$. But this transformation has generated a too strong theorem and it is in fact not true. (For example, an instance $\forall U \exists B' append(0, [U], B')$ is wrong.) In order to keep the theorem right, we need to add type information as antecedants,i.e. when we derive a subgoal assuming $reverse(C, [V|B])$ true, we have

information $list(B)$. Our new subgoal should be
$$\forall U, V, B \; (list(B) \supset \exists B' \; append([V|B], [U], [V|B']))$$
This is provable by induction and we complete the proof.

5. Discussions

Several works are done for type inference in Prolog [3],[8],[9] from different point of views. In our approach, both syntactical and semantical concepts appear. It is semantical whether a type inference I covers a success set, while it is syntactical and closely related to the well-typedness in [3],[9] whether a restriction J is closed. Moreover they are related strongly through the crucial condition that J must be closed for I to be computed. Though our approach is still monomorhic, it is new in the following respects.

(a) Our type inference describes a superset of the success set by associating a type substitutions with each definite clause, which gives some accuracy to the types infered.

(b) Our approach solves the problem under a syntactical restriction, which is utilized to infer types more minutely.

(c) Our type inference is not restricted to that for arguments. Type inference can be done for any variables in any procedure call which is not necessarily in general form.

6. Conclusions

We have shown a type inference method for Prolog programs and its application to verification. This type inference method is an element of our verification system for Prolog programs developed in 1984.

Acknowledgements

Our verification system is a subproject of the Fifth Generation Computer System(FGCS) project. The authors would like to thank Dr.K.Fuchi (Director of ICOT) for the chance of this research and Dr.K.Furukawa(Chief of ICOT 2nd Laboratory) and Dr.T.Yokoi(Chief of ICOT 3rd Laboratory) for their advices and encouragements.

References

[1] Apt,K.R. and M.H.van Emden, "Contribution to the Theory of Logic Programming",J.ACM, Vol.29,No.3,pp 841-862,1982.

[2] Boyer,R.S. and J.S.Moore, "A Computational Logic",Chap. 6., Academic Press,1979.

[3] Bruynooghe,M.,"Adding Redundancy to Obtain More Reliable and More Readable Prolog Programs", Proc.1st International Logic Programming Conference,pp.129-133,1982.

[4] van Emden,M.H. and R.A.Kowalski,"The Semantics of Predicate Logic as Programing Language",J.ACM,Vol.23,No.4, pp.733-742,1976.

[5] Kanamori,T.,"Verification of Prolog Programs Using An Extension of Execution",ICOT TR-096,1984.

[6] Kanamori,T.and H.Fujita, "Formulation of Induction Formulas in Verification of Prolog Programs",ICOT TR-094,1984.

[7] Kanamori,T.and K.Horiuchi,"Type Inference in Prolog and Its Applications",ICOT TR-095,1984.

[8] Mishra,P.,"Towards a Theory of Types in Prolog",Proc. 1984 International Symposium on Logic Programming,pp.289-298,1984.

[9] Mycroft,R.and R.A.O'Keefe,"A Polymorphic Type System for Prolog", Artificial Intelligence 23,pp.295-307,1984.

[10] Pereira,L.M.,F.C.N.Pereira and D.H.D.Warren,"User's Guide to DECsystem-10 Prolog", Occasional Paper 15,Dept.of Artificial Intelligence, Edinburgh,1979.

Term Description:
A Simple Powerful Extension to Prolog Data Structures

Hideyuki Nakashima

Electrotechnical Laboratory
Umezono 1-1-4, Ibaraki, Japan

ABSTRACT

Term description is a simple, powerful extension of terms. For example, functional notation and lazy execution of a program is introduced in a very natural manner without changing the basic mechanism of the computation, such as unification and backtracking. Especially, the readability of functional languages is introduced without actually introducing functional concepts.

I Introduction

A. Term Description

A term description is an extension to Prolog data structure. A term description is a term with some description (constraints) on it:

    <term> : <description>

It means that <term> must satisfy <description> which is a predicate. In other words, whenever the term is unified with another term, the substitution must satisfy the description.

B. Motivation

Although unification in Prolog is a useful tool for manipulating structures, it lacks the ability to express complex patterns and operations over them. In Prolog, dividing a list into its first element and the rest, and constructing a list from its first element and the rest are very easy. There is no need to call a procedure to perform the operation. A simple list notation, [Car Cdr] does both of them. However, it is not so easy to divide a list into two lists or construct a single list from two lists. This operation is usually called "append" and requires a special program.

Some operations are expressed as patterns and others are expressed as procedures. This destroys the readability and coherence of program notations. The distinction is not the essential part of the programming.

Using term description, a pattern for "cons" is described as:

    Z:cons(X,Y,Z)

as well as a pattern for the concatenation of two lists, X and Y:

    Z:append(X,Y,Z)

The definition of "cons" is:

    cons(X,Y,cons(X,Y)).

And the definition of "append" is:

    append(nil,X,X).
    append(cons(A,X),Y,cons(A,Z):append(X,Y,Z)).

I did not use the list notation, [X Y], in this example on purpose. The notation is simply a syntax sugar for a term cons(X,Y). We could similarly give a syntax sugar for Z:append(X,Y,Z), eg. X::Y.

II Semantics of Term Description

When a term description, <term>:<constraints> is unified with another term T, <term> is first unified with T and then <constraints> is checked. A constraint is described as a Prolog program, and executed as if it were written at the top-level. If the execution of the constraint fails, the unification also fails.

A constraint is executed only when it is necessary, ie., only when the term description is unified with non-variable terms.

When two term descriptions are unified, only one of them is executed first. For example, when two term descriptions: X:p(X,Y) and Z:q(Z) are unified, X is unified with Z:q(Z) first*, and p(Z:q(Z),Y) is executed. Then Z:q(Z) is in turn unified with the first argument of 'p'.

A term description may be used to produce a value. For example, X:plus(1,3,X) behaves just as 4.

The term description is similar to the macro in ESP [Chikayama 83] in its effect. ESP provides two different expansion orders to distinguish value-constraining macros and value-generating macros. The same effect is achieved implicitly in term descriptions because of its demand driven execution.

---

* The selection is arbitrary and implementation dependent.

III Features Provided by the Term Description

A. Typed Variables

We could type variables by adding a constraint as:

    X:integer(X)

The above term description is unifiable only with integers.   Hence we could regard X as having the type integer.

B. Functional Notations

The term description is useful to simulate "functional" notations. for example, a sequence of function applications:

    (h (g (f x)))

is written as:

    W:h(Z:g(Y:f(X,Y),Z),W)

If we follow the convention to place the result at the last argument position, we can further introduce a special syntax:

    !f(X)

which stands for

    Y:f(X,Y).

Now the previous example becomes:

    !h(!g(!f(X)))

This form is translated into a normal term description at read-in time. A unique variable names are attached to each pattern.

Using the notation, a function factorial is defined as:

    factorial(0,1).
    factorial(N,!times(N,!factorial(!sub1(N)))).

C. Equality for Terms

1. Equality and Reducibility

Term descriptions introduce equality for terms in a very efficient way compared with other approaches [Kahn 81, Kornfeld 83]. Checking the equality is nothing more than executing a program.

Let us consider defining more than two terms equal.   To assert that morning_star and evening_star in fact refer to the same object "Venus", we may say:

    morning_star(venus).
    evening_star(venus).

Then the three terms: "!morning-star", "!evening-star" and "venus" become unifiable. A term description !p may be thought of as an intention of p (thus ! may be regarded as an intentional operator).

Let us consider another example.   What is expressed by a program such as:

    animal(X):-bird(X).
    animal(X):-mammal(X).
        ...
    bird(X):-penguin(X).
    bird(X):-canary(X).
        ...

    penguin(p001).
        ...

is not *equality* but *reducibility* [Tamaki 84, Shibayama 84].   A term, !animal is reducible to !bird, which is further reducible to !penguin, which is finally reducible to p001. A set of reducible terms (intentions) of !animal is a super set of the set of reducible terms of !bird.

In the case of "morning_star" and "evening_star", two different terms are unified through a unique individual "venus". This can be done very efficiently.   In the case of "birds" on the other hand, the numbers of individual is much larger than the original terms. Therefore unifying !animal and !bird usually requires lots of backtracking.   Further research is required here.

2. Equations

In KRC [Turner 81], equations in which the same term appear on both sides such as

    integers = 1:(add1 integers)

are allowed*.   The term description also covers this kind of equations.   Since "integers" is a function with no argument, it is translated into Prolog predicate with one argument to return its value:

    integers([1: !map(add1,!integers)]).

"Map" is used to apply "add1" to all the elements of a list, and defined as:

    map(Pred,[X: Y],[!Pred(X): !map(Pred,Y)]).

The computation is infinite and hence we need "lazy execution."

D. Lazy Execution and Infinite Data Structure

A demand driven lazy execution is realized naturally as "lazy unification" of term descriptions.   Since a variable is unifiable to any term, it is also unifiable to any term descriptions.   Therefore, there is no need to execute the constraint when a term description is unified with an uninstantiated variable. The description is executed only when the result is actually necessary.

As the direct consequence of the lazy execution, indefinite data structure is manipulatable. The following example depicts the use of the infinite list in "Sieve of Eratosthenes".

The predicate "integers" produces an infinite list of integers beginning N.

    integers(N,[N: !integers(!add1(N))]).

Note the recursive call of "integers" itself as the term description in the second argument. If this call is moved to the body, a call for "integers" runs infinitely and never returns. When the term description is used, only the minimum part required is computed (demand driven computation).

---

* ":" is the concatenation operator.

The predicate "sift" filters a list of integers using "sieve". Only those which are not products of the previous elements remain in the second argument.

```
sift([P! Rest],[P! !sift(!sieve(P,Rest))]).
```

"Sieve" removes those which are products of P.

```
sieve(P,[X:remainder(X,P,0)! Y], !sieve(P,Y)).
sieve(P,[X! Y],[X! !sieve(P,Y)]).
```

Now a call

```
integers(2,I),sift(I,P).
```

returns P an infinite list of prime numbers.

There are other, special purpose, primitives to deal with infinite data structures: Prolog-II [Colmerauer 1982] has 'geler' (freeze) to manipulate infinite data structures; Parlog [Clark and Gregory 1984] and Concurrent Prolog [Shapiro 1983] have read only annotations for variables which provides synchronization among processes.

IV Implementation

A subset of the term description is implemented on Uranus, a successor of Prolog/KR [Nakashima 82]. Only those which is written in functional notations are supported. A term description !p(X) is written in Uranus as [p *x].

This notation is extended to the top-level of Uranus. A user can type in a predicate call just as if it is a function. For example,

```
[+ 1 3]
```

echoes back 4. If we define primitive lisp functions as predicates, then the user can use the system just as if it were Lisp, just by using "[" and "]" instead of "(" and ")". Here are some examples:

```
[cons 1 2]            -->    (1 . 2)
[car [cons 1 2]]      -->    1
[car (cons 1 2)]      -->    cons
[append (1 2) (3 4)]  -->    (1 2 3 4)
```

Note that we do not need "'". We can simply use "(" and ")" to denote a quoted list.

In usual, the description is replaced by the result once it is executed. Thus the multiple execution of the same description is avoided. However, in some cases, it is impossible to optimize the execution automatically. User should be careful and responsible for the efficiency.

As the final comment on implementation, it is worth noting that the implementation of lazy unification on Prolog with structure sharing is efficient. Since the form is shared, delaying the unification does not require extra storage. The storage required for saving the environment is just as large as is required for backtracking.

V. Conclusion

Prolog with term description may not be pure Prolog any more. However, the basic mechanism of the computation such as unification and backtracking are the same.

If Prolog ever needs any extension such as introducing functions, it should be kept as small as possible and that the term description is one of the smallest solutions.

ACKNOWLEDGMENTS

The author gives many thanks to Satoru Tomura and Kokichi Futatsugi at ETL, Koichi Furukawa at ICOT, Taku Takeshima at Fujitsu, Kazunori Ueda at NEC, and members of ICOT WG2, especially Etsuya Shibayama, for their detailed discussions.

REFERENCES

[1] Takashi Chikayama: *ESP -- Extended Self-contained PROLOG -- as a Preliminary Kernel Languages of Fifth Generation Computers* New Generation Computing, Vol. 1, No. 1, pp.11-24 (1983)

[2] Keith L. Clark, Steve Gregory: *PARLOG: Parallel Programming in Logic*, Research Report, Dept. of Computing, Imperial College (1984)

[3] Kenneth M. Kahn: *Uniform -- A Language Based upon Unification which Unifies (Much of) LISP, Prolog and Act 1*, IJCAI-VII, pp. 933-939, (1981)

[4] William A. Kornfeld: *Equality for Prolog*, Proc. of IJCAI-VIII, pp. 514-519 (1983)

[5] Hideyuki Nakashima: *Prolog/KR - Language Features*, Proc. of the First International Logic Programming Conference, pp. 65-70 (1982)

[6] Ehud Shapiro: *A Subset of Concurrent PROLOG and Its Interpreter*, ICOT TR-003 (1983)

[7] Etsuya Shibayama: personal communication (1984)

[8] Hisao Tamaki: *Semantics of a Logic Programming Language with a Reducibility Predicate*, Proc. of the 1984 International Symposium on Logic Programming, pp. 259-264 (1984)

[9] D. A. Turner: *The Semantic Elegance of Applicative Languages*, Proc. Conf. on Functional Programming Languages and Computer Architecture, pp. 85-96 (1981)

[10] David H. D. Warren: *Higher-Order Extensions to Prolog - Are they Needed?*, D.A.I. Research Paper No.154, University of Edinburgh (1981)

INTERPRETING DESCRIPTIONS IN A PROLOG-BASED KNOWLEDGE REPRESENTATION SYSTEM

Randy Goebel

Logic Programming and Artificial Intelligence Group
Computer Science Department
University of Waterloo
Waterloo, Ontario
Canada N2L 3G1

Abstract

Descriptions provide a syntactic device for abbreviating expressions of a formal language. We discuss the motivation for descriptions in a system called DLOG. We describe two approaches to specifying their semantics, and a method for implementing their use. We explain why some descriptions should be given a higher order interpretation, and explain how such descriptions can be interpreted in the simpler logic of Prolog. The essential idea is to constrain the domain of descriptions so that an extended unification procedure can determine description equivalence within the Prolog framework.

Introduction

A description is a syntactic device for abbreviating expressions of a formal language. For example, "The king of America is an old cowboy" might be rendered in first order predicate calculus as

$$\exists x \forall y [[king-of-America(y) \equiv x = y] \wedge old-cowboy(x)]$$

and paraphrased as "there is an x who is the unique king of America, and that x has the property 'old-cowboy'." This expression can be abbreviated, in the classical way, as $old-cowboy(\iota x[king-of-America(x)])$; we say that "$\iota$" is used to form a definite description. In first order logic, predicate arguments denote individual objects; the description operator ι has syntactically "objectified" a portion of the original sentence.

The description operator has created a new syntactic object, but the meaning or denotation of that object may not be well-defined. In this particular case, the existence and uniqueness properties presupposed by the above description have been the issue of much debate (e.g., see [Kaplan75]).

Another example of descriptive abbreviation relaxes the uniqueness assumption. For example, the expression "there is a person who is an old cowboy, and who is a Republican" might be rendered as $\exists x[person(x) \wedge old-cowboy(x) \wedge Republican(x)]$. We might use another description operator, say ξ (read "an"), to provide the following abbreviations:

$person(\xi x[old-cowboy(x) \wedge Republican(x)])$.
$old-cowboy(\xi x[person(x) \wedge Republican(x)])$.
$Republican(\xi x[person(x) \wedge old-cowboy(x)])$.

Each such abbreviation uses the description operator "ξ" to focus syntactic attention on the predicate "person," "old-cowboy," and "Republican," respectively. Again we must be concerned with the meaning of such descriptions. It is somewhat natural to treat all of the above abbreviations are semantically synonymous—that all assert the existence of an individual object with the three properties. But this creates the need to explain their obvious syntactic differences in some other way. One hint comes from Hilbert and his use of description operators (e.g., see [Leisenring69, Robinson79]). Hilbert used the transformations

$$\forall x I(x) \rightarrow I(\epsilon x \neg I(x))$$
$$\exists x I(x) \rightarrow I(\epsilon x I(x))$$

to simplify derivations. In other words, the transformations provided a computational advantage even though their meanings are identical. Robinson nicely expresses the intuition:

> "It would seem that Hilbert terms...do capture a certain intuitive manoeuvre, which is worth formalizing: to introduce a unique name for an entity whose *existence* has been established by some previous part of an argument, so as to continue with the argument and be able conveniently to refer to it if need arises." [Robinson79, p. 291]

This rationalization of the syntactic differences is related to the object-orientation of AI representation systems, where the ability to refer to and manipulate objects is argued to be of conceptual advantage in specifying symbolic representations of domains (e.g., [Moore76, Schubert76, Norman79, Bobrow77a, Bobrow77b, Hewitt80, Steels80, Attardi81]). (Descriptions have also been used within the logic database literature (e.g., [Dilger78, Dahl80, Dahl82]).)

In AI, part of the reluctance to adopt a logical interpretation of descriptions must be attributed to the long-standing confusion and controversy about their meaning—logicians do not generally agree on the semantics of descriptive terms (e.g., see [Carroll78]). The reluctance to analyze descriptions in a logical framework probably results from a traditional misunderstanding of the role of logic (cf. [Hayes77]).

Descriptive terms in DLOG

DLOG is a representation system implemented in Prolog. It is a "system" in the sense that it provides a general representation language (including various kinds of descriptions), a query evaluation mechanism, a simple integrity maintenance scheme, and an abstract description of the intended semantics of the representation language independent of implementation. Although originally developed to to help describe concepts in the Department Database (DDB) domain, the DLOG system is domain independent in the sense of traditional data base management systems.

The descriptions in DLOG are motivated by a desire for brevity in describing undergraduate degree program requirements in the DDB. For example, suppose that "CS115 or a 1.5 unit elective" is a requirement. The desire is to avoid an expression like

$$requirement(BScCS, CS115)$$
$$\vee [\exists x [requirement(BScCS, x)$$
$$\wedge units(x, 1.5) \wedge elective(BScCS, x)]]$$

in favour of something like

$$requirement(BScCS,$$
$$\kappa x [x = CS115$$
$$\vee x = \kappa y [elective(BScCS, y)$$
$$\wedge units(y, 1.5)]]])$$

by using some appropriately defined description operator "κ." Similarly, descriptions of sets were seen to be useful. For example, the expression "at least 12 CS courses" might suggest the use of an expression like that in fig. 1. where the components grouped by the left brace must be written once for each set of twelve CS courses. This is clearly a tiresome way to express the assertion, and furthermore, would require extensive modification after any new CS course was created (e.g., by adding an assertion like "CS-course(CS123)"). We would prefer something like

$$requirement(BScCS,$$
$$\kappa x[set(x)$$
$$\wedge cardinality-of(x)=12$$
$$\wedge \forall y[y \in x \supset CS-course(y)]])$$

where "κ" is another appropriate description forming operator.

Similar motivations have given rise to the following description forms in DLOG.

Definite individuals. DLOG's definite individual provides a shorthand syntax for referring to a unique individual whose name is unknown. Intuitively, the variable binding symbol 'ι' can be read as the English definite article "the." For example, we might refer to "the head of Computer Science" as

$$\iota x[head-of(x,ComputerScience)]$$

If our description distinguished the intended individual, then we need never know which individual constant actually names that domain individual. We normally expect that the variable bound with the symbol 'ι' appears somewhere in the formula that constitutes the body of the description.

Indefinite individuals. When we need to refer to "any old α" with some property specified by a formula '$\Phi(\alpha)$', we can use an indefinite individual. We use the variable binding symbol 'ϵ' as the English indefinite article "a" or "an." For example, "a course with course number greater than 300" might be referred to by the indefinite individual

$$\epsilon x_1[course(x_1)\wedge \exists x_2[course-no(x_1,x_2)\wedge x_2 \geq 300]]$$

As for definite individuals, we normally expect that the variable bound with the symbol 'ϵ' appears somewhere in the formula that constitutes the body of the description.

Definite sets. A definite set is used to refer to a set consisting of all individuals that satisfy some property. The name "definite" is used to correspond to its use in "definite individual." A definite set is "definite" because it refers to all individuals *in the current knowledge base* that satisfy the specified property. For example, "the set of all numerical analysis courses" might be designated as

$$\{x_1:course(x_1)\wedge topic-of(x_1,NA)\}$$

Here the braces "{ }" serve as the description forming symbol.

Indefinite sets. Indefinite sets are "indefinite" in the sense that they refer to one of a set of sets. Like indefinite individuals, they are intended to be used to refer to "any old set" that is an element of *the set of sets* that satisfy the specified properties. For example, the indefinite set

$$\{x_1,X_1:course(x_1)\wedge cardinality-of(X_1,3)\}$$

is the DLOG term that represents an arbitrary set that is a member of the set of "all 3 element sets of courses."

Lambda constants. Lambda constants were introduced to capture a kind of individual occurring naturally in the DDB domain: regulations. For example, in describing a typical degree program, we must classify all kinds of requirements for that program, e.g., "nobody can register if they're under 16 years old" refers to a regulation that uses the lambda constant

$$\lambda x_1[\exists x_2[age-of(x_1,x_2)\wedge x_2 \geq 16]]$$

Figure 1. "...at least 12 CS courses"

In this way regulations can be placed in relation to other individuals and sets, e.g.,

$$program-prerequisite(BScMajors,$$
$$first,$$
$$\lambda x_1[\exists x_2[age-of(x_1,x_2)\wedge x_2 \geq 16]])$$

says "one of the regulations for the first year of a BScMajors program is that an individual be at least 16 years old."

Semantics of descriptions

We have suggested that there is more to the meaning of descriptions than their denotation in a first order language. In DLOG (and, we claim, in any representation system) there are at least two aspects to the meaning of descriptions.

One important aspect is the traditional specification of denotational semantics along Tarskian lines: given a well-defined class of formal expressions, one specifies a systematic way in which expressions and their parts can be attributed denotations in an interpretation. Two assumptions underlying this methodology are (1) that the expressions in question are being evaluated as to their truth; and (2) that the denotation of complete expressions depends solely on the denotations of their parts.

Another important aspect, often overshadowed by concerns of the former, is the *intended meaning* of such formal expressions when they are being formed (e.g., by a user), during their use in assertions (e.g., when adding facts to a knowledge base), and during their use in queries (e.g., when requesting that facts be verified with respect to a knowledge base). In this regard, the use of descriptive terms impinge on philosophical problems associated with names and their use (e.g., [Donnellan66, Brinton77, Katz77, Linsky77]). A most common example is the difference between referential and attributive use of descriptions. The issue is whether a description is intended to refer to a known referent (referential), or unknown referent (attributive). Apparently only a few AI researchers have considered the problem (e.g., [Schubert76, Ortony77]). These and related issues are further discussed in [Goebel84, Goebel85]

Approaches to specifying DLOG's semantics

To attempt a coherent description of a Prolog-based mechanism for proving existential formulas in DLOG, one must first select a methodology for specifying the meaning of descriptions. The most common method is Russell's contextual definition [Kaplan75]. Contextual definition is essentially macro definition, e.g., any string of the form $\Phi(\iota x[\Psi(x)])$ is replaced with

$$\exists x \forall y[[\Psi(y)\equiv x=y]\wedge\Phi(x)].$$

The meaning of the description is specified by the logic from which the definition is taken.

A related issue is the meaning of descriptive terms when their proof-theoretic preconditions fail. For example, a constructive proof of $\exists x\Phi(x)\wedge\Psi(x)$ will produce a referent of the description in $\Phi(\xi[\Psi(x)])$, but what does the latter mean when a proof of the former fails? Under one popular theory [Kaplan75, p. 215], the meaning of such descriptions whose logical preconditions fail have been specified by convention, e.g., a failing description refers to a designated null constant that lies outside the domain of discourse.

First order semantics

One possible choice for the description defining language is first order logic. The overwhelming advantage of first order semantics is simplicity; an abstract, implementation independent specification of semantics is worthwhile in that it provides a simple way to understand the complexity of the actual system.

Using first order logic, most of the intended meaning of DLOG descriptions can be specified in a relatively straightforward way. The individual descriptions (definite and indefinite) are specified as above; sets can be axiomatized with a *set* relation and a set membership relation "$\in$" (DLOG set theory is finite, thus very simple). However, lambda terms rely on semantic notions foreign to first order logic; their definition here requires the use of meta language concepts.

Contextual definitions for set descriptions are defined as follows. The sentence

$$\Phi(\{x_1:\Psi(x_1)\}) \tag{1}$$

contains no set variables—the term $\{x_1:\Psi(x_1)\}$ describes a set consisting of *all* individuals α such that $\Psi(\alpha)$ is true. In a first order language that distinguishes set variables X_1, X_2, X_3,..., the definition of sentence (1) is rendered as

$$\exists X_1.[\Phi(X_1)\wedge\forall x_1.[x_1\in X_1\equiv\Psi(x_1)]]$$

This can be read as "there is a set X_1 that has property Φ, and all individuals x_1 in the set have property Ψ." Because the only defining property of a definite set is the property attributed to each of its members, its uniqueness is easy to establish. In contrast to definite individuals, there is only one extension for each definite set so a further specification of uniqueness is not required.

The contextual definition of indefinite sets can be approached in a similar way. We can view

$$\Phi(\{x_1,X_1:\Psi(x_1)\wedge\Omega(X_1)\})$$

as having the definition

$$\exists X_1\forall x_1[[x_1\in X_1\supset\Psi(x_1)]\wedge\Omega(X_1)\wedge\Phi(X_1)]$$

This says that "some set X_1 that has the property Ω and whose elements each have property Ψ, also has property Φ." Intuitively, the indefinite set construction specifies a set that fits the description, similar to the way that an indefinite individual specifies an individual that fits its description.

DLOG lambda constants provide the user with a method of asserting axioms about unary predicate abstractions, intuitively interpreted as regulations. For example, the assertion

$$\Phi(\lambda x_1\Psi(x_1))$$

can be interpreted as asserting that the property Φ is true of the regulation named by $\lambda x_1\Psi(x_1)$. These terms are useful because they allow a user to assert relations about properties. Intuitively, lambda constants are most reasonably interpreted as a special kind of constant, indexed for retrieval by the terms they appear with. However, they cannot be manipulated without the definition of an application mechanism. This definition relies on a meta relation *satisfies*, which is defined in terms of the provability meta relation *derivable* (cf. [Bowen82]). The *satisfies* meta predicate then provides a method for testing whether an individual satisfies the relation denoted by a DLOG lambda constant. That is,

$$\forall x_1[satisfies(x_1,\lambda x_2\Psi)\equiv derivable(DB,\Psi(x_1))]$$

For any individual constant α of a DLOG database DB, $satisfies(\alpha,\lambda x_1\Psi(x_1))$ holds if and only if $\Psi(\alpha)$ holds in DB. An assertion of the form

$$satisfies(\alpha,\lambda x_1\Phi(x_1)) \tag{2}$$

is interpreted to mean that, in the current database,

$$\Phi(\alpha) \tag{3}$$

is derivable. Indeed (2) is a clumsy alternative to (3), but by using lambda constants in this way, we not only provide a way of asserting axioms about regulations, but also a way of using those regulations in question answering. The *satisfies* predicate provides the mechanism for applying lambda constants as unary predicates of the current database.

An example will illustrate. The experimental DDB domain requires the description of degree requirements, which can often be expressed as lambda constants, e.g., the assertion

$$enrolment-requirement(BScCS, \tag{4}$$
$$\lambda x[\exists y[age-of(x,y)\wedge y\geq 16]])$$

states that "an enrolment requirement of the BScCS degree is that the candidate's age is greater than or equal to sixteen." The lambda constant format allows the requirement to be asserted and queried, and the *satisfies* predicate provides the mechanism to pose a query like

$$\exists x[enrolment-requirement(BScCS,x) \tag{5}$$
$$\wedge satisfies(John,x)]?$$

that can be read as "Has John satisfied an enrolment requirement for the BScCS program?"

Notice that, in the DDB domain, degree requirements are most naturally conceived as conditions which must be satisfied. Since degree programs are distinguished by their various requirements, it is most straightforward to describe degree program requirements as relations on degree names and conditions to be satisfied—in DLOG, as lambda terms.

Of course there are alternatives to the use of this special term. For example, the meaning of sentence (4) might be rephrased in terms of a standard first order language as

$$\forall x[satisfied-requirements(x,BScCS) \tag{6}$$
$$\supset\exists y[age-of(x,y)\wedge y\geq 16]]$$

where we would use BScCS as the name of a degree program and modify the predicate *satisfies* to correspond more closely to our intuition regarding what one must do with degree requirements. This alternative has a more straightforward meaning since there are no "special" forms. But now there is no way of asking what the requirements of the BScCS program are, short of providing another non-first order primitive for manipulating sentences. For example, to answer the equivalent of query (5) in the alternative notation, we require an operation that retrieves a sentence of the form (6) from the current database, and then returns the consequent of that sentence as an answer.

Lambda terms can be manipulated with a standard (sorted) proof procedure to answer existential queries about requirements; they are simply retrieved and bound to existential lambda variables as in normal answer extraction. Furthermore, they can be used in conjunction with the *satisfies* predicate to determine if an individual has satisfied a particular requirement.

The case for higher order semantics

The clear disadvantage of first order semantics is an inability to directly deal with higher order concepts. Though DLOG domains are restricted to be finite and no abstraction is permitted in the DLOG proof mechanism, the specification of certain DLOG expressions in a first order way is contorted and mitigates against the desired semantic simplicity. This is most obvious in the way that lambda terms must be explained in terms of meta relations.

One alternative is to use a second-order intensional logic, as used by Montague to explain such concepts as "obligation," "event," and "task." For example, Montague's formalization of the concept of obligation [Montague74, p. 151ff.] corresponds well with the use of lambda terms in the DDB application of DLOG.

Montague's system provides a natural semantics for DLOG's lambda terms, and is obviously powerful enough to be used to describe the rest of DLOG's descriptive terms (individuals, sets). Only DLOG lambda terms require this treatment, but Montague's system provides a rather more uniform treatment of DLOG's semantics than is possible in weaker systems.

The complete picture of Montague's system requires careful study, but the essence can be explained in a relatively straightforward manner. An essential concept is the classification of individuals into categories of two different kinds. Each n place predicate constant has an associated type $<s_0, s_1, \cdots s_{n-1}>$ that indicates the kind of object that can appear in each term position: $s_i = -1$ specifies a standard* individual; $s_i = 0$ specifies a proposition; and $s_i \geq 1$ specifies a s_i-place predicate.**

For example, a predicate constant P of type $<-1,1>$ takes individual constants in its first position and unary predicates in its second. In the Department Data Base domain, the *satisfies* predicate constant has type $<-1,1>$, e.g., the assertion

$$satisfies(fred, \lambda x\,[completed(x, cs\,115)])$$

has an individual constant 'fred' in the first argument position, and a lambda constant in the second argument position. The first denotes an individual object (the person with name 'fred'), and the second denotes a predicate specifying the property of "x completing the course CS115."

The meaning of the above assertion is assigned in a way that introduces the second and most important difference of Montague's system. The assignment of truth values to sentences is an inherently two phase process. As Montague explains [Montague74, p. 157], an *interpretation* assigns *intensions* to symbols, and a *model* assigns *extensions*. Extensions include the standard objects well-known from traditional Tarksian semantics, as well as sets of sequences of individuals. Intensions are functions from possible worlds to the universe of individuals. They are introduced in order to distinguish the sense or abstract meaning of a predicate from its denotation in a particular possible world.

The complexity of Montague's complete system can be perplexing, the essence of the system provides a rich specification language for DLOG's complex objects. Some of the complexity dissolves because of the simplicity of DLOG theories: they are finite, and the

---

* Here "standard individual" means the usual notion of an individual in a first order model.
** See [Montague74, p. 150]. The notion of predicate used in this context is sometimes called a "relation in intension."

intended interpretation is over a highly restricted domain. This simplicity constrains the number of possible worlds that can serve as interpretations for DLOG theories (thus, for example, providing a restricted interpretation of "□"). In the DDB example, the intended interpretation together with partial knowledge of each particular student identifies *the* intended possible world for semantic interpretation.

In Montague's second order logic, the meaning of DLOG lambda expressions is given by expressing them as unary predicate constants. For example, the DLOG formula

$$requirement(BScCS, \lambda x\,[completed(x, CS\,115)]) \qquad (10)$$

is written as

$$requirement(BScCS, \hat{x}completed(x, CS\,115)) \qquad (11)$$

In general, the '$\hat{u}\Phi$' syntax is shorthand for

$$\top Q \wedge u \Box (Q\,[u] \equiv \Phi)$$

Montague uses the symbols '$\wedge$' and '$\vee$' for '$\forall$' and '$\exists$', respectively. He also uses brackets where parentheses are typical, e.g., P[x] for P(x). In addition Montague employs the symbols '$\top$' and '$\Box$', read as "the" and "necessarily," respectively. These latter symbols are used to form names of predicates. DLOG's lambda symbol 'λ' plays the same role as Montague's '$\hat{\ }$' symbol.

Formula (11) is intended to mean "a requirement of the BScCS program is to bear the relation *completed* to the course CS115." The intensional semantics provides a way of admitting different intensions for the *completed* relation, e.g., completing a course might have different meanings in different possible worlds. In the case of DLOG, the particular possible world in which symbols are assigned extensions is *fixed* to be the Departmental Database.

The second order power of Montague's logic provides the expressive ability to assert relations on predicates: it is the property of completing $CS115$ that bears the *requirement* relation to the program $BScCS$, and not any particular extension of the property.

Again, the application of lambda terms can be explained with the aid of a relation called *satisfies*. However, in Montague's language *satisfies* is a predicate constant of type $<-1,1>$ and is interpreted (in a possible world i in a structure $<I,U,F>$) as a relation $<I,U,<I,U>>$ where I is the set of possible worlds and U the universe of possible individuals. (So $<I,U>$ is a unary relation, $<I,U,U>$ is a binary relation, etc.)

Computing with descriptions by extended unification

The mechanism for manipulating DLOG descriptions is implemented in the Horn clause logic of Prolog. Adopting one of the above approaches to semantics means to adopt the corresponding view of what the DLOG proof procedure is doing. The simplest way to view the DLOG proof procedure is as a Horn clause prover extended with meta relations to handle the non-Horn features of DLOG. However, we speculate that the theoretical foundation of a higher-order proof procedure based on unification due to Jensen and Pietrzykowski [Jensen75] will provide the corresponding view for the Montague system. Here the intuition is to consider the DLOG implementation as a restricted implementation of their unification procedure for general type theory. We have not yet investigated the possibility of adapting Jensen and Pietrzykowski's procedure for use in an intensional logic.

Instead of extending Prolog's Horn clause theorem prover to handle the expressions that arise from any method of contextual definition, the unification algorithm can be augmented to provide the correct matching of descriptive terms. As others have observed (e.g., [Clark78, van Emden84]), any assertion of the form

$$\Phi(t_1, t_2, \cdots t_n)$$

where t_i, $1 \leq i \leq n$ are terms, can be rewritten as

$$\Phi(x_1,x_2,\cdots x_n)\subset x_1{=}t_1{\wedge}x_2{=}t_2{\wedge}\cdots\wedge x_n{=}t_n$$

and implications

$$\Phi(t_1,t_2,\cdots,t_n)\subset\Psi_1{\wedge}\Psi_2{\wedge}\cdots\wedge\Psi_m$$

can be rewritten as

$$\Phi(x_1,x_2,\cdots,x_n)\subset x_1{=}t_1{\wedge}x_2{=}t_2{\wedge}\cdots\wedge x_n{=}t_n$$
$$\wedge\Psi_1{\wedge}\Psi_2{\wedge}\cdots\wedge\Psi_m$$

where the x_i, $1{\le}i{\le}n$ are new variables not occuring in the original formulas. In DLOG, the equality expressions arising from this transformation are determined from within unification. In a sense, some of the complexity of derivation is off-loaded to the "pattern matcher" (cf. [Reiter75]).

The idea of extending a resolution proof procedure's power by augmenting unification was first suggested by Morris [Morris69], who proposed that equality be manipulated with so-called "E-unification." There have been many other related proposals including Stickel [Stickel75], Morgan [Morgan75], and Kahn [Kahn81]. Of related interest is the representation language KRL [Bobrow77a, Bobrow77b, Bobrow79], which relies on a complex "mapping" process on several different kinds of object descriptions called "descriptors." We argue elsewhere that KRL's mapping can best be understood as a elaborated unification scheme [Goebel85].

Returning to the handling of descriptive terms by augmenting unification, we cite Rosenschein on the advantage of embedded terms:

...the data object is kept small and "hierarchical" so that where an exhaustive match must be performed, failure can occur quickly. That is, deep, heterogeneous structures are preferred to broad, homogeneous structures. For example, {()\{()()}} is better than {{}{}{}}.†

We view Rosenschein's claim as support for the interpretation of descriptions as embedded terms, rather than as their contextual definition by rewriting.

The DLOG unification algorithm is invoked by the DLOG *derivable* predicate, similar to the way Prolog's derivation procedure uses a built-in unification algorithm. Intuitively, whenever a unification must be performed and there are special DLOG terms to be matched, standard unification is intercepted, and DLOG unification is used. For example, suppose that the two terms $\xi x\,\Phi(x)$ and *Fred* are to be unified. The applicable DLOG *unify* axiom is

$$unify(\xi x\,\Phi(x),Fred){\leftarrow}apply(\lambda x\,\Phi(x),Fred)$$

where apply binds the symbol "*Fred*" to the lambda variable "x" and invokes *derivable*.

The DLOG unification definition uses an organization similar to the LOGLISP system of Robinson and Sibert [Robinson80, Robinson82]. LOGLISP consists of a logical proof theory embedded within LISP, and allows the invocation of LISP by the theorem-prover, and the theorem-prover by LISP. Similarly, the DLOG *derivable* procedure can invoke the standard Prolog proof procedure, and both are accessible from with DLOG's unification matcher.

In general, the correct "unification" of the DLOG extensions requires a derivation procedure more powerful than that provided by Prolog. For example, the equivalence of two lambda expressions, e.g., $\lambda x\,\Phi(x)$ and $\lambda y\,\Psi(y)$ can only be established if it can be shown that $\forall x\,\Phi(x){\equiv}\Psi(x)$ follows from the current database. The current DLOG unification procedure uses a local context mechanism to derive this equivalence. It is also the case that disjunctive terms require a more general proof mechanism, since a proof of $\exists x\,\Phi(x){\vee}\Psi(y)$ cannot be handled by the current implementation, although a special heuristic will use a notion of partial proof to retrieve facts relevant to such a query [Goebel85].

† [Rosenschein78, p. 534].

Bobrow and Winograd's description of KRL's matching framework (see [Bobrow77a, §2.5]) also uses the notion of partial match. Their discussion about what is deductive and what is heuristic is sufficiently interesting to pursue here because DLOG already provides some of the features of KRL's "flexible" matching.

Recall that the basic data type of KRL is a frame-like structure called a "unit." A unit is a collection of "descriptors" that attribute various properties to the unit in which they appear. Of interest here are the various ways in which units can be related by matching their descriptors. For example, consider KRL's matching by "using properties of the datum elements" [Bobrow77a, pps. 23-24]:

Consider matching the pattern descriptor *(which Owns (a Dog))* against a datum which explicitly includes a descriptor *(which Owns Pluto)*. The SELF description in the memory unit for Pluto contains a perspective indicating that he is a dog. In a semantic sense, the match should succeed. It can only do so by further reference to the information about Pluto.

This form of matching already exists in DLOG. For example, the KRL descriptors *(which Owns (a Dog))* and *(which Owns Pluto)* might be rendered as $\exists x[Owns(x,\epsilon y[dog(y)])]$ and $\exists x[Owns(x,Pluto)]$, respectively. If we have the fact that Pluto is a dog (i.e., the assertion $dog(Pluto)$), DLOG unification will successfully unify the above pair by recursively proving that $dog(Pluto)$ follows from the knowledge base.

Several other forms of KRL matching fall into similar categories, where a recursive proof will provide the inferences required to demonstrate the equality of descriptions. The only clear instance in which partial matches arise are due to resource limitations. Again the partial results determine whether the current line of reasoning is to continue (perhaps given further resources), or to be abandoned.

Concluding remarks

We have argued that there may be more to the meaning of descriptions than their traditional Tarskian semantics, especially as regards the way that they are manipulated within a logic-based representation language. We briefly outlined the kinds of descriptive terms included in the Prolog-based DLOG representation system, and discussed various ways in which those terms could be interpreted. Lambda terms, useful in a particular application, do not have an obvious formal meaning and suggest the need for higher-order semantics. Regardless of which semantic specification is selected, the notion of extended unification can be used to manipulate embedded descriptions. With some effort, the extended procedure can be viewed as providing either metalogical or higher-order proof theory extensions.

Finally, it is important for representation systems to exploit the computational as well as the traditional denotational meaning of descriptions. The proceduralists have been saying this for years; we claim that logic can contribute to an understanding of the computational use of certain kinds of descriptions.

Acknowledgements

David Poole suggested many improvements to an earlier draft of this paper. Richard Robinson pointed out the relationship between DLOG's lambda terms and Montague's formalization of obligation.

References

[Attardi81] G. Attardi and M. Simi (1981), Consistency and completeness of Omega, a logic for knowledge representation, *Proceedings of the Seventh International Joint Conference on Artificial Intelligence*, August 24-28, The University of British Columbia, Vancouver, British Columbia, 504-510.

[Bobrow77a] D.G. Bobrow and T. Winograd (1977), An overview of KRL-0, a knowledge representation language, *Cognitive Science* **1**(1), 3-46.

[Bobrow77b] D.G. Bobrow and T. Winograd (1977), Experience with KRL-0, one cycle of a knowledge representation language, *Proceedings of the Fifth International Joint Conference on Artificial Intelligence*, August 22-25, MIT, Cambridge, Massachusetts, 213-222.

[Bobrow79] D.G Bobrow and T. Winograd (1979), KRL, another perspective, *Cognitive Science* **3**(1), 29-42.

[Bowen82] K. Bowen and R.A. Kowalski (1982), Amalgamating language and metalanguage in logic programming, *Logic Programming*, A.P.I.C. Studies in Data Processing 16, K.L. Clark and S.-A. Tarnlund (eds.), Academic Press, New York, 153-172.

[Brinton77] A. Brinton (1977), Uses of definite descriptions and Russell's theory, *Philosophical Studies* **31**, 261-267.

[Carroll78] J.M. Carroll (1978), Names and naming: an interdisciplinary view, Research Report RC7370, IBM Watson Research Center, Yorktown Heights, New York, October.

[Clark78] K.L. Clark (1978), Negation as failure, *Logic and Data Bases*, H. Gallaire and J. Minker (eds.), Plenum Press, New York, 293-322.

[Dahl80] V. Dahl (1980), Two solutions for the negation problem, *Proceedings of the Logic Programming Workshop*, July 14-16, Debrecen, Hungary, S.-A. Tarnlund (ed.), 61-72.

[Dahl82] V. Dahl (1982), On database systems development through logic, *ACM Transactions on Database Systems* **7**(1), 102-123.

[Dilger78] W. Dilger and G. Zifonun (1978), The predicate calculus-language KS as a query language, *Logic and Data Bases*, H. Gallaire and J. Minker (eds.), Plenum Press, New York, 377-408.

[Donnellan66] K.S. Donnellan (1966), Reference and definite descriptions, *Philosophical Review* **75**(3), 281-304.

[van Emden84] M.H. van Emden and J.W. Lloyd (1984), A logical reconstruction of Prolog II, *Proceedings of the Second International Logic Programming Conference*, July 2-6, Uppsala University, Uppsala, Sweden, 115-125.

[Goebel84] R.G. Goebel (1984), DLOG: a logic-based data model for the machine representation of knowledge, *ACM SIGART Newsletter* **87**, 45-46 [reprinted, with corrections, from *ACM SIGART Newsletter*, **86**, 69-71].

[Goebel85] R.G. Goebel (1985), A logic-based data model for the machine representation of knowledge, Ph.D. dissertation, Computer Science Department, The University of British Columbia, Vancouver, British Columbia, (accepted with revisions in February), 247 pages.

[Hayes77] P.J. Hayes (1977), In defence of logic, *Proceeding of the Fifth International Joint Conference on Artificial Intelligence*, August 22-25, MIT, Cambridge, Massachusetts, 559-565.

[Hewitt80] C. Hewitt, G. Attardi, and M. Simi (1980), Knowledge embedding in the description system Omega, *Proceedings of the First American Association of Artificial Intelligence Conference*, August 18-21, Stanford University, Stanford, California, 157-163.

[Jensen75] D.C. Jensen and T. Pietrzykowski (1975), Mechanizing ω-order type theory through unification, *Theoretical Computer Science* **3**(2), 123-171.

[Kahn81] K. Kahn (1981), UNIFORM - a language based upon unification which unifies (much of) LISP, PROLOG and ACT1, *Proceedings of the Seventh International Joint Conference on Artificial Intelligence*, August 24-28, Vancouver, British Columbia, 933-939.

[Kaplan75] D. Kaplan (1975), What is Russell's theory of descriptions?, *The Logic of Grammar*, D. Davidson and G. Harman (eds.), Dickenson, Encino, California, 210-217.

[Katz77] J.J. Katz (1977), A proper theory of names, *Philosophical Studies* **31**, 1-80.

[Leisenring69] A.C. Leisenring (1969), *Mathematical Logic and Hilbert's E-symbol*, MacDonald Technical & Scientific, London, England.

[Linsky77] L. Linsky (1977), *Names and descriptions*, The University of Chicago Press.

[Montague74] R. Montague (1974), On the nature of certain philosophical entities, *Formal Philosophy*, R.H. Thomason (ed.), Yale University Press, 148-187 [reprinted from *The Monist* **53**(1960), 159-194].

[Moore76] R.C. Moore (1976), D-SCRIPT, a computational theory of descriptions, *IEEE Transactions on Computers* C-**25**(4), 366-373.

[Morgan75] C.G. Morgan (1975), Automated hypothesis generation using extended inductive resolution, *Advance Papers of the Fourth International Joint Conference on Artificial Intelligence*, September 3-8, Tblisi, USSR, 351-356.

[Morris69] J.B. Morris (1969), E-resolution: extension of resolution to include the equality relation, *Proceedings of the Internationl Joint Conference on Artificial Intelligence*, May 7-9, Washington, D.C., 287-294.

[Norman79] D.A. Norman and D.G. Bobrow (1979), Descriptions: an intermediate stage in memory retrieval, *Cognitive Psychology* **11**(1), 107-123.

[Ortony77] A. Ortony and R.C. Anderson (1977), Definite descriptions and semantic memory, *Cognitive Science* **1**(1), 74-83.

[Reiter75] R. Reiter (1975), Formal reasoning and language understanding systems, *Proceedings of the First Conference on Theoretical Issues in Natural Language Processing*, June 10-13, MIT, Cambridge, Massachusetts, 175-179.

[Robinson79] J.A. Robinson (1979), *Logic: Form and Function*, Artificial Intelligence Series 6, Elsevier North Holland, New York.

[Robinson80] J.A. Robinson and E.E. Sibert (1980), Logic programming in LISP, Report 8-80, School of Computer and Information Science, Syracuse University, Syracuse, New York, December.

[Robinson82] J.A. Robinson and E.E. Sibert (1982), LOGLISP: an alternative to PROLOG, *Machine Intelligence*, vol. 10, J.E. Hayes, D. Michie, and Y-H Pao (eds.), Ellis-Horwood, 399-419.

[Rosenschein78] S.J. Rosenschein (1978), The production system: architecture and abstraction, *Pattern-Directed Inference Systems*, D.A. Waterman and F. Hayes-Roth (eds.), Academic Press, New York, 525-538.

[Schubert76] L.K. Schubert (1976), Extending the expressive power of semantic networks, *Artificial Intelligence* **7**(2), 163-198.

[Steels80] L. Steels (1980), Description types in the XPRT-system, *Proceedings of the AISB-80 Conference on Artificial Intelligence*, July 1-4, Amsterdam, Holland, (STEELS 1-9).

[Stickel75] M.E. Stickel (1975), A complete unification algorithm for associative-commutative functions, *Advance Papers of the Fourth International Joint Conference on Artificial Intelligence*, September 3-8, Tblisi, USSR, 71-76.

RETROSPECTIVE ZOOMING:
A KNOWLEDGE BASED TRACING AND DEBUGGING METHODOLOGY FOR LOGIC PROGRAMMING

Marc Eisenstadt
Human Cognition Research Laboratory
The Open University
Milton Keynes, England

ABSTRACT

This paper describes new tracing and debugging facilities for logic programmming (Prolog in particular), based on a selective retrospective analysis of an exhaustive run-time trace. The tracer uses an enriched repertoire of program success/failure 'symptoms' to improve the clarity of the trace, and identifies characteristic 'symptom clusters' in order to work out the true cause of a bug.

INTRODUCTION

In the course of debugging Prolog programs, the user can easily be overwhelmed by a plethora of tracing information. An overview of the behaviour of the user's program is sorely needed before engaging in any kind of single-stepping activity, even when a 'skip/retry' facility is provided. In addition, users can benefit from some intelligent tracing and debugging assistance, as amply demonstrated by the work of Shapiro (1982). The progression towards intelligent tracing facilities involves three main facets:

a) Symptomatic behaviour: A more detailed analysis of the behaviour of Prolog programs needs to be provided. This is because the four behaviours ('call', 'exit', 'fail', 'redo') provided by existing trace packages are insufficient to provide clear signposts indicating the most likely cause of program failure.

b) Zooming: Once the behaviours are elaborated, the user needs to be protected from gory details on the one hand, yet allowed easy and rapid access to the relevant details as needed.

c) Suspicious symptom clusters: Characteristic 'symptom clusters' in the program trace need to be identified, so that particular kinds of behaviour can be singled out as being highly suspect.

SYMPTOMATIC BEHAVIOUR

The 'PTP' Prolog trace package (Eisenstadt, 1984) distinguishes among several different types of Prolog program failure (e.g. subgoals failed, no more backtrack solutions, backtrack encountered cut, no definition, wrong arity, variable unification failed, system primitive failed). In addition, PTP displays resolving clause numbers along with variables instantiated when the clause is attempted (rather than just when it exits).

In general, of course, the user may not want to observe program execution in such detail. The point of PTP's original 'symptomatic trace' facility was to develop a detailed analysis of Prolog program behaviour so that it could then be subjected to semi-automated inspection. The following sections describe how the latest implementation of PTP hides these details from the user while still capitalizing on the information contained therein.

ZOOMING

In the new PTP, the user sees the end results in advance, and can then 'zoom' in successively greater detail on subgoals of interest. Consider the following (buggy) quicksort program:

```
qsort([], []).
qsort([X|Xs], Result) :-
    split(Xs, X, Lo, Hi),
    qsort(Lo, Sorted_Lo),
    qsort(Hi, Sorted_Hi),
    append(Sorted_Lo, [X|Sorted_Hi], Result).

split([X|Xs], Crit, [X|Lo], Hi) :-
    X < Crit,
    split(Xs, Crit, Lo, Hi).
split([X|Xs], Crit, Lo, [X|Hi]) :-
    Crit > X,
    split(Xs, Crit, Lo, Hi).
split([], Crit, [], []).

append([X|Xs],Ys,[X|Zs]):-
    append(Xs,Ys,Zs).
append([],Ys,Ys).
```

Let's run the code through PTP. The symbol '?' below means 'attempting subgoal'. Failure due to inner subgoal failure is indicated by '-'. The symbol '><' is a concatenation of the symbol '>' ('Entering the body of resolving clause whose head is shown') and the symbol '<' ('This clause didn't work, looking for next resolvent'). The notation 'S1/S2' refers to an invocation starting at trace step number S1 and finishing at trace step number S2. A number enclosed in braces, e.g. {2}, indicates which specific clause has been considered. User input to the 'PTP:' tracer prompt is shown underlined. Output from PTP is as shown, with '%' comments added retrospectively.

```
PTP:  qsort([2,1,3],R).
  1: ? qsort([2,1,3],_275)
 38: - qsort([2,1,3],_275) {2}
% Bombed out, 38 steps. Only clause 2 used.

SUBGOAL FAILURES:
  7/16: split([3],2,_184,_185)
  3/36: split([1,3],_2,_184,_185)
  1/38: qsort([2,1,3],_275)
% Why should 'split', invoked at step 7,
% bomb out? Let's invoke the zoomer:

PTP:  zoom(7).  % home in on trace step 7
  7:    ? split([3],2,_127,_128)
 8/11: ><split([3],2,[3|_127],_128) {1}
12/15: ><split([3],2,_127,[3|_128]) {2}
 16:    - split([3],2,_127,_128)

% Clause 1 is tried at step 8, and loses (OK).
% Notice the partly-instantiated third arg shown
% at step 8. But why did clause 2 of 'split' fail?

PTP:  zoom(12).  % clause 2 of split is at step 12
 12: >  split([3],2,_127,[3|_128]) {2}
 13:    @ 2>3        % '@' means system prim
 14:    --2>3        % '--' means prim loses
 15: <  split([3],2,_127,[3|_128]) {2}

% why did I test 2 > 3 at step 13?  Aha...
% that was my mistake... so it loses
% and of course bails out of clause 2
```

Notice that the user has had to direct the process only twice to get to the culprit, by invoking 'zoom(7)' and 'zoom(12)'. This would have been true regardless of recursion depth, i.e. independent of the length of the list input to qsort at the top level. This 'constant zoom time' depends upon (a) the user being informed of 'suspect' subgoal failures from the innermost one outwards, and (b) the user deciding which of these failures is worthy of further perusal.

The retrospective zoom facility allows the user to catch a glimpse of overall program behaviour, and to make an informed decision on the basis of this selective view. The next section describes how PTP takes some of the debugging burden away from the programmer.

SUSPICIOUS SYMPTOMS

Two classes of suspicious code are pinpointed automatically by PTP for the user's benefit: (a) 'singleton suspects', which can be derived directly from symptoms exhibited in single lines of the trace, and (b) 'cluster suspects', which are suggested by the occurrence of characteristic clusters of symptoms distributed appropriately through the trace.

Singleton Suspects

The 'singleton suspect' analyser is automatically invoked when top-level goals are presented to the 'PTP:' prompt. The analyser walks over the full (internally stored) trace, and looks for missing definitions, wrong arity, unresolved goals, subgoal failures, and false (or wrong) successes. There is

a one-to-one mapping from tracer symbols to singleton suspects, so these are easy to collect and point out to the user. False or wrong successes are pointed out if PTP is given prior assertions such as 'expect(qsort([2,1,3],[1,2,3]))'. The analysis becomes more interesting for 'cluster suspects', since the interaction of failure and success patterns needs to be considered.

Cluster Suspects

The complete trace sequence, with its symptom symbols and indenting pattern, forms a characteristic 'trace footprint', which can be analysed empirically to identify particular causes underlying observed program behaviour. The empirical analysis is done by using the PTP 'symptom' and 'zoom' facilities described above, and noting which patterns are indicative of deeper causes of failure. This analysis uses a repertoire of 'bug-cliches' representing PTP's best guess about particular program failures. These cliches are used to invoke a message frame instantiated with the specifics of the goal sequence to help the user identify the source of the problem.

To illustrate cluster symptoms, and PTP's explanation thereof, let's fix the offending line of code discovered earlier in clause 2 of 'split', so that it reads 'X > Crit' instead of 'Crit > X', and try another test run:

```
PTP:  qsort([2,1,3,2],R).
  1: ? qsort([2,1,3,2],_331)
 38: - qsort([2,1,3,2],_331) {2}

SUBGOAL FAILURES:
 15/24: split([2],2,_224,_225)
  7/28: split([3,2],_2,_224,_225)
  3/36: split([1,3,2],_2,_224,_225)
  1/38: qsort([2,1,3,2],_331)

PTP:  why(24).
I.E. WHY DID THE INVOCATION OF 'split'
AT STEP 15 FAIL AT STEP 24?

A SHARED FAILURE PATTERN HAS BEEN OBSERVED IN:
  (A) CLAUSE 1 OF split/4 (STEPS 16/19),
  (B) CLAUSE 2 OF split/4 (STEPS 20/23)

THE FAILURE PATTERN IS: "FAILED PRIMITIVE".
IN (A) THE SUSPECTED TROUBLESOME INVOCATION WAS:
 17:  2<2
IN (B) THE SUSPECTED TROUBLESOME INVOCATION WAS:
 21:  2>2

POSSIBLE UNDERLYING CAUSES ARE:
 i) (SOME OF) THE TROUBLESOME INVOCATIONS ARE WRONG
ii) ADDITIONAL CASES HAVEN'T BEEN CATERED FOR
%End of running example
```

Cause (ii) above is the culprit: a '>=' test is needed to catch the missing case. Here is how the 'cluster suspect' is identified:

a) The user's request 'why(24)' is taken at expressing displeasure at the subgoal invocation/failure between steps 15 and 24. Therefore, it is assumed that the subgoal 'split([2],2,_139,_140)' should have succeeded.

b) The 'singleton suspect' subgoal failures (aside from the top level goal) differ only in terms of the list-lengths of their first arguments. Therefore, it is assumed that the root cause of all these failures is identical.

c) A 'zoom' of steps 15-24 is performed internally. The displayed version would have looked like this:

```
15:    ? split([2],2,_139,_140)
16/19: ><split([2],2,[2|_139],_140) {1}
20/23: ><split([2],2,_139,[2|_140]) {2}
24:    - split([2],2,_139,_140)
```

d) At this point, a characteristic symptom cluster is detected. The kernel of this cluster is the following four element collection:

```
['?', '>< {1}', '>< {2}', '-']
```

This kernel matches a known cluster pattern named 'subgoal fails after all resolving clauses tried and failed'.

e) The detection of the cluster invokes a set of rules which try to see whether there is a shared pattern underlying the failure of each clause. Intuitively, the analyser is looking for why a Prolog rule, viewed abstractly as a 'cases statement', has 'fallen off the end'. A further internally-performed zoom reveals the following kernel pattern:

```
[ '?',
  ['> {1}', ['@', '--'], '< {1}'],
  ['> {2}', ['@', '--'], '< {2}'],
  '-' ]
```

(Line 3 of the above pattern corresponds to trace steps 20-23, which are analogous to steps 12-15 of the trace presented earlier in the ZOOMING section.) This pattern provides sufficient grounds for the remainder of the messages displayed in the example. The declarative nature of this analysis enables it to work on more perverse definitions of 'split', such as ones where the greaterthan and lessthan tests come after the recursive invocation! The analysis can be performed even in the latter case because the internal zoomer inspects behaviour in terms of the program's declarative reading (which looks very similar in both the normal and perverse cases) before delving into sequence details.

Other cluster symptoms currently recognized are shown below:

* uncatered-for-case-with-bad-ordering (appropriate rule exists, but is not encountered due to misordering)

* uncatered-for-case-with-rule-missing (like the 'uncovered goal' of Shapiro, 1982, but has specialists to identify missing tests for (a) null list, (b) atom, (c) last element)

* under-specified-unification (occurs for example when a variable accidentally can unify with either a list or an atom)

* infinite-loop-caused-by-loop-in-db (asserting 'tallerthan(joe,joe)' will cause problems for naive transitivity code)

* infinite-loop-caused-by-left-recursive-rule, e.g. foo(X,Y):-foo(X,Z),foo(Z,Y).

CONCLUSIONS

'Retrospective zooming' enables a trace to remain faithful to the purely declarative reading of a logic program, yet allows appropriate probing of the procedural aspects as well. Suspect code can be identified by an empirical investigation of both single-line symptoms and, more importantly, clusters of co-occurring symptoms.

Our earlier work on automated program debugging (Laubsch & Eisenstadt, 1982) relied on the notion of a 'canonical effect description' which could be used to compare actual program behaviour with desired behaviour. In contrast to this, PTP, (like the system of Shapiro, 1982) leaves the notion of 'desirabililily' of program behaviour up to the programmer during debugging. PTP differs from Shapiro's work in maintaining an a priori repertoire of 'suspect' program behaviour, which itself is based upon a 'bug taxonomy' developed in the course of pilot studies of experienced Prolog programmers. The 'cluster suspects' detectable by PTP, while still in their earliest incarnation, have enabled the rapid development of a practical and empirically-motivated tracing and debugging facility for Prolog.

ACKNOWLEDGEMENTS

This work is supported by the UK Science and Engineering Research Council, Grant number GR/C/69344.

REFERENCES

[1] Eisenstadt, M. A powerful Prolog trace package. In T. O'Shea (Ed.), Advances in Artificial Intelligence (ECAI-84). Amsterdam: Elsevier/North-Holland, 1984.

[2] Laubsch, J., & Eisenstadt, M. Using temporal abstraction to understand recursive programs involving side effects. Proceedings of the National Conference on Artificial Intelligence (AAAI-82), Pittsurgh, PA. 1982.

[3] Shapiro, E.Y. Algorithmic program debugging. Cambridge, MA: MIT Press, 1982.

PROLOG CONTROL RULES

Lee Naish

Department of Computer Science
University of Melbourne
Parkville 3052
Australia

ABSTRACT

We present an overview of the many control constructs and heuristics used by PROLOG systems with extra control facilities. Two features of computations rules are used to evaluate and classify them. They are detecting failure quickly (where it is unavoidable) and avoiding failures. By examining current systems in this light, we reach conclusions concerning deficiencies in performance, and how they may be overcome. We propose an idealized computation rule which uses a hierarchy of goals and a breadth first component.

1. INTRODUCTION

There are now many PROLOG systems with more control facilities than conventional implementations. The design of these systems has been justified by examples of how programmers can implement efficient algorithms using simple logic. [Naish 85b] went a step further and showed how some control can be generated automatically. In this paper, a shortened version of [Naish 84a], we take a much broader view. We examine many proposed and implemented control primitives and heuristics to identify their strengths and weaknesses. We use the term *control rule* for these individual components of complete computation rules. Our attention is restricted to control rules for SLD resolution. We hope the discussion and conclusions here will contribute to the design of logic programming systems with better control components in the future.

The main part of this paper introduces some general properties that we should like computation rules to exhibit. The extent to which each control rule contributes to these properties is discussed and used for a simple classification. Finally, an idealized combination of control rules is suggested. First, however, we give some programming examples which will be referred to in the discussion.

2. PROGRAM EXAMPLES

The following selection of programming examples from the literature illustrates the kinds of problems that can be solved efficiently by using a flexible control strategy.

    perm([ ], [ ]).
    perm(X.Y, U.V) :- perm(Z, V), delete(U, X.Y, Z).

    delete(A, A.L, L).
    delete(X, A.B.L, A.R) :- delete(X, B.L, R).

These procedures define the permutation relation on lists. [Elcock 83] shows how difficult it is to write a definition of *perm* which works with either argument bound using conventional PROLOG. If *perm* is called with the second argument a variable, the execution of *delete* should proceed ahead of *perm* but if the first argument is a variable, *perm* should proceed ahead of *delete*.

    queen(X) :- perm(1.2.3.4.5.6.7.8.[ ], X), safe(X).

    safe([ ]).
    safe(N.L) :- safe(L), nodiag(N, 1, L).

    nodiag(_, _, [ ]).
    nodiag(B, D, N.L) :- D =\= N–B, D =\= B–N,
                         D1 is D + 1, nodiag(B, D1, L).

Using *perm*, we can write a program to solve the eight queens problem. The desirable form of control discussed most is for *perm* and *delete* to generate the list of queen positions one at a time and for *safe* and *nodiag* to test if the new queen position is safe. If the arguments in the initial call to *perm* are swapped, it is more efficient to delay calls to *delete* and =\= until the end, then do the calls to *delete*, resuming the instantiated calls to =\= at each stage.

    sameleaves(T1, T2) :- leaves(T1, L), leaves(T2, L).

    leaves(leaf(X), [X]).
    leaves(t(leaf(X), T), X.L) :- leaves(T, L).
    leaves(t(t(LL,LR),R), L) :- leaves(t(LL,t(LR,R)), L).

This program can be used to check whether two trees have the same list of leaf tags. The desired form of control is for the two calls to *leaves* to coroutine. Whenever one further instantiates the list of leaf tags, the other should check if the newly added tag is the next tag in the other tree. Either call can be the generator at each stage. This program can easily be extended to any number of trees.

    grandparent(G, C) :- parent(P, C), parent(G, P).

    ancestor(P, C) :- parent(P, C).
    ancestor(A, D) :- parent(P, D), ancestor(A, P).

Here we define the *grandparent* and *ancestor* procedures using *parent*, which we assume is defined with a collection of facts. *Grandparent* can be used to find the grandparents or grandchildren of a given person. However, it is most efficient to reverse the calls to *parent* when finding grandchildren.

Ancestor poses some rather difficult optimization problems. For finding the ancestors of someone, *parent* should always be called first. Calling *ancestor* first causes an infinite loop. In fact, infinite loops can always occur if someone is their own ancestor. There are even more difficulties using the program for finding descendants. [Naish 84a] discusses this further.

3. FEATURES OF COMPUTATION RULES

(1) The one obvious overriding property that we wish computation rules to exhibit is to **minimize the size of the search tree**. Unfortunately, there are very few cases where we can even find heuristics directly related to the size of the tree. Therefore, in the next two paragraphs we introduce heuristics which are reasonably general, but are useful for the design and classification of implementable control rules.

(2) For goals which can finitely fail, computation rules should select atoms which lead to **detecting failure quickly**. Several heuristics and some theoretical work have contributed to this area.

(3) There is a slightly more subtle rule which applies more to goals which have solutions. Although the success branches of the SLD tree are fixed, the number and length of other branches is not.

The rule, therefore, is to **avoid creation of failure branches** (and infinite branches) as much as possible.

4. CONTROL RULES

We now discuss many of control rules mentioned in the literature. They are put into three groups, according to the features mentioned above.

4.1. MINIMIZING THE SEARCH TREE SIZE

Unsurprisingly, this section is fairly small, though with more special case analysis, it could probably be expanded in the future.

4.1.1. Select Calls Which Fail

Sub-goals which match with no clauses should clearly be selected immediately. This rule was implemented in METALOG [Dincbas 80], which continually tested whether any atoms had no matching clauses. No method has yet been found for implementing this rule without significant overheads.

4.1.2. Select Deterministic Calls

By deterministic calls, we mean those which match with only one clause. Selecting deterministic calls is optimal for goals with some solution(s). [Naish 85b] shows how control information can increase determinism which can be detected at compile time. We discuss this further in the section on wait declarations.

4.1.3. Database Queries

Given a goal consisting of calls to database procedures (which only contain facts), [Naish 85b] gives a formula for the number of calls needed to find all solutions. It is a heuristic, based on some assumptions about probabilities of various matches being independent, etc. This formula can be generalized to take account of the number of unifications performed, which depends on the form of indexing used [Naish 85a]. It can be minimized to find the best computation rule. Calls to large database procedures should generally be delayed until less expensive calls have been done. This generalizes the methods of [Warren 81] and [Stabler 83] and produces the best form of control for *grandparent*.

4.2. DETECTING FAILURE

4.2.1. Call Tests as Soon as Possible

Tests fail more often than other calls. Thus, to detect failure quickly, they should be called as soon as possible. Programmers generally have a good idea of what calls are tests and [Naish 85b] and [Naish 85a] suggest ways of recognising tests automatically. The proposed definition is that a *test* is a) deterministic and does not construct any variables when it is sufficiently instantiated and b) has an infinite number of solutions otherwise. One problem is that if tests are called too soon, they usually create failure branches. This is normally solved by delaying the call if certain variables are uninstantiated. When they become bound, the test should be resumed quickly.

4.2.2. Eager Consumers

IC-PROLOG's *eager consumer* annotations [Clark 79] can be used to call tests quickly without creating extra failure branches. Placing an eager consumer annotation on some variable in a sub-goal prevents that sub-goal constructing the variable. The whole computation of the subgoal is delayed if an attempt is made to further instantiate the annotated variable. This has the unfortunate consequence of delaying instantiated tests in cases where the annotated sub-goal calls several tests. For example, if *safe* is made an eager consumer in the eight queens program, only one call to *nodiag* is called when a new queen is added. A similar problem is caused by the restriction that only one sub-goal can be a designated consumer of a particular variable. One advantage of *eager*

consumers is the "inheritance" of the annotation to sub-terms. This is useful for the *sameleaves* program.

4.2.3. Fairness

[Lassez 84] shows that SLD resolution is complete with respect to finite failure, assuming a fairness condition. Depth first rules and rules for most primitives which delay calls are unfair. There are two aspects of fairness which could affect practical systems. The first concerns avoiding infinite loops and detecting failure where possible. A fair computation rule could be used when no better heuristics can be found. The second aspect concerns completeness. Several control primitives can delay calls indefinitely, causing incompleteness. With a fair computation rule, all calls would be done eventually.

4.2.4. Breadth First

The simplest way to ensure fairness is to use a *breadth first* computation rule. Usually, generators and tests produce and consume (respectively) data structures at similar rates. Typically, one level of recursion corresponds to one level of functor nesting. This implies that a breadth first rule would have a fairly small delay between generating and testing, so failures are found relatively quickly. Unfortunately, a strict breadth first rule is very poor at avoiding failure, especially when tests are called before generators.

4.2.5. Pseudo Parallelism

IC-PROLOG's // connective has a declarative reading of "and", but the two (or more) sub-goals it connects are computed in pseudo-parallel. The computation rule alternates between selecting atoms from each of the different sub-computations. The same control has also been used as an example of the power of the meta-interpreter approach to control used by Two-Level PROLOG [Porto 84]. If // is used for all and-connectives, the result is a fair computation rule. However, if one sub-computation is a generator and the other contains several tests, the execution of the tests tends to lag behind the generator.

4.2.6. Avoid Left Recursion

This is a goal ordering heuristic, suggested for MU-PROLOG in [Naish 85b]. Actually, left recursion is desirable in some situations, such as *perm* in our alternative eight queens example. The problem is that left recursion is a pathological case for failure detection with a depth first rule, which most current systems use. With a breadth first control rule, failure detection is improved and left recursion is not a problem.

4.3. AVOIDING FAILURE

4.3.1. Freeze

The main reason for delaying sub-goals in PROLOG is to avoid creating failure branches and there are very many primitives which enable this. The simplest is *geler* (freeze) of PROLOG II [Colmerauer 82]. *Freeze* is used to delay a sub-goal until a particular variable is bound to a non-variable. Because it only delays a single call, the eight queens can be made more efficient than with eager consumers, though freeze is needed for four different sub-goals. However, because the control is not inherited to sub-terms of the variable, the same leaves program cannot easily be made efficient. Also, because freeze only waits for one variable, it is less useful for multi-use procedures and cannot make perm work in both ways.

4.3.2. Lazy Producers

IC-PROLOG's *lazy producers* provide a powerful method of avoiding failure and, to a lesser extent, detecting failure. A lazy producer annotation on a variable in a sub-goal prevents all other calls from constructing the variable. When another call attempts to construct the annotated variable, that call is delayed. The producer is then executed until it binds the variable, then the delayed call is resumed. The choice of which call is resumed does not help avoid failure but, if the call is a test, the choice helps detect failure. This overlaps with the control provided by *eager consumers* and means that coroutining between a generator and multiple tests is still difficult to implement.

4.3.3. Wait Declarations

Under this heading, we include the wait declarations of MU-PROLOG [Naish 84b] and the algorithm used for generating them automatically [Naish 85b]. We believe it is a major contribution to avoiding failure. The effect of wait declarations is local, like freeze, but they can be used to delay a call until one of several argument sets is sufficiently instantiated. This added flexibility makes it possible for procedures such as *perm* to work in multiple ways. The heuristic also produces the best form of control in goals like the following. The failure producing subgoals (*safe*, *nodiag* and *perm*) are delayed by automatically generated wait declarations whereas *delete* is not.

?- safe(L), nodiag(N, 1, L), perm(Z, L), delete(N, [1,2,3,4,5,6,7,8], Z).

Automatically generated wait declarations also interact very favourably with the rule for selecting deterministic calls first. With the eight queens program, calls to all procedures except *delete* are forced to be deterministic and this can easily be detected by a pre-processor. Using this information, our alternative eight queens control can be automated. However, there are situations where generated wait declarations delay calls unnecessarily or where wait declaration cannot be generated at all (such as *ancestor*). Both these problems can be overcome by fairness. The calls should just be given a very low priority, rather than being delayed indefinitely or not handled at all. With this control, *parent* would always be called before *ancestor*.

4.3.4. Delaying System Predicates

In IC-PROLOG, partially instantiated calls to system predicates such as < act as generators, often creating failure branches. In MU-PROLOG, they delay instead, allowing our alternative eight queens control. For completeness, it would be preferable for the system tests to be called eventually, if possible.

5. DISCUSSION

With most systems, the methods available for avoiding failure are not flexible enough. To delay the calls which create failure branches, other calls must be delayed also. This is manifest is two ways. Firstly, IC-PROLOG delays whole sub-computations. Secondly, most primitives only allow sub-goals to wait for a single variable to be bound, even though many procedures can work efficiently consuming several different subsets of their arguments. Wait declarations are an exception. They only delay single calls and are flexible enough to enable multi-use procedures. Partly because of this, they can also be generated automatically. The deficiencies in the algorithm can be partially compensated for by having a fair computation rule, so calls delayed by wait declarations are still done eventually.

There are also other deficiencies with failure detection, despite this being well understood. Because of delaying whole sub-computations and the single eager consumer limitation in IC-PROLOG, failure detection is impaired when multiple tests are needed. With other systems especially, multiple (potential) generators, such as the same leaves program, are not handled well. Left recursion also causes problems. Both these areas can be improved by using a breadth first rule. This performs slightly worse than a more controlled coroutine approach but requires no programmer intervention.

Our idealized system has three major features. Firstly, calls which are likely to create extra failure branches are delayed. Secondly, other calls which are likely to fail are called first. Thirdly, the computation rule is fair, so even calls likely to create failure branches are called eventually. We propose a hierarchy of calls as follows:

(1) Tests.
(2) Other deterministic calls.
(3) Nondeterministic calls.
(4) Calls to database procedures.
(5) Calls to procedures for which wait declarations cannot be generated.
(6) Calls delayed by wait declarations.
(7) Delayed calls to system predicates.

The optimal order in which to call the database procedures can be determined and other types of calls should be done in a breadth first manner, for failure finding and fairness. Furthermore, it is desirable that a lower priority call be done after some number of calls (say 1000) of the next higher priority, to ensure fairness.

6. CONCLUSIONS

Current PROLOG systems with extra control facilities have been designed in a fairly ad hoc manner, relying mostly on a few example programs. We have introduced some more general principles on which control rules can be judged. This shows the weaknesses and strengths of current control rules more clearly and should be of use in designing future systems which further exploit the advantages of flexible control strategies.

7. REFERENCES

[Clark 79]
K. L. Clark and F. McCabe, The Control Facilities of IC-Prolog, in *Expert Systems in the Microelectronic Age*, D. Michie, (ed.), University of Edinburgh, Scotland, 1979, 153-167.

[Colmerauer 82]
A. Colmerauer, Prolog-II Manuel de Reference et Modele Theorique, Groupe Intelligence Artificelle, Univerisite d'Aix-Marseille II, 1982.

[Dincbas 80]
M. Dincbas, The METALOG Problem-Solving System: An Informal Presentation, in *Workshop on Logic Programming*, S. A. Tarnlund, (ed.), Debrecen, Hungary, July 1980, 80-91.

[Elcock 83]
E. W. Elcock, The Pragmatics of Prolog: Some Comments, *Proceedings of Workshop on Logic Programming*, Algarve, Portugal, 1983.

[Lassez 84]
J. L. Lassez and M. J. Maher, Closures and Fairness in the Semantics of Programming Logic, *Theoretical Computer Science 29*, (1984), 167-184.

[Naish 84a]
L. Naish, Prolog Control Rules, Technical Report 84/13, Department of Computer Science, University of Melbourne, 1984.

[Naish 84b]
L. Naish, MU-Prolog 3.1db Reference Manual, Internal Memorandum, Department of Computer Science, University of Melbourne, 1984.

[Naish 85a]
L. Naish, Negation and Control in PROLOG, Ph.D. Thesis (in preparation), Department of Computer Science, University of Melbourne, 1985.

[Naish 85b]
L. Naish, Automating Control for Logic Programs, *The Journal of Logic Programming (To appear)*, 1985.

[Porto 84]
A. Porto, Two-Level Prolog, *International Conference On Fifth Generation Computer Systems*, November 1984.

[Stabler 83]
E. Stabler and E. W. Elcock, Knowledge Representation in an Efficient Deductive Inference System, *Proceedings of Workshop on Logic Programming*, Algarve, Portugal, 1983.

[Warren 81]
D. H. D. Warren, Efficient Processing of Interactive Relational Database Queries Expressed in Logic, *Proceedings Seventh International Conference on Very Large Data Bases*, Cannes, France, 1981, 272-281.

A LOGIC PROGRAM SCHEMA AND ITS APPLICATIONS

Takashi Yokomori
International Institute for Advanced Study of
Social Information Science, Fujitsu Limited
140 Miyamoto, Numazu, Shizuoka 410-03 JAPAN

ABSTRACT

In this paper we consider a specific type of logic programs called recursive-schema programs and show that the class of recursive-schema programs has sufficient expressive capability, which provides an alternative simple proof for the result by Tärnlund concerning the computational power of Horn clause programs. Further, it is shown that any Turing computable logic program can be expressed as a conjunctive formula of three recursive-schema programs. Some application issues are also discussed in the contexts of program transformation and synthesis.

1. INTRODUCTION

In reference to recent attempts concerning what is called the fifth generation computer project, the research area of logic programming languages has lately been attracting considerable attention. Since a logic programming language Prolog was initiated by the work of Colmeraure(Colmeraure 1970) and Kowalski(Kowalski 1974), intensive work on Prolog has been done this decade because of its great feasibility as an AI language. Among others, there are a few papers devoting to the theoretical issues on logic programming languages. It was shown by Tärnlund (Tärnlund 1977) that any Turing computable function is computable in binary Horn clauses, which ensures the sufficient computational power of Horn logic programs.

This paper concerns a subclass of Horn logic programs. First we introduce a certain type of a logic program called "recursive-schema", and then define a class of "recursive-schema programs" in a recursive manner. A recursive-schema program has very simple structure and property common to many conventional logic programs, and it is explained by the following example.

Suppose one wish to define the concept "ancestor", then he may express it as a binary predicate as follows :

ancestor(X,Y) holds true if and only if
X is a parent of Y, or there exists Z such that
X is a parent of Z and ancestor(Z,Y) holds true.

In a conventional logic formula this is represented, using a "parent" predicate, like

    ancestor(X,Y) <- parent(X,Y)
    ancestor(X,Y) <- parent(X,Z), ancestor(Z,Y).

On the other hand, one may also express the concept in a different fashion, that is,

    ancestor(X,Y) <- transitive-closure(parent,(X,Y))
where
    transitive-closure(P,(X,Y)) <- P(X,Y)
    transitive-closure(P,(X,Y)) <- P(X,Z),
                      transitive-closure(P,(Z,Y)).

The introduction of a recursive-schema program is motivated by the latter viewpoint of formulating a concept.

In the next section we introduce a fixed logic program called "recursive-schema" which is a simple generalization of "transitive-closure" mentioned above, and define a class of recursive-schema programs. It is shown that the class of recursive-schema programs has sufficient expressive power in that any recursively enumerable language can be computed by a recursive-schema program. This result gives an alternative simple proof for the Tärnlund's result previously mentioned. Preceding concluding remarks in Section 4, in reference to program transformation and synthesis, some application issues are discussed in Section 3.

2. A CLASS OF LOGIC PROGRAMS —— RECURSIVE SCHEMAS

It is generally understood that Prolog, a logic programming language, is one of nonprocedural programming languages. Nonprocedural programming has many desirable features, because it can suppress unnecessary details of low-level constructs the procedures bears, and it enables one to write programs in more concise manner (Leavenworth 1975). The simpler a program is, the easier it is understood, debugged, and modified.

Now, let a predicate "recursive-schema" be defined as follows:

(1) recursive-schema(A,B,F,G,X) <- A(X)
(2) recursive-schema(A,B,F,G,X) <-
            recursive-schema(A,B,F,G,F(X)),B(G(X))

where A,B are predicate names; $X=(X_1,...,X_n)$, X_i: term($1 \leq i \leq n$), $F = (f_1,...,f_m)$, $G = (g_1,...,g_k)$ are tuples of mappings f_i, g_j from the set of terms to the union of the set and the logical constants {true, false}, and $F(X) = (f_1(X),..., f_m(X))$, $G(X) = (g_1(X),...,g_k(X))$.

Since we are concerned with logic programs, it should be noted that the second clause (2) is logically equivalent to
(2') recursive-schema(A,B,F,G,X) <-
        B(G(X)),recursive-schema(A,B,F,G,F(X)).

Hence, in either case we simply refer to it as "recursive-schema".

A class of logic programs denoted by REC is defined in a recursive fashion as follows: (In what follows we identify a predicate with its program implied. Further, a predicate is sometimes identified with its predicate name.)
(i) a finite number of predicates called primitive(including true,false,unif) are in REC,
(ii)if p is in REC, then not(p) is in REC,
(iii)if $p_1,...,p_n$ are in REC and p <- $p_1,...,p_n$, then p is in REC,
(iv)if p_1,p_2 are predicate (names) in REC and p <- recursive-schema(p_1,p_2,F,G,X), then p is in REC,
(v) nothing else is in REC.
A logic program in REC is termed "recursive-schema program".

[Notes]
(1) A predicate unif(X,Y) is the unification predicate. Predicates "true", "false" are logical costants holding true and false, respectively.
(2) not(p) is the logical negation of p.
(3) The class REC is the smallest class of Horn logic programs constructed from primitive predicates by rules (ii)- (v).

Property

Let a predicate "or" be defined by the following two clauses:
        or(P,Q) <- P
        or(P,Q) <- Q.
One can transform it into a recursive-schema program as follows :
    or(P,Q)<-recursive-schema(call1,call2,F,id,(P,Q))
where call1((P,Q)) <- P,   call2((P,Q)) <- Q,
    F = (f_1,f_2), $f_1 = f_2$ = true, id((P,Q))=(P,Q).
Thus, or(P,Q) is in REC, provided that P and Q are in REC. This implies that a program which is defined by a finite set of recursive-schema programs is also a recursive-schema program.

Now, we shall show that the class of recursive-schema programs has sufficient expressive capability, which gives an alternative simple proof for the result that any Turing computable function can be computed in Horn logic programs.(Tärnlund 1977)

It is well known that for a given language L over some finite alphabet T, there exists a Turing machine accepting L if and only if L is a recursively enumerable language. Let L be a recursively enumerable language over T. We show that there exists a logic program P(X) in REC such that for a given x=$a_1 \cdots a_m$ in T^*, x is in L if and only if P(x) succeeds, where P(x) denotes P([$a_1,...,a_m$]). We assume the reader to be familiar with the rudiments in the formal language theory(e.g.,Salomaa 1973, Harrison 1978).

Lemma 1.

A recursively enumerable language L can be represented by L = $f(L_1 \cap L_2)$, where L_1, L_2 are context-free languages, f is a mapping such that for each symbol a, f(a) is a symbol or empty. (See, e.g.,Harrison 1978)

Lemma 2.

Let p be a logic program defined by a set of clauses {p(a), p(X) <- $p(X_1)$,..., p(X) <- $p(X_m)$}, where a, $X,X_1,..,X_m$ are n-tuples of terms for some n $\geq$ 1. Then, p is in REC.
Proof.

Let $p_i(X)$ <- recursive-schema(unif1,true, Fi, id, X), where unif1(X) <- unif(X,a) and Fi(X)=X_i, for i=1,...,m. Obviously, p(X) can be represented by {$p_1(X)$,...,$p_m(X)$}. □

Theorem.

For a given recursively enumerable language L over T, there exists a recursive-schema program P(X) such that P(x) succeeds if and only if x is in L.
Proof.

By Lemma1,there exist context-free grammars G_1,G_2 and f such that L = $f(L(G_1) \cap L(G_2))$, where $L(G_i)$ denotes the language generated by G_i, and f is a mapping from T^* to T^*. We may assume that G_i = (V, T', P_i, S_i) is in Greibach's normal form, i.e., each rule in P_i is either
    A —> $aB_1 \cdots B_m$ (a in T',A,B_j in V;1$\leq j \leq m$), or
    A —> a   (a in T', A in V),
where V:nonterminal alphabet, T':terminal alphabet.
Construct a logic program cfg-i as follows :
    cfg-i(X) <- grammar-i(X,[S_i])
    grammar-i([],[])
 for all A —> $aB_1 \cdots B_m$ in P_i,
    grammar-i([a|X],[A|Y]) <-
            grammar-i(X,[$B_1,...,B_m$|Y])
  and for all A —> a in P_i,
    grammar-i([a|X],[A|Y]) <- grammar-i(X,Y)
Further, define a predicate homomorphism by :
    homomorphism([],[])
  for all x in T' such that f(x) is non-empty,
    homomorphism([f(x)|X],[x|Y]) <- homomorphism(X,Y)
  and for all x in T' such that f(x) is empty,
    homomorphism(X,[x|Y]) <- homomorphism(X,Y).
It is easily seen that
(i) x is in $L(G_i)$ if and only if cfg-i(x) succeeds,
(ii) f(y) = x if and ony if homomorphism(x,y) succeeds. (In the definition of grammar-i above, the 2nd argument is used to simulate the left-most derivation for the input in the 1st argument, and when the two become empty at the same moment, the predicate succeeds and the input is accepted.)
Finally, let a program P(X) be defined as follows :
    P(X) <- homomorphism(X,Y), cfg-1(Y), cfg-2(Y).
Assume that P(x) succeeds, then there exists y such that homomorphism(x,y), cfg-1(y) and cfg-2(y) succeed. Hence, we have f(y)=x, y is in $L(G_1)$ and $L(G_2)$, that is, x is in $f(L(G_1) \cap L(G_2))$ = L. Conversely, it is almost obvious that x is in L implies P(x) succeeds. By the definition of REC and Lemma 2, we have that P(X) is in REC. □

3. PROGRAM TRANSFORMATION AND SYNTHESIS

One can argue the issues on recursive-schema programs from the view points of program transformation and synthesis. As we have already seen, the class of recursive-schema programs REC has sufficient expressive capability, and any program in REC can be constructed from a small set of primitive predicates by using some rules.

It would be useful to point out the following facts :
(1) any program in REC can be transformed into several assertions and one fixed program, and
(2) starting with the fixed program and translating those assertions, one can synthesize a program in REC.
This is illustrated by Figure 1.

When we compare the two databases, it is easily seen that DB2 consisting of one fixed rule (recursive-schema program) and assertions of facts is much simpler and more effective than DB1 in the following sense. That is, each program in DB2 is demand-driven, so that it is not until when called that it is embodied. Hence, DB2 can save much space.

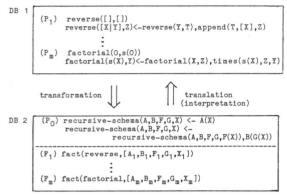

Figure 1

Another aspect of transformation concerning recursive-schema programs is brought when we pay our attention to the common or similar structure of data domains of programs.

Consider the program "plus" defined in terms of recursive-schema programs :

plus(X,Y,Z) <-
    recursive-schema(unif1,true,F1,id,(X,Y,Z))
where unif1(X,Y,Z) <- unif(X,0),unif(Y,Z)
    $F1 = (f_1,f_2,f_3)$, $f_1((X,Y,Z)) = pre(X)$,
    $f_2((X,Y,Z)) = Y$, $f_3((X,Y,Z)) = pre(Z)$.
    id: identity, pre: predicessor operator.
This representation is quite similar to the one for "append" :

append(X,Y,Z) <-
    recursive-schema(unif2,true,F2,id,(X,Y,Z))
where unif2(X,Y,Z) <- unif(X,[]),unif(Y,Z)
    $F2 = (f_1',f_2',f_3')$, $f_1'((X,Y,Z)) = cdr(X)$,
    $f_2'((X,Y,Z)) = Y$, $f_3'((X,Y,Z)) = cdr(Z)$.

Let a mapping T be defined as follows :
    $T(cdr) = pre$, $T(car) = suc$, $T([]) = 0$,
    $T(X) = X$(X: variable), suc: successor operator.
Then, we have $T(F2) = F1$ and $T(unif2) = unif1$.

Thus, a program "plus" can be obtained from "append" by one-to-one mapping T. This means that any program in REC whose domain is the set of natural numbers can be obtained by using only the transfer mapping T and a few primitives in the "List world". In general, the same thing goes to the recursive-schema programs whose domain world has a one-to-one mapping to the List world.

4. CONCLUDING REMARKS

By introducing a specific logic program called "recursive-schema", we have defined the class of "recursive-schema programs" in a recursive fashion. A recursive-schema program was proposed to capture the common and simple structural property of logic programs, and it has been shown that the class of recursive-schema programs has sufficient computational power to compute any recursively enumerable language. It should be noted that from the way of constructing the class of recursive-schema programs and the result on computational power just mentioned above, one can conclude that any Turing computable logic program can be obtained from a small set of primitive predicates and the "recursive-schema" by applying a few rules.

Further, we have discussed some application issues of recursive-schema programs from rather new view-points of program transformation and synthesis. It was demonstrated that a program transformation in terms of "recursive-schema" can provide a spacially efficient method for database design, while a program systhesis in our sense can be useful for generating new predicates.

The proposed methods in this paper can be easily implemented in Prolog and incorporated in the phase of database design.

ACKNOWLEDGEMENTS

The author would like to express his gratitude to Dr. Tosio Kitagawa, the president of IIAS-SIS, Fujitsu Ltd., for warm encouragement and useful suggestion he has been giving through his work.

Also many thanks to Hajime Sawamura for very constructive comment.

REFERENCES

[1]Burstall,R.M. and Darlington, "A Transformation System for Developing Recursive Programs", J. of ACM 24:1(1977) 44-67.
[2]Colmeraurer,A., "Les systèmes-Q ou un formalisme pour analyser et synthétiser des phrases sur ordinateur, Internal publication no.43, Département d'Informatique, Université de Montreal, Canada, September, 1970.
[3]Harrison,M.A., Introduction to Formal Language Theory, Addison-wesley, 1978.
[4]Kowalski,R., "Predicate logic as a programming language," in Proc. IFIP-74, 1974, 569-574.
[5]Leavenworth,B.M.,"NonproceduralProgramming",in Lecture Note in Computer Science 23, Springer, 1975,362-385.
[6]Salomaa,A., Formal Languages, Academic Press, 1973.
[7]Sato,T. and Tamaki,H.,"Transformational logic program synthesis", in Proc. of Interna. Conf. on Fifth Generation Computer Systems '84,Tokyo, November, 1984, 195-201.
[8]Tärnlund,S.A.,"Horn clausecomputability", BIT 17:2 (1977) 215-226.
[9]Yokomori,T., "Using higher-order inference for knowledge generation", in Proc. of Information System Symposium, at IIAS-SIS, Fujitsu Ltd., November, 1984, 6-13.

CONCURRENCY IN PROOF NORMALIZATION
AND LOGIC PROGRAMMING

Shigeki Goto

Computer Science Department, Stanford University
Stanford, California 94305 USA

and

NTT Musashino Electrical Communication Laboratory
3-9-11 Midori-cho, Musashino-shi, Tokyo 180 Japan [from Sept. 85]

ABSTRACT

Proof normalization manipulates formal proofs. It also provides a computation mechanism which belongs to the logic programming family.

Although proof normalization can treat full predicate calculus, it is less practical than the well-known programming language, Prolog.

In this paper, we propose a new technique of attaching proofs to Skolem functions. This technique enables one to nomalize a proof eagerly; that is, one can get a partial answer before the proof is totally normalized. This improves the usability of proof normalization. Partial answers are also useful in normalizing proofs concurrently. We compare our method with computation in Concurrent Prolog.

1. Introduction

Proof normalization has a long history in mathematical logic [Prawitz 1965]. The significant result for computer science is as follows: *If there is a proof of the formula $\exists z(A(z))$, one can get an answer* t, *which satisfies* $A(t)$, *after normalizing the proof.*

This realizes a computation, which is appropriately called logic programming. However, it is less efficient than Prolog.

[Goad 1980] proposes an extended λ-calculus, named p-calculus, to represent proofs. P-calculus terms are executed efficiently. [Hagiya 1982] noticed that most part of a proof is irrelevant for the computation. He introduces new notions to eliminate the unnecessary normalization steps.

This paper describes a new approach to improve the usefulness of the proof normalization. Our method is to attach proofs to Skolem functions, which enables us to normalize eagerly. Eager normalization produces a partial answer in advance. Using this capability, proof normalization can be performed concurrently rather than one proof at a time. Concurrency here means the same as in Concurrent Prolog [Shapiro 1983]. We apply our method to an example from Concurrent Prolog [Takeuchi 1984] and compare this to computation in Concurrent Prolog.

2. Logical Framework

Proof normalization is elegantly explained using a natural deduction system. Figure 1 summarizes the inference rules for natural deduction, which are used in this paper.

A typical proof in natural deduction is illustrated in Figure 2. This proof includes a rule of induction (IND). The proof concludes $\exists z(t + y = z)$. The assumptions are: (1) $0 + y = y$ and (2) $\forall xw(x + w = z \supset s(x) + w = s(z))$. Two other formulas enclosed in brackets, $[a + y = c]$ and $[\exists z(a + y = z)]$, are not considered to be assumptions. The formal definition is given below.

Definition 1 *At applications of* $\supset$I, $\exists$E, *and* IND *rules, certain assumptions (indicated by brackets in figure 1) are said to be* "discharged" *by the rule. The conclusion of a proof is said to depend on the assumptions that have not been discharged.*

```
A   B          A∧B         A∧B          [A]         A  A⊃B
------ ∧I      --- ∧E      --- ∧E       ---         ------ ⊃E
 A∧B            A           B            B            B
                                        --- ⊃I
                                        A⊃B
                                                              [A(a)]
                                                              ------
  A(a)         ∀x(A(x))        A(t)       ∃x(A(x))  C
------- ∀I     -------- ∀E    ------- ∃I  ----------- ∃E
∀x(A(x))         A(t)         ∃x(A(x))          C


             [A(a)]
             ------
  A(0)       A(s(a))        Function symbol "s" in IND
  ---------------- IND      means the successor function:
        A(t)                        s(x)=x+1
```

Figure 1: Inference rules in natural deduction

Sometimes, it is important to distinguish between variables. In Figure 2, there are five variables: x, y, z, w, a and c. Variables x, z and w are called *bound* variables. Variable y is a *free* variable. Two variables a and c are both called proper parameters, which are defined below.

Definition 2 *In applications of the rule* $\forall$I, $\exists$E *and* IND, *the variable* "a" *(see Figure 1) is called the* **proper parameter** *of the inference rule.*

The proper parameters look like free variables, however, they are bound not by the quantifiers ($\forall$ and $\exists$), but by the inference rules. The precise definition of the **bound variable** is given by the formulae_as_types approach [Goad 1980].

3. Computation by normalization

In short, proof normalization reduces the redundant part

```
                      ∀xw(x+w=z ⊃ s(x)+w=s(z))
                      ------------------------------ ∀E
          [a+y=c]     a+y=c ⊃ s(a)+y=s(c)
          ------------------------------------- ⊃E
                      s(a)+y=s(c)
                      ----------- ∃I
  0+y=y     [∃z(a+y=z)]    ∃z(s(a)+y=z)
  -------- ∃I  ----------------------------- ∃E
  ∃z(0+y=z)            ∃z(s(a)+y=z)
  ----------------------------------------- IND
              ∃z(t+y=z)
```

Figure 2: Proof using a rule of induction

in natural deduction proofs ([Prawitz 1965] and [Troelstra 1973]). Here, we explain only two reduction rules which are relevant to this paper.

Reduction rules

1. **E-reduction rule:** If a proof has an ∃I-rule immediately followed by an ∃E-rule, the proof is simplified by cancelling both applications of rules. Here, Π and Π'(a) stand for subproofs. a in Π'(a) indicates a proper parameter.

$$
\begin{array}{c}
\Pi \\
A(t) \qquad [A(a)] \\
\hline
\exists x(A(x)) \quad \Pi'(a) \\
\qquad\qquad C \\
\hline
C
\end{array}
\quad\text{is reduced to}\quad \Rightarrow \quad
\begin{array}{c}
\Pi \\
[A(t)] \\
\Pi'(t) \\
C
\end{array}
$$

with ∃I, ∃E labels.

2. **IND-reduction rule:** IND-reduction rule simplifies the term t if the term is of the form 0 or $s(t)$.

$$
\begin{array}{c}
\qquad\quad [A(a)] \\
\Pi_0 \qquad \Pi(a) \\
A(0) \qquad A(s(a)) \\
\hline \qquad\qquad\qquad \text{IND} \\
A(0)
\end{array}
\quad\Rightarrow\quad
\begin{array}{c}
\Pi_0 \\
A(0)
\end{array}
$$

or

$$
\begin{array}{c}
\qquad\quad [A(a)] \\
\Pi_0 \qquad \Pi(a) \\
A(0) \qquad A(s(a)) \\
\hline \qquad\qquad\qquad \text{IND} \\
A(s(t))
\end{array}
\quad\Rightarrow\quad
\begin{array}{c}
\qquad\quad [A(a)] \\
\Pi_0 \qquad \Pi(a) \\
A(0) \qquad A(s(a)) \\
\hline \qquad\qquad\qquad \text{IND} \\
[A(t)] \\
\Pi(t) \\
A(s(t))
\end{array}
$$

Definition 3 *A proof Π is said to be normal, if no reduction rule is applicable to Π.*

Before stating the key property of a normal proof, the concept of the *Harrop* formula should be introduced.

Definition 4 *The class of Harrop formulas is defined inductively as follows:*

1. *Every atomic formula is a Harrop formula.*
2. *If A and B are Harrop formulas, then $A \wedge B$ and $\forall x A(x)$ are Harrop formulas.*
3. *If B is a Harrop formula, then $A \supset B$ is a Harrop formula, regardless of the form of A.*

The Harrop formula has no positive ∨ nor ∃, except in the left hand side of the implications (⊃).

Proposition 1 *A normal proof of $\exists z A(z)$, where assumptions are only Harrop formulas, contains a subproof of $A(\mathbf{t})$ for a suitable term **t**.*

We can normalize the proof in Figure 2 to calculate the sum of two numbers because the two assumptions are both Harrop formulas, and the proof satisfies the condition of Proposition 1.

4. Attaching proofs

Although proof normalization provides a theoretically justified computation, it does not always produce a satisfactory answer. Consider the example in Figure 3, in which A(x,z) stands for (x+y=z). The uppermost applications of ∀E and ⊃E are abridged to $\pi(a)$. We want to add two terms $s(\alpha)$ and y, where α is some term. Normalization cannot give the answer because the term α does not take the form of $s(t)$ nor 0. The IND-reduction rule cannot be applied further.

```
STEP 1: original proof            [A(a,c)]
        substituted t←s(α)          π(a)
                                  A(s(a),s(c))
                                  ------------ ∃I
   A(0,y)        [∃z(A(a,z))]     ∃z(A(s(a),z))
   ---------- ∃I ----------------------------- ∃E
   ∃z(A(0,z))           ∃z(A(s(a),z))
   --------------------------------------- IND
              ∃z(A(s(α),z))


STEP 2: apply IND-reduction       [A(a,c)]
        (t=s(α))                    π(a)
                                  A(s(a),s(c))
                                  ------------ ∃I
   A(0,y)        [∃z(A(a,z))]     ∃z(A(s(a),z))
   ---------- ∃I ----------------------------- ∃E
   ∃z(A(0,z))           ∃z(A(s(a),z))
   --------------------------------------- IND
              ∃z(A(α,z))
                   ↓          [A(α,c)]
 ↓ indicates the   ↓            π(α)
 ↓ same formula    ↓          A(s(α),s(c))
                   ↓          ------------ ∃I
              [∃z(A(α,z))]    ∃z(A(s(α),z))
              --------------------------- ∃E
                   ∃z(A(s(α),z))

STEP 3: cannot apply IND-reduction, because α is
        not 0 nor s(t). GET STUCK!
```

Figure 3: Addition of two terms, $s(\alpha)$ and y

We solve the problem by attaching proofs to Skolem functions. The new method is as follows:

Attaching proofs:

1. Eliminate the existential quantifiers in the conclusion of an IND rule, using Skolem functions.

In the example, $\exists z(A(\alpha,z))$ is converted into $A(\alpha,\mathbf{f}(\alpha))$, where $\mathbf{f}$ is a Skolem function.

2. Attach the proof of the conclusion to the Skolem function. It means that one can use proof normalization in the future to get the value of the Skolem function. In the example, the proof of $\exists z(A(\alpha,z))$ is attached to $\mathbf{f}$.

Now we can continue the normalization and get the answer $z = s(\mathbf{f}(\alpha))$ in figure 4. The answer is called partial because it contains a Skolem function.

The method of attaching proofs is similar to the semantic attachment in FOL [Weyhrauch 1980]. In FOL, a Lisp function can be attached to a predicate. Whereas, in our method, a proof is attached instead of a Lisp function. Our attachment is performed inside the logic programming world.

Theoretical consideration

1. Syntactically, the elimination of the existential quantifiers converts a non-Harrop formula into a Harrop formula, which becomes an assumption of the proof. This assures the condition of Proposition 1, and normalization can proceed further.

2. The method is applicable to the formula of the form $\forall x \exists z(A(x,z))$. This type of formula appears everywhere in computer science.

3. The reason for the special treatment of the conclusion of IND is that it has the similar properties to the assumptions in a proof. For further details, see the definition of "spine" in [Troelstra 1973].

```
STEP 3: using Skolem function

                     ∃z(A(α,z))      The proof of ∃z(A(α,z))
                     converted       is attached to "f".
                         ·
                         ·
                      A(α,f(α))
                     ----------- ∃I      [A(α,c)]
                      ∃z(A(α,z))           π(α)
   ↓ indicates the        ↓            A(s(α),s(c))
   ↓ same formula         ↓           -------------- ∃I
                     [∃z(A(α,z))]     ∃z(A(s(α),z))
                     ---------------------------------- ∃E
                             ∃z(A(s(α),z))

STEP 4: applying ∃-reduction

                      A(α,f(α))
                        π(α)
                    A(s(α),s(f(α)))
                   ---------------- ∃I
                   ∃z(A(s(α),z))       get the answer z=s(f(α))
```

Figure 4: Addition of two terms (continued)

5. Concurrent normalization

Using the notion of partial answer, proof normalization can be performed concurrently. In this section, the example given in Concurrent Prolog [Takeuchi 1984] is computed, using proof normalization.

Example 1 *Concurrent Prolog*

```
1) integers(N,[N|S]) :- N1:=N+1 | integers(N1,S).
2) outstream([N|S]) :- write(N),outstream(S?).
3) :- integers(0,S),outstream(S?).
```

First, we treat clauses (1) and (2) separately. Each clause provides an assumption, which is used in the proof.

Example 2 *Proof of integer stream*
The rightmost assumption is equivalent to clause (1).

```
                 ∀xw(integers(s(x),w) ⊃ integers(x,[x|w]))
                ----------------------------------------------- ∀E
[integers(s(x),b)]   integers(s(x),b) ⊃ integers(x,[x|b])
-------------------------------------------------------- ⊃E
                                integers(x,[x|b])
                                ----------------- ∃I
              [∃z(integers(s(x),z))]    ∃z(integers(x,z))
              ------------------------------------------- ∃E
∃y∃z(integers(y,z))              ∃z(integers(x,z))
---------------------------------------------------- IND↓
                    ∃z(integers(0,z))
```

The leftmost assumption, $\exists y \exists z(integers(y,x))$, asserts that "*integers*" is not an empty relation and it is taken as an axiom. The proof uses the going-down induction (IND↓) which is a variation of the usual induction rule [Manna and Waldinger 1971]. The reduction rule for IND↓ is defined

```
                     [A(s(a))]
                     ---------
         ∃y(A(y))        A(a)
        ------------------------- IND↓
                   A(0)
```

analogously to the usual induction IND. If the attachment technique is used, one can normalize the proof in Example 2 to get an answer $z = [0|g(1)]$, where $g(x)$ is a Skolem function for $\exists z(integers(x,z))$, and "1" means $s(0)$. Further normalization of the attached proof gives $g(1) = [1|g(2)]$, $g(2) = [2|g(3)]$ and so on. This type of infinite list is called a *stream*.

The second proof corresponds to clause (2). It uses linear list induction (IND[ ]). Linear list induction is another variation of the IND rule, obtained through identifying $0 \leftrightarrow [\ ]$ i.e. NIL-list, and $s(y) \leftrightarrow [x|y]$ i.e. CONS(x,y). The reduction rule for IND[ ] is straightforward and treats the induction term $[x|y]$ as $s(t)$.

```
                  [A(d)]
                  --------
         A([])    A([a,d])
        ------------------- IND[]     "a" and "d" are
                A(t)                  proper parameters.
```

Example 3 *Proof of outstream*
The rightmost assumption is equivalent to clause (2).

```
      ∀x(write(x)) ∀xy(write(x)⊃(outstream(y)⊃outstream([x,y]))
  ∀E----------- -------------------------------------------------- ∀E
         write(a)   write(a) ⊃ (outstream(d)⊃outstream([a,d]))
        -------------------------------------------------------- ⊃E
      [outstream(d)]        outstream(d) ⊃ outstream([a,d])
      -------------------------------------------------------- ⊃E
  outstream([])               outstream([a,d])
  ------------------------------------------------- IND[]
                    outstream(t)
```

The upper left assumption, $\forall x(write(x))$, always holds because "*write*" can print any term. (For simplicity, we ignore errors in printing.) The other assumption, $outstream([])$, is a termination condition for "*outstream*" and taken as an axiom. It should be noted here that predicate "`write(N)`" is a built-in predicate in Concurrent Prolog, and it has a side effect to write the term N. How should it be handled in normalization? Again, the attaching technique solves the problem. This time a program is attached to a Skolem function. We do not specify any programming language here. To attach a program, there should be an existential quantifier. Thus, `write(x)` is modified to have an explicit output variable: `write@(x,z)`. The new predicate is considered "built-in"; that means that $\forall x \exists z(write@(x,z))$ is an axiom. Formally, `write(a)` in Example 3 is replaced by the subproof below:

```
∀x∃z(write@(x,z))         A certain program is
   converted             attached to "p".
      :
∀x(write@(x,p(x)))
------------------- ∀E
  write@(a,p(a))        ∀x(∃z(write@(x,z)) ⊃ write(x))
  --------------- ∃I    ------------------------------ ∀E
  ∃z(write@(a,z))        ∃z(write@(a,z)) ⊃ write(a)
  --------------------------------------------------- ⊃E
                    write(a)
```

In the subproof, a Skolem function p(a) is used. A certain program is attached to function p(a) to print the term "a" when "a" is substituted by some term. This requires more explanation:

When a term is printed?

> A term can be printed anytime unless it is **bound**. That is, no bound variables in the scope of $\forall$ or $\exists$, or no proper parameters can be printed.

In the example, "a" is printed after it is substituted. If the proof is normalized after giving $t = [foo|bar]$, "foo" will be printed, because it is substituted for "a" in the proof.

At last, two proofs are combined to produce the same effect as clause (3) in Concurrent Prolog. Figure 5 illustrates only a few steps of the normalization. However, it is easy to see that computation is performed concurrently. The IND↓ subproof produces the list, and IND[ ] subproof consumes the list. The condition on the print function protects the proper parameter from being printed before it is substituted. This realizes a kind of synchronization, which is attained by the read-only annotation in Concurrent Prolog [Shapiro 1983] [Takeuchi 1984].

6. Conclusion

In this paper we propose a new method of proof normalization, which utilizes Skolem functions to normalize a proof eagerly. Each Skolem function represents an existential variable ($\exists z$), and the relation is preserved by attaching proofs to Skolem functions.

Our method facilitates concurrent normalization. Concurrent Prolog is formally well-explained by our method.

It is easy to see that Prolog itself is closely related to proof normalization because: (1) Prolog always generates normal proofs, and (2) A Horn clause is necessarily a Har-

```
STEP 1: original combined proof
                                                    :
                                             ----- IND[]
              [∃z(A(s(a),z))]    [A(0,b)]       B(b)
              --------------    ---------------------- ∧I
∃yz(A(y,z))   ∃z(A(a,z))            A(0,b)∧B(b)
-------------------------- IND↓   ------------------- ∃I
      ∃z(A(0,z))                    ∃z(A(0,z)∧B(z))
      ------------------------------------------------- ∃E
                    ∃z(A(0,z)∧B(z))
```

```
STEP 2: after getting [0|g(1)]
                                                    :
                                             ----- IND[]
                                   [A(0,b)]       B(b)
         A(0,[0|g(1)])             ---------------------- ∧I
         ------------- ∃I              A(0,b)∧B(b)
         ∃z(A(0,z))               ------------------- ∃I
                                    ∃z(A(0,z)∧B(z))
         ------------------------------------------------- ∃E
                    ∃z(A(0,z)∧B(z))
```

```
STEP 3: after ∃-reduction
                                            :
                                      ----------- IND[]
         A(0,[0|g(1)])                  B([0|g(1)])
         ------------------------------------------- ∧I
            A(0,[0|g(1)])∧B([0|g(1)])
            ------------------------ ∃I
              ∃z(A(0,z)∧B(z))
```

STEP 4: IND[]-reduction for [0|g(1)]

Figure 5: The combined proof

rop formula. Thus, Prolog computation can be considered as a special kind of proof normalization.

ACKNOWLEDGEMENT

I would like to thank Dr. Carolyn Talcott at Stanford University for many valuable comments.

REFERENCES

[1] C.Goad, Computational Use of the Manipulation of Formal Proofs, *PhD Thesis, Department of Computer Science*, Stanford University, 1980.

[2] M.Hagiya, A Proof Description Language and Its Reduction System, *Department of Information Science, Tech. Report 82-03*, University of Tokyo, Feb. 1982.

[3] Z.Manna and R.J.Waldinger, Toward Automatic Program Synthesis, *Comm. ACM*, **14, no.3**, 151–165, 1971.

[4] D.Prawitz, Natural Deduction, Almquist and Wksell, Stockholm, 1965.

[5] E.Shapiro, A subset of Concurrent Prolog and Its Implementation, *Technical Report TR-003*, ICOT.

[6] A.Takeuchi, Concurrent Prolog, *Computer Today, No.***1**, pp.48–55, 1984. (in Japanese)

[7] A.S.Troelstra, Metamathematical Investigation of Intuitionistic Arithmetic and Analysis, *Lecture Notes in Mathematics Vol.***344**, Springer-Verlag 1973.

[8] R.Weyhrauch, Prolegomena to a theory of mechanized Formal Reasoning, *Artificial Intelligence* **13**, North-Holland, 1980.

PROLOG EXTENSIONS BASED ON TABLEAU CALCULUS

Wolfgang Schönfeld
Heidelberg Science Center
IBM Germany
Tiergartenstr. 15
D-6900 Heidelberg

Abstract

The intention of this paper is to help bridging the gap between logic programming and theorem proving. It presents the design of a Gentzen type proof search procedure, based on classical tableau calculus, for knowledge bases consisting of arbitrary first order formulas. At each proof search step, when a new formula is to be chosen from the knowledge base, the procedure chooses in such a way that the search space is small. When applied to a Horn clause knowledge base and an atomic goal, it performs the same proof search steps as any PROLOG interpreter would do. Hence, PROLOG can be viewed as a special Gentzen type procedure just as it is a special (namely, linear input) resolution procedure.

1. Introduction

Problem description. Expert systems are able to draw conclusions from data they contain. This deductive process can adopt different forms. There is the tradition of automated theorem proving, there are the many expert systems working with a production rule formalism, and there is PROLOG, a programming language which, at the same time, is a logical language.

PROLOG has proven very successful though it has some limitations. One of them is that it only accepts Horn clauses as rules and atomic formulas as goals. This restriction makes proof search simple and effective. But some properties cannot be expressed by Horn clauses, e.g. the linearity of an order relation. There are application domains where this handicap is not severe. In the LEX (linguistics and logic based Legal EXpert system) project at Heidelberg Science Center where the paper in hand was worked out, we consider the expressiveness of PROLOG to be too low. Only about 80 % of the knowledge in legal applications can be formulated. For the rest, we need negation, disjunction etc.

Existing solutions. Resolution calculus ([Robinson65]) is able to accept arbitrary first order formulas, even in non-clausal form if the extensions described in [Murray82] are used. Some of its defects when applied in its pure form to proving mathematical theorems are discussed in [Bledsoe77]. Bledsoe points out that heuristics should play an important role. Another defect is ([Clocksin81], p.221): 'Resolution tells us how to derive a consequence from two clauses, it does not tell us either how to decide which clauses to look at next or which literals to match.'

As compared with resolution based systems, Gentzen type systems did not yet attract much attention. An important theoretical article is [Beth59] where the notion of a *tableau* is introduced to present a Gentzen type system in a more natural way. This tableau method has been mainly used to prove completeness of various logic calculi such as modal logic [Rautenberg79]. It has been used to test equivalence of relational expressions [Sagiv81]. And it has drawn some attention in the legal domain where it is regarded as a natural formalization of legal reasoning [Herberger80].

To implement *tableau calculus* as described in [Beth59] is impossible since it is not *invertible* [Richter78]. This is because any Herbrand term can be substituted for the universal variables. It is the idea of Bowen [Bowen82] and (probably independently) of Wrightson [Wrightson84] to use unification in order to find the necessary substitutions. (TABLOG [Malachi84] is *not* based on tableau calculus though its name might suggest. It uses non-clausal resolution as in [Murray82].)

Solution proposed in this paper. Regardless which calculus we use, one problem still remains: In which way should possible applications of rules be ordered ? This is important in case of a very large knowledge base. In each state of proof search, the inference engine can choose among a huge set of formulas. PROLOG uses a rather simple and efficient strategy to make this choice: It tries to unify the current predicate with the head of some rule. The purpose of the paper in hand is to extend the PROLOG idea to non-Horn formulas. More precisely, it presents a strategy with the following properties:

- It accepts arbitrary formulas of first order predicate logic.
- When given a Horn clause knowledge base and a provable atomic goal, it finds the same proof in the same way as any PROLOG interpreter would do.

The paper starts with a (slightly non-traditional) description of tableau calculus for single formulas. The next chapter contains the description of a goal oriented, depth-first strategy with backtracking, as mentioned above, for propositional formulas. How this extends to predicate logic and some further extensions are described in the final chapter.

An implementation of this procedure is under work. Instead of mere first order formulas, it will accept so called discourse representation structures, a modification of predicate logic to cope with linguistic phenomena.

2. Tableaux for propositional formulas

Tableau calculus as developed in [Beth59] is a formalization of the search for counterexamples or, equivalently, for models. Assume e.g. that the formula $\gamma =$

$$((\neg R \& \neg S)|S) \& ((R \& \neg S)|(\neg R \& S)) \& \neg R$$

is satisfiable. ('&', '|', '¬' mean 'and', 'or', 'not' resp.) Satisfiability can be visualized by drawing a *logic diagram*.

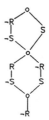

Figure 1

γ is satisfiable if and only if there is a *non-contradictory path* through its diagram, i.e. a path containing no complementary pair of literals.

This method to represent formulas is used in [Bibel83]. It should be compared with the usual and-or-graphs. Bibel describes a procedure which directly checks for the existence of non-contradictory paths. A better way to get an overview of all paths is to arrange them into a tree.

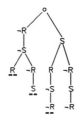

Figure 2

More precisely, we call the smallest tree containing the same paths as the diagram of γ the *tree* of γ. A *tableau* for γ is a tree for γ where any contradictory branch is cut off as soon as a complementary pair occurs. (In [Beth59], a tableau does not only contain literals but also the initial formula as well as all intermediate steps. Since these steps are 'straightforward', it suffices to represent only the final result.) A *proof* for the unsatisfiability of γ is a tableau for it in which all branches are contradictory. γ is satisfiable if and only if its tree is no proof. Hence, any procedure which, given a formula, generates a tableau and checks whether it is a proof is *correct* and *complete*.

3. Tableaux for sets of propositional formulas

Let Γ be a set of formulas which is to be checked for satisfiability. One way to do that is to proceed as above as if Γ were given by the conjunction of its elements in a fixed, but arbitrarily chosen order. For example, suppose that $\Gamma = \{\gamma_i | i = 1, 2, 3\}$ where $\gamma_1 = (\neg R \ \& \ \neg S)|S$, $\gamma_2 = (R \ \& \ \neg S)|(\neg R \ \& \ S)$, $\gamma_3 = \neg R$. Then Figure 2 may be called a tableau for Γ. If Γ is infinite, its tableau may be infinite. Again, Γ is not satisfiable if and only if the tableau is a proof, i.e. all its branches are closed by contradiction. Note that a proof is necessarily finite.

If the order of Γ is not fixed, in which way can a tableau for Γ be composed by the tableaux of its elements so that completeness still holds ? Suppose that a tree T is composed of the tableaux of the elements of Γ. A branch of T is said to *cross* (a tableau of) a formula $\gamma \in \Gamma$ if it contains as a

subpath a branch of the tableau for γ. T is called a *tableau for* Γ if each non-contradictory branch crosses each $\gamma \in \Gamma$ at least once. If T is no proof, then it contains at least one non-contradictory branch. The interpretation determined by such a branch satisfies each $\gamma \in \Gamma$ (since it crosses it). If T is a proof, then no interpretation can satisfy Γ. Hence, Γ is unsatisfiable if and only if there is a tableau for Γ which is a proof.

Choosing the next formula. To make search effective, it is necessary to keep the tableau as small as possible. First, no path should cross a formula twice. Second, branches should be cut off by a complementary pair as soon as possible. For example, a better tableau than Figure 2 on page 3 is

Figure 3

Two literals are *linked* if they form a complementary pair. Furthermore, a literal is *linked to a formula* γ if it is complementary to some literal in γ. Suppose that a set Γ of formulas contains an element α singled out for some reason. α is called the *goal*. Furthermore, suppose that a tableau for Γ is being generated, starting with α, and suppose that this process is now in a state where the tableau of another $\gamma \in \Gamma$ has to be appended to a certain non-contradictory branch B.

The idea is to choose a $\gamma \in \Gamma$ so that at least one of the resulting branches contains a complementary pair. To this end, let δ be the last formula crossed by B, and let B$|\delta$ be the restriction of B to δ, i.e. that subpath of B which is part of the tableau for δ. Furthermore, let C (for 'choices') be the set of all $\gamma \in \Gamma$ with the following properties.

1. γ is linked to some literal on B$|\delta$.
2. γ is not crossed by B.

C is ordered in a certain way, e.g. by respecting a given order of Γ. This is used to organize backtracking. If backtracking occurs, the subtableau starting with the actually chosen $\gamma \in C$ is removed, and a new subtableau is generated starting with the next $\gamma \in C$. We say that the *choice at δ is altered*. Backtracking means that we go upwards on B up to the next δ where such an altering of a choice is possible.

The following gives the whole algorithm, called SEARCH.

1. Start with the tableau for α .
2. Mark contradictory paths.
3. If all paths are contradictory, stop with 'succeed'.
4. Otherwise, let B be the leftmost non-contradictory path.
5. Let C be as above.
6. If C is empty, then check whether any choice can be altered along B.
   a. If yes, then backtrack.
   b. Otherwise, choose a $\gamma \in \Gamma$ which is not yet crossed by B and go to 8. If there is none, then stop with 'fail'.
7. Otherwise, choose a $\gamma \in C$.

8. Append its tableau to B.
9. Goto 2.

This strategy is again correct and complete. Correctness follows from the fact that any tableau (found by a strategy whatsoever) with all branches closed by contradictions is a correct proof. To see completeness, note that 6.b. guarantees that all formulas in Γ are crossed exactly once by each non-contradictory branch. If it is applied to the above Γ with γ_3 as a goal, then Figure 3 on page 4 results.

Comparison with PROLOG. It is claimed that algorithm SEARCH, when applied to propositional Horn clauses, is very close to PROLOG's search strategy. Some remarks will help to understand the claim.

The δ as considered above corresponds to the current predicate. C is the set of rules with which this predicate matches (with the above mentioned exception that matches leading to loops are avoided). Step 4 means that the first predicate on the right hand side of a rule is chosen.

One important difference is that SEARCH does never get into a loop. This comes from the fact that C as defined above does not contain any formula crossed previously by branch B. Such loop checking is essential when definitions of the form $P(x) \equiv \alpha(x)$ are evaluated. Note what PROLOG interpreters do when given the data base $a \leftarrow b, b \leftarrow a$.

The main difference comes in with 6.b. PROLOG stops at this point with 'fail'. SEARCH will in general go on and eventually generate a satisfying interpretation. This is necessary since it may e.g. happen that Γ contains a contradiction which cannot be reached from the goal by chaining through linked formulas. Note that no PROLOG knowledge base can be inconsistent. Furthermore, note that resolution calculus captures this situation by working breadth-first.

Predicate logic Suppose Γ consists of arbitrary predicate logic formulas. A naive implementation of the tableau calculus would be to substitute all Herbrand terms for all universal variables in a fixed order and then to generate a tableau from the resulting set of variable-free formulas (*level saturation*). It is one of the key observations in [Bowen82] and in [Wrightson84] that only those substitutions need to be performed which produce complementary pairs. The combination of their idea (they do not worry about the propositional case, e.g. backtracking) with those of this paper is not difficult and yields a strategy for full first order logic extending PROLOG.

4. Extensions

Our strategy may be refined in many ways. E.g. we could extend the definition of the choice set C in such a way that more than one link is taken into account. This would lead far beyond PROLOG.

Another point to be mentioned is the following. SEARCH composes tableaux starting with the root. But we might equally well try to compose them starting from the leaves. This is nothing else than resolution calculus. Using this unified view of different proof procedures, the following can be said.

- Resolution calculus generates a *theory*, i.e. a deductively closed set of formulas, and stops when it derives the empty clause.

- Tableau calculus generates *models* and stops when all cases lead to contradiction.
- In the PROLOG case, both calculi coincide since the theory to be generated consists of atomic formulas only, describing the 'minimal' model.
- Resolution may make multiple use of the same inference, of lemmas, and so reduce *proof length*.
- Tableau calculus may be extended to recognize loops in the generation of models and so reduce *proof search length* [Schönfeld83].

Both proof search approaches formalize different reasoning principles, and it seems useful to combine them. Mathematicians work this way: When given an open problem, they start by deriving some relevant facts from known theorems (resolution!). But then, they disbelieve their hypothesis and try to construct counterexamples (tableau!). They may switch back to the theorems and so on. I do not claim that their reasoning principles are the ultima ratio. But this shows that a combination of different principles can be useful. (In addition, we should not forget Bledsoe's claim for heuristics.)

To draw a final conclusion from all these considerations - I believe that tableau calculus is not a substitute for other calculi, but a useful complement.

References

[Beth59] E.W. Beth, The foundations of mathematics, North-Holland Pub. Co., Amsterdam 1959,

[Bibel83] W. Bibel, Matings in Matrices, Communications of the ACM 26(1983), 844-852,

[Bledsoe77] W.W. Bledsoe, Non-resolution theorem proving, Artificial Intelligence 9(1977), 1-35,

[Bowen82] K.A. Bowen, Programming with full first order logic, Machine Intelligence 10(1982), 421-440,

[Clocksin81] W.F. Clocksin, C.S. Mellish, Programming in Prolog, Springer, New York 1981,

[Herberger80] M. Herberger, D. Simon, Wissenschaftstheorie für Juristen, Alfred Metzner Verlag, Frankfurt 1980,

[Malachi84] Y. Malachi, Z. Manna, R. Waldinger, TABLOG: The deductive-tableau programming language, SRI Technical Note 328 (1984),

[Murray82] N.V. Murray, Completely non-clausal theorem proving, Artificial Intelligence 18(1982), 67-85,

[Rautenberg79] W. Rautenberg, Klassische und nichtklassische Aussagenlogik, Vieweg 1979,

[Richter78] M.M. Richter, Logikkalküle, Teubner, Stuttgart 1978,

[Robinson65] J.A. Robinson, A machine-oriented logic based on the resolution principle, J. ACM 12(1965), 23-41,

[Sagiv81] Y.C. Sagiv, Optimization of queries in relational databases, UMI Research Press, Ann Arbor 1981,

[Schönfeld83] W. Schönfeld, Proof search for unprovable formulas, 7th German Workshop on Artif. Int. GWAI-83, Springer, 1983, 207-215,

[Wrightson84] G. Wrightson, Semantic tableaux, unification, and links, Technical Report CSD-ANZARP-84-001, University of Wellington, 1984,

A Predicate Connection Graph Based Logic With Flexible Control

Richard Whitney, Darrel J. VanBuer, Donald P. McKay,
Dan Kogan, Lynette Hirschman, Rebecca Davis

System Development Corporation
Santa Monica, California and Paoli, Pennsylvania

Abstract

The FDE has been designed to support multiple search strategies for logic programs. This machine represents the knowledge base in a strategy independent fashion as a predicate connection graph which encodes potential unifications between predicates. It facilitates knowledge representation in the language of full first order predicate calculus. Immediate developments include implementation of various database access strategies and addition of evaluable predicates and functions to the language. Long-term research will focus on exploration of search strategies, especially for parallel logic machines.

I. Introduction

The *Flexible Deductive Engine* (FDE), is designed to serve as the deductive core for both logic programming environments and knowledge management systems involving database access. The intent is to create a single module which supports the full functionality of logic programming, as well as alternate forms of deduction appropriate to a knowledge management system [Kellogg, 1982]. Support of logic programming applications and deductive querying of databases in a single environment requires flexibility in search strategy through control customized to the application. Such flexibility results in a highly modular search engine, operating on a strategy-independent representation of the search space.

One goal of the FDE is to provide an experimental framework where the issues of control of inference, database access, and function evaluation are treated as part of a general problem of search control. For this reason, we have designed the core of the FDE with a set of well-defined interfaces; the person developing a logic system then specifies the search strategy by choosing a set of control functions, which can be augmented as needed to fit the application. The current repertoire of strategies includes at one extreme Prolog-style depth-first left-to-right search and at another Loglisp-style breadth-first search with cost functions for limiting depth-first expansions. Other strategies may combine depth-first and breadth-first expansion at different points in the deduction cycle depending on heuristic choice functions.

The FDE draws upon previous research carried out at SDC over the past several years in the general area of Knowledge Management and specifically in DADM, the Deductively Augmented Data Management project [Kellogg & Travis, 1981]. The FDE preserves the general Knowledge Management architecture underlying DADM [Kellogg, 1982; Kogan, 1984] through decomposition of computational functions into an inference engine, with its associated intensional set of rules, and a search engine, with its associated external extensional DBMSs. This division of relations into those with intensional support and those with extensional support has been a central feature of the DADM architecture [cf. Klahr, 1978] as well as other logic-based systems attempting to deal with external DBMSs [Chang, 1981; Henschen & Naqvi, 1982]. The intensional rules are encoded in a predicate connection graph (PCG) which records both the possible resolvents for each rule and the relations which have extensional database support. Our implementation of the PCG is the main topic of this report.

The FDE provides:

—uniform interface to a collection of diverse relational DBMSs with different query languages, data presentation strategies, and functionalities;

—alternative views to the data in extensional DBs by hiding irrelevant fields or defining new relations derived from the stored data via shallow deductions;

—an interface to the extensional DB allowing external relations to act as ground clauses to the logic programming environment.

The core of the FDE consists of four main parts (figure 1):

(1) The **knowledge base** contains a rule base (the collection of procedures of a logic program or the set of definitions of virtual relations for a high-order query language) and a collection of database facts maintained in multiple relational DBs external to the deductive core. The **predicate connection graph** encodes the *rule base* in the deductive core and also identifies the points of contact to the relations represented in the database components. To support the relational DB component of the knowledge base, the FDE maintains its own internal relational DBMS as well as communication links to external intelligent DB systems. As much as possible, the specialized functions of the external DBMSs will be exploited by the deductive core.

(2) The **unification engine**, central to any logic-based system, supports multiple parallel breadth-first search processes in the FDE. It is based on the unification algorithm of Loglisp [Robinson & Sibert, 1982], extended to allow for multiple simultaneous contexts, i.e. multiple collections of variable bindings in force for a deduction. Each search state has its own associated context to represent the variable bindings in effect in that state [McKay & Travis, 1984].

(3) The **search engine** explores the search space by constructing an AND/OR tree from the PCG representation of the rule base. A list of search states keeps track of the different search paths concurrently under investigation. The search engine proceeds through a deduction cycle which performs reduction on a particular search state. If this search state represents a solution, the deduction cycle returns it and its continuation; otherwise, the deduction cycle continues exploring the search space.

(4) The **search control strategy** is invoked by the search engine to control its deduction cycle through a suite of functions which stipulate how to choose and prune states from the search space. It is this set of functions which allows the control strategy to vary with the application.

The following sections describe our implementation of the predicate connection graph and its representation of first order predicate calculus. The FDE is implemented in Interlisp-D on Xerox 1100-series Lisp Machines.

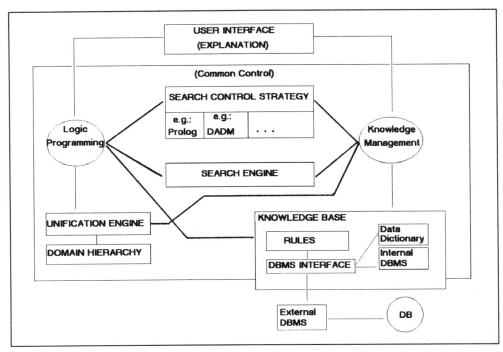

Figure 1. Organization of the FDE

II. The predicate connection graph in the FDE

The purpose of any PCG is to encode the potential unifications between the predicates (literals) as used in rules [Kowalski, 1975; Sickel, 1976]. As the internal specification in the FDE of the logic program, it represents an extended form of indexing. The rules submitted to the FDE are normalized and encoded in the PCG; growth of a proof tree through the deductive cycle is determined by the deductive interactions contained in the PCG.

We chose a predicate connection graph to represent the rules of a logic program primarily because such a formulation lends itself to the central design consideration of flexibility in search strategy. Also, we have substantial prior experience with such structures in database question answering; the present implementation of the predicate connection graph form of rule representation is a refinement of the PCG of DADM.

Our PCG facilitates a language with the expressive power of first order predicate calculus. Its inner representation of a rule set is a Skolem normal form of conjuncts which in turn comprise disjunctions of literals or negations of literals. Simple syntactic transformations reduce a given formula to an equivalent set of normalized PCG entries. The availablility of full first order predicate calculus allows convenient expression of complicated rules and submission of queries involving hypothetical or counterfactual antecedents. Moreover, divorcing the language from a limited canonical form is important when a range of search strategies is available: Horn clauses may be appropriate for Prolog's depth-first left-to-right strategy, but such forms should not prejudice search control in the general case.

One example of the kind of problem that the FDE simplifies is a general treatment of negation. As a database question answering system, the FDE allows for both *open* and *closed* worlds [Reiter, 1978]. Domains where the open world assumption is in effect require that we express and use negated literals in our rule base, since the Prolog technique of negation as failure is inadequate and logically incorrect in such cases. But even in closed worlds, where negation as failure yields desired results, a more robust language

provides additional benefits. Consider the definition of *bachelor* as *unmarried male*. A straightforward Prolog interpretation of this definition would be:

$$bachelor(X):-not(married(X)),male(X).$$

With ground clauses *married(b)* and *male(a)*, however, the particular goal *bachelor(a)?* will succeed while the general goal *bachelor(X)?* will fail, due to the combination of Prolog's search strategy and the handling of negation as failure. In order to compute the relative complement of a database relation, the FDE will first determine which individuals satisfy the positive relations (in this case, which are males). Then it will determine which individuals satisfy the negated relations in a positive sense (i.e. which are married). The relative complement of the first set with respect to the second (members of the set of males which are not members of the married set) then determines the answer. The delayed negation is a feature of the database operations, unlike the more general solution of MU-Prolog [Naish, 1983], where it is a function of search control.

The solution in Prolog is to reorder the defining literals:

$$bachelor(X):-male(X),not(married(X)).$$

Now, with the ground clause *male(a)*, the goal *bachelor(X)?* will succeed for individual *a*. However, asserting *bachelor(a)* does not allow any conclusion to be drawn about a's marital status. In the FDE, we can express the definition in biconditional form,

$$bachelor(X) \Leftrightarrow male(X) \wedge not(married(X))$$

and infer, from the assertion *bachelor(a)*, the conclusion *not(married(a))*. And this is achieved within a depth-first left-to-right search strategy simply through the flexibility of the language provided by rule and query encoding in the PCG.

A. The rationale of the PCG

The PCG is composed of two kinds of abstract objects: relations and occurrences. Relations correspond to symbols used as the name of a relation, e.g. P in $P(a)$. Occurrences represent instances of literals in rules; they also represent instances of literals in queries. Since a single relation may occur many times in a collection of rules, we distinguish the properties pertinent to the relation itself from those pertinent to the occurrences of it.

Relations are objects with two properties, namely, ordered sets of the uses of this relation in literals in (1) a positive sense and (2) a negative sense. The ordering reflects the order in which rules are made known to the system, to preserve the sequential nature needed for Prolog-style programming. For some alternate modes of deduction, it will be possible to express the measure of confidence in each rule by means of a plausibility factor. This factor can then be used to control deduction by ordering the rule set or the uses of rules according to the strength of the plausibility factors.

Literal occurrences are objects with a number of properties. These properties are:

SIGN: whether usage is (P --) or (NOT(P --)),

LITERAL: the literal exclusive of any negation, e.g. (P --),

ORMATES: links of this occurrence to other parts of the rule containing this occurrence,

UNIFIERS: links to occurrences which represent potential resolvents when this occurrence is a goal.

The internal representation of a rule set as a conjunctive normal form expects each rule to be convertible to a disjunction of literals and negated literals. Pure Horn clause rules, which consist of a conjunction of literals as antecedent and a single literal as conclusion, meet this expectation by using the transformation:

$$A_1 \wedge ... \wedge A_n \rightarrow B \Leftrightarrow \neg(A_1 \wedge ... \wedge A_n) \vee B$$

De Morgan's law then converts the conjunctive antecedent to a disjunction:

$$\neg A_1 \vee ... \vee \neg A_n \vee B$$

Other logical forms are transformed by the generation of new, unique literals to replace complex forms in the disjunction and the creation of new rules connecting the new literals with the forms replaced. Such a situation is encountered with the PCG representation of the rule defining bachelorhood previously mentioned (figure 2):

$$bachelor(X) \Leftrightarrow male(X) \wedge not(married(X))$$

In the *only-if* ($\Leftarrow$) direction of the biconditional, the Horn clause equivalent of the Prolog definition is simply transformed as represented in the upper branch of the tree from **BACHELOR** (figure 2). Distribution of negation by De Morgan's law causes the reversal of sign in the components of the original conjunct, so the equivalent disjunctive form would read: x is a bachelor *or* x is not male *or* x is married.

In the *only-if* ($\Leftarrow$) direction of the biconditional, the Horn clause equivalent of the Prolog definition is simply transformed as represented in the upper branch of the tree from **BACHELOR** (figure 2). Distribution of negation by De Morgan's law causes the reversal of sign in the components of the original conjunct, so the equivalent disjunctive form would read: x is a bachelor *or* x is not male *or* x is married.

In the case of the *if* ($\Rightarrow$) direction of the biconditional, a new literal, *not(GPred0(X))*, is generated to represent the conjunction in the consequent of the rule, so we first rewrite the original as two rules:

$$bachelor(X) \Rightarrow not(GPred0(X))$$

and

$$not(GPred0(X)) \Rightarrow male(X) \wedge not(married(X))$$

(Negation of generated literals is introduced to minimize negated terms in the ultimate normal forms.)   The first of these is equivalent to the normal form:

$$not(bachelor(X)) \vee not(GPred0(X))$$

The second is rewritten into two more rules,

$$not(GPred0(X)) \Rightarrow male(X)$$

and

$$not(GPred0(X)) \Rightarrow not(married(X))$$

which find equivalent normal forms in

$$GPred0(X) \vee male(X)$$

and

$$GPred0(X) \vee not(married(X)).$$

This situation can now be read off from the lower branch of the tree from **BACHELOR**. (Since the UNIFIERS field of a given occurrence represents potential unifications for the purpose of resolution, there is a difference of sign between occurrences so connected).

Queries are also treated as occurrences of relations which are connected to the PCG. Because the FDE uses resolution as its main technique and resolution is a form of proof by contradiction, the negation of a query is actually entered into the PCG. For queries, resolution is done primarily by backchaining, and exclusively so when emulating Prolog, so unifications for queries are actually connected in only one direction (from query occurrence to PCG occurrence) instead in the bidirectional form of the PCG proper. The main reason for using the unidirectional links is robustness of the implementation. Because there are no links from the PCG to the query, abnormal termination of query processing never leaves any unwanted connections. Another reason for avoiding reverse links is to avoid begging the question, since queries are not rules, so they should not be backchaining resolvents.

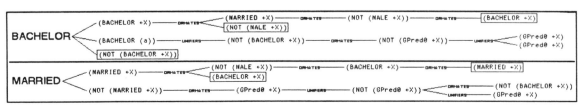

Figure 2. The PCG from **BACHELOR** and **MARRIED**

B. The PCG and the deduction cycle

The search engine of the FDE uses an AND/OR tree to represent progress through the knowledge base. Growth of this tree is governed by the suite of functions which encode the control strategy. The tree contains alternating levels of AND nodes and OR nodes. An OR node represents a literal to be resolved. Each OR node contains a list of alternate potential unifiers obtained from the PCG; the AND-node children of the OR node represent the resolvents of the goal literal obtained from the alternates.

Submitting a query causes it to be conjoined to the PCG and a root AND-node initialized with its children OR-nodes. Resolution of an OR-node causes a new branch to be added to the tree if the alternative unified with has ORMATES. In that case, the resolved OR acquires a child AND-node representing each alternative. If there are no ORMATES, then the OR-node is solved.

A trace of the deduction cycle and the AND/OR tree for the sample query NOT(MARRIED(←X))? are shown in figure 3 and illustrate some of the details of this process, and can be compared with the PCG structure of figure 2. The goal under And-1 in figure 3 corresponds to the PCG node (NOT(MARRIED ←X)) connected to the root of the PCG display for MARRIED (fig. 2), and is the first chosen goal node. The immediate subgoal is found by following the ORMATES arc to the single goal (GPred0 ←X). The goal under And-2 is one of the UNIFIERS (in this case, the only) of this node, (NOT(GPred0 ←X)). From here, we again follow the ORMATES arc of (NOT(GPred0 ←X)) to its immediate subgoal (NOT(BACHELOR ←X)). The goal under And-3 (fig. 3) is the only unifier of the node (BACHELOR a). Since this node has no ORMATES, it is resolved. This represents deducing NOT(MARRIED(a)) from BACHELOR(a).

III. Work in progress

One of the primary targets of the current development is an effective solution to problems of aggregation and the related problems associated with the *setof* and *bagof* predicates of Prolog, as well as a general treatment of evaluable predicates and functions. One case concerns the problem of determining a value for, e.g., the *number* of bachelors in our database. In line with the overall adaptability of the FDE, we intend to allow different strategies for different predicates: a Prolog style for computing this number would abort the inference procedure if an evaluable predicate were called with not all of its arguments instantiated. The DADM strategy would be to check the status of the arguments routinely during the course of deduction until all are instantiated, and then perform the computation.

We are also developing a more general treatment of database access than exists in DADM. The FDE will allow for a relation to be defined in both the intensional rule base and in the extensional database. A special choice function will control the point at which database access is performed: eagerly, as in Prolog, or in batched, deferred mode as in the current DADM.

IV. Bibliography

Chang, C.-L., "On evaluation of queries containing derived relations in a relational data base." *Advances in Data Base Theory, vol. 1*, H. Gallaire, J. Minker, and J. Nicolas (eds.), Plenum, New York, 1981.

Henschen, L. J. and Naqvi, S., "Representing infinite sequences of resolvents in recursive first-order horn databases." *6th Conference on Automated Deduction*, G. Goos and J. Hartmanis (eds.), New York, 1982.

Kellogg, C. and Travis, L., "Reasoning with Data in a Deductively Augmented Data Management System." *Advances in Data Base Theory, vol. 1*, H. Gallaire, J. Minker and J. M. Nicholas (eds.), Plenum, New York, 1981.

Kellogg, C., "Knowledge Management: a Practical Amalgam of Knowledge and Data Base Technology." *Proceedings of the Second National Conference on Artificial Intelligence*, 1982.

Klahr, P., "Planning Techniques for Rule Selection in Deductive Question-Answering." *Pattern-Directed Inference Systems*, D. A. Waterman and F. Hayes-Roth (eds.), Academic Press, New York, 1978.

Kogan, D., "The Manager's Assistant: an Application of Knowledge Mangement." In *IEEE International Conference on Data Engineering Proceedings*, Los Angeles, April 1984.

Kowalski, R., "A Proof Procedure Using Connection Graphs," *JACM*, **22**:4, October, 1975, pp. 572-595.

McKay, D.P. and Travis, L., *Unification Engine*, LBS Technical Memo, System Development Corporation, Paoli, PA, April, 1984.

Naish, L., *An Introduction to MU-Prolog*, Technical Report 82/2, Department of Computer Science, University of Melbourne, January, 1983.

Reiter, R., "Deductive question answering on relational data bases." *Logic and Data Bases*, H. Gallaire and J. Minker (eds.), 1978.

Robinson, J. A. and Sibert, E. E., "LOGLISP: Motivation, design and implementation." *Logic Programming*, K.L. Clark and S-A Tarnlund (eds.), Academic Press, New York, 1982.

Sickel, S., "A Search Technique for Clause Interconnectivity Graphs." *IEEE Transactions on Computers* C-**25**:8, August, 1976.

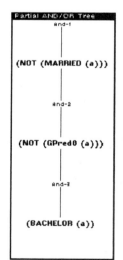

-> NOT(MARRIED(←X))?

CHOSEN GOAL NODE:
NOT(MARRIED ←X)
CHOSEN ALTERNATIVE:
NOT(MARRIED ←X) < -NOT(GPred0 ←X)
** SUCCESS **

CHOSEN GOAL NODE:
NOT(GPred0 ←X)
CHOSEN ALTERNATIVE:
NOT(GPred0 ←X) < -(BACHELOR ←X)
** SUCCESS **

CHOSEN GOAL NODE:
(BACHELOR ←X)
CHOSEN ALTERNATIVE:
(BACHELOR a) < -
** SUCCESS **

BACHELOR(a)
NOT(GPred0(a))
NOT(MARRIED(a))

Figure 3. The AND/OR tree and trace of the deduction cycle for NOT(MARRIED(←X))?

INCORPORATING GENERALIZATION HEURISTICS

INTO VERIFICATION OF PROLOG PROGRAMS

Hirohisa SEKI

Mitsubishi Electric Corporation
Central Research Laboratory
Tsukaguchi-Honmachi 8-1-1
Amagasaki,Hyogo,JAPAN 661

ABSTRACT

This paper is concerned with the problem of generalization heuristics, which are incorporated into our verification system for Prolog programs. Two kinds of generalization are discussed, that is, a *mechanical generalization* and an *intelligent generalization*. We show that the mechanical generalization used in Boyer-Moore's theorem prover (BMTP) can be performed by the simplification rule of our verification system, as well as in the case of cross-fertilization. To the intelligent generalization heuristic, which is not employed in BMTP, we give a generalization scheme which is naturally incorporated into our inference system of the extended-execution style of the Prolog interpreter, and which proves to be effective also for flawed induction schemes.

I. INTRODUCTION

This paper is concerned with a verification system for Prolog programs which is currently under development, as one of the subprojects of the FGCS "Intelligent Programming System"[1].

Logic programming is often advocated as a desirable choice for the verification problem because of its clear semantics (e.g., [2]). In the design of our verification system, we have tried to take advantage of Prolog's characteristics and present first order inference in an extended execution style of a Prolog interpreter [3]. Not only first order inference but induction is indispensable as a means of proving interesting properties of Prolog programs such as termination and correctness. In the case of functional language, Boyer-Moore's theorem prover (BMTP) [4] is famous for its automatic application of induction and many sophisticated heuristics constructing inductive proofs. Into our verification system, various kinds of heuristics have been integrated, most of which are inspired by BMTP and are developed to suit the verification of Prolog programs (e.g.,[5]).

In this paper, special attention is paid to "Generalization Heuristics" which are applied when a theorem to be proved is too weak and it is necessary and easier to prove a theorem that is stronger than the original weak one. We deal with two kinds of generalization heuristics. The first generalization heuristic (we call it *mechanical generalization* in this paper) corresponds to the one used in BMTP, and the second (called *intelligent generalization*) is one that is not employed in BMTP but is left to the user. Some work has been done with respect to functional language to mechanize the intelligent generalization heuristic (e.g.,[6],[7]). Our main purpose lies in an attempt to clarify how these two kinds of generalization heuristics can be incorporated into the verification of Prolog programs.

After summarizing some preliminary materials in section II, we present our verification methods for Prolog programs in section III. In section IV, we explain two kinds of generalization heuristics ; first, we illustrate that the mechanical generalization is naturally incorporated by the simplification rule of our verification system ; secondly, we show some examples which cannot be proved by simply applying first order inference and induction, and therefore motivate us to incorporate the intelligent generalization heuristic. In section V, we discuss in detail how the intelligent generalization is performed in the framework of our verification system of Prolog programs. Lastly in section VI, we discuss the relation to other work and some implementation issues.

II. FORMULATION OF VERIFICATION

In this section, we give our formulation of the verification of Prolog programs. In the following, we follow the syntax of DEC-10 Prolog [8] and assume some familiarity to the terminology of Prolog and first order logic(see e.g.,[9], [10]).

In our verification system, we treat only pure Prolog, i.e., we impose the following 3 conditions on Prolog programs :
- (i) no negative clauses and no "not" in programs.
- (ii) no executable primitives.
- (iii) no "cut" symbol (!).

On the other hand, our specification language is a subclass of first order logic formulas. That is, a specification is expressed by a closed formula which can be transformed into the following prenex form (we call it an *S-formula*) :
$$\forall X_1 \cdots \forall X_m \exists Y_1 \cdots \exists Y_n \ F \ (m, n \geq 0),$$
where F contains no quantifiers.

Let S be a specification and P be a Prolog program and P^* be the completion of P in the sense of Clark [11]. Then we adopt a formulation that *verification* of S with respect to P proves that $P^* \vdash S$. This means that S is a logical consequence of P^* by first order inference and induction, which are explained in the next section.

We use the following definitions and notations. First, we use the notion of *polarity* (see [9], [10]). The positive and negative subformulas are defined as follows :

(i) F is a positive subformula of F.
(ii) When $\neg G$ is a positive (negative) subformula of F, then G is a negative (positive) subformula of F.

(iii) When $G \wedge H$ or $G \vee H$ is a positive (negative) subformula of F, then G and H are positive (negative) subformulas of F.

(iv) When $G \supset H$ is a positive (negative) subformula of F, then G is a negative (positive) subformula of F and H is a positive (negative) subformula of F.

Next, variables which appear in a specification are distinguished in the following way. Let F be a closed first order formula. When $\forall X G$ is a positive subformula or $\exists X G$ is a negative subformula of F, then X is called a *free variable* of F. On the other hand, when $\forall Y H$ is a negative subformula or $\exists Y H$ is a positive subformula of F, then Y is called an *undecided variable* of F. In other words, when F is transformed into prenex normal form, free variables are variables quantified universally, and undecided variables are those quantified existentially.

A *goal formula* is a formula which is obtained from an S-formula by replacing each undecided variable Y with $?Y$ and deleting all quantifications. Furthermore, a substitution σ for a goal formula G is called a *deciding substitution* when σ instantiates no free variable in G.

Example : An S-formula :
$$\forall X (list(X) \supset \forall Y \exists Z \; append(X, Y, Z))$$
is represented by a goal formula :
$$list(X) \supset append(X, Y, ?Z),$$
where $list(X)$ is negative and $append(X, Y, ?Z)$ is positive.

A replacement of an occurrence of a term t in a formula F by s is denoted by $F_t[s]$, and a replacement of all occurrences of a term t in a formula F by s is denoted by $F_t(s)$. Formula F is said to be in a reduced form [10] with respect to logical constants *true* and *false*, if F is either (i) *true* or (ii) *false*, or (iii) if neither *true* nor *false* occur in F. The reduced form of a formula F is denoted by $F \downarrow$.

III. INFERENCE RULES

In this section, we give a brief description of our verification procedure for a specification (for a detailed explanation, see [3]).

A. Extended Execution

Since a specification is not restricted in a Horn clause but is expressed in an S-formula, we need some extension of the usual Prolog interpreter. For this purpose, our verification system uses the following four inference rules.

(1) Case Splitting

Let G be a goal formula and H either (i) an outermost positive subformula of the form $H_1 \wedge \cdots \wedge H_k$ or (ii) an outermost negative subformula of the form $H_1 \vee \cdots \vee H_k (k > 1)$. Then, if each undecided variable appearing in H_i appears only in $H_i (1 \leq i \leq k)$, we generate new k AND-goals $G_H[H_1], \cdots, G_H[H_k]$.

The following two rules are an extension of a Prolog interpreter using polarity.

(2) Definite Clause Inference (DCI)

Let A be a positive atom in a goal formula G and let "$B :\!\!- B_1, \cdots, B_m$" be any definite clause in P. When A is unifiable with B by a deciding m.g.u.(most general unifier) σ, we generate new OR-goals for all such definite clauses : $\sigma(G_A[B_1 \wedge \cdots \wedge B_m]) \downarrow$ ($\sigma(G_A[true]) \downarrow$ when m=0). All newly introduced variables are treated as fresh undecided variables.

(3) Negation as Failure Inference(NFI)

Let A be a negative atom in a goal formula G and let "$B :\!\!- B_1, \cdots, B_m$" be any definite clause in P. When A is not unifiable with a head of any definite clause in P, we generate a goal : $G_A[false] \downarrow$. When A is unifiable with B of a definite clause by an m.g.u. σ, we generate new AND-goals for all such definite clauses : $\sigma(G_A[B_1 \wedge \cdots \wedge B_m]) \downarrow$ ($\sigma(G_A[true]) \downarrow$ when m=0). All newly introduced variables are treated as fresh free variables.

(4) Simplification

Let G be a goal formula. When $A_1, \cdots, A_m$ are positive atoms and $A_{m+1}, \cdots, A_n$ are negative atoms unifiable to A by a deciding m.g.u. σ, we generate new AND-goals : $\sigma(G)_A(true) \downarrow$ and $\sigma(G)_A(false) \downarrow$.

These four inference rules are repeatedly applied to a given goal formula until it is reduced to *true* or *false*. If these rules cannot be applied any more, then we appeal to the following induction.

B. Induction

Our verification system utilizes inductive proofs which are based on structural induction schemes. Those induction schemes are also used in [12],[13],[14] for the verification of Prolog programs. For example, the following is an induction scheme for list X :

$$\frac{Q([\,]) \qquad \forall A, X \; (Q(X) \supset Q([A|X]))}{\forall X : list \; Q(X)}$$

where $Q(X)$ is a theorem to be proved, $Q([\,])$ is a base case, and $\forall A, X \; (Q(X) \supset Q([A|X]))$ is an induction step.

IV. GENERALIZATION HEURISTICS

In the following, we discuss two kinds of generalization heuristics incorporated into our verification system.

A. Mechanical Generalization

The generalization employed in BMTP is a heuristic by which a term in a formula is replaced by a variable under an appropriate condition [4]. For example, when the generalization heuristic is applied to a formula in functional language :

$$reverse(reverse(L))=L$$
$$\supset reverse(append(reverse(L), [X]))=[X|L],$$

then the following formula is obtained :

$$reverse(N)=L \supset reverse(append(N, [X]))=[X|L],$$

where term $reverse(L)$ in the first formula is replaced by a new variable N and thus a more general formula is obtained. On the other hand, let G be a goal formula :

$$(reverse(L, M) \supset reverse(M, L))$$
$$\supset (\underline{reverse(L, M)} \wedge append(M, [X], N) \supset reverse(N, [X|L]))$$

When we apply the simplification rule to the above underlined positive and negative $reverse(L, M)$ in G, then we generate the following AND-goals :

$$[(true \supset reverse(M, L))$$
$$\supset (true \wedge append(M, [X], N) \supset reverse(N, [X|L]))] \downarrow,$$
$$[(false \supset reverse(M, L))$$
$$\supset (false \wedge append(M, [X], N) \supset reverse(N, [X|L]))] \downarrow,$$

which are immediately reduced to :

$$reverse(M, L) \supset (append(M, [X], N) \supset reverse(N, [X|L]))$$

and *true*, respectively. This inference exactly corresponds to the above-mentioned generalization heuristic employed in BMTP.

Likewise, the inference of cross-fertilization in BMTP also corresponds to the one performed by simplification [3]. In this way, generalization and cross-fertilization, which are treated as different heuristics in BMTP, are performed in a unified way by the simplification rule in our verification system.

Furthermore, the heuristic of eliminating destructors in BMTP can be considered as a kind of generalization heuristic. For example, selectors for data structure like $car(L)$ and $cdr(L)$ appearing in the goals of BMTP are eliminated and replaced by variables. In Prolog programs, we usually don't use such selectors explicitly ; we do without them by using unification. Hence, Prolog programming style sometimes makes unnecessary such a generalization heuristic as eliminating destructors.

B.   Intelligent Generalization

The second generalization heuristic differs from the above one, and BMTP intentionally does not employ it because it requires "creative" insight (chap.XII in [4]). In the verification of Prolog programs, however, there are also some cases where, in proving an induction step goal, we cannot use its induction hypothesis because of *mismatching* with its conclusion. As an example of such a case, consider the proof of the following theorem.

theorem(*reverse-reverse*).
$\forall XY \; reverse(X, [\,], Y) \supset reverse(Y, [\,], X) \quad \cdots (G_0)$
end.

where program *reverse* is defined as follows :

$$reverse([\,], X, X).$$
$$reverse([A|X], Y, Z) :- reverse(X, [A|Y], Z).$$

First, we try to prove the above theorem by induction and the induction scheme in section III-B is generated for $list : X$, where $Q(X)$ is $\forall Y \, reverse(X, [\,], Y) \supset reverse(Y, [\,], X)$.

The proof of its base case, $Q([\,])$, is trivial. The proof of the induction step goal, however, is not easily performed

because of those underlined mismatched literals shown below :

[induction step] $(Q(X) \supset Q([A|X]))$

$$(reverse(X, [\,], ?Y_0) \supset reverse(?Y_0, [\,], X))$$
$$\supset (reverse([A|X], [\,], Y) \supset reverse(Y, [\,], [A|X]))$$
$$\Downarrow \text{ NFI for } reverse([A|X], [\,], Y)$$
$$(reverse(X, [\,], ?Y_0) \supset reverse(?Y_0, [\,], X))$$
$$\supset (\underline{reverse(X, [A], Y)} \supset reverse(Y, [\,], [A|X]))$$

Here, since we cannot apply simplification because of mismatching between "$[\,]$" and "$[A]$" in the above underlined parts, there is no way to use the induction hypothesis. These "phenomena" often happen to the verification of Prolog programs containing a "accumulator" [6] like the second argument of *reverse*, which, though they make the computation linear order, cause at the same time mismatching between an induction hypothesis and its conclusion. Hence, in order to solve these kinds of mismatching, it is necessary to incorporate some heuristics in order to generate a generalized goal. Our verification system generates the following goal mechanically :

theorem (*generalized reverse-reverse*).
$\forall XSMT \; reverse(X, S, M) \wedge reverse(S, X, T)$
$$\supset reverse(M, [\,], T) \qquad \cdots (G_{gen})$$
end.

We call such kind of generalization an "*intelligent generalization.*" It is easily known that the above theorem is actually a generalized goal of G_0 and its proof can be rather straightforwardly performed.

V.   INTELLIGENT GENERALIZATION HEURISTIC

In this section, we state how the intelligent generalization heuristic is applied to the proof of an induction step goal and give the intelligent generalization scheme which mechanically generates its generalized goal. We then go on to show that its scheme is also effective for flawed induction schemes [4].

A.   Intelligent Generalization Scheme

At first, for ease of understanding, we illustrate the intelligent generalization heuristic by using the previous example.

$$(reverse(X, [\,], ?Y_0) \supset reverse(?Y_0, [\,], X))$$
$$\supset (\underline{reverse(X, [A], Y)} \supset reverse(Y, [\,], [A|X]))$$

The first step of intelligent generalization is to find those *mismatching arguments* which make it impossible to use the induction hypothesis. In the above example, those mismatching arguments are "$[\,]$" and "$[A]$" in $reverse(X, [\,], ?Y_0)$ and $reverse(X, [A], Y)$, respectively.

Next, we replace the mismatching arguments in the induction conclusion by new variables. In the above, "$[A]$" is replaced by a new variable, say, T. We call those variables contained in the mismatching arguments "*mismatching variables,*" and those arguments in the induction conclusion which contain mismatching variables are called "*arguments relating to mismatching.*" In this case, "A" is a mismatching variable and "$[A|X]$" is an argument relating to mismatching. These arguments relating to mismatching are also replaced by new distinct variables. In this case, we replace "$[A|X]$" by a new variable, say, U, and the induction conclusion becomes the following formula :

$$\forall XYTU\ reverse(X,T,Y) \supset reverse(Y,[\ ],U) \quad \cdots (G_1).$$

Clearly, the above goal G_1 is not a correct specification but an "over-generalized" goal of the original theorem G_0, and an appropriate constraint condition should be imposed on G_1 in order to obtain a correct generalized goal. Hence, we assume some "*constraint relation*" between freshly introduced variables and those variables which appear in arguments relating to mismatching. In this case, a constraint relation, say, $\mathcal{R}(T,X,U)$, is imposed, because T and U are newly introduced variables and X is a variable which appears in the argument relating to mismatching, i.e., $[A|X]$. We assume the following goal as a generalized goal of the original one :

$$reverse(X,T,Y) \wedge \mathcal{R}(T,X,U) \supset reverse(Y,[\ ],U) \quad \cdots (G_2),$$

where $\mathcal{R}(T,X,U)$ is some relation whose precise form is not determined yet ; and we call such a goal that contains an unspecified relation a "*temporary goal.*"

The third step is to infer the constraint relation mentioned above. Our current system infers such a relation from the following two conditions. The first inferring condition is called a "*generalization condition,*" which is a necessary condition for a temporary goal to be actually a generalized goal of the original one. In this case, by comparing G_0 and G_2, it follows that X equals U when T is $[\ ]$, which imposes the following constraint on $\mathcal{R}(T,X,U)$:

$$\mathcal{R}([\ ],X,X). \quad \cdots (CR_1)$$

The second inferring condition is that derived from "*pseudo verification,*" which means that we apply the inference rule mentioned in section III to the temporary goal. For example, if we apply induction on G_2, we get the following verification process for the induction step : $\forall AX\ P(X) \supset P([A|X])$, where $P(X)$ is :
$\forall YTU\ reverse(X,T,Y) \wedge \mathcal{R}(T,X,U) \supset reverse(Y,[\ ],U)$.

$(reverse(X,?T_0,?Y_0) \wedge \mathcal{R}(?T_0,X,?U_0) \supset reverse(?Y_0,[\ ],?U_0))$
$\supset (reverse([A|X],T,Y) \wedge \mathcal{R}(T,[A|X],U) \supset reverse(Y,[\ ],U))$
$\Downarrow$ NFI for $reverse([A|X],T,Y)$
$(reverse(X,?T_0,?Y_0) \wedge \mathcal{R}(?T_0,X,?U_0) \supset reverse(?Y_0,[\ ],?U_0))$
$\supset (reverse(X,[A|T],Y) \wedge \mathcal{R}(T,[A|X],U) \supset reverse(Y,[\ ],U))$
$\Downarrow$ simplification w.r.t
$\Downarrow \quad reverse(X,?T_0,?Y_0)$ and $reverse(X,[A|T],Y)$
$(\mathcal{R}([A|T],X,?U_0) \supset reverse(Y,[\ ],?U_0))$
$\supset (\mathcal{R}(T,[A|X],U) \supset reverse(Y,[\ ],U))$
$\Downarrow$ simplification w.r.t
$\Downarrow \quad reverse(Y,[\ ],?U_0)$ and $reverse(Y,[\ ],U)$
$\mathcal{R}(T,[A|X],U) \supset \mathcal{R}([A|T],X,U). \quad \cdots (CR_2)$

Similarly, as for the base case of the induction scheme for $P(X)$, we obtain the following constraint relation :

$$\mathcal{R}(Y,[\ ],U) \supset reverse(Y,[\ ],U). \quad \cdots (CR_3)$$

Then, from these constraint relations, (CR_1), (CR_2) and (CR_3), we try to identify the unknown relation $\mathcal{R}(T,X,U)$. Our verification system searches for an already defined Prolog

program which satisfies those constraint relations. Actually, we rewrite those constraint relations into formulas in Horn clauses ;

$$\mathcal{R}([\ ],X,X). \quad \cdots (CR_1^*)$$
$$\mathcal{R}([A|T],X,U) :\text{-}\ \mathcal{R}(T,[A|X],U). \quad \cdots (CR_2^*)$$
$$reverse(Y,[\ ],U) :\text{-}\ \mathcal{R}(Y,[\ ],U). \quad \cdots (CR_3^*),$$

and then find a definite clause which can be "unified" with those (CR_i^*)'s whose heads are the unknown constraint relation. If there are no such clauses defined in the system, we consider all the permutations of the arguments of the constraint relation. That is, for example in this case, we consider all the permutations of $\{T,X,U\}$ and check each case for $\mathcal{R}(T,U,X)$, $\mathcal{R}(U,T,X)$, $\mathcal{R}(U,X,T)$, etc. In the above example, from (CR_1^*) and (CR_2^*), we can find that

$$\mathcal{R}(T,X,U) \equiv reverse(T,X,U), \quad \cdots (G_3)$$

and it is easily confirmed to satisfy (CR_3). From G_2 and G_3, we finally obtain the generalized goal G_{gen} mentioned in section IV-B.

To sum up, the intelligent generalization scheme consists of the following 4 steps :

(1) Find out mismatching arguments in literals to which the induction has been applied.
(2) Replace those arguments relating to the mismatching by new variables in the induction conclusion (and obtain an "over-generalized goal").
(3) On the over-generalized goal, impose an appropriate constraint relation by generalization condition and by the pseudo verification.
(4) From the restrictions derived in (3), infer the constraint relation.

As for the inference method in step (4) above, our current implementation deals only with those constraint relations which can be reduced into Horn clauses as mentioned in the examples.

B. Application to Flawed Induction Schemes

The application of the intelligent generalization scheme is not restricted to the above-mentioned proofs, but it is sometimes effective also for a "flawed" induction scheme [4]. For example, consider the following example which is a corollary of the associativity of *append*.

theorem(*corollary-of-append-associativity*)
$\forall XDR\ append(X,X,D) \wedge append(X,D,R) \supset append(D,X,R)$
end.

From the definition of *append*, we note that the predicate $append(X,Y,Z)$ recursively changes its first and third argument and leaves its second argument fixed. If we use the terminology of BMTP, the first and third arguments are *changing variables* and the second argument is an *unchanging variable*. The above example shows a case where an induction scheme suggested by an atom and another induction scheme suggested by a different atom, are mutually flawed. That is, the induction scheme suggested by $append(X,D,R)$ recursively changes X, which is an unchanging variable in

$append(D, X, R)$, while the induction scheme suggested by $append(D, X, R)$ recursively changes D, which is an unchanging variable in $append(X, D, R)$ (and note that the induction scheme suggested by $append(X, X, D)$ is flawed by itself).

In this case, our intelligent generalization scheme generates the following generalized goal :

$$append(X, V, D) \wedge append(X, U, R) \wedge append(V, V, U)$$
$$\supset append(D, V, R),$$

where $append(V, V, U)$ is a constraint relation obtained ; we know that the above goal is easily proved by an "unflawed" induction.

VI. CONCLUDING REMARKS & RELATED WORK

This paper has shown how generalization heuristics are incorporated into the verification system of Prolog programs. Two kinds of generalization, mechanical generalization and intelligent generalization, are discussed. We have shown that the mechanical generalization used in BMTP can be performed by simplification in our verification system, as well as in the case of cross-fertilization. To the intelligent generalization heuristic we have given a generalization scheme which is naturally incorporated into our inference system of the extended-execution style, and which has proved to be effective also for flawed induction schemes.

We owe our heuristics to BMTP and other related work by Moore [6] and Aubin [7], although there is a difference in target languages and deduction methods. As for the inferring constraint relation mentioned in section V, we find some relevance to Shapiro's [15] Model Inference System which is a general theory to infer a Prolog predicate satisfying given facts. Our intelligent generalization scheme differs in that it gives a Prolog predicate some constraint relations to be satisfied.

The generalization heuristics presented here have been examined by numerous hand proofs and their first versions have been implemented in DEC-10 Prolog on DEC-2060 as one of the heuristics of our verification system for Prolog programs. We intend to implement our verification system on PSI [16] as a basis for "Intelligent Programming Environment" for Prolog programming on which we can perform various kinds of experiments such as program transformation and synthesis.

Acknowledgments

The author appreciates K. Fuchi(Director of ICOT) , K. Furukawa (Chief of ICOT 2nd Laboratory) and T. Yokoi(Chief of ICOT 3rd Laboratory) for the chance of doing this research. He is greatly indebted to T. Kanamori for valuable comments, especially on the extended execution. He would also like to thank A. Fusaoka, H. Fujita and K. Suzuki for their useful discussions and help.

References

[1] Furukawa, K. and T. Yokoi, "Basic Software System" In Proc. FGCS-84. Tokyo, Japan, November, 1984, pp. 37-57.

[2] Bowen, K. A. "Programming with Full First-Order Logic" In Machine Intelligence 10 (1982) 421-440.

[3] Kanamori, T. "Verification of Prolog programs Using an Extension of Execution," ICOT Technical Report, TR-096, 1984.

[4] Boyer, R. S. and J. S. Moore. Computational Logic, New York: Academic Press, 1979.

[5] Kanamori, T. et al. "Formulation of Induction Formulas in Verification of Prolog Programs," ICOT Technical Report, TR-094,1984.

[6] Moore, J. S., "Introducing iteration into the pure LISP theorem prover." IEEE Trans. Software Eng. 1:3 (1975) 328-338 .

[7] Aubin, R. "Some Generalization Heuristics in Proofs by Induction" In Proc. IRIA Colloq. on Proving and Improving Programs. Arc et Senans, France, July, 1975, pp. 197-208.

[8] Pereira, L. M., F. C. Pereira and D. H. Warren "User's Guide to DECsystem-10 PROLOG," Techical Report, Univ. of Edinburgh, September 1978.

[9] Prawitz, D. Natural Deduction, A Proof-Theoretical-Study Stockholm: Almqvist & Wiksell, 1965.

[10] Murray, N. V., "Completely Non-Clausal Theorem Proving", Artificial Intelligence, 18:1 (1982) 67-85.

[11] Clark, K. L. "Negation as Failure" In Logic and Database, Gallaire. H and J. Minker. Eds., (1978) 293-322.

[12] Clark, K. L. and S-Å. Tärnlund "A First Order Theory of Data and Programs" In IFIP-77. Toronto, Canada, August, 1977, pp. 939-944.

[13] Clark, K. L. "Predicate Logic as a Computational Formalism," Technical Report 59, Imperial College, December 1979.

[14] Stering, L. and A. Bundy "Meta-Level Inference and Program Verification" In 6th Conf. on Automated Deduction. Lecture Notes in Computer Science 138, 1982, pp. 144-150.

[15] Shapiro, E. Y. "An Algorithm that Infers Theories from Facts" In Proc. IJCAI-81. Vancouver, Canada, August, 1981, pp. 446-451.

[16] Yokoi, T., S. Uchida, et al. "Sequential Inference Machine : SIM" In Proc. FGCS-84. Tokyo, Japan, November, 1984, pp. 70-81.

A Logic Programming and Verification System
for Recursive Quantificational Logic

Frank M. Brown

Dept. of Computer Science
The University of Kansas
Lawrence, Kansas 66045

Peiya Liu

Dept. of Computer Sciences
The University of Texas
Austin, Tx 78713

ABSTRACT

In this paper, we describe a logic programming and program verification system which is based on quantifier elimination techniques and axiomatization rather than on more common method of doing logic programming using the Herbrand-Prawitz-Robinson unification algorithm without occur-check.

This system is shown to have interesting properties for logic programming and includes a number of advanced features. Among these features are user-defined data objects, user-defined recursive relations and functions, either of which may involve quantifiers in the body of their definitions, and automatic termination and consistency checking for recursively defined concept. In addition, it has a correct implementation of negation in contrast to PROLOG implementation of negation as failure, a smooth interaction between LISP-like functions and PROLOG-like relations, and a smooth interaction between specifications and programs. Finally, it provides a method of mathematical induction applicable to recursive definitions involving quantifiers.

I. INTRODUCTION

Quantified Computational Logic(QCL) is a programming and program verification language for programs written in recursive quantificational logic. The language can be used both for logic programming and program specification.

A QCL program consists of sequences of recursively defined data objects declarations and recursive quantificational logic function definitions. Programs written in QCL are both executed and verified by a single automatic deduction system called the symbolic evaluator using a system of axioms and rules called the symmetric logic. The essence of the symmetric logic technique is to push quantifiers to the lowest scope possible in the hope of finding a way to eliminate them. The symbolic evaluator and the symmetric logic are described in detail[Brown 83].

A prototype system for QCL has been implemented in Interlisp.

II. QCL PROGRAMMING

A. Recursively Defined Data Objects

Although many logic programming languages provide system-defined data objects, they provide only a poor capability for user-defined data objects. QCL adopts the shell principle[Boyer&Moore 79] as a method to recursively define some useful user-defined data objects. Since the shell principle was invented, not much attention has been paid to it in logic programming. However, it is very valuable in modelling logic programs and verifying logic programs. Although many of the axioms produced by the shell principle of QCL are similar to those described in[Boyer&Moore 79], some are quite different in order to satisfy the **fundamental deduction principle** described in[Brown 83]. This principle requires that almost all steps in the automatic deduction should take place by a method of replacing expressions by an equivalent but simpler expressions.

The syntax of user-defined data object is: **(SHELLCREATE constructor bottom recognizer selectors types defaults).** The constructor is a name of new function which constructs objects of the new types. The bottom is the bottom object or T if there is no bottom object. The recognizer is a name of new function which recognizes objects of the new type. The selectors are a list of functions which are accessors of the data structure. The types are a list of type restrictions on each shell. Each restriction is an arbitrary formula in QCL consisting of symbols defined at time. The defaults are a list of the default values for each shell. Data objects are easily declared. For examples, Lists are produced by the declaration (SHELLCREATE 'CONS 'T 'LISTP '(CAR CDR) '(T T) '(NIL NIL)) and Trees are produced by the declaration (SHELLCREATE 'TREE 'BTM 'TREEP '(LEFT ROOT RIGHT) '(T T T) '(0 0 0)).

B. A Safe Definition Principle

Most existing logic programming languages have syntax checking but few perform **logic checking** for properties such as **termination** and **consistency**. Suppose P is a logic program and R is a goal we wish to solve. Then, executing P to solve R is the same as deducing R from P in logic program execution. Therefore, any answer will be correct if the logic program P consists of inconsistent logic statements. But the user might get one of the answers because of deduction strategy. Thus user forces his program to produce some answer. QCL on the other hand has logic protection capability to detect inconsistent or non-terminating statements in logic programs. In addition, it stores vital verification information during the checking.

S is a **term** if it is a variable, a sequence of a function symbol of n arguments followed by n terms, or a sequence of a universal quantifier ALL or existential quantifier EX of m+1 arguments followed by a variable and m terms. A variable is **free** in the term if at least an occurrence of it is not within the scope of a quantifier employing the variable. Note that our definition of term is not standard in classical first order logic. QCL intends to blur the distinction between the predicates and functions. And a term t **governs** an occurrence of term s if either there is a subterm (IF t p q) and the occurrence of s is in p, or (IF t' p q) and the occurrence of s in q, where t is (NOT t'). (ALL_LIST $(x_1 \ldots x_n)$ p) is an abbreviation for (ALL x_1(ALL x_2(... (ALL x_n p)))), (EX_LIST$(x_1 \ldots x_n)$ p) for (EX x_1(EX x_2(...(EX x_n p)))) and (ALL_EX$_i$ $(x_1 \ldots x_n)$ p) for a specific n mixed quantifiers over p, its negated form (EX_ALL$_i$$(x_1 \ldots x_n)$(NOT p)).

Formally speaking, a safe definition principle is: **(DEFLQ (EQUAL(f x_1 ... x_n) body)), where**

(A) f is a new function symbol of n arguments.

(B) $x_1, ..., x_n$ are distinct variables.

(C) body is a term and only mentions free variable symbols in $x_1 ... x_n$.

(D) There is a well-founded relation r and a measure function m of n arguments.

(E) For each occurrence of a subterm of the form (f y_1 ... y_n) in the body, the governing terms $t_1 ... t_k$ and the governing variables which are the free variables $z_1 ... z_j$ in the governing terms and (f y_1 ... y_n) but not in $x_1 ... x_n$, it is a theorem that

(ALL_LIST $(x_1 ... x_n)$(ALL_LIST $(z_1 ... z_j)$
(IMPLIES(AND $t_1 ... t_k$)
(r $(m y_1 ... y_n)(m x_1 ... x_n)$))))).

The definition principle is shown by proving that the axiom constitutes a recursive definition of some concept. An axiom of the form:(f x_1 ... x_n)=body can be shown to be recursive if according to some measure M the complexity of the arguments of any occurrence of f in the body, assuming the hypotheses governing f in the body, is less than the complexity of x_1 ... x_n.

Some examples:
```
(DEFLQ                    (DEFLQ
(EQUAL(AND X Y)             (EQUAL(NOT X)
  (IF X                      (IF X
     Y                          NIL
     NIL)))                     T))
```

NIL is considered as false and T denotes true. The function IF is a primitive operator. Informally speaking, if X is NIL, then (IF X Y Z) is equal to Z. and if X is not NIL, then (IF X Y Z) is equal to Y.

```
(DEFLQ                    (DEFLQ
(EQUAL(ADJ X Y)            (EQUAL(ADJDL X Z)
  (IF(LISTP X)              (IF(EQUAL X Z)
    (IF(ADJW(CAR X))          T
      (EQUAL Y(CDR X))        (EX Y(IF(ADJ X Y)
      NIL)                       (ADJDL Y Z)
    NIL)))                      NIL)))))
```

The (ADJDL X Z) says that two things X and Y make an adjective difference list if two things are identical or there is an adjective (ADJ X Y) followed by an adjective difference list (ADJDL Y Z). The defining equation for ADJDL is added to our theory by the following instantiation of definition principle: f is the function symbol ADJDL; n is 2; x_1 is X and x_2 is Z; body is the term (IF(EQUAL X Z) T(EX Y(IF(ADJ X Y)(ADJDL Y Z) NIL))); r is PLESSP; m is the function symbol LENGTH1, where (LENGTH1 X Y) is defined to be (LENGTH X); governing terms are (NOT(EQUAL X Z)) and (ADJ X Y); a governing variable is Y. One theorem required by (E) is: (ALL X(ALL Z(ALL Y(IMPLIES(AND(NOT(EQUAL X Z))(ADJ X Y)) (PLESSP(LENGTH1 Y Z)(LENGTH1 X Z)))))))). The above theorem can be proved from definitions ADJ and LENGTH1.

```
(DEFLQ
(EQUAL(DIFFL X Z A)
  (IF(EQUAL X Z)
    (EQUAL A NIL)
```

```
    (IF(LISTP X)
      (EX B(IF (EQUAL A(CONS(CAR X) B))
         (DIFFL (CDR X) Z B)
         NIL))
      NIL)))
)
```

(DIFFL X Z A) follows the recursive definition principle because (ALL X(ALL Z(ALL A(ALL B(IMPLIES (AND(NOT(EQUAL X Z))(LISTP X)) (PLESSP(LENGTH2 (CDR X) Z B)(LENGTH2 X Z A))))))) is a theorem. (LENGTH2 X Y Z) is defined to be (LENGTH X).

```
(DEFLQ                    (DEFLQ
(EQUAL(ADJL A)             (EQUAL(ADJDIFFL X Z)
  (IF(LISTP A)              (EX A(IF(DIFFL X Z A)
    (IF(ADJW(CAR A))           (ADJL A)
      (ADJL(CDR A))            NIL))))
      NIL)
    (EQUAL A NIL))))
```

(ADJL A) is recursive because (ALL A(IMPLIES(LISTP A)(PLESSP(LENGTH (CDR A))(LENGTH A))) is a theorem.

The principle of definition for this advanced programming language extends previous research[Boyer&Moore 79] in the following ways: The first way is that existential and universal quantifiers are allowed in the body of the defining equation. The second way is that the measured arguments of the recursive calls of a function are not necessarily some function of the formal parameters, but may simply be related to them by an arbitrary relation. For example, ADJDL is recursive because the ADJ relation makes Y smaller than X. In this case there is no obvious selector function car or cdr which, when applied to (ADJDL X Z), results in (ADJDL Y Z).

Theorem D There is a unique total function satisfying the recursive defining equation (f x_1 ... x_n)=body.

Proof: The details are shown in [Brown&Liu 84].

Thus, system guarantees consistency and termination for each new defined function.

C. Relationship to Horn Clauses

In Prolog and some other logic programming languages, Horn clauses are the main type of logic statements. Based on the closed world assumption[Reiter 78], QCL can easily translate these clauses into the quantified IF-form formulas. Thus Horn clauses are essentially a subset of QCL. For example, the following Horn clause style definition of ADJL is automatically translated to the above definition of ADJL.

(ADJL NIL) <-
(ADJL (CONS A1 A)) <- (ADJW A1)(ADJL A).

II. FEATURES OF QCL PROGRAMMING SYSTEM

A. Combining Programming with Verification System

QCL mixes programming and verification system in the natural manner. The output form of the command (PV r), which might **compute** or **prove** relations and functions, should be equivalent to the original expression. The meaning of (PV r)=output_form is (ALL_LIST $(x_1$ ... x_n) r=output_form) if r has n free variables. Otherwise, r= output_form.

The command (PV r) asks the system to generate any n-tuples satisfying the relationship r, where r contains n free variables. The command (PV r) may also be used to ask system to make deduction from the relation in the case that r has no free variables. The command simply tries to prove r. Usually, the output form is true, false, its equivalent but simplified form or a conjunctive form of some equalities and inequalities about remaining arguments and their binding values.

The deduction techniques of PV are based on the fundamental deduction principle, which makes it possible that QCL logic programming interpreter is the same as its verification system interpreter.

B. Explanation Capability

It is worthwhile embedding an explanation capability inside an automated reasoning system. Currently, the system can produce all tracing information whenever a rule, axiom, or definition is applied. This information consists of three parts: an input expression I which is being evaluated, an intermediate expression M and a name of rule which produces M from I, an output expression O obtained by recursively evaluating the M expressions. Thus a trace will generally be of the form:

I1:exp
> by use of: a name of rule, axiom or definition.

M1:exp
> I2:exp
> > by use of: ...

> M2:exp

> ....

> O2:exp

O1:exp

where the number immediately following I, M, or O is the level at which the application of an rule, axiom, or definition takes place. At a given level number i, O_i and M_i are always associated with the preceding I_i.

The debugging principle is this: if I_i does not equal to M_i, then the definition, axiom or rule used in that application is incorrect. if M_i does not equal O_i then one must recursively examine the i+1 level(ie. I_{i+1}, M_{i+1}, O_{i+1}) to find the error.

C. Negation Is Not A Failure

The negation-as-failure rule is an operational connection between negative and positive terms. The soundness and completeness of a restricted form has been shown in [Clark 78][Jaffar 83]. There are still some fundamental limitations on that rule if there is no **logical connection** between them. The following program uses negation-as-failure to define a term (NDIFFL X Y Z), which is supposed to be equivalent to (NOT(DIFFL X Y Z)). The cut symbol "/" makes a commitment for all subgoals since the parent goal. Hence any attempt to resatisfy any previous subgoal will fail. NIL is a predicate defined in such a way that as a goal it always fails and causes backtracking to take place. But when NIL is encountered after cut, the normal backtracking behavior will be altered by the cut and will cause the effect that whenever (DIFFL X Y Z) is successful, (NDIFFL X Y Z) is failed.

(DIFFL X X NIL)<-
(DIFFL(CONS X1 X)Z(CONS X1 A))<-(DIFFL X Z A)
(NDIFFL X Y Z)<-(DIFFL X Y Z)/NIL
(NDIFFL X Y Z)<-

A correct answer can be deduced by failing with NIL or rather false on the query (NDIFFL '(LARGE MANY) '(MANY) '(LARGE)). But it also returns a failure on the following question which is true for any Z not equal to MANY: (NDIFFL

'(LARGE MANY) Z '(LARGE)). This relation involves a variable Z in the NDIFFL. In general, the rule is not complete and has to restrict its queries and either deduction strategy or program statements in order to work[Clark 78]. The negative query is often restricted to the ground term. Thus, much negative information simply can't be queried.

Even worse, it should be noted that the above set of clauses are inconsistent if (NDIFFL X Y Z) really is (NOT(DIFFL X Y Z)). QCL takes a logically correct approach towards handling negative information. Any negative term (NOT tm) is defined as the term (IF tm NIL T) by system. If DIFFL is defined as before, (PV (NOT(DIFFL'(LARGE MANY) Z '(LARGE))) will result (IF (EQUAL Z '(MANY)) NIL T). This means that answer is any Z which is not equal to '(MANY). The details of computing this relation are given as follows:

Example A:
(PV (NOT(DIFFL '(LARGE MANY) Z '(LARGE))))
The expression to be recursively simplified is:
(NOT (DIFFL (QUOTE (LARGE MANY))
        Z
        (QUOTE (LARGE))))
I1:(DIFFL (QUOTE (LARGE MANY))
      Z
      (QUOTE (LARGE)))
    by use of: DIFFL
M1:(IF (EQUAL (QUOTE (LARGE MANY))
          Z)
      (EQUAL (QUOTE (LARGE))
          NIL)
      (IF (LISTP (QUOTE (LARGE MANY)))
        (EX *1 (IF (EQUAL (QUOTE (LARGE))
                (CONS (CAR (QUOTE (LARGE MANY)))
                  *1))
            (DIFFL (CDR (QUOTE (LARGE MANY)))
              Z *1)
            NIL))
        NIL))
  I2:(DIFFL (QUOTE (MANY))
        Z NIL)
      by use of: DIFFL
  M2:(IF (EQUAL (QUOTE (MANY))
            Z)
        (EQUAL NIL NIL)
        (IF (LISTP (QUOTE (MANY)))
          (EX *2 (IF (EQUAL NIL
                  (CONS (CAR (QUOTE (MANY)))
                    *2))
              (DIFFL (CDR (QUOTE (MANY)))
                Z *2)
              NIL))
          NIL))
  O2:(EQUAL (QUOTE (MANY))
        Z)
O1:(EQUAL (QUOTE (MANY))
      Z)

The result of recursive simplification is:
(IF (EQUAL (QUOTE (MANY))
      Z)
  NIL T)
end of deduction

Input I2 is due to variable *1 in M1 being replaced by NIL under the if-condition (EQUAL '(LARGE)(CONS(CAR '(LARGE MANY)) *1)).

Example B:
(PV (DIFFL '(LARGE MANY) Z '(LARGE)))
The expression to be recursively simplified is:
(DIFFL (QUOTE (LARGE MANY))
       Z
       (QUOTE (LARGE)))
I1:(DIFFL (QUOTE (LARGE MANY))
        Z
        (QUOTE (LARGE)))
   by use of: DIFFL
   M1:(IF (EQUAL (QUOTE (LARGE MANY))
               Z)
          (EQUAL (QUOTE (LARGE))
               NIL)
          (IF (LISTP (QUOTE (LARGE MANY)))
              (EX *1 (IF (EQUAL (QUOTE (LARGE))
                             (CONS (CAR (QUOTE (LARGE MANY)))
                                   *1))
                         (DIFFL (CDR (QUOTE (LARGE MANY)))
                                Z *1)
                         NIL))
              NIL))
   I2:(DIFFL (QUOTE (MANY))
          Z NIL)
      by use of: DIFFL
      M2:(IF (EQUAL (QUOTE (MANY))
                  Z)
             (EQUAL NIL NIL)
             (IF (LISTP (QUOTE (MANY)))
                 (EX *2 (IF (EQUAL NIL
                                (CONS (CAR (QUOTE (MANY)))
                                      *2))
                            (DIFFL (CDR (QUOTE (MANY)))
                                   Z *2)
                            NIL))
                 NIL))
      O2:(EQUAL (QUOTE (MANY))
                Z)
   O1:(EQUAL (QUOTE (MANY))
             Z)

The result of recursive simplification is:
(EQUAL (QUOTE (MANY))
       Z)
end of deduction

D. Relational vs. Functional

There are currently two really good ways of programming based on formal logic, namely: (1) programs based on recursive functions, such as the LISP. (2) programs based on NON-NEGATIVE recursive relations, such as HCPRVR and PROLOG.

QCL takes a different approach from LOGLISP[Robinson 82], QUTE[Sato 83] and TABLOG[Malachi 84]towards combining these two formalisms. Our concern focuses on the unique formalism and a smooth interaction between relations and functions.

Each type of programming system, of course, has many additional features (eg. assignment statements, goto's etc.), but it is the logical features: **recursive functions** or **recursive relations** which make it so easy to express, understand, and debug programs written in these systems. Some programs are more easily expressed, understood, and debugged as functions than relations and vice-versa. In particular combinations of **deterministic** programs returning unique outputs should be written as functions. For example, to APPEND the

REVERSE of a list A onto the result of APPENDing the REVERSE of a list B onto the REVERSE of a list C is written as functions as: (APPEND (REVERSE A) (APPEND (REVERSE B) (REVERSE C))) whereas it is rewritten as relations with many extra symbols as:

(EX X1(EX X2(EX X3(EX X4(AND(REVERSE A X1)
            (REVERSE B X2)
            (REVERSE C X3)
            (APPEND X2 X3 X4)
            (APPEND X1 X4 ANSW))))))

X1,X2,and X3 are respectively the results of reversing A, B, and C, X4 is the result of appending X2 to X3, and the answer: ANSW is the result of appending X1 to X4. In such a case the lack of nesting in relational notation makes it resemble assembler notation (where the variables are registers and the assembler operations are REVERSE and APPEND) rather than a high level language.

On the other hand, combinations of **non-deterministic** programs are more naturally expressed as relations. For example, a program which parses English(and translates it into another language) is naturally made up of a number of non-deterministic programs. The definition of a declarative transitive sentence is easily written in relational notation as:

(EX X1(EX X2(EX X3(AND(NP I1 I2 X1)
            (VG I2 I3 X2)
            (NP I3 I4 X3)
            (COMBINE X1 X2 X3 ANSW)))))

where I1 is the input text, I2 is the rest of the text after a noun phrase is parsed, I3 is the rest of the text of I2 after a verb group is parsed, I4 is any remaining unparsed text, X1 is the translation of the first noun phrase, X2 is the translation of the verb group, X3 is the translation of the second noun phrase, and ANSW is the translation of the entire sentence. Such a program can not be rewritten in functional notation as: (COMBINE(NP I1 I2)(VG I2 I3)(NP I3 I4)) because the NP and VG relations are not deterministic on their third arguments. For example, there may be many different parses of the the first noun phrase each giving a different answer. Furthermore, I2 is another non-deterministic output of (NP I1 I2) which must be passed an input to (VG I2 I3). Likewise, if insisting on functional notation, an assembly-like program can not be avoided.

These considerations also apply to advanced database technology. Data can be represented relationally as in relational databases [Codd 72] or functionally. For example, a request for the salary of the president of the university of the largest state in the united states could be written as:

(EX X1(EX X2(EX X3
(AND(LARGEST_STATE_OF(UNITED_STATES) X1)
     (UNIVERSITY_OF X1 X2)
     (PRESIDENT_OF X2 X3)
     (SALARY_OF X3 ANSW)))))

However, it can be written in the simpler functional notation as: (SALARY_OF (PRESIDENT_OF (UNIVERSITY_OF (LARGEST_STATE_OF (UNITED_STATES)))))) because each of these predicates is deterministic on its last argument. On the other hand, in an example with non-deterministic outputs, the relational representation is better.

Two distinct programming systems have been developed based on formal logical notation(recursive functions, recursive relations) and each is especially useful for representing a particular type of programs(deterministic and non-deterministic). Furthermore, the more facilities of formal logic that are provided in a programming system, the less one needs to use constructs such as GOTO and assignment which are harder to use, understand and debug. Therefore, it follows that a significantly better programming system could be achieved by amalgamating these formal notations into a single formal system provided that effici...e interpreted and/or compiled inference systems could be designed.

E. Specification vs. Program

In QCL, specifications and programs are considered as different styles to express logic expressions for their own purposes within the same framework. Specifications are **descriptively useful** logic forms and their **computationally useful** forms are programs.

We believe that automatic derivation, verification and synthesis of logic programs are made easier, provided that specifications and programs have a smooth interaction. Two important relationships between logic programs and their specifications are correctness and completeness. **Correctness** is a property that for any n-tuple x, if x is computed as a solution satisfying a relation R, then x belongs to the relation specified by S. It can be formalized as $\forall x(S\vdash R(x)\Leftarrow P\vdash R(x))$. **Completeness** is a property that for all members of the specified relation R are computable from program P. It can be represented as $\forall x(S\vdash R(x)\Rightarrow P\vdash R(x))$. One way to show these relationships is to use meta-level deduction to prove those formulas[Brown 78]. Another way is that, if finding a good specification S such that $S\vdash P$ or $P\vdash S$, we get same correctness proof or completeness proof by exploiting the transitivity of logical implication $\vdash$.

The second approach is the cornerstone of logic program derivation, verification and synthesis investigated in[Clark 77][Hogger 81]. One advantage in this approach towards verification is that the object-level deduction from S to P or from P to S is sufficient to show their relationships without meta-level deduction and concerning goal relation R(x). Another advantage is that for proving any property of P, it may be much easier to show that S has that property and P is complete with respect to S. In the Hogger study, specifications expressed in "if-and-only-if" and "first-order recursive" styles are crucial in this approach. Since QCL intend to bring specifications and programs together, it provides a good opportunity to investigate good specifications and program styles in order to automate the derivation, synthesis, and verification of logic programs. For example,

```
(DEFLQ
(EQUAL(PICK.S U V Z)
    (IF(MEMBER.S U Z)
      (IF(MEMBER.S V Z)
        (PLESSP U V)
        NIL)
      NIL))
)
```

Informally stated, (PICK.S U V Z)=(MEMBER.S U Z)∧ (MEMBER.S V Z)∧(PLESSP U V).

```
(DEFLQ
(EQUAL(MEMBER.S U L)
(EX X(EX Y(IF(EQUAL L (CONS X Y)))
      (IF(EQUAL U X)
        T
        (MEMBER.S U Y))
      NIL))))
```

Informally, (MEMBER.S U L)=∃x∃y(L=(CONS x y)∧ (U=x∨(MEMBER.S U y))).

The specification S:{PICK.S MEMBER.S} is for the following program P:{PICK.P MEMBER.P}. It said to pick any two numbers U and V from a list Z of numbers, not necessarily distinct, such that U is less than V. The relationships can be shown by object-level deduction, that is, $S\vdash P$ and $P\vdash S$.

```
(DEFLQ
(EQUAL(PICK.P U V Z)
    (IF(LISTP Z))
      (IF(EQUAL U(CAR Z))
        (IF(MEMBER.P V (CDR Z))
          (PLESSP U V)
          NIL)
        (IF(EQUAL V(CAR Z))
          (IF(MEMBER.P U (CDR Z))
            (PLESSP U V)
            NIL)
          (PICK U V(CDDR Z))))
      NIL)
)
(DEFLQ
(EQUAL(MEMBER.P X L)
    (IF(LISTP L)
      (IF(EQUAL X (CAR L))
        T
        (MEMBER.P X (CDR L)))
      NIL))
)
```

IV. QCL VERIFICATION

A. A Generalized Noetherian Induction Principle

In logic programming verification, we often need induction to rearrange the conjecture into a systematic way to prove. The induction principle we use is a generalized version of Noetherian induction[Burstall 69][Boyer&Moore 79]. Existential and universal quantifiers are allowed both in the base case and in the induction steps.

Formally stated, the induction principle is:

Suppose:

(A) p is a term with t's distinct free variables x_1, $...,x_n,x_{n+1}, ...,x_t$;

(B) r is a well-founded relation;

(C) m is a measure function of n arguments;

(D) $b_1, ..., b_k$ are non-negative integers;

(E) For each i $1\leq i\leq k$, $z_{i,1}, ...,z_{i,b_i}$ are distinct bound variables;

(F) $q_1, ...,q_k$ are terms;

(G) $h_1, ...,h_k$ are positive integers; and

(H) For $1\leq i\leq k$ and $1\leq j\leq h_i$, $s_{i,j}$ is a substitution and it is a theorem that

$$\text{ALL\_LIST } (x_1 ... x_t)(\text{ALL\_LIST}(z_{i,1} ... z_{i,b_i})$$
$$(\text{IMPLIES } q_i$$
$$(r(m x_1 ... x_n)/s_{i,j}(m x_1 ... x_n))))).$$

Then

(I). (ALL_LIST $(x_1 \ldots x_t)$ p) is a theorem if

for the base case,
(ALL_LIST$(x_1 \ldots x_t)$
  (IMPLIES(AND(NOT(ALL_EX$_1(z_{1,1} \ldots z_{1,b_1})q_1$))

   ...,
   (NOT(ALL_EX$_k(z_{k,1} \ldots z_{k,b_k})q_k$)))
     p))
is a theorem **and**

for each $1\leq i\leq k$ induction step,
(ALL_LIST$(x_1 \ldots x_t)$
  (IMPLIES (ALL_EX$_i(z_{i,1} \ldots z_{i,b_i})$
    (AND q_i p/$s_{i,1} \ldots$ p/s_{i,h_i}))
      p))
is a theorem.

(II). (EX_LIST $(x_1 \ldots x_t)$ p) is a theorem if

for the base case,
(EX_LIST$(x_1 \ldots x_t)$
  (AND(AND(NOT(ALL_EX$_1(z_{1,1} \ldots z_{1,b_1})q_1$))

   ...,
   (NOT(ALL_EX$_k(z_{k,1} \ldots z_{k,b_k})q_k$)))
     p))
is a theorem **or**

for some $1\leq i\leq k$ induction step,
(EX_LIST$(x_1 \ldots x_t)$
  (AND (ALL_EX$_i(z_{i,1} \ldots z_{i,b_i})$
    (AND q_i (NOT p)/$s_{i,1} \ldots$(NOT p)/s_{i,h_i}))
      p))
is a theorem.

We adopted a Boyer&Moore's definition here before proving soundness of this induction principle. $<X1 \ldots Xn>$ is *RM-smaller* than $<Y1 \ldots Yn>$ if there is a measure function M and a well-founded relation R such that (R (M X1 ... Xn)(M Y1 ... Yn)).

Theorem I. Soundness for Universal Quantifiers Case
Proof:

Supposed there is a t-tuples $<X1, \ldots,Xt>$ such that (P X1 ... Xt)=NIL where (P X1 ... Xt) stands for p/s, s is substitution $\{<x1, X1> \ldots <xt, Xt>\}$. Let it be a RM-minimal such t-tuples.

Case I. Suppose
(NOT(ALL_EX$_1(z_{1,1} \ldots z_{1,b_1})$(Q1 X1 ... Xt)))$\neq$NIL
...,
and
(NOT(ALL_EX$_k(z_{k,1} \ldots z_{k,b_k})$(Qk X1 ... Xt)))$\neq$NIL,
where (Qi X1 ... Xt) is abbreviated for q_i/s, and s is a substitution $\{<x1, X1> \ldots <xt, Xt>\}$.

Then by base case, (P X1 ... Xt)$\neq$NIL contradicting the assumption that (P X1 ... Xt)=NIL.

Case II. Suppose

Some i (NOT(ALL_EX$_i(z_{i,1} \ldots z_{i,b_i})$(Qi X1 ... Xt)))=NIL, where (Qi X1 ... Xt) abbreviated for q_i/s, s is a substitution $\{<x1, X1> \ldots <xt, Xt>\}$.

Then (ALL_EX$_i(z_{i,1} \ldots z_{i,b_i})$(Qi X1 ... Xt))$\neq$NIL.

Since $<X1, \ldots,Xt>$ is an RM-minimal t-tuples such that (P X1 ... Xt)=NIL and condition (H), we have (ALL_EX$_i(z_{i,1} \ldots z_{i,b_i})$ (AND(Qi X1 ... Xt) (P $d_{i,1,1} \ldots d_{i,1,t}$) ... (P $d_{i,h_i,1} \ldots d_{i,h_i,t}$)))$\neq$NIL, where for each $1\leq v\leq t$, the substitution s_{i,h_i} replaces Xv with some $d_{i,h_i,v}$. But we know the ith induction step is a theorem. Hence, we get (P X1 ... Xt)$\neq$NIL, contradicting the assumption that (P X1 ... Xt)=NIL.

Q.E.D.

Theorem II. Soundness for Existential Quantifiers Case
Proof: Theorem II is only a symmetric case of Theorem I. Its validity is obvious after proving Theorem I.

Q.E.D.

An application of this induction principle is illustrated below. In the proof (PV (ALL X(ALL Z(EQUAL(ADJDL X Z)(EX A(AND(DIFFL X Z A) (ADJ A))))))), an induction is obtained by instantiation of the principle as follows: p is (EQUAL(ADJDL X Z) (EX A(AND(DIFFL X Z A)(ADJL A)))); r is PLESSP; m is LENGTH; n is 2; k is 1; b_1 is 1; $z_{1,1}$ is Y; h_1 is 1; q_1 is the term (AND (NOT(EQUAL X Z))(ADJ X Y)); the theorem required by (H) is: (ALL X(ALL Z(ALL Y(IMPLIES(AND (NOT(EQUAL X Z))(ADJ X Y))(PLESSP(LENGTH1 Y Z)(LENGTH1 X Z)))))). The induction is:

Base case :
(ALL X(ALL Z(IMPLIES(OR(EQUAL X Z)
              (NOT (EX Y(ADJ X Y))))
       (p X Z))))
Induction step:
(ALL X(ALL Z(IMPLIES(AND(NOT(EQUAL X Z))
              (EX Y(AND(ADJ X Y)
                 (p Y Z))))
       (p X Z))))

B. Induction Schemes and A Proof Example

The recursive first-order function definition suggests plausible induction schemes. Thus, the induction schemes for each of these recursive functions can now be produced. Suppose we try to prove two notions of adjective different list are equivalent, **(PV (ALL X(ALL Z(EQUAL(ADJDL X Z)(ADJDIFFL X Z)))).**

The mechanical proof of this conjecture begins by unraveling the non-recursive function ADJDIFFL and then examining the induction schemes for each recursive function.

(ALL X(ALL Z(EQUAL(ADJDL X Z) (EX A(AND(DIFFL X Z A)(ADJ A)))))) (by opening up the function ADJDIFFL)

The system examines the induction scheme for each recursive function.

The scheme for (ADJL A) is:
(EQUAL(ALL A(p A))
(AND(ALL A(IMPLIES(NOT(LISTP A))(p A)))
  (ALL A(IMPLIES(AND(LISTP A)(p (CDR A)))(p A)))))

The scheme for (DIFFL X Z A) is:
(EQUAL(ALL X(ALL Z(ALL A(p X Z A))))
(AND(ALL X(ALL Z(ALL A(IMPLIES(OR(NOT(LISTP X))
                 (NOT(EX B(EQUAL A(CONS(CAR X) B)))))
                 (p X Z A)))))
      (ALL X(ALL Z(ALL A(IMPLIES(AND(LISTP X)
                 (EX B(AND(EQUAL A(CONS(CAR X) B))
                 (p (CDR X) Z B)))))
                 (p X Z A)))))))

The scheme for (ADJDL X Z) is:
(EQUAL(ALL X(ALL Z(p X Z)))
(AND(ALL X(ALL Z(IMPLIES(OR(EQUAL X Z)
                 (NOT(EX Y(ADJ X Y))))
                 (p X Z))))
      (ALL X(ALL Z(IMPLIES(AND(NOT(EQUAL X Z))
                 (EX Y(AND(ADJ X Y)(p Y Z))))
                 (p X Z))))))

The induction scheme for (ADJL A) is ignored since it has a measured argument which is a bound variable. The induction scheme for (DIFFL X Z A) is subsumed by the induction scheme for (ADJDL X Z); so the ADJDL induction scheme is used. The system uses heuristics and follows the induction principle to split the original conjecture into two cases as above. The details of the mechanical proof are generated in [Brown&Liu 84].

V. CONCLUSIONS

A new logic programming language has been developed which is based on quantifier elimination techniques and axiomatization. Unlike other logic program systems, it does not involve any unification algorithm. This system handles a number of problems better than unification-based logic programming system. For example, this system allows the proper axiomatization of negation, a smooth interaction between functions and relations, and an ability to write specifications and to verify the correctness of programs using a generalized Noetherian induction rule. Also, it extends previous work in program verification to the problem verifying recursively defined relations whose definition bodies contain quantifiers.

ACKNOWLEDGEMENTS

The work described here has been supported in part by the Army Research Office under Grant DAAG 29-83-K-0103 and in part by the National Science Foundation under Grant DCR-8320340.

The authors would like to thank Prof. Norman Martin and Ruey-Juin Chang for their helpful comments to earlier drafts of this paper. Our thanks also go to the referees for their useful suggestions. Finally, we thank Ching-Hua Chow and Chin-Laung Lei for their tips on using text editor.

REFERENCES

1. Boyer, R.S., and J S. Moore, *A Computational Logic*, New York, Academic Press, 1979.
2. Brown, F.M., "Semantic theory for Logic Programming", *Coloquia Mathematica Society Janos Bolyai, 26 Mathematical Logic in Computer Science* , Salgotarjan, Hungary, 1978.
3. Brown, F.M., "Experimental Logic and the Automatic Analysis of Algorithms", *Proceedings of the Army Conference on Application of AI to Battlefield Information Management*, Maryland, 1983, pp 217-281. (To appear AI Journal).
4. Brown, F.M., and P. Liu, "Foundations of QCL Programming System" The University of Texas at Austin, Computer Science Department, Technical Report, May 1984.
5. Burstall, R. M., "Proving Properties of Programs by Structural Induction", *Computer Journal*, vol. 12, no. 1, February 1969.
6. Clark, K.L., "Negation as Failure" in *Logic and Databases*, eds. Gallarire, H.J. and J. Minker, Plenum Press, 1978.
7. Clark, K.L. and S. Stickel "Predicate Logic: A Calculus for Deriving Programs", *IJCAI-77*.
8. Codd, E.F. "Relational Completeness of Data Base Sublanguages", *Data Base Systems* ed. R. Rustin, Prentice-Hall, 1972.
9. Hogger, C.J. "Derivation of Logic Programs", *JACM* Vol.28, No.2, April 1981.
10. Jaffar, J. Lassez, and J. Lloyd, "Completeness of the Negation as Failure Rule", *IJCAI-83*, pp 500-506.
11. Malachi, Y., Manna, Z., and Waldinger, R., "TABLOG: The Deductive-Tableau Programming Language", *Proceedings of 1984 Lisp and Functional Programming Conference*, Austin, Texas, pp 323-330.
12. Reiter, R., "On Closed World Data Bases" in *Logic and Databases*, eds. Gallarire, H.J. and J. Minker, Plenum Press, 1978.
13. Robinson, J.A. and E.E. Sibert, "LOGLISP: An Alternative to Prolog", *Machine Intelligence 10*, 1982.
14. Sato, M. and T. Sakurai, "QUTE: A Prolog/Lisp Type Language for Logic Programming", *IJCAI-83*, pp 508-513.

A NEW KIND OF FINITE-STATE AUTOMATON:
REGISTER VECTOR GRAMMAR

Glenn David Blank

Lehigh University
CSEE Department
Packard Lab 19
Bethlehem, PA 18015

ABSTRACT

Register Vector Grammar is a new kind of finite-state automaton that is sensitive to context--without, of course, being context-sensitive in the sense of Chomsky hierarchy. Traditional automata are functionally simple: symbols match by identity and change by replacement. RVG is functionally complex: ternary feature vectors (e.g. +-±+-±+) match and change by **masking** (± matches but does not change any value). Functional complexity--as opposed to the computational complexity of non-finite memory--is well suited for modelling multiple and discontinuous constraints. RVG is thus very good at handling the permutations and dependencies of syntax (wh-questions are explored as example). Because center-embedding in natural languages is in fact very shallow and constrained, context-free power is not needed. RVG can thus be guaranteed to run in a small linear time, because it is FS, and yet can capture generalizations and constraints that functionally simple FS grammars cannot.

I INTRODUCTION

Lately there has been considerable impetus among natural language researchers to restrict the computational complexity required by an adequate theory (cf. Gazdar 1981, Church 1982, Langendoen 1984). Whereas FS languages guarantee linear recognition time, those calling for more computational power give rise to a combinatorial explosion with respect to worst recognition time. Certainly, were there no other factors (such as those mentioned by Berwick and Weinberg 1982, Perrault 1983, Pullum 1983 and 1984), grammars with less computational complexity would be preferred, because they are more easily parsed, and probably also learned (see Berwick 1984).

Until recently, however, it has been supposed that grammars with a more desirable recognition time are cursed by a proliferation of rule structures when it comes to representing generalities and particularities of natural languages. The dilemma of computational complexity vs. linguistic generality has resisted a satisfactory solution ever since Chomsky 1957 argued that competence for natural languages requires at least context-free power in order to

handle embedding of clauses. Moreover, to capture generalizations about categories that participate in variations of order, he introduced transformations of phrase structure--further increasing computational complexity (cf. Peters and Ritchie 1973). Similarly, Woods 1970 justified recursion plus the manifold tests and registers of ATNs, which make his scheme "equivalent to a Turing machine in power," because "the actions which it performs are 'natural' ones for the analysis of language."

But natural languages can be modelled by a kind of finite-state device that is quite compact. We can avoid excessive duplication of categories, and having to approximate unbounded memory resources. This is possible--<u>if</u> we are willing to abandon the functional simplicity implied by symbols in rule patterns.

II TABLE-DRIVEN FS AUTOMATA

Below are two essentially equivalent ways to design a simple FS grammar: table-driven and network.

Simple (regular) FS automata

Production table   Transition Network

Cond	Cat	Result
N1	DET	N2
N1	ADJ	N3
N1	N	N4
N1	N	N4
N2	PRON	N5
N2	ADJ	N3
N2	N	N4
N2	N	N5
N3	ADJ	N3
N3	N	N4
N5	N	N5
N4	PREP	N1

Examples: production table-driven

word	CSSR	cat	word	CSSR	cat
	N1	init		N1	init
a	N2	DET	she	N5	PRON
sad	N2	ADJ			
old	N3	ADJ			
dwarf	N4	N			
in	N1	PREP			
rags	N5	N			

The table-driven implementation consists of 1) a register (here called the Current Syntactic State Register, or **CSSR**), 2) a table of syntactic productions (the **Synindex**) and 3) a machine which initializes the CSSR, makes transitions from state to state, and responds to a final state. The Synindex is a list associating: i) a category symbol, ii) a condition state symbol and iii) a result state symbol. A machine that recognizes sentences makes transitions by first matching a Synindex category symbol with a word's lexical category and the production's condition symbol with the CSSR; it then replaces the symbol in the CSSR with the production's result symbol. Following the example grammar, a transition from N1 to N2 is possible because the CSSR has been initialized to N1, and the category of a is DET. The CSSR then gets that production's result symbol, N2. So long as the list of productions is finite, it is a FS grammar. Such a machine has a finite number of possible states, though it can run on indefinitely. The category PREP, for example, iterates back to N1.

A FS grammar requires that every category be determined as possible by a function of the immediately preceding category. Space for the register and index are pre-allocated; no external memory is available. This is as true of the equivalent RVG:

RVG Synindex for simple NPs

Cond	Cat	Result	Feature Key:
1222	DET	0222	1-DET
2122	ADJ	0222	2-ADJ
2212	N	0002	3-HEAD
0001	PREP	1112	4-PREP
1111	PRON	0000	

Examples

word	CSSR	cat	word	CSSR	cat
	1111	init		1111	init
a	0111	DET	she	0000	PRON
sad	0111	ADJ			
old	0111	ADJ			
dwarf	0001	N			
in	1111	PREP			
rags	0001	N			

In a RVG, the symbols become vectors of features, each capable of three possible values (+,-,±, or "on", "off", "mask", or henceforward 1,0,2). The match function allows either identity or ambiguity (2 matches any value); the change function allows either literal or masked replacement (2 doesn't change anything). For example, if the CSSR is initialized to 1111, the condition vector of DET (1222) matches, and the result of DET (0222) can be applied, yielding 0111. This is what is meant by _functional_ _complexity_: whereas in a simple FS automaton match is identity and change is wholesale replacement, in RVG match and change allow ambiguity and masking. Nevertheless the ternary functions are quite simple and determinate.

Note that the RVG Synindex is considerably more compact than the equivalent FS table. Whereas the FS table has three productions for the category ADJ and six for N, the RVG Synindex has just one production per category. The savings--not only of space in the table, but time trying alternatives-- will multiply as more permutations of order are introduced.

How do RVGs achieve their efficiency? Functional complexity confers two properties that functionally simple grammars do not have: multiplicity and masking. Condition vectors can convey multiple constraints. For example, PREP (condition 0001) cannot occur until the first three features have been reversed in value. Moreover, result vectors can produce multiple effects: PREP (result 1112) re-enables all NP-opening productions. Note also that disjoint categories (e.g. N and PRON) share the same position in ordering vectors, so that they mutually exclude each other. That is, the result of N and PRON both disable the same feature (governing the HEAD position). (PRON (result 0000) also rules out having a post-modifying prepositional phrase.)

Masking is a consequence of ternary values. The third possible value (2) matches any value and does not change any value. Thus constraints may be passed through intervening states. For example, the category N is oblivious to whether or not the categories DET or ADJ have already occurred, since its condition vector (2212) matches the initial state (1111) or the state after DET (0111) or after ADJ (0011). Thus we can represent options as well as obligations. (Note that the ordering of optional productions is enforced by having successive categories also disable the constraining features, e.g. the result of N is 0002.) Moreover, iteration may be treated as a special case of optionality. Whereas a one-occurrence category disables itself (e.g. the result of DET is 0111), an iterative category does not (the result of ADJ is 0211). Like an optional category, an iterative category is disabled by successive categories up to the next obligatory category (e.g. the result of N is 0002). Finally, masking features allows constraints to be held through any number of intervening states--as will be demonstrated when we consider long-distance dependencies.

Finite functional complexity can thus increase the expressiveness of a grammar considerably. It is not to be confused with "complex symbols" found elsewhere in linguistic theory. The subcategorization symbols of Chomsky 1965 allow for context-sensitive power; the features of Gazdar and Pullum 1982 call for recursive elaboration of symbols. Features attached to GPSG phrase structure nodes themselves take the form of open-ended trees or directed graphs. The feature vectors of RVG, on the other hand, are finite and do not expand. Moreover, RVG is not an attribute-value system requiring piecemeal interpretation of individual features. Whole vectors (a ternary vector can be implemented as a pair of bit vectors), rather than lists of symbols, are the operational unit of on-line processing.

In any case, other researchers have used complex features to govern categorization, but never to describe _syntactic_ _states_.

III   WH-QUESTIONS

Wh-questions are perhaps the long-distance dependency par excellence. A wh-word (_who_, _what_, etc.) provokes the grammar to watch and wait for a 'gap'--an expected but missing noun phrase. The gap may be filled wherever a noun phrase is expected in a clause:

What is the robot seeking?
WH:what; AUX:is; SUBJ:NP:DET:the; N:robot;
VTRANS:seeking; OBJ:NGAP:CCLOSE:?;

What is the wrench on?
WH:what; AUX:is; SUBJ:NP:DET:the;
N:wrench; PREP:on; NGAP:CCLOSE:?;

What did the robot find the wrench on?
WH:what; AUX:did; SUBJ:NP:DET:the;
N:robot; VTRANS:find; OBJ:NP:DET:the;
N:wrench; PREPPOST:on; NGAP:CCLOSE:?;

What is a robot?
WH:what; AUX:is; SUBJ:NP:DET:a; N:robot;
PREDNP:NGAP:CCLOSE:?;

What did the robot find the wrench?
Synindex search fails at: ?

Delaying, for the moment, discussion of embedded clauses, we can see that wh-questions can be modelled straightforwardly.

Synindex for Wh-Questions

Label	Condition		Result		L?
WH	11111	00002	22222	22211	L
SUBJ	12111	00022	02222	12222	n
AUX	21111	00022	20222	22222	L
VTRANS	02111	00022	20022	22222	L
PREDNP	00111	00022	22000	12222	n
PREP	00111	00022	22000	12222	L
OBJ	00011	00022	22202	12222	n
PREPPOST	00001	00022	22222	12222	L
NP	22222	12222	22222	01122	n
DET	22222	01122	22222	20122	L
N	22222	02122	22222	20022	L
NGAP	00222	12212	22222	02202	n
CCLOSE	00002	00002	11111	00000	L

Feature Key: 1-SUBJ 2-AUX 3-PRED 4-OBJ
   5-PREPPOST 6-NP 7-DET 8-N 9-GAP 10-WH
L?: 'L' - consume a lexeme; 'n' - don't

The result of production WH, among other things, switches "on" a feature GAP. Only the production NGAP can turn this feature "off." NGAP can occur in quite a number of places--in fact, just about wherever an NP can occur (except SUBJ). But sooner or later NGAP _must_ occur, inasmuch as

CCLOSE requires that GAP have been turned off. The last sentence above fails because GAP is never disobligated.

It should be observed that in RVG the recurrence of noun phrases at various positions within a clause does not involve calling a subnetwork. Eschewing recursion, we instead allocate separate sections of the ordering vector type to deal with clause matters and phrase matters. Ternary masking allows the CSSR to preserve its clause-level status while it traverses a phrase. A number of boundary productions--SUBJ, OBJ, IOBJ, PREP, etc.--set a feature which at once temporarily disables subsequent clause-level productions and enables the boundary production NP. If NP is chosen-- there are other possibilities--all of the features ordering a phrase will be reset. One alternative is NGAP, whose condition requires that both the NP and GAP be on, and its result turns both of these features off. Thus NP and NGAP are disjoint.

IV   EMBEDDING

Clause embedding was the primary evidence cited by Chomsky 1957 for claiming that natural languages are at least context-free. He discusses, for example, the following kinds of structures:

if S1 then S2
if [either S3 or S4]$_{S1}$ then S2
if [either [George said that S5]$_{S3}$
   or S4]$_{S1}$ then S2

The argument goes: i) finite-state automata cannot handle $a^n b^n$ (or "mirror image") grammars because they do not have the memory to keep track of n; ii) if..then, either..or constructions suggest that natural languages are of this type; iii) therefore natural languages cannot be finite-state.

There are, however, severe constraints on embedding. The most well-known case is that of object relative constructions:

The mouse the cat chased squeaked.
The mouse the cat the dog bit chased squeaked.

Embedding object relatives once is not unusual, but twice is boggling. The most common explanantion for this problem is that center-embedding causes an overload of short-term memory processing. But as Kac 1980 has pointed out, this cannot be the whole story. For if it were we would expect embedding to break down at a predictable depth. But it does not. For example, though one clause can embed another of a _different_ type, there is _no_ _self-embedding_:

If if the Pope is Catholic then pigs have
   wings then Napoleon loves Josephine.
That that Dan likes Sue annoys Bob bothers me.

These sort of constructs are plausible, of course,

in truly context-free languages such as Pascal or LISP.

Nor are relative clauses a uniform phenomena. First of all, subject relatives are possible indefinitely:

> The fellow who saw the dog that bit the cat
> that chased the mouse is willing to testify.

Object relatives appear to be limited to a depth of one, but combinations of an object relative and a noun complement are not:

> The statement that the election which he lost
> ended his career dismays him.
> The only one who the fact that George resigned
> pleased was Tom.

Embedding also goes to deeper levels in order to attach suspended arguments or adverbial adjuncts:

> A teacher who wants students who persuade
> their classmates who don't know the material
> to help them to ask him instead must make
> himself available.
> Do you see why I wanted to deny that grammar
> is recursive so vehemently now?

In the first sentence, each infinitive clause is projected as an argument of an earlier predicate (wants, persuade). All of the relatives are subject relatives, so for each no gap is suspended, only an argument. In the second sentence, adverbs are attached to predicates after intervening complement clauses--so vehemently to deny and now all the way back to the main clause's predicate, see.

Though short-term memory is related to the shallowness of center-embedding generally, it is not an adequate account for the variety of specific constraints. Typically, memory limitations have been regarded as an aspect of performance rather than competence. The performance processor, with limited memory, is said to "approximate" competence, which is said to "idealize" the unlimited memory of a CF automaton. Thus when Church 1982 talks about finite-state processing, his aim is just "to design a parser that approximates competence with realistic resources." But one wonders: since memory constraints are universal to the species, why aren't they of import to models of competence? The various constraints on center-embedding argue against the functionally simple notation for denoting clauses (e.g. S or S-bar), which seems to imply that all clauses are (almost) alike. The versatility possible with the finite functional complexity of RVG re-opens the question whether CF power is needed.

If..then and either..or are better treated as discontinuous constraints than as "mirror-image" syntax. A single feature allocated for each paired construct can give us the obligations and options we want, with the help of a production to enforce the closure of discourse-level units:

Paired Particles

Label	Cond	Result	Feature Key:
IF	00	12	1: if..then
THEN	20	02	2: either..or
EITHER	20	21	
EITH-OR	21	20	
DCLOSE	00	22	

This fragment effectively enforces these constraints: i) IF obligates a THEN clause before Dclose; ii) EITHER obligates an EITH-OR clause before DCLOSE; iii) IF forbids another IF until a THEN re-options it; iv) EITHER forbids another EITHER until EITH-OR re-options it; v) EITHER forbids IF until EITH-OR re-options it. The last case ensures a constraint that Kac 1980 notes but cannot explain:

> Either if [clause] then [clause] or [clause]

(A possible explanation for this constraint is that it avoids many ambiguities that might otherwise be brought on by the conjunction or.)

In general, embedding can be modelled by any FS automata so long as the maximum depth is finite. Conceivably even a simple FS automaton can manage embedding, by duplicating clause syntax at every possible entry point. But such a grammar would be enormous, and is perhaps justifiably scorned as lacking "explanatory adequacy."

But ternary vectors can consolidate matters considerably. Rather than having to respecify for every possible site of embedding, an RVG need only keep track of the current level of embedding.

The data reviewed in this paper can be managed by keeping track of up to three levels of embedding. The top, or main clause level, is treated differently from the bottom two. Where the grammar does allow us to embed more deeply (e.g. right-embedded complements, subject relatives, etc.), it will begin to iterate in the space of the bottom two clauses. Thus we can adjoin arguments or adverbials to the current clause, or one clause higher, or to the main clause, which is always kept. E.g.:

> Do you see [why I wanted [to deny [that
> grammar is recursive] so vehemently]] now?

The adverbial so vehemently is attached back over an intervening clause; now to the main clause.

There are two styles in which one might implement clause embedding in RVG. They are virtually equivalent in terms of computational efficiency, but reviewing both will perhaps elucidate RVG methodology. The first is in the same spirit as NP embedding. Just as ordering of phrasal constituents is managed by a segment of the complete ordering vector, so each clause level might be treated as a separate segment of a long ordering vector type. Just as several boundary productions (SUBJ, PREP, etc.) suspend further clause-level productions while enabling NP, so other boundary productions may shift attention from one clause level to another. All of the segments are part of the same vector type, so that there is no need for storage beyond the CSSR, which holds a complete vector. Yet it is possible, because of ternary masking, for boundary productions to, as it were, open and close "windows" on relevant segments. The drawback of this technique is that, for each level, the grammar must replicate the features for clauses (the ordering vectors all get wider), and also replicate most of the clause-level productions (the Synindex table gets longer). Replicating productions such as SUBJ, CADJ, et al., is necessary in order to apply different condition and result vectors at each clause level. Increased size is not necessarily a clinching drawback, since it is by a factor somewhat less than three (phrasal and discourse-level features and productions need not be replicated). The alternative approach makes for a smaller Synindex, to be manipulated by a slightly more complicated algorithm.

Instead of widening the ordering vector, we add depth to the CSSR. The new CSSR is multi-leveled:

```
                         CSSR
ClauseLevel -->  ┌────────────────────┐
                 │ Main clause vector │
                 │ 1st embedded vector│
                 │ 2nd embedded vector│
                 └────────────────────┘
```

The state register is still finite and fully visible; no external memory is needed. Only now it has ordered levels as well as features. It is as if we broke up a long vector, masking inactive segments with an array subscript rather than ternary values. To embed a clause, the shifting facility increments ClauseLevel, and initializes the lower clause from the higher (so that features like GAP can be passed down). To return, it simply decrements ClauseLevel.

This scheme captures generalizations about what clause levels hold in common. It also allows specialized productions to distinguish clause types--with different result vectors. E.g., the complementizer that sets up a complete clause, but the infinitive particle to arranges for a clause starting with a non-finite verb. Similarly, the complex NP constraint (Ross 1967) is easily modelled by different result codes. After shifting clause level, change applies as usual. Complement productions allow feature GAP to be passed down (by masking), whereas relatives reset it:

What did you think that the robot which found?
Synindex search fails at: ?

What did you hope to find?
WH:what; TENSE:-past,DO:do; SUBJ:NP:PRON:you
NPCLOSE: NONFIN:-inf,VTRANS:hope; OBJ:
COMPINF:to; NONFIN:-inf,VTRANS:find;
OBJ:NGAP:FILLEDGAP:CCLOSE:?;

Who were you persuaded to find the wrench by?
WH:who; TENSE:-past,BE:be; SUBJ:NP:PRON:you;
NPCLOSE: PASSIVE:-pastpart,VDITRANS:persuade;
COMPINF:to; NONFIN:-inf,VTRANS:find; OBJ:NP:
DET:the; NUMBER:-sing,N:wrench; NPCLOSE:
PASSGAP: PASSIVEBY:by; NGAP:CCLOSE:?;

Clause-closing productions may or may not insist that GAP be off. RELCLOSE makes this requirement, but does not affect the higher clause, whereas FILLEDGAP does turn off GAP in the higher clause, and PASSGAP leaves GAP alone.

After the shifting facility has embedded two clauses, it resorts to re-use. That is, the second embedded clause is shifted up to the first. Thus right-embedding can iterate in two registers, but preserves the main clause. Two embedded clause registers are enough to allow the parser to resume suspended arguments or adverbials, as in

A teacher who wants students who persuade their classmates who don't know the material to help them to ask him instead must make himself available.

But its center-embedding capacity has now has been reached. The parser is baffled by this sentence:

Pamela persuaded the robot who wanted to give the pyramid which was on the blocks which it found to her very much to find a wrench instead.

By the time it encounters very much, the clause to which the adverbial might have been attached (wanted...) has been lost to re-use. But such a sentence is beyond the tolerance of many human speakers as well.

Superficially this embedding scheme resembles a bounded stack. But there are some crucial differences. First of all, a bounded stack scheme (such as that of Church 1982) typically calls for a great deal more storage than just three registers, since it will have to keep track of the full gamut of embedding implied by PS rules--NPs, VPs, X-bars and the like. Second, whereas functionally simple systems treat every level of embedding alike, in RVG each level of embedding is marked--main clause, first embedded, re-usable. Thus in RVG there is no self-embedding. Third, CSSR levels are not really organized like a stack, since the lower two registers are re-used iteratively, and the main clause register is always preserved. In fact there is nothing which prevents a RVG from accessing clause levels in another order. For example, we could model cross-serial dependencies in Dutch (see Bresnan et al. 1982), by allowing boundary productions to access storage registers in a queue-like order. (Assuming that cross-serial dependency, like center-embedding, is limited.)

V   TOWARD A COMPLETE RVG SYSTEM

RVG syntax may be thought of a **general-purpose scheduler**, with potential applications wherever such a device would be desirable. Generally, non-syntactic procedures can be scheduled by association with Synindex productions. Indeed, syntactic productions are motivated by non-syntactic requirements. For example, nouns, pronouns and names are very similar positionally, but they are treated as distinct categories because of semantics. In this section I will briefly describe how an RVG can, while maintaining modular autonomy to a considerable degree, support integration of processes.

Categories. In earlier versions of RVG, categories, like syntactic ordering and semantic constraints, were represented in terms of ternary feature vectors. Ternary values supported cross-categorization well--lexemes in more than one category could allow them with 2's. But since RVG holds down duplication of productions, it is feasable to associate, with each lexeme, a list of Synindex production numbers. Moreover it is possible, with some pre-processing, to let these production numbers be generated from labels, and also to infer the set of non-lexical productions that could precede each lexical production. Thus, for example, the lexeme _kitten_ is categorized by the label N, which is converted to a production number; the non-lexical production numbers for SUBJ, OBJ, NP, etc., are kept in a **precedes set** associated with the Synindex entry for N. This approach is at once more convenient, because categories are kept functionally simple with respect to notation, and more efficient, because the lexicon is 'wired' directly to the Synindex, obviating any on-line processing of categories.

Semantics. RVG syntax can in fact support just about any form of semantics. But I present our biases. Since RVG permits a relatively flat, direct treatment of permutations of order, there is no reason to complicate matters--as trees do, since they imply recursion. Rather than transform syntactic structures, or propose meta-rules or lexical-dependency subtrees which have similar effect, why not let categorized actions operate upon semantic structures directly? The problem of mapping constituent structures into lexical structures is simplified by just eliminating context-free constituent structures. There is no need to move or unify sub-trees in RVG; there are no trees at all. Moreover, semantic and morphological agreement can be simplified: there is no need to 'percolate' or 'inherit' features up and down trees, nor to design special filters or powerful constraints to regulate such activity. Functional complexity allows RVG to be **sensitive to context** without being **context-sensitive** in the sense of the Chomsky hierarchy.

In RVG, we allocate a fixed configuration of registers (the Current Predication State Registers, or CPSR) for managing grammatical relations. The CPSR and CSSR together comprise the state of a clause (or a phrase in a clause), and as shown above, RVG keeps track of up to three clauses. Permanent semantic representation is built up dynamically (it is here that we allow open-ended structures); CPSR slots hold addresses of proposed semantic referents.

Categorized actions (associated with syntactic productions) have the responsibility of mapping new lexical material into existing semantic structure. In the spirit of RVG, lexemes are viewed as standardized in structure. All semantic features are organized in a single vector type, the first-order semantic vector. Every lexeme has an INTRINSIC first-order code. Constraints on arguments of predicates are specified, as needed, in terms of additional first-order vectors. First_Order_Pred, a generalized procedure called by many categorized actions, for all arguments, first matches vectors (thus checking selectional restrictions), then unifies them. E.g., 22201 matches 01202 and yields 01201. Thus in RVG features are not used merely to validate, but also to _define_ semantic structures.

Morphology. Kunst and Blank (1982) show that morphology can be efficiently implemented as a retrieval tree, with provision for morphological paradigms as nodes encountered during lexical lookup. Currently, we represent morphemes as lexemes in their own right, each with its own list of Synindex production numbers and semantic structure. Thus, for example, lookup recognizes _cats_ as two lexemes: -_plur_ and _cat_. The lexeme -_plur_ has an INTRINSIC vector (distinguishing it from -_sing_). It also lists the subscript for the Synindex production NUMBER, which maps the INTRINSIC of the lexeme (-_plur_) to CPSR[Head], and then calls First_Order_Pred: thus enforcing number agreement. Another morphologically categorized production, TENSE, enforces 'subject-verb' agreement. Actually, The _kittens_ _is_ _playing_ fails at TENSE, whereas The _bricks_ _are_ _playing_ violates constraints at VTRANS. But note that _all agreement_ is managed by uniform operations upon a single vector type.

Letters must have been being written.
SUBJ:NP:NUMBER:-plur,N:letter; NPCLOSE:
TENSE:-pres,MODAL:must; NONFIN:-inf,HAVE:have;
PERF:-pastpart,BE:be; PROG:-progpart,BE:be;
PASSIVE:-pastpart,VTRANS:write; CCLOSE:.;

Discourse, etc. RVG does not require that 'S' be the root of syntax. The examples in this paper suggest that a discouse-level syntax could be integrated as part of the Synindex, or as a separate production table interfacing with the Synindex. Paired particles were modelled as discourse-level discontinuity, and wh-questions are marked by a feature switched on by the production WH. Generalizations about syntax, expressed by features in vectors rather than by complex rule patterns, are thus more readily available to other systems.

RVGs are highly reversible. A parser and a

generator can be implemented (and have been) using the same Synindex and basic table-driving algorithm. Indeed, all of the major data structures of RVG work in either direction as is; only the procedures need actually be reversed. While parsing, discourse-level features are set by syntax for higher-level consideration. While generating, discourse-level features are set from above to choose particular sentence forms.

RVGs are computationally simple and compact. The basic algorithm is that of a table-driven finite-state device, modified to invoke ternary match and change functions. Ternary vectors can be represented on a binary computer by paired bit vectors. Ternary match and change are implemented by combining logical operations (exploiting the low-level parallelism of bits in computer words). The most recent version of RVG, in Pascal (earlier versions were in SNOBOL and Icon), does so, with great gains in speed. On a DEC-20, the syntactic parser averages about 5 milliseconds per lexeme. Further improvement is possible--on ternary circuitry.

Expansion to fuller coverage (a substantial fragment of English syntax has been implemented) will have a minimal slowing effect, since each new category motivates one new production, rather than many new rules (or a meta-rule that generates many rules). Each revision is on features already allocated in all productions. Occasionally new features must be allocated, but most frequently early in grammar-making, and least frequently late.

Ambiguous parsing to be sure slows processing down, though not unbearably. The combination of well-specified category vectors, semantic constraints and possibly a form of bounded parallelism (under investigation) can hold syntactic processing time to a small linear time. Thus parsing of natural languages appears to be feasable by machines in real time. Indeed, syntax should be fast, if it is to facilitate the many other processes--from phonology to reasoning-- which all go on in real time.

ACKNOWLEDGEMENT

RVG originates in unpublished work by A. E. Kunst, to whom I am also grateful for help with this paper. In an unpublished paper, Professor Kunst compares RVGs to **Petri nets** (rather than simple transition networks). Petri nets also allow functional complexity. Specifically, he compares of **safe** Petri nets (which are known to be weakly equivalent to FS automata) and RVGs.

REFERENCES

[1] Berwick, R. & A. Weinberg. Parsing efficiency and the evaluation of grammatical theories. Linguistic Inquiry 13:4 (1982) 135-191.

[2] Berwick, R. Bounded context parsing and easy learnability. Proc. 22nd ACL, Stanford, Palo Alto, 1984, pp. 20-23.

[3] Blank, G. Lexicalized metaphors: A cognitive model in the framework of Register Vector semantics. PhD thesis, University of Wisconsin-Madison, 1984.

[4] Bresnan, J., R. Kaplan, S. Peters and A. Zaenan. Cross-serial dependencies in Dutch. Linguistic Inquiry 13:4 (1982) 613-35.

[5] Chomsky, N. Syntactic structures. Mouton, The Hague, 1957.

[6] Chomsky, N. Aspects of the theory of syntax. MIT Press, Cambridge, MA, 1965.

[7] Church, K. On memory limitations in natural language processing. IU Linguistics Club, Bloomington, Indiana, 1982.

[8] Gazdar, G. & G. K. Pullum. Generalized phrase structure grammar: a theoretical synopsis. IU Linguistics Club, Bloomington, Indiana, 1982.

[9] Kac, M. On the recognition of complex NP's. Workshop on Language Processing and Acquisition. Brown University, Providence, RI, 1980.

[10] Kunst, A. E. Petri net theory and the representation of natural languages. Unpublished paper, Comparative Literature, University of Wisconsin-Madison, 1983.

[11] Langendoen, D. T. and Y. Langsam. The representation of constituent structures for finite-state parsing. Proc. 22nd ACL. Palo Alto, 1984, pp. 24-27.

[12] Perrault, C. On the mathematical properties of linguistic theories. Proc. 21st ACL, MIT, Cambridge, MA, 1983, pp. 98-104.

[13] Peters, P. S. and R. W. Ritchie. On the generative power of transformational grammars. Information Science 6 (1973) 49-63.

[14] Pullum, G. Context-freeness and the computer processing of human languages. Proc. 21st ACL MIT, Cambridge, MA, 1983.

[15] Pullum, G. Syntactic and semantic parsability. Proc. 22nd ACL, 1984, pp. 112-22.

[16] Ross, J. Constraints on variables in syntax. PhD thesis, MIT, 1967.

[17] Woods, W. Transition network grammars for natural language analysis. CACM 13:10 (1970) 591-606.

An Efficient
Context-free Parsing Algorithm
For Natural Languages[1]

Masaru Tomita
Computer Science Department
Carnegie-Mellon University
Pittsburgh, PA 15213

Abstract

This paper introduces an efficient context-free parsing algorithm and emphasizes its practical value in natural language processing. The algorithm can be viewed as an extended LR parsing algorithm which embodies the concept of a "graph-structured stack." Unlike the standard LR, the algorithm is capable of handling arbitrary non-cyclic context-free grammars including ambiguous grammars, while most of the LR parsing efficiency is preserved. The algorithm seems more efficient than any existing algorithms including the Cocke-Younger-Kasami algorithm and Earley's algorithm, as far as practical natural language parsing is concerned, due to utilization of LR parsing tables. The algorithm is an all-path parsing algorithm; it produces all possible parse trees (a parse forest) in an efficient representation called a "shared-packed forest." This paper also shows that Earley's forest representation has a defect and his algorithm cannot be used in natural language processing as an all-path parsing algorithm.

1 Introduction

In past decades, many context-free parsing algorithms have been developed, and they can be classified into two groups: algorithms for programming languages and algorithms for general context-free languages. The former group of algorithms are intended to handle only a small subset of context-free grammars sufficient for programming languages. Such algorithms include the LL parsing algorithm, the operator precedence parsing algorithm, the predictive parsing algorithm and the LR parsing algorithm. They can handle only a subset of context-free grammars called LL grammars, operator precedence grammars, predictive grammars and LR grammars, respectively [1]. These algorithms are tuned to handle a particular subset of context-free grammars, and therefore they are very efficient with their type of grammars. In other words, they take advantage of inherent features of the programming language.

The other group of algorithms, often called general context-free parsing algorithms, are designed to handle arbitrary context-free grammars. This group of algorithms includes Earley's algorithm [9] and the Cocke-Younger-Kasami algorithm [19, 11]. General context-free languages include many difficult phenomena which never appear in programming languages, such as ambiguity and cycle. Algorithms in this group have not been widely used for programming languages, because their constant factors are too large to be used in practical compilers, as Earley admitted in his thesis [8]. This is not surprising,

because those algorithms are not tuned for any particular subset of context-free grammars, and must be able to handle all difficult phenomena in context-free grammars. In other words, they do not take advantage of inherent features of the programming language. Intuitively speaking, algorithms in this group are efficient for "hard" grammars by sacrificing efficiency on "easy" grammars.

No parsing algorithm has been designed that takes advantage of inherent features of natural languages. Because natural languages include slightly more difficult phenomena than programming languages, we cannot simply use the first group of algorithms for natural languages. Natural languages are a little "harder" than programming languages, but they are still much "easier" than general context-free languages. As we have seen above, we have context-free parsing algorithms at two extremes. The one is very efficient but not powerful enough to handle natural languages. The other is too powerful and it turns out to be inefficient. We need something in between.

This paper introduces such a context-free parsing algorithm, which can be viewed as an extended LR parsing algorithm which embodies the concept of a "graph-structured stack." The fragile point of the standard LR parsing algorithm is that it cannot handle a non-LR grammar, even if the grammar is almost LR. Unlike the standard LR parsing algorithm, our algorithm can handle non-LR grammars with little loss of LR efficiency, if its grammar is "close" to LR. Fortunately, natural language grammars are considerably "close" to LR, compared with other general context-free grammars.

A primitive version of the algorithm was described in the author's previous work [15]. Because the primitive algorithm used a "tree-structured stack", exponential time was required, whereas the current algorithm uses the "graph-structured stack" and runs in polynomial time. Also, the primitive algorithm was a recognizer; that is, it did not produce any parses, while the current algorithm produces all possible parses in an efficient representation. A "graph-structured stack" was proposed in the author's more recent work [16]. The algorithm was previously called the *MLR* parsing algorithm. All ideas presented in those two previous papers are included in this paper, and the reader does not need to refer to them to understand the current discussion.

2 The Standard LR Parsing Algorithm

The LR parsing algorithms [1, 2] were developed originally for programming languages. An LR parsing algorithm is a shift-reduce parsing algorithm which is deterministically guided by a parsing table indicating what action should be taken next. The parsing table can be obtained automatically from a context-free phrase structure grammar, using an algorithm first developed by DeRemer [6, 7]. I do not describe the algorithms here, referring the reader to chapter 6 in Aho and Ullman [3]. I assume that the reader is familiar with the standard LR parsing algorithm (not necessarily with the parsing table construction algorithm).

[1]This research was sponsored by the Defense Advanced Research Projects Agency (DOD), ARPA Order No. 3597, monitored by the Air Force Avionics Laboratory Under Contract F33615-81-K-1539. The views and conclusions contained in this document are those of the authors and should not be interpreted as representing the official policies, either expressed or implied, of the Defense Advanced Research Projects Agency or the US Government.

The LR paring algorithm is one of the most efficient parsing algorithms. It is totally deterministic and no backtracking or search is involved. Unfortunately, we cannot directly adopt the LR parsing technique for natural languages, because it is applicable only to a small subset of context-free grammars called LR grammars, and it is almost certain that any practical natural language grammars are not LR. If a grammar is non-LR, its parsing table will have multiple entries[2] ; one or more of the action table entries will be multiply defined.

Figures 1 and 2 show an example of a non-LR grammar and its parsing table. Grammar symbols starting with "*" represent preterminals. Entries "sh *n*" in the action table (the left part of the table) indicate the action "shift one word from input buffer onto the stack, and go to state *n*". Entries "re *n*" indicate the action "reduce constituents on the stack using rule *n*". The entry "acc" stands for the action "accept", and blank spaces represent "error". Goto table (the right part of the table) decides to what state the parser should go after a reduce action. The exact definition and operation of the LR parser can be found in Aho and Ullman [3].

We can see that there are two multiple entries in the action table; on the rows of state 11 and 12 at the column labeled "*prep". It has been thought that, for LR parsing, multiple entries are fatal because once a parsing table has multiple entries, deterministic parsing is no longer possible and some kind of non-determinism is necessary. However, in this paper, we extend a stack of the LR parsing algorithm to be "graph-structured," so that the algorithm can handle multiple entries with little loss of LR efficiency.

3 Handling Multiple Entries

As mentioned above, once a parsing table has multiple entries, deterministic parsing is no longer possible and some kind of non-determinism is necessary. We handle multiple entries with a special technique, named a *graph-structured stack*. In order to introduce the idea of a graph-structured stack, I first give a simpler non-determinism, and make refinements on it. Subsection 3.1 describes a simple and straightforward non-determinism, i.e. pseudo-parallelism (breath-first search), in which the system maintains a number of stacks simultaneously. I call the list of stacks *Stack List*. A disadvantage of the stack list is then described. The next subsection describes the idea of stack combination, which was introduced in my earlier research [15], to make the algorithm much more efficient. With this idea, stacks are represented as trees (or a forest). Finally, a further refinement, the graph-structured stack, is described to make the algorithm even more efficient; efficient enough to run in polynomial time.

3.1 With Stack List

The simplest idea is to handle multiple entries non-deterministically. I adopt pseudo-parallelism (breath-first search),

maintaining a list of stacks called a *Stack List*. The pseudo-parallelism works as follows.

A number of *processes* are operated in parallel. Each process has a stack and behaves basically the same as in standard LR parsing. When a process encounters a multiple entry, the process is split into several processes (one for each entry), by duplicating its stack. When a process encounters an error entry, the process is killed, by removing its stack from the stack list. All processes are synchronized; they shift a word at the same time so that they always look at the same word. Thus, if a process encounters a shift action, it waits until all other processes also encounter a (possibly different) shift action.

Figure 3 shows a snapshot of the stack list right after shifting the word "with" in the sentence "I saw a man on the bed in the apartment with a telescope" using the grammar in figure 1 and the parsing table in figure 2. For the sake of convenience, I denote a stack with vertices and edges. The leftmost vertex is the bottom of the stack, and the rightmost vertex is the top of the stack. Vertices represented by a circle are called *state vertices*, and they represent a state number. Vertices represented by a square are called *symbol vertices*, and they represent a grammar symbol. Each stack is exactly the same as a stack in the standard LR parsing algorithm. The distance between vertices (length of an edge) does not have any significance, except it may help the reader understand the status of the stacks.

We notice that some stacks in the stack list appear to be identical. They are, however, internally different because they have reached the current state in different ways. Although we shall describe a method to compress them into one stack in the next section, we consider them to be different in this section.

A disadvantage of the stack list method is that there are no interconnections between stacks (processes) and there is no way in which a process can utilize what other processes have done already. The number of stacks in the stack list grows exponentially as ambiguities are encountered. For example, these 14 processes in figure 3 will parse the rest of the sentence "the telescope" 14 times in exactly the same way. This can be avoided by using a tree-structured stack, which is described in the following subsection.

3.2 With a Tree-structured Stack

If two processes are in a common state, that is, if two stacks have a common state number at the rightmost vertex, they will behave in exactly the same manner until the vertex is popped from the stacks by a reduce action. To avoid this redundant operation, these processes are unified into one process by combining their stacks. Whenever two or more processes have a common state number on the top of their stacks, the top vertices are unified, and these stacks are represented as a tree, where the top vertex corresponds to the root of the tree. I call this a tree-structured stack. When the top vertex is popped, the tree-structured stack is split into the original number of stacks. In general, the system maintains a number of tree-structured stacks

[2] They are often called *conflict*.

```
--------------------------------
  (1)  S  --> NP VP
  (2)  S  --> S PP
  (3)  NP --> *n
  (4)  NP --> *det *n
  (5)  NP --> NP PP
  (6)  PP --> *prep NP
  (7)  VP --> *v NP
--------------------------------
```

Figure 1: An Example Non-LR Grammar

State	*det	*n	*v	*prep	$		NP	PP	VP	S
0	sh3	sh4					2			1
1				sh6	acc			5		
2			sh7	sh6				9	8	
3		sh10								
4			re3	re3	re3					
5				re2	re2					
6	sh3	sh4						11		
7	sh3	sh4						12		
8				re1	re1					
9			re5	re5	re5					
10			re4	re4	re4					
11			re6	re6,sh6	re6			9		
12			re7	re7,sh6	re7			9		

Figure 2: LR Parsing Table with Multiple Entries

in parallel, so stacks are represented as a forest. Figure 4 shows a snapshot of the tree-structured stack immediately after shifting the word "with".

Although the amount of computation is significantly reduced by the stack combination technique, the number of branches of the tree-structured stack (the number of bottoms of the stack) that must be maintained still grows exponentially as ambiguities are encountered. The next subsection describes a further modification in which stacks are represented as a directed acyclic graph, in order to avoid such inefficiency.

3.3 With a Graph-structured Stack

So far, when a stack is split, a copy of the whole stack is made. However, we do not necessarily have to copy the whole stack: Even after different parallel operations on the tree-structured stack, the bottom portion of the stack may remain the same. Only the necessary portion of the stack should therefore be split. When a stack is split, the stack is thus represented as a tree, where the bottom of the stack corresponds to the root of the tree. With the stack combination technique described in the previous subsection, stacks are represented as a directed acyclic graph. Figure 5 shows a snapshot of the graph stack. It is easy to show that the algorithm with the graph-structured stack does not parse any part of an input sentence more than once in the same way. This is because if two processes had parsed a part of a sentence in the same way, they would have been in the same state, and they would have been combined as one process.

So far, we have focussed on how to accept or reject a sentence. In practice, however, the parser must not only simply accept or reject sentences, but also build the syntactic structure(s) of the sentence (parse forest). The next section describes how to represent the parse forest and how to build it with our parsing algorithm.

4 An Efficient Representation of a Parse Forest

Our parsing algorithm is an *all-path parsing* algorithm; that is, it produces all possible parses in case an input sentence is ambiguous. Such all-path parsing is often needed in natural language processing to manage temporarily or absolutely ambiguous input sentences. The ambiguity (the number of parses) of a sentence grows exponentially as the length of a sentence grows. Thus, one might notice that, even with an efficient parsing algorithm such as the one we described, the parser would take exponential time because exponential time would be required merely to print out all parse trees (parse forest). We must therefore provide an efficient representation so that the size of the parse forest does not grow exponentially.

This section describes two techniques for providing an efficient representation: sub-tree sharing and local ambiguity packing. It should be mentioned that these two techniques are not completely new ideas, and some existing systems already adopted these techniques, either implicitly or explicitly. To the author's knowledge, however, no existing system has explicitly adopted both techniques at the same time.

4.1 Sub-tree Sharing

If two or more trees have a common sub-tree, the sub-tree should be represented only once. For example, the parse forest for the sentence "I saw a man in the park with a telescope" should be represented as in figure 6. Our parsing algorithm is very well suited for building this kind of shared forest as its output, as we shall see in the following.

To implement this, we no longer push grammatical symbols on the stack; instead, we push pointers to a node[3] of the shared

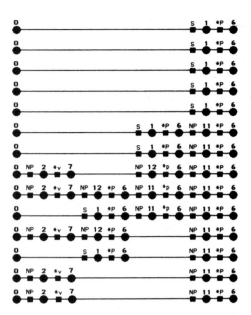

Figure 3: Stack List (simple parallelism)

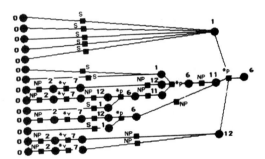

Figure 4: Tree-Structured Stack

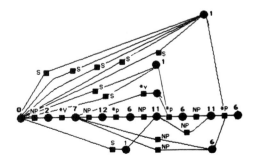

Figure 5: Graph-Structured Stack

---

[3]The term node is used for forest representation, whereas the term **vertex** is used for the graph-structured stack representation.

forest. When the parser "shifts" a word, it creates a leaf node labeled with the word and the pre-terminal, and instead of pushing the pre-terminal symbol, a pointer to the newly created leaf node is pushed onto the stack. If the exact same leaf node (i.e. the node labeled with the same word and the same pre-terminal) already exists, a pointer to this existing node is pushed onto the stack, without creating another node. When the parser "reduces" the stack, it pops pointers from the stack, creates a new node whose successive nodes are pointed to by those popped pointers, and pushes a pointer to the newly created node onto the stack.

Using this relatively simple procedure, our parsing algorithm can produce the shared forest as its output without any other special book-keeping mechanism, because the algorithm never does the same reduce action twice in the same manner.

4.2 Local Ambiguity Packing

I define that two or more subtrees represent *local ambiguity* if they have common leaf nodes and their top nodes are labeled with the same non-terminal symbol. That is to say, a fragment of a sentence is locally ambiguous if the fragment can be reduced to a certain non-terminal symbol in two or more ways. If a sentence has many local ambiguities, the total ambiguity would grow exponentially. To avoid this, we use a technique called *local ambiguity packing*, which works in the following way. The top nodes of subtrees that represent local ambiguity are merged and treated by higher-level structures as if there were only one node. Such a node is called a *packed node*, and nodes before packing are called *subnodes* of the packed node. Examples of a shared-packed forest is shown in figure 7.

Local ambiguity packing can be easily implemented with our parsing algorithm as follows. In the graph-structured stack, if two

or more symbol vertices have a common state vertex immediately on their left and a common state vertex immediately on their right, they represent local ambiguity. Nodes pointed to by these symbol vertices are to be packed as one node. In figure 5 for example, we see one 5-way local ambiguity and two 2-way local ambiguities.

The algorithm will be made clear by an example in the next section.

5 The Example

This section gives a trace of the algorithm with the grammar in figure 1, the parsing table in figure 2 and the sentence "I saw a man in the park with a telescope."

At the very beginning, the stack contains only one vertex labeled 0, and the parse forest contains nothing. By looking at the action table, the next action "shift 4" is determined as in standard LR parsing.

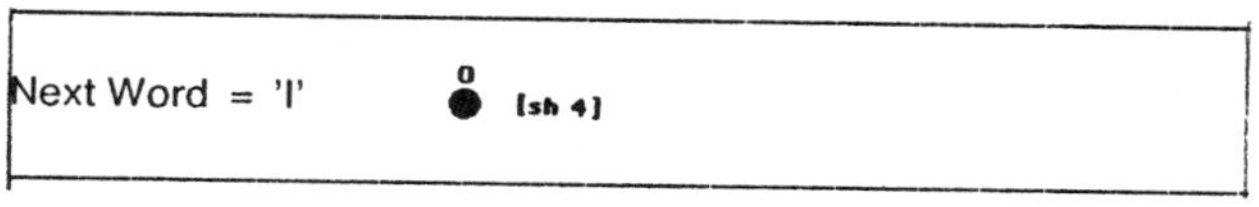

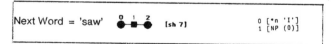

Figure 8: Trace of the Parser

When shifting the word "I", the algorithm creates a leaf node in the parse forest labeled with the word "I" and its preterminal "*n", and pushes a pointer to the leaf node onto the stack. The next action "reduce 3" is determined from the action table.

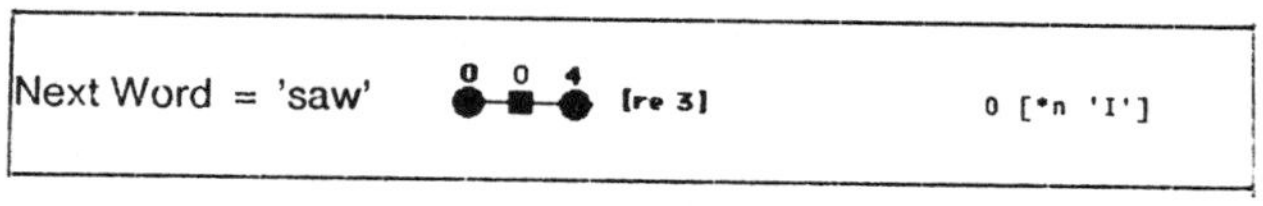

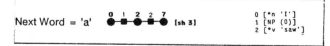

Figure 9: Trace of the Parser (cont.)

We reduce the stack basically in the same manner as standard LR parsing. It pops the top vertex "4" and the pointer "0" from the stack, and creates a new node in the parse forest whose successor is the node pointed to by the pointer. The newly created node is labeled with the left hand side symbol of rule 3, namely "NP". The pointer to this newly created node, namely "1", is pushed onto the stack. The action "shift 7" is determined as the next action. Now, we have figure 10.

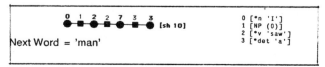

Figure 10: Trace of the Parser (cont.)

After executing "shift 7", we have figure 11.

Next Word = 'a'   0 1 2 2 7 [sh 3]   0 [*n 'I']
1 [NP (0)]
2 [*v 'saw']

Figure 11: Trace of the Parser (cont.)

After executing "shift 3", we have figure 12.

Next Word = 'man'   0 1 2 2 7 3 3 [sh 10]   0 [*n 'I']
1 [NP (0)]
2 [*v 'saw']
3 [*det 'a']

Figure 12: Trace of the Parser (cont.)

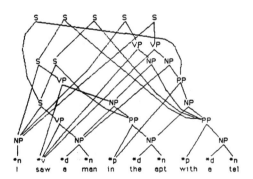

Figure 6: Shared Forest

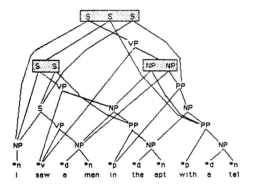

Figure 7: Shared-Packed Forest

After executing "shift 10", we have figure 13.

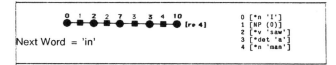

Figure 13: Trace of the Parser (cont.)

The next action is "reduce 4". It pops pointers, "3" and "4", and creates a new node in the parse forest such that node 3 and node 4 are its successors. The newly created node is labeled with the left hand side symbol of rule 4, i.e. "NP". The pointer to this newly created node, "5", is pushed onto the stack. We now have figure 14.

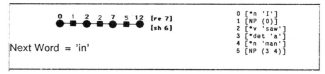

Figure 14: Trace of the Parser (cont.)

At this point, we encounter a multiple entry, "reduce 7" and "shift 6", and both actions are to be executed. Reduce actions are always executed first, and shift actions are executed only when there is no reduce action to execute. After executing "reduce 7", the stack and the parse forest look like the following. The top vertex labeled "12" is not popped away, because it still has an action which is not yet executed. Such a top vertex, or more generally, vertices with one or more actions yet to be executed, are called *active*. Thus, we have two active vertices in the stack above: one labeled "12", and the other labeled "8". The action "reduce 1" is determined from the action table, and is associated with the latter vertex.

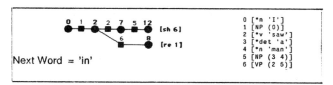

Figure 15: Trace of the Parser (cont.)

Because reduce actions have a higher priority than shift actions, the algorithm next executes "reduce 1" on the vertex labeled "8". The action "shift 6" is determined from the action table.

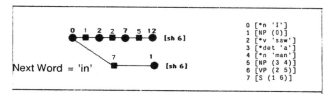

Figure 16: Trace of the Parser (cont.)

Now we have two "shift 6"'s. The parser, however, creates only one new leaf node in the parse forest. After executing two shift actions, it combines vertices in the stack wherever possible. The stack and the parse forest look like the following, and "shift 3" is determined from the action table as the next action.

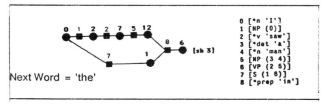

Figure 17: Trace of the Parser (cont.)

After about 20 steps (figure 18), the action "accept" is finally executed. It returns "25" as the top node of the parse forest, and halts the process. The final parse forest is shown in figure 19.

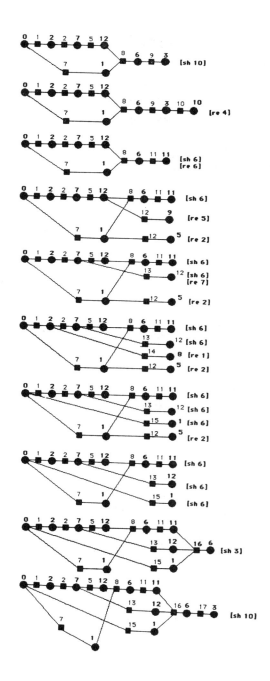

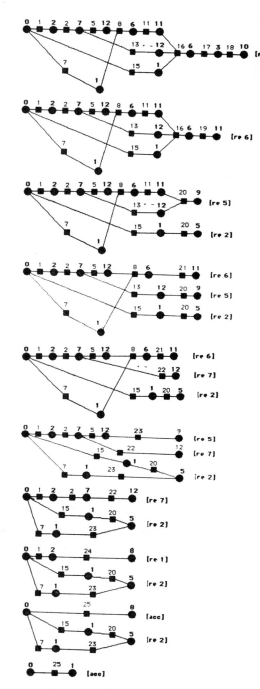

Figure 18: Trace of the Parser (cont.)

```
0 [*n 'I']        10 [*n 'park']
1 [NP (0)]        11 [NP (9 10)]      20 [PP (16 19)]
2 [*v 'saw']      12 [PP (6 11)]      21 [NP (11 20)]
3 [*det 'a']      13 [NP (5 12)]      22 [NP (13 20)]
4 [*n 'man']      14 [VP (2 13)]      23 [PP (8 21)]
5 [NP (3 4)]      15 [S (1 14)  (7 12)]  24 [VP (2 22)]
6 [VP (2 5)]      16 [*prep 'with']   25 [S (1 24) (15 22) (7 23)]
7 [S (1 6)]       17 [*det 'a']
8 [*prep 'in']    18 [*n 'scope']
9 [*det 'the']    19 [NP (17 18)]
```

Figure 19: Final Parse Forest

6 Comparison with Other Algorithms

There have been several general parsing algorithms that run in polynomial time. Theoretically speaking, the fastest algorithm at present is Valiant's algorithm. Valiant [18] reduced the context-free parsing problem to the Boolean Matrix Multiplication problem [10], and his algorithm runs in time $O(n^{2.81})$. This algorithm is, however, of only theoretical interest, because the coefficient of $n^{2.81}$ is so large that the algorithm runs faster than conventional n^3 algorithms only when an input sentence is tremendously long. Practically speaking, on the other hand, the most well-known parsing algorithm is Earley's algorithm [9, 8, 1, 11], which runs in time $O(n^3)$.

All other practical algorithms seem to bear some similarity with or relation to Earley's algorithm. Another algorithm which is as well-known as Earley's algorithm is the Cocke-Younger-Kasami (CYK) algorithm [19, 11, 1]. Graham *et al.* [12], however, revealed that the CYK algorithm is "almost" identical to Earley's algorithm, by giving an improved version of the CYK algorithm which is very similar to Earley's algorithm. The *chart parsing algorithm* is basically the same as the CYK algorithm. The *active chart parsing algorithm* is basically the same as Earley's algorithm, although it does not necessarily have to parse from left to right. Bouckaert *et al.* [4] extended Earley's algorithm to perform tests similar to those introduced in LL and LR algorithms. *Improved nodal span* [5] and LINGOL [13] are also similar to Earley's algorithm, but both of them require grammars to be in Chomsky Normal Form (CNF).

These all practical general parsing algorithms seem to be like Earley's algorithm, in that they employ the tabular parsing method; they all construct *well-formed substring tables* [14]. In chart parsing, such tables are called *charts*. The representation of one well-formed substring is called an "edge" in active chart parsing, a "state" in Earley's algorithm, a "dotted rule" in Graham's algorithm and an "item" in Aho and Ullman [1]. Throughout this paper, we call a well-formed substring an *item*.

6.1 Recognition time

No existing general parsing algorithm utilizes LR parsing tables. All of the practical algorithms mentioned above construct *sets of items* by adding an item to a set, one by one, during parsing. Our algorithm, on the other hand, is sufficiently different; it precomputes sets of items in advance during the time of parsing table construction, and maintains pointers (i.e., state numbers) to the precomputed sets of items, rather than maintaining items themselves.

Because of this major difference, our algorithm has the following three properties.

- It is more efficient, if a grammar is "close" to LR: that is, if its LR parsing table contains relatively few multiple entries. In general, less ambiguous grammars tend to have fewer multiple entries in their parsing table. In an extreme case, if a grammar is LR, our algorithm is as efficient as an LR parsing algorithm, except for minor overheads.

- It is less efficient, if a grammar is "densely" ambiguous as in figure 20. This kind of grammar tends to have many multiple entries in its LR parsing table. Our algorithm may take more than $O(n^3)$ time with "densely" ambiguous grammars.

$$S \longrightarrow S\ S\ S$$
$$S \longrightarrow S\ S\ S$$
$$S \longrightarrow S\ S$$
$$S \longrightarrow x$$

sentence = 'xxxxxx'

Figure 20: Heavy Ambiguity

- It is not able to handle infinitely ambiguous grammars and cyclic grammars[4] (figure 21 and 22), although it can handle e-grammars and left-recursive grammars. If a grammar is cyclic, our algorithm never terminates. The existing general parsing algorithms can parse those sentences (figure 20, 21 and 22) still in time proportional to n^3.

```
S --> S S
S --> e
S --> x

sentence = 'xxx'
```

Figure 21: Infinite Ambiguity

```
S --> S
S --> x

sentence = 'x'
```

Figure 22: Cyclic Grammar

It is certain that no natural language grammars have infinite ambiguity or cyclic rules. It is also extremely unlikely that a natural language grammar has dense ambiguity such as that shown in figure 20. It is therefore safe to conclude that our algorithm is more efficient than any existing general parsing algorithms in terms of recognition time as far as practical natural language grammars are concerned.

6.2 Parse Forest Representation

Some of the existing general parsing algorithms leave a well-formed substring table as their output. In my opinion, these well-formed substring tables are not appropriate as a parser's final output, because it is not straightforward to simply enumerate all possible parse trees out of the tables; another search must be involved. Thus we define a *parse forest* as a representation of all possible parse trees out of which we can trivially enumerate all trees without any substantial computation.

For most natural language grammars, our shared-packed forest representation, described in section 4, takes less than or equal to $O(n^3)$ space. This representation, however, occasionally takes more than $O(n^3)$ space with densely ambiguous grammars. For example, it takes $O(n^5)$ space with the grammar in figure 20.

Earley, on the other hand, gave in his thesis [8] a parse forest representation which takes at most $O(n^3)$ space for arbitrary context-free grammars. However, the next subsection shows that his representation has a defect, and should not be used in natural language processing.[5]   There exist some other algorithms that produce a parse forest in $O(n^3)$ space, but they require their grammars to be Chomsky Normal Form (CNF). Theoretically speaking every context-free grammar can be mechanically transformed into CNF. Practically speaking, however, it is usually not a good idea to mechanically transform a grammar into CNF, because the parse forest obtained from a CNF grammar will make little sense in practical applications; it is often hard to figure out a parse forest in accordance with its original grammar.

6.3 Defect of Earley's Forest Representation

This subsection identifies the defect of Earley's representation. Consider the following grammar G1 and the sentence in figure 23. Figure 24 is the parse forest produced by Earley's algorithm. The individual trees underlying in this representation are shown in figure 25. They are exactly what should be produced from the grammar and the sentence.

```
S --> e
S --> S J
J --> F
J --> I
F --> x
I --> x

sentence = 'xx'
```

Figure 23: Grammar G1

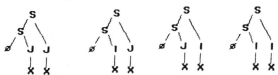

Figure 24: Earley's Parse Forest

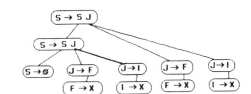

Figure 25: Underlying Parse Trees

Next consider the grammar G2 and the sentence in figure 26.

```
S --> S S
S --> x

sentence = 'xxx'
```

Figure 26: Grammar G2

The two possible parse trees out of this sentence are shown in figure 27.

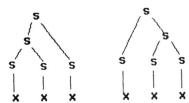

Figure 27: Correct Parse Trees

However, Earley's parsing algorithm produces the following representation.

---

[4]Those two kinds of grammars are equivalent.

[5]Several existing chart parsers seem to build a parse forest by adding pointers between edges. Since none of them gave a specification of the parse forest representation, we cannot make any comparisons. In any event, however, if they adopt Earley's representation then they must have the defect, and if they adopt my representation then they must occasionally take more than $O(n^3)$ time.

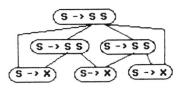

Figure 28: Defective Representation

This representation over-represents the trees; it represents not only the intended two parse trees, but also two other incorrect trees which are shown in figure 29.[6]

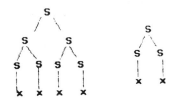

Figure 29: Wrong Parse Trees

Similarly, out of the sentence 'xxxx' with the same grammar G2, the algorithm produces a representation which over-represents 36 trees including 31 wrong trees along with 5 correct parse trees.

A grammar like G2 is totally unrealistic in the domain of programming language, and this kind of defect never appears as a real fault in that context. Productions like

```
S -> SS
```

in G2 look rather tricky and one might suspect that such a problem would arise only in a purely theoretical argument.

Unfortunately, that kind of production is often included in practical natural language grammars. For example, one might often include a production rule like

```
N -> NN
```

to represent compound nouns. This production rule says that two consecutive nouns can be compounded as a noun, as in 'file equipment' or 'bus driver.' This production rule is also used to represent compound nouns that consist of three or more nouns such as 'city bus driver' or 'IBM computer file equipment.' In this case, the situation is exactly the same as the situation with the grammar G2 and the sentence 'xxx' or 'xxxx', making the defect described in the previous section real in practice.

Another defective case is that using conjunctive rules such as

```
NP -> NP conj NP
VP -> VP conj VP
```

which are even more often included in practical grammars. The same problem as that above arises when the algorithm parses a sentence with the form:

```
NP and NP and NP.....
```

Yet another defective case which looks slightly different but which causes the same problem is that with the following productions:

```
NP -> NP PP
PP -> prep NP
```

These represent prepositional phrase attachment to noun phrases. The fault occurs when the algorithm parses sentences with the form:

```
NP prep NP prep NP.....
```

As we have seen, it is highly likely for a practical grammar to have defective rules like those above, and we conclude that Earley's representation of a parse forest cannot be used for natural languages.

7 Concluding Remarks

Our algorithm seems more efficient than any of the existing algorithms as far as practical natural language parsing is concerned, due to its utilization of LR parsing tables. Our shared-packed representation of a parse forest seems to be one of the most efficient representations which do not require CNF.

The following extensions of this paper can be found in my doctorate dissertation [17]:

- The algorithm is implemented and tested against four sample English grammars and about 50 sample sentences, to verify the feasibility of the algorithm to be used in practical systems.
- Earley's algorithm is also implemented and practical comparisons are made. The experiments show that our parsing algorithm is about 5 to 10 times faster than Earley's algorithm, as far as natural language processing is concerned.
- The algorithm's precise specification, as well as the source program, is presented.
- Multi-part-of-speech words and unknown words are handled by the algorithm without any special mechanism.
- An interactive disambiguation technique out of the shared-packed forest representation is described.
- An application to natural language interface, called *left-to-right on-line parsing*, is discussed, taking advantage of the algorithm's left-to-right-ness.

Acknowledgement

I would like to thank Jaime Carbonell, Phil Hayes, Herb Simon and Ralph Grishman for thoughtful comments on an earlier version of this paper, and Cynthia Hibbard for helping to produce this document.

---

[6]We could think of an algorithm that takes the defective representation as its argument, and enumerate only the intended parse trees, by checking the consistency of leaf nodes of each tree. Such an algorithm would, however, require the non-trivial amount of computation, violating our definition of parse forest.

References

[1]   Aho, A. V. and Ullman, J. D.
        The Theory of Parsing, Translation and Compiling.
        Prentice-Hall, Englewood Cliffs, N. J., 1972.

[2]   Aho, A. V. and Johnson, S. C.
        LR parsing.
        Computing Surveys 6:2:99-124, 1974.

[3]   Aho, A. V. and Ullman, J. D.
        Principles of Compiler Design.
        Addison Wesley, 1977.

[4]   Bouckaert, M., Pirotte, A. and Snelling, M.
        Efficient Parsing Algorithms for General Context-free
            Grammars.
        Inf. Sci. 8(1):1-26, Jan, 1975.

[5]   Cocke, J. and Schwartz, J. I.
        Programming Languages and Their Compilers.
        Courant Institute of Mathematical Sciences, New York
            University, New York, 1970.

[6]   Deremer, F. L.
        Practical Translators for LR(k) Languages.
        PhD thesis, MIT, 1969.

[7]   DeRemer, F. L.
        Simple LR(k) grammars.
        Comm. ACM 14:7:453-460, 1971.

[8]   Earley, J.
        An Efficient Context-free Parsing Algorithm.
        PhD thesis, Computer Science Department, Carnegie-
            Mellon University, 1968.

[9]   Earley, J.
        An Efficient Context-free Parsing Algorithm.
        Communication of ACM 6(8):94-102, February, 1970.

[10]   Fischer, M. J. and Meyer, A. R.
        Boolean Matrix Multiplication and Transitive Closure.
        In *IEEE Conf. Rec. Symp. Switching Automata Theory*,
            pages 129-131. 1971.

[11]   Graham, S. L. and Harrison, M. A.
        Parsing of General Context-free Languages.
        Academic Press, New York, 1976, pages 77-185.

[12]   Graham, S. L., Harrison, M. A. and Ruzzo, W. L.
        An Improved Context-free Recognizer.
        *ACM Transactions on Programming Languages and
            Systems* 2(3):415-462, July, 1980.

[13]   Pratt, V. R.
        LINGOL -- A Progress Report.
        In *Proc. of 4th IJCAI*, pages pp.327-381. August, 1975.

[14]   Sheil, B.
        Observations on context-free parsing.
        Statistical Methods in Linguistics :71-109, 1976.

[15]   Tomita, M.
        LR Parsers For Natural Languages.
        In *COLING'84*. 1984.

[16]   Tomita, M.
        *An Efficient All-Paths Parsing Algorithm for Natural
            Langauges.*
        Technical Report CMU-CS-84-163, Computer Science
            Department, Carnegie-Mellon University, Oct., 1984.

[17]   Tomita, M.
        *An Efficient Context-free Parsing Algorithm for Natural
            Languages and Its Applications.*
        PhD thesis, Computer Science Department, Carnegie-
            Mellon University, May, 1985.

[18]   Valiant, L.
        General Context-free Recognition in Less than Cubic
            Time.
        J. Comput Syst. Sci. 10:308-315, 1975.

[19]   Younger, D. H.
        Recognition and Parsing of Context-free Languages in
            time n^3.
        Information and Control 10(2):189-208, 1967.

Table of Contents

UNRESTRICTED GAPPING GRAMMARS[*]

Fred Popowich

Natural Language Group
Laboratory for Computer and Communications Research
Computing Science Department
Simon Fraser University
Burnaby, B.C., CANADA   V5A 1S6

ABSTRACT

Since the introduction of *metamorphosis grammars* (MGs) (Colmerauer, 1978), with their associated *type 0*-like grammar rules, there has been a desire to allow more general rule formats in logic grammars. *Gaps*, which refer to strings of unspecified symbols, were added to the MG rule, resulting in *extraposition grammars* (XGs) (Pereira, 1981) and *gapping grammars* (GGs) (Dahl and Abramson, 1984). *Unrestricted gapping grammars*, which provide an even more general rule format, possess rules of the form "$\alpha \rightarrow \beta$" where α and β many contain any number of terminal nonterminal or gap symbols in any order. FIGG, a Flexible Implementation of Gapping Grammars, is an implementation of a large subset of unrestricted GGs which allows either bottom-up or top-down parsing of sentences. This system provides more built in control facilities than previous logic grammar implementations, which allows the user to restrict the applicability of the rules, and to create grammar rules that will be executed more efficiently.

1. INTRODUCTION

Gaps have been introduced into logic grammars, resulting in *extraposition grammars* (Pereira, 1981) and *gapping grammars* (Dahl and Abramson, 1984), to express a more general grammar rule that can be interpreted with "reasonable" efficiency by a computer. The rules of these grammars are of the form "$nt, \alpha \rightarrow \beta$", where nt is a nonterminal symbol called the *head*, and α and β may contain terminal symbols, nonterminal symbols, procedure calls, and gap symbols.[**] Extraposition grammars are able to provide concise descriptions for left extraposition as found in sentences like *the mouse that the cat chased squeaked*. However, extraposition grammar rules are more restrictive than those of gapping grammars, since the gaps referenced on the left hand side of the rule must be

repositioned in the same order at the end of the right hand side. Also, the contents of multiple gaps must be nested (one gap totally contained within another), or non-intersecting. With gapping grammars, concise descriptions of coordination, free word order, and right extraposition can be obtained (Dahl, 1984).

Unrestricted gapping grammars extend gapping grammars by the removal of the restriction that the left hand side of all rules must start with a nonterminal symbol. Consequently, the unrestricted gapping grammar rules resemble "$\alpha \rightarrow \beta$", where α and β may contain terminals, nonterminals, gaps and procedure calls in any order. This type of rule facilitates easier description of unrestricted left movement of symbols.

Unfortunately, the use of gaps can result in less efficient computer processing of the rules. Consequently, many applications of gapping grammars have not been explored except from a theoretical point of view. One method to circumvent this "efficiency problem" is to add procedural control to the otherwise declarative grammar rules. (The *cut* facility of Prolog (Clocksin and Mellish, 1981) is an example of this procedural intervention). FIGG, a *Flexible Implementation of Gapping Grammars*, is a programming language that incorporates procedural control to process many unrestricted gapping grammars with *tolerable* response time in an interactive environment. Using FIGG, the different forms of procedural control can be examined for their uses with unrestricted gapping grammars.

2. UNRESTRICTED GAPPING GRAMMARS

Unrestricted gapping grammars, like other logic grammars, use *logic terms* as grammar symbols. A *logic term* consists of a *functor*, which may possess zero or more *arguments*. Each *functor* possesses an *order*, which corresponds to the number of arguments, and is an element of some finite set **F**. The *arguments*, which are enclosed in parenthesis and separated by commas, may be *logic terms*, or *variables*. $\hbar$ [**F**] is used to refer to the set of logic terms that can be constructed from **F**. In this paper, elements of **F** will be represented by words starting with a lower case letter, or enclosed in single quotes. Words which start with an upper case letter or an *under score* "_", will represent *variables*. A *list*, which is

[*]This work was supported by the Natural Sciences and Engineering Research Council of Canada under Operating Grant no. A4309, Installation Grant no. SMI-74 and Postgraduate Scholarship #800.

[**]Gap symbols are used to reference sequences of unspecified symbols.

a logic term of the form $'.'(\alpha_1, '.'(\alpha_2,....'.'(\alpha_n,nil)...))$, is usually represented as $[\alpha_1, \alpha_2, ...\alpha_n]$. Also, $[t\|l]$ is a shorthand for $'.'(t,l)$. During a derivation according to the grammar, variables may be *unified* with other logic terms (Clocksin and Mellish, 1981). Logic grammars also tend to possess facilities for handling *procedure calls* appearing within the grammar rules.

An unrestricted gapping grammar can be defined as a quintuple $(V_N, V_T, \Gamma, \Sigma, P)$ where: V_N is the set of nonterminal symbols, $V_N \subset \check{H}$ [F]; V_T is the set of terminal symbols, $V_T \subset \check{H}$ [F], with $V_N \cap V_T = \phi$; Γ is the set of gap symbols, $\Gamma \subset \check{H}$ [F], with $\Gamma \cap V = \phi$, where $V = V_N \cup V_T$; Σ is the set of starting symbols, with $\Sigma \subset V_N$, and P is the set of productions of the form

$$(2.1) \quad \alpha_0, gap(G_1), \alpha_1, \ldots, gap(G_m), \alpha_m$$
$$--> \beta_0, gap(G'_1), \beta_1, \ldots, gap(G'_n), \beta_n$$

with $m, n \geqslant 0$, $0 \leqslant i \leqslant m$, $0 \leqslant j \leqslant n$, $\alpha_i, \beta_j \in V^*$,*** and $gap(G_i), gap(G'_j) \in \Gamma$. The rewrite relation, $==>$, between elements of V^* may be defined as

$$(2.2) \quad \alpha_0 \gamma_1 \alpha_1 \ldots \gamma_m \alpha_m ==> \beta_0 \gamma'_1 \beta_1 \ldots \gamma'_n \beta_n$$

for a production (2.1) where $\gamma_i, \gamma'_j \in V^*$. Ignoring variable substitution, the language, $L(G)$, associated with this grammar is

$$(2.3) \quad L(G) = \{\omega \in V_T^* \mid s ==>^* \omega \text{ for } s \in \Sigma\}****$$

Unrestricted GGs can provide simpler description of some forms of left extraposition than was possible using GGs. To illustrate this point, let us examine a language, L, described in (Joshi, 1983). This language is obtained from $\{(ba)^n c^n \mid n \geqslant 1\}$ by "dislocating some a's to the left." Using an unrestricted gapping grammar, this language can be described by the following productions.

(2.4)   (a) s --> [b], a, s, [c].
        (b) s --> [b], a, [c].
        (c) gap(G), a --> [a], gap(G).

The rules are constructed to allow an a to be moved only once. An equivalent grammar using GG rules, that does not shift b's to the right, requires the addition of at least one production.

(2.5)   (a) s --> target, [b], target, a, s, [c].
        (b) s --> target, [b], target, a, [c].
        (c) target, gap(G), a --> [a], target, gap(G).
        (d) target --> ε.

In (2.5), the nonterminal *target* represents a location where an a may be moved to, while epsilon, ϵ, corresponds to the empty string.

***For any set S, $S^* = \cup_{i=0}^{\infty} S^i$.

****$==>^*$ is the reflexive transitive closure of $==>$.

Along with easier description of left relocation of symbols, there is another phenomenon that follows from the removal of the nonterminal head restriction. The definition of rules resembling "$\epsilon --> \beta$" is no longer prohibited. With this style of production, rule (2.4c) could be replaced by the following two rules.

(2.6)   (a) target, gap(G), a --> [a], gap(G).
        (b) ε --> target.

Any *target*s introduced somewhere to the left of an a by (2.6b), can be replaced by an a which is dislocated to the left according to (2.6a).

To facilitate further study of unrestricted gapping grammars, and to examine mechanisms for introducing procedural control to provide more efficiently *executable* productions, the FIGG programming language was developed. FIGG is a Prolog programme that implements a large subset of unrestricted gapping grammars.

3. FIGG

FIGG currently consists of a bottom-up shift-reduce parser and a top-down depth-first parser which can operate (independently) on a set of unrestricted GG rules. The system also provides built-in control operators which allow the user to create efficiently executable grammar rules. The top-down depth-first backtrack parser incorporates these procedural control mechanisms in a parser which is based on one described in (Dahl and Abramson, 1984). It differs from its predecessor by allowing left recursion in its grammar rules, and by being more efficient, although not as general. Rules are still required to have a nonterminal as the head. The shift reduce parser used with FIGG is a variation of a context free shift reduce parser (Aho and Ullman, 1972) (Stabler, 1983) extended to allow non-context-free rules and gaps. To mirror the left to right processing of the top-down parser, the shift reduce parser processes a sentence from right to left. Details about the syntax and implementation of FIGG can be found in (Popowich, forthcoming).

The implementations of many previous logic grammars incorporated clumsy mechanisms for procedural control. Unless one resorted to arbitrary procedure calls, the only options available for such control were rule order, the introduction of marker symbols, or the *cut* operation. Increased control facilities provided in FIGG include control of gap processing, more sophisticated variations of *cut*, and restrictions on applicability of rules. For example, when the FIGG parser is processing a gap symbol, gap(G), it initially assumes an empty gap and then attempts to parse the next symbol. Through *backtracking*, the gap size is increased. However, a *decreasing gap*, gap(-,G), is initially assumed to contain the rest of the sentence, and is decreased in size during backtracking. Also, although the *cut* behaves as in Prolog during top-down parsing, it behaves differently during bottom-up parsing since the top-down parser operates on terminal symbols — like the definite clause grammar parser (Pereira and Warren, 1980) — while the shift reduce parser works with sentential forms. For bottom-up processing, each rule is converted into a single Prolog clause that modifies a *list* which corresponds to a *sentential form*. When the right hand side of a rule matches part of a sentential form, the matched region can be replaced by the left hand side of the rule. Consequently, cuts — and other control mechanisms — that appear in the right hand of a rule affect the left to right matching of the rule to a sentential form. Once the portion of a rule to the left of a cut has matched a sentential form, a subsequent failure in the match occurring to the right of the cut cannot force the match to the left of the cut to be reattempted. A cut found in the left hand side of a rule, R, will prevent any subsequent rule, R', from matching a region entirely to the right of the cut. That is, the application of R' to the sentential form resulting from the application of R must include at least one symbol to the left of the cut. If a rule, R, is entirely enclosed in a cut, $(R)!$, then the decision to apply R to a sentential form cannot be revoked once the rule has been successfully applied.

4. USE OF PROCEDURAL CONTROL

Unrestricted gapping grammars, as implemented in FIGG, can be considered as a programming language, and can be used to provide parsers for languages, given a grammatical specification. Few studies have been done to examine the applicability of gapping grammars as a programming tool, since the earlier implementations were either inefficient or processed too small of a subset of these grammars. We will examine some ways to control the processing of unrestricted GG specifications to improve the efficiency of the parsing, and to restrict the language described. In this section, we shall use a selection of familiar formal languages to examine the use of the various control mechanisms. The use of FIGG with natural languages is examined in (Popowich, 1985) and (Popowich forthcoming).

Consider the context sensitive language $L_1 = \{a^m b^n c^m d^n \mid m,n \geq 0\}$. A set of productions (Dahl, 1984) of a grammar, G_1, that describes this language is provided in (4.1).

(4.1) (a) s --> as, bs, cs, ds.
       (b) as, gap(G), cs --> [a], as, gap(G), [c], cs.
       (c) bs, gap(G), ds --> [b], bs, gap(G), [d], ds.
       (d) as, gap(G), cs --> [a], gap(G), [c].
       (e) bs, gap(G), ds --> [b], gap(G), [d].

Behaviour of FIGG with this grammar and with strings of increasing length is summarised in Table 4-1. Times are in CPU seconds for a SUN Workstation running C-Prolog (Pereira, 1984) under UNIX.[*****] The first number represents the time required for a successful parse, and the second number includes the time spent looking for all

---

[*****]UNIX is a trademark of Bell Laboratories.

other possible parses. The results expose a severe parsing problem for G_1 with increasing sentence length. However, closer examination of (4.1) illustrates that the *gaps* should result in the ith a matching the ith c, and similarly for the b's and d's. If a decreasing gap is used in the productions, then the first successful gap followed by a c (or d, depending on the rule) will result in the correct matching. A cut can then prevent the other alternatives from being tried. Thus, G_1' is obtained by modifying (4.1b-e) as shown in (4.2), resulting in much improved performance as illustrated in Table 4-1.

(4.2) (b) as, gap(-,G), cs --> [a], as, gap(-,G), [c], !, cs.
       (c) as, gap(-,G), cs --> [a], gap(-,G), [c], !.
       (d) bs, gap(-,G), ds --> [b], bs, gap(-,G), [d], !, ds.
       (e) bs, gap(-,G), ds --> [b], gap(-,G), [d], !.

While G_1 and G_1' are processed by the top-down parser, G_1'' in Table 4-1 represents a grammar equivalent to G_1' that is processed by the bottom-up parser. In this case, the bottom-up processing takes about two and a half times longer than top-down parsing.

Table 4-1: Parse and total analysis times for $a^m b^m c^m d^m$

grammar	m=1	m=5	m=10	m=15	m=20	m=25	m=30
G_1	0.1	1.4	9.8	32.			
	0.2	6.3	85.	420.			
G_1'	0.1	0.5	1.6	3.2	5.4	8.4	11.8
	0.2	0.7	1.9	3.6	6.0	9.0	13.
G_1''	0.2	1.4	4.0	8.2	14.	22.	30.
	0.3	1.5	4.3	8.7	15.	22.	31.

Now consider the productions that describe the language $L_2 = \{a^n b^n c^n \mid n > 0\}$.

(4.3) (a) s --> [a], bs, [c].
       (b) s --> [a], s, b, [c].
       (c) bs, gap(G), b --> [b], bs, gap(G).
       (d) bs --> [b].

Unfortunately, a gapping grammar containing these productions would be ambiguous. The ambiguity can be removed through modification of (4.3b-c), as shown in (4.4), resulting in a new gapping grammar G_2'.

(4.4) (b) s --> [a], s, b, c.
       (c) bs, gap(-,G), b, c --> [b], bs, gap(-,G), [c], !.

An unambiguous unrestricted gapping grammar, G_2'', which has one less production and one less nonterminal symbol than G_2', can also be provided for this language.

(4.5) (a) s --> [a], [b], [c].
       (b) s --> [a], s, b, c.
       (c) ([b], !, gap(-,G), b, c --> [b], [b], gap(-,G), [c])!.

The parse times for various sentences, where G_2' and G_2'' are processed by the top-down and bottom-up parsers respectively, are summarised in Table 4-2. This time, the bottom-up parser is slower by a constant multiple of three However, its slowness is offset by the fact that it can process many more grammars than its top-down counterpart. An unrestricted gapping grammar can be used by the bottom-up parser as long as it does not result in *bottom-up cycles*. For example, any grammar containing the rule *"nt --> ϵ"*, can not be used by this parser. Further development on this Prolog parser may improve its efficiency.

Table 4-2:   Parse and total analysis times for $a^m b^m c^m$

grammar	m=1	m=5	m=10	m=15	m=20	m=25	m=30
G_2'	0.1	0.2	0.7	1.3	2.3	3.5	5.0
	0.1	0.3	0.9	1.7	2.7	4.0	5.7
G_2''	0.1	0.5	1.7	3.7	6.5	11.	15.
	0.1	0.7	2.2	4.5	7.9	12.	18.

Thus, the results illustrate that the introduction of some limited procedural control can be done simply with very beneficial results. Without its introduction, the processing time may be intolerable in some cases. It will not always be possible though, to introduce simple restrictions on gaps and parsing. The effect of a control mechanism is also very dependent on the grammar itself. As illustrated in the examples, the same operator — the cut — can result in more efficient parsing, or can restrict the language described by the grammar. The determination of which control to use, and how to use it, is the responsibility of the person who contructs the grammar. Obviously, more study of procedural control is required.

5. SUMMARY

Unrestricted gapping grammars provide more concise grammatical descriptions than previous logic grammar formalisms for many languages due to the more general rule format allowed. However, with such a general rule format, caution must be taken to insure that the grammar is restricted, by some form of control, to describe the required language. Control facilities provided in FIGG permit refined control mechanisms while maintaining a high degree of descriptiveness in the grammar rules. These control facilities can be used either to restrict the language described by the grammar, or to obtain more efficient parsing The parsers of FIGG have successfully combined processing efficiency along with a large subset of unrestricted gapping grammars to produce a programming environment to study grammars and their languages.

ACKNOWLEDGEMENTS

I would like to thank Nick Cercone and the referees for their comments and suggestions. Facilities for this research were provided by the Laboratory for Computer and Communications Research.

REFERENCES

Aho, A.V. and Ullman, J.D. **The Theory of Parsing, Translation and Compiling.**   Englewood Cliffs, N.J :Prentice Hall Inc., 1972.

Clocksin, W.F. and Mellish, C.S. **Programming in Prolog.** Berlin-Heidelberg-NewYork:Springer-Verlag, 1981.

Colmerauer, A. Metamorphosis Grammars. In L. Bolc (Ed.). **Natural Language Communication with Computers,** Springer Verlag, Berlin, 1978.

Dahl, V. **More On Gapping Grammars.** Proceedings of the International Conference on Fifth Generation Computer Systems, Institute for New Generation Computer Technology, Tokyo, 1984.

Dahl, V. and Abramson, H. **On Gapping Grammars.** Proceedings of the Second International Joint Conference on Logic, University of Uppsala, Sweden, 1984.

Joshi, A.K. **Factoring Recursion and Dependencies: An Aspect of Tree Adjoining Grammars (TAGs) and a Comparison of Some Formal Properties of TAGs, GPSGs, PLGs and LPGs,** pages 7-15. Proceedings of the 21th Annual Meeting of the Association for Computational Linguistics, June, 1983.

Pereira, F.C.N. Extraposition Grammars. **American Journal of Computational Linguistics,** 1981, 7(4), 243-256.

Pereira, F.C.N.(ed). **C-Prolog User's Manual.** Technical Report, SRI International, Menlo Park, California, 1984.

Pereira, F.C.N. and Warren, D.H.D. Definite Clause Grammars for Language Analysis. **Artificial Intelligence,** 1980, 13, 231-278.

Popowich, F. **Unrestricted Gapping Grammars for ID/LP Grammars.** Proceedings of Theoretical Approaches to Natural Language Understanding, Dalhousie University, Halifax Canada, 1985.

Popowich, F. **Effective Implementation and Application of Unrestricted Gapping Grammars.** Master's thesis, Department of Computing Science, Simon Fraser University, forthcoming.

Stabler, E.P. (Jr). **Deterministic and Bottom-Up Parsing in Prolog,** pages 383-386. Proceedings of the American Association for Artificial Intelligence, August, 1983.

PARSING WITH ASSERTION SETS AND INFORMATION MONOTONICITY[*]

G. Edward Barton, Jr. and Robert C. Berwick

M.I.T. Artificial Intelligence Laboratory
545 Technology Square
Cambridge, MA 02139

ABSTRACT

We propose a new approach to parsing ambiguity in which a parser always moves forward with the common elements of competing syntactic analyses. The approach involves *assertion sets* constrained so that information is monotonically preserved throughout a parse. Assertion sets have several advantages over trees as a parsing representation. They may also lead to better computational understanding of the attention-shifting mechanism.

I INTRODUCTION

Recent linguistic theories divide linguistic constraints into subsystems each having its own character. The complex surface character of a language is ultimately generated by the interactions among a few fundamental processes and constraints. We are most interested in the GB-theory framework of Chomsky (1981), which identifies subtheories concerned with locality, government, assignment of semantic roles, pronoun binding, case, control, and $\overline{X}$-constraints, but some developments in other frameworks also tend toward modularity. For instance, Shieber (1983:2ff) describes a version of the GPSG formalism that separates immediate-dominance rules, linear-order constraints, and metarules, while the TAG formalism (Kroch and Joshi, 1985) factors recursion apart from co-occurrence restrictions.

The surface complexity of parsing should be decomposed in the same way as the surface complexity of language. Principles that are common to all languages should not have their effects repeatedly redescribed in the descriptions of particular languages, but should instead be exploited as part of parser design. Similarly, a single underlying process within an individual language should not have its effects spelled out separately in each surface manifestation; ideally the process should be encoded just once, in such a way that the parser can work out what surface appearances to look for. Beyond syntactic theory, parser design provides additional opportunities for such factoring; not only linguistic principles but also aspects of parser control structure may be factored out. However, the general effect on the description of a language is the same: Less information is needed to describe a language, if redundancy can be factored out and if control-structure elements can be removed from the grammar and incorporated in basic parser design.

Our goal is thus a dual one. We aim to build a parser that bases its operation on modular subcomponents instead of a welter of surface-oriented rules; in so doing, we will reduce the amount of language-particular syntactic information that must be supplied by the designer of a natural-language system.[**] As one component of this effort, we are considering possible ways to use a "stripped-down" parsing representation that is based as much as possible on the predicates of linguistic theory. We hope to reduce the amount of grammatically extraneous information that the parser manipulates.

II ASSERTION SETS

It is doubtful that traditional parse trees are ideal for representing syntactic structure, for in general the range of structural information that a tree makes explicit may not correspond to the information that is grammatically relevant. For example, $\overline{X}$-theory suggests that the head-projection relationship may be more important grammatically than the immediate-domination relationship that a tree displays. In a different vein, it has been hypothesized (Lasnik and Kupin, 1977:178f) that linguistic theory is insensitive to characteristics of trees that cannot be recovered from information about the range of terminals spanned by each constituent.

We are investigating the use of *monotonically growing assertion sets* as a parsing representation. A constituent is represented by a triple $(\varphi\ i\ j)$, where φ is a bundle of syntactic features (*e.g.* one that we might abbreviate with the usual label NP) and i, j are the input positions defining the left and right edges of the constituent.[*] For example, if we assume that Adj⁻ N forms a constituent that we will call NBAR, the structure of the NP *the red block* might be represented by the assertion set

$$\{(NP\ 0\ 3),(Det\ 0\ 1),(Adj\ 1\ 2),(N\ 2\ 3),(NBAR\ 1\ 3)\}.$$

With this representation, parsing is the construction of such an assertion set — closely akin to a "phrase-marker" in the sense of Chomsky's (1955) early work. (In the early stages of parsing, the assertion should actually appear as (NP 0 *) to indicate that the right edge of the constituent has not yet been encountered.)

An assertion-set parser develops its analyses *deterministically* if changes in its (global) assertion set are always *refinements* in the information-theoretic sense — that is, if information is monotonically preserved. Under determinism, the only possible refinements are adding a new assertion, changing a * to a specific value, and adding features to an underspecified category. For example, operating under a rudimentary $\overline{X}$-theory, it would be possible to change the features of a constituent from [+N] to [+N, −V, +max], *i.e.* from an underspecified category to NP, but impossible to change NP to VP. Monotonicity would also rule out the usual notion of nondeterministic chart parsing; the parser would be unable to remove initially plausible analyses that failed to pan out.

Monotonically growing assertion sets are attractive in several ways for representing syntactic structure. For example, beyond the device of using initially underspecified feature bundles, there are some useful *structural modifications* that are information-preserving when applied to assertion sets, but not when applied

---

[*] This report describes research done at the Artificial Intelligence Laboratory of the Massachusetts Institute of Technology. Support for the Laboratory's artificial intelligence research has been provided in part by the Advanced Research Projects Agency of the Department of Defense under Office of Naval Research contract N00014-80-C-0505. During a portion of this research Ed Barton's graduate studies were supported by the Fannie and John Hertz Foundation.

[**] See Barton (1984) for more information on this general research program.

---

[*] This representation takes a cue from Lasnik and Kupin as well as from the representations used in chart parsing. Nirenburg and Attiya (1984) use a similar representation, but do not add the constraint of information monotonicity. Although we use numeric input indices here for simplicity, a representation based instead on the actual words of the terminal string is better in cases of movement and, under an new analysis by Goodall (1984), in cases of conjunction.

to trees.* Changing the tree for *I told John a ghost story* into the tree for *I told John a ghost story was the last thing I wanted to hear* requires (non-monotonically) breaking the link between VP and [$_\text{NP}$ *a ghost story*] and replacing it with a link between VP and S. In the same way, a tree link is deleted when *John* is moved one level deeper in going from *see John* to *see John and Bill*. In the assertion-set representation, each of these changes can be described as the addition of an assertion. An S assertion is added in the first change, an NP assertion in the second; in each case all previous structure assertions remain valid when the new assertion is added, if the change is made before the right edge of VP has been declared. Assertion sets can thus allow a deterministic parser to be *partially noncommittal* about the exact attachment level of a constituent.**

The ability of assertion sets to represent partial information can also be useful in handling PP-attachment ambiguity. If it is not clear whether to attach an adjunct PP under NP or VP, for instance, the various structural possibilities will still agree on the existence and internal structure of PP. If NP with adjunct PP is analyzed as [$_\text{NP}$ NP PP], they will also agree on the lower NP.*** This example illustrates the fact that assertion sets support co-called Chomsky-adjunction more naturally than sister-adjunction. For example, on some analyses of the rightward movement called Heavy NP Shift, NP is Chomsky-adjoined to the end of VP to produce the structure [$_\text{VP}$ VP NP]. With assertion sets, the representation of the lower VP is (monotonically) preserved when the assertion is added that describes the upper VP. Some linguists have argued that the preservation of information about constituent structure makes this form of adjunction the appropriate one for describing the structural changes wrought by transformations.**** With trees, it is *sister*-adjunction that is information-preserving, as in a hypothetical replacement of [$_\text{VP}$ V *t* PP] with [$_\text{VP}$ V *t* PP NP].

III THE THEORY OF ATTENTION-SHIFTING

Because of its atomistic character, the assertion-set representation may also pave the way to a better understanding of the attention-shifting mechanism of the deterministic Marcus parser (Marcus, 1980:175). The attention-shifting mechanism implements a "wait-and-see" strategy for dealing with some of the cases in which the parser cannot tell which possible step to take next. Interpreted abstractly, the strategy allows the parser to move forward with those elements of the structural analysis that it can be sure of. When attention-shifting rules begin to build a constituent, it may be unclear how it will fit into the final parse tree. However, a deterministic parser cannot be justified in building the constituent unless all competing analyses agree on its existence and internal structure.*****

The possibility exists that a parser could deal with parsing ambiguity by explicit observing the operating principle: always go ahead with the *common elements* of competing syntactic analyses. Under this principle, it would not be necessary to write attention shifts into the rule system explicitly; attention-shifting, when necessary, would be automatic. Such a parser could *explain*

attention-shifting behavior by deriving it from a principled treatment of parsing ambiguity, could validate the informal characterization of attention-shifting as the implementation of a *wait-and-see* strategy, and would clarify the *computational problem* that is solved by the attention-shifting mechanism. In brief, it would contribute to the *computational theory* of the Marcus parser — in Marr's (1980:25) sense — in addition to serving the goal of removing control-structure elements from language descriptions.

Assertion sets are superior to trees for use in such a parser. It is unclear how to *intersect* trees in order to take the common elements of different analyses, while ordinary set intersection roughly suffices for assertion sets because of their atomistic character.* It is also unclear how the tree representing common elements of analysis could be *partially noncommittal* about attachment point in the cases mentioned earlier. Finally, in the presence of left-recursion as with possessive NPs, there will be an *infinite number* of ways to extend a tree downward to encompass a new element; with at most bounded lookahead, it is impossible to say how many tree nodes lie between the new input and the point of attachment to the existing tree. It will thus be difficult to envision all possible syntactic analyses in a tree-based parser. Left-recursion causes no more of a problem with assertion sets than it does with the related representation of a chart parser, since the *-notation collapses an infinite number of nodes into a single assertion.

Several issues must be addressed in the design of any parser that proceeds by moving ahead with those elements of the syntactic analysis that are known for certain. The parsing representation must be *decomposable* into smaller elements that have meaning when separated; assertion sets fit the bill here. Different aspects of parsing rules and actions must also be *separable* in the sense that some parsing actions can still be licensed even when knowledge is insufficient to license all of them. It should sometimes be possible for parsing ambiguity to be eventually *resolved* when disambiguating evidence is encountered; elements of analysis that are correct but were initially discarded because of uncertainty should not remain forever absent. A decision must be made about the *stringency* of rule matching; it is customary to require the parsing representation to explicitly list the features mentioned in a rule, but because taking the common elements of competing analyses will result in feature underspecification, it may be better to require only feature compatibility between the rule pattern and the parsing representation. One must ensure that the implementation strategy does not allow *combinatorial blowup* to creep into the rule-matching process. Finally, it will be necessary to impose some *coherence* requirement on the collection of analytic possibilities; if they diverge too widely, the parser cannot sensibly integrate their common elements.

IV SHAPE COMPATIBILITY

The application of this parsing method is not completely worked out, either in the Marcus framework or in a standard context-free parsing framework. However, some of the intent can be suggested by sketching out a simplified model based on CFGs. The basic parsing cycle is to involve three steps: matching rules against the parsing representation, running the matching rules to produce several possible extensions of the representation, and intersecting the possibilities to produce the next parsing representation. The fundamental problem is to intertwine analysis and control in such a way that the monotonically growing syntactic analysis is always sufficient to support rule matching, while the control component always runs a set of rules that will advance the analysis one step further in a coherent way — all the while operating under the strategy of taking the common elements of competing syntactic analyses.

As an initial approximation, suppose predictions define the unit of licensed parse continuation. Then if *a* is ambiguously either A_1 or A_2 and the rules $S \rightarrow A_1 B x$ and $S \rightarrow A_2 B y$ are being considered while parsing a string that begins with *a*, it will

---

* Marcus *et al.* (1983) describe a parsing representation that also differs from trees in its possibilities for information-preserving structural modification.

** This should be especially helpful in devising a data-driven treatment of conjunction that does not predict conjoined NPs except when prompted by specific cues. The close relation between some variant of assertion sets and the monostrings that Lasnik and Kupin have described also makes assertion sets promising for the implementation of Goodall's new (1984) monostring-based theory of conjunction.

*** The assertion-set framework is compatible with having the assertion sets filtered by extrasyntactic information in order to ultimately resolve the attachment ambiguity.

**** Chomsky (1981:141), among others, has tentatively argued this. However, "Chomsky-adjunction" as a name for this operation is historically accidental.

***** Marcus's actual mechanism includes nothing to guarantee such agreement, with consequences that become more severe as lexical ambiguity increases.

---

* Some modification is necessary in order to accommodate analyses that disagree only on node features.

initially be unclear whether to reduce a as A_1 or A_2. However, in either case it is predicted that a B will come next in the input. This common prediction can license the construction of a B and eventually allow the parser to see the disambiguating x at the end of the string. The same principle operates in a more complex way when parsing the VP *know that big red blocks* ... given a determiner-noun agreement mechanism; if *that* can be either Comp or Det, it is initially unclear which interpretation to take. However, the competing syntactic analyses agree that an NBAR is possible after *that*. Thus the construction of NBAR is licensed, and the agreement mechanism can rule out the determiner interpretation once the NBAR is built.

Closer scrutiny reveals that intersection of predictions is not actually the appropriate operation here. Suppose B above surfaces as $k^\sim b$, another constituent C surfaces as $k^\sim c$, and the rule $S \rightarrow A_1 C z$ is possible. The construction of either B or C should be licensed after the initial a; in fact, B and C can always be distinguished by the time they have been completely scanned. However, only B is licensed if we take the intersection of all predictions. In seeming contradiction to the principle of taking common elements of competing analyses, predictions should be subject to *union* rather than intersection.

The contradiction is resolved by noticing that in any deterministic parser, it is necessary to say what counts as part of the syntactic analysis subject to determinism. In Marcus's parser, packet activations don't count; in contrast to features, they may be both added and removed. Packet activation *licenses* the interpretation of certain elements in certain ways if they occur, but it does not *commit* the parser to expecting those elements. (Node creation and attachment, on the other hand, *are* subject to determinism.) Predictions in the CFG framework license possible interpretations in the same way, hence they should not be subject to intersection; rather, the interpretations that are actually imposed should be intersected.

If some operations involve the union rather than the intersection of possibilities, an immediate question is why the parsing method does not degenerate to the full Earley algorithm. In this sketch, that question is where the *coherence* requirement comes in. In the assertion-set framework, the simplest requirement to impose is one of *shape compatibility*. In the case of *that*-ambiguity, even though we cannot initially decide whether *that* is a complementizer or a determiner, in either case it bears the same structural relationship to the next constituent (commanding the NBAR of NP, or commanding the S of SBAR).* If different analyses must place constituent boundaries in the same place but may disagree about constituent identity, dotted-rule items will not require a return address as they do in the full Earley algorithm. In the above example, the possibilities $(A_1\ 0\ 1)$ and $(A_2\ 0\ 1)$ are shape-compatible and can intersect to the featureless lump $(*\ 0\ 1)$. When the end of a dotted rule is reached, such lumps can be back-traversed to find the left edge of the completed constituent. Thus the coherence requirement of shape compatibility allows the parser to use a *finite* "packet structure," as indeed it must if information monotonicity is not to be vacuous.

Preliminary investigation suggests that shape compatibility can help in many troublesome cases, *e.g. that*-ambiguity and *for*-ambiguity. Other cases such as PP-attachment ambiguity will require mechanisms to be extended. As one possibility, limited lookahead promotes coherence by filtering out shape-incompatible possibilities that would die soon anyway. Extensions will also be required for full attention-shifting behavior.

Ideally, CFGs and dotted rules should be dispensed with and the feature bundles of assertions should drive the entire analysis. By separability, this is feasible only if the feature system that is used can support a parsing interpretation for individual features. A feature system under development by Reuland (1984) is especially interesting in this regard, since each of his features describes a separate aspect of the combinatorial possiblities of a syntactic category. However, the standard $\overline{X}$ features $[\pm N, \pm V]$ also are individually relevant to Case-assignment rules and other

---

* The possibilities share the same skeleton, in the sense of Levy and Joshi (1978).

constraints that could be exploited in parsing. In addition, some cases of parsing ambiguity that have been thought to require attention-shifting might be analyzed in terms of other common elements between competing analyses besides those mentioned here. For example, a fact closely related to shape compatibility is that English *that* must *begin* some kind of $\overline{X}$ projection, whether it is the specifier (Det) or the head (Comp) of that projection.

REFERENCES

[1] Barton, E. (1984). "Toward a Principle-Based Parser," A.I. Memo No. 788, M.I.T. Artificial Intelligence Laboratory, Cambridge, Mass.

[2] Chomsky, N. (1955). *The Logical Structure of Linguistic Theory*, published in 1975 by Plenum Press (New York).

[3] Chomsky, N. (1981). *Lectures on Government and Binding*. Dordrecht, Holland: Foris Publications.

[4] Goodall, G. (1984). "Coordination," PhD dissertation, Department of Linguistics, University of California at San Diego.

[5] Kroch, A., and A. Joshi (1985). "The Linguistic Relevance of Tree Adjoining Grammars," Technical Report No. MS-CIS-85-16, Department of Computer and Information Science, Moore School, University of Pennsylvania, Philadephia, Penn.

[6] Lasnik, H., and J. Kupin (1977). "A Restrictive Theory of Transformational Grammar," *Theoretical Linguistics* 4:3, 173–196.

[7] Levy, L., and A. Joshi (1978). "Skeletal Structural Descriptions," *Information and Control* 39:192–211.

[8] Marcus, M. (1980). *A Theory of Syntactic Recognition for Natural Language*. Cambridge, Mass.: M.I.T. Press.

[9] Marcus, M., D. Hindle, and M. Fleck (1983). "D-Theory: Talking about Talking about Trees," ACL '83 proceedings.

[10] Marr, D. (1982). *Vision*. San Francisco: W. H. Freeman and Company.

[11] Nirenburg, S., and C. Attiya (1984). "Interruptible Transition Networks," COLING '84 proceedings, pp. 393–397.

[12] Reuland, E. (1984). "Features for the Set of Categorial Heads," ms.

WEIGHTED INTERACTION OF SYNTAX AND SEMANTICS
IN NATURAL LANGUAGE ANALYSIS

Leonardo Lesmo and Pietro Torasso

Dipartimento di Informatica - Universita' di Torino
Via Valperga Caluso, 37 - 10125 TORINO - ITALY

ABSTRACT

The present paper discusses the extensions to the parsing strategies adopted for FIDO (a Flexible Interface for Database Operations). The parser is able to deal with ill-formed inputs (syntactically ill - formed sentences, fragments, conjunctions, etc.) because of the strict cooperation among syntax and semantics. The syntactic knowledge is represented by means of packets of condition-action rules associated with syntactic categories. The non-determinism is mainly handled by means of rules which restructure the parse tree (called "natural changes") so that the use of backtracking is strongly limited.

In order to deal with difficult cases in which no clear-cut mechanism exists for excluding an interpretation, a weighting mechanism has been added to the parser so that it is possible to explore few different hypotheses in parallel and to choose the best one on the basis of complex interaction among syntax and semantics.

INTRODUCTION

If one considers the evolution of computerized natural language understanding systems (Charniak, 1981), it becomes apparent that the role of syntactic knowledge can vary from being the basis of the process to being completely neglected. In the first case, the conversion fom a linear sequence of words to a corresponding structured representation (parse tree) is guided only by the syntactic knowledge, whereas the other knowledge sources (mainly semantics) have the task to translate the parse tree into a meaning representation; within the other approach the understanding process is viewed as a whole and no special role is played by syntactic knowledge (given that such a knowledge is assumed to exist).

As regards purely semantic approaches, they present some problems with respect to the perspicuity of the model. In particular, the structural information (e.g. the fact that in English the adjectives precede the noun necessarily, whilst in Italian they do not) has to be duplicated for the different entities or represented in procedural form within the analysis program. Since we believe that structural information is fundamental in the analysis process, and that its explicit representation increases the understandability (and the modifiability) of the systems, we will take in the following the opposite view, trying to start from syntactic approaches and to justify the increasing

role of semantics within them.

The aim of this introduction is to discuss how the semantics can be used to increase the effectiveness of N.L. analysis. In particular, three points will be set forth:
- from the point of view of efficiency of processing, the grammar-based approaches have to use semantic information as soon as possible
- the human ability to understand ill-formed fragments suggests to reduce the predominance of syntactic knowledge and, again, to use more heavily semantic information
- the phenomenon of garden paths shows that two different modes of operation exist: normal and backup. However, purely syntactic approaches fail to account for the phenomenon in a perspicuous way.

If we consider a grammar only from the point of view of expressive power, of course we can, after a thorough analysis of the phenomena occurring in natural language use, hope to find a grammar that characterizes all and only the sequences of words that constitute "acceptable" sentences. The study of the required power of N.L. grammars received considerable attention in the past (for a recent and thorough overview see (Pullum, 1984); some prominent positions are described in (Perrault, 1984)).

However, it has often pointed out that a comprehensive (and useful) N.L. understanding system should also take into account higher-level problems; in particular, it should also provide the researcher with some insights about the relationships existing between syntactic structures and semantic interpretation.

Most classical studies, both within the field of formal languages and within the field of natural languages viewed the semantic interpretation as a process "appended" to the syntactic analysis. It is widely accepted that this way of using semantics is highly inefficient: the number of alternative parses is often so high (especially when prepositional phrases are present), that it is not cost effective to delay the intervention of semantics (Sagalowicz, 1980); on the contrary, it is preferable to use semantics both as a meaning-construction process and as a source of further constraints for the analysis, as soon as possible during the analysis itself (Woods, 1980).

However, some other problems deserve attention. The first of them concerns the idea of "correctness" that, as stated above, is at the basis of the grammar-based approach. It is well known that in most cases, humans are able to understand the meaning of sentence fragments that are syntactically ill-formed without any apparent difficulty. It's worth observing that the locution "ill-formed sentences" does not refer exclusively to sentences that can reasonably be rejected on syntactic grounds. For example, the existence of a conjunction (Huang, 1984) can result in a sentence fragment that is ill-formed, although the entire sentence must be considered correct under any plausible definition of syntactic correctness. The problem of parsing ill-formed inputs has become very popular recently; a number of papers appeared in a special issue of the ACL Journal (AJCL, 1983). It must be noted that the approaches can be roughly categorized in two classes: extensions of grammatical formalisms and semantic-based analyzers. As stated above, we will not discuss here the semantic approaches; as regards the other ones, we can say that an extension of a grammatical formalism lends itself rather well to the relaxation of some syntactic constraints (e.g. number agreement), less well to others (e.g. the absence of a required constituent) and meets big difficulties in handling ordering problems (out of order constituents). This is obviously due to the fact that formal grammars have the task of describing "strings" of symbols, i.e. objects where the order is fundamental. It is not sufficiently proved that in natural language sentences, in their aspect of information conveying tools, the order of constituents is as fundamental. This observation leads to a last remark: in languages where the order is not as strict as in English (almost free word-order languages as Italian or Japanese) grammars that are not based on the common concept of rewrite rules (mainly related with case systems) are receiving greater and greater attention (Nitta et al., 1984; Sakamoto et al., 1984).

Another problem that should be mentioned is based on psychological motivations. Although this paper is not intended to present a psychologically valid model of natural language processing, we believe that some well known phenomena cannot be disregarded, because they help in making more clear what should (or should not) happen in a N.L. analyzer. The phenomenon we will consider here is that of garden paths. It gives a hint about the existence of two processing modes in the interpretation of a sentence: normal analysis and backup. At first sight, this remark confirms the adoption of standard, non-deterministic parsing methods, where backtracking is a usual technique. On the other hand, the number of times a normal ATN parser (to consider a well known tool) backtracks is not justified by the relative rarity of garden paths. The efforts in the development of deterministic parsing (Marcus, 1980) tried to characterize the normal processing mode, by stating that PARSIFAL would fail to analyze a sentence in cases where a person would garden path. However, it has been shown (Milne, 1982) that the three-constituent-buffer approach adopted by Marcus does not predict with sufficient accuracy the occurrence of garden paths. Again this can be seen as a failure of approaches based only on syntactic knowledge (a grammar-based one - ATN - and a rule-based one - PARSIFAL) to account for a linguistic phenomenon: the solution should be looked for in a more effective cooperation between syntax and semantics.

It is not possible to close this introduction without quoting a recent paper, which addresses some of the problems mentioned above in a thorough way. In (Schubert, 1984) the section 2.3 deserves attention. It is entitled "Lack of provision for integration with semantic/pragmatic preference principles". What is shown in the paper is that human reaction to sentences that have exactly the same syntactic structure may vary considerably depending on the semantics of occurring words. Although the analysis is carried on in a way different from ours, the concept of "potential" as a means to balance the syntactic and semantic information is similar to our weighting of alternative hypotheses.

Another work closely related with the present one is reported in (Pazzani, 1984). In that case also, the need of a strict cooperation between syntax and semantics is explicitly acknowledged. On the other hand it seems that the absence of a weighting mechanism could make the LAZY parser fail in some cases where no clear-cut choice is possible.

In the second section of the present paper we will describe the structure of the syntactic processor included in the FIDO system. Although the system (which is fully implemented in FRANZ LISP on a VAX 11/780 computer) does not handle all the phenomena discussed in this introduction, the presentation will allow us to clarify the basic operating principles, in order to describe in the third section the extensions of the parser we are currently implementing.

SYNTACTIC ANALYSIS IN FIDO

FIDO (a Flexible Interface for Database Operations) is a prototypal system that allows the user to access in N.L. (Italian) the data stored in a relational database. After a previous approach to building natural language interfaces (Lesmo, Magnani, Torasso 1981), we realized that one of the main concerns had to be to guarantee the portability of the system; this was achieved by adopting a strongly modular approach. Some efforts have been made to develop efficient methods to store semantic information (Lesmo, Siklossy, Torasso 1983) and to optimize the resulting query, expressed in relational algebra (Lesmo, Siklossy, Torasso 1985). The organization of the parser was described in (Lesmo, Torasso 1983) and its suitability to the analysis of ill-formed sentences in (Lesmo, Torasso 1984); in particular, the extensions introduced to deal with conjunctions are decribed in (Lesmo & Torasso, 1985). We will overview here the basic design choices.

The syntactic knowledge source is composed of a set of condition-action rules, where the condition examines the current status of the analysis, i.e. the parse tree that has already been built, whereas the action extends in some way the parse tree, hypothesizing the attachment point and the syntactic role of a new constituent. The parse tree is built according to the head and modifier approach and an example is reported in fig.1.

Six node types have been defined; each node label in fig.1 has the form TYPEi: the node labelled XXj is the j-th instance of the type XX that has been built during the analysis. The types appearing in the figure are: REL (standing for RELation, normally associated with verbs); REF (REFerents: nouns and pronouns); CONN (CONNectors, mainly for prepositions; it can happen that the filler of the node is UNMARKED: it means that the corresponding verb case is not marked by a preposition); DET (mainly DETerminers). The other node types are ADJ (ADJectives) and MOD (MODifiers, e.g. adverbs).

The syntactic rules are grouped in packets associated with syntactic categories. When an input word is syntactically ambiguous, different packets are activated and all conditions are tested. If just one of them succeeds, then the action is executed and the analysis goes on deterministically. Otherwise, the status of the analysis is saved to allow for possible backups in a subsequent phase, and the first action is executed (the different rules are ordered manually). Facilities are provided in the lexicon to handle canned phrases (e.g. "di corsa" - on the run) and compound words (e.g. "dammelo" - give it to me). It must be noted that some conditions require a lookahead (2 words maximum); this is done in order to increase the discriminating power of the conditions and to reduce the number of choice points.

In order to give an idea of the control structure of the analysis, let us see what happens when the first word of the example in fig.1 is found (we must stress again that FIDO works on commands in Italian: we will go on with English examples in order to increase the readability of the paper. In Italian the most direct translation of "which" is "quale", though its use differs slightly when it is used as a relative pronoun).

There are three different lexical entries for "which", each of which is associated with a different syntactic category: QADJ (interrogative adjective), QPRON (interrogative pronoun), and RELPRON (relative pronoun). The analysis begins with an empty REL node (REL1) as current node. Roughly speaking, all conditions of QADJ rules require that the next word is an adjective or a noun, the QPRON rules apply in the remaining cases, whereas the RELPRON rules can be activated just in case a previous REF node can be used as an attachment point for the relative clause. In our case the QADJ

interpretation is selected and, among the rules of the packet, the one is chosen that applies when the current node is an empty REL node. That rule builds a CONN node (and fills it with UNMARKED), a REF node (and leaves it empty) and a DET node (and fills it with the current word, i.e. "which"). The resulting structure is shown in fig.2. Then, the controller of the parsing process is awaken; it looks for another word and finds it in the lookahead buffer (it was used to discriminate between QADJ and QPRON). The NOUN packet is activated and a rule is selected, which fills the empty REF (REF1) with "course". We leave at this point the example, assuming that it gave an idea about how he analysis of a sentence is carried on.

Instead, some more specific points have to be made clear. The nodes in the figures have been represented very sketchily. Each node is actually a complex data structure, with various slots and some procedures attached to the prototype. For example, a REL node includes slots as HEAD (the verb), FORM (active vs. passive), TENSE, NUMBER, MOOD (indicative, conjunctive, etc.), ROLES (the case frame) and others. Notice that the slot AUX indicates the presence of an auxiliary verb in the sentence. The actual form of the auxiliary is not reported since it can be inferred by taking into account the values of MOOD, FORM, TENSE, etc. The associated procedures are called RELHEADPROC (operations to be done when the HEAD slot is filled, e.g. computing the tense of the verb), RELAGREEPROC (checking the number agreement with the subject), and RELSEMPROC (checking the acceptability of the actual case frame and beginning to build the semantic interpretation). When a node is operated upon, one or more procedures can be scheduled for execution. They can accept or reject the operations done by the parser (syntactic hypothesis). A simple way to make the parser more robust is to relax some of the constraints embodied in the procedures. For instance, an agreement failure can produce just a warning message, without requesting a reorganization of the parse tree, a reorganization which is always attempted in case of semantic failure. Such relaxation techniques can also be introduced in other formalisms, such as ATN (Kwasny & Sondheimer, 1981). More interesting, the proposed formalism handles easily also ordering errors. In fact, the attachment of cases to verbs and of adjectives to nouns is always allowed (in Italian the adjectives can occur both before and after the noun) and only

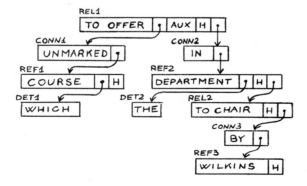

Fig.1 - Parse tree resulting from the analysis of the sentence: "Which courses are offered in the department chaired by Wilkins?".

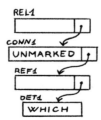

Fig.2 - Partial structure built after the analysis of the first word ("Which") of the sentence in fig.1.

when the node is closed (a node is closed, i.e. it is considered to be complete, when an attachment is proposed to a node above it in the tree) the CHECKORDER procedure verifies that the rules which govern the ordering of constituents are respected. Also in this case, a failure of CHECKORDER results in the issuing of a warning message, without any reorganization of the parse tree.

It has probably been noted the use of the term "reorganization of the tree" in the discussion above. In fact, such modifications, that we call "natural changes" to point out their simplicity and naturalness, are the primary tool for handling non-determinism. The brief presentation of the structure building rules failed probably to make clear one important point: when the action part of a rule is executed, it usually adds a subtree to the current tree; the attachment point of the new subtree is the nearest node of the required type that is above the current node. Of course, this choice is made only on syntactic grounds, so it may happen that it is not acceptable from a semantic point of view. In a standard ATN framework, this problem is solved backtracking: the subnets allowing, for example, PP modifiers include an implicit choice point (in correspondence with the position where a PP could be present or absent) and a semantic failure would involve backing up to such a previous choice point. Although the introduction of some special tools (of the kind of well-formed substring tables or chart parsers) allows the system to avoid the re-analysis of the PP component, some bookkeeping is needed to save the status of the analysis at the choice points. The natural changes mechanism makes that work useless, in that the choice points are implicitly available in the structure of the parse tree and can be easily looked for by the modification rules. A further advantage is the high flexibility of the tool: the natural changes are expressed in the form of pattern-action rules (as the standard rules) so that, in principle, an action could restructure the tree in a very complex way. In fact, we use them also to handle some problems related with the analysis of conjunctions (Lesmo & Torasso, 1985) and with some special forms of relative clauses. As often happens, the natural changes are actually too powerful; at this time we have not pursued the study of what are the reasonable constraints that must be put on the operations of the changes. We want to stress, however, that the introduction of the natural changes does not substitute the backup completely: this remark is in agreement with the discussion about the existence of different processing modes in the analysis of N.L. sentences. Although we are not able to state now the correspondence between the use of backup and the occurrence of garden paths, we can notice that the saving of the status is limited (in most cases) to syntactically ambiguous words such that more than one syntactic category is acceptable in the current context: this strongly reduces the number of choice points, as predicted by the garden path phenomenon.

EXTENSIONS TO THE PARSER

Before going on we have to make clear an important point: whereas the parser embodied in

FIDO works on Italian sentences, in order to perform the tests that led to the version described in this section, we had to develop a small set of rules for English. The reason why we did this was to have at disposal a wide corpus of thoroughly analyzed examples (i.e. the ones appearing in the referenced papers by Milne and Schubert). This approach to testing has both an advantage and a disadvantage: the adaptability of the parser to a different language is partially demonstrated, but the number of syntactic phenomena that has been taken into account in building the English rules is not very high, so that some ad-hoc solutions could have been adopted.

We can now start by seeing what happens when syntactically ambiguous sentences are processed by FIDO (old version). A first example is drawn from Schubert's paper:

(1) John bought the book which I had selected for Mary

After the analysis of the first portion of the sentence (as far as the word "selected") the status of the tree is the one of fig.3. Upon encountering the preposition "for", a rule would propose its attachment (in a CONN node) to the node REL2 (i.e. as a verb modifier). The subsequent attachment of a REF node (containing "Mary") to the newly created connector would trigger the semantic check procedures, which give a positive answer (case frame: TO SELECT; SUBJ: PERSON, OBJ: THING, FOR: PERSON) and allows the system to confirm the proposed analysis.

On the contrary, in the example below:

(2) John bought the book which I had selected at a lower price

after a sequence of steps analogous to the one described above (extended to handle the determiner and the adjective), the semantics would reject the syntactic hypothesis. The natural changes would be triggered, the attachment of the PP to "book" would be tried and again rejected on semantic bases. Finally, the attempt to attach "at a low price" to "buy" succeeds and the analysis is completed.

It is apparent that this process does not work in cases such as:

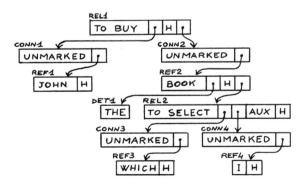

Fig.3 - Analysis of the sentence fragment: "John bought the book which I had selected ...".

(3) John carried the groceries for Mary

The attachment of "for Mary" to "groceries" would be attempted; it cannot be rejected by the semantics, thus the final analysis is the one reported in fig.4 (contrarily to the expected one).

Another example concerns a pair of garden path sentences. In

(4) The building blocks the sun

we obtain the structure reported in fig.5. If the actual input sentence were

(5) The building blocks the sun faded are red

then the analyis would be blocked at "are" (in fact, "faded" would be used as a modifier for "sun"; see (6)) and a backup would make the system build the right structure.

(6) The building blocks the sun faded behind the hills

Again, although the model predicts the correct behavior in the examples above, it fails to characterize the difference between (7) and (8):

(7) The table rocks during the earthquake

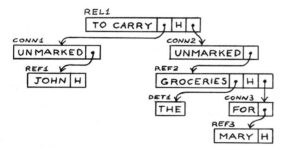

Fig.4 - Analysis of the sentence "John carried the groceries for Mary".

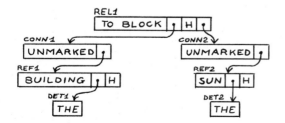

Fig.5 - Analysis of the sentence "The building blocks the sun".

(8) The granite rocks during the earthquake

In these sentences we assume, according to the results of Milne's experiments that (8) makes people garden path, whilst (7) does not. In fact, the only way FIDO has at disposal to express preferences (lexical, in this case) is to take into account the order of the lexical entries. Thus, we are able to say that "rock" is more commonly used in its nominal sense than in its verbal sense, but not to say that (to use Milne's words) "people like granite rocks, but don't like table rocks". In other words, FIDO is not able to express preferences on the basis of the context.

The solution we adopted to overcome the problems mentioned above was to introduce a limited degree of parallelism in the analysis, and to evaluate and update the weights of the different alternatives that are being carried on in parallel, until a definite decision can be taken. Notice that we don't claim that the chosen alternative is always the right one, nor we would like to get such a result: in some cases the system can take the wrong way, as humans do when they garden path.

In implementing such a model, we took advantage of our research on expert systems based on fuzzy production rules (Lesmo, Saitta, Torasso 1985): in fact, the weighting mechanism we adopted is based on possibility theory (Zadeh, 1979). We will not analyze here the advantages of a possibility based approach with respect to approaches based on probability theory or on heuristic methods (the interested reader can see (Lesmo, Saitta, Torasso 1985)), but, as we did in the previous section, we will try to let the reader understand how the weighting mechanism has been merged with the facilities previously available in FIDO. We have only to say that the weight (that, from now on, will be called Confidence Degree - CD) is a value ranging from 0 to 1, where 0 means that the hypothesis cannot be accepted at all and 1 means that the hypothesis is surely the right one.

The basic design choices that must be made concern:
- What alternatives must be considered (how much parallelism should be supported)?
- How long must the different paths be pursued (when should the final decision be taken)?
- What knowledge sources contribute to the weighting (and how can the weights be adjusted)?

It is interesting to note that the structure of the parser described in the previous section gives a hint about the first choice. In fact, two sources of ambiguity are present: more than one rule may be activated at the same time and the attachment point of a constituent is not uniquely determined. Thus, to test the validity of the proposed approach we had to change the basic control structure in only two ways:
1) The different rules whose conditions are satisfied are executed in parallel. Although there is no a-priori upper limit to the amount of parallelism, the constraints embodied in the conditions keep low the number of alternative hypotheses (according to the observation made in the previous section about the reduction of the number of choice points).
2) Instead of waiting for the results of the semantic checks, the natural changes are scheduled as

soon as an attachment is proposed. The natural changes have been modified in a simple way: no detachment is made, but the different alternatives are added to the proposed one (note that this is just a first, low-cost solution: what we are studying now is the possibility to eliminate the natural changes mechanism; this can be done if all attachment points can be found at a glance by the linking procedures).

As regards the second choice (when should the final decision be taken?), we decided to distinguish again the sources of ambiguity described above. The reason why different solutions were reasonable stood in the different computational cost of carrying on alternatives: whereas the rule ambiguity seemed to require a real maintenance of different trees, the role (attachment) ambiguity implied only that different links are included in the same tree. In the first case, after trying different alternatives (no lookahead, one-word lookahead, just the lookahead required by the conditions) we had the pleasant surprise that in most cases the different states had not to be maintained. In fact, the only thing we had to do was to defer the decision about the rule to apply after the execution of the semantic check procedures: they provided the parser with the information about the semantic preferences that was lacking in the previous version of the system. As regards the role ambiguity, we let the analysis go on until the filler of the node which is the root of the attached subtree has been found: this means that we wait until the semantic checks can be done. For example, if sentence (1) were changed into:

(9) John bought the book that I selected for the nice blond-haired girl that you know

then the choice would be delayed until the word "girl" is found.

Note that in both cases, though the behavior of the parser is different, the parser pursues different paths until the system allows the semantics to provide it with some evidence about the most reasonable choice.

Finally, the third problem concerns the knowledge sources involved in the weighting process. Apparently, we had to attach CD's to lexical entries, syntactic rules, and semantic information. On the other hand, the semantic information (which in FIDO consists in a semantic net representing the selectional restrictions, see (Lesmo, Siklossy, Torasso 1983)) overcomes the information that could be attached to lexical entries. In fact, the choice is made on the basis of the possibility of attachment of a pair of "concepts": this provides the system with more detailed information than the possibility of occurrence of a single interpretation. That is, if the system knows that CD (TO ROCK, SUBJ:TABLE) = 0.8 and CD (ROCK, MODIF:TABLE) = .1, CD (TO ROCK, SUBJ:GRANITE) = 0.6 and CD (ROCK, MODIF:GRANITE) = 0.9, it can disregard the fact that CD (TO ROCK [CAT:VERB]) = 0.7 and CD (ROCK [CAT:NOUN]) = 0.9. The solution we adopted is to associate with the arcs appearing in the semantic net a CD expressing the preference of the system. It is not possible here to discuss the details of the implementation (actually, not all arcs have a CD), because such a discussion would

require a description of the semantic net. It must be noted, however, that this solution requires the explicit introduction of all possible semantic connections. This is consistent with a database interface, because the associations carry the information about the correspondence with the database schema. In a general N.L. understanding system this is quite expensive and some way to propagate the CD's according to the degree of match with the declared selectional restrictions should be included in the system.

As regards the syntactic knowledge source, we attached CD's to the structure building rules and we decided to compute the CD's of the attachment points on the basis of their distance (number of nodes to traverse) from the "current" node. In particular, the current node is assigned a CD equal to 1 and, for each node that is traversed to find an alternative, the CD is decreased by a constant factor (currently 0.1). Apart from this latter, all CD's (both in the net and in the rules) have been assigned manually. This allowed the system to succeed on a wide set of examples; of course, a less heuristic determination of CD values would be useful, but it requires a large research effort per se.

CONCLUSIONS

As Winograd states in (Winograd, 1983), the research on N.L. understanding is being carried on today within a new paradigm: the computational paradigm. Its main differences with respect to the previous (generative) one, stands in the "attention to process organization" and the "relevance of non-linguistic knowledge".

It is not the aim of this paper to take into account all the problems that non-linguistic knowledge conveys into N.L. analysis, but to make clear that the in-depth understanding of the respective roles of syntactic and semantic knowledge sources and the clarification of the way they interact to construct the interpretation of natural language sentences is fundamental to building N.L. interpreters. We claim that neither syntax nor semantics can be assigned the role of "guide" of the interpretation process, but they must operate on a parity basis. Both of them provide the analyzer with information about the choices that must be made during the interpretation.

The approach outlined in the paper is just a first attempt to satisfy these principles: many problems must be examined and some substantial changes can be introduced, but we maintain the fundamental role of the "rule" concept in the construction of N.L. analyzers and the necessity of being able to weight the contributions of different knowledge sources: the interpretation is not a categorical (yes/no) process, but it must be based on the idea of preference (Wilks, 1975) (or subjective evidence).

The paper shows how a rule-based approach has been modified to take into account both syntactic and semantic preferences. We hope to have given a feeling about the ease with which the required modifications were embodied in the previous system. The available space did not allow us to consider some other phenomena that FIDO is able to handle quite easily: they concern the analysis of ill-formed sentences. Although many aspects of ill-formedness were already handled by the old version of the system, the introduction of CD's and the modifications of the natural changes are useful also to characterize in a more perspicuous way the analysis of conjunctions: also in this case, the CD's are used to compare the different alternatives regarding the role the second conjunct can assume.

REFERENCES

[1] A.A.V.V.: Special Issue on Ill-Formed Parsing, AJCL 9, no.3-4 (1983).

[2] E.Charniak: Six Topics in Search of a Parser. Proc. 7th IJCAI , Vancouver (1981),1079-1087.

[3] X.Huang: Dealing with Conjunction in a Machine Translation Environment. Proc. COLING 84, Stanford (1984), 243-246.

[4] S.C.Kwasny, N.K.Sondheimer: Relaxation Techniques for Parsing Grammatically Ill-Formed Input in Natural Language Understanding. AJCL 7 (1981), 99-108.

[5] L.Lesmo, D.Magnani, P.Torasso: A Deterministic Analyzer for the Interpretation of Natural Language Commands. Proc. 7th IJCAI, Vancouver (1981), 440-442.

[6] L.Lesmo, L.Saitta, P.Torasso: Evidence Combination in Expert Systems. Int. J. of Man-Machine Studies, vol.22 (1985).

[7] L.Lesmo, L.Siklossy, P.Torasso: A Two Level Net for Integrating Selectional Restrictions and Semantic Knowledge. Proc. IEEE Int. Conf. on Systems, Man and Cybernetics, India (1983), 14-18.

[8] L.Lesmo, L.Siklossy, P.Torasso: Semantic and Pragmatic Processing in FIDO: a Flexible Interface for Database Operations. Information Systems 10, n.2 (1985).

[9] L.Lesmo, P.Torasso: A Flexible Natural Language Parser based on Two-Level Representation of Syntax. Proc. 1st Conf. ACL Europe, Pisa (1983), 114-121.

[10] L.Lesmo, P.Torasso: Interpreting Syntactically Ill-Formed Sentences. Proc. COLING 84, Stanford (1984), 534-539.

[11] L.Lesmo, P.Torasso: Analysis of Conjunctions in a Rule-based Parser. Proc. 23rd ACL Meeting, Chicago (1985).

[12] M.Marcus: A Theory of Syntactic Recognition for Natural Language. MIT Press (1980).

[13] R.W.Milne: Predicting Garden Path Sentences. Cognitive Science 6, 349-373 (1982).

[14] Y.Nitta et al.: A Proper Treatment of Syntax and Semantics in Machine Translation. Proc. COLING 84, Stanford (1984), 159-166.

[15] M.J.Pazzani: Conceptual Analysis of Garden-Path Sentences. Proc. COLING 84, Stanford (1984), 486-490.

[16] C.R.Perrault (ed.): Special Issue on Mathematical Properties of Grammatical Formalisms. Computational Linguistics 10 (1984), 165-202.

[17] G.K.Pullum: Syntactic and Semantic Parsability. Proc. COLING 84, Stanford (1984), 112-122.

[18] Y.Sakamoto et al.: Lexical Features for Japanese Syntactic Analysis in MU-Project-JE. Proc. Coling 84, Stanford (1984), 42-47.

[19] D.Sagalowicz: Mechanical Intelligence: Research and Applications. Final Tech. Report, SRI Int., Menlo Park (December 1980).

[20] L.K.Schubert: On Parsing Preferences. Proc. Coling 84, Stanford (1984), 247-250.

[21] Y.A.Wilks: A Preferential Pattern-Seeking Semantics for Natural Language Inference, Artificial Intelligence 6 (1975), 53-74.

[22] T.Winograd: Language as a Cognitive Process. Vol.1: Syntax, Addison Wesley (1983).

[23] W.A.Woods: Cascaded ATN Grammars. AJCL 6 (1980), 1-12.

[24] L.A.Zadeh: A Theory of Approximate Reasoning. In E.Elcock, D.Michie, L.Mikulich (eds.): Machine Intelligence 9, Ellis Horwood (1979), 149-194.

Syntax, Preference and Right Attachment

Yorick Wilks, Xiuming Huang & Dan Fass

Computing Research Laboratory
New Mexico State University
Las Cruces, NM, USA 88003

ABSTRACT

The paper claims that the right attachment rules for phrases originally suggested by Frazier and Fodor are wrong, and that none of the subsequent patchings of the rules by syntactic methods have improved the situation. For each rule there are perfectly straightforward and indefinitely large classes of simple counter-examples. We then examine suggestions by Ford et al., Schubert and Hirst which are quasi-semantic in nature and which we consider ingenious but unsatisfactory. We offer a straightforward solution within the framework of preference semantics, and argue that the principal issue is not the type and nature of information required to get appropriate phrase attachments, but the issue of where to store the information and with what processes to apply it. We present a prolog implementation of a best first algorithm covering the data and contrast it with closely related ones, all of which are based on the preferences of nouns and prepositions, as well as verbs.

1. Syntactic Approaches

Recent discussion of the issue of how and where to attach right-hand phrases (and more generally, clauses) in sentence analysis was started by the claims of Frazier and Fodor (1979). They offered two rules :

(i) Right Association

which is that phrases on the right should be attached as low as possible on a syntax tree, thus

JOHN BOUGHT THE BOOK THAT I HAD BEEN TRYING TO OBTAIN (FOR SUSAN)

which attaches to OBTAIN not to BOUGHT.

But this rule fails for

JOHN BOUGHT THE BOOK (FOR SUSAN)

which requires attachment to BOUGHT not BOOK.

A second principle was then added :

(ii) Minimal Attachment

which is that a phrase must be attached higher in a tree if doing that minimizes the number of nodes in the tree (and this rule is to take precedence over (i)).

So, in :

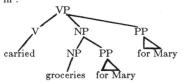

as part of

JOHN CARRIED THE GROCERIES (FOR MARY)

attaching FOR MARY to the top of the tree, rather than to the NP, will create a tree with one less node. Shieber (1983) has an alternative analysis of this phenomenon, based on a clear parsing model, which produces the same effect as rule (ii) by preferring longer reductions in the parsing table; i.e., in the present case, preferring VP <-- V NP PP to NP <-- NP PP.

But there are still problems with (i) and (ii) taken together, as is seen in :

SHE WANTED THE DRESS (ON THAT RACK)

rather than attaching (ON THAT RACK) to WANTED, as (ii) would cause.

2. Semantic Approaches

(i) Lexical Preference

At this point Ford et al. (1981) suggested the use of lexical preference, which is conventional case information associated with individual verbs, so as to select for attachment PPs which match that case information. This is semantic information in the broad sense in which that term has traditionally been used in AI. Lexical preference allows rules (i) and (ii) above to be overridden if a verb's coding expresses a strong preference for a certain structure. The effect of that rule differs from system to system: within Shieber's parsing model (1983) that rule means in effect that a verb like WANT will prefer to have only a single NP to its right. The parser then performs the longest reduction it can with the strongest leftmost stack element. So, if POSITION, say, prefers two entities to its right, Shieber will obtain :

THE WOMAN WANTED THE DRESS (ON THE RACK)

and

THE WOMAN POSITIONED THE DRESS (ON THE RACK).

But this iterative patching with more rules does not work, because to every example, under every rule (i, ii and lexical preference), there are clear and simple counter-examples. Thus, there is :

JOE TOOK THE BOOK THAT I BOUGHT (FOR SUSAN)

which comes under (i) and there is

JOE BROUGHT THE BOOK THAT I LOVED (FOR SUSAN)

which Shieber's parser must get wrong and not in a way that (ii) could rescue. Under (ii) itself, there is

JOE LOST THE TICKET (TO PARIS)

which Shieber's conflict reduction rule must get wrong. For Shieber's version of lexical preference there will be problems with :

THE WOMAN WANTED THE DRESS (FOR HER DAUGHTER)

which the rules he gives for WANT must get wrong.

(ii) Schubert

Schubert (1984) presents some of the above counter-examples in an attack on syntactically based methods. He proposes a syntactico-semantic network system of what he calls preference trade-offs. He is driven to this, he says, because he rejects any system based wholly on lexically-based semantic preferences (which is part of what we here will call preference semantics, see below, and which would subsume the simpler versions of lexical preference). He does this on the grounds that there are clear cases where "syntactic preferences prevail over much more coherent alternatives" (Schubert, 1984, p.248), where by "coherent" he means interpretations imposed by semantics/pragmatics. His examples are :

MARY SAW THE MAN WHO HAD LIVED WITH HER (WHILE ON MATERNITY LEAVE)

(where full lines show the "natural" pragmatic interpretations, and dotted ones the interpretations that Schubert says are imposed willy- nilly by the syntax). Our informants disagree with Schubert : they attach as the syntax suggests to LIVE, but still insist that the leave is Mary's (i.e. so interpreting the last clause that it contains an elided (WHILE) SHE WAS (ON....). If that is so the example does not split off semantics from syntax in the way Schubert wants, because the issue is who is on leave and not when something was done. In such circumstances the example presents no special problems.

JOHN MET A TALL SLIM AUBURN HAIRED GIRL FROM MONTREAL THAT HE MARRIED (AT A DANCE)

Here our informants attach the phrase resolutely to MET as commonsense dictates (i.e. they ignore or are able to discount the built-in distance effect of the very long NP). A more difficult and interesting case arises if the last phrase is (AT A WEDDING), since the example then seems to fall withing the exclusion of an "attachment unless it yields zero information" rule deployed within preference semantics (Wilks, 1973), which is probably, in its turn, a close relative of Grice's (1975) maxim concerned with information quantity. In the (AT A WEDDING) case, informants continue to attach to MET, seemingly discounting both the syntactic indication and the information vacuity of MARRIED AT A WEDDING.

JOHN WAS NAMED (AFTER HIS TWIN SISTER)

Here our informants saw genuine ambiguity and did not seem to mind much whether attachment or lexicalization of NAMED AFTER was preferred. Again, information vacuity tells against the syntactic attachment (the example is on the model of :

HE WAS NAMED AFTER HIS FATHER

Wilks 1973, which was used to make a closely related point), but normal gendering of names tells against the lexicalization of the verb to NAME+AFTER.

Our conclusion from Schubert's examples is the reverse of his own : these are not simple examples but very complex ones, involving distance and (in two cases) information quantity phenomena. In none of the cases do they support the straightforward primacy of syntax that his case against a generalized "lexical preference hypothesis" (i.e. one without rules (i) and (ii) as default cases, as in Ford et al.'s lexical preference) would require. We shall therefore consider that hypothesis, under the name preference semantics, to be still under consideration.

(iii) Hirst

Hirst (1984) aims to produce a conflation of the approaches of Ford et al., described above, and a principle of Crain and Steedman (1984) called The Principle of Parsimony, which is to make an attachment that corresponds to leaving the minimum number of presuppositions unsatisfied. The example usually given is that of a "garden path" sentence like :

THE HORSE RACED PAST THE BARN FELL

where the natural (initial) preference for the garden path interpretation is to be explained by the fact that, on that interpretation, only the existence of an entity corresponding to THE HORSE is to be presupposed, and that means less presuppositions to which nothing is the memory structure corresponds than is needed to opt for the existence of some THE HORSE RACED PAST THE BARN. One difficulty here is what it is for something to exist in memory: Crain and Steedman themselves note that readers do not garden path with sentences like :

CARS RACED AT MONTE CARLO FETCH HIGH PRICES AS COLLECTOR'S ITEMS

but that is not because readers know of any particular cars raced at Monte Carlo. Hirst accepts from (Winograd 1972) a general Principle of Referential Success (i.e. to actual existent entities), but the general unsatisfactoriness of restricting a system to actual entities has long been known, for so much of our discourse is about possible and virtual ontologies (for a full discussion of this aspect of Winograd, see Ritchie 1978).

The strength of Hirst's approach is his attempt to reduce the presuppositional metric of Crain and Steedman to criteria manipulable by basic semantic/lexical codings, and particularly the contrast of definite and indefinite articles. But the general determination of categories like definite and indefinite is so shaky (and only indirectly related to "the" and "a" in English), and cannot possibly bear the weight that he puts on it as the solid basis of a theory of phrase attachment.

So, Hirst invites counter-examples to his Principle of Referential Success (1984, p.149) adapted from Winograd: "a nongeneric NP presupposes that the thing it describes exists.....an indefinite NP presupposes only the plausibility of what it describes." But this is just not so in either case :

THE PERPETUAL MOTION MACHINE IS THE BANE OF LIFE IN A PATENT OFFICE

A MAN I JUST MET LENT ME FIVE POUNDS

The machine is perfectly definite but the perpetual motion machine does not exist and is not presupposed by the speaker. We conclude that these notions are not yet in a state to be the basis of a theory of PP attachment. Moreover, even though beliefs about the world must play a role in attachment in certain cases, there is, as yet, no reason to believe that beliefs and presuppositions can provide the material for a basic attachment mechanism.

(iv) Preference Semantics

Preference Semantics has claimed that appropriate structurings can be obtained using essentially semantic information, given also a rule of preferring the most densely connected representations that can be constructed from such semantic information (Wilks 1975, Fass & Wilks 1983).

Let us consider such a position initially expressed as semantic dictionary information attaching to the verb; this is essentially the position of the systems discussed above, as well as of case grammar and the semantics- based parsing systems (e.g. Riesbeck 1975) that have been based on it. When discussing implementation in the last section we shall argue (as in Wilks 1976) that semantic material that is to be the base of a parsing process cannot be thought of as simply attaching to a verb (rather than to nouns and all other word senses)

In what follows we shall assume case predicates in the dictionary entries of verbs, nouns etc. that express part of the meaning of the concept and determine its semantic relations. We shall write as [OBTAIN] the abbreviation of the semantic dictionary entry for OBTAIN, and assume that the following concepts contain at least the case entries shown (as case predicates and the types of argument fillers) :

[OBTAIN]   (recipient hum)   recipient case, human.

[BUY]   (recipient hum)   recipient case, human.

[POSITION]   (location *pla)   location case, place.

[BRING]   (recipient human)   recipient case, human.

[TICKET]   (direction *pla)   direction case, place.

[WANT]   (object *physob)   object case, physical object.

             (recipient hum)   recipient case, human.

The issue here is whether these are plausible preferential meaning constituents: e.g. that to obtain something is to obtain it for a recipient;
to position something is to do it in association with a place; a ticket (in this sense i.e. "billet" rather than "ticket" in French) is a ticket to somewhere, and so on. They do not entail restrictions, but only preferences. Hence, "John brought his dog a bone" in no way violates the coding [BRING]. We shall refer to these case constituents within semantic representations as semantic preferences of the corresponding head concept.

3. A First Trial Attachment Rule

The examples discussed are correctly attached by the following rule :

Rule A : moving leftwards from the right hand end of a sentence, assign the attachment of an entity X (word or phrase) to the first entity to the left of X that has a preference that X satisfies; this entails that any entity X can only satisfy the preference of one entity. Assume also a push down stack for inserting such entities as X into until they satisfy some preference. Assume also some distance limit (to be empirically determined) and a DEFAULT rule such that, if any X satisfies no preferences, it is attached locally, i.e. immediately to its left.

Rule A gets right all the classes of examples discussed (with one exception, see below): e.g

JOHN BROUGHT THE BOOK THAT I LOVED (FOR MARY)

JOHN TOOK THE BOOK THAT I BOUGHT (FOR MARY)

JOHN WANTED THE DRESS (ON THE RACK)(FOR MARY)

where the last requires use of the push-down stack. The phenomenon treated here is assumed to be much more general than just phrases, as in:

PÂTE DE CANARD TRUFFÉ

(i.e. a truffled pate of duck, not a pate of truffled ducks!) where we envisage a preference (POSS STUFF) ----i.e. prefers to be predicated of substances -- as part of [TRUFFÉ]. French gender is of no use here, since all the concepts are masculine.

This rule would of course have to be modified for many special factors, e.g. pronouns, because of :

SHE WANTED { THE DRESS / IT } (ON THE SHELF)

A more substantial drawback to this substitution of a single semantics- based rule for all the earlier syntactic complexity is that placing the preferences essentially in the verbs (as did the systems discussed earlier that used lexical preference) and having little more than semantic type information on nouns (except in cases like [TICKET] that also prefers associated cases) but, most importantly, having no semantic preferences associated with prepositions that introduce phrases, we shall only succeed with rule A by means of a semantic subterfuge for a large and simple class of cases, namely:

JOHN LOVED HER (FOR HER BEAUTY)

or

JOHN SHOT THE GIRL (IN THE PARK)

Given the "low default" component of rule A, these can only be correctly attached if there is a very general case component in the verbs, e.g. some statement of location in all "active types" of verbs (to be described by the primitive type heads in their codings) like SHOOT i.e. (location *pla), which expresses the fact that acts of this type are necessarily located. (location *pla) is then the preference that (IN THE PARK) satisfies, thus preventing a low default.

Again, verbs like LOVE would need a (REASON ANY) component in their coding, expressing the notion that such states (as opposed to actions, both defined in terms of the main semantic primitives of verbs) are dependent on some reason, which could be anything.

But the clearest defect of Rule A (and, by implication, of all the verb- centered approaches discussed earlier in the paper) is that verbs in fact confront not cases, but PPs fronted by ambiguous prepositions, and it is only by taking account of their preferences that a general solution can be found.

4. Preposition Semantics: Preplates

In fact rule A was intentionally naive: it was designed to demonstrate (as against Shubert's claims in particular) the wide coverage of the data of a single semantics-based rule, even if that required additional, hard to motivate, semantic information to be given for action and states. It was stated in a verb-based lexical preference mode simply to achieve contrast with the other systems discussed.

For some years, it has been a principle of preference semantics (e.g. Wilks 1973, 1975) that attachment relations of phrases, clauses etc. are to be determined by comparing the preferences emanating from all the entities involved in an attachment: they are all, as it were, to be considered as objects seeking other preferred classes of neighbors, and the best fit, within and between each order of structures built up, is to be found by comparing the preferences and finding a best mutual fit. This point was made in (Wilks 1976) by contrasting preference semantics with the simple verb-based requests of Riesbeck's (1975) MARGIE parser. It was argued there that account had to be taken of both the preferences of verbs (and nouns), and of the preferences cued from the prepositions themselves.

Those preferences were variously called paraplates (Wilks 1975), preplates (Boguraev 1979) and they were, for each preposition sense, an ordered set of predication preferences restricted by action or noun type. (Wilks 1975) contains examples of ordered paraplate stacks and their functioning, but in what follows we shall stick to the preplate notation of (Huang 1984b).

We have implemented in CASSEX (see below) a range of alternatives to Rule A : controlling both for "low" and "high" default; for examination of verb preferences first (or more generally those of any entity which is a candidate for the root of the attachment, as opposed to what is attached) and of what-is-attached first (i.e. prepositional phrases). We can also control for the application of a more redundant form of rule where we attach preferably on the conjunction of satisfactions of the preferences of the root and the attached (e.g. for such a rule, satisfaction would require both that the verb preferred a prepositional phrase of such a class, and that the prepositional phrase preferred a verb of such a class).

In the next section we describe the algorithm that best fits the data and alternates between the use of semantic information attached to verbs and nouns (i.e. the roots for attachments as in Rule A) and that of prepositions; it does this by seeking the best mutual fit between them, and without any fall back to default syntactic rules like (i) and (ii).

5. The CASSEX Strategy

This strategy, implemented within Huang's (1984a, 1984b) CASSEX program, correctly parses all of the example sentences in this paper. CASSEX, which is written in Prolog on the Essex GEC-63, uses a definite clause grammar (DCG) to recognize syntactic constituents and Preference Semantics to provide their semantic interpretation.

For PP attachment CASSEX uses the case preferences of verbs, nouns and prepositions. The case information for verbs and nouns is encoded into their semantic formulas. The formula for one sense of the verb POSITION contains a location case :

sem(position1, ... , preps([prep(at,on,in,by), prep-obj(*pla), case(loc-static)])).

The formula for one sense of the noun TICKET has a direction case, as in "ticket to Paris" :

sem(ticket1, ... , preps([prep(to), prep-obj(*pla), case(direction)])).

The case information for prepositions is encoded into lists of preplates, stored under the names of individual prepositions. Each preplate is comprised of four elements. Below is the list of preplates for ON :

preplates(on, [[move, instrument, thing, on1],
              [be, loc-static, *pla, on2],
              [strik, loc-dynamic, *physob, on3],
              [*do-dynamic, loc-static, point, on4],
              [*ent, location, *physob, on5],
              [*do-dynamic, time, event, on6]]).

The first element represents the preferred semantic class of the head noun or verb preceding the prepositional phrase to be attached; the second element is the case of the preposition; the third is the preferred semantic class of the head noun of the prepositional phrase.

In CASSEX, the strategy (Rule B) is contained within the prolog goal pp_ attachment which is called by the grammar after the subject, verb and object of a sentential clause has been recognized. pp_attachment consists of seven clauses (see below) which are tried sequentially until one succeeds. There are three stages or phases to the strategy. The first stage (clauses 1, 2 and 3) attempts PP attachment using verb and noun case preferences, starting with the element immediately to the left of the PP and working leftwards. The second phase (clauses 4 and 5) attempts PP attachment using the case preferences of the preposition, starting with the main sentence verb and working rightwards. The third stage (clauses 6 and 7) is a default : preferences of the preposition for some classes of action primitives are relaxed and the PP is attached to the main sentence verb.

pp_attachment(Verb_sense, Object, Obj_Head_Noun, Rebuilt_Object, Verb_Modifier) -->

   % Clause 1

   prepositional_phrase(Prep, Preplates, Noun_phrase, Head_noun),

      % Find PP. Get the preplates listed for the preposition;
      % identify the head noun of the PP.

   check_noun_cases(Object, Preplates, Noun_phrase, Head_noun, Rebuilt_Object).

      % Check the noun phrase immediately preceding the pp for
      % any case preferences. If its preferences are satisfied then
      % attach the pp to the (Object) np, producing Rebuilt_
      % Object.

pp_attachment(Verb_sense, Object, Obj_Head_Noun, Rebuilt_Object, Verb_Modifier) -->

   % Clause 2

   prepositional_phrase(Prep, Preplates, Noun_phrase, Head_noun),
   check_verb_cases(Verb_sense, Preplates, Head_noun, Verb_Modifier).

      % Check the sense of the verb preceding the pp to see for
      % any case preferences. If its preferences are satisfied then
      % attach the pp to the verb as a Verb_Modifier.

pp_attachment(Verb_sense, Object, Obj_Head_Noun, Object,[]) --> [].

      % Clause 3. No pp attachment is made. The Verb-sense and
      % the Object of the sentential clause is returned unaltered.
      % CASSEX will then try to attach the pp at the next sent-
      % ence level up, starting with the rightmost constituent, by
      % calling pp_attachment again. If no attachment is possible
      % at that level, CASSEX tries attachment at the next level
      % up. If no attachment is made then CASSEX remains at
      % that level and tries clauses 4-7 of pp_attachment, one of
      % which must succeed.

pp_attachment(Verb_sense, Object, Obj_Head_Noun, Rebuilt_Object, Verb_Modifier) -->

   % Clause 4

   prepositional_phrase(Prep, Preplates, Noun_phrase, Head_noun),
   verb_pp_match(Preplates, Noun_phrase, Head_noun, Verb_sense, Verb_Modifier).

   % Try to attach the pp to the verb.

pp_attachment(Verb_sense, Object, Obj_Head_Noun, Rebuilt_Object, Verb_Modifier) -->

   % Clause 5

   prepositional_phrase(Prep, Preplates, Noun_phrase, Head_noun),
   noun_pp_match(Preplates, Noun_phrase, Head_noun, Object, Rebuilt_Object).

   % Try to attach the pp to the (Object) noun phrase.

```
pp_attachment(Verb_sense, Object,Obj_Head_Noun, Rebuilt_
    Object, Verb_Modifier) -->
    % Clause 6
    prepositional_phrase(Prep, Preplates, Noun_phrase, Head_
        noun),
    {relax_preplates(Preplates, Preplates0)},
    % Relax certain restrictions in the preplates
    verb_pp_match(Preplates0, Noun_phrase, Head_noun, Verb_
        sense, Verb_Modifier).
    % Try to attach the pp to the verb.


pp_attachment(Verb_sense, Object,Obj_Head_Noun, Rebuilt_
    Object, Verb_Modifier) -->
    % Clause 7
    prepositional_phrase(Prep, Preplates, Noun_phrase, Head_
        noun),
    {relax_preplates(Preplates, Preplates0)},
    noun_pp_match(Preplates0, Noun_phrase, Head_noun, Object,
        Rebuilt_Object).
    % Try to attach the pp to the noun phrase.
```

Below, by way of illustration, we show how our strategy correctly attaches PPs in four of the example sentences in this paper :

(1) JOHN LOVED THE GIRL (IN THE PARK)

(2) JOHN STABBED THE GIRL (IN THE PARK)

(3) JOE BOUGHT THE BOOK THAT I HAD BEEN TRYING TO OBTAIN (FOR SUSAN)

(4) JOE BOUGHT THE BOOK THAT I LOVED (FOR SUSAN).

Whenever pp-attachment is called, its first three arguments are always instantiated. In (1), for example, Verb_sense is instantiated to LOVE; Object to THE GIRL, and Obj_Head_Noun to GIRL. The first clause of pp_attachment calls check_noun_cases (i.e. the noun is checked first) to see if GIRL has any case preferences. GIRL has none so check_noun_cases fails, failing clause 1. The second clause of pp_attachment is called which calls check_verb_cases to see if LOVE has any case preferences. LOVE has none so check_verb_cases fails, causing the second clause of pp_attachment to fail. The third clause of pp_attachment returns the v and np with the pp not attached to either. CASSEX tries to attach the pp at the next level up, but the sentence has no higher level so clause 3 of pp_attachment eventually fails. The fourth clause of pp_attachment calls verb_pp_match (during this, the second stage of the strategy, the verb is matched first). verb_pp_match matches LOVE against the preplates for IN but does not find a match so verb_pp_match fails and so does clause 4. Clause 5 calls noun_pp_match which matches GIRL against the preplates for IN. The preplate [*physob, location, *pla, in3] matches so noun_pp_match succeeds, clause 5 succeeds, and the PP is attached to the np THE GIRL.

For (2), the strategy's first stage (clauses 1, 2 and 3) fails again, failing to find a match for either GIRL or STAB. In the second stage, verb_pp_match (clause 4) finds a preplate ([*do_dynamic, loc_static, *pla, in4]) that matches STAB (which belong to the *do_dynamic verb group) to IN THE PARK, so the pp is attached to the v STAB.

For (3), pp_attachment is called while CASSEX is parsing the sentence's relative clause so it tries to attach the PP to that clause. The second clause of pp_attachment looks to see if OBTAIN has any case preferences. Its formula includes a recipient case ([prep(for), prep-obj(*hum), case (recipient)]) so the PP is successfully attached to OBTAIN.

For (4), pp_attachment is also called while CASSEX is parsing the sentence's relative clause. Clause 2 of pp_attachment fails because LOVE does not have suitable case preferences. Clause 3 causes returns the pp unattached, along with the sentence Object THE BOOK THAT I LOVED. Processing continues one level up, at sentence level, and pp_attachment is called again. The second clause of pp_attachment looks to see if BUY has any case preferences. Like OBTAIN, the semantic formula for BUY includes a recipient case, so the pp is attached to BUY.

Apart from Rules A and B, we tried three other PP attachment rules -- C, D and E -- and implemented them in CASSEX. The rules varied in their use of case information for PP attachment. Rule A uses only verb and noun-based case information, as does Rule C. Rules D and E use only preposition-based information. We also varied the order of application of information and the nature of the default, trying both "high" and "low." The five strategies are summarized below.

Strategy	Noun & Verb Case Information	Preposition Case Information	Default
A	Move from PP leftwards	None used	Attach to immediate left of PP
B	Move from PP leftwards	Move from main verb rightwards	Attach to main verb
C	Move from PP leftwards	None used	Attach to main verb
D	None used	Move from PP leftwards	Attach to immediate left of PP
E	None used	Move from main verb rightwards	Attach to main verb

Earlier we gave reasons for rejecting an approach like Rule A i.e. it fails to provide the correct attachment for sentences like

JOHN LOVED HER (FOR HER BEAUTY)

or

JOHN SHOT THE GIRL (IN THE PARK).

Rule C gets these right but fails on

MARY SAW THE MAN WHO HAD LIVED WITH HER (WHILE ON MATERNITY LEAVE)

and

THE WOMAN WANTED THE DRESS (ON THE RACK)

because it gets the wrong default attachment. Rules D and E are also inadequate. Rule D gets wrong

THE WOMAN POSITIONED THE DRESS (ON THE RACK)

and

THE WOMAN WANTED THE DRESS (FOR HER DAUGHTER)

because Rule D defaults low (correct attachment relies on the verb preferences of POSITION and WANT). Rule E gets wrong sentences like

JOHN LOST THE TICKET (TO PARIS)

Only Rule B correctly attaches all the sentences.

6. Conclusions

We suggest that correct PP attachment is possible with only semantic information (ignoring, for the purposes of this paper, situations of pragmatic override and exceptional uses of world knowledge, of the Crain and Steedman type) and without syntactic rules, provided the system of preferences allows the interaction of not only verb-based but also noun and preposition-based preference. CASSEX has explored a number of alternative arrangements of default and order, and we have presented a best-fit algorithm for the data, without needing syntactic rules or complex syntactico-semantic weighting.

7. References

Boguraev, B.K. (1979) "Automatic Resolution of Linguistic Ambiguities." Technical Report No.11, University of Cambridge Computer Laboratory, Cambridge.

Crain, S. & Steedman, M. (1984) "On Not Being Led Up The Garden Path : The Use of Context by the Psychological Parser." In D.R. Dowty, L.J. Karttunen & A.M. Zwicky (Eds.), **Syntactic Theory and How People Parse Sentences**, Cambridge University Press.

Fass, D.C. & Wilks, Y.A. (1983) "Preference Semantics, Ill-Formedness and Metaphor," **American Journal of Computational Linguistics**, 9, pp. 178-187.

Ford, M., Bresnan, J. & Kaplan, R. (1981) "A Competence-Based Theory of Syntactic Closure." In J. Bresnan (Ed.), **The Mental Representation of Grammatical Relations**, Cambridge, MA : MIT Press.

Frazier, L. & Fodor, J. (1979) "The Sausage Machine: A New Two-Stage Parsing Model." **Cognition**, 6, pp.191-325.

Grice, H. P. (1975) "Logic & Conversation." In P. Cole & J. Morgan (Eds.), **Syntax and Semantics 3 : Speech Acts**, Academic Press, pp. 41-58.

Hirst, G. (1983) "Semantic Interpretation against Ambiguity." Technical Report CS-83-25, Dept. of Computer Science, Brown University.

Hirst, G. (1984) "A Semantic Process for Syntactic Disambiguation." **Proc. of AAAI-84**, Austin, Texas, pp. 148-152.

Huang, X-M. (1984a) "The Generation of Chinese Sentences from the Semantic Representations of English Sentences." **Proc. of International Conference on Machine Translation**, Cranfield, England.

Huang, X-M. (1984b) "A Computational Treatment of Gapping, Right Node Raising & Reduced Conjunction." **Proc. of COLING-84**, Stanford, CA., pp. 243-246.

Riesbeck, C. (1975) "Conceptual Analysis." In R. C. Schank (Ed.), **Conceptual Information Processing**, Amsterdam : North Holland.

Ritchie, G. (1978) **Computational Grammar**. Hassocks : Harvester.

Shieber, S.M. (1983) "Sentence Disambiguation by a Shift-Reduced Parsing Technique." **Proc. of IJCAI-83**, Kahlsruhe, W. Germany, pp. 699-703.

Shubert, L.K. (1984) "On Parsing Preferences." **Proc. of COLING-84**, Stanford, CA., pp. 247-250.

Wilks, Y.A. (1973) "Understanding without Proofs." **Proc. of IJCAI-73**, Stanford, CA.

Wilks, Y.A. (1975) "A Preferential Pattern-Seeking Semantics for Natural Language Inference." **Artificial Intelligence**, 6, pp. 53-74.

Wilks, Y.A. (1976) "Processing Case." **American Journal of Computational Linguistics**, 56.

Winograd, T. (1972) **Understanding Natural Language**. New York : Academic Press.

Controlling Search in Flexible Parsing

Steven Minton[1], Philip J. Hayes, and Jill Fain

Computer Science Department, Carnegie-Mellon University
Pittsburgh, PA 15213, USA

Abstract

Most natural language parsers require their input to be grammatical. This significantly constrains the search space that they must explore during parsing. Parsers which attempt to recover from extragrammatical input contend with a search space that is potentially much larger, since they cannot necessarily prune branches when grammatical expectations are violated. In this paper we discuss the control structure of the experimental MULTIPAR parser, which directs its search by exploring potential parses in order of their degree of grammatical deviation.[2]

1 Introduction

Most natural language processing systems parse their input by searching through a space of partial parses. They operate this way because, even though complete utterances alone or in context may be quite unambiguous, natural language is highly ambiguous locally. For instance, individual words can be ambiguous in their meaning or part of speech (e.g. "bank"), or components of utterances can fit together in more than one way (e.g. "look at the man with the telescope"). A parser's search space for a given input is defined by the relevant set of local ambiguities. A search succeeds if a globally acceptable parse is found that accounts for all the input. There are various techniques to reduce search in parsing, including looking ahead to resolve local ambiguities [5], or ignoring local alternatives that are inconsistent with domain-specific semantic constraints [2, 4]. However, no techniques can completely eliminate search from natural language parsing.

The search problem becomes much worse if we require a parser to cope with extragrammatical input. For practical natural language interface systems, this requirement is a real one [1]. Such interfaces must contend with the grammatical errors that inevitably arise when people use natural language interactively. Moreover, they also must cope with input that is correct, but outside their domain-restricted grammars.[3] We use the term *flexible parser* for a parser that can handle extragrammatical input.

The major search problem in flexible parsing lies in the criterion for identifying failing branches of the search — normally the violation of some syntactic or semantic expectation. While parsers that require grammatical input can employ this constraint to prune the search tree, flexible parsers must act more cautiously. If a candidate parse violates an expectation, it may mean that the candidate parse is incorrect and should be abandoned, or it may mean that the input really does violate the parser's expectations in the way that has been detected. In the latter case, the parser should not abandon the branch, but should try to recover from the deviation and complete the parse along that branch.

One approach to this problem is to abandon a search branch only when the flexible parser has run out of correction techniques to apply. This, in effect, enlarges the grammar of the parser to cover not only the inputs originally considered grammatical, but also those that can be recognized by any combination of available recovery methods. Although straightforward, this approach is unlikely to produce acceptable results. First, given the range of possible recovery techniques [1], the search space will quickly become unmanageably large. Second, the recovery techniques may generate spuriously "corrected" parses of grammatical input. Finally, the described approach provides no way to distinguish between parses that involve widely varying degrees of correction (e.g. simple spelling corrections versus hypothesization of entire phrases).

What is needed, then, is a control structure that allows the normal criterion of extragrammaticality to cut off failing searches, but also accommodates the application of recovery techniques to reactivate failed search branches if no grammatical parse can be found. Moreover, the recovery techniques should be ordered across all search branches according to the degree of ungrammaticality their use implies, i.e. the simpler ones (like spelling correction) must be tried in all branches of the parse before the more complex and unlikely ones (like missing word insertion) are tried in any branch.

This paper presents a control structure which satisfies these goals. The next section describes the control structure from the point of view of the programmer constructing a parser that uses it. Section 3 discusses some efficiency issues that arose in implementing the control structure.

2 A Programmer's View of the Control Structure

The control structure described in this paper was developed in the context of a restricted domain parser consisting of a collection of caseframe instantiation strategies. We have previously used the phrases multi-strategy [3] and entity-oriented [2] to describe this approach. There is no space here to describe this parser, called MULTIPAR, in detail. The most important characteristic of MULTIPAR from the control structure point of view is that its caseframe interpretation strategies are programmed directly, rather than being driven by a declarative formalism such as a transition network. We will refer to the person who writes strategies as the strategy programmer. In some sense, the strategy programmer is the user of the control structure.

Each strategy is an expert at parsing certain types of constructs. Strategies cooperate by calling upon each other to parse sections of the input sentence. When a strategy encounters particular difficulties (violated expectations) while parsing its input, several options are typically available. The options always include simply

---

[1] AT&T Bell Laboratories Scholar

[2] This research was sponsored in part by the Air Force Office of Scientific Research under Contract AFOSR-82-0219.

[3] We use the term grammar broadly here to cover the semantic expectations used by many restricted domain systems in addition to syntactic ones.

reporting failure, but may also include recovery methods to resolve the violated expectation. The MULTIPAR control structure provides the programmer with a method of specifying the alternative ways of proceeding, and indicating how much of a deviation each option would represent, without requiring him to schedule the investigation of the options explicitly. This scheduling is taken care of by the control structure automatically

The construct provided[4] by the control structure to specify alternative ways of proceeding in the face of violated expectations is the SPLIT statement. A SPLIT statement splits the computation into parallel branches — one branch for each option. For each branch, the programmer specifies a *flexibility increment* indicating the degree of grammatical deviation implied by producing a successful parse via that branch. For instance, if a violated expectation could be resolved by a spelling correction or by hypothesizing a missing word, these two options would be specified as different branches of a SPLIT. The control structure would then pursue the two options independently. However, the spelling correction option would have a lower flexibility increment than the missing word hypothesization, and so it would be pursued first. If it led to a complete parse, the missing word hypothesization would never be tried.

A stylized example of a split statement is:

```
(Split (+0 actionA)
       (+1 actionB)
       (+3 actionC) ....)
```

Execution of this SPLIT statement produces a three-way branch in the search tree. Action A has a zero flexibility increment, implying no grammatical deviation along this branch. Actions B and C have flexibility increments of 1 and 3 respectively. This means that Actions B and C would be scheduled for later investigation, while Action A would be pursued immediately.

The system maintains a global Current-Flexibility-Level whose value is equal to the flexibility level of the least deviant partial parse that remains to be investigated. In this way, the control structure can guarantee that parses are attempted in strict flexibility order and can generate all and only parses at the lowest flexibility level at which a global parse succeeds. In particular, if a grammatical parse can be found, then all and only grammatical parses will be generated.

It is important to note that the flexibility level of a parse is the sum of all flexibility increments of all SPLIT statement branches used to achieve the parse. In terms of the stylized example above, this means that other branches in entirely different parts of the tree may be tried between trying Actions B and C. It also means that Actions B and C may be tried, even if Action A succeeds locally, so long as the parse fragment produced by Action A does not participate in a complete global parse. This global comparison of the sums of the local flexibility increments is crucial in ensuring that recovery techniques are attempted in order of drasticness across the entire search space of a parse. It also ensures that improbable combinations of recovery techniques are not applied if simpler parses can be found.

Another advantage provided by the SPLIT statement is that recovery actions can be closely integrated with the normal parsing process. Instead of having a separate recovery phase that occurs independently of normal parsing, recovery actions occur within the local context of strategies. Therefore, only recovery actions appropriate to the context need be applied. This is important for recovery strategies such as spelling correction, where availability of the local context can provide information that constrains the range of possible corrections.

Let us now look at a less stylized use of SPLIT. The following algorithm is a simplified version of the strategy MULTIPAR uses for parsing imperative sentences.

Imperative Caseframe Strategy

1. *Find the head verb of the sentence.*

2. *Retrieve an uninstantiated caseframe for the action associated with this verb.*

3. *Identify the semantic type of the syntactic direct object. Call the Nounphrase Strategy to find an object of that type at the beginning of the unparsed segment.*

4. *Determine the unfilled marked cases and SPLIT*

   + 0   *Alternative1: Recognize next word as a case-marker for an unfilled marked case; attempt to fill that case with the remaining segment.*

   + 5   *Alternative2: Hypothesize that a case-marker for an unfilled marked case is missing; attempt to fill the case with the remaining segment.*

5. *If sentence has not been completely parsed, go to 4.*

Let us assume that MULTIPAR is being used as the front-end to a mail system, and that the user has just composed a message to be sent. To parse a command such as "Mail message to Paul@CMUA", the strategy would first identify "Mail" as the head verb, and SEND as its corresponding action, and then call the Nounphrase Strategy to recognize a potential **MSG-OBJECT** as the direct object. Assuming this lower level strategy parses "message" correctly, the imperative strategy then reaches the SPLIT statement. At this point, two branches of the search tree are created with flexibility levels equal to the sum of the Current-Flexibility-Level (which is 0) and the corresponding flexibility increments. The branch corresponding to Alternative2 is scheduled by the control structure at flexibility level 5 (0 plus 5). The branch corresponding to Alternative1 still has flexibility level 0 (0 plus 0), and so it continues immediately. Alternative1 would successfully recognize "to" as a marker for SEND's destination case, and call a lower-level strategy to parse "Paul@CMUA" as the **MSG-DESTINATION**. Thus, this branch of the parse succeeds and the other branch spawned by the SPLIT is never tried.

A common error in spontaneous input is to omit case markers, so let us suppose now that the input reads "Mail message Paul@CMUA". As before, after "message" is recognized as the direct object, the SPLIT statement is encountered. However, this time Alternative1 reports failure. If the control structure finds no other branches of the tree suspended at flexibility level 0 (the Current-Flexibility-Level), it will look for suspended branches at higher flexibility levels. In our present example, it will find the branch suspended earlier at level 5. The Current-Flexibility-Level is set to 5, and computation is restarted at Alternative2. This means that the imperative strategy will now hypothesize that a case-marker has been omitted, and will try to parse "Paul@CMUA" as one of the unfilled cases for SEND. When "Paul@CMUA" is recognized as a possible **MSG-DESTINATION**, the input will have been completely accounted for, and the parse would be the same as for the first example.[5] Notice that this recovery action is specific to the violated

---

[4]MULTIPAR is implemented in Common Lisp.

[5]A complete interface system might want to confirm its interpretation with the user.

expectation of finding a case marker. Because the action is context-dependent, it would have been more difficult to achieve in a completely separate recovery phase

Even with this simple example, it will be clear that the size of the search tree can grow rapidly when recovery is attempted. If "Paul@CMUA" qualified as both a **MSG-SOURCE** and a **MSG-DESTINATION**, Alternative2 above would have to split again, and two alternative corrected parses would be produced. Then too, Paul@CMUA might be the name of a misspelled message-header. Exploring this alternative would be the responsibility of one of the strategies called while parsing the direct object. Note that spelling correction can potentially generate many alternatives, especially if words in the parser's lexicon can be considered as potential misspellings of other words in the lexicon (perhaps the user intended "Make" instead of "Mail").

These examples may make clearer the importance of exploring all potential parses at lower flexibility levels before any of those at higher levels. Witness the computational expense inherent in recovering a missing case marker, i.e. trying all unfilled cases. If there is still a possibility that branches of the search requiring less drastic recovery techniques might yet succeed, they must be attempted first. For example, the sentence "Mail message should be saved" will be recognized by a strategy for declarative sentences that is invoked in a branch parallel to the imperative strategy. Since this branch succeeds at level 0, it should be examined in its entirety before the imperative strategy attempts to hypothesize a missing case marker

This best-first order of exploring the search tree implies that grammatical parses will be discovered relatively quickly. (A disadvantage, of course, is that ungrammatical, but recoverable parses may be produced significantly more slowly.) Equally important, the use of flexibility levels imposes a partial order on deviant parses, so parses that are highly undesirable will never be discovered if better alternatives exist. For example, a parse with two spelling corrections will not be generated if a parse with a single spelling correction can be found. At times, the ordering may be rather arbitrary (e.g. is a missing case marker worse than a single spelling mistake?). However, such arbitrary judgments tend to overconstrain the search rather than underconstrain it, which seems appropriate.

3 Implementing the Multipar Control Structure Efficiently

In order for the control structure outlined in the previous sections to be of practical use, it must implement the best-first search in an efficient manner, and it must be convenient for the strategy programmer to use. In this section we outline some of the engineering considerations that proved to be crucial in achieving these goals.

- *Usability*: MULTIPAR consists of many communicating strategies, each of which may involve a complex computation. The control structure provides a standard interface for one strategy to call upon another and controls the pseudo-parallel exploration of the search tree. An important attribute of the control structure is its unobtrusiveness; the strategy writer is provided with a small set of facilities for executing strategy calls and parallel actions

- *Efficient Context Re-creation*: To return to an alternative on the agenda, the local context at the SPLIT statement must be re-created. Rather than saving the complete state of the computation, context re-creation is effected by re-executing the local strategy from its inception. This seemingly inefficient mechanism is quite practical due to two factors: most scheduled alternatives are never attempted during a

typical parse, and a caching mechanism is used to store substrategy results.

- *Sharing Strategy Results*: It is often the case that parallel branches will duplicate each other's work, since they may differ only in a few respects. This is especially true when recovery actions are initiated, since the number of branches tends to grow dramatically as higher flexibility levels are reached. Because of this, the mechanism for caching substrategy results has a dual purpose. In addition to enabling rapid context re-creation, it makes the overall operation of the parser more efficient by allowing strategies to share results.[6] For example, to recover from a missing case marker, the lower-level case filler strategy has to be called once for each case that could possibly be filled. Each time it is called it may have to operate somewhat differently depending on the constraints for that case (e.g. call a name-recognizing sub-strategy or check to see whether the input can be found among current message headers). However, much of the work may be identical in each instance, and so caching produces considerable savings.

4 Conclusion

All natural language parsers must perform some search, but when a parser is intended to handle ungrammatical as well as grammatical input, its search space becomes very large. The control structure described in this paper allows a large, complex search space of this kind to be explored in an orderly manner. Efficiency is improved by a caching mechanism that takes advantage of the significant amount of redundancy present in the search space. The control structure provides convenient facilities for specifying the search space, while automatically performing the bookkeeping necessary for an efficient search.

We have built a version of MULTIPAR that parses natural language commands to an operating system. Experience with both grammatical and deviant sentences in this domain suggests that the control structure adequately fulfills the requirements for a flexible parser outlined earlier.

5 Acknowledgements
We thank Jaime Carbonell for his help and participation in all phases of this project.

References

1. Carbonell, J. G. and Hayes, P. J. "Recovery Strategies for Parsing Extragrammatical Language." *Computational Linguistics* 10 (1984).
2. Hayes, P. J. Entity-Oriented Parsing. COLING84, Stanford University, July, 1984.
3. Hayes, P. J. and Carbonell, J. G. Multi-Strategy Parsing and its Role in Robust Man-Machine Communication. Carnegie-Mellon University Computer Science Department, May, 1981.
4. Hendrix, G. G. Human Engineering for Applied Natural Language Processing. Proc. Fifth Int. Jt. Conf. on Artificial Intelligence, MIT, 1977, pp. 183-191.
5. Marcus, M. A.. *A Theory of Syntactic Recognition for Natural Language*. MIT Press, Cambridge, Mass., 1980.

[6]A relatively sophisticated caching mechanism is required to support this functionality. Due to the parallelism introduced by the SPLIT statement, a strategy may return different results at different flexibility levels, or even at the same flexibility level. The caching mechanism must not only record the various results, but also keep track of which strategies access the cache. This allows the control structure to create appropriate additional branches of the search tree if the cached set of results for a strategy is updated (with a new value at a higher flexibility level) after it has been previously accessed by one or more other strategies.

GRAMMATICAL RELATIONS AS THE BASIS FOR NATURAL
LANGUAGE PARSING AND TEXT UNDERSTANDING*

Samual Bayer, Leonard Joseph, Candace Kalish

A045
Mitre Corporation
Bedford, MA 01730

ABSTRACT

The KING KONG parser described by this paper attempts to apply the principles of relational grammar to the parsing of English in order to overcome the problems encountered by syntactic and semantic parsers. Specifically, this parser uses relational categories such as subject, direct object, and instrument to map syntactic constituents onto semantic roles within CD-like structures. Thus, the parser makes use of both syntactic and semantic information to guide its parse.

I BACKGROUND

A. Syntactic Parsing

During the 1970's, Woods, and Bresnan and Kaplan among others developed syntax driven parsers based on various kinds of ATNs, whose theoretical base derived more or less from transformational grammar and its offshoots. A more recent approach to syntax driven parsing is represented by the Marcus parser, which, unlike ATN's, does no backtracking and builds permanent structure. One of the principal difficulties with the type of parser represented by Woods's work and Marcus's work, and also to a lesser extent of Bresnan's and Kaplan's, is illustrated by the problems associated with garden path sentences, which require extended backtracking, or, in the case of the Marcus parser, more lookahead than his theory permits.

Prepositional phrase attachment represents another problem for syntactic parsers, since this phenomenon is primarily semantic and as such does not lend itself to syntactic solutions. More abstractly, one can say that syntactic parsers generally have trouble dealing with sentences with multiple interpretations, where the ambiguity involves the placement of constituents. Marcus uses a related problem, that of locating the source of a moved WH-phrase, to argue that semantic as well as syntactic information is necessary for an accurate syntactic parse and appeals to the procedure in (Woods 1973) of Selective Modifier Placement, although he does not formally incorporate it.

One syntactic parser, the CHART parser developed by Kay for the MIND system, dealt extensively with this type of problem. The solution chosen was to keep several possibilities open at once by building constituents and, in effect, treating them as building blocks which could be put together in a variety of ways. The final parse would be the result not only of the identification and analysis of the constituents but also of the choice of how to put them together. The CHART parser relied on some semantic knowledge to make this choice and was in a way a hybrid of syntactic and semantic approaches to parsing.

B. Semantic Parsing

Another approach to ambiguity is offered by members of the semantic school of parsing, among them the developers of CDs: Schank, Abelson, and their students. The developers of such parsers recognized multiple senses of of a word from the start. Attachment problems were resolved either by reference to larger meaning structures such as a scripts or by lexical expectations.

The ability to handle ambiguity is the great advantage of semantic parsers, but this ability comes at a high price. Such a parser has great difficulty capturing generalizations between transformationally related sentences, and it also has to work harder in dealing with problems that are better analyzed in terms of constituent structure, such as gapping. Furthermore, there is no graceful way to retarget a word-based parser to another language, since such parsers ignore cross-linguistic generalizations. Finally, error handling is often easier in a syntactic parser both because knowledge of constituent structure can often aid in correction and because syntactically based error messages are far more intelligible to the user.

II THE NEED FOR RELATIONAL GRAMMAR

The parser being developed at MITRE differs from most parsers in that it recognizes not two but three levels of representation: the level of structure, the level of meaning, and the level of grammatical relations (subject, object, indirect object), which mediates between the first two for the purpose of identification of semantic roles. This notion is based mainly on work in (Bayer 1984), although a similar approach in a different framework has been suggested in (Wasow 1978). The premise of this approach is that there is no straightforward mapping between structural information (which, in typical CD approaches, seems to amount to no more than appeals to position) and semantic roles. This is clear even in English, a language whose structure is quite rigid and yields more clues than most languages about the mapping between structure and semantic roles.

An approach in terms of grammatical relations may be justified by i) simplification of syntactic generalizations, ii) simplification of identification of semantic roles, and iii) generality with respect to complex sentences.

A. Simplification of Syntactic Generalization

In English, as in other languages, various syntactic facts are best expressed in terms of grammatical relations. The facts of verb agreement, for example, are most elegantly captured through appeals to the categories subject, object, and indirect object (in English as well as languages with richer case marking). Semantic subcategorization facts, such as the requirement that the verb "walk" be predicated of an animate being, are also most easily expressed in terms of grammatical relations. Since final grammati-

---

*This research was sponsored by Rome Air Force Development Center under Contract F19628-84-C-001, project #6070.

cal relations are deduced from surface structure almost solely by positional and morphological information, one might claim that a statement of the facts of verb agreement and subcategorization in terms of this sort of information would be adequate. While it is true that this sort of description can be made, its awkwardness calls its intuitiveness and usefulness into question. The term "subject" in English is isomorphic with the phrase "the NP directly preceding the verb in an uninverted clause, or the NP directly following the initial verb in an inverted clause", but the fact that this disjunction must be employed in all those references where the word "subject" would be naturally used suggests that an important generalization is being missed, even in a language where structure is strict and fairly unambiguous; in a language where case-marking and word-order combine to identify the subject, the description of the above phenomena in structural and morphological terms becomes much harder.

B. Simplification of Identification of Semantic Roles

Analogously, the explicit identification of subject aids in the identification of semantic roles. Generalizations or defaults, such as the mapping into the ACTOR slot, can be greatly simplified by referring to the notion of subject rather than to the positions the NP in question may occupy. The mapping properties of classes of exceptions can also be described easily, when the group of np´s conveniently labeled "subject" map into the OBJECT slot instead, for example.

C. Generality with Respect to Complex Sentences

We referred earlier to the notion of final grammatical relations. This phrase hints at the idea that grammatical relations may CHANGE. This is why, in the passive sentence "John was struck by Mary", the surface subject is mapped into the same semantic slot that receives the direct object of an active sentence such as "Mary struck John". The operation of Passive makes a direct object a subject, with concomitant displacement of the original subject (into the "by"-phrase in English, for example). In order to identify the original relations, we apply the operation BACKWARD in order to "undo" the application of Passive. Although English has relatively few rules which change grammatical relations, these few rules interact to derive complicated multi-clause sentences which positional approaches are hard-pressed to analyze elegantly or easily.

Consider two more of these relation-changing rules: Subject-to-Subject Raising, which makes the subject of a clause in subject position the subject of the dominating clause, relating "That John will go is likely" and "John is likely to go", and Subject-to-Object Raising, which makes the subject of a clause in direct object position the direct object of the dominating clause, relating "I believe that John left" and "I believe John to have left". These two rules, combined with the rule of Passive above, may cooperate in their application to yield quite complex sentences. For example,

John is believed by Mary to be likely to have left.

is derived by Subject-to-Subject Raising in the most embedded clause, followed by Subject-to-Object Raising in the next clause up, and finally Passive in the matrix clause. While a relational approach can, having identified and extracted those NPs which bear the relevant grammatical relations, simply change the grammatical relations of the NPs involved when they undo these operations, a positional/structural approach must physically move the NPs or try to develop a set of complicated conditions which alter the slot-mappings for a verb. These approaches are unwieldy alternatives to the relational approach; the intuitive appeal of grammatical relations is demonstrated even in the names of the raising operations just described, names which were coined not by relational grammarians but by the classical transformational grammarians of the ´50´s and ´60´s, notably Noam Chomsky, for whom grammatical relations were (and still are) derivative.

III   Implementation of the KING KONG Parser

The current implementation of the KING KONG parser contains a Marcus-type syntactic parser coupled with mechanisms for manipulating grammatical relations and semantic roles. It also relies on a semantic representation scheme in which CD type structures are embedded in a semantic net. As the parse progresses, the grammatical relations of the terms in the sentence are identified, and the changes in grammatical relations are undone. Once the initial relations have been reached, the function FILL-CD takes the relational network, along with a set of slot-mappings (which are produced by modifying a set of global defaults, such as SUBJ -> ACTOR, DOBJ -> OBJECT, with whatever verb-specific mappings are appropriate) and maps in the values for the CD.

```
(defkong fly
  (make-word newform ´fly
     semantics (make-kernel
                     part-of-speech ´v
                     cd fly-family)
     features (copylist *VERB-DEFAULT*)
     gr<->slots ´(((subject actor command))
                  ((intrans-subject obj))
                  ((trans-subject instr
                     instrumentality))
                  ((trans-subject obj neither)
                   (dobj instr
                     instrumentality)))
     slot-completions ´((obj instr
                          instrumentality)
                         (instr actor control))
                    ))
```

Figure 1.

The dictionary entries for KING KONG, although based on CD-like kernels, look quite different from standard CD´s. Figure 1 contains an example of a typical verb entry, for the word "fly". The "part-of-speech" slot for the verb contains subcategorization information, and the "features" slot specifies syntactic and morphological properties. The two fields "gr<->slots" and "slot-completions" contain crucial information which ties the semantic properties of "fly" to its syntactic properties. The former maps from relational categories to semantic slots; the latter fills empty semantic slots based on already filled slots. Each can rely on the functional/semantic notions of "command" and "instrumentality" to guide the slot-filling. An actor must be able to command an action in the sense that he must be able to cause the action to occur; an instrument must be a tool useable by the commander to accomplish the action; an object is the entity primarily affected by the action. An example may clarify this.

The various senses of "fly" are illustrated in Table 1; we consider the semantic roles of these sentences to be as in Table 2.

1. The businessman flew the plane to Cairo. –
    The businessman was a passenger.

2. The pilot flew the plane to Cairo. –
    The pilot actually manipulated the plane's
    controls.

3. The mummy flew to Cairo. –
    The mummy was cargo.

4. The plane flew to Cairo. –
    The plane was the instrument of its own mo-
    tion.

5. The pigeon flew to Cairo. –
    The bird was both the instrument and com-
    mander of the action.

Table 1.

1. fly: actor nil
         object businessman
         instrument plane
2. fly: actor pilot
         object plane
         instrument plane
3. fly: actor nil
         object mummy
         instrument
4. fly: actor nil
         object plane
         instrument plane
5. fly: actor pigeon
         object pigeon
         instrument pigeon

Table 2.

IV   TESTING AND RESULTS

The parser, with a dictionary of 72 words, was tested on a set of 120 sentences to verify that it recognized the morphology of the words and syntactic constructions of the clauses properly, and that the mapping from structure to grammatical relations and from grammatical relations to semantic roles was correct.

KING KONG worked correctly under the full range of tenses, voices, and under many transformations on sentence structure including unbounded movement rules like WH movement, relation-changing rules like Passive, Dative Movement and Raising, deletion rules such as Equi, and insertion rules such as There-insertion and Extraposition (see a sampling in Table 3). However, there were some limitations on the capabilities of the parser arising from its insufficient handling of coordination. We are currently implementing KING KONG as an expert systems approach to parsing in order better to handle decisions about ambiguity. Even with these limitations, the range of sentence constructions it could parse was very wide. Most crucially, KING KONG successfully recognized grammatical relations. It was always able to identify the subject, object and indirect object of each verb, even when these were shifted away from the verb by transformations of the base sentence.

Finally, within the restrictions imposed by lack of context and only the most rudimentary suggestions of a semantic component, KING KONG was always able to map from grammatical relations of entities to actions, to the semantic roles of actor, instrument, and object.

A pilot flew the plane.

The good plane could quickly be flown by a good pilot.

Who flew the plane?

What plane is the pilot flying?

Are planes destroying boxes?

He gave the box to John.

Refuel the plane at the airbase.

I am trying to believe that John seemed to promise me to want the ecm to jam the radar.

Does John go quickly?

Table 3.

V   CONCLUSION

We have demonstrated that the use of relational grammar as a mapping between syntax and semantics overcomes many of the weaknesses associated with other parsing strategies. We realize, of course, that a parser is only one component of an interface; we are currently developing a representation of context using scripts and semantic networks. The latter should provide a capability for understanding simple word extensions, while the former will aid in understanding ill-formed but "meaningful" input. A last hope is that by making use of universal relational categories we can attempt the retargetting of KING KONG to another language.

REFERENCES

[1] Bayer, Samuel. A Theory of Linearization in Relational Grammar. Senior essay, Yale U., New Haven, CT., 1984

[2] Dyer, Michael. In-Depth Understanding. Cambridge: MIT Press, 1983.

[3] Kaplan, R. M. "Augmented Transition Networks as Psychological Models of Sentence Comprehension". Artificial Intelligence 3 (1972) 77 – 100.

[4] Kay, Martin. "The MIND System". In Rustin (1973).

[5] Marcus, Mitchell. A Theory of Syntactic Recognition for Natural Language. Cambridge. Ma.: MIT Press, 1980.

[6] Pazzani. Mike. "APE – A Parsing Example" (unpublished research) MITRE Corp., Bedford, Ma., 1980-83.

[7] Perlmutter, David, ed., Studies in Relational Grammar 1. Chicago: U. Chicago Press, 1983.

[8] Rustin. R. ed., Natural Language Processing. New York: Algorithmics Press, 1973.

[9] Wasow, Tom. "Remarks on Processing, Constraints, and the Lexicon" In D. Waltz, ed., Theoretical Issues in Natural Language Processing, N.Y.: ACM, 1978

[10] Woods, Bill. The Lunar Sciences Natural Language Information System. BBN Report No. 2378. Bolt Beranek and Newman, Cambridge. MA., 1972.

[11] Woods, Bill. "An Experimental Parsing System for Transition Network Grammars," in Rustin (1973).

THE ROLE OF PERSPECTIVE IN RESPONDING TO PROPERTY MISCONCEPTIONS*

Kathleen F. McCoy
Department of Computer & Information Science
University of Pennsylvania
Philadelphia, PA 19104

Abstract

In order to adequately respond to misconceptions involving an object's properties, we must have a context-sensitive method for determining object similarity. Such a method is introduced here. Some of the necessary contextual information is captured by a new notion of *object perspective*. It is shown how object perspective can be used to account for different responses to a given misconception in different contexts.

1. Introduction

As a user interacts with a database or an expert system, s/he may attribute a property or property value to an object that that object does not have. For instance, imagine the following query to a database.

U. Give me the HULL-NO of all DESTROYERS whose MAST-HEIGHT is above 190.

If a system were to evaluate such a query, it might find that there are no such ships in the database. The reason for this is that the user has queried a value of the property MAST-HEIGHT that it cannot have for the object DESTROYER. I term this error a *property misconception*. Upon encountering such a query, even a very cooperative system could only respond:

S. There are no DESTROYERS in the database with a MAST-HEIGHT above 190. Would you like to try again?

In most cases, however, this is not the way a human would respond. A study of human/human transcripts reveals that a human conversational partner often tries to get at the cause of the misconception and offer additional information to correct the wrong information. The additional information often takes the form of a correct query that is a possible alternative to the user's query. In this paper I describe some of the knowledge and reasoning that are necessary for a natural language interface to a database or expert system to mimic this human behavior.

In the above query, since there is an object similar to a DESTROYER that has the value of HULL-NO given, the user's misconception may result from his/her confusing the two objects. Hence a reasonable response would be:

S. All DESTROYERS in the database have a MAST-HEIGHT between 85 and 90. Were you thinking of an AIRCRAFT-CARRIER?

Notice the strategy used to correct the misconception is to (1) deny (implicitly) the property/value given, (2) give the corresponding correct information, (3) suggest an alternative query containing the object the user may have confused with the misconception object.

In other situations, a reasonable alternative query might involve the same object the user asked about, with a different property/value pair. This is the case in the following query.

U. Give me the HULL-NO of all DESTROYERS whose MAST-HEIGHT is above 3500.
S. All DESTROYERS in the database have a MAST-HEIGHT between 85 and 90. Were you thinking of the DISPLACEMENT?

This response is similar to the one given above except that the alternative query suggests an attribute rather than an object which may have been confused.

In general, there can be two major reasons why a wrong attribution may occur. Either (1) the user has the wrong object — that is, s/he has confused the object being discussed with a similar object or has reasoned (falsely) by analogy from a similar object; or (2) the user has the wrong attribute — that is, s/he has confused the attribute being discussed with a similar attribute. If one of these two can be seen as likely in a given situation, then a revised query can be suggested which mentions the similar object or the similar attribute.

To propose alternative queries, a system must have a method for determining similarity of objects and attributes. In this paper I will focus on responses involving object confusion; thus I will examine a similarity metric for objects. In the next section such a similarity metric is introduced. The following section introduces a new notion of object perspective which is needed to provide the similarity metric with some necessary contextual information, in particular, attribute salience ratings. Finally, an example of how perspective information and the similarity metric can be used to give reasonable responses to misconceptions involving object properties is given.

2. Object Similarity

As was shown above, in order to respond effectively to property misconceptions, we must have a method for determining object similarity. Object similarity has previously been shown to be important in tasks such as organizing explanations [6], offering cooperative responses to pragmatically ill-formed queries [2], and identifying metaphors [9]. In the above systems the similarity of two objects is based on the distance between the objects in the generalization hierarchy. One problem with this approach is that it is *context invariant*.** That is, there is no way for contextual information to affect similarity judgments.

However, Tversky [8] proposes a measure of object similarity based on common and disjoint features/properties of the objects involved, which enables contextual information to be taken into account. Tversky's similarity rating for two objects a and b, where **A** is the set of properties associated with object a and **B** is the set of properties associated with object b, can be expressed as:
$$s(a,b) = \theta f(A \cap B) - \alpha f(A - B) - \beta f(B - A)$$
for some $\theta, \alpha, \beta \,)= 0$. This equation actually defines a family of similarity scales where θ, α, and β are parameters which alter the importance of each piece of the equation, and f maps over the features and yields a salience rating for each. The equation states

---
*This work is partially supported by the NSF grant #MCS81-07290 and by the ARO grant DAA20-84-K-0061.

**See [5] for additional problems and discussion of this point.

that the similarity of two objects is some function of their common features minus some function of their disjoint features. The importance of each feature involved (determined by the function f) and the importance of each piece of the equation (determined by θ, α, and β) may change with context.

Previous work [4, 7] has discussed the effect of "focus" on the prominence of objects. Focusing algorithms can be adapted to set the values of θ, α, and β. For instance, if object a is "in focus" and object b is not, then the features of a should be weighted more heavily than the features of b. Thus we should choose $\alpha > \beta$ so that the similarity is reduced more by features of a that are not shared by b than vice versa.

The problem then is to determine f. Other work [3, 9] has hand encoded salience values for the attributes of individual objects in the knowledge base, effectively setting the f function once and for all. This approach, however, is not sufficient since salience values must change with context. The following examples in which two objects (Treasury Bills and Money Market Certificates) are compared in two different circumstances, illustrate the importance of context on the similarity rating.

Consider someone calling an expert financial advisor to see if she can better invest her money. She begins by telling the expert where her money is:

U. We have $40,000 in money market certificates. One is coming due next week for $10,000... I was wondering if you think this is a good savings...

E. Well, I'd like to see you hold that $10,000 coming due in a money market fund and then get into a longer term money market certificate.

U. Hm... well I was just wondering, what about a treasury bill instead?

E. That's not a bad idea but it doesn't replace your money market certificate in any way — it's an exact duplicate. They're almost identical types of instruments - so one, as far as I'm concerned, is about the same as another.

Now consider how the same two objects can be seen quite differently when viewed in a different way. Imagine the following conversation:

U. I am interested in buying some US Government Securities. Now I was thinking of Money Market Certificates since they are the same as Treasure Bills.

E. But they're not - they are two very different things. A Treasury Bill is backed by the U.S. Government: you have to get it from the federal reserve. A Money Market Certificate, on the other hand, is backed by the individual bank that issues it. So, one is a Government Security while the other is not.

In the first example the objects are viewed as savings instruments. This view highlights attributes such as interest-rates and maturity-dates that are common to Treasury Bills and Money Market Certificates. This highlighting causes the two instruments to be seen as "identical". In contrast, the second example views the objects as instruments issued by a particular company or organization. In this case attributes such as issuing-company and purchase-place are highlighted. Since these highlighted attributes are different for the two objects, the objects are seen as being quite different.

As the examples illustrate, a context-free metric of similarity is not sufficient; contextual information is needed. A notion of object perspective, introduced below, can capture the needed contextual information. In particular, perspective accounts for how the f function (the assignment of salience values to various attributes) changes with context.

3. Perspective

[4, 1] note that the same object may be viewed from different perspectives. For instance a particular building may be viewed as an architectural work, a home, a thing made with bricks, etc. According to this work, an object viewed from a particular perspective is seen as having one particular superordinate, although in fact it may have many superordinates. The object inherits properties only from the superordinate in perspective. Therefore different perspectives on the same object cause different properties to be highlighted.

Although this notion of perspective is intuitively appealing, in practice its use is rather difficult since it hinges on the use of a limited inheritance mechanism. The problem is that attributes may be inherited from the top of the generalization hierarchy, not just from immediate superordinates. So, an object's perspective involves not just one superordinate but a chain of superordinates. Therefore one must not only determine what perspective a particular object is being viewed from, but also what perspective its superordinate is viewed from, and so on. As one continues up the hierarchy in this fashion, the definition of perspective as viewing an object as a member of a particular superordinate becomes less and less appealing.

In addition, this notion of object perspective says nothing about the density of the generalization hierarchy. That is, in some situations the immediate superordinate of an object (and the properties it contributes) may be ignored. For example, even though a whale is a cetacean (a class of aquatic mammals including whales and porpoises), this classification (and all attributes contributed by the classification) may be ignored in some situations in which the important attributes instead are inherited from a superordinate of cetacean, say, mammal. In other situations, the class "cetacean" may be central. The notion of object perspective outlined above has no way of determining whether or not certain superordinates should be ignored or included.

Here I introduce a new notion of perspective which is able to handle both the assignment of differing salience values and the density problem. In this notion, perspectives sit orthogonal to the generalization hierarchy. Each comprises a set of properties and their salience values. A number of perspectives must be defined a priori for the objects in a particular domain. The specification of perspectives, just like the specification of an object taxonomy, must be done by a domain expert. Knowledge of useful perspectives in a domain then, is part of the domain expertise.

With this new notion of perspective, when an object is viewed through a particular perspective, the perspective essentially acts as a filter on the properties which that object inherits from its superordinates. That is, properties are inherited with the salience values given by the perspective. Thus properties of the object which are given a high salience rating by the perspective will be highlighted, while those which are given a low salience value or do not appear in the perspective will be suppressed. The density problem is handled by ignoring those superordinate concepts which contribute only attributes suppressed by the current perspective.

4. Using Perspective to Determine Responses

Perspective information can be used with Tversky's similarity metric to help determine alternative queries to a query containing a misconception. To see how this works, consider a domain containing the following three objects with the attributes shown:

Money Market Certificates
  Maturity: 3 months
  Denominations: $1,000
  Issuer: Commercial Bank
  Penalty for Early Withdrawal: 10%
  Purchase Place: Commercial Bank
  Safety: Medium

Treasury Bills
    Maturity: 3 months
    Denominations: $1,000
    Issuer: US Government
    Purchase Place: Federal Reserve
    Safety: High

Treasury Bond
    Maturity: 7 years
    Denominations: $500
    Issuer: US Government
    Penalty for Early Withdrawal: 20%
    Purchase Place: Federal Reserve
    Safety: High

and the following perspectives:

Savings Instruments
    Maturity -- high
    Denominations -- high
    Safety -- medium

Issuing Company
    Issuer -- high
    Safety -- high
    Purchase Place -- medium

Notice that the perspective of Savings Instruments highlights Maturity and Denominations, and somewhat highlights Safety. This indicates that when people are discussing securities as savings instruments, they are most interested in how long their money will be tied up and in what denominations they can save their money. The perspective of Issuing Company, on the other hand, highlights different attributes. When securities are discussed from this perspective, things like who the issuer of the security is and how safe a security issued from that company is, become important.

Suppose the perspective is Savings Instruments and the user says:

U. What is the penalty for early withdrawal on a Treasury Bill?

This query indicates that the user has a misconception since s/he has attributed a property to Treasury Bills that they do not have. One reasonable correction to the query would contain an alternative query which to replaces Treasury Bills with another object that has the property specified and is similar to Treasury Bills. The system may reason that both Money Market Certificates and Treasury Bonds have the penalty specified, and so check to see if either of these objects is similar to Treasury Bills. Notice that the Savings Instruments perspective highlights attributes common to Treasury Bills and Money Market Certificates (they have the same Maturity and Denominations), as well as attributes disjoint to Treasury Bills and Treasury Bonds (they have different Maturity and Denominations). Using these salience values, the similarity metric will find that Money Market Certificates are very similar to Treasury Bills while Treasury Bonds are very different. Thus Money Market Certificates will be deemed a probable object of confusion and the following correction may be offered:

S. Treasury Bills do not have a penalty for early withdrawal. Were you thinking of a Money Market Certificate?

Notice that if the perspective had instead been Issuing Company, which highlights attributes common to Treasury Bills and Treasury Bonds and disjoint to Treasury Bills and Money Market Certificates, the most reasonable response would be:

S. Treasury Bills do not have a penalty for early withdrawal. Were you thinking of a Treasury Bond?

Selecting the appropriate perspective is in itself a difficult question which is currently under investigation and will be reported in [5]. Certainly important in the selection procedure will be the attributes that have entered into the conversation so far: these attributes should be of fairly high salience in the selected perspective. Other clues to the selection process include the objects under discussion, the superordinates which contribute the attributes under discussion to these objects, and the current goals of the user.

5. Conclusion

In this paper we have seen that a context-dependent similarity metric is needed in order to respond adequately to misconceptions involving the properties of an object. Such a metric has been suggested and a notion of perspective has been introduced to account for some of the contextual information required by the metric. These notions have been shown to account for differences in the way a particular misconception is best corrected in two different circumstances.

6. Acknowledgements

I would like to thank Julia Hirschberg, Aravind Joshi, Martha Pollack, Ethel Schuster, and Bonnie Webber for their many comments and discussions concerning the direction of this research and the content and style of this paper.

7. References

[1] Bobrow, D. G. and Winograd, T. "An Overview of KRL, a Knowledge Representation Language." *Cognitive Science 1*, 1 (January 1977), 3-46.

[2] Carberry, Sandra M. Understanding Pragmatically Ill-Formed Input. 10th International Conference on Computational Linguistics & 22nd Annual Meeting of the Association of Computational Linguistics, Coling84, Stanford University, Ca., July, 1984, pp. 200-206.

[3] Carbonnell, Jaime R. & Collins, Allan M. Mixed-Initiative Systems For Training and Decision-Aid Applications. Tech. Rept. ESD-TR-70-373, Electronics Systems Division, Laurence G. Hanscom Field, US Air Force, Bedford, Ma., November, 1970.

[4] Grosz, B. Focusing and Description in Natural Language Dialogues. In *Elements of Discourse Understanding*, A. Joshi, B. Webber & I. Sag, Ed.,Cambridge University Press, Cambridge, England, 1981, pp. 85-105.

[5] McCoy, K.F. Correcting Object-Related Misconceptions. 1985. Forthcoming University of Pennsylvania doctoral thesis

[6] McKeown, K. . *Generating Natural Language Text in Response to Questions About Database Structure*. Ph.D. Th., University of Pennsylvania, May 1982.

[7] Sidner, C. L. Focusing in the Comprehension of Definite Anaphora. In *Computational Models of Discourse*, Michael Brady and Robert Berwick, Ed.,MIT Press, Cambridge, Ma, 1983, pp. 267-330.

[8] Tversky, A. "Features of Similarity." *Psychological Review 84* (1977), 327-352.

[9] Weiner, E. Judith. "A Knowledge Representation Approach to Understanding Metaphors." *Computational Linguistics 19*, 1 (January - March 1984), 1-14.

Tailoring Explanations for the User[1]

Kathleen R. McKeown
Dept. of Computer Science
Columbia University
New York, N.Y. 10027
212-280-8194
MCKEOWN@COLUMBIA-20

Myron Wish
AT&T Bell Laboratories
600 Mountain Ave.
Murray Hill, N.J. 07974
201-582-7630

Kevin Matthews
Dept. of Computer Science
Columbia University
New York, N.Y. 10027
212-280-8180
MATT@COLUMBIA-20

Abstract

In order for an expert system to provide the most effective explanations, it should be able to tailor its responses to the concerns of the user. One way in which explanations may be tailored is by point of view. A method is presented for representing the knowledge to support different points of view in the current domain. In addition, we present a method for determining the point of view to take by inferring the user's goal within a brief discourse segment. The advising system's response to the derived goal depends on the strength of its belief in the inference, for which a method of determination is also provided. This information enables the system to decide what answer to give to a question, which kind of justification is relevant, and when to provide it. Some details of the current implementation are included.

1 Introduction

While research on explanation for expert systems has addressed some important issues in identifying the kind of knowledge needed to provide acceptable explanations (e.g., Swartout 81; Clancey 79), one main problem with existing systems is their inability to tailor an explanation adequately to the needs or perspective of a particular user. In this paper, we show how information about the current user can and should influence the type of explanation provided.

In past artificial intelligence research, there have been two main approaches to user modelling: classifying users according to *a priori* types often by direct interrogation (e.g., Rich 79, Swartout 81, Wallis 82) or deriving information about the current state of the user's goals, beliefs, and desires from the ongoing discourse itself (e.g., Allen and Perrault 80; Carberry 83). Our work draws from the second of these two main approaches; but while previous research has emphasized the derivation of a user's goal in order to interpret an utterance correctly, we are interested in making use of derived goals to generate appropriate explanations. This difference in emphasis has required the development of techniques for handling four specific tasks: representing different points of view in a knowledge base to support different explanations, identifying *which* of several possible goals underlying the current discourse should be addressed, determining *when* the derived goal should be taken into account, and specifying *how* a generation system can relate the derived goal to different points of view to determine explanation content. This extends Allen and Perrault's (80) approach by showing how a goal can be derived to represent a sequence of utterances as opposed to a single utterance, and goes beyond Carberry's (83) approach by showing how a system can decide to respond to such goals.

This work is being done within the context of an ongoing project to develop a dialogue facility for computer-aided problem solving. A student advising system is being developed which can provide information about courses and advice about whether a student can or should take a particular course. The system is currently structured as a question-answering system which invokes an underlying expert system on receiving "can" questions (e.g., "Can I take natural language this semester?") and "should" questions (e.g., "Should I take data structures?"). This production system uses its rule base to determine the advice provided (i.e., *yes* or *no*) and the trace of rule invocations is used to provide a supporting explanation of the advice.

The Advisor system consists of an ATN parser (Woods 70), a KL-ONE knowledge base (Brachman 79) with access functions, a goal inferencer, an underlying production system, and a surface generator to produce responses and explanations in natural language (Derr and McKeown 84). Currently the system can produce responses to information questions by accessing the knowledge base and to "can" questions by invoking the underlying production system. Certain aspects of response generation and inferencing for "should" questions have been implemented.

In the following sections, we first show the different types of explanations required and then describe in some detail the techniques we have developed.

2 Different Explanations

In this paper, we focus on how the content of an explanation must vary according to the perspective or point of view taken on the underlying problem domain. For example, in the student advisor domain there are a number of points of view the student can adopt for selecting courses. It can be viewed, among others, as a process of meeting requirements (i.e., "*how do courses tie in with requirement sequencing?*"), as a state model process (i.e., "*what should be completed at each state in the process?*"), as a semester scheduling process (i.e., "*how can courses fit into schedule slots?*"), or as a process of maximizing personal interests (as in "*how will courses help me learn more about AI?*"). Given these different points of view, alternative explanations of the same piece of advice (i.e., *yes*) can be generated in response to the question, "*Should I take both discrete math and data structures this semester?*":

1. **Requirements**: Yes, data structures is a requirement for all later Computer Science courses and discrete math is a co-requisite for data structures.
2. **State Model**: Yes, you usually take them both first semester, sophomore year.
3. **Semester Scheduling**: Yes, they're offered next semester, but not in the spring

---

[1]The work described in this paper was partially supported by ONR grant N00014-82-K-0256 and by AT&T Bell Laboratories.

and you need to get them out of the way as soon as possible.

4. Personal Interests (e.g., AI:) Yes, if you take data structures this semester, you can take Introduction to AI next semester, and you must take discrete math at the same time as data structures.

One of these explanations may be more appropriate than others depending upon the user's goal in pursuing the dialogue. For example, we might supply explanation (1) above if the user's goal were to complete requirements as soon as possible and explanation (2) if the user's goal were to keep apace with the normal rate of progress. Thus to address the problem of selecting a perspective to use in an explanation, we must develop techniques that allow a system to infer a user goal from a discourse segment as well as techniques that can indicate information that is relevant for any given perspective.

3 Knowledge Representation

In order to identify information that is relevant to a user's goal, we are using intersecting multiple hierarchies to represent different points of view in the underlying knowledge base. The hierarchies are cross-linked by entities or processes (often courses in the student advisor domain) which can be viewed from different perspectives (and thus occur in more than one hierarchy). Hence to construct the content for explanation (1) above, the system would extract information about the relation between **data structures** and **discrete math** from the *requirements* hierarchy, and for explanation (2) extracts information from the *state model* hierarchy. A diagram of a portion of these two hierarchies containing information for the two points of view is shown in Figure 1 below.

The partitioning of the knowledge base by intersecting hierarchies allows the generation system to distinguish between different types of information that support the same fact. From this partitioning, the system can select the portion that contains the information relevant to the current request and user goal.

4 Deriving the User Goal

The system must also be able to reason about the appropriateness of one perspective versus others. Since the perspective taken is related to the user's goal in pursuing the dialogue, the large body of work on goal inference techniques (Allen and Perrault 80; Carberry 83; Litman and Allen 84) is applicable for deriving the user's goal. We have drawn heavily from Allen and Perrault's (80) work, making use of their plausible inference rules, representation of domain plans, and representation of speech acts as plans. While their work has been extremely useful, it falls short for our purposes in several ways. For example, their inferencing procedure derives a plausible goal for a user based on a single utterance, while we are interested in deriving a goal based on the current sequence of utterances[2].

Consider the discourse shown in (6) below. Assuming that a database of domain plans common to the student advising domain is maintained, Allen and Perrault's techniques could be used to derive the domain goal shown following each question. But the explanation shown in (6c) addresses not the derived goal of (6c), nor any of the derived goals of the previous utterances, but instead addresses the higher level goal indicated by the derived goals of (6a) and (6b). The problem for responding to such goals in an explanation, then, is to be able to derive a higher level goal relating the goals of individual utterances.

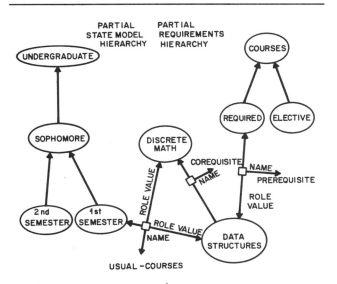

Figure 1:   Representing Points of View

6a. S: I've read about the field of AI and I'm interested in learning more about it eventually. Is natural language offered next semester?
   Plausible goal = take natural language

   A: Yes.

b. S: Who is teaching artificial intelligence?
   Plausible goal = take AI

   A: Lebowitz this semester.

c. S: I haven't taken data structures yet. Should I take it this semester?
   Plausible goal = take data structures

   A: Yes, if you take data structures this semester, you can take AI next semester which is necessary for all later AI courses.

We use Allen and Perrault's rules to derive the domain goal of each individual utterance, which we term the *current goal*. We also identify a goal representing the discourse sequence which we term the

---

[2]In this work, we restrict ourselves to a discourse segment that deals with a single or related set of goals. Over a longer sequence of discourse, topics may shift and the user may reveal very different goals across such boundaries. Detecting topic shifts and radical changes in goals is a difficult problem that we are not addressing.

relevant goal since it will be used to generate later explanations. Intuitively, the relevant goal is a higher level goal, if there is one, relating the goals of several utterances.

The process of determining the relevant goal involves the following steps. The current goal is first derived from the initial utterance. All higher level domain goals are then derived from the current goal using Allen and Perrault's *body-action* inference rule (i.e., if the user wants a step in the body of a plan to hold, it is plausible that s/he wants the action to hold). Any one of these is a candidate for the relevant plan. A derivation of the higher level plans for the utterance "Is natural language offered next semester?" is shown in Figure 2. Note that the action **take natural language** is a step in two separate plans, **concentrate-on-ai** and **fulfill electives**, and thus two parent paths are formed.

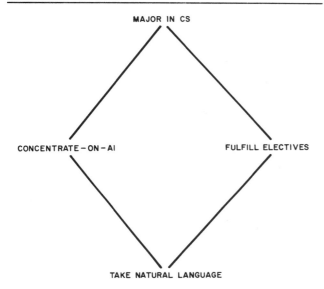

"Is natural language offered next semester?"

Figure 2:   Current and Higher Level Goals
for Utterance 1

When the second utterance "Who is teaching artificial intelligence?" is entered, the current goal **take ai** is derived and all higher level goals derived (see Figure 3) from that using the body-action rule. The lowest level node where the two paths intersect becomes the relevant plan (**concentrate-on-ai** in this case). If the second utterance had been "When is operating systems offered?," the higher level goal **fulfill electives** would have been inferred since this is the only relation between the goals **take operating systems** and **take natural language**.

This method is essentially a search for the lowest common ancestor of the current goals of two

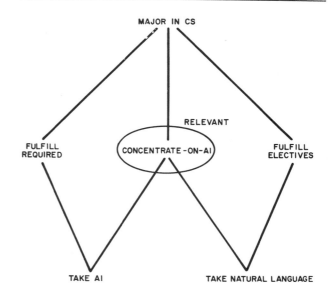

1: "Is natural language offered next semester?"
current goal = take natural language
2: "Who is teaching artificial intelligence?"
current goal = take ai
relevant goal = concentrate-on-ai

Figure 3:   Relevant Goal for Utterances 1 and 2

consecutive utterances. When the third, or any subsequent utterances are encountered, the relevant goal is determined by performing the search for common ancestor using the previous relevant goal and the current goal of the new utterance.

Carberry (83) does present a method for tracking user goals over a sequence of discourse, building in the process a hierarchical model of user plans for the discourse. She uses this hierarchy and a set of focus heuristics to determine for the next incoming utterance which of several plausible plans the user could be focusing on. She does not specify which plan in the hierarchy best represents the overall discourse purpose and therefore should be addressed in succeeding explanations. Our model thus augments hers by providing this information.

5 When to Respond
The goal inference techniques just described allow the system to infer what a user's goal *might* be, but this inference may be so tentative that explanations which always address such goals will be as undesirable as those that never take a goal into account. Allen and Perrault themselves term their rules *plausible* inference rules since the goals they attribute to the user are only possibilities and not definite. However, goals derived from some discourse sequences seem intuitively more definite than those derived from other sequences.

If the user directly asserts his/her goal (as in 7)

then it can be definitely inferred. The plausible inference rules, however, will infer the same goal for an utterance like that shown in (8). Unless we have further indication that the user actually has the goal **take natural language**, then on receiving a follow-up question such as (9a), a neutral explanation as shown in (9b) is preferable to the tailored explanation in (9c). One problem for a system that generates tailored explanations, then, is being able to determine *when* to respond to a derived goal.

---

7. S: I'm planning on taking nlp in the future. What are the prerequisites?
    plausible goal = take natural language

---

8. S: Is natural language offered this semester?
    Plausible goal = take natural language

9.a. S: I'm thinking of taking computability this semester. Would that be a good idea?
    plausible goal = take computability

  b. A: Yes, it's your last requirement and it's a good idea to get it out of the way before going on to electives.

  c. A: Yes, computability is particularly important for nlp since it covers grammars so it's a good idea to take it first.

To handle this problem we use three levels of likelihood of derived user goals. If we can distinguish between derived user goals that can *definitely* be attributed to the user, derived goals that are *likely*, and derived goals that are only *plausible*, then we have a basis for determining when to generate tailored explanations. Tailored explanations can be generated for *definite* and *likely* goals and a neutral explanation generated for *plausible* goals.

A goal is *definite* if a user states that s/he has that goal, as in "I want to concentrate in AI.", "I'd like to concentrate in AI.", or "I'm interested in taking as much AI as possible.". If not stated, it is difficult to infer without doubt that a user has a given goal, but there are cases where it is more *likely* than others. Space prohibits providing details, but we note that a goal is more likely if it has been repeatedly derived from consecutive utterances as well as in cases where it is one step in a plan that the user has partially completed. The system is currently capable of deriving current and relevant goals for a discourse segment and classifying them as *plausible* or *definite*. Classification of goals as *likely* has been designed, but must still be implemented.

We have ignored, in this paper, the possibility of responding in other ways than providing explanations. In some cases, in fact, it may be preferable for the system to ask the user to clarify his/her goal or to take the initiative in some other way. Determining when and how to take the initiative as an alternative to providing explanations is a topic addressed elsewhere (see Matthews 85).

6 How to Respond

Finally, the system must be able to make use of the derived goal in constructing an explanation when a "should" question follows a dialogue sequence. The underlying mini production system, consisting of working memory, rule base, and inference engine, is invoked in this process.

To construct the explanation, the hierarchy representing the proper perspective is determined directly from the relevant goal, and information retrieved about the questioned object[3] from that hierarchy is placed in working memory. The production system uses this information to derive the response, that is whether the user should or should not pursue the queried action. The trace of the reasoning is then available to provide the basis for the explanation, as is the case in traditional expert systems. Note that the information extracted from one hierarchy will allow a different set of rules to fire than will information extracted from another, thus producing different explanation content.

As an example, consider again the question "Should I take both data structures and discrete this semester?". Assume that the system has determined that the user's goal is **take required** and that the goal should be taken into account in the explanation. After deducing that the student *can* take these courses[4], the production system will attempt to prove that the queried action helps the user achieve his/her goals. The information shown in Figure 4, extracted from the requirements hierarchy (refer back to Figure 1), enables rules 1 and 2 to fire with **?x** instantiated as **data structures**, **?y** as **discrete math**, and **?course** as **required**. The extracted fact that **discrete math** is a co-requisite for **data structures** enables rule 2 to fire. Its consequence and the extracted fact that **data structures** is a prerequisite to **required** enables rule 1 to fire, which concludes that **required** can be taken. Thus, the advice is *yes* since **take required** is the user's goal and these two instantiated rules can then be used as the basis for the hypothetical explanation given earlier and reproduced in Figure 4. Other rules in the rule base (such as "A course should be taken if the student is at the right year to take it") do not fire since information necessary to fire that rule does not exist in working memory. This processing is partially implemented, but much work is needed before the full explanation can be produced.

---

[3]The questioned object is the course the user is inquiring about (e.g., **data structures** in "Should I take data structures?").

[4]Regardless of whether the user's queried action helps him/her achieve the relevant goal, if it is not permissible or will prevent the student from completing the major, the advice is always negative. Rules encoding such absolute constraints include "a course cannot be taken before its prerequisite", or "a course should not be taken if it prevents the student from completing requirements by the time s/he is a senior". Here, we assume, for convenience, that the student has already taken the prerequisites to data structures and discrete math and is early enough in his/her program that s/he will be able to finish on time, and thus the absolute rules are satisfied.

Information Extracted:

```
(prerequisite required data-structures)
(co-requisite data-structures discrete-math)
```

Rule 1:

```
(taken ?x) and (prerequisite ?course ?x)
        --> (can-take ?course)
```

Rule 2:

```
(co-requisite ?x ?y)
    and
(taking ?y)  --> (can-take ?x)
```

Yes, data structures is a requirement for all later Computer Science courses and discrete math is a co-requisite for data structures.

Figure 4:   Constructing Explanation Content

7 Future Directions

More research is needed on explanation, plan recognition, and user modelling for our approach to be effective for a broad range of human-computer dialogue. As for explanation, in the current implementation the production system needs to be developed further and its reasoning trace interfaced to the operational surface generator for English output. On the theoretical side, we are investigating the use of discourse strategies to control the organization of the explanation. The plans in the current implementation were selected by examining transcripts of actual student advising sessions, but it would be desirable to have a much larger set of plans, knowledge about their base rates and importance, and additional criteria for tracking their relevance and likelihood during the interaction. It seems likely, also, that better explanations will require a more complete user model incorporating static, global characteristics of the user as well as those dynamic, local characteristics available from the ongoing dialogue itself. Additionally, while we have touched on one way of representing and using point of view, others will doubtless be necessary. Such a comprehensive attack on the topics of explanation, plan recognition, and user modelling offers promise from both a theoretical and practical perspective.

8 Conclusion

We have demonstrated the need for tailoring explanations to users in consultative or problem solving dialogues with a computer, and have addressed this problem with a new approach integrating research in plan recognition, user modelling, and explanation generation. Derivation of goals, or plans, is based on an extension of Perrault and Allen's (80) work which handles discourse segments rather than isolated utterances. Our model and implementation provide mechanisms for assessing which goal is relevant to the user at any moment during the discourse, as well as when that point of view should be addressed in an explanation. It also makes progress toward the determination of how to tailor the explanation to the user's goal. In addition to enhancing previous work on goal inferencing, this report shows how research in natural language processing on goal derivation can be applied to generate explanations sensitive to the user's current perspective in expert system interactions.

Acknowledgments
We would like to thank Michael Lebowitz for his suggestions on an earlier draft of this paper.

References
(Allen and Perrault 80). Allen, J. F. and C. R. Perrault, "Analyzing intention in utterances," *Artificial Intelligence 15*, 3, 1980.

(Brachman 79). Brachman, R., "On the epistemological status of semantic networks." in N. Findler (ed.) *Associative Networks: Representation and Use of Knowledge by Computer*, Academic Press, N. Y., 1979.

(Carberry 83) Carberry, S., Tracking user goals in an information-seeking environment, in *Proceedings of the National Conference on Artificial Intelligence*, Washington D.C., August 1983, pp. 59-63.

(Clancey 79) Clancey, W.J., Tutoring rules for guiding a case method dialogue, *International Journal of Man-Machine Studies 11*, 1979, pp. 25-49.

(Derr and McKeown 84). Derr, M.A. and K.R. McKeown, Using focus to generate complex and simple sentences, *Proceedings of COLING-84: Tenth International Conference on Computational Linguistics*, Stanford, July 1984, pp. 319-26.

(Litman and Allen 84) Litman, D.J., and J.F. Allen, A plan recognition model for clarification subdialogues, *Proceedings of COLING-84: Tenth International Conference on Computational Linguistics*, Stanford, July 1984, pp. 302-11.

(Matthews 85) Matthews, K., Initiatory and reactive system roles in human computer discourse, unpublished manuscript, AT&T Bell Laboratories, 1985.

(Rich 79) Rich, E.A., User modelling via stereotypes, *Cognitive Science*, Vol. 3, 1979, pp. 329-54.

(Swartout 81) Swartout, W.R., Producing explanations and justifications of expert consulting programs, Technical Report MIT/LCS/TR-251, MIT, Cambridge, Mass., January 1981.

(Wallis 82) Wallis, J.W. and E.H. Shortliffe, Explanatory power for medical expert systems: studies in the representation of causal replationships for clinical consultation. Technical Report STAN-CS-82-923, Stanford University, 1982.

(Woods 70). Woods, W. A., "Transition network grammars for natural language analysis." *Communications of the ACM*, Vol. 13, No. 10, October, 1970, pp. 591-606.

Description-Directed Natural Language Generation

David D. McDonald and James D. Pustejovsky

Department of Computer and Information Science
University of Massachusetts at Amherst

1. Abstract

We report here on a significant new set of capabilities that we have incorporated into our language generation system MUMBLE. Their impact will be to greatly simplify the work of any text planner that uses MUMBLE as its linguistics component since MUMBLE can now take on many of the planner's text organization and decision-making problems with markedly less hand-tailoring of algorithms in either component. Briefly these new capabilities are the following:

(a) **ATTACHMENT.** A new processing stage within MUMBLE that allows us to readily implement the conventions that go into defining a text's intended prose style, e.g. whether the text should have complex sentences or simple ones, compounds or embeddings, reduced or full relative clauses, etc. Stylistic conventions are given as independently stated rules that can be changed according to the situation.

(b) **REALIZATION CLASSES** are a mechanism for organizing both the transformational and lexical choices for linguistically realizing a conceptual object. The mechanism highlights the intentional criteria which control selection decisions. These criteria effectively constitute an "interlingua" between planner and linguistic component, describing the rhetorical uses to which a text choice can be put while allowing its linguistic details to be encapsulated.

The first part of our paper (sections 2 and 3) describes our general approach to generation; the rest illustrates the new capabilities through examples from the UMass COUNSELOR Project. This project is a large new effort to develop a natural language discourse system based on the HYPO system [Rissland & Ashley 1984], which acts as a legal advisor suggesting relevant dimensions and case references for arguing hypothetical legal cases in trade-secret law. At various relevant points we briefly contrast our work with that of Appelt, Danlois, Gabriel, Jacobs, Mann and Mattheissen, and McKeown and Derr.

2. Major Components of the Generation Process

As nearly everyone who has worked on generation from an AI perspective will agree, it is the character of the decision-making involved, and not any *a priori* division by linguistic level, that dictates how the process divides into components. Decision-making varies in at least the three dimensions listed below, with the clustering patterns of groups of decisions along these dimensions deterining what different components there should be.

o What information does the decision draw on: properties of lexical items? Conceptual attributes? Details of planned rhetorical structures? Details of surface structures?

o What is the decision dependent on: what other generation decisions, if made differently, would force a change in this decision? If the generation process is to be indelible (i.e. never retracting its decisions) then this dependency structure will have to be respected.

o How should the decision's conclusions be represented: does a conclusion dictate linguistic actions or just constrain other decisions? Can it be acted on immediately or must it be scheduled for later?

On the basis of such considerations, we have determined that generation as a whole involves three different kinds of activities: two that are dominated by conceptual (typically domain-specific) criteria and decisions, and one that is dominated by linguistic criteria and has a correspondingly wider applicability. These three activities are:

1. determining what goals to (attempt to) accomplish with the utterance;

2. deciding what information the utterance should convey and what rhetorical force it should have in order to satisfy those goals;

3. realizing those conceptual "specifications" as a grammatical text that is cohesive with the discourse that precedes it.

We see these activities as intermingled and ongoing throughout the duration of a text's generation. Goals are only partially formulated when one starts speaking, and may even emerge opportunistically as the linguistic structure of the text is incrementally planned and produced. We presume that in people these activities are carried out in parallel, though in our discourse system for the COUNSELOR project they are treated as strictly gated co-routines.

It is the last of these activities, the linguistically most demanding, that is our concern in this paper. This aspect of our research has two goals, one pragmatic, the other scientific. First, for researchers who need capable natural language interfaces, we have developed a versatile *linguistic component* ("LC"), implemented as the Zetalisp program MUMBLE, that can be interfaced to domain specific systems, where it handles all of the linguistic considerations that occur during generation. The domain specific system supplies a specification of what it wants said, couched in its own internal representation, and is then realized by our LC as a grammatical text.

Our second goal is to project from the computational architecture of our LC to hypotheses about the actual generation process in human beings. To this end we have disciplined ourselves in the design of the computer program to employ only devices with specific, very narrow capacities. This influences our choice of linguistic analyses, in that only a few of the analyses that one could imagine (and appear in the literature) are plausible in our generator, allowing us to develop linguistic and psycholinguistic hypotheses that are predictive and falsifiable. We will not discuss this aspect of our research in this paper; some of our earlier conclusions are described in [McDonald 1984].

3. Our Approach to Generation

In this section we describe our approach in general terms and outline the separate components of our system; detailed examples will be given in the section following.

3.1 Goal-directed Generation

In our view, research on the production of text is most revealing when it considers how the text advances the goals of a speaker. A generation program should produce texts for an audience that is situated in a concrete discourse context working from a particular plan of information to be communicated with specific rhetorical goals. Furthermore, we believe (and it is here that we part company with researchers such as Mann and Matthiessen [1983], whose aims we otherwise share) that the demands placed on an LC by the need to work efficiently from a plan have overriding implications for the LC's architecture. This can require it to take a form very different from what is developed when working on the form/function relationship in isolation. Generation programs like Mann and Matthiessen's NIGEL that have so far been used only to produced well-formed texts in isolation from computationally represented situations or speakers' goals may tell us a great deal about the structure of grammars and linguistic *competence*, but it does not follow that they are therefore *models* of the generation process.

In accordance with this methodology, our LC has always been developed in the context of one or more *underlying programs* which have been responsible for dictating the communicative goals. Each program has included a *text planning system*, of varying (sometimes trivial) sophistication. (For example the program GENARO developed by Jeff Conklin [1983] and the programs listed in

[McDonald 1983].) The text planners react to their associated programs' communicative goals and construct a conceptual level "plan"—a non-linguistic specification of what it wants said—which is given to the LC as its input.

Although we are presently working with text planners that we are designing ourselves, we expect that the place we have picked for the division between planning what to say and determining how to say it is a natural one; consequently our Linguistic Component should be able to be used to advantage with text planners of very different internal design than the ones we happen to have used.

3.2 Multiple levels in the linguistic component

An ongoing trend in our research has been to introduce more and more levels within the generation processes between originating the goals and ultimately producing the text. At the present time we employ three sucessive levels of processing within the LC: **attachment, realization**, and **phrase structure execution**. We will briefly define each of these levels later in this section and will expound on their functional organization and give illustrations of the structures they use in the second half of the paper.

At each processing level there is a shift in the vocabulary of the rules, the representations that are used, and the character of the reasoning that is brought to bear. Each level is narrowly restricted in the kind of information that it can draw on and the textual horizon it is able to work within. Each is a specialized activity within the "virtual machine" that we have developed for generation, and works according to its own computational principles and therefore with the high degree of efficiency that is possible through specialization of the mechanism to the task (provided, of course, that the "boundaries" between the levels are in fact well placed). Decisions at each level are simpler than if the levels were folded together, since less linguistic detail is determined at a time.

In this regard we disagree with Appelt [1980, 1985] about the benefits of maintaining a single computational paradigm throughout the generation process (in his case axiomatic planning): his point that all of the generation processes involve planning is very well taken, yet this need not imply a homogeneous design. Indeed, one of the implications of homogeneity is that all information is equally available at any point in the process, which we do not believe is the case in generation by people or is of any advantage in machine systems. With our multi-level design we can specify quite exactly when a given kind of information becomes available, whether it is available "early" in some more abstract form (i.e. before the representation that would normally carry that information has been instantiated), and when it later becomes inaccessible.

It is crucial to understand that while we speak loosely of these different reasoning engines and representations as constituting "levels", they are in fact not strictly ordered in the process as a whole. All of them are active simultaniously, including the planner that supplies their input; they operate as closely coordinated co-routines, precisely synchronized to the "point of speech", passing information (in the form of progressively more refined specifications and eventually syntactic and lexical stuctures) from one to the other along a well defined path or "pipeline".

Setting goals and planning content.   Generation starts when the underlying program sets the goals of the utterance. In our own work this is done by the decisions of a "discourse controller" designed after Woolf [1984]. The goals direct the actions of a conceptual or "information" level planner that makes decisions about what information to actually communicate (versus leave for the audience to infer), how to structure it as a text, and what rhetorical or discourse effects to achieve. The planner also occasionally selects key lexical items (anticipating and preempting later choices) when this allows the combination of basic information units into a more useful "package" (e.g. merging an object's temporal BEGINNING and ENDING fields by using the word "between", or using a term such as "get revenge" rather than simply stating the underlying events of a story [Cook, Lehnert, & McDonald 1984].) Figure 3 shows an example of a plan of the sort we are presently using.

To the LC, the output of the text planner appears as a sequence of kernal information units (i.e. objects from the internal conceptual representation of the underlying program, typically pointers to frames or relations extracted from them, see Figures 2 and 3). Each unit is typically accompanied by a rhetorical annotation, put there by the text planner, which describes some perspective or emphasis that the unit's textual realization is to reflect.

SURFACE STRUCTURE   While there are four processes in our model of generation (planning, attachment, realization, and phrase structure execution), there are only two reference structures: the plan, and surface structure. This second representational level is the only linguistic level we support; its representational vocabulary is abstract and for the most part syntactic and phrasal. It corresponds to the level in generative grammars that is the input to the phonological component and incorporates many of the devices of modern linguistic theory such as "traces" and X-bar categories.

The surface structure is the core of our LC's design. It defines the action sequence (program) carried out by Phrase Structure Execution, absorbs the output (in sucessive chunks) of Realization, and is the target of Attachment. The fact that a linguistically motivated description of an utterance in progress can take on such a controlling, coordinating role in the generation process is to us too striking to be a fortuitous accident of our skills as computer programmers, rather it reflects something crucial about the nature of the generation process operating in people. Space does not permit a proper technical description of our surface structure or of PSE; interested readers should see [McDonald 1984].

The ATTACHMENT PROCESS   The first thing that must happen to the units in the plan is for them to be assigned ("attached") to positions within the surface structure. This extends the surface structure by instantiating one of the "attachment points" that have been assigned to it according to the grammatical structure it currently has (e.g. next-sentence, additional-adjective embedded-discourse-unit etc.).

The process does not attach all of the units in a plan at once; instead attachment is interleaved with Phrase Structure Execution so that most earlier units will have been realized and their text spoken before the last one is positioned. To judge where to attach a unit, the process considers first the syntactic form of the various text choices that could be made in realizing the unit, filtering out any that are incompatible with the available attachment points (e.g. one cannot position an adjective to serve the syntactic function of a new sentence). It then employs a set of rules to order the remaining points according to the designated prose style.

The REALIZATION PROCESS   Once a unit has been positioned within the surface structure, the next thing that happens to it is the selection of a text that will adequately "realize" its information content. This requires sensitivity to its functional role within the knowledge base and the plan (e.g. topic versus instrument), to the desired perspective, and to the grammatical constraints emposed by the surface structure at that position.

The association of objects (or object types) from the underlying system's knowledge base with the texts that could be used to realize them is made by assigning them to predefined "realization classes". Realization classes are highly parameterized and annotated lists of "choices" where each choice defines a possible syntactic structure and wording. Each choice is annotated by a set of "characteristics" which summarize the linguistic nature of the choice and the functional uses to which it may be put. The characteristics can also be viewed as predicates against the current state of the surface structure and plan and thus provide the backbone of the decision procedure that makes the realization choices. Linguistically, the pattern of choices in a realization class most strongly resembles the "transformation families" of Harris [1951, 1952].

Choices are defined in terms of a schematically described phrase structure plus a "mapping" that takes the parameters of the choice into positions in the phrase. This parameterization reflects the compositionality of the units in the plan: most units can be viewed as relations over other units; a typical realization is then the selection of a verb to realize the relation with the argument units mapped into the verb's thematic roles.

PHRASE STRUCTURE EXECUTION   The phrase structure defined by a choice consists of a labeled tree of constituents with English words and some units as its leaves. The depth-first traversal of this tree defines a path that will enumerate the words and embedded units (which will then be realized and replaced by a phrase) in their natural left to right order as a text.

Using this path as its controlling representation, Phrase Structure Execution ("PSE") carries the whole LC forward: Words at the leaves of the surface structure are morphologically specialized and spoken as soon as they are reached. When embedded units are reached they are passed to the Realization Process; the sub-tree selected and instantiated by that process is then passed back to PSE and incorporated at the position of the unit, replacing the unit and thereby defining an extension of the traversal path. When a potential attachment point is reached the Attachment Process is awakened to determine whether it wishes to use that point for positioning the next unit in the plan.

4.   Some Examples

Consider the text below, which our LC generates from the plan in Figure 3 (as fleshed out by later subplanning). This text was originally produced by a human lawyer as the initial description of the legal case on which he was seeking advice; our research goal has been to reproduce it (and the rest of the dialogue it was part of—work which is not yet complete) in a generalizable way as a precursor to having the full COUNSELOR system eventually plan other such texts on its own.

" I represent a client named RCAVICTIM who wants to sue SWIPEINC and Leroy Soleil for misappropriating trade secrets in connection with software developed by my client. RCAVICTIM markets the software known as AUTOTELL, a program to automate some of a bank teller's functions, to the banking industry. In !982, Leroy Soleil, one of RACVICTIM's personnel, left RCAVICTIM and began working for SWIPEINC on a competing product, TELLERMATIC, also an automated teller program. SWIPEINC has begun marketing TELLERMATIC in competition with AUTOTELL. "

Figure 1   Output text from the LC

4.1   Rhetorically-annotated Input from the Planner

At the moment, this paragraph is generated from the plan in Figure 2. This structure specifies the following. (1) The purpose of the utterance, i.e. to inform the audience of the intention to bring suit and the basic facts of the case. (2) Its information content—the frames from the knowledge base that will be the proximal sources for the wording of the text (given in the "#<...>" notation used to indicate flavor instances in ZetaLisp, the implementation language of our homebrew frame system). (3) Any special perspectives that are to govern the realization of those frames (indicated by the keyword ": perspective"). The specification of perspective is crucial because of the potentially enormous range of realizations most of the frames in this domain may have (e.g. a "neutral" perspective on this Legal-case should probably be realized as something like "RCAVICTIM is the plaintiff and SWIPEINC and Leroy Soleil are the defendants").

```
Inform
  : discourse-bridge
        #<Lawyer-Client-Relationship
              #<lawyer the-speaker>
              #<corporate-party RCAVICTIM>>
        : perspective establish-relation-of-speaker
  : head
        #<legal-case "RCAVICTIM vs. SWIPEINC">
        : perspective #<action-taken-by
                        #<corporate-party RCAVICTIM>>
  : motivation-behind-head
        #<claim misappropriation-of-trade-secret
                  #<knowledge-of #<product AUTOTELL>>>)
  : elaboration
      (event-history #<legal-case RCAVICTIM-us-SWIPEINC>)
      : perspective misapropriation-script
```

Figure 2   A Rhetorically-Annotated Plan

4.2   Incremental Planning

The text planning process has two problems: (1) to decide what information and rhetorical organization will best render the communicative intent of the underlying system, and (2) to bridge the gap between the way information is organized in that system's knowledge base and what is possible in the natural language being used (i.e. what are the words and grammatical constructions of the language). In our COUNSELOR project this gap is nontrivial, as illustrated by the frames in Figure 3. The dominating problem is the considerable difference in "packaging": the unit frames hold considerably more information than should be communicated at one time, making selection of perspective and other culling criteria quite important if what is said is to be relevant.

```
#<Legal-case
    name    "RCAVICTIM-vs-SWIPEINC"
    status   intended-but-not-brought-to-court
    party-list (#<corporate-party RCAVICTIM>
                 #<corporate-party swipeinc>
                 #<individual-party leroy-Soleil>)
    claim-or-defense-list
        (#<misappropriation-of-ts
              #<knowledge-of #<AUTOTELL>>) >

#<Corporate-party
    name `RCAVICTIM'
    case RCAVICTIM-vs-SWIPEINC
    case-role plaintiff
    employee-list (#<individual-party leroy-Soleil>)
    product-list (#<product autotell>)
    competitor-product-alist
        '((#<corporate-party rcavictim>
             #<product tellermatic>)) >
```

Figure 3   Example Frames from the Knowledge Base

Our planner, a program we are calling "CICERO", is presently quite limited. It is organized as a set of specialists with names like **Describe-legal-case, Describe-a-party-to-a-case,   Describe-corporate-party** (a specialization of **Describe-a-party-to-a-case**) and so on. The procedure used now is a simple contextual discrimination between alternative, precompiled "scripts", which are then instantiated and passed to the LC in the form shown before in Figure 2. That plan is the standard one for unmarked descriptions of cases except for the addition of the first unit (indicating the relation of the speaker to the case), which was included because the utterance is the first one in the conversation and that relation cannot yet be deduced from context. We recognize that this use of scripts is quite limiting, and are in the midst of developing more versatile techniques.

One key part of CICERO's design which we expect to retain, however, is the fact that it operates incrementally. It would be neither psychologically plausible nor computationally economical to have a planner make all of the decisions about the information in an utterance (especially a long one) in "one pass", and then completely relinquish control to the LC until it was time to plan the next utterance. Instead, planning should proceed incrementally, leaving the details of references or elaborations as conceptual "stubs" in the larger plan to be worked out in detail later once that plan has been partially realized and a linguistic characterization of that position of the stub becomes available. A recursive invocation of CICERO then uses that characterization, as well as the stub's position in the original plan, to aid it in deciding what information and perspectives to use. The resulting "subplan" is then passed back to the LC which continues where it left off.

So for example the plan in Figure 2 was constructed by Describe-legal-case. This specialist knows to mention the party (#<corporate-parth Rcavictim>) that the lawyer is representing, but does not itself know how to describe that party, leaving that decision to be made later by Describe-corporate-party once PSE reaches the its position in the surface structure.

4.3 Attachment and Prose Style

The Attachment Process is a transducer from the stream of annotated units in the plan to assignments of active "attachment points" within the surface structure. These assignments modify the surface structure at the time they are made, in effect "splicing in" additional phrase structure to accomodate the new unit. What points are active at any moment is determined by the details of the surface structure already in place and the position of the PSE process. Deliberations over which attachment points to select are mediated by preferences which are characterized in terms of "stylistic rules".

At the beginning of an utterance, there is only one attachment point active, namely First-sentence. The first unit of the plan will be positioned here, and then almost immediately will be reached by PSE and passed to Realization. Realization will select a phrase for it (in this case a clause), and then knit the phrase into the surface structure in place of the unit.

[S #<speaker>
  [VP represent
    [NP #<corp.-party Rcavictim>]]]

(The actual representation of surface structure is considerably more elaborate than this simplified presentation suggests.) Once this replacement occurs new attachment points are made active, as dictated by the form of the clause. These include New-sentence, various conjunctions such as Reduced-on-common-subject and Reduced-on-common-predicate, and especially various syntactic extensions to the final NP such as additional adjectives, postnominal phases, or quantifiers which would refine the characterization of Rcavictim, as well as non-restrictive attachments relating some of its attributes or activities. What attachments are allowed is a function of the syntactic configuration of the surface structure ahead of the point of speech; the relevant criteria are discussed in [McDonald & Pustejovsky 1985b].

With the realization of the first unit, the attachment possibilities for the second can be considered. These are narrowed by ignoring all possibilities that demand a syntactic realization for a unit at their position that is not found in the second unit's realization class (which in the present case are essentially just variations on clauses involving the verb "sue"). At present this leaves only three points still in the running:

New-sentence: *"I represent a client named Rcavictim. They want to sue Swipelnc and Leroy Soleil."*

Simple-conjunction: *"I represent a client named Rcavictim, and they want to sue Swipelnc and Leroy Soleil."*

Non-restrictive-relative-chaining-off-final-NP: *"I represent a client named Rcavictim, who wants to sue Swipelnc and Leroy Soleil."*

Figure 4   Variations due to alternative attachments

We contend that the decision between these three is a matter only of the prose style one prefers: long sentences or short, simple syntax or complex. Lawyers have very definite preferences in their prose style which we can capture as a set of "ordering rules". These rules of prose style are used to order the alternatives, each rule accompanied by a predicate characterizing the linguistic contexts in which it applies. Our algorithms for this process are described in [McDonald & Pustejovsky 1985a].

```
(define-stylistic-rule  Always-prefer-extension-with-Relative-clause
  ordering-on-attachment-points
    (absolute-preference-for
        Non-restrictive-relative-chaining-off-final-NP )
  applicability-condition
    (not (is-more-than-one-sentence-before-point-of-speech
          (relative-text-position
              (most-recent-use
                  'Non-restrictive-relative-chaining-off-final-NP)))))
```

Figure 5   A simple Stylistic Rule

After the non-restrictive-relative is selected, the surface structure will look approximately like this:

```
[s #<speaker>
    [vp represent
        [NP [NP #<corp.-party Rcavictim> ]
            [s #<legal-case ...> ] ] ] ]
```

The standard technique for combining a sequence of conceptual units into a text has been "direct replacement" (see discussion in [Mann et al. 1982]), in which the sequential organization of the text is identical to that of the message because the message is used directly as a template. Our use of Attachment dramatically improves on this technique by relieving the message planner of any need to know how to organize a surface structure, letting it rely instead on explicitly stated stylistic criteria operating after the planning is completed.

Derr and McKeown [1984] also improve on direct replacement's one-proposition-for-one-sentence forced style by permitting the combination of individual information units (of comparable complexity to our own) into compound sentences interspersed with rhetorical connectives. They were, however, limited to extending sentences only at their ends, while our Attachment Process can add units at any grammatically licit position ahead of the point of speech. Furthermore they do not yet express combination criteria as explicit, separable rules.

Dick Gabriel's program Yh [1984] produced polished written texts through the use of critics and repeated editing. It maintained a very similar model to our own of how a text's structure can be elaborated, and produced texts of quite high fluency. We differ from Gabriel in trying to achieve fluency in a single online pass in the manner of a person talking off the top of his head; this requires us to put much more of the responsibility for fluency in the pre-linguistic text planner, which is undoubtedly subject to limitations.

4.4 Realization Classes

We have said that language generation is a problem of how to organize decision making: first of what information to convey (done incrementally within the Text Planner), then of how to textually capture the relation of the units in a plan to each other (done by the Attachment Process), and finally of how to express—"realize"—the information in a conceptual unit, which is the task of Realization.

Realization is the selection of one of a predefined set of alternative text specifications ("choices") subject to grammatical constraints according to the position within the surface structure at which the realization occurs. The predefined choices are organized into "realization classes" such as shown in Figure 6. At the time this is written, these classes either organize alternative wordings, as in the concept-specific class or when wording has been determined, organize the structural (e.g. transformational) alternatives that the language permits, as in Transitive-Latinate-verbs.

The selection decision is based on the "characteristics" that accompany each choice (e.g. in-focus(arg), expresses-result(verb)). These symbols have attached procedures which test for prerequisites, and also may be

```
(define-realization-class   establish-relation-of-speaker-o-lawyer-to-client
   :parameters  (lawyer client)
   :choices
   ((((represent-o-SVO lawyer client)
      ; I represent a client
      clause initial-mention(self) )
    ((relation-expressed-as-genitive ; my client
        lawyer (instance-of(client next-plan-step))))
    np instance-of(client (next-plan-step)) )) ))
(define-realization-class  transitive-latinate-verbs-forming-nominalization
   : parameters  (verb subj obj)
   : choices
   ((((ddefault-active-form verb subj obj)
      ; A misappropriates B
      clause )
    ((passive-form verb subj obj)
      ; B is misappropriated by A
      clause in-focus(obj) )
    ((gerundive-with-subject verb subj obj)
      ; A misappropriating B
      np)
    ((gerundive-passive-with-subject verb subj obj)
      ; B being misappropriated by A
      np in-focus(obj))
    ((nominalization (nominal verb) subj obj)
      ; A misappropriation of B
      np expresses-result(verb) express(subj))
    ((definite-nominalization-with-subject nominal(verb) subj obj)
      ; the misappropriation of B by A
      np expresses-result(verb) )
    ((bare-nominalization-with-subject nominal(verb) subj obj)
      ; misappropriation of B by A
      np untensed-situation(self) ) ))
```

Figure 6   Two Realization Classes

tested for presence or absence by the grammatical constraints. Much of our ongoing research involves determining what reasonable characteristics are and what predicates they should be allowed to use; this will dictate the amount and character of the linguistic knowledge we allow our text planner to have, since all further information about a candidate text (for example the information used by PSE and morphology) is encapsulated in the choice.

It is appropriate at times to think of the choices in a realization class as items in a "phrasal lexicon" [Becker 1975], i.e. as productive, frozen turns of phrase that we use not because of their compositional, literal meaning, but because they are a conventional phrase rather like an idiom. Our mechanism of associating conceptual units directly with choices (rather than mediating the concepts-text relationship with sets of abstract features, as for example done by Matthiessen [1983]) permits us to capture these conventional relationships easily, while noting those abstract relations that we do understand by labeling the choices with characteristics.

Linguistically, our choices are more versatile than the phrasal entries in use at Berkeley where phrasal lexicons are a common part of language processing programs, e.g. [Jacobs 1983]. Ours are transparent to the addition of other modifying or elaborating concepts within the phrase because of the thoroughness of the linguistic specification given with a choice and the use of the Attachment Process.

As one of the two loci of decision-making within the LC (the other being Attachment), we think of the process of Realization as simultaneously drawing on knowledge from syntactic, semantic, and pragmatic levels, which, as we stated at the very beginning of this paper is a natural property of the generation process. In this we agree with Danlois [1984], and see a familial resemblance between our realization classes and the sets of cross-level alternatives she describes. We do, however, believe that a greater *a priori* ordering among decision classes is possible than Danlois would permit. In particular it appears to us as more than just programmer´s convenience is involved in our design decision to reduce the combinatoric complexity of realization classes by having the lexicalization decisions for phrasal heads made <u>before</u> alternative arrangements of thematic arguments are considered; we suspect that Danlois´ motivation for her "flatter" design (i.e. more classes of alternatives combined into a single decision) stems from the fact that she works from an underlying representation (Conceptual Dependency) that is less differentiated and more expression-based than ours.

5. Conclusions and Future Research

Our generation design now uses a significantly richer computational architecture than it has in the past; in particular, we have introduced the notions of an attachment process and realization classes, both operating within a Description-Directed control structure coordinated by the Phrase Structure Execution Process. This has allowed us to produce a greater variety of texts with an intuitively more satisfying modularity in design (that is, the effects of stylistic rules, attachment points and realization classes are limited and well-defined).

Our experience with this new architecture is still small, and our designs continue to evolve, especially as we now begin to work out a control structure for text planning that is not script based and to develop an executable statement of the competence grammar that underlies the linguistic knowledge in the realization classes and PSE. We do expect though, that the major outlines of what we have described will remain the same at least over the next several years. A robust, well documented version of the system is under development for general release in the fall of 1986; preliminary versions are available now to people doing research on generation.

6. Acknowledgments

Funding for this research has been provided by DARPA under order number N00014-85-K-0017, by NSF grant IST 8104984 and Atari Corporation. We would like to thank Kevin Gallagher and Marie Vaughan for help in the preparation of the text.

7. References

Appelt D. (1980) "Problem Solving Applied to Language Generation", Proceedings of the 18th Annual Meeting of the Association for Computational Linguistics, June 19-22, 1980, University of Pennsylvania, pp.59-63.

Appelt D. (1981) "Planning Natural Language Utterances to Satisfy Multiple Goals" Ph.D. Thesis, Stanford University. Available as SRI Technical Note 259.

Becker J. (1975) "The Phrasal Lexicon" BBN Report No. 3081, Bolt Beranek and Newman, Inc., Cambridge, MA.

Conklin E.J. (1983) "Data-Driven Indelible Planning of Discourse Generation Using Salience" Ph.D. Thesis, Department of Computer and Information Science, University of Massachusetts at Amherst; available as COINS Technical Report 83-13.

Cook M., Lehnert W., and McDonald D. (1984) "Conveying Implicit Context in Narrative Summaries" Proc. of COLING-84, Stanford University, pp.5-7.

Danlos L. (1984) "Conceptual and Linguistic Decisions in Generation", Proceedings of COLING-84, Association for Computational Linguistics, pp.501-504.

Derr M., & McKeown K., (1984)"Using Focus to Generate Complex and Simple Sentences" Proceedings of COLING-84, pp.319-326.

Gabriel R., (184) Ph.D. thesis, Computer Science Department, Stanford University.

Harris Z. (1951) Methods of Structural Linguistics, Chicago, University of Chicago Press.

Harris Z. (1952) "Discourse Analysis: a sample text", Language 28, pp.474-494.

Jacobs P. (1983) "Generation in a Natural Language Interface," Proc. Eigth IJCAI, pp.610-612.

Joshi A. (1983) "How much context-sensitivity is required to provide reasonable structural descriptions: Tree Adjoining Grammars" in Dowty, Karttunen, & Zwicky (eds) Natural Language Processings: Psychology, Computational, and Theoretical Perspectives, Cambridge University Press.

Mann W., Bates M., Grosz G., McDonald D., McKeown K., Swartout W., "Report of the Panel on Text Generation" Proceedings of the Workshop on Applied Computational Linguistics in Perspective, American Journal of Computational Linguistics, 8(2), pgs 62-70.

Mann W, & Matthiessen C., (1983) "A Systemic Grammar for Text Generation" ISI Technical Report RR-83-105.

Matthiessen C., (1983) "How to make grammatical decisions in text generation" ISI Technical Report RS-83-120.

McDonald D. (1983) "Natural Language Generation as a Computational Problem: an Intrduction" in Brady and Berwick, eds. Computational Problems in Discourse, MIT Press.

McDonald D. (1984) "Description-Directed Control: Its Implications for Natural Language Generation" in Cercone, ed. Computational Linguistics, Pergamon Press.

McDonald D., & Pustejovsky J. (1985a) "Samson: A computational Theory of Prose Style", Proceedings of the Conference of the European Association for Computational Linguistics, University of Geneva.

McDonald D., & Pustejovsky J. (1985b) "TAGs as a Grammatical Formalism for Generation", Proceedings of the 23rd Annual Meeting of the Association for Computational Linguistics, University of Chicago.

Rissland E., Valcarce E., & Ashley K., "Explaining and Arguing with Examples" Proceedings of AAAI-84, pgs.288-294.

Woolf B. (1984) "Context Dependent Planning in a Machine Tutor" Ph.D. thesis, University of Massachusetts.

Tense, Aspect and the Cognitive Representation of Time

Kenneth Man-kam Yip

Artificial Intelligence Laboratory
Massachusetts Institute of Technology
545 Technology Square
Cambridge, MA 02139.

ABSTRACT

This paper explores the relationships between a computational theory of temporal representation (as developed by James Allen) and a formal linguistic theory of tense (as developed by Norbert Hornstein) and aspect. It aims to provide explicit answers to four fundamental questions: (1) what is the computational justification for the primitives of a linguistic theory; (2) what is the computational explanation of the formal grammatical constraints; (3) what are the processing constraints imposed on the learnability and markedness of these theoretical constructs; and (4) what are the constraints that a linguistic theory imposes on representations. We show that one can effectively exploit the interface between the language faculty and the cognitive faculties by using linguistic constraints to determine restrictions on the cognitive representations and *vice versa*.

Three main results are obtained: (1) We derive an explanation of an observed grammatical constraint on tense -- the Linear Order Constraint -- from the **information monotonicity property** of the constraint propagation algorithm of Allen's temporal system; (2) We formulate a principle of markedness for the basic tense structures based on the computational efficiency of the temporal representations; and (3) We show Allen's interval-based temporal system is not arbitrary, but it can be used to explain independently motivated linguistic constraints on tense and aspect interpretations.

We also claim that the methodology of research developed in this study -- "cross-level" investigation of independently motivated formal grammatical theory and computational models -- is a powerful paradigm with which to attack representational problems in basic cognitive domains, e.g., space, time, causality, etc.

1. Objectives and Main Results

One major effort in modern linguistics is to limit the class of possible grammars to those that are psychologically real. A grammar is psychologically real if it is (a) **realizable** - possessing a computational model that can reproduce certain psychological resource complexity measures, and (b) **learnable** - capable of being acquired (at least, in principle) despite the poor quality of input linguistic data. A shift of emphasis from the pure characterization problem of grammar to the realization and learnability problems naturally brings linguistics closer to AI work in natural language understanding concerned with computational models of language use and language acquisition. Computational study is in principle complementary to more formal and abstract grammatical theory. Each should contribute to the other.

The purpose of this paper is to work out an example of how formal grammatical theory and computational models can effectively constrain each other's representations. In particular, I seek to explore four fundamental issues:

1. How is the choice of primitive structures in grammatical theory to be justified?

2. What is the explanation of the rules and constraints that have to be stipulated at the grammatical level?

3. How are these knowledge structures acquired?

4. What are the theoretical constraints imposed by the grammar on the representational scheme of the computation theory?

What I hope to show is that structures and principles that have to be *stipulated* at the grammatical level fall out naturally as consequences of the properties of the algorithms and representations of the underlying computational model. In so doing, I will also restrict the class of *plausible* computational models to those that can explain or incorporate the constraints imposed by the formal grammatical theory.

There are a number of requirements that must be met in order for such "cross-level" study to succeed. First, there is a sizable collection of facts and data from the target domain to be explained. Second, there is independent motivation for the theory of grammar -- it is empirically adequate. And, third, the computational model is also independently motivated by being sufficiently expressive and computationally efficient.

With these considerations, I have chosen two domains: (1) tense and (2) aspect. Tense concerns the chronological ordering of situations with respect to some reference moment, usually the moment of speech. Aspect is the study of situation types and perspectives from which a particular situation can be viewed or evaluated (cf. Comrie76) The point of departure of this study is two papers: (1) for the theory of tense, Hornstein's "Towards a theory of Tense" (Hornstein77) and (2) for the cognitive theory of time, James Allen's "Towards a General Theory of Action and Time" (Allen84).

In the following, I shall list the main results of this study:

1. A better theory of tense with revised primitive tense structures and constraints.

2. We derive an explanation of Hornstein's Linear Order Constraint, an observed formal constraint on linguistic tense, from properties of the constraint propagation algorithm of Allen's temporal system. This shows this formal grammatical constraint need not be learned at all. We also show that the rule of R-permanence follows from the hypothesis that *only the matrix clause and the subcategorizable SCOMP or VCOMP can introduce distinct S and R points*. Finally, we prove that certain boundedness condition on the flow of information of a processing system leads directly to the locality property of a constraint on sequences of tense.

3. A principle of markedness for tense structures based on the computational efficiency of the temporal representation. The principle predicts that (1) of the six basic tenses in English, future perfect is the only marked tense, and (2) the notion of a distant future tense, just like the simple future, is also unmarked.

4. A better account of the state/event/process distinction based on Allen's interval-based temporal logic and the idea that the progressive aspect specifies the perspective from which the truth of a situation is evaluated.

5. An account of theoretical constraints on the representation of time at the computational level, e.g., three distinct time points are necessary to characterize an elementary tensed sentence, and the distinction between instantaneous and non-instantaneous time intervals.

2. Tense

We begin by first outlining Hornstein's theory of tense. In section 2.1, we describe the primitives and constraints on tense of his theory. In sections 2.2 and 2.3, we show how the primitives and constraints can be derived from computational considerations.

2.1 Revisions to Hornstein's Theory of Tense

Hornstein develops a theory of tense within the Reichenbachian framework which postulates three theoretical entities: S (the moment of speech), R (a reference point), and E (the moment of event). The key idea is that certain linear orderings of the three time points get grammaticalized into the six basic tenses of English.[1] The following is the list of *basic* tense structures:

1. SIMPLE PAST	E,R__S
2. PAST PERFECT	E__R__S
3. SIMPLE PRESENT	S,R,E
4. PRESENT PERFECT	E__S,R
5. SIMPLE FUTURE	S__R,E
6. FUTURE PERFECT	S__E__R

The notation here demands some explanation. The underscore symbol "__" is interpreted as the "less-than" relation among time points whereas the comma symbol "," stands for the "less-than-or-equal-to" relation. As an illustration, the present perfect tense denotes a situation in which the moment of speech is either cotemporaneous or precedes the reference point, while the moment of event is strictly before the other two moments. Note that Hornstein also uses the term "association" to refer to the comma symbol ",".

Given the basic tense structure for a simple tensed sentence, the interpretation of the sentence that arises from the interaction of tense and time adverbs is represented by the modification of the position of the R or E points to form a new tense structure which we call a *derived tense structure*. In two papers (Hornstein77 & Hornstein81), Hornstein proposes three formal constraints that limit the class of derived tense structures that can be generated from the basic tense structures in such a way as to capture the acceptability of sentences containing temporal adverbs (e.g., now, yesterday, tomorrow), temporal connectives (e.g., when, before, after), and indirect speech. In the rest of this section, I shall examine the adequacy of these constraints.

2.1.1 Linear Order Constraint

The Linear Order Constraint (LOC) states that (p.523-4):

(1) The linear order of a derived tense structure must be the same as the linear order of the basic structure.
(2) No new association is produced in the derived tense structure.

LOC is stipulated to account for examples consisting of a single temporal adverb such as (4a) and those with two time adverbs such as (32).[2]

```
4a. John came home i. *now, at this very moment
                   ii. yesterday
                  iii. *tomorrow
```

```
32 a. John left a week ago [from] yesterday.
   b. [From] Yesterday, John left a week ago.
   c. *A week ago, John left [from] yesterday.
```

The basic tense structure for 4(ai) is:

E,R__S   (simple past: *John came home*)

Now modifies E or R so that they become cotemporaneous with the moment of speech S with the derived tense structure as

---

1. Hornstein actually listed nine basic tenses, but I think the progressive belongs to the province of aspect rather than tense.

2. The numberings are Hornstein's.

follows:

```
E,R,S    (BAD: violates LOC since new
          association is produced)
```

On the other hand, 4(aii) is acceptable because the modifier *yesterday* leaves the tense structure unchanged:

```
          yesterday
E,R__S   →    E,R__S   (OK: does not
                        violate LOC)
```

The crucial example, however, is 5(c):[3]

```
5c. John has come home  i.  ?right now
                        ii. *tomorrow
                       iii. yesterday.
```

LOC predicts (wrongly) that 5cii is good and 5ciii bad.[4] But LOC gives the wrong prediction only on the assumption that the basic tense structures are correct. To account for 5c, I propose to save the LOC and change the following SRE association with the present perfect:

```
PRESENT PERFECT    E__R,S
```

With the modified basic tense structure for present perfect, LOC will give the correct analysis. 5cii is bad because:

```
          tomorrow
E__R,S  →  E__S__R   (linear order
                      violated)
```

5ciii is acceptable since:

```
          yesterday
E__R,S  →  E__R__S
```

(OK: no new linear order and no new comma)

The question that naturally arises at this point is: Why does Hornstein not choose my proposed SRE structure for the present perfect? The answer, I believe, will become apparent when we examine Hornstein's second constraint.

2.1.2 Rule for Temporal Connectives

The rule for temporal connectives (RTC) states that (p.539-40):

For a sentence of the form P_1-conn-P_2, where "conn" is a temporal connective such as "when", "before", "after" etc., line up the S points of P_1 and P_2, that is, write the tense structure of P_1 and P_2, lining up the S points. Move R_2 to under R_1, placing E_2 accordingly to preserve LOC on the basic tense structure.

It can be easily seen that my proposed tense structure for present

perfect does not work with RTC since it produces the wrong predictions for the following two sentences:

[1] *John came when we have arrived.
[2] John comes when we have arrived.

For [1] the new analysis is:

```
E,R__S   →   E,R__S
  |            |
E__R,S       E__R__S
```

which does not violate the RTC and hence predicts (wrongly) that [1] is acceptable. Similarly, for [2], the new analysis is:

```
S,R,E    →    S,R,E     (violates RTC)
  |             |
E__R,S        E__S,R
```

which predicts (wrongly) that [2] is bad.

This may explain why Hornstein decides to use E__S,R for the present perfect because it can account for [1] and [2] with no difficulty. However, I suggest that the correct move should be to abandon RTC which has an asymmetrical property, i.e., it matters whether P_1 or P_2 is put on top, and does not have an obvious semantic explanation. (See Hornstein's footnote 20, p.543). My second proposal is then to replace RTC with a Rule of R-permanence (RP) stating that:

(RP): Both the S and R points of P_1 and P_2 must be *aligned* without any manipulation of the tense structure for P_2.

Thus sentence [3]:

[3] John came when we had arrived.

is acceptable because its tense structure does not violate RP:

```
E,R__S   (OK: S and R points are
E__R__S   already aligned)
```

Now, let us reconsider sentences [1] and [2]. Sentence [1] is not acceptable under RP and the new tense structure for present perfect since:

```
E,R__S   (violates RP: the two R's
E__R,S    are not aligned)
```

Sentence [2] is still a problem. Here I shall make my third proposal, namely, that the simple present admits *two* basic tense structures:

```
SIMPLE PRESENT        S,R,E and E,R,S
```

Given this modification, sentence [2] will now be acceptable since:

```
E,R,S    (S and R points are aligned)
E__R,S
```

---

3. See footnote 7 and 11 of Hornstein's paper.
4. There may be doubts as regards the acceptability of 5ciii. An equivalent form of 5ciii is acceptable is Danish (Jespersen65, p.271). Also, in French, the present perfect can be used for a situation that held not more than 24 hours before the present moment (Comrie76, p.61).

To examine the adequacy of RP, let us look at more examples:

```
[4] John has come when i.   *we arrived
                       ii.  *we had arrived
                       iii.  we arrive
                       iv.   we have arrived
                       v.   *we will arrive
```

The corresponding analysis is as follows:

```
[4'] i.  E__R,S        (BAD)
         E,R__S

     ii. E__R,S        (BAD)
         E__R__S

     iii. E__R,S       (OK)
          E,R,S

     iv. E__R,S        (OK)
         E__R,S

     v.  E__R,S        (BAD)
         S__R,E
```

We can see that the proposed theory correctly predicts all of the five cases. There is, however, an apparent counter-example to RP which, unlike RTC, is symmetrical, i.e., it does not matter which of the P_i's is put on the top. Consider the following two sentences:

```
[5] i.  John will come when we arrive.
    ii. *John arrives when we will come.
```

RP predicts both 5i and 5ii will be unacceptable, but 5i seems to be good. It is examples like 5i and 5ii, I believe, that lead Hornstein to propose the asymmetrical rule RTC. But I think the data are misleading because it seems to be an idiosyncrasy of English grammar that 5i is acceptable. In French, we have to say an equivalent of "John will come when we will arrive" with the temporal adverbial explicitly marked with the future tense (Jespersen65, p.264). Thus, the acceptability of sentences like 5i can be explained by a principle of Economy of Speech allowing us to omit the future tense of the temporal adverbial if the matrix clause is already marked with the future tense.

2.1.3 Sequences of Tense

Now, we describe the third and final grammatical constraint on sequences of tense. Consider the following sentences:

```
[6] John said a week ago that Mary
              (a) will   leave in 3 days.
              (b) would
```

In the (a) sentence, the temporal interpretation of the embedded sentence is evaluated with respect to the moment of speech. Thus, for instance, [6a] means that Mary's leaving is 3 days after present moment of speech. On the other hand, the (b) sentence has the temporal interpretation of the embedded sentence evaluated with respect to the interpretation of the matrix clause, i.e., [6b] means that Mary's leaving is 4 days before the moment of speech.

To account for the sequence of tense in reported speech, Hornstein proposes the following rule:

(SOT): For a sentence of the form "P_1 that P_2", assign S_2 with E_1.

In general, for an n-level embedded sentence, SOT states that: assign S_n with E_{n-1} (Hornstein81, p.140). With the SOT rule, [6a] and [6b] will be analyzed as follows:

```
[6a'] a week ago
        |
      E_1,R_1__S_1
            S_2__R_2,E_2      ==> E_2 is 3 days
                  |                    after S_1
            in three days

[6b'] a week ago
        |
      E_1,R_1__S_1
        |
      S_2__R_2,E_2            ==> E_2 is 4 days
            |                        before S_1
      in three days
```

The local property of SOT, i.e., linking occurs only between nth and (n-1)th level, has a nice consequence: it explains why a third level nested sentence like [7]:

```
[7] John said a week ago                              (a)
    that Harry would believe in 3 days               (b)
    that Mary
        (i) will   leave for London in 2 days        (c)
        (ii) would
```

has only two temporal readings: (1) in 7(ci), Mary's leaving is two days after the moment of speech, and (2) in 7(cii), Mary's leaving is two days before the moment of speech. In particular, there is not a temporal reading corresponding to the situation in which Mary's leaving is five days before the moment of speech. We would obtain the third reading if SOT allowed non-local linking, e.g., assigned S_3 with E_1.

2.2 Explanations of the Formal Constraints

In the previous section, we have examined three formal constraints on the derivation of complex tense structures from the basic tense structures: (1) LOC, (2) RP, and (3) SOT. Now, I want to show how the LOC falls out naturally from the computational properties of a temporal reasoning system along the line suggested by Allen (Allen84, Allen83), and also how the RP and SOT constraints have intuitive computational motivation.

The basis of Allen's computational system is a temporal logic based on intervals instead of time points. The temporal logic consists of seven basic relations and their inverses (Allen84, p.129, figure 1):

Relation	symbol	symbol for inverse	meaning
X before Y	<	>	XXX YYY
X equal Y	=	=	XXX YYY
X meets Y	m	mi	XXXYYY
X overlaps Y	o	oi	XXX YYY
X during Y	d	di	XXX YYYYY
X starts Y	s	si	XXX YYYY
X finishes Y	f	fi	XXX YYYY

The reasoning scheme is a form of constraint propagation in a network of event nodes linked by temporal relationships. For instance, the situation as described in the sentence "John arrived when we came" is represented by the network:

where A = John's arrival and B = Our coming

This network means that both event A and event B are before *now*, the moment of speech, while A can be before, after or simultaneous with B.

When new temporal relationships are added, the system maintains consistency among events by propagating the effects of the new relationships via a *Table of Transitivity Relationships* that tells the system how to deduce the set of admissible relationships between events A and C given the relationships between A and B, and between B and C. Thus, for instance, from the relationships "A during B" and "B < C", the system can deduce "A < C".

One property of the constraint propagation algorithm generally is that further information only causes removal of members from the set of admissible labels, i.e., temporal relationships, between any two old events (Allen83, p.835). No *new* label can be added to the admissible set once it is created. Let us call this property of the constraint propagation algorithm the Delete Label Condition (DLC). DLC can be interpreted as a kind of **information monotonicity condition** on the temporal representation.

Let us further restrict Allen's temporal logic to instantaneous intervals, i.e., each event corresponds to a single moment of time. The restricted logic has only one primitive relation, $\leq$, and three other derived relations: $<$, $>$, and $\geq$. There is a straightforward translation of Hornstein's SRE notation into the network representation, namely, replace each comma symbol "," by $\leq$ (or $\geq$ with the event symbols reverse their roles) and each underscore symbol "_" by $>$ (or $<$ with similar adjustment on the event symbols). Thus, a tense structure such as: E__R,S can be represented as:

```
S -(>)->E
 \       ↗
(> =)   (>)
   ↘   ↙
     R
```

With this representation scheme, we can prove the following theorem:

(T1) DLC → LOC

Proof

Let A and B range over { S, R, E } and A ≠ B. There are five basic types of violations of the LOC:

1. A__B → B__A
2. A__B → A,B
3. A__B → B,A
4. A,B → B,A
5. A,B → B__A

We can see that each of these cases is a violation of the DLC. To spell this out, we have the following operations on the constraint network corresponding to the above violations of the LOC:

1'. A -(<)-> B → A -(>)->B
2'. A -(<)-> B → A -(< =)->B
3'. A -(<)-> B → A -(> =)->B
4'. A -(< =)-> B → A -(> =)->B
5'. A -(< =)-> B → A -(>)->B

In each of these cases, the operation involves the addition of new members to the admissible set. This is ruled out by DLC. Thus, we have the result that if LOC is violated, then DLC is violated. In other words, DLC → LOC.[5] ⊣

The second constraint to be accounted for is the RP which effectively states that (a) the S points of the matrix clause and the temporal adverbial must be identical, and (b) the R points of the matrix clause and the temporal adverbial must be identical. One hypothesis for this rule is that:

(H1) Only the matrix clause introduces distinct S and R points.

In other words, the non-subcategorizable temporal adjuncts do not add new S and R points.

H1 has to be modified slightly to take the case of embedded sentence into account, namely,

(Revised RP): Only the matrix clause and the subcategorizable SCOMP or VCOMP can introduce distinct S and R points.
where SCOMP and VCOMP stand for sentential complement and verbal complement respectively. The interesting point is that both the revised RP and the locality property of SOT can be easily

---

5. The converse of this theorem is not true.

implemented in processing systems which have certain *boundedness* constraint on the phrase structure rules (e.g., information cannot move across more than one bounding node). To illustrate this, let us consider the following tense interpretation rules embedded in the phrase structure rules of the Lexical-Functional Grammar:

```
S   → NP VP
(↓ S-POINT) = NOW
VP  → V (NP) (ADVP) (S')
          (↓ S-POINT) =
            ⎰ (↑ E-POINT) if (↓ tense) = PAST
            ⎱ NOW          otherwise
ADVP → Adv S
S'  → COMP S
Adv → when
        (↑ T-REL) = { <,>,=,m,mi }
        before
        (↑ T-REL) = { > }
```

The S rule introduces a new S point and sets its value to *now*. The VP rule has two effects: (1) it does not introduce new S or R points for the temporal adverbial phrase, thus implicitly incorporating the revised RP rule, and (2) it looks at the tense of the embedded sentential complement, setting the value of its S point to that of the E point of the higher clause if the tense is *past*, and to *now*, otherwise. Thus, in this way, the second effect accomplishes what the SOT rule demands.

2.3 Implications for Learning

If the revisions to Hornstein's theory of tense are correct, the natural question to be asked is: How do speakers attain such knowledge? This question has two parts: (1) How do speakers acquire the formal constraints on SRE derivation? and (2) How do speakers learn to associate the appropriate SRE structures with the basic tenses of the language?

Let us consider the first sub-question. In the case of LOC, we have a neat answer -- the constraint need NOT be learned at all! We have shown that LOC falls out naturally as a consequence of the architecture and processing algorithm of the computational system. As regards the constraint RP, the learner has to acquire something similar to H1 But H1 is a fairly simple hypothesis that does not seem to require induction on extensive linguistic data. Finally, as we have shown in the previous section, the boundedness of the flow of information of a processing system leads directly to the locality property of the SOT. The particular linking of S and E points as stipulated by the SOT, however, is a parameter of the Universal Grammar that has to be fixed.

What about the second sub-question? How do speakers learn to pair SRE configurations with the basic tenses? There are 24 possible SRE configurations seven of which get grammaticalized. Here I want to propose a principle of markedness of SRE structures that has a natural computational motivation.

Let us recall our restrictive temporal logic of instantaneous interval with one primitive relation, $\leq$, and three derived relations:

$<, >$, and $\geq$. Represent a SRE configuration as follows:

The admissible labels are among { $<, <=, >, >=$ }. So there are altogether 64 possible configurations that can be classified into three types:

(1) Inconsistent labelings (16), e.g.,

(2) Labelings that do not constrain the SE link given the labelings of SR and RE (32), e.g.:

(3) Labelings that are consistent and the SE link is constrained by the SR and RE link (16), e.g.,

S -(<)-> E

If we assume that labelings of the third type correspond to the unmarked SRE configurations, the following division of unmarked and marked configurations is obtained:

UNMARKED		MARKED	
E__R__S	PAST PERFECT	E__S__R	
E,R__S	SIMPLE PAST	E,S__R	
E__R,S	PRESENT PERFECT	E__S,R	
E,R,S	SIMPLE PRESENT	E,S,R	
S,R,E	SIMPLE PRESENT	S__E__R	FUTURE PERFECT
S,R__E			
S__R,E	SIMPLE FUTURE	S__E,R	
S__R__E		S,E__R	
		S,E,R	
		R__S__E	
		R__S,E	
		R__E__S	
		R__E,S	
		R,E__S	
		R,S__E	
		R,E,S	
		R,S,E	

There are only eight unmarked tense structures corresponding to the sixteen SRE network configurations of type 3 because a tense structure can be interpreted by more than one network representations, e.g., the Past Perfect (E__R__S) has the following two configurations:

The interesting result is that five out of the six basic tenses have unmarked SRE configurations. This agrees largely with our pretheoretical intuition that the SRE configurations that correspond to the basic tenses should be more "unmarked" than other possible SRE configurations. The fit, however, is not exact because the future perfect tense becomes the marked tense in this classification.

Another prediction by this principle of markedness is that both the simple future (S__R,E) and distant future (S__R__E) are unmarked. It would be interesting to find out whether there are languages in which the distant future actually gets grammaticalized.

The final point to be made is about the second type of labelings. There are two other possible ways of grouping the labelings: (1) given SR and SE, those labelings in which RE is constrained, and (2) given SE and RE, those in which SR is constrained. But these types of grouping are less likely because they would yield the simple present tense as a marked tense. Thus, they can be ruled out by relatively few linguistic data.

3. Verb Aspect

In considering the problem of tense, we have restricted ourselves to a subset of Allen's temporal logic, namely, using a temporal structure $\langle T, \leq \rangle$ with linear ordering of time points. To make use of the full power of Allen's temporal logic, we now turn to the problem of verb aspect.

The two main problems of the study of verb aspect are the correct characterization of (1) the three fundamental types of verb predication according to the situation types that they signify -- state, process and event, and (2) the perspectives from which a situation is viewed, or its truth evaluated -- simple or progressive.[6] In the first part of his paper, Allen attempts to provide a formal account of the state/process/event distinction using a temporal logic. However, I believe that his characterization fails to capture well-known patterns of tense implications, and does not make the distinction between situation types and perspective types fundamental to any adequate account of verb aspect. In the next section, I will present some data that any theory of verb aspect must be able to explain.

3.1 Data

3.1.1 Tense Implications

1. Statives rarely take the progressive aspect[7], e.g.,
   I know the answer.
   *I am knowing the answer.

2. For verb predications denoting processes, the progressive of the verb form entails the perfect form, i.e.,
   x is V-ing → x has V-ed.
For instance,
   John is walking → John has walked.

3. For verb predications denoting events, the progressive of the verb form entails the negation of the perfect form, i.e.,
   x is V-ing → x has not V-ed.
For instance,
John is building a house → John has not built the house.

3.1.2 Sentences containing When

Sentences containing clauses connected by a connective such as "when" have different aspect interpretations depending on the situation types and perspective types involved.

[9] John laughed when Mary drew a circle.
   Situation/Perspective type:
   X = process/simple; Y = event/simple
   Interpretation:
   X can be before, after or simultaneous with Y

[10] John was laughing when Mary drew a circle.
   Situation/Perspective type:
   X = process/progressive; Y = event/simple
   Interpretation:
   Y occurs during X.

[11] John was angry when Mary drew a circle.
   Situation/Perspective type:
   X = state/simple; Y = event/simple
   Interpretation:
   X can be before, after, simultaneous with or during Y.

[12] John was laughing when Mary was drawing a circle.
   Situation/Perspective type:
   X = process/progressive; Y = event/progressive
   Interpretation:
   X must be simultaneous with Y.

3.2 Formal Account of the State/Process/Event distinction

Define:

---

6. Some of the better works are: Vendler67, Comrie76, Mourelatos78.

7. It has often been pointed out that some statives do take the progressive form. E.g., "I am thinking about the exam.", "The doctor is seeing a patient." However, a statistical study has shown that the familiar statives rarely occur with the progressive aspect -- less than 2% of the time (Ota63, section 2.2)

(a) $X \subset Y \leftrightarrow X d Y \vee X s Y \vee X f Y$

(b) $X \subseteq Y \leftrightarrow X \subset Y \vee X$ equal Y

(c) mom(t) $\leftrightarrow$ t is an instantaneous interval, i.e., consists of a single moment of time

(d) per(t) $\leftrightarrow$ t is a non-instantaneous interval[8]

where X and Y are generic symbols denoting state, event or process.

3.2.1 Progressive

(PROG): OCCUR(PROG(v,t)) $\leftrightarrow$ mom(t) $\wedge \neg$ OCCUR(v,t) $\wedge$ ($\exists$ t')(t d t' $\wedge$ OCCUR(v,t'))[9]

The progressive aspect is the evaluation of a situation from an interior *point* t of the situation which has the property that though the sentence is not true at that instantaneous interval, it is true in a non-instantaneous interval t' properly containing t.

3.2.2 State

(S1): OCCUR(s,t) $\leftrightarrow$ ($\forall$ t')(mom(t') $\wedge$ t' $\subseteq$ t $\rightarrow$ OCCUR(s,t'))

A state verb is true at every instantaneous interval of t. The definition is similar to Allen's H.1 (Allen84, p.130).

The following theorem shows that state verbs do not occur with the progressive aspect.

(S-THEOREM): *OCCUR(PROG(s,t))

Proof

OCCUR(PROG(s,t))
   $\leftrightarrow$ mom(t) $\wedge \neg$ OCCUR(s,t) $\wedge$ ($\exists$ t')(t d t' $\wedge$ OCCUR(s,t'))
   $\rightarrow$ OCCUR(s,t') for some t' containing t
   $\rightarrow$ OCCUR(s,t)   (by S1)
   $\therefore$ contradiction. $\dashv$

This theorem raises the following question: Why do some statives occur with the progressive? I think there are two answers. First, the verb in question may have a use other than the stative use (e.g. "have" is a stative when it means "possession", and not a stative when it means "experiencing" as in "John is having a good time in Paris.") Second, the English progressive may have a second meaning in addition to that characterized by PROG above. A frequent usage of the progressive is to indicate short duration or temporariness, e.g., in "They are living in Cambridge"/"They live in Cambridge".

---

8. This section benefits from the insights of Barry Taylor (Taylor77).
9. A reviewer of this paper points out that the PROG axiom seems to imply that if something is in progress, it must complete. Thus, if Max is drawing a circle, then at some future time, he must have drawn the circle. This inference is clearly false because there is nothing contradictory about "Max was drawing a circle but he never drew it." For instance, Max might suffer a heart attack and died suddenly. This inference problem of the progressive form of an event verb is known as the *imperfective paradox* in the literature. One way out is to deny that Max was really drawing a circle when he died. Rather he was drawing something which *would have been* a circle had he not died. This type of analysis would involve some machinery from Possible World semantics.

3.2.3 Process

A process verb can be true only at an interval larger than a single moment. This property differs crucially from that of the statives.

(P1): OCCUR(p,t) $\rightarrow$ per(t)

(P2): OCCUR(p,t) $\rightarrow$ ($\forall$ t')(per(t') $\wedge$ t' $\subseteq$ t $\rightarrow$ OCCUR(p,t'))

The following theorem shows that for a process verb, the progressive verb form entails the perfect form.

(P-THEOREM) OCCUR(PROG(p,t)) $\rightarrow$ ($\exists$ t')(per(t') $\wedge$ t' $<$ t $\wedge$ OCCUR(p,t'))

Proof

OCCUR(PROG(p,t))
   $\rightarrow$ mom(t) $\wedge \neg$ OCCUR(p,t) $\wedge$ ($\exists$ t')(t d t' $\wedge$ OCCUR(p,t'))
   $\rightarrow$ OCCUR(p,t') for some t' such that t d t'
   $\rightarrow \exists m_1 \in$ t'. $m_1 < t$ (since t d t')
   $\rightarrow \exists m_2 \in$ t'. $m_1 < m_2 < t$ (by density of time points)

Let t" be the interval $[m_1, m_2]$. Then, we have t" $<$ t and t" $\subseteq$ t'. By (P2), we have OCCUR(p,t"). That is, p has occurred. $\dashv$.

The characterization of process verb by Allen (his O.2) is less satisfactory because it combines both the notion of progressive aspect (his "OCCURRING") and the process verb into the same axiom. Furthermore, the difference between the predicate "OCCUR" and "OCCURRING" is not adequately explained in his paper.

3.2.4 Event

An event verb shares an important property with a process verb, namely, it can be true only at a non-instantaneous interval.

(E1): OCCUR(e,t) $\rightarrow$ per(t)

(E2): OCCUR(e,t) $\rightarrow$ ($\forall$ t')(per(t') $\wedge$ t' $\subseteq$ t $\rightarrow \neg$ OCCUR(e,t'))

The following theorem shows that the progressive form of an event verb entails the negation of the perfect form.

(E-THEOREM): OCCUR(PROG(e,t)) $\rightarrow \neg$($\exists$ t')(per(t') $\wedge$ t' $<$ t $\wedge$ OCCUR(e,t'))

Proof

As in the proof of (P-THEOREM), we can find a non-instantaneous interval t" such that t" $<$ t and t" $\subseteq$ t'. But for any such t", we have $\neg$ OCCUR(e,t") because of (E2). That is, it cannot be the case that e has occurred. $\dashv$.

Again the crucial property (E1) is not captured by Allen's characterization of events (his O.1).

3.3 Constraint on temporal interpretations involving When

To account for the variety of aspect interpretations as presented in section 3.1.2, I propose the following constraint on situation/perspective type:

(C-ASPECT): Let "dynamic" stand for a process or event.

(a) simple/dynamic $\rightarrow$ mom(t)
(b) simple/state $\rightarrow$ per(t)
(c) progressive/dynamic $\rightarrow$ per(t) $\wedge \subseteq$

Perspective is a way of looking at the situation type. For process or event, the simple aspect treats the situation as an instantaneous interval even though the situation itself may not be instantaneous. For state, the simple aspect retains its duration. The progressive aspect essentially views a process or event from its interior, thus requiring a stance in which the situation is a non-instantaneous interval and the admissible temporal relationship to be the $\subseteq$ relations, i.e., *s, si, f, fi, d, di, equal*.

Let me show graphically how C-ASPECT accounts for the aspect interpretations of sentences [9] to [12].

[9'] simple/process WHEN simple/event

Admissible relations:

```
   <        m       =        mi       >
  X   Y    XY       X        YX      Y   X
                    Y
```

[10'] progressive/process WHEN simple/event

Admissible relations:

```
   si        di        fi
  XXX       XXX       XXX
   Y         Y         Y
```

[11'] simple/state WHEN simple/event

Admissible relations:

```
     >        mi        si        di        fi
   Y XXX     YXXX       XXX       XXX       XXX
                        Y         Y         Y
     m         <
   XXXY      XXX Y
```

[12'] prog/process WHEN prog/event

Admissible relations:

```
   =         f        fi        s        si
  XXX       XXX      XXXX      XXX      XXXX
  YYY       YYYY     YYY       YYYY     YYY
  d         di
   XX       XXXX
  YYYY      YY
```

4. Conclusion

In this paper, I have examined two problems regarding linguistic semantics: tense and aspect. Important relationships between abstract constraints governing linguistic behavior and a computational scheme to reason about temporal relationships are discussed. In particular, I have shown that certain formal constraints, such as the Linear Order Constraint on tense, fall out naturally as a consequence of some computational assumptions. The interesting result is that this formal constraint need not be learned at all.

Another important role of a representation scheme in explaining phenomena that exist on a entirely different -- linguistic -- level is illustrated by the formulation of the C-ASPECT constraint to account for interpretations of sentences containing temporal connectives.

The study of linguistic semantics also sheds light on a representation of time by revealing the fundamental distinctions that must be made, e.g., a tensed sentence involves three distinct time points, and the aspectual interpretations require instantaneous/non-instantaneous interval distinction.

Acknowledgments

I would like to thank Prof. Robert C. Berwick for his insightful suggestion that the relationship between a cognitive theory of time and a linguistic theory of tense is a fruitful and important area for research. He also contributed substantially to the presentation of this paper. Finally, I also thank Norbert Hornstein who provided useful comments during the revision of this paper.

5. References

[Allen84]   James Allen, "Towards a General Theory of Action and Time", <u>AI Journal</u>, Vol 23, No. 2, July, 1984.

[Allen83]   "Maintaining Knowledge about Temporal Intervals", <u>CACM</u> Vol 26, No. 11, Nov. 1983.

[Comrie76]   Bernard Comrie, <u>Aspect</u>, Cambridge University Press, 1976.

[Hornstein81]   Norbert Hornstein, "The study of meaning in natural language", in: <u>Explanation in Linguistics</u>, Longman, 1981.

[Hornstein77]   "Towards a Theory of Tense", <u>Linguistic Inquiry</u>, Vol 8, No. 3, Summer 1977.

[Jespersen65]   Otto Jespersen, <u>The Philosophy of Grammar</u>, Norton Library 1965.

[Mourelatos78]   A.P.D. Mourelatos, "Events, processes and states", <u>Linguistics and Philosophy 2</u>, 1978.

[Ota63]   Kira Ota, <u>Tense and Aspect of Present Day American English</u>, Tokyo, 1963.

[Taylor77]   Barry Taylor, "Tense and Continuity", <u>Linguistics and Philosophy 1</u>, 1977.

[Vendler67]   Zeno Vendler, <u>Linguistics and Philosophy</u>, Cornell University Press.

LEXICAL AMBIGUITY AS A TOUCHSTONE

FOR THEORIES OF LANGUAGE ANALYSIS

Lawrence Birnbaum

Yale University
Department of Computer Science
New Haven, Connecticut

Abstract

This paper assesses several broad approaches to language analysis with respect to the problem of lexical ambiguity. The impact of the problem on both syntactic and semantic analysis is discussed, and several common methods for disambiguation, including the use of selectional restrictions and scriptal lexicons, are analyzed. Their shortcomings illustrate the need for complex inference to resolve ambiguity, which forms one of the key functional arguments in favor of integrating language analysis with memory and inference. However, it has proven surprisingly difficult to realize such an integrated approach in practice: An assessment of lexical disambiguation within some recent models which attempt to do so reveals that they rely largely on the traditional techniques of selectional restrictions and scriptal lexicons, with all their drawbacks. The difficulty is shown to stem primarily from the theories of memory and inferential processing utilized. The implications for recent approaches to language analysis based on connectionist mechanisms are explored. Finally, the requirements imposed by lexical disambiguation on theories of memory and inferential processing are discussed.

Introduction

The problem of natural language analysis, or "parsing," has been approached in many different ways and from the perspective of many different theoretical traditions. Because these theoretical traditions often differ quite radically in their basic assumptions about the goals of language analysis and the methods that ought to be employed, it can be quite difficult to compare the different approaches. But regardless of these differences, there are certain characteristics of the input that must be dealt with. Natural language is elliptic, ambiguous, and vague, to name just three of these problematic features. Any language analyzer must contend with some or all of these problems. This suggests that one good way to try and make sense out of the variety of approaches is to examine their various strengths and weaknesses with regard to such characteristics.

In this paper, I propose to evaluate several broad approaches to parsing with respect to one of the most basic of these problematic characteristics, lexical ambiguity. Lexical ambiguity is one of the chief sources of ambiguity in language, so the problem is undeniably important. It is, further, widely recognized to be a far more pervasive phenomenon than it intuitively seems to be. Because people are not consciously aware of most of the ambiguities in what they read or hear, the fact that most of what they read or hear *is* ambiguous is not immediately apparent. However, a glance at any ordinary dictionary should make it plain that lexical ambiguity is extremely common.

Lexical ambiguity is, finally, a problem the importance of which has long been appreciated. It was one of the rocks on which the early work in machine translation foundered. Bar-Hillel (1960), in his critique of that work, showed that determining the correct sense of an ambiguous word depends, in general, on plausible inferences from extremely complex features of the context in conjunction with arbitrary facts about the world. He gave as an example the problem of choosing the correct meaning of the word "pen" in the sentence "The box is in the pen." In this sentence, the pen in question is probably an enclosure, such as a play-pen, rather than a writing implement. Bar-Hillel argued that in order to determine this, a language analyzer would need access to knowledge of the functions and relative sizes of these two different kinds of objects, as well as some means of using that knowledge to determine the plausibility of the various possible interpretations of the sentence.

Of course, lexical ambiguity is not just a problem for *semantic* analysis. It is also one of the chief causes of structural ambiguity, and it is, therefore, an issue with which syntactic analyzers must contend as well. This aspect of the problem has also long been appreciated. In the well-known example "Time flies like an arrow," (Kuno, 1965), much of the structural ambiguity of the sentence stems from the part-of-speech ambiguity of the words "time," "flies," and "like," which in turn reflects their semantic ambiguity.

In sum, the problem of lexical ambiguity can indeed serve as a touchstone by which theories of language analysis can be assessed. The problem is basic and pervasive. The issues implicated in its solution, and the problems to which it gives rise, have long been appreciated. It arises regardless of whether one is trying to construct a syntax-based parser or a semantics-based one. Despite its importance, however, surprisingly little progress has been made on the problem. In this paper, I will attempt to provide a critical survey of what has been accomplished. No new solutions will be presented. However, the critique will reveal some of the requirements for a solution, and some of the consequences for the understanding process as a whole will be explored.

Lexical ambiguity and syntactic analysis

In syntactic analysis, the problem of lexical ambiguity is not the problem of choosing the correct sense of a word, but simply the correct part of speech. However, as the last example demonstrated, these problems are not unrelated. Word-sense ambiguity very often entails part-of-speech ambiguity as well. Thus, correctly disambiguating the part of speech of a word will in general depend on complex semantic and pragmatic processing. Syntactic analyzers cannot, therefore, be expected to solve by themselves the problem of lexical ambiguity, even just part-of-speech ambiguity. It is not unreasonable, however, to expect that they might contribute to its solution.

The chief approach to resolving syntactic ambiguity, lexical or otherwise, is simply to try each alternative, while being prepared to back up in case it should prove mistaken. This is the approach taken in ATN parsers and descendant models (see, e.g., Thorne, Bratley, and Dewar, 1968; Bobrow and Fraser, 1969; Woods, 1970; Pereira and Warren, 1980). When such a parser encounters an ambiguous word, it simply tries each possible choice for that word's part of speech which will enable a transition, and which therefore offers the possibility of successfully parsing the input sentence according to the grammar utilized. If the choice does not lead to a successful syntactic analysis, then it will be discarded when the parser backs up. (By performing an incremental semantic analysis on structures proposed by the syntactic analyzer, it is possible to rule out choices on semantic grounds as well; see, e.g., Bobrow and Webber, 1980.) This process will be repeated for a given word each time the parser encounters it when driving forward in the network. All and only the choices that lead to successful analyses will be output with those analyses. Further disambiguation is the responsibility of the semantic and pragmatic components of the understanding process.

More recently, however, Marcus (1980) has criticized this approach to resolving ambiguities, and has argued instead that syntactic analysis can normally be accomplished without resorting to unlimited back-up. In particular, he claims that syntactic structural ambiguities must and can be resolved with limited look-ahead and highly restricted use of semantic information. Since much of the structural ambiguity in language arises as a result of lexical ambiguity, lexical ambiguity is clearly one of the crucial issues which must be faced in making such a claim. Nevertheless, Marcus's theory barely addresses the problem: with only one or two exceptions, words are taken to be syntactically unambiguous in his work. At the very least, this failure to confront the issue makes it difficult to evaluate the status of the theory.

In fact, the one or two cases of lexical ambiguity which Marcus does attempt to resolve within the framework of his theory simply serve to show how profound the impact of the problem actually is. For example, in order to disambiguate whether the word "have" is used as an auxiliary or a main verb, Marcus introduces a diagnostic rule which is arguably the most complex in his entire grammar. Nevertheless, as Marcus himself points out, the rule fails on many obvious examples. How well such rules would work in the context of many *other* ambiguous words is highly questionable. Indeed, Milne's (1982) attempt to address lexical ambiguity within the framework of Marcus's theory led to a substantially greater reliance on semantics. One need not agree with the details of his proposals to find this result suggestive.

Lexical ambiguity and semantic analysis

We have seen that syntactic analyzers, alone, cannot be expected to do very much about lexical ambiguity. It is, after all, primarily a question of word-sense ambiguity rather than just part-of-speech ambiguity, and so primarily a semantic problem rather than a syntactic one. Quite naturally, therefore, it is an issue which has received far more attention in semantic analyzers than in syntactic ones. At first glance, there seem to be a variety of different semantic approaches to the problem. In fact, however, most approaches turn out to share only one or two fundamental mechanisms.

The major semantic approach to the solution of lexical ambiguity involves the use of *selectional restrictions* (Katz and Fodor, 1963). These are semantic requirements associated with the structures representing the meanings of words or phrases, which must be met by another semantic structure before the two can be combined. For example, an action like eating might require that its actor be animate. In general, selectional restrictions are one-place predicates that test for the presence or absence of some semantic feature, or some boolean function of such predicates.

The use of selectional restrictions in disambiguation is, in principle at least, quite straightforward. One simply chooses the sense (or senses) of a word that selectional restrictions will allow to combine with other semantic structures in the sentence, either because it meets the requirements of those other structures, or because they meet its own requirements. To paraphrase a simple example from Katz and Fodor (1963), consider the word "ball." This can mean, among other things, either a fancy party with dancing, or a round object used as a toy. In the sentence "John hit the ball," the use of selectional restrictions would result in choosing the round object sense of "ball," since the action of hitting can be applied to a physical object but not to a social gathering.

A variety of different methods have been developed for applying selectional restrictions in the resolution of lexical ambiguity; I will briefly mention just a few of them here. Winograd (1972) proposed that they be used by semantic interpretation specialists associated with functional syntactic constituents such as noun groups and clauses. Riesbeck (1975) proposed encoding selectional restrictions in the tests of the lexically indexed productions that represent, in his theory, the different meanings of a word. Rieger and Small's (1979) theory of word experts and Hirst and Charniak's (1982) theory of Polaroid words are based on more sophisticated versions of this idea. Wilks (1976) has proposed that selectional restrictions should not be absolute requirements, but simply *preferences*. In his model, one picks the sense of each word that maximizes the total number of preferences satisfied in a given sentence.

The other major approach to handling lexical ambiguity involves the use of a *scriptal lexicon* (Schank and Abelson, 1977; Cullingford, 1978; Riesbeck and Schank, 1978; Charniak 1981). This idea is based on the observation that many words have special meanings in particular contexts. Thus, in a sense, each script or frame used in understanding a text should have an associated lexicon in which words are assigned their frame-specific meaning. For example, the frame for a baseball game would have an associated lexicon in which the word "home" would be defined as the plate in the ground over which batters stand, and which a player must touch to score a run. By itself, this idea is not very useful for disambiguation, except insofar as it keeps frame-specific meanings out of consideration unless the relevant frame is "active." The crucial simplifying assumption which is usually made, therefore, is that if a given frame is "active," all words in its scriptal lexicon can be presumed to have their frame-specific meaning.

Although both selectional restrictions and scriptal lexicons are very useful up to a point, especially in domain-limited applications, it should be clear that they have severe limitations. The simplifying assumption which underlies the scriptal lexicon approach, that words will not be used in other than their frame-specific sense, is clearly not true. For example, consider the following sentence in the context of a story about a baseball game: "The game was so lopsided that Fred got bored and walked home after the seventh inning." Here, the home in question is probably Fred's residence, not home plate.

The use of selectional restrictions has similar limitations. Consider the following variant of Bar-Hillel's example: "The pen is in the box along with assembly instructions." Here, the pen in question is probably a play-pen, and almost certainly not a writing implement. Determining this requires recognizing that the assembly instructions are probably for the assembly of the pen, and knowing that play-pens often require assembly by the consumer after purchase, whereas writing implements do not. Using this knowledge in turn requires inferring that since the pen is in a box with assembly instructions, it has probably just been purchased by the consumer. The point here is that these are simply not the kinds of rules that can be represented and employed as selectional restrictions, except at the risk of precluding the correct analysis of other examples. We cannot, for example, just invent a feature "objects that can be assembled" as a selectional restriction on the object of "assemble," and which would be a property of play-pens but not writing implements. Writing pens certainly *are* assembled, in factories, and they may even be assembled by the consumer, as in "John assembled the pen after cleaning it

and putting in a new cartridge."

Lexical ambiguity and integrated analysis

The above discussion makes it clear that what must be brought to bear on the problem of lexical ambiguity are the general inference and memory processes used in understanding. Thus, lexical ambiguity is one of the key problems which motivates an integrated approach to language analysis, one in which inference and memory processing play an important role in the analysis process itself (Schank, Lebowitz, and Birnbaum, 1980; Schank and Birnbaum, 1984). Although it plays a key role in motivating this approach, however, and would therefore seem crucial to theories of integrated analysis, surprisingly little attention has been devoted to it.

For example, consider the approach taken in the model proposed by Dyer (1983), which explicitly aims to be a model in which memory and inference are intimately entwined in the language analysis process. Despite this intent, the discussion of lexical disambiguation in the model is limited to the use of selectional restrictions and scriptal lexicons. Both are implemented as the tests of lexically indexed productions, in a manner similar to Riesbeck (1975). We can best see how this works by looking at a representative example. For instance, here is the procedure which disambiguates the phrase "run into," slightly paraphrased for readability:

```
If the actor is a VEHICLE or
    the SCENARIO is TRANSITIONAL
        with a VEHICLE instrument,
Then interpret "run into" as VEHICLE-ACCIDENT;
Else If the object is
        a HUMAN who has an INTERPERSONAL
        RELATIONSHIP with the actor,
    Then interpret "run into" as
        RENEW-INTERPERSONAL-RELATIONSHIP.
```

Let's analyze how this is intended to work. The test for whether or not the actor is a vehicle is simply a selectional restriction. The test for whether "the SCENARIO is TRANSITIONAL with a VEHICLE instrument" is perhaps more puzzling. However, its purpose would seem to be to handle examples such as "While I was driving home, I ran into a parked car," in which the actor of "run into" is not a vehicle, but the proper interpretation is nevertheless vehicle accident. In effect, this is an implementation of the scriptal lexicon idea: if the vehicle travel frame is active, then "run into" means vehicle accident. Both of these rules are subject to the limitations described in the last section. For example, this use of the scriptal lexicon approach would fail on the following text:

While I was driving home, I remembered I needed some milk. I ran into a Seven-Eleven and picked up a half-gallon.

Finally, let's consider the test for a human who has some interpersonal relationship with the actor. Here, the model begins to employ knowledge beyond simple selectional restrictions, which are technically just one-place predicates. The problem is, it still *employs* this knowledge exactly as if it were just a selectional restriction. Although the presence of such a relationship (or, in fact, any semantic feature) is indeed the sort of knowledge that may be *relevant* in determining the correct meaning of a word, its use as a sufficient condition in a non-inferential, lexically-indexed rule of this variety is entirely misplaced. The point is that such knowledge must be represented and indexed in a way that makes it available for use by the general inferential capabilities of the understander.

To be more specific about what is required, consider *how* the fact that two people have an interpersonal relationship might be relevant to determining the appropriate interpretation of "run into." If two people who knew each other happened to have a fortuitous encounter, then social rules such as politeness, and personal goals stemming perhaps from friendship, might *cause* them to pursue their interpersonal relationship at that juncture. They might, for example, engage in conversation, go to a bar, or arrange a subsequent meeting. Knowledge of this causal relationship would enable an understander to explain why people who knew each other would exhibit such behavior, and thus enable the understander to construct a causally coherent representation of a textual fragment describing such an episode. It is the attempt to construct such a causally coherent representation that determines the proper interpretation of "run into." A particular interpretation, such as "social encounter," is preferred to the extent that it promotes such coherence.

But the rule cited above does not explicitly represent such causal knowledge, nor does its choice of an interpretation for "run into" depend on the attempt to infer a causally coherent representation. Instead, the inference process is "short circuited" by directly linking some (but not all) of the relevant features with some (but not all) of the possible interpretations. Such a rule simply cannot work in general. Consider, for example, the following text:

John was racing down the street trying to catch a bus. All of a sudden, his neighbor Fred stepped out of a doorway into his path. John ran into Fred and knocked him down. Fortunately, he wasn't hurt.

What both this example and the previous one demonstrate, to repeat, is that the proper interpretation of "run into" should be determined on the basis of the attempt by memory and inference to construct a causally coherent representation of the text as a whole -- which is, after all, one of the chief functions of memory and inference in understanding. In a language analyzer which is truly integrated with memory and inference, it must be on the basis of these sorts of inferential considerations that language analysis problems, such as lexical ambiguity, are resolved. Instead, in Dyer's model we find

that such inferential processing occurs *after* a word has already been disambiguated by means of selectional restrictions and scriptal lexicons.

The model of integrated partial parsing proposed by Schank, Lebowitz, and Birnbaum (1980) and substantially extended by Lebowitz (1980) also depends, primarily, on the scriptal lexicon approach. In fact, most words are simply unambiguous as far as the model is concerned, since it presumes that input stories will involve only a single domain (terrorist incidents). To some extent, however, this model does make more serious use of memory and inference in disambiguation as well. In order to construct coherent representations of input stories, the model employs a version of script application (Schank and Abelson, 1977; Cullingford, 1978), in which an action or state is interpreted by matching a scriptal expectation. The model can then use these expectations to disambiguate a word by choosing the meaning that satisfies one of them. (This method was originally proposed by Riesbeck and Schank, 1978.)

This method is clearly a step in the right direction. It is, however, subject to severe limitations, because it assumes, first, that if a script is active, then an ambiguous word *must* have the meaning that matches an expectation from that script, and second, that only one meaning will match an expectation. But consider what would happen if more than one script were active, or if the scripts were larger and more detailed, or if expectations from sources other than scripts were utilized. Under these conditions, it seems quite likely that more than one meaning of an ambiguous word would match an expectation, or to put this another way, that more than one interpretation could be coherently interpreted within the context. Thus, this method for using scriptal expectations will not work in many situations; it will either fail to disambiguate, or else simply choose in a way which guarantees a high probability of error. The method can only be employed reliably when only one script is active, and when only one sense of the word matches an expectation from that script. As a result, this use of scriptal expectations is virtually equivalent, in the power and scope of its disambiguation capabilities, to the use of a scriptal lexicon. For all practical purposes, one might just as well stipulate that the given word will have a given meaning if the given script is active.

Conclusions

How can the the use of scriptal expectations, or more generally of contextual expectations from varying sources, be extended to handle those cases in which more than one meaning of an ambiguous word might seem at first to fit the context? Several factors must be taken into account beyond the mere occurrence of a match between a potential word meaning and an expectation. First, which expectations are more important, or more likely to be satisfied at this point in the text? To put this in more general terms, which of the explanations for the different possible interpretations is more plausible or more salient? Second, does the text supply any additional clues? For example, a candidate semantic structure may be the right sort of action to satisfy an expectation, but may nevertheless be inappropriate because its potential actor, as specified in the text, does not match the binding already assigned to the actor in that expectation. The use of such information is essential to exploit the full potential of memory and inference in lexical disambiguation.

In fact, this requirement poses the greatest challenge to recent models of language analysis employing connectionist mechanisms (see, e.g., Small, Cottrell, and Shastri, 1982; Cottrell, 1984; Waltz and Pollack, 1984). The manipulation of variables and variable bindings is a difficult issue in the connectionist framework (J. Feldman, personal communication), and as currently formulated these models do not seem capable of utilizing such information in disambiguation. Thus, their use of contextual information in disambiguation seems subject to the limitations described at the end of the last section. Whether the clever manipulation of parameters such as weights and activation levels can overcome these limitations remains to be seen. One possible solution is to use connectionist methods simply to suggest potential inference chains, and employ more traditional inference mechanisms, capable of manipulating variable bindings, to check over the suggestions (Charniak, 1983). Another possibility, requiring a more radical change in the connectionist framework, is to allow variable bindings to be passed between the units in a memory network (Riesbeck and Martin, 1985).

More broadly, however, the apparent difficulties in applying memory and inference to lexical disambiguation reflect not so much on the state of theories of language analysis as on theories of memory and inference. Here, the lesson of lexical ambiguity is that the knowledge needed to draw inferential connections in understanding cannot be packaged in isolated rules that commit the understander to certain inferences irrespective of what other rules may propose. It is true that one possible interpretation of someone "running into" another person is as a fortuitous encounter leading to a social interaction. It is also true that one explanation for why two people would care to engage in such an interaction would be if they already knew each other. Thus, the knowledge that two people knew each other would provide support for interpreting "run into" as a social encounter, since such an interpretation would enable the understander to explain certain aspects of the situation. But, as we have seen, the decision that this is the *correct* interpretation cannot be made without considering the need to explain *other* aspects of the situation, aspects which may have nothing to do with social interactions and to which rules explaining such interactions cannot be expected to attend.

This last point bears particular attention. No single explanatory inference rule can be expected to attend to all the aspects of a situation which might affect the truth or relevance of the explanation it offers, and hence the validity of the interpretation it prefers for some vague or ambiguous linguistic element. Thus, determining which explanations to accept, and hence which interpretations to prefer, cannot be left to the inference rules themselves.

Rather, there must be a more general inferential mechanism that determines which explanations to accept, taking into account the need to explain diverse aspects of a situation, and the evidence of diverse rules.

Probably the most ambitious attempt in this direction has been McDermott's (1974) model, which is capable of considering several potential explanations for a situation in parallel as it unfolds and choosing among them when evidence is available, as well as patching or replacing explanations that prove erroneous. Granger (1980) and O'Rorke (1983) propose models with this last capability as well, and Granger, Eiselt, and Holbrook (1984) have proposed a model of language understanding (including lexical disambiguation) which makes use of such techniques. The most salient feature of these models is that they *explicitly* employ criteria, however crude, for deciding whether an explanation is adequate, when one explanation is preferable to another, and when an explanation has gone awry. For example, McDermott's criteria are, basically, coherence -- an explanation must fit the facts -- and parsimony -- an explanation with fewer unjustified assumptions is preferred. The use of such criteria would seem to be a crucial aspect of any inferential mechanism capable of fulfilling the requirements set out above, and thus capable of resolving lexical ambiguity in a general manner.

Acknowledgments: I thank Beth Adelson, Gregg Collins, and Alex Kass for useful discussions and for comments on an earlier draft of this paper. This work was supported in part by the Defense Advanced Research Projects Agency, monitored by the Office of Naval Research under contract N00014-85-K-0108.

References

Bar-Hillel, Y. 1960. The present status of automatic translation of languages. In F. Alt, ed., *Advances in Computers 1*, Academic Press, New York, pp. 91-163.

Bobrow, D., and Fraser, B. 1969. An augmented state transition network analysis procedure. *Proceedings of the First IJCAI*, Washington, DC, pp. 557-567.

Bobrow, R., and Webber, B. 1980. Knowledge representation for syntactic/semantic processing. *Proceedings of the 1980 AAAI Conference*, Stanford, CA, pp. 316-323.

Charniak, E. 1981. Six topics in search of a parser: An overview of AI language research. *Proceedings of the Seventh IJCAI*, Vancouver, B.C., pp. 1079-1087.

Charniak, E. 1983. Passing markers: A theory of contextual influence in language comprehension. *Cognitive Science*, vol. 7, pp. 171-190.

Cottrell, G. 1984. A model of lexical access of ambiguous words. *Proceedings of the 1984 AAAI Conference*, Austin, TX, pp. 61-67.

Cullingford, R. 1978. Script application: Computer understanding of newspaper stories. Research report no. 116, Yale University, Dept. of Computer Science, New Haven, CT.

Dyer, M. 1983. *In-Depth Understanding: A Computer Model of Integrated Processing for Narrative Comprehension.* MIT Press, Cambridge, MA.

Granger, R. 1980. When expectation fails: Towards a self-correcting inference system. *Proceedings of the 1980 AAAI Conference*, Stanford, CA, pp. 301-305.

Granger, R., Eiselt, K., and Holbrook, J. 1984. The parallel organization of lexical, syntactic, and pragmatic inference processes. *Proceedings of the First Annual Workshop on Theoretical Issues in Conceptual Information Processing*, Atlanta, GA, pp. 97-106.

Hirst, G., and Charniak, E. 1982. Word sense and case slot disambiguation. *Proceedings of the 1982 AAAI Conference*, Pittsburgh, PA, pp. 95-98.

Katz, J., and Fodor, J. 1963. The structure of a semantic theory. *Language*, vol. 39, pp. 170-210.

Kuno, S. 1965. The predictive analyzer and a path elimination technique. *Communications of the ACM*, vol. 8, pp. 453-462.

Lebowitz, M. 1980. Generalization and memory in an integrated understanding system. Research report no. 186, Yale University, Dept. of Computer Science, New Haven, CT.

Marcus, M. 1980. *A Theory of Syntactic Recognition for Natural Language.* MIT Press, Cambridge, MA.

McDermott, D. 1974. Assimilation of new information by a natural language-understanding system. Technical report no. 291, Massachusetts Institute of Technology, Artificial Intelligence Laboratory, Cambridge, MA.

Milne, R. 1982. Predicting garden path sentences. *Cognitive Science*, vol. 6, pp. 349-373.

O'Rorke, P. 1983. Reasons for beliefs in understanding: Applications of non-monotonic dependencies to story processing. *Proceedings of the 1983 AAAI Conference*, Washington, DC, pp. 306-309.

Pereira, F., and Warren, D. 1980. Definite clause grammars for language analysis -- A survey of the formalism and a comparison with augmented transition networks. *Artificial Intelligence*, vol. 13, pp. 231-278.

Rieger, C., and Small, S. 1979. Word expert parsing. *Proceedings of the Sixth IJCAI*, Tokyo, pp. 723-728.

Riesbeck, C. 1975. Conceptual analysis. In R. Schank, ed., *Conceptual Information Processing*, North-Holland, Amsterdam, pp. 83-156.

Riesbeck, C., and Schank, R. 1978. Comprehension by computer: Expectation-based analysis of sentences in context. In W. Levelt and G. Flores d'Arcais, eds., *Studies in the Perception of Language*, John Wiley, Chichester, England, pp. 247-293.

Riesbeck, C., and Martin, C. 1985. Direct memory access parsing. Research report no. 354, Yale University, Dept. of Computer Science, New Haven, CT.

Schank, R., and Abelson, R. 1977. *Scripts, Plans, Goals, and Understanding.* Lawrence Erlbaum, Hillsdale, NJ.

Schank, R., and Birnbaum, L. 1984. Memory, meaning, and syntax. In T. Bever, J. Carroll, and L. Miller, eds., *Talking Minds: The Study of Language in the Cognitive Sciences*, MIT Press, Cambridge, MA, pp. 209-251.

Schank, R., Lebowitz, M., and Birnbaum, L. 1980. An integrated understander. *American Journal of Computational Linguistics*, vol. 6, pp. 13-30.

Small, S., Cottrell, G., and Shastri, L. 1982. Toward connectionist parsing. *Proceedings of the 1982 AAAI Conference*, Pittsburgh, PA, pp. 247-250.

Thorne, J., Bratley, P., and Dewar, H. 1968. The syntactic analysis of English by machine. In D. Michie, ed., *Machine Intelligence 3*, American Elsevier, New York, pp. 281-309.

Waltz, D., and Pollack, J. 1984. Phenomenologically plausible parsing. *Proceedings of the 1984 AAAI Conference*, Austin, TX, pp. 335-339.

Wilks, Y. 1976. Parsing English II. In E. Charniak and Y. Wilks, eds., *Computational Semantics*, North-Holland, Amsterdam, pp. 155-184.

Winograd, T. 1972. *Understanding Natural Language.* Academic Press, New York.

Woods, W. 1970. Transition network grammars for natural language analysis. *Communications of the ACM*, vol. 13, pp. 591-606.

VOX--An Extensible Natural Language Processor

Amnon Meyers

Artificial Intelligence Project
Computer Science Department
University of California
Irvine, California

ABSTRACT

VOX is a Natural Language Processor whose knowledge can be extended by interaction with a user.

VOX consists of a text analyzer and an extensibility system that share a knowledge base. The extensibility system lets the user add vocabulary, concepts, phrases, events, and scenarios to the knowledge base. The analyzer uses information obtained in this way to understand previously unhandled text.

The underlying knowledge representation of VOX, called Conceptual Grammar, has been developed to meet the severe requirements of extensibility. Conceptual Grammar uniformly represents syntactic and semantic information, and permits modular addition of knowledge.

1. INTRODUCTION

The ability to learn is one of the most important characteristics of intelligent systems. To approach such an ability, we first must build systems that can accept new knowledge automatically. By continually enhancing the extensibility capabilities of such systems, we can begin to address the problems of general learning.

Critical to extensibility is the underlying knowledge representation. The more powerful and flexible the knowledge representation, the more easily extensibility capabilities can be built and improved.

VOX (Vocabulary Extension System) is a Natural Language Processing system that emphasizes automatic extensibility. In VOX, extensibility capabilities are developed hand-in-hand with the knowledge representation. The knowledge representation, called Conceptual Grammar [5], supports a bottom-up study of language, by representing both very general and very specific knowledge. As generalizations about language are discovered, they are incorporated into the representation.

Currently, VOX allows automatic addition of vocabulary and action-oriented events and scenarios. The user may build knowledge hierarchies of scenarios, events, nouns, verbs, adjectives, and other parts of speech, as well as specifying a variety of semantic and syntactic information

about these objects. The VOX analyzer uses information obtained in extensibility sessions to analyze novel text.

1.1 EXAMPLES

We will illustrate how VOX works by adding the sequence of events for a simple Naval 'attack' scenario:

> ship searches for ship.
> ship sights ship.
> ship approaches ship.
> ship attacks ship.
> ship damages ship.

We will add the words, the individual events, and the entire scenario to the system. Then, we will show a text analysis example that uses this knowledge. [User inputs are in boldface, in the examples below.]

MACRO NOUN EXAMPLE:

Enter singular form of noun: **ship**
Enter plural   form of noun: **ships**
Enter synonym or more general concept: **platform**

Macro noun is an extensibility capability for adding nouns. The words 'ship', 'ships', as well as the more abstract concepts ship(noun) and ship(np) are added to the knowledge base by macro noun. A phrase like "the 3 green ships" will be found to be equivalent to ship(np), for example. By specifying 'platform', the user places 'ship' into a conceptual hierarchy of nouns already containing 'platform'. ('Platform' is a Navy word for anything that a missile can be fired from. Thus, a base, a submarine, and an aircraft are all platforms.)
Macro verb is similar to macro noun. In addition to concepts for words, verb, and verb phrase levels, macro verb creates concepts for the event and frame level. For example, in adding the verb search, the concepts search(event) and search(frame) will be created.

Assume that all the word-level items in the simple attack scenario have been added using macro noun, macro verb, and macros for other parts of speech. Next, we add an event:

This work is supported by the Naval Ocean Systems Center, under NOSC Grant N66001-83-C-0255.

MACRO EVENT EXAMPLE:

Enter an event:

ship search location for ship
1   2   3   4   5

Semantic information

Enter position of the following:
actor = **1**
act = **2**
object = **5**
instrument = __
location = **3**
time = __
Enter a concept that the event suggests: **search**

Syntax information

Enter position of subject: **1**
Enter voice of act (active or passive): **active**

Optionality information

Enter starting points of event: **1**
Enter end points of event: **5**
Enter skipping points for event:
Element 1 can skip to: __
Element 2 can skip to: **4**
Element 3 can skip to: __

Entry for new event = ship-search

Macro event lets the user add standard events to the knowledge base. These events are templates, and will match much more than the literal words "ship search location for ship". Macro event uses the abstract concepts ship(np), search(vp), rather than the word-level concepts. The event added is treated not just as a semantic restriction, but as a full-fledged concept. The concept <ship-search-location-for-ship> is stored in the knowledge base under the entry 'ship-search'. We can use concepts such as this to add new scenarios, as will be shown below. This specific event-concept is added to a hierarchy of events by suggesting the generic 'search' event.

The user specifies the semantic case (actor, act, location, etc.) of each element in the event. The user specifies that the phrase starts with element 1 and ends with element 5. The syntactic component of VOX's grammar handles incomplete forms such as "ship searched the area", so the user need not specify that element 3 is a possible end of the event phrase. The user specifies that element 3 can be skipped over; that is, "The ship searched for the submarine", omitting a location element, is correct English. The user specifies this because it varies on a case-by-case basis. For example, in the sentence "Ship conducted attack on submarine", "attack" could not be omitted.

Assume that all events of the simple attack scenario have been entered using macro event. Next, we invoke macro frame to add the entire scenario.

MACRO FRAME EXAMPLE:

Enter the events of the frame:
1 **ship-search**
2 **ship-sight**
3 **ship-approach**
4 **ship-attack**
5 **ship-damage**

Briefly describe the frame: **ship attacks ship**

Semantic information

Enter the main event: **4**
Enter events needed in a complete text: **2 4 5**
Enter concept suggested by frame: **attack**

Enter number of actor roles: **2**
Enter a word for actor 1: **ship**
Actor 1 is subject in which events? **1 2 3 4 5**
Actor 1 is object in which events? __

Enter a word for actor 2: **ship**
Actor 2 is subject in which events? __
Actor 2 is object in which events? **1 2 3 4 5**

Optionality information

Enter starting points for frame: **1 2 3 4 5**
Enter end points for frame: **4 5**
Enter skipping points for frame:
Element 1 can skip to: **3 4 5**
Element 2 can skip to: **4 5**
Element 3 can skip to: **5**

Entry for frame = ship-attack

Macro frame is similar in many ways to macro event. In particular, this specific scenario is given full concept status, and is placed under the entry 'ship-attack' (Note: the entry 'ship-attack' holds both events and scenarios.) We entered it into a hierarchy of scenarios by having it suggest the generic attack(frame) concept.

Optionality information: The user specifies that the description of the scenario could start with any of the events in it and skip over any events. For example, a complete text might read "damaged sub". On the other hand, we require that an attack scenario end with an attack or damage event (event 4 or 5).

Having entered this scenario into the system, we can make use of it to understand texts that deal with a 'ship attacking ship' scenario. Here is an example of the kind of text VOX analyzes using the scenario just entered.

VOX TEXT ANALYSIS EXAMPLE

(Constellation is message sender.)

Type message:

at 1235T had searched area. damaged sub.

INTERPRETATION 1 OF 1.
MESSAGE FEATURES

> ERROR: missing event = attack
> ERROR: missing event = sight
> ERROR: missing object = sub
> ERROR: missing actor = constellation
> ERROR: missing actor = constellation

REWORDED MESSAGE

> constellation had searched area for sub
> at 1235 t. constellation damaged sub.

Frame = ship attacks ship

When analyzing text, VOX builds a frame-based representation of the underlying meaning, which is used for checking and correcting syntactic and semantic problems. VOX reports errors found and produces a reworded version of the input text. VOX's use of extensibility session information in the above example is fairly straightforward.

2. CONCEPTUAL GRAMMAR

We describe the Conceptual Grammar knowledge representation, which forms the foundation of the extensibility and analysis capabilities of VOX.

2.1 INTRODUCTION

Conceptual Grammar (CG) is a framework for the representation of conceptual information. The unit of knowledge in CG is the *concept*. A concept is an atomic representation of anything that can be verbalized. In our notation, a concept is depicted by a description of the concept enclosed in angle brackets. For example,

<aircraft carrier (noun)>

is an atomic representation of the concept "aircraft carrier". We often omit the angle brackets and hyphenate the description, for simplicity:

aircraft-carrier   or   <aircraft-carrier>

Concepts can be combined to form *phrases*. Most phrases have associated concepts to represent their meaning. Concepts and phrases *suggest*, or *reduce to*, other concepts by means of grammar rules. Some typical rules in CG are shown in Figure 1.

(A)	aircraft carrier	----->	aircraft-carrier
(B)	aircraft-carrier	----->	ship
(C)	attack (vp)	----->	attack (event)
(D)	ship	----->	noun
(E)	det quan adj noun	----->	<specific np>

FIGURE 1

In rule (A), a phrase suggests its atomic representation. The phrase "aircraft carrier" has no corresponding single English word, yet it is a well-defined object, so we represent it with an atomic concept.

Rule (B) is an example of a hierarchical rule. The *hierarchy* is an important organizing principle of CG. CG has semantic hierarchies of nouns, adjectives, and some other parts of speech, as well as events and scenarios. For example, a scenario where a ship attacks a submarine is a more specific instance of one where a platform attacks a platform, which is a more specific version of the generic attack scenario, and so on. ('platform' is a Navy word for anything that missiles can be fired from.)

Rule (C) illustrates a second organizing principle of CG -- *conceptual levels*. When we speak of 'attack', we may be talking about the word itself, the verb, the action, the event, or an entire scenario. CG treats all of these facets as explicit concepts. The lower-level semantic concepts correspond to the syntactic concepts word, verb, verb phrase, and so on. The higher semantic levels of event and frame (or scenario) have no precise syntactic equivalent. A frame could correspond to a sentence, a paragraph, or even a novel.

The different levels of semantic concepts allow semantic phrases to be represented unambiguously in CG. Note how the concept of 'ship' is used in

(1) <ship(np)>   <attack(vp)>   <submarine(np)>
(2) <ship(noun)>   <ahoy(word)>   <'!'>
(3) <ship(word)>   <hyphen>   <shape(word)>

Phrase (1) would match a text like "The 3 US destroyers will attack the enemy sub". Phrase (2) matches only "ship ahoy!", "destroyers ahoy!", etc. Phrase (3) matches only "ship-shape". Conceptual levels allow semantic phrases to be represented with a high degree of precision.

An important class of rules in CG is concerned with the transitions between semantic and syntactic phrases. In Figure 1 above, rule (D) shows a semantic concept suggesting a syntactic concept, while rule (E) shows the reverse. Rule (E) is an example of a *restriction rule*. It suggests a specific noun-phrase concept corresponding to the noun on the left-hand-side of the rule. We will discuss this kind of rule in more detail in the next section.

2.2. EXAMPLE

We show, step-by-step, how CG analyzes

"Green ship will fire 2 missiles at 1230pm at submarine".

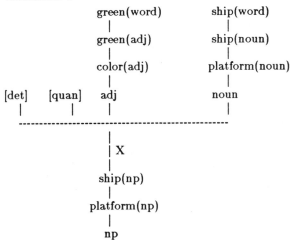

```
        green(word)        ship(word)
           |                  |
        green(adj)         ship(noun)
           |                  |
        color(adj)        platform(noun)
           |                  |
[det]  [quan]  adj          noun
  |      |      |             |
  ----------------------------------------
                    |
                    | X
                    |
                 ship(np)
                    |
               platform(np)
                    |
                    np
```

Most important here is step X, which uses the rule:

det quan adj noun -------> <specific np>

Since <ship (noun)> gave rise to the noun in the left-hand-side of the above rule, this rule suggests <ship (np)>. In essence, "green ship" has been condensed to the *semantic* concept <ship (np)>.

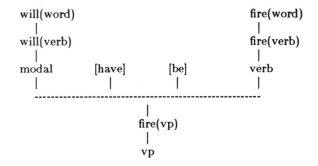

```
will(word)                    fire(word)
   |                             |
will(verb)                    fire(verb)
   |                             |
modal    [have]     [be]        verb
  |        |         |           |
  -------------------------------------
                 |
              fire(vp)
                 |
                 vp
```

Here again, we are using a semantic restriction rule:

modal have be verb ------> <specific vp>

This rule finds the most specific possible semantic instance of the verb, and suggests its corresponding vp-level.

"2 missiles" is analyzed similarly to "green ship".

The detailed analysis of the prepositional phrases "at 1230pm" and "at submarine" is omitted for simplicity. Both will suggest the concept <adv>, which corresponds to prepositional and adverbial phrases. Also, we represent

a list of adverbial phrases by <x>, for short.

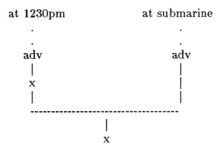

```
   at 1230pm          at submarine
      .                    .
      .                    .
      .                    .
     adv                  adv
      |                    |
      x                    |
      |                    |
      -------------------------
                |
                x
```

Now, we try to merge the elements found for the given sentence:

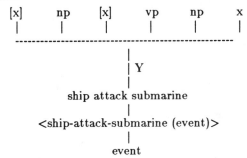

```
[x]     np    [x]     vp     np      x
 |       |     |       |      |       |
 -------------------------------------------
                    |
                    | Y
                    |
            ship attack submarine
                    |
         <ship-attack-submarine (event)>
                    |
                  event
```

Rule Y looks like

(Y)   x np x vp np x ------> <specific event>

The task of rule Y is to find specific events in the database; in this case, it found the event "ship attack submarine". Now, rule Y is highly sophisticated, and we will describe some of the actions that it took. First, note that "ship fired missile at submarine" is syntactically ambiguous. "At submarine" could be analyzed as a prepositional phrase, or "fire ... at" could be recognized as a prepositional verb with its associated particle. Rule Y knows about both of these possibilities. It checks the kind of verb, and uses one of the rules A or B accordingly:

A
x np x vp-prep np x prep np x --> <specific event>

B
x np x vp-regular np x   --> <specific event>

If the verb can be prepositional, rule Y looks for rules such as

<fire(vp)> <weapon(np)> <at> --> <attack(vp)>

In our case, it will find and use this rule. Having found that "will fire 2 missiles at" corresponds to an 'attack' concept, rule Y looks for the most specific possible event of the type

<ship> <attack> <submarine>

or

<platform> <attack> <platform>

and so on. Once the most specific possible event is found, rule Y suggests it. Note that rule Y has to search through the adverbial-list to find possible prepositional particles for the prepositional verb, and that it rejected the time adverbial because the knowledge base has no information about attacks on 'time'.

Rules like Y form a critical part of CG. They not only provide a mapping from surface text to underlying concepts, but also handle syntactic ambiguity in a unified and non-combinatorially explosive fashion. (Using rules A and B instead of Y would always result in two interpretations, whereas Y chooses the best one.)

Another example of such a rule is

  x np x <vp (passive)> x --> <specific event>

which handles forms like

> The ship was attacked by the submarine
> Missiles were fired at ship by submarine
> Missiles were fired by submarine at ship

again, in non-combinatorially explosive fashion. Furthermore, this rule is able to search for active-voice events, thus allowing most event knowledge to be stored in active voice. If desired, this rule can transform passive voice sentences to active voice. Another critical rule is

  <event-list> -----> <specific frame>

The task of this rule is to find a single frame (or scenario) which will unify a sequence of events, and to try to determine the causal relationship of all the events. This rule embodies some of the analyzer's frame-selection mechanisms.

3. RELATED WORK

VOX is a revised version of NOMAD [1].

CG developed from our attempt to reconcile the PHRAN approach [6] with traditional syntax theories, and to systemize the representation of phrasal knowledge.

We know of several efforts to build automatically extensible NLP systems: The Teacher component of UC [7],

LIFER [4], KLAUS [3], TEAM [2], and others. The success of these efforts depends, ultimately, on the underlying knowledge representation, including both conceptual and linguistic knowledge. We find that CG provides a framework for both productive and nonproductive linguistic knowledge, while the other systems mentioned tend to concentrate on one type or the other. Also, CG alone provides for automatic addition of scenarios.

ACKNOWLEDGMENT

Thanks to Richard Granger for his support and for critiquing this paper, Karin Klein for proofreading it, and Laura Yoklavich for formatting it.

REFERENCES

[1] Granger, R.H. (1984). The NOMAD System: Expectation-Based Detection and Correction of Errors during Understanding of Syntactically and Semantically Ill-Formed Text. *American Journal of Computational Linguistics.* v.9, no.3-4.

[2] Grosz, Barbara J. (1983). TEAM: A Transportable Natural Language Interface System. *Conference on Applied Natural Language Processing*, Santa Monica.

[3] Grosz, Barbara J. and Mark E. Stickel (1984). Research on Interactive Acquisition and Use of Knowledge. SRI Technical Report.

[4] Hendrix, Gary G. (1977). The LIFER Manual: A Guide to Building Practical Natural Language Interfaces. SRI Technical Note 138.

[5] Meyers, Amnon (1983). Conceptual Grammar. AI Project, ICS Department, Irvine, California. UC Irvine Technical Report 215.

[6] Wilensky, Robert and Yigal Arens (1980). PHRAN - A Knowledge Based Approach to Natural Language Analysis. UC Berkeley. Electronic Research Laboratory Memorandum No. UCB/ERL M80/34.

[7] Wilensky, Robert, Yigal Arens, and David Chin (1984). Talking to UNIX in English: An Overview of UC. *CACM* vol. 27, no. 6, pp.574-593.

PARTIAL CONSTRAINTS IN CHINESE ANALYSIS

Yiming YANG, Shuji DOSHITA and Toyoaki NISHIDA

Department of Information Science
Kyoto University
Sakyo-ku, Kyoto 606, Japan

ABSTRACT

In this paper, we describe a method using semantic constraints to reduce the ambiguities and generate case structure from phrase structure in Chinese sentence analysis.

Semantic constraints written on semantic markers indicate the plausible case structure. Different sets of semantic markers are chosen according to the purpose. A priority evaluation scheme steers the analysis towards the most plausible structure first, without trying all possibilities.

1. INTRODUCTION

Chinese is written with characters that don't admit formal inflections to indicate the grammatical categories of words. Also, there are few functional words, so few cues are available to indicate the grammatical structure.

Automatic parsing of Chinese runs immediately into an explosive growth of possible structures due to ambiguity, so syntactic and semantic constraints must be introduced as soon as possible in the analysis to restrict the search.

Knowledge that can be used for this purpose is mostly of a partial nature that leads to "plausible" interpretations. As such, it is difficult to manage, because several possibilities occur at each step.

In a previous paper (Yang et al. 1984), we show how to use the knowledge associated with "characteristic words" in a preprocessor designed to precede syntactical analysis.

Here we describe a system that uses the semantic categories of words to obtain case structure.

2. CASE STRUCTURE ANALYSIS

In Chinese, we cannot derive the phrase structure from the syntactic categories of the words and phrases, because cues such as conjunctions and inflexions are for most part lacking.

Fig 1 shows three examples of Chinese sentences:

Example 1

The children laugh at him for being a big fatso.

Example 2

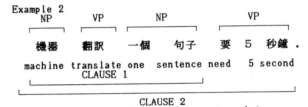

It needs 5 seconds for machine to translate one sentence.

Example 3

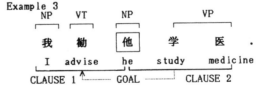

I advised him to study medicine.

Figure 1

All three examples show the same sequence NP-VT-NP-VP. The NP, VP, etc., are the partial results of a phrase structure analysis stage, but the analysis cannot proceed from here on. All the examples consist of two clauses, but the relationship between them is different in each case. In Example 2, the clause is embedded, whereas Examples 1 and 3 have both a "pivotal structure" (Li and Thompson 1981), that is, the second NP is both the object of the preceding clause and the subject of the following clause. These differences only emerge if one considers the meaning of the words.

In our system we try to apply semantic knowledge to lift this kind of ambiguity. We do not attempt to provide at some step a complete syntactic phrase structure. Instead, we use a case stucture to represent the result of semantic analysis.   We chose a set of case labels identical to that of the Mu-machine translation project (Nagao et al. 1983, 1984), for compatibility and to enable comparison.

Fig 2 shows the case structures for the two of the previous sentences:

(a) case structure of Example 1

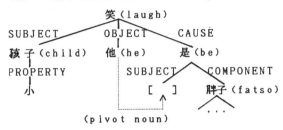

(b) case structure of Example 2

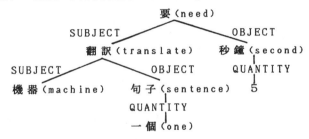

[ ] : absent component
( ) : caption
capital letter : case label

Figure 2

3. SEMANTIC CONSTRAINTS FOR CASE STRUCTURE

We determine the case structure from the partial syntactic structure using semantic markers.   The semantic markers (for nouns, verbs, etc.) used for writing the constraints are organized in hierarchies of semantic categories. Multiple hierarchies are used, according to the purpose (the particular ambiguity to be lifted) and the subject domain of the text.

Consider the examples above.   We choose the case structure according to the semantic category of the verbs.   Seven types of case structure are defined for the NP-VT-NP-VP sequence (including the two types shown in figure2).   Likewise, verbs are classified into seven groups named LET, EMOTION, HAVE, KNOW, NEED, TEACH and OTHER, each of which corresponds to one type of structure.   Note however that one verb can belong to several groups.

The rules are like the following:
"if the preceding verb belongs to the EMOTION group,   then use the "pivot construction" (as in Example 1), with a CAUSE relation;
 if the posterior verb (in VP) belongs to the NEED group, then the preceding part, NP-VT-NP is a clause which is the subject of VP (as in Example 2); ..."
 In some cases, the rules give contradictory conclusions.   In Example 1, the verb "笑" belongs to the EMOTION group, but "是" belongs to the "NEED" group. We must find a way of managing such multiple possibilities and choosing among them. This is done by means of the priority calculus scheme that we describe further on.

Consider, as another example,   the sentence "A是B".   Like the sentence "A is B" in English,   "A是B" is a very common sentence in Chinese,   but it is difficult to decide its scope,   that is,   where A begins and where B finishes.   As above, we lift the ambiguity by using the semantical properties of A and B,   to choose from several possible phrase structures.

For this particular problem we use a semantic hierarchy containing about 60 semantic markers for nouns,   borrowed from the Mu-project.   However, we add cross relationships that link some categories that are not sub-categories one of the other.   For example, in the physics text-books that we tested our system with,   the need appeared for relationships linking "physical phenomenon" with "relation", "standard" with "unit" etc.. This kind of add-on relationship is domain-dependant.

In the case where either A or B is an embedded clause,   a quite different classification is appropriate,   grouping for example the words that would most frequently stand   opposite an event like "原因" (reason), "問題"(problem), "状態" (state), "作用 " (function), etc..

Thus the semantical hierarchies are both domain and problem (ambiguity) dependant.

4. PRIORITY

As we mentioned above, our semantic constraints use knowledge which is
- not 100% correct (only statistically probable),
- not complete (described for parts of structure, or only written for typical situations).
This often results in some wrong decisions when a local analysis is done, so at some stages several possibilities must be retained.   We use a priority scheme to

evaluate the plausibility of each case structure and find the best choice.

In calculation:
a) Partial priority is calculated by constraint rules. It is determined experimentally.
b) Positive priority indicates a likely structure, negative priority an unlikely structure, 0 is indifferent.
c) Priority of the whole structure is the sum of partial priorities.

Consider the two plausible structures in Example 1, for example. Their scores are both given as +1 when the semantic constraints are checked with NP-VT-NP-VP. However, the score for "A is B" in the structure of Figure 1 is +1 because both A ("he") and B ("fatso") belong to the same group HUMAN. The score for the other interpetation, "It is a big fatso that the childrens laugh at him.", is -1 because A, an embeded clause, and HUMAN B ("fatso"), form an unlikely pair. The two partial scores above are added together, and the correct structure(in Figure 1) has the higher score.

5. OTHER FEATURES

For describing the knowledge used in semantic analysis, a complete set of rules comprising both general and word specific rules would be clumsy to write, use and modify. Instead, we use an object-oriented scheme to separate the rules into independent modules (objects) according to their operational properties, and organize them into layers of classes. More then one parent, or a set of parents are allowed. The object-oriented interpreter supports a nondeterministic search mechanism for the multiple heritage.

A priority-driven parser is designed to make the searching efficient. The parser does a phrase structure analysis following context-free grammar rules, in a bottom-up way. It evokes an object-oriented interpreter, like calling a procedure, to generate case structure and calculate priority for each hypothesis it makes. Only the partial result with the highest priority is expanded. The others are saved, so the searching direction can be adjusted each time the priority is changed.

This system is in the course of being developed and is only partially completed. As a preliminary evaluation, we tested the system against 20 typical sentences selected from grammar books and science and technology books in Chinese (Li and Thompson 1981, Lu 1980, Zhu 1982). The correct case structures are obtained as first choice 70% of the time, and as first or second 100% of time. We also did a hand simulation with 160 sentences from a physics book in Chinese, resulting in 70% success rate in the first choice.

6. SUMMARY

In this paper, we described a technique for semantical analysis in our Chinese analysis system.

Rules of partial semantic constraints built on a limited set of concepts are used to reduce the ambiguities in case structure generation.

The priority scheme gives us a way to write incomplete knowledge into our rules. The priority-driven parser guides the global analysis through the search space heuristically, so a combinatorial explosion of computation can be avoided.

The object-oriented scheme makes it easy to modularize, access and modify different kinds of knowledge.

In conclusion, we hope this method to be useful for natural language processing, where very complex semantical information must be managed in an efficient way.

ACKNOWLEDGEMENTS

I wish to thank Associate Professor Jun-ichi Tsujii and Dr. Jun-ichi Nakamura of Kyoto University for their help and fruitful discussions, and Dr. Alain de Cheveigne for help with the English.

REFERENCES

[1] Yang, Y., Nishida, T., Doshita, S. (1984), "Use of Heuristic Knowledge in Chinese Language Analysis", COLING-84, 222-225.
[2] Nagao, M. (1983), "Summary of Machine Translation Project of Science & Technology Agency (of Japanese Government)" (科技庁機械翻訳プロジェクトの概要), technical report of WG on Natural Language Processing of IPSJ, 38-2 (in Japanese).
[3] NAKAMURA, J., TSUJII, J.,and NAGAO, M. (1984), "Grammar writing system (GRADE) of Mu-machine translation project and its characteristics", COLING-84, 338-343.
[4] Li, C., Thompson, S. (1981) "MANDARIN CHINESE --- A Functional Reference Grammar", University of California Press.
[5] Lu, S. (1980), "800 Mandar in Chinese Words" (現代漢語八百詞), Beijing (in Chinese).
[6] Zhu, D. (1982) "Lecture of grammar" (語法講義), Beijing (in Chinese).

Grammatical Functions, Discourse Referents and Quantification

Uwe Reyle
Department of Linguistics
University of Stuttgart
West Germany

ABSTRACT

A new algorithm is proposed which transforms f-structures into discourse representation structures (DRSs). Its primary features are that it works bottom up, that it is capable of translating f-structures without preimposing any arbitrary order on the attributes occurring in it, and that it handles indeterminacy of scoping by using sets of translations. The approach sheds light on how an efficient interaction of different components of a natural language processing model can be achieved.

I INTRODUCTION *)

The informational content of a sentence is determined not only by its linguistic form, but also by a number of contextual factors. Thus within any compositional approach to semantics the control structure for the functional composition must not be determined exclusively by the syntactic structure of the phrase. The present approach is based on two levels of representation, that 'mediate' between the linguistic form of a sentence and its denotation(s) (in a model).

F-structures constitute the first level. They have the property that the unraveling of the grammatical roles of a sentence is already achieved, while the quantifier scope relations are not yet represented. This is basically due to the use of grammatical functions as theoretical primitives ([1],[3]).

The second level accounts for the dependency of (the construction of the interpretation) of a sentence on factors which are not purely syntactic. It consists of DRSs in which the scope relations will be treated. The central property of DRSs is that the part of sentence or text from which they derive acts as a context which guides the interpretation of the parts following it. This property of DRSs is based mainly on their containing discourse referents ([4]). It leads to a dynamic creation of interpretations of sentences.

We will show how to formulate a translation mechanism which allows for arbitrary scope relations not only within the limit of a clause nucleus but also within the various clause nuclei in which an NP can play a role by means of functional control. Possible non-syntactic scope restrictions can thus be licensed by additional constraints derived from various other features of the surface string, the semantics, or pragmatics.

The central feature of the translation algorithm is, loosely speaking, to replace the grammatical functions in the f-structure by the discourse referents which have been made available (for subsequent reference) by the values of the grammatical functions, i.e. the f-structures representing NPs. These f-structures themselves are translated into DRSs which are partial in the sense that there are (in general) still

*) This work has been supported in part by DFG under grant R0245/13 and ESPRIT under grant ACORD.

conditions or sub-DRSs missing in order to be interpretable. We will define some principles for the translation into and completion of partial DRSs.

II EXAMPLE

But before stating the exact definitions let us illustrate the algorithm by

(1) Every boy loves a girl

In order to give a graphic representation of the interplay between syntax and semantics we will represent f-structures as directed acyclic graphs (dag), the nodes C_i of which are associated with the translations of the f-structures rooted in C_i. The procedure works bottom-up (i.e. from inside the f-structures out). First, we associate with every leaf node a partial DRS as follows (making use of some λ-notation):

After ordinary λ-conversion of the SPEC-PRED combinations in the sub-dags of SUBJ and OBJ we get

Transformation of this dag into a tree is achieved by splitting the nodes which are the values of the grammatical functions and ARGi so that the discourse referents occurring in the partial DRSs are associated with the new nodes of the ARGi attributes and the partial DRSs themselves with the nodes of the grammatical functions:

After pruning the attributes we get the following set of expressions which is to be associated with the root node of the tree.

(2) $\left\{\lambda Q \begin{array}{|c|} \hline \fbox{$\begin{array}{|c|}\hline v \\ \hline boy(v) \\ \hline\end{array}$} \Rightarrow \fbox{Q} \\ \hline\end{array}\right.$, love(v,u), $\lambda Q \begin{array}{|c|}\hline u \\ \hline girl(u) \\ Q \\ \hline\end{array}\right\}$ *)

This set allows for two different sequences of λ-conversion, yielding the two desired readings

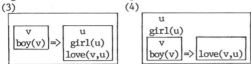

(3)   (4)

The example shows that we have to formulate two principles, one for the transduction of the dag into a tree, the other for calculating the partial translation of an arbitrary non-terminal tree node given the partial translations associated with its daughter nodes. Both principles will be local in the sense that only local trees and dags are used in their formulation.

III THE ALGORITHM

First we have to give the precise definition of partial DRSs. The usual definition of a DRS K as a pair consisting of a set of discourse referents U(K) and a set of conditions CON(K), together with Kamp's accessibility relation (cf. [4]), allows for the abstraction of discourse referents, predicates and (sets of) conditions. We therefore define partial DRSs inductively as follows.

Def. (a) Every DRS K = ⟨U(K),CON(K)⟩ is a partial DRS .
(b) If u is a discourse referent occurring in conditions c1,...,cn of CON(K) but not in any of the universes that are accessible from K, then
λuK = ⟨U(K),λuCON(K)⟩ is a partial DRS, where
λuCON(K) = {λuci|i=1,...n} ∪ CON(K)\{ci|i=1,...,n}.
(c) If P is a variable over partial DRSs of the form λuK´ with u and c1,...,cn as under (b), then λPK = λP⟨U(K), CON(K) ∪ P(u)⟩ is a partial DRS.
(d) If Q is a variable over DRSs, then
λQ = λQ⟨U(K),CON(K) ∪ Q⟩ is a partial DRS.

Suppose now we have a semantic interpretation schema with attribute names ATTR1,...,ATTRn

(SIS1)

ATTR1 ATTRn ⟹ ATTR1 ATTRn
o,C1´ ... o,Cn´   o,C1´ ... o,Cn´

where the translations C1´,...,Cn´ are already given as sets of partial DRSs. Suppose further that C1´,...,Cn´ are singletons, i.e. contain exactly one partial DRS. Then CO´ is calculated from them by the following principle.

Functional application principle for sets of partial DRSs
Given a set KK = {K1,...,Kn} of partial DRSs, then the set FA(K1,...,Kn) consists of those elements which belong to the

*) In contrast to the set of at least two s-structures which Halvorsen's algorithm ([3]) would produce, we have still just one representation of the sentence. The reason is that in [3] the attributes (corresponding to the arguments of the verb) are linearly ordered in the s-structures, and therefore, a quantifying-in device is used.

transitive closure of KK under the operation of functional application fa defined by:
(a) fa(λuK,v) = fa(λuCON(K),v) = K[v/u], where u and v are discourse referents and K[v/u] is the result of replacing every occurrence of u in CON(K) by v.
(b) fa(λPK,λu´K´) =
⟨ U(K) ∪ U(K´), CON(K)\P(u) ∪ fa(λu´CON(K´),u) ⟩, where P is a variable over partial DRSs of the form λuK and u and u´ are discourse referents.
(c) fa(λQK,K´) = ⟨U(K) ∪ U(K´), CON(K) ∪ CON(K´)⟩, where Q is a variable over DRSs.

Def. (a) A DRS K is closed if all discourse referents occurring in CON(KO) for some sub-DRS KO of K are introduced in some universe U(K1) accessible form KO.

This allows us to finish the interpretation of (SIS1): We supposed that all C1´,...,Cn´ were singletons. If we now admit non-singletons among the Ci´ then CO´ is calculated as the union of all FA(C1´´,...,Cn´´) with Ci´´ belonging to Ci´. But we restrict the occurrence of non-singletons to such sets Ci´ for which all Ci´´ are closed.

What we have not explained yet is how the semantic predicate gets the correct discourse referent as its value.

Def. A DRS with distinguished discourse referent u is a pair ⟨u,K⟩, where u is a discourse referent introduced in K and K is a partial DRS.

This allows us to formulate the second interpretation schema. Its task is to disambiguate the role of the nodes in the dag which are values of more than one attribute. In every such configuration at least as many grammatical functions Fj occur as there are ARGi. We will restrict ourselves to the treatment of grammatical functions and argument positions ([2]).
Suppose first that the node is the value of a subcategorizable function and is of NP-type, i.e. the associated translation is a partial DRS with distinguished discourse referent u. Then for m ≼ n and 1 ≼ k ≼ n we have

(SIS2)   F1 ... Fn ⟨u,K⟩ ⟹ Fk o, K
          ARG1 ... ARGm   ARG1 ... ARGm o,u

That is, every argument position is filled up by the distinguished discourse referent, and only one of the grammatical functions gets the content of the NP, i.e. determines the position of the introduction of the discourse referent in the hierarchy of the whole DRS. The edges of the other grammatical functions are erased. This allows for the introduction of the content of the NP exactly in those clause nuclei in which it plays a semantic role by force of controlling an unexpressed constituent in them. If the node is the value of a subcategorizable function the value of which is a clause nucleus, then the corresponding node in the dag has been associated with a set of closed DRSs KK. In order to disambiguate this node we take one K out of KK, associate it with the ARGi attribute, and prune the grammatical function F.

(SIS3)   F
          o ,KK ⟹ o , K
          ARGi   ARGi

Of course the translation of the PRED has to introduce a discourse referent p specified by K. For the interpretation of (5) we translate the

(5) Every boy expects an American to win

entry for <u>expect</u> by

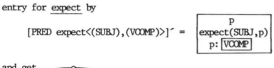

and get

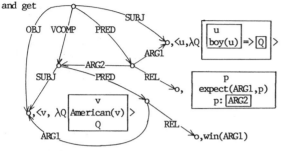

After two applications of (SIS2), where we choose Fk to be the SUBJ (in both cases), we have

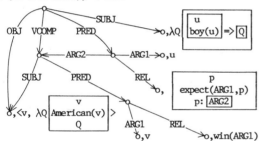

which yields just as in the introductory example by (SIS1)

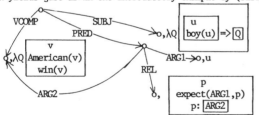

This is further reduced by (SIS3)

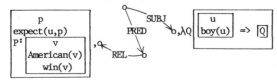

so that we finally get

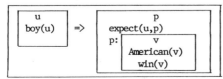

Before we calculate the other two readings for (5) we want to note that in the case of Equi verbs the requirement that only closed DRSs are accepted as a translation excludes the

derivation just outlined. Remember that the lexical entry for e.g. persuade also subcategorizes for the OBJ and hence yields the translation

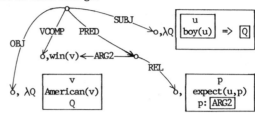

in which the object position would not have been bound by the discourse referent v introduced by <u>an American</u>. Only the following two calculations will be applicable to both types of verbs. If we had taken the OBJ in the application of (SIS2) above we would have got

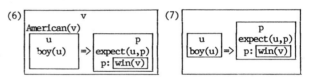

and then (6), if the value of the PRED is converted with the value of the SUBJ first; or, if one converts the value of the PRED first into the value of the OBJ one gets the third and last reading (7) of this sentence.

IV   CONCLUSION

It has been shown how grammatical functions and discourse referents can be used in the translation process from linguistic form to discourse representations. The algorithm described accounts for the dynamics of the construction of interpretations of sentences, determined not only by syntactic configurations, but also by contextual means, semantics, or pragmatics.

REFERENCES

[1] Bresnan, J.W. (1982), The Mental Representation of Grammatical Relations, MIT Press, Cambridge, Massachusetts.

[2] Frey, W. (1985), "Syntax and Semantics of Some Noun Phrases", in: Laubsch, J. (ed.) Proceedings of GWAI 1984, Springer, 1985.

[3] Halvorsen, P.-K. (1983), "Semantics for Lexical-Functional Grammar", in: Linguistic Inquiry 14.

[4] Kamp, H. (1981), "A Theory of Truth and Semantic Representation", in: Groenendijk, J.A., et al. (eds.), Formal Semantics in the Study of Natural Language, Vol.I, Amsterdam.

Discourse Structure
and the Proper Treatment of Interruptions

Barbara J. Grosz
AI Center
SRI International
Menlo Park, CA
& CSLI, Stanford University
Stanford, CA

Candace L. Sidner
BBN Laboratories
Cambridge, MA

Abstract

This paper reports on the development of a computational theory of discourse. The theory is based on the thesis that discourse structure is a composite of three structures: the structure of the sequence of utterances, the structure of intentions conveyed, and the attentional state. The distinction among these components is essential to provide adequate explanations of such discourse phenomena as clue words, referring expressions and interruptions. We illustrate the use of the theory for four types of interruptions and discuss aspects of interruptions previously overlooked.

1. Introduction

This paper reports on the development of a computational theory of discourse structure that simplifies and extends previous work. As we develop it, the theory will be seen to be intimately connected with two nonlinguistic notions, namely intention and attention. Attention and intention are crucial to accounting for the processing of utterances in discourse. Intentions will be seen to play a primary role not only in providing a basis for explaining discourse structure, but also in defining discourse coherence, and providing a coherent notion of the term "discourse" itself.

The theory is a further development and integration of two lines of research: work on focusing in discourse [6], [7], [8], and more recent work on intention recognition in discourse [[2], [20], [22], [23]]. Our goal has been to generalize properly to a wide-range of discourse types the notions of focusing and task structure shown by Grosz to be necessary for processing task-oriented dialogue. One of the main generalizations of previous work will be to show that discourses generally are in some sense "task-oriented," but the kinds of "tasks" that can be achieved are quite varied--some are physical, others mental, others linguistic. As a result, the term "task" is unfortunate, and we will use the more general terminology of intentions--speaking for example of discourse purposes--for most of what we say.

Our main thesis is that the structure of any discourse is a composite of three distinct but interacting constituents: the structure of the actual sequence of utterances in the discourse, a structure of intentions, and an attentional state. The distinction among these constituents is essential to providing an explanation of interruptions (see Section 3), as well as the use of certain types of referring expressions and of various expressions that affect discourse segmentation and structure (discussed in [10]). Most related work on discourse structure (including Reichman [17], Linde [12],

Linde and Goguen [11], and Cohen [4]) conflates at least two of these constituents. As a result, significant generalizations are lost, and the computational mechanisms proposed are more complex than needed. By carefully distinguishing the constituents, we are able to account for the significant observations in this related work while simplifying the explanations given and computational mechanisms used. Related work by Polanyi and Scha ([16], [14], [15]) concentrates on a single component, the linguistic one, and examines in more detail various aspects of its internal structure.

In addition to its use in explaining these linguistic phenomena, the theory provides an overall framework in which to answer questions about the relevance of various segments of discourse to each other, and to the overall purposes of the discourse participants. Various properties of the intentional component have implications generally for work in natural-language processing. In particular, the range of intentions that underlie discourse is such that approaches to discourse coherence based on selecting discourse relationships from a fixed set of alternative rhetorical patterns are unlikely to suffice in general. Furthermore, this study makes evident several problems that must be confronted in extending speech-act related theories (e.g., [1], [3], [2], etc.) from coverage of individual utterances to coverage of extended sequences of utterances in discourse.

Although a definition of "discourse" must await the development of the theory laid out in the remainder of this paper, some properties of the phenomena we want to explain must be specified now. In particular, we take a discourse to be a piece of language behavior that typically involves multiple utterances and multiple participants. The discourse may be produced by one or more speakers (or writers) and the audience may comprise one or more hearers (or readers). Each *conversational participant* brings to the discourse a set of beliefs, goals, intentions, and other mental attitudes. These attitudes affect a conversational participant's participation in the discourse; they influence both how utterances are produced and how they are understood. Where necessary, we use *initiating conversational participant* (ICP) and *other conversational participant* (OCP) to distinguish participants.

2. The Basic Theory

Discourse structure is a composite of three interacting components: a linguistic structure, an intentional structure, and an attentional state. These three components of discourse structure deal with different aspects of the utterances in a discourse. Utterances--the actual saying or writing of particular sequences of phrases and clauses--are the basic elements in the linguistic structure. Note that this use of linguistic structure to refer to the structure of a sequence of utterances rather than to single sentence syntactic structure. Intentions of a particular sort, namely those whose recognition (by the OCP) is intended (by the ICP) and which provide the basic reason for the discourse are the basic elements of the intentional structure. Attentional state contains information about the objects, properties, relations, and discourse-intentions that are most salient at any given point in a discourse; it summarizes information from previous utterances crucial for processing subsequent ones so that a complete history need not be kept.

Together the three constituents of discourse structure provide the information needed by the conversational participants to determine how an individual utterance fits with the rest of the discourse——in essence to figure out why it was said, and what it means, in the context in which it was uttered. The context provided by these constituents also forms the basis for certain expectations about what is to come; these expectations too play a role in fitting in new utterances. The attentional state serves an additional role, namely it provides the means for actually using the information in the other two structures in the generation and interpretation of individual utterances.

2.1. Linguistic Structure

The first component of discourse structure is the structure of the sequence of utterances that form a discourse. Just as the words in a single sentence form constituent phrases, the utterances in a discourse are naturally aggregated into *discourse segments*. The utterances in a segment, like the words in a phrase, serve particular roles with respect to that segment. In addition, the discourse segments, like the phrases, fulfill certain functions with respect to the overall discourse. Although two neighboring utterances may be in the same discourse segment, it is also possible for them to be in different segments. Likewise two utterances that are not in linear sequence may be in the same segment.

The factoring of discourses into discourse segments has been observed across a wide range of discourse types. Grosz [6] showed this for task-oriented dialogues. Linde [12] found it held for descriptions of apartments; Linde and Goguen [11] describe such structuring in the Watergate transcripts. Reichman [17] observed it in informal debates, explanations, and therapeutic discourse. Cohen [4] found similar structures in essays in rhetoric texts.

There is a two-way interaction between the discourse segment structure and the utterances constituting the discourse: linguistic expressions affect the discourse structure; they are also constrained by it. Not surprisingly, linguistic expressions are among the primary indicators of discourse segment boundaries. Explicit use of certain words and phrases (e.g., "in the first place"), and more subtle clues like changes in tense and aspect are among the repertoire of linguistic devices that function wholly or in part to indicate these boundaries ([4], [16], [17]). These linguistic devices can be divided according to whether they indicate changes in the intentional structure or the attentional state of the discourse (or both). The differential use of these linguistic markers provides one piece of evidence for the separation of these two components of discourse structure. In addition, because these linguistic devices function explicitly as indicators of discourse structure, it becomes clear that they are best seen as providing information at the discourse, and not the sentence, level

and hence that certain kinds of questions (e.g., about their truth conditions) do not make sense.

Just as linguistic devices affect structure, so does the discourse segmentation affect the interpretation of linguistic expressions in a discourse. Referring expressions provide the primary example of this effect. The segmentation of discourse constrains the use of referring expressions by delineating certain points at which there is a significant change in what entities are being discussed. In particular, pronouns and reduced definite noun phrases act differently within a segment than they do across segment boundaries. While discourse segmentation is not the only factor governing the use of referring expressions, it is important for capturing one of the constraints on their use. Section 2.3 contains some simple examples of the effects of segmentation on referring expressions; more detail can be found in [10].

2.2. Intentional Structure

A rather straightforward property of discourses, namely that they——or, more accurately, those who participate in them——have an overall purpose, turns out to play a fundamental role in the theory of discourse structure. In particular, some of the purposes that underlie discourses, and the discourse segments they comprise, provide the means of individuating discourses and of distinguishing coherent discourses from incoherent ones.

Although typically the participants in a discourse may have more than one aim in participating in the discourse (e.g., a story may entertain its listeners as well as describe an event; an argument may establish someone's brilliance as well as convince that some claim is true), we distinguish one of these purposes as primary to the discourse. We will refer to this particular purpose as the *discourse purpose*, or *DP*. Intuitively, this discourse purpose is the reason for engaging in this particular discourse.* For each of the discourse segments, we can also single out one intention, the *discourse segment purpose*, or *DSP*. Intuitively, the DSP says how this segment contributes to achieving the overall discourse purpose.**

Typically, an ICP will have a number of different kinds of intentions that lead to initiating a discourse. One kind of intention might include intentions to speak in a particular language or to utter particular words. Another might include intentions to amuse, or to impress. The kinds of intentions that can serve as discourse purposes or discourse segment purposes are distinguished from other intentions because they are intended to be recognized (c.f. [1], [23]), whereas other intentions are private; that is, the recognition of the DP (or DSP) is essential to its achieving its (intended) effect. Discourse purposes and discourse segment purposes share this property with certain utterance-level intentions that Grice [5] uses in defining utterance meaning.

---

*That is, both why a discourse—a linguistic act—and not some other behavior, and why the particular content of this discourse, and not some other information, is being conveyed.

**We will assume here a single DP for discourses and DSP for segments. The consequences for the theory of loosening this assumption are discussed in [10].

It is important to distinguish this property from that of being the main intention behind a discourse, a property which the discourse purpose may well not have. Some other intention might be the primary reason for the uttering of a sequence of utterances. For example, when on-stage a comedian's main intention may be to amuse. He might do this in a variety of ways. Some of these could require linguistic behavior--e.g., relate an event sequence, describe a funny object. In all of these cases the discourse purpose is the main intention that is *intended to be recognized* (e.g., the intention that the hearers' beliefs come to include some particular beliefs about the sequence of events--those told in the relating--and their relationship to one another) whereas the intention to amuse is private and need not be recognized by the audience in order for the discourse to succeed.

The range of intentions that can serve as discourse, or discourse segment, purposes is open-ended (c.f. [25], para. 23), much like the range of intentions that underlie purposeful action more generally. There is no finite list of discourse purposes, as there is of, say, syntactic categories. Thus a theory of discourse structure cannot depend on choosing the DP and DSPs from a small fixed list (as in [17], [19] or [13]), nor on the particulars of individual intentions. The particulars of individual intentions are, of course, crucial to understanding any particular discourse, but this is a different issue. What is essential for discourse structure is that such intentions bear certain kinds of structural relationships to one another. Since the conversational participants can never know the whole set of intentions that might serve as DPs and DSPs, what they must determine are the relevant structural relationships among intentions.

Two structural relationships play an important role: *dominance* and *satisfaction precedence*. An action that satisfies one intention, say DSP1, may (be intended to) provide part of the satisfaction of another, say DSP2. When this is the case, we will say that DSP1 *contributes to* DSP2; conversely, we will say that DSP2 *dominates* DSP1. For some discourses, including task-oriented ones, the order in which the DSPs are satisfied may be intended to be recognized. DSP1 *satisfaction precedes* DSP2 in the dominance hierarchy whenever its intention must be satisfied before the other.

The following are some examples of the types of intentions that could serve as DPs or DSPs, followed by one particular instance of each type.

1. intend that some agent intend to do some physical task; intend that Ruth intend to fix the flat tire.

2. intend that some agent (come to) believe some fact; intend that Ruth believe the campfire is started.

3. intend that some agent believe one fact provides support for another; intend that Ruth believe the smell of smoke supports that the campfire is started.

4. intend that some agent intend to identify an object (existing physical object, imaginary object, plan, event, event sequence); intend that Ruth intend to identify my bicycle

5. intend that some agent know some property of an object; intend that Ruth know that my bicycle has a flat tire

DPs and DSPs are basically the same sorts of intentions. Whether an intention is a DP or a DSP depends on whether it is the reason for initiating the discourse (in which case it is a DP) or its satisfaction contributes in some way to achieving this main discourse purpose (in which case it is a DSP). Any of the intentions on the preceding list could be either a DP or a DSP. Furthermore, particular instances of any one of them could contribute to another, or to a different instance of the same type. For example, the intention that someone identify some object might dominate several intentions that that person know some property of that object; likewise, the intention to get someone to believe some fact might dominate a number of contributing intentions that that person believe other facts.

2.3. Attentional State

The third component of discourse structure, the attentional state, is an abstraction of the focus of attention of the discourse participants as the discourse unfolds. It is inherently dynamic, recording the changes in what objects, properties, and relations are salient at each point in the discourse. The attentional state can be modeled by a set of *focus spaces*; changes in the attentional state are modelled by transition rules for adding and deleting spaces. The collection of focus spaces available at any one time we call the *focusing structure*, and the process of manipulating spaces is called *focusing*. A focus space is associated with each discourse segment; this space collects together representations of those entities that are salient either because they have been mentioned explicitly in the segment or because they became salient in the process of producing/comprehending the utterances in the segment. The focus space also includes the discourse segment purpose; the inclusion of the purpose reflects the fact that the conversational participants are focused on not only what they are talking about but also why they are talking about it.

Figure 2-1 illustrates how the focusing structure serves to coordinate the linguistic and intentional structures, as well as capturing the attentional state. The discourse segments (on the left of the figure) are tied to focus spaces (in the middle of the figure). The focusing structure is a stack. We illustrate that stack in Figure 2-1 with a pointer between individual focus spaces. Information in each space is accessible to other spaces higher in the stack unless otherwise notated with a hash line.

The stacking of the focus spaces shown reflects the relative salience of the entities in each space during the corresponding segment's portion of the discourse. The stack relationships arise from the ways in which the various DSPs relate, information captured in the hierarchy of DSPs (depicted on the right in the figure). The depiction of spaces shown in the figure is a static representation of what results from a sequence of operations such as pushes onto and pops from a stack. A push occurs when the DSP for a new segment contributes to the DSP for the immediately preceding segment. When the DSP contributes to some intention higher in the DSP hierarchy, some number of focus spaces are "popped" from the stack before inserting the new one.

Part one of figure 2-1 shows the state of focusing when the paragraph P2 is being processed. Paragraph P1 gave rise to FS1 and had as its discourse purpose DP$_1$. The properties, objects, relations and purpose

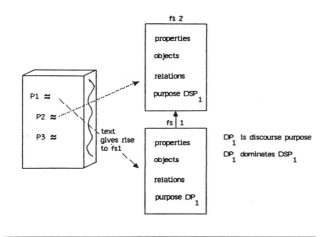

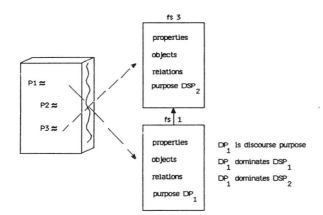

Figure 2-1:   Discourse segments, focus spaces
and purpose hierarchy.

represented in FS1 are accessible but less salient than those in FS2. P2 yields a focus space that is stacked relative to FS1 because DP_1 in FS1 dominates P2's DSP, DSP_1. As a result of the relationship between FS1 and FS2, reduced noun phrases will be interpreted differently in P2 than in P1. For example, if some red balls exist in the world and are represented in both FS2 and FS1, "the red ball" used in P2 will be understood to mean that red ball that is represented in FS2. If, however, there is a green truck and it is represented only in FS1, "the green truck" occurring in P2 will be understood as that green truck.

Part two of figure 2-1 shows the state of focusing when paragraph P3 is processed. Because the DSP of FS3, DSP_2, is dominated only by DP_1 and not by DSP_1, FS2 has been popped from the stack, and FS3 has been pushed on.

Two essential properties of the focusing structure are now clear. First, the focusing structure is parasitic on the intentional structure. The relationship among DSPs determines pushes and pops. Note however, that which operation is relevant may sometimes be indicated

in the language itself. For example, the clue word "first" indicates the start of a segment whose DSP contributes to the DSP of the previous segment. Second, the focusing structure, like the intentional and linguistic structures, evolves as the discourse proceeds. None of them exists a priori[***].

The discussion here should also clarify some misinterpretations of focus-space diagrams and task structure in [6], [8]. The focus-space hierarchies in that work are best seen as special cases of the attentional state, and the task structure as a special case of the intentional structure we stipulate in this paper. Several researchers (e.g., Linde and Goguen [11], Reichman [17]) misinterpreted the original research in an unfortunate (and unintended) way--they took the focus-space hierarchy to include (or be identical with) the task structure. The conflation of these two structures forces a single structure to contain information about attentional state and intentional relationships. It prevents a theory from adequately accounting for certain aspects of discourse, including interruptions (see Section 3).

A second confusion was that the task-structure is necessarily a prebuilt tree. Taking the task-structure to be a special case of intentional structure makes it clear that the tree structure is simply a more constrained structure than one might require for other discourses; the nature of the task that generates a task-oriented discourse has both dominance and ordering relations,[****] while other discourses may not have significant ordering constraints among the DSPs. Furthermore there has never been reason to assume that the task structures in task-oriented dialogues are pre-built. Rather the task of discourse theory is to explain how the hearer builds up a task structure using information conveyed in the discourse.

Figure 2-1 illustrates some fundamental distinctions between the intentional and attentional aspects of discourse structure. First, the DP hierarchy provides, among other things, a complete record of the discourse-level intentions and their dominance (and, where relevant, precedence) relations, whereas the focusing structure at any one time can contain only information relevant to a single branch of the hierarchy. Second, at the conclusion of a discourse, if the discourse completes normally, the focus stack will be empty while the DP hierarchy will be fully constructed. Third, when the discourse is being processed, only the attentional state can directly constrain the interpretation of referring expressions.

It is possible to confuse the DSP with the notion of

[***]Although there are some rare cases in which one conversational participant has a complete plan for the whole discourse prior to uttering a single word, much more typically, the DSP hierarchy is constructed as the conversational participants create the discourse and need not exist prior to it. It may be more obvious this is true for speakers and hearers of spoken discourse than for readers and writers of texts, but in fact even for the writer, the DSP hierarchy is often developed as the text is written.

[****]Even in the task case the orderings may be partial. In fact, the systems built for task-oriented dialogues ([18], [24]) did not use a prebuilt tree, but constructed the tree—based on a partially-ordered model—only as a particular discourse evolved.

center [9]. The DSP and center differ in two ways. First, the center is an element only of the attentional state, whereas the DSP plays a role in both the attentional and intentional structures. Second, the center may shift within a discourse segment (it almost always shifts across segment boundaries); the DSP does not: a change in DSP is what underlies a segment boundary. Although in some cases the intention that is the DSP may be the object that is the center, more typically these do not coincide.

In short, the focusing structure is the central repository for the contextual information needed to process utterances at each point in the discourse. It contains those objects, properties, and relations most salient at that point——distinguishing the center from others——and also contains links to those parts of the linguistic structure and the intentional structure that are relevant. The ability to identify relevant discourse segments, the entities they make salient, and their DSPs becomes especially important as the amount of information grows over the course of a discourse.

3. Application of the Theory: Interruptions

Interruptions in discourses provide an important test of any theory of discourse structure. Because processing an utterance requires figuring out how it fits with previous discourse, it is crucial to figure out which parts of the previous discourse are relevant to it, and which cannot be. Thus, the treatment of interruptions has implications for the treatment of the normal flow of discourse. Interruptions may take many forms——some are not at all relevant to the main flow of the discourse, others are quite relevant, and many fall somewhere inbetween these extremes. A theory must differentiate these cases and explain (among other things) what connections there are between the main discourse and the interruption and how the relationship between them affects the processing of the utterances in both.

The importance of distinguishing between intentional structure and attentional state is evident in the first three examples we consider in this section. The distinction also permits us to explain a type of behavior considered by others to be similar——so-called semantic returns——an issue we consider at the end of the section.

The three examples that follow do not exhaust the types of interruptions that can occur in discourse. There are additional ways to vary the explicit linguistic and nonlinguistic indicators used to indicate boundaries, the relations among DSPs, and the combinations of focus-space relationships present. These examples illustrate interruptions that fall at different points on the spectrum of relevancy to the main discourse. They can be explained more adequately by the theory of discourse structure given here than by previous theories, and hence provide evidence for the necessity of the distinctions we have drawn.

3.1. Type 1: True Interruptions

The first kind of interruption is the true interruption, a discourse segment whose purpose is distinct from the purpose of the discourse in which it is embedded. In the example below, from [15], there are two (separate) discourses, D1 indicated in normal type, and D2 in italics.

John came by
and left the groceries
Stop that

you kids
and I put them away
after he left

These two discourses have distinct purposes and convey different information about properties, objects, and relations. Since D2 is embedded within D1, one expects the discourse structures for the two segments to be somehow embedded as well. The theory described in this paper differs from Polanyi and Scha's [14] (and other more radically different proposals as well; e.g., [17], [4]; [11]) in that the embedding occurs *only* in the attentional structure: the focus space for D2 is pushed onto the stack, above (i.e., as more salient than) the focus space for D1, until D2 is completed, as shown in Figure 3-1. The intentional structures for the two segments are distinct. There are two DP/DSP structures for the utterances in this sequence. It is not necessary to relate these two——and indeed intuitively they are not related.

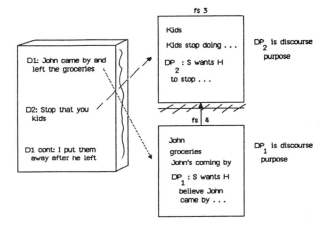

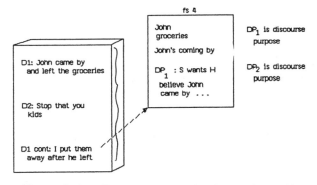

Figure 3-1:   The structures of a true interruption.

The focusing structure for true interruptions is different from that for the normal embedding of segments, in that the focusing boundary between the discourse in progress and the interruption is non-penetrable (depicted with a hashed line between focus spaces). The boundary between the focus spaces prevents entities in the one from being available to the other. Because the second discourse totally shifts attention to a new purpose (and may shift who the intended hearers are), the speaker cannot use referential expressions in it that depend on the accessibility of entities from the first discourse. Because the boundary between the focus space for D1 and that for D2 is non-penetrable, if D2 were to include an utterance like, "put them away", the word "them" would have to refer to something deictically present, and could not be used to refer anaphorically to the groceries.

As the discourse stands however, D1 is resumed almost immediately. The word "them" in "and I put them away" cannot refer to the kids,***** but only to the groceries. The focus space for D2 has been popped from the stack. Note for this to be clear to the hearer, the speaker must indicate a return to D1 explicitly. Two indicators of the "stop that" interruption are assumed to have been present at the time of the discourse—a change of intonation and a change of eye gaze. The linguistic indicators are the change of mood to an indicative, and the use of the vocative [16].

Unlike previous accounts, the theory is not forced to integrate these two discourses in terms of a single grammatical structure, nor must the theory provide answers to questions about the specific relationship between segments D2 and D1, as in [14] . Instead, the intuition readers have of an embedding in the discourse structure is captured in the attentional state by the stacking of focus spaces, which thus accounts for the manner in which the utterances are processed. Further, what is intuitively distinct about the two segments is captured in their different intentional (DP/DSP) structures.

3.2. Type 2: Flashbacks and Filling in missing pieces

Sometimes a speaker interrupts his or her own flow of discussion because some purposes, propositions or entities need to be brought into the discourse but have not been: the speaker forgot to include those entities first, and now must go back and fill in the missing information. A flashback or a filler segment results at that point in the discourse. These segments contain additional DSPs that must be satisfied before the current DSP can be. This type of interruption differs from true interruptions in several ways: the DSP for the flashback or filler bears some relationship to the DP for the whole discourse, even though it may not have a close relationship to the DSP of the current segment or to any of the DSPs dominating the current DSP; the linguistic indicator of the flashback or filler typically includes a comment about something going wrong; and the audience always remains the same.

In the example below, from [21], the speaker is instructing a mock-up system, played by a person, about how to define and display some knowledge-representation information. Again, the interruption is indicated by italics.

OK. Now how do I say that Bill is
Woops I forgot about ABC.
I need an indivdual concept for the company ABC

...[remainder of discourse segment on ABC]...

*****Because this is so clearly the case on other grounds, the segment boundary is clear even to a reader after the fact.

Now back to Bill. How do I say that Bill is an employee of ABC?

The DP for the whole larger discourse from which this sequence was taken is to provide information about various companies (including ABC) and their employees. The outer segment in this example--*D-Bill*--has a DSP--*DSP-Bill*--to tell about Bill, while the inner segment--*D-ABC*--has a DSP--*DSP-ABC*--to convey certain information about ABC. Because of the nature of the information being told, there is order to the final structure of the DP/DSPs: information about ABC must be conveyed before all of the information about Bill can be. The speaker in this instance does not realize this constraint until after he begins. The "flashback" interruption allows him to satisfy DSP-ABC while suspending satisfaction of DSP-Bill (which he then resumes). Hence, as shown in Figure 3-2, there is an intentional structure rooted at DP and with DSP-ABC and DSP-Bill as <u>ordered</u> sister nodes.

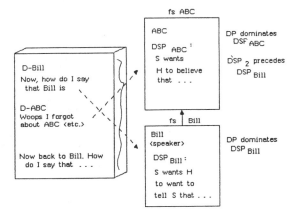

Figure 3-2:   The structures of a flashback.

The available linguistic data permit two possible attentional states as appropriate models for flashback-type interruptions. The simpler model has a focusing structure identical to the one that would ensue if the flashback segment were a normally embedded segment, as depicted in Figure 3-2. The focus space for the flashback--*FS-ABC*--is pushed onto the stack above the focus space for the outer segment--*FS-Bill*, and all of the entities in both focus spaces are normally accessible for reference. The more complex model uses an auxiliary stack. FS-Bill (and possibly some additional spaces) are put onto the auxiliary stack for the duration of the interruption. After an explicit indication that there is a return to work on DSP-Bill (e.g., the "Now back to Bill" used in this example), any focus spaces left on the stack from the flashback are popped off, and all spaces on the auxiliary stack (including FS-Bill) are returned to the main stack.

The major difference between these two models is that the first allows entities relevant to the interrupted material to be accessible during the interruption whereas in the second they are not. Which model is correct depends on whether in the embedded segment (D-ABC) the speaker can refer to Bill or other entities in FS-Bill using less than full definite descriptions.

Because the use of pronouns seems to be connected much more with centering than with focus space boundaries, the appropriateness of pronominal reference to Bill ("he") is not an adequate test; as a result the current example--is not an adequate test--and other data available--do not indicate a clear choice between these models. However, the explicit return to D-Bill in this example suggests the more complex model is needed.

This kind of interruption is distinct from true interruptions because there is a connection, although indirect, between the DSPs for the two segments. Further the linguistic markers of the start of the interruption indicate that there is a precedence relation between these DSPs (and hence the need for the correction). Flashbacks are also distinct from normally embedded discourses by the precedence relationship between the DSPs for the two segments, and the order in which the segments occur. The second attentional model further distinguishes flashbacks from normal discourse because it provides for information being saved but not accessible (in the auxiliary stack) during the interruption.

3.3. Type 3: Digressions

The third type of interruption we consider, which we call a digression, is a segment that is linked to the segment it interrupts by some entity that is salient in both, but that has a DSP unrelated to the DP to which the interrupted segment's DSP contributes. For example, if while discussing Bill's role in company ABC, one conversational participant interrupts with, "Speaking of Bill, that reminds me, he came to dinner last week," Bill remains salient, but the DSP changes. The salient object on which the digression is based might be the DSP, but more typically is some object, relation, or property in the focus space for the interrupted segment. A typical means of beginning such digressions are phrases like "speaking of John" and "that reminds me."

In processing digressions, the DSP for the digression forms the base of a separate intentional structure just as in the case of true interruptions. A new focus space is formed and pushed onto the stack, but it contains at least one--and possibly other--entities from the interrupted segment's focus space. Like the flashback-type interruption, the digression usually must be closed with an explicit closing utterance such as "getting back to ABC..."

3.4. Noninterruptions--"semantic returns"

One case of discourse behavior which we must distinguish are the so-called "semantic returns" discussed by Polanyi and Scha [16]. In all the interruptions we have considered there is a need to pop the stack when the interruption is over, and the main flow of the discourse is resumed. The focus space for the interrupted segment is "returned to." In the semantic return case, entities and DSPs previously salient are taken up once again, but they are explicitly reintroduced. The state of the focus stack is not a factor in constraining such "returns." For example, suppose yesterday two people had discussed how badly Jack behaved at the party, and then today one says "Remember our discussion about Jack at the party? Well, a lot of other people thought he acted just as badly as we thought he did." The utterances today call up, or return to, yesterday's conversation through the intention that more be said about Jack's poor behavior, but the return is not a return to a previous focus space.

Anything that can be talked about once, can be talked about again later. However, if there is no focus space on the stack corresponding to the segment and DSP being discussed further, then, as Polanyi and Scha [16] point out, there is no popping of the stack. The separation of attentional state and intentional structure makes clear what is occurring in such cases, and the intuitions that lie behind the use of the term "semantic return." In re-introducing some entities from a previous discourse, conversational participants are establishing some connection between the DSP of the new segment and the intentional structure of the original discourse. It it not a return to a previous focus space because the focus space is gone from the stack and the items to be referred to must be explicitly re-established. It is a return, at least in some sense, to a previous intentional structure.

4. Conclusions and Future Research

The theory of discourse structure presented in this paper generalizes from theories of task-oriented dialogues. It differs from previous generalizations in carefully distinguishing three components of discourse structure--one linguistic, one intentional, and one attentional. The distinctions are crucial for an explanation of interruptions, clue words, and referring expressions.

The particular intentional structure used also differs from the analogous aspect of previous generalizations. Although, like them it provides the backbone for the discourse segmentation and determines structural relationships for the focusing structure (part of the attentional state), unlike them it does not depend on the particular details of any single domain or discourse-type.

Although (obviously) not complete, the theory provides a solid basis for investigating not only discourse structure, but also discourse meaning, and for constructing discourse-processing systems. Several difficult research problems remain to be addressed. Of these, we take the following two to be of primary importance:

1. What is the relationship between discourse-level (DP/DSP) and utterance-level (speech acts) intentions?

2. What information do discourse participants use to recognize these intentions, and how do they do it?

Finally, the theory suggests two important conjectures. First, that a discourse is coherent only when its discourse purpose is shared among the conversational participants, and when each of the utterances of the discourse contributes to achieving this purpose, either directly or indirectly by contributing to the satisfaction of a discourse segment purpose. Second, that the notion of "topic" is primarily an intentional notion; it is best seen as referring to the DP, and DSPs. Previous discussions of the "topic" of an utterance or discourse have been confused because uses of the term "topic" have variously referred to notions that are essentially syntactic (e.g., the "wa" marking in Japanese; surface subject in English), attentional (the center of an utterance), and intentional (the DSP of a segment).

Acknowledgments

The research reported in this paper has been made

possible by a gift from the System Development Foundation, and by a grant from the Defense Advanced Research Project Agency under contract N00014−77−C−0378.

References

[1]   Allen, J.F., and Perrault, C.R.
       Analyzing intention in dialogues.
       Artificial Intelligence 15(3):143−178, 1980.

[2]   Allen, J.F.
       Recognizing Intentions from Natural Language
           Utterances.
       In M. Brady and R.C. Berwick (editors),
           Computational Models of Discourse, pages
           107−166.Massachusetts Institute Technology
           Press, 1983.

[3]   Cohen, P.R. and Levesque, H.L.
       Speech Acts and the Recognition of Shared Plans.
       In *Proc. of the Third Biennial Conference*, pages
           263−271. Canadian Society for Computational
           Studies of Intelligence, Canadian Society for
           Computational Studies of Intelligence, Victoria,
           B. C., May, 1980.

[4]   Cohen, R.
       *A Computational Model for the Analysis of
           Arguments.*
       Technical Report CSRG−151, Computer Systems
           Research Group, University of Toronto,
           October, 1983.

[5]   Grice, H.P.
       Utterer's Meaning and Intentions.
       Philosophical Review 68(2):147−177, 1969.

[6]   Grosz, B.J.
       Discourse Analysis.
       In D. Walker (editor), *Understanding Spoken
           Language*, chapter IX, pages 235−268.Elsevier
           North−Holland, New York City, 1978.

[7]   Grosz, B.J.
       Focusing in Dialog.
       In *Theoretical Issues in Natural Language
           Processing−2*, pages 96−103. The Association
           for Computational Linguistics, University of
           Illinois at Urbana−Champaign, July, 1978.

[8]   Grosz, B.J.
       Focusing and Description in Natural Language
           Dialogues.
       In A. Joshi, B. Webber, I. Sag (editors), *Elements of
           Discourse Understanding*, pages
           84−105.Cambridge University Press, 1981.

[9]   Grosz, B.J., Joshi, A.K., Weinstein, S.
       Providing a Unified Account of Definite Noun
           Phrases in Discourse.
       In *Proceedings of the 21st Annual Meeting of the
           Association for Computational Linguistics.*
           Association for Computational Linguistics, June,
           1983.

[10]   Grosz, B.J. and Sidner, C.L.
       The Structures of Discourse Structure.
       In *Discourse Structure.*Ablex Publishers, 1986.

[11]   Linde, C. and Goguen, J.
       Structure of Planning Discourse.
       J. Social Biol. Struct. 1:219−251, 1978.

[12]   Linde, C.
       Focus of Attention and the Choice of Pronouns in
           Discourse.
       In T. Givon (editor), *Syntax and Semantics, Vol.
           12 of Discourse and Syntax*, pages
           337−354.Academic Press, Inc., 1979.

[13]   Mann, W.C. and Thompson, S.A.
       Relational Propositions in Discourse.
       Technical Report Information Sciences Institute−
           RR−83−115, Information Sciences Institute,
           November, 1983.

[14]   Polanyi, L. and Scha, R.
       A Syntactic Approach to Discourse Semantics.
       In *Proceedings of Int'l. Conference on
           Computational Linguistics.* Stanford
           University, Stanford, CA, 1984.

[15]   Polanyi, L. and Scha, R.
       A Model of Natural Language Discourse.
       In *Discourse Structure.*Ablex Publishers, 1986.

[16]   Polanyi, L., and Scha, R. J. H.
       On the Recursive Structure of Discourse.
       In *Proceedings of the January 1982 Symposium on
           Connectedness in Sentence, Text, and
           Discourse.* The Catholic University of Tilsburg,
           Tilsburg, The Netherlands, 1983.
       In press.

[17]   Reichman−Adar, R.
       Extended Person−Machine Interface.
       Artificial Intelligence 22(2):157−218, March, 1984.

[18]   Robinson, A.
       Interpreting verb phrase references in dialogs.
       In *Proceedings of the Third Biennial Conference
           of the Canadian Society for Computational
           Studies of Intelligence.* Victoria, May, 1980.

[19]   Schank, R.C., Collins, G.C., Davis, E., Johnson, P.N.,
           Lytinen, S., Reiser, B.J.
       What's the Point?
       Cognitive Science 6(3):255−275, July−September,
           1982.

[20]   Sidner, C.L., and Israel, D.J.
       Recognizing intended meaning and speaker's
           plans.
       In *Proceedings of the International Joint
           Conference in Artificial Intelligence*, pages
           203−208. IJCAI, IJCAI, Vancouver, B.C., August,
           1981.

[21]   Sidner, C.L.
       *Protocols of Users Manipulating Visually
           Presented Information with Natural Language.*
       Technical Report 5128, Bolt Beranek and Newman
           Inc., September, 1982.

[22]   Sidner, C.L.
       What the Speaker Means: The Recognition of
           Speakers' Plans in Discourse.
       Computers and Mathematics with Applications 9(1),
           1983.
       Special Issue on Computational Linguistics − Nick
           Cercone, guest editor.

[23]   Sidner, C.L.
       Plan parsing for intended response recognition in
           discourse.
       Computational Intelligence 1(1):1−10, February,
           1985.

[24]   Walker, D.
       Understanding Spoken Language.
       Elsevier North−Holland, New York City, 1978.

[25]   Wittgenstein,L.
       Philosophical Investigations.
       Oxford Press, 1953.

EVALUATING IMPORTANCE: A STEP TOWARDS TEXT SUMMARIZATION

Danilo Fum[*], Giovanni Guida[†], Carlo Tasso[‡]
Istituto di Matematica, Informatica e Sistemistica
Università di Udine
Udine, Italy

ABSTRACT

The paper deals with the problem of evaluating importance of descriptive texts and proposes a procedural, rule-based approach which is implemented in a prototype experimental system operating in the specific domain of text summarization. Importance evaluation is performed through a set of rules which are used to assign importance values to the different parts of a text and to resolve or explain conflicting evaluations. The system utilizes world knowledge on the subject domain contained in an encyclopedia and takes into account a goal assigned by the user for specifying the pragmatic aspects of the understanding activity. In the paper some examples of the system operation are presented by following the evaluation of a small sample text.

INTRODUCTION

Understanding a written text is a complex process that exploits different capabilities including, among others, linguistic competence, common sense reasoning, and domain specific inference. This process can be divided into three main activities (Fum, Guida, and Tasso, 1984a):

1. understanding the literal meaning of every single sentence of the text (including reference, quantification, and time);

2. inferring and expliciting the macro-structure of the text that accounts for its global meaning and organization (including coherence, rhetoric, and stylistic relations);

3. evaluating the relative importance of the different conceptual units that constitute the text.

In recent years we have been working at developing a system (SUSY - a SUmmarizing SYstem) that can show some basic capabilities in performing

----

(*) also with: Laboratorio di Psicologia E.E., Universita' di Trieste, Trieste, Italy
(†) also with: Milan Polytechnic Artificial Intelligence Project, Milano, Italy
(‡) also with: CISM - International Center for Mechanical Sciences, Udine, Italy

the above mentioned activities in the specific domain of descriptive text summarization (Fum, Guida, and Tasso, 1982). In this paper we focus on the third activity only, namely importance evaluation, and we discuss the basic features and mode of operation of a module of the SUSY system devoted to this task.

The topic of importance evaluation has been dealt with, although often only in a quite indirect way, by several authors and in many different contexts. A conceptual unit of a text can be considered important in relation to other units according to several criteria that include, among others, relevance for explaining discourse coherence (Kintsch and van Dijk, 1978; Hobbs, 1982), relation to the topic (Lehnert, 1982) or topic-focus articulation (Hajičova' and Sgall, 1984) of the text, reference to semantically relevant concepts in the subject domain (Schank, 1979; van Dijk and Kintsch, 1983), relevance to a given goal (Fum, Guida, and Tasso, 1982).

In the paper we propose a new approach to importance evaluation (Fum, Guida, and Tasso, 1985) that integrates the above mentioned points of view into a unitary and flexible framework.

A RULE-BASED APPROACH

Two basic kinds of knowledge are involved in the process of evaluating importance in a text:

- linguistic knowledge, that makes possible to understand the meaning and structure of the text;

- world knowledge (including both common sense and domain specific knowledge) that is used for reasoning and inferencing.

In addition to this knowledge, we may assume that importance evaluation always relies on the (explicit or implicit) consideration of a goal. Furthermore, whenever the goal with which a text is read changes, the parts of the text that are judged important vary accordingly. Finally, knowledge about how to use linguistic knowledge, world knowledge, and goals in the process of importance evaluation, i.e. the criteria on which humans ground their judgment capabilities, has a crucial role too.

The complexity and expanse of knowledge involved in importance evaluation and the multifaceted nature of the processes that underly it, strongly suggest to resort to the powerful techniques offered by the rule-based system approach. In fact, the concept of importance seems to escape a simple, explicit, algorithmic definition. A procedural, knowledge-based approach comprising a set of rules that can assign relative importance values to the different conceptual units of a text seems more viable. This standpoint can supply the conceptual and computational tools needed for taking into account in a flexible and natural way the variety of knowledge sources and processing activities that are involved in importance evaluation. Moreover, it is expected to be well founded from a cognitive point of view (Anderson, 1976), as it allows close and transparent modeling of several processes that occur in human mind.

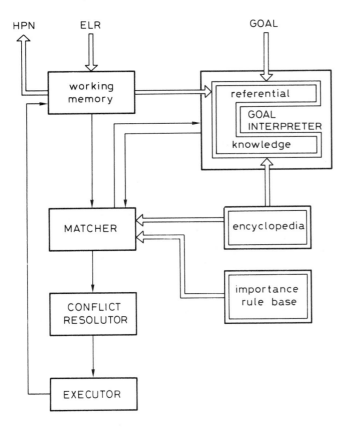

Figure 1 - Basic architecture of the evaluator.

On the basis of the above analysis, a prototype implementation of an experimental system, called importance evaluator, has been developed. This system is a functional module of SUSY and concentrates on the importance evaluation task only. It receives in input the internal representation of a natural language text (supplied by another SUSY module, namely the parser) expressed in the ELR (Extended Linear Representation) formalism (Fum, Guida, and Tasso,

1984b), and produces in output a new representation called HPN (Hierarchical Propositional Network). In HPN integer importance values are assigned to the basic conceptual units of the ELR (concepts and propositions), in such a way as to account for the different importance of the constituents of the text. Moreover, the importance evaluator takes in input an explicit, declarative representation of a goal to be considered for its own activity.

The overall architecture of the evaluator is shown in Figure 1. It features a core rule-based structure with a forward-chaining control regime that includes a specialized module, namely the goal interpreter, devoted to make it fit the specific task of importance evaluation.
Two main knowledge bases are available to the evaluator:

1. the importance rule base, that contains knowledge (mostly of empiric nature) on the mechanisms that are supposed to be used by man in evaluating importance, expressed through IF-THEN production rules;

2. the encyclopedia, that contains specific world knowledge on the subject domain (mostly of structured, taxonomic, descriptive nature), represented through a network of frames.

The importance rule base includes several classes of rules:

- referential-structural (RS) rules that derive importance values from the structure of references among conceptual units of the text, taking into account, for example, concepts referenced in several propositions, propositions embedded into others, etc.;

- rhetoric-structural (TS) rules, that take into account the overall argumentational and stylistic organization of the text and derive importance relations from rhetoric-predicates of the ELR;

- structural-semantic (SS) rules, that rely on the analysis of some specific structural features of the text that have a definite semantic role, such as ISA relations, macro-predicates of the ELR, etc.;

- semantic-encyclopedic (SE) rules, that refer to world knowledge contained in the encyclopedia concerning the specific subject domain dealt with by the text under consideration;

- explicit evaluation (EE) rules, that rely on explicit statements concerning importance evaluation that sometimes are purposely inserted in the text by the author in order to make reading and understanding easier;

- meta (MT) rules, that embody higher-level knowledge that concern reasoning about importance rules and that are used by the system mainly for solving conflicts between rule applications, i.e. for deciding which rule to use first among several applicable ones, or which rule to trust among several conflicting ones.

The IF-part of a rule contains conditions that are evaluated with respect to the current HPN (initially the ELR) contained in the working memory. The THEN-part specifies either an importance evaluation or an action to be performed to further the analysis (e.g., a strategic choice concerning rule activation, a criterion to solve conflicting evaluations, the activation of a frame of the encyclopedia, etc.).
The evaluation of importance contained in the THEN-part of a rule takes usually the form of an ordering relation among importance values of concepts or propositions of the ELR, or it specifies ranges of importance values (VERY HIGH, HIGH, MEDIUM, LOW, VERY LOW). Thus, rules only assert relative importance of different parts of the text: a constraint propagation algorithm will eventually transform these relative evaluations into absolute importance values according to a given scale, after the evaluator has terminated its activity.

The encyclopedia is the second knowledge source employed by the evaluator and it contains domain specific knowledge. Encyclopedic knowledge is represented through a net of frames. Frames embody, in addition to a header, two kinds of slots:

- knowledge slots, that contain domain specific knowledge, represented in a form homogeneous with the propositional language of the ELR;

- reference slots, containing pointers to other frames that deal with related topics in the subject domain.

The operation of the evaluator obeys the basic recognize-act cycle shown below:

```
INITIALIZE working memory with ELR
CYCLE
    matcher activation
    MATCH the current working memory
        WITH the LHS of importance rules
            IF    the LHS of the considered rule
                  refers to the goal
            THEN  activate goal the interpreter
        DETERMINE the set of all applicable rules
            IF    this set is empty
            THEN  EXIT CYCLE
    conflict resolution activation
    SELECT the rule to be applied next
    executor activation
    EXECUTE the RHS of the selected rule and update
            the working memory
END CYCLE
```

The above non-deterministic program deviates from the usual recognize-act cycle of a rule-based system because of the novel structure of the matcher that can invoke the goal interpreter whenever the goal is mentioned in a rule.

The goal is a chunk of variable knowledge expressed in a specific goal definition language (GDL). It is assigned by the user taking into account the pragmatic aspects of the understanding activity, and it defines the motivations and objectives that are behind the reading process. The role of the goal is twofold:

- exerting control on the activation of importance rules that operate on the working memory, thus allowing implementation of evaluation mechanisms triggered by the current goal (goal-directed evaluation);

- enabling the evaluator to choose from the encyclopedia the pieces of knowledge which are expected to be relevant to the current importance evaluation activity, thus allowing the same pieces of world knowledge to be used differently in different situations according to the current goal (selective focusing).

The specific way in which the goal influences operation of the matcher is determined by the goal interpreter. The motivation for having an interpreter for this activity can be found in the diversity between the language utilized by the user for stating a goal (the GDL) and the language in which the content of the text and the encyclopedia are represented (the ELR formalism) that does not allow a direct and meaningful matching between pieces of knowledge expressed in these two languages. To this purpose the goal interpreter must have at its disposal an explicit representation of the semantic relationships existing between the worlds of the user goals and the knowledge on the subject domain. This additional knowledge is called referential knowledge as it can relate goals to specific topics in the subject domain. It takes the form of a network of conceptual chunks of knowledge (in the most usual cases, simple concepts) whose entry nodes represent items in the goal world and whose terminal nodes directly refer to frames of the encyclopedia or conceptual units of the ELR. The task of the goal interpreter is that of skillfully navigating in this network to find out the relevant relationships between the current goal and parts of the encyclopedia and HPN according to the conditions stated in the LHS of the rule being currently processed by the matcher.

The goal interpreter serves two basic functions that have a crucial role in the global architecture of the system. First, it allows to implement the encyclopedia without bothering of importance: no a-priori evaluation of importance is contained in it and full responsibility about importance evaluation is left to the rules. Second, it clearly separates the representation of world knowledge contained in the encyclopedia from the representation of goals, thus making any possible extension of the GDL easy and feasible without the need for restructuring knowledge in the encyclopedia.

THE IMPORTANCE EVALUATOR AT WORK

In this section we illustrate through the analysis of a sample text some of the most basic mechanisms of operation of the importance evaluator. The current prototype version of the evaluator (Fum, Guida, and Tasso, 1985) operates on scientific and technical computer science literature on operating systems. It contains about 40 importance rules and it comprises a small encyclopedia of about 30 frames. The goal definition language has been assigned a very simple structure: it allows to logically combine key-terms chosen in a predefinite vocabulary, that represent possible points of view of a reader (e.g., KNOW, USE, BUY, EVALUATE PERFORMANCE, etc.).

Let us consider the following fragment of a sample text:

"... An operating system is constituted by a set of programs which are used to monitor the execution of the user programs and the use of resources. One of the main reasons for utilizing operating systems is that they allow several processes to run at the same time. ..."

The ELR representation of the first sentence of this text is:

```
    010 CONSTITUTE (VV1, OP-SYSTEM, P)
    020 *PROGRAM (VV1)
    030 USE-FOR (NIL, VV1, 40, P)
  035 MACRO-GOAL (40, 30)
    040 MONITOR (VV1, 50, P)
    050 AND (60, 80)
    060 EXECUTE (NIL, VV2)
    070 *USER-PROGRAM (VV2)
    080 USE (NIL, VV3)
    090 *RESOURCE (VV3)
```

The importance evaluator usually tries to apply referential-structural rules first. An example of an RS rule is:

Rule RS4 - Highly Referenced Concept:
  IF   there is a concept X which is at least
       K-referenced
  THEN set w(X) = high.

This rule guesses that a concept which is highly referenced in a text is probably important. In our example (where the parameter K is set equal to 5), the concept OP-SYSTEM is considered important as it is highly referenced in the ELR of the complete text.

After rule RS4 has been applied, the following structural-semantic rule can fire:

Rule SS5 - Definitional Predicate:
  IF   there is a proposition   P A(... X ...)
       such that A ISA DEFINITIONAL,
       X is the 'definiendum' of A,
       w(X) >= high
  THEN set w(P) = w(X).

Predicates of type DEFINITIONAL are used to describe the nature, properties, or essential qualities of a concept (e.g., DEFINE, EQUAL, CONSTITUTE, FORM, etc.). Rule SS5 conveys the idea that a proposition which defines a concept that is considered important inherits the importance value assigned to that concept. As a result of the application of this rule, proposition 10 receives the importance value w(10) = high.

After rule SS5 has been triggered, the following rule can fire:

Rule SS2 - ISA Proposition Extension:
  IF   there is a proposition P A(X)
       such that X ISA A,
       the argument X of A appears in another
       proposition Q B(... X ...) with importance
       value w(Q) >= high
  THEN set w(P) = w(Q).

This rule says that the proposition which specifies the type to which a concept contained in another important proposition belongs (ISA relation), is also important. In our example, proposition 20, which states that the variable VV1 represents a concept of type PROGRAM, receives the same importance value as proposition 10, i.e. w(20) = high.

It is interesting to note that the same result (i.e., w(20) = high) can be obtained, if we assume the current goal KNOW, through the successive application of rules SS6 and SS7. Let us examine both of them:

Rule SS6 - Goal-Directed Definitional Predicate:
  IF   there is a proposition P A(... X ... Y ...)
       such that A ISA DEFINITIONAL,
       X is the 'definiendum' of A,
       Y is the 'definiens' of A,
       w(X) >= high,
       the current goal is KNOW
  THEN set w(Y) = w(X).

Rule SS7 - ISA Proposition:
  IF   there is a proposition P A(X)
       such that X ISA A,
       X has importance value w(X)
  THEN set w(P) = w(X).

Rule SS6 shows a case of goal-directed evaluation. The rule says that if the current goal is to know something about a concept which is important, the concept which is used to define it to be considered important too. In our example, w(VV1) is set to high. This allows, in turn, application of rule SS7 which asserts that a proposition stating an ISA relation about an important concept is important too. Thus w(20) = high.

Propositions 30 and 40 receive a low importance value by the application of the following rule:

Rule SS12 - USE Propositional Inference:
  IF   there exist propositions   P A(NIL ... X ...)
                                   M MACRO-GOAL(P, Q)
                                   Q B(... X ...)

       such that A ISA USE,
                 X is the 'object' of A,
                 Q ISA ACT,

                    X is the 'agent' of B
THEN set w(P) = low, w(M) = low, w(Q) > low.

Rule SS12 implements a case of propositional inference (Graesser, 1981) that asserts that if something is used to do a certain action then it does that action, and only this is what matters.

Using the result previously obtained through rule RS4 (i.e., w(OP-SYSTEM) = high), we can now apply rule SE3:

Rule SE3 - Definitional Frame Activation:
  IF   there is a proposition   P A(... X ...)
        such that X ISA DEFINITIONAL,
        X is the 'definiendum' of A,
        w(X) >= high,
        X is the header of a frame F
  THEN activate F.

The idea on which SE3 is grounded is that, in order to understand a segment of text defining a concept which is judged important, it is necessary to have available the encyclopedic knowledge related to that concept, i.e., in our example, to activate the OP-SYSTEM frame. Note that rule SE3 does not directly state whether a proposition or a concept has to be considered important or not, but it specifies which frames are to be considered relevant to the current context. The mechanism of frame activation is commonly used in the operation of the evaluator. It models the well-known phenomenon of spreading activation that automatically occurs in human cognitive processes (Anderson, 1976).

In order to examine the use of the frame OP-SYSTEM above activated, let us introduce now the ELR of the second sentence of our sample text:

        100 MAIN (VV4, P)
        110 *REASON (VV4)
        120 *VV4 (V5)
        130 EQUAL (V5, 160, P)
        140 REASON-FOR (160, 150, P)
    145 MACRO-RESULT (160, 150)
        150 USE (NIL, OP-SYSTEM)
        160 ALLOW (OP-SYSTEM, 170, P)
        170 RUN (VV6)
        180 *PROCESS (VV6)
        190 SEVERAL (VV6, P)
        200 SIMULTANEOUSLY (170, P)

We can now apply the following rule:

Rule SE25 - Goal-Directed Matching:
  IF   there are propositions P1,...,Pn that match
        a pattern of a knowledge slot K of an
        active frame F,
        the current goal matches K
  THEN set w(P1) = ... = w(Pn) = high.

This rule states that if a piece of the ELR contained in the working memory matches the content of a knowledge slot of an active frame and the goal interpreter can relate the current goal to the content of this slot, then that piece of ELR is important. In our example, the knowledge slot TECHNICAL-FEATURES of the OP-SYSTEM frame includes,

among others, the following fragment of knowledge:

    10 RUN (VVx: PROCESS)
    20 CONCURRENTLY (10)
    30 DEFINE (MULTI-TASKING, 20)

Propositions 10 and 20 of the TECHNICAL-FEATURES knowledge slot match (indirectly through inferencing via ISA relations) propositions 170, 180, and 200 of the ELR, and, furthermore, the goal interpreter evaluates the slot TECHNICAL-FEATURES as relevant to the current goal KNOW. This yields w(170) = w(180) = w(200) = high.

REFERENCES

1. Anderson J.R. (1976). Language, Memory, and Thought, Hillsdale, NJ: Lawrence Erlbaum.
2. Fum D., Guida G., and Tasso C. (1982). Forward and Backward Reasoning in Automatic Abstracting. In J. Horecky (Ed.), COLING-82, Amsterdam, NL: North-Holland, 83-88.
3. Fum D., Guida G., and Tasso C. (1984a). A Rule-Based Approach to Natural Language Text Representation and Comprehension. In R.Trappl (Ed.), Cybernetics and Systems Research 2, Amsterdam, NL: Elsevier Science, 727-732.
4. Fum D., Guida G., and Tasso C. (1984b). A Propositional Language for Text Representation. In B.G. Bara and G. Guida (Eds.), Computational Models of Natural Language Processing, Amsterdam, NL: North-Holland, 121-163.
5. Fum D., Guida G., and Tasso C. (1985). A Rule-Based Approach to Evaluating Importance in Descriptive Texts. Proc. 2nd Conf. of the European Chapter of the Association for Computational Linguistics, Geneva, Switzerland.
6. Graesser A.C. (1981). Prose Comprehension Beyond the Word. New York, NY: Springer-Verlag.
7. Hajičova' E. and Sgall P. (1984). From Topic and Focus of a Sentence to Linking in a Text. In B.G. Bara and G. Guida (Eds.), Computational Models of Natural Language Processing, Amsterdam, NL: North-Holland, 151-163.
8. Hobbs J.R. (1982). Towards an Understanding of Coherence in Discourse. In W.G. Lehnert and M.H. Ringle (Eds.), Strategies for Natural Language Processing, Hillsdale, NJ: Lawrence Erlbaum, 223-244.
9. Kintsch W. and van Dijk T.A. (1978). Toward a Model of Text Comprehension. Psychological Review 85, 363-394.
10. Lehnert W.G. (1982). Plot Units: A Narrative Summarization Strategy. In W.G. Lehnert and M.H. Ringle (Eds.), Strategies for Natural Language Processing, Hillsdale, NJ: Lawrence Erlbaum, 375-414.
11. Schank R.C. (1979). Interestingness: Controlling Inferences. Artificial Intelligence 12, 273-297.
12. van Dijk T.A. and Kintsch W. (1983). Strategies of Discourse Comprehension. New York, NY: Academic Press.

UNDERSTANDING ANALOGIES IN EDITORIALS

Stephanie E. August *
Michael G. Dyer

Artificial Intelligence Laboratory
Computer Science Department, 3531 BH
University of California
Los Angeles, California 90024
net address: AUGUST@UCLA-LOCUS.ARPA

ABSTRACT

The widespread use of analogy in human communication underscores the need for a system which can recognize and understand analogies. This paper presents a theory of analogy recognition and comprehension, using as a domain letters to the editor of a weekly news magazine. Some of the issues facing a system which understands analogies in this domain are identified, initial work on this program is reviewed, and work in progress is discussed.

I Introduction

People often rely on analogy as a vehicle for conveying ideas. Researchers in linguistics, education, psychology and other academic disciplines have studied this use of analogy and metaphor in depth (Lakoff and Johnson, 1980) (Ortony, 1979) (Sternberg, 1977). Recent investigations by AI researchers into computational models of analogical reasoning include (Carbonell, 1983), in which Carbonell outlines extensions to means-ends analysis which make use of past experience in solving new problems, thus integrating skill refinement and plan acquisition processes. There are few computational theories on the use of analogy in editorials, conversations, debates, narratives or other natural language text. Two examples of work in this area are Winston's work on learning by analogy (Winston, 1982) and Lebowitz' IPP (Lebowitz, 1980).

In Winston's system, a teacher supplied a precedent setting story to the system and then gave the system as an exercise a second story and a conclusion which was known to be true about the precedent. The system was able to reason why the conclusion was true for the precedent, and show how it was also true for the second story. While Winston's system was able to perform some analogical reasoning on the narratives, it did not recognize the narratives as being analogous without the assistance of the teacher.

IPP compared new wire service stories to similar events previously stored in memory. Lebowitz used in frame-like structures (Minsky, 1975) to index events in memory according to their similarities and differences. IPP was successful in finding events similar to the new one and was able to form generalizations allowing it to learn about its domain. However, IPP did not form specific analogical mappings and did not deal with disputes, arguments, or beliefs.

JULIP is a computer program which is part of the OpEd project (Alvarado, Dyer, and Flowers, 1985). The goal of OpEd is to develop a theory about the process of reasoning comprehension in the domain of editorials. The focus of JULIP is on the use of analogies in editorials. In contrast to the work by Winston and Lebowitz, the objective of JULIP is to implement a theory of analogy recognition, representation, and access for question answering. A completed JULIP system will accept as input a letter to the editor in English containing an analogy. Our challenge will be to recognize the presence of the analogy in the letter to the editor, map analogous elements together, and perform any transformations needed to complete the analogy. Our system will demonstrate that it understands the analogy via an English language question answer session with the user.

II The Issues Facing JULIP

Consider the following hypothetical letter to an editor:

HIGH-TECH-1

Some people are against computers because computers eliminate people's jobs. However, the automobile industry did the same thing to people in the horse carriage industry. Yet consumer demand for autos was strong enough that eventually more jobs were created in the auto industry than were lost in the horse carriage industry. In the end, the economy benefitted by the introduction of the new technology.

Informal protocols show that readers give the following answers when questioned on their understanding of this text:

Q1: To what is the computer industry being compared?

A1: THE COMPUTER INDUSTRY IS BEING COMPARED TO THE AUTOMOBILE INDUSTRY.

Q2: What did the auto industry do to people in the horse carriage industry?

A2: PEOPLE IN THE HORSE CARRIAGE INDUSTRY LOST JOBS.

A3: Why is the computer industry being compared to the auto industry?

Q3: BOTH INDUSTRIES INITIALLY ELIMINATED JOBS BUT ULTIMATELY CREATED MORE JOBS THAN THEY ELIMINATED.

Q4: What will happen as computers eliminate jobs?

A4: AN EVEN GREATER NUMBER OF NEW JOBS WILL BE CREATED.

Both the textual clues and an understanding of the mechanics of editorials and arguments are used in recognizing and following an analogy. Since JULIP's domain is letters to the editor, work on JULIP also encompasses a theory of editorial comprehension and draws upon previous work on argument structures and rules (Flowers, McGuire, and Birnbaum, 1982).

How can all these elements -- analogical reasoning, editorial comprehension, and argumentation -- be combined with natural language understanding? Our approach is to base the natural language comprehension component on BORIS (Dyer83), an integrated natural language understanding system for narratives. The work by Flowers et al. on representation of beliefs and the structure of arguments is a key part of our representation of an editorial letter (Flowers, McGuire, and Birnbaum, 1982). Memory organization and causal rea-

This work is supported in part by the Artificial Intelligence Center, Hughes Aircraft Company, Calabasas CA, and by a grant from the W.M. Keck Foundation.

* Also affiliated with the Software Engineering Division, Electro-Optical and Data Systems Group, Hughes Aircraft Company, El Segundo, CA 90245.

soning components are based upon Schank's work (Schank, 1982) (Schank, 1977). Our implementation of JULIP'S question answer processing draws upon Lehnert's work in this area (Lehnert, 1978).

III How Do You Know the Analogy Is There?

Understanding an editorial requires that the reader identify the dispute being presented, and the technique being used to support or refute the author's arguments. Analogy is one of these techniques. There are two main indicators of the presence of an analogy: 1) textual clues, and 2) conceptual similarities. JULIP relies upon both of these indicators to identify the presence of an analogy.

A. Textual Clues

Use of textual clues provides the most direct technique for introducing an analogy into an editorial letter. In this case, the author uses a phrase such as "the same thing" or "similar to" or "so it is" to link the source to the target. This technique is used in the following letter:

REVOLUTION

The Soviets are **doing the same thing** in Lebanon that they did in Viet Nam. By supplying the Syrians and the Druze with weapons, the U.S.S.R. is fostering internal feuds and abetting the downfall of Lebanon. (Christison, 1983)

In REVOLUTION, the reader is explicitly called upon to map the Soviets' role in Viet Nam in the past to the Soviets' role in Lebanon today. It is assumed that the reader has prior knowledge of what the Soviets did in Viet Nam.

B. Conceptual Similarities

People can readily detect the presence of an analogy even in the absence of textual clues, as seen in the following example:

DESTRUCTION

The Soviets are bombing people in Afganistan. But the U.S. killed people in Vietnam. What does labelling the Soviet's actions as despicable say about our own action?

A reader identifies both events as instances of destruction. This indicates that the concepts representing the text are categorized in memory by type. To provide this capability in a computer program, conceptual representations must be categorized as they are built, and linked together in the order in which they are encountered. The contents of these groups must be checked as new elements are added to them. When similar conceptual representations are encountered, similarity measures and other heuristics must be employed to determine whether an analogy is intended.

IV Constructing a Representation of the Analogy in an Editorial Letter

HIGH-TECH-1 serves as a typical editorial letter containing an analogy. Here we present the analysis that JULIP is being designed to perform in building the representation of HIGH-TECH-1 in memory.

The author of HIGH-TECH-1 first brings up the issue (ARG-1) of introduction of computers into manufacturing, where robots are being used on the assembly lines. The author makes the point that this automation is causing people who would normally work on the assembly lines to lose their jobs. This is understood as a belief that computer aided manufacturing (CAM) is bad. This belief is justified by the fact that computers cause people to suffer job loss, and that losing a job is something bad.

Since this is a letter to an editor, JULIP must expect the author of the article to either defend or attack the original point. JULIP sees the author's argument begin to unfold in the second sentence, when the conjunction "however" provides a lexical clue that a dispute regarding the argument is about to be introduced.

In sentence 2, JULIP is introduced to a new topic, the automobile industry and its relationship to the horse carriage industry. Encountering the phrase "did the same thing" must cause JULIP to search memory for the most recent causal structure (CAM leads to job loss) and try to make a mapping to it. JULIP must map the auto industry to CAM and infer that the auto industry caused people in the horse carriage industry to lose jobs. Comparison links between the first causal structure and the second, and between the antecedents of both and the consequents of both will be added to these structures to reflect the mapping. By analogy to ARG-1, JULIP must form the second argument, ARG-2, reflecting the belief that manufacturing of automobiles was bad.

JULIP must interpret the concepts represented by sentence 3 as a contradiction to ARG-2. Flowers et al. note that an argument can be contradicted by an attack on the belief espoused, by attack on the justification given for that belief, or by attack on the claim that the justification supports the belief. Lack of a value judgement on manufacturing of autos, and lack of a contradiction to the claim that job loss is bad rule out the first and second attack strategies. JULIP's knowledge of the consumer demand/manufacturer supply cycle and its relationship to an increased job market must guide it to the realization that manufacturing automobiles actually led to the creation of additional new jobs. This contradiction of the justification given for ARG-2 must cause JULIP to recognize that ARG-2 is invalid. The comparison links indicate that ARG-2 is parallel to ARG-1, so justification for ARG-1 as well as ARG-1 itself must now be viewed as suspect.

After reading sentence 4, JULIP must to build ARG-2' as an alternate to ARG-2, reflecting the belief that manufacturing of automobiles is good, justified by the fact that the economy ended up actually improving as a result of the introduction of automobiles to the marketplace. By analogy, a representation for an alternate argument to ARG-1 must now be built, reflecting the belief that computer aided manufacturing is actually good, since it too will lead to new jobs and an improved economy. Thus the conceptual representation for this analogy has been completed in memory.

Figure 1 depicts the basic elements of the completed representation of HIGH-TECH-1.

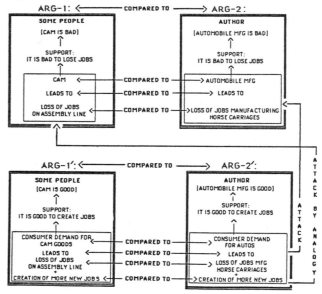

Figure 1. Argument Graph for HIGH-TECH-1.

V Answering Questions About the Analogy

JULIP is being designed to answer questions related to the mapping of source and target in the analogy, the transforms required to complete the analogy, and the basis of the analogy. Techniques for answering these types of questions draws upon Lehnert's theory of question answering (Lehnert, 1978), which is being augmented to handle questions peculiar to accessing the conceptual representation of an analogy. For example, questions regarding analogical mapping such as Q1 above, are basically concept completion questions that require traversing a new type of link; in this case, the comparison link.

VI Work in Progress

Work on JULIP up to this point has concentrated on developing a conceptual representation of the text of HIGH-TECH-1. We examined the text of this letter in detail in an effort to identify the lexical items, demons, and domain knowledge that must be available to the parser in order to develop a plausible conceptual representation of HIGH-TECH-1 in memory. This approach enabled us to test the robustness of the representation, without being distracted by parser and coding implementing details.

JULIP currently works with a hand coded conceptual representation of the HIGH-TECH-1 analogy built in memory using ARF (Edwards, 1984), a knowledge representation tool which supports both static and dynamic property inheritance. JULIP accepts queries in conceptual representation form. It searches the completed graph in memory and returns a conceptual representation of its findings to the user. The question answer session is implemented via ARF queries on the representation.

VII Future Work

We are now developing the parsing and generation components of JULIP to enable it to handle verbatim input.

The next step for JULIP is to translate our theory into the demons and lexical entries needed to support analogy recognition and comprehension in DYPAR, the parsing component of BORIS (Dyer, 1983). Our theory will continue to develop as we collect additional examples of letters to the editor containing analogies and human protocols for understanding them. JULIP's current objective is to demonstrate understanding of editorial analogies given to the program in English through a natural language question answer session with the user. Future objectives of the project will address the issues of incorporation of conclusions drawn from the analogies into long term memory, and generation of analogies.

VIII Conclusions

JULIP draws upon knowledge of editorial comprehension, argumentation, and integrated natural language understanding systems to develop a theory of analogy comprehension in the domain of letters to the editor. We have shown how both lexical cues and comparison of conceptual similarities trigger recognition of analogies in editorials letters. Our conceptual representation of an analogy in memory utilizes comparison links to map analogous elements to each other and to tie together parallel arguments. These links must be created and traversed during understanding as the representation of the completed analogy is built in memory. Question answer processing utilizes these links to demonstrate the system's understanding of the completed analogy.

REFERENCES

Alvarado, S.J., Dyer, M.G., Flowers, M. "Understanding Editorials: The Process of Reasoning Comprehension," Technical Report UCLA-AI-85-3, University of California, Los Angeles, 1985.

Carbonell, J.G. "Learning by Analogy: Formulating and Generalizing Plans from Past Experience", in *Machine Learning*, R.S. Michalski, J.G. Carbonell, and T.M. Mitchell, eds., Tioga, Palo Alto CA, 1983.

Dyer, Michael G. *In-Depth Understanding: A Computer Model of Integrated Processing for Narrative Comprehension*. MIT Press, Cambridge MA, 1983.

Edwards, Gary R. *A Rule and Frame System, Version 2.2.* Hughes Artificial Intelligence Center, Calabasas CA, 1984.

Flowers, M., McGuire, R., and Birnbaum, L. "Adversary Arguments and the Logic of Personal Attacks", in *Strategies for Natural Language Processing*, Wendy G. Lehnert and Martin H. Ringle, eds., Lawrence Erlbaum Associates, Hillsdale NJ, 1982.

Lakoff, G. and Johnson, M. *Metaphors We Live By*. Chicago University Press, 1980.

Lebowitz, Michael. "Generalization and Memory in an Integrated Understanding System", Research Report #186, Yale University Computer Science Department of Computer Science, November 1980.

Lehnert, W.G. *The Process of Question Answering*. Lawrence Erlbaum Associates, Hillsdale NJ, 1978.

Minsky, M. "A Framework for Representing Knowledge", in *The Psychology of Computer Vision*, P. Winston, ed., McGraw-Hill, NY, 1975.

Ortony, A. (Ed.) *Metaphor and Thought*. Cambridge University Press, Cambridge, 1979.

Schank, R., and Abelson, R. *Scripts Plans Goals and Understanding*. Lawrence Erlbaum Associates, Hillsdale NJ, 1977.

Schank, R.C. *Dynamic Memory*. Cambridge University Press, Cambridge, 1982.

Sternberg, R.J. *Intelligence, Information Processing and Analogical Reasoning: the Componental Analysis of Human Abilities*. Lawrence Erlbaum Associates, Hillsdale NJ, 1977.

Christison, Robert. From "Letters", in TIME, 24 October 1983.

Winston, P.H. "Learning new principles from precedents and examples", *Artificial Intelligence*, 19:3, November 1982, p.321.

Integrating Text Planning and Production in Generation

Eduard H. Hovy

Yale University
Artificial Intelligence Project
2158 Yale Station
New Haven, CT 06520

Abstract

While the task of language generation seems to separate quite naturally into the two aspects of language generation (text planning and text production), it is necessary to have the planning and the production interact at generator decision points in such a way that the former need not contain explicit syntactic knowledge, and that the latter need not contain explicit goal-related information. This paper describes the decision points, the types of plans that are used in making the decisions, and a process that performs the task. These ideas are embodied in a program.[1]

1 Introduction: the Problem

Our current understanding of language generation includes text planning and text production. In generation work of a decade ago (Simmons & Slocum 72; Goldman 75), no text planning phase ever appeared. In the last few years, much work has been done developing text planners. The issue of interaction between planning and production phases was addressed in various ways. This paper suggests a better way to achieve the necessary interaction.

In the simplest systems, planners make only very high-level decisions, such as selecting appropriate speech acts (Cohen 78; Jacobs 85), and play no further role in text expansion.

In systems with more elaborate plans, the text can be planned out in considerable detail before actual production is started. In this approach, there is a one-way flow of information from the planner to the generator (McDonald (personal communication); McDonald 80; Appelt 81). The production process requires this information whenever it must decide how to expand a generator instruction into a series of more detailed instructions. If the decision criteria are based purely on syntactic and rhetorical grounds (using notions such as sentence focus and stress); it is comparatively easy to build them into a pre-expansion planner, since they are relatively simple and only impinge on expansion at a small number of points (such as subject choice and clause content).

However, when you want the decisions to take into account pragmatic considerations such as speaker intentions, conversational setting, and hearer characteristics, it is much more difficult to plan all the decisions before commencing actual expansion. For example, suppose the generator wants to create in the hearer sympathy for a 65-year old beggar. In the sentence "the [*say-age* AGE-INSTANCE-23] woman is homeless", *say-age* should return "old" or even "ancient" rather than "65-year old". For the planner to precompute this decision, it will have to compute all the decisions (via *say-sentence* and *say-subject*, etc.), such as selecting a subject, a head noun, and adjectives, before it will be in a position firstly to realize that AGE is to be said as an adjective, and secondly to determine what the options are in this case. In order to do this computation, the planner will have to have access to information which one would like to claim is properly the exclusive concern of expansion, such as syntactic and lexical knowledge. (For instance, Appelt's planner contains grammatical knowledge spread throughout. Appelt alludes to the problems that this causes in (Appelt 81).) Furthermore, if the planner is going to do this computation down to the level of individual words, it may as well do the generation simultaneously. One can try to get around this problem by having the planner assemble a set of injunctions upon which the expansion can base its decisions. To do so, the injunctions would have to span the space of possible locutions arising from the representation; assembling them would be a very large task.

A better solution is to perform planning only when necessitated by the expansion. This approach is characterized by a two-way communication at decision points. As the example in section 3 shows, five decision points enable a generator to produce flexible yet good text. These decision points are: topic choice; sentence content; sentence organization; clause organization; and word choice.

---

[1]This work was supported in part by the Advanced Research Projects Agency monitored by the Office of Naval Research under contract N00014-82-K-0149.

There are good reasons why this approach is desirable:

- **modularity:** the planner need not precompute all generator decisions, but must simply be able to furnish answers when required by the generator. That means it need not contain knowledge about the generation process itself.

- **parsimony:** it is unnecessary to make more decisions than exactly and only those the generator requires.

- **opportunism:** it should be possible opportunistically to take advantage of possibilities of locution that arise due to syntax (of which the planner should have no knowledge) and which the production mechanism cannot decide by itself. This can be done only if the planner can make decisions during the actual production.

2 Plans

The generator described here tries to satisfy multiple pragmatic goals. It can be given a goal to affect the hearer in each of the following areas: his knowledge; beliefs (affective values attached to knowledge); future behaviour; emotional state (aspects: hearer's own; toward topic; toward conversation); relation wrt the speaker (aspects: social; emotional). It requires a set of hearer characteristics, and is able to reason about relatedness of concepts to those in the model. Unfortunately it is impossible to describe the goal structure and plan selection process here. (Related work was done in (Cohen 78) and (Hermann & Laucht 78).)

Some of the plans this program contains are sets of injunctions (among others, DESCRIBE-OBJECT, DESCRIBE-CAUSE/HISTORY, CORRECT-MISCONCEPTION, CONVINCE); they are similar to McKeown's (McKeown 82) generational scripts (schemata). These plans are used by a depth-first network traversal planner to make topic-related decisions and instructions. For example, the CONVINCE plan serves the goal to get the hearer to attach a certain affective connotation to some concept. To do this, it directs the story representation traversal by selecting for consideration and, if further criteria are met, for inclusion in the text, concepts that help to support the connotation. Analysis of various written arguments (taken from communist newspapers, pro- and anti- labour strike leaflets, etc.) indicates that the CONVINCE plan contains, at least, the following suggestions about a topic:

- consider the topic if speaker and hearer agree over its connotation

- consider the topic if it opposes a concept accepted by both

- consider concepts the topic is a subgoal to

- consider concepts the topic is an instance of

- consider the topic's results

- consider the current state of affairs relating to the topic

- minimize difference between speaker's desire/interpretation and reality, if it is small

- minimize difference between hearer's desire/interpretation and reality, if it is small

- find someone hearer respects who agrees with speaker's interpretation

This plan is described further in the next section.

Other plans are suggestions for achieving a goal. For example, the relation plan *make the hearer dominant* contains, amongst others, the instructions:

- topic choice: don't change the topic; follow his lead (i.e., don't select unrelated topics)

- sentence content: don't include in a sentence clauses about concepts he doesn't know

- sentence organization: focus on what he deems important

- sentence organization: make questions rather than assertions; ask his opinion

- word choice: use words he knows

whereas the increase-knowledge plan *teach the hearer* contains:

- topic choice: change the topic when required

- sentence content: don't include in a sentence concepts he doesn't know, unless they are the topic

- sentence organization: make short, simple sentences

- word choice: use words he knows

Clearly, there is a potential conflict in the two plans given: one calls for never changing the topic and the other explicitly calls for the opposite. For planners such as NOAH (Sacerdoti 77) this poses a serious problem. However, this is what gives generation its spice! People holding contradictory goals and plans can speak; a generator must be able to hold conflicting plans and merge their instructions into one sensible generator instruction or decision.

The integrated method of generation proposed here is well suited to manage such contradictory demands.

Rather than being mandatory instructions, an activated plan's steps become suggestions on suggestion lists. Since the guidance which the expansion process requires from the planner always takes the form of selecting one of a number of options, a suggestion is some criterion for evaluating a list of alternatives and preferring one (or more). For example, if the speaker's goal is to teach the hearer, one of his plan-suggestions is to use words that the hearer knows. Given a list of possible words, the suggestion will select only such word(s). If none exist, no suggestion is made, and the decision is made by whatever other criteria apply. Thus, when the expansion has to make a word-choice decision, a query containing the syntactically obtained alternatives is sent to the appropriate suggestion list for pragmatic and rhetorical evaluation.

Merging conflicting preferences can be achieved in various ways. Some alternatives are: most popular option; result of the suggestion serving least recently served goal; using some fixed ranking of goals. Woolf's program (Woolf & McDonald 84) contains "meta-rules" to guide the planner through its network of plans (in effect, a planner planner!); similar criteria can be defined in this scheme under which one of the active suggestions will be preferred over other, conflicting ones. My program currently uses the (simplistic) first alternative.

3 An Example

Tracing through an example will make clear the decisions and the planning criteria required to produce text. The example is part of a story denoting one of the primary elections in the Carter-Kennedy Presidential nomination contest in 1980. OUTCOME-4 is one of the results of the election. A similar result, OUTCOME-5, denotes Kennedy's getting 218 delegates. In the conversation, the hearer has been defined to be antipathetic toward Carter and sympathetic toward Kennedy, while the program has the opposite sympathies. (This is accomplished by including the relevant concepts among the interlocutors' sympathy and antipathy characteristics.) The program's goal is to convince the hearer that, even though Kennedy won, Carter didn't do badly. This goal activates the CONVINCE plan.

```
(OUTCOME-4
  (INSTANCE-OF : VOTE-OUTCOME)
  (VOTING : ELECTION-12)
  (ACTOR : CARTER-15)
  (AMOUNT-GOT : 215)
  (UNIT : DELEGATE)
  (CONNOTATION-VALUE : FAIL)
  (DIFF-AMOUNT : 3))
```

where VOTE-OUTCOME, CARTER-15, ELECTION-12, etc., are concepts further defined in a property inheritance network.

3.1 Topic Choice and Change

OUTCOME-4 was nominated for consideration by the CONVINCE plan's fifth rule during scrutiny of the representation of the election. When OUTCOME-4 itself is considered by the topic choice suggestions, the seventh rule fires and builds a *say-sentence* instruction to make a sentence that stresses the small difference between the actual outcome, OUTCOME-4, (to which the hearer is sympathetic) and the speaker's desired outcome (a hypothetical outcome, also represented, to which the hearer is antipathetic). The stress information *min* will enable *say-stress* to generate an appropriate adverb or adjective. In more detail, rule 7 contains:

```
IF the speaker is antipathetic to the topic
  AND there is a hypothetical equivalent
      to the topic
  AND the speaker is sympathetic to the
      equivalent
  AND the difference between these two is
      not large
THEN make a sentence expressing the
     difference, with stress: min
```

3.2 Sentence Content

Since both OUTCOME-4 and OUTCOME-5 are selected by the CONVINCE plan, and since their sentence instructions are both sent to the expander only when a satisfactory end to the line of argumentation has been found, the expansion has the options of making two sentences, or of combining them into a relational sentence such as:
"While Kennedy got 218 delegates, Carter got 215"
"Carter only got 3 delegates fewer than Kennedy"
The decision is made by the planner's sentence content suggestions. If most suggestions call for long or complex sentences, the relation will be said; otherwise, two sentences will be formed. Typically, suggestions to make long or complex sentences are activated by the goals to confuse or bore the hearer, or to make him feel inferior. Similar criteria decide whether or not to include the clause "in the election on Feb 20".

3.3 Sentence Organization

In a typical sentence, you can usually select almost any clause to be the sentence subject. McKeown describes rules concerning focus or stress in order to make subject choices which resulted in natural, flowing text. Additional criteria you can take into account are pragmatic; for example, if it is your intention to anger the hearer, and you know he does not like some aspect of the topic, you may select that aspect as the subject, to give it prominence.

The example contains at least three possible sentence subjects (the ACTOR, AMOUNT-GOT, DIFF-AMOUNT aspects):

"Carter lost the election"
"215 delegates were won by Carter"
"3 delegates was the margin by which Carter lost"

3.4 Clause Organization

Within a clause, the generator has to decide which aspects of the representation to say and how to order them. For example, when making a noun group, it must select the head noun and then decide whether to describe it in full, only give unsaid information, or give an abbreviated version. It then has to select and order the modifiers, both pre- and post-nominal (and some modifiers can appear in both positions), before it can return a form from which the eventual noun group will be built.

Some possibilities are ruled out by text flow rules (one doesn't say "the Georgian male 65-year old Jimmy Carter, the President"); other decisions can be based upon goal-related criteria, and therefore can form another point of interaction between planner and generator. For example, if your goal is to calm the hearer, you should not explicitly include aspects about an object that you know he disapproves of.

3.5 Word Choice

This decision must be made in any representation system rich enough to associate more than one word with a concept. Like (Goldman 75), the program uses discrimination nets attached to the representational primitives; here the discriminations depend both on features of the particular instance of the concept, and on the pragmatic issues mentioned (for example, interaction of word affect with the hearer's sympathies: saying "terrorist" to an IRA soldier may get you shot; saying "freedom fighter" certainly will not!).

Selecting a verb has implications for sentence content and organization. For example, when the subject has been said, *say-predicate* has to select a verb and build up *say*-function instructions for the rest of the sentence. The discrimination net for the concept VOTE-OUTCOME contains, among others, the verbs "win", "lose", and "get". While "win" is inappropriate, either of the others can be said:

"Carter got 215 delegates"
"Carter lost the election"
The two verbs are passed to the word-choice suggestions of the planner, which (in this case) prefer the former option, since the CONVINCE plan's sugggestions call for preferring words with connotations that match the speaker's interpretations. (Since OUTCOME-4 is the failure of an event which the program was sympathetic to, and since "lose" has negative connotations which would oppose the sympathy, it is rejected.)

4 Conclusion

The final text, generated from the whole representation, is:
KENNEDY ONLY GOT A SMALL NUMBER OF DELEGATES IN THE ELECTION ON 20 FEBRUARY. CARTER JUST LOST BY A SMALL NUMBER OF DELEGATES.   HE HAS SEVERAL DELEGATES MORE THAN KENNEDY IN TOTAL.

5 Acknowledgements

Thanks to Lawrence Birnbaum and Rod McGuire.

6 References

1. Appelt, D.E., *Planning Natural Language Utterances to Satisfy Multiple Goals*, Ph.D. dissertation, Stanford, 1981.

2. Cohen, P.R., *On Knowing What to Say: Planning Speech Acts*, Ph.D. dissertation, University of Toronto, 1978.

3. Goldman, N.M., *Conceptual Generation*, in R.C. Schank (ed.), **Conceptual Information Processing**, Elsevier North-Holland, 1975.

4. Herrmann, T. & Laucht, M., *Planung von Aeusserungen alsSelektion von Komponenten Implikativer Propositionsstrukturen*, Universitaet Mannheim Technical Report no. 3, 1978.

5. Jacobs, P.S., *PHRED: a Generator for Natural Language Interfaces*, University of California (Berkeley) Technical Report, 1985.

6. McDonald, D., *Natural Language Production as a Process of Decision Making under Constraint*, Ph.D. dissertation, MIT, 1980.

7. McKeown, K.R., *Generating Natural Language Text in Response to Questions about Database Queries*, Ph.D. dissertation, University Of Pennsylvania, 1982.

8. Sacerdoti, E., **A Structure for Plans and Behavior**, Elsevier North-Holland, 1977.

9. Simmons, R.F. & Slocum, J., *Generating English Discourse from Semantic Networks*, Communications of the ACM, Vol 15, No 10, 1972.

10. Woolf, B. & McDonald, D.D., *Context-Dependent Transitions in Tutoring Discourse*, AAAI Proceedings, 1984.

BE BRIEF, BE TO THE POINT, ... BE SEATED

or RELEVANT RESPONSES IN MAN/MACHINE CONVERSATION

Anne Vilnat, Gérard Sabah

GR22, Paris VI, 4,Place Jussieu, 75230 Paris Cedex 05

ABSTRACT

In the dialogue part of our system, we have tried to increase the user's possibilities to criticize the machine's results and require explanations of them. The system must then provide a clear justification : either by furnishing the chain of reasoning or by asking a "good question" when it failed. The system must also be able to engage in a real dialogue, with more than one question / one answer. To do that, the system must build and use several kinds of representation : the reasoning, the topics and a model of the user, which is used to tailor the system's responses.

I. Introduction.

Artificial Intelligence systems developed during the 70's were based on Knowledge Representation. The applications were supposed to showcase the different types of representation, such as frames, scripts, scenarios, or expert-systems. The dialogue problem was partly neglected. Some programs (6) were then related to written dialogues; their primary purpose was to really understand the attitudes of both participants, but they didn't mind engaging in dialogue. At the same time, theoretical research has been pursued on this point, but has not always given rise to practical applications (5), (2),...

Following this path, we have tried to determine the types of knowledge implicated in human conversation. Even if they are not always well defined, there are some rules which govern the elaboration of the sentences uttered in conversation. In this paper we will focus on the knowledge a program needs to cooperate in a dialogue. After a brief overview of the works that have influenced our research, the paper presents examples of possible dialogues. We then describe how the different kinds of knowledge representations are built and used.

II. The role of the machine in a dialogue.

Most studies in the theory of Speech Acts (11), (1) agree on Grice's cooperation principle for analysis of human dialogues (4). A conversation is a relational act in which each participant is required to take an active part : else it would be a monologue or a dictatorial lecture! Each interlocutor must take into account the other's goal. No one can be engaged in a dialogue if he can't explain his own utterances, or cannot specify what he couldn't understand in someone else's previous statements.

To detail his principle, Grice proposes some axioms that must be respected, otherwise, as your interlocutor assumes your statement was intentional, he will make incorrect inferences.

We have established that to be considered as a help, a question-answering system must respect the three following principles :
- be able to participate in a real dialogue, with more than just "one question - one response",
- be able to restart the dialogue when some problem prevents the successful operation of the system
- be able to justify itself,i.e. the chain of reasoning it used to produce a previous answer.

III. Examples of dialogues.

In this paper, we describe dialogues where both participants are involved; the user expects from the machine a well-formed answer (i.e. not in some jargon), and the machine doesn't limit the user's part to a choice among a set of predefined questions. We are currently working on an application in which a program takes the place of the"yellow pages" of the french telephone directory (the professional listings : suppliers of goods and services).

This system assumes that the user's goal is to obtain a phone number; when a problem is posed, it searches for someone who might solve it. The system has a deterministic parser (7) which analyzes the user's utterances; it uses a semantic network with different kinds of links. Each listing is represented by its name, i.e. a concept and a list of sentences describing the activity of the supplier (8).

Example E1 (illustrates the explanation process)

U1 : I would like to move my safe.
S1 : I suggest an art mover or a piano mover.
U2 : Why a piano mover ?
S2 : Because, both your safe and a piano are very heavy.
U3 : Why an art mover ?
S3 : Because your safe may contain valuable objects, and an art mover handles things of value.

In U1, the topic recognized is "to move a safe". Then, the reasoning process (REASON) looks for an answer to this request : first it chooses the listings whose name contains the concept "move" or the concept "safe", then it searches the list of sentences describing the activity of the supplier. Here it finds nothing, so it uses the "synonym" reasoning process (it examines the links between the concepts in the semantic network, and their possible combinations, e.g. "sort of" and "part of" give "part of"). REASON finds that safe is the "approximate synonym" of "piano" (both heavy) and "valuables" (safe may contain objects of value). Then it verifies that the listing "piano mover" and the listing "art mover" contain information which agrees with the question the user asks, and generates S1. The user suprised (and he has reason to be!) questions in U2. The internal representation of this question is passed to the dialogue process (DIALOG). It recognizes a causal question, concerning a prior topic : to move a piano. Then it must find the path that led it to this result and it must constitute an explanation which is, as much as possible, tailored for the user. In order to carry on the dialogue with good results, the system must incorporate the following three representations : the topics that have already been mentioned, the different chains of reasoning the system has used, and the knowledge level we suppose the user has. We will develop below the methods used to build these representations. Using them, the system can give coherent explanations. When it is asked about the piano mover, it uses its topic knowledge to selection only the relevant information from the reasoning (S2), and the same process with S3. In building these answers, the system must take into account the knowledge we suppose the user to have, so as to avoid an overly detailed explanation.

Example E2 (underlines the capacities to follow the changes of subject, and restart the dialogue).

U1 : I would like the phone number of an oriental restaurant.
S1 : Would you prefer a vietnamese, a japanese or a chinese one?
U2 : I don't care.
S2 : In which part of town?
U3 : First give me a phone number for a radio taxi
S3 : You have the following listings under Taxi : Hello Taxi (111-11-11), Night Taxi(222-22-22).
U4 : In that case, I would like a restaurant in the 5th district.
S4 : You have :
    chinese restaurant :"The Mandarin" 333-33-33
    japanese restaurant :"The rising sun"444-44-44

After analysis, we know that U1 is an "object" demand for an oriental restaurant. REASON works only on the couple (predicate, object): dine at a restaurant. Thus, it finds the following listings : chinese, russian, japanese restaurant, fast food,... DIALOG obtains this list. To make a selection, it begins by looking for a modifying criterion in the user's request. It finds : oriental, which qualifies the type of restaurant. There remain the chinese, vietnamese restaurants, which are proposed to the user (S1). As he refuses to make a choice, another question must be constituted. First, we try to use the criteria (topics) which allowed us to determine the current listings. Then we make a search on the information known about the listings. But these procedures fail. If the system contained the fact that vietnamese food was "spicy" and japanese food was "non-spicy", the system would have been able to offer a further choice. In this case, the criteria were "richer" than the first choices presented; but not in our example E2. The last solution we have foreseen is to ask a question about the restaurant location (S2). In U3, the user changes the topic,

he asks for a radio taxi. After a new search, REASON finds the listing taxi. DIALOG verifies that it operates by radio call, and proposes S3. The user may then answer S2, and asks for a restaurant in the 5th district. The system then recognizes a topic already discussed, it doesn't make a new search, but makes a selection among three types of restaurant chosen before. It is possible to compose S4.

IV. The representations built by the system.

The first representation we show here is the chronological record (CR). It connects all the others which we present below. It establishes the link between the different utterances and indicates "who" says "what", and in which context an utterance has been said.

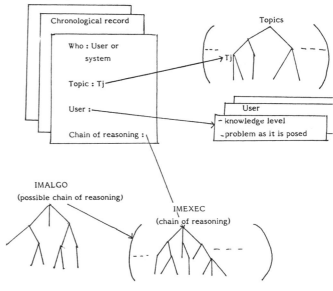

Fig 1 : Chronological record

In this structure, we find, for each utterance :

1) who said it, the user or the system.

2) the topics developed in this utterance. By topic, we mean the subject of the dialogue, what we are speaking about. In this part, we used the results obtained by Grau's system (3). In her work, the topic is represented by a set of schemas which are connected by different kinds of links (hierarchical, descriptive,..) Her system offers the possibility of integrating a sentence in its context, that is to relate it to the topics which have already been discussed. During the dialogue, the different topics are developed both by the user, when he introduces a request or further specifies it, and by the system when REASON makes approximations. Among these topics, we establish a hierarchy, which underlines the fact that some "detours" may appear after a user request without a complete change of subject. This hierarchy leads us to build a tree whose root is the user's initial request. We have considered that REASON can't introduce a completely new topic; it can only produce different kinds of "detours". The topics developed during the dialogue constitute a list of trees (cf Fig 1). Each entry of CR points to a node inside one of these trees.

3) the system's chain of reasoning. In the examples we demonstrate the necessity of different levels of detail in the chain of reasoning so as to present a "good" justification. In an order to obtain those levels, we have represented the reasoning as a tree. The sets of procedures which form REASON constitute an implicit hierarchy; this hierarchy is reflected in the structure of the "reasoning tree" we produce. As a one-time procedure (for each version of REASON) we build a tree which represents all the possibilities of REASON (the image of the algorithm : IMALGO). Each time REASON is called, a new sub-tree is extracted, corresponding to the particular execution (the image of the execution : IMEXEC). IMEXEC is the trace of the reasoning used to solve a certain problem. It will be used by the explanation process (EXPLAIN).

4) the user's representation. In CR, we store a pointer towards a representation of the user as we currently define it (it is dynamic). It is composed of two elements : the knowledge level the system attributes to the user, and our current definition of the user's problem. The knowledge level is used to avoid to drown the user in details when the system explains its reasoning. It is based on IMALGO. The representation of the user's problem is composed of the couple (predicate, object) which was used to call REASON. Joined to this is a list of concepts which modify one of the couple's two elements. We see in E2 that it is used to solve some cases of ambiguity.

It is the set of all these representations interconnected byCR which allow us to manage a dialogue, taking into account as best we can the three points underlined above :
- participation in more than "one question - one answer" dialogue,
- restart the dialogue,
- self-justification.

V. The use of these representations for the dialogue

To enable us to accept questions regarding the whole dialogue, the CR is updated at each utterance, A new entry is created showing who spoke, the topic developed, the user's representation as it is currently perceived and the chain of reasoning.

Let us examine what happens when a user's utterance is addressed to the system. It is first analyzed. Then DIALOG acts in different ways, depending on the kind of question and the topic developed. If the question contains a topic change, REASON is called to search the knowledge base (in E2 : U1 and U3). If it is a question concerning a prior topic, EXPLAIN is called (in E1 : U2). Otherwise it is treated as information to resolve an ambiguous point (in E2 : U4). At the end of the reasoning process, a good answer either has or has not been found.DIALOG will then transmit the good answer to the generation process, otherwise it tries to determine a question, in order to pursue the dialogue (see E2).

When EXPLAIN is called, it first decides, by referring to topic and CR,where this problem has been solved. Then it retrieves the part of IMEXEC concerned by the question, and taking into account the knowledge we assumes the user has, it builds an explanation. After that, the user's representation is modified so if he asks again for an explanation we may give him more details.

We find in the following diagram a resume of this process.

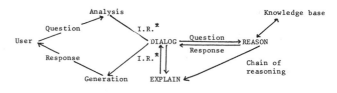

DIALOG : manages the dialogue
REASON : searches the knowledge base
EXPLAIN : explains the reasoning

(∗) Internal
     representation

Fig 2 Representation of the system

VI. Conclusion

Our goal is to give control of the dialogue back to the user, to permit him to change the subject, to backpedal, and to question the system's responses. In any case, if the system can't solve the whole problem, it must be able to efficiently aid the user to modify the request. To this end, the system's questions take into account the work already accomplished and indicate to the user the various paths possible to arrive at their goal.

During a conversation, each participant assumes an enormous amount of knowledge on the part of the other(s). This is what is shown in Grices's maxims. He points out that the violation of any of the axioms derived from the cooperation principle is given significance equal to that of the actual contents of the utterance. This is why our system is constructed to act in accordance with these principles. The system's utterance must be clear so that the user doesn't have to search for hidden meanings.

References :

(1) J.F.Allen,C.R.Perrault "Analyzing intention in Utterances", AI n°15,p.143-178, 1980.
(2) J.Bien,Y.Wilks "Beliefs,Points of view and Multiple environments" CS,Vol.7 n°2, 1983.
(3) B.Grau "Stalking coherence in the topical jungle" FGCS 84,Tokyo.
(4) H.P.Grice "Logic and Conversation",In Cole and Morgan,EdSyntax and Semantics,Speech Acts, Academic Press,New-York,1975.
(5) P.Hayes,R.Reddy,"An anatomy of graceful interaction in spoken and written man-machine communication" Dpt of Computer Science,CMU,79.
(6) W.G.Lehnert 'Human and computational question-answering",CS I (1),1977.
(7) M.Rady,G.Sabah "A deterministic syntactic-semantic parser",IJCAI 83,Karlsruhe.
(8) G.Sabah "Un système de questions-réponses sur les rubriques professionnelles",Pub 31,CNRS GR22,83.
(9) G.Sabah "Différentes notions de synonymie liées à la compréhension automatique du Langage", Congrès ARC 84, Orsay.
(10)R.C.Schank,W.G.Lehnert "The conceptual content of conversation", IJCAI 79, Tokyo.
(11) J.R.Searle "Expression and Meaning",Cambridge University Press, 1979.
(12) A.Vilnat "L'élaboration d'informations pertinentes dans une conversation homme-machine",Thèse 3ème cycle,Paris 6,1984.

SAPHIR+RESEDA, A NEW APPROACH TO INTELLIGENT DATA BASE ACCESS

Bernard Euzenat
Bernard Normier
Antoine Ogonowski
ERLI, 72 quai des Carrières, 94220 Charenton, France

Gian Piero Zarri
Centre National de la Recherche Scientifique, Paris, France
and
TECSIEL, via Barnaba Oriani 32, 00197 Rome, Italy

ABSTRACT

This paper describes a transportable natural language interface to databases, augmented with a knowledge base and inference techniques. The inference mechanism, based on a classical expert system's type of approach, allows, when needed, to automatically convert an input query into another one which is "semantically close". According to RESEDA's theory, "semantically close" means that the answer to the transformed query implies what could have been the answer to the original question. The presented system integrates natural language processing, expert system and knowledge representation technology to provide a cooperative database access.

I. INTRODUCTION

Most of the existing natural language interfaces (NLIs) to databases - too numerous to be cited - free the user from learning the cumbersome and difficult syntax of formal database query languages. Still they impose a very strict semantic model, which corresponds to the way a real world domain is represented in a particular database (DB).

It is therefore difficult to produce a "valid question" without being aware of the structure of the database concerned. This issue is the main concern of the SAPHIR+RESEDA (Euzenat et al., 1984a, 1984b) research project at ERLI.* SAPHIR (Normier, 1984, Normier et al., 1984) our transportable, domain independent NLI to databases, is in the course of being provided with a relatively general knowledge base (KB) and associated inference mechanisms.

Before going into the technical details of this new system, let us show a typical problem that SAPHIR+RESEDA will be able to handle.

Suppose that you want to ask a question such as "who has ever been in the US", and that your staff management database does not contain any information concerning the employees' excursions. Suppose further that the DB knows instead where each one of them was born and what their degrees are.

Using simple common sense knowledge, without accessing the database, we can tell the user that although we do not explicitly know who has been in the USA, we can nevertheless look for people born there and/or having an American degree. If the user accepts this proposal then we transmit the modified query to the DBMS.

_____

* This research was supported in part by the "Agence de l'Informatique" research contract ADI-84-068.

II. THE ARCHITECTURE OF THE SYSTEM

Figure 1 contains a simplified flowchart of our system capable of such rational behaviour.

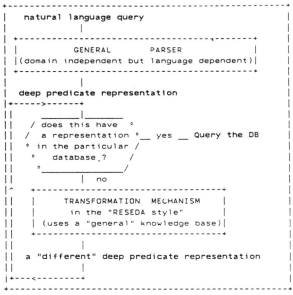

Figure 1

First of all the natural language (i.e. French) query is parsed and partially disambiguated, using structure rules (Gross, 1975) and a syntactical grammar of French. In some cases the parser resorts to simple clarifying dialogues. As the result of this analysis, a predicate representation is produced. It carries the meaning of the user's query. Due to space limitations the parser will not be presented here.

The system has at its disposal a model of the structure of the database being accessed (a special predicate calculus description, close to the conceptual schema), so it can check whether this query is a meaningful request to the database. If it is meaningful, then the system translates the deep predicate representation into a corresponding formal query language formula (this is how our existing NLI - SAPHIR proceeds; currently we can produce QBE, SQL, Adabas and Clio translations).

However, in many cases the query will not map directly onto the database.

Instead of simply telling the user that his question is not "the question to ask", we will try to transform his request into something meaningful in the particular database and **semantically close** to the original request - this part of the system is based on G.P. Zarri's RESEDA system (Zarri, 1983, 1984a, 1984b, 1984c). We define "question1" to be **semantically close** to "question2" iff the answer to "question1" is implied by the answer to "question2".

III. THE KNOWLEDGE BASE

To achieve this, we need of course the knowledge of what is "semantically close".

In the example presented above the system was able to transform the original question, because it knew that "if a person is born in a particular place then that person must have been in that place at least for a short period of time".

The second alternative of the transformed query is produced because the system knows that "in order to obtain a degree, a person has to attend courses at a particular university or do some research work at that university" and that "in both cases the person had to be physically present there at one time or another" (to simplify the presented example we deliberately ignore all the cases of exception to this rule).

It follows from the example that the system manipulates rather general common sense knowledge.

We decided to take the domain of staff management as our test-bed. However we still need to represent some more general, extra-domain knowledge.

From a technical point of view, our overall knowledge base is divided into a number of smaller knowledge bases, as illustrated in Figure 2.

```
+---------------------------------------------------+
|                                             |     |
|| Knowledge Base                    |        |     |
||                                   |        |     |
||  _____         | ex: a human being |
||  |KB1 (most general)    |        |     has a sex     |
||  -----------------------         |        |     |
||                                   |        |     |
||  _____         | ex: the staff     |
||  |KB2 (domain specific) |        |     management     |
||  -----------------------         |     legislation   |
||                                   |        |     |
||  _____         | ex: particular rules |
||  |KB3                   | |       |     of staff manage- |
||  |(application specific)| |       |     ment for a parti- |
||  ----------------------- |        |     cular company  |
||  _____|        |     |
|                                             |     |
+---------------------------------------------------+
```

Figure 2

KB1 contains bits of knowledge that are usable in any application (of course, it will never be complete).

KB2 contains general knowledge for a particular domain. We hope to develop a certain number of KB2s (with a common KB1 nucleus) for each real world domain that our system will have to deal with.

Each KB1 + KB2 couple is transportable "as is", as long as we do not switch to a completely different domain.

Note that KB3 is not specific of a particular database, the system can use the same KB3 in order to access different personnel databases of the same company.

The model of the database itself (the most specific level of knowledge) is not included here since it does not take part directly in the transformation process.

IV. TYPES OF KNOWLEDGE.

Any one of the KBs mentioned above may contain two types of knowledge: factual knowledge and rules (represented in a formalism based on RESEDA).

A. Factual knowledge

A fact such that "a university is in a city...", which is a piece of factual knowledge, is represented by the highlighted part of Figure 3.

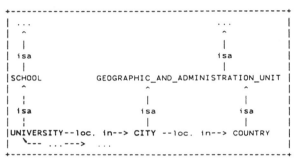

```
+----------------------------------------------------+
| ...                              ...               |
|  ^                                ^                 |
|  |                                |                 |
| isa                              isa                |
|  |                                |                 |
|SCHOOL        GEOGRAPHIC_AND_ADMINISTRATION_UNIT     |
|  ^                   ^                  ^           |
|  |                   |                  |           |
| isa                 isa                isa          |
|  |                   |                  |           |
|UNIVERSITY--loc. in--> CITY --loc. in--> COUNTRY     |
|  `--- ...--->   ...                                 |
+----------------------------------------------------+
```

Figure 3

This frame-like network describes "specific-generic" type of relations ("isa" links; we allow polyhierarchies) used as matching criteria when applying rules (cf below). Other specific relations (used in the rules, for example topological ones) are also present in the network.

This representation does not have the full power of frame systems since presently there is no procedural knowledge represented in the network.

B. Rules

Currently we have two types of rules:

1. Transformation rules.
2. Standardization rules.

A fact such as "if a person (x) has received ("BE-AFFECTED-BY") a degree in a particular place (y) then that person has been ("BE-PRESENT") in that place", which is a transformation rule, is represented as in Figure 4.

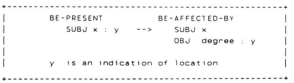

```
+----------------------------------------------------+
|      BE-PRESENT           BE-AFFECTED-BY           |
|        SUBJ x : y   -->      SUBJ x                |
|                              OBJ  degree : y       |
|                                                    |
|      y  is an indication of location              |
+----------------------------------------------------+
```

Figure 4

Note that:

a. This is a deep case representation with a limited number of predicates ("deep verbs").

b. The direction of the arrow is following RESEDA's convention. From a practical point of view the arrow indicates that the right-hand side schema is allowed to replace something that matches the left-hand side schema. Conceptually it means that the information possibly retrieved using the right-hand side schema implies the information searched for, by the (original) left hand side schema.

Rules can place restrictions on variables (as is the case in RESEDA). For instance, the rule shown above could have required that "x" be a human being. This rule would then apply for "x = y", where "y" is known to be a teacher. The match (between x and y) is made possible, because we have stored in the factual knowledge representation the fact that "teacher 'is_a' human_being".

Standardization rules are used to translate the parser's output (containing surface verbs) into a more canonical form, i.e. usable by transformation rules. All of the standardization rules belong to the KB1 level, as they are absolutely general.

V. THE INFERENCE ENGINE

We are in the course of developing (December 84) a prototype version with an "exhaustive" engine, meaning that all the possible transformations are executed (with simple destructive chronological backtracking) until a representation is found. This approach is very close to the RESEDA inference engine (see Zarri, 1984c, for a description of the later one)

This simplistic approach is justified since our current knowledge base contains only "KB3" types of knowledge.** We are planning to move onto more sophisticated approaches (ex. choosing among several representations in the database of the same question, a.s.o...) after the prototype has been well tested.

VI. CONCLUSIONS

The presented NLI system is designed to tackle issues such as **transportability** and **"helpful understanding"** of a naive user.

Transportability, the first issue, has been examined in many research systems, however all of these seem to lack a clear distinction between different levels of transportability of the knowledge represented (HAM-ANS, Hoeppner et al., 1983 seems to be an exception).

In addition SAPHIR+RESEDA is using **general common sense** knowledge (reference Hemphill and Rhyne, 1978, describes a project where the use of Schank's general formalism in DB queries has been explored, but its goals seem to be more limited than ours).

The second issue is somewhat close to " **cooperation**" as defined in the CO-OP system (Kaplan, 1982). Kaplan

---

** Our rules (temporarily) have a very specific content, i.e. they have not been "factored out". This is due to the fact that only a limited number of queries have been tested on a single database (we are beginning the implementation phase, following a one year study period).

however seems to consider only the case where the DB produces a null answer. We believe his and our approach to be complementary.

Our system uses rules to produce a DB query, this is similar to a deductive DBMS approach. However our rules are not formal and we never access the database in the course of transformation (because in most real world cases it is prohibitively expensive).

REFERENCES

<1> Gross, M. Méthodes en syntaxe. Paris: Hermann, 1975.

<2> Hoeppner, W., T. Christaller, H. Marburger, K. Morik, B. Nebel, M. O'Leary and W. Wahlster, "Beyond Domain-Independence", in Proc. of IJCAI-83, Karlsruhe, W. Germany, 1983.

<3> Hemphill L. and J. Rhyne, A Model for Knowledge Representation in Natural Language Query Systems, Research Report Laboratory RJ 2304(31046), IBM Research Laboratory, San Jose, September 1978.

<4> Kaplan, S. J. "Cooperative Responses from a Portable Natural Language Query System". Artificial Intelligence, vol 19 (1982) 165-187.

<5> Normier, B. SAPHIR - Présentation générale, ERLI, Janvier 1984.

<6> Normier, B., M-E. Aubert, G. Clemencin, B. Euzenat, S. Lacep, N. Lellouche, A. Ogonowski and J. Vega, Extension de la gestion du dialogue, Rapport final (Marché DRET 83/234), ERLI, Décembre 1984.

<7> Euzenat, B., B. Normier, A. Ogonowski and G. P. Zarri, Les mécanismes d'inférence dans l'interrogation de bases de données relationnelles en langage naturel, Convention ADI-84-068 rapport intermédiaire N.1, ERLI, Juin 1984a.

<8> Euzenat, B., B. Normier, A. Ogonowski and G. P. Zarri, Les mécanismes d'inférence dans l'interrogation de bases de données relationnelles en langage naturel, Convention ADI-84-068 rapport final, ERLI, Décembre 1984b.

<9> Zarri, G. P. "An Outline of the Representation and Use of Temporal Data in the RESEDA System". Information Technology: Research and Development, vol 2 (1983) 89-108.

<10> Zarri, G. P. "Expert Systems and Information Retrieval: an Experiment in the Domain of Biographical Data Management", in Developments in Expert Systems, Coombs M.J. ed. London: Academic Press, 1984a.

<11> Zarri, G. P. "Constructing and Utilizing a Large Fact Database Using AI Techniques", in Proc. of the First International Workshop on Expert Database Systems, Univ. of South Carolina, College of Business Administration, Kerschberg L. ed., 1984b.

<12> Zarri, G. P. "Intelligent Information Retrieval: an Interesting Application Area for the New Generation Computer Systems", in Proc of the International Conference on Fifth Generation Computer Systems, Tokyo, Japan, 1984c.

RESEARCHER: AN EXPERIMENTAL INTELLIGENT INFORMATION SYSTEM*

Michael Lebowitz
Department of Computer Science
Computer Science Building, Columbia University
New York, NY 10027, USA

Abstract

The development of very powerful intelligent information systems requires the use of many techniques best derived by studying human understanding methods. RESEARCHER is a system that reads, remembers, generalizes from, and answers questions about complex technical texts, patent abstracts in particular. In this paper we discuss three current areas of research involving RESEARCHER -- the generalization of hierarchically structured representations; the use of long-term memory in text processing, specifically in resolving ambiguity; and the tailoring of answers to questions to the level of expertise of different users.

1 Introduction

In [Lebowitz 83a] we described the first stages of development of RESEARCHER, a prototype intelligent information system. RESEARCHER is intended to accept natural language input, patent abstracts in particular, and 1) understand the text, 2) add the acquired information to a long-term memory, generalizing as it does so, and 3) answer questions from its memory. In this paper, we will present an overview of the new areas that we are using RESEARCHER to study. In each of these areas we apply techniques derived from cognitive modelling approaches to language and learning. We are using people as our model to help us achieve better performance on very hard tasks (which, in return, gives us insight into the human processing methods).

2 Generalizing hierarchies

The patent abstracts that we have been looking at describe the physical structure of complex objects. Since such objects are most naturally represented as hierarchies of parts, our learning research has addressed the generalization of hierarchically structured descriptions. EX1 is part of a typical patent abstract.

> **EX1** - P81; U. S. Patent #4306258; Higashiyama Nobor et al.
>
> A magnetic head supporting mechanism equipped with a magnetic head positioning carriage of a interchangeable double side type flexible disc drive apparatus comprising a carriage having a pair of arms which is rotated in detachable to a double side type flexible disc and arms ...

*This research was supported in part by the Defense Advanced Research Projects Agency under contract N00039-84-C-0165. Many people have contributed to RESEARCHER. In particular, the work on generalizing hierarchies has largely been conducted by Kenneth Wasserman and the work on question answering by Cecile Paris, co-advised by Professor Kathleen McKeown.

Our representation of patent abstracts such as this one includes three classes of information: 1) *a parts hierarchy*, that illustrates the components of each part; 2) *interpart relations*, physical and functional relations between various components; and 3) *properties* of the objects. We have concentrated on the parts hierarchy and physical relations [Wasserman and Lebowitz 83]. We are currently working on classification schemes for functional relations and object properties (such as size and composition).

Full understanding requires that we integrate new representations with existing knowledge in memory. RESEARCHER has as one of its goals the incremental generalization of hierarchical descriptions of objects such as EX1 by finding similar examples in memory, comparing them with the new example, and abstracting out the similarities.

Generalizing hierarchical representations presents a number of difficult problems. Typical problems are: deciding how the components in the objects being compared correspond; dealing with differing levels of description of objects; and structuring memory so that maximally efficient inheritance of the sort used in semantic networks and frame systems (see [Barr et al. 82]) can be achieved automatically. In this paper, we will only give examples of how the generalization process works, and refer the reader to [Wasserman 85] for more details.

We can break generalization into two phases -- 1) when a new example is presented, deciding what other objects to compare it to (since RESEARCHER is not given examples designed to teach a specific concept), and 2) the comparison process itself, which abstracts out similarities.

We will look at the comparison process first, as it is involved in the search process. EX2 and EX3 are two simplified disc drive patents.

> **EX2** - A disc drive comprising an enclosure surrounding the disc drive, said disc drive including a spinning assembly, a disc and a readwrite head, said spinning assembly including a spindle connected to a motor, said enclosure comprising a cover on top of a support member.

> **EX3** - A disc drive comprising an enclosure surrounding the disc drive, said disc drive including a spinning assembly, a magnetic assembly and a readwrite head, said spinning assembly including a spindle connected to a motor, said magnetic assembly comprising a disc, said enclosure comprising a cover on top of a support member.

As human understanders, we can easily see that patents EX2 and EX3 describe similar objects. However, to begin to generalize the similarities, RESEARCHER must decide how the parts of the representations correspond -- for example, that the enclosure in EX2 corresponds to the enclosure in EX3, and not to the spinning assembly, the magnetic assembly or the readwrite head, which are all parts of the disc drive in EX3. Here this is relatively easy, as the enclosures are identical, but we must be able to identify less perfect matches. RESEARCHER does this with a numerical scoring algorithm, similar to the one in [Winston 80].

Figure 1 shows RESEARCHER's generalization of these objects, taken from [Wasserman 85]. When RESEARCHER makes correspondences of the sort mentioned above, one problem arises in dealing with the discs. The disc in EX2 is described as part of the disc drive, while in EX3 the disc is part of a magnetic assembly which is part of the disc drive. To make the representations match, RESEARCHER must insert a "null" part, which may or may not actually exist in any given object. The two input representations are stored as variants of the generalized object, recording only how they differ from it (basically, in this case, how the null object is resolved; in real examples there would usually be more differences).

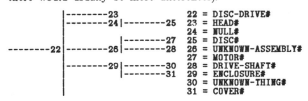

Figure 1:   Generalization of EX2 and EX3

Even with just two hierarchical descriptions to compare, the matching process involves a number of problems in determining how the components of the hierarchies correspond. One such problem is the need to insert levels in a hierarchy to obtain a good match, as described above. (While the insertion of a null level by itself decreases the goodness of a match, it may increase the value of lower level matches.) The problem is that there are an exponentially large number of places where null levels can be inserted, each requiring a complex recursive match to test. We have used RESEARCHER to experiment with a variety of different algorithms for deciding where null levels should be inserted for optimal matching, concentrating on ones that only try the most obvious places near the top of the hierarchy.

Since the examples given RESEARCHER are not expressly designed for learning specific concepts (as they would be for a system being taught concepts), the program must decide which examples to compare for the purpose of generalization. This is done using a generalization-based memory of the sort in [Lebowitz 83b]. A hierarchy of concepts is created in memory (a hierarchy of hierarchies, in this case) that organizes specific examples.

In using its generalization-based memory, RESEARCHER takes each new example and searches down the tree for the example or generalized concept most similar to it. This process involves matching generalized concepts with the new example in much the same way as EX2 and EX3 were matched. We begin by matching the new example with each of the children of the generalization tree's root. RESEARCHER selects the best match and looks at that node's children. As long as one of the children produces a better match than the parent node, RESEARCHER continues down the tree. Eventually, it either reaches a leaf (an instance already in memory) or a maximally good generalization (i.e., all of the subordinate nodes contain factors that decrease the quality of the match).

Once the most similar previous example or existing generalization is found, RESEARCHER "factors out" similarities between these representations, and, if need be, creates a new generalization node. In any case, the new example is stored by recording how it differs from the generalizations in memory. This is an optimally space-efficient method of storage, which also captures significant generalizations about the objects in the domain.

The current implementation of RESEARCHER's generalization scheme works quite well on modest-sized examples. In addition to disc drive patents, a modified version of the program (CORPORATE-RESEARCHER [Wasserman 85]) has been tested on hierarchical descriptions of corporate organizations.

3 Text processing using memory

Since intelligent information systems such as RESEARCHER have available many examples in memory, it seems natural to make use of this information for text processing (beyond identifying lexical items). Patent abstracts, despite being written in legalese are, like the rest of natural language, quite ambiguous. We can use memory to help resolve many ambiguities.

We feel that the best way to use detailed memory information during text understanding in the context of current systems is to identify specific tasks where a piece of information from memory will be useful. More general methods, such as using memory to determine the interesting aspects of a text to focus processing, we leave for the future. We have identified a set of "questions" that arise during text processing that can most easily be answered (and often can *only* be answered) by accessing long-term memory.

It is important to keep in mind that we are proposing using *memory* for understanding, as opposed to general semantic information about words or concepts. While such general information is crucial for our conceptually-based understanding methods, in order to resolve many ambiguities it will be necessary to look at very detailed information in memory -- in our case, how the objects described in patent abstracts are constructed and how their pieces relate to each other. The use of the information base also reduces the need to initially hand-code information for RESEARCHER.

EX4 illustrates two kinds of ambiguities that arise in patent abstracts.

EX4 - A disc head supporting a spindle made of magnetic material.

The first ambiguity in EX4 involves "disc head". Although not syntactically ambiguous, an understanding system such as RESEARCHER must determine the conceptual relationship between the nouns. The phrase "made of magnetic material" is ambiguous in that we do not know whether it refers to the head or the spindle. Both of these ambiguities can only be resolved by looking at memory. In fact, it would be easy to construct scenarios where different states of memory would cause this example to be understood differently (e.g., whether we knew about magnetic heads or magnetic spindles).

RESEARCHER makes use of relatively simple, but heavily memory-based, techniques for handling ambiguities of the sort in EX4. Its conceptual analysis type text processing algorithm (described in [Lebowitz 83a; Lebowitz 84]), involves identifying object descriptions (usually noun groups) and connecting them with various relational words (usually prepositions -- patent abstracts are quite short of verbs) which indicate the various physical, functional and assembly-component relations mentioned in Section 2. Within this processing algorithm, we have identified places where ambiguity can be identified and memory queried for resolution. Memory is asked which of two possible physical constructions is more likely or what relation is likely to occur between two objects. Questions in both classes are answered by looking for examples of the possible configurations that already exist in memory.

Figure 2 lists some of the questions that RESEARCHER can currently ask memory for purposes of disambiguation. They primarily involve prepositional phrase attachment and noun groups with multiple nouns.* Our analyses of these ambiguities shares much with the linguistic work of [Levi 78] and the application of this work to AI in [Finin 82]. However, our method of resolving the ambiguities -- the use of a dynamic, long-term memory -- is rather different.

Form: object-word1 object-word2
Example: **An actuator housing ...**
Question: **What is the relation between object-word1 and object-word2?**

Form: modifier object-word1 object-word2
Example: **A metal drive cover ...**
Question: **Does the modifier better apply to object-word1 or object-word2?**

Form: object-word1 relation-word1 object-word2 relation-word2 object-word3
Example: **A coating on a disc touching a spindle ...**
Question: **Does relation-word2 connect object-word3 with object-word1 or object-word2?**

Figure 2:   Some disambiguation questions

The search for possible examples that answer a given question is a relatively simple one. RESEARCHER uses its dynamically created device hierarchies to look for possible constructions and relations. It begins its search with general object descriptions and searches through more specific descriptions until a relevant example is found. If several possible constructions (or relations) are found, the one associated with the most general description is used, as that represents RESEARCHER's most widely applicable information. RESEARCHER's memory search disambiguation process is described in more detail in [Lebowitz 84].

_____

*The word types used in Figure 2 are functional, rather than syntactic. However, object words are usually nouns and relation words are usually prepositions, although not always in either case.

Our disambiguation methodology bears resemblance to that of [Small 80] and [Hirst 83], except, crucially, it relies on information from a detailed, dynamic memory. Our algorithm does have the side-effect of making understanding subjective, in the sense of [Abelson 73; Carbonell 81], since new examples will be interpreted to correspond to old ones, but we view this as inevitable if we wish to achieve robust understanding.

As an illustration of RESEARCHER's use of memory in text processing, we will show how it processes part of a real patent abstract, EX1, seen earlier.

Although it may not be immediately obvious, the beginning of EX1 is extremely ambiguous. (It may not be obvious because people are so good at resolving ambiguity.) The internal structures of the various noun phrases and the determination of what is a part of what could all be resolved in several ways. Without any information in memory, RESEARCHER would have to rely on general heuristics which might or might not work, and would, in any case, be quite ad hoc. Instead, we will provide RESEARCHER with a few (admittedly somewhat artificial) examples that it can use. Specifically, we will give it the following descriptions:

An apparatus with a support mechanism.

An interchangeable double sided floppy disc within a drive which has a magnetic head.

Having given RESEARCHER examples of support mechanisms and double sided floppy disc drives, we let it read EX1 (Figure 3).

A number of aspects of RESEARCHER's text processing are shown in Figure 3. We will focus on its use of memory. Each memory access is indicated by ">>>". The first such use occurs when processing the initial noun group, "A magnetic head supporting mechanism". RESEARCHER uses a "save and skip" strategy for noun groups -- it saves words in a short term memory stack until the head noun is reached. Then it works backwards processing the stacked words. Here, it easily sets up two relations between the head and the mechanism, both from the word "supporting", indicating that the mechanism supports and is connected to the head.

Next RESEARCHER must process "magnetic". It is syntactically ambiguous here whether the modifier applies to the head or the mechanism. (To see the other case, consider, "a complicated head supporting mechanism".) So, RESEARCHER searches its memory for examples of magnetic heads or magnetic mechanisms. It finds the former, and appropriately resolves the ambiguity.

The processing of the next part of EX3, "equipped with a magnetic head positioning carriage" is relatively sedate. "Magnetic" is again ambiguous, but this time refers to an object already described in the patent. Memory again becomes important in processing "a interchangeable double side type flexible disc drive apparatus".

The first problem arises in determining the relation between the drive and the apparatus (remember, noun groups are processed, in effect, backwards). Here, since RESEARCHER has no examples in memory, it uses a

```
Running RESEARCHER at 6:03:19 PM

(A MAGNETIC HEAD SUPPORTING MECHANISM EQUIPPED WITH A
MAGNETIC HEAD POSITIONING CARRIAGE OF A INTERCHANGEABLE
DOUBLE SIDE TYPE FLEXIBLE DISC DRIVE APPARATUS COMPRISING ..

Processing:

A            : New instance word -- skip
MAGNETIC     : Memette modifier; save and skip
HEAD         : Memette within NP; save and skip
SUPPORTING   : Purpose word within NP; save and skip
MECHANISM    : MP word -- memette UNKNOWN-ASSEMBLY#

New UNKNOWN-ASSEMBLY# instance (&MEM6)
New HEAD# instance (&MEM7)
Establishing R-CONNECTED-TO; SUBJECT: &MEM6 ('MECHANISM');
   OBJECT: &MEM7 (HEAD#) [&REL2]
Establishing P-SUPPORTS; SUBJECT: &MEM6 ('MECHANISM');
   OBJECT: &MEM7 (HEAD#) [&REL3]
>>> Select memette modified by DEV-TYPE/MAGNETISM from
   &MEM6 ('MECHANISM') &MEM7 (HEAD#)
Augmenting &MEM7 (HEAD#) with feature: DEV-TYPE = MAGNETISM

EQUIPPED WITH : Parts of &MEM6 to follow
A            : New instance word -- skip
MAGNETIC     : Memette modifier; save and skip
HEAD         : Memette within NP; save and skip
POSITIONING  : Purpose word within NP; save and skip
CARRIAGE     : MP word -- memette CARRIAGE#

New CARRIAGE# instance (&MEM8)
Establishing P-GUIDES; OBJECT: &MEM8 (CARRIAGE#);
   SUBJECT: &MEM7 (HEAD#) [&REL4]
Recognized instance of &MEM7 (HEAD#)
Assuming &MEM8 (CARRIAGE#) is part of &MEM6 ('MECHANISM')
OF (OF1)     : Part of indicator
Assuming &MEM8 or &MEM6 is part of the following

A            : New instance word -- skip
INTERCHANGEABLE : Memette modifier; save and skip
DOUBLE SIDE  : Memette modifier; save and skip
TYPE         : Skip (SKIP)
FLEXIBLE     : Memette modifier; save and skip
DISC         : Memette within NP; save and skip
DRIVE        : Memette within NP; save and skip
APPARATUS    : MP word -- memette UNKNOWN-ASSEMBLY#

New UNKNOWN-ASSEMBLY# instance (&MEM9)
>>> Looking for relation between DRIVE# and
   &MEM9 ('APPARATUS')
New DRIVE# instance (&MEM10)
Assuming &MEM10 (DRIVE#) is part of &MEM9 ('APPARATUS')
>>> Looking for relation between DISC# and one of
   &MEM9 ('APPARATUS') &MEM10 (DRIVE#)
New DISC# instance (&MEM11)
Establishing R-INSIDE-OF; SUBJECT: &MEM11 (DISC#);
   OBJECT: &MEM10 (DRIVE#) [&REL5]
>>> Select memette modified by RIGIDITY/NONE from
   &MEM9 ('APPARATUS') &MEM11 (DISC#)
Augmenting &MEM11 (DISC#) with feature: RIGIDITY = NONE
>>> Select memette modified by NUMBER-OF-SIDES/2 from
   &MEM9 ('APPARATUS') &MEM11 (DISC#)
Augmenting &MEM11 (DISC#) with feature: NUMBER-OF-SIDES = 2
>>> Select memette modified by DEV-PURPOSE/MANY from
   &MEM9 ('APPARATUS') &MEM11 (DISC#)
Augmenting &MEM11 (DISC#) with feature: DEV-PURPOSE = MANY
>>> Selecting comp for &MEM9 ('APPARATUS') from among
   &MEM8 (CARRIAGE#) &MEM6 ('MECHANISM')
Assuming &MEM6 ('MECHANISM') is part of &MEM9 ('APPARATUS')

COMPRISING   : Parts of &MEM9 or &MEM6 to follow
...
```

Figure 3:   RESEARCHER using memory

heuristic to assume that since "apparatus" describes a rather vague assembly, the drive is probably a part of it. When "disc" is reached, the problem is more complex, since RESEARCHER must determine both whether the disc is related to the drive or the apparatus, and what the relation is. Here, as always, memory is used. Since RESEARCHER does not have an example of a relation between a disc and an apparatus, but knows of an example of a disc being

inside a drive, it assumes that the disc is inside the drive here.

When the modifiers, "flexible", "double side" (RESEARCHER has a phrasal lexicon) and "interchangeable" are processed, the program must attach them to either the apparatus or the disc. (The drive is ruled out by syntactic considerations.) The processing is similar to the first noun group, using memory to resolve the conflict. Note that the disambiguation search has a semantic basis, so that the "floppy" disc in memory resolves the ambiguity over "flexible".

Finally, RESEARCHER must decide whether the apparatus has as a part the carriage or the mechanism. (The "part of" relation is indicated by the word "of".) Once again, the routine is the same -- search memory for examples and find one that resolves the ambiguity in favor of the mechanism. Different examples in memory would lead to a different resolution.

We have much left to do in our integration of text processing and memory. However, we feel our general approach is quite promising, as our work in building up memory has a positive synergistic effect on text processing robustness. The identification of specific questions to ask memory seems to be much more effective than looking for more general applications of memory to understanding.

4 Q/A in RESEARCHER

Once a substantial knowledge base has been built up by RESEARCHER, it is important that it can be queried intelligently. In [Lebowitz 83a; Paris 84] we described an early question answering module. Recently, our work has concentrated on how RESEARCHER might tailor its answers for individual users. There are many elements to such tailoring, the goal of the user, for example, but here we will concentrate on just one factor -- the user's expertise. We have tried to determine the sorts of basic answering strategies that would be appropriate for expert and naive users of the system.* Eventually, we will also look at how expertise affects other levels of processing (such as word choice) as well as other factors on answering.

In order to get an idea about the kinds of strategies that might be appropriate for various users, we have looked at texts that describe objects that are aimed at readers with different levels of expertise -- several adult and junior encyclopedias. As described fully in [Paris 85], the strategies used in the adult and junior encyclopedias are quite different -- the adult encyclopedias, presumably aimed at relative experts, tend to describe the part structure of objects, while the junior encyclopedias describe the processes that take place in the device. EX5 and EX6 show this distinction for descriptions of telephones.

EX5 - The hand-sets introduced in 1947 consist of a receiver and a transmitter in a single housing available in black or colored plastic. The transmitter diaphragm is clamped rigidly at its edges to improve the high frequency response. The diaphragm is coupled to a doubly resonant system -- a cavity and an air chamber -- which

---

*Actually, user expertise falls into two areas -- familiarity with the system and familiarity with the domain. We are concerned here with the latter.

broadens the response... (Collier's Encyclopedia, 1962)

As we can see, EX5, taken from an adult encyclopedia, describes a telephone by presenting its parts. The description continues in this vein. It is using a construction quite similar to the constituency schema that McKeown used in her question answering work [McKeown 82], providing an almost tree-like description of the parts of the object. This is in contrast with a description aimed at younger readers, EX6.

EX6 - When one speaks into the transmitter of a modern telephone, these sound waves strike against an *aluminum disk or diaphragm* and cause it to vibrate back and forth in just the same way the molecules of air are vibrating... (Britannica Junior, 1963)

Here the description is process-oriented. It traces the process of transmitting sound, introducing part descriptions only when necessary. This is clearly a different presentation strategy, one that our study of texts indicates is much more widely used in texts aimed at less experienced readers. We feel that a process-oriented answer would be appropriate for RESEARCHER to use when dealing with a novice user not likely to know what various parts are used for.

We are currently in the early stages of implementing these two different strategies for describing the same object. We have implemented simple techniques for producing "expert" type responses using McKeown's constituency schema (although our low-level generation, even here, is quite basic). In addition to looking at the different generation strategies, we are also studying ways to determine the expertise of a user as well as mixed strategies that make use of elements of each generation technique.

5 Conclusion

We have described here three areas of investigation in the study of intelligent information systems focused around the program RESEARCHER. The generalization of hierarchical representations allows the system to learn about a wide range of complex objects and build up a rich memory. This memory is used extensively in text processing, primarily for disambiguation, to achieve robust performance. Finally, awareness of the expertise level of a user will allow RESEARCHER to tailor it answers to each user. The sum of these three related areas of investigation should lead towards the development of powerful intelligent information systems.

References

[Abelson 73] Abelson, R. P. The structure of belief systems. In R. C. Schank and K. Colby, Ed., *Computer Models of Thought and Language*, W. H. Freeman Co., San Francisco, 1973.

[Barr et al. 82] Barr, A., Cohen, P. R. and Feigenbaum, E. A., eds. *The Handbook of Artificial Intelligence, Volumes 1 - 3.* William Kaufmann, Inc., Los Altos, California, 1982.

[Carbonell 81] Carbonell, J. G. *Subjective Understanding: Computer Models of Belief Systems.* UMI Research Press, Ann Arbor, Michigan, 1981.

[Finin 82] Finin, T. W. The interpretation of nominal compounds in discourse. Technical Report MS-CIS-82-3, Moore School of Engineering, University of Pennsylvania, 1982.

[Hirst 83] Hirst, G. *Semantic interpretation against ambiguity.* Ph.D. Thesis, Department of Computer Science, Brown University, 1983.

[Lebowitz 83a] Lebowitz, M. RESEARCHER: An overview. Proceedings of the Third National Conference on Artificial Intelligence, Washington, DC, 1983, pp. 232 - 235.

[Lebowitz 83b] Lebowitz, M. Concept learning in a rich input domain. Proceedings of the 1983 International Machine Learning Workshop, Champaign-Urbana, Illinois, 1983, pp. 177 - 182. To appear in *Machine Learning II*.

[Lebowitz 84] Lebowitz, M. Using memory in text understanding. Proceedings of ECAI-84, Pisa, Italy, 1984.

[Levi 78] Levi, J. N. *The Syntax and Semantics of Complex Nominals.* McGraw Hill, New York, 1978.

[McKeown 82] McKeown, K. R. *Generating natural language text in response to questions about database structure.* Ph.D. Thesis, University of Pennsylvania, 1982.

[Paris 84] Paris, C. L. Determining the level of expertise. Proceedings of the First Annual Workshop on Theoretical Issues in Conceptual Information Processing, Atlanta, Georgia, 1984.

[Paris 85] Paris, C. L. Description strategies for naive and expert users. Proceedings of the 23rd Annual Meeting of the Association for Computational Linguistics, Chicago, 1985.

[Small 80] Small, S. Word expert parsing: A theory of distributed word-based natural language understanding. Technical Report TR-954, University of Maryland, Department of Computer Science, 1980.

[Wasserman 85] Wasserman, K. *Unifying representation and generalization: Understanding hierarchically structured objects.* Ph.D. Thesis, Columbia University Department of Computer Science, 1985.

[Wasserman and Lebowitz 83] Wasserman, K. and Lebowitz, M. "Representing complex physical objects." *Cognition and Brain Theory 6*, 3 (1983), 333 - 352.

[Winston 80] Winston, P. H. "Learning and reasoning by analogy." *Communications of the ACM 23* (1980), 689 - 702.

A Parallel-Process Model of On-Line Inference Processing

Kurt P. Eiselt

Irvine Computational Intelligence Project
Computer Science Department
University of California
Irvine, California 92717

Abstract

This paper presents a new model of on-line inference processes during text understanding. The model, called ATLAST, integrates inference processing at the lexical, syntactic, and pragmatic levels of understanding, and is consistent with the results of controlled psychological experiments. ATLAST interprets input text through the interaction of independent but communicating inference processes running in parallel. The focus of this paper is on the initial computer implementation of the ATLAST model, and some observations and issues which arise from that implementation.

1.0 Introduction

This paper describes a new theory of inference processing developed at the Irvine Computational Intelligence Project, and an initial computer implementation of that theory. The research described here integrates inference processing at the lexical, syntactic, and pragmatic levels, and is consistent with the results of controlled psychological experiments. The theory centers upon a parallel-process model of text understanding which explains inference behavior at the different levels as the result of interactions between three independent but communicating inference processes. Though there are three processes operating at three different levels of language understanding, there is no direct correspondence between the levels and the processes. Inference decisions at all levels are made through the combined actions of the three processes running in parallel. We call this model ATLAST (A Three-level Language Analysis SysTem).

ATLAST represents a real departure from most previous models of language understanding and inference processing [e.g., Schank, 1975; Cullingford, 1978; Wilensky, 1978; DeJong, 1979], though there are models which integrate some of the levels of inference processing. For example, IPP [Lebowitz, 1980] and BORIS [Dyer, 1982] integrate the syntactic and pragmatic levels, while the model of Small, Cottrell, and Shastri [1982] integrates lexical access and syntactic parsing. Finally, Charniak's model, as

This research was supported in part by the National Science Foundation under grant IST-81-20685 and by the Naval Ocean Systems Center under contracts N00123-81-C-1078 and N66001-83-C-0255.

does ATLAST, seeks to integrate lexical, syntactic, and pragmatic inference processing [Charniak, 1983], though his model differs from ATLAST in other respects.

2.0 Background: The Theory in Brief

The theory behind ATLAST is described in detail in [Granger, Eiselt, & Holbrook, 1985], but a brief review of the theory is provided here to aid in understanding the program.

ATLAST is a direct descendant of earlier work on inference decision processes at the pragmatic level. Specifically, it came about as an attempt to address word-sense ambiguity problems which arose during research into different pragmatic inference strategies used by human subjects while reading text, and the development of a program, called STRATEGIST, which modelled that behavior [Granger, Eiselt, & Holbrook, 1983; Granger & Holbrook, 1983]. As we worked on STRATEGIST, we observed that lexical and pragmatic inference processes appeared to have much in common. Many pragmatic inferences seemed to be triggered by individual words. This is hardly new news, of course, as there exist integrated models of language understanding in which higher-level inferences are directly activated by input text (FRUMP [DeJong, 1979] and IPP [Lebowitz, 1980] are notable examples). We believed, though, that the relationship was even closer than described by previous models—that the inference decision mechanisms themselves were in some way interdependent at the very least. For example, in the text

The CIA called in an inspector to check for bugs. The secretaries had reported seeing roaches.

the first sentence alone has an unambiguous interpretation: the "hidden microphone" sense of "bugs" is more appropriate than the "insect" sense. Upon reading the second sentence, the "insect" sense is obviously more appropriate, and the initial choice of word-sense for "bugs" must be supplanted. To explain this process, we theorize that "CIA" triggers a pragmatic inference about espionage which in turn influences the choice of the "hidden microphone" word-sense for "bugs". Later, the word "roaches" generates higher-level inferences which suggest that the "insect" sense of "bugs" is correct and that the Central Intelligence Agency, in this case at least, is more appropriately viewed as a generic employer trying to rid itself of pests rather than as an espionage agency protecting its secrets. Thus, the context generated by "CIA" determined the selection of a word-sense for "bugs", while the context generated by "roaches" resulted in an entirely new interpretation of "bugs" and a slightly modified interpretation of "CIA". Because of this interdependence between inference levels, theories about pragmatic inference mechanisms must include theories about **lexical access** processes.

Lexical access is the process by which a word's meaning is extracted from its written (or spoken) form. Recent research into lexical access has led to the counter-intuitive conclusion that when an ambiguous word is presented in context (i.e., a sentence or phrase), all meanings of the word are initially accessed, and context is subsequently consulted to determine the most appropriate meaning [Swinney & Hakes, 1976; Tanenhaus, Leiman, & Seidenberg, 1979; Lucas, 1983; Granger, Holbrook, & Eiselt, 1984]. This happens regardless of the syntactic category of the word, or whether the context is biased toward one meaning or another.

If the lexical access process does in fact work as described above, and if individual words trigger the higher-level pragmatic inferences, then it is likely that the pragmatic inference decision process is much the same as the lexical inference decision process. Work on ATLAST goes under the assumption that, when more than one interpretation (i.e., pragmatic inference) of an input text is possible, all possible interpretations are pursued in parallel, and those interpretations which do not fit well with the existing context are "de-activated" or inhibited.

3.0 How ATLAST Works
3.1 Memory

ATLAST is built around a high-level episodic memory structure which contains two kinds of memory organization packets (MOPs) [Schank, 1982; Kolodner, 1984]. For each word in ATLAST's vocabulary there is a MOP which represents that word. Most lexical-entry MOPs contain a one-way link to one or more word-senses directly associated with that word, and syntactic information about the word-senses. Function words, such as "a" and "the", are not linked to other MOPs and serve only to aid in syntactic decisions. The word-senses are an example of the other kind of MOP in ATLAST's memory: those which represent events or objects. These MOPs are interconnected through a network of two-way links which serve to define the relationships between the MOPs. These MOPs can be, but are not necessarily, directly linked to lexical entries.

The inference decisions in ATLAST are carried out by three primary components: the **Capsulizer**, the **Proposer**, and the **Filter**. Theoretically, these processes run in parallel. However, ATLAST is written in UCI-LISP on a DECSYSTEM-20, so the parallelism which is so important

to the theory is necessarily simulated in its implementation. This simulation is accomplished by repeatedly cycling through the three processes. Thus, the Capsulizer runs for a pre-determined amount of time, followed by the Proposer, then the Filter, then the Capsulizer again, and so on. The amount of time each process is allocated is an important issue with respect to the accuracy of the model. This issue has not yet been fully explored.

3.2 Capsulizer

The Capsulizer contains the first stage of a **two-stage syntactic analysis process** similar in some respects to that described by Frazier and Fodor [1978]. The Capsulizer makes **intra-phrasal**, as opposed to inter-phrasal, syntactic decisions about the words in the input text (again, see [Granger, Eiselt, & Holbrook, 1985] for a discussion of the theory behind two-stage syntactic analysis). As the Capsulizer encounters each new word in the input text, it retrieves the syntactic category information associated with that word (e.g., "this word can be used as a noun and a verb") and activates any word-senses associated with that word. The word-senses are not used in any decisions made by the Capsulizer, though pointers to the word-senses are retained. The activated word-senses serve as a starting point for the search carried out by the Proposer, which is described below.

As the Capsulizer processes the input words, it accumulates the syntactic information it retrieves and makes initial decisions about syntactic relationships within the phrases of the input text. These intra-phrasal decisions, along with the pointers to the word-senses which comprise the phrases, are passed along to the Filter as "capsules" of information. The Filter then makes decisions about the syntactic relationships between the phrases (i.e., **inter-phrasal** syntax). If an input word activates more than one word-sense (i.e., a word-sense ambiguity), the pointers to the multiple word-senses are all passed on to the Filter, which will eventually select the "best" word-sense. This process is also described in more detail below.

3.3 Proposer

The Proposer gets its name from the idea that it "proposes" possible inference paths which might explain the input text. Essentially, it is a search mechanism which employs spreading activation to traverse the links between the MOPs in memory and find connections between word-senses which have been activated by the Capsulizer.

The Proposer maintains pointers to the most recently activated MOPs in memory, and to the word-senses which are the origins of the spreading activation search. Each time the Proposer is invoked, it traverses the links leading away from the recently activated MOPs, activates the adjacent MOPs at the end of those links, and updates its list of pointers. If the spread of activation from one point of origin intersects the spread of activation from some other point of origin, then the Proposer has found some plausible relationship, by way of links and MOPs, between two (and possibly more) of the word-senses activated by the input text. The Proposer then passes information about this newly-discovered pathway to the Filter; in this way, the Proposer "proposes" possible inference paths for evaluation by the Filter.

Spreading activation has been employed in a number of models [e.g., Quillian, 1968; Fahlman, 1979; Anderson, 1983; Charniak, 1983; Norvig, 1983; Riesbeck & Martin, 1985]. Spreading activation allows ATLAST to pursue multiple inference paths in parallel. Were this process allowed to continue unchecked, it would lead to a combinatorial explosion of inference paths. To prevent this from happening in ATLAST, the third major process, the Filter, constantly evaluates or "filters" inference paths and inhibits pursuit of those which appear to be poor explanations of the input text. Though the idea of beginning pursuit on all inference paths instead of just the "appropriate" ones may seem both counter-intuitive and counter-productive, there are two arguments for using this approach. One is that it would seem impossible to determine which inferences may be appropriate without first evaluating all inference possibilities. The other is that this approach is consistent with experimental studies of human behavior [Tanenhaus, Leiman, & Seidenberg, 1979; Seidenberg, Tanenhaus, Leiman, & Bienkowski, 1982; Granger, Holbrook, & Eiselt, 1984].

The Proposer is implemented in ATLAST as a separate process, but from a theoretical perspective it might be more appropriately viewed as an emergent property of a human memory organization. Computer memory seems to work somewhat differently than human memory, though, so it was necessary to provide a separate process to make the spreading activation possible.

3.4 Filter

The Filter performs two functions; the first is that of inter-phrasal syntax. As capsules are passed from the Capsulizer to the Filter, the Filter makes decisions about the relationships between the phrases represented by the capsules. Inter-phrasal syntax rules enable the Filter to fill the Actor, Action, and Object slots, for example. Future work on the ATLAST program will add rules about modifying phrases, keeping track of referents across phrases, and agreement of tense, number, and gender, among other rules.

The Filter's other function is the evaluation of inference paths. When two competing inference paths are proposed (e.g., different paths connecting the word-senses of two words from the input text), the Filter attempts to select the more appropriate path through the application of three inference evaluation metrics.

First, the Filter evaluates the inference paths according to the **specificity** metric [Wilensky, 1983]. If one path is determined to be less specific than the other, the less specific path is inhibited; that is, the spread of activation

from nodes on the path is stopped, and that path is no longer considered as a plausible explanation for the input text. Specificity is determined by the links in the path: a path which includes a "viewed-as" link (from the "view" relationship defined in [Wilensky, 1984]) is less specific than a path which does not contain such a link. In the example of Section 3.5, the CIA is a special case of a spy agency, but a spy agency can also be viewed as an employer; an inference path which describes the CIA only as a spy agency is more specific than one which explains it as a spy agency and an employer.

If the specificity metric fails to make a decision between two competing paths, the Filter applies two variations of the **parsimony** metric [Granger, 1980]. The first of these variations (the "length" metric) gives precedence to the inference path with fewer links. Failing this, the Filter applies the other variation of the parsimony metric (the "explains more" metric), which examines the "intermediate" MOPs (those which are not the endpoints) of the two competing paths. This variation then selects the inference path that contains more intermediate MOPs which are intersection points with other inference paths. In other words, the intermediate MOPs can be either endpoints or intermediate MOPs of paths other than the two being evaluated.

It is with the Filter that the implementation of ATLAST diverges most from the theory. In some sense, this is to be expected, since the Filter is the most complex of the three processes. In theory, ATLAST should be able to evaluate and inhibit pursuit of apparently implausible inference paths almost as soon as pursuit has begun, thus preventing problems of combinatorial explosion. ATLAST would accomplish this by comparing the multiple, possibly incomplete, inference paths which begin with a specific word-sense to the context it has built up to that point in the processing of the input text, and determining which of the paths fit "best" with that context. This would be in agreement with experimental results in lexical access research [Tanenhaus, Leiman, & Seidenberg, 1979; Lucas, 1983; Granger, Holbrook, & Eiselt, 1984]. At this time, the ATLAST model can only evaluate complete inference paths (i.e., those which connect two or more word-senses activated by the Capsulizer) without regard to the existing context. Though this simple inference evaluation mechanism seems to work for sentences such as the one presented in the following example, it will not be sufficient to properly interpret longer, more complicated texts. This problem will be rectified in the near future.

3.5 An Example

What follows is actual (though abbreviated) annotated run-time output from the ATLAST prototype program. This example illustrates primarily how ATLAST disambiguates between two possible meanings of the word "bugs" in the text, "The CIA checked for bugs." In the interest of brevity and clarity, we use a very short text and just enough of a knowledge base to process this example. Due to space limitations, we will concentrate primarily on the operation of the Filter. Also, we have abbreviated the names of some of the memory structures, again due to space limitations. The following legend should make the program trace more readable:

```
GEN-EMPLOYER = GENERIC-EMPLOYER
GET-SECRETS = GET-OTHERS-SECRETS
MPHONE = MICROPHONE
P-HEALTHY-ENVT = PRESERVE-HEALTHY-ENVIRONMENT
P-SECRETS = PRESERVE-OWN-SECRETS
PLANT-LISTEN-DEV = PLANT-OWN-LISTENING-DEVICE
REM-HEALTH-HZRD = REMOVE-HEALTH-HAZARD
REM-LISTEN-DEV = REMOVE-OTHERS-LISTENING-DEVICE
```

After processing "The CIA" and activating associated memory structures, ATLAST processes "checked", which terminates the noun phrase and begins a verb phrase. Capsulizer sends a capsule consisting of the word-senses initially activated by the noun phrase (i.e., C-I-A) to Filter. Filter, looking for an actor for this sentence, fills the slot with this noun-phrase capsule. ATLAST then processes "for":

```
Filter:
  New path discovered: IPATH0
    Path from C-I-A to SEARCH
      C-I-A is special case of SPY-AGENCY
      SPY-AGENCY has goal P-SECRETS
      P-SECRETS has plan REM-LISTEN-DEV
      REM-LISTEN-DEV is special case of REMOVE
      REMOVE has precondition SEARCH
  ACTION slot filled by SEARCH
```

The preposition "for" does not activate any new memory structures, but it does begin a modifying prepositional phrase. Capsulizer sends the verb component of the verb phrase (SEARCH) to Filter, which then assigns the capsule to the action slot.

Proposer, looking for intersections among the "wavefronts" of spreading activation, finds a connection, or inference path (IPATH0), between C-I-A and SEARCH, and notifies Filter. Filter knows of only one inference path at this time, so there is no basis for comparison and evaluation of inference paths yet. ATLAST then moves on to "bugs":

```
Filter:
  New path discovered: IPATH1
    Path from C-I-A to SEARCH
      C-I-A is special case of SPY-AGENCY
      SPY-AGENCY can be viewed as GEN-EMPLOYER
      GEN-EMPLOYER has goal P-HEALTHY-ENVT
      P-HEALTHY-ENVT has plan REM-HEALTH-HZRD
      REM-HEALTH-HZRD is special case of REMOVE
      REMOVE has precondition SEARCH
  New path discovered: IPATH2
    Path from C-I-A to INSECT
      C-I-A is special case of SPY-AGENCY
```

```
      SPY-AGENCY can be viewed as GEN-EMPLOYER
      GEN-EMPLOYER has goal P-HEALTHY-ENVT
      P-HEALTHY-ENVT has plan REM-HEALTH-HZRD
      REM-HEALTH-HZRD has role-filler INSECT
  New path discovered: IPATH3
    Path from C-I-A to MPHONE
      C-I-A is special case of SPY-AGENCY
      SPY-AGENCY has goal GET-SECRETS
      GET-SECRETS has plan PLANT-LISTEN-DEV
      PLANT-LISTEN-DEV has role-filler MPHONE
  New path discovered: IPATH4
    Path from C-I-A to SEARCH
      C-I-A is special case of SPY-AGENCY
      SPY-AGENCY has goal GET-SECRETS
      GET-SECRETS has plan PLANT-LISTEN-DEV
      PLANT-LISTEN-DEV has role-filler MPHONE
      MPHONE is role-filler of REM-LISTEN-DEV
      REM-LISTEN-DEV is special case of REMOVE
      REMOVE has precondition SEARCH
  New path discovered: IPATH5
    Path from SEARCH to MPHONE
      SEARCH is precondition of REMOVE
      REMOVE has special case REM-LISTEN-DEV
      REM-LISTEN-DEV has role-filler MPHONE
  New path discovered: IPATH6
    Path from SEARCH to INSECT
      SEARCH is precondition of REMOVE
      REMOVE has special case REM-HEALTH-HZRD
      REM-HEALTH-HZRD has role-filler INSECT
  New path discovered: IPATH7
    Path from MPHONE to C-I-A
      MPHONE is role-filler of REM-LISTEN-DEV
      REM-LISTEN-DEV is plan of P-SECRETS
      P-SECRETS is goal of SPY-AGENCY
      SPY-AGENCY has special case C-I-A
  Parsimony: IPATH7 explains more than IPATH3
  Specificity: IPATH4 more specific than IPATH1
  Parsimony: IPATH0 shorter than IPATH4
```

Capsulizer reads the ambiguous word "bugs", which results in the activation of two word-senses: INSECT and MPHONE. Proposer's search has uncovered several new inference paths. When two different inference paths connect the same two word-senses, Filter applies inference evaluation metrics to the two paths to determine which of the two provides the better explanation of the input text. The rejected paths are de-activated until later text results in activating that path again. Finally, ATLAST encounters the end of the text:

```
Filter:
  OBJECT has competing slot fillers:
    INSECT vs. MPHONE
  Specificity: IPATH7 more specific than IPATH2
  Parsimony: IPATH5 explains more than IPATH6
  Lexical ambiguity resolution:
    MPHONE vs. INSECT
```

```
All paths through INSECT de-activated
Ambiguity resolved: MPHONE selected
OBJECT slot filled by MPHONE
```

Capsulizer sends to Filter a capsule containing the word-senses activated by the prepositional phrase. Filter determines that the capsule contains the object of the action SEARCH, and that this object is ambiguous. Filter attempts to resolve this ambiguity by applying the inference evaluation metrics to the remaining active inference paths. Because MPHONE and INSECT are now known to be competing word-senses, Filter treats IPATH7 and IPATH2 as competing inference paths. That is, although IPATH7 connects MPHONE to C-I-A and IPATH2 connects INSECT to C-I-A, the two different paths are evaluated as if they connected the same two word-senses because INSECT and MPHONE were activated by the same lexical entry ("bugs"). For this same reason, IPATH5 is evaluated against IPATH6. This evaluation results in the two remaining inference paths containing INSECT to be de-activated, so Filter resolves the ambiguity in favor of MPHONE. Below is the active memory structure after all processing has ended, followed by the pointers into the structure.

```
Processing completed
  Active memory structure:
    Path from MPHONE to C-I-A
      MPHONE is role-filler of REM-LISTEN-DEV
      REM-LISTEN-DEV is plan of P-SECRETS
      P-SECRETS is goal of SPY-AGENCY
      SPY-AGENCY has special case C-I-A
    Path from SEARCH to MPHONE
      SEARCH is precondition of REMOVE
      REMOVE has special case REM-LISTEN-DEV
      REM-LISTEN-DEV has role-filler MPHONE
    Path from C-I-A to SEARCH
      C-I-A is special case of SPY-AGENCY
      SPY-AGENCY has goal P-SECRETS
      P-SECRETS has plan REM-LISTEN-DEV
      REM-LISTEN-DEV is special case of REMOVE
      REMOVE has precondition SEARCH
  Pointers to memory structure:
    Actor: C-I-A
    Action: SEARCH
    Object: MPHONE
```

3.6 An Observation on the Ordering of Inference Metrics

While testing the ATLAST program, it became apparent that the order of application of the pragmatic inference metrics affected ATLAST's eventual interpretation of the input text. As mentioned earlier, ATLAST applies its specificity metric first, followed by the "length" metric, and then the "explains more" metric. For the example of Section 3.5, this ordering of the inference metrics results in the interpretation that the CIA was looking for hidden microphones. On the other hand, if the order of application of the two parsimony metrics is reversed, ATLAST arrives at a different, nonsensical interpretation.

Though this observation does not lead us to any meaningful conclusions at this time, it provides an example of how ATLAST can serve not only as a "proving ground" for theories, but also as a source of new and interesting ideas worthy of further investigation.

4.0 Open Questions and Future Work

The initial implementation of ATLAST raised a myriad of implementation issues, many of which are yet to be resolved. More importantly, the implementation again raised some open questions which have been encountered by other researchers.

One question has to do with the timing of the three inference processes running in parallel. We do not yet know how much work each of the three processes should do in a given cycle, though we have made arbitrary initial decisions. For the Proposer in particular, there are issues which have been addressed by some of the previous models utilizing spreading activation [Quillian, 1968; Fahlman, 1979; Anderson, 1983]: How far does activation spread? Does activation decay with time? Is there reinforcement when paths intersect? Though we do not have answers to the questions now, ATLAST is designed to allow us to change timing parameters easily, possibly enabling us to "tune" the model for cognitive accuracy as work proceeds.

Another question is concerned with the content of ATLAST's memory. Currently, ATLAST runs with a high-level abstraction of episodic memory: the relationships between the MOPs are fairly well defined, but the details of the episodes themselves are almost non-existent. Thus, information is stored in the links, not in the nodes. The eventual addition of lower-level detail to the episodes will require the application of yet unknown qualitative, as opposed to quantitative, inference metrics.

Additionally, there is the issue of memory organization. Whenever researchers assume that specific concepts are organized in specific ways in human memory (i.e., "this MOP is connected to that MOP by this relationship"), it is nothing more than an educated guess. Currently, ATLAST's metrics depend more on the specific organization of memory, rather than on the content of memory, for correct operation. If the memory had been organized differently, so that there were a different number of links between certain MOPs, for example, ATLAST's interpretation of the input text would have been different. This particular realization of the metrics is not necessarily inaccurate, nor does the metrics' reliance on a particular organization of memory invalidate ATLAST, any more than similar educated guesses invalidate any other models of human understanding. This issue does remind us, however, that our implementation decisions can have as great an impact as our scientific theories on the perceived accuracy of our cognitive models, and that we should remain aware of where theoretical issues end and implementation issues begin.

Obviously, much work remains to be done on AT-LAST. The current implementation has been applied only to short texts. In the future, we will process longer texts, and different types of texts, in order to discover additional rules for inference processing. The ATLAST model provides a framework for testing theories, as well as for making predictions which can be verified experimentally.

5.0 Conclusion
5.1 Summary

To some extent, ATLAST is a unification and refinement of ideas from previous models of human inference processes at the lexical, syntactic, and pragmatic levels. Yet, while ATLAST shares common features with each of these models, in many ways it is different from each of these same models. The features which distinguish the AT-LAST model from others are discussed in greater detail in [Granger, Eiselt, & Holbrook, 1985]. A brief summary of those features follows:

- ATLAST unifies inference processing at three distinct levels: the lexical, syntactic, and pragmatic levels.

- The separation of intra-phrasal and inter-phrasal syntactic analysis enables ATLAST to process texts which humans understand and to make the same mistakes a human understander makes.

- The use of a spreading-activation memory model allows ATLAST to pursue competing inference paths simultaneously until syntactic or semantic information suggests otherwise. Previous models of inference decision processes either left a loose end or chose a default inference when faced with an ambiguity [De-Jong, 1979; Granger, 1980; Lebowitz, 1980; Granger, 1981; Dyer, 1982; Wilensky, 1983].

- The concurrent operation of ATLAST's Capsulizer, Proposer, and Filter permits pragmatic interpretations to be evaluated independently of syntactic decisions. This parallel organization also allows immediate evaluation and inhibition of competing inference paths, thus minimizing combinatorial explosion effects.

- ATLAST conforms to the results of controlled experiments on human subjects.

5.2 Final Comment

This paper describes how ATLAST attempts to understand only a five-word sentence. At first glance, this hardly seems like progress when one considers, for instance, that earlier systems understood hundreds of newspaper stories; in fact, it might even appear that work in natural language understanding is going backwards, at least from a performance perspective. What is really indicated by this phenomenon, though, is that we are becoming more aware of the great quantity of knowledge and the complexity of the processes which language understanders, both human

and otherwise, must bring to bear in understanding even the simplest text. In this light, we should not measure the validity of any model of understanding in terms of how many stories it understands, how many words are in its vocabulary, or how fast it runs. More appropriately, we should ask such questions as: Is the model extensible? Does it compare favorably with experimental data? Is it learnable? Does it make testable predictions? In other words, cognitive models should be evaluated on the robustness of the theory which they embody. Only when that metric is satisfied will the engineering issues become relevant. From this perspective, it is safe to say that ATLAST is a step in the right direction.

6.0 Acknowledgments

Special thanks to Rick Granger and Jen Holbrook, whose efforts have made this work possible.

7.0 References

Anderson, J.R. *The Architecture of Cognition.* Cambridge, MA: Harvard University Press, 1983.

Charniak, E. Passing markers: A theory of contextual influence in language comprehension. *Cognitive Science,* **7,** 171-190, 1983.

Cullingford, R.E. *Script Application: Computer Understanding of Newspaper Stories.* Ph.D. thesis. Research Report #116. Department of Computer Science. Yale University, New Haven, CT, 1978.

DeJong, G.F. *Skimming Stories in Real Time: An Experiment in Integrated Understanding.* Ph.D. thesis. Research Report #158. Department of Computer Science. Yale University, New Haven, CT, 1979.

Dyer, M.G. *In-Depth Understanding: A Computer Model of Integrated Processing for Narrative Comprehension.* Cambridge, MA: MIT Press, 1983.

Fahlman, S.E. *NETL: A System for Representing and Using Real-World Knowledge.* Cambridge, MA: MIT Press, 1979.

Frazier, L., & Fodor, J.D. The sausage machine: A new two-stage parsing model. *Cognition,* 6, 291-325, 1978.

Granger, R.H. When expectation fails: Towards a self-correcting inference system. *Proceedings of the First Annual National Conference on Artificial Intelligence,* Stanford, CA, 1980.

Granger, R.H. Directing and re-directing inference pursuit: Extra-textual influences on text interpretation. *Proceedings of the Seventh International Joint Conference on Artificial Intelligence,* Vancouver, B.C., Canada, 1981.

Granger, R.H., Eiselt, K.P., & Holbrook, J.K. STRATEGIST: A program that models strategy-driven and content-driven inference behavior. *Proceedings of the National Conference on Artificial Intelligence,* Washington, D.C., 1983.

Granger, R.H., Eiselt, K.P., & Holbrook, J.K. Parsing with parallelism: A spreading-activation model of inference processing during text understanding. In J.L. Kolodner and C.K. Riesbeck (eds.), *Memory, Experience and Reasoning*. Hillsdale, NJ: Erlbaum, 1985 (to appear).

Granger, R.H., & Holbrook, J.K. Perseverers, recencies, and deferrers: New experimental evidence for multiple inference strategies in understanding. *Proceedings of the Fifth Annual Conference of the Cognitive Science Society*, Rochester, NY, 1983.

Granger, R.H., Holbrook, J.K., & Eiselt, K.P. Interaction effects between word-level and text-level inferences: On-line processing of ambiguous words in context. *Proceedings of the Sixth Annual Conference of the Cognitive Science Society*, Boulder, CO, 1984.

Kolodner, J.L. *Retrieval and Organizational Strategies in Conceptual Memory: A Computer Model*. Hillsdale, NJ: Erlbaum, 1984.

Lebowitz, M. *Generalization and Memory in an Integrated Understanding System*. Ph.D. thesis. Research Report #186. Department of Computer Science. Yale University, New Haven, CT, 1980.

Lucas, M. Lexical access during sentence comprehension: Frequency and context effects. *Proceedings of the Fifth Annual Conference of the Cognitive Science Society*, Rochester, NY, 1983.

Norvig, P. Six problems for story understanders. *Proceedings of the National Conference on Artificial Intelligence*, Washington, D.C., 1983.

Quillian, M.R. Semantic memory. In M. Minsky (ed.), *Semantic Information Processing*. Cambridge, MA: MIT Press, 1968.

Riesbeck, C.K., & Martin, C.E. *Direct Memory Access Parsing*. Research Report #354. Department of Computer Science. Yale University, New Haven, CT, 1985.

Schank, R.C. *Conceptual Information Processing*. Amsterdam: North-Holland, 1975.

Schank, R.C. *Dynamic Memory: A Theory of Reminding and Learning in Computers and People*. New York: Cambridge University Press, 1982.

Seidenberg, M.S., Tanenhaus, M.K., Leiman, J.M., & Bienkowski, M. Automatic access of the meanings of ambiguous words in context: Some limitations of knowledge-based processing. *Cognitive Psychology*, 14, 489-537, 1982.

Small, S., Cottrell, G., & Shastri, L. Toward connectionist parsing. *Proceedings of the National Conference on Artificial Intelligence*, Pittsburgh, PA, 1982.

Swinney, D.A., & Hakes, D.T. Effects of prior context upon lexical access during sentence comprehension. *Journal of Verbal Learning and Verbal Behavior*, 15, 681-689, 1976.

Tanenhaus, M., Leiman, J., & Seidenberg, M. Evidence for multiple stages in processing of ambiguous words in syntactic contexts. *Journal of Verbal Learning and Verbal Behavior*, 18, 427-440, 1979.

Wilensky, R. *Understanding Goal-Based Stories*. Ph.D. thesis. Research Report #140. Department of Computer Science. Yale University, New Haven, CT, 1978.

Wilensky, R. *Planning and Understanding*. Reading, MA: Addison-Wesley, 1983.

Wilensky, R. Knowledge representation—A critique and a proposal. *Proceedings of the First Annual Workshop on Theoretical Issues in Conceptual Information Processing*, Atlanta, GA, 1984.

New Approaches to Parsing Conjunctions Using Prolog

Sandiway Fong
Robert C. Berwick
Artificial Intelligence Laboratory
M.I.T.
545 Technology Square
Cambridge MA 02139, U.S.A.

Abstract

Conjunctions are particularly difficult to parse in traditional, phrase-based grammars. This paper shows how a *different* representation, not based on tree structures, markedly improves the parsing problem for conjunctions. It modifies the union of phrase marker model proposed by Goodall [1984], where conjunction is considered as the linearization of a three-dimensional union of a non-tree based phrase marker representation. A PROLOG grammar for conjunctions using this new approach is given. It is far simpler and more transparent than a recent phrase-based extraposition parser conjunctions by Dahl and McCord [1984]. Unlike the Dahl and McCord or ATN SYSCONJ approach, no special trail machinery is needed for conjunction, beyond that required for analyzing simple sentences. While of comparable efficiency, the new approach unifies under a single analysis a host of related constructions: *respectively* sentences, right node raising, or gapping. Another advantage is that it is also completely reversible (without cuts), and therefore can be used to generate sentences.

Introduction

The problem addressed in this paper is to construct a grammatical device for handling coordination in natural language that is well founded in linguistic theory and yet computationally attractive. The linguistic theory should be powerful enough to describe all of the phenomenon in coordination, but also constrained enough to reject all ungrammatical examples without undue complications. It is difficult to achieve such a fine balance - especially since the term *grammatical* itself is highly subjective. Some examples of the kinds of phenomenon that must be handled are shown in fig. 1

The theory should also be amenable to computer implementation. For example, the representation of the phrase marker should be conducive to both clean process description and efficient implementation of the associated operations as defined in the linguistic theory.

The goal of the computer implementation is to produce a device that can both generate surface sentences given

John and Mary went to the pictures
Simple constituent coordination

The fox and the hound lived in the fox hole and
kennel respectively
Constituent coordination with the 'respectively' reading

John and I like to program in Prolog and Hope
Simple constituent coordination but can have a collective or respectively reading

John likes but I hate bananas
Non-constituent coordination

Bill designs cars and Jack aeroplanes
Gapping with 'respectively' reading

The fox, the hound and the horse all went to market
Multiple conjuncts

*John sang loudly and a carol
Violation of coordination of likes

*Who did Peter see and the car?
Violation of coordinate structure constraint

*I will catch Peter and John might the car
Gapping, but component sentences contain unlike auxiliary verbs

?The president left before noon and at 2. Gorbachev

Fig 1: Example Sentences

a phrase marker representation and derive a phrase marker representation given a surface sentences. The implementation should be as efficient as possible whilst preserving the essential properties of the linguistic theory. We will present an implementation which is transparent to the grammar and perhaps cleaner & more modular than other systems the execution time of both systems for some sample sentences will be presented. Furthermore, the advantages and disadvantages of our device will be discussed in relation to the MSG implementation.

Finally we can show how the simplified device can be extended to deal with the issues of extending the system to handle multiple conjuncts and strengthening the constraints of the system.

The RPM Representation

The phrase marker representation used by the theory described in the next section is essentially that of the *Reduced Phrase Marker (RPM)* of Lasnik & Kupin [1977]. A reduced phrase marker can be thought of as a set consisting of monostrings and a terminal string satisfying certain predicates. More formally, we have (fig. 2) :-

> Let Σ and N denote the set of terminals and non-terminals respectively.
>
> Let $\varphi, \psi, \chi \in (\Sigma \cup N)^*$.
> Let $x, y, z \in \Sigma^*$.
> Let A be a single non-terminal.
> Let P be an arbitrary set.
>
> Then φ is a monostring w.r.t. Σ & N if $\varphi \in \Sigma^*.N.\Sigma^*$.
>
> Suppose $\varphi = xAz$ and that $\varphi, \psi \in P$ where P is a some set of strings. We can also define the following predicates :-
>
> y isa* φ in P if $xyz \in P$
>
> φ dominates ψ in P if $\psi = x\chi y$. $\chi \neq \emptyset$ and $\chi \neq A$.
>
> φ precedes ψ in P if $\exists y$ s.t. y isa* φ in P. $\psi = xy\chi$ and $\chi \neq z$.
>
> Then :-
>
> P is an RPM if $\exists A, z$ s.t. $A, z \in P$ and $\forall \{\psi, \varphi\} \subseteq P$ then
>
> ψ dominates φ in P or φ dominates ψ in P or ψ precedes φ in P or φ precedes ψ in P.

Fig 2: Definition of an RPM

This representation of a phrase marker is equivalent to a proper subset of the more common syntactic tree representation. This means that some trees may not be representable by an RPM and all RPMs may be re-cast as trees. (*For example, trees with shared nodes representing overlapping constituents are not allowed.*) An example of a valid RPM is given in fig. 3 :-

Sentence: *Alice saw Bill*

RPM representation.

> {S. Alice.saw.Bill. NP.saw.Bill. Alice.V.Bill,
> Alice.VP,Alice.saw.NP}

Fig 3: An example of RPM representation

This RPM representation forms the basis of the linguistic theory described in the next section. The set representation has some desirable advantages over a tree representation in terms of both simplicity of description and implementation of the operations.

Goodall's Theory of Coordination

Goodall's idea in his draft thesis [Goodall??] was to extend the definition of Lasnik and Kupin's RPM to cover coordination. The main idea behind this theory is to apply the notion that *coordination results from the union of phrase markers* to the reduced phrase marker. Since RPMs are sets, this has the desirable property that the union of RPMs would just be the familiar set union operation. For a computer implementation, the set union operation can be realized inexpensively. In contrast, the corresponding operation for trees would necessitate a much less simple and efficient union operation than set union.

However, the original definition of the RPM did not envisage the union operation necessary for coordination. The RPM was used to represent 2-dimensional structure only. But under set union the RPM becomes a representation of 3-dimensional structure. The admissibility predicates dominates and precedes defined on a set of monostrings with a single non-terminal string were inadequate to describe 3-dimensional structure.

Basically, Goodall's original idea was to extend the **dominates** and **precedes** predicates to handle RPMs under the set union operation. This resulted in the relations **e-dominates** and **e-precedes** as shown in fig. 4 :-

> Assuming the definitions of fig. 2 and in addition let $\omega, \Omega, \Theta \in (\Sigma \cup N)^*$ and $q, r, s, t, v \in \Sigma^*$. then :-
>
> φ e-dominates ψ in P if φ dominates ψ' in P. $\chi x \omega = \psi'$. $\Theta y \Omega = \psi$ and $x \equiv y$ in P.
>
> φ e-precedes ψ in P if y isa* φ in P. v isa* ψ in P. $qyr \equiv svt$ in P. $y \neq qyr$ and $v \neq svt$
>
> where the relation $\equiv$ *(terminal equivalence)* is defined as :-
> $x \equiv y$ in P if $\chi x \omega \in P$ and $\chi y \omega \in P$

Figure 4: Extended definitions

This extended definition, in particular - the notion of equivalence forms the basis of the computational device described in the next section. However since the size of the RPM may be large, a direct implementation of the above definition of equivalence is not computationally feasible. In the actual system, an optimized but equivalent alternative definition is used.

Although these definitions suffice for most examples of coordination, it is not sufficiently constrained enough to reject some ungrammatical examples. For example, fig. 5 gives the RPM representation of "*John sang loudly and a carol*" in terms of the union of the RPMs for the two constituent sentences :-

$$John\ sang\ loudly \begin{cases} \{John.sang.loudly, S, \\ \quad John.V.loudly, John.VP, \\ \quad John.sang.AP, \\ \quad NP.sang.loudly\} \end{cases}$$

$$John\ sang\ a\ carol \begin{cases} \{John.sang.a.carol, S, \\ \quad John.V.a.carol, John.VP, \\ \quad John.sang.NP, \\ \quad NP.sang.a.carol\} \end{cases}$$

(When these two RPMs are merged some of the elements of the set do not satisfy Lasnik & Kupin's original definition - these pairs are :-)

{John.sang.loudly, John.sang.a.carol}

{John.V.loudly, John.V.a.carol}

{NP.sang.loudly, NP.sang.a.carol}

(None of the above pairs satisfy the **e-dominates** *predicate - but they all satisfy* **e-precedes** *and hence the sentence is accepted as an RPM.)*

Fig.5: An example of union of RPMs

The above example indicates that the extended RPM definition of Goodall allows some ungrammatical sentences to slip through. Although the device presented in the next section doesn't make direct use of the extended definitions, the notion of equivalence is central to the implementation. The basic system described in the next section does have this deficiency but a less simplistic version described later is more constrained - at the cost of some computational efficiency.

Linearization and Equivalence

Although a theory of coordination has been described in the previous sections - in order for the theory to be put into practice, there remain two important questions to be answered :-

- How to produce surface strings from a set of sentences to be conjoined?

- How to produce a set of simple sentences *(i.e. sentences without conjunctions)* from a conjoined surface string?

This section will show that the processes of *linearization* and *finding equivalences* provide an answer to both questions. For simplicity in the following discussion, we assume that the number of simple sentences to be conjoined is two only.

The processes of *linearization* and *finding equivalences* for generation can be defined as :-

Given a set of sentences and a set of candidates which represent the set of conjoinable pairs for those sentences, *linearization* will output one or more surface strings according to a fixed procedure.

Given a set of sentences, *finding equivalences* will produce a set of conjoinable pairs according to the definition of equivalence of the linguistic theory.

For generation the second process (*finding equivalences*) is called first to generate a set of candidates which is then used in the first process (*linearization*) to generate the surface strings. For parsing, the definitions still hold - but the processes are applied in reverse order.

To illustrate the procedure for linearization, consider the following example of a set of simple sentences (fig. 6) :-

{ John liked ice-cream, Mary liked chocolate}
set of simple sentences

{{John, Mary}, {ice-cream, chocolate}}
set of conjoinable pairs

Fig 6: Example of a set of simple sentences

Consider the plan view of the 3-dimensional representation of the union of the two simple sentences shown in fig. 7 :-

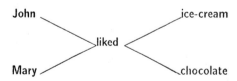

Fig 7: Example of 3-dimensional structure

The procedure of linearization would take the following path shown by the arrows in fig. 8 :-

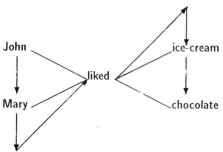

Fig 8: Example of linearization

Following the path shown we obtain the surface string "John and Mary liked ice-cream and chocolate".

The set of conjoinable pairs is produced by the process of *finding equivalences*. The definition of equivalence as given in the description of the extended RPM requires the generation of the combined RPM of the constituent sentences. However it can be shown [Fong??] by considering the constraints imposed by the definitions of equivalence and linearization, that the same set of equivalent terminal strings can be produced just by using the terminal strings of the RPM alone. There are considerable savings of computational resources in not having to compare every element of the set with every other element to generate all possible equivalent strings - which would take $O(n^2)$ time - where n is the cardinality of the set. The corresponding term for the modified definition *(given in the next section)* is $O(1)$.

The Implementation in Prolog

This section describes a runnable specification written in Prolog. The specification described also forms the basis for comparison with the MSG interpreter of Dahl and McCord. The syntax of the clauses to be presented is similar to the Dec-10 Prolog [Bowen et al.1982] version. The main differences are :-

- The symbols ":-" and "," have been replaced by the more meaningful reserved words "if" and "and" respectively.

- The symbol "." is used as the list constructor and "nil" is used to represent the empty list.

- An an example, a Prolog clause may have the form :-

  a(X Y ... Z) if b(U V ... W) and c(R S ... T)

  where a,b & c are predicate names and R,S,...,Z may represent variables, constants or terms. *(Variables are distinguished by capitalization of the first character in the variable name.)* The intended logical reading of the clause is :-

  > "a" *holds if* "b" *and* "c" *both hold for consistent bindings of the arguments* X,Y,...,Z, U,V,...,W, R,S,...,T

- Comments *(shown in italics)* may be interspersed between the arguments in a clause.

Parse and Generate

In the previous section the processes of *linearization* and *finding equivalences* are described as the two compo-

nents necessary for parsing and generating conjoined sentences. We will show how these processes can be combined to produce a parser and a generator. The device used for comparison with Dahl & McCord scheme is a simplified version of the device presented in this section.

First, difference lists are used to represent strings in the following sections. We can now introduce two predicates **linearize** and **equivalentpairs** which correspond to the processes of *linearization* and *finding equivalences* respectively (fig. 9) :-

> linearize(*pairs* S1 E1 *and* S2 E2 *candidates* Set *gives* Sentence)
>
> **Linearize** *holds when a pair of difference lists ({S1, E1} & {S2, E2}) and a set of candidates (Set) are consistent with the string (Sentence) as defined by the procedure given in the previous section.*
>
> equivalentpairs(X Y *from* S1 S2)
>
> **Equivalentpairs** *holds when a substring* X *of* S1 *is equivalent to a substring* Y *of* S2 *according to the definition of equivalence in the linguistic theory.*

Fig 9: Predicates **linearize** & **equivalentpairs**

Additionally, let the meta-logical predicate **setof** as in "setof(Element Goal Set)" hold when Set is composed of elements of the form Element and that Set contains all instances of Element that satisfy the goal **Goal**. The predicates **generate** can now be defined in terms of these two processes as follows (fig. 10) :-

```
generate(Sentence from S1 S2)
if   setof(X.Y.nil in equivalentpairs(X Y
              from S1 S2) is Set)
and linearize( pairs S1 nil and S2 nil
              candidates Set gives Sentence)

parse( Sentence giving S1 E1)
if   linearize(pairs S1 E1 and S2 E2
              candidates SubSet gives Sentence)
and setof(X.Y.nil in equivalentpairs(X Y
              from S1 S2) is Set)
```

Fig 10: Prolog definition for **generate** & **parse**

The definitions for parsing and generating are almost logically equivalent. However the sub-goals for parsing are in reverse order to the sub-goals for generating - since the Prolog interpreter would attempt to solve the sub-goals in a left to right manner. Furthermore, the subset relation rather than set equality is used in the definition for parsing. We can interpret the two definitions as follows (fig. 11) :-

> **Generate** *holds when Sentence is the conjoined sentence resulting from the linearization of the pair of difference lists (S1, nil) and (S2, nil) using as candidate pairs for conjoining, the set of non-redundant pairs of equivalent terminal strings (Set).*

> **Parse** *holds when Sentence is the conjoined sentence resulting from the linearization of the pair of difference lists (S1, E1) and (S2, E2) provided that the set of candidate pairs for conjoining (Subset) is a subset of the set of pairs of equivalent terminal strings (Set).*

Fig 11: Logical reading for **generate & parse**

The subset relation is needed for the above definition of parsing because it can be shown [Fong??] that the process of *linearization* is more constrained (*in terms of the permissible conjoinable pairs*) than the process of *finding equivalences*.

Linearize

We can also fashion a logic specification for the process of linearization in the same manner. In this section we will describe the cases corresponding to each Prolog clause necessary in the specification of linearization. However, for simplicity the actual Prolog code is not shown here.

In the following discussion we assume that the template for predicate **linearize** has the form "linearize(*pairs* S1 E1 *and* S2 E2 *candidates* Set *gives* Sentence)" shown previously in fig. 9. There are three independent cases to consider during linearization :-

1. **The Base Case.**
   If the two difference lists ({S1, E1} & {S2, E2}) are both empty then the conjoined string (Sentence) is also empty. This simply states that if two empty strings are conjoined then the result is also an empty string.

2. **Identical Leading Substrings.**
   The second case occurs when the two (non-empty) difference lists have identical leading non-empty substrings. Then the conjoined string is identical to the concatenation of that leading substring with the linearization of the rest of the two difference lists. For example, consider the linearization of the two fragments "likes Mary" and "likes Jill" as shown in fig. 12

:-

{likes Mary, likes Jill}

which can be linearized as :-

{likes X}
where X is the linearization
of strings {Mary, Jill}

Fig.12: Example of identical leading substrings

3. Conjoining.

The last case occurs when the two pairs of (non-empty) difference lists have no common leading substring. Here, the conjoined string will be the concatenation of the conjunction of one of the pairs from the candidate set, with the conjoined string resulting from the linearization of the two strings with their respective candidate substrings deleted. For example, consider the linearization of the two sentences "John likes Mary" and "Bill likes Jill" as shown in fig. 13 :-

{John likes Mary, Bill likes Jill}
Given that the selected candidate pair is {John, Bill}, *the conjoined sentence would be :-*
{John and Bill X}
where X
    is the linearization of strings {likes Mary, likes Jill}

Fig.13: Example of conjoining substrings

There are some implementation details that are different for parsing to generating. However the three cases are the same for both.

We can illustrate the above definition by showing what linearizations the system would produce for an example sentence. Consider the sentence "John and Bill liked Mary" (fig. 14) :-

{John and Bill liked Mary}

would produce the strings:-

{John and Bill liked Mary,
 John and Bill liked Mary}
    with candidate set {}

{ John liked Mary, Bill liked Mary}
    with candidate set {(John, Bill)}

{John Mary, Bill liked Mary}
    with candidate set {(John, Bill liked)}

{John, Bill liked Mary}
    with candidate set {(John, Bill liked Mary)}

Fig.14: Example of linearizations

All of the strings are then passed to the predicate

findequivalences which should pick out the second pair of strings as the only grammatically correct linearization.

Finding Equivalences

Goodall's definition of equivalence was that two terminal strings were said to be equivalent if they had the same left and right contexts. Furthermore we had previously asserted that the equivalent pairs could be produced without searching the whole RPM. For example consider the equivalent terminal strings in the two sentences "Alice saw Bill" and "Mary saw Bill" (fig. 15) :-

{Alice saw Bill, Mary saw Bill}

would produce the equivalent pairs :-

{Alice saw Bill, Mary saw Bill}

{Alice, Mary}

{Alice saw, Mary saw}

Fig.15: Example of equivalent pairs

We also make the following restrictions on Goodall's definition :-

- If there exists two terminal strings X & Y such that $X=\chi x\Omega$ & $Y=\chi y\Omega$, then χ & Ω should be the strongest possible left & right contexts respectively - provided x & y are both nonempty. In the above example, χ=nil and Ω="saw Bill", so the first and the third pairs produced are redundant.

  In general, a pair of terminal strings are redundant if they have the form (uv, uw) or (uv, xv), in which case - they may be replaced by the pairs (v, w) and (u, x) respectively.

- In Goodall's definition any two terminal strings themselves are also a pair of equivalent terminal strings (when χ & Ω are both null). We exclude this case as it produces simple string concatenation of sentences.

The above restrictions imply that in fig. 15 the only remaining equivalent pair ({Alice, Mary})is the correct one for this example.

However, before finding equivalent pairs for two simple sentences, the process of *finding equivalences* must check that the two sentences are actually grammatical. We assume that a recognizer/parser (e.g. a predicate parse(S E)) already exists for determining the grammaticality of simple sentences. Since the process only requires a yes/no answer to grammaticality, any parsing or recognition system for simple sentences can be used.

We can now specify a predicate findcandidates(X Y

S1 S2) that holds when {X, Y} is an equivalent pair from the two grammatical simple sentences {S1, S2} as follows (fig. 16) :-

findcandidates(X *and* Y *in* S1 *and* S2)
if parse(S1 nil)
and parse(S2 nil)
and equiv(X Y S1 S2)

where equiv is defined as :-

equiv(X Y X1 Y1)
if append3(Chi X Omega X1)
and terminals(X)
and append3(Chi Y Omega Y1)
and terminals(Y)

where append3(L1 L2 L3 L4) holds when L4 is equal to the concatenation of L1,L2 & L3. terminals(X) holds when X is a list of terminal symbols only

Fig.16: Logic definition of Findcandidates

Then the predicate findequivalences is simply defined as (fig. 17) :-

findequivalences(X *and* Y *in* S1 *and* S2)
if findcandidates(X *and* Y *in* S1 *and* S2)
and not redundant(X Y)

where redundant implements the two restrictions described above

Fig.17: Logic definition of Findequivalences

A Note on SYSCONJ

It is worthwhile to compare the phrase marker approach to the ATN-based SYSCONJ mechanism. Like SYSCONJ, our analysis is extragrammatical: we do not tamper with the basic grammar, but add a new component that handles conjunction. Unlike SYSCONJ, our approach is based on a precise definition of "equivalent phrases" that attempts to unify under one analysis many different types of coordination phenomena. SYSCONJ relied on a rather complicated, interrupt-driven method that restarted sentence analysis in some previously recorded machine configuration, but with the input sequence following the conjunction. This captures part of the "multiple planes" analysis of the phrase marker approach, but without a precise notion of equivalent phrases. Perhaps as a result, SYSCONJ handled only ordinary conjunction, and not *respectively* or gapping readings. In our approach, a simple change to the linearization process allows us to handle gapping.

Comparison with MSGs

The following table (fig. 18) gives the execution times in milliseconds for the parsing of some sample sentences mostly taken from Dahl & McCord [1983]. Both systems were executed using Dec-20 Prolog. The times shown for the MSG interpreter is based on the time taken to parse and build the syntactic tree only - the time for the subsequent transformations was not included.

Sample sentences	MSG system	RPM device
Each man ate an apple and a pear	662	292
John ate an apple and a pear	613	233
A man and a woman saw each train	319	506
Each man and each woman ate an apple	320	503
John saw and the woman heard a man that laughed	788	834
John drove the car through and completely demolished a window	275	1032
The woman who gave a book to John and drove a car through a window laughed	1007	3375
John saw the man that Mary saw and Bill gave a book to laughed	439	311
John saw the man that heard the woman that laughed and saw Bill	636	323
The man that Mary saw and heard gave an apple to each woman	501	982
John saw a and Mary saw the red pear	726	770

Fig.18: Timings for some sample sentences

From the timings we can conclude that the proposed device is comparable to the MSG system in terms of computational efficiency. However, there are some other advantages such as :-

- Transparency of the grammar - There is no need for phrasal rules such as "S → S and S". The device also allows non-phrasal conjunction.

- Since no special grammar or particular phrase marker representation is required, *any* parser can be used - the device only requires an accept/reject answer.

- The specification is not biased with respect to parsing or generation. The implementation is reversible allowing it to generate any sentence it can parse and vice versa.

- Modularity of the device. The grammaticality of sentences with conjunction is determined by the definition of equivalence. For instance, if needed we can filter the equivalent terminals using semantics.

Extensions to the Basic Device

The device described in the previous section is a simplified version for rough comparison with the MSG interpreter. However, the system can easily be generalized to handle multiple conjuncts. The only additional phase required is to generate templates for multiple readings. Also, *gapping* can be handled just by adding clauses to the definition of *linearize* - which allows a different path from that of fig. 8 to be taken.

The simplified device permits some examples of ungrammatical sentences to be parsed as if correct (fig. 5). The modularity of the system allows us to constrain the definition of equivalence still further. The extended definitions in Goodall's draft theory were not included in his thesis [Goodall84] presumably because it was not constrained enough. However in his thesis he proposes another definition of grammaticality using RPMs. This definition can be used to constrain equivalence still further in our system at a loss of some efficiency and generality. For example, the required additional predicate will need to make explicit use of the combined RPM. Therefore, a parser will need to produce a RPM representation as its phrase marker.

Acknowledgements

This work describes research done at the Artificial Intelligence Laboratory of the Massachusetts Institute of Technology. Support for the Laboratory's artificial intelligence research has been provided in part by the Advanced Research Projects Agency of the Department of Defense under Office of Naval Research contract N00014-80-C-0505. The first author is also funded by a scholarship from the Kennedy Memorial Trust.

References

Bowen et al: D.L. Bowen (ed.), L. Byrd, F.C.N. Pereira, L.M. Pereira, D.H.D. Warren. *Decsystem-10 Prolog User's Manual.* University of Edinburgh. 1982.

Dahl & McCord: V. Dahl and M.C. McCord. *Treating Coordination in Logic Grammars.* American Journal of Computational Linguistics. Vol. 9, No. 2 (1983).

Fong??: Sandiway Fong. To appear in S.M. thesis - "Specifying Coordination in Logic" - 1985

Goodall??: Grant Todd Goodall. Draft - *Chapter 2 (sections 2.1. to 2.7)- Coordination.*

Goodall84: Grant Todd Goodall. *Parallel Structures in Syntax.* Ph.D thesis. University of California, San Diego (1984).

Lasnik & Kupin: H. Lasnik and J. Kupin. *A restrictive theory of transformational grammar.* Theoretical Linguistics 4 (1977).

On The Use of A Taxonomy of Time-Frequency Morphologies for Automatic Speech Recognition

Renato De Mori and Mathew Palakal

Concordia University, Department of Computer Science,
1455, de Maisonneuve Blvd, Montreal, Quebec. H3G 1M8

Abstract

A computer vision approach based on skeletonization and hierarchical description of speech patterns is proposed. Learning hierarchical descriptions of phonetic events is discussed. Experimental results are reported showing the power of the approach in the recognition of dipthongs in connected letters and digits.

1. Introduction

Most of the popular techniques used today for Automatic Speech Recognition (ASR) are based on comparisions between prototypes and speech data [1]. When the recognition task involves simple vocabularies, word prototypes are used. For complicated tasks, syllable prototypes or centisecond prototypes are used[2]. In the latter case, a comparision between data and prototypes allows one to assign a label to segments of speech having fixed duration. The label of a speech segment is one of the prototype that best matches that segment. Matching is usually context-free.

Whether knowledge about speech analysis, synthesis and perception should be taken into account or not in ASR is still the object of discussions among the researchers in the field. Automatic recognition of connectedly spoken letters and of large vocabularies is still an unsolved problem.

As an attempt to solve this problem, a system of plans for extracting and using acoustic properties has been proposed and a general framework for its implementation has been described[3].

The system allows to segment continuous speech into pseudo-syllabic segments. Each segment is not necessarily a syllable, but an acoustic unit to be described. Some portions of this unit can act as contextual constraints for the description of other portions.

The purpose of this paper is that of introducing a novel approach for the description of acoustic segments characterized by spectral lines.

A skeletonization algorithm is applied to digital spectrograms. A variable number of lines with different durations inside an acoustic segment are thus obtained avoiding the errors and the difficulties of tracking formants. A pattern of spectral lines is represented by a hierarchical description.

For the application described in this paper there are only four levels in the hierarchy taxonomy but the levels as well as the relations at each level can be expanded in order to make the taxonomy reliable enough for a given recognition task.

Experimental results on the characterization of dipthongs in connected digits and letters are discussesd.

2. A Taxonomy for Spectral Lines

Spectral lines are extracted with a skeletonization algorithm from the time-frequency-energy patterns obtained by considering the 0-4 kHz portions of spectra computed with the Fast Fourier Transform (FFT) algorithm applied to the preemphasized speech signal. A hierarchical description of spectral lines is then obtained.

The time-frequency-energy pattern for a given pseudo-syllabic segment is processed by a skeletonization algorithm whose details are given in [4].

2.1 The description hierarchy for spectral lines.

The description hierarchy for spectral lines is based on acoustic properties that are known or are expected to be perceptually significant.

The hierarchy follows an open taxonomy that can be expanded to incorporate new items and new classes.

At level-0 of the taxonomy spectral lines are described by vectors V_j of triplets (t_{ji}, f_{ji}, e_{ji}) $(j = 1,...J; i = 1,..., I_j)$ where t_{ji} is a time reference in centiseconds, f_{ji} is a frequency value in Hz and e_{ji} is an energy value in dB.

At level-1 spectral lines are described by morphology symbols $x_k \in \Sigma 1$ and a sequence of attributes, consisting of time and frequency values. $\Sigma 1$ is an alphabet obtained by concatenating two symbols belonging to alphabets $\Sigma 1a$ and $\Sigma 1b$. $\Sigma 1a$ describes temporal events and is defined as follows:

$\Sigma 1a$: $\{$A:ascendent, H:horizontal, D:descendent$\}$

$\Sigma 1b$ gives a rough indication of the frequency location of the mid-point of the line:

$\Sigma 1b$: $\{$LO:low, LA:low-average, A:average, AH:average-high, HI:high, VH:very-high$\}$

Notice that level-1 descriptions contain pointers that allows one to exactly pick-up the triplets of values at the level-0 desription.

Level-2 descriptions refer to local temporal relations of level-1 descriptions representing lines that are close in frequency. They are of the following type:

$$b_m : \Re_m \ (y_{m1}, y_{m2})$$

where $\Re_m$ is a relation symbol, y_{m1} and y_{m2} are line descriptions like a_k.

$\Re_m$ symbols belong to an alphabet $\Sigma 2$ whose elements are defined in Table I.

Table I

Symbol	Description	Definition
$I(y_1, y_2)$	y_1 includes y_2	
$LI(y_1, y_2)$	y_1 includes on the left y_2	
$RI(y_1, y_2)$	y_1 includes on the right y_2	
$F(y_1, y_2)$	y_1 follows y_2	
$FD(y_1, y_2)$	y_1 follows down y_2	
$FU(y_1, y_2)$	y_1 follows up y_2	
LCL	clusters in low frequency range	
MCL	clusters in medium frequency range	
HCL	clusters in high frequency range	

Level-3 descriptions capture important frequency relations in a broad frequency range of level-1 and level-2 descriptions. They are of the type:

$$C_n = Q_n(Z_{n1}, Z_{n2})$$

where Z_{n1} and Z_{n2} can be level-1 or level-2 descriptions.

Q_n symbols belong to an alphabet $\Sigma 3$ that contains, at the moment, three symbols.

$$\Sigma 3 : \left\{ \begin{array}{l} \text{BF:the back feature, CF:the central feature,} \\ \text{and FF:the front feature} \end{array} \right\}$$

In this way, spectral morphologies relevent for computer perception are extracted and described through subsequent levels of abtraction without loosing detail of the original spectra. Fig. 1 shows an example of the description obtained for the dipthong /æi/ in /k/.

3. Hypothesis Generation Using Hierarchical Descriptions

Expressions of predicates whose arguments are elements of hierarchical descriptions are used as preconditions for actions of various types. Some actions consider, for example, the concatenation of spectral lines through a low energy transition with possible gaps as in the case of /ju/ as represented in Fig. 2. Here the detection of an FF followed by a BF is a precondition for searching the above mentioned low energy transition which is circled in Fig. 2. Once descriptions at all levels have

been obtained, then specific parameters relating elements of different descriptions can also be extracted and a-priori probabilities of them can be collected.

The entire descriptor can be seen as an expert system that contains a set of operators. Operators are clustered and clusters are ordered so that there will be a cluster of operators for each level of descriptions. Possible chains of operators are specified by the Expert System Knowledge. The specific chain of operators that is applied on a given pattern depends on the matching between Knowledge and data.

Vector Quantization (VQ) can be considered as one of the operators making this system more general than the ones just based on VQ.

Part of the Expert's Knowledge is used for hypothesis generation and may contain a-priori probabilities.

Let $\Phi(k)$ be the hierarchical description of the k-th syllabic segment. Hypothesis H(k) are generated by matching $\Phi(k)$ with the system knowledge.

H(k) may contain ambigous hypotheses. For example, a vowel can be identified as a front vowel, but a doubt may remain whether the vowel is /i/ or /e/. Hypotheses are linked with the descriptions that generated them and a summary about hypotheses and descriptions is kept.

As k increases, the summary is updated and consistencies are evaluated and used for pruning ambigous hypotheses.

For example it is well known that spectral lines are related to formant frequencies and that formant frequencies of vowels are among the acoustic properties mostly affected by speaker variability. In the case of connected pronounciations of letters, it is difficult to distinguish between /i/ and /e/ until a dipthong /æi/ is hypothesized. At this point, the system control knows better what are the differences between /e/ and /i/ for a particular speaker and can put this knowledge into the summary and use it for disambiguating hypotheses already considered. The knowledge written into the summary about a speaker or its mood remains in the summary frame until new evidence makes it change.

The idea of using a summary frame for checking consistencies has been applied to the simple example that will be described in Section 4. It appears to be promising especially because relaxation methods are applicable inside the summary frame thus allowing to check consistencies among acoustic data of the same speaker collected in a short period of time.

Maintaining in time the belief contained into the summary frame is not an easy task because it is difficult to establish when a belief has to be considered obsolete. It is certainly worth keeping into the summary frame acoustic information collected in a frame during the pronounciation of a sentence.

A system for inductive learning of discriminent descriptions involving acoustic properties of phonetic events has been developed[5]. This system is based on principles presented in [6] and can be adapted to the case of heirarchical descriptions.

4. Experimental Results and Conclusions

The experiment reported in this section refers to the use of hierarchical descriptions for improving the recognition accuracy of connectedly spoken letters belonging to the so called E1 set defined below:

$$E1 = \{E,G,P,3,V,K,C,B,T,D\}$$

From previous experiments reported in [3], the confusion between /k/ and the other elements of the set is responsible for more than 10% of the overall error rate. As /k/ is the only letter containing a dipthong, it is expected that the detection of the dipthong /æi/ will improve the recognition of the E1 set.

For this purpose samples from 5 anglophone speakers were selected (3 male and 2 female); each one pronounced 20 sequences of five letters each.

Knowledge for the /æi/ of /k/ contains an FF with a descendent line or a *follows-down* feature on the first element of the relation and an ascendent line or a *follow-up* feature on the second element. For the other letters, the /i/ vowel was characterized by the FF feature without the *follows-down* or descendent feature considered for /æi/.

The results shown in Table II allows to reduce to zero the errors involving the letter /k/.

Table II

Speakers	Letter	Features				
		FD	FF	$\Delta F1/æ/$	$\Delta F1/i/$	$\Delta F2$
#1	/k/	100%	100%	425-450	325-345	1950-2250
	others	0	100%	-----	345-525	2125-2375
#2	/k/	100%	100%	475-525	350-375	2125-2250
	others	0	100%	-----	425-525	2175-2350
#3	/k/	100%	100%	375-450	300-325	1800-2200
	others	0	100%	-----	300-500	2100-2350
#4	/k/	100%	100%	575-650	325-350	2025-2300
	others	0	100%	-----	355-610	2100-2325
#5	/k/	100%	100%	475-525	275-300	2175-2400
	others	0	100%	-----	325-550	2200-2475

The strong evidence of *follow-down* feature and 100% presence of FF in letter /k/ allows to distinguish the dipthong /æi/ and to unambiguously recognize the letter /k/. Table II shows also the frequency intervals in which spectral lines of /æ/ and /i/ involved in the FF relation were detected. As these intervals overlap, it appears doubtful that context-free recognition algorithm can be efficient in a multi-speaker detection of the dipthong /æi/ as opposed to the vowel /i/.

Pronounciations of connected dipthongs in $\{1,I,U,9,5\}$ pronounced connected were analyzed. Sentences from 5 male and 5 female speakers were considered.

Temporal relations involving disjunctions of conjunctions of descriptions were infered. These relations allowed to correctly segment and unambiously characterize more than 90% of the data. Work is in progress for disambiguating the most difficult data and for analyzing more speakers.

The results obtained show that heirarchical descriptions are powerful tools for detecting and recognizing dipthongs as opposed to single vowels. The research will continue towards the goal of the multi-speaker recognition of connectedly spoken letters and numbers.

Acknowledgements

This work was supported by the Natural Science and Engineering Council of Canada.

Bibliography

[1] L. R. Rabiner and S. E. Levinson
Isolated and Connected Word Recognition. Theory and Selected Applications, IEEE Transactions on Communications,vol.COM-29. no. 5,pp. 621-659, 1981.

[2] L. R. Bahl, F. Jelinek and R. L. Mercer
A maximum likelihood Approach to Continuous Speech Recognition, IEEE Trans. on Pattern Analysis and Machine Intelligence, vol. PAMI-5, no. 2, pp. 179-190, 1983.

[3] R. De Mori, P. Laface and Y. Mong
Parallel Algorithms for Syllabic Recognition In Continuous Speech,IEEE Trans. on Pattern Analysis and Machine Intelligence, vol. PAMI-7, no.1, January, 1985.

[4] R. De Mori and M. Palakal
On The Use of Computer Vision Techniques for Automatic Speech Recognition, proc. IEEE-CVPR'85, LA, 1985.

[5] R. De Mori and M. Gilloux
Inductive Learning of Phonetic Rules for Automatic Speech Recognition,Proc.CSCSI-84, London,Ont., pp. 103-105, 1984.

[6] R. S. Michalski, J. G. Carbonell, and T. M. Mitchell
eds., Machine Learning: An Artificial Intelligence Approach, Tioga Press, Palo Alto, CA, 1983.

FF: (FDN(B,9), FUP(A,C))

Fig 1. Spectrogram Skeleton of /æi/ in /k/.

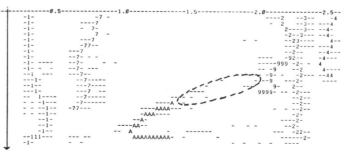

Fig 2. Example of Concatenation of Spectral lines.

REVERSIBLE AUTOMATA AND INDUCTION OF THE ENGLISH AUXILIARY SYSTEM

Robert C. Berwick
Samuel F. Pilato

MIT Artificial Intelligence Laboratory*
545 Technology Square
Cambridge, MA 02139, USA

ABSTRACT

In this paper we apply some recent work of Angluin (1982) to the induction of the English auxiliary verb system. In general, the induction of finite automata is computationally intractable. However, Angluin shows that restricted finite automata, the *k-reversible* automata, can be learned by efficient (polynomial time) algorithms. We present an explicit computer model demonstrating that the English auxiliary verb system can in fact be learned as a 1-reversible automaton, and hence in a computationally feasible amount of time. The entire system can be acquired by looking at only half the possible auxiliary verb sequences, and the pattern of generalization seems compatible with what is known about human acquisition of auxiliaries. We conclude that certain linguistic subsystems may well be learnable by inductive inference methods of this kind, and suggest an extension to context-free languages.

I   INTRODUCTION

Formal inductive inference methods have rarely been applied to actual natural language systems. Linguists generally suppose that languages are easy to learn because grammars are highly constrained; no "general purpose" inductive inference methods are required. This assumption has generally led to fruitful insights on the nature of grammars. Yet it remains to determine whether *all* of a language is learned in a grammar-specific manner. In this paper we show how to successfully apply one computationally efficient inductive inference algorithm to the acquisition of a domain of English syntax. Our results suggest that particular language subsystems can be learned by general induction procedures, given certain general constraints.

The problem is that these methods are in general computationally intractable. Even for regular languages induction can be exponentially difficult (Gold, 1978). This suggests that there may be general constraints on the design of certain linguistic subsystems to make them easy to learn by general inductive inference methods. We propose the constraint of *k-reversibility* as one such restriction. This constraint guarantees polynomial time inference (Angluin, 1982). In the remainder of this paper, we also show, by an explicit computer model, that the English auxiliary verb system meets this constraint, and so is easily inferred from a corpus. The theory gives one precise characterization of just where we may expect general inductive inference methods to be of value in language acquisition.

*This paper describes research done at the Artificial Intelligence Laboratory of the Massachusetts Institute of Technology. Support for the laboratory's artificial intelligence research is provided in part by the Advanced Research Projects Agency of the Department of Defense under the Office of Naval Research Contract N00014-80-C-0505.

II   LEARNING *K*-REVERSIBLE LANGUAGES FROM EXAMPLES

The question we address is, If a learner presumes that a natural language domain is systematic in some way, can the learner intelligently infer the complete system from only a subset of sample sentences? Let us develop an example to formally describe what we mean by "systematic in some way," and how such a systematic domain allows the inference of a complete system from examples. If you were told that *Mary bakes cakes*, *John bakes cakes*, and *Mary eats pies* are legal strings in some language, you might guess that *John eats pies* is also in that language. Strings in the language seem to follow a recognizable pattern, so you expect other strings that follow the same pattern to be in the language also.

In this particular case, you are presuming that the to-be-learned language is a zero-reversible regular language. Angluin (1982) has defined and explored the formal properties of reversible regular languages. We here translate some of her formal definitions into less technical terms.

A regular language is any language that can be generated from a formula called a regular expression. For example the strings mentioned above might have come from the language that the following regular expression generates:

(Mary|John) (bakes|eats) [[very* delicious] (cakes|pies)]

A complete natural language is too complex to be generated by some concise regular expression, but some simple subsets of a natural language can fit this kind of pattern.

To formally define when a regular language is reversible, let us first define a prefix as any substring (possibly zero-length) that can be found at the very beginning of some legal string in a language, and a suffix as any substring (again, possibly zero-length) that can be found at the very end of some legal string in a language. In our case the strings are sequences of words, and the language is the set of all legal sentences in our simplified subset of English. Also, in any legal string say that the suffix that immediately follows a prefix is a tail for that prefix. Then a regular language is *zero-reversible* if whenever two prefixes in the language have a tail in common, then the two prefixes have all tails in common.

In the above example, prefixes *Mary* and *John* have the tail *bakes cakes* in common. If we presume that the language these two strings come from is zero-reversible, then *Mary* and *John* must have all tails in common. In particular, the third string shows that *Mary* has *eats pies* as a tail, so *John* must also have *eats pies* as a tail. Our current hypothesis after having seen these three strings is that they come not from the three-string language expressed by (Mary|John) bakes cakes | Mary eats pies, which is not zero-reversible, but rather from the four-string language (Mary|John) (bakes cakes | eats pies), which is zero-reversible. Notice that we have enlarged the corpus just enough to make the language zero-reversible.

A regular language is *k-reversible*, where *k* is a non-negative integer, if whenever two prefixes *whose last k words match* have a tail in common, then the two prefixes have all tails in common. A higher value of *k* gives a more conservative condition for inference. For example, if we presume that the aforementioned strings come from a 1-reversible language, then instead of presuming that whatever *Mary* does *John* does, we would presume only that whatever *Mary bakes*, *John bakes*. In this case the third string fails to yield any inference, but if we were later told that *Mary bakes pies* is in the language, we could infer that *John bakes pies* is also in the language. Further adding the sentence *Mary bakes* would allow 1-reversible inference to also induce *John bakes*, resulting in the seven-string 1-reversible language expressed by (*Mary*|*John*) *bakes* [*cakes*|*pies*] | *Mary eats pies*.

With these examples zero-reversible inference would have generated (*Mary*|*John*) (*bakes*|*eats*) (*cakes*|*pies*)* by now, which overgeneralizes an *optional* direct object into *zero or more* direct objects. On the other hand, two-reversible inference would have inferred no additional strings yet. For a particular language we hope to find a *k* that is small enough to yield some inference but not so small that we overgeneralize and start inferring strings that are in fact not in the true language we are trying to learn.

III   AN INFERENCE ALGORITHM

In addition to formally characterizing *k*-reversible languages, Angluin also developed an algorithm for inferring a *k*-reversible language from a finite set of positive examples, as well as a method for discovering an appropriate *k* when negative examples (strings known not to be in the language) are also presented. She also presented an algorithm for determining, given some *k*-reversible regular language, a minimal set of shortest possible examples (a "characteristic" or "covering" sample) sufficient for inducing the language. We have implemented these procedures on a computer in MACLISP and have applied them to all of the artificial languages in Angluin's paper as well as to all of the natural language examples in this paper.

To describe the inference algorithm, we make use of the fact that every regular language can be associated with a corresponding deterministic finite-state automaton (DFA) which accepts or generates exactly that language.

Given a sample of strings taken from the full corpus, we first generate a prefix-tree automaton which accepts or generates exactly those strings and no others. We now want to infer additional strings so as to induce a *k*-reversible language, for some chosen *k*. Let us say that when accepting a string, the last *k* symbols encountered before arriving at a state is a *k-leader* of that state. Then to generalize the language, we recursively merge any two states where any of the following is true:

- Another state arcs to both states on the same word. (This enforces determinism.)
- Both states have a common *k*-leader and either
  - both states are accepting states or
  - both states arc to a common state on the same word.

When none of these conditions obtains any longer, the resulting DFA accepts or generates the smallest *k*-reversible language that includes the original sample of strings. (The term "reversible" is used because a *k*-reversible DFA is still deterministic with lookahead *k* when its sets of initial and final states are swapped and all of its arcs are reversed.)

This procedure works incrementally. Each new string may be added to the DFA in prefix-tree fashion and the state-merging algorithm repeated. The resulting language induced is independent of the order of presentation of sample strings.

If an appropriate *k* is not known *a priori*, but some negative as well as positive examples are presented, then one can try increasing values of *k* until the induced language contains none of the negative examples.

IV   INFERENCE OF THE ENGLISH AUXILIARY SYSTEM

We have chosen to test the English auxiliary system under *k*-reversible inference because English verb sequences are highly regular, yet they have some degree of complexity and admit to some exceptions. We represent the English auxiliary system as a corpus of 92 variants of a declarative statement in third person singular. The variants cover all standard legal permutations of tense, aspect, and voice, including *do* support and nine modals. We simply use the surface forms, which are strings of words with no additional information such as syntactic category or root-by-inflection breakdown. For instance, the present, simple, active example is *Judy gives bread*. One modal, perfective, passive variant is *Judy would have been given bread*.

We have explored the *k*-reversible properties of this natural language subsystem in two main steps. First we determined for what values of *k* the corpus is in fact *k*-reversible. (Given a finite corpus, we could be sure the language is *k*-reversible for all *k* at or above some value.) To do this we treated the full corpus as a set of sample strings and tried successively larger values of *k* until finding one where *k*-reversible inference applied to the corpus generates no additional strings. We could then be sure that any *k* of that value or greater could be used to infer an accurate model of the English auxiliary system without overgeneralizing.

After finding the range of values of *k* to work with, we were interested in determining which, if any, of those values of *k* would yield some power to infer the full corpus from a proper subset of examples. To do this we took the DFA which represents the full corpus and computed, for a trial *k*, a set of sample strings that would be minimally sufficient to induce the full corpus. If any such values of *k* exist, then we can say that, in a nontrivial way, the English auxiliary system is learnable as a *k*-reversible language from examples.

We found that the English auxiliary system can be faithfully modeled as a *k*-reversible regular language for $k \geq 1$. Only zero-reversible inference overgeneralizes the full corpus as well as the active and passive corpora treated as separate languages. For the active corpus, zero-reversible inference groups the forms of *do* with the other modals. The DFAs for the passive and full corpora also contain loops and thereby generate infinite numbers of illegal variants.

Does treating the English auxiliary system as a 1-or-more-reversible language yield any inferential power? The English auxiliary system as a 1-reversible language can in fact be inferred from a cover of only 48 examples out of the 92 variants in the corpus. The active corpus treated separately requires 38 examples out of 46 and the passive corpus requires 28 out of 46. Treating the full corpus as a 2-reversible language requires 76 examples, and a 3+-reversible model cannot infer the corpus from any proper subset whatsoever.

For 1-reversible inference, 45 of the verb sequences of length three or shorter will yield the remaining nine such strings and none longer. Verb sequences of length four or five can be divided into two patterns, <modal> *have been giv*(*ing*|*en*) and ... *be*[*en*] *being given*. Adding any one (length-four) string from the first pattern will yield the remaining 17 strings of that pattern. Further adding two length-four strings from the awkward second pattern will yield the remaining 18 strings of that pattern, nine of which are of length five. This completes the corpus.

V   DISCUSSION

The auxiliary system has often been regarded as an acid test for a theory of language acquisition. Given this, we are encouraged that it is in fact learnable via a computationally efficient general method. It is significant that at least in this domain we have found a k (of 1) that is low enough to generate a good amount of inference from examples yet high enough to avoid overgeneralization. Even more conservative 2-reversibility generates a little inference.

This inductive power derives from the systematic sequential structure of the English auxiliary system. In an idealized form (ignoring tense and inflections) the regular expression

[DO | [<modal>] [HAVE] [BE]] [BEpassive] GIVE

generates all English verb sequence patterns in our corpus.

Zero-reversible inference basically attempts to simplify any partial, disjunctive permutation like $(a|b)x \mid ay$ into an exhaustive, combinatorial permutation like $(a|b)(x|y)$. Since the active corpus (excluding *BE-passive* from the idealized regular expression) in fact has such a simple form except for the *DO* disjunction, zero-reversible inference productively completes the three-place permutation but also destroys the disjunction, by overgeneralizing what patterns can follow both *DO* and *<modal>*. One-reversible inference requires that disjuncts share some final word to be mergeable, so that *DO* cannot merge with any auxiliary triplet, yet the permutation of *<modal> HAVE* by *[BE]* is still productive. Similar considerations obtain in the passive case, as well as for the joint corpus.

In complex environments, rather than reduce the inferential power by raising k one could instead embed this algorithm within a larger system. For example, a more realistic model of processing English verb sequences would have an external, more linguistically motivated mechanism force the separate treatment of active versus passive forms. Then if, say on considerations of frequency of occurrence, *do* exceptions were externally handled and the infrequent ... *BE being* ... cases were similarly excluded from the immature learner, then one could apply the more powerful zero-reversible inference to the remaining active and passive forms without overgeneralizing. In such a case the active system can be induced from 18 examples out of 44 variants and the passive system from 14 out of 22. The entire active system is learnable once examples of each form of each verb and each modal have been seen, plus one example to fix the relative order of *have* vs. *be*, and one example each to fix the order of modal vs. *have* or *be*.

Though a more complex model must ultimately represent a domain like the English auxiliary system, the way k-reversible inference in itself handles a complex territory satisfies some conditions of psychological fidelity. Especially zero-reversibility is a rather simple form of generalization of sequential patterns with which we believe humans readily identify. In general the longer, more complex cases can be inferred from simpler cases. Also, there is a reasonable degree of play in the composition of the covering sample, and the order of presentation does not affect the language learned.

Children evidently never make mistakes on the relative order of auxiliaries, which is consistent with the reversibility model, but they do mistakenly combine *do* with tensed verb forms (Pinker, 1984). Given that the appearance of *do* in declarative sentences is also fairly rare, one might prefer the aforementioned zero-reversible system that handles *do* support as an exception, rather than opt for a 1-reversible inference which is flawless but a slower learner.

The ... *BE being* ... cases are systematically related to the rest, but also have a natural boundary: 1-reversible inference from simpler cases doesn't intrude into that territory, yet only a few such examples allow one to infer the remainder. Very rare sequences like *could have been being given* will be successfully acquired even if they are not seen. This seems consistent with human judgments that such phrasing is awkward but apparently legal.

k-Reversibility is essentially a model of simplicity, not of complexity. As such, it induces not linguistic structure but the substitution classes that linguistic structures typically work with, building these by analogy from examples. In the linguistic structure for which k-reversibility is defined — regular grammars — it functions to induce the classes that fill "slots" in a regular expression, based on the similarity of tail sets. Increasing the value of k is a way of requiring a higher degree of similarity before calling a match. (See Gonzalez and Thomason, 1978, for other approaches to k-tail inference that are not so efficient.)

The same principle can apply to the induction of substitution classes in other linguistic domains including morphological, syntactic, and semantic systems. For a particularly direct example, consider the right-hand sides of context-free rewrite rules. Any subset of such rules having the same left-hand side constitutes a regular language over the set of terminal and nonterminal symbols, and is therefore a candidate for induction. One might thus infer new rewrite rules from the pattern of existing ones, thereby not only concluding that words are members of certain simple syntactic classes, but also simplifying a disjunctive set of rules into a more concise set that exhibits systematic properties. Berwick's *Lparsifal* system (1982) is an example of this kind of extension.

We believe that k-reversibility illustrates a psychologically plausible pattern induction process for natural language learning that in its simplest form has an efficient computational algorithm associated with it. The basic principle behind k-reversible inference shows some promise as a flexible tool within more complex models of language acquisition. It is encouraging that, at least in a simple case, computational linguistic models can suggest formal learnability constraints that are natural enough to be useful in the learning of human languages.

REFERENCES

Angluin, D., "Inference of reversible languages," *Journal of the Association for Computing Machinery*, 29(3), 741–765, 1982.

Berwick, R., *Locality Principles and the Acquisition of Syntactic Knowledge*, PhD, MIT Department of Electrical Engineering and Computer Science, 1982.

Gold, E., "Complexity of Automaton Identification from Given Data," *Information and Control*, 37, 1978.

Gonzalez, R., and Thomason, M., *Syntactic Pattern Recognition*, Reading, MA: Addison-Wesley, 1978.

Pinker, S., *Language Learnability and Language Development*, Cambridge, MA: Harvard University Press, 1984.

DP-MATCHING: WITH OR WITHOUT PHONEMES?

Shigeyoshi Kitazawa*, Masa-aki Ishikawa** and Shuji Doshita**

* Shizuoka University,Hamamatsu-shi,432,Japan
** Kyoto University, Sakyo-ku, Kyoto-shi,606,Japan

ABSTRACT

Attempts at automatic speech recognition have known several waves.

Early efforts were based on the faith that speech is a string of phonemes that can be isolated and recognized one by one. This wave broke when it became clear that the physical realization of a phoneme is smeared in time and mingled with that of its neighbors, and also context and speaker-dependent.

Next came the invention of the highly successful time-warping DP-matching methods, in which whole words are matched by templates. This wave is still going strong, at least in Japan, but it may have reached a high mark.

To probe this question, we investigate the case of the "jion", a subset of character readings that "generates" a large subset of Japanese. This set has low redundancy and contains many minimal pairs. Error analysis of DP-matching shows that most errors occur between pairs that differ only in their initial consonant, especially if it belongs to groups such as plosives or nasals.

Combining DP-matching with limited-scope phoneme recognition could break through present limits.

I INTRODUCTION

When we listen to speech in an analytic frame of mind, we hear it, or we think we hear it, as a succession of phonemes. It seems to us that we could pick out each "phoneme" if only they didn't flow past quite so quickly. This view now seems naive (Repp 1981), but it was natural enough when speech recognition began.

Systems based on phoneme recognition run into a variety of troubles. First, the boundary between successive "phonemes" is elusive (the segmentation problem).

Second, once a phoneme segment is fenced off, it is found that it bears little ressemblance to the same phoneme uttered elsewhere in the speech stream, or in isolation (the co-articulation problem). Worse still, the range of possible realizations may overlap that of a different phoneme. Finally, even if a taxonomy of all phonemes in context is attained, it proves different from speaker to speaker (the speaker-dependency problem).

The task of designing systems to reliably extract and sort out all "phoneme" cases and cues is thus formidable. It drained the energy of early researchers, and the results were disappointing.

The invention of Dynamic Programming time-warp matching came as a relief because it provided a simple, elegant, and immediately appliable method of recognizing whole words. Many variants of DP-matching have been proposed (continuous, multiple level, augmented, etc.) and its efficiency has been improved to cope with large vocabulary, multiple speakers, etc..

DP-matching continues to be the object of much research in Japan (27 papers out of 200 on speech at the 1984 meetings of the ASJ). However, it may be that the efficiency of DP-matching has reached its maximum. The fundamental drawback is that the discriminating distance is calculated over a whole word. If two words differ by just one phoneme (minimal pair), the difference is "diluted" and may be masked by small variations over the rest of the word.

This is particularly so for "short" phonemes (eg plosives) in long words. These are likely to cause problems if they occur in an application's word list.

DP-matching scores are often evaluated on lists of city names. The results cannot easily be extrapolated because of the inhomogeneity and redundancy of cues in such sets. For this reason, we chose instead to perform our experiments on a set of words, the "jion", that are highly representative and have low redundancy.

The word "jion" means "character sound", and designates the sounds that the "chinese" readings of Sino-Japanese characters can assume. Many words in Japanese are built up of "jion", so combinations of "jion" cover most of the language. Many "jion" are minimal pairs, and these are representative of longer minimal pairs in which they occur.

The "jion" set is thus a good evaluation set, and we used it to try to situate the limits of DP-matching recognition methods. As expected, the score attained by DP-matching on the jion set is much lower than on a city name list. In addition, an analysis of the errors provided interesting results that we discuss here.

II   PHONOLOGICAL STRUCTURE OF "JION"

The "jion" correspond originally to an old chinese syllabary consisting of 403 kinds of sounds (excluding toneme difference). This syllabary was japanized and reduced when Chinese characters were introduced in Japanese.

Each "Jion" consists of two to four phonemes, forming one or two syllables. When the first phoneme is a vowel, it is assumed that it is actually preceded by a glottal stop /?/. Not all combinations of can occur, and the phonological structure is confined to the following four types: /CV/, /CVN/, /CVV/ and /CVCV/, where /N/ designates the mora-nasal and /C/ is a consonant (McCawley,1968).

Table 1.   Phonological structures of "jion" (ignoring initial phoneme), and number of occurences of each:

CV		CVN		CVV	
group	number	group	number	group	number
Ca	19	CaN	13	Cai	13
Ci	11	CiN	11	Cui	6
Cu	17	CuN	8	Cuu	13
Ce	10	CeN	12	Cei	12
Co	20	CoN	12	Cou	23
				Cii	1
total	77	total	56	total	68

CVCV					
group	number	group	number	group	number
Caku	23	Cuku	4	Coku	18
Catu	12	Cutu	6	Cotu	9
Cati	7	Cuti	3	Coti	6
Ciku	6	Ceku	1	Citi	6
Citu	10	Cetu	12	Ceti	8
Ciki	5	Ceki	9		
total		145			

The "jion" set has thus the following chacteristics :
  a) the number of segments is limited;
  b) there are only 33 kinds of phonological structures (if one excepts initial phoneme);
  c) there are many minimal pairs, (for example, /baku/ and /daku/).

III   DP-MATCHING OF 346 "JION"S

One male speaker produced the set of 346 "jion"s twice. We made the first set of them the templates and the second set the object of recognition. Waveforms were first low-pass filtered at 8.9 KHz and then sampled at 18.5 KHz. The parameterization, a 20th-order LPC analysis, was carried out over 20.8-ms Hamming windows shifted every 6.92-ms.

LPC cepstrum distance is used as inter-frame distance. Using these local distances, the distance between the input pattern and the reference pattern is calculated by means of a dynamic programming time warping technique. As a result 43.9% recognition rate was achieved.

Table.2   Classification of recognition errors:

type	errors	examples
initial consonant only	164 (84.5%)	a-ma, ran-nan,ta-a, mei-rei,satu-zatu, den-gen, batu-matu, bi-ri, bo-go, etc.
vowel in initial syllable	7 (3.61%)	kotu-katu,sun-son, sei-sai, sen-san, syaku-syoku, dan-don, etc.
consonant & vowel in initial syllable	14 (7.22%)	katu-hutu,kan-ton, sii-tui,siti-keti, sui-zai,seti-zati, soti-zati,nai-rui, nan-mon,ratu-botu, bati-oti, etc.
others	9 (4.64%)	so-son,syuu-syu, tyu-tyuu, hu-huu, me-men, yu-yuu, ryu-gyuu, etc.

Errors in the initial syllable account for 95.4% of all errors, of which 88.6% were errors in the initial consonant only. The recognition rate is low compared to the rate currently achieved on sets of city names, but this is precisely attributable to the low redundancy of "jion".

To illustrate this point, suppose we build a system that can recognize only the vowel parts of a word. If we input the sounds of the 346 "jion"s, the average number of symbols confused (recognized as the same word) is 19.8. If we input instead a set of 641 city names, the average number of confusions is 2.75.

Table 3 shows the recognition rates of distinctive features in the morpheme-initial consonant. The rate for "strident" was 100%, and that for "sharp" and "flat" were comparatively good. "Compact" was the worst, at 81.3%. However this result does not necessarily reflect the recognizability of the initial consonant, as there are constraints within the set that aid recognition. For example "strident" is a feature which opposes affricates /ts/ and /dz/ to simple stops /t/ and /d/. But /ts/ and /dz/ can precede only /u/, and /t/ and /d/ only a vowel among /a/, /e/ and /o/.

Table.3 Recognition rate of distinctive-features in initial consonant:

features	%	samples
1. strident	100.0	10
2. sharp	93.1	346
3. flat	90.9	11
4. consonantal	90.5	346
5. continuant	87.7	114
6. obstruent	85.7	294
7. grave	83.3	239
8. voiced	82.7	185
9. nasal	82.1	67
10. compact	81.3	80

IV   CONCLUSION AND PROSPECTS FOR RECOGNITION

The "jion" set experiment showed that DP-matching scores can be rather low on a word set containing many minimal pairs. It is not a worst-case set, and one could expect performance to be even worse if the set contained more minimal pairs or longer words, as might occur in an application.

However, the experiment also showed that the errors occur in a very limited number of configurations: mainly confusions of minimal pairs differing by initial consonants belonging to the same group (for example nasals or plosives). This suggests that combining a limited-scope phoneme discrimination method with DP-matching might drastically improve recognition scores.

Over the last few years our laboratory has been working on obtaining high quality discrimination of consonants. Our first results were on plosive discrimination (Kitazawa et al 1982), and nasals (Kitazawa et al 1984).

The method used is based on statistical analysis of spectral parameters gathered over several consecutive frames. The method calculates canonical vectors that can be considered as optimal linear combinations of the parameters. The reader interested in the details should refer to the papers quoted. Discrimination results are typically 92% and 80% for plosives and nasals, respectively.

Developing similar discrimination methods for all possible distinctive features, and combining them into a phoneme recognition system would be impractical. However, by concentrating on a limited set of features, it should be possible to improve results of DP-matching.

It can be argued that speech features are designed to be recognized by humans rather than by machines. A human relies heavily on syntax, semantics and context to supplement the acoustic cues, and a machine that cannot do the same is sure to be limited in performance.

However, our opinion is that there is still much that can, and should be improved in bottom-up speech recognition before we should give up and let top-down methods take over.

ACKNOWLEDGEMENTS

Authors wish to express their thanks to Dr.Alain de Cheveigne for his criticism and suggestions.

REFERENCES

[1] Repp,B.H. "On Levels of Description in Speech Research," JASA 69, 1981, 1462-1464.

[2] McCawley,J.D. The Phonological Component of a Grammar of Japanese, The Hague,1968.

[3] Kitazawa,S. and S.Doshita, "Discriminant Analysis of Burst Spectrum for Japanese Initial Voiceless Stops", Studia Phonologica XVI, 1982,48-70.

[4] Kitazawa,S. and S.Doshita, "Speaker and Vowel Independent Recognition of CV Initial Plosives by Reduction and Integration of Running Spectra" In Proc. ICPR-84. Montreal, Canada, 1984, pp.179-181.

[5] Kitazawa,S. and S.Doshita, "Nasal Consonant Discrimination by Vowel Independent Features," Studia Phonologica XVIII,1984, 49-61.

STRUCTURE FROM MOTION WITHOUT CORRESPONDENCE: GENERAL PRINCIPLE

Ken-ichi Kanatani*

Center for Automation Research
University of Maryland
College Park, MD 20742

ABSTRACT

A general principle is given for detection of the 3D structure and motion from an image sequence without using point-to-point correspondence. The procedure consists of two stages: (i) determination of the "flow parameters" from "features" without using correspondence and (ii) computation of the 3D structure and motion from these flow parameters. The first stage is done by solving equations of functionals, and the second stage is described in analytical expressions.

I INTRODUCTION

Schemes to recovery the 3D structure and motion from a 2D image sequence have been studied by many people, e.g., [1 - 6], but most of them are based on the point-to-point correspondence, which requires a large amount of implementation effort. There do exist methods which do not require the correspondence [7 - 9], but they can be used only to trace the motion along time, starting from a given initial information, and the results are obtained only numerically.

In this paper, we present a general mathematical principle to detect the 3D structure and motion without using correspondence. Yet, the solution at particular time is given in analytical expressions, giving geometrical interpretations and proving the existence of the spurious solution [6], etc. The procedure consists of two stages. First, we extract, without using correspondence, the "flow parameters" which completely characterize the viewed motion for each planar region of the object. This is done by measuring "features" of the image. The next stage is the computation of structure and motion from these flow parameters, and the solution is given in the form of analytical expressions.

II OPTICAL FLOW AND FLOW PARAMETERS

Take a Cartesian xy-coordinate system on the image plane and the z-axis perpendicular to it. Consider a plane moving in the scene. Let $z = px + qy + r$ be its equation. Let $(0, 0, r)$, the

intersection between the plane and the z-axis, be a reference point. The motion is instantaneously specified by translation velocity (a, b, c) at the reference point and rotation velocity $(\omega_1, \omega_2, \omega_3)$ around it (i.e., with rotation axis orientation $(\omega_1, \omega_2, \omega_3)$ and angular velocity $\sqrt{(\omega_1)^2 + (\omega_2)^2 + (\omega_3)^2}$ (rad/sec) screwwise around it). Our goal is to compute p, q, r, a, b, c, ω_1, ω_2 and ω_3 from an image sequence without using point-to-point correspondence.

Let $(0, 0, -f)$, the point away from the image plane by f on the negative side, be the viewpoint. A point (X, Y, Z) in space is projected to $(fX/(f + Z), fY/(f + Z))$ on the image plane. If the point is on the plane $z = px + qy + r$ moving as described above, it induces the following "optical flow" at point (x, y) on the image plane (cf. Kanatani [8, 9]):

$$u = u_0 + Ax + By + (Ex + Fy)x,$$
$$v = v_0 + Cx + Dy + (Ex + Fy)y, \qquad (1)$$

where 8 parameters u_0, v_0, A, B, C, D, E and F are given by

$$u_0 = fa/(f + r), \qquad v_0 = fb/(f + r),$$
$$A = p\omega_2 - (pa + c)/(f + r),$$
$$B = q\omega_2 - \omega_3 - qa/(f + r),$$
$$C = -p\omega_1 + \omega_3 - pb/(f + r), \qquad (2)$$
$$D = -q\omega_1 - (qb + c)/(f + r),$$
$$E = (\omega_2 + pc/(f + r))/f,$$
$$F = (-\omega_1 + qc/(f + r))/f.$$

In other words, what we are viewing is a very restricted form of motion whose velocities are specified only by 8 parameters u_0, v_0, A, B, C, D, E and F. If these parameters are the same, motions seem identical to the viewer. Hence, our procedure is divided into two stages. First, we will show how to detect the "flow parameters" u_0, v_0, A, B, C, D, E and F from an image sequence without using point-to-point correspondence. Next, we will show how to solve simultaneous non-linear equations (2) for p, q, r, a, b, c, ω_1, ω_2 and ω_3 not simply "numerically" but also "analytically." Here, the "focal length" f of the camera is assumed to be a known constant.

If we take the limit $f \to \infty$ of a large focal length f, we obtain the following "orthographic approximation"

$$u_0 = a, \qquad v_0 = b,$$

---

* On leave from the Department of Computer Science, Gunma University, Kiryu, Gunma 376, Japan.

$$A = p\omega_2, \qquad\qquad B = q\omega_2 - \omega_3,$$
$$C = -p\omega_1 + \omega_3, \qquad Q = -q\omega_1, \qquad\qquad (3)$$
$$E = 0, \qquad\qquad\qquad F = 0,$$

and if we omit terms of $O(1/f^2)$ but retain terms of $O(1/f)$, we obtain the following "pseudo-orthographic approximation"

$$u_0 = fa/(f + r), \qquad v_0 = fb/(f + r),$$
$$A = p\omega_2 - (pa + c)/(f + r),$$
$$B = q\omega_2 - \omega_3 - qa/(f + r),$$
$$C = -p\omega_1 + \omega_3 - pb/(f + r), \qquad (4)$$
$$D = -q\omega_1 - (qb + c)/(f + r),$$
$$E = \omega_2/f, \qquad\qquad F = -\omega_1/f.$$

Here, we consider only the planar motion. However, if the object is not planar, we can decompose the object surface image into small planar or almost planar regions by fitting the form of eqns (1) to the observed flow, say by the least square error method. Thus, the subsequent analysis applies to objects of arbitrary shape.

III   ESTIMATION OF FLOW PARAMETERS FROM FEATURES

Let $X(x, y)$ represent an image. For example, if the image consists of gray-levels, $X(x, y)$ denotes its intensity at point (x, y). If the image consists of colors, $X(x, y)$ may be a vector value function corresponding to R, G and B. If the image consists of points and lines, $X(x, y)$ has delta-function-like singularities. In any case, we define a "feature" $F[X]$ of image $X(x, y)$ as a "functional," *i.e.*, a map $F[.]$ from the set of images $X(x, y)$ to real numbers.

Consider the time change when there exists an optical flow $(u(x, y), v(x, y))$ on the image plane. If $X(x, y)$ is an image at time t, it changes at time $t + \delta t$ after a short time interval into

$$X(x - u(x, y)\delta t, y - v(x, y)\delta t) = X(x, y)$$
$$- X_x(x, y)u(x, y)\delta t - X_y(x, y)v(x, y)\delta t + \ldots, \quad (5)$$

where X_x and X_y are partial derivatives. Then, the corresponding feature $F[X]$ becomes $F[X] + DF[X]\delta t + \ldots$, where in general the "change rate" $DF[.]$ is a "linear functional" in $u(x, y)$ and $v(x, y)$. In view of the optical flow of eqns (1), this means that we have a "linear" equation of the form

$$DF[X] = C_1[X]u_0 + C_2[X]v_0 + C_3[X]A + C_4[X]B$$
$$+ C_5[X]C + C_6[X]D + C_7[X]E + C_8[X]F. \quad (6)$$

Here, $C_1[.], \ldots, C_8[.]$ are functionals derived from the given feature $F[.]$, so that they are known functionals. The change rate $DF[.]$ can be estimated by difference schemes. For example, observe an image at time t and compute its feature $F(t)$. Next, observe the image at time $t + \delta t$ after a short time interval and compute its feature $F(t + \delta t)$. Then, $DF[X]$ is approximated by $(F(t + \delta t) - F(t))/\delta t$ or by other higher order difference schemes. Thus, all quantities except u_0, v_0, A, B, C, D, E and F in eqn (6) are directly computed from the image sequence without using point-to-point

correspondence. Hence, if we prepare 8 or more independent functionals $F_1[.]$, $F_2[.]$, $\ldots$, we obtain a set of simultaneous "linear" equations in u_0, v_0, A, B, C, D, E and F of the form of eqn (6) to determine them.

The idea of using features was already introduced by Amari [10, 11] and Kanatani [7 - 9]. However, they did not divide the process into two stages as described here but tried to compute p, q, r, a, b, c, ω_1, ω_2 and ω_3 directly. This leads to a set of simultaneous "non-linear" equations, which is difficult to solve. Kanatani [7 - 9] proposed an iterative method which traces the motion along time, starting from known initial values of p, q and r. Here, however, we divide the process into two stages and first determine the "flow parameters," which can be computed by solving a set of "linear" equations. This poses no computational problem. The desired p, q, r, a, b, c, ω_1, ω_2 and ω_3 are given in terms of the flow parameters as is shown subsequently.

As for the feature functionals, we can choose those used by Amari [10, 11] and Kanatani [7 - 9]. Amari [10, 11] used weighted integral (or "filter") $F[X] = \iint m(x, y)X(x, y)dxdy$ of various $m(x, y)$ over a fixed window for gray-level images. Invoking a mathematics called "stereology," Kanatani [7] used, for textured surfaces, Fourier coefficients of function $N(\theta)$, where $N(\theta)$ is the number of intersections, per unit length, between parallel lines of orientation θ and the texture on the image plane. When no texture exists and only circumference contours are available, Kanatani [8] used Fourier coefficients of $D(\theta)$, which is the caliper diameter of the contour measured by two parallel lines of orientation θ. Kanatani [9] also used line integral $\int m(x, y)ds$ of various $m(x, y)$ along the contour and surface integral $\iint m(x, y)dxdy$ of various $m(x, y)$ inside the contour. In any case, a set of linear equations of the form of eqn (6) is obtained, and the flow parameters are determined immediately. However, the accuracy and reliability heavily depends on the choice of the features.

IV   STRUCTURE AND MOTION FROM FLOW PARAMETERS

Suppose we have already computed the flow parameters u_0, v_0, A, B, C, D, E and F by the method described in the previous section. Or, if the point-to-point correspondence happens to be available, they are immediately determined, say by the least-square-error fitting of eqns (1). What we want is p, q, r, a, b, c, ω_1, ω_2 and ω_3. First, compute

$$U_0 = u_0 + iv_0, \quad T = A + D, \quad R = C - B,$$
$$S = (A - D) + i(B + C), \quad K = E + iF, \quad (7)$$

where i is the imaginary unit, and hence U_0, K and S are complex numbers. Define complex variables $V = a + ib$, $P = p + iq$ and $W = \omega_1 + i\omega_2$. Then, V, c, P, r, W and ω_3 are given as follows.

In the case of the orthographic approximation, we get

$$V = U_0, \qquad \omega_3 = (R \pm \sqrt{SS* - T^2})/2,$$
$$W = ke(\pi/4 + \arg(S)/2 - \arg(2\omega_3 - (R+iT))/2), \qquad (8)$$
$$P = Se(\pi/4 - \arg(S)/2 + \arg(2\omega_3 - (R+iT))/2)/k,$$

where $e(.)$ denotes $\exp(i.)$, arg the argument and $*$ the complex conjugate. Here, k is an indeterminate scale factor. Thus, (i) the absolute depth r and the velocity c in the z-direction are indeterminate, (ii) an indeterminate scale factor k is involved, and (iii) there exist two types of solutions, one is the true one and the other a spurious one. They are indistinguishable because they yield identical flow parameters. However, if we observe two or more planar regions of the same rigidly moving object, we can pick up the true one because ω_1, ω_2 and ω_3 must be common to all. The fact that an indeterminate scale factor k is necessarily involved was already pointed out by Sugihara and Sugie [5], but the existence of the spurious solution and the explicit forms of eqns (8) have not been known.

In the case of the pseudo-orthographic approximation, we get

$$V/(f + r) = U_0/f, \qquad W = ifK, \qquad P = S/(fK - U_0/f),$$
$$\omega_3 = (R + \mathrm{Re}[P(W* + iU_0*/f)])/2, \qquad (9)$$
$$c/(f + r) = - (T + \mathrm{Im}[P(W* + iU_0*/f)])/2,$$

where $\mathrm{Re}[.]$ and $\mathrm{Im}[.]$ designate the real and the imaginary part, respectively. Hence, (i) the absolute depth r is indeterminate, but (ii) $a/(f + r)$, $b/(f + r)$, $c/(f + r)$, p, q, ω_1, ω_2 and ω_3 are uniquely determined.

In the case of the pure central projection, we obtain

$$V/(f + r) = U_0/f, \qquad c/(f + r) = c',$$
$$P(c') = (fK - U_0/f \pm \sqrt{(fK-U_0/f)^2 - 4c'S})/2c',$$
$$W(c') = i(fK - U_0/f \mp \sqrt{(fK-U_0/f)^2 - 4c'S})/2 + iU_0/f, \qquad (10)$$
$$\omega_3 = (R + \mathrm{Re}[P(c')(W(c')* + iU_0*/f)])/2,$$
$$c' = - (T + \mathrm{Im}[P(c')(W(c')* + iU_0*/f)])/2. \qquad (11)$$

Here, P and W are given as functions of c', and c' is determined from eqn (11). Eqn (11) is proved to have only one non-zero solution. Since the uniqueness of the solution is guaranteed, a simpliest solution method is to assume an appropriate value of $c' = c/(f + r)$, say by the pseudo-orthographic approximation (9), compute the right-hand side of eqn (11) and repeat the process, using the new value of c', until convergence. We see that (i) the absolute depth r is indeterminate, (ii) $a/(f + r)$, $b/(f + r)$ and $c/(f + r)$ are uniquely determined and (iii) there exist two sets of solutions for p, q, ω_1, ω_2 and ω_3, one is the true one and the other a spurious one, and they are indistinguishable because they yield the same flow parameters. The spurious solution is eliminated by observing two or more planar regions of the same rigidly moving object because ω_1, ω_2 and ω_3 must to be common to them.

Numerical schemes of recovering 3D structure and motion from point-to-point correspondence pairs have been known [1 - 4], and the existence of the spurious solution was pointed out by Longuet-Higgins [6]. However, analytical expressions like eqns (10) and (11) have not been known. The parameters of eqns (7) have physical meanings: U_0 "translation," T "divergence," R "rotation," S "shearing," and K "fanning." They are transformed by a coordinate rotation by θ on the image plane as

$$U_0 \to U_0 e(- \theta), \qquad T \to T, \qquad R \to R,$$
$$S \to Se(- 2\theta), \qquad K \to Ke(- \theta), \qquad (12)$$

i.e., U_0 and K (as well as V, P and W) are (relative) invariants of "weight" $- 1$ (or "vectors"), S is an (relative) invariant of weight $- 2$ (or a "tensor"), and T and R (as well as r, c and ω_3) are (absolute) invariants of weight 0 (or "scalars").

REFERENCES

[1] Ullman, S. *The Interpretation of Visual Motion.* Cambridge, Mass.: MIT Press, 1979.

[2] Nagel, H.-H. "Representation of moving rigid objects based on visual observations." *Computer* 14:8 (1981) 29 - 39.

[3] Longuet-Higgins, H. C. "A computer algorithm for reconstructiong a scene from two projections." *Nature* 239:10 (1981) 133 - 135.

[4] Tsai, R. Y. and T. S. Huang, "Uniqueness and estimation of three dimensional motion parameters of rigid objects with curved surfaces." *IEEE Trans.* PAMI-6 (1984) 13 - 27.

[5] Sugihara, K. and N. Sugie, "Recovery of rigid structure from orthographically projected optical flow." *Computer Vision, Graphics, and Image Processing* 27 (1984) 309 - 320.

[6] Longuet-Higgins, H. C. "The visual ambiguity of a moving plane." *Proc. R. Soc. Lond.* B-223 (1984) 165 - 175.

[7] Kanatani, K. "Detection of surface orientation and motion from texture by a stereological technique." *Artificial Intelligence* 23 (1984) 213 - 237.

[8] Kanatani, K. "Tracing planar surface motion from projection without knowing correspondence." *Computer Vision, Graphics, and Image Processing* 29 (1985) 1 - 12.

[9] Kanatani, K. "Detecting the motion of a planar surface by line and surface integrals." *Computer Vision, Graphics, and Image Processing* 29 (1985) 13 - 22.

[10] Amari, S. "Invariant structures of signal and feature spaces in pattern recognition problems." *RAAG Memoirs* 4 (1968) 553 - 566.

[11] Amari, S. "Feature spaces which admit and detect invariant signal transformations" In *Proc. 4th Int. Conf. Pattern Recognition, Tokyo, 1978,* pp. 452 - 456.

UNIQUE RECOVERY OF MOTION AND OPTIC FLOW VIA LIE ALGEBRAS

A. Peter Blicher*
Computer Science Department, Stanford University, Stanford, CA 94305
and *Mathematics Department, University of California, Berkeley*
and
Stephen M. Omohundro**
Physics Department, University of California, Berkeley

ABSTRACT

We use some ideas from the theory of Lie groups and Lie algebras to study the problem of recovering rigid motion from a time-varying picture. We are able to avoid the problem of finding corresponding points by considering only what can be determined from picture point values and their time derivatives. We do not assume that we can track individual points in the image, nor that we are given any of their velocities (i.e., the optic flow). Among our results are:

The **6 point** df/dt **theorem**, showing that generically*** the values of df/dt at 6 points of the monochrome image f are necessary and sufficient to specify the motion of a given object.

The **2-color theorem for optic flow**, which states that the optic flow vector is uniquely specified at a generic point of the image if there are 2 or more color dimensions.

Also, we get the color version of the 6 point theorem, the **2 colors, 3 points corollary**, which reduces the number of points required to 3, if there are at least 2 color dimensions.

I INTRODUCTION

For the past several years, many researchers have been investigating problems of moving objects and observers (see e.g., [Tsai and Huang 1984], [Prazdny 1983], [Nagel 1983], [Horn and Schunck 1980], [Bruss and Horn 1983], [Ullman 1979]). A conventional paradigm is to consider 2 subproblems: finding the optic flow in the image, then computing 3-dimensional motion. Finding the optic flow in monochrome images by point tracking is, however, degenerate except for special points, just as for the point matching problem [Blicher 1983, Blicher 1984]. E.g. at a single point, the image function and its time derivative tell us nothing about motion perpendicular to the gradient of the image function.

We consider a rigid object undergoing an arbitrary motion in space. Our data is a time-varying image, i.e. a map $f : I \times M^2 \to \mathbf{R}^n$, where I is a time interval, M^2 is some 2-dimensional manifold, specifically the image plane, and n is the number of independent color dimensions; $n = 1$ for monochrome pictures. We concern ourselves here with the problem of finding the motion of the object, particularly, how much data is necessary and sufficient. Rather than make assumptions about first finding point correspondences or optic flow, we consider the full situation of a map from the rigid motion group to the time-varying image (but only for the interior of a single object), and we develop the differential theory, based on the data of the picture and its time derivative.

We regret that space limitations preclude defining mathematical terms. A fuller presentation, as well as more extensive references, can be found in [Blicher 1984].

II THE MATHEMATICAL STRUCTURE

The situation is that of Fig. (*'), just as in [Blicher 1983], except now the nature of the transformation g will be paramount.

We are interested in rigid motions in $\mathbf{R}^3$, so $g \in E(3)$, the Euclidean (rigid motion) group of $\mathbf{R}^3$. The time evolution of the mo-

tion is then given by $\gamma : \mathbf{R} \to E(3)$, i.e., as a path in the transformation group. In fact, γ defines a 1-parameter family of transformations. Since we are interested only in small changes from the current state, we take $\gamma(0) = I$, the identity in $E(3)$ (we could have done this anyway by using the group structure to translate back to the identity). For every t, γ gives a rigid motion of $\mathbf{R}^3$, since we are identifying $E(3)$ with the rigid motions of $\mathbf{R}^3$, i.e. $\gamma(t) : \mathbf{R}^3 \to \mathbf{R}^3$. Each point of $\mathbf{R}^3$ is carried along with this motion, and describes a path in $\mathbf{R}^3$ (defined by $\gamma_p(t) = (\gamma(t))(p)$, $p \in \mathbf{R}^3$). In particular, every point of our surface of interest, embedded in $\mathbf{R}^3$, has such a path. Now apply the imaging projection, and restrict attention only to the visible surface of the embedded object. By composition, this leads to a path through each point that gets hit in the image. (defined by $\hat{\gamma}_q(t) = \pi((\gamma(t))(p))$, $q \in M^2$). Now consider only a single time, $t = 0$. The structure we have presented thus far is summarized in Fig. (flow).

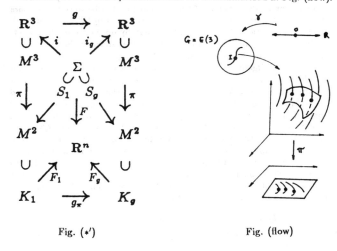

Fig. (*')   Fig. (flow)

Each such path in the picture has a velocity vector, and each point in the image has a path, so there is a vector field defined on the image. This is usually called the *optic flow*, but it is more consistent with mathematical terminology to call its integral, i.e. the paths in the image, the optic *flow*. We will reserve the term *optic flow* for this integral, i.e. the map $\varphi_t : U \to \mathbf{R}^2$ which specifies the paths of corresponding points in the picture with initial points in the region U, while using *optic velocity field* or *optic vector field* for its instantaneous velocities, the vectors $d\varphi_t/dt$. Similarly, the paths in $\mathbf{R}^3$ define a vector field on $\mathbf{R}^3$, and the path γ in $E(3)$ defines a tangent vector at the identity in $E(3)$.

The available data, however, is not the optic flow or vector field, but the time-varying picture function f_t which is just the projection of the intrinsic surface function F, which we assume is carried along with the motion, i.e. we neglect changes in f due purely to photometric effects, such as specular reflection. Since we are considering only the differential theory, we regard our data as telling us only the instantaneous value f_0, and all the time derivatives at $t = 0$. This is the same as knowing the Taylor series for f_t. We will only use the 1st

*This work was supported in part by DARPA contracts N00039-82-C-0250 and N00039-84-C-0211.

**Present address: Thinking Machines, Cambridge, Mass.

***A *generic* property is one which is true for a *typical* element of a space, i.e for a very dense subset of the space. For this paper, we take this to mean an open dense subset. See [Blicher 1984] for a discussion of genericity.

derivative. At a point p of the image, call the optic flow vector v. Then in a frame with velocity v at p in the image, f_t does not appear to change; the optic flow specifies the motion of corresponding points. Thus if we leave the frame fixed, we see that

$$\frac{d}{dt} f_t(p) = -D_v(f_t)(p) = -v \cdot \nabla f_t(p), \qquad (*)$$

where D_v means differentiation by the vector v, equivalent to $v \cdot \nabla$. (This is well-known in the context of optic flow; see e.g. [Horn and Schunck 1980], [Ballard and Brown 1982].) Equation $(*)$ shows how it is that we only have partial information about v: we only know 1 component. We can immediately see, also, that if f had multiple dimensions, i.e. if there were more than 1 color dimension, we would have information about multiple components, and v would be uniquely determined for generic f. This is the differential version of the 2-color theorem we have proved earlier [Blicher 1983, Blicher 1984]. Finding optic flow, like matching, is much easier with color. We formalize this in

Theorem. (2-color theorem for optic flow) For a generic time-varying image function $f_t : M^2 \to \mathbf{R}^n$, the optic flow vector is uniquely specified at a generic point of the image if $n \geq 2$, i.e. for 2 or more color dimensions.

When we fix $t = 0$, each side of equation $(*)$ is just a number, so for each p we have a map $D_.(f)(p) : v \mapsto a$ real number. We have thus defined a string of linear mappings (v.f. stands for vector field, v.b. for vector bundle):

tangent vector on $E(3) \mapsto$ v.b. section on object $\mapsto$

v.f. on image $\mapsto$ vector at $p \mapsto$ real number

(We must consider sections of a vector bundle on the object rather than vector fields (sections of the tangent bundle) because the vectors we are interested in are tangent vectors to paths in $\mathbf{R}^3$ going through points of the object. Since the paths generally do not lie in the object, their tangent vectors needn't be in the tangent space of the object, but rather are merely tangent vectors in $\mathbf{R}^3$.)

The Lie algebra $\mathfrak{g}$ of a Lie group G is a vector space which can be identified with the tangent space of G at the identity. $E(3)$ is a Lie group, and therefore associated with it is the Lie algebra $\mathfrak{e}(3)$; and since $E(3)$ is a 6-dimensional manifold, $\mathfrak{e}(3)$ is a 6-dimensional vector space. The tangent vector $\gamma'(0)$, which is the instantaneous motion, can therefore be thought of as an element of the Lie algebra $\mathfrak{e}(3)$.

We can do this for every path γ, hence for every element of $\mathfrak{e}(3)$, giving us a homomorphism from the Lie algebra $\mathfrak{e}(3)$ to sections of the vector bundle on the object, and likewise again to a Lie algebra of vector fields on the image of the object in the image plane. The composition of these is a Lie algebra homomorphism. The sequence of linear maps can therefore be written

Lie algebra $\mathfrak{e}(3) \to$ v.b. sections on object $\to$

v.f.'s on image $\to$ vectors at $p \to$ real numbers

This defines a map $\mathfrak{e}(3) \to \mathbf{R}$, i.e. an element of $\mathfrak{e}^*(3)$, the dual of $\mathfrak{e}(3)$.

Now we have enough machinery to attack some questions. The first question is whether there is enough information in df/dt to uniquely specify the instantaneous motion, for generic f. The instantaneous motion is an element of $\mathfrak{e}(3)$. As we just saw, for each point p of the image, the geometry defines an element of $\mathfrak{e}^*(3)$. The question then becomes whether we can span all of $\mathfrak{e}^*(3)$ by ranging over all points of the image, for knowing the value of applying a dual basis in $\mathfrak{e}^*(3)$ uniquely specifies the original vector in $\mathfrak{e}(3)$. $\mathfrak{e}^*(3)$ is 6-dimensional, so if this is possible, it is possible for 6 points corresponding to a dual basis. This doesn't say anything yet about finding the shape or position of the object; we only want to know whether we can recover the motion for fixed shape and position.

Theorem (6 point df/dt theorem). Let

$$f : \mathbf{I} \times U \to \mathbf{R}$$
$$(t, p) \mapsto f(t, p)$$

be a time-varying picture for some time interval $\mathbf{I}$ around 0, and some

neighborhood U in the image plane of regular values of the imaging projection of some 2-dimensional object (i.e. a 2-manifold) embedded in $\mathbf{R}^3$. If f comes from the projection of a generic intrinsic function on an object undergoing rigid motion in $\mathbf{R}^3$, then the values of $\partial f / \partial t$ $(0, p)$ at 6 generic points $p \in U$ are necessary and sufficient to uniquely specify the instantaneous motion of the object.

Proof. We are in effect measuring the optic velocity field with our image function; this is what equation $(*)$ says. To be able to tell the difference between different elements of $\mathfrak{e}(3)$, i.e. different motions, the mapping from $\mathfrak{e}(3)$ to velocity fields on the picture must be 1-1. Since the mapping is a vector space homomorphism, this is the same as saying it has no (nontrivial) kernel. The homomorphism $\mathfrak{e}(3) \to$ v.b. sections on object has no kernel, because any kernel would leave the entire object fixed, but a rigid motion of $\mathbf{R}^3$ can leave at most a line fixed. So $\mathfrak{e}(3)$ is mapped 1-1 to sections of bundles on the object. Now we must show that the kernel of the homomorphism v.b. sections on object $\to$ v.f.'s on image doesn't contain anything that comes from the previous map from $\mathfrak{e}(3)$. The kernel of the current map is just the sections whose vectors lie along the rays of projection to the picture. For orthogonal projection, vertical translation would of course be in this kernel, but we are assuming a projective projection, i.e. that the rays all meet at a point; for a planar retina this is the usual perspective projection.

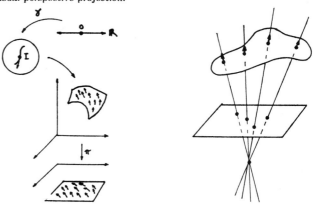

Fig. (vector fields)   Fig. (kernel-rays)

We have to show that any such motion, where points move only along rays, cannot come from a rigid motion. This is easy to see; take 3 points a, b, c on the object not all on the same line in $\mathbf{R}^3$. Since a rigid motion of $\mathbf{R}^3$ can only leave a single line axis (or nothing) fixed, at least 1 of the points must move, say a. If a moves down (toward the image plane), b must move up, to keep their distance constant (rigid motion). Since b is moving up, c must move down. But then a and c are both moving down and therefore narrowing their distance, showing that the motion cannot be a rigid motion, i.e. the kernel of v.b. sections on object $\to$ v.f.'s on image is not in the image of $\mathfrak{e}(3) \to$ v.b. sections on object (except for 0, of course). So we know that the composition $\mathfrak{e}(3) \to$ v.f.'s on image has no kernel, i.e. is 1-1. This means that every rigid motion gives a unique optic velocity field, and the vector space of such fields is 6-dimensional.

Fig. (3 points)   Fig. (3 fibers)

Actually, we showed more than that. We showed that a generic set of 3 points cannot stay fixed in the image—we didn't even have to consider the whole vector field. The set of vectors at 3 such points in the image make up a 6-dimensional vector space, so what we showed is that the map $e(3) \to$ *vectors at 3 given points in image* has no kernel, i.e. is 1-1.

That means that to specify a motion, i.e. an element of $e(3)$, we only have to figure out the optic velocity vectors at 3 points. A generic function, via equation $(*)$, tells us 1 component of each of the vectors (by genericity, the gradient is nonzero at all 3 points). If we had 2 generic functions, then we could recover both components of each of the 3 vectors by using equation $(*)$ for both functions (generically, the gradients will be linearly independent, i.e. in different directions at the 3 points). Parenthetically, we have just proved

Corollary (2 colors, 3 points). For generic f taking values in 2 or more color dimensions, the values of $\partial f / \partial t (0, p)$ at 3 noncollinear points $p \in U$ are necessary and sufficient to uniquely specify the instantaneous motion of the object.

Now we must show that 1 component at each of 6 points is as good as 2 components at each of 3 points. We saw earlier that df defines an element of $e^*(3)$. Thus the geometry defines a map $T^*\mathbf{R}^2 \to e^*(3)$. What we saw earlier is

Lemma (3 fiber lemma). If we choose 3 generic points in $\mathbf{R}^2$, and 2 linearly independent covectors in each fiber over those points, the 6 resulting points of $T^*\mathbf{R}^2$ are mapped to a spanning set in $e^*(3)$.

What we will now show is that we can choose *any* 6 generic points in $T^*\mathbf{R}^2$, i.e. 6 generic points in the image, and 6 generic values of df at those points (i.e. a generic f). This is pretty easy by making use of the 3 fiber lemma. The lemma still applies for any neighborhood of $\mathbf{R}^2$, i.e. we can choose the 3 points arbitrarily close together. This gives us

Lemma (local spanning). Every neighborhood of every point in $T^*\mathbf{R}^2$ contains 6 points which are mapped to a spanning set in $e^*(3)$.

Proof. Choose a point and neighborhood in $T^*\mathbf{R}^2$. It projects to a neighborhood of $\mathbf{R}^2$, in which we can choose 3 generic points. We can then choose 6 points in $T^*\mathbf{R}^2$, 2 to a fiber, by the 3 fiber lemma. QED (local spanning).

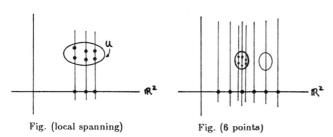

Fig. (local spanning)   Fig. (6 points)

Now we can see what happens when we choose 6 points in the image. df gives us 6 points in $T^*\mathbf{R}^2$. We can perturb these points to guarantee that $df \neq 0$. Now since every neighborhood of each point maps to a spanning set of $e^*(3)$ (local spanning lemma), we can always perturb the nth point so that it is mapped to something outside the span of the first $n-1$ points (at least through $n = 6$, anyway). This gives a perturbation of the 6 points which maps to a spanning set. Since spanning sets are open, these points will still span under sufficiently small perturbation. (In general, one might need a perturbation of both the location of the points and of f to guarantee a spanning set. The degenerate situation occurs when the optic velocity vector is in the direction of constant f.) QED

III   AFTERWORD

By virtue of the local spanning lemma and the 3 fiber lemma, our results are local, i.e. they hold in an arbitrarily small neighborhood—generically every neighborhood has 6 points yielding sufficient data. This is significant because it implies that an estimate of the motion can be obtained from any neighborhood. In practice, of course, using a very small neighborhood would lead to a very bad estimate. One would

rather use many points over a large region to obtain a least squares estimate. But the localness means that estimates can be made over a range of scales, and that a procedure for segmentation based on local estimates is well-founded.

ACKNOWLEDGMENTS

We are grateful to Tom Binford for his help and encouragement throughout the period of this work.

REFERENCES

[Ballard and Brown 1982]
Ballard, Dana Harry and Christopher M. Brown, **Computer Vision**, Prentice-Hall, Englewood Cliffs, 1982. [TA1632.B34, ISBN 0-13-165316-4].

[Blicher 1983]
Blicher, A. Peter, "The Stereo Matching Problem from the Topological Viewpoint," *Proceedings of the Eighth International Joint Conference on Artificial Intelligence*, 1983, 1046–1049.

[Blicher 1984]
Blicher, A. Peter, "Edge Detection and Geometric Methods in Computer Vision," Ph.D. thesis, Mathematics Department, University of California, Berkeley, December 1984. Also Stanford University Computer Science Department technical report STAN-CS-85-1041 and AI memo AIM-352, February 1985.

[Bruss and Horn 1983]
Bruss, Anna R. and Berthold K.P. Horn, "Passive Navigation," *Computer Vision, Graphics, and Image Processing*, 21, 1983, 3–20.

[Horn and Schunck 1980]
Horn, Berthold K.P. and Brian G. Schunck, "Determining Optical Flow," MIT AI Memo 572, MIT Artificial Intelligence Laboratory, April 1980; also *Artificial Intelligence*, 17, 1981, 185–203.

[Nagel 1983]
Nagel, Hans-Hellmut, "Displacement Vectors Derived from Second-Order Intensity Variations in Image Sequences," *Computer Vision, Graphics, and Image Processing*, vol. 21, 1983, 85–117.

[Prazdny 1983]
Prazdny, K., "On the Information in Optical Flows," *Computer Vision, Graphics, and Image Processing*, vol. 22, 1983, 239–259.

[Tsai and Huang 1984]
Tsai, Roger Y. and Thomas S. Huang, "Uniqueness and Estimation of Three-Dimensional Motion Parameters of Rigid Objects with Curved Surfaces," *IEEE Transactions on Pattern Analysis and Machine Intelligence*, vol. PAMI-6, no. 1, 1984, 13–27.

[Ullman 1979]
Ullman, Shimon, **The Interpretation of Visual Motion**, MIT Press, Cambridge, 1979. [BF241.U43 ISBN 0-262-21007-X].

COARSE–TO–FINE CONTROL STRATEGY
FOR MATCHING MOTION STEREO PAIRS

Gang Xu, Saburo Tsuji and Minoru Asada

Department of Control Engineering
Osaka University
Toyonaka, Osaka 560, Japan

ABSTRACT

This article proposes a slider stereo matching method, which employs a coarse-to-fine control strategy to overcome the false targets problem. At first, a stereo pair is taken at a short baseline, and a match is assigned to it. The resulting disparity map is then used to restrict search range and to predict occlusion for efficiently and reliably matching the succeeding stereo pair taken at a longer baseline. The system iterates the sliding and matching to obtain an enough disparity range.

1. INTRODUCTION

It has been pointed out by the early researches[1,2] on stereopsis that at the heart of the matching problem lies the problem of false targets, whose severity is enhanced by both a wide disparity range and a fine resolution. To obtain both, which are necessary for accuracy, Marr and Poggio [2] proposed a zero-crossing algorithm (implemented by Grimson [3]) based on the coarse-to-fine strategy. The stereo images were filtered at different scales, yielding a set of primitive image pairs of different resolutions. A match of a wide disparity range but of a coarse resolution was assigned first, and this result was then used to reduce search space, for matching the finer detailed primitive pairs. While the algorithm was successfully applied to a variety of images, it resulted in incorrect matches along occluding zero-crossings, because the continuity constraint was used along those depth-discontinuous contours.

In this paper, we present a new stereo matching method, which is based upon a different coarse-to-fine strategy. A camera is slid along a straight line to take stereo pairs at different baselines, resulting in a set of stereo pairs of different disparity ranges. Images are convolved with a small-sized Laplacian-Gaussian operator, which assures us of a fine resolution, and the zero-crossings in the filtered images are extracted along horizontal scan lines. Then the matching process proceeds in a coarse-to-fine iterative manner. The pair taken at the shortest baseline is matched first; the matching is easy, at the expense of reduced disparity range. This result, a narrow range disparity map, can then be used to reduce search space for matching the longer baseline pair, again making the process easier. We iterate the sliding, imaging and matching several times to obtain a wide disparity range. One important advantage of our method over the conventional ones is that we can predict occlusion, helping avoid mismatches.

Motion stereo methods have been studied for a long time by Moravec and Nevatia. The idea, however, was used to make reliable depth measurement[4] and to save computing time[5], while the disparity information available from the already matched pairs was not utilized in matching the other pairs.

2. COARSE-TO-FINE RULE

Both our algorithm and Marr and Poggio's are based on the coarse-to-fine control strategy, aiming at obtaining both a wide disparity range and a fine resolution at last. The two algorithms, however, take different routes to reach the goal. Fig.1 helps to understand the difference. While the depth accuracy in Marr and Poggio's algorithm is improved by making the resolution finer over a wide disparity range, that in ours is improved by widening the disparity range in a fine resolution.

It is important to note that, the only physical constraint we use here is that features should not disappear, nor features newly appear, through the sliding, because the scene and the illumination condition are supposed not to change during this period. In general, it is satisfied except the cases where some feature points are occluded, as

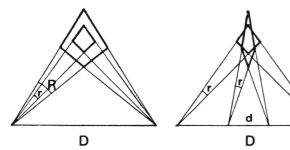

Fig.1 There are two routes leading to the final goal, the accurate depth measurement. The diamonds indicate the possible errors in estimates of location of a point in scene. (a) The vertical diagonal of the diamond becomes shorter with the finer resolutions (R→r), while a wide disparity range(D) remaining unchanged. (b) The vertical diagonal becomes shorter with the disparity range getting wider(d→D), while a fine resolution(r) remaining unchanged.

the camera is slid. These feature points, however, are assigned with disparities before occluded and the probability of occlusion is predicted from the disparity information obtained already. As a consequence, not only can we avoid the incorrect matches due to occlusion, but it is also possible to obtain more disparity information about the feature points occluded finally than the other stereo matchers.

3. SLIDING AND MATCHING

A camera is slid from left to right along a straight line, taking a sequence of images at predetermined intervals. The sliding is kept parallel to the horizontal axis of the camera coordinate system, so that the epipolar lines, on which correspondences can be found, are completely horizontal. Let the first image be the only left image and the remainders right ones. Note that such an arrangement is purely for simplifying our description, and the following matching algorithm can be easily modified for other arrangements.

Images are convolved with the Laplacian-Gaussian filter, and zero-crossings in the filtered images are found. For a fine resolution, we have chosen 4 as the filter's central region width W. Besides the location, an attribute of the zero-crossings, the contrast sign, is also recorded, and used as a criterion for matching.

The first stereo pair, due to its reduced disparity range, can be easily matched by simply searching a small region without encountering false targets. Below, we discuss how to use the obtained disparity information for matching the second stereo pair. Suppose that the baseline of the second stereo pair is k times that of the first one. Then for a zero-crossing in the left image at position (x,y), whose disparity obtained by matcing the first stereo pair is $D(x,y)$, its correspondence's position in the right image is estimated by
$$(x-kD(x,y),y).$$
Taking into account the error ΔD in the disparity obtained already, the position is revised as
$$(x-kD(x,y)+k\Delta D,y).$$
Therefore, we can constrain the search for the corresponding zero-crossing in the right image of the second stereo pair to the region
$$\{(x',y)\mid x-kD(x,y)-k\Delta D_{max} \leq x' \leq x-kD(x,y)+k\Delta D_{max},$$
$$\Delta D \leq \Delta D_{max}\}.$$

The size of search region should be selected so that the probability for double targets in one search region is not high. A conservative value, 7 pixels, is selected for the width of the search region. Then the worst case probability of double targets is 0.5 (estimated from the result by Grimson [3]), and true matches can found by utilizing "pulling effect" [2].

Now let us consider how long we can slide the camera in each step of the successive imaging. Given ΔD_{max}, We can determine k, the ratio of the baselines, as $3/\Delta D_{max}$. ΔD results from many factors, such as errors in locating zero- crossings in quantized images and the physical inaccuracy in sliding the camera. We have not estimated all these

factors yet. The experimental results, however, indicate that ΔD_{max} does not exceed 1.5 pixels in most cases; 2 is currently selected for k. Clearly, we need less sliding times for obtaining an enough disparity range than conventional motion stereo methods [4,5], which take pictures at equal intervals.

4. OCCLUSION PREDICTION

In this section, we consider how the occlusions in the successive stereo pair is predicted from the disparity map obtained already. Suppose that there are two zero-crossings P_1 and P_2 at (x_1,y) and (x_2,y) on a scan line in the left image. If they are predicted as changing to the opposite order in the right image, i.e.,
$$x_1 < x_2,$$
$$x_1 - kD(x_1,y) > x_2 - kD(x_2,y),$$
then the probability for P_1 being occluded is high.

The prediction is not always true, because of the error in estimating the zero-crossing positions. Therefore, the following method is used to avoid mismatches. If the estimated distance between the occluding and occluded zero-crossings is above a threshold, then the occlusion is certain and we search for only P_1. If below, we search for both. In the latter case, if there is only one matchable zero-crossing, then it is considered as corresponding to P_2, the one closer to the camera.

5. EXPERIMENTS AND DISCUSSION

We have tested the described method for a blocks-world and an indoor scene. Fig.2 (a), (b) and (c) illustrate the first, second and fifth images of an image sequence of the blocksworld, respectively. Fig.2 (d) shows the zero-crossing contours of Fig.2 (c). The contours are displayed as bright if the contrast sign is positive, and as dark if negative. Fig.2 (e) shows the differences between the estimated zero-crossing positions and the real ones. It can be seen that they agree with each other quite well. The dark points indicate the estimated locations of zero-crossings and those predicted as occluded are displayed with larger spots. The bright points are the actual positions in the image. Fig.2 (f) shows the top view obtained by matching Fig.2 (a) to Fig.2(e). Fig.3(a) shows an input image of the indoor scene, and Fig.3(b) shows the disparity map, in which the disparity is displayed as proportional to the brightness.

The experiments indicate that most zero-crossings appear in the search pools, provided that the camera sliding is accurate enough. The disparities obtained along occluding zero-crossing contours also demonstrate that there are few mismatches resulting from occlusion.

One difficulty in matching the stereo pair is that the contrast sign along occluding zero-crossing contours sometimes changes as the camera is slid. Therefore, the contrast sign, which played a significant role in the implementation of Marr and Poggio's algorithm by Grimson, results in mismatches in this method. We consider that our method can be improved to accomodate such cases by predicting the changes in the background's intensity.

At present, the camera motion is along a straight line. We can, however, modify the method so as to move the camera more freely in space, and give the system intelligence to plan motion by observing the coarse disparity map obtained already.

REFERENCES

[1] Marr, D. and Poggio, T. "Cooperative Computation of Stereo Disparity" Science, N.Y.194, 1976, pp.283-287
[2] Marr, D. and Poggio, T. "A Computational Theory of Human Stereo Vision" Proc. R. Soc. Lond. B204, 1979, pp.301-328.
[3] Grimson, W. E. L. "From Images To Surfaces: A Computational Study of the Human Early Vision System", Cambridge, MA., MIT Press, 1981
[4] Moravec, H. "The Stanford Cart and the CMU Rover" Proc. of IEEE, Vol.71,No.7,1983 pp.872-884
[5] Nevatia, R. "Depth Measurement by Motion Stereo" Comput. Graphics & Image Proc., Vol.6, 1976.

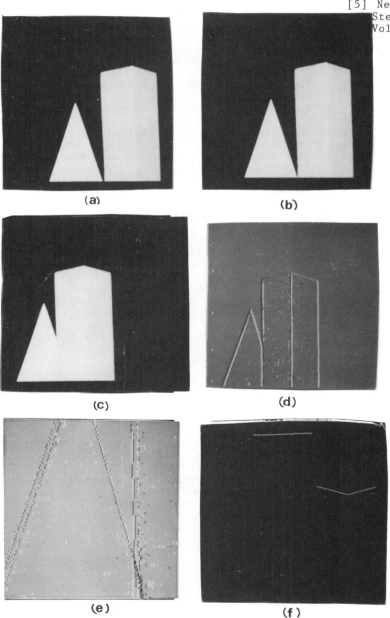

(a)

(b)

(c)

(d)

(e)

(f)

Figure 2

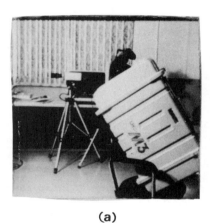

(a)

(b)

Figure 3

UTILIZATION OF A STRIPE PATTERN
FOR DYNAMIC SCENE ANALYSIS

Minoru Asada and Saburo Tsuji

Department of Control Engineering

Osaka University

Toyonaka, Osaka 560, Japan

ABSTRACT

This paper describes a new idea to project a stripe pattern onto a time-varying scene to find moving objects and acquire scene features in the consecutive frames for estimating 3-D motion parameters. At first, a simple temporal difference method detects objects moving against a complex background. A 2(1/2)D representation of moving objects at each frame is then obtained by estimating surface normals from the slopes and intervals of stripes in the image. The 2(1/2)D image is further divided into planar or singly curved surfaces by examining the distribution of the surface normals in the gradient space. Then, the rotational motion parameters of the objects are estimated from changes in the geometry of these surfaces between frames. Determining translational ones is also discussed.

1. INTRODUCTION

Determining of 3-D motion parameters in a time-varying scene is a current problem in computer vision. Interesting theories have been presented to estimate 3-D motion of objects from a sequence of images taken by a camera [1-3]. They, assuming the rigidity of objects, analyze changes in geometry of object's images in the consecutive frames to obtain 3-D motion cues. The results of applying these theories to real scenes, however, are very sensitive to noise and unsatisfactory in most cases. We, therefore, need a reliable method to obtain scene features from each frame in the image sequence.

A method useful for acquiring 3-D information is to project the structured light to the scene. Since the time for scanning a slit light [4] is too long for the dynamic scene analysis, we use a dense stripe pattern as the structured light. One advantage of this method is that a simple temporal difference method can easily detect objects moving against a very complex background, saving a considerable computing time.

If the stripe is dense, finding of correspondence between each stripe pattern in image and light stripes in scene is difficult, especially when the scene contains many concave objects or discontinuous boundaries. As a result, our method cannot provide with the range information at each image point. Surface normals as important scene features, however, are available at a number of points distributed densely in the image.

The image acquisition system is arranged such that all light stripes in scene are almost parallel and the projection from scene to image is orthographic. Thus, we can obtain a 2(1/2)D representation of the moving objects at each frame by estimating the surface normals from the slopes and intervals of the stripe.

The 2(1/2)D image is further segmented into planar or singly curved surfaces by finding and examining clusters of the surface normals mapped onto the gradient space. Although the estimate of each surface normal is somewhat inaccurate, we can obtain much better estimates of geometrical parameters of these surfaces by utilizing the continuity in each surface. The rotational movements of the objects are determined from changes in these parameters between consecutive frames. The estimation of the translational components from these changes is difficult, however, we could utilize cues to get the range

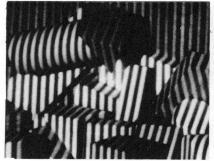 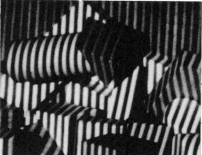

(a) The 2nd frame.   (b) The 5th frame.

Fig.1 Examples of input images.

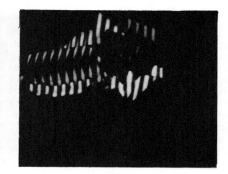

Fig.2 The difference picture between (a) and (b) in Fig.1.

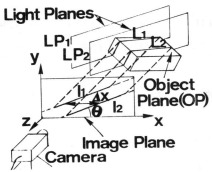

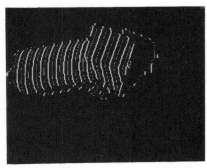

Fig.3 The moving object at the 5th frame.

Fig.4 The principle of measurement.

Fig.5 Edge picture of Fig.3.

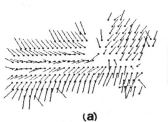

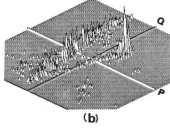

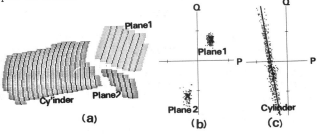

Fig.6 The obtained surface normals, (a) needle map and (b) histogram of them on the gradient space.

Fig.7 The result of segmentation, (a) region map, (b) planar and (c) cylindrical surfaces on the gradient map.

information as discussed in the final chapter.

2. METHODS

We apply the method to a real scene shown in Fig.1. Input images consist of 256*240 pixels, 8bits/pixel. Many blocks are stacked up, and a cylinder with a wedge is moving above them. It seems difficult to extract moving objects because of complexity of background.

2.1 Extraction of Moving Objects

The first step of dynamic scene analysis is to separate non-stationary portions from the stationary background. In our case, a difference picture of gray values between two consecutive frames shows most parts of moving objects, because the stripe pattern on an object surface is changed in its position, slope or intervals in image by the object motion in most cases.

Fig.2 shows a difference picture of gray values between the 2nd and the 5th frames, which displays the absolute value of difference. We can see the region covers almost whole parts of moving objects while, by ordinary lighting, overlapping part of moving objects in those frames will not be detected. In order to extract the moving object at the 5th frame, we take one more difference picture between the 5th and the 8th frame, and take the AND picture of two difference pictures, then the region of moving object at the 5th frame is left (frame interval is arbitrarily chosen). Small holes and cracks are eliminated by region growing. As a result, the moving object at the 5th frame is extracted (See Fig.3).

2.2 Determination of Surface Orientation

The surface orientation is determined locally from the slope and intervals of each stripe in image.

Fig.4 shows the geometrical relations among light planes and an object plane in the camera-centered coordinate system. We define the equations of two light planes LP1 and LP2 parallel to each other and of an object plane OP on which a stripe pattern is projected, as

$$LP1 : P_sX + Q_sY + Z = D1,$$
$$LP2 : P_sX + Q_sY + Z = D2,$$

and

$$OP : P_oX + Q_oY + Z = C,$$

where P_s and Q_s are parameters which represent the direction of light source in a projector and (P_o, Q_o) is the surface orientation. The object plane OP and the light plane LP1 (LP2) intersect in a line L1 (L2). The projection of two lines L1 and L2 onto the image plane (the x-y plane) are defined as l1 and l2, respectively. The slope of these lines ($\tan\theta$) and the distance between them (Δx) in the x-direction are easily measured in image since we assume the orthographic projection.

The geometrical relation among these variables leads to the following equations,

$$\tan\theta = -(Q_s - Q_o) / (P_s - P_o),$$
$$\Delta x = (D2 - D1) / (P_s - P_o).$$

From these equations,

$$P_o = (D1 - D2) / \Delta x + P_s$$

and,

$$Q_o = -(D1 - D2) / \Delta x * \tan\theta + Q_s.$$

That is, the surface orientation (P_o, Q_o) of a point on an object is calculated locally from the slope $(\tan\theta)$ and intervals (Δx) of the stripe in the image.

In order to obtain the surface normal, the system detects edge segments from the striped image of moving objects (See Fig.5). The location of edge point is estimated in a sub-pixel order by using the Linear Mixing Model [5] of intensity around the boundary between dark and bright regions to reduce the effect of digitizing error. The system fits a line segment to seven successive edge points. Those segments whose fitting error exceeds a threshold are discarded as discontinuous boundaries. From the slope and intervals of these line segments, we can calculate the surface orientations. Fig.6 (a) shows sampled surface normals on the moving objects obtained at the 5th frame. A histogram of these surface normals in the gradient space are shown in Fig.6 (b).

2.3 Motion Analysis

Let us consider how we can utilize the 2(1/2)D images to estimate the 3-D motion parameters. At first, we map the obtained surface normals onto the gradient space in order to segment the 2(1/2)D image into planar or singly curved surfaces (see Fig.6 (b)). Surface normals on a plane make a cluster in the gradient space. By mapping them from the gradient space into the 2(1/2)D image reversely, we obtain the planar region. Its orientation is precisely estimated by calculating again with longer line segments and wider intervals.

Also, surface normals on a singly curved surface, for example, a cylindrical surface make a line-like cluster in the gradient space. The line parameters obtained by fitting a line to the cluster gives us the orientation of generating line of the cylindrical surface. Its orientation makes the surface parameters more precise.

Since the lower surface of wedge is parallel to the generating line of the cylindrical surface, the cluster corresponding to it is merged in a line-like cluster (See Fig.6 (b)). Therefore, we cannot detect the lower surface of wedge in the gradient space at first. The line-like cluster, however, is segmented into two surfaces by examining the surface continuity on the 2(1/2)D image. Fig.7 shows the results of the segmentation.

Since each 2(1/2)D image is segmented into planar or singly curved surfaces, it is easy to find correspondence of these surfaces between consecutive frames. Table 1 indicates the angles between the surfaces at the 4th and the 5th frames. The orientation of cylindrical surface is represented as the direction of generating line. Little changes of them between frames shows the rigidity of object. Assuming it, we determine the accurate rotation parameters from the precisely obtained surface properties at each frame.

3. DISCUSSIONS

We have determined the rotational movement of object from the changes of surface geometry between frames. They, however, can provide us with little information on the translational movement. Thus, let us consider how we can get the range information from such images as shown in Fig.1 to determine the translation.

Shadow parts give us a very important cue to extract the depth information. Utilizing the projections of light lines onto the image plane, which are equivalent to the epipolar line in stereo vision, we can label each stripe in image between two surfaces which are discontinuous as shown in Fig.8. This figure displays the upper surface of the wedge and its shadow on the back wall in Fig.1 (b). Then, the relative distance between them is obtained from the equations of light stripes in scene.

If two surfaces are continuous, stripe edges in image are connected across their boundary. Therefore, we hypothesize that the range is continuous between two surfaces where stripe edges in image are connected, although it is not always true.

Most parts of the image would be interpreted by propagating the consistent labeling of stripes with the shadow information and the cue of surface continuity. There would remain several candidates of interpretation for unknown portion of the image.

REFERENCES

[1] S.Ullman ,The interpretation of visual motion, MA: M.I.T. Press, 1979.
[2] M.Asada and S.Tsuji, "Representation of three-dimensional motion in dynamic scenes," C.V.G.I.P., vol.21, pp.118-144, 1983.
[3] J.-Q.Fang and T.S.Huang, "Some experiments on estimating the 3-D motion parameters of a rigid body from two consecutive image frames," IEEE Trans. Pattern Anal. Machine Intell., vol.PAMI-6, pp.545-554, 1984.
[4] M.Ohshima and Y.Shirai, "A scene description method using three-dimensional information," Pattern Recognition, vol.11, pp.9-17, 1979.
[5] M.Mericlel, J.Lundgram and T.Sorensen, "Cascade, an algorithm to reduce the effect of mixed pixels," Proc. of CVPR-83, pp.53-58, 1983.

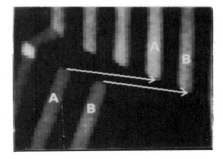

Fig.8 Consistent labeling of stripes with shadow information.

inter-surface \ frame	4th	5th
Plane1 <-> Cylinder	40.9(deg.)	40.9
Cylinder <-> Plane2	89.7	88.1
Plane2 <-> Plane1	89.5	88.6

Table 1 Angles between the surfaces.

Determining 3–D Motion of Planar Objects from Image Brightness Patterns

S. Negahdaripour and B.K.P. Horn

Artificial Intelligence Laboratory
Massachusetts Institute of Technology
Cambridge, Massachusetts 02139

Abstract: The brightness patterns in two successive image frames are used to recover the motion of a planar object without computing the optical flow as an intermediate step. Based on a least-squares formulation, a set of nine nonlinear equations are derived. A simple iterative scheme for solving these equations is presented. Using a selected example, it is shown that in general, the scheme may converge to either of two possible solutions depending on the initial condition. Only in the special case where the translational motion vector is perpendicular to the surface does our algorithm converge to a unique solution.

1. Introduction

The problem of determining rigid object motion and surface structure from a sequence of image frames has been the topic of many recent research papers in the area of machine vision. Much of the theoretical work has been restricted to using the optical flow, the apparent velocity of brightness patterns in the image. Three types of approaches, discrete, differential, and least-squares, have been commonly pursued.

In the discrete approach, information about a finite number of points is used to reconstruct the motion [3,7,11–13]. To do this, one has to identify and match feature points in a sequence of images. The minimum number of points required depends on the number of image frames. In the differential approach, one uses the optical flow and its first and second derivatives at a single point [8,15]. In the least-squares approach, the optical flow is used at every image point [1,2,16].

In general, to compute the optical flow, one exploits a constraint equation between the optical flow and the image brightness gradients. Locally, the brightness variations in time varying images only provide one constraint on the two components of the optical flow. Therefore, an additional constraint will be required to compute the local flow field. For instance, one may assume that the flow field varies smoothly [5,6], or that it is locally quadratic [15].

In this paper, we restrict ourselves to planar surfaces where only three parameters are needed to specify the surface structure. We determine the motion and surface parameters directly from the image brightness gradients, without having to compute the optical flow as an intermediate step.

2. Problem Formulation

Horn and Schunk [6] have derived a constraint equation between the optical flow (u, v), the apparent velocity of brightness patterns in the image, and the spatial-temporal gradients of the brightness patterns (E_x, E_y, E_t), when the incident illumination is uniform across the surface. This constraint equation is of the form:

$$E_x u + E_y v + E_t = 0. \qquad (1)$$

In practice, the brightness gradients are estimated from the gray levels in consecutive image frames using finite difference methods.

Any rigid body motion can be decomposed into translational and rotational components. We can either consider the motion of an object relative to a stationary camera, or equivalently the motion of a camera relative to a stationary object (navigation). In either case, the relative motion between the object and the camera and the object structure are to be determined from sequences of image frames. Let $\mathbf{t} = (U, V, W)^T$ and $\omega = (A, B, C)^T$ denote the vectors of translational and rotational velocity, respectively (T denotes the transpose of a vector), and let the point $\mathbf{r} = (x, y, 1)^T$ in the image plane be the perspective projection of the point $\mathbf{r} = (X, Y, Z(X, Y))^T$ on the rigid object. It can be shown that the optical flow generated in the image plane by the relative motion between the camera and the object is given by[2]:

$$
\begin{aligned}
u &= A\,xy - B(x^2 + 1) + C\,y + (-U + xW)/Z, \\
v &= A\,(y^2 + 1) - B\,xy - C\,x + (-V + yW)/Z.
\end{aligned}
\qquad (2)
$$

Substituting equations (2) into (1), and simplifying the results, we obtain the brightness change constraint equation for the case of rigid body motion:

$$c + \mathbf{v} \cdot \omega + \frac{1}{Z}\,\mathbf{s} \cdot \mathbf{t} = 0, \qquad (3)$$

where $c = E_t$, and

$$
\mathbf{v} = \begin{pmatrix} E_x xy + E_y(y^2 + 1) \\ -E_x(x^2 + 1) - E_y xy \\ E_x y - E_y x \end{pmatrix}, \quad
\mathbf{s} = \begin{pmatrix} -E_x \\ -E_y \\ E_x x + E_y y \end{pmatrix}.
$$

For a planar surface, $(\mathbf{r} \cdot \mathbf{n}) Z = 1$, where $\mathbf{n} = (p, q, r)^T$ is the normal to the surface. Substituting for Z into equation (3) yields:

$$c + \mathbf{v} \cdot \boldsymbol{\omega} + (\mathbf{r} \cdot \mathbf{n})(\mathbf{s} \cdot \mathbf{t}) = 0. \qquad (4)$$

This is the brightness change constraint equation for a rigid planar object undergoing 3-D motion. We will exploit it to recover the motion and surface parameters.

3. Least-Squares Formulation

Given perfect data, only a few points are sufficient to determine the nine unknowns (three components of $\boldsymbol{\omega}$, $\mathbf{t}$, and $\mathbf{n}$)—or rather, eight, since we can only recover the distance to the plane and the translational velocity up to a scale factor (Equation (4) will remain invariant if $\mathbf{n}$ is multiplied by a scale factor and $\mathbf{t}$ is divided by the same factor). In practice, this constraint equation will not be satisfied at each image point due to additive sensor noise, quantization of the image brightness levels and finite difference approximaation used to estimate the brightness gradients. Therefore, a least-squares formulation seems appropriate in developing a robust algorithm.

A suitable choice of surface and motion parameters should minimize some measure of error in equation (4) for every image point. We will formulate the following unconstrained optimization problem:

Find the surface $\mathbf{n}$, and motion parameters $\boldsymbol{\omega}$ and $\mathbf{t}$, that minimize the expression:

$$J = \iint_\Omega [c + \mathbf{v} \cdot \boldsymbol{\omega} + (\mathbf{r} \cdot \mathbf{n})(\mathbf{s} \cdot \mathbf{t})]^2 \, dx \, dy, \qquad (5)$$

where the integration is performed over the relevant region Ω of the image plane. Necessary conditions for minimizing equation (5) with respect to $\boldsymbol{\omega}$, $\mathbf{t}$, and $\mathbf{n}$ include:

$$\frac{\partial J}{\partial \boldsymbol{\omega}} = \mathbf{0}, \quad \frac{\partial J}{\partial \mathbf{t}} = \mathbf{0}, \quad \text{and} \quad \frac{\partial J}{\partial \mathbf{n}} = \mathbf{0}. \qquad (6)$$

Performing the indicated differentiations in (6) we get:

$$\iint_\Omega [c + \mathbf{v} \cdot \boldsymbol{\omega} + (\mathbf{r} \cdot \mathbf{n})(\mathbf{s} \cdot \mathbf{t})] \, \mathbf{v} \, dx \, dy = \mathbf{0}, \qquad (7a)$$

$$\iint_\Omega (\mathbf{r} \cdot \mathbf{n}) [c + \mathbf{v} \cdot \boldsymbol{\omega} + (\mathbf{r} \cdot \mathbf{n})(\mathbf{s} \cdot \mathbf{t})] \, \mathbf{s} \, dx \, dy = \mathbf{0}, \qquad (7b)$$

$$\iint_\Omega (\mathbf{s} \cdot \mathbf{t}) [c + \mathbf{v} \cdot \boldsymbol{\omega} + (\mathbf{r} \cdot \mathbf{n})(\mathbf{s} \cdot \mathbf{t})] \, \mathbf{r} \, dx \, dy = \mathbf{0}. \qquad (7c)$$

These comprise nine nonlinear simultaneous equations that can be solved for the six motion parameters, $\mathbf{t}$ and $\boldsymbol{\omega}$, and the three surface parameters, $\mathbf{n}$.

4. An Iterative Solution Procedure

We now present an iterative solution procedure for solving the nine simultaneous equations defined previously. First, some observations about equations (7) are in order:

1. Equation (7a) is linear in $\boldsymbol{\omega}$, $\mathbf{t}$, and $\mathbf{n}$.
2. Equation (7b) is linear in $\boldsymbol{\omega}$ and $\mathbf{t}$, but quadratic in $\mathbf{n}$.
3. Equation (7c) is linear in $\boldsymbol{\omega}$ and $\mathbf{n}$, but quadratic in $\mathbf{t}$.

Several iterative schemes for solving equations (7) can be considered. The two we have implemented are as follows:

1. Solve the linear equations in (7a) and (7b) for $\boldsymbol{\omega}$ and $\mathbf{t}$ in terms of $\mathbf{n}$, and the linear equations in (7c) for $\mathbf{n}$ in terms of $\boldsymbol{\omega}$ and $\mathbf{t}$ in an iterative procedure.
2. Solve the linear equations in (7a) and (7b) for $\boldsymbol{\omega}$ and $\mathbf{t}$ in terms of $\mathbf{n}$, and the linear equations in (7a) and (7c) for $\boldsymbol{\omega}$ and $\mathbf{n}$ in terms of $\mathbf{t}$ in an iterative procedure.

The second scheme involves more computation, but converges faster. We will only describe the first scheme here (see [10] for more details on both schemes).

Expanding equations (7), collecting terms, and simplifying the results yield:

$$\begin{pmatrix} \mathbf{M}_1 & \mathbf{M}_2 \\ \mathbf{M}_2^T & \mathbf{M}_4 \end{pmatrix} \begin{pmatrix} \boldsymbol{\omega} \\ \mathbf{t} \end{pmatrix} = -\begin{pmatrix} \mathbf{d}_1 \\ \mathbf{d}_2 \end{pmatrix}, \qquad (8)$$

$$\mathbf{N}\mathbf{n} = -\mathbf{g}, \qquad (9)$$

where

$$\mathbf{M}_1 = \iint_\Omega (\mathbf{v}\mathbf{v}^T) \, dx \, dy \quad \mathbf{M}_2 = \iint_\Omega \mathbf{n}^T \mathbf{r}(\mathbf{v}\mathbf{s}^T) \, dx \, dy$$

$$\mathbf{M}_4 = \iint_\Omega \mathbf{n}^T (\mathbf{r}\mathbf{r}^T)\mathbf{n}(\mathbf{s}\mathbf{s}^T) \, dx \, dy$$

$$\mathbf{N} = \iint_\Omega \mathbf{t}^T (\mathbf{s}\mathbf{s}^T)\mathbf{t}(\mathbf{r}\mathbf{r}^T) \, dx \, dy$$

$$\mathbf{d}_1 = \iint_\Omega c\mathbf{v} \, dx \, dy \quad \mathbf{d}_2 = \iint_\Omega c(\mathbf{s}\mathbf{r}^T)\mathbf{n} \, dx \, dy$$

$$\mathbf{g} = \iint_\Omega \left[c(\mathbf{r}\mathbf{s}^T)\mathbf{t} + \mathbf{t}^T \mathbf{s}(\mathbf{r}\mathbf{v}^T)\boldsymbol{\omega} \right] \, dx \, dy.$$

Given the surface parameters $\mathbf{n}$, the motion parameters $\boldsymbol{\omega}$ and $\mathbf{t}$ can be determined from equation (8). Similarly, given the motion parameters $\boldsymbol{\omega}$ and $\mathbf{t}$, equation (9) can be solved for the surface parameters $\mathbf{n}$. Based on these observations, we adopt the following iterative scheme:

1. Start with an initial guess for the surface parameters.
2. Solve the matrix equation (8) for motion parameters.
3. Solve the matrix equation (9) for surface parameters.
4. Evaluate the improvement in the solution to either go to (2) for the next iteration or stop if the solution has not improved.

The solution of equation (8) for $\boldsymbol{\omega}$ and $\mathbf{t}$ can be determined analytically, and can be written in many forms. For example, if $\mathbf{M}_1$ is invertible, we have

$$\mathbf{t} = \left(\mathbf{M}_4 - \mathbf{M}_2^T \mathbf{M}_1^{-1} \mathbf{M}_2 \right)^{-1} \left(\mathbf{M}_2^T \mathbf{M}_1^{-1} \mathbf{d}_1 - \mathbf{d}_2 \right), \qquad (10a)$$

$$\boldsymbol{\omega} = -\mathbf{M}_1^{-1} \left(\mathbf{d}_1 + \mathbf{M}_2 \mathbf{t} \right). \qquad (10b)$$

900 S. Negahdaripour and B. Horn

Similarily, the solution of equation (9) is given by:

$$\mathbf{n} = -\mathbf{N}^{-1}\mathbf{g}. \qquad (11)$$

Since all arrays in equations (10) and (11) are either 3×3 matrices or vectors of length 3, the solutions for ω, $\mathbf{t}$, and $\mathbf{n}$ can be determined easily.

5. Implementation

Let us consider the computations involved during one iteration. Using tensor notation (implicit summation over repeated indeces), we have:

$$\{\mathbf{M}_1\}_{i,j} = \iint_\Omega v_i v_j\, dx\, dy \quad \{\mathbf{M}_2\}_{i,j} = \left[\iint_\Omega r_k v_i s_j\, dx\, dy\right] n_k$$

$$\{\mathbf{M}_4\}_{i,j} = \left[\iint_\Omega r_k r_l s_i s_j\, dx\, dy\right] n_k n_l$$

$$\{\mathbf{N}\}_{i,j} = \left[\iint_\Omega s_k s_l r_i r_j\, dx\, dy\right] t_k t_l \qquad (12)$$

$$\{\mathbf{d}_1\}_i = \iint_\Omega c v_i\, dx\, dy \quad \{\mathbf{d}_2\}_i = \left[\iint_\Omega c s_i r_j\, dx\, dy\right] n_j$$

$$\{\mathbf{g}\}_i = \left[\iint_\Omega c r_i s_j\, dx\, dy\right] t_j + \left[\iint_\Omega s_k r_i v_j\, a x\, dy\right] t_k w_j.$$

In the above equations, $(c v_i)$, $(v_i v_j)$, $(c s_i r_j)$, $(r_k v_i s_j)$, and $(r_k r_l s_i s_j)$ depend only on x, y, E_x, E_y, and E_t, and so can be integrated over the image once. Therefore, the updating of the coefficients at each iteration only involves 27 multiplications to compute $\mathbf{M}_2$, 9 to compute $\mathbf{d}_2$, and 42 to compute each of $\mathbf{M}_4$, $\mathbf{N}$, and $\mathbf{g}$ (note that $\mathbf{M}_4$ and $\mathbf{N}$ are symmetric). This gives a total of 162 multiplications per iteration. Further, solving equations (10) and (11) for ω, $\mathbf{t}$, and $\mathbf{n}$ requires a total of 117 multiplications.

This iterative scheme has been implemented and tested for many cases. We will present a selected example in section 7.

6. Uniqueness

Our analytical as well as simulation results show (see [10] for proof) that there exists at most two solutions that generate the same optical flow (The existance but not necessarily the uniqueness of a dual solution has been shown in several papers [4,9,12,14]). The two solutions are related as follows:

$$\mathbf{n}' = k\mathbf{t}, \qquad \mathbf{t}' = k^{-1}\mathbf{n}, \quad \text{and} \quad \omega' = \omega + \mathbf{n} \times \mathbf{t}, \quad (13)$$

where k is any arbitrary constant chosen to scale the surface and translational motion parameters. Note that when the translational motion is perpendicular to the planar surface, a unique solution is obtained. Further, when the component of translational motion along the line of sight (Z-axis) is zero, the planar surface for the dual solution is parallel to the line of sight. In this case, the dual solution can be viewed as a degenerate one.

7. Experimental results

In the following example, we will demonstrate the sensitivity of the scheme to the initial condition. The image brightness function was generated using a multiplicative sinusoidal pattern (one that varies sinusoidally in both x and y directions), a 45° field of view was assumed, and the brightness gradients were computed analytically to avoid errors due to quantization and finite differencing of brightness values (In practice, the brightness values in two image frames are discretized first, and are then used to compute the brightness gradients using finite difference methods). Table 1 shows the results of two tests using different initial conditions. In each case, the algorithm converges to one of the two possible (true or dual) solutions. The results show that the error in each parameter after less than 30 iterations is within 10% of the true value.

In similar tests, with various motion and surface parameters, accurate results have been obtained in less than 40 iterations with a variety of initial conditions. More importantly, the algorithm eventually converged to one of the two possible solutions. The results have not been as satisfactory for the particular case where the translational motion component is (almost) perpendicular to the planar surface (The solution is unique in this case). In these cases, several hundred iterations were required to achieve reasonable accuracy. It appears that the behavior resembles that observed when the Newton-Raphson method is applied to a problem where two roots are very close to one another.

8. Summary

The problem of recovering the orientation of a planar surface and its motion from a sequence of images was investigated and formulated as one of unconstrained optimization. Using conditions for optimality, the problem was reduced to solving a set of nine nonlinear algebraic equations and an implemented procedure based on an iterative scheme for solving these equations was presented. Through a selected example, it was shown that the algorithm could converge to either of two possible solutions (or the only solution when the translational motion vector is perpendicular to the surface). In practice, once a solution is obtained, the dual solution can be computed from equation (13). In several other cases tested, solutions with good accuracy have been obtained after 10–40 iterations.

9. Acknowledgments

This report describes research done at the Artificial Intelligence Laboratory of the Massachusetts Institute of Technology. Support for the Laboratory's Artificial Intelligence research is provided in part by the System Development Foundation.

Table 1. Test Results for a Selected Example

True Rotational Motion	A = .003	B = .001	C = -.01
True Translational Motion	U = .0005	V = -.005	W = .0125
True Surface Parameters	p = .2	q = .4	r = 1.

Dual Rotational Motion	A = .013	B = -.001	C = -.0112
Dual Translational Motion	U = .0025	V = .005	W = .0125
Dual Surface Parameters	p = .04	q = -.4	r = 1.

Initial Guess   p = -.5   q = -1.5   r=1

Itr	A	B	C	U	V	W	p	q
10	.00531	.00260	-.01016	-.00069	-.00284	.01301	.35524	.192?
15	.00429	.00178	-.01008	-.00006	-.00384	.01291	.27623	.2742
20	.00353	.00137	-.01002	0.00024	-.00454	.01270	.23725	.3448
25	.00318	.00117	-.01000	0.00038	-.00485	.01257	.21718	.3814
30	.00305	.00107	-.01000	0.00045	-.00495	.01252	.20755	.3945
35	.00302	.00103	-.01000	0.00048	-.00499	.01250	.20323	.3984
40	.00300	.00101	-.01000	0.00049	-.00500	.01250	.20137	.3996
45	.00300	.00101	-.01000	0.00050	-.00500	.01250	.20058	.3999
50	.00300	.00100	-.01000	0.00050	-.00500	.01250	.20024	.4000
55	.00300	.00100	-.01000	0.00050	-.00500	.01250	.20010	.4000

Initial Guess   p = -10(q= -5   r=1

Itr	A	B	C	U	V	W	p	q
10	.01302	-.00120	-.01118	.00266	.00503	.01247	.01941	-.4021
15	.01299	-.00108	-.01119	.00256	.00500	.01249	.03220	-.3992
20	.01299	-.00103	-.01120	.00253	.00500	.01250	.03692	-.3993
25	.01300	-.00101	-.01120	.00251	.00500	.01250	.03876	-.3996
30	.01300	-.00101	-.01120	.00250	.00500	.01250	.03950	-.3998
35	.01300	-.00100	-.01120	.00250	.00500	.01250	.03980	-.3999
40	.01300	-.00100	-.01120	.00250	.00500	.01250	.03992	-.4000
45	.01300	-.00100	-.01120	.00250	.00500	.01250	.03997	-.4000
50	.01300	-.00100	-.01120	.00250	.00500	.01250	.03999	-.4000

Note that without loss of generality, we have set $r = 1$, since the distance to the plane and the translational motion component can only be recovered up to a scale factor.

10. References

[1] Adiv, G., "Determining 3-D Motion and Structure from Optical Flow Generated by Several Moving Objects," COINS TR 84-07, Computer and Information Science, University of Massachusetts, Amherst, MA, April 1984.

[2] Bruss, A.R., Horn, B.K.P., "Passive Navigation," *Computer Vision, Graphics, and Image Processing*, Vol. 21, pp. 3–20, 1983.

[3] Fang, J.Q., Huang, T.S., "Solving Three–Dimensional Small–Rotation Motion Equations: Uniqueness, Algorithms, and Numerical Results," *Computer Vision, Graphics, and Image Processing*, Vol. 26, pp. 183–206, 1984.

[4] Hay, C.J., "Optical Motion and Space Perception, an Extension of Gibson's Analysis," *Psychological Review*, Vol. 73, pp. 550–565, 1966.

[5] Hildreth, E.C., *The Measurement of Visual Motion*, MIT Press, 1983.

[6] Horn, B.K.P., Schunck, B.G., "Determining Optical Flow," *Artificial Intelligence*, Vol. 17, pp. 185–203, 1981.

[7] Longuet-Higgins, H.C., "A Computer Algorithm for Reconstructing a Scene from Two Projections," *Nature*, Vol. 293, pp. 131–133, 1981.

[8] Longuet-Higgins, H.C., Prazdny, K., "The Interpretation of a Moving Retinal Image," *Proceedings of the Royal Society of London*, Series B, Vol. 208, pp. 385–397, 1980.

[9] Maybank, S.J., "The Angular Velocity Associated with the Optical Flow Field Due to a Single Moving Rigid Plane," *Proceedings of the Sixth European Conference on Artificial Intelligence*, pp. 641–644, September 1984.

[10] Negahdaripour, S., Horn, B.K.P., "Direct Passive Navigation," A.I. Memo 821, MIT A.I. Lab, February 1985.

[11] Sugihara, K., Sugie, N., "Recovery of Rigid Structure from Orthographically Projected Optical Flow," TR 8304, Department of Information Science, Nagoya University, Nagoya, Japan, October 1983.

[12] Tsai, R.Y., Huang, T.S., Zhu, W.L., "Three-Dimensional Motion Parameters of a Rigid Planar Patch, II: Singular Value Decomposition," *IEEE Trans. on Acoustics, Speech, and Signal Processing*, Vol. ASSP-30, No. 4, August 1982.

[13] Tsai, R.Y., Huang, T.S., "Uniqueness and Estimation of Three-Dimensional Motion Parameters of Rigid Objects with Curved Surfaces," *IEEE Transactions on Pattern Analysis and Machine Intelligence*, Vol. PAMI-6, No. 1, January 1984.

[14] Waxman, A.M., Ullman, S., "Surface Structure and 3-D Motion from Image Flow: A Kinematic Analysis," CAR-TR-24, Comp. Vis. Lab, Center for Automation Research, Univ. of Maryland, College Park, MD, October 1983.

[15] Waxman, A.M., Wohn, K., "Contour Evolution, Neighborhood Deformation and Global Image Flow: Planar Surfaces in Motion," CAR-TR-58, Comp. Vis. Lab, Center for Automation Research, Univ. of Maryland, College Park, MD, April 1984.

[16] Wohn, K., Davis, L.S., Thrift, P., "Motion Estimation Based on Multiple Local Constraints and Nonlinear Smoothing," *Pattern Recognition*, Vol. 16, No. 6, pp. 563–570, 1983.

A New Method of 3-D Motion Analysis
Using
A Concept of Projective Geometry

Tadahiro Kitahashi

Dept. of Infor. & Comp. Sciences
Toyohashi Univ. of Technology
Toyohashi, 440, JAPAN

Hiroyuki Endo

Fujitsu Ltd.
Kawasaki, 210, JAPAN

ABSTRACT

This paper describes a method of interpreting three dimensional motion of an object by making use of rigidity assumption and orientation of its edge. We employ a vanishing point to determine the orientation. We propose a new idea of using cross ratio, i.e. one of the most fundamental concepts in projective geometry to find a vanishing point of a line. This allows to calculate the location of a vanishing point with a known sequence of points on it without another parallel line required by the conventional method.

1. Introduction

These years a number of researchers working on the computer vision come to be interested in the analysis of three dimentional motions of an object for the application to improving industrial robots and some intelligent systems. Three major approaches have been taken for this problem, optical flow analysis, algebraic geometry and projective geometry. These methods have their own advantages.

Some robots, for example mobile robots, require visual systems providing a standard (not long focus) lens for getting a rather wide scope. Perspective distortions appear in the image, since projection through such a lens yields an image of central projection. Perspective geometry is useful to deal with the image. The most advantageous point of it is that it enables to calculate relative distance between the camera and arbitary points on a line could be calculated by a simple ratio of the one (or two) dimensional distances between the images of the points and the vanishing point of the line. The difficulty in the procedure is to find the vanishing point by means of image processing. Hence it has been given a priori in most of the scene analysis using vanishing points. In case of utilizing image processing it has been determined an intersection of several edges in an image assumed to be parallel in the orginal space. However we often encounter the cases to analyze images which involve no parallel edges or lines.

In this paper we propose a method which does not require the existence of parallel lines for finding the vanishing point of a line. It is expected to extend application areas of projective geometry in the field of computer vision and scene analysis. We describe an application to interpreting the 3-D motion of an object moving freely in space.

2. Preliminary

In this paper the vanishing point is used to know the orientation of an object and the rigidity assumption is also used to calculate position of the object at each instance of the motion. Below will be presented several fundamental properties of algebraic geometry which are necessary to the discussion.

2.1 Coordinates and Central projection

Cartesian coordinates to express three dimensional location of an object are fixed to a camera. The origin is set on the eyepoint, i.e. the center of the lens and the z-axis is aligned to the optical axis. A focal distance is denoted by f.

An image plane with coordinates (ξ, ℓ) is defined by an equation z=f, that is, to be parallel to the xy plane at a distance f in front of the eyepoint such that the z-axis pierces the coordinate axes origin. As illustrated in Fig.1, ξ and ℓ axes on the image plane are defined to be parallel to the x and y axes, respectively. Since a point P(x,y,z) is projected to a point p(ξ,ℓ) on

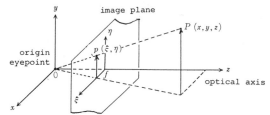

Fig. 1 Coordinates and Central Projection

the image plane by the central projection, the following equations hold.

$$\xi = \frac{x}{z} f , \qquad \ell = \frac{y}{z} f \qquad (1)$$

When a line with a directional cosine (n_1, n_2, n_3) is projected onto the image plane, the coordinates (ξ_∞, ℓ_∞) of its vanishing point is represented by the following equations.

$$\xi_\infty = \frac{n_1}{n_3} f , \qquad \ell_\infty = \frac{n_2}{n_3} f \qquad (2)$$

Inversely, a line with the vanishing point (ξ_∞, ℓ_∞) on the image plane is pointing in the direction (n_1, n_2, n_3) in the 3-D space, where

$$\text{and} \quad \begin{cases} n_1 = k\xi_\infty , \quad n_2 = k\ell_\infty , \quad n_3 = k \cdot f \\ k = \frac{1}{\sqrt{\xi_\infty^2 + \ell_\infty^2 + f^2}} \end{cases} \qquad (3)$$

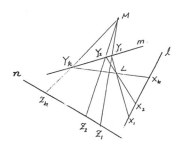

Fig. 5 Total Edge Images
of the Sequence

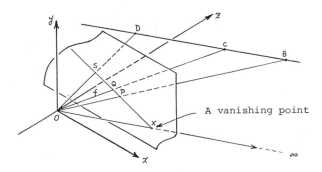

Fig. 3 A Contral Projection

2.2 Rigidity-assumption and central projection

Let r denote the distance between two points $P_1(x_1,y_1,z_1)$ and $P_2(x_2,y_2,z_2)$ on an object and (n_1,n_2,n_3) denote the orientation of the line P_1P_2 running on these points. We get the following relations.

$$\left.\begin{array}{l} x_2 = x_1 + r n_1 \\ y_2 = y_1 + r n_2 \\ z_2 = z_1 + r n_3 \end{array}\right\} \quad (4)$$

If these points change the position to $P_1'(x_1',y_1',z_1')$ and $P_2'(x_2',y_2',z_2')$ after a motion of the object, the distance between them is invariant from the rigidity-assumption of the object. Thus the similar relations to eq.(4) hold as follows.

$$\left.\begin{array}{l} x_2' = x_1' + r n_1' \\ y_2' = y_1' + r n_2' \\ z_2' = z_1' + r n_3' \end{array}\right\} \quad (5)$$

where (n_1',n_2',n_3') also represents the orientation of the line $P_1'P_2'$.

On the other hand, suppose that these points P_1, P_2, P_1' and P_2' are projected to the points $p_1(\xi_1,\eta_1)$, $p_2(\xi_2,\eta_2)$, $p_1'(\xi_1',\eta_1')$ and $p_2'(\xi_2',\eta_2')$ on the image plane, respectively. Then, the following equations are derived from the equations (1), (4) and (5).

$$\left.\begin{array}{l} z_1' = \dfrac{\xi_2' n_3' - f n_1'}{\xi_2 n_3 - f n_1} \cdot \dfrac{\xi_1 - \xi_2}{\xi_1' - \xi_2'} \\[2mm] = \dfrac{\eta_2' n_3' - f n_2'}{\eta_2 n_3 - f n_2} \cdot \dfrac{\eta_1 - \eta_2}{\eta_1' - \eta_2'} \cdot z_1 \end{array}\right\} \quad (6)$$

When the value of z is given, the coordinates of P_1' can be calculated with eq.'s (6) and (1) and those of P_2' as well. In this process it is assumed that the orientations of the lines $\overline{P_1P_2}$ and $\overline{P_1'P_2'}$ are also given. In the next section we propose a new approach to know the vanishing point of a line from its image.

3. Projective Geometry

Equations (3) shows that a vanishing point is a key to know the orientation of a line from its image. Conventional methods to find vanishing points have utilized parallelpiped structures of objects. However, there are not always parallels in the scene and moreover even if there are any, we do not have means how to verify them now. This is the greatest problem in employing vanishing points to recover 3-D structures. Consequently if

we could obtain an algorithm to find the vanishing point of a line without using other lines parallel to it, we could extend applicable fields of the method using vanishing points to much more scenes as well as reduce the load of image processing.

3.1 Cross ratio of a range of points

We have solved this problem by introducing the cross ratio, to calculate the position of the vanishing point of a line with the locations of a sequence of points.

We describe several definitions and properties about the concept of the cross ratio below.

[Def.1] The cross ratio R_{ABCD} of the ordered four points A,B,C and D on a line is defined by the following equation.

$$R_{ABCD} = \dfrac{\overline{AB}}{\overline{AD}} : \dfrac{\overline{CB}}{\overline{CD}} = \dfrac{\overline{AB}}{\overline{AD}} \cdot \dfrac{\overline{CD}}{\overline{CB}} \quad (7)$$

where XY denotes the line segment directing from X to Y.

[Prop.1] The cross ratio is invariant through projective transformation of a range of points.

[Prop.2] If a point A in a range of points A,B,C and D locates at the infinite (∞) and the others do not, the following equation holds.

$$R_{\infty BCD} = \dfrac{\overline{CD}}{\overline{CB}} \quad (8)$$

By the central projection, a point located at the infinite in the 3-D world is projected to a vanishing point on an image plane. Suppose that a range of points ∞,B,C and D in the 3-D world is projected to a range of points X,P,Q and S on an image plane, and that their cross ratios are denoted by $R_{\infty BCD}$ and R_{XPQS}, respectively.

Then from [Prop.1] and [Prop.2] we can readily obtain the following relation.

$$\dfrac{\overline{CD}}{\overline{CB}} = \dfrac{\overline{XP}}{\overline{XS}} \cdot \dfrac{\overline{QS}}{\overline{QP}} \quad (9)$$

The relation (9) is immediately interpreted as a relation among the coordinates of the points in the 3-D world as follows.

$$\dfrac{\zeta_X - \zeta_P}{\zeta_X - \zeta_S} \cdot \dfrac{\zeta_Q - \zeta_S}{\zeta_Q - \zeta_P} = \dfrac{k_C - k_D}{k_C - k_B} \quad (10)$$

,where $\left\{\begin{array}{l} \zeta = \xi \sim \eta \quad (\text{ordered}) \\ k = x \sim y \end{array}\right.$, $\left\{\begin{array}{l} U=(\xi_U,\eta_U) \quad U=X,P,Q,S \\ V=(x_V,y_V,z_V) \quad V=B,C,D \end{array}\right.$

This is the relation that we have pursued for the purpose of calculating the location of a vanishing point without the assumption of an existence of parallel edges and detection of them.

Fig. 4
A Picture Sequence
of a Twisted Motion
of an Object

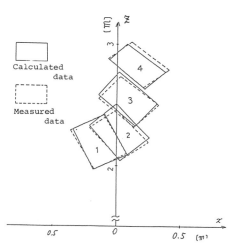

Calculated
data

Measured
data

Fig. 6   Results of Experiment
compared with Measured Data

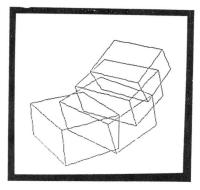

Fig. 5
Total Edge Images
of the Sequence

4.   Experiment

The   concept of the cross ratio enables us to
calculate   a location of a vanishing point with   a
simple   formula   by   imposing   rather   easy
restrictions satisfied in most of the applications
as   described   in   the   previous   section.   Thus
together   with the discussion in chapter 2 now   we
have   a   new method for the analysis of   free   3-D
motion of an object.

We have experimentally applied this method to
an   analysis of a motion of a simple shaped object,
i.e.   a   carton.   We move it 4 feet from 7 feet in
front of a fixed camera tilting gradually   to realize   taken,   although   pictures in Fig.3 are displayed   128x128 in size and 8 levels   in intensity
for convenience.

The   requirement   of   the proposed   method   is
satisfied   by   three points on a diagonal   of   the
top-surface of the box, that is both end-points of
the   diagonal   and   the   intersection   of   diagonals.
Since   a   pair of facing edges of the   top-surface
could be assumed parallel, the intersection is the

middle point of each diagonal.   In this case   and
the cross ratio becomes as simple as equal to -1.

The   computed   results of the experiment   are
shown in Fig.6 and the measured data are added for
comparison.   The   relative errors in the   position
are lower than 2%. This is well acceptable to most
of the actual applications.

5.   Conclusion

In   this   paper,   we   have   proposed   a   new
method   to analyze non-restricted 3-D   motions   by
introducing   a   simple   but   fundamental   concept
useful   to   deal with actual problems.   Results   of
the   experiments proved its validity for a variety
of   applications.   Our method is also relevent   to
the   recovery of three dimensional   structures   of
static   scenes   although   it   may   fail   to   analyze
structures   of small objects.   The accuracy for the
estimation   should   be   well   considered   in   such
applications.

Acknowlegement

We   thank   Dr.   K.   Murase   for his   suggesting
improvements in presentation.

REFERENCES

(1)   Ullman,   S.   The   Interpretation   of   Visual
      Motion, MIT Press, 1979
(2)   Horn,   B. K. P., et al.,   "Determining optical
      flow", Artif. Intell., 17 1981
(3)   Prazdny,   K.   "Egomotion and relative depth map
      from optical flow", Biol. Cybern. 36 1980
(3)   Kender,   J.   R.   "Shape from texture",   DARPA,
      Image Understanding Workshop, 1979
(4)   Huang,   T.   S.   Ed.,   Image Sequence Analysis,
      Springer-verlag, 1981

USING DISCRIMINATION GRAPHS TO REPRESENT VISUAL INTERPRETATIONS THAT ARE HYPOTHETICAL AND AMBIGUOUS

by
Jan A. Mulder

Department of Mathematics, Statistics, and Computing Science
Dalhousie University
Halifax, Nova Scotia
Canada B3H 4H8[1]

Abstract

The use of specialization hierarchies in model-based vision systems may cause problems with uniformity in representation and efficiency. The concept of a discrimination graph is introduced. Such a graph facilitates the representation of hypothetical and ambiguous interpretations in a uniform and efficient way. We describe the implementation of Mapsee-3, a sketch map interpretation program that uses discrimination graphs in combination with a hierarchical constraint propagation algorithm.

1. Introduction

A key issue in Computational Vision is the proper mapping from image features to interpretations. Image features are often highly ambiguous with respect to interpretation. As a result, alternative interpretations for a single feature have to be represented as hypotheses. These hypotheses are instantiations of scene objects and they can be represented by means of an interpretation graph in which each variable (node) represents a hypothesis and the arcs represent constraints between different hypotheses. In a computational vision system the number of hypotheses can be quite large. Hence, the propagation of constraints over the interpretation graph can be a complex and cumbersome operation, because the addition of new hypotheses and invalidation of existing ones requires a continuous restructuring of the graph.

Most model-based vision systems use specialization hierarchies[2] in an attempt to alleviate this problem. These hierarchies can be used to replace sets of elementary interpretations with a similar appearance in the image by a smaller set of more abstract interpretations. These interpretations are not only hypothetical, they are also ambiguous. They reduce the number of hypotheses that the system has to deal with. Unfortunately, specialization hierarchies only offer a partial solution to the interpretation explosion problem. They are natural categorization schemes and many image features allow for interpretations that do not fit into such schemes. For example, a grassy area seen from low altitude could be farm land as well as a golf course and there is no specialization hierarchy that joins both concepts into one.

The use of specialization hierarchies may therefore cause some interpretations to be hypothetical, whereas others are both hypothetical and ambiguous. Hypothetical interpretations are *explicitly* represented in an interpretation graph by means of different variables, whereas ambiguous interpretations are *implicitly* represented by means of a single variable. Such a representation is not uniform.

The efficiency of the system is also affected, in particular, with respect to constraint propagation. Most images allow only one globally consistent interpretation for each image primitive. At the start of the interpretation process, however, each image feature has many possible interpretations, most of which are explicitly represented in the interpretation graph. Once, more global constraints are found, most hypotheses have to be deleted from the interpretation graph.

Both the problems of uniformity and efficiency can be alleviated, if discrimination graphs are used. Such graphs permit the representation of all interpretations, hypothetical or ambiguous, by means of a single variable which is never deleted from the interpretation graph, once it is constructed. The use of a hierarchical constraint propagation algorithm in combination with discrimination graphs further increases the efficiency of the system. We have designed a model-based vision system that uses discrimination graphs in combination with such an algorithm. This system has been implemented as a schema-based sketch map interpretation program.

2. Discrimination graphs

The idea of discrimination graphs is based on the assumption that we can classify image features with respect to a particular characteristic (e.g. shape, texture) the result of which is a finite number of categories. As well, we assume that there is only a finite number of scene objects whose image appearance falls in a particular category. Discrimination graphs are based on a categorization of object classes that belong to a particular image feature category. The source node of the graph is an abstract object class that intensionally represents all the elementary object classes described by a particular image feature category. The leaves of this graph are the elementary object classes. Elementary object classes can belong to more than one image feature category. As a result, discrimination graphs can become tangled hierarchies with multiple source nodes.

Discrimination graphs differ from specialization

---

[1]The research reported in this paper was carried out in the Laboratory for Computational Vision at the University of British Columbia.

[2]For a review of different uses of specialization hierarchies, see [1]

hierarchies in at least two respects. An abstract class often represents elementary classes that cannot be joined in a natural specialization hierarchy. As well, the tangled structure of the graph means that not all members of a subclass are automatically a member of a superclass as well (i.e. no universal implication). At the source nodes, discrimination graphs represent object classes which are unique with respect to a particular image appearance, but highly ambiguous with respect to interpretation. At the leaves, on the other hand, we find elementary classes which are unique with respect to interpretation, but ambiguous with respect to their physical appearance.

Discrimination graphs permit the construction an interpretation graph in which each image feature is represented by means of a single variable. This variable is an instance of an abstract object class which intensionally represents the whole range of possible (elementary) interpretations for the feature concerned. The elementary interpretations can be represented *explicitly* as a set of labels in the domain of the variable, or, if we use discrimination graphs, *implicitly* by an abstract label. As the interpretation progresses, we can expect an invalidation of some of these labels. The variables, however, only represent information that is true for all interpretations. Thus, invalidation of one label only requires its deletion or replacement. This can be done without changing the structure of the interpretation graph. As well, all interpretations, hypothetical or ambiguous, are now represented as labels in the domain of a *single* variable.

3. Mapsee-3

Mapsee-3, the sequel to Mapsee-2 [2], is a schema-based program for interpreting sketch maps. Its schema-based format has been inherited from Mapsee-2. Each object class is represented as a list of attribute-value pairs. The attributes determine its internal structure and its relations to other object classes. For example, each class has a "components" and "super-components" attribute which determines its location in a composition hierarchy of objects. The object's location in a discrimination graph, on the other hand, is determined by its "discriminations" and "generalizations" attributes. An "instances" attribute lists the current instantiations of the object class. Each instance of an object class inherits the attributes of its parent. A special attribute "label" is used to store the current interpretation of the instance.

Mapsee-3 interprets sketch maps such as the one in figure 1. Both line segments and regions have meaning. Line segments can be interpreted in terms of elementary object classes such as roads, rivers, shores, towns, mountains, and bridges, whereas regions can be land or water. The input consists of a set of plotter commands which indicate the exact location of each line segment in the image.

The Mapsee-3 control is subdivided into three stages: segmentation, image-to-scene mapping, and interpretation. A segmentation process results in the creation of sets of connected line segments (called chains) and regions. The chains form the image features that need interpretation. Mapsee-3 has a fixed number of shape categories for describing chains. The image-to-scene process observes the shape of each individual chain and selects a category in which the chain is placed. Different categories are characterized by features such as closure, mountain-shape, bridge-shape, and blobs.

Discrimination graphs form a key feature in the Mapsee-3 design. Each shape category allows for many different elementary interpretations. The discrimination graphs are constructed such that there is a single (abstract) object class for the set of elementary classes allowed by each shape category. Figure 2 shows a simplified example of a Mapsee-3 discrimination graph. This graph would result from the existence of two shape categories. A closed chain depicts a coastline, lakeshore, or road. Any other line segment depicts a road or river. The leaves of the graph are elementary object classes (e.g. *lakeshore*, *road*), the other nodes represent more abstract classes, some of which are unnatural (e.g. *road/shore*). All descendents of *road/shore* can have the same appearance in the image. The nodes in the graph with more than one parent can have different appearances in the image. A road, for example, may or may not be depicted by a closed line segment. Thus, not all roads are road/shores, some may be road/rivers instead.

The image-to-scene process instantiates the appropriate scene object for each chain. Only one instance is created for every chain. A closed chain, for instance, gets represented by an instance of the class *road/shore*. The interpretation of this chain is represented by the "label" attribute of the instance. This label is also *road/shore*, which indicates that all of *road/shore*'s successors in the discrimination graph are valid interpretations. The image-to-scene process also creates the beginning of the interpretation graph. The instances are the variables, their label the domain. Finding the constraints between instances, however, is the responsibility of the interpretation process.

This paper does not address the question of the construction of the interpretation graph. For such a discussion the reader is refered to [3]. We therefore only discuss the component of the interpretation process that is concerned with constraint propagation. In Mapsee-3 this process is called discrimination, and it uses the discrimination graphs.

Discrimination is an implementation of a network consistency algorithm called hierarchical arc consistency (h.a.c.). This algorithm is a derivative of arc consistency as described in [4]. It maintains consistency between labels in the domain of adjacent variables in a constraint graph. Two adjacent variables are considered consistent if all labels in the domain of one variable are consistent with at least one label in the domain of the other. If this is not the case then the inconsistent label is replaced. In case of replacement the test is repeated for all variables adjacent to the one in the domain of which the replacement took place. H.a.c. assumes a hierarchical organization of the domain of each variable as is the case in discrimination graphs. If a label is inconsistent then h.a.c. will recursively replace it by one of its descendents in the hierarchy until a consistent descendent is found.

As an example, the *road/shore* label of an instance becomes inconsistent if both regions surrounding the closed chain are constrained to be *land*. *Road/shore* is valid only as long as all of its descendents (see figure 2) are valid. The new constraint invalidates the shore interpretation. H.a.c. replaces this label by using the principle of least commitment, introduced to Computational Vision by Marr and Nishihara [5]. First, *road/shore* is replaced by *road* and *shore*. Next, the consistency of each of these labels is tested. Consistent labels are kept, inconsistent labels are replaced by their successors. In this example, *shore*, *lakeshore* and *coastline* are all inconsistent. Thus *road* is the only label that remains. A more detailed discussion of h.a.c. is provided in [3].

Mapsee-3 solves the problem of uniformity and efficiency as described in the introduction. Competing interpretations are all represented as labels in the domain of a *single* variable. Efficiency is achieved in several ways. First, invalidation of a particular label does not result in a structural change in the interpretation graph. Second, the number of labels in the domain of each variable can be kept very small, thanks to the use of discrimination graphs and the principle of least commitment. Specialization hierarchies do not offer this capability to such an extent. Third, h.a.c. does not maintain an explicit administration of the compatibility between the labels of adjacent variables. Only if a label change in a neighboring variable took place, will a variable test its labels. It will stop this test as soon as a compatible label is found in the domain of a neighbor. In interpretation graphs with competing interpretations represented by different variables, the compatibility between the interpretation of adjacent variables is represented explicitly. As mentioned before, most interpretations tend to be eliminated during the course of the interpretation process.

4. Conclusions

We have described the concept of discrimination graphs as a uniform and efficient way for representing interpretations that are hypothetical and ambiguous. We have also described a hierarchical constraint propagation algorithm that uses discrimination graphs in an efficient manner to propagate constraints in an interpretation graph. Discrimination graphs and hierarchical constraint propagation have been implemented in Mapsee-3, a schema-based vision system that interprets sketch maps.

References

[1] R.J. Brachman, "What IS-A is and Isn't", *Proc. of the 4th Nat. Conf. of the Can. Soc. for Comp. Studies of Intelligence*, pp. 212-221, Saskatoon, Canada, 1982.

[2] W.S. Havens and A.K. Mackworth, "Representing Knowledge of the Visual World", *IEEE Computer*, vol. 16, no 10, pp. 90-98, 1983.

[3] J.A. Mulder, "Representing Ambiguity and Hypotheticality in Visual Knowledge", Forthcoming Ph.D. Thesis, Department of Computer Science, University of British Columbia.

[4] A.K. Mackworth, "Consistency in Networks of Relations", *Artificial Intelligence*, vol. 8, no 1, pp. 99-118, 1977.

[5] D. Marr and H.K. Nishihara, "Representation of the Spatial Organization of Three Dimensional Shapes", Report 377, A.I. Lab, M.I.T., 1976.

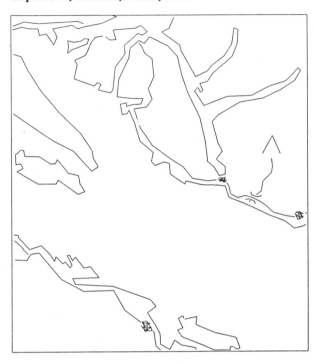

Figure 1: Sketch of Georgia Strait (B.C.)

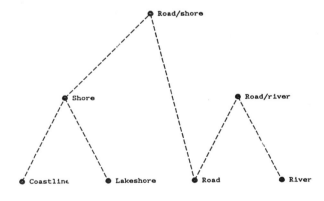

Figure 2: A Discrimination Graph

SIGMA : A FRAMEWORK FOR IMAGE UNDERSTANDING
- INTEGRATION OF BOTTOM-UP AND TOP-DOWN ANALYSES -

Takashi MATSUYAMA

Department of Electrical Engineering

Kyoto University

Sakyo, Kyoto 606 JAPAN

Vincent HWANG

Center for Automation Research

University of Maryland

College Park, Maryland 20742 U.S.A.

ABSTRACT

The framework and control structure of an image understanding system SIGMA are presented. SIGMA consists of three experts: Geometric Reasoning Expert (GRE) for spatial reasoning, Model Selection Expert (MSE) for appearance model selection, and Low Level Vision Expert (LLVE) for knowledge-based picture processing. This paper mainly describes the control mechanism for the spatial reasoning by GRE, where bottom-up and top-down analyses are integrated into a unified reasoning process.

1. INTRODUCTION

Many experimental image understanding systems have been developed to test the feasibility of image understanding[1-7]. The followings are some problems in building an image understanding system which have not yet been treated successfully.

(1)Segmentation

There are many methods of segmenting an image to extract objects. Each method has its advantage and disadvantage. How to select and/or combine appropriate methods is a basic problem in image understanding.

(2)Diversity in Appearance

2D appearances of a 3D object vary greatly depending on viewing angles. On the other hand, an object has many diverse appearances. For example, houses in a suburban area have many possible shapes, sizes, and colors. How to limit the number of possible appearances and intelligently select the ones to try (search) is another problem.

(3)Representation and Utilization of Domain Knowledge

An image understanding system needs to have domain knowledge to construct an interpretation of the image. Usually, the sources of knowledge are diverse and redundant. Requirements that must be satisfied by an object are specified in many different ways, and each of them gives only a weak constraint. Knowing that only some of the constraints for an object are satisfied is not enough to assign the object label to an image feature(e.g. region). On the other hand, failure to satisfy some of the constraints does not indicate that the image feature cannot be an object. How to organize and use domain knowledge is another problem.

In this paper, we describe the framework and control structure of an image understanding system SIGMA. The followings are the basic ideas incorporated into SIGMA to solve the above three problems.

(1)Knowledge-Based Segmentation

It is advantageous to use a knowledge-based segmentation system to process an image[8][9][10]. Many studies have been done on picture processing operators. Their characteristics have been well studied, such as effectiveness in extracting given types of image features(e.g. region, line) in a given environment, required cost of computation, and possible artifacts caused by the operators. A knowledge-based segmentation system uses such knowledge about the operators to realize efficient and reliable extraction of required image features.

(2)Evidence Accumulation for Spatial Reasoning

An image understanding system builds interpretations by establishing relations among objects, and searching for missing objects by analyzing the image. Objects found (object instances) can be used to predict missing objects by generating hypotheses. Hypotheses from various sources can be combined to guide the searching process[5, 6]. Such accumulation of evidence from different sources decreases the total amount of effort spent in the search and increases the reliability of the analysis.

(3)Appearance Model Selection Based on Contextual Information

As described above, an object can have many diverse appearances. When an image understanding system searches for a missing object, it should use contextual information to predict the most likely appearance(s) of the object. Given an appropriate description of the context where the target object is embedded, its possible appearance(s) in the image can be predicted.

2. OVERVIEW OF THE SYSTEM

Fig. 1 shows the organization of the entire system. It consists of the following three experts.

(1)Geometric Reasoning Expert (GRE)

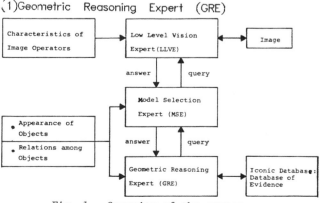

Fig. 1   Overview of the system

This expert is the central reasoning module in the system, and utilizes a symbolic hierarchical model for the possible spatial organization of objects in the world. The geometric reasoning performed by this expert (evidence accumulation) integrates both bottom-up and top-down analysis processes into a unified reasoning process. All of the partial evidence obtained during the interpretation are stored in a common database (Iconic Database in Fig. 1), where consistent pieces of evidence are accumulated. GRE first establishes local environments (contexts) using the accumulated evidence. Then, either the bottom-up analysis to establish a relation between objects or the top-down analysis to find a new object are activated depending on the nature of a focused local environment. In the top-down analysis, GRE first reasons about its goal (the target object to be detected) and where to analyze the image. Then it asks Model Selection Expert to perform the analysis.

(2)Model Selection Expert (MSE)

This expert reasons about the most promising appearance models to use in searching for the object in the image. This model selection is performed based on the contextual information provided by GRE. Knowledge about objects is represented at several levels of specificity. For example, an object class "house" is a generalization of many specifically shaped types of houses. GRE determines the general class of objects to search for (e.g. "house") while MSE determines which specialization (e.g. rectangular house) should be looked for. In addition to this reasoning, MSE performs geometric transformation from the scene domain to the image domain.

(3)Low Level Vision Expert (LLVE)

The appearance model determined by MSE is given to this expert. LLVE performs picture processing to extract the image feature corresponding to the specified appearance model. It selects appropriate picture processing operators and determines efficient and effective process sequences based on the knowledge about picture processing methods(as for details of LLVE, see[10]).

3. EVIDENCE ACCUMULATION FOR SPATIAL REASONING

It is widely accepted that image understanding systems should incorporate both bottom-up and top-down analyses. The use of geometric relations, however, is very different in the two analysis processes: consistency verification in bottom-up analysis and hypothesis generation in top-down analysis. An important characteristic of our evidence accumulation method is that it enables the system to integrate both bottom-up and top-down processes into a single flexible spatial reasoning process.

3.1 Principle of Evidence Accumulation

The spatial reasoning using the evidence accumulation method is perfomed by the Geometric Reasoning Expert. Its principle is as follows.

Let REL(O1,O2) denote a binary geometric relation between two classes of objects, O1 and O2. This relation can be represented using two functional expressions:

$$O1 = f(O2) \quad \text{and} \quad O2 = g(O1).$$

Given an instance of O2, say s, function f maps it into a description of an instance of O1, f(s), which satisfies the geometric relation, REL, with s. The analogous

interpretation holds for the other function g.

In SIGMA, knowledge about a class of object is represented by a frame [9], and a slot in that frame is used to represent a function such as f or g. A slot contains a group of production rules, each of which consists of a precondition and an action. A precondition represents a set of conditions specifying when the function can be activated. An action represents a computational procedure corresponding to the function, which produces the description of the related object.

Whenever an instance of an object is created and the conditions are satisfied, the function is applied to the instance to create a "hypothesis" (expectation) for another object which would, if found, satisfy the geometric relation with the original instance (Fig. 2(a)). A hypothesis is associated with (Fig. 2(b))
(i) a prediction area (locational constraint) where the target object instance may be located, and
(ii) a set of constraints on the target object instance.

All pieces of evidence (hypotheses and object instances) are stored the iconic database(Fig. 1), where accumulation of evidence (i.e. recognition of consistent hypotheses and instances) is performed. This database contains an iconic data structure (i.e. two dimensional array for 2D scene analysis) to represent locational constraints associated with the stored pieces of evidence. They are represented as regions on this array. GRE uses overlaps among the regions to index mutually consistent pieces of evidence. Note that this array represents the world under analysis and its coordinate system is defined independently of that of the image. Besides this locational information, symbolic information such as relations among and properties of object instances is also stored in this database.

Suppose object instance s creates hypothesis f(s) (based on relation REL) for object O1, which overlaps with an instance of O1, t (Fig. 3(a)). If the set of constraints associated with f(s) is satisfied by t, these two pieces of evidence are combined to form what we call a "situation". That is, a situation is defined by a set of mutually consistent pieces of evidence. GRE unifies f(s) and t, and establishes the relation REL from s to t as the result of resolving the situation. This is the bottom-up process to establish a geometric relation between a pair of object instances.

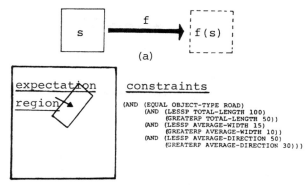

iconic data structure   (b)

Fig. 2   (a)Hypothesis generation
(b)Description of a hypothesis

On the other hand, a situation may consist of overlapping hypotheses alone(Fig. 3(b)). Then their unification leads GRE to search for an instance of the required object in the image. The expert asks MSE to detect the instance, which in turn activates LLVE. If the instance is detected, it is inserted into the iconic database, and the relations between the new instance and the "source" instances, which generated the hypotheses, are established. This process is the top-down analysis to find a missing object. Fig. 4 shows goal specifications to MSE and LLVE in the top-down analysis.

3.2 Handling Part—Whole Relations

Two types of geometric relations are used in our system: "spatial relation" (SP) and "part-whole relation" (PW). These two types of relations are used differently in the system. PW relations specify hierarchies which represent objects with complex internal structures, while SP relations represent geometric relations between different classes of objects. While hypothesis generation by an SP relation is done as explained above, the use of PW relations is different.

Suppose the PW hierarchy illustrated in Fig. 5(a) is given. The system uses PW relations both to group parts into a whole and to predict missing parts. In general, the objects corresponding to leaf nodes in the hierarchy are instantiated first, because their appearances are simple and correspond directly to primitive image features. The presence of a higher level object instance is represented symbolically by an instantiated hierarchy. This implies that no iconic description (i.e. region) representing higher level object instances is stored in the iconic database. (Note that hypotheses for higher level objects have iconic representations and as a result, can interact with other pieces of evidence.)

Let s denote an instance of object class O1 (Fig. 5(a)). Then, it can directly instantiate its parent object through the PW relation instead of generating a hypothesis as in case of SP relations(Fig. 5(b)).

This bottom-up instantiation through a PW hierarchy is controlled by a "kernel list" associated with each object class. An object instance in our system is in one of two instantiation states: fully-instantiated and partially-instantiated. The kernel list is used to discriminate these two states. The list consists of a set of sublists. Suppose object O is composed of part

objects P1, P2,...,Pn. Each sublist in the kernel list of O specifies a subset of {P1, P2,...,Pn}. Object O is fully instantiated if all parts objects in at least one sublist are fully instantiated. Otherwise it is partially instantiated. Only a fully instantiated object can instantiate its parent object via a PW relation.

When a parent object is instantiated, it may then generate hypotheses for its missing part objects (Fig. 5(c)). That is, no instantiated part object generates hypotheses for the other part objects at the same level of the PW hierarchy.

PW relations are represented in the same way as SP relations. That is, a PW relation is represented by

```
((GOAL    (AND (EQUAL OBJECT-TYPE HOUSE)
              (AND (LESSP AREA 475)
                   (GREATERP AREA 250)))
 (LOCATION (AND (LESSP X 1000)
                (GREATERP X 100)
                (LESSP Y 2000)
                (GREATERP Y 300)))
 (CONTEXT (HOUSE-GROUP002, HOUSE-GROUP006, ROAD005)))
```

(a) Goal specification to MSE
(unit is square feet and (X,Y) is in the world coordinate)

```
((GOAL   (AND (EQUAL OBJECT-TYPE RECTANGLE-HOUSE)
              (AND (LESSP AREA 400)
                   (GREATERP AREA 200)))
 (LOCATION (AND (LESSP X 1000)
                (GREATERP X 100)
                (LESSP Y 2000)
                (GREATERP Y 300))))
```

(b) Goal specification after selecting a specific object model

```
((GOAL    (EQUAL IMAGE-FEATURE-TYPE RECTANGLE)
          (AND (LESSP AREA 230)
               (GREATERP AREA 125)))
 (LOCATION (AND (EQUAL START-I 24)
                (EQUAL START-J 30)
                (EQUAL END-I 120)
                (EQUAL END-J 230))))
```

(c) Goal specification to LLVE
(unit is number of pixels and (I,J) is in the picture coordinate)

Fig.4 Goal specification in a top-down analysis

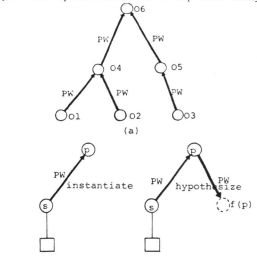

Fig. 5 (a)PW hierarchy (b)Bottom-up instantiation
(c)Top-down hypothesis generation

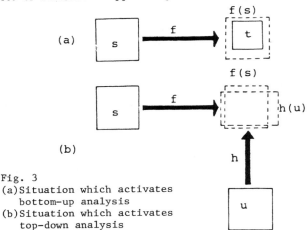

Fig. 3
(a)Situation which activates bottom-up analysis
(b)Situation which activates top-down analysis

a slot in a frame, where a set of production rules are stored. Conditions for both the bottom-up instantiation and top-down hypothesis generation through a PW hierarchy are represented by preconditions of the production rules. Computational procedures to generate parent instances and hypotheses for part objects are represented as actions of the rules. (The interpretation process to construct instantiated PW hierarchies (i.e. recognition of complex objects) will be described in Section 4.5.)

4. AERIAL IMAGE UNDERSTANDING BY A PROTOTYPE SYSTEM

This section describes the knowledge organization and analysis process of a prototype system for aerial image understanding. The system is implemented on VAX 780 and is written in FLAVOR, LISP, and C. The model selection and low level vision experts in this system are realized by simple functions written in LISP and C.

4.1 Knowledge Representation

Fig. 6 illustrates the knowledge organization used in the prototype system. As described above, an object class is represented by a frame, which consists of slots. Information stored in the slots includes attributes of the object and its relations to other objects. Besides these slots, a set of constraints among object attributes are stored in a frame to represent their allowable value ranges[7]. These constraints are basic requirements to be satisfied in object recognition.

The relations used to associate frames are:
(1)PW :represent geometric structures of objects with complex internal structures
(2)SP :geometric relations between objects
(3)AKO :specialization/generalization relations among objects
(4)IO :represent instances of a class of object
(5)ICW :Some pairs of objects cannot occupy the same location in an image. For instance, a region cannot be interpreted as both house and road at the same time. Pairs of frames representing object classes which cannot occupy the same location are linked with an in-conflict-with (ICW) relation.
(6)APO :represent appearance of object

4.2 Initial Segmentation

The first analysis of an image is initiated by MSE. At the very beginning of the analysis, there is no object instance in the system. MSE examines the knowledge stored in the system and selects objects with simple appearances. Then, it asks LLVE to extract image features which match the selected appearances. The basic constraints on object attributes are associated with the goal specification to LLVE. All image features found by LLVE are returned to MSE, which then instantiates corresponding object instances and inserts them into the iconic database. These instances are seeds for reasoning by GRE.

Fig. 7(a) shows an aerial photograph (black and white) used in the experiment (250 X 140 and six bits for each pixel). Figs. 7(b)(c) illustrate the instances of house and road-piece extracted by the initial segmentation. Note that the segmentation in our system is dynamically performed on request and that no fixed set of image features (e.g. regions) to be interpreted are formed by the initial segmentation.

4.3 Interpretation Cycle of GRE

GRE iterates the following steps until no change is done in the iconic database.

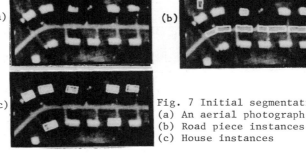

(a)
(b)
(c)

Fig. 7 Initial segmentation
(a) An aerial photograph
(b) Road piece instances
(c) House instances

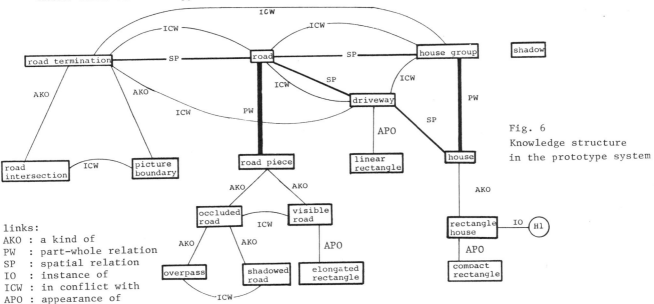

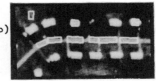

Fig. 6
Knowledge structure
in the prototype system

links:
AKO : a kind of
PW : part-whole relation
SP : spatial relation
IO : instance of
ICW : in conflict with
APO : appearance of

(1) Each instance of an object generates hypotheses about related objects using functions stored in the object model. Object instances in PW hierarchies instantiate their parent objects, which then generate hypotheses for missing parts.

(2) All pieces of evidence (both hypotheses and instances) are stored in the iconic database.

(3) Consistent pieces of evidence are combined to establish "situations".

(4) Focus of attention : since there are many situations, the most reliable situation is selected. Each piece of evidence has a reliability value, and the reliability of a situation is computed from those of its constituent pieces of evidence.

(5) The selected situation is resolved, which results either in verification of predictions on the basis of previously detected/constructed object instances or in top-down image processing to detect missing objects.

The system has one additional post-processing: During the analysis by GRE, conflicting pieces of evidence may be generated. Comparing Figs. 7 (b) and (c), for example, two road-piece instances overlap with house instances. These interpretations are considered as conflicting. GRE maintains all possible interpretations throughout the analysis. The final interpretation process then selects the maximal consistent interpretation. At this stage, all partially instantiated objects and their parts are removed, because enough evidence to support their existence has not been obtained from the analysis.

4.4 Consistency Examination among Evidence

The consistency among pieces of evidence is examined based on:

(1) prediction areas of hypotheses and locations of instances

(2) object categories of evidence

(3) constraints imposed on properties of hypotheses and instances

(4) relations among sources of evidence.

4.4.1 Intersection of Prediction Areas

Fig. 8(a) shows all intersections formed from four pieces of evidence E1, E2, E3, and E4 in the iconic database. A partial ordering on intersections can be constructed on the basis of region containment. Intersection OP1 is less than OP2 if region OP1 is contained in region OP2. Fig. 8(b) shows the lattice representing the partial ordering among the intersections in Fig. 8(a). Each intersection consists of some set of hypotheses and instances. Situations are only formed among intersecting pieces of evidence (i.e. satisfying locational constraints). In other words, this lattice is an index to search for consistent pieces of evidence. To examine the consistency among pieces of evidence, it is sufficient to examine all intersections containing only a pair of pieces of evidence and then to propagate the results through the lattice.

4.4.2 Conflicting Evidence

Let OP be the intersection arising from evidence {E1, E2} and let OBJ1 and OBJ2 denote the object categories of E1 and E2, respectively. If OBJ1 and OBJ2 are linked by an ICW relation, then E1 and E2 are said to be conflicting, and OP is removed from the lattice. The removal of OP is propagated through the lattice, and any intersections contained in OP are also removed.

In the above case, if both E1 and E2 are instances, GRE records them as conflicting interpretations and performs independent analyses based on them. (See Section 4.4.4.)

4.4.3 Constraint Consistency

After eliminating all conflicting intersections from the lattice, the remaining intersections are checked to determine if their associated sets of constraints are consistent. Let E1 and E2 denote the non-conflicting evidence under consideration. One of the following conditions must hold:

(a) The object categories of E1 and E2 are the same,

(b) there is a path between the two categories consisting of PW relations,

   or

(c) one of the two categories is a subcategory of the other, according to the AKO hierarchy.

As shown in Fig. 9, suppose a grandparent object in a PW hierarchy has been instantiated by an instance of a leaf node object s. Let p and q denote instances of the parent and grandparent objects. q as well as p generates hypotheses for its missing parts, say g(q). Suppose that g(q) itself has parts and one of them has already been instantiated. Let t denote that instance.

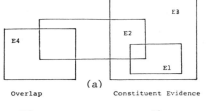

(a)

Overlap	Constituent Evidence
OP1	E1
OP2	E2
OP3	E3
OP4	E4
OP5	E1, E2
OP6	E1, E3
OP7	E2, E3
OP8	E2, E4
OP9	E1, E2, E3

Fig. 8

Lattice to represent overlaps among regions

(b)

Fig. 9

Accumulation of evidence of different object classes

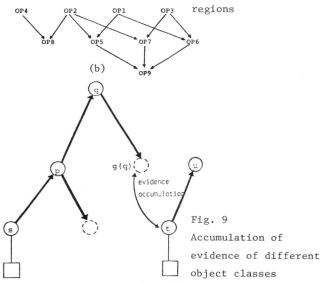

Then, if instances s and t are really parts of the same object, regions of g(q) and t will overlap with each other and will be consistent. (Note that instance u cannot intersect with g(q) directly since no iconic description is associated with u in the database.) In this case, although the object classes of g(q) and t are different, they can be consistent since their object categories are linked by a sequence of PW relations.

In such a case, since the names of the attributes used in the constraints associated with E1 (g(q) in Fig. 9) and E2 (t in Fig. 9) are different, they cannot, in general, be directly compared. In this case, the constraints associated with the lower level object (i.e. t) are translated into those for the higher level object (i.e. g(q)) by using PW relations. Currently, this translation is done simply by rewriting the attributes (slot names) of the lower level object into appropriate attributes of the higher level object using a "attribute translation table" for the PW relation (Fig. 10). The similar attribute translation is used between object categories linked by AKO relations.

The properties of and/or constraints associated with both pieces of evidence must be consistent. Both constraints associated with a hypothesis and properties associated with an instance represented by a set of linear inequalities in one variable. A simple constraint manipulation system[7] is used to check the consistency between the sets of inequalities.

4.4.4 Relations between Sources of Evidence

Sources of accumulated evidence involved in a situation must not be conflicting. Let S1 and S2 denote the source evidence of E1 and E2, respectively. If a piece of evidence is a hypothesis, its source evidence is the instance which generated the hypothesis. An instance is the source evidence for itself. It is possible that S1 and S2 are mutually conflicting (belonging to conflicting interpretations), but that E1 and E2 themselves are consistent. In such a case, we do not combine E1 and E2 into a situation; analysis based on such conflicting interpretations should be performed independently.

4.5 Resolving a Situation

As described in Section 3.1, one of two actions is taken in order to resolve a situation: confirm relation between instances or activate top-down analysis. After the action is taken, GRE provides a description of its proposed solution to the situation to all instances involved in that situation. Each instance then evaluates the proposed solution according to its specific

expectations.

4.5.1 Resolution Process

In what follows, the process of resolving a situation is described by using the example shown in Fig. 11. Suppose GRE selected the overlapping region between two hypotheses generated from two road instances RD1 and RD2 (Fig. 11(a)). In the symbolic data structure, RD1 and RD2 are linked to their part (road-piece) instances RP1 and RP2 by PW relations, respectively.

Since this situation consists only of hypotheses, the system activates top-down analysis to find a road-piece in the overlapping region. This request is issued to MSE together with the supporting evidence (i.e. RD1 and

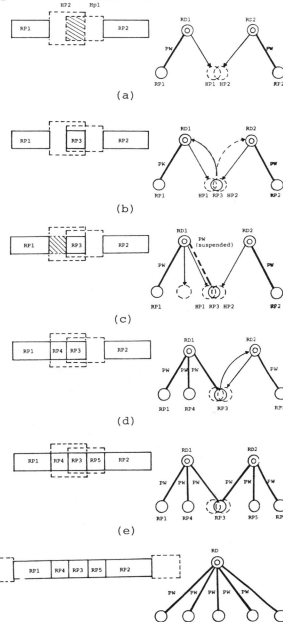

Fig. 11 (see text)

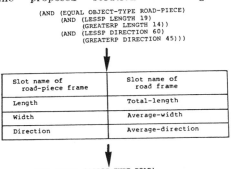

```
(AND (EQUAL OBJECT-TYPE ROAD-PIECE)
     (AND (LESSP LENGTH 19)
          (GREATERP LENGTH 14))
     (AND (LESSP DIRECTION 60)
          (GREATERP DIRECTION 45)))
```

Slot name of road-piece frame	Slot name of road frame
Length	Total-length
Width	Average-width
Direction	Average-direction

```
(AND (EQUAL OBJECT-TYPE ROAD)
     (AND (LESSP AVERAGE-LENGTH 19)
          (GREATERP AVERAGE-LENGTH 14))
     (AND (LESSP AVERAGE-DIRECTION 60)
          (GREATERP AVERAGE-DIRECTION 45)))
```

Fig. 10
Attribute translation

RD2), so that the expert can use any available contextual information of such supporting evidence.

Assume that a new road-piece instance, RP3, is created (Fig. 11(b)). Then, GRE provides this result to the instances involved in the situation, RD1 and RD2.

Suppose RD1 is the first to be informed of the proposed solution. RD1 examines whether or not RP3 satisfies all constraints required to establish the PW relation with itself. In this case, however, RP3 fails, because RP3 is not adjacent to RP1. (The constraints associated with the hypothesis do not include this type of relational constraints.) This failure activates an exception handler, which is also a production rule stored in the corresponding slot in the road frame. Then it issues a top-down request to find a road-piece between RP1 and RP3 (see Fig. 11(c)).

Assume that another new road-piece instance, RP4, is detected (Fig. 11(d)). Since RP4 is adjacent to RP1, RD1 establishes a PW relation to RP4, and then to RP3.

Fig. 11(e) shows the interpretation after the same analysis is performed by RD2. In this case, however, when RD2 establishes a PW relation to RP3, an exception handler in RP3 is triggered, because RP3 has two different parents. More specifically, after RD2 establishes a PW relation to RP3, RD2 asks RP3 to ckeck its reverse relation from RP3. An exception handler is activated as a result of this checking process. This handler issues a request to GRE to examine the consistency between two parents. If they are consistent, GRE merges the two PW hierarchies below them into one (Fig. 11(f)).

The hypotheses generated by RD1 and RD2 are removed from the iconic database. The resultant new road instance in Fig. 11(f) generates new hypotheses for its adjacent road-pieces at the beginning of the next interpretation cycle.

Figs. 12 and 13 illustrate an example of this process. First top-down analysis is performed to extract a house instance. Then, parent house group instances sharing

a common house instance (i.e. a new detected house instance) are merged into one instance.

4.5.2 Error Analysis
There are several stages in the above example where the top-down request might have failed.

In general, MSE has the ability to deal with such failures. For example, MSE analyzes the request to find RP3 (Fig. 11(a)) by first assuming the road-piece to be detected is a visible road(Fig. 6), and issues a request to LLVE. If this request fails, MSE switches to the other appearance of a road-piece, i.e. an occluded-road (Fig. 6). The selection between overpass and shadowed road is done based on the cause of the failure returned from LLVE.

If all efforts by MSE fail, this is reported to GRE. Then, GRE reports this to RD1 and RD2, which trigger their relevant exception handlers (if any). Since different new hypotheses may be generated by such exception handlers, no immediate further analysis is activated.

Fig. 14 illustrates an example of this, where a road instance is reported that its hypothesis for an adjacent road-piece cannot be verified. Then it removes that hypothesis and newly generates a hypothesis for a road terminator (Fig. 6), assuming that it comes to an termination.

If a top-down request issued by an instance fails, the instance reports this to GRE. Then GRE activates another instance involved in the focused situation. In the prototype system, failures of this type are not taken into accout in any way.

4.5.3 Merging a Pair of Partial PW Hierarchies
If a part instance is shared by two parent instances, the part issues a request to check the similarity between the parents. If they are similar, the system merges them into one.

Similarity examination involves checking whether or not the two parents instances denote (perhaps different pieces of) the same object. For example, RD1 and RD2 in Fig. 11(e) should be merged into one, although they do not denote the same (portion of) road.

In practice, according to the request from the system, the more reliable of the two parent instances to be merged ckecks whether or not the part instances of the other instance are consistent with that more reliable parent. The more reliable parent may decide to merge with the other parent, that such a merge is not (and will never be) possible, i.e. both parents are mutually conflicting, or that sufficient information is not available to make a decision.

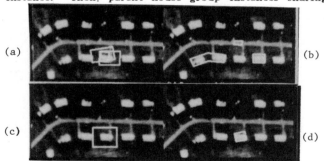

Fig. 12 Top-down detection of a house
(a)Selected situation (b)Source instances
(c)Composite hypothesis (d)Proposed solution

Fig. 13 Unification of house group instances
left:House group instances before the analysis
right:House group instances after the analysis

Fig. 14 Changing hypothesis
(a)Road instance
(b)Road segment hypothesis
(c)Road terminator hypothesis

Fig. 15 illustrates an example of the third case. Suppose that definition of a house group is a group of regularly arranged houses which face the same side of the same road. As shown in Fig. 15, if two house group instances share a house instance, the similarity examination is performed. If both house group instances face the same side of the same road instance, then they are similar and merged into one. On the other hand, if one (or both) of them has not established such a "facing" relation, then it is not possible to verify the similarity between them. Moreover, even if the two house group instances have established "facing" relations to different road instances, it is still possible for them to be similar, because those road instances may be merged later.

If the result of the similarity examination is "inconclusive", the system records its causes and suspends the action of establishing a new PW relation from a parent instance to the shared part instance. In the case shown in Fig. 15, the relation between HG1 and H3 is suspended. The system records all suspended actions together with their causes. The suspended action can be reactivated if its cause is resolved by analyzing other situations.

At the final stage of the analysis, the system makes copies of shared part instances involved in the suspended actions, and separates overlapping interpretations. The system does not regard these interpretations as conflicting, but considers them as possible interpretations.

5. CONCLUDING REMARKS

Fig. 16 shows the final results of analyzing the aerial photograph shown in Fig. 7. Although there are several mis-interpretations, they can easily be removed since such interpretations are isolated and/or conflicting with the correct (maximally consistent) interpretation.

SIGMA is not a completed system and has several problems to be solved. First, no negative sources of evidence are considered in assessing the reliability of a situation. Introduction of negative evidence requires a more general method of combining evidence. The most difficult problem would be how to coordinate interpretations excecuted in parallel in local areas. In our system, the interpretation of an object with many parts can be initiated from any part in parallel, and

partial interpretations are merged into one global interpretation if they are consistent. This merging process is triggered by a local interpretation shared by multiple partial interpretations. The complication explained in Section 4.5.3 in merging partially instantiated PW hierarchies arises from the intrinsic parallelism involved in our reasoning process. Since the current global control is sequencial, the suspension of the reasoning process was introduced to cope with the parallelism. More general and powerful control scheme is necessary to manage such parallel reasoning.

ACKNOWLEDGEMENT

The authors sincerely appreciate helphul comments and constructive discussions by Profs. A. Rosenfeld and L.S. Davis of University of Maryland. The first author thanks Prof. M. Nagao of Kyoto University for giving him this research opportunity. The support of the U.S. Air Force Office of Science Research under Contract F-49620-83-C-0082 is gratefully acknowledged.

REFERENCES

[1] Binford, T.O., "Survey of model-based image analysis systems," The International Journal of Robotics Research, Vol. 1, No. 1, pp.18-64, 1982.

[2] Nagao, M. and Matsuyama, T., "A structural analysis of complex aerial photographs," Plenum, 1980.

[3] Tsotsos, J.K., "Temporal event recognition: an application to left venticular performance," Proc. of 7th IJCAI, pp.900-907, 1983.

[4] Havens, W. and Mackworth, A., "Representing knowledge of the visual world," IEEE Computer, Vol. 16, No. 10, pp.90-96, 1983.

[5] Russell, D.M., "Where do I look now? : modeling and inferring object location by constraints," Proc. of Pattern Recognition and Image Processing, pp.175-183, 1979.

[6] Selfridge, P.G., "Reasoning about success and failure in aerial image understanding," Ph.D. Thesis, TR 103, Univ. of Rochester, 1982.

[7] Brooks, R.A., "Symbolic reasoning among 3D models and 2D images," Artificial Intelligence, Vol. 17, pp.285-348, 1981.

[8] Nozif, A.M. and Levine, M.D., "Low level image segmentation: an expert system," IEEE Trans. Vol. PAMI-6, No. 6, pp.555-577, 1984.

[9] Minsky, M.L., "A framework for representing knowledge," in The Psychology of Computer Vision (P.H. Winston ed.), McGraw-Hill, 1975.

[10] Matsuyama, T. et al, "An expert system for top-down image segmentation," (in Japanese) Technical Report of Working Group on Computer Vision of IPS Japan, WGCV-36-3,1985.

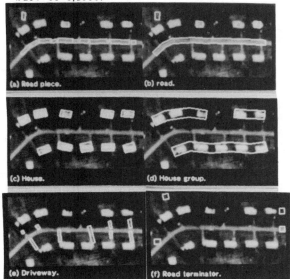

Fig. 16 Final object instances

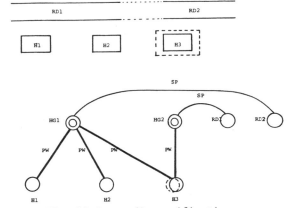

Fig. 15 Suspending unification process

PROBLEM-SOLVING STRATEGIES IN A MUSIC TRANSCRIPTION SYSTEM

Bernard Mont-Reynaud

CCRMA, Stanford University

ABSTRACT

Music transcription is a significant problem in machine perception. The system discussed in this paper, MANA, takes as input either the sound of a recorded performance, or data captured using a musical keyboard. It produces conventional musical notation as output. It has successfully handled pieces ranging from 18th-century piano music to improvisations on conga drums, in the Afro-Cuban style.

The paper describes the key ideas and techniques found in the temporal analysis component of MANA, the goal of which is to assign a rhythmic value to each note played.

Perception seems to result from the interplay of sensory evidence and pre-existing mental structures, data-driven agents pitted against model-driven agents in the formation of hypotheses that seem tolerable to our prejudices and not too distant from the data. To this first order view one must add a second order one, which allows the system to notice patterns among partially elaborated hypotheses, and to use these patterns to alter confidence ratings, according to "peer pressure" rules.

Concerning the use of multiple criteria for hypothesis evaluation and pruning, which necessary in the context of perception systems, it is argued that the use of partial orders over multi-dimensional spaces of natural criteria yield more robust methods that approaches based on combining criteria down to scalars.

I INTRODUCTION

An ongoing research project at CCRMA (Stanford University) is concerned with exploring an AI approach to the recognition of musical structures in sound and other forms of data. The effective integration of numerical processing and symbolic processing towards the goal of machine perception is a central technical theme, while music transcription is the task goal.

Automatic transcription from sound is clearly more difficult than transcription from keyboard strokes. It requires, prior to the musical analysis which is needed in both cases, an initial stage of acoustic analysis. Further refinements may be obtained by feeding information gathered from the musical context back to acoustic levels of the analysis system.

It is perhaps less obvious that transcription from keyboard strokes alone presents a significant challenge. The problem is trivial if one either forbids expressive performance and rhythmic complexity, requiring strict metronomis accuracy in timing; or if one accepts musically

absurd (but physically accurate) transcriptions, as may be obtained by setting the tempo and the metrical grid resolution to fixed values, and rounding durations to the nearest grid point. But one should keep in mind that, for example, an eighth note (1/2 of a beat) may be played shorter than a triplet eighth (1/3 of a beat) without confusing human listeners, provided the appropriate musical context. How to provide sufficient context mechanisms to reach correct decisions, often in spite of the physical evidence, without carrying context-driving to excess, may well be the most sensitive question in the design of robust perception systems.

In this paper, the discussion will be limited to the musical analysis component of MANA, and further restricted to the temporal aspects of the analysis. The reader is referred to [FOS82a-b, SCH84] for a discussion of acoustic analysis, and to [CHA82, MON84] for a more comprehensive account of the methods used in musical analysis. Section II of the paper provides an overview of the system, and presents some of the key ideas and techniques used in temporal analysis. Section III discusses some of the problem-solving strategies whose compounded effect is a carefully measured dose of context-driving. Section IV draws some conclusions and outlines the direction of future research, in which learning issues will play an increasing role.

II MUSICAL ANALYSIS

The performance goal initially set for the system was to exhibit a fair degree of musical wisdom while transcribing expressively played 18th-century music. The input was restricted to a single musical voice. A first redesign of the temporal analysis permitted opening up the range of musical styles without having to train specific styles into the program. Another redesign, which is is progress, is aimed at dealing with polyphonic sound. However, the system as discussed here only with one voice at a time.

Further progress towards increased grasp of the musical structure, including more robust methods for tempo tracking and meter determination, require moderately powerful learning techniques, of the "unsupervised" type. The idea is to uncover the most significant musical patterns in a piece, and to use the temporal patterns of pattern occurences as hints to the tempo and meter. Near-misses also offer important possibilities, notably for error detection. near-missed to initiate self-doubt.

A Rational Approximation Generation

Note values, metrical intervals and metrical positions are rational numbers, expressed in terms of a reference unit. Given (say) a note duration X and the duration R of the metrical reference unit, both in seconds, one wishes to generate rational approximations of X/R as candidate note values for the given note, in terms of the given unit. The choice of rational approximations must take into account at least two criteria: closeness to the data (or *fit*), and simplicity of the fraction. The latter must be understood in terms of how simple or natural the resulting musical notation would be. The techniques of multi-criteria filtering (section III-B) come into play at this point, to limit the number of answers retained.

The program relies on the same generator for a variety of different tasks, but it varies parameters such as the set of acceptable numerators and denominators, and the error thresholds. The most obvious use is in the generation of hypotheses for individual note values. There are others, and they use different tunings.

Finally, the complexity measure for metric fractions is allowed to change over time. For example, fractions such as 1/3 and 2/3 may become *simpler* than 1/4 or 1/2 after sufficient statistical evidence of ternary meter has been gathered. This is an applications of *peer pressure* (cf. III-A).

B   Approach to the rhythmic value problem

The goal is to express note values as rational fractions of a whole note. It turns out that this goal must be approached in a round-about manner, which goes in 4 steps as follows: (a) choose a reference unit R; (b) express note values as fractions of a reference unit R; (c) analyze the patterns of note values in order to determine values for metrical divisions like beat, bar and (at least) the whole note; and (d) convert from R-values to whole-note values.

Problem (b) is the rhythmic value problem. Problem (c) is the meter problem, which is not discussed here. From a formal point of view, it appears that the value of R in step (a) is arbitrary. This is not so: the behavior of the rational approximator depends very much on the reference unit used. A first set of rules is used to determine R. Statistical clustering of note values plays a role there.

The next key idea is to localize the problem, to regions where the tempo is supposedly held constant. This factors out the global tempo fluctuation, which can be represented by a piecewise linear correspondence between musical time and physical time. The slope of each linear segment is a tempo value, and the list of successive segments is regarded as the *tempo line* of the piece. A second set of rules, based on simple rhythmic and melodic patterns is used to determine the *structural anchors*. These notes are singled out as likely candidates to occupy strong positions in the (as yet undetermined) metric grid. For instance, these notes might occur at downbeats, or at least at beat boundaries. The endpoints of the tempo line segments, on the physical time axis, are placed at these structural anchor points.

A third set of rules determines the metrical duration of each tempo line segment, in terms of R. This completes the construction of the tempo line. Once the tempo is known within each segment, it is possible to use the rational approximation generator to associate with each note a set of candidate rational values, in terms of R. Among the combination of approximations which add up to the desired metric length it is possible to select one that represents the best compromise between musical simplicity and closeness to the data, for this segment.

In terms of search paradigms, choosing the tempo line before assigning individual note values is a special case of solving a problem in a much smaller *abstract space*. Once an abstract solution S is obtained, one returns to solving the original problem under the constraints imposed by S.

III   PROBLEM-SOLVING STRATEGIES

MANA operates primarily in a bottom-up fashion, but it does use top-down constraints. The important point is that very few *a priori* top-down constraints are used. In other words, the program tries to refrain from having too strong a notion of what music "must" be like. On the other hand, *a posteriori* constraints are heavily relied upon. Such context-driving operates in a top-down manner, but the context is acquired during previous bottom-up hypothesis generation. The idea is to promote homogeneity, or self-consistency. In other words, the program operates under the assumption that a piece defines its own "style" and then wants to see more of the same "style". This feedback mechanism, termed *peer pressure*, is further examined in section III-A.

Instead of backtracking, the system relies on a multiple-value technique, whereby a set of alternatives is operated on parallel. Techniques of *multi-criteria filtering* (cf III-B) are used to to prune the sets of alternatives whenever evaluation criteria are added or modified.

A   Peer pressure

The system uses several levels of abstraction in its description of the data. It combines data-driven and context-driven methods of hypothesis generation and evaluation. Data-driven methods use features obtained at one level to generate hypotheses at the next level. Context-driven methods use information gathered at higher levels to re-evaluate and possibly re-generate lower-level hypotheses. A key problem is to arrange that feedback loops between the bottom-up and top-down modes either converge rapidly, either to a stable consensus, or to no effect at all. This problem is adressed by the *peer pressure* strategy, a method that allows a collection of hypotheses (obtained using statistics, clustering or pattern discovery methods) to promote hypotheses with similar contextual features.

Using rather broad terms here, let us call "data" some collection of hypotheses at a given level of description, and "partial model" some description of the the set of data. The partial model might be a set of patterns found in the data, or a statistical summary of some aspect of the data.

Peer pressure, which may be viewed as a noise reduction technique, operates in two steps. The first step extracts a partial model from the data. The model must be "safe" before proceeding: under poor conditions, peer pressure may amplify noise! The second step modifies the data to create a better agreement with the partial model. Each data point is re-examined in terms of this agreement. If the agreement is weak, the data point becomes a candidate for modification, that is, deletion, replacement by one or more other data points, or simple adjustment. Strong patterns always get stronger by the use of this technique, which decreases the perceived disorder in the interpretation of the data.

B   Multi-criteria filtering

In an attempt to achieve robustness over a wide range of examples and styles, MANA relies on a variety of independent methods for hypothesis generation, and also on a multiplicity of evaluation criteria. Rather than using backtracking, MANA usually carries a small number of hypotheses in parallel. Excessive pruning of a set of hypotheses, most likely to occur during early stages of analysis, may cause a system to overlook a good solution whose value is not yet obvious at that stage of the game. Too little pruning, on the other hand, not only slows things down, but leaves noisy points which may affect the operation of peer pressure. Thus, it is important to maintain a balanced degree of indecision.

In a multiple-criteria situation, a popular approach is to use a weighting scheme to produce a scalar from all the criteria. MANA considers this method to be one of last resort, as it all too often leads to erroneous decisions. Trying to improve the approach by making the weighting scheme dependent on context leaves the problem unchanged for initial decisions, which must be made before sufficient context is established. It also forces one to develop ways of changing the weights as a function of context, a rather hazardous enterprise.

It seems better to deal with the original multiplicity of criteria directly, especially during pruning stages. The intuition behind the scheme we use is quite simple: if hypothesis A is no worse than hypothesis B in any of the criteria, and better in at least one criterion, then (and only then) B should be pruned. This idea immediately generalizes to an arbitrary partial orderings in the space of criteria. We say that an hypothesis is *dominated* if it is larger than some other hypothesis, with respect to the chosen partial ordering. *Undominated* hypotheses are those that correspond to minimal elements in the space of criteria. They are the only ones retained past a pruning stage.

Since the retained hypotheses are minimal in the partial ordering, they trade one criterion for another: one hypothesis might be close to the observed data while the other is simpler but farther away, and a third is intermediate in both respects. The scheme is uniform, but leaves much flexibility in the choice of the partial ordering. In our application, this technique has been found extremely effective.

IV CONCLUSIONS

Elements of a methodology for achieving robustness in perception tasks have been gathered, along with some ideas more specific of the transcription domain. In terms of performance, the automatic transcription system described has also produced some rather interesting results. Naturally, there is much more work to be done, both to improve robustness in single-voice examples, and to deal with polyphonic data.

Experiments underway suggest that the response to these challenges will be based on (a) extending the use of adaptive feedback strategies into the acoustic levels of the system, so that signal processing and reasoning work hand-in-hand, and (b) developing the techniques for pattern discovery and selection to the point where second-order patterns become a reliable source of information.

In fact, in the process of this research, it has become more and more apparent that the musical domain provides an ideal setting for in-depth studies in machine perception and machine learning. Statistical pattern recognition and unsupervised inductive learning [MIC83] both have important roles to play in a flexible musical understanding system.

REFERENCES

[CHA82] Chafe, C., B. Mont-Reynaud and L. Rush. Toward an Intelligent Editor of Digital Audio: Musical Construct Recognition, Computer Music Journal 6:1 (1982), 30-41.

[FOS82a] Foster, S., J. Rockmore and W. Schloss. Toward an Intelligent Editor of Digital Audio: Signal Processing Methods, Computer Music Journal 6:1 (1982), 42-51.

[FOS82b] Foster, S. and A. Joseph Rockmore. Signal Processing for the Analysis of Musical Sound, ICASSP Proceedings, Paris. May 3-5, 1982.

[MIC83] Michalsky, R., J. Carbonell, and T. Mitchell, eds. *Machine Learning*. Tioga Publishing Co., Palo Alto, 1983.

[MON84] Bernard Mont-Reynaud, et. al. *Intelligent Systems for the Analysis of Digitized Acoustic Signals, Final Report*. Technical Report STAN-M-15, Department of Music, Stanford University, Stanford, California (1984)

[SCH84] Schloss, W. On the Automatic Transcription of Percussive Music, PhD thesis, Department of Speech and Hearing, Stanford University, Stanford, California (in preparation)

----

* This work was supported by the National Science Foundation under Contracts NSF MCS-8012476 and DCR-8214350.

LandScan: A Natural Language and Computer Vision System for Analyzing Aerial Images

Ruzena Bajcsy

Aravind Joshi

Eric Krotkov

Amy Zwarico

CIS Dept/D2
University of Pennsylvania
Philadelphia, Pennsylvania 19104

Abstract

LandScan (LANguage Driven SCene ANalysis) is presented as an integrated vision system which covers most levels of both vision and natural language processing. Computations are both data-driven and query-driven. In the report we focus on the design of the vision and control modules. Future work will investigate in more detail the design of the natural language interface. The data-driven system employs active control of stereo cameras for image acquisition, and dynamically constructs a surface model from multiple aerial views of an urban scene. The query-driven system allows the user's natural language queries to focus analysis to pertinent regions of the scene. This is different than many image understanding systems which present a symbolic description of the entire scene regardless of what portions of that picture are actually of interest.

1. Introduction

The aim of our research on LandScan (LANguage Driven SCene ANalysis) is to develop a system capable of dynamically updating and maintaining a model of an urban world over multiple aerial views. The system will have a natural language front end through which users can query the system about a scene, and interactively assist the vision processing by restricting the analysis to those areas of the scene which are of current interest. A unique contribution of the work is that processing is both data-driven (bottom up, determined by sensor data) and query-driven (top down, determined by user queries). The integration of both methods into one system can help overcome the shortcomings of each method employed independently. For example, if data-driven processing were able to segment a graph of edges derived from the image into *several* different connected components, query-driven information about what the system *should* be looking for can help impose structure, and a unique segmentation, upon the otherwise ambiguous data.

The data-driven processing starts with stereo aerial images and reconstructs the surfaces in the scene. The query-driven processing constructs a logical representation of the scene using the queries to guide analysis. High-level scene analysis is performed using an Augmented Transition Network (ATN).

This research was supported by the following grants: ARO DAA6-29-84-k-0061 AfOSR 82-NM-299 NSF MCS-8219196-CER NSF MCS 82-07294 AVRO DAABO7-84-K-FO77 NIH 1-RO1-HL-29985-01.

As an example, suppose the user asks, "Is there a car on the street?" The output from this query would be: the objects to be recognized, car and street; the relation ON which must hold between them; and an indication that this query is responded to by a yes/no answer with some explanation. The vision system would then be called to find a car and a street in the relation ON. The car and street would then be added to the Scene Model (if not there already) and the system would reply with an affirmative response.

This paper will describe some related research, the implementation of the data-driven and query-driven portions of the LandScan system, and our plans for future work. A later paper will detail how natural language queries will interface with LandScan to guide the scene analysis.

2. Related Research

A large corpus of research on aerial image understanding *per se* exists, and many general vision techniques are applicable to the aerial domain. Large aerial projects have been undertaken at USC [Nevatia 83], CMU [Herman 83] and SRI [Fischler 83]. However, very few integrated systems have been successfully implemented, and the best system architecture is still an open question. In particular, the problem of providing high-level feedback to the vision system has not been adequately addressed.

ATN's have been used primarily in the domain of natural language [Bates 81], [Winograd 83]. A notable exception is the system designed by Tropf and Walter [Tropf 83] which uses an ATN model for the recognition of 3D objects with known geometries.

The work of Talmy [Talmy 83] and Herskovits [Herskovits 82] influenced the design of both the topological relations in the models and the choice of linguistic attributes which must be associated with objects in order to ensure a robust and reliable natural language interface.

3. Data-driven System Implementation and Results

This section will describe the data-driven vision modules, which must be effective in an urban world, seen from above. Urban scenes are characterized by an abundance of straight lines and planar surfaces. Under these constraints, the scene may usefully be approximated as polyhedra.

We have tested the modules on real, highly complex aerial images; it is very difficult to present these results. We show results derived from imaging a subset of the scale model depicted in Figure 6-2: a "mock up" of an urban scene. One advantage of using the scale model is the clarity of the results, and the ease of verifying their compatibility with reality.

3.1. Vision Modules

A stereo pair of images is acquired. The gradient ∇f of the images blurred at multiple resolutions is computed, and the Canny operator is used to locally suppress non-maxima in the gradient magnitude $\| \nabla f \| = SQRT(f_x^2 + f_y^2)$. We call the surviving pixels "edgels". To find corners, the variance σ^2 in the gradient directions $\theta = \tan^{-1}(f_y)/(f_x))$ is computed over a local neighborhood. The cornerness of an edgel is proportional to the product $\sigma^2 \| \nabla f \|$.

Corresponding edgels in the two images are matched using 2-sided correlation at multiple scales. In images of parts of the scene in Figure 5-1, 83% of the vertically oriented edgels are matched, and the disparity at each is computed. The resultant sparse depth map is refined by linear interpolation (acceptable under the constraints of this domain), first across columns and then across rows. Figure 5-2 depicts the interpolated depth map (corresponding to only the more distant objects in Figure -1).

Figure 5-1:   Scale model.

3.2. Surface Model

A graph is constructed to serve as the surface model [Krotkov 84]. The construction algorithm converts a set of contours into a set of closed contours represented as a graph (a linked list of vertices, edges, and faces) by traversing edges and at trihedral junctions choosing the path making the most acute angle with respect to the present path.

Surface attributes and relations are computed in the

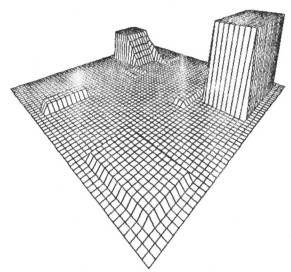

Figure 5-2:   Depth map of partial view of 5-SurfsUP [Radack, et al 84] geometrical modelling system. Attribute values for each face in the surface graph are computed: compactness, centroid, normal, area, type (building, sidewalk, field, street, and unknown), and number of sides. These values are computed once and stored on an attribute list. Computed topological relations are *above*, *adjacent* (touching), *contiguous* (sharing an edge), *contains* (proper inclusion), *looksadjacent*, *lookscontiguous* (respectively adjacent and contiguous under perspective transformations). Relations (and indirectly their complements) are computed once and stored as Boolean arrays.

4. Query-driven System Implementation and Results

This section describes the design and implementation of the query-driven processes. These include object recognition and scene modelling [Zwarico 84], high level reasoning processes, and query handling.

4.1. Object Recognition

The ATN formalism has been chosen as the paradigm for object recognition in LandScan. It is composed of three parts: the grammar, a dictionary, and an interpreter. The grammar represents the *a priori* or world knowledge that the system must have in order to recognize objects. The dictionary represents the actual data: a list of all of the faces which have been segmented by vision and the relations between them. The third component is a Lisp program which provides the control structure for the process. Figure 5-3 shows the results of running the recognizer on the scene in Figure 5-1.

4.2. The Scene Model

The Scene Model is composed of two components: a list of objects currently known to be in the scene and a set of matrices representing the primitive relations. The objects on the object list have already been recognized. Each object has associated with it a list of surfaces, its location, and a subtype. The relations which are the same as in the surface model, are represented by their adjacency matrices because the adjacency matrix is easily updated and makes composition of relations a simple matter of Boolean matrix multiplication.

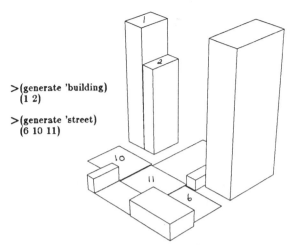

>(generate 'building)
(1 2)

>(generate 'street)
(6 10 11)

Figure 5-3: Reconstructed planar surfaces.

The Scene Model is dynamic because information can be added to it as further image analysis occurs. A new object is added to the head of the list. The relations are updated by calculating the relations between the new entity and the current object list.

4.3. Linguistic Analyzer

Given a query, the Linguistic Analyzer will symbolically represent this utterance so that it can be used by the reasoning process to analyze the image. The Linguistic Analyzer will parse the query, determine the query type, and categorize all implicit subqueries in the actual utterance. Its output will contain a list of the objects to be found, the relations which must hold between these objects, and the query type (so that an appropriate response can be generated). This is not yet implemented.

4.4. Reasoning

The Reasoner analyzes the query, determines the strategy for obtaining an answer to the query, and provides feedback to the vision system. In order to obtain the information necessary for the generation of the response the Reasoner must have both runtime data (the current Scene Model and the query) and global knowledge (the World Model and the Object Model).

The World Model describes the features and relations of the objects in the domain, buildings, streets, sidewalks, etc. The world is represented by a labelled directed multigraph in which the nodes are the objects in the domain and the arcs are labelled with the relation which can hold between them. The Object Model represents the expected physical features (subparts) and linguistic properties (features which affect the usage and interpretation of a spatial construct) of the objects in the domain.

If the reasoning processes fail to produce a positive response (the query fails to have an answer), the Reasoner performs two types of query failure analysis. The first type of query failure involves a query violating the global knowledge. In this case, the system will respond with a message indicating why the query is conceptually ill-formed in this domain. The other type of failure involves not finding the information requested in the scene model. In this case, rather than simply responding "not present",

the system may ask the user whether a new view of the scene should be analyzed.

5. Discussion

This paper has presented LandScan, a prototype integrated system under development that covers most of the different levels of vision and natural language processing. It may be used both to guide the low-level vision processing, and to provide communication of visual information to a user. While LandScan is not complete in the sense that all of it is successfully implemented, it provides a computational model for a vision system guided by natural language.

In summary, the data-driven subsystem of LandScan takes stereo images and builds a surface graph representing three-dimensional geometric and topological attributes. The query-driven modules recognize objects and build a Scene Model which represents the user's interest in the image.

The natural language interface which uses the scene representation still has to be designed. It must be able to apply locative linguistic constructs to some representation of visual data and reason about this data. When this is operative, the scene analysis will be truly query-driven and the goals of the system will have been reached.

References

[Bates 81]   Bates, Madeleine. The Theory and Practice of Augmented Transition Network Grammars. In Leonard Bolc (editor), *Natural Language Communication with Computers*. Springer-Verlag, 1981.

[Fischler 83]   Martin Fischler. *Image Understanding Research and its Application to Cartography and Computer-Based Analysis of Aerial Imagery*. Technical Report, SRI International, September, 1983.

[Herman 83]   Herman, Martin, Takeo Kanade, Shigeru Kuroe. The 3D MOSAIC Scene Understanding System. In *Proceedings of the 8th International Joint Conference on Artificial Intelligence*. 1983.

[Herskovits 82]   Herskovits, Annette. *Space and the Prepositions in English: Regularities and Irregularities in a Complex Domain*. PhD thesis, Department of Linguistics, Stanford University, 1982.

[Krotkov 84]   Krotkov, Eric. *Construction of a Three Dimensional Surface Model*. Technical Report MS-CIS-84-40, CIS Department, University of Pennsylvania, 1984.

[Talmy 83]   Talmy, Leonard. *How Language Structures Space*. Technical Report 4, Berkeley Cognitive Science Report, January, 1983.

[Tropf 83]   Tropf and Walters. An ATN for 3-D Recognition of Solids in Single Images. In *Proceedings of the 8th International Joint Conference on Artificial Intelligence*. 1983.

[Winograd 83]   Winograd, Terry. *Language as a Cognitive Process*. Addison-Wesley Publishing Co., 1983.

[Zwarico 84]   Amy Zwarico. *The Recognition and Representation of 3D Images for A Natural Language Driven Scene Analyzer*. Technical Report MS-CIS-84-29, University of Pennsylvania, 1984.

LEARNING SHAPE DESCRIPTIONS

Jonathan H. Connell and Michael Brady

Massachusetts Institute of Technology, Artificial Intelligence Laboratory
545 Technology Square, Cambridge MA 02139

ABSTRACT

We report on initial experiments with an implemented learning system whose inputs are images of two-dimensional shapes. The system first builds semantic network shape descriptions based on Brady's *smoothed local symmetry* representation. It learns shape models from them using a modified version of Winston's *ANALOGY* program. The learning program uses only positive examples, and is capable of learning disjunctive concepts. We discuss the learnability of shape descriptions.

1. Introduction

We report on initial experiments with an implemented system that learns two-dimensional shapes from images. The system first builds semantic network descriptions of the imaged shape based on Brady's *smoothed local symmetry* representation [Brady and Asada 1984, Heide 1984]. It learns shape models from the descriptions using a modified version of Winston's *ANALOGY* program [Winston 1980, 1981, 1982; Winston, Binford, Katz, and Lowry 1984]. The inputs to the program are grey-scale images of real objects, such as tools, model airplanes, and model animals. The outputs of the program are production rules that constitute a procedure for recognising subsequent instances of a taught concept.

Figure 1a shows the gray-scale image of (a model of) a Boeing 747, Figure 1b shows the results of Brady's smoothed local symmetries program, and Figure 1c shows a portion of the semantic network that is computed from them by our program. The semantic network is transformed into a set of associative triples [Doyle and Katz 1985] and input to our learning program. The 747 generates 239 associative triples. Similarly, Figure 2a shows the subshapes found from the smoothed local symmetries of a tack hammer and Figure 2b shows the full semantic net for this image. The tack hammer generates 51 associative triples.

The learning program is a modification of Winston's *ANALOGY* [Connell 1985]. It is capable of learning concepts containing disjunctions. The program learns shape models using positive examples only. Figure 3b shows the concept *hammer* that is learned from the three positive instances shown in Figure 3a.

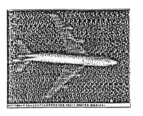

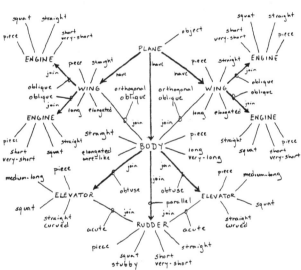

Figure 1. a. The input image. b. The smoothed local symmetries of the plane. c. A portion of the hierarchical semantic network that is computed from the information in b. The full network generates 239 associative triples.

The novelty of our work is the ability to learn visual shape representations from real visual data. Previous work has not been based on real data because such data was unavailable or too complex and unstructured for existing learning algorithms. However, recent developments in edge-detection [Canny 1983] and middle-level vision [Brady and Asada 1984] have provided a solid base on which to build a robust vision system. Using this system we can generate shape descriptions in a form amenable to learning. Furthermore, although the descriptions typically comprise between fifty and three hundred assertions, various forms of abstraction keep this volume of data manageable.

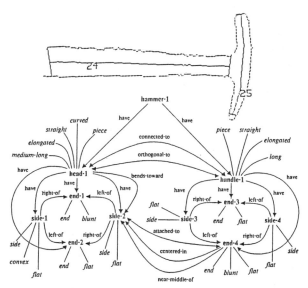

Figure 2. a. The main smoothed local symmetries computed from the results of Brady's program. b. The semantic network that is computed from the information in a.

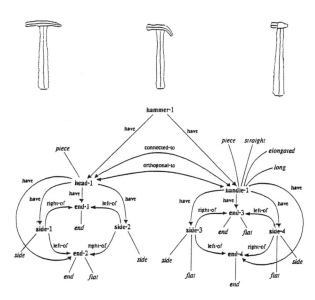

Figure 3. The concept *hammer* that is learned from the three positive instances shown above.

2. Representing Shape

To describe an object it is necessary to first segment it into separate subshapes. In terms of the mathematical analysis in [Brady and Asada 1984], a subshape is defined as maximal with respect to smooth variations in the defining parameters. For example, the portions of fuselage in front of and behind the wings of the B747 in Figure 2 are joined, but the handle and blade of a screwdriver are perceived as separate pieces. Once a part has been found, its shape is specified by three numbers: the aspect ratio, the curvature of the axis, and the change in width along the axis.

Joins between subshapes are determined by examining the spines of the regions and the adjacency of the contour segments. A join is specified by the relative angle and sizes of the pieces, and the location of join with respect to each piece. Few previous representations of shape have described subshape joins. For example, *ACRONYM* [Brooks 1981, Brooks and Binford 1980] specified the coordinate transformation between two joined pieces, but did not explicitly describe the join.

Once we break the image into pieces and find the joins we must somehow represent this information. Images are noisy, so it is necessary to develop representations that are stable, in the sense of being invariant under localized changes such as image noise. However, tasks involving visual representations, for example inspection, often require that programs be sensitive to fine detail. A variety of techniques for simultaneously achieving stability and sensitivity have been proposed, each expressing some aspect of hierarchical description. The underlying idea is that gross levels of a hierarchy provide a stable base for the representation, while finer levels increase sensitivity.

A vision program needs to maintain several different representational hierarchies, including the following:

• Numeric values and symbolic descriptors

Specifying a shape parameter of interest, say a measure of the elongation of a shape, by a numerical value is sensitive, but highly unstable. Symbolic names that correspond to an interval of numeric values are (usually) more stable but less sensitive. Our representation employs symbolic descriptors that have overlapping ranges. For example, an end which is determined to be on the borderline between blunt and sharp is declared to be both blunt and sharp. Overlaps like this help to combat the quantization error introduced by encoding a continuous range as a set of discrete symbolic values. A small change in value leads to a small change in the representation.

• Structural approximations to shapes

Marr and Nishihara [1978] proposed summarizing the lesser subparts of an object, leaving them unspecified until they are needed. For example, all airplanes have a fuselage, with pairs of symmetrically attached wings and elevators. Upon closer examination, a wing of a B747 has two attached engine pods, a DC10 has one, and an L1011 none. Suppressing mention of the engine subshapes, as well as summarizing the parameters that describe the shapes of the wings and fuselage, enables the descriptions of the three airplanes to closely match each other.

In general, larger subshapes tend to determine gross categorization, and so they tend to appear higher in the structural hierarchy. Conversely, smaller subshapes tend to allow finer discrimination and occur lower in the hierarchy. The smaller subparts of a tool typically determine the specific function of the tool. For example, deciding whether a tool is an awl, a gimlet, or a Phillips screwdriver involves looking closely at the end of the blade; the relatively localized *context* of the business end of the blade is established by the grosser levels of the hierarchy, where it is recognized (for example) that the tool is not a hammer or wrench. In this way, the Marr-Nishihara proposal tends (heuristically) to relate large scale geometric structure to gross functional use.

● **A-kind-of hierarchies**

Family hierarchies are ubiquitous, and apply as much to visual shape representations as to the more cognitive situations in which they were developed in Artificial Intelligence. *ACRONYM* represents the fact that the sets of B747-SPs, B747s, wide-bodied jets, jets, and aircraft, are ordered by subset inclusion. Similarly, a claw hammer is a-kind-of framing hammer, which is a-kind-of hammer. In general, a subset hierarchy is a partially-ordered set, but not a tree. From the domain of tools, for example, a shingle ax is both a-kind-of ax, and a-kind-of hammer.

3. Learning

The commonest form of inductive generalization used to learn concepts from positive examples is the *drop condition* heuristic [Dietterich and Michalski 1981, Winston 1984, page 398]. This is the method used in our program. Through careful design of the representation the method has been extended to allow generalizations of intervals and structural graphs.

The idea behind the heuristic is that if two things belong to the same class then the differences between them must be irrelevant. Accordingly, when we have a partial model of a concept and receive a new example, we modify the model by deleting all the differences between it and the example. This can be seen by comparing Figure 2b with Figure 3b. Notice that the network in Figure 3 puts very little constraint on the size or shape of the head. This is because the shapes of the heads in the examples vary widely. For instance, the heads of the first and third hammer are straight while the head of the second hammer is curved. Note also that the manner in which the handle joins the head is only loosely specified. This is because the handle is joined to the side of the head in the first two examples but to the end of the head in the third example.

This is a simplified explanation of the learning algorithm. The matching involved is not graph isomorphism nor is it merely counting the number of required features an object has. Rather it is a complex local matching scheme. Consider using the semantic net shown in Figure 1 as the model for the *airplane* concept. For an object to match this model, at the top level it must have three pieces which look similar to the three in the model. A piece of the example is similar to the wing model if, first of all, it has the shape specified in the network and, second, it has two things which look like engines attached to it. Suppose that a certain piece has the right shape for a wing but has only one engine attached to it. At the level

of the wing model the program notices that there is a discrepancy yet judges that the piece is still close enough to the description to be called a wing. When the top level of the matcher asks if the piece in question looks like a wing the answer is "yes". No mention is made of the fact that the wing is missing an engine. The difference only matters locally and is isolated from the higher levels of matching.

Another important concern is limiting the scope of generalizations made. Imagine that the program is shown a positive example that is substantially different from its current model. Altering the model by the usual induction heuristics typically leads to gross over-generalization. This, in turn, runs counter to what Winston [1984, page 401] has dubbed *Martin's law*, namely: learning should proceed in small steps. Therefore our program creates a new, separate model based on the new example, splitting the concept being taught into a disjunction.

In some cases, the disjunction will be replaced by a single model as positive examples are taught that are intermediate to the disjuncts. For example, suppose that the first example of a hammer shown to the program is a claw hammer, and that the second is a sledge hammer. The program will create a disjunction as its concept of hammer, but it will be consolidated into a single model once it has seen such examples as a mallet and ballpein hammer.

Even though the program only generalizes a concept using an example that is structurally similar, it is sometimes deceived and must recover from over-generalization. We follow Winston [1984] and provide censors that override the offending rule. Censors can be generalized and there can be disjunctive censors; in fact this is the usual case. Since censors can be generalized they also have the possibility of being over-generalized. This is countered by putting censors on the censors. In general, a concept is not represented by a single model but by a group of models. There can be several positive models corresponding to the disjuncts as well as several negative non-models summarizing the exceptions to the other models.

4. Current Work

The goals of our research are not limited to learning. The work reported here forms part of the *Mechanic's Mate* project [Brady, Agre, Braunegg, and Connell 1984], which is intended to assist a handyman in generic assembly and construction tasks. The primary goal of that project is to understand the interplay between reasoning that involves tools and fasteners and representations of their shape.

For example, instead of learning that a certain geometric structure is called a hammer, we learn that something which has a graspable portion and a striking surface can be used as a hammer. These two functional concepts are then defined geometrically in terms of the shape representation. Reasoning from function as well as from form allows more flexibility. For instance, faced with a hammering task, but no hammer, one might try mapping the hammer structure onto that of any available tool. A screw driver provides a good match, identifying the blade of a screw driver with the handle of the hammer, and the (assumed flat) side of the screw driver handle with the striking surface of the head of the hammer. In this way, the Mechanic's Mate can suggest improvisations, like using a screw driver as a hammer.

Our initial goal was to learn shape models cast in the representation described previously. Eventually, the *Mechanic's Mate* will have to learn about the non-geometric properties of objects: weight, material type, and the processes that use them. Currently we are using Katz's English interface [Katz and Winston 1983] to tell our program such things. This is not satisfactory. Instead, we hope to teach dynamic information using a robot arm and hand.

Another area of interest is inducing structural subclasses from examples. Since the subclasses that form the a-kind-of hierarchy are an important part of the shape representation, they should be learnable. However, in learning subclasses there is a danger of combinatorial explosion. Learning subclasses requires a suitable similarity metric. Feature-based pattern recognition systems learn subclasses as clusters in feature space, and clusters are sets that are dense with respect to the Euclidean metric. Part of our research in learning shape descriptions has been to determine what makes objects look similar. This suggests using the metric employed in the learning procedure to form subclasses through a process analogous to feature space clustering. This is the focus of our current work.

5. Acknowledgements

This report describes research done at the Artificial Intelligence Laboratory of the Massachusetts Institute of Technology. Support for the Laboratory's Artificial Intelligence research is provided in part by the the System Development Foundation, the Advanced Research Projects Agency of the Department of Defense under Office of Naval Research contract N00014-80-C-0505, and the Office of Naval Research under contract number N00014-77-C-0389. We thank the people who have commented on the ideas presented in this paper, particularly Phil Agre, Steve Bagley, Bob Berwick, Ben DuBoulay, Alan Bundy, Margaret Fleck, Scott Heide, Boris Katz, Tomás Lozano-Pérez, John Mallery, Tom Mitchell, Sharon Salveter, Dan Weld, and Patrick Winston.

References

Brady, Michael, and Asada, Haruo, [1984], "Smoothed Local Symmetries and their Implementation," *Int. J. Robotics Research*, **3** (3) .

Brady, Michael, Agre, Philip, Braunegg, David J., and Connell, Jonathan H., [1984], The Mechanic's Mate, **ECAI 84: Advances in Artificial Intelligence**, O'Shea, T. (ed.), Elsevier Science Publishers B.V. (North-Holland).

Brooks, Rodney A., [1981], "Symbolic Reasoning Among 3-D Models and 2-D Images," *Artif. Intell.*, **17**, 285 – 348 .

Brooks, Rodney A., and Binford, Thomas O., [1980], Representing and Reasoning About Partially Specified Scenes, *Proceedings, DARPA Image Understanding Workshop*, Baumann, Lee S. (ed.), Science Applications Inc., 150 –156.

Canny, John Francis, [1983], Finding Edges and Lines in Images, MIT Artificial Intelligence Laboratory, Cambridge Mass., AI-TR-720.

Connell, Jonathan H., [1985], forthcoming SM thesis, MIT Department of Electrical Engineering.

Dietterich, T. G., and Michalski, R. S, [1981], "Inductive Learning of Structural Descriptions," *Artif. Intell.*, **16** .

Doyle, Richard J., and Katz, B, [1985], Exploring the Boundary Between Natural Language and Knowledge Representation, MIT Artificial Intelligence Laboratory, Forthcoming AI Memo.

Heide, S, [1984], A Hierarchical Representation of Shape, SM thesis, MIT Department of Mechanical Engineering.

Katz, Boris, and Winston, Patrick H, [1983], A Two-way Natural Language Interface, *Integrated Interactive Computing Systems* P. Degano and Erik Sandewall (eds.), North-Holland, Amsterdam.

Marr, D., and Nishihara, H. K, [1978], "Representation and Recognition of the Spatial Organisation of Three Dimensional Shapes," *Proc. Roy. Soc. Lond. B*, **200** , 269 – 294.

Winston, Patrick H., [1980], "Learning and Reasoning by Analogy," *Comm. ACM*, **23** , 689 – 703.

Winston, Patrick H., [1981], "Learning New Principles from Precedents and Exercises," *Artif. Intell.*, **19** , 321 – 350.

Winston, Patrick H., [1982], Learning by Augmenting Rules and Accumulating Censors, MIT Artificial Intelligence Laboratory, AIM-678.

Winston, Patrick H., [1984], *Artificial Intelligence, 2nd. Ed.*, Addison-Wesley, Reading, Ma..

Winston, Patrick H., Binford, Thomas O., Katz, B., and Lowry, M., [1984], Learning Physical Descriptions from Functional Definitions, examples, and precedents, Robotics Research, Michael Brady and Richard Paul (eds.), MIT Press, Cambridge, 117 – 135.

Shape from texture

John Aloimonos and Michael J. Swain
Department of Computer Science
The University of Rochester
Rochester, N.Y. 14627

Abstract

Measurements on image texture interpreted under an approximate perspective image model can be used with an iterative constraint propagation algorithm to determine surface orientation. An extension of the ideas allows their robust application to natural images of textured planes. The techniques are demonstrated on synthetic and natural images.

1. Introduction

The recovery of 3-D (shape) information from a two dimensional image is an important task in image understanding. "Shape from ..." algorithms exist for intensity, motion, contour, and texture. This work extends work on *Shape from Texture*. The shape from texture problem has been studied extensively. Gibson (1950) first proposed the texture density gradient as the primary basis of surface perception by humans. Following Gibson's ideas, Bajcsy and Lieberman (1976) tried a heuristic use of the two dimensional Fourier spectrum to detect the gradient.

To formalize the shape from texture problem requires a model for the image formation system. Up to now three kinds of projections have been used: orthographic, perspective and spherical projection. Kender (1980), Kanade (1979) and Witkin (1981) studied the problem under orthographic projection, and Kender (1980) and Ohta (1981) address the problem under perspective projection. Ikeuchi (1984) used spherical projection. In his work the texture elements had to be **known** and **symmetrical**.

Our algorithm determines surface orientation from the apparent distortion of patterns on the image, provided that:

(1) The surface in view is smooth and is covered with uniformly repeated texture elements. All the texture elements on the surface are identical. These texture elements we call texels. The shape of the texels is of no importance for our theory.

(2) Each texture element is assumed to lie on a plane (i.e. we assume that the surface in view is locally planar). This means that the size of the texels on the surface has to be small compared with a change of surface orientation there.

(3) The scene texture is imaged under an approximation to perspective projection similar to that of Ohta (1981). This projection preserves important perspective distortions but is computationally tractable.

Under the above assumptions, we develop a new gradient map that will enable us to define a "textural reflectance function.". Our theory is very similar to earlier work on Shape from Shading (Horn, 1977; Ikeuchi, 1981), with the image intensity at a point replaced with the area of the image texel at that point.

2. Mathematical preliminaries

In this section we define a way to approximate the distortion of a texel under perspective projection by a 2-D affine transformation.

2.1 Approximation of the perspective projection by a 2-D affine transformation

Let a coordinate system OXYZ be fixed with respect to the camera, with the -Z axis pointing along the optical axis, and O the nodal point of the eye (center of the lens). The image plane is assumed to be perpendicular to the Z axis at the point (0,0,-1), (i.e. focal length = 1).

Under perspective projection, a point of the object surface is projected onto the image plane by a projecting ray defined by that point and the center of the lens.

Our approximation is done by dividing the projection process into two steps. (See figure 1). Consider a textured surface S in the world and a texel T on the surface, lying in a local plane Q with orientation given by the surface gradients (p,q). Consider also a plane γ, parallel to the image plane and just in front of the surface S. The plane γ has distance β from the origin, (i.e. its equation is $-Z = \beta$).

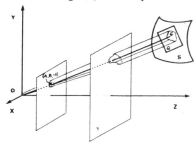

Figure 1

The steps of the projection process of the texel T onto the image plane are as follows:

(1) The surface texel is projected onto the plane γ. This projection is performed parallel to the ray OG, where G is the mass center of the texel T. (Thus the image of the mass center of the texel is on the projected mass center of the texel, and the projection is parallel to the direction (A,B,-1) where (A,B) is the image of the mass center of the texel T).

(2) The image on the plane γ is projected perspectively onto the image plane. Since the plane γ is parallel to the image plane, this perspective transformation is just a reduction by a factor of $1/\beta$.

Step 1 skews the image to account for foreshortening, and step 2 scales the image in a location-depth dependent manner, as does perspective. The combined process is an affine transformation.

To represent the original pattern of the surface texel, we use an (a,b,c) coordinate system, with its origin at the mass center of the texel and the (a,b) plane identical to the plane Q. To represent the pattern of the image texel, we use an (a',b',c') coordinate system, with its origin the point (A,B,-1), i.e. the mass center of the image texel, and the axes a',b',c' parallel to the axes X,Y,Z respectively. Then the transformation from (a,b) to (a',b') with the two step projection process of previous section is given by the affine transformation.

$$\begin{bmatrix} a' & b' \end{bmatrix} = \begin{bmatrix} a & b \end{bmatrix} \frac{1}{\beta} \begin{bmatrix} \dfrac{-1+pA}{\sqrt{1+p^2}} & \dfrac{pB}{\sqrt{(1+p^2)}} \\ \dfrac{q(p+A)}{\sqrt{(1+p^2)(1+p^2+q^2)}} & \dfrac{qB-p^2-1}{\sqrt{(1+p^2)(1+p^2+q^2)}} \end{bmatrix}$$

It is clear that this transformation is the relation between two 2-D patterns, one in the 3-D space and the other its image on the image plane. We now use the above affine transformation to develop the desired constraint.

2.2   The constraint

The determinant of the matrix of an affine transformation is equal to the ratio of the areas of the two patterns before and after the transformation. Specifically, if S_W is the area of a world texel that lies on a plane with gradient (p,q) and S_I is the area of its image that has mass center (A,B), then we have:

$$\frac{S_I}{S_W} = \frac{1}{\beta^2} \det \begin{bmatrix} \dfrac{-1+pA}{\sqrt{1+p^2}} & \dfrac{pB}{\sqrt{(1+p^2)}} \\ \dfrac{q(p+A)}{\sqrt{(1+p^2)(1+p^2+q^2)}} & \dfrac{qB-p^2-1}{\sqrt{(1+p^2)(1+p^2+q^2)}} \end{bmatrix}$$

or

$$S_I = \frac{S_W}{\beta^2} \cdot \frac{1-Ap-Bq}{\sqrt{1+p^2+q^2}} \tag{1}$$

Equation (1) relates the area of a world texel S_W, its gradient (p,q), the area S_I of its image and its mass center (A,B). If we call the quantity S_I "textural intensity," and the quantity S_W/β^2 "textural albedo," then equation (1) is very similar to the image irradiance equation

$$I = \lambda \frac{1+Ap+Bq}{\sqrt{1+p^2+q^2}}$$

where I is the intensity, (p,q) the gradient of the surface point whose image has intensity I, λ is the albedo at that point and (A,B,1) the direction of the light source (Horn, 1977; Ikeuchi, 1981).

Thus equation (1) can be used to recover surface orientation, using methods that have been discovered for the solution of the shape from shading problem (Ikeuchi, 1981).

2.3   A gradient map

Equation (1) of the previous section can be written as :

$$I = R(p,q) \tag{2}$$

where I is the textural intensity, i.e. the area of an image texel with mass center (A,B), and

$$R(p,q) = \lambda \cdot \frac{1-Ap-Bq}{\sqrt{1+p^2+q^2}}$$

with λ the textural albedo, i.e. the quantity S_W/β^2, and (p,q) the gradient of the plane on which the world texel lies. The function R(p,q) we call **textural reflectance**. If we fix the albedo λ, and the position (A,B) of the texel on the image, then equation (2) can be represented conveniently as a series of contours of constant textural intensity. Figure 2 illustrates such a simple textural reflectance map.

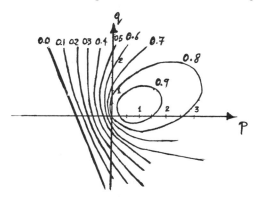

Fig. 2: The textural reflectance map for a point $(A,B) = (-.7,-.3)$ with textural albedo $\lambda = 1$. The reflectance map is plotted as a series of contours spaced one unit apart.

2.4   Recovering the textural albedo

We use equation (2) of the previous section to recover the local surface orientation. No matter what method we use we must know the textural albedo $\lambda = S_W/\beta^2$.

We cannot know β from a static monocular view; neither can we know S_W in general. But it turns out that we can compute approximately the ratio S_W/β^2, i.e. the textural albedo λ.

Consider three neighboring image texels T_1, T_2 and T_3 with areas I_1, I_2 and I_3 and we suppose that the world texels whose images are the texels T_1, T_2 and T_3 lie on the same plane with gradient (p,q). Then the following equations arise:

$$I_1 = \lambda \ (s_1.n) \qquad (3)$$

$$I_2 = \lambda \ (s_2.n) \qquad (4)$$

$$I_3 = \lambda \ (s_3.n) \qquad (5)$$

where $n = (p,q,1)/ \sqrt{1 + p^2 + q^2}$ and $s_i = (-A_i, -B_i, 1)$ for $i = 1,2,3$ and (A_i, B_i) the mass center of texel T_i. Eliminating the textural albedo λ from the equations (3), (4) and (5) we get:

$$n = k[I_1(s_2 \times s_3) + I_2(s_3 \times s_1) + I_3(s_1 \times s_2)]. \qquad (6)$$

$$\lambda = 1/ \ k[s_1, s_2, s_3], \qquad (7)$$

for some constant k that makes n a unit vector, where

$$[s_1, s_2, s_3] = s_1(s_2 \times s_3)$$

and provided that $[s_1,s_2,s_3] \neq 0$, i.e. the vectors s_1, s_2, s_3 are not coplanar (linearly dependent).

The result of equation (7) is approximate due to the hypothesis that three neighboring texels lie on the same plane. But, if we perform this process in all the triples of neighboring points, and we take the average value for the albedo, then the result is highly improved. At the same time, we can get an approximate value for the surface normals at all the texels in the image (equation (6)). Then we can use these initial approximations to start the iterative algorithm that will be introduced in the next section.

2.5 Another way to recover the albedo

Following Ohta *et al.* (1980) and assuming local planarity, i.e. three neighboring texels belong to the same plane which we call Q, we have that:

$$\frac{f_1}{f_2} = \left(\frac{s_1}{s_2}\right)^{\frac{1}{3}}$$

where f_1, f_2 are the distances from two texels to the vanishing line of the plane Q along the line joining the two texels and s_1, s_2 are the areas of the two texels in the image. Since $|f_1 - f_2|$ is just the distance between the two texels in the image and it is known, a point on the vanishing line may be determined. With a third texel, two points may be determined, which give the equation of the vanishing line. Since the equation of the vanishing line of the plane Q is $px + qy = 1$, the orientation of the plane Q can be determined, and from that an approximation of the textural albedo is found.

3. Additional constraints and propagation of the constraints

In this section we introduce the smoothness constraint (Ikeuchi, 1981) and we present an iterative algorithm of the same flavour as the one introduced by Ikeuchi.

3.1 An iterative propagation algorithm

We have already proved that every distortion value (image texel area) for a specific image position corresponds to a contour in the gradient space (See section 3.4). So, the problem has infinite solutions (is "ill-posed") and this is the reason that we introduce the smoothness assumption (a "regularization condition"). A smoothness constraint can be used to reduce the locus of possible orientations to a unique orientation, through an iterative algorithm.

Trying to develop a global error function that should be minimized in order to give the desired value, we measure the departure from smoothness and the error in the textural reflectance equation (equation 2). The error in smoothness we measure (after Ikeuchi, 1981) as follows:

$$s_{i,j} = \frac{(p_{i+1,j}-p_{i,j})^2+(p_{i,j+1}-p_{i,j})^2+(q_{i+1,j}-q_{i,j})^2+(q_{i,j+1}-q_{i,j})^2}{4}$$

where p_{ij} and q_{ij} denote the orientation at the surface point whose image is the point (i,j). The error in the textural reflectance equation, can be given by :

$$e_{i,j} = (I_{i,j} - R(p_{i,j},q_{i,j}))^2$$

where $I_{i,j}$ is the distortion value (texel area) at the point (i,j) and R the textural reflectance.

An acceptable solution should minimize the sum of the error terms in all the grid nodes. If E is such a global error function, then

$$E = \sum_i \sum_j (s_{i,j} + \omega e_{i,j})$$

and the factor ω gives a weight to the errors in the textural gradient map relative to the "distance" from smoothness. To minimize E, we differentiate with respect to $p_{i,j}$ and $q_{i,j}$, and setting the resulting derivatives to zero and rearranging the equations we obtain:

$$p_{i,j} = pa_{i,j} + \omega \ [I_{i,j} - R(p_{i,j},q_{i,j})] \ \partial R/\partial p$$

$$q_{i,j} = qa_{i,j} + \omega \ [I_{i,j} - R(p_{i,j},q_{i,j})] \ \partial R/\partial q$$

where $pa_{i,j}$ and $qa_{i,j}$ are the average values of p and q around the point (i,j) respectively. The above equations suggest an adjustment of p and q in the direction of the gradient of the textural reflectance function, by an amount that is proportional to the error in the textural reflectance equation (equation 2). So it is natural to use the following iterative rule for the estimation of the p and q everywhere in the image:

$$p_{i,j}^{n+1} = pa_{i,j}^n + \omega \ [I_{i,j} - R(p_{i,j}^n, q_{i,j}^n)] \ \partial R/\partial p$$

$$q_{i,j}^{n+1} = qa_{i,j}^n + \omega \ [I_{i,j} - R(p_{i,j}^n, q_{i,j}^n)] \ \partial R/\partial p$$

In the above equations the partial derivatives of the textural reflectance are evaluated on the values of p and q of the n-th iteration. Finally, to avoid numerical instabilities we modify the above formulas to the following form (Ikeuchi & Horn, 1981):

$$p_{i,j}^{n+1} = pa_{i,j}^n + \omega \ [I_{i,j} - R(pa_{i,j}^n, qa_{i,j}^n)] \ \partial R/\partial p$$

$$q_{i,j}^{n+1} = qa_{i,j}^n + \omega \ [I_{i,j} - R(pa_{i,j}^n, qa_{i,j}^n)] \ \partial R/\partial p$$

$R(p_{i,j}, q_{i,j})$ is a function on a four-dimensional space, unlike the R(p,q) of orthographic Shape from Shading. The shading R(p,q) can be determined empirically, but the textural reflectance $R(p_{i,j}, q_{i,j})$ is an analytic, geometrical entity arising from imaging geometry, and thus only the global constant (texture) albedo varies from texture to texture and scene to scene.

4. Experiments

The algorithm was tested on artificial images of a plane, cylinder and sphere. There are four distinct steps into which the program may be broken down:

1)   Location of texels

2)   Minimum triangulation of the texel centers

3)   Calculation of initial orientations and textural albedo.

4)   Iterative process.

In 1), the connected regions in the image are detected. Their centers of gravity are taken to be the locations of the texels. Their size is recorded and the texels which are in the boundary are marked (Ballard & Brown, 1982). In 2), the points denoting the centers of the texels are triangulated so that the sum of the length of the lines is minimum (Aho, Hopcroft & Ullman). In 3), the initial orientations were calculated using the method in Section 3.6. The estimate of λ was calculated from the local orientation with the lowest value of p and q. Due to curvature of the surface, convex objects tend to give an overestimate of λ while concave objects tend to give an underestimate. These errors are minimized when the surface of the object is most nearly perpendicular to the image plane. The algorithm is quite insensitive to initial orientations given to texels whose orientations were allowed to vary through the iterative process. Boundary texels were not allowed to change. The error in calculating their values was the predominant factor in influencing the total error. The iterative process took under 10 iterations. The process always converged for our synthetic images. The final error values were

	fractional error
plane	negligible
sphere	.005
cylinder	.015

The errors in the above table denote the average percent error at each texel. The error at each texel was taken to be

$$1/4\pi \cdot \varphi \;,$$

where φ = solid angle subtended by rotating the calculated orientation about the actual orientation. Figure 3 gives a pictorial description of the error at each texel.

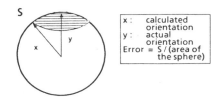

Figure 3.

Finally, azimuthal equidistant coordinates (AEC) were used through the iterative process instead of the gradient space p and q, since AEC change linearly with change in orientation. Figure 4 shows the image of a sphere which is covered with a repeated pattern, Figure 5 shows the reconstructed sphere using the algorithms of Sections 3.5 and 3.6, and Figure 6 shows the reconstructed sphere after the relaxation. Figures 7, 8, and 9 and 10, 11, and 12 show the analogous pictures for a cylinder and plane respectively.

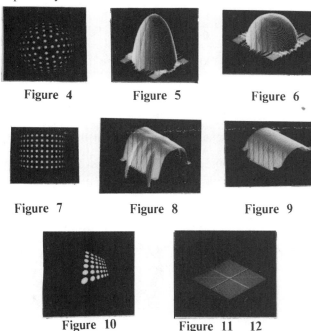

Figure 4   **Figure 5**   **Figure 6**

Figure 7   **Figure 8**   **Figure 9**

Figure 10   **Figure 11   12**

5. An extension to natural images

In natural images, the assumption that the world surface is covered with the same texels is not very realistic. This section refers to recent work by Aloimonos and Chou (1985) on shape from the images of textured planes, based on the uniform density assumption under strong segmentation (identification of texels) and weak segmentation (edge finding). Consider a world plane - z = px + qy + c, and the plane γ passing through the center of mass of a small area s of the world plane. If we consider an area s_I in the image, then in order to find the area in the world plane whose projection is s_I, we must multiply the area s_I with the factor

$$R_I = abs(\frac{c^2\sqrt{1+p^2+q^2}}{(1-Ap-Bq)^3})$$

where (A,B) is the center of gravity of the image area S_I.

5.1 Exploiting the uniform density assumption

The uniform density assumption states that if K, $\wedge$ are any two regions in the world plane and they contain K_1 and K_2 texels respectively, then $K_1/area(K) = K_2/area(\wedge)$. So considering any two regions s_1 and s_2 in the image with areas S_1 and S_2 that contain K_1 and K_2 texels respectively, then under the assumption that the world texels are uniformly distributed, we have $K_1/S_1 R_1 = K_2/S_2 R_2$ with

$$R_1 = abs(\frac{c^2\sqrt{1+p^2+q^2}}{(1-A_1p-B_1q)^3}) \quad and \quad R_2 = abs(\frac{c^2\sqrt{1+p^2+q^2}}{(1-A_2p-B_2q)^3})$$

and (A_1,B_1), (A_2,B_2) the centers of gravity of the image regions S_1 and S_2 respectively.

From this we get:

$$\left[(\frac{K_2}{K_1}\frac{S_1}{S_2})^{\frac{1}{3}}A_2-A_1\right]p+\left[(\frac{K_2}{K_1}\frac{S_1}{S_2})^{\frac{1}{3}}B_2-B_1\right]q = (\frac{K_2}{K_1}\frac{S_1}{S_2})^{\frac{1}{3}}-1,$$

The above equation represents a line in p-q space. Any two regions in the image constrain (p,q) to lie on a line in the gradient space. Thus, taking any two pairs of regions we can solve explicitly for p and q. (To overcome undesirable results due to errors from the digitization process and the density fluctuations of the regions, we employed a least-square-fit mechanism by considering several image pairs. A Hough transform estimation method might also be appropriate.) Figure 13 is the image of a plane parallel to the image plane, covered with random dots (texels). Figure 14 is the image of the dotted plane rotated and translated with tilt = 135° and slant = 30°. Our program, based on the scheme described above, recovered tilt = 134.4° and slant = 29.75°.

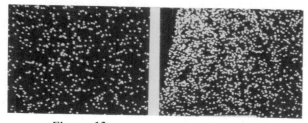

Figure 13   **Figure 14**

5.2 Solving the problem with a weaker segmentation

In the previous section a method was developed to recover the orientation of a textured plane from its image, based on the assumption of uniform texel density; by uniform density, we mean that the number of texels per unit area of the world plane is the same. Application of this method to natural images did not seem to work very well, because no good methods have been developed up to now that can identify texels in an image, and this algorithm depends critically on the number of texels per unit area. On the other hand, in the recent literature

(Bandyopadhyay, 1984; Ballard & Brown, 1982; Marr, 1979) there are several methods for the computation of partial boundaries of the texels (edges) at every point in a textured image. Let us redefine density to be the total length of the texel boundaries per unit area. The uniform density assumption states that this density is the same everywhere in the world plane. This assumption is not far from the previous one and seems to be true for a large subset of natural images, in contrast with Witkin's isotropy assumption, which does not seem to hold true for many natural images. Aloimonos & Chou (1985) describe a method that finds the orientation of the world plane under the new assumption and below we describe expriments based on that method. Figure 15 presents the image of a plane parallel to the image plane, covered with random line segments. Figure 16 presents the image of this plane rotated with tilt = 135° and slant = 30°. The program recovered tilt = 133.77° and slant = 30.40°. Figure 17 presents the image of a plane (parallel to the image plane) covered with randomly generated small circles. Figure 18 presents the image of this plane rotated with tilt = 135° and slant = 30°. The program recoverd tilt = 135.54° and slant = 29.77°. The natural images used were first preprocessed to find the boundaries of texels (edges) by applying the modified Frei-Chen operators introduced by Bandopadhyay (1984). Figure 19 shows the photograph of a textured floor with slant $\simeq$ 45° and tilt $\simeq$ −108°. Figure 20 shows the edges after the proprocessing. The algorithm produced slant = 45.87° and tilt = −109.43°. Finally, Figure 21 shows the photograph of a part of a grass field with slant = 60° and tilt = 0°. Figure 22 shows the images of its edges after the preprocessing. The program recovered slant = 63.057° and tilt = −1.076°.

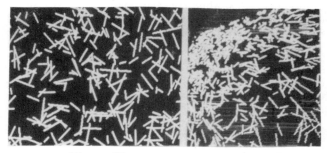

Figure 15   **Figure 16**

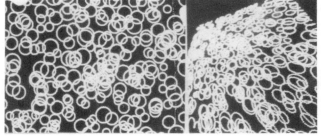

Figure 17   **Figure 18**

Figure 19

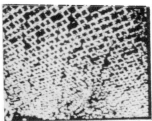

Figure 20

Figure 21

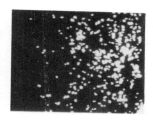

Figure 22.

Aloimonos and Chou (1985) present a theoretical analysis of the error introduced by the affine approximation to the perspective projection.

Conclusion

In this paper we gave a method for "shape from texture" computation that extends results in the literature. Our algorithm can work in a richer domain than already published methods. For reasons involving the cosine foreshortening law, the result here is similar to the original Shape from Shading constraint applied to lambertian surfaces. We believe that this may have some important implications, since for example the same hardware may be used for shape recognition, regardless of whether we use shading or texture. Finally, an extension of the algorithm to a form that works well for many natural images was presented.

Acknowledgments

We would like to thank Christopher Brown for his constructive criticism. Our thanks also go to Dana Ballard, Amit Bandyopadhyay and Paul Chou for their help during the preparation of this paper. This research was sponsored by the National Science Foundation under Grant MCS-8302038.

References

[1] Aho, A.V., Hopcroft, J.E. and Ullman, J.D., *The Design and Analysis of Computer Algorithms*, Addison-Wesley Publishing Co., Reading, MA., 1974.

[2] Aloimonos, J. and Chou, P., "Detection of surface orientation and motion from texture," forthcoming Technical Report, Dept. of Computer Science, Univ. of Rochester.

[3] Bandyopadhyay, A., "Interesting points, disparities and correspondence," *Proceedings*, DARPA Image Understanding Workshop, October 1984.

[4] Bajcsy, R. and Lieberman, L., "Texture gradients as a depth cue," *Comp. Graphics and Image Processing* 5, 1976, 52-67.

[5] Ballard, D.H. and Brown, C.M., *Computer Vision*, Prentice-Hall, Inc., Englewood Cliffs, NJ, 1982.

[6] Gibson, J.J., *The Perception of the Visual World*, Houghton Miffin, Boston, 1950.

[7] Horn, B.K.P., "Understanding image intensities," *Artificial Intelligence* 8, (2), 1977, 201-231.

[8] Ikeuchi, K., "Shape from regular patterns." *Artificial Intelligence* 22, 1984, 49-75.

[9] Ikeuchi, K. and Horn, B.K.P., "Numerical shape from shading and occluding boundaries," *Artificial Intelligence* 17, 1981, 141-184.

[10] Kanade, T., "Recovery of the three dimensional shape of an object from a single view," CMU-CS-79-153, Dept. of Comp. Science, Carnegie-Mellon Univ., 1979.

[11] Kender, J.R., "Shape from texture: an aggregation transform that maps a class of textures into surface orientation," *Proceedings*, IJCAI, 1980, 475-480.

[12] Kender, J.R, "Shape from texture: A computational paradigm," *Proceedings*, DARPA Image Understanding Workshop, April 1979, 79-84.

[13] Marr, D. and Hildreth, H., "A theory of edge detection," AI Memo 518, MIT, 1979.

[14] Ohta, Y., Maenobu, K., and Sakai, T., "Obtaining surface orientation of from texels under perspective projection," *Proceedings*, IJCAI, 1980, 746-751.

[15] Witkin, A., "Recovering surface shape and orientation from texture," *Artificial Intelligence* 17, 1981, 17-45.

SHAPE AND SOURCE FROM SHADING

Michael J. Brooks*
Berthold K.P. Horn

Artificial Intelligence Laboratory
Massachusetts Institute of Technology
Cambridge, Massachusetts, 02139, U.S.A.

Abstract

Well-known methods for solving the shape-from-shading problem require knowledge of the reflectance map. Here we show how the shape-from-shading problem can be solved when the reflectance map is not available, but is known to have a given form with some unknown parameters. This happens, for example, when the surface is known to be Lambertian, but the direction to the light source is not known.

We give an iterative algorithm which alternately estimates the surface shape and the light source direction. Use of the unit normal in parameterizing the reflectance map, rather than the gradient or stereographic coordinates, simplifies the analysis. Our approach also leads to an iterative scheme for computing shape from shading that adjusts the current estimates of the local normals toward or away from the direction of the light source. The amount of adjustment is proportional to the current difference between the predicted and the observed brightness. We also develop generalizations to less constrained forms of reflectance maps.

I. Introduction

Given an image, E, and a reflectance map, R, the shape-from-shading problem may be regarded as that of recovering a smooth surface, $z(x, y)$, satisfying the image irradiance equation

$$E(x, y) = R\left(\frac{\partial z}{\partial x}, \frac{\partial z}{\partial y}\right)$$

over the domain Ω of E. Any given boundary conditions on $z(x, y)$ should also be satisfied. The problem takes the form of a first-order partial differential equation (Horn, 1970 & 1975).

Implicit in this formulation are a number of assumptions, the principal one being that the brightness of a surface patch does not depend on its position in space. Another is that an image depicts a smooth surface of homogeneous reflectance. Several algorithms have been devised to tackle the problem, notably those of Horn (1975), Strat (1979), and Ikeuchi & Horn (1981).

---

*   On leave from:

School of Mathematical Sciences,
Flinders University of South Australia,
Bedford Park, SA 5042, Australia.

One of the many difficulties these schemes face in practice is that the reflectance map is typically not known. The reflectance map specifies how the brightness of a surface patch depends on its orientation under given circumstances. It therefore encodes information about the reflecting properties of the surface, and information about the distribution and intensity of the light sources. In fact, the reflectance map can be computed from the bidirectional reflectance-distribution function and the light source arrangement, as shown by Horn & Sjoberg (1979).

When encountering a new scene, the information required to determine the reflectance map is usually not available. Yet without this information, the shape-from-shading problem cannot be formulated, much less solved. We may resolve this dilemma if a calibration object of known shape appears in the scene, since the reflectance map can be computed from its image. Here we wish to consider the situation where we are not that fortunate.

It is interesting to evaluate how some basic assumptions can resolve this impasse. Pentland (1984) has looked at the problem of recovering shape from shading under the assumption that the image depicts a Lambertian surface illuminated by a point source whose direction is unknown. Under the additional assumption that the surface is locally umbilical, surface normals are shown to be recoverable by a local operation. This method does not depend on the iterative propagation of information across the image.

There are some serious drawbacks to the local approach, however. One problem is that the umbilical assumption is very restrictive. In fact, spheres are the only surfaces whose points are all umbilical. So this method naturally computes incorrect normals for other shapes, although the errors for approximately spherical surfaces, such as ellipsoids of low eccentricity, may be acceptable. Further, the constraining effect of known occluding boundary normals cannot be incorporated into the local method. This is unfortunate because these normals provide powerful boundary conditions on the shape-from-shading problem, as shown by Bruss (1983). Finally, because a local method does not take into account neighbors when calculating the normal at a point, nearby normals may differ a great deal, particularly in the presence of noise.

We now present an alternative approach that does not suffer from these disadvantages.

II. An iterative scheme for shape and source

The task is to recover the shape of a smooth surface depicted in an image, E, that is defined over a region Ω in the xy-plane. Let the shape of the surface be characterized by the function, $\mathbf{n}$, that associates a unit normal with each point in Ω. The problem is therefore to find $\mathbf{n}(x, y)$ over Ω. Assume for now that the object has a Lambertian surface, and that it is illuminated by a single point source. If the vector $\mathbf{s}$ points to the source, and $\mathbf{n}(x, y)$ is the unit normal of a surface patch, then the apparent brightness of the patch is given by the reflectance map

$$R_{\mathbf{s}}(\mathbf{n}(x, y)) = \mathbf{n}(x, y)\cdot\mathbf{s}.$$

We do not, by the way, force $\mathbf{s}$ to be a unit vector; this allows for the possibility that the intensity of the source may be unknown. This way we can also deal with unknown sensor sensitivity and unknown surface albedo, provided it is uniform.

Our problem is now to find a smooth shape, $\mathbf{n}$, and source direction, $\mathbf{s}$, satisfying the image irradiance equation

$$E(x, y) = \mathbf{n}(x, y)\cdot\mathbf{s} \qquad \forall (x, y) \in \Omega.$$

In practice, brightness cannot be determined with perfect accuracy, and so it appears reasonable to transform this into a minimization problem (Ikeuchi & Horn, 1981; Horn & Brooks, 1985). There is another reason to consider this as a minimization problem: if we simply try to solve the image irradiance equation as it stands, we obtain a set of differential equations equivalent to the characteristic strip equations. Here, however, we seek an iterative scheme lending itself to a parallel implementation on a grid, as originally suggested by Horn (1970). Further, a shape-from-shading problem that has noisy image data may well not have a theoretical solution. A minimization approach will, however, enable the recovery of a shape that fits the given data best, in a sense determined by the functional chosen.

We seek a smooth shape, $\mathbf{n}$, and a source direction, $\mathbf{s}$, that minimize

$$\iint_{\Omega} (E(x, y) - \mathbf{n}(x, y)\cdot\mathbf{s})^2 \, dx\, dy.$$

If a solution exists, and there are no errors in brightness measurements, then the image irradiance equation will have been satisfied (although there is no guarantee that the resulting $\mathbf{n}$ will be integrable; see Horn & Brooks, 1985). We adopt a regularizing component (Poggio & Torre, 1984) by incorporating the expression

$$\iint_{\Omega} (\mathbf{n}_x^2(x, y) + \mathbf{n}_y^2(x, y)) \, dx\, dy,$$

which is intended to select a particularly smooth solution from a possibly infinite set of candidates. Note that a subscript here denotes partial differentiation, and that squaring a vector is equivalent to taking the dot-product with itself. Finally, we wish to insist that normals have unit length. This is accomplished with the constraint

$$\mathbf{n}^2(x, y) = 1 \qquad \forall (x, y) \in \Omega.$$

Combining the three terms gives the composite functional

$$I(\mathbf{n}, \mathbf{s}) = \iint_{\Omega} (E - \mathbf{n}\cdot\mathbf{s})^2 + \lambda(\mathbf{n}_x^2 + \mathbf{n}_y^2) + \mu(x, y)(\mathbf{n}^2 - 1) \, dx\, dy$$

which is to be minimized with respect to $\mathbf{n}$ and $\mathbf{s}$. Here, λ is a scalar that weights the relative importance of the regularization term, while $\mu(x, y)$ is a Lagrangian multiplier function used to impose the constraint that $\mathbf{n}(x, y)$ be a unit vector (see Horn & Brooks, 1985).

Minimizing I is a problem in the calculus of variations. First assume that $\mathbf{s}$ is known and that minimization is to be achieved by a suitable choice of $\mathbf{n}$. Extrema of functionals are obtained by examining solutions to the associated Euler equations (see Courant & Hilbert, 1953). The functional

$$\iint_{\Omega} F(x, y, \mathbf{n}, \mathbf{n}_x, \mathbf{n}_y) \, dx\, dy$$

has the Euler equation

$$F_{\mathbf{n}} - \frac{\partial}{\partial x} F_{\mathbf{n}_x} - \frac{\partial}{\partial y} F_{\mathbf{n}_y} = \mathbf{0}.$$

So, by substitution, it follows that I has the Euler equation

$$(E - \mathbf{n}\cdot\mathbf{s})\mathbf{s} + \lambda\nabla^2\mathbf{n} - \mu\mathbf{n} = \mathbf{0},$$

where

$$\nabla^2 = \frac{\partial^2}{\partial x^2} + \frac{\partial^2}{\partial y^2}.$$

Now, a discrete approximation to the Laplacian operator is given by

$$\left\{\nabla^2\mathbf{n}\right\}_{ij} \approx \frac{4}{\epsilon^2}(\bar{\mathbf{n}}_{ij} - \mathbf{n}_{ij}),$$

in which ϵ is the distance between adjacent picture cells in the image, and $\bar{\mathbf{n}}_{ij}$ is the local average of normals

$$\bar{\mathbf{n}}_{ij} = \tfrac{1}{4}(\mathbf{n}_{i,j+1} + \mathbf{n}_{i,j-1} + \mathbf{n}_{i+1,j} + \mathbf{n}_{i-1,j}).$$

Hence we may translate the Euler equation into the discrete form

$$(E_{ij} - \mathbf{n}_{ij}\cdot\mathbf{s})\mathbf{s} + \frac{4\lambda}{\epsilon^2}(\bar{\mathbf{n}}_{ij} - \mathbf{n}_{ij}) - \mu_{ij}\mathbf{n}_{ij} = \mathbf{0}.$$

Rearranging this in order to isolate $\mathbf{n}_{ij}$ on one side yields the iterative scheme

$$\mathbf{n}_{ij}^{k+1} = \frac{1}{1 + \mu_{ij}(\epsilon^2/4\lambda)}\left(\bar{\mathbf{n}}_{ij}^k + \frac{\epsilon^2}{4\lambda}(E_{ij} - \mathbf{n}_{ij}^k\cdot\mathbf{s})\mathbf{s}\right),$$

which computes shape given direction of the light source. Other approximations for the Laplacian may lead to improved results, at the cost of increased computation. For example, if we use the more accurate 9-point approximation for the Laplacian, in which

$$\bar{\mathbf{n}}_{ij} = \tfrac{1}{20}[4(\mathbf{n}_{i,j+1} + \mathbf{n}_{i,j-1} + \mathbf{n}_{i+1,j} + \mathbf{n}_{i-1,j})$$
$$+ (\mathbf{n}_{i-1,j-1} + \mathbf{n}_{i-1,j+1} + \mathbf{n}_{i+1,j+1} + \mathbf{n}_{i+1,j-1})],$$

then twice as many array accesses are needed (and the constant multiplier $\epsilon^2/4\lambda$ becomes $3\epsilon^2/10\lambda$). The simple 5-point approximation was adequate for our purposes.

Note that we have yet to solve for μ, the Lagrangian multiplier. This can be avoided, however, by observing that the division of the right hand side by $(1 + \mu(\epsilon^2/4\lambda))$ does not change the direction of the vector being computed.

Since μ is intended to ensure that the result is normalized, we can simply do this explicitly, as in

$$\begin{cases} \mathbf{m}_{ij}^{k+1} = \bar{\mathbf{n}}_{ij}^k + \dfrac{\epsilon^2}{4\lambda}(E_{ij} - \mathbf{n}_{ij}^k\!\cdot\!\mathbf{s})\mathbf{s} \\[2mm] \mathbf{n}_{ij}^{k+1} = \mathbf{m}_{ij}^{k+1}/|\mathbf{m}_{ij}^{k+1}|. \end{cases}$$

Now consider the problem of minimizing I with respect to $\mathbf{s}$, given that $\mathbf{n}$ is known. This is a problem in conventional calculus. Computing the partial derivative of I with respect to $\mathbf{s}$, we have

$$\frac{\partial I}{\partial \mathbf{s}} = -\iint_\Omega 2(E - \mathbf{n}\!\cdot\!\mathbf{s})\mathbf{n}\,dx\,dy = \mathbf{0},$$

and so

$$-\iint_\Omega E\,\mathbf{n}\,dx\,dy + \iint_\Omega (\mathbf{n}\!\cdot\!\mathbf{s})\mathbf{n}\,dx\,dy = \mathbf{0}.$$

Noting that

$$(\mathbf{n}\!\cdot\!\mathbf{s})\mathbf{n} = (\mathbf{n}^T\mathbf{s})\mathbf{n} = \mathbf{n}(\mathbf{n}^T\mathbf{s}) = (\mathbf{n}\mathbf{n}^T)\mathbf{s},$$

then by substitution we have

$$\iint_\Omega E\,\mathbf{n}\,dx\,dy = \left[\iint_\Omega \mathbf{n}\mathbf{n}^T\,dx\,dy\right]\mathbf{s},$$

where $(\mathbf{n}\mathbf{n}^T)$, and also the integral of $(\mathbf{n}\mathbf{n}^T)$, are 3×3 matrices. From this we finally obtain the desired equation

$$\mathbf{s} = \left[\iint_\Omega \mathbf{n}\mathbf{n}^T\,dx\,dy\right]^{-1} \iint_\Omega E\,\mathbf{n}\,dx\,dy.$$

Here $^{-1}$ denotes the inverse of a matrix. A discrete version of this formula, in which the integrals are replaced by sums, is easily obtained. An iterative scheme in both $\mathbf{n}$ and $\mathbf{s}$ is then within grasp:

$$\begin{cases} \mathbf{m}_{ij}^{k+1} = \bar{\mathbf{n}}_{ij}^k + \dfrac{\epsilon^2}{4\lambda}(E_{ij} - \mathbf{n}_{ij}^k\!\cdot\!\mathbf{s}^k)\mathbf{s}^k \\[2mm] \mathbf{n}_{ij}^{k+1} = \mathbf{m}_{ij}^{k+1}/|\mathbf{m}_{ij}^{k+1}| \\[2mm] \mathbf{s}^{k+1} = \Big[\displaystyle\sum_{i,j\in\Omega} \mathbf{n}_{ij}^{k+1}\mathbf{n}_{ij}^{k+1\,T}\Big]^{-1} \displaystyle\sum_{i,j\in\Omega} E_{ij}\,\mathbf{n}_{ij}^{k+1}. \end{cases}$$

This takes advantage of the fact that $\mathbf{s}$ need not be a unit vector. If the brightness of the source is known, we can normalize $\mathbf{s}$ so that it is a unit vector. Then the determination of $\mathbf{s}$ becomes slightly more complex, since it involves a constrained minimization.

III. Properties and performance of the scheme

The iterative scheme has two components: one concerned with the recovery of shape, the other concerned with the determination of the source direction. The shape-recovery component has an intuitively satisfying form. In essence, a new normal is computed by taking a local average, and adjusting this either toward or away from the source. The magnitude and sign of the adjustment is determined by the brightness error of the current estimate.

For a given shape, a new source direction is computed by a single pass through the image; unlike shape-recovery,

no iteration is necessary. The 3×3 matrix $(\mathbf{n}\mathbf{n}^T)$ is summed across the image, as is the vector $(E\,\mathbf{n})$. The source direction can then be computed using Gaussian elimination or even Cramer's method (see Korn and Korn, 1968). The source-recovery component has been tested on a number of images and shapes. When the data are free of noise, the estimate of source direction is extremely accurate. Furthermore, estimates remain very good in the face of significant noise. For example, a synthetic image was generated of a sphere illuminated by a point source in the direction $(-4, 3, 8)^T$. The image was quantized at 255 irradiance levels, and the correct surface normal was given for each of the 1250 image points. Gaussian noise was added to the image giving an average perturbation in irradiance values of 34. Despite this, the source-finder computed an estimate of source direction that was only $2.7°$ in error. Further trials gave similar results.

The source-direction estimates are robust because the whole image is used. Theoretically, the problem is highly over-determined as source direction can be recovered from brightness values of only three different surface orientations. Using the whole image ensures, however, that noise effects are significantly reduced.

The shape-and-source-from-shading problem for a point light source and Lambertian surface has a natural two-way ambiguity. If the image irradiance equation is satisfied over Ω by the shape $\mathbf{n}_1$ and the source direction $\mathbf{s}_1$, it will also be satisfied by the dual shape $\mathbf{n}_2$ and source direction $\mathbf{s}_2$ where

$$\mathbf{n}_2 = 2\hat{\mathbf{z}}(\mathbf{n}_1\!\cdot\!\hat{\mathbf{z}}) - \mathbf{n}_1 \qquad \text{and} \qquad \mathbf{s}_2 = 2\hat{\mathbf{z}}(\mathbf{s}_1\!\cdot\!\hat{\mathbf{z}}) - \mathbf{s}_1,$$

and $\hat{\mathbf{z}}$ is the viewing direction. Here, both source direction and surface normals are reflected about the viewing direction. This is easily verified by observing that

$$\begin{aligned} \mathbf{n}_2\!\cdot\!\mathbf{s}_2 &= (2\hat{\mathbf{z}}(\mathbf{n}_1\!\cdot\!\hat{\mathbf{z}}) - \mathbf{n}_1)\!\cdot\!(2\hat{\mathbf{z}}(\mathbf{s}_1\!\cdot\!\hat{\mathbf{z}}) - \mathbf{s}_1) \\ &= 4(\hat{\mathbf{z}}\!\cdot\!\hat{\mathbf{z}})(\mathbf{n}_1\!\cdot\!\hat{\mathbf{z}})(\mathbf{s}_1\!\cdot\!\hat{\mathbf{z}}) - 2(\mathbf{n}_1\!\cdot\!\hat{\mathbf{z}})(\mathbf{s}_1\!\cdot\!\hat{\mathbf{z}}) \\ &\quad - 2(\mathbf{s}_1\!\cdot\!\hat{\mathbf{z}})(\mathbf{n}_1\!\cdot\!\hat{\mathbf{z}}) + \mathbf{n}_1\!\cdot\!\mathbf{s}_1 \\ &= \mathbf{n}_1\!\cdot\!\mathbf{s}_1. \end{aligned}$$

Given some initial values for the normals, the shape-and-source scheme will head for one or the other of these solutions. The dual shape and source direction can then be determined immediately using the equations given above.

We now present two examples of the program at work. Synthetic images were used, each of which depicted a Lambertian surface illuminated by a point source in the direction $(3, 2, 9)^T$. The images each contained more than 1000 points at which normals were to be determined. Normals were assigned an initial value of $(0, 0, 1)^T$, as was the source direction. Occluding boundary normals were given. The equations for $\mathbf{n}_{ij}$ could be solved sequentially using the Gauss-Seidel algorithm. Since we are ultimately interested in parallel implementation on a grid, we used the Jacobi method instead (despite the fact that the Gauss-Seidel method has slightly better convergence properties).

The first image portrayed a hemisphere viewed from

directly overhead. After 100 iterations with $\lambda = 0.005$, the average angular difference between estimated and correct normals was less than $3°$. The maximum such deviation was less than 2.5 times the average value. The estimate of the light source direction, at this time, had errors in azimuth and zenith angles of $1.4°$ and $1.6°$ respectively.

The second image depicted a cylinder with rounded, hemispherical ends, viewed from a direction perpendicular to its axis. After 60 iterations, this time with $\lambda = 0.003$, the average angular error in surface-normal was less than $5°$. A further 30 iterations brought this value down to $4°$. The maximum error remained somewhat larger, however, due to the scheme's tendency to smooth the intersections of the cylinder and the hemispheres. The errors in azimuth and zenith angles for the source were $7.3°$ and $1.1°$ respectively, achieved after 90 iterations. These, too, improved slowly with further processing.

The scheme was sometimes slow in converging. After rapid initial improvements, the rate of progress would decrease appreciably. However, one might expect the scheme to be slower than some of the current iterative methods given the disadvantage of not knowing the light source direction. Convergence could be accelerated by employing multigrid techniques that propagate information across the image more quickly (see Terzopoulos, 1984). Interestingly, in the examples considered, a reasonable estimate for the source direction was obtained after only a few iterations. Subsequent processing just improved the estimate.

IV. Iterative schemes for other reflectance maps

We now present two more new iterative schemes: the first extends the shape-and-source finder to cover situations in which a simple model of the sky is also included; the second uses methods developed above to find shape from shading, given a general reflectance map, but does not recover source direction.

A. Incorporating a sky component

The reflectance map

$$R_{sky}(\mathbf{n}) = \tfrac{1}{2}(1 + \mathbf{n} \cdot \hat{\mathbf{z}})$$

captures the situation in which a Lambertian surface is illuminated by a hemispherical source of uniform radiance (Brooks, 1978; Horn & Sjoberg, 1979). A point source may be added to the map to give

$$R_{ss}(\mathbf{n}) = \alpha(\mathbf{n} \cdot \mathbf{s}) + \tfrac{1-\alpha}{2}(1 + \mathbf{n} \cdot \hat{\mathbf{z}})$$

Here, α controls the relative intensity of the sun and the sky. We can now generate a method of shape-and-source recovery, under the assumption that the image was formed in accordance with the reflectance map R_{ss}.

We seek to minimize

$$\iint_\Omega \left(E - \alpha(\mathbf{n} \cdot \mathbf{s}) - \tfrac{1-\alpha}{2}(1 + \mathbf{n} \cdot \hat{\mathbf{z}})\right)^2 +$$

$$\lambda(\mathbf{n}_x^2 + \mathbf{n}_y^2) + \mu(x, y)(\mathbf{n}^2 - 1) \; dx \, dy,$$

with respect to both $\mathbf{n}$ and $\mathbf{s}$. Fixing $\mathbf{s}$ for the time being, we are required to minimize the above functional with respect to $\mathbf{n}$ alone. The Euler equation for this problem is

$$\left(E - \alpha(\mathbf{n} \cdot \mathbf{s}) - \tfrac{1-\alpha}{2}(1 + \mathbf{n} \cdot \hat{\mathbf{z}})\right)(\alpha \mathbf{s} + \tfrac{1-\alpha}{2}\hat{\mathbf{z}}) + \lambda\nabla^2\mathbf{n} - \mu\mathbf{n} = 0.$$

Treating μ as before, the following scheme is obtained:

$$\begin{cases} \mathbf{m}_{ij}^{k+1} = \bar{\mathbf{n}}_{ij}^k + \dfrac{\epsilon^2}{4\lambda}(E_{ij} - R_{ss}(\mathbf{n}_{ij}^k))(\alpha \mathbf{s}^k + \tfrac{1-\alpha}{2}\hat{\mathbf{z}}) \\ \mathbf{n}_{ij}^{k+1} = \mathbf{m}_{ij}^{k+1}/|\mathbf{m}_{ij}^{k+1}|. \end{cases}$$

Here, the reflectance map, R_{ss}, has been substituted back into the equation to improve the presentation.

We now assume $\mathbf{n}$ to be fixed and minimize the functional with respect to $\mathbf{s}$. This we do, as before, by differentiating with respect to $\mathbf{s}$ and equating the result to zero. Thus we have

$$-2 \iint_\Omega \left(E - \alpha(\mathbf{n} \cdot \mathbf{s}) - \tfrac{1-\alpha}{2}(1 + \mathbf{n} \cdot \hat{\mathbf{z}})\right)\alpha \mathbf{n} \; dx \, dy = 0.$$

Expanding,

$$\iint_\Omega (E - \tfrac{1-\alpha}{2}(1 + \mathbf{n} \cdot \hat{\mathbf{z}}))\mathbf{n} \; dx \, dy = \iint_\Omega \alpha(\mathbf{n} \cdot \mathbf{s})\mathbf{n} \; dx \, dy.$$

Noting as before that $(\mathbf{n} \cdot \mathbf{s})\mathbf{n} = (\mathbf{n}\mathbf{n}^T)\mathbf{s}$, the equation becomes

$$\iint_\Omega (E - \tfrac{1-\alpha}{2}(1 + \mathbf{n} \cdot \hat{\mathbf{z}}))\mathbf{n} \; dx \, dy = \alpha \left[\iint_\Omega \mathbf{n}\mathbf{n}^T \; dx \, dy\right] \mathbf{s}.$$

Thus we obtain the equation in $\mathbf{s}$ given by

$$\mathbf{s} = \frac{1}{\alpha} \left[\iint_\Omega \mathbf{n}\mathbf{n}^T \; dx \, dy\right]^{-1} \iint_\Omega (E - \tfrac{1-\alpha}{2}(1 + \mathbf{n} \cdot \hat{\mathbf{z}}))\mathbf{n} \; dx \, dy.$$

This we may write in discrete form and combine with the iterative scheme for $\mathbf{n}$ derived previously to give

$$\begin{cases} \mathbf{m}_{ij}^{k+1} = \bar{\mathbf{n}}_{ij}^k + \dfrac{\epsilon^2}{4\lambda}(E_{ij} - R_{ss}(\mathbf{n}_{ij}^k))(\alpha \mathbf{s}^k + \tfrac{1-\alpha}{2}\hat{\mathbf{z}}) \\ \mathbf{n}_{ij}^{k+1} = \mathbf{m}_{ij}^{k+1}/|\mathbf{m}_{ij}^{k+1}| \\ \mathbf{s}^{k+1} = \dfrac{1}{\alpha}\Big[\sum_{i,j\in\Omega} \mathbf{n}_{ij}^{k+1}\mathbf{n}_{ij}^{k+1\,T}\Big]^{-1} \times \\ \qquad\qquad \sum_{i,j\in\Omega}\Big(E_{ij} - \tfrac{1-\alpha}{2}(1 + \mathbf{n}_{ij}^{k+1} \cdot \hat{\mathbf{z}})\Big)\mathbf{n}_{ij}^{k+1}. \end{cases}$$

Note that α is assumed to be known. Interestingly, the computation of $\mathbf{s}$ proceeds as before, except that the contribution of the sky is subtracted from E. This does not render the scheme trivial, however, as the calculation of shape does not follow suit.

B. Recovery of shape for the general reflectance map

Recall that the iterative scheme for shape and source direction is composed of two parts. Either component of the scheme may stand alone in the event that shape is required from source, or source is required from shape. Indeed, if used in this way, the shape-recovery component may be generalized to incorporate any reflectance map, $R(\mathbf{n})$. In minimizing the functional

$$\iint_\Omega \left(E(x,y) - R(\mathbf{n}(x,y))\right)^2 + \lambda(\mathbf{n}_x^2 + \mathbf{n}_y^2) + \mu(x,y)(\mathbf{n}^2 - 1)\, dx\, dy,$$

we obtain the Euler equation

$$(E - R)R_\mathbf{n} + \lambda\nabla^2\mathbf{n} - \mu\mathbf{n} = 0,$$

from which we derive the scheme

$$\begin{cases} \mathbf{m}_{ij}^{k+1} = \bar{\mathbf{n}}_{ij}^k + \dfrac{\epsilon^2}{4\lambda}(E_{ij} - R(\mathbf{n}_{ij}))R_\mathbf{n}(\mathbf{n}_{ij}) \\ \mathbf{n}_{ij}^{k+1} = \mathbf{m}_{ij}^{k+1}/|\mathbf{m}_{ij}^{k+1}|. \end{cases}$$

This is perhaps the most appealing of the current shape-from-shading schemes that deal with a general reflectance map. It is simply derived, and is expressed elegantly in terms of unit-normals, rather than a two-parameter system such as the stereographic fg space of Ikeuchi and Horn.

V. Summary

Most current methods for obtaining shape from shading assume complete knowledge of the reflectance map. Here, we considered the situation in which a Lambertian surface is illuminated by a point light source from an unknown direction. Thus we dealt with a parameterized, rather than a fixed, reflectance map. The local approach to recovering shape from shading, which is also intended to deal with unknown source direction, was found to have several drawbacks, notably its restrictive assumption that surfaces are locally umbilical.

The adoption of unit normal vectors for describing surface orientation was important to the development of our method. It led to simple derivations and elegant presentations. The problem was cast as one of minimizing a positive-definite functional incorporating a brightness error term, a regularizing term, and a Lagrangian multiplier to enforce the condition that the normal be of unit length. The Euler equation for this calculus of variations problem was shown to be a second-order partial differential equation in the unknown surface-normal function. A convergent iterative scheme solved it in the discrete domain.

The direction of the light source can be determined in closed form if the surface shape is known. At any iteration, a source-direction estimate can be obtained using the current estimate of the surface shape. The iterations for obtaining increasingly accurate estimates of the surface shape can be interlaced with estimation of the light-source direction.

We implemented and tested this method for recovering shape and source direction. We also discussed a two-way ambiguity that can appear in the solution. Further, we showed how to extend the shape-from-shading component of the iterative scheme to more general reflectance maps.

Acknowledgements

We thank Alan Yuille for many useful discussions. Comments on a draft by Steve Bagley, Eric Grimson, Tomás Lozano-Pérez, Bruce Nelson and, especially, Demetri Terzopoulos were much appreciated. Mike Brooks wishes to express gratitude to the MIT AI laboratory for the opportunity to spend some months there, and to Flinders University for granting leave. Support for the laboratory's artificial intelligence research is provided in part by the System Development Foundation.

References

Brooks, M.J., "Investigating the Effects of Planar Light Sources," CSM 22, Dept. Computer Science, Essex University, 1978.

Bruss, A.R., "Is What You See What You Get?", *Proceedings of the International Joint Conference on Artificial Intelligence*, Karlsruhe, August, 1983, pp. 1053–1056.

Courant, R & Hilbert, D, *Methods of Mathematical Physics, Vol. 1*, Interscience Publishers, Inc., New York, 1953.

Horn, B.K.P, "Shape-from-Shading: A Method for Obtaining the Shape of a Smooth Opaque Object from one View," MAC-TR-79 and AI-TR-232, M.I.T., November 1970.

Horn, B.K.P., "Obtaining Shape from Shading Information," in *The Psychology of Computer Vision*, P.H.Winston (Ed.), McGraw-Hill, 1975.

Horn, B.K.P & Sjoberg, R.W, "Calculating the Reflectance Map," *Applied Optics*, Vol. 18, 11, June 1979, pp. 1770–1779.

Horn, B.K.P. & Brooks, M.J., "A Variational Approach to Shape from Shading," A.I.M. 813, Artificial Intelligence Lab., M.I.T., January, 1985.

Ikeuchi, K. & Horn, B.K.P., "Numerical Shape from Shading and Occluding Boundaries," *Artificial Intelligence*, 17, 1981, pp. 141–185.

Korn, G.A & Korn, T.M., *Mathematical Handbook for Scientists and Engineers*, 2nd edition, McGraw-Hill, 1968.

Pentland, A.P., "Local Shape Analysis," *IEEE Transactions on Pattern Analysis and Machine Intelligence*, March, 1984, pp. 170–187.

Poggio, T. & Torre, V., "Ill-posed Problems and Regularization Analysis in Early Vision," A.I.M. 773, Artificial Intelligence Lab., M.I.T., 1984.

Strat, T.M., "A Numerical Method for Shape from Shading from a Single Image," M.S. thesis, Department of E.E.C.S., M.I.T., 1979.

Terzopoulos, D., "Efficient Multiresolution Algorithms for Computing Lightness, Shape from Shading, and Optical Flow," *Proceedings of the A.A.A.I. Conference*, Austin, Texas, August, 1984, pp. 314–317.

One-Eyed Stereo: A General Approach to Modeling 3-D Scene Geometry

Thomas M. Strat and Martin A. Fischler
Artificial Intelligence Center
SRI International
Menlo Park, California 94025

Abstract

A single 2-D image is an ambiguous representation of the 3-D world—many different scenes could have produced the same image—yet the human visual system is extremely successful at recovering a qualitatively correct depth model from this type of representation. Workers in the field of computational vision have devised many distinct schemes that attempt to duplicate this ability of human vision; these schemes are collectively called "shape from ...." methods (e.g., shape from shading, shape from texture, shape from contour). In this paper we argue that the distinct assumptions employed by each of these different schemes must be equivalent to providing a second (virtual) image of the original scene, and that all of these different approaches can be translated into a conventional stereo formalism. In particular, we show that it is frequently possible to structure the problem as that of recovering depth from a stereo pair consisting of a conventional perspective image (the *original* image) and an orthographic image (the *virtual* image). We provide a new algorithm of the form required to accomplish this type of stereo reconstruction task.

1 Introduction

The recovery of 3-D scene geometry from one or more images, which we will call the scene modeling problem (SMP), has solutions that appear to follow one of three distinct paradigms: stereo; optic flow; and shape from shading, texture, and contour.

In the stereo paradigm, we match corresponding world/scene points in two images, and, given the relative geometry of the two cameras (eyes) that acquired the images, we can use simple trigonometry to determine the depths of the matched points [1].

In the optic flow paradigm, we use two or more images to compute the image velocity of depicted scene points. If the camera's motion and imaging parameters are known, we can again use simple trigonometry to convert velocity measurements in the image to depths in the scene [20].

In the shape from shading, texture, and contour (SSTC) paradigm, we must either know, or make some assumptions about the nature of the scene, the illumination, and the imaging geometry. Reference [2] contains an excellent collection of papers, many of which address the problem of how to recover depth from the shading, texture, and contour information visible in a single image. Two distinct computational approaches have been employed in the SSTC paradigm: (a) integration of partial differential equations describing the relation of shading in an image to surface geometry in a scene, and (b) back-projection of planar image facets to undo the distortion in an image attribute (e.g., edge orientation) induced by the imaging process on an assumed scene property (e.g., uniform distribution of edge orientations).

Our purposes in this paper are to provide a unifying framework for the scene modeling problem, and to present a new computational approach for recovering scene geometry from the shading, texture, and contour information present in a single image. Our contribution is based on the following observation: regardless of the assumptions employed in the SSTC paradigm, if a 3-D scene model has been successfully derived, it will generally be possible to establish a large number of correspondences between image and scene (model) points. From these correspondences we can compute a collineation matrix [10] and extract from the matrix the imaging geometry [3] [18]. We can now construct a second image of the scene as viewed by the camera from some arbitrary location in space. It is thus obvious that any technique that is competent to solve the SMP must either be provided with at least two images, or must make assumptions that are equivalent to providing a second image. We can unify the various approaches to the SMP by converting their associated assumptions and auxiliary information into the implied second image and employ the stereo paradigm to recover depth. In the case of the SSTC paradigm, our approach amounts to "one-eyed stereo."

2 Shape from One-Eyed Stereo

Most people viewing Figure 1 get a strong impression of depth. We can recover an equivalent depth model by assuming that we are viewing a projection of a uniform grid and employing the computational procedure to be described. In the remainder of this paper we will show how various simple modifications and variations of the uniform grid, as the implied second image, allow us to recover depth from shading, texture, and contour.

The one-eyed stereo paradigm can be described as a five-step process, as outlined in the paragraphs below. Differences in the scenes and the image-formation processes will require variations in the particular procedures to be used, but the general approach will remain the same.

2.1 Partition the image

As with all approaches to the SMP, the image must be segmented into regions prior to the application of a particular algorithm on any individual portion of the image. Before the one-eyed stereo computation can be employed, the image must be segmented

The work reported herein was supported by the Defense Advanced Research Projects Agency under Contract No. MDA903-83-C-0027.

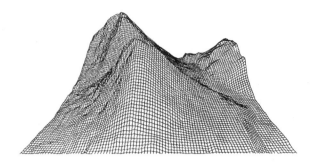

Figure 1: A synthetic image

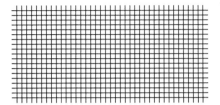

Figure 2: The virtual image of Figure 1

into regions that can be described by a single underlying model. The computation can then be carried out independently in each region, and the results knitted together.

2.2   Select a model

For each region identified by the partitioning process, we must determine the underlying model that explains that portion of the image. Surface reflectance functions and texture patterns are examples of such models. Partitioning the image and selecting the appropriate models are difficult problems that are not addressed in this paper. Witkin and Kass [22] are exploring a new class of techniques that promises to provide answers to these questions. It will not be possible to recover depth where no single model can be associated with a particular image region. Similarly, inaccurate or incorrect results can be expected if the partitioning or modeling is performed incorrectly.

2.3   Generate the virtual image

The key to one-eyed stereo is using the model to fabricate a second (virtual) image of the scene. The idea is that the model often allows one to construct an image of the scene that is independent of the actual shape of the imaged surface. This allows the virtual image to be determined solely from knowledge of the model without making use of the original image. For example, the markings on the surface of Figure 1 could have arisen from a projection of a uniform grid upon the surface (Figure 2). For all images that fit this model, we can use a uniform grid as the virtual image. The orientation, position, and scale of this grid will typically be unknown, and we will show how this information can be recovered from the original image. Other models give rise to other forms of virtual images.

2.4   Determine correspondences

In order to apply stereo techniques to determine depths, we must first establish correspondences between points in the real image and the virtual image. When dealing with textures, the process is typified by counting texels in each image from a chosen starting point. With shading, the general approach is to integrate intensities. Several variations are described in the next section, and the difficulty of the procedure will depend on the nature of the model.

2.5   Compute depths using stereo

With two images and a number of point-to-point correspondences in hand, the techniques of binocular stereo are immediately applicable. At this point, the problem has been reduced to computing the relative camera models between the two images and using that information to compute depths by triangulation. The fact that the virtual image will normally be an orthographic projection required reformulation of existing algorithms for performing this computation. The appendix describes a new algorithm that computes the relative camera model and reconstructs the 3-D scene from eight point-correspondences between a perspective and an orthographic image.

The problem of recovering scene and imaging geometry from two or more images has been addressed by workers in both binocular stereo and monocular perception of motion (where the two projections are separated in time as well as space). Various approaches have been used to derive equations for the 3-D coordinates and motion parameters; these equations are generally solved by iterative techniques [4] [7] [12] [13]. Ullman [20] presents a solution for recovering 3-D shape from three orthographic projections with established correspondences among at least four points. His "polar equation" allows computation of shape when the motion of the scene is restricted to a rotation about the vertical axis and arbitrary translation. Nagel and Neumann [9] provide a compact system of three nonlinear equations for the unrestricted problem when five point-correspondences between the two perspective images are known. More recently, Huang [19] and Longuet-Higgins [8] have independently derived methods that only require the solution of a set of eight simultaneous linear equations when eight point-correspondences are known between two perspective images. In our formulation we are faced with a stereo problem involving a perspective and an orthographic image, and while the aforementioned references are related, none provides a solution to this particular problem.

The derivation described in the appendix was inspired by the formulation of Longuet-Higgins for perspective images. When either image nears orthography, Longuet-Higgins' method becomes unstable and is undefined if either image is truly orthographic. Moreover, his approach requires knowledge of the focal length and principal point in each image. Our method was specifically derived for one orthographic and one perspective image whose internal imaging parameters may not be fully known.

3   Variations on the Theme

In this section we illustrate how our approach is used with several models of texture, shading, and contour. Where these models

 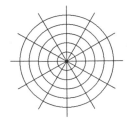

Figure 3: (a) The original image   (b) The virtual image

Figure 4: The streets in this scene resemble a projected texture.

don't match given scene characteristics, they may require additional modification. However, a qualitatively correct answer might still be obtainable by applying one of the specific models we discuss in the following subsections to what appears to be an inappropriate situation, or a situation where the validity of the assumptions cannot be established.

3.1   Shape from texture

Surface shapes are often communicated graphically to humans by drawings like Figure 1. These drawings can also be interpreted by one-eyed stereo. In this case, there is no need to partition the image; the underlying model of the entire scene is that the intersections of the lines are distributed in the form of a square grid. When viewed from directly above at an infinite distance, the surface would appear as shown in the virtual image of Figure 2 regardless of the shape of the surface. This virtual image can be construed as an orthographic projection of the object surface from an unknown viewing direction. Correspondences between the original and virtual images are easily established if there are no occlusions in the original image. Select any intersection in the original image to be the reference point and pair it with any intersection in the virtual image. A second corresponding pair can be found by moving to an adjacent intersection in both images. Additional pairs are found in the same manner, being careful to correlate the motions in each image consistently in both directions. When occlusions are present, it may still be possible to obtain correspondences for all visible junctions by following a non-occluded path around the occlusion. If no such path can be found, the shape of each isolated region can still be computed, but there will be no way to relate the distances without further information. Other techniques used to graphically represent images of 3-D shapes may require other virtual images. Figure 3a, for example, would imply a virtual image as shown in Figure 3b. Methods for recognizing which model to apply are needed, but are not discussed here.

Once correspondences have been determined, we can use the algorithm given in the appendix to recover depth. We have presumably one perspective image and one orthographic image whose scale and origin are still unknown. The depths that will be recovered will be scaled according to the scale chosen for the virtual image[1]. The choice of origin for the orthographic image is arbitrary, and will result in the same solution regardless of the point chosen as the origin. The appendix shows how to compute the orientation of the orthographic coordinate system relative

[1]Recall that the original image does not contain the information necessary to recover the absolute size of the scene.

to the perspective imaging system as well as the displacement between the two, given the choice of origin for the orthographic view. 3-D coordinates of each matched point are then easily computed using back-projection. A unique solution will be obtained whenever the piercing point of the perspective image is known. A minimum of eight pairs of matched points are required to obtain a solution; depths can be computed for all matched points.

There exists a growing literature on methods to recover shape from natural textures [6][11][17][21]. We will now show how the constraints imposed by one particular type of natural texture can be exploited to obtain similar results by using one-eyed stereo.

Consider the pattern of streets in Figure 4. If this city were viewed from an airplane directly overhead at high altitude, the streets would form a regular grid not unlike the one used as the virtual image in Figure 2. There are many other scene attributes that satisfy this same model. The houses in some cities would appear to be distributed in a uniform grid if viewed from directly overhead. In an apple orchard growing on a hillside, the trees would be planted in rows that are evenly spaced when measured horizontally.

Ignoring the nontrivial tasks of partitioning these images into iso-textural regions, verifying that they satisfy the model, and identifying individual texels, it can be seen how these images can be interpreted using the same techniques as in the previous section. The virtual image in each case will be a rectangular grid, and can be considered as an orthographic view from an unknown orientation. Correspondences can be determined by counting street intersections, rooftops, or apple trees. As before, one can solve for the relative camera model and compute depths of matched points. Obviously, for the situations discussed here, we must be satisfied with a qualitatively-correct interpretation due to the difficulty of locating individual texels reliably and accurately, as well as the numerical instabilities arising from the underlying nonlinear transformation.

3.2   Shape from shading

For our purposes, surface shading can be considered the limiting case of a locally uniform texture distribution, as the texels approach infinitesimal dimensions (as seen near the horizon in Figure 1). To compute correspondences, we need to appropriately integrate image intensities in place of counting lines, since

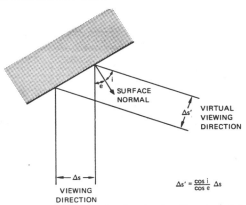

Figure 5: The geometry along a line in the direction of the light source

Figure 6: (a) An image of contours [16]   (b) Its virtual image

the image intensities can be seen to be related to the density of lines projected on the surface. The feasibility of this procedure depends on the reflectance function of the surface.

What types of material possess the special property that allows their images to be treated like the limit of the projected texture of the previous section? It must be the case that the integral of intensity in an image region is proportional to the number of texels that would be projected in that region. This can be described in terms of i and e, where i is the angle between the local surface normal and the light source, and e is the angle between the surface normal and the viewpoint. It can be seen that the number of texels projected onto a surface patch will be proportional to $\cos i$, the cosine of the incident angle. At the same time, the surface patch (as seen from the viewpoint) will be foreshortened by $\cos e$, the cosine of the emittance angle. Thus, the integral of reflected light intensity over a region will be proportional to the flux of the light striking the surface if the intensity of the reflected light at any point is proportional to $\cos i/\cos e$. Horn [5] has pointed out that the material in the maria of the moon, and other rocky, dusty objects when viewed from great distances, possess a reflectance function that allows recovery of the ratio $\cos i/\cos e$ from the imaged intensities. This surface property has allowed unusually simple algorithms for computing shape-from-shading, so it is not surprising that it easily submits to one-eyed stereo as well.

To interpret this type of shading, we can construct a virtual image whose direction of view is the lighting direction (i.e., taken from a "virtual camera" located at the light source). When the original shaded image is orthographic, we consider a family of parallel lines that lie in planes that include both the light source and the (distant) view point. When viewed from the light source, the image of the surface corresponding to these lines will also be a set of parallel lines regardless of the shape of the surface. These parallel lines constitute the virtual image. We will use the image intensities to refine these line-to-line correspondences to point-to-point correspondences. Figure 5 shows the geometry for an individual line in the family. A little trigonometry shows that

$$\Delta s' = \frac{\cos i}{\cos e}\Delta s \qquad (1)$$

where Δs is a distance along the line in the real image and $\Delta s'$ is the corresponding distance along the corresponding line in the virtual image. Integrating this equation produces the following expression, which defines the point correspondences in the two

images along the given line.

$$s' = s'_o + \int_0^s \frac{\cos i}{\cos e}\Delta s \qquad (2)$$

To use this equation we must first compute $\frac{\cos i}{\cos e}$ from the intensity value at each point along the line. This will, of course, be possible only when the reflectance function is constant for constant $\frac{\cos i}{\cos e}$. With these point-to-point correspondences in hand, it is a simple matter of triangulation to find the 3-D coordinates of the surface points, given that we know the direction to the light source. We can explore the remainder of the surface by repeating the process for each of the successive parallel lines in the image. It still remains to tie each of the adjacent profiles together, as the scale factor of each profile has not been determined. Knowledge of the actual depth of one point along each profile provides the necessary additional information. It is important to note that our assumptions and initial conditions are those used by Horn; the fact that he was able to obtain a solution under these conditions assured the existence of a suitable virtual image for the one-eyed stereo paradigm.

3.3 Shape from contour

It is sometimes possible to extract a line drawing, such as shown in Figure 6, from scene textures. Parallel streets like those encountered in Figure 4 give rise to a virtual image consisting of parallel lines when the cross streets cannot be located; terraced hills also produce a virtual image of parallel lines. Correspondences between real and virtual image lines can be found by counting adjacent lines from an arbitrary starting point. This matches a virtual image line with each point in the real image. Point-to-line correspondences are not sufficient to employ the stereo computation of the appendix to reconstruct the surface. Knowledge of the relative orientation between the two images (equivalent to knowing the orientation of the camera of the real image relative to the parallel lines in the scene) provides the necessary additional constraint; the surface can then be reconstructed uniquely through back-projection. Without knowledge of the relative orientation of the virtual image, heuristics must be employed that relate points on adjacent contours so that a regular grid can be used as the virtual image. The human visual system is normally able to interpret images like Figure 6 although just what assumptions are being made remains unclear. Further study into this phenomenon may lead to the extraction of models suitable to the employment of one-eyed stereo on this type of image without requiring prior knowledge of the virtual orientation.

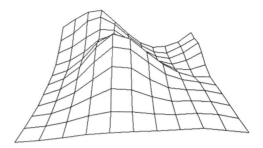

Figure 7: This simple drawing has two reasonable interpretations. It is seen as curved roller-coaster tracks if the lines are assumed to be the projection of a rectangular grid, or as a volcano when the lines are assumed to be the projection of a circular grid.

Figure 8: View of surface reconstructed from Figure 1.

3.4 Distorted Textures and Unfriendly Shading

We have already noted that image shading can be viewed as a limiting (and, for our purposes, a degenerate) result of closely-spaced texture elements. In order to recover depth from shading, we must use integration to replace counting the texture elements that define the locations of the "grid lines" of our virtual image. The integration process depends on having a "friendly" reflectance function and an imaging geometry that allows us to convert distance along a line in the actual image to a corresponding distance along a line in the virtual image.

The recovery of lunar topography from a single shaded image [5], as discussed in Section 3.2, is one of the few instances in which "shape from shading" is known to be possible without a significant amount of additional knowledge about the scene; and even here we are required to know the actual reflectance function, the location of the (point) source of illumination, the depths along a curve on the object surface, and be dealing with a portion of the object having constant albedo. Further, the reflectance function had to have just the property that we require to replace direct counting, i.e., the reflectance function had to compensate exactly for the "foreshortening" of distance due to viewing points on the object surface at an unknown tangent-plane orientation angle. Most of the commonly encountered reflectance functions, such as Lambertian reflectance, do not have this friendly property, and it is not clear to what extent it is possible to recover depth from shading in such cases (e.g., see Pentland [11] and Smith [14]). Additional assumptions will probably be needed and the qualitative nature of the recovery will be more pronounced. Just as in the case where a complex function can be evaluated by making a local linear approximation and iterating the resulting solution, it may be possible to deal with unfriendly, or even unknown, reflectance functions by assuming that they are friendly about some point, directly solving for local shape using the algorithm applicable to the friendly case, and then extending the solution to adjacent regions. We are currently investigating this approach.

The uniform rectangular grid and the polar grid that we used as virtual images to illustrate our approach to one-eyed stereo are effective in a large number of cases, because there are processes operating in the real world that produce corresponding textures (i.e., grid-like textures that appear to be orthographically projected onto the surfaces of the scene). However, there are also textures that produce similar-appearing images, but are due to different underlying processes. For example, a uniform grid-like texture might have been created on a flat piece of terrain, which

then underwent geologic deformation—in this case the virtual image needed to recover depth (or the recovery algorithm) must be different from the projective case. We have already indicated the problem of choosing the appropriate model for the virtual image, and as noted above, image appearance is probably not sufficient to make this determination—some semantic knowledge about the scene is undoubtedly required. Figure 7 shows an example in which two completely different interpretations of scene structure result, both believable, depending on whether we use the rectangular grid model, or the polar grid model.

4 Experimental Results

The stereo reconstruction algorithm described in the appendix has been programmed and successfully tested on both real and synthetic imagery. Given a sparse set of image points and their correspondence in a virtual image, a qualitative description of the imaged surface can be obtained.

Synthetic images were created from surfaces painted with computer-generated graphic textures. Figure 1 shows a synthetic image constructed from a piece of a digital terrain model (DTM). The intersections of every 20th grid line constitute the set of 36 image points made available to the one-eyed stereo algorithm. Their correspondences were determined by selecting an arbitrary origin and counting grid lines to obtain virtual image coordinates. Processing these pairs by the algorithm in the appendix yields a set of 3-D coordinates in either the viewer-centered coordinate space, or the virtual image coordinate space (which, if correct, is aligned with the original DTM). Figure 8 was obtained from the 3-D coordinates in the virtual image space by fitting a surface to these points using Smith's surface interpolation algorithm [15]. This gives a dense set of 3-D coordinates that can then be displayed from any viewpoint. The viewpoint that was computed by one-eyed stereo was used to render the surface as shown in Figure 8. Its similarity to the original rendering of the surface (Fig. 1) illustrates the successful reconstruction of the scene.

The same procedure was followed when working with real photographs. Using the photo of San Francisco in Figure 4, the intersections of 31 street intersections were extracted manually. Those that were occluded or indistinct were disregarded. Virtual image coordinates were obtained by counting city blocks from the lower-left intersection. The one-eyed stereo algorithm was then used to acquire 3-D coordinates of the corresponding image points in both viewer-centered and grid-centered coordinate systems. A continuous surface was fitted to both representations of these points. The location and orientation of the camera relative

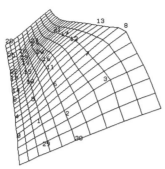

Figure 9: Perspective view of surface reconstructed from photograph of San Francisco (Figure 4)

to the grid were also computed. Figure 9 shows the reconstructed surface from the derived location of the viewpoint of the original photo. The numbers superimposed are the computed locations of the original 31 points. While several of the original points were badly mislocated, the general shape of the landform is apparent.

There are several reasons why the algorithm can only provide a qualitative shape description. First, the problem itself can be somewhat sensitive to slight perturbations in the estimates of the piercing point or focal length. This appears to be inherent to the problem of recovering shape from a single image. How humans can determine shape monocularly without apparent knowledge of the piercing point or semantic content of the scene remains unresolved. The second factor precluding precise, quantitative description of shape is the practical difficulty of acquiring large numbers of corresponding points. While the algorithm can proceed with as few as eight points, the location of the object will only be identified at those eight points. If a more complete model is sought, then additional points will be required to constrain the subsequent surface interpolation.

The task remains to evaluate the effectiveness of the iterative technique, described in Section 3.4, for recovering (a) shape from shading in the case of scenes possessing "unfriendly" reflectance functions, and (b) shape from nonprojective and distorted textures. Our experience with the process indicates that the key to these problems lies in the ability to establish valid correspondences with the virtual image. Once these are available, reconstruction of the surface can proceed as outlined.

5   Conclusion

In this paper we have shown that, in principle, it is possible to employ the stereo paradigm in place of various approaches proposed for modeling 3-D scene geometry—including the case in which only one image is provided. We have further shown that, for the case of a single image, the approach could be implemented by:

(1) Setting up correspondences between portions of the image and variations of a uniform grid;

(2) Treating each image portion and its grid counterpart as a stereo pair, and employing a stereo technique to recover depth. (We present a new algorithm necessary to accomplish this step.)

Automatic procedures to partition the image, select the appropriate form of the virtual image, and establish the correspondences, are all difficult problems which were not addressed in this paper. Nevertheless, we have unified a number of apparently distinct problems, which, individually, would still have to contend with these same pervasive problems (*i.e.*, partitioning, model selection, and matching).

References

[1] Barnard, S. T., and Fischler, M. A., "Computational Stereo," Computing Surveys, Vol. 14, No. 4, December 1982.

[2] Brady. M., ed., Artificial Intelligence (Special Volume on Computer Vision), Volume 17, Nos. 1–3, August 1981.

[3] Ganapathy, S., "Decomposition of Transformation Matrices for Robot Vision," International Conference On Robotics, (IEEE Computer Society), March 13-15 1984, pp. 130–139.

[4] Gennery, D. B. "Stereo Camera Calibration," Proceedings of the IU Workshop, November 1979, pp. 101–107.

[5] Horn, B. K. P., "Image Intensity Understanding," MIT Artificial Intelligence Memo 335, August 1975.

[6] Kender, J. R., "Shape from Texture," PhD thesis, Carnegie-Mellon University, CMU-CS-81-102, November, 1980.

[7] Lawton, D. T., "Constraint-Based Inference from Image Motion," Proc. AAAI-80, pp. 31-34.

[8] Longuet-Higgins, H. C., "A Computer Algorithm for Reconstructing a Scene from Two Projections," Nature, Vol. 293, September 1981, pp. 133–135.

[9] Nagel, H., and Neumann, B., "On 3-D Reconstruction from Two Perspective Views," Proc. IEEE 1981.

[10] Nitzan, D., Bolles, R.C., it et. al., "Machine Intelligence Research Applied to Industrial Automation," 12th Report SRI Project 2996, January 1983.

[11] Pentland, A. P., "Shading into Texture" Proceedings AAAI-84, August 1984, pp. 269–273.

[12] Prazdny, K., "Motion and Structure from Optical Flow," Proc. IJCAI-79, pp. 704-704.

[13] Roach, J. W., and Aggarwal, J. K., "Determining the Movement of Objects from a Sequence of Images," IEEE Trans. on Pattern Analysis and Machine Intelligence, Vol. PAMI-2, No. 6, November 1980, pp. 554-562.

[14] Smith, G. B., "The Relationship between Image Irradiance and Surface Orientation," Proc. IEEE CVPR-83.

[15] Smith, G. B., "A Fast Surface Interpolation Technique," Proceedings: DARPA Image Understanding Workshop, October 1984, pp. 211-215.

[16] Stevens, K. A., "The Line of Curvature Constraint and the Interpretation of 3-D Shape from Parallel Surface Contours," AAAI-83, pp. 1057-1061.

[17] Stevens, K. A., "The Visual Interpretation of Surface Contours," Artificial Intelligence Journal Vol. 17, No. 1, August 1981, pp. 47-73.

[18] Strat, T. M., "Recovering the Camera Parameters from a Transformation Matrix," Proceedings: DARPA Image Understanding Workshop, October 1984, pp. 264-271.

[19] Tsai, R.Y. and Huang, T.S., "Uniqueness and Estimation of Three-Dimensional Motion Parameters of Rigid Objects with Curved Surfaces," IEEE Trans. on Pattern Analysis and Machine Intelligence, vol. PAMI-6, No. 1, Jan 1984, pp. 13-27.

[20] Ullman, S., The Interpretation of Visual Motion, The MIT Press, Cambridge, Mass., 1979.

[21] Witkin, A. P., "Recovering Surface Shape and Orientation from Texture," Artificial Intelligence Journal Vol. 17, No. 1, August 1981, pp. 17–45.

[22] Witkin, A., and Kass, M., "Analyzing Oriented Patterns," in this proceedings.

Appendix

This appendix shows how 3-dimensional coordinates can be computed from point correspondences between a perspective and an orthographic projection when the relation between the imaging geometries is unknown.

We will use lower-case letters to denote image coordinates and capital letters to denote 3-D object coordinates. Unprimed coordinates will refer to the geometry of the perspective image, and primed coordinates to the orthographic image. Let x_1 and x_2 be the image coordinates of a point in the perspective image relative to an arbitrarily selected origin. Let $-d_1$ and $-d_2$ be the (unknown) image coordinates of the principal point and f (> 0) be the focal length. The object coordinates associated with an image point are (X_1, X_2, X_3) where the origin coincides with the center of projection and the X_3 axis is perpendicular to the image plane. The X_3 coordinates of any object point will necessarily be positive.

The imaging geometry is given by the following standard perspective equations:

$$x_1 + d_1 = f\frac{X_1}{X3}; \qquad x_2 + d_2 = f\frac{X_2}{X_3} \qquad (3)$$

For the orthographic image, x_1' and x_2' are the image coordinates (relative to an arbitrary origin) and (X_1', X_2', X_3') is the world coordinate system defined such that

$$x_1' = X_1'; \qquad x_2' = X_2'. \qquad (4)$$

We use the unknown scale factor between orthographic image coordinates and the scene as our unit of measurement.

The two world coordinate systems can be related as follows.

$$X' = R(X - T) \qquad (5)$$

where X is the column vector $[X_1, \ X_2, \ X_3]^T$
X' is the column vector $[X_1', \ X_2', \ X_3']^T$
R is a 3x3 rotation matrix and
T is a translation vector from the center of perspective projection to the origin of the world coordinate system associated with the orthographic projection.

By substituting Equations 3 and 4 into the above, and eliminating X_3 from the two resulting equations, we get

$$
\begin{aligned}
0 = \ & x_1' x_1 R_{21} + x_1' x_2 R_{22} + x_1' R_2 \cdot D \\
& - x_2' x_1 R_{11} - x_2' x_2 R_{12} - x_2' R_1 \cdot D \\
& + x_1(R_{21} R_1 \cdot T - R_{11} R_2 \cdot T) + x_2(R_{22} R_1 \cdot T - R_{12} R_2 \cdot T) \\
& + R_1 \cdot T R_2 \cdot D - R_2 \cdot T R_1 \cdot D
\end{aligned}
\qquad (6)
$$

where D is the vector $[d_1, \ d_2, \ f]$ and R_i is the i-th row of R.

The above equation relates image coordinates for corresponding points in both images. The following unknowns can be found by using eight corresponding pairs and solving the system of eight linear equations.

$$
\begin{aligned}
C_1 &= \frac{R_{21}}{R_{11}} \\
C_2 &= \frac{R_{22}}{R_{11}} \\
C_3 &= \frac{R_2 \cdot D}{R_{11}} \\
C_4 &= \frac{R_{12}}{R_{11}} \\
C_5 &= \frac{R_1 \cdot D}{R_{11}} \\
C_6 &= \frac{R_{21}}{R_{11}} R_1 \cdot T - R_2 \cdot T \\
C_7 &= \frac{R_{22}}{R_{11}} R_1 \cdot T - \frac{R_{12}}{R_{11}} R_2 \cdot T \\
C_8 &= R_1 \cdot T R_2 \cdot D - R_2 \cdot T R_1 \cdot D
\end{aligned}
\qquad (7)
$$

$$
\begin{bmatrix}
x_1' x_1 & x_1' x_2 & x_1' & -x_2' x_2 & -x_2' & x_1 & x_2 & 1 \\
\cdot & \cdot & \cdot & \cdot & \cdot & \cdot & \cdot & \cdot \\
\cdot & \cdot & \cdot & \cdot & \cdot & \cdot & \cdot & \cdot
\end{bmatrix}
\begin{bmatrix}
C_1 \\ C_2 \\ C_3 \\ C_4 \\ C_5 \\ C_6 \\ C_7 \\ C_8
\end{bmatrix}
=
\begin{bmatrix}
x_2' x_1 \\ \cdot \\ \cdot
\end{bmatrix}
\qquad (8)
$$

Once we have the C_is in hand, we can solve for the components of the rotation matrix R using Equations 7 and the following properties of rotation matrices: $\| R_1 \| = 1$; $R_1 \cdot R_2 = 0$; and $R_1 \times R_2 = R_3$.

The origin of the primed coordinate system in unprimed coordinates is found to be

$$T = [C_7 \frac{R_{11}}{R_{33}}, \ -C_6 \frac{R_{11}}{R_{33}}, \ 0]. \qquad (9)$$

If the location of the principal point is known but the focal length (the scale factor of the perspective image) is not, f can easily be computed from Equation 7.

$$f = \frac{C_5 R_{11} - R_{11} d_1 - R_{12} d_2}{R_{13}} \qquad (10)$$

If the focal length is known, the principal point of the perspective image is found using the third and fifth expressions of Equation 7:

$$
\begin{aligned}
d_1 &= f\frac{R_{31}}{R_{33}} + \frac{C_5 R_{11} R_{22} - C_3 R_{11} R_{12}}{R_{33}} \\
d_2 &= f\frac{R_{32}}{R_{33}} + \frac{C_3 R_{11}^2 - C_5 R_{11} R_{21}}{R_{33}}
\end{aligned}
\qquad (11)
$$

We are now in a position to compute the world coordinates of all points for which we have correspondences. There may, of course, be many more than the 8 points used so far. The following expression is derived from Equation 5:

$$X_3 = \frac{f(x_1' + R_1 \cdot T)}{R_{11} x_1 + R_{12} x_2 + R_1 \cdot D} \qquad (12)$$

Equation 3 gives the other unprimed world coordinates:

$$X_1 = \frac{X_3}{f}(x_1 + d_1); \qquad X_2 = \frac{X_3}{f}(x_2 + d_2) \qquad (13)$$

If desired, the primed coordinates are found with Equation 5.

ANALYZING ORIENTED PATTERNS

Michael Kass
Andrew Witkin

Schlumberger Palo Alto Research
3340 Hillview Ave.
Palo Alto, CA 94304

ABSTRACT

Oriented patterns, such as those produced by propagation, accretion, or deformation, are common in nature and therefore an important class for visual analysis. Our approach to understanding such patterns is to decompose them into two parts: a flow field, describing the direction of anisotropy, and the residual pattern obtained by describing the image in a coordinate system built from the flow field. We develop a method for the local estimation of anisotropy and a method for combining the estimates to construct a flow coordinate system. Several examples of the use of these methods are presented. These included the use of the flow coordinates to provide preferred directions for edge detection, detection of anomalies, fitting simple models to the straightened pattern, and detecting singularities in the flow field.

I   Introduction

A central focus in recent computational vision has been the decomposition of the original intensity image into intrinsic images (Horn 1977; Barrow & Tenenbaum, 1978; Marr, 1982), representing such properties as depth, reflectance, and illuminance. These intrinsic properties are believed to be more meaningful than image intensity because they describe basic independent constituents of the image formation process. Thus, for example, in separating shape from illumination, we can recognize an invariance of shape regardless of changing illumination.

The advantages of decomposing what we see into its more-or-less independent parts extends beyond the image formation process to the shapes and patterns on which that process operates. For instance, decomposing a bent rod into a straight rod and a bending transformation reveals the similarity between a bent rod and one that hasn't been bent, or some other solid that's been bent the same way (Barr, 1984).

Just as we need to understand the image-forming process to decompose an image into intrinsic images, we need to understand the processes that generate patterns to decompose them into their intrinsic parts. But, while there is only one image-forming process, a staggering variety of processes shape and color the world around us. Our only hope of dealing with this complexity is to begin with some basic pattern classes that recur in nature, and understand how to decompose and describe them.

One such class are oriented patterns, notably those produced by propagation, accretion, or deformation. To understand an oriented pattern we must be able to say (1) what is propagating, accreting, or deforming, and (2) which way and how much. More precisely, we must estimate everywhere the direction and magnitude of anistropy (which we will call the flow field,) and describe the residual pattern, independent of that field. Why this decomposition leads to simpler, more regular descriptions is best illustrated by example:

- A typical oriented pattern created by propagation is the streaked trail left by a paint brush dipped in variegated paint. The flow field describes the trajectory of the brush, the residual pattern depending only on the distribution of paint on the brush.

- Accretion typically results in laminar structures, such as wood grain. Here, the flow field gives isochrones (the moving accretion boundary,) and the residual pattern describes the change in color or brightness of the accreting material over time.

- If an isotropic body is deformed, the flow field principally describes the bending and stretching it has undergone, while the residual pattern describes the undeformed body.

In all these cases, separate descriptions of the flow field and the residual pattern are appropriate because they describe different processes. The path of propagation for many physical processes is controlled by very different mechanisms than control the coloration of the trail left behind. Similarly, the mechanisms which control the shape of an accretion boundary are frequently unrelated to the processes controlling the color of the accreted material. Finally, the forces which deform a piece of material are often completely unrelated to the process which created the piece of material in the first place. By separately describing these processes, we can create descriptions of the whole which are often simpler than is possible without the separation because each of the pieces may have different regularities.

Orientation selective mechanisms have been extensively studied by physiologists since Hubel and Wiesel's (1962) discovery of orientation selective cells in mammalian visual cortex (see Schiller et. al. (1976) for a comprehensive example). There has also been considerable interest among psychologists in the perception of oriented patterns, particularly dot patterns (Glass, 1969). Only recently have the computational issues involved received attention. Stevens (1978) examined the grouping of tokens in Glass patterns based on orientation. While successful with Glass patterns, his methods were never extended to natural imagery. Zucker (1983) investigated the estimation of orientation by combining the outputs of linear operators. Zucker's estimation method for what he calls "Type II" patterns, while differing in many respects, is quite close in spirit to our own.

Little progress has been made in using local orientation estimates to interpret patterns, perhaps because reliable estimates have proved difficult to obtain. The key difference between our work and earlier efforts lies in our use of the flow field to build a natural coordinate system for analyzing the pattern.

The remainder of the paper covers the computation of the flow field by local estimation of orientation, the construction of a coordinate system using the flow field, and some examples of analysis and description using flow coordinates.

In Section 2 we develop an estimator for the local flow direction, that direction in which intensity tends to vary most slowly due to an underlying anisotropic process. The estimator, based on the direction of least spatial variance in the output of an oriented filter, is computed as follows: After initial filtering, the intensity gradient is measured at each point in the image. The gradient angle, θ, is then doubled (by treating the gradient vectors as complex numbers and squaring them) to map directions differing by π into a single direction. The transformed vectors are then summed over a weighted neighborhood around the point of interest. The angle of the summed vector is halved, undoing the previous transformation. This gives an estimate for the direction of *greatest* variance, which is then rotated by $\pi/2$ to yield the flow direction.

In section 3, we describe the construction and use of coordinate systems based on the result of local estimation. Integral curves in the flow field are computed numerically, by following the estimated vectors from point to point. A coordinate system is constructed in which the integral curves are parameter lines. Transforming the image into these "flow coordinates" straightens the pattern, removing the effects of changing orientation. We present several examples of analysis and description of the flow field and the straightened pattern.

II   Flow Computation

For intensity patterns created by anisotropic processes such as propagation, accretion, or deformation, variation in the flow direction is much slower than variation in the perpendicular direction. Anisotropy in such patterns will be evident in the local power spectrum. The high frequency energy will tend to cluster along the line in the Fourier domain perpendicular to the flow orientation.

A simple way to detect this clustering is to sum the energy in an appropriate region of the power spectrum and examine how the sum is affected by rotations. This can be done by examining the energy in the output of an appropriate orientation-selective linear filter. The orientation at which the energy is maximal can be expected to be perpendicular to the flow orientation.

Selection of the filter involves a number of tradeoffs. Very low spatial frequencies are affected more strongly by illumination effects than surface coloration, so they are inappropriate for measuring textural anisotropy. Very high spatial frequencies are sensitive to noise and aliasing effects so they too are inappropriate. Hence some type of roughly bandpass filtering is required. The orientation specificity of the filter is also quite important. If the filter is too orientation-specific then a large spatial neighborhood will be required in order to make a reliable measurement of the energy. Conversely, if the filter responds over a wide range of orientations then it will be difficult to localize the orientation very accurately. Thus there is a trade-off between angular- and spatial- resolution.

One reasonable choice for the frequency response of the filter is

$$F(r, \theta) = [e^{r^2 \sigma_1^2} - e^{r^2 \sigma_2^2}] 2\pi i r \cos(\theta). \qquad (1)$$

The filter is bandpass with passband determined by σ_1 and σ_2. In our experience, ratios of the sigmas in the range of 2.0 to 10.0 work well. The orientation specificity or *tuning curve* is provided by the cosine dependence of the filter on θ. This appears to strike a reasonable balance between angular- and spatial- resolutions for the range of patterns we have examined. The filter's power spectrum is shown in figure 1

The cosine orientation tuning-curve of the filter has some unusually good properties for computing the filter output at different orientations. The impulse response $S(x, y)$ of the filter

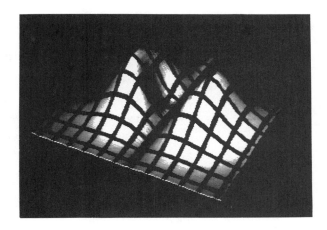

Figure 1: The power spectrum of the filter in equation 1 for $\sigma_2 = 2\sigma_1$.

is

$$S(x, y) = \frac{\partial}{\partial x} H(x, y)$$

where

$$H(x, y) = [\sigma_1^{-2} e^{r^2/\sigma_1^2} - \sigma_2^{-2} e^{r^2/2\sigma_2^2}]$$

is an isotropic filter. Let $C = H * I$ and let $R_\theta[S]$ denote a counter-clockwise rotation of S by an angle θ. Then the convolution $R_\theta[S] * I$ is just the directional derivative of $H * I$ in the θ direction. The directional derivative can easily be written in terms of the gradient so we have

$$R_\theta[S] * I = (\cos\theta, \sin\theta) \cdot \nabla H * I. \qquad (2)$$

Thus a single convolution suffices for all orientations.

Since the filter S severely attenuates very low frequencies $R_\theta[S] * I$ can be safely regarded as zero-mean. Thus the variance in its output can be estimated by the expression

$$V(\theta) = W * (R_\theta[S] * I)^2$$

where $W(x, y)$ is a local weighting function with unit integral. We use Gaussian weighting functions $W(x, y)$ because approximate Gaussian convolutions can be computed efficiently (Burt 1979).

Using the gradient formulation of the filter output in equation 2, we can write the variance $V(\theta)$ as

$$V(\theta) = W * [\cos(\theta)C_x + \sin(\theta)C_y]^2. \qquad (3)$$

A.   Interpretation of Filter Output

There remains the issue of interpreting $V(\theta)$. Assume that there is only one axis of anisotropy. Then $V(\theta)$ will have two extrema π apart corresponding to that axis. Let $V_2(\theta) = V(\theta/2)$. Then $V_2(\theta)$ will have a single extremum in the interval $0 < \theta < 2\pi$. A computationally inexpensive way of estimating the position of this extremum is to consider V_2 as a distribution and compute its mean. Since θ is periodic, V_2 should be considered as a distribution on the unit circle. Hence its mean is the vector integral $(\alpha, \beta) = \int_0^{2\pi} V_2(\theta)(\cos\theta, \sin\theta)d\theta$. The angle $\tan^{-1}(\beta/\alpha)$ is an estimate of the angle of the peak in V_2 and hence twice the angle of the peak in V. Thus the angle ϕ of *greatest* variance can be written

$$\phi = \tan^{-1} \frac{\beta}{\alpha}$$

$$= \tan^{-1} \left(\frac{\int_0^{2\pi} V_2(\theta) \sin(\theta) d\theta}{\int_0^{2\pi} V_2(\theta) \cos(\theta) d\theta} \right) / 2 \qquad (4)$$

$$= \tan^{-1} \left(\frac{\int_0^{\pi} V(\theta) \sin(2\theta) d\theta}{\int_0^{\pi} V(\theta) \cos(2\theta) d\theta} \right) / 2$$

These integrals are evaluated in Appendix A to show that the angle of anisotropy ϕ can be written

$$\phi = \tan^{-1} \left(\frac{W * 2C_x C_y}{W * (C_x^2 - C_y^2)} \right) / 2 \qquad (5)$$

which directly yields a simple algorithm for computing ϕ.

B.   Combining Gradient Orientations

Notice that the right hand side of equation 5 can be regarded as the orientation of a locally weighted sum of the vectors of the form $J(x,y) = (C_x^2 - C_y^2, 2C_x C_y)$. These vectors are related in a simple way to the gradient vectors $G(x,y) = (C_x, C_y)$. The magnitude of $J(x,y)$ is just the square of the magnitude of $G(x,y)$ and the angle between $J(x,y)$ and the x-axis is twice the angle between $G(x,y)$ and the x-axis. This follows easily from the observation that $(C_x + C_y i)^2 = C_x^2 - C_y^2 + 2C_x C_y i$.

One might be tempted to believe that smoothing the gradient vectors $G(x,y)$ would be nearly as good a measure of anisotropy as smoothing the rotated squared gradient vectors $J(x,y)$. This is emphatically not the case. Consider an intensity ridge such as $I(x,y) = \exp(-x^2)$. The gradient vectors on the left half-plane all point to the right and the gradient vectors on the right half-plane all point to the left. Adding them together results in cancellation. By contrast, if they are first rotated to form the J vectors, they reinforce. The types of oriented patterns we are concerned with often have nearly symmetric distributions of gradient directions around the axis of anisotropy. In such patterns, if the gradients are added together directly, the cancellation is so severe that the result often has little relation to the direction of anisotropy. Thus the difference between rotating the gradient vectors or leaving them be is often the difference between being able or unable to detect the anisotropy. Note also that smoothing the image first and then computing the gradients is exactly the same as computing the gradients and then smoothing. It will not avoid the difficulties of cancellation.

C.   Coherence

In addition to finding the direction of anisotropy, it is important to determine how strong an anisotropy there is. If the orientation of the local J vectors are nearly uniformly distributed between 0 and 2π, then the orientation ϕ of slight anisotropy is not very meaningful. Conversely, if all the J vectors are pointing the same way then the indication of anisotropy is quite strong and ϕ is very meaningful. A simple way of measuring the strength of the peak in the distribution of J vectors is to look at the ratio $\chi(x,y) = |W * J| / W * |J|$ which we will call the *coherence* of the flow pattern. If the J vectors are close to uniformly distributed, then the ratio will be nearly zero. If the J vectors all point the same way, the ratio will be one. In between, the ratio will increase as the peak gets narrower.

D.   Summary

The computation of the flow direction and local coherence can be summarized as follows.   First the image $I(x,y)$ is

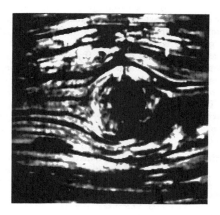

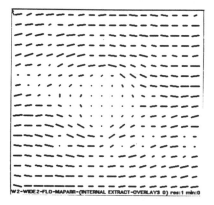

Figure 2: An image of wood grain with its flow field. Estimated flow directions are given by the black needles. The length of the needle encodes coherence. Notice that coherence is low within the knot at the center.

convolved with the isotropic portion $H(x,y)$ of the filter response. The result $C(x,y)$ is then differentiated (by finite differences) to form $C_x(x,y)$ and $C_y(x,y)$.   The resulting vectors $(C_x(x,y), C_y(x,y))$ are rotated by computing $J_1(x,y) = 2C_x(x,y)C_y(x,y)$ and $J_2(x,y) = C_x^2(x,y) - C_y^2(x,y)$. The gradient magnitude $J_3(x,y) = [C_x^2(x,y) + C_y^2(x,y)]^{1/2}$ also has to be computed in order to measure the coherence. The next step is to convolve $J_1(x,y), J_2(x,y)$, and $J_3(x,y)$ with the weighting function $W(x,y)$ to obtain $J_1^*(x,y), J_2^*(x,y)$, and $J_3^*(x,y)$. The angle $\phi(x,y)$ of anisotropy and the coherence $\chi(x,y)$ can then be computed from the formulas

$$\phi(x,y) \approx \tan^{-1}(J_1^*(x,y)/J_2^*(x,y))/2$$

and

$$\chi(x,y) = (J_1^*(x,y)^2 + J_2^*(x,y)^2)^{1/2}/J_3^*(x,y).$$

An example of this computation applied to a picture of a piece of wood is shown in figure 2. The flow direction $\phi(x,y) + \pi/2$ is displayed by the orientation of small needles superimposed on the image. The lengths of the needles is proportional to the coherence $\chi(x,y)$. Note that the pattern is strongly oriented except near the knot in the middle.

E.   Relation To Prior Work

The flow computation just described bears an interesting relation to an early proposal of David Marr that information about local distributions of oriented edge elements be included in the *primal sketch* (Marr 76). If this proposal is combined with his later work with Hildreth on edge detection (Marr & Hildreth, 1980) it results in a special case of the above computation. Marr and Hildreth define edges as zero-crossings in the Laplacian of the Gaussian smoothed image. The natural combination of Marr's proposal with this definition of edge elements calls for examining the local density of zero crossings as a function of orientation. For stationary zero-mean Gaussian processes the square of the oriented zero-crossing density is approximately $V(\theta)$ (see appendix B). Thus in the special case where the point spread function of the filter is $S = (\partial/\partial x)\nabla^2 \exp(-(x^2+y^2)/2\sigma^2)$ our computation can be viewed as computing the direction of minimal edge density in the Marr-Hildreth theory.

Zucker's work on flow (Zucker 1983) is also related to a special case of the above computation. For biological reasons, he prefers to use oriented second derivatives of Gaussians as the initial filters. These have $F(r,\theta) = r^2 \exp(-r^2/2)\cos^2(\theta)$. Instead of looking at the variance of the filter outputs as the orientation is changed, he combines the outputs in a biologically motivated relaxation process. Although quite different in detail, the computation described here has much in common with his technique.

III   Flow coordinates.

The orientation field is an abstraction from the anisotropic pattern that defines it. We can, for example, get the same spiral field from a pattern composed of bands, irregular streaks, dot pairs, etc. In addition to measuring the orientation field, it is useful to be able to produce a description of the underlying pattern independent of the changing direction of anisotropy. Such a description would make it possible to recognize, for example, that two very different orientation fields are defined by the same kind of bands or streaks.

A powerful way to remove the effects of changing orientation is to literally "straighten" the image, subjecting it to a deformation that maps the flow lines into straight, parallel lines in a canonical (e.g. horizontal) orientation. Performing this deformation is equivalent to viewing the image in a coordinate system (u,v), with $u = u(x,y)$ and $v = v(x,y)$ that everywhere satisfies

$$\nabla u \cdot (\sin \phi, -\cos\phi) = 0. \qquad (6)$$

Equation 6 does not determine a unique coordinate system. An additional constraint may be imposed by choosing lines of constant v orthogonal to those of constant u, i.e,

$$\nabla v \cdot (\cos \phi, \sin \phi) = 0 \qquad (7)$$

which has the desirable effect of avoiding the introduction of spurious shear in the deformation.

Even with equation 7, an additional constraint is needed, because we are free to specify arbitrary scaling functions for the u and v axes. In the spirit of equation 7, we want to choose these functions to avoid the introduction of spurious stretch or dilation. Although difficult to do globally (one might minize total stretch,) we will usually want to construct a fairly local coordinate frame around some point of interest. For this purpose, it suffices to take that point as the origin, scaling the axes $u = 0$ and $v = 0$ to preserve arc-length along them.

Intuitively, the flow field describes the way the pattern is bent, and viewing the image in these *flow coordinates* straightens the

Figure 3: A flow coordinate grid obtained for the image of figure 2.

pattern out. Figure 3 shows the flow coordinate grid for the wood-grain image from figure 1. The grid lines were computed by taking steps of fixed length in the direction $(cos\phi, sin\phi)$ or $(-sin\phi, cos\phi)$ for lines across and along the direction of flow respectively, using bilinear interpolation on the orientation field. Since ϕ is always computed between 0 and π, we must assume that there are no spurious discontinuities in direction to track smoothly.

For many purposes it is unnecessary to compute the deformed image explicitly, but doing so vividly illustrates the flow coordinates' ability to simplify the pattern. Figure 4 shows the deformation from image coordinates to flow coordinates in several stages. As the grain lines straighten the knot shrinks and finally vanishes. The deformed images were anti-aliased using texture-map techniques (Williams, 1983) The deformed image shows, to a reasonable approximation, what the grain would have looked like had it not been subjected to the deforming influence of the knot.

Thus far, we have separated the image into a flow field, and a pattern derived by viewing the image in flow coordinates. We argued earlier that the advantage of this decomposition, like the decomposition of an image into intrinsic images, is that the components are liable to be simpler and more closely tied to independent parts of the pattern-generating process than is the original image. To exploit the decomposition, we need ways of analyzing, describing, and comparing both the flow field and the straightened pattern. These are difficult problems. In the remainder of this section, we present several examples illustrating the utility of the decomposition.

A.   A coordinate frame for edge detection.

Oriented measurements have been widely used in edge detection. For example Marr & Poggio (1979) employed directional second derivative operators, whose zero-crossings were taken to denote rapid intensity changes. Due to the difficulty in selecting an orientation, Marr & Hildreth (1980) later abandoned this scheme, in favor of zero-crossings of the Laplacian, a non-directional operator.

The flow field provides two meaningful directions—along and across the direction of flow—in which to look for edges within an oriented pattern. Zero-crossings in the second directional derivative in the direction of ϕ (against the grain) should highlight edges that contribute to defining the flow field, while zero-

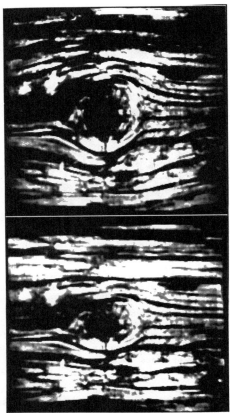

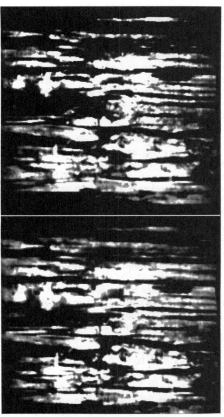

Figure 4: Deformation, in stages, from image coordinates to flow coordinates. Upper left: the original image; Lower left, upper right: two intermediate stages, in which the grain's curvature has diminshed, and the knot compressed; Lower right: the image as seen in flow coordinates: the grain lines are straight and the knot has vanished, showing approximately what the grain would have looked like had it not been deformed by the intrusion of the knot.

crossings in the second derivative perpendicular to ϕ (with the grain) should highlight anomalous elements or terminations. The sum of these two derivatives is the Laplacian.

The two directional derivatives of the wood grain image are shown, with the Laplacian, in figure 5. Indeed, the derivative against the grain captures all the elements comprising the grain pattern, while the derivative with the grain does not appear meaningful. The Laplacian confuses these very different signals by adding them together.

The derivative along the grain can also be meaningful, where anomalous elements are present. In addition to being perceptually salient, such anomalies are often physically significant, with origins such as cracks, intrusions, or occlusions, that are distinct from those of the main pattern. In man-made structures, anamolies are often important because they indicate some variety of flaw.

Figure 6 shows a pattern of aligned elements (straw) with some anomalous elements. The directional second derivatives along and across the flow direction are shown, together with their sum (which is just the Laplacian.) Differentiating along the grain highlights anomalous elements, attenuating the rest (thus finding the "needles" in the haystack.) Differentiating across the grain supresses the anomalies. The Laplacian shows both.

A related demonstration is shown in figure 7, in which the anomalous elements have actually been removed by directional median filtering in the flow direction.

B.   Singularities.

We have shown several ways in which viewing an oriented pattern in flow coordinates facilitates analysis and description of the pattern. Describing and anlyzing the flow field itself is the other side of the coin. The topology of a flow field, as of any vector field, is determined by the structure of its singularities, those points at which the field vanishes. Identifying and describing singularities is therefore basic to describing the flow field. The singularities provide the framework around which metric properties, such as curvature, may be described. Singularities are also perceptually salient (see figure 8.)

A robust basis for identifying singularities is the index or winding number (Spivak, 1979.) Suppose we follow a closed curve on a vector field. As we traverse the circuit, the vector rotates continuously, returning to its original orientation when the circuit is completed. The index or winding number of the curve is the number of revolutions made by the vector in traversing the curve. The index of a point is the index of a small circle as we shrink it around the point:

$$\mathrm{ind}(x,y) \;= \lim_{\epsilon \to 0} \tfrac{1}{2\pi} \int_0^{2\pi} \tfrac{\partial}{\partial \theta} \phi(x + \epsilon \cos\theta, y + \epsilon \sin\theta)\, d\theta$$
$$= \lim_{\epsilon \to 0} \tfrac{1}{2\pi} \int_0^{2\pi} (-\sin\theta, \cos\theta)$$
$$\cdot \nabla \phi(x + \epsilon \cos\theta, y + \epsilon \sin\theta)\, d\theta.$$

To compute the winding number numerically, we divide the flow field into suitably small rectangles, summing the rotation of ϕ around each rectangle. As in computing the flow lines, we assume

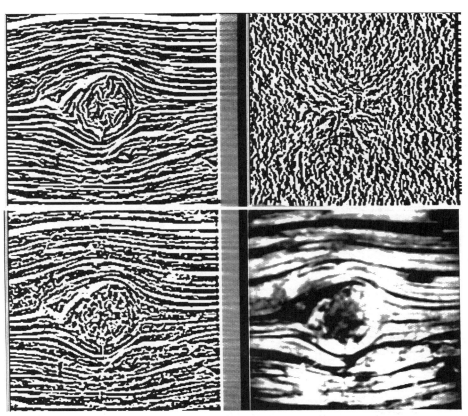

Figure 5: Using flow coordinates for edge detection. Upper left: 2nd directional derivative across the flow direction. Upper right: 2nd directional derivative along the flow direction. The first of these highlights the oriented structure, the second supresses it. Lower left: the sum of the directional derivatives is the Laplacian.

that ϕ has no spurious discontinuities. Where the result is non-zero, the rectangle surrounds a singularity. Figure 9 shows an example of the detection of singularities using winding number, for a fingerprint. We are currently working on classifying the singularities, and using them to describe the topology of the flow field.

IV   Conclusion

We addressed the problem of analyzing oriented patterns by decomposing them into a flow field, describing the direction of anisotropy, and describing the pattern independent of changing flow direction.

A specific computation for estimating the flow direction was proposed. The computation can be viewed as a) finding the direction of maximal variance in the output of a linear filter, b) combining gradient directions locally, or c) finding the direction of maximal edge density. The computation has been applied to a number of natural and man-made patterns with consistent success.

The flow field was then used to form a coordinate system in which to view the pattern. Two orthogonal families of curves—along and across the direction of flow—form the coordinate system's parameter lines. Viewing the pattern in these flow coordinates amounts to deforming the pattern so that the flow lines become parallel straight lines. This deformation produces a pattern that is simpler, more regular, and therefore more amenable to analysis and description than the original one.

Several examples of the use of this decomposition were presented. These included the use of the flow coordinates to provide preferred directions for edge detection, detection of anomalies, fitting simple models to the straightened pattern, and detecting singularities in the flow field.

Our ongoing work focuses on the analysis of patterns with multiple axes of anisotropy, statistical modeling and resynthesis of straightened patterns, and richer description of the structure of the flow field.

Appendix A: Derivation of Equation 5

The integrals in equation 4 can be evaluated fairly easily by expansion using equation 3 for V. The numerator of $\tan(2\phi)$ can be written

$$\int_0^\pi V(\theta)\sin(2\theta)d\theta = W * [2C_x^2 \int_0^\pi \sin(\theta)\cos^3(\theta)d\theta$$
$$+ 4C_x C_y \int_0^\pi \sin^2(\theta)\cos^2(\theta)d\theta$$
$$+ 2C_y^2 \int_0^\pi \sin^3(\theta)\cos(\theta)d\theta].$$

The first and third integrals are zero and the middle integral is $\pi/8$. Hence

$$\int_0^\pi V(\theta)\sin(2\theta)d\theta = (\pi/2)W * C_x C_y$$

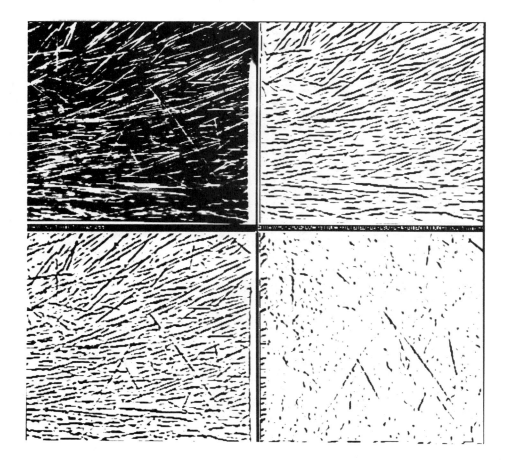

Figure 6: "Finding the needle in the haystack." In this straw pattern, directional derivatives across the flow direction show elements aligned with the pattern (upper right.) Those along the flow direction show anomalous elements (lower right.) The Laplacian (lower left) shows both.

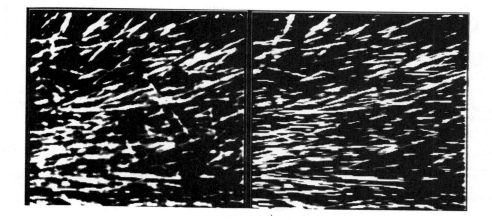

Figure 7: Left: the straw picture from figure 6. Right: the anomalous elements have been removed by directional median filtering in the flow direction. (Following a suggestion by Richard Szeliski.)

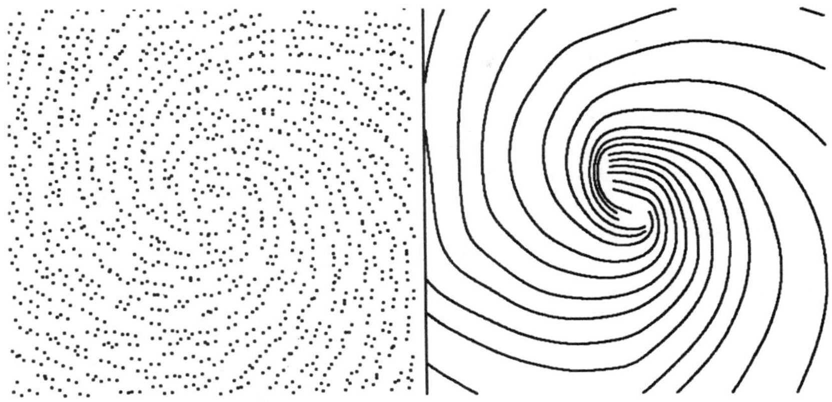

Figure 8: A spiral Glass pattern and its flow lines. The pattern is perceptually dominated by the singularity at the center. Since the flow field vanishes at a singularity, the flow lines obtained by integrating the flow field tend to become ill behaved as they approach one.

The denominator of $\tan(2\phi)$ similarly is

$$\int_0^\pi V(\theta)\cos(2\theta)d\theta = W * 2C_x^2 \int_0^\pi 2\cos^4(\theta) - \cos^2(\theta)d\theta$$

$$+ 4C_x C_y \int_0^\pi \sin(4\theta)d\theta$$

$$+ 2C_y^2 \int_0^\pi 2\cos^2(\theta)\sin^2(\theta) - sin^2(\theta)d\theta].$$

Here the first integral is $\pi/4$, the second integral is zero and the third is $-\pi/4$. Hence the above expression can be simplified to

$$\int_0^\pi V(\theta)\cos(2\theta)d\theta = (\pi/4)W * (C_x^2 - C_y^2).$$

Substituting for both the numerator and denominator of $\tan(2\phi)$ in equation 4 yields

$$\phi = \tan^{-1}\left(\frac{W * 2C_x C_y}{W * (C_x^2 - C_y^2)}\right)/2$$

There is a close connection between the flow computation described in section 2 and the density of edges in the Marr-Hildreth theory of edge detection. Suppose the image $I(x,y)$ is a stationary zero-mean Gaussian process and let $D(x,y)$ be the Laplacian of a Gaussian. The density of zero-crossings in $B_\theta(x,y) = D * R_\theta[I]$ along the x-axis can be approximated by (Papoulis, 1965; Rice, 1944-45)

$$\lambda^2(\theta) \approx \frac{1}{\pi^2}\frac{\int \omega^2 K(\omega)d\omega}{\int K(\omega)d\omega}$$

where $K(\omega)$ is the power spectrum of a slice through B_θ along the x-axis. Using Papoulis' Fourier transform conventions, the numerator can be converted to a spatial integral through the identity

$$\int B_x^2 dx = \frac{1}{2\pi}\int \omega^2 K(\omega)d\omega.$$

Similarly, the denominator can be converted with the identity

$$\int B^2 dx = \frac{1}{2\pi}\int K(\omega)d\omega.$$

If the integrals are computed locally with the windowing function W, then we have the following estimate for zero crossing density:

$$\lambda^2(\theta) \approx \frac{1}{\pi^2}\frac{W * B_x^2}{W * B^2}$$

If W is radially symmetric, $W * B^2$ will not depend on θ so the maximum zero-crossing density will occur at the maximum of $W * B_x^2$. By assumption, the mean of the process is zero, so $W * B_x^2$ is the variance of $D_x * R_\theta[I]$. Thus, for stationary zero-mean Gaussian processes, if $S = D_x$, $\lambda^2(\theta) \approx V(\theta)$.

References

Horn, B.K.P "Understanding image intensities," *Aritificial Intelligence*, **8**, 1977, 201–231.

Barrow, H., & Tenenbaum, J. M. "Recovering intrinsic scene charactristics from images. In Hanson & Riseman (Eds.), *Computer Vision Systems*. New York: Academic Press, 1978.

Marr, D. *Vision*, 1982, Freeman, San Fransisco CA.

Barr, A. "Global and local deformation of solid primitives." *Computer Graphics*, **18**, pp. 21–30, July 1984.

Brodatz, P. Textures. New York: Dover, 1966.

Glass, L. "Moire effect from random dots." *Nature*, 1969, **243**, 578-580.

Hubel, D. H. & Wiesel, T. N. "Receptive fields, binocular interaction and functional architecture in the cat's visual cortex." *J. Physiol., Lond.*, 1962, **166**, 106–154

Papoulis, *Probability, Random Variables and Stochastic Processes*. New York: McGraw-Hill, 1965.

Marr, D. "Early processing of visual information." *Proc. Royal Soc.*, 1976, **B 275**, 484-519.

Marr, D., & Hildreth, E. "Theory of edge detection." *Proc. Royal Soc.*, 1980, **B 207**, 187-217.

Marr, D., & Poggio, T. "A computational theory of human stereo vision." Proc. Royal Soc., 1979, **204**, 301-328.

Rice, S. O. "Mathematical Analysis of Random Noise." *Bell Sys. Tech. J.*, **23-24**, 1944-1945.

Schiller, P. H., Finlay, B. L. & Volman, S. F. "Quantitative studies of single-cell properties in monkey striate cortex. II. Orientation specificity and ocular dominance." *J. Neurophysiology* **39**, 1976, 1320-1333.

Spivak, *Differential Geometry*. Berkely, California: Publish or Perish, 1979.

Stevens, K. "Computation of locally parallel structure." *Biological Cybernetics*, 1978, **29** 29-26.

Williams, L. "Pyramidal Parametrics" *Computer Graphics,* **17** No. 3, 1983

Zucker, S. "Computational and psychophysical experiments in grouping." In Beck, Hope, Rosenfeld (Eds.),*Human and Machine Vision*, New York: Academic Press, 1983.

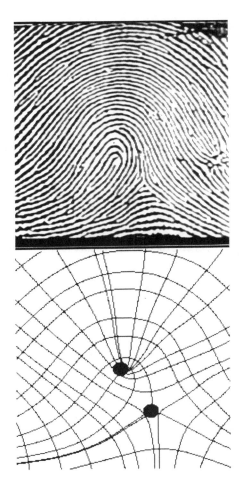

Figure 9: A fingerprint and its flow coordinate grid. The two white circles represent the major singularities, which were detected by measuring the flow field's winding number.

VISUAL RECOGNITION FROM SPATIAL CORRESPONDENCE AND PERCEPTUAL ORGANIZATION

David G. Lowe

Courant Institute of Mathematical Sciences
New York University
251 Mercer St., New York, NY 10012

Abstract

Depth reconstruction from the two-dimensional image plays an important role in certain visual tasks and has been a major focus of of computer vision research. However, in this paper we argue that most instances of recognition in human and machine vision can best be performed without the preliminary reconstruction of depth. Three other mechanisms are described that can be used to bridge the gap between the two-dimensional image and knowledge of three-dimensional objects. First, a process of perceptual organization can be used to form groupings and structures in the image that are likely to be invariant over a wide range of viewpoints. Secondly, evidential reasoning can be used to combine evidence from these groupings and other sources of information to reduce the size of the search-space during model-based matching. Finally, a process of spatial correspondence can be used to bring the projections of three-dimensional models into direct correspondence with the image by solving for unknown viewpoint and model parameters. These methods have been combined in an experimental computer vision system named SCERPO. This system has demonstrated the use of these methods for the recognition of objects from unknown viewpoints in single gray-scale images.

Introduction

The standard model for much recent research in computer vision has been based on the reconstruction of depth information from the image prior to recognition. However, in this paper we will argue that this is not the primary pathway used for most instances of recognition in human vision. Although depth measurement has an important role in certain visual problems, it is often not available and is not needed for typical instances of recognizing familiar objects. Instead, we will propose that the primary bottom-up descriptive analysis of the image can best be performed by a process of perceptual organization. This process leads to the formation of significant groupings and structures directly from the two-dimensional image data. These groupings are partially invariant to viewpoint and can be matched directly against three-dimensional object models. The verification of these matches can be performed by spatially mapping the projection of three-dimensional object models onto the image data, through a process of viewpoint and model-parameter determination.

These methods have been combined in a vision system named SCERPO (for Spatial Correspondence, Evidential Reasoning, and Perceptual Organization). While seemingly solving a more difficult problem—the direct recognition of objects from unknown viewpoints in two-dimensional images—the approach is shown to be apparently simpler and more flexible than those that rely upon depth reconstruction. While it is true that the appearance of a three-dimensional object can change completely as it is viewed from different viewpoints, it is also true that many aspects of an object's projection remain invariant over large ranges of viewpoints (examples include instances of connectivity, collinearity, parallelism, repetitive textures, and certain symmetries). It is the role of perceptual organization to detect those image groupings that are unlikely to have arisen by accident of viewpoint or position. Once detected, these groupings can be matched to corresponding structures in the objects through a knowledge-based process of evidential reasoning. These methods for evidential reasoning were initially developed for combining probabilistic information in diagnostic expert systems, but they can be readily adapted to combining information regarding probabilistic associations between particular image features and object models. This probabilistic information is used to order the search strategy so that the most reliable and informative information is tested first.

The reliability of the search process depends upon the the final verification of each hypothesized interpretation. SCERPO uses a quantitative method to simultaneously determine the best viewpoint and object parameter values for fitting the projection of a three-dimensional model to given two-dimensional features. It allows a few initial hypothesized matches to be extended by making exact predictions for the locations of other object features in the image. This provides a highly reliable method for verifying the presence of a particular object, since it can make use of the spatial information in the image to the full degree of available resolution.

The role of depth recovery in human vision

A substantial fraction of recent computer vision research has been aimed at the bottom-up derivation of depth or surface orientation from image data, using information such as stereo, motion, shading or texture. This has come to be known as the "Shape from X" paradigm. Marr [12] suggested that these sources of information could be combined in a representation known as the $2\frac{1}{2}$-D sketch that would allow one source of information to compensate for the absence of another. The depth representation would then be used to determine correspondence with three-dimensional object representations, the assumption being that it would be easier to match a three-dimensional model to a depth representation than to two-dimensional image data.

Human vision contains many of these components for recovering depth, and they presumably have important functions. However, biological visual systems have many objectives, so it does not follow that these components are central to the problem of visual recognition. In fact, the available evidence would seem to indicate the opposite. The first problem with these methods is that depth information is often unavailable or requires an unacceptably long interval of time to obtain. Stereo vision is only useful for objects within a restricted portion of the visual field and range of depths for any given degree of eye vergence, and is never useful for distant objects. Motion information is available only when there is sufficient relative motion between observer and object, which in practice is also usually limited to nearby objects. Recognition times are usually so short that it seems unlikely that the appropriate eye vergence movements or elapsed time measurements could be taken prior to recognition even for those cases in which they may be useful. Depth measurements from shading or texture are apparently restricted to special cases such as regions of approximately uniform reflectance or regular texture, and they lack the quantitative accuracy or completeness of stereo or motion.

Secondly, human vision exhibits an excellent level of performance in recognizing images—such as line drawings—in which there is very little potential for the bottom-up derivation of depth information. Whatever mechanisms are being used for line-drawing recognition have presumably developed from their use in recognizing three-dimensional scenes. The common assumption that line-drawing recognition is a learned or cultural phenomena is not supported by the evidence. In a seemingly definitive experiment, Hochberg and Brooks [6] describe the case of a 19-month-old human baby who had had no previous exposure to any kinds of two-dimensional images, yet was immediately able to recognize ordinary line drawings of known objects.

Finally, there has been no clear demonstration of the value of depth information for performing recognition, even when it is available. The recognition of objects from complete depth images, such as those produced by a laser scanner, has not been shown to be much easier than for systems that begin only with the two-dimensional image. This paper will describe methods for directly comparing the projection of three-dimensional representations to the two-dimensional image without the need for any prior depth information.

Of course, none of this is meant to imply that depth recovery is an unimportant problem or lacks a significant role in human vision. Depth information may be crucial for the initial stages of visual learning or for acquiring certain types of knowledge about unfamiliar structures. It is also clearly useful for making precise measurements as an aid to manipulation or obstacle avoidance. However, it seems likely that the role of depth recovery in common instances of recognition has been overstated.

Matching 3-D knowledge to the image

Although knowledge of object shape, context, and surface properties must naturally be represented in three-dimensional form, this knowledge can be matched directly against the two-dimensional image through the use of projection. A major practical difficulty is in using image measurements to determine the unknown projection parameters. Six parameters are needed to specify an arbitrary position and orientation of an object with respect to the camera, and there may be other unknown parameters internal to the object. However, each match between a point in the image and a point on the object allows us to solve for two parameters. Therefore, only three or four hypothesized matches between the image and an object model are typically needed to solve for the projection parameters. Once these parameters have been determined, it is straightforward to carry out the projection and extend the match by making accurate predictions for the locations of other model features in the image. These further matches may be used to solve for any remaining model parameters, but their most important function is to provide reliable confirmation for the correctness of an interpretation.

The author has previously presented a mathematical technique [7, 9] for solving for viewpoint and model parameters given some matches between image and model. Briefly, this method linearizes the projection equations and uses Newton-Raphson iteration to solve simultaneously for the unknown parameters. Since the projection equations are very smooth (consisting of linear combinations of *sin* and *cos* functions of viewpoint), the method has quadratic convergence and typically requires only 3 iterations to achieve high accuracy. This basic technique has been extended to perform least-squares solution of over-determined systems, and to allow matching of image lines to model lines (without concern for the location of line terminations). Given these methods, the problem of verification is largely solved for well-specified objects, and the remaining problems of recognition are those of reducing the size of the search space to produce the few initial matches.

There is experimental evidence that human recognition also relies upon the determination of viewpoint parameters for projecting a three-dimensional object description onto the image. Cooper & Shepard [4] describe experiments in which subjects are asked to compare images at varying orientations to previously memorized shapes. They found that the recognition time varied linearly in the angle of rotation between the image and the orientation of the original memorized shape. In conjunction with their other work on mental rotation, this would seem to indicate that recognition is performed by bringing a prior representation into spatial correspondence with image data by manipulating viewpoint parameters.

Allowing for variations in object models

The capability for recognizing objects from their two-dimensional projections is possible only because of previous knowledge regarding the objects. However, recognition does not imply that we must know every aspect of an object's appearance prior to recognition. Object models may be parameterized with variable sizes, angles, or articulations between components, with expected bounds given for each parameter. As already mentioned, it is possible to back-solve for these parameters using the same methods as when solving for viewpoint. Just as important is the fact that there is no precise boundary between what is an object and what is a component. It is possible to recognize commonly-occurring components, such as cylinders, rectangular solids, or repeated patterns, as parameterized objects in their own right. The only requirement is that there be fewer unknown parameters to the description than there are useful measurements to be made from the image data. These recognized components—even if the identification is only tentative—can then be used to suggest the identity of the more specific structure of which they are a part. If the identification of the components is quite certain, then they can even be combined into previously unknown or very loosely parameterized relationships. Most objects can be represented both in terms of their overall shape and in terms of a combination of components, and different images can best make use of each type of description depending upon such variables as image resolution, viewpoint, and occlusion.

Previous work on model-based vision

There is a considerable body of previous research in model-based vision. The remarkable early work of Roberts [13] demonstrated the recognition of certain polyhedral objects by precisely solving for viewpoint and object parameters. Unfortunately, this work was poorly incorporated in later vision research, which tended to emphasize less quantitative methods. The ACRONYM system of Brooks [1] used a general symbolic constraint solver to calculate bounds on viewpoint and model parameters from image measurements. These bounds could then be used to check the consistency

of interpretations produced by general matching operations, and were capable of handling wide classes of generic object descriptions. Goad [5] describes the use of automatic programming methods to precompute a highly efficient search path and viewpoint-solving technique for each object to be recognized. This research has been incorporated in an industrial computer vision system by Silma Inc. which has the capability of performing all aspects of recognition within as little as 1 second. Because of their runtime efficiency, these precomputation techniques are likely to remain the method of choice for industrial systems dealing with small numbers of objects. Other closely related research on model-based vision has been performed by Shirai [14] and Walter & Tropf [16].

Perceptual organization in SCERPO

Unlike previous model-based systems, SCERPO makes use of perceptual organization as the central process for bottom-up analysis of an image. Perceptual organization refers to a basic capability of the human visual system to derive relevant groupings and structures from an image without prior knowledge of its contents. For example, people will immediately detect clustering, connectivity, collinearity, parallelism, and repetitive textures when shown an otherwise randomly distributed set of image elements. This grouping capability of human vision was studied by the early Gestalt psychologists [17] and is related to research in texture description [10]. A major function of perceptual organization is to distinguish non-accidental groupings from the background of groupings that arise through accident of viewpoint or random positioning [18, 8]. Those groupings that are non-accidental in origin will also be partially invariant with respect to viewpoint and be most suited to model-based recognition (see [9] for a much more detailed discussion).

In order to provide image features for input to perceptual organization, the first few levels of image analysis in SCERPO use established methods of edge detection, as shown in Figures 1–3. The 512-by-512-pixel image shown in Figure 1 was convolved with a Laplacian of Gaussian function ($\sigma = 1.8$ pixels) as suggested by the Marr-Hildreth [11] theory of edge detection. The zero-crossings of this function are shown in Figure 3. Of course, many of these zero-crossings do not correspond to significant edges in the image. We remove those corresponding to insignificant intensity changes by applying the Sobel gradient operator to the $\nabla^2 G$ convolution. Only those points that are above a chosen gradient threshold and lie on a zero crossing are retained in Figure 5. These remaining zero-crossings are linked into lists of points on the basis of connectivity.

The first stage of perceptual organization is to group the linked lists of points into perceptually significant curve segments. The author has previously described a method for finding straight-line and constant-curvature segmentations at multiple scales and for measuring their significance [9, Chap. 4]. However, here we use a simplified method that selects only the single highest-significance line representation at each point along the curve. The significance of a straight line fit to a list of points is measured as the ratio of its length divided by the maximum deviation of a point from the line. This provides a scale-independent measure of significance that places no prior bounds on the allowable deviations. This is then used in a modified version of the recursive endpoint subdivision method. A segment is subdivided at the point with maximum deviation from a line connecting its endpoints. If the maximum significance of any of the subsegments is greater than the significance of the complete segment, then the subsegments are returned. Otherwise the single segment is returned. This procedure is applied recursively until each segment contains fewer than 3 points. The procedure will return a segment covering every point along the curve, but those with a length-to-deviation ratio less than 4 are discarded. This method is implemented in only 40 lines of Lisp code, yet does a reasonable job of detecting the most perceptually significant straight line groupings in the linked point data. The results are shown in Figure 4.

The straight line segments are indexed according to endpoint locations and orientation. Then a sequence of procedures is executed to detect instances of collinearity, endpoint proximity (connectivity), and parallelism. A region around each endpoint or segment is examined to determine candidates for grouping. Each potential grouping is assigned a significance value that is roughly inversely proportional to the likelihood that it is accidental in origin. This is done in a scale-independent manner (i.e., measurements of endpoint proximity or separation of parallel lines are divided by the length of the shortest of the two line segments). After the execution of this grouping process, the many groupings are ranked in order of significance. Unfortunately, it is difficult to display the results of this grouping process without showing a separate image for each grouping that has been detected. Although several hundred significant groupings were detected in the line segments of Figure 4, we show in Figure 5 only the two sets of highly-ranked groupings that were actually used for successful recognition.

Evidential reasoning

Evidential reasoning refers to the combination of different sources of information or evidence in order to reach a conclusion with a specified level of certainty. This form of reasoning has been developed for use in diagnostic expert systems, among other applications. It can be used, for example, to calculate the likelihood that a particular disease is present given a number of symptoms. We are faced with a very similar problem in vision when we wish to calculate the likelihood that a particular object is present in an image given a number of detected features and other sources of information. The performance requirements for evidential reasoning in vision are much less stringent than in medical expert systems, since we have a reliable procedure for final

verification and only need to use the evidential reasoning to suggest the most efficient ordering for our search.

In order to minimize the search time, we would like to order our consideration of hypotheses according to decreasing values of P_k/W_k, where P_k is the probability that a particular hypothesis for the presence of object k is correct, and W_k is the amount of work required to verify or refute it. Evidence can come from many sources: we may have initial expectations for the presence of certain objects, contextual expectations resulting from the presence of already-detected objects, and information from many forms of image data such as perceptual groupings, texture, color, or metric measurements. The initial researchers in medical expert systems rejected the use of Bayesian methods for combining evidence [15], since they assumed that it would either require unrealistic independence assumptions or an impossibly large number of known statistical parameters. However, recent work by Charniak [2] has shown that it is possible to formalize the previous apparently ad-hoc methods within a Bayesian framework. The application of Charniak's methods to ordering search during recognition is discussed in [9, Chap. 6]. An important aspect of evidential reasoning is that it offers a strong basis for building learning systems in which the required statistical parameters are moved towards their correct values as the system gains experience.

The evidential reasoning component of SCERPO has not yet been developed as fully as other parts of the system. Since the system has only been used with a single object under consideration, the performance requirements for minimizing search have not been great. The system makes use of a list of perceptual groupings and the model features that could give rise to them. This list is entered by the user at the same time as model specification. For example, the groupings shown in Figure 5 consist of particular combinations of parallelism and endpoint proximity that could be matched to various parts of the object model. The probabilities of non-accidentalness for the image relations that make up a grouping are multiplied together to calculate the probability for the grouping as a whole. This is multiplied by an estimate of the likelihood of correctness for the match (assuming a non-accidental grouping) that has been entered for each element of the association list, and these final values are used to order the search. We plan to explore methods for incrementally learning the required probability values in future research.

Verification of interpretations

The verification component of SCERPO is able to take a tentative match between a couple of image features and model features and return a reliable answer as to whether the match is correct. If the object is present, this module will extend the match as much as possible and determine the precise viewpoint.

Given the initial set of correspondences, the iterative

Figures 1–6: The original image of some desk staplers is shown in Fig. 1. This image was convolved with a $\nabla^2 G$ function ($\sigma = 1.8$ pixels). The zero-crossings of this function are shown in Fig. 2. The gradiant of the convolved image was measured, and Fig. 3 shows only those zero-crossings at locations where the function had a gradient above a selected threshold value. Fig. 4 shows the segments that resulted from linking of zero-crossings and selection of the most significant straight-line segmentations (shown superimposed on the original image). Fig. 5 shows the two perceptual groupings that were actually used to initiate successful recognition. After solving for model viewpoint, selecting new segments most consistent with model predictions, and iterating, the segments shown in Fig. 6 were selected as being consistent with one viewpoint.

7.   8.

Figures 7–8: These final figures show the object model projected onto the image from the two final calculated viewpoints. The slight orientation error in one direction in Fig. 8 is due to small inaccuracies in the model and image measurements as well as the small amount of data being used to determine viewpoint.

viewpoint-solving procedure described earlier is used to determine the best viewpoint that would project the model features onto the image features. The current implementation solves only for viewpoint and does not allow variable model parameters. If large errors remain following the least-squares fit, the solution is rejected as inconsistent. All edge features from the model are then projected onto the image using the calculated viewpoint, and the image data structure is searched for segments that are close to the predictions. Matches are evaluated according to the degree of agreement in transverse location, orientation, and length with the prediction, and according to the lack of ambiguity between competing matches for a single object feature. This evaluation is used to rank the potential matches and only those above a high threshold value, or else the single highest-ranked match, is selected. The selected matches are combined with the original matches and the least-squares viewpoint determination is repeated. An estimate is maintained of the error bounds, based upon the number of matches and the least-squares deviations, so that instances of ambiguity become less likely as the viewpoint estimate improves. The set of matches is repeatedly extended until no more can be found. The final result of this process is the selection of a set of segments, as shown in Figure 6, that are consistent with a single viewpoint of the model, as shown in Figure 7.

The current verification process in SCERPO could clearly be extended to include many other aspects of verification than just the matching of line segments. For example, the viewpoint determination for the model instance shown in Figure 8 has a small error in orientation, due to errors in image measurements and the small number of segments

being used for the least-squares matching. However, given this degree of recognition, it would now be straightforward to go back to the original image data or zero-crossings and make further image measurements.

Implementation details

SCERPO is written in several different languages. The image processing components are executed on a VICOM image processor under the *Vsh* software facility developed by Robert Hummel and Dayton Clark [3]. The VICOM can perform a 3x3 convolution against the entire image in a single video frame time. However, our edge detection method uses an 18x18 convolution that is performed by 36 of the 3x3 convolutions and the appropriate image translations and additions. The steps up to figure 5 are performed on the VICOM, after which the zero-crossing image is transferred to a VAX 11/750 running UNIX 4.2 for subsequent processing. A program written in C reads the original image and produces a file of linked edge points (requiring about 30 seconds of CPU time). All other components are written in Franz Lisp. Segmentation into straight line segments requires 40 seconds, indexing and grouping operations require about 1 minute and the later stages of matching and verification took 40 seconds for this example.

The object models used by the system consists merely of a set of straight 3-D line segments. Each segment has a simple visibility specification, listing viewpoint ranges over which it is visible. A full hidden-line algorithm and more complete object models would improve the performance of the system.

Conclusions and future research

The current capabilities of SCERPO provide a framework that could be used to incorporate numerous additional capabilities, each of which would improve the generality of the system or its level of performance. A brief list of these possible extensions might include the following: incorporation of a wider range of perceptual grouping operations, the ability to handle variable model parameters, the recognition of object components and their subsequent combination, more complete modeling with surface information and hidden-line algorithms, the use of color and texture information, the expanded use of evidential reasoning, the incremental learning of associations and probabilities, the detection of curve segments as well as straight lines, and more detailed verification in terms of the original image data.

Perceptual organization and the methods for achieving spatial correspondence offer an alternative to the use of depth reconstruction and matching in three-dimensions. It has been argued in this paper that most instances of recognition in human vision also work directly from two-dimensional data. It should be possible to provide a definitive answer to this question by designing psychophysical experiments that test human recognition capabilities with different combinations of available information. A final answer to this question would carry many implications for the future design of knowledge-based vision systems.

Acknowledgments

Implementation of the SCERPO system relied upon the extensive facilities and software of the NYU vision laboratory, which are due to the efforts of Robert Hummel, Jack Schwartz, and many others. Robert Hummel, in particular, provided many important kinds of technical and practical assistance during the implementation process. Mike Overton provided help with the numerical aspects of the design. Much of the theoretical basis for this research was developed while the author was at the Stanford Artificial Intelligence Laboratory, with the help of Tom Binford, Rod Brooks, Chris Goad, David Marimont, Andy Witkin, and many others.

References

[1] Brooks, Rodney A., "Symbolic reasoning among 3-D models and 2-D images," *Artificial Intelligence,* **17** (1981), 285-348.

[2] Charniak, Eugene, "The Bayesian basis of common sense medical diagnosis," *Proceedings of AAAI-83* (Washington, D.C., August, 1983), 70-73.

[3] Clark, Dayton and Robert Hummel, "VSH user's manual: an image processing environment," *Robotics Research Technical Report,* Courant Institute, New York University (September 1984).

[4] Cooper, Lynn A., and Roger N. Shepard, "Turning something over in the mind," *Scientific American,* **251**, 6 (December 1984), 106–114.

[5] Goad, Chris, "Special purpose automatic programming for 3D model-based vision," *Proceedings ARPA Image Understanding Workshop* (1983).

[6] Hochberg, Julian E. and Virginia Brooks, "Pictorial recognition as an unlearned ability: A study of one child's performance," *American Journal of Psychology,* **75** (1962), 624-628.

[7] Lowe, David G., "Solving for the parameters of object models from image descriptions," *Proc. ARPA Image Understanding Workshop* (College Park, MD, April 1980), 121–127.

[8] Lowe, David G. and Thomas O. Binford, "Perceptual organization as a basis for visual recognition," *Proceedings of AAAI-83* (Washington, D.C., August 1983), 255–260.

[9] Lowe, David G., *Perceptual Organization and Visual Recognition* (Boston, Mass: Kluwer Academic Publishers, 1985).

[10] Marr, David, "Early processing of visual information," *Philosophical Transactions of the Royal Society of London, Series B,* **275** (1976), 483-524.

[11] Marr, David, and Ellen Hildreth, "Theory of edge detection," *Proc. Royal Society of London, B,* **207** (1980), 187-217.

[12] Marr, David, *Vision* (San Francisco: W.H. Freeman and Co., 1982).

[13] Roberts, L.G., "Machine perception of three-dimensional objects," in *Optical and Electro-optical Information Processing,* Tippet *et al.,* Eds. (Cambridge, Mass.: MIT Press, 1966), 159-197.

[14] Shirai, Y., "Recognition of man-made objects using edge cues," in *Computer Vision Systems,* A. Hanson, E. Riseman, eds. (New York: Academic Press, 1978).

[15] Shortliffe, Edward H. and Bruce G. Buchanan, "A model of inexact reasoning in medicine," *Mathematical Biosciences,* **23** (1975), 355-356.

[16] Walter, I. and H. Tropf, "3-D recognition of randomly oriented parts," *Proceedings of the Third International Conf. on Robot Vision and Sensory Controls* (November, 1983, Cambridge, Mass.), 193-200.

[17] Wertheimer, Max, "Untersuchungen zur Lehe von der Gestalt II," *Psychol. Forsch.,* **4** (1923). Translated as "Principles of perceptual organization" in *Readings in Perception,* David Beardslee and Michael Wertheimer, Eds., (Princeton, N.J.: 1958), 115-135.

[18] Witkin, Andrew P. and Jay M. Tenenbaum, "On the role of structure in vision," in *Human and Machine Vision,* Beck, Hope & Rosenfeld, Eds. (New York: Academic Press, 1983), 481-543.

DETERMINING OBJECT ATTITUDE FROM EXTENDED GAUSSIAN IMAGES

James J. Little[*]

Department of Computer Science
The University of British Columbia
Vancouver, B.C., Canada V6T 1W5

Abstract

The Extended Gaussian Image (EGI) of an object records the variation of surface area with surface orientation, uniquely representing convex objects. The inversion problem for polyhedra (from an EGI to a description in terms of vertices and faces) has been solved, by an iterative algorithm [Little, 1983]. The algorithm depends upon the mixed volume, a geometric construction linking the areas and positions of the faces of an object. A robust method for determining object attitude from the EGI is developed here, using this construction. Experiments show the method's insensitivity to small attitude differences.

1 Introduction

Orientation maps can be generated by binocular stereo [Baker and Binford, 1981] [Grimson, 1981], photometric stereo [Woodham, 1980], shape from shading [Horn, 1975], or by differentiation of laser range images[Brou, 1984]. By translating the surface normals of an object to a common point, a representation of the distribution of surface orientation is formed, called the Extended Gaussian Image (EGI) [Horn, 1984]. Figure 1 shows the Extended Gaussian Image of a polyhedron and the corresponding object.

Horn and Ikeuchi[1984] demonstrated the feasibility of using EGIs for attitude determination, comparing the EGI of a prototype with a sensed EGI. The reconstruction method using the mixed volume suggests a new method for attitude determination. This method is practical and more robust than direct comparison of EGIs. A detailed discussion of this method is presented in [Little, 1985].

[*] This research was supported in part by a UBC University Graduate Fellowship and by the Natural Science and Engineering Research Council of Canada grant A3390.

2 Object Models

Objects will have surfaces tiled with planar facets. The intersection of half-spaces forms a convex polyhedron. A bounded convex polyhedron is a *polytope*. The direction of the outward facing normal ω on a face of the polytope is the surface *orientation*, which can be identified with a point on the unit sphere U. The set of orientations of the faces of a polytope, Ω, is referenced by indices $1 \ldots n$.

A plane J *supports* a convex body C if C lies on one side of the plane and C has at least one point in common with J. For any orientation ω there is a unique support plane J for C with equation $\langle \omega, x \rangle = c$. A support function of orientation can be defined:

$$\mathcal{H}(\omega) = c, \text{where } \langle \omega, x \rangle = c \text{ is a supporting plane}$$

A polytope in this setting can be represented by $H = (h_1, h_2 \ldots h_n) = (\mathcal{H}(\omega_1), \mathcal{H}(\omega_2) \ldots \mathcal{H}(\omega_n))$, the values of the support function at Ω.

Two polytopes P and Q in R^3 are *homothetic* if

$$P = \{x \mid x = \lambda * y + t, y \epsilon Q, \lambda \epsilon R, \lambda > 0, t \epsilon R^3\}$$

Homotheticity is invariance under translation and scaling.

The areas and orientations of the faces describe a function $\mathcal{A}(\omega)$; if the polytope has a face with orientation ω, its value is the area of the face, otherwise, zero. This function is represented as a vector A of the values of $\mathcal{A}(\omega_i)$.

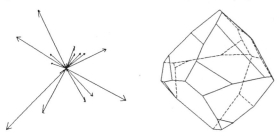

Figure 1: Extended Gaussian Image and Object

The Extended Gaussian Image of a polytope P can be represented as a set of vectors N: $\{n_i | n_i = \omega_i A_i, A_i = \mathcal{A}(\omega_i)\}$. Minkowski[1897] showed that when N sums to 0, N uniquely represents a polytope, up to translation.

1 Recovering Shape from an EGI

The reconstruction method derives from Minkowski's theorem[1897], arising from the study of mixtures(convex sums) of convex bodies. The *mixed volume* of polytopes P and Q, $V(P,Q)$, is the product of the support function of P and the area function of Q:

$$V(P,Q) = 1/3 \langle H_P, A_Q \rangle$$

As a consequence of the theory of mixtures of polytopes:

$$V(P,Q)^3 \geq V(Q)^2 V(P) \qquad (1)$$

where $V(P)$ is the volume of P. Equality holds only when P and Q are homothetic.

Minkowski's theorem states that, among all polytopes P of fixed volume, the P which minimizes $V(P,Q)$ is homothetic to Q. The reconstruction method[Little,1983] minimizes the mixed volume to recover object shape.

2 Determining Attitude

Determining the attitude of a known object is equivalent to finding a rotation R, such that $R(EGI_{prototype}) = EGI_{sensed}$. Attitude in R^3 can be identified with a rotation $R(\theta, n)$, where θ is the angle by which an object is rotated about an axis n in R^3.

To access the area function it is necessary to quantize orientation, tesselating U. The projection of the icosahedron onto U generates a tesselation. The number of facets in a tesselation U can be increased by subdividing the triangular faces of the icosahedron into smaller triangles. At frequency i, each face is mapped into i^2 triangles.

Attitude is quantized by the rotation group Γ_{60} which brings the vertices of the icosahedron into correspondence. The difference between two attitudes is the angle of the rotation taking one into the other. The minimum difference among the 60 attitudes in Γ_{60} is 72°. For a detailed discussion of methods for representing and quantizing attitude in R^3 and quantizing orientation on U, see Brou [1984].

2.1 Comparing Area Functions

To determine object attitude from the EGI, Horn and Ikeuchi [Horn and Ikeuchi,1984] match the prototype EGI and the sensed EGI at a discrete set of attitudes. At each sample attitude the matching measure between two area distributions is:

$$\sum_{i=1}^{m}(A_{R(i)} - A_i)^2 \qquad (2)$$

where A_i is the sensed EGI area function at direction ω_i and $A_{R(i)}$ is the prototype area function evaluated at the direction to which ω_i is transformed by R. This amounts to maximizing the correlation of A and A. The attitude which minimizes the measure in Equation 2 is selected.

Area matching can fail when the object attitude is offset from a sample attitude[Brou, 1984]. A polytope with m faces fills at most m cells on U. As the resolution of orientation increases, the number of empty cells increases. If the attitude offset is near the cell resolution, the faces of the prototype and the object may not lie in the same cells, even at the correct attitude (the attitude in Γ_{60} nearest the actual attitude). The minimum matching error increases and the minimum may not indicate the correct attitude.

2.2 Mixed Volumes

Reconstruction builds a polytope whose area function fits the EGI; attitude determination seeks an attitude which rotates the sensed EGI into correspondence with the prototype EGI. Both determine a fit between an EGI and a model. Rotating a polytope preserves volume, so among all P' which are rotated versions of P, that P' which has the same attitude as P minimizes the mixed volume. To determine object attitude, minimize the mixed volume:

$$1/3 \sum_{i=1}^{m} (H_{R(i)} * A_i)$$

H_i is the prototype support function and A_i the sensed area function.

2.3 Support and Area Functions

For polytopes, the area function $\mathcal{A}(\omega)$ is discontinuous; in contrast, the support function $\mathcal{H}(\omega)$ is continuous on U. The comparative smoothness of the support function can be seen by examining its relation to the area function, most easily for polygons. The area function of a polygon, for example, consists of a finite set of non-zero points in the interval $0 - 2\pi$. Its autocorrelation is 0 almost-everywhere. Not surprisingly, when the attitude of the sensed object is slightly different from the prototype (or any attitude in the sample set), the value of the area matching is maximum. Discretizing A by sampling U is helpful, as Brou remarks, introducing a smoothing effect, widening each of the pulses to the resolution. With discretization, small changes in attitude do not affect the area function, until the size of the attitude difference exceeds the resolution on U, when the errors recur.

The support function for a polygon can be written in terms of the area function A:

$$H(\omega) = cos(\omega)\int_0^\omega -A(\psi)sin(\psi)d\psi + sin(\omega)\int_0^\omega A(\psi)cos(\psi)d\psi$$

when the point on the polygon where $\omega = 0$ coincides with the origin. The support function is an integral transform of A and is much smoother. Because A varies rapidly, shifting A by a small rotation changes its correlation with the prototype A significantly. The support function varies less and the error rate is correspondingly lower. For a polygon, the support function is piecewise sinusoidal, as is the mixed volume.

3   Experiments

Initials tests employ the complete EGI, the total spherical distribution, to demonstrate feasibility. To examine the effects of attitudes different from the test set, at a specified resolution, the attitude difference between the object and the prototype was varied. The results can be evaluated under two criteria: the magnitude of the rotation between the selected attitude and the correct attitude, and, where the method ranks the correct attitude (it should have rank 0 – lower is better).

The EGI of the polytope shown in Figure 1 was rotated about the coordinate axes by angles of 5, 10, 15 and 20 degrees and its attitude determined by both methods. At frequency 2, the area matching method fails at angles as small as 15.0°; both fail sometimes when the angle is 20.0°. When the mixed volume method fails, its failure is less severe in two respects: the attitude selected is closer to the correct attitude and the rank of the correct attitude is lower. Area matching fails in 4 out of 12 cases and MV in only 1 out of 12.

The results for the 20° rotation are shown in another form in Figure 2. The graph shows, on the vertical axis,

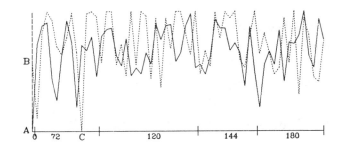

Figure 2: Mixed volume (solid) vs. area (dotted)

the values of area matching, in a dotted line, and mixed volume, in a solid line; the horizontal axis shows the attitudes (from Γ_{60}) at which the matchings were evaluated. The horizontal axis is separated by tick marks into regions which are 0, 72, 120, 144 and 180° from the prototype attitude. Point A is the minimum found by MV, correctly identifying the object attitude. Point B, the value of the area matching method for the correct attitude, is rather high; there are 21 attitudes with lower values. The area function achieves a minimum (point C) at an attitude in the 72° set.

At frequency 3, the MV method errs in 2 out of 12 cases (both at 20° offset), while the area matching method fails for 6 out of 12 cases (some as little as 10° offset). In general, the area matching method performs worse at a finer resolution. Finally, at frequency 5, the number of errors increases, for area matching, from 6 out of 12 to 8/12, while the mixed volume method fails twice. Three other objects, of varying eccentricity, were tested. The MV method succeeded for all offsets, while area matching failed 8 times at frequency 3 and 14 times at frequency 5.

In all cases, MV ranks the correct attitude in the top 5, suggesting that more sophisticated procedures can be applied to these to determine correct attitude. Area matching performs much more poorly at ranking the correct attitude. The better behaviour of MV at lower resolutions also suggests that MV would be useful in a coarse-to-fine search strategy.

3.1   Visible Subsets of EGIs

In practice, the sensed portion of a surface corresponds to a single visible hemisphere of the EGI. With only partial information, experiments with several prototypes contrasted the MV technique with the area method. In no case does the MV method fail where the area method succeeds; in all cases, the ranking of the MV method is lower than the

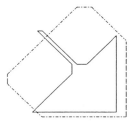

Figure 3: Non-convex polygon and its reconstruction

area method. There were 3 times as many errors by the area matching method.

Using MV for attitude determination depends on the fact that volume $V(P)$ remains constant (see Equation 1). Ignoring this effect incurred no penalty in these experiments, because the contribution of invisible faces to the mixed volume is negligible. A reconstruction method makes possible construction of suitable invisible faces.

4 Non-Convexity and Attitude

To extend the use of EGIs for non-convex objects, consider using the support function of the convex object reconstructed from the area function of a non-convex object. Dashed lines in Figure 3 delimit the convex polygon corresponding to the area function of this non-convex polygon. If, hypothetically, the entire area function of the sensed object were available, then recovering the attitude of the non-convex polygon would be indistinguishable from recovering attitude of the convex polygon. Using complete EGIs and ignoring the effects of self-occlusion, this method proved effective for a set of sample polygons, including the polygon in the Figure 3. This holds the promise that mixed volume method can be applied to attitude determination for non-convex objects, especially where the effects of self-occlusion are small.

5 Conclusions

An EGI supplies the sensed area function for an object. The object model permits calculation of the support function. The mixed volume combines these two functions; it is minimized when the attitude of the model matches that of the sensed object. Because of the smoothness of the support function, the mixed volume technique is robust for determining the attitude of convex objects. The experiments described here demonstrate its effectiveness and its insensitivity to small changes in attitude which affect other methods. This method can also be applied to non-convex objects when the effects of self-occlusion are small.

References

[1] H.H. Baker and T.O. Binford, "Depth From Edge and Intensity Based Stereo", *Proceedings of the Seventh IJCAI*, pp. 631-636, Vancouver, 1981

[2] P. Brou, "Using the Gaussian Image to Find the Orientation of Objects", *The International Journal of Robotics Research*, vol. 3, no. 4, pp. 89-125, Winter, 1984

[3] W.E.L. Grimson, "From Images to Surfaces: A Computational Study of the Human Early Visual System", MIT Press, Cambridge, Mass, 1981

[4] B.K.P. Horn, "Obtaining Shape From Shading Information", *The Psychology of Computer Vision*, ed. P.H. Winston, pp. 115-155, McGraw-Hill, New York, 1975

[5] B.K.P. Horn, "Extended Gaussian Images", *Proceedings of the IEEE*, pp. 1671-1686, December, 1984

[6] B.K.P. Horn and K.I. Ikeuchi, "The Mechanical Manipulation of Randomly Oriented Parts", *Scientific American*, August 1984

[7] J.J. Little, "An Iterative Method for Reconstructing Convex Polyhedra from Extended Gaussian Image", *Proceedings of AAAI-83*, pp. 247-250, 1983

[8] J.J. Little, "Recovering Shape and Determining Attitude from Extended Gaussian Images", Ph.D. Thesis, University of British Columbia, Vancouver, April 1985

[9] Herman Minkowski, "Allgemeine Lehrsatze uber die konvexe Polyeder ", *Nachr. Ges. Wiss. Gottingen*, pp. 198-219, 1897

[10] R.J. Woodham, "Photometric Method for Determining Surface Orientation from Multiple Images", *Optical Engineering*, vol. 19, pp. 139-144, 1980

Transformational Form Perception in 3D: Constraints, Algorithms, Implementation

Dana H. Ballard
Computer Science Department
University of Rochester

Hiromi Tanaka
Department of Control Engineering
Osaka University

Abstract

Most of the geometric information in a scene is captured by local coordinate frames oriented according to local geometric features. In polyhedral worlds these features are faces, vertices and edges. Such features lead naturally to parallel algorithms for building such a scene description from stereo input that are insensitive to noise and occlusion. This representation can be used for object location, object recognition, and navigation.

1. Introduction

The critical problem of form perception is that of picking the right representation. In previous papers we have argued that if *frame primitives* are picked as the underlying geometric representation, then many problems related to form perception can be solved in an elegant way [2,3,4,5,6,7,23]. Frame primitives are geometric coordinate frames that can be extracted from more primitive image features. These primitives play a dual role: they can be regarded as features in their own right and used in the form matching process directly, or they can be used to specify transformations between themselves and other features.

In this paper, frame primitives are developed with respect to a polyhedral model of the geometric environment. The advantage of a polyhedral model is that the polyhedral primitives are intimately related to the frame primitives. However, any substrate related to coordinate frames such as symmetries [8] may be used as well.

Frame primitives express the fundamental nature of rigidity: two shapes are equivalent if there exists a rigid transformation that maps one into the other. This idea can also be extended to the matching of a prototype with portions of a scene. A portion of a scene is said to represent an instance of a prototype if there exists a rigid transformation mapping the prototype into portions of the scene. The use of rigidity distinguishes the approach from topoplogical matching [11,17,24].

The problem of matching a 3d prototype to an image can be hierarchically organized into: (1) the recovery of 3d lines from stereo image data (for monocular approaches, see [21,11]); (2) the construction of a 3d polyhedral scene model; and (3) the matching of portions of that model to a library of stored prototypes. This hierarchical strategy is similar to that of [9] and has several advantages over the methods that try to match the image to the 3d prototype in one step. For example, [19,20] try to match the 3d prototype directly with the 2d line drawing.

The computation is implemented in a connectionist architecture, motivated by biological information processing systems [2]. The complete processes of extracting 3d structure and matching is carried out by a parallel probabilistic relaxation algorithm.

2. Basic Concepts

2.1. Geometrical Primitives

A *3d plane* is defined by $aX + bY + cZ + d = 0$ where $\mathbf{n} = (a, b, c)$ is a unit normal to the plane surface and d is the distance of closest approach to the origin.

A *3d line* is defined by the equation $\mathbf{x} = \mathbf{D} + s\mathbf{e}$ where $\mathbf{D}$ is the closest point to the origin that the line passes through, $\mathbf{e}$ is the unit vector direction of the line, and $s \geq 0$ is a scalar parameter.

Each of the above can be seen as the *partial specification of local coordinate frames* where the frame parameters are synonymous with geometric features. In other words, these geometrical entities provide *natural* choices for the orientation of local geometric features.

2.2. Frame Descriptions

A coordinate frame is defined by a transformation with respect to a *base coordinate frame* which has vectors $(\mathbf{v}_1, \mathbf{v}_2, \mathbf{v}_3) = ((1,0,0)(0,1,0)(0,0,1))$. This transformation is specified by scale factor s, a rotation of the frame by an angle θ about a unit vector $\mathbf{w}$ with respect to a base coordinate frame, and a translation of the origin by $\mathbf{x}_0$. Notationally we will refer to the complete frame as F, the rotation part as E. Thus $F = (E, \mathbf{x}_0)$, where $E = (\mathbf{e}_1, \mathbf{e}_2, \mathbf{e}_3)$ is an orthonormal basis.

A virtue of the geometric primitives is that the transformation itself allows one to change the point of view. Thus to make an arbitrary frame $F = (\mathbf{e}_1, \mathbf{e}_2, \mathbf{e}_3, \mathbf{x}_0)$ the base frame, one need only apply the transformation in reverse to all the frame primitives. That is, $T = (\mathbf{w}, -\theta, -\mathbf{x}_0)$, where $\mathbf{w}$ and θ are determined from $\mathbf{e}_1, \mathbf{e}_2$, and $\mathbf{e}_3$ (we show how this is done in Section 3.3).

This extremely important point is the main virtue of frame primitives: *frame primitives contain all the information necessary to change the point of view.* Any particular primitive may be chosen as a reference for all the other primitives by applying the reference transformation to each primitive.

2.3. Matching Different Frame Descriptions

An instance of an object in the viewer-centered frame may be related to a prototypical internal representation in an object-centered frame by a *viewing transformation*, but this problem is generally underdetermined [5]. Furthermore, the image usually contains many features that belong to different objects, and these tend to confound the perception of a particular shape.

A key simplifying assumption is that the internal representation contains only a single object. In this case the viewing transformation can generally be computed and parts of the object in the image can be identified despite other image clutter [3,6]. The task of determining if a known object is in an image is posed as: is there a transformation of a subset of image features such that the transformed subset can be explained as the object? If the answer to this question is no, then the object is not present. If yes, then the transformation provides all the necessary information about the object.

The principal feature of our method is that it decouples the computations for orientation and translation. In other words, the orientation of the object can be detected without knowing its translation.

3. Specification of Constraints

3.1. Matching Two-Dimensional Stereo Lines

A line in the image plane defines a plane which passes through the focal point ($Z = 0$) as well as the line itself (this development is similar to that of [12]). Consider the intersection of this plane with the image plane. At the intersection locus: $X = x$, $Y = y$, and $Z = 1$, so that the equation of the line in the image plane is

$$ax + by + c = 0$$

The different imaging geometries of stereo images will produce two different lines, and correspondingly, two different planes. In order to relate these two planes, they must be expressed in the same coordinate frame. For the simple case of parallel views separated by Δ, the equation of the second plane (a_2, b_2, c_2) in terms of the first frame is simply

$$a_2 X + b_2 Y + c_2 Z - a_2 \Delta = 0$$

The two planes, when intersected, define a 3d line $(\mathbf{D}, \mathbf{e})$. Given the two normals $\mathbf{n}_1$ and $\mathbf{n}_2$, $\mathbf{e}$ can be readily calculated as

$$\mathbf{e} = \langle \mathbf{n}_1 \times \mathbf{n}_2 \rangle \tag{3.1}$$

where the operator $\langle \ \rangle$ normalizes its vector argument. The vector from the origin $\mathbf{D}$ may be calculated by solving:

$$\mathbf{D} = N^{-1}\mathbf{d} \tag{3.2}$$

where

$$N = \begin{bmatrix} n_{1x} & n_{1y} & n_{1z} \\ n_{2x} & n_{2y} & n_{2z} \\ e_x & e_y & e_z \end{bmatrix} \quad \text{and} \quad \mathbf{d}^T = (0, d_2, 0)$$

3.2. Building Polyhedral Scene Descriptions

Given a collection of 3d lines, the problem now becomes one of recovering additional 3d structure. To do this one can exploit an instance of Barlow's notion of "suspicious coincidences." Applied to a polyhedral world, this idea is as follows: *it is unlikely that two three-dimensional lines will happen to be coplanar or meet at a vertex accidentally.* Thus we consider constraints between all pairs of 3d lines, assuming that intersections usually reflect rigid polyhedral structure. The constraints are simple applications of vector geometry of R^3 [7,23] and are as follows.

I. Two planes define a concave or convex edge. Pairs of planes $P_1 = (\mathbf{n}_1, d_1)$ and $P_2 = (\mathbf{n}_2, d_2)$ produce edges which have an associated coordinate frame ($\mathbf{e}_1, \mathbf{e}_2, \mathbf{e}_3$) where

$$(\mathbf{e}_1, \mathbf{e}_2, \mathbf{e}_3) = (\langle \mathbf{n}_1 \times \mathbf{n}_2 \rangle, \mathbf{e}_3 \times \mathbf{e}_1, \langle \mathbf{n}_1 + \mathbf{n}_2 \rangle) \tag{3.3}$$

The distance of closest approach of the edge to the origin, $\mathbf{D}$, can be calculated from the following three equations:

$$\mathbf{n}_1 \cdot \mathbf{D} = d_1, \mathbf{n}_2 \cdot \mathbf{D} = d_2, \mathbf{e}_1 \cdot \mathbf{D} = 0$$

II. Two edges can determine a plane. Coplanar 3d lines with orientations $\mathbf{e}_{11}$ and $\mathbf{e}_{12}$ must lie in a plane $(\mathbf{n}, d)$, where

$$\mathbf{n} = \mathbf{e}_{11} \times \mathbf{e}_{12} \tag{3.4}$$

and d is specified by

$$\mathbf{n} \cdot \mathbf{D}_1 = \mathbf{n} \cdot \mathbf{D}_2 = -d \tag{3.5}$$

III. Two edges can determine a vertex. If two coplanar 3d lines intersect, then the intersection points can be determined by solving two equations from

$$\mathbf{D}_2 - \mathbf{D}_1 = \alpha \mathbf{e}_{12} - \beta \mathbf{e}_{11} \tag{3.6}$$

IV. Two planes and a 3d line can define an edge. A 3d line only has a direction $\mathbf{e}$, but additional orientation information can be computed in the case where the line is also the intersection locus of two planes. In this case a frame can be specified that has the orientation given by (3.3) where $\mathbf{n}_1$ and $\mathbf{n}_2$ are the normals of the two planes.

3.3. Matching a Scene Frame with a Prototype

I. Rotational Constraint. To develop the rotational constraint, we show how given two orientation frames E_p and E_s from the prototype and scene, we can compute the rotation θ about a unit vector $\mathbf{w}$. The mathematics of quaternions, e.g., [25], states that the rotation of one unit vector, $\mathbf{u}$, into another unit vector, $\mathbf{v}$, around a unit vector axis, $\mathbf{w}$, is given by:

$$R = \sqrt{-(\mathbf{w} \times \mathbf{v})(\mathbf{w} \times \mathbf{u})} \tag{3.7}$$

We will use the orientation vectors $\mathbf{e}_i$ from both the model and image as $\mathbf{u}$ and $\mathbf{v}$, respectively. How do we define $\mathbf{w}$? Since $\mathbf{w}$ must be perpendicular to both $\mathbf{u}$ and $\mathbf{v}$, it can be defined in terms of the two orientation frames as

$$\mathbf{w} = (\mathbf{e}_{1p} - \mathbf{e}_{1s}) \times (\mathbf{e}_{2p} - \mathbf{e}_{2s}) \tag{3.8}$$

In the special case of where $\mathbf{e}_{1p}$ equals $\mathbf{e}_{1s}$ and $\mathbf{e}_{2p}$ equals $\mathbf{e}_{2s}$, we arbitrarily set $\mathbf{w} = (1, 0, 0)$ and $\theta = 0$. This procedure and (3.7) specify the axis of rotation.

The next step is to compute θ for the general case. The rotation from $\mathbf{u}$ to $\mathbf{v}$ is also given by

$$R = \cos(\theta/2) + \sin(\theta/2)\mathbf{w} \tag{3.9}$$

where θ is the angle of rotation around the unit vector axis $\mathbf{w}$. Thus the angle θ can be computed from (3.7) and (3.9).

II. Rotating the Model. Once the rotation between the prototype and scene has been established, then the origins of the prototype frames can be appropriately rotated by (for details, see [25]):

$$\mathbf{x}'_p = R \mathbf{x}_p R^{-1} \tag{3.10}$$

This results in a new set of origins that only differ from their counterparts in the scene by a translation vector.

III. Translational Constraint. The translational constraint is trivially computed if the correspondence between a scene frame origin $\mathbf{x}_s$ and a rotated prototype frame origin $\mathbf{x}'_p$ is known. The answer is the difference vector

$$\Delta\mathbf{x} = \mathbf{x}'_p - \mathbf{x}_s \tag{3.11}$$

4. Algorithms

4.1. Energy Minimization

The parallel algorithm uses a form of relaxation developed for binary threshold units by [15,14]. Each unit has a state, s, which is either on (s = 1) or off (s = 0). In the case of ternary constraints, a unit k will receive a weighted input from pairs of other value cells i and j in an amount given by $w_{ijk}s_i s_j$. Each unit turns on according to the following computation:

1) Compute the input

$$p_k = \sum_{i, j \text{ connected to } k} w_{ijk} s_i s_k$$

2) Substract a threshold

$$p_k := p_k - \theta_k$$

3)   Turn s_k on if $p_k > 0$, else turn it off.

Units are turned on and off acording to steps 1 through 3 until convergence is achieved. Formally, if all the weights w_{ijk} are symmetrical ($w_{ijk} = w_{jik} = w_{kij}$) then the converged set of states will minimize the energy function $E = - \Sigma w_{ijk} s_i s_j s_k$. In practice, the examples that we have tried are well conditioned, so that convergence is achieved in one iteration.

If the algorithm takes one iteration to converge, it is roughly equivalent to *correlation*. If more than one iteration is required, i.e., a sequence of states s^k converges to a fixed point s^* then the algorithm specified by steps 1-3 is equivalent to *gradient search*. Gradient search will work if the constraints have a single minimum. The case where E has more than one local minimum can be handled by *simulated annealing* [13,14,10].

4.2. Value Cells

The constraints are represented using special connectionist architecture based on *value cells*. In the value cell approach, a particular vector variable is represented as a discrete collection of cells where the central location of the cell is a particular value for the variable and the width of the cell is its accuracy. For example, representing edges in an image requires a three-dimensional cell type with location (x_0, y_0, θ_0) and width ($\Delta x, \Delta y, \Delta \theta$). Collections of these cells cover the range of all possible edge positions and orientations.

Since value cells are described in terms of threshold units, they can be either *off* or *on*. An on value signifies the presence of an edge at the associated position and orientation. Additional accuracy and the avoidance of certain computational problems can be achieved through the use of overlapping cells. The technical details of overlapping cells strategies are discussed in a separate paper [22]. Value cells representing different variables are related via constraints. In the familiar example of line detection, an edge cell (x_0, y_0, θ_0) is related to the line cell (ρ_0, θ_0) through the constraint $x_0\cos\theta_0 + y_0\sin\theta_0 = \rho_0$.

The previous line constraint was binary in that a value cell for a specific edge value was connected to a cell for a specific line. A special kind of constraint is a *ternary constraint*, in which three value cells are related. A ternary constraint can improve the accuracy of line detection by using two edges, (x_1, y_1, θ_1) and (x_2, y_2, θ_2), that are on the same line iff $\theta_1 \tilde{} \theta_2 \tilde{} \arctan(y_2-y_1, x_2-x_1)$. If this constraint is satisfied, then the (ρ, θ) cell is determined by

$$\theta = \arctan(y_2-y_1, x_2-x_1) \qquad (4.1)$$

$$\rho = x_1\cos\theta + y_1\sin\theta$$

4.3. The Overall Network

Representative value cells in the overall network are shown in the following Figure. Part A) denotes the prototype frame primitives, B) shows the cells related to the view transformation, C) shows the polyhedral network, and D) shows the stereo network. Ternary constraints are denoted with an arc connecting pairs of inputs. In each parameter network, only representative cells are shown.

5. Implementation

5.1. Data Structures

The overall algorithm is conceptually simple: asynchronously, each cell evaluates its input and turns on or off. When the entire network converges, the on units represent the solution to the particular problem. This simple description can lead to inefficient implementations, since most of the cells are off in any given instant [4].

Thus when a processor checks its input pairs (in the case of a ternary constraint), most of the cells will be off. To take advantage of this, we use pairs of *on* units to calculate incremental inputs, and when all such pairs have been considered for any network, subtract thresholds and determine whether to turn the units on or off. This strategy is repeated for all the ternary constraints in the network. The only differences are: (1) the different constraints that relate different value cells; and (2) the set of on units at any given instant. The above strategy requires a data structure that only records on cells.

We use hash tables with collision resolution via chaining, e.g., [16, pp. 462-469].

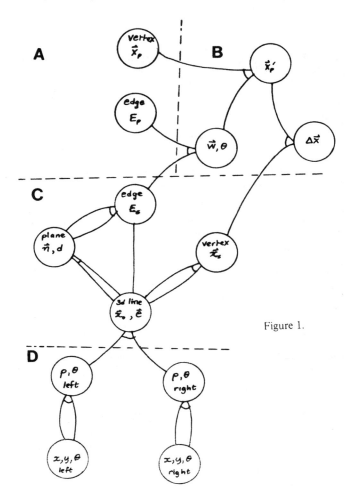

Figure 1.

5.2. Generic Relaxation Structures

For each ternary constraint, two tables must be indexed to compute the index of a third. Then the input is added to the appropriate cell, as follows.

```
Foreach u in T₁ do
  Foreach v in T₂ do
    {
      w := rule (u, v, T₁, T₂)
      Increment (w, T₃)
    }
```

The function of *Increment* is to add the appropriate weight to the *p* field of the entry in the T.linetable. If there is no previous entry, an appropriate cell is added. Next the entries are thresholded, and if below threshold, deleted from the table:

> Foreach u in T do
>   if u < threshold then
>   delete (u);

Given the generic format, we can specify the network of computations by specifying collections of three tables, each group having an associated update rule. The following summary table represents this information.

T_1	T_2	T_3	rule
edge	edge	line	Eq. 4.1
line	line	3d line	Eqs. 3.1, 3.2
3d line	3d line	plane	Eqs. 3.4, 3.5
3d line	3d line	vertex	Eq. 3.6
plane	plane	possible edge	Eq. 3.3
possible edge	3d line	edge	Eq. 3.3, Sec. 2B
scene edge	prototype edge	orientation	Eqs. 3.8, 3.9
orientation	model vertex	rotated vertex	Eq. 3.10
rotated vertex	image vertex	translation	Eq. 3.11

5.3. Implementation

The status of the current implementation is that the constraints for matching an object in two coordinate frames have been shown to work by [23]. The stereo portion of the constraints are currently being implemented. Figure 2 shows the result for a simulated three-dimensional wrench. In these first tests, the data for the wrench is rotated and translated to obtain a scene copy and there is no self occlusion.

This is then matched against the original using the constraints described in Section 3.3, implemented as described in Sections 4 and 5. The figure shows: A) the wrench, B) values for the direction of rotation(magnitude not shown) and C) values for the direction of translation(magnitude not shown). The multiple values are the result of false pairings between scene frame primitive and prototype.

Although the greyscale does not emphasize this, the correct transformation is found easily in this case.

6. High-Level Control

The prototype frames form a generic basis set. In order to represent a particular object, an appropriate subset of value units must be turned on. One way to do this is to represent objects as specific links between an object token space and the prototype frame space. This arrangement forms a basic architecture that can be used in several different ways.

I. Object Location. If a particular object is sought, its prototype frame description is turned on by activating its object token. This turns on the appropriate frame primitives. Then if a match between the object and a subset of the scene exists, a rotation and a translation unit will be turned on in the transformation network.

II. Object Recognition. If an object has been segmented (by other methods, e.g., range, color, etc.) and its identity is sought, the prototype frame can be loaded with several candidate objects. If the matching process can build a transformation between any of these objects and the segmented object, appropriate rotation and translation units will be turned on.

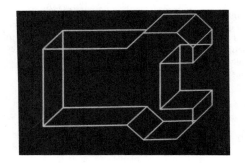

A

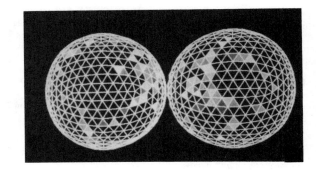

B

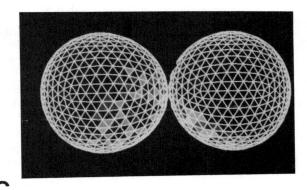

C

Figure 2.

III. Navigation. This architecture can also be used for navigation in the following way. At some initial time t_0 the current scene is loaded into the prototype frame by activating the identity units in the transformation space. This has the effect of turning on units in the prototype frame that are a copy of the scene units at that instant. Henceforth, as the observer moves around, these units are locked on. The result is that at any instant the transformation units will reflect the transformation between the current scene and that at t_0. The inverse of this transform corresponds to the observer motion.

7. Conclusions

In this paper we have developed a number of interdependent ideas. The main point is that geometric frames provide a natural way of talking about shape. This idea has been present in psychology and differential geometry for a long time. Our contribution has been to develop the particular constraints for polyhedra and show how they lead naturally to algorithms for extracting frame information from the scene and matching it against stored prototypes.

The particular focus of the paper was on the extraction of linear features from edge data and the matching of these features to obtain three-dimensional information.

It is extremely important to note that these algorithms all use relaxation as the computing engine and value cells as the representation. The fact that all these problems can be handled in the same way argues for the generality of the approach.

8. Acknowledgements

Shmuel Tomer, Matt Curtis and Owen Kimball provided invaluable programming support in developing the geodesic package and testing two-dimensional versions of the algorithms. Peggy Meeker prepared the many drafts of this manuscript. This research was supported by NSF under Grant MCS-8203290.

9. References

1. Attneave, F., "Some informational aspects of perception," *Psychological Review 61*, 1954.

2. Ballard, D.H., "Cortical connections: Structure and function," TR 133, Computer Science Dept., U. Rochester, July 1984b; to appear, *Brain and Behavioral Sciences*.

3. Ballard, D.H., "Generalizing the Hough transform to detect arbitrary shapes," TR 55, Computer Science Dept., U. Rochester, 1979; *Pattern Recognition 13*, 2, April 1981.

4. Ballard, D.H., "Parameter networks: Towards a theory of low-level vision," TR 75, Computer Science Dept., U. Rochester, 1981; *Proc., 7th IJCAI*, Vancouver, August 1981; *Artificial Intelligence 22*, 235-267, 1984a.

5. Ballard, D.H. and L.M. Hrechanyk, "A connectionist model for shape perception," Computer Vision Workshop, Ringe, NH, August 1982; also appeared as "Viewframes: A connectionist model of form perception," *DARPA Image Understanding Workshop*, Washington, D.C., June 1983.

6. Ballard, D.H. and D. Sabbah, "On shapes," *Proc., 7th IJCAI*, Vancouver, Canada, August 1981; also appeared as "Viewer independent shape recognition," *IEEE Trans. on Pattern Analysis and Machine Intelligence 5*, 6, 653-660, November 1983.

7. Ballard, D.H., A. Bandyopadhyay, J. Sullins, and H. Tanaka, "A connectionist polyhedral model of extrapersonal space," *Proc., IEEE Conference on Computer Vision*, Annapolis, MD, 1984.

8. Brady, M. and A. Haruo, "Smoothed local symmetries and their applications," *Int. Journal of Robotics Research 3*, 3, 1984.

9. Faugeras, O.D., "Representation and matching techniques for range data," Rank Price Funds Symposium on Representation and Control in Visual Processing, Malvern, England, April 1985.

10. Geman, S. and D. Geman, "Stochastic relaxation, Gibbs distributions, and the Bayesian restoration of images," TR, Brown U., September 1983; also appeared in *IEEE Trans. PAMI*, January 1985.

11. Kanade, T., "Recovery of the three-dimensional shape of an object from a single view," *Artificial Intelligence 17*, 409-460, 1981.

12. Kanade, T., presentation at the University of Rochester, November 1984.

13. Kirkpatrick, S., C.D. Gelatt, and M.P. Vecchi, "Optimization by simulated annealing," *Science 220*, 671-680, 1983.

14. Hinton, G.E. and T.J. Sejnowski, "Optimal perceptual inference," *Proc., IEEE Computer and Pattern Recognition Conference*, 448-453, June 1983.

15. Hopfield, J.J., "Neural networks and physical systems with collective computational abilities." *Proc., Nat'l Acad. Sciences USA 79*, 2554-2558, 1982.

16. Horwitz, E. and S. Sahni. *Fundamentals of Data Structures*. Computer Science Press, 1976.

17. Mackworth, A.K., "Interpreting pictures of polyhedral scenes," *Artificial Intelligence 4*, 2, 121-137, June 1973.

18. Sabbah, D., "Computing with connections in visual recognition of origami objects," to appear, *Cognitive Science*, Special Issue on Connectionism, Winter 1985.

19. Silberberg, T.M., D. Harwood, and L.S. Davis, "Object recognition using oriented model points," CAR-TR-56 and CS-TR-1387, Center for Automation Research, U. Maryland, April 1984.

20. Stockman, G.C. and J.C. Esteva, "3D object pose via cluster space stereo," TR 84-05, Computer Science Dept., Michigan State U., 1984.

21. Sugihara, K., "An algebraic approach to shape-from-image problems," *Artificial Intelligence 23*, 1, May 1984.

22. Sullins, J., "Coarse coding in connectionist networks," forthcoming TR, Computer Science Dept., U. Rochester, 1985.

23. Tanaka, H., D.H. Ballard, M. Curtiss, and S. Tusji, "Parallel

3-D SHAPE REPRESENTATION BY CONTOURS

ISAAC WEISS*

Massachusetts Institute of Technology

ABSTRACT

The question of 3-D shape representation is studied on the fundamental and general level. The two aspects of the problem, (i) the reconstuction of a 3-D shape from a given set of contours, and (ii) finding "natural" coordinates on a given surface, are treated by the same theory. We first set a few basic principles that should guide any shape reconstruction mechanism, regardless of its physical implementation. Second, we propose a new mathematical procedure that complies with these principles and offers several advantages over the existing ad hoc treatments. Some general results are derived from this procedure, which conform very well with human visual perception.

I. Introduction

A major component of Image Understanding is associating 3-D shapes with contours. First, given a set of contours, such as may be provided by some image processing device, one wants to infer the shape of the surface that they most likely describe. In the complementery problem, given the surface, one seeks its "natural parametrization", namely contours that will convey its essential characteristics in the most economical, yet reliable way. One known mechanism that performs these tasks well is the human visual system. A few drawn lines can create a surprisingly vivid and convincing impression of a 3-D shape [Barrow & Tannenbaum, 1981].

In this report, we address this problem on the fundamental and general level, finding the principles that must guide any process of representing a surface by contours, regardless of its physical implementaton, and second, we propose a mathematical mechanism that can perform these tasks, conforming with our principles. Nevertheless, as the eye is the most successful image processing system we have, we shall test the performance of our abstract procedure against it. In the following we shall summarize the requirements that we impose on a surface reconstruction mechanism, and their relation to previous work.

1) A mechanism should build a surface in accordance with the information it has available about it, like boundary or other contours on it, but it should not add extraneous information of its own. It is qualitatively clear that information is closely related to the smoothness of the curve or the surface. A straight line can be described by the coordinates of the end points only, while a more complicated shape will require more informaton. Thus it is reasonable, and mathematically convenient, to associate minimal information with minimal curvature, and to assume that a surface reconstruction mechanism will look for a surface that will have a minimum overall curvature while fitting the given contours.

2) The reconstruction mechanism should be invariant to rotations and translation, i.e. if the input image is rotated or translated, the output should move by the same amount but not change its shape. The principle of mininimal "energy", assuming that the overall scalar curvature $\int \bar{k}^2$ is minimal, satisfies requirement (1) and (2), but not the following demands, which our proposed measure does.

3) Dimensionlessness, or scale invariance: When the distance between an object and a viewer changes, the object's apparent size changes, but not its shape. Thus, a reconstruction mechanism should yield the same output shape from an input image, regardless of its size. Thus the mathematical method of reconstruction must be dimensionless, or invariant to scale. The minimum energy principle does *not* satisfy this important demand. A simple remedy, examined later, is to multiply the energy by the total length of the contour, but this will not satisfy the rest of our requirements. The principle of maximum compactness, which seeks to maximize the ratio of the area to the square of the perimeter, is dimensonless, but it has only been successfully applied to closed planar curves.

4) Handling of different scales of variations: A variation in the tangent occuring over a small length results in a large curvature. A small bump, or "noise", will have considerable effect on the integral. A sharp corner will totally dominate it, with the integrals value being determined by the exact way the corner is formed, which should be immaterial for determining the shape of it. Thus, the energy principle is only applicable for very smooth curves, while the compactness criterion is inherently quite insensitive to noise. The energy principle also tends to be insensitive to slowly changing, large scale features, and it will completely ignore straight sections of the curve. Our procedure deals with both small- and large-scale variations quite successfully.

5) We would prefer the same mechanism to handle both aspects of the problem mentioned above, namely finding both the surface and a suitable set of coordinates on it. While previously suggested mechanisms only attempt to find the surface, ours also lead to a "natural" parametrization of it.

This report is an abbreviation of a paper (to appear) which contains the mathematical details.

II. Smooth Contours

As we want to represent the amount of information contained in a curve by its curvature, the natural mathematical quantities to deal with are the derivatives of the tangent vector, such as the curvature vector $\bar{k} = d\bar{t}/ds$. As we demand rotational invariance, we have to use a scalar product of these vectors. This has led to the suggestion of the principle of minimum energy, by which one wants to minimize the integral $\int k^2 ds$, with the integral taken over the whole curve, and to its 3-D generalizations. This may be implemented in several ways: first, given the coordinates and tangents of two points on the curve, one can find the curve that will pass through them and will minimize this integral. Second, given a closed boundary such as an ellipse, one can try to interpret it as a projected image of a surface in 3-D. The human eye will usually regard an ellipse as a slanted circle, and we would like an extremum principle to yield

*Now at the Center for Automation Research, University of Maryland, College Park, MD 20742.

1

2

the circle as an extremum over the set of all curves compatible with the projected ellipse. Limiting ourselves to planar curves (zero tortion). this means the set of ellipses (produced by different slant angles). with the same major axis as the apparent one.

The energy principle fails in this task as it does not extremize the circle over the set of ellipses. Even worse. as it is not dimensionless, the extremum will depend on the apparent size of the image, contrary to to our demands. We now propose a modification of the energy principle, which will work for smooth curves.

Letting Δs be the total length of the curve, we can define the dimensionless variable:

$$l = \frac{s}{\Delta s}$$

where s is the length of the curve lying between a point on the curve and one of its ends. l is a measure of the relative position of a point on the curve, regardless of the curve's length. We define the "action", in analogy to the physical quantity, as the integral:

$$A = \int_0^1 \frac{d\vec{t}}{dl} \cdot \frac{d\vec{t}}{dl} dl$$

This is equivalent to mutiplying the "energy" by Δs. As both l and $\vec{t}$ are dimensionless, so is A. (Unlike the physical action). Another advantage of this normalization is related to the way the extremum is found. In general, one can use the Euler-Lagrange equations to obtain a differential equation for $\vec{t}(l)$. But this requires that both the dependent and the independent variables will have fixed values at the end points. Our normalization provides that, as l always runs between 0 and 1, unlike s.

The extremum problem is easily solved in the simple case of a curve with two boundary points. It is convenient to use a polar coordinate system, with the angle ϕ defined as the angle between the tangent $\vec{t}$ and (say) the x axis. We thus have:

$$t_x = \cos\phi, \qquad t_y = \sin\phi$$

The action now reads:

$$A = \int_0^1 \left(\frac{d\phi}{dl}\right)^2 dl$$

We shall now show that given two end points with the tangent there. the curve that passes through them is a circular arc. As a special case. extremizing over the set of ellipses with their extreme points fixed. will yield a circle. Our variational variable is now $\phi(l)$. with the boundary conditions $\phi(0) = \phi_1$ and $\phi(1) = \phi_2$. where ϕ_1, ϕ_2 are the inclinations of the curve at the end points. The EL equations yield:

$$\frac{d^2\phi}{dl^2} = 0$$

with the unique solution:

$$\phi = (\phi_2 - \phi_1)l - \phi_1$$

which is a circular arc.

III.   Large- and Small-scale Variations

The simple minimum energy principle. our modification notwithstanding. suffers from a severe shortcoming: It cannot handle sharp turns in the curve. A sharp corner will completely dominate the curve, and the value of the integral will depend on the exact shape of the corner, with point-like edges leading to infinities. Even a small bump will have a considerable influence, and in fact. the smaller the bump, the greater its effect on the integral will be (keeping its shape similar). This makes the energy principle inapplicable for curves with edges, or noise, without elaborate filtering techniques. On the other hand. straight lines are ignored by this principle, regardless of how long they may be.

We propose a new kind of an extremum principle, one of whose advantages is essentially solving this small (and large) scale variation problem. (Another advantage will become apparent when we go over to 3-D). First, we parametrize the curve by a new coordinate α, running along the curve with its limits being 0 and 1. Then we define a new "action" A:

$$A = \int_0^1 \left[\left(\frac{d\vec{t}}{d\alpha}\right)^2 + \left(\frac{dl}{d\alpha}\right)^2\right] d\alpha$$

Intuitively, one can regard α as a variable which is affected by two forces, generated by the fact that the extremizing drives α to follow l and $\vec{t}$, in analogy to an inertia effect. The second term in A pushes α to be as close as possible to l. In the absence of the first term (i.e. a straight line) α will coincide with l. This makes the first term as close as possible to the notion of curvature. On the other hand, the first term drives α to follow $\vec{t}$, (or ϕ) to some extent and concentrate in regions where $\Delta\vec{t}$ is large (such as a corner), so that $\Delta\vec{t}/\Delta\alpha$ does not get out of control.

As a "physical" analogy, one may think of a spring which can be stretched and bent unevenly along its length. The variable "α" will represent the amount of mass from a point on the spring to one end (as opposed to the spatial length l). The analogy is not perfect, though, as an actual spring usually does not have a dimensionless A. The spring is "ideal" in the sense that it, or part of it, can shrink to an infinitesimal length (like an ideal gas). This is what will happen in a corner. A finite "mass" $\Delta\alpha$ will concentrate in an infinitesimal corner, allowing the finite bending $\Delta\phi$ to spread over it.

In extremizing A, the unknowns are the functions $l(\alpha)$ and $\vec{t}(\alpha)$ (or equivalently $\phi(\alpha)$). Solving for them will give us both $\alpha(l)$, (the distribution of the "mass" along the mass, and $\vec{t}(l)$, which defines the curve. These unknown functions are not always completely independent. which may reduce the number of unknowns. or they may depend on a parameter such as the slant. that will become an unknown to be found by the extremization process. As we shall see, the first term will be rather dominant in sections of the curves having rapid curvature changes over short length, such as bumps, corners, or saw-teeth. The second term will be the major contributer in the large-scale features, having slow variations in curvature, such as the other boundaries of the saw. Thus we have obtained a "natural" way of treating curves with two very different scales of curvature change, without having to use arbitrarily preset filtering widths, as is commonly done.

A simple demonstration of the workings of this procedure can be made for a simple corner. We shall now examine the influence of a corner on our new A, as compared to its contribution to the energy.

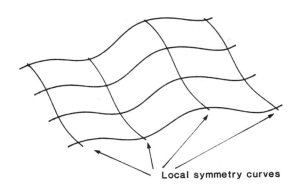

Figure 1. Local symmetry curves

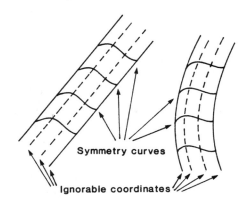

Symmetry curves

Ignorable coordinates

Figure 2. Ribbons with symmetry curves

We can build a corner from two "sticks" of length l, making an angle $\Delta\phi$ between themselves. We keep $\Delta\phi$ fixed, and we are only interested now in finding the distribution of the α along this corner. This turnes out to be a quite simple extremum problem. The increments of α along the sticks and on their joint is, respectively.

$$\Delta\alpha_{stick} = \frac{l}{2l - \Delta\phi}. \qquad \Delta\alpha_{joint} = \frac{\Delta\phi}{2l + \Delta\phi}$$

As we noted before, the second quantity is indeed finite. (In fact, we derived this result by treating the joint as a small circular arc, with length l_{joint}, which tends to a point.) Substituting these quantities in A we obtain in the extremum:

$$A = (1 + \Delta\phi)^2$$

which is independent of the exact shape and size of the corner, only on the total turn $\Delta\phi$.

In comparison, the (modified) energy principle will give for this corner:

$$A_{energy} = \frac{\Delta\phi^2}{\Delta l_{joint}}$$

which tend to infinity as the length of the corner goes to zero.

A bump can be regarded as a series of relatively sharp turns. Thus, given our expression for A at a corner, it is clear that its contribution is not dominating. With filtering, that will reduce the turns $\Delta\phi$ along the bump to small values, the influence of the bump will be quite negligible.

IV.   Skew-symmetry

We now collect 4 corners to form a parallelogram, which is a skew-symmetric shape. We shall allow the $\Delta\phi$-s of the corners to vary, in accordance with with interpreting the parallelgram as a shape with a slant in 3-D. We want to extremize A in respect to these $\Delta\phi$-s, to find the slant. The problem is complicated slightly by the fact that there is a constraint, namely that the sum of the angle of the 4 corners is equal to 2π. this can be handles by the method of Lagrange multipliers, and the result is that all the corner angles are equal, namely equal to $\pi/2$. Hence, the parallelogram is interpreted by our extremum principle as a slanted rectangle, which is consistent with human perception. This result can be extended to general skew-symmetric shapes.

V.   General Surfaces in 3-D

So far we have dealt with planar surfaces that can be described by a one-parameter boundary curve. We now turn to

the general case of a (reasonably) arbitrary surface in 3-D. such a surface can be parametrized by two coordinates α_1, α_2. Our action A will now be a double integral:

$$A = \int_0^1 \int_0^1 \sum_i \left[\left(\frac{d\vec{t}}{d\alpha_i}\right)^2 + \left(\frac{dl}{d\alpha_i}\right)^2 \right] d\alpha_1 d\alpha_2$$

where the summation is on $i = 1, 2$.

Given a set of known contours, either on the boundary or otherwise. we construct the surface that best fits these contours as the one that extremizes the above integral. Moreover, the α_i will now have a more tangible meaning then in the one-parameter case: they will be the natural coordinates parametrizing the surface. This is another advantage of the new procedure over the energy principle. It is interesting that the variables α_i can serve the dual purpose of both handling bumps (and straight lines) and provide a set of 3-D natural coordinates.

it is easy to prove, for example, that a circular boundary will give rise to a sphere. complete with its longitudinal and latitudinal coordinates. Rather then do that, we shall state a general theorem about curves on surfaces, which will be very useful in finding natural coordinates as well as the surfaces themselves (including the sphere).

We first define a curve of local symmetry, Γ as one which divides the surface in two parts that are symmetric in the vicinity of the curve. Put another way, a reflection, say of the surface lying to right side of Γ will match the left side, near Γ. An example is the center line of any fold, ridge, valley or corrugation on a surface (fig 1), if this line is planar. Another example is the three symmetry lines on an ellipsoid (this is a global symmetry).

Theorem 1: A curve of local symmetry is planar.

proof: Trivial. A reflection of the right side of Γ will not match the left side if Γ is not planar. (fig 1).

Theorem 2: A local network of coordinates, consisting of a local symmetry curve Γ and curves that are orthogonal to it, locally extremizes the action A.

By "locally extremize" we mean that an infinitesimal variation of these curves, in the vicinity of Γ, will leave A unchanged.

We shall discuss consequences of the last theorem. (The proof is ommited.) A very interesting class of surfaces to which our theorem is easily applicable is the one having an "ignorable coordinate", namely, its curvatures will not change as we move along this coordinate. As sub-classes one can mention (a) strips, or pipes, of arbitrary cross section, whether straight, circularly or helically bent, (fig 2), in which the ignorable coordinate is the length of the pipe. and (b) surfaces of revolution. in which the

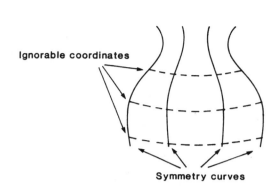

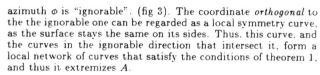

Figure 3. A surface of revolution.

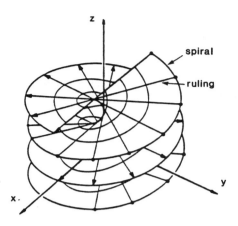

Figure 4. A helicoid

azimuth ϕ is "ignorable". (fig 3). The coordinate *orthogonal* to the the ignorable one can be regarded as a local symmetry curve, as the surface stays the same on its sides. Thus, this curve, and the curves in the ignorable direction that intersect it, form a local network of curves that satisfy the conditions of theorem 1, and thus it extremizes A.

As we can see from the figures, these curves are exactly the ones that our visual intuition would expect as natural, so that we are justified in calling the curves extremizing A the "natural coordinates".

A further consequence of theorem 2 is the ability to make predictions about surfaces when they are not known in advance, without having to actually extremize A using the EL equations. It is clear that generally, the greater the number of extremal local sections a surface has, the more "extremal" the global 2-dimensional integral A will be. (This would be clearer if this "extremum" were a "minimum", which it usually is, but as we have not examined here the second derivatives, we shall stick to the term "extremum".) Thus, a surface that extremizes A will contain as many symmetry curves as are compatible with the initial data. As a consequence, we will tend to obtain surfaces containing planar, spherical or cylindrical parts, exact or approximate, rather than bumpy ones. As a particular example, we can use this general result to conclude, without having to solve the EL equations, that a circular boundary will give rise to a sphere. This is because a sphere is the most symmetric surface, thus having the greatest amount of symmetry curves. More generally, boundary contours such as of fig. 3 will give rise to a surface of revolution, as this surface consists of a collection of local networks (the meridians and parallels) which fits those contours, and similarly for other surfaces.

It is reasonable to assume, that when the conditions of the theorem are satisfied only approximately, e.g. when the curve is only approximately symmetric, a similar parametrization will still take place, with the natural coordinates approximately following the quasi-symmetry curves. Thus our theory is applicable to shapes like generalized cones, as long as the flutings vary slowly on the lenth-scale of the cone's radius. This also is consistent with human perception.

VI.   Relation to Other Work

We have already noted the intrinsic flaws of the energy principle, and its derivatives (such as Barrow and Tenenbaum's), as surface reconstruction mechanisms. The compactness measure of Brady and Yuille [1984] does not suffer from these deficiencies. It has been applied successfully to closed planar curves, but it is hard to see how it can be made a general theory. It should be best viewed, perhaps, as a good measure of global symmetry.

Brady & Asada [1984] have studied local symmetries in planar shapes. Strictly speaking, our definition of "local" applies to an infinitesimal vicinity around a curve. In this sense, every straight line on a plane is a local symmetry curve, except at it edges. Brady examined larger vicinities, that extend to the nearby boundaries of the curve, so we shall elevate the type of symmetry he treated to a "regional" symmetry. The fact that Brady's curves are also natural coordinates indicate that the notion of symmetry is of fundamental importance at all spatial scales (global, regional, and local) of shape representation.

In differential geometry terms, our local symmetry curves are planar geodesic ones. Brady *et al* [1984] have shown that planar geodesics are usually "natural" coordinates. However, not all natural coordinates are planar geodesics. For example, the parallels on a surface of revolution, and the spirals on a helicoid (fig. 4), are not planar geodesics. The question why these look natural was left open, as they did not seem to fit any consistent rule. In our theory, these curves are natural coordinates by virtue of their being *orthogonal at each point of their length to planar geodesics*, namely the meridians and the rulings, respectively. Moreover, unlike the previous works, our results come out as a part of a general theory of shape representaton derived from sound first principles.

Acknowledgements

The author thanks Michael Brady of MIT's AI Lab for carefully reading earlier drafts of this paper and making very valuable comments and suggestions.

References

Barrow, H. G. and J. M. Tenenbaum, [1981], "Interpreting line drawings as three-dimensional surfaces", *Artif. Intell.*, **17**, 75–117.

Brady, Michael, J. Ponce, A. Yuille, H. Asada, [1984], "Describing surfaces". To be published.

Brady, Michael, and H. Asada, [1984], "Smooth local symmetries and their implementation", A. I. Memo No. 757.

Brady, Michael, and A. Yuille, [1984], "An extremum principle for shape from contour", *IEEE Patt. Anal. & Mach. Int.*, PAMI-6.

SPECULAR STEREO

A. Blake

Computer Science Department,
Edinburgh University,
Scotland.

ABSTRACT

A glossy highlight, viewed stereoscopically, can provide information about surface shape. For example, highlights appear to lie behind convex surfaces but in front of concave ones.

A highlight is a distorted, reflected image of a light source. A ray equation is developed to predict the stereo disparities generated when a point source of light is reflected in a smooth, curved surface. This equation can be inverted to infer surface curvature properties from observed stereo disparities of the highlight. To obtain full information about surface curvature in the neighbourhood of the highlight, stereo with two different baselines – or stereo with motion parallax – is required.

The same ray equation can also be used to predict the monocular appearance of a distributed source. A circular source, for instance, may produce an elliptical specular patch in an image, and the dimensions of the ellipse help to determine surface shape.

1 INTRODUCTION

When the reflectance of a surface has a specular as well as a diffuse component, the viewer may see highlights. Highlights can give extra information about surface shape. Ikeuchi [8] uses photometric stereo with specular surfaces to determine surface orientation. Beck [1] notes that stereo vision might be able to perceive highlights on a convex surface as lying beneath the surface. Grimson [7] incorporated lambertian and specular components of reflectance into stereo. But he found that the computation of surface orientation could be numerically unstable.

Here a computation is proposed that is less ambitious than Grimson's, in that it attempts to determine only local surface geometry, at specular points. But it avoids relying on precise assumptions about surface reflectance.

Instead, the only assumption is that a specularity can be detected in an image, and its position measured. For instance a method like that of Ullman [15] could be used. Thereafter specularities are matched in the same way as features in conventional stereo [6,9,10]. The disparity of a stereo-matched specular point is then compared with the disparity of any nearby surface features.

The basic principle of the surface shape estimation relies on the properties of curved mirrors (fig 1).

To interpret specular stereo, both horizontal and vertical disparities are used. Ideally, three non-collinear eyes are needed to obtain full information about local curvature. Alternatively, parallax from a known vertical motion of a viewer, combined with conventional stereo geometry, is just as good. If only a static, stereo view is available then this still yields partial information. This could be combined

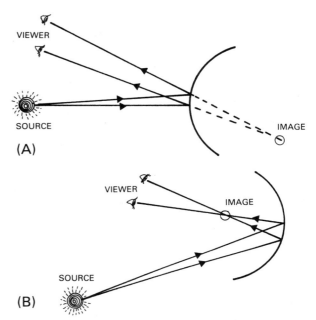

Figure 1: *Viewing geometry. In a convex mirror (a) the image of a distant point source appears behind the mirror surface. In a concave one (b) the image may appear in front. Study of the ordinary domestic soup spoon should confirm this.*

with *a priori* knowledge or measurements from other sources (stereo, shape-from-shading or specular reflection of a distributed source) to fully determine local surface shape.

Finally, observe that the path of a light ray from source to viewer can be reversed. Analysis developed to show the effect of moving the viewer also serves for movement of the source. The resulting equation is used to predict the appearance in an image of a distributed source under specular reflection in a curved surface. For instance a circular source generally produces an elliptical specularity in the image. The orientation and length of its major and minor axes, in principle, determine local surface shape.

2 IMAGING EQUATIONS

Equations are given to describe the process of formation of images of specular reflections. Details of derivations are given in [3]. These predict the dependence of observed stereo disparities on surface and viewing geometry. Certain assumptions about the geometries are made, for the sake of mathematical simplicity. Then the equations are inverted so that, given viewing geometry and disparities, local surface geometry can be inferred.

2.1 Viewing, surface and reflection geometry

The stereo viewing geometry is shown in fig 2.

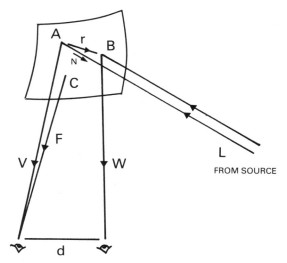

Figure 2: *Stereo viewing geometry.*
*Illumination comes from a distant point source,
in direction L. Rays to left and right eyes lie
along vectors V,W, and strike the surface at
points A,B respectively. Surface normals at
A,B are N,N' respectively. The vector from A to
B is r, and the baseline lies along vector d. A
surface feature is assumed to be present
nearby, at C, with position vector F relative to
the left eye.*

It is assumed that the curved surface is locally well
approximated by terms up to 2nd order in a Taylor
series (see eq. (4)). The vectors $V,d,-W,-r$ form a
closed loop, so that

$$V + d - W - r = 0. \tag{1}$$

A coordinate frame is chosen with origin at A,
with $N=(0,0,1)$, and with L,V lying in the x–z plane,
so that

$$V = (V\sin\sigma,0,V\cos\sigma), \; L = (-\sin\sigma,0,\cos\sigma) \tag{2}$$

where σ is the slant of the tangent plane at A. Its
tilt direction lies in the x–z plane. Note that if
viewing geometry and light–source direction L are
known (and the latter could be obtained as in [11])
then surface slant and tilt are known: the surface
normal lies in the plane of V,L and bisects them.

It is assumed that some feature at point C on
the surface, is available near to the specular points
A,B (fig 2) and that stereo is able to establish the
position of C. Its position vector F is used to
estimate V, the length of the vector V. Assuming
that C is not too far away from A, so that C lies,
approximately, in the tangent plane at A,

$$(V-F).N = 0 \text{ so that}$$

$$V\cos\sigma = F.N. \tag{3}$$

Since the choice of coordinate frame ensures
that gradients vanish $(\partial z/\partial x = \partial z/\partial y = 0)$, the
surface, in the neighbourhood of A, is described by

$$z(x,y) = (1/2)x.(Hx) + O(|x|^3). \tag{4}$$

where $r=(x,y,z)$, $x=(x,y)$ and H is the (symmetric)
hessian matrix [4] of the surface. Note that r,d
etc. are 3-dimensional vectors but x is a 2-
dimensional vector, in the xy-plane. Similarly H is
a 2×2 matrix operating on x.

The law of reflection at A is that

$$2(V.N)N - V \parallel L, \tag{5}$$

where $\parallel$ denotes "is parallel to". Similarly for the
other eye, at B,

$$2(W.N')N' - W \parallel L. \tag{6}$$

Combining (1) (5) (6) gives (see [3] for details):

$$MHx = x + w \tag{7}$$

where $w_x= -d_x+d_z\tan\sigma$, $w_y= -d_y$ and

$$M = \begin{pmatrix} 2(V\sec\sigma+d_z+d_x\tan\sigma) & 2d_y\tan\sigma \\ 0 & 2(V\cos\sigma+d_z) \end{pmatrix} \tag{8}$$

The approximations used above hold good
provided $|\delta N| \ll \cos\sigma$ and $|x| \ll V\cos\sigma$. This means that
surface slant σ must not be close to 90°, and that
both vergence angle and (angular) disparity should
be small. It can be shown that these conditions will
usually be satisfied when the stereo baseline is
short, so that $|d| \ll V\cos\sigma$.

To solve equation (7), we note also that

$$\det(M) = 4(V\sec\sigma+d_z+d_x\tan\sigma)(V\cos\sigma+d_z)$$

so that, provided surface slant σ is not near 90° as
above, and provided $|d| \le (1/2)V$ (baseline length
less than half viewing distance), then $\det(M) \ne 0$. In that
case, equation (7) can be inverted to give

$$Hx = v \text{ where } v=M^{-1}(w+x) \tag{9}$$

which, in general, can be expected to impose 2
constraints on the 3 variables of H. If something is
known already about H – say, that the surface is
locally cylindrical at A – then it might be possible
to determine H completely.

2.2 Disparity measurement

The equations just derived require the vector x
to be determined from disparity measurements, as
shown in fig 3.

Having obtained from the stereo images the
angular disparity δ of the specularity as in fig 3, it
can be "back-projected" onto the surface to obtain
the length x. The assumption that $|\delta N|$ is small is
used again to obtain

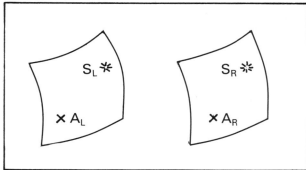

Figure 3: *Disparity measurements.* *The
specular point is imaged at angular positions
S_L,S_R in the left and right images respectively.
A nearby surface feature is imaged at A_L,A_R
and provides a disparity reference point on
the surface. From these measured positions in
the image, $\delta = (S_R-A_R)-(S_L-A_R)$ is computed
– the difference between the angular disparities
of the 2 points. Then $x = (x,y) = V(\delta_x\sec\sigma,\delta_y)$.*

$$x = (x,y) = VP\delta, \text{ where} \tag{10}$$

$$P = \begin{pmatrix} \sec\sigma & 0 \\ 0 & 1 \end{pmatrix}$$

2.3 Focusing effects

Equation (7) predicts that imaging of a
specularity can become degenerate (fig 4). The
equation can be rewritten as

$$(MH{-}I)x = w \qquad (11)$$

and the condition for degeneracy is that $\det(MH{-}I)=0$.

The focusing effect may produce either a line or a blob in the image:

1. If the rank of $(MH{-}I)$ is 1 the specularity will appear in the image as a line. Or else, there may be no solution for x in (7), and nothing of the specularity will be visible. Stevens [13] observes that, with infinitely distant source and viewer, any line specularity must lie on a plane curve in the surface – a special case of the rank 1 focusing effect.

2. If the rank of $MH{-}I$ is zero, that is $MH{-}I{=}0$, then either the specular reflection is invisible as above, or it is focussed in 2 dimensions onto the imaging aperture, and appears in the image as a large bright blob.

3. It can be shown that if the surface patch is convex, the effect cannot occur. This corresponds to physical intuition. Only concave mirrors focus distant light sources.

2.4 A source at a finite distance

If the source is at a finite distance L, rather than infinite as assumed so far, the imaging equation (7) becomes:

$$(MH - (1{+}p)I)x = w. \qquad (12)$$

The constant $p=(d_z\sec\sigma+V)/L$ and clearly, as $L\to\infty$,

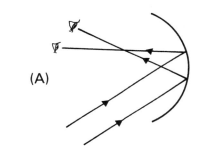

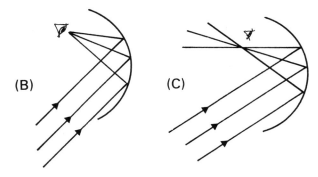

Figure 4: *Degenerate imaging of a specularity.* Normal imaging of a specularity (a) becomes degenerate because of the focusing action of the curved surface. The surface may focus onto the viewing aperture (b) to produce a bright blob or line in the image, or away from the aperture (c) in which case nothing is visible in the image.

$p\to0$ which gives the infinite source equation (7).

Suppose the infinite source computation of surface shape is performed, when in fact the source is at a finite distance L, how great is the resulting error? The answer is that the error in the curvature (along a given direction in the xy-plane) is of the order of $\pm1/L$. The error is negligible if, assuming σ not to be close to 90°, either

– the light source distance is large compared with the viewing distance: $L{\gg}V$, or
– the surface has *high curvature*: for *both* principal curvatures, $\kappa_i{\gg}1/L$, $i{=}1,2$.

The first case is intuitively reasonable; if the light source is distant compared with the observer distance V, then equations for an infinite light source can be used with little error. What is perhaps less obvious is the second condition that, for highly curved objects, the source need *not* be further away than the observer.

2.5 Distributed sources

The mathematical model that has been used so far assumes a point source. In practice the source may be distributed, so that it subtends some non-zero solid angle, at the surface.

Equation (12), for a source at a finite distance, is used but source and viewer positions are interchanged. The light ray is reversed. Vector d now represents the movement of *source* for a fixed *viewer* position. After some rearrangement, this yields a new equation, looking rather like (12) but with a factor V/L on the right hand side:

$$(MH - (1{+}p)I)x = (V/L)w. \qquad (13)$$

It would be most convenient to express the shape of the image specularity (using angular position in the image, δ) in terms of source distribution (using a new angular variable α). From (10) $x=VP\delta$, and it is straightforward to show that $w=LP\alpha$. So now

$$T\delta = \alpha \text{ where } T=P^{-1}MHP - (1{+}p)I. \qquad (14)$$

What equation (14) says is that the viewer sees an image of the source that has undergone a linear transformation T^{-1}. The effect of the transformation depends on surface shape. For a planar mirror for example, $H{=}0$ so that $\delta=-\alpha/(1{+}p)$ – an isotropic scaling that preserves the shape of the source. Note that if the source is very distant, $p{\approx}0$ and the scaling factor is unity.

If the angular dimensions of the source are known then, in principle, surface shape may be recovered completely by monocular observation. For a circular source with slant $\sigma{=}0$, the ellipse axes coincide with the principal curvature directions of the surface. In general, when $\sigma{\neq}0$, measuring the length and direction of ellipse axes enables T and hence H to be found from (14). Note that for a circular source, because of its symmetry, principal curvatures are determined only up to sign inversion (approximately).

3 INFERRING LOCAL SURFACE SHAPE

3.1 Locally cylindrical surface

On a surface that is *known* to be locally cylindrical, equation (7) is sufficient to recover both parameters of local surface shape. For instance, when the source is distributed, a strip shape image-specularity indicates that the surface may be cylindrical – or at least that one principal curvature may be much larger than the other. (This can be deduced from (14).)

The parameters to be determined are: the direction of the cylinder axis θ and the radius R. Using (9):

$$\tan\theta = v_y/v_x$$

$$R = (x\cos^2\theta+y\sin\theta\cos\theta)/v_x.$$

3.2 Spherical surface

The knowledge that the surface is locally spherical could be derived monocularly, from (14), as in the cylindrical case except that rather more must be known about the source – for example, that it is circular.

On a spherical surface there is only one parameter to specify – the radius of curvature R, and from (9):

$$R = x/v_x = y/v_y$$

- the second equality being available as a check for consistency of assumptions.

3.3 Known orientation of principal axes

If the orientation of principal axes about the surface normal, is known then the complete local surface geometry can be obtained. Orientation could be derived monocularly (assuming source shape known) from (14).

Rotating coordinates about the z axis, a primed (') frame can be obtained in which H in (9) becomes diagonal:

$$H'x' = v'$$

Now, in general, the two diagonal components of H' can be obtained immediately. Experiments with computer generated images have obtained curvature to an accuracy of 10%.

3.4 General case

In the general case, the surface curvature at the specular point is described by 3 parameters, but the specular stereo measurements yields only 2 constraints. However two additional constraints – 4 in all – are available if a second baseline is used. The extra baseline could be derived either from a third sensor, suitably positioned, or from known motion of the viewer (parallax).

Suppose now that there are 2 baselines $d^{(i)}, i=1,2$ with corresponding $x^{(i)}, M^{(i)}, w^{(i)}, v^{(i)}$. Now equation (9), applied once for each baseline, gives

$$HX = V \quad \text{where} \tag{15}$$

$$X = \begin{pmatrix} x^{(1)} & x^{(2)} \\ y^{(1)} & y^{(2)} \end{pmatrix} \quad V = \begin{pmatrix} v_x^{(1)} & v_x^{(2)} \\ v_y^{(1)} & v_y^{(2)} \end{pmatrix}$$

and H can be recovered provided X is non-singular.

It appears to be impossible to suggest baselines that guarantee to generate a non-singular X, for *all* viewing geometries and surfaces. This is because $\det(X)$ depends on the surface and the viewing geometry, as well as on the baselines. This is probably best achieved (see [3]) by making the baselines $d^{(i)}$ fairly near orthogonal, and certainly nowhere near collinear.

The disparity measurements give 4 constraints. If H is the only unknown, it is now overdetermined. One could test either

1. Test whether the H obtained from (15) is indeed symmetric as a check on validity of assumptions (for example, the validity of the local approximation of (4), over the range of movement of the specular point on the surface)
2. Use a least-squares error method to find the symmetric H that fits the data best. Then H is the solution of linear equations:

$$HXX^T + XX^TH = VX^T + XV^T.$$

The error measure $\|HX-V\|$, if it is too large, indicates that some assumptions were not valid.

4 CONCLUSION

Is specular stereo actually useful? We argue that it is. Of course the presence of specularities in the image cannot be guaranteed; specular stereo is not an autonomous process in the sense that conventional stereo is. Indeed specular stereo itself *relies* on conventional stereo to provide a disparity reference. In the case of a densely textured surface, conventional stereo with surface fitting [2,5,6,12,14] would be able to give an accurate estimate of surface shape. But for a smooth surface, stereo features may be relatively sparse, and fitting a surface to disparity measurements may be difficult and inaccurate. Then, provided at least one nearby surface feature is available as a disparity reference, specular stereo, together with monocular analysis of specularity, provides valuable surface shape information.

Acknowledgement

This work was supported by SERC grant GR/D 1439.6 and by the University of Edinburgh. Thanks are due to G. Brelstaff, A. Zisserman and R. Fisher for valuable discussion.

REFERENCES

1. Beck, J. (1972). *Surface color perception.* Cornell University Press, Ithaca, U.S..

2. Blake, A. (1984). Reconstructing a visible surface. *Proc AAAI conf.* 1984, 23–26.

3. Blake, A. (1984). Inferring surface shape by specular stereo. Report CSR-179-84, Dept. Computer Science, Edinburgh University.

4. do Carmo, M.P. (1976). *Differential geometry of curves and surfaces.* Prentice Hall, Englewood cliffs, USA.

5. Faugeras, O.D. and Hebert, M. (1983). A 3-D recognition and positioning algorithm using geometrical matching between primitive surfaces. *IJCAI 83*, 996–1002.

6. Grimson, W.E.L. (1982). *From images to surfaces.* MIT Press, Cambridge, USA.

7. Grimson, W.E.L. (1982). Binocular shading and visual surface reconstruction. *AI Lab. Memo.* 697, MIT, Cambridge, USA.

8. Ikeuchi,K. (1981). Determining surface orientations of specular surfaces by using the photometric stereo method. *IEEE trans. PAMI,* 3, 6, 661–669.

9. Marr, D. and Poggio, T. (1979). A computational theory of human stereo vision. *Proc. R. Soc Lond. B,* 204, 301–328.

10. Mayhew, J.E.W and Frisby, J.P. (1981). Towards a computational and psychophysical theory of stereopsis. *AI Journal,* 17, 349–385.

11. Pentland, A.P. (1984). Local shape analysis. *IEEE trans. PAMI,* March 1984, 170–187.

12. Potmesil, M. (1983). Generating models of solid objects by matching 3D surface segments. *IJCAI 83*, 1089–1093.

13. Stevens,K.A. (1979). *Surface perception from local analysis of texture and contour.* Ph.D. thesis, MIT, USA.

14. Terzopoulos, D. (1983). Multilevel computational processes for visual surface reconstruction, *Computer Vision Graphics and Image Processing,* 24, 52–96.

15. Ullman, S. (1976). On visual detection of light sources. *Biol. Cybernetics,* 21, 205–212.

A PARALLEL MATCHING ALGORITHM FOR STEREO VISION

Y. Nishimoto

Asada Research Laboratory
Kobe Steel, Ltd.
53-3, Maruyama, Gomo, Nada-ku, Kobe, Japan

and

Y. Shirai

Automatic Control Division
Electrotechnical Laboratory
1-1-4, Umezono, Sakura-mura Niihari-gun, Ibaraki, Japan

ABSTRACT

This paper proposes a parallel matching algorithm for feature-based stereo vision. Features are zero-crossing (ZC) points detected with various sizes of Laplacian-Gaussian filters. In order to obtain candidate intervals of disparity, the disparity histogram is computed all over the image. The image is, then, divided into small areas and the disparity histogram in each local area is computed within the candidate intervals. The local disparity histograms in all the channels are fed to the fusion evaluator and the most probable disparity is detected in each local area. Once the most probable disparity is detected, disparities for all the finest ZC points are determined in the local area to obtain a high resolution disparity map. The matching pairs are removed from a set of ZC points. A series of processes are iterated until no more disparities are determined.

Experiments with a sample scene reveals that the algorithm has advantages in efficiency and performance.

I INTRODUCTION

Among various types of range finding methods, stereo vision is worthy of notice since it needs no active media. However, it is so difficult to match corresponding points in the two images that the stereo vision has not been fully established as a computer vision system.

There have been many matching algorithms proposed, which may be classified into feature-based method and area-based method.

In feature-based method, Marr and Hildreth introduced the convolution operator $\nabla^2 G$, where ∇^2 is the Laplacian operator and G stands for the two-dimensional Gaussian distribution, and adopted the zero-crossing (ZC) of the $\nabla^2 G$-filtered image as the features to be matched (Marr and Hildreth, 1980). A problem with matching the ZC is that ZC points may appear randomly in the region of little intensity change. If we try to match ZCs including such random ones, the probability of false matching becomes large.

Another problem is concerned about how to match corresponding points. Marr and Poggio proposed the hierarchical matching algorithm, in which matching process is started in the coarsest channel of ZC and followed by finer ones (Marr and Poggio, 1979). As was successfully implemented by Grimson the algorithm is quite reasonable for a scene where the depth change smoothly (Grimson, 1981). However, it turns out to be inefficient in certain cases. The first is a case where a scene includes many objects at different positions as observed in usual room scenes. The inheritance of disparity information from a coarser channel to a finer one frequently fails, especially at the discontinuities of depth. The second is a case where the main feature consists of high spatial frequency component alone. A white wall with small scratches is one of the examples. In that case the matching process can not start in the coarsest channel.

In order to solve problems mentioned above, we have developed and implemented a parallel matching algorithm.

II OUTLINE OF ALGORITHM

The general block diagram of the parallel matching algorithm is shown in Figure 1.

Features are the ZC points detected with various sizes of $\nabla^2 G$. In order to obtain candidate intervals of disparity, the disparity histogram is computed all over the image. The image is, then, divided into small areas and the disparity histogram in each local area is computed within the candidate intervals. The local disparity histograms in all the channels are fed to the fusion evaluator and the most probable disparity is detected in each local area. Once the most probable disparity is detected, disparities for all the finest ZC points are determined in the local area to obtain a high resolution disparity map. A series of processes are iterated until no more disparities are determined.

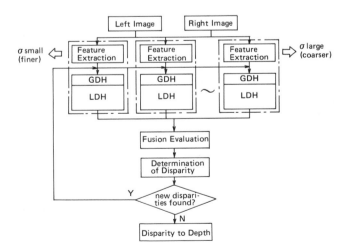

FIGURE 1   BLOCK DIAGRAM OF PARALLEL MATCHING ALGORITHM

$$\begin{pmatrix} \text{GDH} : \text{Global Disparity histogram} \\ \text{LDH} : \text{Local Disparity histogram} \end{pmatrix}$$

III   FEATURE EXTRACTION

Let the input image and ∇^2G-filtered image be denoted by $E^{(x)}(i,j)$ and $B_\sigma^{(x)}(i,j)$, where σ is the standard deviation of G and x means either right (R) or left (L). $B_\sigma^{(x)}(i,j)$ is given by the following equation:

$$B_\sigma^{(X)}(i,j) = \nabla^2(G*E^{(X)}(i,j)) = (\nabla^2G)*(E^{(X)}(i,j)) \ ,$$

where "$*$" denotes the convolution operation. The filtered image $B_\sigma^{(x)}(i,j)$ has no dc component and can be equally divided into positive and negative regions. The boundaries between the two regions turn out to be the ZC. Here, we define the ZC as unit vector $r_\sigma^{(x)}(i,j)$ along the boundary.

A ZC point corresponding to a small contrast is removed on the basis of the gradient value of the G-filtered image on that ZC, that is,

if $|\nabla(G*E^{(X)}(i,j))| < G_o$,
then the ZC is removed,

where G_O is a predetermined threshold value.

IV   DISPARITY HISTOGRAMMING

The calculation of disparity histogram is generally the most time-consuming process in the matching operation. Here, the global disparity histogram (GDH) is first computed to find an approximate disparity distribution. The GDH is defined as:

$$GDH_\sigma^{(R)}(d) = \frac{\sum\limits_{(i,j)\in A} r_\sigma^{(R)}(i,j)\cdot r_\sigma^{(L)}(i+d,j)}{\sum\limits_{(i,j)\in A} r_\sigma^{(R)}(i,j)\cdot r_\sigma^{(R)}(i,j)} \ ,$$

where d stands for a disparity and A is the whole image plane. Since points on the physical surface constitute clusters in space, the true matches tend to fall in some intervals of disparity, while the false matches randomly scatter. The GDH consequently gives the approximate disparity distribution of objects in the scene.

Now let the peak value of $GDH_\sigma^{(x)}(d)$ be H. Intervals S determined in the following equation is the disparity intervals for the local disparity histogram (LDH) to be calculated in.

$$S = \{ \ d \mid GDH_\sigma^{(X)}(d) > a\cdot H \ \} \ ,$$

where a is a constant value and $0<a<1$. S may generally consist of multiple intervals corresponding to objects in the scene. In this way we can limit the candidate intervals of disparity and greatly improve the efficiency of the LDH process.

The LDH represents the disparity distribution of true and false matches within window W_σ of $M_\sigma \times M_\sigma$ around ZC point $P(i,j)$, where M_σ is determined as the average pitch of ZCs, that is, a function of σ. The LDH for a fixed window on the right image is defined as:

$$LDH_\sigma^{(R)}(d;i,j) = \frac{\sum\limits_{(i',j')\in W_\sigma} r_\sigma^{(R)}(i',j')\cdot r_\sigma^{(L)}(i'+d,j')}{\sum\limits_{(i',j')\in W_\sigma} r_\sigma^{(R)}(i',j')\cdot r_\sigma^{(R)}(i',j')} \ ,$$

where $d \in S$.

V   FUSION EVALUATION

Now the fusion for each window area is evaluated using LDHs of all channels. The best fusion channel is first selected as the one such that the difference between the first and second largest peaks in LDH is the largest. Let the difference of the peaks in the best channel be $F^{(x)}(d;i,j;\sigma)$. The local fusion is established if the following condition is satisfied for a certain disparity d*:

$$F^{(R)}(d^*;i,j;\sigma) > F_o \quad \text{and} \quad F^{(L)}(d^*;i+d^*,j;\sigma) > F_o \ ,$$

where F_O is a predetermined threshold value. Disparity d* can be regarded as the most probable disparity in W_σ.

VI   DETERMINATION OF DISPARITY MAP

Once the most probable disparity d* is obtained in W_σ, disparities for all ZC points in W_σ are determined in the following manner. Let the disparities between a ZC point in the right image and matching candidates in the left image be $d_1, d_2, ..., d_n$ in the finest channel, and the disparity which is the nearest to d* among $d_1, d_2, ... d_n$ be d_{op}.

If $|d_{op} - d^*| < d_o$, then the disparity for the ZC is finally determined to be d_{op}, otherwise, the determination is postoponed,

where d_O is the predetermined value. Once the pair $Q(P_m,P_n)$ is determined as a true match, pairs $Q(P_k,P_n)$ $(k\neq m)$ and pairs $Q(P_m,P_k)$ $(k\neq n)$ are regarded false matches and removed in the succeeding iterations, where P_m and P_n are a ZC point in the right and left image.

The processes from GDH calculation to this process are iterated until no more disparities are determined. The disparities are transformed to depths by means of predetermined geometrical relations and camera parameters in a straightforward manner.

VII   EXPERIMENT

The parallel matching algorithm was tested with the scene shown in Figure 2, with the Prime 750 in the Information Computer System of Electrotechnical Laboratory. The scene has many objects such as a plaster figure, a telephone, a book, plant, and a coffee cup in front of a shelf, white paper, and a calendar. The telephone has a glossy surface and the plant has quite a complex profile. In addition, the calendar has a periodical pattern which is, in principle, unsuitable for stereo vision.

The ZC points in the fine, middle, and coarse channel are shown in Figure 3, and the filtered ZC points in the fine channel is shown in Figure 4. The global disparity histogram from the right at the first iteration is shown in Figure 5. The disparities finally obtained are shown in Figure 6, where the larger disparities (nearer to the camera) are displayed by the brighter points. There are 9424 ZC points in all in the right image, of which about 6500 ZC points have correspondences and the left are those in the occluding or uncommon regions. Most of the disparities of 6500 ZC points were reasonably determined.

It is revealed that the ZC points whose correspondences are detected by a finer channel, mainly lie in the region near edges of objects, that is, the area of discontinuous depth, while the ZC points whose correspondences are detected by a coarser channel lie in the region of little change of depth, or in the periodical pattern on the calendar.

The cpu time is about 20 minutes except the calculation of feature extraction which could be quickly executed with special hardware.

(c) $\sigma = 6$ pixel (coarse)

FIGURE 3   ZC POINTS

FIGURE 2   ORIGINAL IMAGE

FIGURE 4   FILTERED ZC (FINE)

(a) $\sigma = 1.5$ pixel (fine)

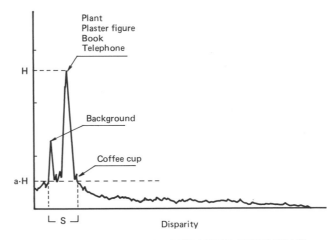

FIGURE 5   GLOBAL DISPARITY HISTOGRAM

(b) $\sigma = 3$ pixel (middle)

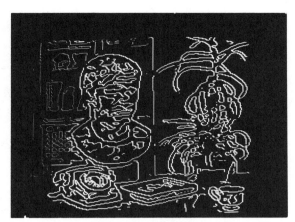

FIGURE 6   FINALLY OBTAINED DISPARITY

VIII   CONCLUSION

A parallel matching algorithm for feature-based stereo vision is proposed.

It has the following features.   Since the algorithm uses the features in the various resolutions evenly and complementally, it can deal with the correspondence problem according to the way how the depth changes on and between the physical surfaces of objects.   For example, if an object has a surface on which the depth changes little, a coarser channel is automatically excited and the disparities over the wide area can be determined at a time.   Introduction of GDH enables us to limit the search intervals of disparity and to reduce the amount of calculations.   In addition, the algorithm is essentially suitable for hardware due to its parallel architecture.

However, there is room for improvement in the details of algorithm.   Especially, the criterion of evaluation of fusion and the procedure of iteration need further refinement through experiments with various types of scenes.

REFERENCES

[1]   Marr, D. and Hildreth, E., "Theory of Edge Detection." Proc. R. Soc. Lond. B. 207 (1980) 187–217.

[2]   Marr, D. and Poggio, T., "A Computational Theory of Human Stereo Vision." Proc. R. Soc. Lond. B 204 (1979) 301–328.

[3]   Grimson, W.E.L., "From Image to Surface." MIT Press, Cambridge (1981).

Optical Navigation by the Method of Differences

Bruce D. Lucas and Takeo Kanade

Computer Science Department
Carnegie-Mellon University
Pittsburgh, PA 15213

Abstract. The *method of differences* refers to a technique for image matching that uses the intensity gradient of the image to iteratively improve the match between the two images. Used in an iterative scheme combined with image smoothing, the method exhibits good accuracy and a wide convergence range. In this paper we show how the technique can be used to directly solve for the parameters relating two cameras viewing the same scene. The resulting algorithm can be used for optical navigation, which has applications in robot arm guidance and autonomous roving vehicle navigation. Because of the regular structure of the algorithm, the prospects of carrying it out with special-purpose hardware for real-time control of a robot seem good. We present experimental results demonstrating the accuracy and range of convergence that can be expected from the algorithm.

1. Introduction

Optical navigation refers to the determination of the position and orientation of a camera analysis of the picture taken by the camera. The objective of such analysis is to determine some or all of the six parameters (three of position and three of orientation) that determine the position of that camera relative to some fixed frame of reference. In our method and in many others the fixed frame of reference is that of a second camera, so that the problem is that of image comparison.

Optical navigation has a number of applications in robotic tasks that require a knowledge of the position and orientation of the robot. This is because mechanical imperfections and environmental uncertainty make it impossible to know exactly how a robot will move in response to the commands sent to it and exactly what it will encounter in its surroundings. Such applications include navigation of autonomous roving vehicles and navigation of a robot arm relative to the object on which it is performing its task.

This research was sponsored by the Defense Advanced Research Projects Agency (DOD), ARPA Order No. 3597, monitored by the Air Force Avionics Laboratory Under Contract F33615-84-K-1520. The views and conclusions contained in this document are those of the authors and should not be interpreted as representing the official policies, either expressed or implied, of the Defense Advanced Research Projects Agency or the US Government.

The approaches to matching for optical navigation may be divided into three categories: sparse two-dimensional matching, continuous two-dimensional matching, and three-dimensional matching. The sparse two-dimensional approach starts with a discrete set of matching points in the two images, and from them deduces the camera motion. The question of how many points are necessary to uniquely solve for the camera parameters has been addressed by Tsai & Huang (1981). With more points, the problem is overspecified and a least-squares approach is required (Gennery, 1980). The continuous two-dimensional matching approach starts with a whole image field of matches (the "optical flow field"); Bruss & Horn (1983) have shown how how to determine the camera motion from the optical flow field, again using a least-squares formulation. Obtaining the optical flow field has been investigated by, for example, Horn & Schunck (1981) and Cornelius & Kanade (1983), among others. In the three-dimensional matching approach, corresponding points in three dimensions (obtained e.g. by stereo) are used to determine the camera motion; this technique was used by Moravec (1980) to navigate a rover.

These approaches all split the process into two steps: finding the matches and using those matches to solve for the camera parameters. In this paper we show how to combine the two steps into one, by applying a generalized image matching technique that we term the *method of differences*. The method of differences directly computes the six camera parameters, or any desired subset of them, much as standard matching techniques compute two parameters (the x and y displacements). That is, the camera parameters are explicitly included in the matching process. The method takes advantage of the fact that, in many applications the approximate position and orientation of the camera are known. Starting from that estimate we compute a better estimate by using the image intensity gradient as a guide. By using an iterative scheme our estimates converge to the correct value. The result is a technique that is fast and free of search.

In the remainder of the paper, we first describe the method of differences in a one-dimensional case, which serves to illustrate many of the issues. Then we show how the same technique can be used for multi-parameter estimation. Finally, we present some experimental results and draw some conclusions.

2.   The technique

Parameter estimation by the method of differences.
The one-dimensional case illustrates the nature of the technique. Given two one-dimensional images $I_1(x)$ and $I_2(x)$ related by a translation, so that $I_1(x) = I_2(x+h)$, we wish to estimate the translation h. We do this by finding that $\hat{h}$ that minimizes the total squared error,

$$E = \sum_x \left(I_2(x+\hat{h}) - I_1(x)\right)^2. \tag{1}$$

Since we want a local, non-searching algorithm, we approximate $I_2(x+\hat{h})$ using $I_2(x)$ on the basis of local information, namely the derivative; this yields the approximation

$$E \approx \sum_x \left(I_2(x) + \hat{h}D_x I_2(x) - I_1(x)\right)^2, \tag{2}$$

where D_x denotes partial differentiation with respect to x. This equation is quadratic in $\hat{h}$, so we can differentiate with respect to $\hat{h}$, set equal to zero, and solve the resulting linear equation for $\hat{h}$, obtaining

$$\hat{h} = \frac{\sum_x \left(I_1(x) - I_2(x)\right) D_x I_2(x)}{\sum_x D_x I_2(x)^2}. \tag{3}$$

We call this the method of differences because it is based on comparing the difference between the images, $I_1(x) - I_2(x)$, with the derivative $D_x I_2(x)$ (which will in fact be implemented as a difference), to obtain an estimate for the parameter h.

We have shown elsewhere (Lucas, 1985) how this method is easily extended to multi-parameter estimation, as required for navigation. Briefly, the scalar disparity h is replaced by a vector of camera parameters; the derivatives become gradients, and the division becomes a matrix inversion. The stability of the matrix inversion is investigated in the work cited above, with the conclusion that the matching points should be well-distributed in three-space to guarantee good numerical accuracy.

Iteration and smoothing.   Two modifications are required to make the method work. First, because the method yields only an approximation $\hat{h}$ to the disparity h, we must use an iterative scheme to obtain an accurate result. The idea is to calculate an estimated disparity, move I_2 by that amount, and calculate again.

Second, to improve the accuracy and range of validity of the linear estimate used in (2), we must smooth the image. This can be thought of as smoothing out purely local bumps and wrinkles in the image intensity profile that would make a linear estimate accurate only over a small range. This can be made more precise by a Fourier analysis of (3); this shows that removing the high frequency

components of the image by smoothing does indeed extend the range of convergence, in rough proportion to the size of the smoothing window (Lucas, 1985). This is because convergence to the correct value with an image consisting of a pure sine wave is possible only for disparities up to one-half the wavelength of the sine wave; for larger disparities, the algorithm will converge to the wrong value.

Since smoothing the image also reduces the accuracy of the method, it is necessary to use an iterative approach in which each successive step uses a less-smoothed image, in a sort of coarse-fine approach. This allows the algorithm to tolerate a large disparity yet yield an accurate answer.

3.   Experimental results

Our experimental data consisted of three views of the same scene taken by a camera mounted on the Stanford cart (Moravec, 1980); they are shown in Figure 1. The camera was mounted on a slider, so we had accurate knowledge of the relative positions of the cameras. The three views were pictures taken by the camera at the left, middle, and right slider positions, with 26 cm separating each position. The left picture was used as the reference image, and a number of points **p** were selected from this image as reference points. These points correspond to the points x that the sum in (1) runs over. Then the right picture was used as the second image of a stereo pair to obtain (essentially by hand) the distances $z(\mathbf{p})$ of the reference points **p**. The method of differences was then used to determine position of the middle camera. Since the exact position of the middle camera was known, we could assess the accuracy of the method. Moreover, we could determine the range of convergence by varying the initial estimate of the middle camera's position around the correct value.

Convergence range.   The convergence range for both the one-dimensional case and the multi-dimensional case was investigated using these pictures. As predicted, the convergence ranged was found to increase in rough proportion to the size of the smoothing window. The range for x and y motions was roughly ± 1 meter, and somewhat more in the z direction. The range for pan and tilt was approximately ± 10 degrees, and about ± 30 degrees for roll. Except for roll, these parameters are limited more by the angle of view of the camera than by the technique. For example, no matching technique could work if there angle of view is so small and the motion between the cameras so large that there is no overlap between the pictures. When this point is reached, the smoothing window required would be so large that each picture would be smoothed to a uniform gray. Nevertheless, these results are useful in that they verify that a useful range of convergence is obtainable using the method.

What is the relationship between these convergence ranges and the convergence ranges in the multi-parameter case? This is shown in Figure 2. We see that if we solve for two parameters (pan and tilt, top graph), the range is smaller than the range that would be expected on the basis of the one-parameter results for pan and tilt alone; and if we solve for all six parameters (bottom graph), it is smaller still. Nevertheless, the range is still quite adequate for the continuous feedback mode. Whether it is adequate for the stop-and-go mode, which involves a larger motion at each step, depends on the accuracy of the arm and on the accuracy of other navigational aids that can provide the initial estimates.

Accuracy. To assess the accuracy under a variety of conditions, we select reference points using a variety of methods, including by hand and by computer, resulting in several sets of data points of various sizes. Then we doubled the number of sets of reference points by either applying or not applying a pruning process to the sets we had. This pruning process, which is described elsewhere (Lucas, 1985), was based on the method of differences and served to improve the accuracy of the stereo matches. It also eliminated some points as being unfit for use by the method, for example because they were in a region of small gradient. The results are shown in Figure 3. Several general trends are observable. First, using more points produces more accurate results. Second, the pruning process can to improve the results, as evidenced by the left endpoints of the lines in the figure being lower than the right endpoints. These two factors are of course in conflict, and the improvement due to the pruning process is apparent only provided the number of points is not reduced too much. Finally, the accuracy does not seem to be affected much by the number of parameters solved for.

Implementation. The implementation may be divided into two parts: smoothing and camera parameter estimation. The smoothing must be done over a relatively large window, up to 65×65 in our experiments. It is the most time-consuming, part even though we implemented it as uniform smoothing over a rectangular region, which by a well-known algorithm takes a constant number of operations (two additions and two subtractions) per pixel, regardless of the size of the smoothing window. However, it is fairly well understood how to build special-purpose hardware for doing smoothing quickly, essentially in real time.

The parameter estimation step is more interesting. Our implementation, in which no attention was paid to efficiency, requires approximately 3 to 4 ms per reference point per iteration on a VAX 11/780. In the continuous feedback mode, only one iteration per time step would be used since only an approximate answer is needed. Thus 50 reference points (the largest number used in the experiments reported above) would require less than 200 ms per time step. This figure could probably be improved several-fold by more careful coding and taking account of the fact that some of the entries in the matrices to be inverted are known *a priori* to be zero. This information, together with the fact that the algorithm has a regular structure free of

decision points that could easily be implemented in special-purpose hardware, suggests that it is feasible for real-time control of a robot.

4. Conclusions

We have demonstrated that the method of differences provides a useful technique for optical navigation. We have shown that the algorithm can successfully determine all six camera parameters. It converges to the correct position given an estimate within something on the order of a meter (less if more parameters are solved for), and converges to a result accurate to a centimeter or so (regardless of the number of parameters solved for). Moreover, it can do so using 50 or less reference points. Because of the regular structure of the algorithm, the prospects of carrying out the calculations in real time with special-purpose hardware seem good.

5. References

A. R. Bruss and B. K. P. Horn, 1983. Passive navigation. *Computer Vision, Graphics, and Image Processing*, **21**, 3-20.

C. Cafforio and F. Rocca, 1979. Tracking moving objects in television images. *Signal Processing*, **1**, 133-140.

N. H. Cornelius and T. Kanade, 1983. Adapting optical-flow to measure object motion in reflectance and x-ray image sequences. Proc. ACM SIGGRAPH/SIGART Workshop on Motion: Representation and Perception, Toronto, 50-58.

D. B. Gennery, 1980. Modeling the environment of an exploring vehicle by means of stereo vision. PhD Thesis, Department of Computer Science, Stanford University.

B. K. P. Horn and B. G. Schunck, 1981. Determining optical flow. *Artificial Intelligence*, **17**, 185-202.

J. O. Limb and J. A. Murphy, 1975. Estimating the velocity of moving images in television signals. *Computer Graphics and Image Processing*, **4**, 311-327.

B. D. Lucas, 1985. Generalized image matching by the method of differences: algorithms and applications. PhD Thesis (in preparation), Computer Science Department, Carnegie-Mellon University.

B. D. Lucas and T. Kanade, 1981. An iterative image registration technique with an application to stereo vision. Proc. Seventh International Joint Conference on Artificial Intelligence, Vancouver.

H. P. Moravec, 1980. Obstacle avoidance and navigation in the real world by a seeing robot rover. Tech. Rept. CMU-RI-TR-3, Robotics Institute, Carnegie-Mellon University.

R. Y. Tsai and T. S. Huang, 1981. Uniqueness and estimation of 3-D motion parameters of rigid objects with curved surfaces. Proc. IEEE Conference on Pattern Recognition and Image Processing.

Figure 1. Experimental data. Left, middle, and right views of the same scene. Reference points are shown on left (reference) image.

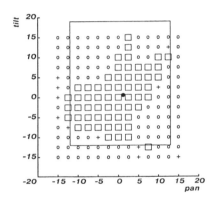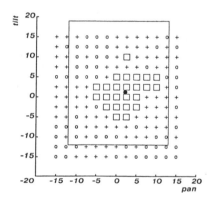

Figure 2. Left graph shows, for each initial value of pan and tilt, whether the algorithm converged to the correct value (large boxes), converged to the wrong value (small circles), or failed to converge (pluses). Solid dot is correct value, big rectangle indicates range predicted by single-parameter results. Right graph is a two-dimensional slice of a similar six-dimensional solid, in which all six parameters were solved for.

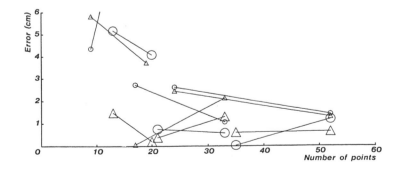

Figure 3. Graph shows the absolute error in x position on images smoothed with 9×9 window. Each point represents the result with a different set of reference points, distinguished by resulting error (in cm) on the vertical axis, and by number of points in the reference set on the horizontal axis. Triangles indicate the case where three parameters were solved for, circles six. The point at the left end of each line represents a reference set in which a pruning process was carried out on the points represented by the right end of the line. Large points represent image pair discussed in text, small points represent a different image pair.

SPECTRAL CONTINUITY AND EYE VERGENCE MOVEMENT

Lance R. Williams

Department of Computer Science
The Pennsylvania State University
University Park, Pennsylvania

ABSTRACT

In the Marr-Poggio model of human stereopsis, eye vergence movement is tightly coupled to the matching process. Any local area of any spatial frequency tuned channel can initiate a vergence movement designed to bring zero crossings within that local area into their range of correspondence. Since, in the human system, the resource of eye movement is limited, the control problem inherent in such a strategy seems intractable. This paper, in contrast, proposes that by requiring spectral continuity of disparity, global disambiguation can occur during the course of any reasonable sequence of vergence movements. The matching process is thus only loosely coupled to the vergence mechanism. A computer implementation has been tested successfully on both a random dot stereogram and a stereo pair of a natural scene.

1. Introduction

The structure of the physical world is constrained by physical laws, which in turn constrain images depicting it. The brain exploits these underlying constraints when it builds its world model from the images it receives from the eyes. An interesting conjecture is that it is able to do this with little or no *a priori* knowledge of semantic content. In this sense, early visual processing is a constructive process of description and is independent of recognition [1]. Perhaps the best example of the success of this approach is the Marr-Poggio model of human stereopsis, and its subsequent computer implementation by E.L. Grimson [2,3]. Marr and Poggio propose that matching is conducted on zero crossings of the $\nabla^2 G$ convolution of the left and right eye image. The results of matching zero crossings from low spatial frequency tuned channels are used to guide vergence movements which bring zero crossings from high spatial frequency tuned channels into their smaller range of correspondence. The vergence control mechanism is local, based on the success or failure of matching in local neighborhoods of each image.

The principal motivation behind this study is the desire to model the control of eye vergence movement in a biologically plausible manner. Grimson's implementation of the Marr-Poggio theory uses the results of matching within local areas of a channel to decide whether or not vergence movement is necessary to bring zero crossings within those local areas into correspondence. Local areas with less than 70% matches are declared out of range, and require vergence movement. The cross channel coupling is through the 2½-D sketch, which stores the results of matching from the low frequency channels. When a local area is out of range, these results are consulted to determine whether a convergent or divergent movement should be initiated.

However, there is an inherent difficulty with this control strategy, since vergence movement is a resource of limited access. Vergence movement is a physical process; the eyes are unable to make both convergent and divergent movements simultaneously. The single access resource of eye movement must however, satisfy the conflicting requirements of hundreds of different local areas within a single channel. The problem is further complicated because requests for eye movement can come from any local area of any channel, and must proceed sequentially from low frequency to high frequency.

This paper proposes a vergence strategy which is independent of the results of matching within local areas. The matching module is designed to take opportunistic advantage of any "reasonable" set of eye vergence movements. A reasonable set of eye vergence movements is defined to be any sequence of movements that spans the disparity range in a scene. In this implementation a single uniform vergence movement carries the eyes through a series of fixation positions, the optimal match over the range of the movement being preserved as in hysteresis. Vergence is thus only loosely coupled to the matching process, perhaps being controlled, as Marr and Poggio have suggested, by relative imbalances in the response of disparity sensitive pools [4], although on a global level. Kidd, Frisby and Mayhew's [5] demonstration that monocular cues can initiate vergence movement also supports the idea of the matching process being relatively independent of a specific vergence mechanism.

If this simple vergence strategy is to prove sufficient, two objectives must be met: 1) A consistent description of depth must be computed for a single vergence fixation; 2) This description must be integrated within the 2½-D sketch with other descriptions computed at other vergence fixations. Additionally, in the human system, the 2½-D sketch must be updated without explicit knowledge of eye position [2,3], which is probably not available. In order that these objectives may be examined properly, a review of the concept of *raw primal sketch* is in order.

2. Spectral Continuity of Disparity

Marr has suggested that one purpose of early visual processing is the creation of a symbolic description of physically meaningful changes in image intensity [6]. He developed a set of primal sketch tokens along with parsing rules based on cross channel combination of zero crossings. The first problem, that of creating the depth description for a single vergence fixation, can be solved by exploiting a binocular extension of Marr and Hildreth's [7] *spatial coincidence assumption:*

> If a zero-crossing segment is present in a set of independent $\nabla^2 G$ channels over a contiguous range of sizes and the segment has the same position, orientation, and *measured disparity* in each channel, then the set of such zero-crossing segments may be taken to indicate the presence of an intensity change in the image that is due to a single physical phenomenon (adapted from [7]).

Matching may occur in a more or less indiscriminate manner within each spatial frequency tuned channel, but only those matches which yield disparities of similar value to spatially coincident matches in neighboring channels are associated with the combined channel descriptor, or raw primal sketch token.

Mayhew and Frisby [8] have proposed that "the process of human binocular combination integrally relate the extraction of disparity information with the construction of raw primal sketch assertions." This work is therefore in great sympathy with their approach. However, it is worth noting the important difference between this proposal and Mayhew and Frisby's proposal that "the patterns of between-channel correspondence... also help disambiguate within-channel fusions." Their program, FRECKLES, uses a cross channel description as an enriched matching primitive, allowing disambiguation of false targets to occur over a larger fusional area. The disambiguating power actually seems to stem from a form of *compatibility constraint;* matches are forbidden between cross-channel descriptions that could not have arisen from the same physical phenomenon [1].

In contrast, this paper proposes that a requirement of continuity of disparity in the frequency domain is used to select the optimal cross channel combination of matches obtained independently within each spatial frequency tuned channel. The intra-frequency matching is conducted in essentially the same manner as in the Marr-Poggio model, and like the Marr-Poggio model, the chief disambiguating power lies in the fact that the size of fusional area is restricted to the small interval in which false targets can be resolved by local neighborhood support [1,4]. Global disambiguation depends on the selection of the optimal cross channel combination during the course of vergence movement.

That there is an optimal cross channel combination of within channel matches follows from the fact that for each spatially localized area of the left or right eye image there will be a specific vergence fixation which will preserve spectral continuity optimally (Fig. 1). Since these matches are associated with a particular primal sketch token, the raw primal sketch provides a frame of reference for the maintenance of disparity values across vergence movements. The solution to the problem of updating the $2\frac{1}{2}$-D sketch without explicit knowledge of eye position is thus implicit in the solution of the problem of correspondence in time between tokens of the primal sketch, a problem examined extensively by Ullman [9].

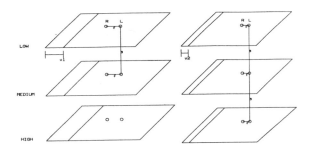

Figure 1. Vergence movement is simulated by increasing the displacement between the left and right images. At the initial vergence position, v_1, only the low and middle frequency channels are in fusion. For this spatially localized area, optimal spectral continuity is obtained at v_2, when all three channels are in fusion. Thus, the matches at v_2 are associated with the combined channel descriptor, or primal sketch token.

This vergence strategy also has the advantage of eliminating the problem Grimson's program had solving images with periodic features [2,3]. The problem arose because the criterion for determining whether or not a vergence movement would be initiated was of a purely local nature. Any area of a channel with more than 70% matches would not initiate a vergence movement, irrespective of the results of matching within spatially coincident areas of lower frequency channels. Thus, different initial vergence positions could produce different matching results. By requiring that disparity remain relatively constant for a given feature through the frequency domain, the more local matches of higher frequency channels are forced to agree with the more global definition of disparity provided

by lower frequency channels. As long as the lowest frequency channel is of lower spatial frequency than the period of the repeating pattern (windows on an office building in the case of Grimson's program) correct disparity values will be assigned.

3. Implementation

The program proceeds by first extracting zero crossings for both eyes at each spatial frequency. This is accomplished by traversing each horizontal raster looking for sign changes in the $\nabla^2 G$ profile. The current implementation uses two spatial frequency tuned channels. Each channel is processed independently, the low frequency channel first (in the human system, intra-frequency matching would be conducted concurrently within all channels). Vergence movement is simulated by incrementally increasing the displacement between the left and right images by an amount equal to half the fusional area of the high frequency channel (the actual amount is not critical). This has the effect of moving the plane of fixation through the disparity range determined by the matches of the low frequency channel. Matching is repeated at each fixation, only matches yielding disparities consistent with those of the lower frequency being accepted. For the two channel implementation, minimal spectral continuity is also optimal spectral continuity.

Matching proceeds within a frequency by first forming "competition" matrices from the cross product of like signed zero crossings from corresponding rasters of the left and right images (Fig. 2). Zero crossings from the right eye form rows while zero crossings from the left form columns. All potential matches are explicitly represented by a unique position in the competition matrix and associated with each row and column is the x-coordinate corresponding to the location of the zero crossing along the raster of the appropriate image. A disparity is assigned to each potential match by subtracting the x-coordinates of all rows and columns. Those potential matches having disparity smaller than 2σ for the channel being processed are marked as targets.

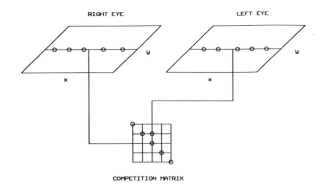

Figure 2. A competition matrix is formed from the cross product of like signed zero crossings from corresponding rasters of the left and right image. Potential matches with disparity less than 2σ are marked with circles. A match is ambiguous when more than one match appears in any given row or column. Ambiguous matches are resolved by the pulling effect, which favors matches of similiar disparity to surrounding ambiguous matches.

Targets are ambiguous when more than one target is present in any given row or column. Two targets in the same column represent ambiguity to the left eye, while two targets in the same row represent ambiguity to the right. Every raster is first processed for unambiguous matches and the results stored in a buffer so that the *pulling effect,* as in the Marr-Poggio model, may use these results to resolve ambiguous targets. Before a match from a high frequency channel is accepted, the majority disparity within a circular region surrounding the spatially coincident area of the low frequency channel is calculated. Only those matches having disparity within a small ϵ (equal to σ for the channel) of the majority disparity are accepted as correct. The entire matching process is then repeated at the next vergence fixation.

4. Conclusion

A computer implementation has been tested on a random dot stereogram (Fig. 3,4) and a stereo pair of a natural scene (Fig. 5,6) with good qualitative results. The vergence strategy was very simple and consisted of moving the plane of fixation through the entire disparity range in a single uniform movement. Global disambiguation was effected by requiring that matches from spatially coincedent areas of adjacent spatial frequencies possess similar disparity. This constraint is a binocular extension of the spectral continuity property of raw primal sketch tokens. Thus it has been shown that there is no need for local control of the vergence mechanism and its associated problems. Additionally, it has been suggested that the raw primal sketch provides a frame of reference for the maintenance of disparity values across vergence movements.

Figure 3. The random dot stereogram used in this study.

Figure 4. The solution for the random dot stereogram.

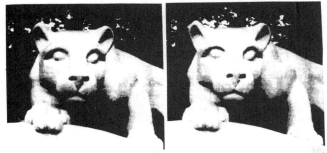

Figure 5. Stereo pair of the Nittany Lion shrine. Each image is 256x256 with 16 grey levels.

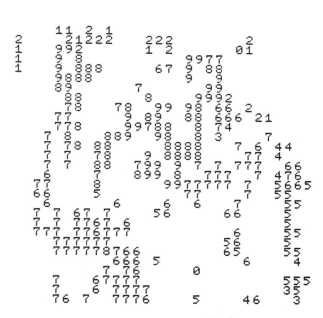

Figure 6. Disparity map for the Nittany Lion image.

ACKNOWLEDGMENTS

Special thanks to Bill Sakoda. Thanks also to Tony Maida, Gordon Shulman, John Sacha, and Jon Crouse. This work was supported in part through a grant from the General Electric Corporation.

REFERENCES

[1]   Marr, D. 1982. *Vision.* San Francisco: W.H. Freeman and Company.

[2]   Grimson, W.E.L. 1980. A computer implementation of a theory of human stereo vision. MIT A.I. Lab. Memo 565. "Phil. Trans. Soc. Lond. B292",217-253.

[3]   Grimson, W.E.L. 1981. *From Images to Surfaces.* Cambridge, Mass.: MIT Press.

[4]   Marr, D., and T. Poggio. 1979. A computational theory of human stereo vision. "Proc. R. Soc. Lond. B204",301-328.

[5]   Kidd, A.L., J.P. Frisby, and J.E.W. Mayhew. 1979. Texture contours can facilitate stereopsis by initiating appropriate vergence eye movements. "Nature 280",829-832.

[6]   Marr, D. 1976. Early processing of visual information. "Phil. Trans. R. Soc. Lond. B275",483-524.

[7]   Marr, D., and E. Hildreth. 1980. Theory of edge detection. "Proc. R. Soc. Lond. B207",187-217.

[8]   Mayhew, J.E.W., and J.P. Frisby. 1981. Psychophysical and computational studies toward a theory of human stereopsis. "Artificial Intelligence 17", 349-385.

[9]   Ullman, S. 1979. *The Interpretation of Visual Motion.* Cambridge, Mass.: MIT Press.

A NEW SENSE FOR DEPTH OF FIELD

Alex P. Pentland

Artificial Intelligence Center, SRI International
333 Ravenswood Ave, Menlo Park, CA 94025
and
Center for the Study of Language and Information
Stanford University, Stanford CA 94038

ABSTRACT

One of the major unsolved problems in designing an autonomous agent [robot] that must function in a complex, moving environment is obtaining reliable, real-time depth information, preferably without the limitations of active scanners. Stereo remains computationally intensive and prone to severe errors, the use of motion information is still quite experimental, and autofocus schemes can measure depth at only one point at a time. We examine a novel source of depth information: focal gradients resulting from the limited depth of field inherent in most optical systems. We prove that this source of information can be used to make reliable depth maps of useful accuracy with relatively minimal computation. Experiments with realistic imagery show that measurement of these optical gradients can potentially provide depth information roughly comparable to stereo disparity or motion parallax, while avoiding image-to-image matching problems. A potentially real-time version of this algorithm is described.

I. INTRODUCTION

Our subjective impression is that we view our surroundings in sharp, clear focus. This impression is reinforced by the virtually universal photographic tradition[**] to make images that are everywhere in focus, i.e., that have infinite depth of field. Unfortunately, both this photographic tradition and our feeling of a sharply focused world seems to have lead vision researchers — in both human and machine vision — to largely ignore the fact that in biological systems the images that fall on the retina are typically quite *badly* focused everywhere except within the central fovea [1,2]. There is a *gradient* of focus, ranging from nearly perfect focus at the point of regard to almost complete blur at points on distant objects.

It is puzzling that biological visual systems first employ an optical system that produces a degraded image, and then go to great lengths to undo this blurring and present us with a subjective impression of sharp focus. This is especially peculiar because it is just as easy to start out with everything in perfect focus. Why, then, does Nature prefer to employ a lens system in which most of the image is blurred?

In this paper we report the finding that this gradient of focus inherent in biological and most other optical systems is a useful source of depth information, prove that these focal gradients may be used to recover a depth map (i.e., distances between viewer and points in the scene) by means of a few, simple transformations of the image, and that with additional computation the reliability of this depth information may be internally checked. This source of depth information (which differs markedly from that used in automatic focusing methods) has not previously been described in the human vision literature, and we have been unable to find any investigation of it in the somewhat more scattered machine vision literature. The performance of a practical technique has been demonstrated on realistic imagery, and an inexpensive, real-time version of the algorithm is described. Finally, we report experiments showing that people make significant use of this depth information.

This novel method of obtaining a depth map is important because there is currently no passive sensing method for obtaining depth information that is simultaneously fast enough, reliable enough, and produces a sufficiently dense depth map to support the requirements of a robot moving in a complex environment. Stereopsis, despite huge investment, remains computationally intensive and prone to severe errors, the use of motion information is still in an experimental stage, and autofocus schemes can measure depth at only one point at a time. We believe that this research, therefore, will prove a significant advance in solving the problem of real-time acquisition of reliable depth maps without the limitations inherent in active scanners (e.g., laser rangefinders).

II. THE FOCAL GRADIENT

Most biological lens systems are exactly focused[*] at only one distance along each radius from the lens into the scene. The locus of exactly focused points forms a doubly curved, approximately spherical surface in three-dimensional space. Only when objects in the scene intersect this surface is their image exactly in focus; objects distant from this surface of exact focus are blurred, an effect familiar to photographers as depth of field.

The amount of defocus or blurring depends solely on the distance to the surface of exact focus and the characteristics of the lens system; as the distance between the imaged point and the surface of exact focus increases, the imaged objects become progressively more defocused. If we could measure the amount of blurring at a given point in the image, therefore, it seems possible that we could use our knowledge of the parameters of the lens system to compute the distance to the corresponding point in the scene.

---

[*] This research was made possible in part by a grant from the Systems Development Foundation, and by a grant from the National Science Foundation, Grant No. DCR-83-12766, and by Defense Advanced Research Projects Agency contract no. MDA 903-83-C-0027

[**] A practice established in large part by Ansel Adams and others in the famous "f/64 Club"

---

[*] "Exact focus" is taken here to mean "has the minimum variance point spread function," the phrase "measurement of focus" is taken to mean "characterize the point spread function."

The distance D to an imaged point is related to the parameters of the lens system and the amount of defocus by the following equation, which is developed in the appendix.

$$D = \frac{Fv_0}{v_0 - F - \sigma f} \quad (1)$$

where v_0 is the distance between the lens and the image plane (e.g., the film location in a camera), f the f-number of the lens system, F the focal length of the lens system, and σ the spatial constant of the point spread function (i.e., the radius of the imaged point's "blur circle") which describes how an image point is blurred by the imaging optics. The point spread function may be usefully approximated by a two-dimensional Gaussian $G(r, \sigma)$ with a spatial constant σ and radial distance r. The validity of using a Gaussian to describe the point spread function is discussed in the appendix.

In most situations, the only unknown on the right-hand side of Equation (1) is σ, the point spread function's spatial parameter. Thus, we can use Equation (1) to solve for absolute distance given only that we can measure σ, i.e., the amount of blur at a particular image point.

Measurement of σ presents a problem, however, for the image data is the result of both the characteristics of the scene and those of the lens system. To disentangle these factors, we can either look for places in the image with known characteristics (e.g., sharp edges), or we can observe what happens when we change some aspect of the lens system. In the following discussion both of these two general strategies for measurement of σ are described: the use of sharp edges, and comparison across different aperture settings. Both approaches require only one view of the scene.

A. Using Sharp Discontinuities

Image data are determined both by scene characteristics and the properties of the lens system, e.g., how fast image intensity changes depends upon both how scene radiance changes and the diameter of the blur circle. If we are to measure blur circle, therefore, we must already know the scenes' contribution to the image. At edges — sharp discontinuities in the image formation process — the rate of change we observe in the image is due primarily to the point spread function; because we can often recognize sharp discontinuities with some degree of confidence [3,4] we can use image data surrounding them to determine the focus. These observations lead to the following scheme for recovering the viewer-to-scene[*] distance at points of discontinuity.

Mathematical Details. To calculate the spatial constant of the point spread function we require a measure of the rate at which image intensity is changing; the wide-spread use of zero-crossings of the Laplacian to find edges [5] suggests using slope of the Laplacian across the zero-crossing as a measure of rate of change.

Consider a vertical step edge in the image of magnitude δ at position x_0. In this case the values $C(x, y)$ resulting from the convolution of image intensities $I(x, y)$ with the Laplacian of a Gaussian $\nabla^2 G(r, \sigma)$ (as in [5]) have the form

$$\begin{aligned} C(x, y) &= \nabla^2 G(r, \sigma) \otimes I(x, y) \\ &= \int \int \nabla^2 G(\sqrt{(x-u)^2 + (y-v)^2}, \sigma) I(u, v) du\, dv \\ &= \delta(dG(x - x_0, \sigma)/dx) \end{aligned} \quad (2)$$

where $G(x - x_0, \sigma)$ is a one-dimensional Gaussian centered at point x_0, and σ is the spatial constant of the point spread function at that point in the image. For such an edge the slope of the function $C(x, y)$ at the

---

[*]When the discontinuity is in depth, as at an occluding contour, the distance measured is to the nearer side of the discontinuity.

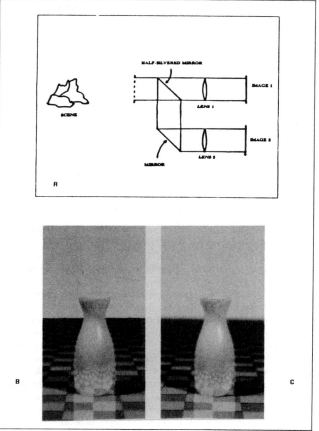

Figure 1. Images Identical Except for Depth of Field. (a) Production: The light from a single view is split into two identical images and directed through two lens systems with different aperture size. Alternatively, one can vary the aperture between alternate frames from a standard video or CCD camera. In either case the two resulting images are identical except for depth of field, as shown in Figure 1 (b) and (c). These images are of a mirrored bottle on a checkered plain.

point of the zero-crossing is equal to the maximum rate of change in image intensity, and so we can use it to estimate σ.

An estimate of σ can be formed as follows:

$$C(x, y) = \delta \frac{dG(x, \sigma)}{dx} = \frac{-\delta x}{\sqrt{2\pi}\sigma} \exp\left(-\frac{x^2}{2\sigma^2}\right) \quad (3)$$

where x, y and δ are as before, and for convenience x_0 is taken to be zero. Taking the absolute value and then the natural log, we find

$$\ln \frac{\delta}{\sqrt{2\pi}\sigma^3} - \frac{x^2}{2\sigma^2} = \ln\left|\frac{C(x, y)}{x}\right| \quad (4)$$

We can formulate Equation (4) as

$$Ax^2 + B = C \quad (5)$$

where

$$A = -\frac{1}{2\sigma^2} \qquad B = \ln \frac{\delta}{\sqrt{2\pi}\sigma^3} \qquad C = \ln\left|\frac{C(x, y)}{x}\right|$$

If we interpret Equation (5) as a linear regression in x^2 we can then obtain a maximum-likelihood estimate of the constants A and B, and thus obtain σ. The solution of this linear regression is

$$A = \frac{\sum_i (x_i^2 - \bar{x}^2)C_i}{\sum_i (x_i^2 - \bar{x}^2)^2} \qquad B = \bar{C} - \bar{x}^2 A \qquad (6)$$

where $\bar{x}$ is the mean of the x_i, and $\bar{C}$ is the mean of the C_i. From A in Equation (6) we can obtain the following estimate of the value of the spatial constant σ:

$$\sigma = (-2A)^{-2}$$

Having estimated σ we can now use Equation (1) to find the distance to the imaged point; note that there are two solutions, one corresponding to a point in front of the locus of exact focus, the other corresponding to a point behind it. This ambiguity is generally unimportant because we can usually arrange things so that the surface of exact focus is nearer to the sensor than any of the objects in the field of view.

B. Comparison Across Differing Apertures

The limiting factor in the previous method is the requirement that we must know the scene characteristics before we can measure the focus; this restricts the applicability of the method to special points such as step discontinuities. If, however, we had two images of exactly the same scene, but with different depth of field, we could factor out the contribution of the scene to the two images (as the contribution is the same), and measure the focus directly.

Figure 1 shows one method of taking a single view of the scene and producing two images that are identical except for aperture size and therefore depth of field. This lens system uses a half-silvered mirror (or comparable contrivance) to split the original image into two identical images, which are then directed through lens systems with different aperture size. Because change in aperture does not affect the position of image features, the result is two images that are *identical* except[*] for their focal gradient (amount of depth of field), and so there is no difficulty in matching points in one image to points in the other. Figures 1 (b) and (c) show a pair of such images. Alternatively, one could rig a video or CCD camera so that alternate frames employ a different aperture; as long as no significant motion occurs between frames the result will again be two images identical except for depth of field.

Because differing aperture size causes differing focal gradients, the same point will be focused differently in the two images; for our purposes the critical fact is that the magnitude of this difference is a simple function of the distance between the viewer and the imaged point. To obtain an estimate of depth, therefore, we need only compare corresponding points in the two images and measure this change in focus. Because the two images are identical except for aperture size they may be compared directly; i.e., there is no matching problem as there is with stereo or motion algorithms. Thus we can then recover the absolute distance D by simple point-by-point comparison of the two images, as described below.

Mathematical Details. We start by taking a patch $f_1(r, \theta)$ centered at (x_0, y_0) within the first image $I_1(x, y)$:

$$f_1(r, \theta) = I_1(x_0 + r\cos\theta, y_0 + r\sin\theta)$$

and calculate its two-dimensional Fourier transform $\mathcal{F}_1(t, \theta)$. The same is done for a patch $f_2(r, \theta)$ at the corresponding point in the second image, giving us $\mathcal{F}_2(t, \theta)$. Again, note that there is no matching problem, as the images are identical except for depth of field.

Now consider the relation of f_1 to f_2. Both cover the same region in the image, so that if there were no blurring both would be equal to the same intensity function $f_0(r, \theta)$. However, because there is blurring

---

(with spatial constants σ_1 and σ_2), we have

$$\frac{f_1(r, \theta)}{f_2(r, \theta)} = \frac{f_0(r, \theta) \otimes G(r, \sigma_1)}{f_0(r, \theta) \otimes G(r, \sigma_2)} \qquad (7)$$

[One point of caution is that Equation (7) may be substantially in error in cases with a large amount of defocus, as points neighboring the patches f_1, f_2 will be "spread out" into the patches by differing amounts. This problem can be minimized by using patches whose edges trail off smoothly, e.g., $f_1(r, \theta) = I(x_0 + r\cos\theta, y_0 + r\sin\theta)G(r, \omega)$ for appropriate spatial parameter ω.]

Noting that

$$f(r, \theta) = e^{-\pi r^2} \qquad \mathcal{F}(\lambda, \theta) = e^{-\pi \lambda^2}$$

are a Fourier pair and that if $f(r, \theta)$ and $\mathcal{F}(\lambda, \theta)$ are a Fourier pair then so are

$$f(\alpha r, \theta) \qquad \frac{1}{|\alpha|}\mathcal{F}\left(\frac{\lambda}{\alpha}, \theta\right)$$

we see that we may use Equation (7) to derive the following relationship between $\mathcal{F}_1$ and $\mathcal{F}_2$ (the Fourier transforms of image patches f_1 and f_2) and $\mathcal{F}_0$ (the transform of the [hypothetical] unblurred image patch f_0):

$$\mathcal{F}_1(\lambda, \theta) = \frac{\mathcal{F}_0(\lambda, \theta)G(\lambda, \frac{1}{\sqrt{2\pi}\sigma_1})}{\sqrt{2\pi}\sigma_1} \qquad \mathcal{F}_2(\lambda, \theta) = \frac{\mathcal{F}_0(\lambda, \theta)G(\lambda, \frac{1}{\sqrt{2\pi}\sigma_2})}{\sqrt{2\pi}\sigma_2} \quad (8)$$

Thus[*] ,

$$\frac{\mathcal{F}_1(\lambda)}{\mathcal{F}_2(\lambda)} = \frac{G(\lambda, \sigma_1)\sigma_2}{G(\lambda, \sigma_2)\sigma_1} = \frac{\sigma_2^2}{\sigma_1^2}\exp(\lambda^2 2\pi^2(\sigma_2^2 - \sigma_1^2)) \qquad (9)$$

where

$$\mathcal{F}(\lambda) = \int_{-\pi}^{\pi}\mathcal{F}(\lambda, \theta)d\theta$$

Thus, given $\mathcal{F}_1$ and $\mathcal{F}_2$ we can find σ_1 and σ_2, as follows. Taking the natural log of Equation (9) we obtain

$$\ln\frac{\sigma_2^2}{\sigma_1^2} + \lambda^2 2\pi^2(\sigma_2^2 - \sigma_1^2) = \ln\mathcal{F}_1(\lambda) - \ln\mathcal{F}_2(\lambda)$$

We may formulate this as $A\lambda^2 + B = C$ where

$$A = 2\pi^2(\sigma_2^2 - \sigma_1^2) \qquad B = \ln\frac{\sigma_2^2}{\sigma_1^2} \qquad C = \ln\mathcal{F}_1(\lambda) - \ln\mathcal{F}_2(\lambda)$$

i.e., as a linear regression equation in λ^2. The solution to this regression equation is the same as shown in the last example, and gives us maximum-likelihood estimates of A and B. Solving A and B for σ_1 and σ_2 yields

$$\sigma_1 = \sqrt{\frac{A}{2\pi^2(e^B - 1)}} \qquad \sigma_2 = \sqrt{\frac{Ae^B}{2\pi^2(e^B - 1)}} \qquad (10)$$

We may now use these estimates of σ_1 and σ_2 to calculate absolute distance to the imaged surface patch. Using Equation (1) for each of the two images, we see that we now have

$$D = \frac{Fv_0}{v_0 - F - \sigma_1 f_1} \qquad D = \frac{Fv_0}{v_0 - F - \sigma_2 f_2} \qquad (11)$$

where f_1 and f_2 are the f-numbers for the two halves of the imaging system.

Figure 2. Accuracy at estimating distance, assuming human visual system parameters, using (a) focal gradient information, and (b) stereopsis.

C. Checking the answer: overconstraint

We may solve either of the two equations in (11) for D, the distance to the imaged surface patch. Thus the solution is overconstrained; *both* solutions must produce the same estimate of distance—otherwise the estimates of σ_1 and σ_2 must be in error. This can occur, for instance, when there is insufficient high-frequency information in the image patch to enable the change in focus to be calculated. The important point is that this overconstraint allows us to check our answer: if the equations disagree, then we know not to trust our answer. If, on the other hand, both equations agree then we can know (to within measurement error) that our answer *must* be correct.

D. Accuracy

Possibly the major question concerning the usefulness of focal gradient information is whether such information can be sufficiently accurate. There are two major issues to be addressed: first, can we estimate the variance σ of the point spread function with sufficient accuracy, and second, does this translate into a reasonable degree of accuracy in the estimation of depth.

Recent research aimed at estimating the point spread function has shown that it may be accurately recovered from unfamiliar images despite the presence of normal image noise [6,7]. Further, it appears that humans can estimate the width of the point spread function to within a few percent [8,9]. These findings, together with the results of estimating σ reported in the next section, show that accurate estimation of σ is practical given sufficient image resolution.

The second issue is whether the available accuracy at estimating σ translates into a reasonable accuracy in estimating depth. Figure 2 (a) show the theoretical error curve for the human eye, assuming the accuracy at estimating σ reported in [4]. It can be seen that reasonable accuracy is available out to several meters. This curve should be compared to the accuracy curve for stereopsis, shown in Figure 2 (b), again assuming human parameters. It can be seen that the accuracies are comparable.

E. Human Perception

We have recently reported evidence demonstrating that people make use of the depth information contained in focal gradients [9]; interestingly, the ecological salience of this optical gradient does not appear to have been previously reported in the scientific literature. The hypothesis that the human visual system makes significant use of this cue to depth has been investigated in two experiments.

In the first experiment, pictures of naturalistic scenes were presented with various magnitude of focal gradient information. It was found that increasing the magnitude of the focal gradient results in increasing subjective depth. In the second experiment, subjects were shown a rightward rotating wireframe (Nekker) cube displayed in perspective on a CRT. Such a display may be perceived as either as a rigid object rotating to the right, or (surprisingly) as wobbling, non-rigid object rotating to the left. Normally subjects see the rigid interpretations most of the time, but when we introduced a focal gradient that favored the non-rigid interpretations, the non-rigid interpretations was seen almost as often as the rigid one.

An experiment demonstrating the importance of depth of field in human perception can be easily performed by the reader. First make a pinhole camera by poking a small, clean hole through a piece of stiff paper or metal. Imposition of a pinhole in the line of sight causes the depth of field to be very large, thus effectively removing this depth cue from the image. Close one eye and view the world through the pinhole, holding it as close as possible to the surface of your eye, and note your impression of depth (for those of you with glasses, things will look sharper if you are doing it correctly). Now quickly remove the pinhole and view the world normally (still using only one eye). The change in the sense of depth is remarkable; many observers report that the change is nearly comparable to the difference between monocular and binocular viewing, or the change which occurs when a stationary object begins to move.

III. IMPLEMENTATION AND EVALUATION

A. Using sharp edges

The first method of deriving depth from the focal gradient, by measuring apparent blur near sharp discontinuities, was implemented in a straightforward manner (convolution values near zero-crossings were employed in Equations (4) - (6)) and evaluated on the image shown in Figure 3. In this image the optical system had a smaller depth of field than is currently typical in vision research; this was done because the algorithm requires that the digitization adequately resolve the point spread function.

Figure 3 also shows the depth estimates which were obtained when the algorithm was applied to this image. Part (a) of this Figure 3 shows all the sharp discontinuities identified [2]. It was found that there was considerable variability in the depth estimates obtained along these contours, perhaps resulting from the substantial noise (3 of 8 bits) which was present in the digitized image values. To minimize this variability the zero-crossing contours were segmented at points of high curvature, and the depth values were averaged within the zero-crossing segments. Figures 3 (b), (c), and (d) show the zero-crossing segments that have large, medium, and small depth values, respectively. It can be seen that the image is properly segmented with respect to depth, with the exception of one small segment near the top of (c). This example demonstrates that this depth estimation technique — which requires little computation beyond the calculation of zero-crossings — can be employed to order sharp edges by their depth values.

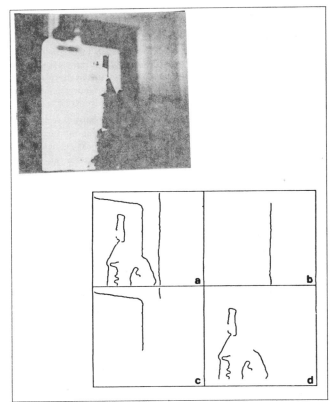

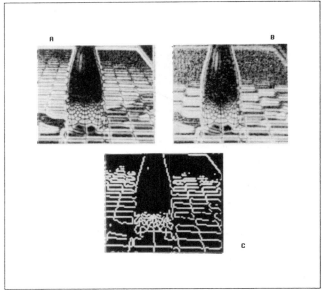

Figure 4.   (a) and (b) show the normalized high-frequency content of Figures 2 (b) and (c), respectively. (c) shows the focal disparity map (analogous to a stereo disparity map) obtained by comparing (a) and (b); brightness is proportional to depth.

Figure 3.   An Indoor Image of a Sand Castle, Refrigerator, and Door, Together with Depth Estimates for its Zero-Crossing Segments. Part (a) of this figure shows all the sharp discontinuities found. Parts (b), (c), and (d) show the zero-crossing segments that have large, medium, and small depth values, respectively. It can be seen that the image is properly segmented with respect to depth, with the exception of one small segment near the top of (c).

B.   Comparison of different apertures

The second technique, comparing two images identical except for aperture, can be implemented in many different ways. We will report a very simple version of the algorithm that is amenable to an inexpensive real-time implementation.

In this algorithm two images are acquired as shown in Figure 1 (a); they are identical except for their depth of field and thus the amount of focal gradient present, as shown in Figures 1 (b) and (c). These images are then convolved with a small Laplacian filter, providing an estimate of their local high-frequency content. The output of the Laplacian filters are then summed over a small area and normalized by dividing them by the mean local image brightness, obtained by convolving the original images with a Gaussian filter. It appears that a region as small as 4 x 4 pixels is sufficient to obtain stable estimates of high-frequency content. Figures 4 (a) and (b) show the normalized high-frequency content of Figures 1 (b) and (c).

Finally, the estimated high-frequency content of the blurry, large-aperture image is divided by that of the sharp, small-aperture image, i.e., each point of Figure 4 (a) is divided by the corresponding point in Figure 4(b). This produces a "focal disparity" map, analogous to a stereo disparity map, that measures the change in focus between the two images and whose values are monotonically related to depth by Equation (1). Figure 4 (c) shows the disparity map produced from Figures 2 (b) and 2 (c); intensity in this figure is proportional to depth.

Areas of 4 (c) that are black have insufficient high-frequency energy in the sharp-focus image to make an estimate of depth.

It can be seen that this disparity map is fairly accurate. Note that points reflected in the bottle are estimated as further than points along the edge of the bottle; this is not a mistake, for these points the distance traveled by the light *is* further than for those along the edge of the bottle. This algorithm, in common with stereo and motion algorithms, does not "know" about mirrored surfaces.

C.   Design for a real-time implementation

A minimum of one convolution per image is required for this technique, together with a left shift and four subtractions for the Laplacian, and three divides for the normalization and comparison. If special convolution hardware is available, one can use two convolutions — one Laplacian and one Gaussian – per image, leaving only three divides[*] for the normalization and comparison. Frame buffers that can convolve image data in parallel with image acquisition are now available at a reasonable price, leaving as few as 3 operations per pixel to calculate the disparity map. For a 256 x 256 image, this can be accomplished in as little as 0.35 seconds with currently available microcomputers.

IV.   DISCUSSION

The most striking aspect of this source of depth information is that absolute range can be estimated from a single view with no image-to-image matching problem, perhaps the major source of error in stereo and motion algorithms. Furthermore, no special scene characteristics need be assumed, so that the techniques utilizing this cue to depth can be generally applicable. The second most striking fact is the simplicity of these algorithms: it appears that a real-time implementation can be accomplished relatively cheaply.

Measurement of the focal gradients associated with limited depth of field appears to be capable of producing depth estimates that are at least roughly comparable to edge- or feature-based stereo and motion

---

[*]which can be done by table lookup.

algorithms. The mathematics of the aperture-comparison technique shows it to be potentially more reliable than stereo or motion — i.e., there is no correspondence problem, and one can obtain an internal check on the answer — although (as discussed above) it has somewhat less accuracy.

The sharp-edge algorithm appears to have potential for useful depth-plane segmentation, although it is probably not accurate enough to produce a depth map. I believe that this algorithm will be of some interest because most of the work — finding and measuring the slope of zero-crossings — is often already being done for other purposes. Thus this type of depth-plane segmentation can be done almost as a side effect of edge finding or other operations.

The aperture-comparison algorithm provides considerably stronger information about the scene because it *overconstrains* scene depth, allowing an internal check on the algorithm's answer. Thus it provides depth information with a reliability comparable to the best that is theoretically available from three-or-more image stereo and motion algorithms, although it has somewhat less depth resolution. The major limitation in measuring focal gradient depth information in this manner appears to be insuring sufficient high-frequency information to measure the change between images; this requires having both adequate image resolution and high-frequency scene content.

Summary. In summary, we have described a new source of depth information — the focal gradient — that can provide depth information at least roughly comparable to stereo disparity or motion parallax, while avoiding the image-to-image matching problems that have made stereo and motion algorithms unreliable. We have shown that the limited depth of field inherent in most optical systems can be used to make depth maps of useful accuracy with relatively minimal computation, and have successfully demonstrated a potentially real-time technique for recovering depth maps from realistic imagery. It is our hope, therefore, that this research will prove to be a substantial advance towards building a robot that can function in complex, moving natural environments.

REFERENCES

[1] H. Crane, *A Theoretical Analysis of the Visual Accommodation System in Humans*, Final Report NAS 2-2760, NASA Ames Research Center (1966).

[2] M. Born and E. Wolf, *Principles of Optics*, Pergamon, London (1965).

[3] A. Pentland, *The Visual Inference of Shape: Computation from Local Features*, Ph.D. thesis, Massachusetts Institute of Technology (1982).

[4] A. Witkin, *Intensity-Based Edge Classification*, Proceedings of the American Association for Artificial Intelligence, August 1982, Pittsburgh, Penn.

[5] E. Hildreth, *Implementation of a Theory of Edge Detection*, M.I.T. AI Laboratory Technical Report 579 (April 1980).

[6] K.T. Knox and B.J. Thomson, *Recovery of Images from Atmospherically Degraded Short-Exposure Photographs*, Astrophys. J. 193, L45-L48 (1974).

[7] J.B. Morton and H.C. Andrews, *A Posteriori Method of Image Restoration*, Opt. Soc. Am. 69, 2 (1979) 280-290.

[8] A. Pentland, *Uniform Extrafoveal Sensitivity To Pattern Differences*, Journal of the Optical Society of America, November 1978.

[9] A. Pentland, *The Focal Gradient: Optics Ecologically Salient*, Supplement to Investigative Opthomology and Visual Science, April 1985.

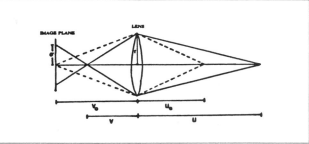

Figure 5.   Geometry of Imaging. v_0 is the distance between the image plane and the lens, u_0 is the distance between the lens and the locus of perfect focus, and r is the radius of the lens. When a point at distance $u > u_0$ is projected through the lens, it focuses at a distance $v < v_0$, so that a blur circle is formed.

APPENDIX

For a thin lens,

$$\frac{1}{u} + \frac{1}{v} = \frac{1}{F} \qquad (12)$$

where u is the distance between a point in the scene and the lens, v the distance between the lens and the plane on which the image is in perfect focus, and F the focal length of the lens. Thus,

$$u = \frac{Fv}{v - F} \qquad (13)$$

For a particular lens, F is a constant. If we then fix the distance v between the lens and the image plane to the value $v = v_0$, we have also determined a locus of points at distance $u = u_0$ that will be in perfect focus, i.e.,

$$u_0 = \frac{Fv_0}{v_0 - F} \qquad (14)$$

We may now explore what happens when a point at a distance $u > u_0$ is imaged. Figure 5 shows the situation in which a lens of radius r is used to project a point at distance u onto an image plane at distance v_0 behind the lens. Given this configuration, the point would be focused at distance v behind the lens—but in front of the image plane. Thus, a blur circle is formed on the image plane. Note that a point at distance $u < u_0$ also forms a blur circle; throughout this paper we assume that the lens system is focused on the nearest point so that u is always greater than u_0. This restriction is not necessary in the second algorithm, as overconstraint on the distance solution allows determination of whether $D = u > u_0$ or $D = u < u_0$.

From the geometry of Figure 5 we see that

$$\tan\theta = \frac{r}{v} = \frac{\sigma}{v_0 - v} \qquad (15)$$

Combining Equations (13) and (15) and substituting the distance D for the variable u we obtain

$$D = \frac{Frv_0}{rv_0 - F(r + \sigma)}$$

or

$$D = \frac{Fv_0}{v_0 - F - \sigma f}$$

where f is the f-number of the lens.

The blurring of the image is better described by the point spread function than by a blur circle, although the blurring is bounded by the blur circle radius in the sense that the point spread function is less than some threshold outside of the blur circle. The point spread function is due primarily to diffraction effects, which for any particular wavelength produce wave cancellation and reinforcement resulting in intensity patterns qualitatively similar to the sinc function, $\frac{\sin r}{r}$, but with different amplitudes and periods for the "rings" around the central peak [2].

The "rings" produced by this function vary in amplitude, width and position with different states of focus and with different wavelengths. As wavelength varies these rings change position by as much as 90 degrees, so that the blue light troughs become positioned over the red light peaks, etc. Further, change in wavelength results in substantial changes in the amplitude of the various rings. Although this point spread function is quite complex, and the sum over different wavelengths even more so, our analysis shows that for white light the sum of the various functions obtained at different wavelengths has the general shape of a two-dimensional Gaussian.

Sampling effects caused by digitization are typically next in importance after the diffraction effects. The effect of sampling may be accounted for in the point spread function by convolving the above diffraction-produced point spread function with functions of the form $\frac{\sin r}{r}$. Other factors such as chromatic abberation, movement, and diffusion of photographic emulsion may also be accounted for in the final point spread function by additional convolutions.

The net effect, in light of the central limit theorem and our analysis of the sum of single-wavelength focus patterns, is almost certainly best described by a two-dimensional Gaussian $G(r, \sigma)$ with spatial constant σ. The spatial constant σ of the point spread function will be proportional to the radius of the blur circle; however, the constant of proportionality will depend on the particulars of the optics, sampling, etc. In this paper the radius of the blur circle and the spatial constant of the point spread function have been treated as identical; in practical application where recovery of absolute distance is desired the constant of proportionality k must be determined for the system and included in Equation (1) as follows:

$$D = \frac{F v_0}{v_0 - F - \sigma k f}$$

WHAT ENABLES A MACHINE TO UNDERSTAND?

Aaron Sloman

Cognitive Studies Programme
University of Sussex
Brighton BN1 9QN, England

Abstract

The 'Strong AI' claim that suitably programmed computers can manipulate symbols that THEY understand is defended, and conditions for understanding discussed. Even computers without AI programs exhibit a significant subset of characteristics of human understanding. To argue about whether machines can REALLY understand is to argue about mere definitional matters. But there is a residual ethical question.

Topic area and keywords

Philosophical foundations, machines, language, meaning, understanding, reference, Strong AI.

Introduction

Filing cabinets contain information but understand nothing. Computers are more active than cabinets, but so are copiers and card-sorters, which understand nothing. Is there a real distinction between understanding and mere manipulation? Unlike cabinets and copiers, suitably programmed computers appear to understand. They respond to commands by performing tasks; they print out answers to questions; they paraphrase stories or answer questions about them. Does this show they attach meanings to symbols? Or are the meanings 'derivative' on OUR understanding them, as claimed by Searle([10])? Is real understanding missing from simulated understanding just as real wetness is missing from a simulated tornado? Or is a mental process like calculation: if simulated in detail, it is replicated?

I argue that there is no clear boundary between things that do and things that do not understand symbols. Our ordinary concept of 'understanding' denotes a complex cluster of capabilities, and different subsets of these may be exhibited in different people, animals or machines. To ask 'which are necessary for REAL understanding?' is to attribute spurious precision to a concept of ordinary language.

Instead of answering either 'YES' or 'NO' to the question whether suitably programmed computers can understand, we note that within the space of possible 'behaving systems' (including animals) there are infinitely many cases, some sharing more features with human minds, some fewer. The important task is to analyse the nature and the implications of these similarities and differences, without assuming existing English words can label the cases adequately.

Dennett [2] thinks we can justifiably take the 'intentional' stance towards any machine or organism whose behaviour thereby becomes easier to predict or explain. Searle [10], [11] retorts that behaviour is not enough, alleging that a suitable program could make a system appear to understand Chinese when it doesn't really, e.g. if Searle is inside executing the programs. In [18] I show that he actually attacks an extreme and implausible thesis, namely that ANY 'instantiation' of a suitable program would understand. But he is right in suggesting that actual behaviour is not what mental concepts refer to. How the behaviour is produced is relevant. There are significantly different ways in which the same behaviour might be generated. For instance a huge lookup table, prepared by an extraordinarily foresightful programmer who anticipated all our questions, could pass a collection of behavioural tests. But it might produce nasty surprises later, because no finite set of actual tests can establish the powers required for passing a wider range of possible tests. Since there are indefinitely many counterfactual conditional statements that are true of us, but which would not be true of such a machine, we would be unwise to rely on it in future simply because it has worked so far, without knowing the basis for success.

Attributions of mentality imply coherent behaviour and reliability, as friends, enemies, colleagues, or goal achievers. There are different kinds of unreliability. One kind would exist in a machine whose computations depended on co-operation of a (speeded up) human interpreter performing millions of steps, as in Searle's experiment. Tiredness, boredom, cussedness, and mere slips could easily interfere. This supports Searle's claim that mentality presupposes machinery with the right causal powers (though not his other conclusions).

The lookup table is unreliable in a deeper way: we cannot rely on it to deal with the unanticipated. The same applies, to a lesser degree, to less rigid programs: human-like performance in any finite set of tests does not justify the assumption that the behaviour would be convincing in other possible situations. This is painfully evident in AI programs to date.

So, taking the intentional stance on purely behavioural grounds (Turing's test), is potentially risky. We must adopt what Dennett calls the 'design stance' for a better justification of our ascriptions of intentionality, understanding, etc. A machine must not merely produce appropriate behaviour, but must satisfy the design requirements for understanding. Could a machine do this?

The main features of human understanding are sketched below. We'll find important aspects of our ordinary concept of 'understanding' in simple computers, even without AI programs. Requirements for richer human-like capacities are also described. There are no reasons for doubting that machines can satisfy them.

The Semantic Linkage Problem

A central issue is the 'semantic linkage problem': how can a person, or machine, take one thing as referring to or describing another? AI work on language and image understanding often relies on translation into some internal representation. But if the machine itself does not understand the internal representation, we have not progressed much beyond filing cabinets. If all understanding requires translation we risk an infinite regress. Ultimately something must be interpreted as meaningful in its own right. How? It is implausible that existing AI story 'understanders' really can think about parties, political events, or passionate murders, despite printing out sentences about them after reading stories. If a symbol-user U uses a symbol S to refer to some object O, then it seems that U must have some other way of relating to O, attending to O, thinking of O, etc., besides using S. This 'semantic linkage' problem pervades recent analytical philosophy (E.g. See [17], [6], [3]). It is ignored in work on formal semantics, and both linguistics and psychology seem to have little to say about it. It is complicated by the fact that O can be remote from U, or even long dead, or imaginary, which rules out direct causal connections between U, S and O, as necessary. We shall see that when O is part of U (e.g. a location in U's memory, an internal action U can perform, an internal pattern U can test for), the link may be a comparatively simple causal relationship. My conjecture is that more sophisticated types of meaning and reference are possible only on the basis of this 'internal' semantics.

What is understanding a language?

I use the word 'language' loosely as equivalent to 'notation', 'representational scheme', 'symbol system' etc. Very roughly, a language L is a system of symbols used by some agent U in relation to a world W. A full analysis would distinguish different kinds of: (a) symbol media, (b) symbol systems, (c) mechanisms for manipulating symbols, (d) symbol users, (e) worlds, and (f) purposes for which symbols might be used. This paper discusses only a subset of this rich array of possibilities.

Symbols are structures that can be stored, compared with other structures, searched for, etc. They may be physical structures, like the marks on a piece of paper, or virtual symbols, i.e. abstract structures in a virtual machine, like 2-D arrays in a computer (See [15]). They may be internal or external. They need not be separable physical objects or events, since a single travelling wave may 'carry' different signals simultaneously, and a network of active nodes may have several patterns superimposed in its current state. Symbols include maps, descriptions, representations, of all kinds, including computer programs, and non-denoting symbols, like parentheses and other syntactic devices. (In fact, anything at all can be used as a symbol.)

A language L contains symbols used by U to represent or refer to entities, properties, relations, events, processes, or actions in some world W. The word 'used' may suggest that U has goals or purposes. However, this is not a necessary condition, since a plant "uses" water in photosynthesis without having any explicit goal, or purpose. We can tell that U uses a symbol S to refer to object O, by discovering that some significant subset of the conditions listed below are satisfied. We shall see that in the more elaborate cases goals are involved.

The symbols need not be used for external communication. Meaning and understanding are often assumed (e.g. [7]) to be essentially concerned with communication between language users. As argued in [13], this is a mistake, since understanding of an external language is secondary to the use of an internal symbolism for storing information, reasoning, making plans, forming percepts and motives, etc. This is prior in (a) evolutionary terms, (b) in relation to individual learning, and (c) insofar as the use of an external language requires internal computations. In short:
'Representation is prior to communication'.

Objects in the world W may be concrete (e.g. physical objects) or abstract (e.g. numbers, grammatical rules). They may be external, or internal to U. Like symbols, the objects may exist in a virtual world, embodied in a lower level world, like a virtual machine implemented in a lower level computer. Many programming languages refer to objects in a virtual world, such as lists, arrays, procedures, etc. Similarly social systems form a virtual world embedded in a psychological and physical world.

The structure of the concept 'understanding'

Instead of fruitlessly trying to identify a set of defining conditions for U to use symbols with understanding, I offer a prototypical set of conditions for saying that U uses some collection of symbols as a language L referring to objects in a world W. Different combinations of these conditions define different concepts of 'language', 'meaning', 'understanding', etc. Asking which is the 'RIGHT' concept is pointless.

For each condition I comment on how it might be satisfied by a machine, ignoring, for brevity, the difference between internal and external representations of computer languages. The discussion will appear to be question-begging, as fragments of evidence will be presented as if the case had been made. The fact that so many fragments can be presented this way, is what makes the case! It shows that events and processes in a machine can constitute a model for a significant subset of the 'axioms' implicitly defining mentalistic concepts. Unlike simulations of (e.g.) tornadoes, people outside the model can relate to the model as to the real thing (though some may find this distasteful). A robot may obey commands, answer questions, teach you things. But a simulated tornado will not make you wet or cold. Anyone who objects that this is not enough can be challenged to describe precisely what is missing. Appeals to mystery, or to unanalysable kinds of mental or spiritual stuff are undiscussable.

We'll see that computers can manipulate internal structures and use them as symbols associated with a world W consisting of both entities within the machine and more abstract entities like numbers and symbol-patterns. Later, the discussion addresses reference to an 'external' world.

Prototypical conditions for U to use L to refer to W

* L is a set containing simple and complex symbols, the latter being composed of the former, in a principled fashion, according to syntactic rules.

This condition is satisfied by most computer languages, though machine codes generally have very simple syntactic rules and structures. Rules may be implicit in procedures.

* U associates some symbols of L with objects in W, and other symbols with properties, relations, or actions in W.

A computer can associate 'addresses' with a world W containing locations in its memory (or in a virtual machine) and their contents and relationships. The symbols cause processes to be directed to or influenced by specific parts of the system. Some of the symbols specify which processes - i.e. they name actions.

Various sorts of properties and relations may be symbolised in a machine language, e.g. equality of content, neighbourhood in the machine, arithmetic relations, having a bit set, etc. Symbols indicating tests that produce a boolean result, name properties and relationships.

So, if U is a simple computer, the basic semantic relation is causal:
  'S refers to O for U' =
    'S makes U's activities relate to or involve O',
where O may be an object, property, relation or type of action.

Instructions have imperative meanings because they systematically cause actions to occur. Roughly,
  'S denotes action A to U' = 'S makes U do A'

Depending on how rich the language is, S and A may have independently variable components, e.g. object, instrument, manner, location, time, etc.

In computers imperative meaning is basic: even denoting expressions are often instructions to compute a value. This low level meaning depends on direct causal connections within the machine. Later we discuss non-imperative denotation.

* Some of the objects referred to in world W are abstract, like numbers.

Computers can use certain symbols to denote numbers because they are manipulated by arithmetical procedures and used as loop counters, address increments, array subscripts etc. Thus the machine can count its own operations, or the elements of a list that satisfy some test. The way a machine does this is typically very close to the core of a young child's understanding of number words - they are just a memorised sequence used in certain counting activities. So:
  'S refers to a number, for U' =
    'S belongs to a class of symbols which U manipulates in a manner characteristic of counting, adding, etc.'

* What a complex symbol S expresses for U depends on its structure, its more primitive components and some set of interpretation rules related to the syntactic rules U uses for L. ([5])

This is true of many computer languages. E.g. what is denoted by a complex arithmetical expression, or a complex instruction, depends on what the parts denote, and how they are put together according to the syntactic rules of the language.

* U can treat the symbols of L as 'objects', i.e. can examine them, compare them, change them, etc., though not necessarily consciously.

This applies to computers. Symbolic patterns used to refer can also be referred to, compared, transformed, copied, etc. E.g. two patterns may be tested for equality, or overlap, or set inclusion. An address can be incremented to get the next location. It is not clear whether other animals can or need to treat their internal symbols as objects. This may be a pre-requisite for some kinds of learning.

* Certain symbols in L express conditionality.

This is the key to much creative thinking or planning, and to flexibility of action. We can distinguish (a) 'if' used in conditional imperatives, (b) 'if' used as the standard boolean (truth-functional) operator and (c) 'if' used in conditional assertions. (c) is not found in the simplest computer languages.

Conditional imperatives are found in machines since 'if' (or some equivalent) when combined with evaluable expressions permits or suppresses actions, depending on the evaluation.

* By examining W, U can distinguish formulas in L that assert something true from those asserting something false.

Computers typically use symbols to denote 'truth-

values' ('true' and 'false' or '1' and '0').
Boolean operations e.g. 'or', 'and', 'not' are also
represented, by symbols that trigger actions
transforming inputs to outputs consistently with
truth-tables. The 'result' is taken as a truth-
value partly because of its role in conditional
imperatives. The sense in which computers can examine their internal states to assign a truth-value
is fairly clear, though how they check arithmetical
statements requires deeper analysis.

If U assigns truth-values to symbols in a manner
that depends on the state of world W, the symbols
can be thought of as representing factual propositions, that so and so is the case in W. More generally,
  'For U, S means P is the case' =
    'in certain contexts the expression S causes U
    to do certain things only if P is the case,
    otherwise not'

We have yet to see how a machine can treat 'true'
and 'false' as more than just formal duals.

* U can detect that stored symbols contain errors
  and take corrective action, e.g. noting that two
  descriptions are inconsistent and finding out
  which to reject.

Something like this occurs in programs that attempt
to eliminate wrong inferences derived from noisy
data, e.g. in vision, and in plan-executors that
check whether the assumptions underlying the
current plan are still true. Here we find support
for a richer conception of a truth-value than just
a pair of arbitrarily chosen symbols, if 'true'
connotes surviving tests, and 'false' rejection.
More on this later.

* A complex symbol S with a boolean value may be
  used for different purposes by U, for instance:
  questioning (specifying information to be found
  by lookup, computation, or external sensing),
  instructing (specifying actions), asserting
  (storing information for future use).

We have seen how, in a computer, S can function as
a primitive question, in a conditional instruction
where action depends on the answer to the question.
In low level machine languages there is not usually
the possibility of using the same symbol to express
the content of an imperative as in "Make S true".
I.e. machine codes do not have 'indirect imperatives' with embedded propositions. However, AI
planning systems have shown how in principle this
can be done, at least in simple cases, assuming the
initial availability of direct imperatives.

Apart from a few exceptions like Planner, Conniver
and Prolog, most computer languages include
requests and instructions, but not assertions: factual statements assimilated to some store of
beliefs. However, it is easy to allow programs to
record results of computations or externally sensed
data, or even results of self-monitoring. Recom-
putable information may be stored simply for easy
access, as people store multiplication tables.

Whether U uses S as a question, an assertion, or an

instruction, will depend on context. S may specify
the content of an assertion in one context
('store(S)'), a question in another ('if S then...'
or 'lookup(S)'), and an instruction in a third
('achieve(S)'). I.e. role is determined by use
rather than form or content.

* U can make inferences by deriving new symbols in
  L from old ones, in order to determine some
  semantic relation (e.g. proofs preserve truth,
  refutations demonstrate falsity).

Work in AI has demonstrated mechanisms for doing
this, albeit in a restricted and mostly uncreative
fashion so far. Human forms of inference require
some of the functional architecture discussed below
in connection with motives, and also require use of
a much wider range of representations than AI has
so far addressed ([15]).

* L need not be a fixed, static, system: it should
  be extendable, to cope with expanding requirements.

One source of language change in people is communication with others using different dialects. A
deeper source is situations that prove hard to
describe.

Many computer languages are extendable. Adaptive
dialogue systems are beginning to show how a
machine may extend its own language according to
need. But deep concept formation is still some way
off. It is not clear which animals can and which
cannot extend their internal languages. Without
this, certain other forms of learning may be impossible. (More on language change below.)

* U may use symbols of L to formulate goals, purposes, or intentions; or to represent hypothetical possibilities for purposes of planning or
  prediction.

Simple versions of this sort of thing are found in
existing AI planning systems.

Without a functional architecture supporting distinctions between beliefs, desires, plans, supposi-
tions, etc., a machine cannot assign meanings in
the way that we do. Merely storing information, and
deriving consequences, or executing instructions,
leaves out a major component of human understanding, i.e. that what we understand matters to us.
For information to matter to a machine it would
have to have its own desires, preferences, likes,
dislikes, etc. This presupposes that there are
modules whose function is to create or modify goals
- motive generators. Full flexibility requires
motive-generator generators. Deciding and planning
require motive comparators and motive-comparator-
generators. This is a complex story, spelled out in
a little more detail in [14]. When desires, intentions, plans, preferences, etc. are generated
through experience, perhaps over many years, this
undermines the claim that a machine can exhibit
only desires of the programmer or user. Such a
machine, unlike existing computers, would use symbols in L for its purposes.

This takes us across yet another boundary in the space of behaving systems. Does a machine 'REALLY' understand without all this? Well, it could 'understand' well enough to be an utterly slavish servant. It could not, however, be entrusted with tasks requiring creativity and drive, like managing a large company or a battle force, or minding children.

* A language may be used for communication between individuals. This adds new requirements [18]), which are irrelevant to our present concerns.

Recapitulation

All the conditions so far listed for U to use a language L in relation to a world W are consistent with U being a computer. Several do not even require AI programs, since modern computers are built able to use symbols to refer to a world W containing numbers, locations in memory, the patterns of symbols found in those locations, properties and relations of such patterns, and actions that change W.

Associations between program elements and things in the computer's world define a primitive type of meaning that the computer itself attaches to symbols. Its use of the symbols has features analogous to simpler cases of human understanding, and quite unmatched by filing cabinets. So, it does not interpret symbols merely derivatively: the causal relations justify our using simplified intentional descriptions, without anthropomorphism.

Reference to inaccessible objects

We have seen how machines can refer to their own internal states, to numbers, and to symbolic patterns, i.e. what Woods [18] calls a 'completely accessible' world. In order to be useful as robots, or friends, they will need to refer to external objects, events, locations, etc. The problem of external semantic linkage is harder to deal with. Can a system use symbols to describe objects, properties, and relationships in a domain to which it has no direct access, and only incomplete evidence, so that it can never completely verify or falsify statements about the domain? (Compare philosophers on unobservables in science, e.g. [8]).

A key idea is that implicit, partial, definitions (e.g. in the form of an axiom system) enable new undefined concepts to be added to a language. (Compare [1]) on 'meaning postulates'. Woods' 'abstract procedures' seem to be the same thing.) For instance, a collection of axioms for Euclidean geometry, in the context of a set of inference procedures, can partially and implicitly define concepts like 'line', 'point', 'intersects', etc. The axioms constrain the set of permissible models. Similarly, a congenitally blind person may attach meanings to colour words not too different from those of a sighted person, because much of the meaning resides in rich interconnections with concepts shared by both, such as 'surface', 'edge', 'pattern', 'cover', 'stripe', 'harmonise', etc.

We can generalise this. In A.I. vision programs, instead of assertions and inference rules we often find data-structures and procedures for manipulating them. If the structures are also used to guide actions and predict their consequences, that implicitly gives them semantic content, by constraining the class of possible environments that could coherently close the feedback loops, just as a set of axioms restricts the set of possible models. As with axioms, the constraints may not define a unique model.

Causal embedding in an environment

Does external reference require external causal links? One may be able to use sensors detecting light, sound or pressure from external objects, and mechanical devices that act on objects. But direct links are often not possible. For instance we can refer to events remote in space and time, and even to hypothetical objects in hypothetical situations. So direct causal connections to X are not necessary for reference to X.

Causal links may differ in kind. Consider two machines running programs P1 and P2, the former connected to TV cameras and mechanical arms, as well as a VDU, and the latter only to a VDU. Suppose P1 is able to use its sensory-motor links in referring to the external world, and P2 contains all of P1 except portions of the program required for interacting with the cameras and arms. P1 can learn about the world either through its cameras, or from another agent through the VDU. P2 has only the VDU, but can think about the same world, like a blind and paralysed person who can talk and listen; and like paleontologists talking about pre-history. Causal links can be more or less direct, and can convey more or less rich information. Communication via another agent is indirect, and generally provides limited but abstract information, but it is still a causal link, like fossil records.

So, using symbols to formulate descriptions of an external world does not require that the world actually be directly sensed and acted on by the specific symbol-user, though the internal symbols and procedures must be rich enough to support such processes. However, some causal link is required if symbols are to refer to particular physical objects, like the Tower of London, or physical properties found in our world, such as magnetism. Without causal connections with the environment a thinker could only think (existentially quantified) thoughts about an abstract possible world, perhaps a generalisation of our world, but not about this world, or things in it. Causal links, whether via sense organs or other agents, can help to pin the reference down to this world. They can reduce the extent of ambiguity of reference, though they never totally remove it, as shown by old philosophical arguments in support of scepticism (see Strawson).

Extending 'mentalese': concept learning

A language may be extended by the addition of new axioms and procedures, partially and implicitly defining some new primitive symbols, and modifying the meanings of old ones. The history of concepts of science and mathematics shows that not all newly-acquired concepts need be <u>translatable</u> into one's previous symbolism. E.g. 'mass' in Einstein's physics is not definable in Newtonian terms. Physicists use concepts not explicitly definable in terms of tests that may be applied to sensory data. Using theories and inconclusive tests, they infer descriptions including symbols that are only partially defined. An intelligent machine or organism is in the same sort of relation to the world as is a scientific community.

So new symbols may be learnt without being <u>translatable</u> into old ones. After such learning, there is no clear functional distinction between the original concepts and the accreted language: we can memorise facts, formulas and instructions in English, instead of always having to translate into 'mentalese'. Hence, contrary to Fodor, different humans (or machines) may use different 'mentalese' even if they all started off the same.

The essential incompleteness of semantics

Not <u>every</u> descriptive or referential symbol U understands must be one to which U can relate reality <u>directly</u>, using perceptual or other causal links. The symbol-system L may make contact with reality, e.g. through U's sense-organs and actions, only at relatively scattered points, and only in indirect ways (like the connection between reality and our concepts of 'atom', 'the remote future', 'another person's mind', 'Julius Caesar', 'the interior of the sun', and so on). People with different points of contact with reality store much the same general information about large chunks of the world, because their inference procedures permit them to extrapolate beyond what they have already learned, and we very likely have biological constraints built into us that, together with social processes, lead us to similar extrapolations from fragmentary evidence. However, convergence is clearly not guaranteed, and its absence may go undetected for some time [9]. If machines are to communicate successfully with us, the designers will have to understand these constraints and how they work.

If a new symbol is introduced using axioms that partially implicitly define it, then it can only be used with a partial meaning, and sentences containing it will not have determinate truth- and falsity-conditions. Such meanings may be inherently incomplete, if the concepts are indefinitely extendable by adding new theoretical assumptions about the nature of the reality referred to. This incompleteness is evident in theoretical concepts of science, but can also be demonstrated in ordinary concepts. This is an inevitable fact about the semantics of a language used to represent information about external objects, concerning which only partial, inferred, information is available, via sense organs, instruments, hearsay, books, fossil records, etc. In a sufficiently complex system, even the language used for describing its own <u>internal</u> state will have this kind of indeterminateness and completeness, because of the problems of internal access sketched in chapter 10 of [12].

How can truth and falsity be distinguished?

Although I have shown that computers can be said to use boolean operations and boolean values, it is not clear how to distinguish a 'true' from a 'false' boolean value, since their roles in a computer may be totally symmetrical. The manual may say that 1 stands for 'true' and 0 for 'false', and that certain symbols are interpreted as 'and', 'or' 'if', etc. But the duality of propositional logic implies that there is as much basis in the formal manipulations for treating 1 as 'false' and 0 as 'true', 'and' as 'or', 'or' as 'and' and 'if' as 'unless'. What else is required for there to be an asymmetry between the symbol for 'true' and the symbol for 'false'?

Assertions can be stored, but mere storage does not introduce an asymmetry between 'true' and 'false', since false as well as true statements could be stored, with explicit boolean indicators, or in different data-bases.

In Prolog-like languages, it might seem that there is a clear distinction between truth and falsity, between 'and' and 'or', and so on, with completed derivations signifying truth, failure signifying falsity. However, this is not sufficient to distinguish truth and falsity, since proving conclusion C on the basis of premises P1 to Pn is equivalent to refuting the disjunction of P1 to Pn on the basis of the falsity of C.

We have seen one source of asymmetry, in mechanisms that can check stored assertions out, instead of always blindly assuming them correct: an elementary form of self-consciousness. Truth of a formula is then associated with having the capacity to survive thorough checking. But the connection is not simple, for the process of checking may include errors.

Another source of asymmetry is a 'redundancy convention'. Instead of storing values of expressions explicitly, adopt a convention that one of the boolean indicators is redundant: it is signified merely by the presence of a formula in an information store or a communication. 'True' and 'false' then drop out of the 'object language' and become partly redundant metalinguistic concepts.

A deeper asymmetry lies in connections between beliefs and autonomous motives. Truth then is the boolean value of those beliefs (stored information) which (generally) enable desires to be satisfied by rational planning. Again the connection is not simple, for a true belief combined with other false premises, or an invalid inference, can lead to a disastrous plan. Moreover, what fulfiles one desire may turn out to subvert another far more important one. I believe that further investigation will show that by adopting the design stance we can replace old and apparently empty philosophical disputes with new fruitful analyses with important implications for the design of intelligent systems.

Conclusion

By adopting a 'design stance', we can begin to

clarify the question whether machines themselves can understand symbols, or whether meanings of symbols in a computer are only derivative. It is not enough that machines appear from the outside to mimic human understanding: there must be a reliable basis for assuming that they can display understanding in an open-ended range of situations, not all anticipated by the programmer. I have briefly described structural and functional design requirements for this, and argued that even the simplest computers use symbols in such a manner that, independently of how PEOPLE interpret the symbols, the machines themselves (unlike cabinets and copiers) associate meanings of a primitive sort with them. Internal uses of symbols are primary.

I have shown that a machine may use symbols to refer to its own internal states and to abstract objects; and indicated how it might refer to a world to which it has only limited access, relying on the use of axiom-systems to constrain possible models, and perception-action loops to constrain possible completions. These constraints leave meanings partly indeterminate and indefinitely extendable. Causal links reduce some of the indeterminacy. (All these topics require far more detailed discussion.)

The full range of meaningful uses of symbols by human beings requires a type of architectural complexity not yet be achieved in AI systems. There is no known obstacle to such developments in principle, though further research may reveal insuperable difficulties.

Instead of listing necessary and sufficient conditions for understanding I argued that there is a complex set of prototypical conditions, different subsets of which may be exemplified in different animals or machines, yielding a complex space of possible systems which we are only just beginning to explore. Our ordinary concepts, like 'understanding' are not suited to drawing global boundaries within such a space. At best we can analyse the implications of various different designs, and the capabilities they produce, or fail to produce.

When we have shown in detail how like or unlike a human being some type of machine is, there remains a residual seductive question, namely whether such a machine really can be conscious, really can feel pain, really can think etc. Pointing inside yourself at your own pain (or other mental state) you ask 'Does the machine really have THIS experience?'. This sort of question has much in common with the pre-Einsteinian question, uttered pointing at a location in space in front of you: 'Will my finger really be in THIS location in five minutes time?' In both cases it is a mistake to think that there really is an 'entity' with a continuing identity, rather than just a complex network of relationships. The question about machines has an extra dimension: despite appearances, it is ultimately an ethical question, not just a factual one. It requires not an answer but a practical decision on how to treat the machines of the future, if they leave us any choice.

Acknowledgements

The author has a fellowship from the GEC Research Laboratories, and has benefitted from discussions with members of and visitors to the Cognitive Studies Programme at Sussex University, especially Margaret Boden, Steve Torrance, and Bill Woods.

BIBLIOGRAPHY

[1] Carnap, R., Meaning and Necessity Phoenix Books 1956.
[2] Dennett, D.C., Brainstorms, Harvester Press 1978.
[3] Evans, Gareth, The Varieties of Reference, Oxford University Press, 1982.
[4] Fodor, J.A., The Language of Thought Harvester Press 1976.
[5] Frege, G., Translations from the philosophical writings, ed. P. Geach and M. Black. Blackwell, 1960.
[6] Hempel, C.G, 'The Empiricist Criterion of Meaning' in A.J. Ayer (Ed.) Logical Positivism, The Free Press, 1959. Originally in Revue Int. de Philosophie, Vol.4. 1950.
[7] Lyons, John, Semantics Cambridge University Press. 1977.
[8] Pap, A., An Introduction to the Philosophy of Science Eyre and Spottiswoode (Chapters 2-3). 1963.
[9] Quine, W.V.O., 'Two Dogmas of Empiricism' in From a Logical point of view 1953.
[10] Searle, J.R., 'Minds, Brains, and Programs', with commentaries by other authors and Searle's reply, in The Behavioural and Brain Sciences Vol 3 no 3, 417-457, 1980.
[11] Searle, J.R., Minds Brains and Science, Reith Lectures, BBC publications, 1984
[12] Sloman, A., The Computer Revolution in Philosophy: Philosophy Science and Models of Mind, Harvester Press and The Humanities Press, 1978.
[13] Sloman, A., 'The primacy of non-communicative language', in The analysis of Meaning: Informatics 5, Proceedings ASLIB/BCS conference Oxford, March 1979, Eds: M.MacCafferty and K.Gray, Published by Aslib.
[14] Sloman, A. and M. Croucher, 'Why robots will have emotions' in Proc. IJCAI Vancouver 1981.
[15] Sloman, A., 'Why we need many knowledge representation formalisms', in Research and Development in Expert Systems, ed M. Bramer, Cambridge University Press, 1985.
[16] Sloman, A., 'Strong strong and weak strong AI', AISB Quarterly, 1985.
[17] Strawson, P. F., Individuals: An Essay in Descriptive Metaphysics, Methuen. 1959.
[18] Woods, W.A., 'Procedural semantics as a theory of meaning', in Elements of discourse understanding Ed. A. Joshi, B. Webber, I. Sag, Cambridge University Press, 1981.

In Defense of Probability

Peter Cheeseman
SRI International
333 Ravenswood Ave., Menlo Park, California 94025

Abstract

In this paper, it is argued that probability theory, when used correctly, is sufficient for the task of reasoning under uncertainty. Since numerous authors have rejected probability as inadequate for various reasons, the bulk of the paper is aimed at refuting these claims and indicating the scources of error. In particular, the definition of probability as a measure of belief rather than a frequency ratio is advocated, since a frequency interpretation of probability drastically restricts the domain of applicability. Other sources of error include the confusion between relative and absolute probability, the distinction between probability and the uncertainty of that probability. Also, the interaction of logic and probability is discusses and it is argued that many extensions of logic, such as "default logic" are better understood in a probabilistic framework. The main claim of this paper is that the numerous schemes for representing and reasoning about uncertainty that have appeared in the AI literature are unnecessary—probability is all that is needed.

1 Introduction

A glance through any major AI publication shows that an overwhelming proportion of papers are concerned with what might be described as the logical approach to inference and knowledge representation. It now widely accepted that many knowledge representations can be mapped into (first order) predicate calculus, and the corresponding inference procedures can be reduced to a type of controlled logical deduction. However, examples of human reasoning (judgements) are full of such terms as "probably", "most", "usually" etc., showing that many patterns of human reasoning are *not* logical in form, but intrinsically probabilistic.

The claim that many patterns of human reasoning are probabilistic does not mean that the underlying "logic" of such patterns cannot be axiomatized. On the contrary, a basis for such an axiomatization is given in section 3. The claim is that when such an exercise is performed, the resulting patterns of inference are different in form from those found in analogous logical deductions. A characteristic difference is that in probabilistic inference all the relevant inference paths ("proofs") connecting the evidence to the hypothesis of interest must be examined and "combined", while in logic it is sufficient to establish a single path between the axioms and the theorem of interest. Also, the output is different, the former includes at least one numerical measure, the latter simply true or false.

Unfortunately, the logical style of reasoning is so prevalent in AI that many have attempted to force intrinsically probabilistic situations into a logical straight-jacket with predictable limited success. Two conspicuous examples of this are "Default Logic" [19] and "Non-Monotonic Logic" [15] discussed in more detail below. These methods are appropriate for dealing with some situations where limited knowledge is available. The same cannot be said for those who invent new theories for reasoning under uncertainty, such as "Certainty Factors", "Schafer/Dempster Theory", "Confirmation Theory", "Fuzzy Logic", "Endorsements" etc.

These theories will be shown below to be at best unnecessary and at worst misleading (not to mention confusing to the poor novice faced with so many possibilities). Each one is an attempt to circumvent some perceived difficulty of probability theory, but as shown below these difficulties exist only in the minds of their inventors. However, these supposed difficulties are common misconceptions of probability, generally springing from the inadequate frequency interpretation. A major aim of this paper is to put forward the older view (Bayes, Laplace etc.), that probability is a measure of belief in a proposition given particular evidence. This definition avoids the difficulties associated with the frequency definition and answers the objections of those who felt compelled to invent new theories.

An analogy can be draw between the situation in AI in the late 1970s, where Pat Hayes, in a paper entitled "In Defence of Logic" [10], found it necessary to take a broadside at the proliferation of new representation languages (with associated inference procedures) that proported to solve difficulties with the logical approach. He showed that far from being "nonlogical" it is possible to cast such languages into an equivalent logical form, and by doing so provide a clear semantics. In addition, he pointed out the obvious but unpopular fact that logic has been around for a long time and has a considerable body of research and experience that no new theory can match. Similarly today we have a set of new theories for dealing with uncertainty, despite the fact that probability theory has been around for three centuries and, as shown below, is sufficient for the task.

Any text on probability presents a formal calculus for manipulating probabilities according to a consistant set of axioms. Many disputes concerning probability are centered on the *interpretation* of the terms in the formal system, since an interpretation (model theory) is necessary if the theory is to be applied. Others dispute that the formal axioms under any interpretation really capture their intuitive expectations for uncertain inference. This paper argues for a particular interpretation of the probability formalism and that the result is sufficient for all uncertain inference in AI. Since Bayes' theorem is integral to the use of probabilities the terms Bayesian and probabilistic are used interchangeably.

2 Some Misconceptions of Probability

This section discusses and hopefully exorcises the most common misconceptions of probability.

2.1 Probability is a Frequency Ratio

Rather than give an historical account of the different theories (interpretations) that have been applied to probability (e.g. [8]), the following definition is put forward as one that withstands all previous criticisms:

The (conditional) probability of a proposition given particular evidence is a real number between zero and one, that is a measure of an entity's belief in that proposition, given the evidence

Several corollaries follow directly from this definition. Firstly, there is no such thing as *the* probability of a proposition, since the probability value depends on the evidence used to derive it. This implies that if new evidence is utilized, the probability value assigned to the proposition will generally change. The only exception to this variability is when the probability is zero or one, because then there is no longer any uncertainty and further evidence makes no difference. Secondly, different observers with different evidence (information) will assign different probabilities. There is no contradiction inherent in this—the apparent contradiction comes from the idea that every proposition has a unique probability. A third consequence of the above definition is that probabilities are inherently subjective in the sense that the value depends on the believer's information, but they are objective in the sense that the same (ideal) believers should arrive at the same value given the same information.

This definition differs sharply from the still commonly held frequency definition of probability:

The probability of an event (hypothesis) is the ratio of the number of occurrences (n) in which the event is true to the total number of such occurrences (m)

This definition has some immediate problems that many other critics have noted. For a start, this definition restricts probability to domains where repeated experiments (e.g., sampling) are possible, or at least conceivable. Also, the probability of an event under this definition is undefined if there are no prior examples ($m = 0$)—thus limiting its usefulness. Even worse are cases where, for example, there has been one success ($n = 1$) and one trial ($m = 1$), giving a probability of one for the next event!—that is on the basis of a single trial the probability of the next event is known with certainty. In most circumstances this is nonsense—those who defend the frequency ratio definition escape into "the law of large numbers" which essentially says that given a large number of (repeatable) trials, the true probability lies within given error bounds with high probability. This restriction bans small sample cases from the realm of probabilistic ("frequency") analysis, but works well for the large sample case. Given the success of the frequency definition in areas where it is applicable, it is fortunate that there is a strong connection between the measure of belief definition of probability and the frequency ratio definition. It has been shown by Jaynes [12] that under certain conditions (e.g., repeatable trials) the *expectation* of the frequency ratio is necessarily equal to the probability. However the measure of belief definition applies to the small sample case as well.

Philosophers have been arguing the "correct" definition of probability for centuries, and some have defined up to five different meanings for probability [8], including: "statistical probability" (i.e., the frequency ratio definition); "probability = propensity" (i.e., probability used for prediction); "logical probability" (i.e., the degree of confirmation of a hypothesis based on logical analysis) and "subjective probability". The measure of belief definition subsumes all these supposedly different concepts. For example, the probability of set membership ("the probability of A being a B") and the probability of future events ("the probability that H will happen, given E") are not different kinds of probability but just the observer's belief in the corresponding proposition given the evidence. Similarly, it makes no difference to the belief in a proposition whether the probability is the result of logical analysis (e.g., the probability of a number being prime) or the result of empirical observations (e.g., the probability of surviving a car accident). The philosophical distinctions and alternative definitions of probability obscure rather than enlighten understanding of probability.

2.2 Bayesian Analysis Requires Vast Amounts of Data

This particular fallacy has appeared so often that its truth is rarely questioned. The reason for this fallacy follows directly from the frequency ratio definition. This says that the probability of a proposition, such as "This patient has a particular infection given his particular set of symptoms", can be computed from the number of patients that have previously exhibited that combination of symptoms. Clearly, in practice, the set of previous patients with a particular combination of symptoms is going to be very small or zero, so by the frequency definition of probability this conditional probability cannot be computed.

In anything but the most trivial cases, the basic problem that the Bayesian (or any other) approach must deal with is that the available information is not sufficient to determine any particular conditional probability, as in the above example. That is, the probability space associated with a particular problem is usually highly under-constrained by the known probabilities, so it is impossible to calculate directly any particular conditional probability [3]. The normal way around this difficulty is to make additional assumptions that supply the missing constraints. The most common assumption is "conditional independence", as advocated in [2], [7] and [16]. The conditional independence assumption has been generalized by Lemmer and Barth [14] to include conditional independence between groups of propositions, and all these forms of independence assumptions are subsumed under the maximum entropy assumption [3], [13].

The use of the maximum entropy assumption (or its specializations) raises the question of its validity. For maximum entropy, it has been shown that the probability generated is the one which has the maximum number of possible worlds consistent with the known information, and in this sense is the "best" value [12]. In some circumstances, such as occur in statistical mechanics, the probability of the system being in a state with entropy significantly less than the maximum is vanishingly small. Maximum entropy implies that if a non maximum value is chosen, then more information is being assumed than was available—i.e., the maximum entropy gives the "least commitment" value or the one that distributes the uncertainty as evenly as possible over the set of possibilities. Conditional independence (the most common form of maximum entropy) is not just another assumption, as implied in [18], it is the only consistant assumption that can be made in the absence of any information about possible interactions. However, these desirable properties do *not* mean that information is being generated out of nothing.

What maximum entropy is doing is providing a neutral background against which any systematic (non-random) patterns can be observed. That is, if the current (probabilistic) information is incomplete, the predictions using this information and maximum entropy will differ significantly from future observations. When such differences are detected the response should not be to throw out maximum entropy (as many authors advocate), but to utilize this additional information. Maximum entropy *is* making stronger predictions than the current information warrants because it is assuming the current information is complete. However, without this prediction it is difficult to detect if the current information is incomplete, and thus difficult to

discover new information. Also many decision making situations require probability values, so that some additional principle, such as maximum entropy, is necessary in these circumstances to select point values even when the value is poorly known. This justification for the maximum entropy assumption is really the old problem associated with the use of prior probabilities in the Bayesian approach as discussed in the next subsection.

2.3 Prior Probabilities Assume more Information than Given

This statement appears in numerous AI publications, especially those expounding the Schafer-Dempster approach to uncertainty. For example:

"Bayesians might attempt to represent ignorance by a function assigning 0.25 to each of the four possibilities, assuming no prior information. ...such a function would imply more information given by the evidence than is truly the case."—[1].

"A Likelihood represented by a point probability is usually an over statement of what is actually known, distorting the available precision".—[9]

Yet those that make these claims fail to show a single unfortunate consequence that follows from this supposed assumed information. To illustrate the situation, consider the following examples. In the first example, you are told there is a normal dice and asked what probability you would assign to the next throw yielding a "6". The Maximum Entropy answer is $\frac{1}{6}$, since this distributes the uncertainty as evenly as possible over the set of possibilities. In the next example you are told there is a *loaded* dice (but not which numeral is favoured) and are asked what is the probability of a "6". Again the answer representing your state of knowledge is to assign $\frac{1}{6}$. The difference between these two situations is that in the first example your knowledge of dice mechanics and symmetry implies that after having seen the outcome of many throws you do not expect to change your state of knowledge (i.e., the probability assignment). However, for the loaded dice, you do expect the probabilities assigned to the different faces to change as a result of further trials.

Those who reject the Maximum Entropy approach argue that in the second example, the initial assignment of $\frac{1}{6}$ was assuming more than you know because after many trials you ended up with a different assignment (i.e., the initial assignment was incorrect). This objection arises from the mistaken idea that there is such a thing a *the* probability of a proposition instead of the idea that probability represents a state of knowledge. Of course the probability assignment to a proposition will change as more information is gained without inconsistency with previous assignments. The idea that there is a unique probability associated with a particular proposition comes from situations where all observers have the same information (e.g., physics), and so they all have the same measure of belief (assuming ideal observers). However, not just any prior probabilities will do. If non-equal priors are chosen, this implies that you have information about the different possibilities. Put another way, the equal prior assignment gives a neutral background against which deviations from your state of maximum uncertainty can be detected. It is because it is *not* assuming more information than given that the maximum entropy assignment is used. Looking at the example in reverse, if someone assigns equal probabilities to a set of possible outcomes, they are telling you they are completely ignorant about the next outcome (apart from how many possibilities there are). Note that in these two examples, our knowledge about our knowledge of the probabilities (i.e., the probability distribution of the probability) is the main difference.

A more subtle criticism of the use of the principle of indifference that has historically plagued probability theory is illustrated by the following example. Assume there are five "concepts" (a, b, c, d, e), then the principle of indifference will assign prior probability $\frac{1}{5}$ to each. If you are now told that concept a is actually f or g, then you should reassign probabilities of $\frac{1}{6}$ to each of (f, g, b, c, d, e). This apparent arbitrariness of the prior probabilities through regrouping and relabelling is put forward as a reason for rejecting use of priors at all. The arbitrariness of the probability assignment only arises in this example because the "concepts" are meaningless, so any grouping is just as meaningless as any other. If the problem is undefined, probability theory (or any other theory) cannot say anything useful. However, as soon as the concepts are identified with possibilities in the real world, the arbitrariness disappears. When each possibility in a problem corresponds to a physically realizable possibility, we no longer have the freedom to count arbitrary groupings of such outcomes as if they are a separate outcome—i.e., we can no longer arbitrarily redefine the problem [11].

For example, consider the famous problem known as Bertrand's Paradox. In this "paradox" we are required to draw lines "at random" that intersect a circle, and wish to know the probability that the length of a chord of such a line is longer than a side of an inscribed equilateral triangle. There appears to be different answers depending how "equally possible" situations are defined. Three possibilities are to assign uniform probability density to: (a) the distance between the centers of the chord and circle, (b) the angle the chord makes with the center, and (c) the center of the chord within the circle; each possibility giving a different answer. Jaynes [11] has shown that only (a) is consistent with the requirement that the answer be invariant under infinitesimal translations and rotations—an obvious requirement coming from our understanding of the physical set-up.

Another example of the invariance argument leading to a definite prior probability assignment is to consider the probability of finding a ship within a particular square mile somewhere in the Atlantic. If this is the only information available, then an invariance argument requires assigning equal probability to equal areas, in agreement with intuition. Since the Atlantic is roughly diamond shaped, this means that the probability of finding the ship at an equatorial latitude is higher than at a polar latitude. If the ship is instructed to move to a particular latitude, but interference completely scrambles our reception of *which* latitude, then after the ship has had time to move, our knowledge is represented by assigning uniform probability to each latitude. This new assignment, based on the new "information" leads to a new probability distribution in which the probability of finding the ship near the equator is now less than near the poles. This example shows that in real problems we cannot arbitrarily assign equal prior probabilities to any dimension or combination of possibilities because to do so implies unequal assignments on other dimensions. In practice, our rich domian background knowledge usually leads to non-uniform priors, even though we may be uncertain of their values. In complex cases, there is no substitute for a careful analysis of each problem to find what the appropriate priors for that problem are.

2.4 Numbers are not Necessary

An unfortunate tendency in AI is to rediscover the wheel but call it something else so it then becomes a "new" paradigm. An example is found in Cohen and Grinberg [5], who shows, convincingly, that in many situations it is necessary to keep track of the evidence that was used to arrive at a particular (conditional probability) judgment, so that the judgment can be revised if new evidence requires it. Their work calls attention to the fact that a computed probability number is just a *summarization* of all the evidence that was used to derive it (for convenience in decision making), and so does not contain information about its origin. However, it still a *conditional* probability and the conditions of its derivation can also be important. This utilization of probabilistic dependencies is unfortunately given the new name "endorsements", and from its success in explaining observed judgements under uncertainty, the conclusion is reached that numbers are not necessary for such judgements at all!

This conclusion has validity in restricted circumstances—in particular, it is possible to construct a theory of *relative* probabilities (e.g., [8]) that only uses information of the form P_1 is-more-probable-than P_2. Deductions in such a theory do not use numbers and can keep track of their dependencies in a style similar to "endorsements". However, the best that such a theory can say is that "this proposition is the most probable given the evidence"—it cannot indicate any absolute strength in its conclusion. It often happens that the most probable alternative is itself highly unlikely, but non-numeric approaches are unable to express such a result. The bottom line is that judgment under uncertainty *can* be done without using numbers if the user is in a decision making situation where he has only to choose among a set of alternatives. If he has the option of not selecting at all (e.g., because the most likely alternative is still too improbable), then non-numeric approaches are not sufficient.

2.5   More than one Number is Needed to Represent Uncertainty

Many of the alternative theories of uncertainty start with the observation that a single number (a probability value) does not represent all the uncertainty about a proposition—in particular, it does not indicate the accuracy with which the probability value itself is known (i.e., the probability of the probability). Similarly, Schafer [20] distinguishes between uncertainty (roughly a probability) and ignorance (no knowledge of the probability). However, even though one can make these distinctions, basic questions about their utility remain. Ultimately, the utility of any theory of uncertainty comes from the coupling it provides between evidence (information) and decision making (or prediction). A theory of uncertainty is useless without a model theory that indicates how to map evidence into an uncertainty measure and how to use this uncertainty measure to make predictions (or decisions). To decide whether particular distinctions of types of uncertainty are useful or not, we must examine whether they make any difference to the theory's decision making behavior.

The theory of optimal decision making using point probability and utility values is well known. This would seem to imply that a point probability is sufficient to represent uncertainty. However, this theory makes the assumption that the probabilities used in the analysis are known to sufficient accuracy. Probability theory can be extended so that a probability density function is assigned to a sentence instead of a point value, or higher order moments of the density function can be given. However, a result of decision analysis is that *exactly the same decision is reached whether a point value or a density function is used*. This situation is similar to that in mechanics, where a complex body can be replaced by a point mass at the center of gravity to give the same results. However, knowledge of the probability density function is important for sensitivity analysis as in the following example.

If you are given a black box and told that it will put out a string of decimal digits and are asked what is the probability that the first digit will be say 7, the standard principle of indifference answer is (.1). If, later, after seeing 10,000 digits of which 1000 were 0, 1000 were 1, etc., in no noticeable order, you are again asked to give the probability that the next digit will be 7, you will still answer (.1). This last answer, by standard information theory, implies that all the evidence gave no information whatever—you are still as uncertain about the probability of the next event as you were before seeing the "evidence". However, something has clearly changed between these two cases—it is the expectation that further evidence will significantly change our probability assignment (i.e., will provide real information). This changed expectation can be captured as a standard deviation about the probability value which is very large initially and becomes quite small (about .003) after seeing the 10,000 trials.

This example implies that if you are in a decision mak-ing (or prediction) situation *and obtaining more evidence is not an option* then a single number (the probability) is a sufficient representation of your uncertainty. However, if obtaining more information is a possible option, then a measure of how informative this information is likely to be (e.g., the standard deviation) is required. Thus, how many numbers are needed to represent uncertainty depends on the questions you are trying to answer with the uncertainty representation. To always calculate two numbers, as done in the Schafer-Dempster approach, is often overkill, and in some cases, under-kill.

2.6   The Bayesian Approach Doesn't Work— So Here is a New Scheme!

As described above, various authors have found fault with Bayesian probability, and their response has been to invent new representations and inference procedures that purport to remove particular difficulties. However, these *ad hoc* theories do not have a well established model theory to show how to go from real data to the internal uncertainty representation and then to map the final uncertainty representation into a well defined decision theory. Because of this missing interpretive framework, and because of their rejection of prior probabilities, they have produced all sorts of misleading conclusions. The following examples are illustrative:

Example 1

"Translated to the notation of conditional probability, this rule $(s_1, s_2, s_3 => h1)$ seems to say $P(h_1|s_1, s_2, s_3) = 0.7$ where h_1 is the hypothesis that the organism is Streptococcus, s_1 is the observation that the organism is gram-positive, s_2 that it is a coccus, and s_3 that it grows in chains. Questioning of the expert gradually reveals, however, that despite the apparent similarity to a statement regarding a conditional probability, the number 0.7 differs significantly from a probability. The expert may well agree that $P(h_1|s_1, s_2, s_3) = 0.7$, but he becomes uneasy when he attempts to follow the logical conclusion that therefore $P(not\ h_1|s_1, s_2, s_3) = 0.3$. He claims that the three observations are evidence (to degree 0.7) in favor of the conclusion that the organism is a Streptococcus and should not be construed as evidence (to degree 0.3) against Streptococcus. We shall refer to this problem as Paradox 1 ..."—[1]

The authors then conclude, on the basis of this "paradox", that one should gather and evaluate separately the evidence for an hypothesis and the evidence against it. This spurious argument only arises by ignoring prior probabilities and the consequent misrepresentation of the situation to the expert. The prior probability of an infection being caused by a particular bacterium is low, for the sake of argument we will assume it to be .01. After seeing the evidence (s_1, s_2, s_3) the expert is willing to update his probability (i.e., his belief) to 0.7. Another way of saying the same thing is that the probability (belief) in the negation of the hypothesis (that the organism is not *Streptococcus*) drops from a prior of .99 to .3. Thus, either way, the evidence is being used to strongly support the hypothesis, and not (as claimed above) being construed as evidence against the hypothesis. Given the misrepresentation of the situation, it is not surprising that the expert felt uneasy with the way his evidence was being used.

This example shows the danger of ignoring prior probabilities when dealing with uncertainty, and also shows its considerable advantages when used properly. As a basic principle of inference one should use whatever information is available, and this includes prior probabilities. Perhaps the main sources of opposition to the use of prior probabilities is that they are subjective estimates of the expert, and it has been shown (e.g., [21]) that people are not very good at estimating probabilities. However, the expert does not necessarily have to supply the priors—once the hypothesis space is defined, the equiprobable assignment (i.e., the principle of indifference) or relevant data can be used instead. If the expert has prior information (e.g., some infections have higher prior probabilities than others) then he should give this information to the system (in the form of non-uniform priors), because to not do so is to ignore useful information. The fact that these subjective estimates will be poorly known is no excuse for not using them. Fortunately, the final probability values calculated on the basis of extensive new information are not very sensitive to the exact value of the priors.

Example 2 (Fuzzy Sets, Fuzzy and Possibilistic Logic)

".., it is a standard practice to rely almost entirely on the techniques provided by probability theory and statistics, especially in applications relating to parameter estimation, hypothesis testing and system identification. It can be argued, however, as we do in the present paper, that such techniques cannot cope effectively with those problems in which the softness of data is nonstatistical in nature–in the sense that it relates, in the main, to the presence of fuzzy sets rather than random measurement errors or data variability."—Zadeh, [23]

This quote captures some of the motivation that underlies fuzzy sets (and their further development—fuzzy and possibility logic)—namely, the fallacy that probabilities are necessarily frequencies. The concept of vague set boundaries has no obvious frequency interpretation, so Zadeh invented fuzzy sets to capture this vagueness idea. Actually, there *is* a probabilistic (degree of belief) model for vague sets that also supplies a computable quantitative measure for the "best" (most informative) vague classification. Normally, a set is defined by a criterion that distinguishes members from non-members without allowing for partial membership. This concept of sets has been widely critisized by philosophers (e.g., Wittgenstein) largely because sets in common use do not have sharp boundaries. The alternative probabilistic model is to define a set by a "prototype" and expectations of divergence from the prototypical features shown by members of the set. That is each object has a numeric "degree of membership" given by how likely it is that the observed features would have occurred given that it is a member of that set. The best classification of the object is that which maximizes the probabilistic "similarity" measure, and it is quite possible for an object to be so dissimilar from any prototype that it forms a new set. Also, an object can be simultaneously probabilistically similar to more than one set. The underlying theory of probabilistic set membership is given in [22].

Other errors found in the AI literature include the notion that the final conditional probability value of a proposition depends on the order in which the evidence is introduced [20]; that hypotheses, such as the possible diseases a patient might have, are mutually exclusive [2]; that a piece of evidence whose conditional probability differs considerably from that of other evidence should be rejected [17] (instead of rejecting the corresponding hypothesis); etc.

2.7   Summary of Conceptual Confusions

The authors that reject probabilities as a formalism for dealing with uncertainty in AI are usually a victim of one or more of the following confusions.

- Relative versus Absolute Probabilities—To decide the most probable of a set of hypotheses is only a relative evaluation sufficient for some tasks, but decision analysis requires (absolute) conditional probability values.

- Separation of Probability and Utility—The importance (utility) of an hypothesis is often confused with its probability, since both are required for decision making.

- Probabilities are a Measure of Belief in a Proposition—This definition does not require a frequency interpretation, but applies to any well defined situation and summarizes all the evidence for that proposition.

- Probability versus Uncertainty about the Probability—The (conditional) probability P of a proposition is the user's measure of belief in that proposition, but information about the accuracy of P is fully expressed by a probability density function over P.

- Probability is not a special case of Logic—Probabilistic reasoning is often cast incorrectly in a logical form, as discusses in Section 3.

- Prior Probabilities should be used—Failure to use prior probabilities can lead to erroneous conclusions, especially when there is a large number of possibilities.

- Ambiguous Probabilities—If they occur, it is a sign that the problem is not fully defined, not that probability theory is inadequate.

3   Logic and Probability

Formally, probability can be regarded as a generalization of predicate calculus, where instead of the truth value of a formula given the evidence (context) having only the values 0 (false) or 1 (true), it is generalized to a real number between 0 and 1. This generalization can be achieved by creating new propositions of the form "The probability of F is X", where F is an arbitary well formed formula in predicate calculus. Once it has been accepted that:

- The generalized truth value (degree of plausibility) of a formula can be represented by a real number.

- The extremes of this scale must be compatible with logic.

- An infinitesimal increase in the plausibility of A given new evidence implies an infinitesimal decrease in the plausibility of $\neg A$.

- The plausibility should not be dependent on the order of evaluation.

- Where possible, all the available evidence should be used in evaluating the plausibility.

- Equivalent problems should have the same plausibility.

then it has been shown by [6] that all the degrees of freedom have been used up. That is, all the standard Kolmogorov "axioms" of probability (Addition, Multiplication, Baye's etc.) follow as logic consequences. This implies that fuzzy set theory (which rejects the additivity axiom) is necessarily violating one or more of the above requirements. Any formalism for representing "plausibility" by a real number is either equivalent to probability theory (but perhaps differing in interpretation) or not satisfying the above basic criterion. Even formalisms that do not use a single real number (e.g., [20]) can be captured by higher order probability theory (i.e., probabilities of probabilities etc.). Probability theory provides the basic procedure for computing uncertainties in real situations, but it is often not obvious how to apply it in a particular situation—in particular, the assignment of prior probabilities has historically been the main sources of difficulty.

Misapplications of probability do not usually arise from dispute or uncertainty about the basic axioms but from the way they are interpreted. A purist would insist that the only propositions that can be known with certainty are tautologies (e.g., 7 is a prime number)—any empirical (contingent) proposition can only be known probabilistically, since it is based on induction. However, this insistence forbids the application of logically reasoning to anything about the real world! A reasonable compromise is to treat propositions whose probability is close to 0 or 1 as if they are known with certainty—i.e., thresholding probability values if they are "beyond reasonable doubt". The result of this approximation is to allow logical reasoning instead of probability, because it is usually easier to use. Many of the difficulties experienced by logicians in applying logic to the real world come from a failure to recognize that logic is only an approximation of probability. In particular, "Default Logic"

and "Non-Monotonic Logic" are mainly concerned with belief revision when new (logically contradictory) evidence is found. While these logics are suitable for such things as theory completion (when one wishes to avoid, say, having to state all negative facts), they often attempt to force into a logical mold a type of reasoning that is *not* logical in nature. One standard example of default reasoning "All birds fly unless proved otherwise" should be "Most birds fly", which can be used as a piece of evidence in evaluating the probability of the proposition "this bird flies", along with any other relevant evidence.

In probabilistic reasoning, different pieces of evidence are combined together to change the reasoner's measure of belief in a particular proposition—a single line of reasoning, such as a logical proof, is not sufficient. In many cases, there is one piece of evidence (or line of reasoning) that dominates the final result, which is usually given as the "reason" for the result ("if there is smoke, there is fire"). Such reasoning resembles logical reasoning and is often mistaken for it, but its non-logical nature becomes clear when "contradictory" evidence is found. In probability, contradictions do not occur—all the evidence is combined to get a final probability value, so there is no need to reject evidence (although evidence can be used to reject hypotheses). Practical reasoning is usually a complex combination of logical reasoning (discovering consequences, finding the possibilities) and probabilistic reasoning (evaluating the evidence, weighting the possibilities). Likewise, AI should be using both methods where appropriate.

4   Subjective Probabilities

An important topic on the border line between AI (especially expert systems), cognitive science, psychology and philosophy is that of subjective probabilities. Given the above emphasis on probability being a measure of belief, it will come as no surprise that this paper advocates that subjective probabilities should be treated the same as any other probability (such as that from a measurement). However, there are a number of caveats that should be observed, particularly the observation [21] that people are poor estimators of probability—largely because they are victims of many of the misconceptions noted above. Rather than just accepting this situation, as the expert system community seem to, and try to work around it by better interviewing techniques and the like, the view advocated here is that we should aim for *artificial* intelligence. In particular, we should infer expert systems directly from data (as in [4]), rather than filter the same information (badly) through an "expert" and accept whatever numbers he provides. Anyone who has observed an expert giving probability estimates and then discovered he will later provide a completely different estimate, must begin to wonder about the quality of the results of such an expert system.

An artificial intelligence system that reasons under uncertainty will probably use many of the mental techniques that people use. One such technique is random sampling in the set of possible worlds (i.e., the set of worlds that is consistent with current knowledge) to find the proportion of those worlds in which the predicate of interest is true (i.e., estimate its probability). For example, if a robot is trying to estimate the probability that a person will enter the work area during a particular operation, it should use its current world knowledge to construct (randomly) scenarios in which the event happens and others in which it does not, then using the probability of these different scenarios, to form an estimate of the events' probability. In doing this construction, logic is used extensively. For example, if is unlikely that any person could reach the work area in the time available, then the event is unlikely. When people perform similar hypothetical reasoning, they are often biased by such things as the most recent relevant events—an artificial intelligent system should be designed to avoid such biases and estimate the required probability to the accuracy desired.

An artificially intelligent system for reasoning under uncertainty should be possible based only on the basic "laws" of probability—Baye's theorem, additivity rule, multiplication rule etc., and additional principles, such as "if there is no known causal connection between two events, then assume they are independent (causal closure)" etc. In underconstrained situations, the principle of indifference (or maximum entropy) should be used to obtain the most unbiased value given the available information. No other representation or calculus is necessary for reasoning under uncertainty. This includes the problem of combining evidence from different sources (use Bayes' theorem). Note that use of Bayes' theorem requires that the system keep track of the information that was used in computing conditional probabilities for belief maintenance, in a manner very similar to truth maintenance in logic.

References

[1] Buchanan, B. G., and E. H. Shortliffe, "Rule-Based Expert Systems", Addison-Wesley, p239, 1984.

[2] Charniak, E., "The Bayesian Basis of Common Sense Medical Diagnosis", Proc. National Conf. Artificial Intelligence, Washington, pp 70-73, Aug., 1983.

[3] Cheeseman, P. C., "A Method of Computing Generalized Bayesian Probability Values for Expert Systems", Proc. Eight International Conference on Artificial Intelligence, Karlruhe, Aug. 1983, pp 198-202.

[4] Cheeseman, P. C., "Learning Expert Systems from Data", Proc. Workshop on Principles of Knowledge-Based Systems, Denver, pp 115-122, Dec. 1984.

[5] Cohen, P. R. and Grinberg, M. R., "A Theory of Heuristic Reasoning About Uncertainty", AI Magazine Vol. 4 No. 2, Summer 1983, pp 17-24.

[6] Cox, R. T., "Of Inference and Inquiry—An Essay in Inductive Logic", In The Maximum Entropy Formalism, Ed. Levine and Tribus, M.I.T. Press, 1979.

[7] Duda, R. O., P. E. Hart, and Nils Nilsson, "Subjective Bayesian Methods for Rule-Based Inference Systems", AFIPS Conf. Proc., National Computer Conf., Vol 45, New York, pp 1075-1082, 1976.

[8] Fine, T. L., "Theories of Probability", Academic Press Inc., 1973.

[9] Garvey, T. D., J. D. Lowrance, and M. A. Fischler, "An Inference Technique for Integrating Knowledge form Disparate Sources", Proc. 7th. International Joint Conf. Artificial Intelligence, Vancouver, pp 319-325, Aug. 1981.

[10] Hayes, P., "In Defence of Logic", Proc. 5th. International Joint Conf. Artificial Inteligence, M.I.T., pp 559-565, Aug. 1977.

[11] Jaynes, E. T., "The Well-Posed Problem", Foundations of Physics, 3, pp 477-493, 1973.

[12] Jaynes, E.T., "Where do we stand on Maximum Entropy", in "The Maximum Entropy Formalism", Levine and Tribus Eds. M.I.T Press 1979.

[13] Konolige, K., "Bayesian Methods for Updating Probabilities", Appendix D in "A Computer Based Consultant for Mineral Exploration", SRI report, Sept. 1979.

[14] Lemmer, J. F., and S. W. Barth, "Efficient Minimum Information Updating for Bayesian Inferencing in Expert Systems", Proc. National Conf. Artificial Intelligence, Pittsburgh, pp 424-427, Aug., 1982.

[15] McDermott, D. and J. Doyle, "Non-Monotonic Logic I," Artificial Intelligence, Vol. 13, Nos. 1,2, pp 41-72, April 1980.

[16] Pearl, J., and Kim, J. H., "A Computational Model for Causal and Diagnostic Reasoning in Inference Systems", Proc. 8th. International Conf. Artificial Intelligence, Karlsruhe, pp 190-193, Aug., 1983.

[17] Quinlan, J. R., "Consistency and Plausible Reasoning", Proc. International Joint Conference on Artificial Intelligence, Karlsruhe, pp 137-144, August 1983.

[18] Rauch, H. E., "Probability Concepts for an Expert System used for Data Fusion", AI Magazine, Vol. 5, No. 3, pp 55-60, Fall 1984.

[19] Reiter, R., and G. Criscuolo, "On Interacting Defaults", Proc. 7th. International Conf. Artificial Intelligence, Vancouver, pp 270-276, Aug. 1981.

[20] Shafer, G. "A Mathematical Theory of Evidence", Princeton University Press, Princeton, N.J., 1976.

[21] Tversky, A., and Kahneman, D., "Judgement under Uncertainty: Heuristics and Biases", Science, 185, pp 1124-31, Sept. 1974.

[22] Wallace, C.S. and Boulton, D.M. "An Information Measure for Classification", Computer Journal, 11, 2, pp 185-194, 1968.

[23] Zadeh, L. A., "Possibility Theory and Soft Data Analysis", In Mathematical Frontiers of the Social and Policy Sciences, Ed. L. Cobb and R. M. Thrall, pp 69-129.

REFINING AND EXTENDING THE PROCEDURAL NET

Mark E. Drummond

Department of Artificial Intelligence
University of Edinburgh
Hope Park Square
Edinburgh, Scotland, U.K.

Abstract

This paper presents a new definition for Plans. The objects defined are called Plan Nets, and are similar in spirit to Sacerdoti's Procedural Nets (1975). It is argued that Plan Nets are more descriptive than Procedural Nets, because they can easily describe iterative behaviour. The Plan Net definition is motivated by providing an operational semantics for the Procedural Net, and noticing that all Procedural Net state spaces are "loop free". This is seen to restrict the behaviours that can be described by the Procedural Net to those which do not include iteration. It is suggested that Plan Net state spaces can contain loops, and thus can describe iterative behaviour.

1. Paper Overview

In the next section we give Sacerdoti's definition of the Procedural Net. A simple method for deriving Procedural Net behaviours is also presented, and it is argued that the Procedural Net cannot describe iteration. Section 3 defines and discusses the Plan Net. Two sample Plan Nets are given. An operational semantics is <u>suggested</u> for the Plan Net, and it is argued that Plan Nets can describe iteration. The Procedural Net and the Plan Net are compared in Section 4. Section 5 concludes.

2. The Procedural Net

A <u>Procedural Net</u> has been defined as "a network of actions at varying levels of detail, structured into a hierarchy of partially ordered time sequences." (Sacerdoti, 1975, p. 10). The basic objects in a Procedural Net are actions, and some ordering relations on the actions. Because of this, we refer to the Procedural Net as an "event space" representation. A net can be drawn as an action-on-node graph, with directed arcs between nodes. An arc running from one node α to another node β means that the action denoted by α must occur "before" the action denoted by β.

We can derive the possible behaviours of a given Procedural Net by analyzing the state space which it describes. A net's state space can be produced by playing a version of the "pebbling game" (Pippenger, 1980). While pebbling was not developed with this application in mind, it does capture our intuition of what "before" means in a Procedural Net. In our version of this game, we place "pebbles" on the nodes of a Procedural Net as they are executed. The net starts out pebble-free, and finishes up pebble-laden — each node must be pebbled; that is, each action must be executed. Pebble placement is carried out according to the rule: A node may be pebbled if all of its immediate predecessors are pebbled.

The Procedural Net has been criticized recently (McDermott, 1983; Rosenschein, 1984). This paper addresses the Procedural Net's inability to describe "iterative" behaviour. Such behaviour is difficult to model in a natural way using a Procedural Net. Since the arcs of a net are taken to mean "before", one cannot simply direct an arc from an action "back into" the net.

It is obvious that all Procedural Net state-spaces will be loop-free, since the number of pebbles on a net must increase monotonically. There will never be an action which removes a pebble; thus never an action which can produce an earlier state. This is due to the strict "before" interpretation of the Procedural Net's arcs.

While Sacerdoti did include a mechanism for dealing with iteration, it hides the notion of "process" inside a special <u>replicate</u> node. His treatment of iteration poses problems. Below, we suggest that by defining an alternative "event space" representation for plans, we <u>can</u> describe iterative behaviour. This new definition follows the belief that iteration must be expressed in terms of the structure of a plan, so that a planner can <u>reason</u> about the iteration.

3. The Plan Net

In this section, we define <u>Plan Nets,</u> using some basic concepts from Net Theory (Brauer, 1979).

Definition 1. A <u>Plan Net</u> is a 6-tuple $\langle P,T,R_a,R_b,R_c,R_e \rangle$, where $P = \{p_1,p_2,...,p_N\}$, a finite set of places; $T = \{t_1,t_2,...,t_M\}$, a finite set of transitions; $N \geq 0$, $M \geq 0$; and $T \cap P = \phi$, the empty set. $R_a = \{(t_i,t_k) \mid \exists p_j \in P \ [(t_i,p_j) \in R_c \ \& \ (p_j,t_k) \in R_e]\}$, the Allow relation. $R_e \subseteq (P \times T)$, the Enable relation; $R_c \subseteq (T \times P)$, the Cause relation. $R_b \subseteq (T \times T)$, the Before relation; R_b must be a strict partial order on T.

Definition 2.   Place p_i is an <u>input</u> <u>place</u> of transition t_j if and only if $(p_i, t_j) \in R_e$. Place p_i is an <u>output</u> <u>place</u> of transition t_j if and only if $(t_j, p_i) \in R_c$.

Definition 3.   A <u>marking</u> of a Plan Net is a mapping $\mu: P \to \{0, 1\}$.

Definition 4.   A transition t_j is <u>enabled</u> if for each input place, p_i, $\mu(p_i) = 1$. A transition t_j may <u>fire</u> when enabled. Firing t_j in a marking μ produces a new marking μ' such that

1) If p_i is an input place of t_j
   then $\mu'(p_i) = 0$;
2) If p_i is an output place of t_j
   then $\mu'(p_i) = 1$;
3) If p_i is not an input place
   and not an output place of t_j
   then $\mu'(p_i) = \mu(p_i)$.

A place is thought of as a "condition", a static thing which does or does not hold. If a place p_i is marked ($\mu(p_i) = 1$) it is considered to be believed [by the planning system], and if it is unmarked ($\mu(p_i) = 0$), it is considered to be not believed [by the planning system].

Transitions are events, the Plan Net counterparts of a Procedural Net's actions. Events are dynamic entities; conditions are static. Events are things which "happen".

The Allow relation (R_a) is an abstraction of two simpler relations: Cause (R_c), and Enable (R_e). Events cause conditions, and conditions enable events. The input places of a transition describe those conditions which must be believed to hold in the world for the event the transition denotes to be enabled. The firing of a transition models the activation of its event. After firing, the output places of the transition describe the new conditions that are believed to hold.

Sample plans in this formalism are given in Figures 1 and 2. The plan of Figure 1 is designed to solve a canonical Blocks World problem. An initial marking is included. The plan of Figure 2 is one for (endlessly) hammering a nail. The plans look large, but this is due to redundant information being included in the formalism. When a plan is drawn as a graph it shrinks to more modest proportions (see Drummond, forthcoming).

4. Comparing the Nets

In this section we argue that the Plan Net representation is more powerful than the Procedural Net because of an explicit epistemological commitment to conditions and events. The Procedural Net makes no <u>clear</u> distinction between them. Using the Allow and Before relations as defined above, we can produce state spaces which contain cycles; that is, ones which correspond to iterative behaviour.

C = <P,T,R_a,R_b,R_c,R_e>

P = { (on c a), (on c t3), (on a t1),
       (on b t2), (on b c), (on a   b),
       (clear t3), (clear a), (clear t1),
       (clear b), (clear t2), (clear c)}

T = { (move c a t3), (move a t1 b),
       (move b t2 c) }

R_c = { ((move c a t3), (clear a)),
       ((move c a t3), (on c t3)),
       ((move c a t3), (clear c)),
       ((move b t2 c), (clear b)),
       ((move b t2 c), (on b   c)),
       ((move b t2 c), (clear t2)),
       ((move a t1 b), (clear a)),
       ((move a t1 b), (clear t1)),
       ((move a t1 b), (on a   b)) }

R_e = { ((on   c a), (move c a t3)),
       ((clear t3), (move c a t3)),
       ((clear c), (move c a t3)),
       ((clear a), (move a t1 b)),
       ((clear b), (move a t1 b)),
       ((on a t1), (move a t1 b)),
       ((clear c), (move b t2 c)),
       ((clear b), (move b t2 c)),
       ((on b t2), (move b t2 c)) }

R_a = { ((move c a t3), (move b t2 c)),
       ((move b t2 c), (move a t1 b)),
       ((move c a t3), (move a t1 b)),
       ((move b t2 c), (move b t2 c)),
       ((move a t1 b), (move a t1 b)),
       ((move c a t3), (move c a t3)) }

R_b = { ((move c a t3), (move b t2 c)),
       ((move b t2 c), (move a t1 b)) }

$\mu(p) = 1$ if $p \in$ {(on   c a), (clear t3),
                 (clear c), (clear b),
                 (on b t2), (on a t1)}
$\mu(p) = 0$ otherwise.

Figure 1:   A plan. (move X Y Z) means "Move block X from Y to Z".

NOAH (Sacerdoti, 1975), and its descendents, such as NONLIN (Tate, 1976), DEVISER (Vere, 1981), and SIPE (Wilkins, 1983) all use plans based on Sacerdoti's original Procedural Net. The following comments are expressed principally in terms of NOAH, but apply equally to these newer planners.

The Allow relation takes the form of a "before" link in a Procedural Net which has been introduced by pattern-directed operator invocation. Such a link might appear, for instance, between an action which must make block **A** clear, and an action which must stack **A** on **B**.

$C = \langle P,T,R_a,R_b,R_c,R_e \rangle$

$P = \{\text{Hammer-Up, Hammer-Down}\}$

$T = \{\text{Lift-Hammer-Up, Pound-Hammer-Down}\}$

$R_a = \{(\text{Pound-Hammer-Down, Lift-Hammer-Up}),$
$(\text{Lift-Hammer-Up, Pound-Hammer-Down})\}$

$R_e = \{(\text{Hammer-Up, Pound-Hammer-Down}),$
$(\text{Hammer-Down, Lift-Hammer-Up})\}$

$R_c = \{(\text{Pound-Hammer-Down, Hammer-Down}),$
$(\text{Lift-Hammer-Up, Hammer-Up})\}$

$R_b = \{\}$

Figure 2:   A plan for hammering a nail.

The Before relation appears in a Procedural Net as a "before" link introduced by the Resolve Conflicts critic. This critic analyzes operator preconditions and effects, and introduces "before" orderings because of unfavourable interactions.

In Section 2, it was shown that one can take a Procedural Net, and through repeated application of the pebbling rule, determine possible net behaviours. The situation is slightly more complex when we consider deriving a Plan Net's possible behaviours. To do this, we require an initial marking of the net, the net itself, and the firing rule as provided in Definition 4. Using the initial net marking, we repeatedly fire transitions until either no enabled transitions remain, or a marking is reached that has been seen previously. A tree or graph structure can be built in this manner, in which the nodes contain states (markings) of the Plan Net, and the arcs are transitions for moving from one state to another. In net Theory, this structure is often called a reachability tree (or graph), and is precisely the sort of behavioural account we generated for the Procedural Net by using the Pebbling rule. (See Peterson, 1980, for more on net reachability.) The important thing is that the state space constructed from a Plan Net need not be loop free. Using these nets, it is possible to model iterative behaviour in a natural way.

A planning system called Selah has been implemented which uses the Plan Net representation. Selah is currently able to solve "Blocks World" problems, and work is underway to extend its construction algorithms to allow it to create iterative plans.

5. Summary

This paper has defined the Plan Net using Sacerdoti's Procedural Net as a starting point. Through the introduction of a simple operational semantics, the Procedural Net was shown to be incapable of describing iterative behaviour. It was argued that the Plan Net can describe such behaviour. The implementation of a planner able to construct iterative plans is underway, and results from it will be reported.

Acknowledgements

Thanks are given to the Edinburgh University AI Planning Group, and to Dave Wilkins for providing useful comment on an earlier version of this paper. I am indebted to Karl Kempf and Barry Fox of the University of Missouri for introducing me to Pebbling. The supervision of Austin Tate has been invaluable.

References

Brauer, W. (ed.). 1979. Springer-Verlag LNCS series. Net theory and applications. Proceedings of the Advanced Course on General Net Theory of Processes and Systems, Hamburg.

Drummond, M. 1985. Ph.D. dissertation, University of Edinburgh. (To appear.)

McDermott, D. 1983. Generalizing problem reduction: a logical analysis. Proceedings of IJCAI-83. pp. 302-308.

Peterson, J.L. 1980. Petri Net theory and the modeling of systems. Prentice-Hall.

Pippenger, N. 1980. Pebbling. RC 8258 (#35937), IBM TJ Watson Research Center, Yorktown Heights, NY.

Rosenschein, S. 1984. Invited lecture at AAAI-84, In Austin, TX: "A perspective on planning".

Sacerdoti, E.D. 1975. A structure for plans and behaviour. SRI Technical Note #109.

Tate, A. 1976. Project planning using a hierarchic non-linear planner. University of Edinburgh, Department of Artificial Intelligence Research Report #25.

Vere, S.A. 1981. Planning in time: windows and durations for activities and goals. Jet Propulsion Laboratory, Information Systems Research section, research report.

Wilkins, D.E. 1983. Representation in a domain independent planner. Proceedings of IJCAI-83. pp. 733-740.

THE USE OF MULTIPLE PROBLEM DECOMPOSITIONS
IN TIME CONSTRAINED PLANNING TASKS[*]

Stephen F. Smith

The Robotics Institute
Carnegie-Mellon University
Pittsburgh, PA 15213 USA

Peng Si Ow

Grad. School of Ind. Admin.
Carnegie-Mellon University
Pittsburgh, PA 15213 USA

ABSTRACT

Problems requiring the synthesis of a collection of plans accomplishing distinct (but possibly related) goals has received increasing attention within AI. Such problems are typically formulated as multi-agent planning problems, emphasizing a problem decomposition wherein individual agents assume responsibility for the generation of individual plans while taking into account the goals and beliefs of other agents in the system. One consequence of such a problem decomposition is a simplified view of resource allocation that assumes avoidance of conflicts to be the sole concern. The validity of this assumption comes into question in time constrained problem domains requiring the allocation of multiple, shared resources. In job shop scheduling, for example, where sequences of manufacturing operations must be determined and scheduled for multiple orders, it is necessary to consider much more than availability to efficiently allocate resources over time. We argue that in such domains, an ability to reason from both resource-based and agent-based perspectives is essential to appropriate consideration of all domain constraints.

I MULTI-AGENT PLANNING AND RESOURCE ALLOCATION

Problems requiring the synthesis of a collection of plans accomplishing distinct (but possibly related) goals has received increasing attention within AI. Systems that address this problem have been called multi-agent planning systems [5], so termed because of the emphasis on a system of loosely-coupled, cooperative planning agents, each responsible for the generation of a single plan but cognizant of, and taking into account, the goals and beliefs of other agents in the system. Work in this area has focused primarily on the issue of goal protection, i.e. the planning of activities to achieve desired goals despite the dynamic nature of the surrounding environment. The issue of allocating resources to such activities has typically been given secondary importance, the assumption being that the avoidance of resource conflicts is the sole concern. The validity of this assumption comes into question in time constrained domains requiring the allocation of multiple, shared resources. In job shop scheduling, for example, where sequences of operations must be determined and scheduled for multiple orders, resource (e.g. machine) assignments to support these operations are influenced by much more than the mere availability of the resource during the time period in question. Other constraints, such as capacity limitations, sequencing preferences, and order splitting preferences, must also be considered. Efficient allocation of resources under such constraints is difficult within the problem decomposition ascribed to multi-agent planning systems above, given the local and incomplete view of resources held by each individual agent. Our experience with the ISIS job shop scheduling system [4], which adopts

such a problem decomposition, confirms this claim. What is needed to directly exploit these types of constraints is an ability to reason from a resource based perspective, suggesting the use of multiple problem decompositions. This paper describes an initial approach to providing such a reasoning capability.

The remainder of the paper is organized as follows. In Section II we briefly review the approach taken by ISIS in reasoning with the large and conflicting set of constraints encountered in the job shop scheduling domain. This is followed in Section III by a closer examination of the limitations of decomposing the problem solely from a order (or agent) based perspective, and issues surrounding the integration of a resource based reasoning capability are explored. An initial system architecture possessing an ability to reason from both perspectives is presented. Finally, in Section IV, some research directions are identified.

II CONSTRAINT-DIRECTED REASONING IN ISIS

The scheduling domain of ISIS is realistically complex, requiring the consideration of such diverse and conflicting factors as due date requirements, cost restrictions, production levels, machine capabilities, alternative production processes, order characteristics, resource characteristics and resource availability. To address this complexity, the ISIS design advocates two key ideas:

- an explicit formalization of the various scheduling influences as constraints in the system's knowledge base, and

- the formulation of schedule construction as a *constraint-directed* heuristic search.

The first point above presumes a fairly broad view of constraints, and it is important to note that the ISIS constraint representation encompasses scheduling objectives, goals, and preferences as well as the range of necessary conditions that delineate the space of admissible schedules. Constraints of the former variety provide a basis for optimization during the evaluation of alternative solutions, by assigning utilities indicative of the degree to which they have been satisfied. The representation also captures other knowledge necessary to effectively reason with the constraints, including constraint importance, constraint relevance, and constraint interdependencies.

The generation of a shop schedule is accomplished in an incremental fashion. For each order to be scheduled, the system proceeds through multiple levels of analysis, principal of which is the heuristic search procedure employed to make detailed selections of operations, resources, and time intervals for production of the order. Working from a set of allowable routings for the order (i.e. a directed graph of operations capturing operation precedence constraints, alternative manufacturing processes and resource substitutability), the search

---

[*]This research was supported in part by the Air Force Office of Scientific Research under contract F49620-82-K-0017, Westinghouse Electric Corporation, and the Robotics Institute.

proceeds either forward from the order's requested start date or backward from the requested ship date. The search space is composed of states that represent alternative partial schedules, and the application of the search operators serves to generate new states that further specify the partial schedules under development (e.g. add another operation to a partial schedule for the order, bind a particular machine to an operation, allocate a particular time interval for the order on a particular machine). Using a beam search, only the best n search states are extended at each iteration of the search, and, as indicated above, the quality of a given state is estimated on the basis of how well it satisfies the objectives, goals, and preferences that are relevant to the scheduling decisions it embodies. The outcome of this search is a particular routing for the order along with an assignment of time bounds to the resources required to produce it. Once refined into the order's final schedule, these commitments serve to additionally constrain any subsequent scheduling that must be performed. [**]

III   REASONING FROM MULTIPLE PERSPECTIVES

The ISIS heuristic search paradigm outlined above attempts to provide a framework for incorporating the full range of constraints that typically influence human scheduler's decisions in the automatic construction of job shop schedules. Unfortunately, its commitment to a particular decomposition of the scheduling problem places undue emphasis on the exploitation of a certain class of constraints to the effective exclusion of others. The "focus on one order at a time" approach employed, while useful in reducing the overall complexity of the problem, does not provide an adequate basis for attending to *inter-order constraints*, i.e. constraints that influence the allocation of resources over a number of orders. One example of how this weakness manifests itself is in the consideration of order sequencing preferences, which arise due to machine setup costs[***]. These preferences relate to the total set of orders requiring a given resource in the shop. Yet, within the ISIS framework, they can be considered only in the context of the partially constructed shop schedule that exists at the time each order is selected for scheduling. As such, the extent of their influence is somewhat coincidental.

We next address the problem of how to cope with these inter-order constraints while preserving the ability to adequately exploit intra-order constraints. Specifically, we explore the use of a resource-based decomposition in conjunction with an order-based decomposition to provide this added ability.

A.   Partitioning the Problem Solving Effort

The primary source of difficulty in constructing good job shop schedules stems from the conflicting nature of the domain's constraints. Constraints are said to be in conflict when a scheduling decision made with respect to satisfying any one affects the extent to which the others may be satisfied. The optimal resolution of a given conflict necessarily requires a problem decomposition in which all constraints involved in the conflict are grouped within the same subproblem. The order-based decomposition utilized by ISIS groups together the constraints surrounding a particular order and, consequently, provides an

opportunity for effectively resolving order-centered conflicts (e.g. conflicts involving precedence constraints). A resource-based problem decomposition, in contrast, produces a grouping of constraints that promotes the resolution of a different set of conflicts. Here the strategy becomes one of scheduling on a resource by resource basis, and the grouping of constraints contained within a given subproblem includes a cross-section of the constraints associated with a number of orders. Conflicts brought to the foreground under this decomposition center around the resource allocation decisions that must be made at a particular resource (e.g. conflicts involving various setup preferences). It is obvious that there are many conflicts that cannot be effectively isolated within either decomposition strategy, and, consequently, conflicts that cannot be optimally resolved from either problem solving perspective. Nonetheless, it is felt that a broadening of the range of constraints that can be meaningfully addressed through the use of multiple perspectives will lead to a more equitable consideration of the domain's constraints.

Given the decision to employ multiple problem decompositions, the task becomes one of how to best partition the problem solving effort between distinct perspectives so as to maximize the number of conflicts that can be directly addressed. Since the formation of specific subproblems (e.g. schedule operations on the milling machine from a resource-based perspective, and schedule the other operations on an order by order basis) will determine which conflicts can be directly resolved, a partitioning that associates essential resource-based conflicts with the resource-based reasoning component and, likewise, essential order-based conflicts with the order-based reasoning component, is highly desirable. Fortunately, the majority of resource-based conflicts can be identified through the detection of *bottleneck* resources, so called because they are scarce resources of the shop. Accordingly, a division of effort in which the resource-based reasoning component is employed to make resource allocation decisions at the bottleneck resources and non-bottleneck resources are scheduled from an order-based perspective is seen as most appropriate.

Despite an ability to derive a fairly useful problem decomposition, interactions amongst subproblems remain an important concern. Resource allocation decisions made with respect to a particular bottleneck, for example, might quite likely limit the extent to which we can effectively resolve conflicts (or satisfy constraints) in subsequent order-based subproblems. It is felt that the harmful effects of these interactions can be minimized somewhat by a judicious ordering the subproblems identified. Specifically, the relative importance of satisfying various constraints is seen as a useful criterion for coordinating the overall effort.

B.   A Specific System Architecture

To gain a better understanding of these issues, a specific system architecture possessing both resource-based and order-based reasoning components has been implemented. Adopting the problem decomposition strategy discussed in Section I.A (i.e. that resource-based reasoning is most critical with respect to bottleneck resources), a simple scheme for coordinating the overall effort has been imposed. Specifically, the system first employs its resource-based reasoning component to establish resource reservations at the bottleneck resources. These resource allocation decisions, which are guaranteed to be feasible, then serve as "islands of certainty" [1] for subsequent exploitation by the order-based reasoning component in developing the remainder of the schedule. The resource based reasoning strategy currently employed is based on a particular OR (Operations Research) heuristic developed in [6]. The order-based reasoning component is a derivative of the strategy employed by ISIS that has been generalized to operate on arbitrary portions of the set of routings associated with a

---

[**] The above description is necessarily brief and omits several important issues that are not directly relevant to the discussion below. The reader is referred to [2, 3, 4, 7] for more detailed accounts of this work.

[***] It is sometimes necessary to prepare or "set up" a machine before an operation can be performed on it. This is typically caused by a change in the type of operation to be performed on the machine and the amount of machine time consumed for setups is dependent on the type of change. A proper sequencing of orders on a machine can greatly increase its throughput.

particular order.

Testing of the system is currently proceeding, and preliminary results using simulated plant data[****] appear promising. Moreover, the reconfiguration of the ISIS scheduling system to treat previously imposed resource reservations as fixed points or islands from which to expand the search has also provided an opportunity to employ the user as the resource-based reasoning component of the system. In experiments where we have manually scheduled bottleneck resources before invoking the order-based reasoning component, the benefits of providing an ability to reason directly about the critical resource allocation decisions that have to be made can be immediately seen, and give considerable credence to the approach we have adopted.

IV DISCUSSION

In this paper we have pointed up the inadequacy of the problem decomposition typically embodied by multi-agent planning systems for certain classes of problems involving the synthesis of multiple plans. In particular, we argue that problems requiring the efficient allocation of a collection of shared resources over time cannot be effectively addressed by relying solely on the incomplete and local knowledge possessed by individual agents attending to the construction of individual plans. The specific focus of our work, the generation of schedules to govern production in a job shop, exemplifies this type of problem wherein efficient allocation of resources requires direct consideration of inter-order constraints, and, hence, an ability to reason globally from a resource-based perspective. Recognizing this, we have proposed a problem solving framework that employs both resource-based and order-based decompositions of the scheduling problem. We have suggested that the division of effort between these distinct perspectives can be usefully guided by an attempt the maximize the range of constraint conflicts that can be meaningfully resolved, and that the harmful effects of the interactions amongst the resulting subproblems can be minimized by an appropriate prioritization of the domain's constraints. A initial system architecture was presented to demonstrate the feasibility of this approach.

The work reported here has only begun to address the larger issues associated with the use of multiple problem decompositions in balancing a large set of conflicting objectives. We have made specific assumptions about the relative importance of satisfying various constraints which have led to a static partitioning of the problem solving effort (i.e. first schedule bottlenecks from a resource based perspective and then schedule non-bottlenecks using an order-based decomposition). While this, in general, might constitute a reasonable guideline for prioritizing the domain's constraints, there are obviously situations in which important constraints will not be appropriately attended to. The improvement of matters requires a more dynamic interplay between the reasoning strategies associated with distinct problem solving perspectives in which decisions made while reasoning from a particular perspective can be questioned and undone in light of the constraints that become relevant as different perspectives are employed. This is an issue that we are currently pursuing.

A second important issue concerns the level of sophistication of the resource-based reasoning strategy. In adopting an OR heuristic as the sole basis for decision making, we have limited the system's attention to the constraint knowledge that is implicitly captured by the heuristic. While the specific heuristic employed does, in fact, attend to several

important inter-order constraints, it nonetheless operates with a restrictive model of the scheduling environment. Ultimately, the reasoning strategy must be capable of exploiting any constraint found to be relevant to the resource allocation decisions under consideration. This implies a strategy that reasons with an explicit characterization of constraint knowledge, analogous to the heuristic strategy currently employed by the system when reasoning from an order-based perspective. The development of such a strategy is also currently under investigation.

ACKNOWLEDGEMENTS

The ideas presented in this paper have benefited greatly from many discussions with Mark Fox.

REFERENCES

[1]   Erman, L.D., F. Hayes-Roth, V.R. Lesser and D.R. Reddy "The HEARSAY-II Speech Understanding System: Integrating Knowledge to Resolve Uncertainty" Computing Surveys 12:2 (June 1980).

[2]   Fox, M.S., B.P. Allen and G.A. Strohm "Jobshop Scheduling: An Investigation in Constraint-Directed Reasoning" In Proc. of the 2nd National Conference on Artificial Intelligence AAAI. August, 1982, pp. 155-158.

[3]   Fox, M.S. Constraint-Directed Search: A Case Study of Job Shop Scheduling Ph.D. Th., Carnegie-Mellon University, 1983.

[4]   Fox, M.S. and S.F. Smith "ISIS: A knowledge-Based System for Factory Scheduling" Expert Systems 1:1 (July 1984) pp. 25-49.

[5]   Konolidge, K., and N.J. Nilsson "Multi-Agent Planning Systems" In Proceedings 1st Conference of the AAAI August, 1980.

[6]   Ow, P.S. Heuristic Knowledge and Search for Scheduling Ph.D Th., Graduate School of Industrial Administration, Carnegie-Mellon University, 1984.

[7]   Smith, S.F. "Exploiting Temporal Knowledge to Organize Constraints" Technical Report CMU-RI-TR-83-12, Robotics Institute, Carnegie-Mellon University, July 1983.

[****]The specific job shop model employed is based on the Westinghouse Turbine Components Plant located in Winston-Salem, North Carolina. The reader is referred to [4] for a discussion of the characteristics and complexities of this specific scheduling environment.

SPLICING PLANS TO ACHIEVE MISORDERED GOALS*

Steven A. Vere
Information Systems Division
Jet Propulsion Laboratory
Pasadena, California 91109

ABSTRACT

Most parallel planners are sensitive to the order in which goals and activity preconditions are specified. A "wrong" ordering can easily cause a solution to be missed. Permuting goals and preconditions on failure in hopes of finding a soluble order is in general computationally unacceptable. Plan splicing is a solution to this problem. Splicing is a violent conflict resolution procedure which involves the cutting of assertion dependencies, recursive demotion or excision of selected activities around the cut, and reinsertion of deachieved goals back into the middle of the planner's goal stack so that they can be replanned later to mend the plan around the splice. In a temporal planner, after an excision it is further necessary to relieve the "temporal stress" induced on surviving activities by the activities which were excised. This is an important capability for two reasons: first, because the order of achievement can of course not always be known in advance, and secondly because it is desirable to be able to present goals in priority order.

I INTRODUCTION

AI planners are beginning to reach the maturity required for real world applications. DEVISER I [Vere, 1983] has been successfully applied to generating command sequences for the Voyager spacecraft. DEVISER I is on the evolutionary path of NOAH [Sacerdoti, 1977] and NONLIN [Tate, 1977]. NOAH was the first planner to deal with parallel activities. NONLIN is an improved parallel planner which is able to recover from bad decisions and which implements a more sophisticated treatment of goal protection. A recent version with a consumable resource management capability [Tate and Whiter, 1984] has been demonstrated on a naval replenishment problem. DEVISER I extended the mechanisms of the 1977 NONLIN to permit planning in time, with arbitrary time constraints on activities, preconditions, and goals. It also

----

*This paper presents the results of one phase of research carried out at the Jet Propulsion Laboratory, California Institute of Technology, and sponsored by the National Aeronautics and Space Administration under contract No. NAS-918.

handles events, scheduled events, and inferences in a uniform manner. Temporal planning has also attracted the attention of a number of other researchers within the last few years [Allen and Koomen, 1983; Cheeseman, 1983; Dean, 1984; McDermott, 1982]. However, time is largely orthogonal to the issue of goal order and splicing, which is the focus of this paper. SIPE [Wilkins, 1984] is another contemporary planner derived from NOAH which has special resource handling features. It has been applied to planning activities on an aircraft carrier.

A common difficulty experienced with most planners is the phenomenon I will call goal protection deadlock, in which the achievement and subsequent protection of an earlier goal can block the achievement of a later goal [Dreussi, 1982, pg. 59]. For example, suppose a robot is in front of a closed door leading into a room. It's goals are to be inside the room with the door closed. Goal protection deadlock is experienced if it first tries to achieve (DOOR CLOSED) (with a null action), and then attempts to achieve (IN ROBOT ROOM). To enter, it must plan to open the door, but this would violate the first goal, (DOOR CLOSED), which is achieved by the start state and is now protected. The problem is that the goals have been attempted in the "wrong" order. Previous parallel planners have avoided this problem by requiring goals to be presented to the planner in an order in which they can be achieved. This problem applies both to the original conjunctive goal set as well as to the ordering of the preconditions of an activity, which become subgoals during plan synthesis. In complex domains it may be impossible to know the correct order in which to attempt goals, and it is computationally unacceptable to try every possible permutation of goals and preconditions.

There are reasons other than ignorance for wanting a planner to be insensitive to goal ordering. A greedy person may try to give a planner many more goals than are logically achievable, due to time or resource limitations. If goal deadlock can be avoided, it then becomes attractive to order the goals by decreasing priority. The most important goals can be planned first and allowed first claim to the finite resources. If possible, activities to achieve goals lower on the list are fitted into the plan later. Otherwise the lower priority goal is discarded. In this way the planner is able to generate a partial solution for insoluble goal sets instead of just just giving up.

It is for these two reasons, to avoid goal deadlock and to allow goal prioritization and discard, that I have investigated and implemented splicing in a new version of my planner designated DEVISER III.

For tutorial purposes, the plan splicing process will be illustrated in this paper on blocksworld and abstract examples. However, splicing has been applied in practice on large plans constructed with a very detailed knowledge base for the Voyager spacecraft consisting of 1800 lines and describing about 140 different actions, inferences, and events.

II PLAN SPLICING

Plan splicing may be regarded as a new variety of conflict resolution in a parallel planner. Figure 1 illustrates a prototypical conflict situation. During parallel plan synthesis, a conflict is said to occur when two parallel nodes, such as Node A and Node B, assert contradictory literals, represented by P and ~P. (You are cautioned not to confuse this usage of "conflict" with the completely unrelated notion of "conflict sets" in forward chaining production rule systems such as OPS5). The dashed lines show that Node C depends on the assertion P from Node A, and Node D depends on the assertion ~P of Node B. These will be called <u>assertion dependencies</u>. They indicate that the truth of the assertion must be protected in the region of the plan between the two nodes. Tate calls these dependency relationships the goal structure. Of course there may be many nodes like Node C depending on P in Node A and many nodes like Node D.

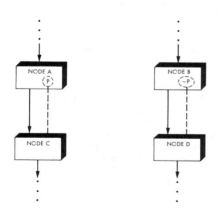

Figure 1. A Conflict Situation in a Plan

There are two possible conflict resolutions, as performed in NONLIN (and DEVISER I): either D must be ordered before A, or C must be ordered before B, so that the assertion dependencies are respected and preserved. This is illustrated in Figures 2a and 2b. Because assertion dependencies are never violated, neither of these two conflict resolutions can overcome the problem of goal protection deadlock.

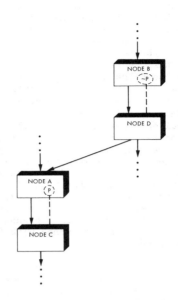

Figure 2a. One Non-Violent Conflict Resolution

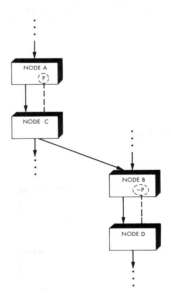

Figure 2b. The Other Non-Violent Conflict Resolution

Plan splicing is a violent form of conflict resolution which is only tried as a last resort, after nonviolent conflict resolution has failed. There are two possible splicings for every

conflict, just as there are two possible ordering
resolutions. Figures 3a and 3b illustrate these
two alternatives. Because of symmetry, only Figure
3a will be discussed. There the assertion
dependency between A and C has been cut, and B has
been ordered between A and C. Simultaneously, C has
been "demoted." Node demotion is a generic term
for an involved process whose details depend on
whether C is a phantom or an activity. (A phantom
node is a null action which signifies that a
precondition has "already" been achieved above in
the plan; an activity node is everything else--an
action, an inference, or a (forward chaining)
event).   Thus splicing literally cuts the Gordian
knot in a goal deadlock situation. The (recursive)
demotion process is responsible for ensuring that
the plan will mend properly around the splice.   At
one extreme, demotion may involve simply changing a
phantom node back to a goal.   At the other extreme,
demotion may trigger the erasure of large sections
of the plan around and below the splice, with many
goals being inserted at a variety of positions
within the goal stack for later replanning.   Most
of this paper is in fact concerned with the details
of the demotion process.

Loosely speaking, one or more goals below the
splice were achieved too early. Demotion sends
these back into the goal stack in exactly the
position which allows interfering later goals a
chance. A solution is then obtained as though the
goals had originally been attempted in the right
order.   In effect, interfering goals are
dynamically reordered during plan synthesis, and
this is accomplished without erasing any more of
the existing plan than is logically necessary.

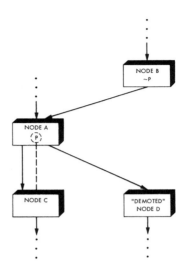

Figure 3b.   The Other Possible Splice

The advantage of splicing is that it renders the
planner insensitive to goal and subgoal ordering.
However, a certain penalty is incurred. The size of
the planner's search tree is enlarged, since there
are now four possible resolutions to every conflict
situation rather than two.   In DEVISER this is
mitigated by discarding the two splicing
alternatives if one of the two nonviolent
resolutions is successful.   Otherwise, in
backtracking the two splicing alternatives can lead
into irrelevant sections of the search tree and
waste time.

As already mentioned, the details of demotion
depend on whether the demoted node is a phantom or
an activity. These two cases will now be
investigated in turn.

III DEMOTING A PHANTOM NODE

Demotion of a phantom node is potentially the
simplest case. If the assertion of the phantom is
P, we simply convert the node back to a goal, and
enter P at the "appropriate place" in the planner's
goal stack. The appropriate place is generally not
the top of the goal stack, but somewhere in the
middle.   Details of the procedure for entering a
goal back in the goal stack will be presented
later, in Section V.

This simple picture is complicated if a
substitution was applied at the time the phantom
node was created. For example, suppose the goal
assertion was (ON .x C). In creating the phantom
node, suppose that the substitution {B/.x} was
applied to cause the goal assertion to match (ON B
C) asserted by an earlier action. This means that
to demote the phantom we must restore the goal
assertion to its original uninstantiated form, (ON
.x C).

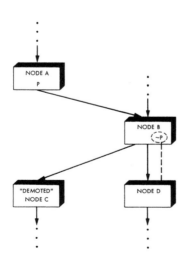

Figure 3a.   One Conflict Resolution by Splicing

A further, more serious complication is encountered if the substitution was in fact also applied to other literals in the plan. If we cannot somehow restore these literals to their uninstantiated state, existing parts of the plan may remain unnecessarily constrained, preventing us from finding a solution plan when in fact one exists. However, in DEVISER it is effectively impossible to deinstantiate an arbitrary literal. Suppose the instantiated literal is (P A A) and the substitution was {A/.x}. Restoring the literal to (P .x .x) can be incorrect if the original literal was actually (P A .x). The alternative of "remembering" precisely which terms were replaced for each substitution application was judged to be unacceptable. The approach I have adopted is to demote all plan nodes having a literal instantiated by the substitution. This only requires "remembering", for each phantom, the list of nodes affected by the substitution (if any) applied when that phantom is created. Thus the demotion of one phantom may in turn call for the demotion of several additional "affected nodes", i.e., those affected by that phantom's substitution. If an affected node is also a phantom it is in turn treated in the manner just described. If the affected node is an activity, it is demoted as described in the next section.

IV DEMOTING AN ACTIVITY NODE

As seen above, splicing may require the demotion of an activity node N back to a goal, either because N is Node C in Figure 3a, or because N was affected by the substitution of a demoted phantom. This in turn calls for the excision (erasure) of selected nodes above N in the plan. The nodes which must be excised are those which exist in the plan exclusively to satisfy preconditions of N. These will be called the <u>activity pyramid</u> above N.

Consider the blocksworld plan in Figure 4. Assertion dependencies are not shown to avoid cluttering the diagram. This plan was generated to achieve the goals (ONTABLE C) (ON B C), given the initial state (CLEAR C) (ON C A) (ONTABLE A) (CLEAR B) (ONTABLE B). N4 achieves the first goal; N5 achieves the second. Suppose that in the course of planning to achieve other additional goals (not shown), we wish to do a splice and demote N5. Should we excise all the nodes above N5 in the plan? No. Nodes N6, N7, and N8 exist to enable the putdown action of N4 , and should be retained. We should excise only nodes N9, N10, N11, and N12. These were backchained into the plan to enable the stack action of N5. Nodes N9, N10, N11, and N12 constitute the activity pyramid above node N5, because they form an inverted pyramid of nodes backchained above N5, with N5 at the apex. Similarly, N6, N7, and N8 form the activity pyramid above N4. Consequently, to demote N5 we must first excise N9, N10, N11, and N12, and then convert N5 back to a goal and insert it into the goal stack.

One key aspect of activity demotion is then the excision of all nodes in the activity pyramid above

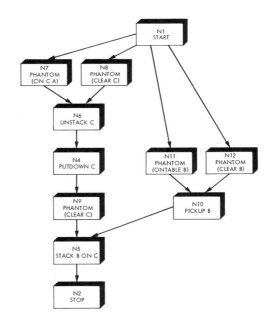

Figure 4. A Blocksworld Plan Illustrating Activity Pyramids

the demoted node. Excision of a set of nodes involves erasure of the nodes from the plan by modification of the successor and predecessor lists of nodes which will remain, removal of the assertions of the excised nodes from the assertion database, and similar bookkeeping activities. Note that this erasure must be reversible, so that if the planner must backtrack, these excised nodes are "unerased" and restored to the plan. In addition, all phantom nodes outside the pyramid which depend on an assertion of an excised node must be demoted, because that assertion is going to disappear.

Having excised the activity pyramid above an activity node, that node is converted back to a goal. Side effect assertions of the activity are deleted, and any nodes below it which depend on one of these side effect assertions must be demoted too. The original goal assertion must be restored as the single assertion of the goal node, and the node must be inserted back into the goal stack as in the case of phantom demotion. Also, as in phantom demotion, other nodes affected by substitutions applied to the activity node or its pyramid must be demoted too.

One minor problem with splicing is that the planner may occasionally go into a search loop consisting of demotion, replanning, demotion, replanning, etc. In my implementation this was cured by keeping a record of demoted nodes and and the activity which caused the demotion. If the demotion subroutine is about to try to demote a node a second time for the same reason, this information causes the demotion to fail, breaking the loop and forcing the planner to backtrack.

Finally, in a temporal planner it is necessary to relieve the temporal stress induced on remaining nodes by those which have been excised. The situation is like a crowded elevator: when some people get off, those that remain can space themselves out more comfortably. In the same way, in a temporally crowded plan the start time windows of many nodes are compressed by the durations of adjacent activities. When some nodes are excised, the remaining nodes may be able to expand their start time windows. One possible approach would be to simply open the windows of all remaining nodes to the maximum interval, and then recompute all the start times based on the ordering and consecutivity constraints. However, this is unacceptable because excisions will be done frequently, and in practice only a small percentage of the nodes in a plan will be under stress from a set of excised nodes. A much more efficient technique is to follow <u>stress chains</u> from nodes on the boundary of the excised pyramid. Two sequential nodes, NA and NB, in a plan are <u>temporally</u> <u>stressed</u> if:

1. they are constrained to be consecutive (cf. [Vere, 1983]), or

2. the earliest finish time of NA equals the earliest start time of NB, or

3. the latest finish time of NA equals the latest start time of NA.

For cases 2 and 3 above it seems natural to say that their windows touch. Figure 5 illustrates a stress chain for an abstract plan. Suppose that node 1 is an activity node to be demoted. An activity pyramid with 1 at its apex is indicated by the dashed lines. Thus nodes 2, 3, 4, 5, and 6 are going to be excised. Nodes 1, 3, 4, 5, and 6 are on the boundary of the pyramid, i.e., they are adjacent to nodes not in the pyramid. The bold lines connect temporally stressed nodes leading away from the pyramid and beginning at boundary nodes. Note that a zig-zag pattern is possible, since nodes 15, 9, 8, 7, and 6 may be a chain of nodes with touching windows. The chain can continue in another direction since nodes 9 and 20, and 22 and 21 are assumed to be consecutive. The "C" label on the arcs indicates a consecutivity constraint. The subgraph connected by the bold lines is the stress chain in this diagram. It is only necessary to recompute start time windows for nodes in this stress chain. The windows of all other nodes outside the pyramid, such as 10, are not affected by the excision of the pyramid nodes. Of course it is possible for a stress chain to exist below the pyramid as well as above it, as in this example.

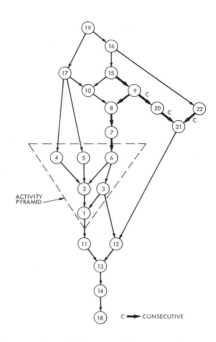

Figure 5. A Temporal Stress Chain

V INSERTING A DEACHIEVED GOAL INTO THE GOAL STACK

We have seen that demotion of both phantoms and activities leads to the creation (or, more accurately, the recreation) of one or more goals, which must then be inserted into the goal stack of the planner. How should such a goal be positioned relative to the existing goals in the stack? The answer is found in an analysis of why a node is demoted: it is demoted to "give another goal a chance." Stated differently, the planner decides that, in effect, the order of two goals must be reversed. Referring back to Figure 3a, Node C was demoted because of Node B. From the diagram we can infer that the goal of C was attempted first and then later the goal of B. If we are compelled to attempt a splice, it means that the goal of B should be "completely achieved" first before going back to work on the goal of C. By completely achieved I mean that all backward chaining above B must be completed before going back to work on C. This can be ensured if the goal of C is inserted into the goal stack just below the lowest goal node in the activity pyramid above B.

Figure 6 illustrates with an example. It shows Figure 3a redrawn with an activity pyramid above B, as well as the associated goal stack. GC is the goal node created by demoting C. G1 and G2 are goal nodes in the pyramid above B. (Here the pyramid serves for analysis, and is not excised). G1 happens to be the lowest in the stack. If we insert GC just below G1 in the stack, then the planner will have completed the section of the plan above Node B before it starts to work on GC.

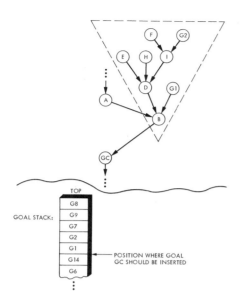

Figure 6. Goal Insertion During Demotion

[4] Dreussi, J. F. *The Detection and Correction of Errors in Problem-solving Systems.* Ph.D. dissertation, Univ. of Texas at Austin, 1982.

[5] McDermott, D. A. "A Temporal Logic for Reasoning About Processes and Plans." *Cognitive Science*, Vol. 6, 1982, 101-155.

[6] Sacerdoti, E. D. *A Structure for Plans and Behavior.* Elsevier North-Holland, 1977.

[7] Tate, A. "Generating Project Networks" In *Proc. IJCAI-77*, 888-893.

[8] Tate, A. and A. M. Whiter, "Planning with Multiple Resource Constraints and an Application to a Naval Planning Problem" In *Proc. 1st. Conf. on AI Applications*, 1984, 410-415.

[9] Vere, S. A. "Planning in Time: Windows and Durations for Activities and Goals." *IEEE trans. Pattern Analysis and Machine Intelligence*, Vol. PAMI-5, No. 3, May 1983, 246-267.

[10] Wilkins, D. E. "Domain-independent Planning: Representation and Plan Generation." *Artificial Intelligence*, April 1984, 269-301.

VI SUMMARY

Planning is inherently sensitive to the order in which goals are accomplished, with failure the possible result of attempting goals in the wrong order. Splicing is a way, in effect, to reorder goals "on the fly" as planning proceeds. It is attempted only when normal conflict resolution fails. A portion of the plan which accomplishes an earlier goal is erased, and the earlier goal is put back into the planner's goal stack in a position which allows the later goal to be accomplished without interference. Through the stack mechanism, the planner's attention later returns to achievement of the demoted goal. The result is that actions to achieve the later goal are spliced into the middle of the plan, and some activities around the splice are replanned. This permits a solution to be found in goal protection deadlock situations where the planner would otherwise fail.

REFERENCES

[1] Allen, J. F. and J. A. Koomen, "Planning Using a Temporal World Model" In *Proc. IJCAI-83*, 741-747.

[2] Cheeseman, P. "A Representation of Time for Planning," Tech. Note 278, AI Center, SRI International, Menlo Park, California, Feb. 1983.

[3] Dean, T. "Planning and Temporal Reasoning under Uncertainty" In *Proc. IEEE Workshop on Principles of Knowledge-Based Systems*, Denver, Colorado, 1984.

NONLINEAR PLANNING: A RIGOROUS RECONSTRUCTION

David Chapman

MIT Artificial Intelligence Laboratory
545 Technology Square Room 709
Cambridge, MA 02139
Net: ZVONA@MIT-MC.ARPA

The problem of achieving several goals simultaneously has been central to domain-independent planning research; the nonlinear constraint-posting approach has been most successful. Previous planners of this type [3, 4, 5, 6] have been complicated, heuristic, and ill-defined. I have combined and distilled the state of the art into a simple, precise, implemented algorithm (TWEAK) which I have proved correct and complete. The simplicity and rigor of this algorithm illuminate the workings of previous planners, the range of applicability of current planning technology, and suggest future directions for research. This paper presents the mathematical foundations for non-linear planning; due to space limitations, I have omitted proofs, some detail, and much discussion. These appear in [1].

This paper begins by presenting a series of necessarily dry and obvious definitions, leading up to that of a plan that solves a problem. I present a "truth criterion" which provides an efficient means of analyzing a plan to determine when a proposition will be true in the world as the plan is executed. The truth criterion also provides a way of making a plan achieve a goal, and this is the basis of the TWEAK algorithm. Finally I state a completeness/correctness theorem and present conclusions.

TWEAK is a constraint posting planner. Constraint posting is the definition of an object, a plan in this case, by successively specifying more and more partial descriptions it must fit. Alternatively, constraint posting can be viewed as a search strategy in which rather than generating and testing specific alternatives, chunks of the search space are progressively removed from consideration by constraints that rule them out, until finally every remaining alternative is satisfactory. The advantage of the constraint posting approach is that properties of the object being searched for do not have to be chosen until a reasoned decision can be made. This reduction of arbitrary choice often reduces the amount of backtracking necessary.

This report describes research done at the Artificial Intelligence Laboratory of the Massachusetts Institute of Technology. Support for the laboratory's artificial intelligence research has been provided in part by the Advanced Research Projects Agency of the Department of Defense under Office of Naval Research contract N00014-80-C-0505, in part by National Science Foundation grants MCS-7912179 and MCS-8117633, and in part by the IBM Corporation. The views and conclusions contained in this document are those of the author, and should not be interpreted as representing the policies, either expressed or implied, of the Department of Defense, of the National Science Foundation, or of the IBM Corporation.

As TWEAK works on a problem, it has at all times an incomplete plan, which is a partial specification of a plan that may solve the problem. This incomplete plan could be completed in many different ways, depending on what constraints are added to it; thus it represents a class of complete plans. The incomplete plan supplies partial knowledge of the complete plan that will eventually be chosen; ideally all possible completions of the current plan should solve the given problem. I will say "necessarily foo" if foo is true of all possible completions of the current plan, and "possibly foo" if foo is true of some completion of the current plan.

A complete plan is a total "time" order on a set of steps, which represent actions. The plan is executed by performing the actions corresponding to the steps in the order given. A step has a set of preconditions, which are things that must be true about the world for it to be possible to execute the action. A step also has postconditions, which are things that will be true about the world after the corresponding action has been executed. Pre- and postconditions are both expressed as propositions. Propositions can be positive or negative, and have a content, which is a tuple of elements. Elements can be variables or constants. Functions, propositional operators and quantification are not allowed.

Plans in TWEAK can be incomplete in two ways: the time order may be incompletely specified, using temporal constraints, and steps may be incompletely specified, using codesignation constraints. A temporal constraint is a requirement that one step be before another; thus a set of temporal constraints is simply a partial order on steps. A completion of a set of temporal constraints C is any total order O on the same set of steps such that sCt implies sOt.

Codesignation is an equivalence relation on variables and constants. In a complete plan, each variable that appears in a pre- or postcondition must be constrained codesignating with a specific constant. In execution, that constant will be substituted for the variable when the action is performed. Distinct constants may not codesignate. Two propositions codesignate if both are positive or both are negative and if their contents are of the same length and if corresponding elements in the contents codesignate.

TWEAK represents the state of the world as a set of propositions. This set changes as steps are executed. A plan has an initial situation, which is a set of propositions describing the world at the time that the plan is to be executed. Associated with each step in a plan is its input situation, which is the set of propositions that are true in the world just before it is executed, and its output situation, which is the set of propositions that are true in the world just after it is executed. In a complete plan, the input situation of each step is required to be the same set as the output situation of the previous step. The final situation of a plan has the same set of propositions in it as the output situation of the last step. The time order extends to situations: the initial and final situations are before and after every other situation respectively. The input situation of a step is before the step and after every other situation that is before the step; the output situation of a step is after the step and before any other situation that is after the step.

Say that a proposition is true in a situation if it codesignates with a proposition that is a member of the situation. Say that a step asserts a proposition in its output situation if the proposition codesignates with a postcondition of the step. Say that a proposition is asserted in the initial situation if it true in that situation. A proposition is denied in a situation if another proposition with codesignating content but opposite truth value is asserted there. It's illegal for a proposition to be both asserted and denied in a situation.

A step can be executed only if all its preconditions are in true in its input situation. In this case, the output situation is just the input situation minus any propositions denied the step, plus any propositions asserted by the step. This model of execution does not allow for indirect or implied effects of actions; any changes in the world must be explicitly mentioned as postconditions.

I will now sketch the derivation of a criterion for when a proposition is necessarily true in a situation. Of course a proposition is necessarily true in situation if it is necessarily asserted in it. Once a proposition has been asserted, it remains true until denied. Thus a proposition p is necessarily true in a situation if there is some previous situation in which it is necessarily true, and there is no possibly intervening step that possibly denies it: for if there is a step that is even possibly inbetween that even possibly denies p, there is a completion in which the step actually is inbetween and actually denies p. (A step possibly denies p by denying a proposition q which possibly codesignates with p). The converse of this criterion is not true; this plan illustrates an exception:

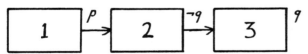

If p and q are possibly codesignating, this plan has two classes of completions: one in which p and q actually codesignate, in which case p is asserted by step 3; and one in which p and q are noncodesignating, so that p is asserted by step 1, and is never denied. In either case, p is true in the final situation, even though no step necessarily asserts p without an intervening step possibly denying it. The complete criterion is as follows:

Truth criterion: A proposition p is necessarily true in a situation s iff two conditions hold: there is a situation t necessarily equal or previous to s in which p is necessarily asserted; and for every step C possibly before s and every proposition q possibly codesignating with p which C possibly denies, there is a step W

necessarily between C and s which asserts r, a proposition such that r and p codesignate whenever p and q codesignate. The criterion for possible truth is exactly analogous, with all the modalities switched (read "necessary" for "possible" and vice versa).

This criterion can be computed in polynomial time, though it does exponentially much "work" by describing properties of the exponentially large set of completions of a plan. The remainder of TWEAK depends heavily on this theorem; its proof is surprisingly complex. It can be usefully viewed as a completeness/soundness theorem for a version of the situation calculus.

Now I will define problems and their solutions. A problem is an initial situation and a final situation, which are two sets of propositions. A plan for a problem is a plan every proposition of whose initial situation is true in the initial situation of the problem. A goal is a proposition which must be achieved (true) in a certain situation. The goals of a plan for a problem are defined to be the propositions in the final situation of the problem, which must be true in the final situation of the plan, and the preconditions of steps in the plan, which must be true in the corresponding input situations. A complete plan for a problem solves the problem if all its goals are achieved. Thus, a complete plan solves a problem if it can be executed in the initial situation of the problem and if the final situation of the problem is a correct partial description of the world after execution. The aim of TWEAK is to produce a plan that necessarily solves the problem it is given. This plan may be incomplete; in this case any of its completions may be chosen for execution.

TWEAK's contract is to produce a plan for a specific problem it is given. TWEAK has at all times an incomplete plan, initially null, which is an approximation to a plan that solves the problem. The top-level loop of the planner nondeterministically chooses a goal that is not already achieved and uses a procedure which I will now describe to make the plan achieve that goal.

The goal-achievement procedure is derived by interpreting the truth criterion as a nondeterministic procedure. Universal quantification over a set becomes iteration over that set; existential quantification a nondeterministic choice from a set; disjunction a simple nondeterministic choice; and conjunction several things that must all be done. Also, an existentially quantified situation can be satisfied by nondeterministically choosing either an existing situation in the plan or a situation belonging to a newly added step. The newly added step must represent an action that is possible to execute in the domain in which the problem is specified; the choice is among those that are allowed in the domain and that possibly assert the desired goal.

To make a situation be before another or to make two propositions codesignating or not codesignating, the procedure just adds constraints. These constraints may be incompatible with existing constraints: for example, you can't constrain s before t if you have already constrained t before s. The constraint maintenance mechanism signals failure in such cases, and the top-level control structure backtracks. Since the set of things of things possibly asserted in a situation can not be changed, to make a proposition necessarily asserted there, the procedure constrains codesignation of the given proposition with one of those asserted.

The following diagram defines the nondeterministic procedure:

Because the truth criterion is sufficient as well as necessary, this achievement procedure encompasses *all* the ways to make a plan achieve a goal. In this respect TWEAK can not be improved upon.

Step addition adds new preconditions to the plan that need to be achieved, and the added step may also deny, and so undo, previously achieved goals. Therefore, TWEAK tries to avoid step addition. This is not always successful. There are three possible outcomes to planning: success, in which a plan is found; failure, when the planner has exhaustively searched the space of sequences of plan modification operations, and every branch fails; and nontermination, when the plan grows larger and larger and more and more operations are applied to it, but it never converges to solve the problem.

The central theorem of this paper is the following:

Correctness/completeness theorem: If TWEAK, given a problem, terminates claiming a solution, the plan it produces does in fact solve the problem. If TWEAK returns signalling failure or does not halt, there is no solution to the problem.

The theorem follows easily from the truth criterion.

The rigor of TWEAK's formulation has several uses. Previous planning research becomes substantially clearer when analyzed with the tools built in constructing TWEAK. In [1] I present a detailed history of planning, showing that the classic planners are more similar than has previously been realized.

Another use of this rigor is that the range of applicability of state-of-the-art planning techniques becomes clear. The correctness of TWEAK and similar planners depends crucially on details of the representation of actions. Useful extensions to this representation, such as range restrictions for variables, non-atomic propositions, derived effects of actions, actions whose effects depend on the situation in which the are applied, and changes in the world due to agencies other than execution of the constructed plan, invalidate the truth criterion, and so the correctness of TWEAK. There seems to be no simple way to extend the criterion to accommodate these effects. The difficulty is just that of the McCarthy frame problem [2]; my thesis suggests an approach to its solution.

ACKNOWLEGEMENTS

This paper incorporates suggestions Phil Agre, Steve Bagley, Alan Bawden, Mike Brady, Gary Drescher, Margaret Fleck, Walter Hamscher, Scott Layson, David McAllester, Kent Pitman, Charles Rich, Mark Shirley, Reid Simmons, and Dan Weld.

REFERENCES

[1] Chapman, David, *Planning for Conjunctive Goals.* MIT Technical Report 802, May, 1985.

[2] McCarthy, John, and Hayes, Patrick, "Some Philosophical Problems from the Standpoint of AI." *Machine Intelligence 4*, B. Meltzer and D. Mitchie, eds. Edinburgh: Edinburgh University Press, 1969.

[3] Sacerdoti, Earl D., *A Structure for Plans and Behavior.* New York: Elsevier North Holland, 1977.

[4] Stefik, Mark Jeffrey, *Planning with Constraints.* Stanford Heuristic Programming Project Memo 80-2.

[5] Tate, Austin, "Project Planning Using a Hierarchic Non-linear Planner." Department of Artificial Intelligence Research Report No. 25, University of Edinburgh, Edinburgh, August 1976.

[6] Wilkins, David E., "Domain-Independent Planning: Representation and Plan Generation." *Artificial Intelligence* 22:3 (1984) pp. 269–301.

INCREASING COHERENCE
IN A DISTRIBUTED PROBLEM SOLVING NETWORK

Edmund H. Durfee, Victor R. Lesser, and Daniel D. Corkill

Department of Computer and Information Science
University of Massachusetts
Amherst, Massachusetts 01003

ABSTRACT

Globally coherent behavior is the holy grail of distributed problem solving network research. Obtaining coherent network activity without sacrificing node autonomy and network flexibility places severe demands on the local control component of each node. We introduce new mechanisms that allow a node to compute an abstracted, high-level description of its local state which it then uses to formulate multi-step plans. Not only do these mechanisms significantly improve local problem solving performance, but they also enable nodes to make dynamic refinements to their long-term network organization knowledge. The coordination decisions made by nodes are thus increasingly responsive to changes in network activity as problem solving progresses. We provide experimental results indicating that these new mechanisms improve the internal control decisions of a node, reduce the communication requirements of the network, and improve network coherence. We believe that these mechanisms would also be useful for control in centralized multi-level blackboard-based problem solving systems.

I. INTRODUCTION

Achieving global coherence in cooperative distributed problem solving networks (DPSNs) is a major problem [4,13]. In a DPSN, each node is an intelligent semi-autonomous problem solving agent that determines its own behavior based on its perception of network activities. Global coherence means that the activities of the nodes should appear to make sense given overall network goals. Nodes should avoid unnecessarily duplicating the work of others, sitting idle while others are swamped with work, or transmitting information that will not improve overall network performance. Because network coordination must be decentralized to improve reliability and responsiveness, the amount of global coherence in the network is dependent on the degree to which each node makes coherent decisions based on its local view of network problem solving activities.

This research was sponsored, in part, by the National Science Foundation under Grant MCS-8300239 and by the Defense Advanced Research Projects Agency (DOD), monitored by the Office of Naval Research under Contract NR049-041.

At any given time, a node will rank its pending tasks based on how it believes each will improve network problem solving. A decision by the node to execute the top ranked task is therefore more or less coherent depending on how highly ranked the task would have been if the node had a completely global view of network problem solving. Full global coherence requires that each node have a complete and accurate view of the past, present, and intended future activities of all other nodes. If this is done by globally predefining a coordinated multi-agent plan at network creation, the network will be inflexible to changing problem solving situations and network characteristics. Alternatively, having nodes broadcast all state changes and future intentions is infeasible due to bandwidth limitations and channel delays. Therefore, we have no practical means to insure full global coherence. The functionally accurate, cooperative approach to distributed problem solving develops a framework in which network goals can be achieved with only partial global coherence [13]. However, since partial coherence wastes resources and degrades performance, we have been developing mechanisms which increase coherence without significant additional communication costs.

Our previous work toward this end developed a decentralized approach to network coordination in which each node is guided by a high-level strategic plan for cooperation among the nodes in the network [3]. This strategic plan, represented as a network organizational structure, specifies in a general way the communication and control relationships among the nodes. The organizational structure increases the likelihood that nodes will be coherent in their behavior by predefining a limited range of options available to a node. Network flexibility is maintained by not limiting these options too tightly. Sophisticated local control plays a key part in this approach because decisions about which of these options to pursue must be based on short-term information about the current situation.

In this paper, we describe new mechanisms that allow a node to refine its perception of the role it currently plays in the organization. This refined view is achieved by providing each node with the ability to reason about its current state of problem solving and to make predictions about its future actions. To accomplish this, these new mechanisms allow a node to compute an abstracted, high-level description of its local state. The node uses this description to formulate high-level goals and to generate plans to achieve them. Since each plan incorporates a sequence of actions, the pursuit of a specific plan allows the node to make reliable predictions about its actions in the near future. These predictions enable the node to make medium-term, dynamic refinements to how it views its role in the network organization, and it may modify its local processing accordingly. Furthermore, if nodes occasionally exchange *meta-level* information about these refined views of the organizational roles they will be playing in the near future, each node will have a more global view of the network problem solving activity, and global coherence will increase.

We have implemented and empirically evaluated our ideas using the Distributed Vehicle Monitoring Testbed. The next section outlines the relevant aspects of the testbed, describes how our mechanisms were incorporated, and discusses experimental results indicating improvement in local problem solving ability. We then study how these mechanisms can be used to improve network coherence, and present results indicating their utility. Finally, we relate our work to other research in distributed problem solving and discuss the implications of the preliminary research we have outlined, along with the directions we will be pursuing in the future.

II.   INCREASING THE SOPHISTICATION OF A PROBLEM SOLVING NODE

The distributed vehicle monitoring testbed (DVMT) is a flexible and fully-instrumented research tool for the evaluation of distributed network designs and coordination policies [14]. The DVMT simulates a network of problem solving nodes attempting to identify, locate and track patterns of vehicles moving through a two-dimensional space using signals detected by acoustic sensors. Each problem solving node is an architecturally-complete Hearsay-II system with knowledge sources and levels of abstraction appropriate for this task. The basic Hearsay-II architecture has been extended to include more sophisticated local control [2], knowledge sources (KSs) for communicating hypotheses and goals among nodes, and data structures called *interest areas* that specify the organizational role of a node [3]. These interest area specifications are used by the local node control in deciding what problem-solving and communication knowledge sources should be instantiated and how these knowledge source instantiations (KSIs) should be rated for possible execution.

In this section, we introduce further modifications to this architecture by providing a node with the capability to generate and reason with a more complete view of its past, present, and future activities. Although nodes generally tend to methodically perform sequences of related actions, they are unable to represent and reason about such sequences. For example, given a highly rated hypothesis, a node typically executes a sequence of KSIs that drive up

low level data to extend the hypothesis. However, the entire sequence of KSIs is never on the queue at once. We have therefore developed a structure, called a *plan*, to explicitly represent a KSI sequence.

A. Blackboards, Plans, and Node Activities

Each *plan* represents a desire to achieve a high-level goal by performing a sequence of activities. To identify plans, the node needs to recognize these high-level goals. Inferring high-level goals based on pending KSIs is an inappropriate strategy; it is like attempting to guess a chess opponents strategy after seeing a single move. Furthermore, the hypothesis and goal blackboards provide information at too detailed a level to infer these high-level goals. What is required is a structure similar to the blackboards that groups related hypotheses and goals into a single structure. We have developed a preliminary version of this structure which we call the *abstracted blackboard*, a multi-level structure reminiscent of the focus-of-control database first used in the Hearsay-II speech understanding system [7]. Our implementation of the abstracted blackboard is incomplete because it does not adequately incorporate the information from the goal blackboard. However, for the type of processing done in the DVMT, hypothesis abstraction is usually effective.

Hypotheses with similar level, time, and region characteristics are grouped together on the abstracted blackboard. This grouping acts as a smoothing operator, obscuring details about individual hypothesis interactions so that broader, long-term interactions between areas of the solution space can be discerned. By transforming the data blackboard into the abstracted blackboard, we explicitly generate a state representation that is uniquely appropriate for planning at a higher level of abstraction. We believe that the significant success of our modified architecture can largely be attributed to having such a representation, and expect that the control components in other multi-level blackboard-based problem solving systems might similarly find such representations useful [9].

In our preliminary implementation, the abstracted blackboard takes the form of a two-dimensional array, with level and time indices. Each hypothesis has associated with it a sequence of time-locations which indicates where the hypothesized vehicle was at various times. When a hypothesis is created, it is incorporated into the abstracted blackboard by stepping through this sequence of time-locations and modifying the appropriate level-time entries in the abstracted blackboard. Each level-time entry contains some number of regions, and if the location associated with the specific time can be included in one of these regions (perhaps by enlarging the region within certain bounds), the hypothesis is associated with that region. Otherwise, a new region is formed for the hypothesis.

Each level-time-region of the abstracted blackboard is summarized into a set of values that are derived from the associated hypotheses. These values include the maximum belief of the hypotheses in the level-time-region, the number of highly believed hypotheses, the number of KSIs stimulated by these hypotheses that have yet to be invoked, the total number of hypotheses in the level-time-region and how many uninvoked KSIs are associated with them, and an indication as to the other level-time-regions that share at least one of the hypotheses. This information allows the *situation recognizer* to develop a higher level view of the problem solving. For example, low maximum belief indicates the problem solving approach in that area should be re-evaluated, a large number of equally rated hypotheses could imply that there is uncertainty that should be resolved, and a large number of pending KSIs indicates the need for making an informed and judicious choice as to which action to take next. Based on this higher-level view, we can begin to form higher level goals. A goal might be to merge hypotheses in adjacent time-regions, to improve the belief of an established hypothesis, or to extend a highly believed hypothesis into a new region.

The detection of these goals, and the subsequent generation and ranking of their respective plans, is in itself a complex problem solving task. Our current implementation is a first step toward this end, in which we only consider very simple but important plans. Given the abstracted blackboard, our planner scans down it, looking for regions of high belief. Having found such a *stimulus region*, the planner determines whether there is any indication that the data in this region can be improved (this is done by determining whether any corresponding lower level regions have higher belief than the upper level regions), and if so indicated, a plan is formed to achieve this improvement. Otherwise, a plan is generated to extend this highly rated region, either by merging a hypothesis in this region with a hypothesis in an adjacent region on the same level (if any), or by driving lower level data in an adjacent area up to a level at which it can be incorporated. If none of these plans can be formed, then a plan to synthesize the hypotheses in this highly rated region up to a higher level of abstraction may be formed.

Plans in our current implementation are not yet fully developed, because a plan should not only involve the specification of an eventual goal, but also of a sequence of actions needed to achieve this goal. Only the next potential step(s) for achieving the plan are currently represented as a priority rated queue of KSIs. In turn, the node maintains a queue of plans, ordered based on their respective ratings. A plan rating is based on a number of factors, including the belief of its stimulus region, the level of its stimulus region, the interest in that region (specified by the interest areas), the ratings of its KSIs, and whether the stimulus region represents hypotheses generated locally or it represents received hypotheses (to reason more fully about potentially distracting information received from outside). Therefore, in choosing its next activity, a node will invoke the highest rated KSI in the highest rated plan.

We have therefore made important modifications to the control structure of a node (Figure 1). As the figure indicates, the creation and ranking of plans requires the planner to integrate the influences of the long-term strategy

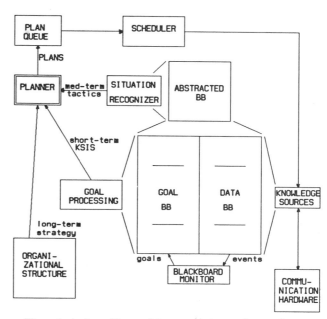

The principal problem solving components of a node are presented. Note that the planner must integrate long-term, medium-term, and short-term information.

Figure 1: The Problem Solving Architecture of a Node.

of the organizational structure (the interest areas), the medium-term higher-level view of the current situation (the abstracted blackboard), and the short-term KSI input indicating actions that can be achieved immediately (the KSI queue). Hence, decisions in a plan-based node are more informed than those in a KSI-based node (a node without plans). Moreover, a plan-based node is no less opportunistic, because plans, unlike KSIs, are interruptable. If an area outside the current plan looks more promising, a plan to work there may temporarily supplant the current plan at the top of the queue. In addition, when plans are introduced, one can begin reasoning about the time invested in a particular area, and whether it is really in the node's best interests to leave this area for another.

B. Experiments with Plan-based Nodes

We now briefly illustrate how problem solving is improved in a plan-based node (we shall consider multi-node networks in the next section). Consider the sensor configuration and input data shown in Figure 2. The vehicle track has two strongly sensed areas divided by a weakly sensed area, while the ghost track is moderately sensed throughout. In the centralized case, a single node receives data from all four sensors. If the node makes only correct decisions, it can generate the solution in 40 time units. However, the presence of moderate ghost data serves to distract the node. This distraction is severe if the node is KSI-based—the solution is found in 213 time units.

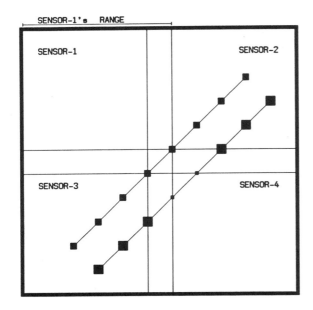

The four sensors have a small amount of overlap. There are eight data points on both the ghost track (upper) and the vehicle track (lower). The size of the data point indicates how strongly it is sensed.

Figure 2: Four Sensor Configuration.

Although a plan-based node is also distracted, its high-level view helps it quickly recognize that the distracting data will not satisfy the high-level goal which drives the plan. For example, the high-level goal may be to create a hypothesis which extends a hypothesis with three time-locations to four time-locations. Distracting data which initially looks like it might satisfy this goal is developed until the planner, using the high-level view, recognizes that the high-level goal will not be achieved. At this point, a plan to develop other data which could satisfy the high-level goal becomes the highest rated plan. Due to the high-level view and the sophistication of the planner, the time spent deviating from the correct solution path is reduced, and the plan-based node can generate the solution in 58 time units.

Plan-based nodes have been used in a number of other environments with similar results. In both the centralized case and the multi-node case where nodes do not exchange meta-level information (see next section), the increased self-awareness afforded by the new mechanisms significantly improves problem solving performance. The experiments thus serve to emphasize the importance of sophisticated local control which recognizes and reacts appropriately to various problem solving situations. We anticipate expanding the repetoire of situations which can be dealt with so that plans can be developed in more complex environments.

III. INCREASING THE COHERENCE OF THE PROBLEM SOLVING NETWORK

We have seen how the performance of a centralized node can be improved by allowing it to reason more fully as to the appropriate activities to perform. We now examine the multi-node case, where each node has a limited local view of network problem solving. In the previous section, we established that the problem solving behavior of a plan-based node is more effective than that of a KSI-based node. Therefore, we can expect that a network of such nodes might have improved performance, not because they display better "teamwork" (their global knowledge does not increase), but rather because each is a better "player".

These expectations were empirically verified on a number of environments. Environment E1 uses the configuration of Figure 2, but assigns a separate node to each sensor, each node being allowed to communicate with its neighbors. A second environment, E2, is a four-node environment identical to E1 except that the positions of the vehicle and ghost tracks are reversed. Note that, in this case, the weakly sensed vehicle data is received by all four nodes, and is the only data received by one of them. A larger sensor and data configuration consisting of ten sensors and eighteen sensed times was developed, patterned after the four sensor configuration [5]. A third environment, E3, consisting of ten nodes was built upon this configuration.

The experimental results are given in Table 1. Note that, in all cases, the multi-node network composed of plan-based nodes is significantly better. Environment E2 approaches optimal results because one node receives only the weakly sensed vehicle data, and so, will drive this data up earlier. In the other environments, however, work on this weakly sensed data is not as timely because the nodes prefer to work redundantly on the more highly sensed vehicle and ghost data in their overlapping sensed areas. This redundancy wastes computation time that could be used to develop the weak vehicle data instead—the network is not behaving coherently.

By transmitting the abstracted blackboards (or portions thereof), nodes can reason about the *past* activities of their neighbors. Furthermore, if a node knows the current plan of its neighbor, it can reason about the *present* actions of its neighbor. Reasoning about the *future* actions of a node, however, is a complex problem. This reasoning involves considering not only the current plans in the node's queue and making estimations about their durations and effects, but also what further information the node may receive (from another node or from its sensor) that could affect its activities. A plan may have associated with it some estimations as to duration and probability of completion, or even more specific information about how its execution could be affected by received information.

Our current implementation assumes that a node can make completely accurate short-term predictions about future activity based solely on the plan queue. We simulate this best-case scenario by allowing a node access

Environment	Type of nodes	Time
E1	KSI-based	49
	Plan-based	36
	Plan-based/MLC	26
	Optimal	23
E2	KSI-based	34
	Plan-based	26
	Plan-based/MLC	26
	Optimal	23
E3	KSI-based	66
	Plan-based	58
	Plan-based/MLC	38
	Optimal	35

Legend:
Time	Earliest time at which a solution was found
MLC	Meta-level Communication

Comparison of performance in multi-node environments. Plan-based nodes work consistently better than KSI-based nodes, resulting in improved performance. Meta-level communication can further improve performance by increasing coherence.

Table 1: Performance of Multi-node Networks.

to the abstracted blackboard and plan queue of another node. Discussion of more realistic scenarios where nodes must transmit this *meta-level* information as they transmit hypotheses, and must therefore reason about relevance, timeliness, and completeness, can be found elsewhere [6].

A node may use meta-level information to avoid redundancy. In developing a plan, a node can determine if the plan represents a redundant derivation of information that another node has either generated (present in the abstracted blackboard) or is in the process of generating (the top plan). By avoiding redundant activity, significant improvements in solution generation rate can result because less highly rated but potentially useful activities will be invoked earlier (rather than redundant invocation of highly rated activities). Hence, the experimental results in Table 1 indicate that network performance can be further improved by the exchange of meta-level information which allows individual nodes to make more coherent local decisions.

A. Coherent Communication

An important aspect of coherent network activity is that limited communication resources should be used intelligently to improve the global state of network problem solving. Flooding the bandwidth with partial results can cause both undesirable delays to important messages and unreasonable amounts of local processing as nodes incorporate the received information. On the other hand, if a node withholds certain partial results, network performance can degrade. It is therefore important that a node have a satisfactory view of both local and network problem solving in order to make coherent communication decisions.

We have developed a number of communication strategies that use the high-level view of node and network activity to guide a node in making these decisions [6]. These strategies extend the ideas first developed by Lesser and Erman [12]. When deciding about sending a partial result, the node might consider whether it will be improving upon that result in the future, and if so, whether by waiting and sending only the better version (conserving bandwidth) it can still fulfill its obligation to provide partial results in a timely manner. Furthermore, the exchange of meta-level information can allow a node to make inferences about how a particular transmission might affect network problem solving, and to decide when to repeat a message if the effects are not seen. In experimental studies, we have found that simple communication strategies that flood the bandwidth can significantly slow down the network, and that these problems become much more pronounced as we experiment with larger networks. For example, in the ten-node environment above (E3), a simple communication strategy results in 279 hypothesis transmissions between nodes. A more intelligent strategy reduces this number to 166 without adversely affecting the solution time. Therefore, indications are that coherence in communication decisions is an important area of study, and will become increasingly so as our environments continue to increase in size.

IV. SUMMARY AND IMPLICATIONS FOR DPSN RESEARCH

We have discussed our experiences in increasing the coherent behavior of the Distributed Vehicle Monitoring Testbed. We modified the blackboard problem solving architecture of the individual nodes to enhance their ability to make predictions about their future activities. Network coherence is increased by allowing a node to refine its organizational role based on these predictions. Exchanging the predictions permits a node to refine its view of the organizational roles of the other nodes.

Coherence is an integral part of distributed problem solving research. In contrast with others [11], we assume that we have only a limited number of highly sophisticated problem solving agents, and so, should coordinate them to make the most effective team possible. Because we assume that communication between agents is potentially slow and unreliable, we regard coordination that requires mutual agreement on contracts before action [1,4] to be insufficiently responsive to changing problem circumstances (indeed, mutual agreement might not even be possible [8]). To insure reliability, we cannot accept centralized coordination [1]. The unpredictable nature of the problem solving environment makes simple game theoretic models of agents unrealizable [15], while more complete models of agent beliefs [10] might require nodes to essentially duplicate each others reasoning.

Our view of distributed problem solving therefore stresses the importance of sophisticated local control which integrates object-level knowledge about the problem domain with meta-level knowledge about network coordination. Such control allows nodes to make rapid, intelligent local decisions based on changing problem characteristics without the overhead of conferring with each other. Coordination decisions are based on a high-level organizational view of individual node activity, so nodes need not have detailed models of the object-level problem solving activity of their compatriots. Dynamic improvements to this organizational view may be achieved with the exchange of meta-level messages which briefly convey high-level coordination information. In short, the nodes initiate their own activities and will take advantage of any local and network knowledge available to form the best "team" possible within the constraints of their environment.

We believe that implementation and experimentation are essential for learning about and understanding distributed problem solving. Our future plans include improving the representation of the state of a node, enhancing the mechanisms to recognize problem solving situations, and extending the plan structures to incorporate more information. Our preliminary experiments indicate that these developments should significantly improve the performance of distributed problem solving networks, and may also be useful in blackboard-based problem solving systems in general.

REFERENCES

[1] Stephanie Cammarata, David McArthur, and Randall Steeb
Strategies of cooperation in distributed problem solving.
In *Proceedings of the Eighth International Conference on Artificial Intelligence*, pages 767–770, August 1983.

[2] Daniel D. Corkill, Victor R. Lesser, and Eva Hudlicka.
Unifying data-directed and goal-directed control: An example and experiments.
In *Proceedings of the Second National Conference on Artificial Intelligence*, pages 143–147, August 1982.

[3] Daniel D. Corkill and Victor R. Lesser
The use of meta-level control for coordination in a distributed problem solving network.
In *Proceedings of the Eighth International Conference on Artificial Intelligence*, pages 748–756, August 1983.

[4] Randall Davis and Reid G. Smith
Negotiation as a metaphor for distributed problem solving.
Artificial Intelligence, 20(1983):63—109.

[5] Edmund H. Durfee, Daniel D. Corkill, and Victor R. Lesser
Distributing a distributed problem solving network simulator.
In *Proceedings of the Fifth Real-time Systems Symposium*, pages 237–246, December 1984.

[6] Edmund H. Durfee, Victor R. Lesser, and Daniel D. Corkill
Coherent Cooperation Among Communicating Problem Solvers.
Technical Report 85-15, Department of Computer and Information Science, University of Massachusetts, April 1985.

[7] Lee D. Erman, Frederick Hayes-Roth, Victor R. Lesser, D. Raj Reddy
The Hearsay-II speech understanding system: Integrating knowledge to resolve uncertainty.
Computing Surveys, 12(2):213—253, June 1980.

[8] Joseph Y. Halpern and Yoram Moses
Knowledge and common knowledge in a distributed environment.
In *Proceedings of the Third ACM Conference on Principles of Distributed Computing*.

[9] Barbara Hayes-Roth and Frederick Hayes-Roth
A cognitive model of planning.
Cognitive Science, 3:275–310, 1979.

[10] Kurt Konolige
A deductive model of belief.
In *Proceedings of the Eighth International Conference on Artificial Intelligence*, pages 377–381, August 1983.

[11] William A. Kornfeld and Carl E. Hewitt
The scientific community metaphor.
IEEE Transactions on Man, Systems, and Cybernetics, SMC-11(1):24–33, January 1981.

[12] Victor R. Lesser and Lee D. Erman.
An experiment in distributed interpretation.
IEEE Transactions on Computers, C-29(12):1144–1163, December 1980.

[13] Victor R. Lesser and Daniel D. Corkill.
Functionally accurate, cooperative distributed systems.
IEEE Transactions on Man, Systems, and Cybernetics, SMC-11(1):81–96, January 1981.

[14] Victor R. Lesser and Daniel D. Corkill.
The Distributed Vehicle Monitoring Testbed: A tool for investigating distributed problem solving networks.
AI Magazine, 4(3):15–33, Fall 1983.

[15] Jeffrey S. Rosenschein and Michael R. Genesereth
Deals among rational agents.
Stanford Heuristic Programming Project Report No. HPP-84-44, December 1984.

AN IMPLEMENTATION OF A
MULTI-AGENT PLAN SYNCHRONIZER

Christopher Stuart

Department of Computer Science
Monash University
Clayton 3168 Australia

ABSTRACT

A program is described which augments plans with synchronizing primitives to ensure appropriate conflict avoidance and co-operation. The plans are particularly suitable for describing the activity of multiple agents which may interfere with each other. The interpretation of a plan is given as a non deterministic finite automaton which exchanges messages with an environment for the commencement and conclusion of primitive actions which take place over a period of time. The synchronized plan allows any and all execution sequences of the original plan which guarantee correct interaction.

1. Introduction

All planning systems operate by combining actions or sub-plans in some way so that the total plan satisfies some constraint – usually to achieve a goal state. Knowledge of how actions interact with each other and the world is used to determine the appropriate combinations. In NOAH[5], for example, consideration of interactions between sub-plans is explicit in the planning process. A plan is a partial order of sub-plans. The planning technique is to expand sub-plans into partial orderings of lower level sub-plans, and then look for and resolve ensuing conflicts. The resolution may impose fixed orderings. This can be unnecessarily restrictive, as in the case where two sub-plans may execute in any order but not at the same time.

This paper considers the use of synchronizing primitives to resolve conflicts and produce a plan which is as unrestrictive as possible. The models of plan and action used are appropriate for simple agents or robots engaged in parallel and or repetitive tasks which may be described at a level not using sensory input to the agents. Use could be made of this technique, for example, in automated assembly lines. Georgeff[2] has also done related work on planning for multiple agents.

2. Underlying theory.

Here we give an informal summary of a fully formalized theory of action and the world, which is described in [6].

2.1. Actions

An agent changes the world by executing *actions*. When multiple agents are operating in parallel, it may be possible for two actions to be executing simultaneously, and so actions must have a beginning and an end. We consider an action to be decomposed into discrete transformations of the world, which are called *events*. An event also has an associated correctness condition, which must be true at the moment it is executed. An action will be a set of possible finite sequences of events.

2.2. The environment

The state of the *environment* in which actions are executed consists of a world state, and a set of actions currently being executed. If an agent executes an action, one of the possible sequences of events for that action is selected non-deterministically and added to the environment state. The environment may at any time take a currently executing action, pop the next event from the event sequence, check for event failure, and change the world state according to that event.

The environment defines a set of symbols called *operators*, and gives each operator an interpretation as a set of event sequences (action). These operators are the means of interaction between an agent and the environment, and are exchanged as messages.

2.3. Agents

The execution of a plan corresponds to some sequence of messages between the environment and an *agent*. Let A be the set of operators. Then a sequence of messages will be denoted by a string over the alphabet $\{begin, end\} \times A$. For any $\alpha \in A$, $(begin\ \alpha)$ corresponds to the agent sending α to the environment to cause the associated action to be executed, and $(end\ \alpha)$ corresponds to the environment sending α to the agent to indicate that the associated action has completed. We refer simply to *strings* and assume them to be over this alphabet.

An *agent* is an acceptor for *strings*. The formal model for an agent is similar to a non-deterministic finite automaton. It has a set of nodes (agent states), and a set of arcs defining allowed state transitions with associated messages. An agent deadlocks if it is in a state from which there are no possible state transitions involving a $(begin\ \alpha)$ message, and the environment has finished executing all the operators sent by the agent.

An agent defines a set of possible strings, and for any string, an environment defines some set of possible world state sequences. The planning problem is to take information about the environment, and find an agent which has some desired effect on the world, such as the ultimate achieving of a goal world state, no matter what choices the environment makes. We say two agents are *equivalent* if in any environment they induce the same set of possible sequences of world states.

An agent is *bounded* if there is a finite upper bound on the number of actions which the environment can be executing at a time. Thus a bounded agent will suffice to represent the concurrent activity of a finite number of multiple real world agents .

2.4. Plans

Given three symbol sets A, M and S being *operators*, *memory states* and *signals* respectively, *plans* are defined recursively.

- For any $\alpha \in A$: α is a plan for executing an single action.

- For any $m \in M$, $s \in S$: (set m), (send s) and (guard $m\ s$) are synchronizing primitives.

- If p_1 and p_2 are two plans, then $p_1;p_2$ is the plan to execute them in sequence, $p_1 || p_2$ is to execute them in parallel, $p_1 | p_2$ is to execute one or the other by non-deterministic selection, and p_1^* executes p_1 an arbitrary number of times.

The semantics for plans is given as a mapping from *plans* to *agents*, which is described in [6]. Intuitively, the agent for the simple plan α is an automaton accepting only the string $\{(begin\ \alpha),(end\ \alpha)\}$. The plan operators build automata in the conventional manner. The synchronizing primitives correspond to arcs in the automaton which have a side effect on plan execution without exchanging any messages with the environment. *Set* changes the *memory state* of the plan, and *guard* and *send* can only be executed simultaneously, and then only when the memory is in the specified state and the signals match. This particular form of primitive is an adaptation of synchronization in the parallel programming language CSP[3], which uses guards which may be a combination of an input/output operation and a normal conditional.

The following two results, given without proof, assert that there is a one to one correspondence between plans and bounded agents.

- Any agent which is given as the semantics of a plan is bounded.

- For any arbitrary bounded agent, there is a plan which has an interpretation equivalent to that agent.

3.   The Interaction problem

The problem addressed here is that of ensuring that a plan does not deadlock, or allow any event to fail. Correctness conditions on events or actions can be used to represent many types of plan correctness. If a plan should achieve some goal state given some initial condition, this is ensured by beginning the plan with an action that asserts the initial condition, and terminating it with an action that will always fail in the absence of the goal condition. A condition which must be maintained during a plan can be enforced with an action in parallel that will fail in the absence of the maintained condition.

A program has been developed which takes a plan and a description of an environment, and generates a revised plan which allows all and only the sequences of communication acts of the first plan that cannot cause failure, and also that will never deadlock.

3.1.   Preventing event failure

For this program we use a very simple form of event, corresponding to the operators of the STRIPS planner[1]. The world is modeled as a set of propositions. Events are constrained to add or delete propositions without reference to the current world state. Also, the correctness condition is a conjunction of propositions or negated propositions. Thus an event is four sets of propositions: a *require true* set, a *require false* set, an *add* set and a *delete* set.

It turns out in this case that to prevent event failure an action is completely defined by five sets of atomic formulae (possibly negated propositions). The five properties are defined by considering the execution of the action in isolation from other actions. An atomic formula is

- *asserted* if it is inevitably true after the execution.

- *retracted* if it could possibly become false after the execution.

- *conflicted* if it could become false at some stage during the execution.

- *a precondition* if it must be true immediately before the action begins to ensure that no event will fail.

- *a during condition* if it must be true for some event in the action.

The necessary and sufficient rules for ensuring no event failure are:

- An action which has a during condition may not run in parallel with an action that conflicts that during condition.

- An action α_p which has a precondition may not begin until some action α_a which asserts that condition has completed, and also no action α_r which retracts that condition may be running from when α_a begins until α_p ends.

3.2.   Synchronizing Plans

We synchronize a plan by inserting send operations, and running it in parallel with a *synchronization skeleton* consisting only of *guard* and *set* operations. The set of possible strings for the resulting plan is a subset of those for the original plan. Manna and Wolper describe an algorithm for generating such a skeleton from propositional temporal logic (PTL) formulae used to express constraints on execution sequences of a plan.[4]

PTL is a logic for reasoning about sequences of states. The interpretation of a PTL formula is the set of sequences for which it is *true*. States give truth values to propositions and hence to non modal formulae, and the temporal connectives of PTL (*always, eventually, until* and *next*) have truth values depending on the successors of a state. We also use a *regular expression* operator equivalent in expressiveness to the grammar operators of Wolper.[7] A regular expression with the basic elements being non modal formulae translates into a set of sequences of non modal formulae, and then to a set of sequences of states.

3.3.   The algorithm

The plan synchronizer has three phases. First, PTL formulae are generated. Correctness constraints, being the two rules defined above, are expressed in standard PTL, using propositions to represent relevant stages in plan execution. A *regular expression* formula corresponding to a simplification of the plan is used to express the constraints imposed by the plan syntax on the order of the relevant stages. The formulae are simplified or ignored depending on orderings already enforced by the plan syntax. This reduces the time spent in the second phase without altering the interpretation of the conjunction of all the PTL formulae generated.

Second, a tableau method of theorem proving is applied. Formulae are decomposed into non modal constraints on the first state of a sequence, and general constraints on the remainder. A graph is constructed, with arcs corresponding to states in plan execution, and nodes labeled with PTL formulae. This graph is pruned to enforce eventuality constraints. Every interpretation for the original PTL formula is a path through the final graph, and every finite path is the prefix of an interpretation.

Finally, the graph is converted directly into a synchronization skeleton, and *send* operations are inserted into the plan for every proposition used. The set of memory states used corresponds to the set of nodes in the graph, and each arc is represented as a guarded command to alter the memory. The resulting plan allows all possible execution sequences of the original which do not permit an event to fail, and which always allow for plan termination.

The current version of the program only handles restricted classes of plans and actions (no loops, no selection, and actions consisting of a single event sequence), but is being extended at the moment to include these.

4.   An example

Consider the problem of three robots all trying to pickup a block and move it clockwise to a location which another robot will clear as it moves, represented by the following unsynchronized plan:

```
( (START (R1 R2 R3) ((A X) (B Y) (C Z)))
  (PARALLEL ( (PICKUP R1 A X) (PUTDOWN R1 A Y))
            ( (PICKUP R2 B Y) (PUTDOWN R2 B Z))
            ( (PICKUP R3 C Z) (PUTDOWN R3 C X))))
```

The start action sets up the initial conditions, and then each robot in parallel executes a pickup and putdown. Clearly collisions might result. The problem is represented pictorially in the following diagram:

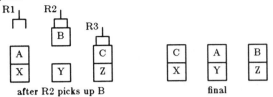

after R2 picks up B   final

The synchronized plan produced by the program is

```
( (PARALLEL
    ( (SEND (BEGIN 1))
      (START (R1 R2 R3) ((A X) (B Y) (C Z)))
    (PARALLEL
      ( (PICKUP R1 A X) (SEND (END 2 1 1))
        (SEND (BEGIN 2 1 2)) (PUTDOWN R1 A Y))
      ( (PICKUP R2 B Y) (SEND (END 2 2 1))
        (SEND (BEGIN 2 2 2)) (PUTDOWN R2 B Z))
      ( (PICKUP R3 C Z) (SEND (END 2 3 1))
        (SEND (BEGIN 2 3 2)) (PUTDOWN R3 C X))))

    ( (RECV (BEGIN 1))
      (SETQ N 2)
      (WHILE (NOT (EQ N 13))
        (SELECT-ONE-OF
          (IF (AND (EQ N 2) (RECV (END 2 3 1)))
            THEN (SETQ N 5))
          (IF (AND (EQ N 2) (RECV (END 2 2 1)))
            THEN (SETQ N 4))
. . . . . . .
          (IF (AND (EQ N 5) (RECV (END 2 1 1)))
            THEN (SETQ N 6)))))))
```

The syntax is close to CSP, and can be translated directly into plans as we have defined them. A large section of the synchronization skeleton has been removed in the example, since it contains 42 guarded commands – one for each arc in the model for the PTL formulae. The final plan has the desired result of holding any putdown until the appropriate pickup has completed. Each *pickup* is followed by a *send* which indicates a block is clear, and each *putdown* is preceded by a *send* which is delayed until the appropriate destination block is clear.

5. Conclusion and Future Work

There are some optimizations possible in the general method by pruning the graph, which in the above example would have reduced the size of the synchronization skeleton, and removed redundant references to (BEGIN 1). It is also worthy of investigation to consider how synchronization primitives could be inserted in the main plan without adding a new parallel branch with the synchronization skeleton, or how the synchronization skeleton could be made more modular, with distinct components to handle particular constraints.

The definition of actions and environments given here enables very strong properties to be given to the synchronized plans: in particular that *all and only* the correct executions of the initial plan are permitted. This is in contrast to previous means of synchronizing plans which prohibit some execution sequences that would succeed.

By extending the definition of actions to include general state transformations in events, a similar algorithm could generate a plan which is still less restrictive than that produced by previous plan modifying techniques, but might still disallow certain correct

executions. There is no simple action description capturing all the essential properties in the same way as can be done in the simple case with five sets of atomic formulae. Also, the PTL formulae might need to reference propositions reflecting world state as well as the stages of plan execution. This problem could be considered in more detail.

There is also the problem of types of non-determinism. The current selection operator corresponds to the case where a plan may proceed in one of two directions, and the synchronizer is permitted to chose one over the other. This is *angelic* non-determinism. However, it may be the case for some plans that the choice is critical, but made at execution time, in which case the synchronizer must allow both cases or none at all. This is *demonic* non-determinism, and implies some additional structure to a plan which restricts the ways in which it may be synchronized. For added complexity, the decision may be based on the state of the world model, and so the synchronizer can determine the choices it must leave open, depending on the possible world models it derives for the moment of choice.

Loops often have a termination condition which is a function of all the activity in the loop, and yet may not easily be derived from the given information. Such a termination condition could be specified if a plan segment were treated as a single hierarchical action, and given properties similar to those for individual actions. Consider a loop of an action that removes a single item from a box until none are left. To represent this in the formalism given here, the entire loop would be given an assert condition that the box become empty. To guarantee termination, the entire loop could be given a during condition that no one places anything in the box.

A version of the program is being designed which will take as input an arbitrary plan as defined above, and will also handle both types of non-determinism, and conditions attached to sub-plans as hierarchical actions. The theoretical justification is being pursued concurrently.

ACKNOWLEDGEMENTS

Much of this investigation was conducted at the AI center at SRI International. Thanks are due to the center and especially to Michael Georgeff for helpful discussion; and to Monash University for financial assistance, and where the work is proceeding.

REFERENCES

[1] Fikes, R.E., Nilsson, N.J. "STRIPS: A new approach to the application of theorem proving in problem solving." *Artificial Intelligence* 2 (1971), pp189-208.

[2] Georgeff, M.P. "Communication and Interaction in Multi-Agent Planning." In *Proc. AAAI-83*, (1983) pp125-129.

[3] Hoare, C.A.R. "Communicating Sequential Processes." In *Communications of the ACM* 21:8 (1978), pp 666-677.

[4] Manna, Z.; Wolper, P. "Synthesis of Communicating Processes from Temporal Logic Specifications." Report STAN-CS-81-872, Stanford University Computer Science Dept, September 1981.

[5] Sacerdoti, E.D. "A Structure for Plans and Behaviour." Tech Note 109, SRI AI Center, Menlo Park, CA 1975.

[6] Stuart, C.J. "An Implementation of a Multi-Agent Plan Synchronizer Using a Temporal Logic Theorem Prover." Report under development, SRI AI Center, Menlo Park, CA, 1985.

[7] Wolper, P. "Temporal Logic Can Be More Expressive." In *Proc. of the 22nd Symposium on Foundations of Computer Science.* Nashville, TN, (1981)

Iterative-Deepening-A*:
An Optimal Admissible Tree Search[1]

Richard E. Korf[2]

Department of Computer Science
Columbia University
New York, N.Y. 10027

Abstract

A serious limitation of the A* algorithm is that in practice it requires space which is exponential in the solution cost. We propose an iterative-deepening extension to A* which only requires linear space. The algorithm is admissible and expands the same number of nodes, asymptotically, as A* for exponential tree searches. This algorithm is the only known algorithm that is capable of finding optimal solutions to randomly generated instances of the Fifteen Puzzle within practical resource limits.

1. Introduction

Heuristic search is ubiquitous in artificial intelligence. The performance of most AI systems is dominated by the complexity of a search algorithm in their inner loops. The best known admissible algorithm, A*, has a serious space limitation, which can be overcome by applying an iterative-deepening technique. This article describes the application of iterative-deepening to A*, proves its optimality for exponential tree searches in terms of time, space, and solution cost, and demonstrates its practicality on the Fifteen Puzzle. A more comprehensive treatment of iterative-deepening, including its application to brute-force, bi-directional, and two-person game searches, can be found in [Korf 85.]

The A* algorithm was first proposed by Hart, Nilsson, and Raphael [Hart 68]. Iterative-deepening has no doubt been rediscovered many times independently. The first use of the technique that is documented in the literature is in Slate and Atkin's Chess 4.5 program [Slate 77]. Pearl[3] initially suggested the iterative-deepening extension of A*, and Berliner and Goetsch [Berliner 84] have implemented such an algorithm concurrently with this work. In addition, Stickel and Tyson [Stickel 85] have independently analyzed iterative-deepening for the special case of brute-force search.

---

[1]This research was supported in part by the Defense Advanced Research Projects Agency under contract N00039-84-C-0165, and by the National Science Foundation under grant IST-84-18879.

[2]Current address: Department of Computer Science, University of California, Los Angeles, Ca. 90024

[3]personal communication, 1984

The complexity of a search algorithm for a given problem will be expressed in terms of two parameters: the cost of a solution to the problem, and the effective branching factor of the algorithm. The *cost* (*c*) of a solution to a problem is the cost of the least expensive sequence of operators that map the initial state into a goal state. The *effective branching factor* (*b*) of a search algorithm is the ratio of the number of nodes that are generated at a given cost compared to those generated at the next smaller cost, and in general depends on the accuracy of the heuristic function. We will assume that the branching factor is constant throughout the problem space. The time complexity of a search algorithm in this model is simply the number of nodes that are generated, since we assume that the amount of time is proportional to the number of nodes generated. Similarly, since we assume that the amount of space required is proportional to the number of states that are stored, the space complexity of an algorithm in this model will be the number of states that must be stored.

Strictly speaking, the results in this paper hold only for trees. The reason is that the iterative-deepening algorithm is inherently depth-first and hence is constrained to explore all paths to a given cutoff. For graphs with cycles, the number of paths can be an exponential function of the number of nodes, and hence a depth-first approach would be dominated by a breadth-first algorithm. The performance of a depth-first algorithm on a graph is a function of the average number of edges that are incident to a given state rather than the number of nodes that are adjacent. For trees the edge and node branching factors are equal but can be quite different for some graphs.

This work is focused on searches which produce optimal solutions. We recognize that for most applications, optimal solutions are not required and that their price is often prohibitive. There are occasions, however, when optimal solutions are needed. For example, in assessing the quality of non-optimal solutions, it is often enlightening to compare them to optimal solutions for the same problem instances.

2. A Limitation of A*

The A* algorithm [Hart 68] works as follows: starting with the initial state, a node is expanded, an evaluation function is applied to its descendents, they are placed in a priority queue, and another node is chosen for expansion. The evaluation function of a node is the sum of the cost so far in reaching that node from the initial state (*g*), plus the heuristic estimate of the cost remaining to reach a goal state from the node (*h*). The next node expanded is always a node of least cost among all those in the queue. To facilitate comparison with the iterative-deepening algorithm, we will assume that ties are broken by expanding the most recently generated node among all those of least cost. The algorithm terminates when a goal state is chosen for expansion.

The disadvantage of A* is its space requirement. Every open node, i.e. those on the frontier of the search tree, must be stored since any one may eventually become the one with the least cost. Pearl has shown that if the heuristic used by A* exhibits even constant relative error, then the number of nodes generated by the algorithm increases exponentially with solution cost [Pearl 84]. He also observes that heuristics with better accuracy almost never occur in practice. For example, most physical measurements are subject to constant relative error. Thus, we can conclude that in practice the number of nodes on the open list is an exponential function of solution cost and as a result is of the same asymptotic order as the total number of nodes generated.

As a practical matter, an A* search of most problem spaces will exhaust the available memory long before an appreciable amount of time is used. The reason for this is that the typical ratio of memory to speed in modern computers is a million words of memory for each million instructions per second (MIPS) of processor speed. For example, if we can generate a million states per minute and require a word to store each state, memory will be exhausted in one minute.

3. Iterative-Deepening-A*

The memory limitation of A* can be overcome by applying iterative-deepening. Iterative-deepening-A* (IDA*) works as follows: Starting from the initial state, perform a depth-first search, cutting off a branch when its total cost $(g+h)$ exceeds a given threshold. Repeat the depth-first search with successively increasing thresholds until a goal state is selected for expansion. The threshold starts at the heuristic estimate of the cost of the initial state. After each iteration, the next threshold is always the minimum cost of all values that exceeded the previous threshold.

A well-known property of A* is that it always finds a cheapest solution path if the heuristic is *admissible*, or in other words never overestimates the actual distance to the goal [Hart 68]. As we will see, his property also holds for iterative-deepening-A*. In addition, since IDA* is a series of depth-first searches, at any given point only the stack of states corresponding to the current search path need be stored, and hence the space complexity of this algorithm is linear in the solution cost. Furthermore, we will show that for tree searches IDA* expands the same number of nodes, asymptotically, as A*.

Theorem 1: Given an admissible heuristic with constant relative error, then heuristic depth-first iterative-deepening is optimal in terms of solution cost, time, and space, over the class of admissible best-first tree searches.

Proof: We first consider solution cost. Since the initial cost cutoff of IDA* is the heuristic estimate of the cost of the initial state, and the heuristic never overestimates cost, the cost of the shortest solution cannot be less than the initial cost cutoff. In addition,

since the cost cutoff for each succeeding iteration is the minimum value which exceeded the previous cutoff, and again the heuristic never overestimates, no paths can have a cost which lies in a gap between two successive cutoffs. Finally, consider an optimal solution path. Since the cost function never overestimates, no node on such a path can have a value exceeding the optimal cost. Therefore, this path will be generated by IDA* when the threshold equals the optimal cost. Furthermore, no greater cost solution will be found first because no nodes with a greater cost will be expanded on that iteration.

To determine the time used by IDA*, consider the final iteration, in other words the one which finds a solution. It must expand all paths from the initial state whose maximum values are less than the optimal solution cost, plus some number of nodes whose cost equals the optimal solution cost. If A* employs the depth-first tie-breaking rule of "most recently generated", it will also expand these same nodes. Thus, the final iteration of IDA* expands the same set of nodes as A* under this tie-breaking rule, and expands each one only once if the graph is a tree.

IDA* must also expand nodes during the previous iterations as well. As mentioned above, if the heuristic used by A* exhibits constant relative error, then the number of nodes generated by the algorithm increases exponentially with cost [Pearl 84]. The branching factor b is determined by the accuracy of the heuristic function. We can use this fact to show that the previous iterations of IDA* do not affect the asymptotic order of the total number of nodes generated, as follows.

Let e be the smallest cost difference between two nodes of different cost, and let d be c/e, or the optimal solution cost expressed as a multiple of this smallest cost difference. In the worst case, the initial cost threshold would be zero and each successive threshold would increase by e. Under these conditions, d represents the "depth" of the solution or the iteration during which the solution is found. Since b was defined as the ratio between the number of nodes whose costs differ by e, the number of nodes at the frontier of iteration d is b^d. These nodes are expanded once during the final iteration of the search. The nodes at the frontier of iteration $d-1$ are expanded twice, once during iteration d, and once during iteration $d-1$. Similarly, the nodes at iteration $d-2$ are expanded three times, during iterations d, $d-1$, and $d-2$, etc. Thus, the total number of nodes expanded in a heuristic depth-first iterative-deepening search with d iterations is

$b^d+2b^{d-1}+3b^{d-2}+...+db$	Factoring out b^d,
$b^d(1+2b^{-1}+3b^{-2}+...+db^{1-d})$	Letting $x=1/b$
$b^d(1+2x^1+3x^2+...+dx^{d-1})$	This is less than
$b^d(1+2x^1+3x^2+4x^3+...)$	which equals
$b^d(1-x)^{-2}$	for $abs(x)<1$

Since $(1-x)^{-2}$, or $(1-1/b)^{-2}$, is a constant that is independent of d, if $b>1$ then the running time of depth-first iterative-deepening is $O(b^d)$.

Thus, IDA* expands the same number of nodes, asymptotically, as A* for exponential tree searches. A recent result of Dechter and Pearl [Dechter 83] shows that A* is optimal, in terms of number of nodes generated, over the class of admissible best-first searches with *monotone* heuristics. A monotone heuristic function is one which never decreases along a path. This is not a serious restriction since given an admissible heuristic, we can trivially construct a monotone one by taking the maximum value along the path so far as the value of each succeeding node on the path [Mero 84]. Therefore, IDA* is asymptotically optimal in terms of time over the class of admissible best-first tree searches.

Finally, we consider the space used by IDA*. Since IDA* at any point is engaged in a depth-first search, it need only store a stack of nodes which represents the branch of the tree it is expanding. Since it finds a solution of optimal cost, the maximum depth of this stack is d, and hence the maximum amount of space is $O(d)$.

To show that this is optimal, we note that any algorithm which uses $f(n)$ time must use at least $k \, log \, f(n)$ space for some constant k [Hopcroft 79]. The reason is that the algorithm must proceed through $f(n)$ distinct states before looping or terminating, and hence must be able to store that many states. Since storing $f(n)$ states requires $log \, f(n)$ bits, and $log \, b^d$ is $d \, log \, b$, any brute-force algorithm must use kd space, for some constant k.   Q.E.D.

As mentioned above, most heuristics in practice exhibit at least constant relative error. Thus, we can conclude that heuristic depth-first iterative-deepening is asymptotically optimal for most best-first tree searches which occur in practice. An additional benefit of IDA* over A* is that it is simpler to implement since there are no open or closed lists to be managed. A simple recursion performs the depth-first search, and an outer loop handles the iterations.

As an empirical test of the practicality of this algorithm, both IDA* and A* were implemented for the Fifteen Puzzle. The implementations were in Pascal and were run on a DEC 2060. The heuristic function used for both was the admissible Manhattan distance heuristic: for each movable tile, the number of grid units between the current position of the tile and its goal position are computed, and these values are summed for all tiles. The two algorithms were tested against 100 randomly generated, solvable initial states. IDA* solved all instances with a median time of 30 CPU minutes, generating over 1.5 million nodes per minute. The average solution length was 53 moves and the maximum was 66 moves. A* solved none of the instances since it ran out of space after about 30,000 nodes were stored. As far as we know, this is the first algorithm to find optimal solutions to randomly generated instances of the Fifteen Puzzle within practical resource limits. An additional observation is that in experiments with the Eight Puzzle, even though IDA* generated more nodes than A*, it actually ran faster than A* on the same problem instances, due to the reduced overhead per node. The actual data from these experiments are reported in [Korf 85].

4. Conclusions

The best known admissible search algorithm, A*, is severely limited by its exponential space requirement. An iterative-deepening version of A* uses only linear space, and is asymptotically optimal in terms of cost of solution, running time, and space required for exponential tree searches. Since almost all heuristic searches have exponential complexity, iterative-deepening-A* is an optimal admissible tree search in practice. In addition, it was easier to implement and ran faster than A* in our experiments.

Acknowledgments

I would like to acknowledge the helpful comments of Mike Lebowitz, Andy Mayer, and Mike Townsend who read an earlier draft of this paper, and several helpful discussions with Hans Berliner and Judea Pearl concerning this research. In addition, Andy Mayer implemented the A* version that was compared with IDA*

References

[Berliner 84]   Berliner, Hans, and Gordon Goetsch. A quantitative study of search methods and the effect of constraint satisfaction. technical report CMU-CS-84-147, Department of Computer Science, Carnegie-Mellon University, Pittsburgh, Pa., July, 1984.

[Dechter 83]   Dechter, Rina, and Judea Pearl.   The optimality of A* revisited.   Proceedings of the National Conference on Artificial Intelligence, Washington, D.C., August, 1983, pp. 95-99.

[Hart 68]   Hart, Peter E., Nils J. Nilsson, and Bertram Raphael.   "A formal basis for the heuristic determination of minimum cost paths."   *IEEE Transactions on Systems Science and Cybernetics SSC-4*, 2 (1968).

[Hopcroft 79]   Hopcroft, John E., and Jeffrey D. Ullman   *Introduction to Automata Theory, Languages, and Computation.* Addison-Wesley, Reading, Mass., 1979.

[Korf 85]   Korf, Richard E.   "Depth-first iterative-deepening: An optimal admissible tree search." *Artificial Intelligence to appear* (1985).

[Mero 84]   Mero, Laszlo.   "A heuristic search algorithm with modifiable estimate."   *Artificial Intelligence 23* (1984).

[Pearl 84]   Pearl, Judea   *Heuristics.* Addison-Wesley, Reading, Mass., 1984.

[Slate 77]   Slate, David J., and Lawrence R. Atkin. CHESS 4.5 - The Northwestern University chess program.   In Frey, Peter W., Ed., *Chess Skill in Man and Machine*, Springer-Verlag, New York, 1977.

[Stickel 85]   Stickel, Mark E., and W. Mabry Tyson. An analysis of consecutively bounded depth-first search with applications in automated deduction. Proceedings of the International Joint Conference on Artificial Intelligence (IJCAI-85), Los Angeles, Ca., August, 1985.

A WEIGHTED TECHNIQUE IN HEURISTIC SEARCH

Zhang, Bo

Dept. of Computer Science
Tsinghua University
Beijing, China

Zhang, Ling

Dept. of Mathematics
Anqing Teachers' College
Anqing, Anhui, China

ABSTRACT

As shown in [1], we examine search as a statistic sampling process. Based on some statistical inference method the probability that a subtree in search tree contains the goal can be decided. Thus some weight is intentionaly added to the evaluation function of those nodes which are unlikely in the solution path so that the search will concentrate on the most promising path. It results in a new weighted algorithm-WSA.

In a uniform m-ary tree, we show that a goal can be found by WSA in the polynomial time, although the computational complexity of A (or A*) may be $O(e^{CN})$ for searching the same space. Where N is the depth at which the goal is located.

INTRODUCTION

Weighted techniques in heuristic search have been investigated by several researchers (e.g., see [2]-[4]). Although thoes methods made the search more efficiency, the improvement is rather limitted because weights are usually added to all nodes undicriminally, for example, in [2] the same weight α_o is applied to each node.

The alternative weighted technique presented here is the following. According to decisions made by some statistic inference method during A (or A*) search a weight will only be added to the evaluation of some nodes which are unlikely in the solution path. It results in a new weighted technique that will provide better results.

A NEW WEIGHTED METHOD

As shown in [1], under certain conditions we examine search as a statistic sampling process so that statistic inference method can be used during the search. Assume the Wald sequential probability radio test (SPRT) is used as a testing hypotheses. In some searching stage, if the hypothesis that some subtree T contains solution path is rejected, from [1] it's known that subtree T contains the goal with lower probability. Rather than pruning T (as in [1]) a fixed weight w is added to the evaluation function of nodes in T, i.e., $f_1(n) = f(n) + w$. If the hypothesis that the subtree T' contains the goal is accepted, the same weight is added to all nodes in the brother-subtrees of T' which roots are the brothers of the root of T'. If no decision can be made the search process is continued as in A search. Thus the search will concentrate on the subtrees which contain the goal with higher probability due to the weighting. This new algorithm is called the weighted SA search—WSA.

THE COMPLEXITY OF WSA

Assume the search space is a uniform m-ary tree, the SPRT is used as the testing hypotheses and the given significance level is (α, β), $\alpha + \beta = b$. The complexity of an algorithm is defined as the expected number of nodes expanded by the algorithm when a goal is found. We have proved the following theorems (the proof is presented in the Appendix).

Theorem 1: Assume $P(A) \sim O(e^{CN})$, $C > 0$ and C is a known constant, N is the depth at which the goal is located, P(A) is the complexity of algorithm A when it searches the same space. Using the weighted function $f_1(n) = f(n) + w_o$, where $w_o = \frac{1}{2C} \ln \frac{1-b}{b}$ (the optimal weight) the complexity of algorithm WSA is

$$P(WSA) \sim O(N).$$

Theorem 2: If $P(A) \sim O(N^a)$, $a > 1$, using the weighted function $f_1(n) = \lambda_o f(n)$ where $\lambda_o = \sqrt[2a]{\frac{1-b}{b}}$, then the complexity of WSA is

$$P(WSA) \sim O(N).$$

Obviously, the new weighted method can improve the computational complexity greatly.

Generally, P(A) is either $\sim O(e^{CN})$ or $\sim(N^a)$, and it's unknown. When an arbitrary weight $w \neq w_o$ is used in WSA search, how about its complexity?

Theorem 3: If $P(A) \sim O(e^{CN})$, $C > 0$ and C is unknown, using the weighted function $f_1(n) = f(n) + w$, $w \neq w_o$, and a monotonously decreased significance level $b_i = \frac{b}{i^2}$ is used for testing T_i-subtrees, then

$$P(WSA) \sim O(N.\ln N)$$

Theorem 4: If $P(A) \sim O(N^a)$, $a > 1$, using the same weighted function $f_1(n) = f(n) + w$, the complexity of WSA search remains in the polynomial time.

ALGORITHM WSA

Given an evaluation function (statistic) f(n) and a testing hypotheses method, the WSA search procedure as follows:

(1) Create a list called OPEN. Expand initial node S_o, generating its m successors, put them on OPEN.

Create a list CLOSED. It's initially empty.

Create a list ROOTS. Put m successors of S_o on it, The node in ROOTS is called a.

(2) LOOP: If OPEN is empty, exit with failure (It's impossible that OPEN is empty when there exists a goal in the search tree).

(3) Select the first node on OPEN, remove it from OPEN, and put it on CLOSED. Call this node n.

(4) If n is a goal, exit successfully with the solution obtained by tracing a path along the pointers which are established in step 5.

(5) Expand node n, generating its m successors, Put them on OPEN.Establish a pointer to n from these successors.

(6) If some subtree T(a) is accepted according to some testing hypothese, add a weight w to the statistics of all nodes in the brother-subtree of T(a), remove the root nodes of T(a) and its brother-subtrees from ROOTS and put their successors on ROOTS.

(7) Reorder the list OPEN according to statistics. Go LOOP.

CONCLUSIONS

A new weighted technique is incorporated in A (or A*) search. While the algorithm A searches a space using evaluation function f(n), some weight w is added to f(n) ($f_1(n)=f(n)+w$) of the nodes which are unlikely in the solution path according to decisions made by some statistic inference method. Thus the paths that contain the goal with higher probability will be expanded more due to the weighting.

In a uniform m-ary tree, we show that a goal can be found by WSA in the polynomial time, although the complexity of A may be $O(e^{CN})$ for searching the same space.

Both algorithm A [3] and SA are special cases of this more general algorithm WSA. Note that when $w \equiv 0$ algorithm WSA is idential to A search. While $w = +\infty$ algorithm WSA degenerates into SA search.

APPENDIX

The proof of Theorem 1:

For simplicity, we assume the search space is a uniform 2-ary tree, m=2, in the following discussion. There is no loss of generality in assuming that $P(A)=e^{CN}$.

If a statistic decision is made in some search stage, a weight w is added to evaluation of nodes of the rejected subtrees. A subtree is called a completely weighted if all its subtrees have been decided to be rejected or accepted. The subtree shown in Fig.1 is completely weighted (Where the rejected subtrees are marked with sign "X").

Obviously, a completely weighted subtree has more expanded nodes than the incompletely weight-

ed one. Thus if an upper estimate of the mean complexity of the completely weighted subtree is computed, it certainly is an upper estimate of the mean complexity in general cases.

Fig. 1.

We now discuss this upper estimate.

Let P_d be a set of nodes at depth d. Given $n \in P_d$. From initial node S_o to n there exists a unique path consisting of d arcs. Among these arcs if there are i($o \leqslant i \leqslant d$) arcs marked by "X", node n is referred to as an i-type node or i-node.

So P_d can be divided into the following subsets:

0-node: there is only one, 1-node: $C_d^1=d$,....,
i-node: C_d^i,..., d-node: $C_d^d=1$.

In considering the complexity for finding a goal, we first ignore the cost of the statistic inference. Assume that the goal belongs in 0-node so that its evaluation is $f_g(n)=N$. From algorithm A, it's known that every node which $f(n) < N$ must be expanded in the searching process.

If node n is an i-node, its evaluation function is $f_1(n)=f(n)+iw$. All nodes which evaluation satisfy the following inequation will be expanded.

$f_1(n)=f(n)+iw N$,   i.e., $f(n) < N-iw$.

Using evaluation function f(n) the complexity of A search is known to be $P(A)=e^{CN}$, thus the complexity corresponding to the evaluation function $f_1(n)=f(n)+iw$ is $e^{C(N-iw)}$. The mean complexity of each i-node (the possibility that an i-node may be expanded) is $\dfrac{e^{C(N-iw)}}{2^{N+1}}=e^{-Ciw}\dfrac{e^{CN}}{2^{N+1}}$

The mean complexity for finding a goal at depth N is at least N. Thus the mean complexity of each i-node is

$$\max\left(\frac{e^{C(N-iw)}}{2^{N+1}}, \frac{N}{2^{N+1}}\right) \leqslant \frac{1}{2^{N+1}}\left(e^{C(N-iw)}+N\right).$$

When the goal is an 0-node, the upper estimate of the mean complexity for computing all d-th depth nodes is the following:

$$\frac{1}{2^{N+1}}\sum_0^d C_d^i\left(e^{C(N-iw)}+N\right)=\frac{e^{CN}}{2^{N+1}}(1+e^{-Cw})^d+\frac{N}{2^{N-d+1}}.$$

On the other hand, if $\alpha+\beta=b$ is a constant, from [1] for making the statistic inference of a node, the mean computational cost of SPRT is a constant Q. When the goal is an 0-node, accounting for this cost, the mean complexity is

$$P_0(WSA) \leqslant Q\left(\frac{e^{CN}}{2^{N+1}}(1+e^{-Cw})^d+\frac{N}{2^{N-d+1}}\right).$$

Similarly, if the goal belongs in i-node, the mean complexity for computing all d-th nodes is

$$P_i(WSA) \leqslant Q\left(\frac{e^{CN}\cdot e^{iwC}}{2^{N+1}}(1+e^{-Cw})^d+\frac{N}{2^{N-d+1}}\right).$$

From algorithm SA [1], the goal falls into an i-node with probability $(1-b)^{N-i}b^i$, if the given level is (α, β), $\alpha+\beta=b$. At depth N there are C_N^i i-nodes, so the probability that the goal belongs in i-node is

$$C_N^i(1-b)^{N-i}b^i, \qquad i=0,1,\ldots,N-1.$$

Accounting for all possible cases of the goal node, the mean complexity for computing all d-th depth nodes is

$$\sum_{i=0}^{N-1} C_N^i(1-b)^{N-i}b^i P_i(WSA)$$

$$\leq \frac{Q}{2^{N+1}}\left[e^{CN}\frac{(1+e^{-Cw})^d}{2}(1-b+be^{Cw})^N\right]+\frac{NQ}{2^{N-d+1}}$$

Let $F(w)=(1+e^{-Cw})\cdot(1-b+be^{Cw})$ (1)

$F(w)$ attains its minimum for a value of w given by

$$w_0=\frac{1}{2C}\ln\frac{1-b}{b}$$
$$F(w_0)=1+2\sqrt{b(1-b)} .$$

Under the optimal weight, the upper bound of the mean complexity of algorithm WSA is

$$P(WSA)\leq Q\left[\frac{e^{CN}}{2^{N+1}}\sum_0^N(1+2\sqrt{b(1-b)})^i+\sum_0^N\frac{N}{2^{N-i}}\right]$$

$$\sim O(N)+\frac{Qe^{CN}}{2\sqrt{b(1-b)}}\left(\frac{1+2\sqrt{b(1-b)}}{2}\right)^{N+1} .$$ (2)

Assume $0<C<\ln2$, we shall show that there exists an b_0 such that $C<\ln(\frac{2}{1+2\sqrt{b_0(1-b_0)}})$.

Let $C=\ln f<\ln2$, i.e., $f<2$.

From $C<\ln(\frac{2}{1+2\sqrt{b_0(1-b_0)}})$ (3)

obtain

$$\frac{f}{2}<\frac{1}{1+2\sqrt{b_0(1-b_0)}} \text{ or } 2\sqrt{b_0(1-b_0)}<\frac{2}{f}-1>0(\because f<2)$$

Let $\frac{1}{2}(\frac{2}{f}-1)=h$, $b_0(1-b_0)=h^2$.

If $4h^2>1$, given any $0<b_0<1$, Form (3) holds.

If $4h^2-1\leq0$, as long as $0<b_0<\frac{1-\sqrt{1-4h^2}}{2}$, Form (3) holds

Substitute (3) into (2), have

$$P(WSA)\leq Q\left\{\frac{1+2\sqrt{b_0(1-b_0)}}{4\sqrt{b_0(1-b_0)}}e^{(C+\ln\frac{1+2\sqrt{b_0(1-b_0)}}{2})N}\right.$$
$$\left.+O(N)\right\}\sim O(N)$$ (4)

Similarly, Theorem 2 can be proved.

The proof of Theorem 3:

We discuss $P(A)\sim O(e^{CN})$ and C is unknown. So the optimal weight w_0 is also unknown.

Assume $w=w_0+\Delta w$,
$$e^{-Cw}=e^{-Cw_0}\cdot e^{-C\Delta w}$$
Let $u=e^{C\Delta w}$

Thus $(1-e^{-Cw})(1-b+b^{Cw})=(1+u\sqrt{\frac{b}{1-b}})(1-b+\frac{1}{u}\sqrt{b(1-b)})$

$$=1+(u+\frac{1}{u})\sqrt{b(1-b)}$$

$$P(WSA)\leq Q\left[\frac{1+(u+\frac{1}{u})\sqrt{b(1-b)}}{2(u+\frac{1}{u})\sqrt{b(1-b)}}\right.$$
$$\left. e^{(C+\ln\frac{1+(u+\frac{1}{u})\sqrt{b(1-b)}}{2})N}+N\right]$$ (5)

In order to obtain $P(WSA)\sim O(N)$, value b must be so small that

$$C\leq\ln\frac{2}{1+(u+\frac{1}{u})\sqrt{b(1-b)}}$$ (6)

But C is unknown, it is unable to select a fixed b so that Form (6) is satisfied. If we use a monotonously deceased value b_i for testing T_i-subtrees as we did in [1][6]. Due to the gradual decrement of $b_i=\alpha_i+\beta_i$, in some search stage, Form (6) must hold.

For example, if $b_i=\frac{b}{i^2}$, b is a constant, for making the statistic inference(SPRT) once, the mean complexity Q is $O(\ln N)$ at most. From (5) obtain $P(WSA)\sim O(N.\ln N)$.

The proof of Theorem 4 is omitted.

REFERENCES

[1]Zhang, Bo and Zhang, Ling, "A New Heuristic Search Technique--Algorithm SA". IEEE Trans. on PAMI, VOL. PAMI-7, NO. 1 (1985) 103-107.

[2]Pearl, J., "Some recent Results in Heuristic Search Theory". IEEE Trans. on PAMI, VOL. PAMI-6, NO. 1, (1984) 1-12.

[3]Nilsson, N.J., Principles of Artificial Intelligence, Palo Alto CA: Tioga Publishing Compary, 1980.

[4]R. Field, K. Mohyeldin-Said & I. Pohl, " An Investigation of Dynamic Weighting in Heuristic Search". In Proc. ECAI-84, Pisa, Italy, Sept. 19 1984, pp.277-278.

[5]S. Zacks, The Theory of Statistic Inference, John Wiley & Sons, Inc., New York, 1971.

[6]Zhang, Ling & Zhang, Bo, "The Successive SA* Search and Its Computational Complexity". In Proc. ECAI-84, Pisa, Italy, Sept. 1984, pp.249-258.

INFORMATION ACQUISITION IN MINIMAL WINDOW SEARCH

Alexander Reinefeld †
Jonathan Schaeffer
T.A. Marsland ††

Computing Science Department,
University of Alberta,
Edmonton,
Canada T6G 2H1

ABSTRACT

The alpha-beta tree search algorithm can be improved through the use of minimal windows. Branches are searched with a minimal window $[\alpha, \alpha+1]$ with the expectancy that this will show the sub-tree to be inferior. If not, then that sub-tree must be re-searched. In this paper, several methods are discussed to minimize the cost of the re-search. Two new algorithms, INS and PNS, are introduced and their performance on practical trees is shown to be comparable to SSS*, but with considerably smaller overhead.

1. Introduction

The use of minimal windows [1] provides an improvement to the alpha-beta tree-searching algorithm (AB) [2]. Minimal window search is based on the assumption that all subtrees are inferior to the best subtree searched thus far, until proven otherwise. Having searched the first branch with a full window $[\alpha, \beta]$, all remaining branches are searched with a minimal window $[\alpha, \alpha+1]$, where α represents the best minimax value found so far. If the value returned is indeed $\leq \alpha$, then our assumption was correct and the sub-tree is inferior. Otherwise, this subtree is superior and usually must be re-searched with a wider window.

The re-search idea originally appeared in Pearl's Scout algorithm [3]. Subsequently, there have been two generalizations, Principal Variation Search [4] and NegaScout [5]. Figure 1 shows the NegaScout (NS) algorithm for searching a tree of width w and depth d. If a node p is terminal, *Evaluate(p)* returns its value. For interior nodes, *Generate(p)* determines the w branches from p. Those branches whose minimal window search produces a better minimax value of v usually must be re-searched. Only when $\alpha < v < \beta$, and the remaining depth of search is greater than 2, is a re-search with a window $[v, \beta]$ necessary.

† Current address: Universitaet Hamburg, Fachbereich Informatik, Schlueterstr.70, D-2000 Hamburg 13, West-Germany.
†† Research reported here was supported in part through Canadian NSERC grants A7902 and E5722.

This paper introduces two new algorithms. These use information acquired from the original search of a subtree to minimize the cost of a possible re-search. **Informed NegaScout (INS)** uses all available information to generate the smallest possible trees, but does so with increased storage overhead. **Partially Informed NegaScout (PNS)** is a compromise between NS and INS. The performance of NS, PNS, and INS is compared with AB and SSS* [6,7]. INS searches trees of size comparable to those traversed by SSS*, but does so with lower overheads.

2. Information Acquisition

When the initial search of a subtree is performed, the values returned by each of the descendants is maintained in a tree-like data structure. This information can be used to minimize the cost of any necessary re-search, otherwise it is discarded.

```
FUNCTION NS (p: POS; α, β, depth: INTEGER):
                                INTEGER;
VAR i, v, a, b : INTEGER;
    succ : array [1..w] of POS;

BEGIN
  IF depth = 0 THEN        { Terminal node? }
    RETURN (Evaluate (p));
  succ := Generate (p);    { Generate succ. }
  a := -∞;
  b :=  β;

  FOR i := 1 TO w DO BEGIN
    v := -NS (succ[i], -b, -MAX(α, a), depth-1);

    IF v > a THEN           { Re-search needed? }
      IF i = 1 OR v ≤ α OR v ≥ β OR depth ≤ 2
      THEN                  { v is accurate enough }
        a := v
      ELSE                  { Re-search required }
        a := -NS (succ[i], -β, -v, depth-1);

    IF a ≥ β THEN RETURN (a); { β cut-off }

    b := MAX (α, a) + 1; { Minimal window }
  END;
  RETURN (a);
END;
```

Figure 1. The NegaScout Algorithm (NS)

Information gathered from the initial search of the subtree is used on a re-search to allow two new types of cut-offs. Figure 2 illustrates the *ignore left* cut-off. In Figure 2a, the subtree has been searched with a minimal-window of [100,101]. The descendant B returned a value of 105 causing a normal beta cut-off. If at some future point it is necessary to re-search this subtree, descendant A need not be looked at again since it has already been shown to be inferior to B, Figure 2b.

Figure 3 illustrates the *prove best* cut-off. At these nodes, a beta cut-off has not occurred and all descendants have been examined. Each of the values returned is an *upper bound* on the subtree's true value, Figure 3a. If a re-search is necessary on this subtree, there are three things that can be done to minimize tree size. First of all, the branches can be re-ordered according to their values from the initial search. By sorting the branches in descending order of value, the branch with the highest upper bound (and therefore with the highest probability of being the root of the best subtree) is searched first, Figure 3b.

Secondly, since the initial value for each subtree represents an upper bound, the re-search can be done with a narrow window instead of a minimal-window. By doing this, no re-searches of re-searches can ever occur.

Finally, if the search of a subtree returns a true value that is greater than the upper bound of any of the other descendants, then those descendants can be discarded without any further work. For example, in Figure 3b, if move B is re-searched and returns a true value of 88, then moves A, and C need not be searched again, since their values can never exceed that of B.

It turns out that *ignore left* cut-offs are just a special case of *prove best* cut-offs. Branches proven inferior can be treated as having value −∞ and the rest of the branches as having a +∞ value. Retrieving this information and performing a stable sort creates the *prove best* condition. The cut-offs are treated differently because in an actual implementation the *ignore left* cut-offs require less storage to maintain the necessary information, e.g. only the number i of the best descendant thus far need be saved. On a re-search, descendants 1 through $i-1$ are ignored and the remainder searched. At *prove best* nodes, the values for all descendants must be saved.

3. Algorithms

NegaScout can be enhanced to use information from the initial search of a subtree to aid in any re-searches. Every time a node is visited, a record is kept of the results obtained from searching each descendant subtree. Either a beta cut-off occurs, and *ignore left* information is available for a re-search, or all descendants are examined, and

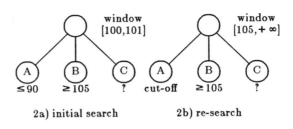

Figure 2. Ignore left cut-offs

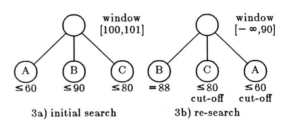

Figure 3. Prove best cut-offs

prove best information is available. In both cases, this information can be linked together to form a map of the subtree just searched. If a re-search is necessary, the map data can be used to achieve *ignore left* and *prove best* cut-offs that are not possible in NegaScout. Informed NegaScout (INS), see Appendix, does exactly this for all nodes in a tree.

The storage overhead in saving all this information is proportional to $\sum_{i=1}^{\lfloor \frac{d-1}{2} \rfloor} w^i$ entries, which is less than for SSS*. Nevertheless this may be too much, even if one reclaims storage whenever possible. As an alternative, Partially Informed NegaScout (PNS) has been implemented, providing a compromise between the complete information of INS and the zero information of NS. One can devise many different compromise algorithms; our version of PNS only retains information about *prove best* cut-offs near the root of each subtree and maintains the *principal variation,* the path to the terminal node that the initial search considered best. This algorithm tries to provide many of the benefits of INS without the storage overhead.

An important point to note is that the information used by INS is not a hash table or a transposition table [4]. Whereas transposition tables are most useful in directed graphs, the methods described here are applicable to any tree structure and do not depend on the properties of the application.

4. Results

Figures 4 and 5 illustrate some results comparing AB, NS, PNS, INS, and SSS*. The number of leaves searched by each algorithm is normalized to the size of the minimal game tree [2]. Each data point represents an average over 20 runs. Random trees, where each descendent has an equal probability of being best, and strongly ordered trees [4], where the first descendent has a 60% probability of being the best, were searched by all algorithms. In Figure 5, data at depths 7 and 8 are not available for SSS* and INS, because of memory constraints.

The graphs provided, as well as results for other widths not reported here, show that the curves oscillate, with SSS* varying the least. The oscillation is normal and occurs because the formula for the minimal tree size depends on whether the tree is of even or odd depth. SSS* fluctuates least since it is a best first search algorithm†; the other algorithms are (partly) directional. For even search depths SSS* visits fewer nodes than INS, but for odd search depths INS is usually better, because INS postpones node expansion until it is proven that the principal variation lies in this part of the tree. Of course, minimal window techniques are favored in strongly ordered trees, since researches are less probable. Here even a modest amount of information is enough to allow PNS to outperform SSS* at odd depths.

Nodes visited is not the only consideration when comparing tree searching algorithms. SSS* and INS have significant overheads when compared to AB and NS. Obviously, any timing results are implementation dependent. Our experience is that a call to INS is, on the average, about twice as expensive as a call to AB, NS, or PNS, and that SSS* is 10 times slower than INS. Whether this overhead is significant or not depends on the application.

5. Conclusions

INS has been shown to be competitive with SSS* in terms of leaf nodes searched. However the data structure to support INS is more efficient. Not only is it slightly smaller, but it can be processed in one tenth the time required by SSS*. Perhaps more importantly, by storing the information acquired during the minimal window search in a hash table, rather than as a map of the re-search tree, the memory needs can be reduced to the space available. The cost for use of such reduced memory is increased search overhead, but the search time is bounded below by NS.

PNS represents a good compromise, yielding significant reductions in tree size with little time and space overhead. In our experience, PNS is the preferred algorithm for large trees, especially under conditions of well ordered interior nodes.

The results reported here show the relative properties of the algorithms. Experiments are continuing to obtain a better measure of the standard deviation. Current work includes empirical performance analyses of these algorithms in practical game playing programs.

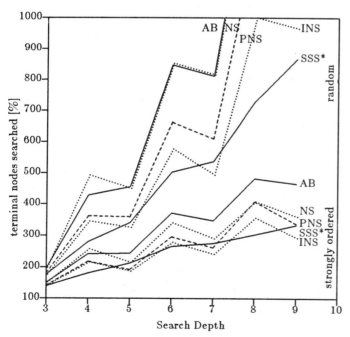

Figure 4. Comparison to minimal tree (w = 5)

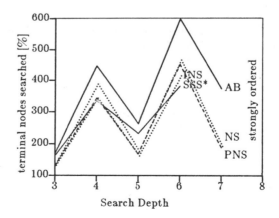

Figure 5. Comparison to minimal tree (w = 20)

† Sometimes the best first data misleads SSS* so that it expands more nodes than NS!

References

1. J.P. Fishburn, Analysis of speedup in distributed algorithms, University of Wisconsin, Tech. Rep. 431, Madison, May 1981.

2. D.E. Knuth and W. Moore, An analysis of alpha-beta pruning, *Artificial Intelligence 6*, (1975), 293-326.

3. J. Pearl, Asymptotic properties of minimax trees and game searching procedures, *Artificial Intelligence 14*, (1980), 113-138.

4. T.A. Marsland and M.S. Campbell, Parallel search of strongly ordered game trees, *ACM Computing Surveys 14*, 4 (1982), 533-552.

5. A. Reinefeld, An improvement of the Scout tree search algorithm, *ICCA Journal 6*, 4 (1983), 4-14.

6. G.C. Stockman, A minimax algorithm better than alpha-beta, *Artificial Intelligence 12*, 2 (1979), 179-196.

7. M. Campbell and T.A. Marsland, A comparison of minimax tree search algorithms, *Artificial Intelligence 20*, (1983), 347-367.

Appendix: Informed NegaScout (INS)

```
FUNCTION INS (p: POS; α, β, depth: INTEGER;
                          research: BOOLEAN): INTEGER;
VAR i, v, a, b: INTEGER; res: BOOLEAN;
    kind : (PROVE_BEST, IGNORE_LEFT);
    score: array [1..w] of INTEGER;
    succ : array [1..w] of POS;

BEGIN
  IF depth = 0 THEN RETURN (Evaluate(p)); { Terminal node? }
  succ[] := Generate(p);          { Generate successors }
  res := research;                { Save research status }
  IF research THEN BEGIN
    kind := GetInfo (p, score[]); { In research mode, }
    Sort (succ[], score[]);       { get scores and sort }
  END
  ELSE kind := PROVE_BEST;
  a := -∞;
  b :=  β;

  FOR i := 1 TO w DO BEGIN        { Start searching }
    v := -INS (succ[i], -b, -MAX(α, a), depth-1, res);

    IF v > a THEN                 { Re-search needed? }
      IF i = 1 OR v ≤ α OR v ≥ β OR depth ≤ 2 THEN
        a := v
      ELSE IF research AND kind = PROVE_BEST THEN
        a := v                    { Narrow window before }
      ELSE                        { Re-search required }
        a := -INS (succ[i], -β, -v, depth-1, YES);

    IF a ≥ β THEN BEGIN
      kind := IGNORE_LEFT;
      GOTO done; END;             { β cut-off }

    IF res AND i < w THEN
      IF MAX (a, α) ≥ score[i+1] THEN BEGIN
        a := MAX (a, score[i+1]);
        GOTO done;                { Prove-best cut-off }
      END ELSE
        b := score[i+1]           { Set narrow window }
    ELSE
      b := MAX (α, a) + 1;        { Set minimal window }

    IF kind = IGNORE_LEFT THEN    { Only 1st subtree has }
      res := FALSE;               { been seen before     }
  END;
done:
  IF NOT research THEN SaveInfo (p, kind, score[]);
  RETURN (a);
END;
```

A HYBRID SSS*/ALPHA-BETA ALGORITHM FOR
PARALLEL SEARCH OF GAME TREES

Daniel B. Leifker
Laveen N. Kanal

Department of Computer Science
University of Maryland
College Park, Maryland 20742

ABSTRACT

This paper explores the issues that arise when SSS*-like search algorithms are implemented in parallel. There is an important implicit assumption regarding the OPEN list of SSS* (and A*-like algorithms): those states which are guaranteed never to become part of an optimal solution are forced down into the OPEN list and never rise to the top for expansion. However, when multiple processors are introduced in a parallel version of SSS*, these buried states become subject to expansion despite their provable suboptimality. If such states are not identified and purged, they may exert an enormous drag on the parallel algorithm because considerable processor effort will be wasted. However, the pruning mechanisms of alpha-beta can be adapted by a parallel SSS*; the resulting algorithm HYBRID is suitable for searching game trees and general AND/OR trees in parallel.

I INTRODUCTION

A. The Alpha-Beta and SSS* Algorithms

The alpha-beta game tree search algorithm offers significant potential for search speedup by "pruning", or ignoring game tree branches that cannot affect the final minimax value of the root. The State Space Search algorithm, or SSS* (Stockman 1977), as originally presented, usually dominated alpha-beta by the "parallel" traversal of subtrees. Whereas alpha-beta was condemned to search strictly in a left-to-right fashion, SSS* sent "probes" simultaneously into the tree, and, in a manner not unlike A* (Nilsson, 1980), maintained an "open" list of partial solutions ordered by descending merits. However, SSS* could also be used to search general problem-reduction representations as well as simple game trees (Stockman and Kanal, 1983). Stockman's original SSS* underwent a few revisions, and the final version (Pearl, 1984) is admissible and always dominates alpha-beta. (We shall henceforth assume that the reader is familiar with the next-state operator G of SSS* as well as list notation for trees.)

B. Essential Components of SSS*

For later comparisons, we give a high-level description of the SSS* algorithm:

ALGORITHM SSS*

(1) Place the start state (i.e., root) on the OPEN list.
(2) If OPEN is empty, exit with failure and halt.
(3) Remove the top state S from OPEN.
(4) If S is final, i.e., represents a complete solution
     then return S with success and halt.
(5) Apply the next-state operator G to S and add G(S)
     to the OPEN list (possibly with changed merits).
(6) Go to (2).

Additional detailed discussions of SSS* can be found in (Leifker and Kanal, 1985).

Our goal is to implement a form of SSS* in parallel, using a generalized alpha-beta pruning process to excise suboptimal states from the OPEN list before any processor effort is wasted. This proposed algorithm, which we call HYBRID, is suitable for use in searching general AND/OR trees as well as game trees. Since any game tree can easily be transformed into an AND/OR tree (with strictly alternating levels of AND-nodes and OR-nodes), general AND/OR trees are used in the discussion which follows, although, as in game trees, only top-down expansion of states will be considered. Our concepts are unlike previous hybrid algorithms (Campbell and Marsland, 1983), in that there is a true coalescence of alpha-beta and SSS*, not simply a juxtaposition of the two in one program.

II INTRODUCTION OF PARALLELISM

A. Where to Introduce Parallelism

The control part (or driver) of SSS* is relatively straightforward. A state is removed from the top of OPEN and examined. If it is final (i.e., its root is solved), it is taken as the solution and the algorithm halts. If not, the "next-state" operator G is applied to the state and the result(s) placed back into the OPEN list. If the number of states in OPEN ever drops to zero, the algorithm halts with failure.

B. A First Possibility

To implement a form of non-partitioned SSS* in parallel, multiple processors obviously must be introduced somewhere. One of two possible locations is shown in Figure 1, where only the top state from OPEN is removed at a time. The processors p_1, p_2, ..., p_N then cooperate to expand this state through the next-state operator G and return the results back to OPEN. If G were a very complex operator having many disjoint tasks, this arrangement would probably be very attractive. The fundamental algorithm would not be changed, and it would still share in all the formal properties enjoyed by SSS*. The only difference would be that the actions of operator G would be accelerated considerably.

This method of "operator parallelism" must be rejected for the following reasons: (1) It forces processors to assume specialized tasks, (2) It can create enormous bottlenecks when work cannot be conveniently partitioned, and (3) it has the potential to cause enormous congestion among the waiting processors because the tasks have been broken down into excessively primitive components.

C. The Alternative

The alternative, shown in Figure 2, overcomes many of these pitfalls and is amenable to parallel processing by N processors, even when N is not specified until runtime. The basic approach is to permit each processor to access the OPEN list.

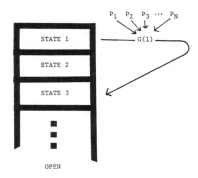

FIGURE 1

Each processor removes the next state from the top of the OPEN list, expands the state by itself, and returns the resulting state(s) back to OPEN. This is the method adopted by HYBRID. As one might expect, HYBRID is not simply a variation of SSS* - it represents a new way of heuristic control using the operator G. Consequently, the formal properties of SSS* do not necessarily hold for HYBRID. The remainder of this section defines HYBRID formally and discusses the ramifications of allowing processors to manipulate states from the interior of the OPEN list.

A special notation must be introduced to facilitate discussion of parallel algorithms. The construction

COBEGIN <statement-list> COEND

indicates concurrent execution (Dijkstra, 1965) in that all statements of <statement-list> are executed simultaneously. The notation is augmented here such that processors may be specified explicitly by attaching their names as labels to statements.

The HYBRID algorithm simply assigns each of the given N processors a copy of the sequential SSS* program. Formally, the preliminary version can be defined as:

Algorithm HYBRID
/* Preliminary version */

(1) Place the start state (i.e., root) on OPEN.

(2) halt := FALSE; /* initialize */

(3) COBEGIN /* Each processor 1 through N begins
identical and concurrent execution.
Only the code for processor p_k
(1 <= k <= N) is shown. */

```
pk: BEGIN
      WHILE NOT halt DO
      IF the OPEN list is not empty
      THEN BEGIN
             Remove a state S from OPEN;
             If S is final
             THEN BEGIN
                    halt := TRUE;
                    return(S);
                  END
             ELSE BEGIN
                    Expand S by operator G;
                    Place results back on
                      the OPEN list by
                      descending merit;
                  END;
           END;
    END;

COEND
```

FIGURE 2

The Boolean variable HALT serves as a global flag to initiate parallel processing and then to terminate it when a solution is found. Presumably the OPEN list and the HALT variable are contained in shared memory and guarded by semaphores. More elaborate synchronization constructs could also be used (Hoare, 1972), but these concerns will not be addressed here. The point to remember is that processors must be in critical sections to change any data in shared memory, and that at most one processor can be in a critical section at a time.

III   ANOMALIES OF THE HYBRID ALGORITHM

A.   Two Problems with the Proposed HYBRID

The proposed version of HYBRID given in Section II is only preliminary because two interesting anomalies occur which must be investigated further: (1) There is no clearly defined time to halt should HYBRID find no solution; and (2) The preliminary version of HYBRID is not admissible (i.e., if HYBRID halts with a solution, that solution cannot be guaranteed to be optimal).

B.   The First Anomaly: When to Halt?

As defined above, the algorithm is simply allowed to enter an infinite loop if no solution exists for the given tree. Although this is hardly desirable in a practical application, it does illustrate a problem that occurs whenever more than one processor is granted access to an OPEN list. Suppose that HYBRID is executed on a given tree with two processors, p_i and p_j, and that the OPEN list contains one start state when execution begins. Processor p_i will enter a critical section, remove the state from OPEN, exit the critical section, and begin generating its successors. Processor p_j will then pursue a similar action, but it will find the OPEN list empty because p_i has not finished expanding the state. If processor p_j is sufficiently naive, it may conclude from the empty list that the given PRR has no solution and then may even attempt to force the entire algorithm to terminate with failure. Since this is clearly not the true state of the computation, HYBRID (as given above) merely instructs all processors to wait idly until (1) a "next" state arrives at the OPEN list for expansion, or (2) the global HALT condition is raised by the discovery of a true solution.

C.   The Second Anomaly: Is HYBRID Admissible?

As N (the number of processors) increases, there is also in increase in the likelihood that the algorithm will halt with a non-optimal solution. To see this, recall that the check for termination is made when the state is removed from OPEN, not after it has been generated and about to be placed back onto OPEN. The inadmissibility of HYBRID, then, although unexpected, is easily demonstrated: as the number of processors increases, the total number of examined states increases, thus raising the probability that a non-optimal solved state hovering near the top of the OPEN list will be selected for expansion and identified as a final solution. This does not occur in sequential

SSS*, for there the OPEN list is kept strictly sorted by merit, and only the top state is examined at a time.

D.   Correcting the Anomalies

Both the anomalies may be easily eliminated. The first anomaly is corrected by halting only when the OPEN list is empty and all processors are idle; the second by maintaining a "tentative optimal merit" (i.e., a running best solution found so far), and halting only when all remaining states on OPEN are below this threshold. Unfortunately, even with these modifications, HYBRID as it stands is grossly inefficient because of the presence of provably suboptimal states on the OPEN list. This issue is discussed in Section IV.

IV   PROVABLY SUBOPTIMAL STATES

A.   Efficient Use of Processor Effort

Very often in the course of execution of SSS* the interior of the OPEN list may contain states which are guaranteed not to be subsumed by any optimal solution. This never causes a problem in sequential SSS*, for there only the top state is examined. However, considerable processor effort will be wasted if any processor is permitted to fetch and expand any of these provably suboptimal states. It is therefore clear that any efficient version of HYBRID requires a decision procedure to "test" states as they are taken off the OPEN list. If the state is provably suboptimal, it is discarded. It is expanded only if it has any potential of becoming an optimal solution.

B.   Another Look at Alpha-Beta

The alpha-beta algorithm, suitably generalized, can be adapted for use in an efficient version of HYBRID. Although alpha-beta evaluates nodes in a strict left-to-right fashion, the use of alpha values and beta values captures very neatly the concept of suboptimality. If these attributes can be managed by HYBRID, they will provide a quick decision procedure for identifying provably suboptimal branches of the search tree. However, for mnemonic purposes, we shall use the names "floor" and "ceiling" in place of "alpha value" and "beta value"; when discussing the attributes of problem #k, it is convenient to write "floor(k)" and "ceiling(k)". It should be emphasized that this notation is not a function in the mathematical sense, but is rather an attribute which can be accessed and changed.

C.   Definitions

Formally, if node #n is terminal and solved with merit m, then $floor(n) = ceiling(n) = m$. If terminal node #n has not yet been expanded, then $floor(n) = 0.0$ and $ceiling(n) = 1.0$. If non-terminal node #n has AND successors, then $floor(n)$ is defined as the minimum of its successors' floors, and $ceiling(n)$ is defined as the minimum of its successors' ceilings. If non-terminal node #n has OR successors, then $floor(n)$ is defined as the maximum of its successors' floors, and $ceiling(n)$ is defined as the maximum of its successors' ceilings. For any given PRR having nodes $p_1, ..., p_n$, we define the set Z of provably suboptimal nodes as follows:

(1)   If any node p_k has an ancestor p_j such that p_j is in Z, then p_k is in Z.

(2)   If any node p_k has an ancestor p_j such that $floor(p_j)$ is greater than $ceiling(p_k)$, then p_k is in Z.

(3)   If any OR node p_k has an ancestor p_j and sibling node p_i such that $floor(p_i)$ is greater than $floor(p_k)$, and $floor(p_i)$ is greater than $ceiling(p_j)$, then pk is in Z (a "don't-care" cutoff).

There is an important implicit assumption regarding the definition of Z. Initially, Z is empty and grows as the algorithm evaluates more and more terminal nodes. However, once a node becomes provably suboptimal, it remains provably suboptimal and is removed from all additional consideration. If this were not the case, rule (3) above would give rise to nodes with only transient suboptimality.

D.   The Final Version of HYBRID

The efficient final version of HYBRID is essentially the same as corrected HYBRID at the end of Section III, with the exception that as each processor removes a state from OPEN, it verifies that no node in the state is a member of Z. If there is such a node, the entire state is discarded and the processor returns to OPEN for another state.

V   REMARKS

This is only a high-level description of the HYBRID concept. The detailed mechanisms for practical implementations and the design of appropriate data structures and algorithms to detect provably suboptimal states are current topics of our research.

REFERENCES

[1]   Campbell, M. and Marsland, T. A. "A Comparison of Minimax Game Tree Search Algorithms", Artificial Intelligence, Volume 20, No. 4, July 1983, p. 347.

[2]   Dijkstra, E. "Cooperating Sequential Processes", Technical Report EWD-123, Technological University, Eindhoven, The Netherlands, 1965.

[3]   Hoare, C. A. R., and Perrot, R. "Toward a Theory of Parallel Programming", Operating Systems Techniques, Academic Press, London, 1972.

[4]   Leifker, D. B., and Kanal, L. N. "Design and Analysis of Parallel SSS* Algorithms", Technical Report (in preparation), Department of Computer Science, University of Maryland.

[5]   Nilsson, N. "Principles of Artificial Intelligence", Tioga Publishing Co., Palo Alto, California, 1980.

[6]   Pearl, J. "Heuristics: Intelligent Search Strategies for Computer Problem Solving", Addison-Wesley Publishing Co., Reading, Massachusetts, 1984.

[7]   Stockman, G. "A Problem-Reduction Approach to the Linguistic Analysis of Waveforms", Ph.D. dissertation, TR-538, Department of Computer Science, University of Maryland, 1977.

[8]   Stockman, G., and Kanal, L. N. "Problem-Reduction Representation for the Linguistic Analysis of Waveforms", IEEE Transactions on Pattern Analysis Machine Intelligence, May 1983.

SPAN: Integrating Problem Solving Tactics

Daniel L.S. Berlin
Computer Science Department
Stanford University
Stanford, CA 94305

Abstract

This paper describes SPAN, a system designed to integrate a variety of problem solving tactics in a coherent package. The paper discusses some of the tactics that had been used in previous systems to overcome the combinatorial explosion that is inherent in any planning problem. It then continues with a description of SPAN architecture. Two case studies are presented. The first, from the blocks world, is already implemented, and the second, from the domain of bridge playing, is in the coding stage. SPAN's limitations are discussed and directions for further research are considered.

I   INTRODUCTION

Much of the activity in artificial intelligence can be thought of as problem solving, so it is not surprising that, over the years, a lot of effort has gone into developing automatic problem-solvers. These efforts at producing domain-independent techniques usually have concentrated on solving simple problems.

In a 1980 revision of an article first published in 1979, Earl Sacerdoti presented an overview of problem-solving tactics [Sacerdoti 79] [Sacerdoti 80]. In that paper he states:

> "To date, there has been no successful attempt known to this author to integrate a significant number of the tactics we have described into a single system."

This failure to integrate these tactics into a coherent package has been one of the main reasons that general domain-independent planning has met with limited success in solving non-trivial problems.

SPAN is a system for integrating a large variety of tactics into a cohesive package. The general architecture, along with those domain-independent parts necessary for planning in the relatively simple domain of the blocks world have been already implemented in the LOOPS programming language on the 1100 series XEROX personal work stations. Other domain-independent parts necessary for planning in more complex domains are currently being added.

SPAN's architecture allows us to combine the insights developed in Sacerdoti's NOAH [Sacerdoti 77], Sussman's HACKER [Sussman 75], and Waldinger's goal regression system (independently developed by Warren [Waldinger 77]

[Warren 74]); all of which were for ordering conjunctive sub-problems. The same framework is used to integrate these methods with tactics for choosing between alternatives. These techniques include splicing alternatives together (when neither is guaranteed to succeed), in addition to domain-specific comparisons of probability. A generalization of Berliner's B* algorithm [Berliner 78] can also be integrated into the system, to facilitate planning in a competitive domain.

II   HANDLING THE COMBINATORIAL EXPLOSION

Typically, the world is modeled by a series of propositions which describe what is true in the world (i.e. its state) at a particular time. An action is usually modeled as a transformation from propositions that hold in one world model to propositions that hold in the new world model after the action has been executed. These transformations are referred to as operators.

It may be the case that an operator requires certain conditions to be true in order for its action to be executable. These conditions are referred to as preconditions. An operator can be viewed as a solved problem, with the initial state specified by the preconditions, and the goal specified by the initial state and the transformation of the propositions.

In the simplest planning case, each operator corresponds to a single action in the real world. These operators are known as primitive operators. Typically, in any one state many different operators can be applied because their preconditions are true. Furthermore, it is not always clear which operator gets one closer to the goal state. For this reason, simple search techniques face a combinatorial explosion, and thus are unable to solve anything other than very elementary problems.

Much of the history of planning has been concerned with getting around this combinatorial explosion, and thus increasing the applicability of automatic problem solvers. Three ideas, in particular, have been useful in dampening the explosion. The first of these is the concept of abstraction. The second is the notion that some sub-problems (particularly the difficult ones) can constrain the number of solutions to other sub-problems, and so should be tackled first. The third is the idea that, if possible, one should always apply the best operator for getting from the initial state to the goal.

The advantage of abstraction is quite simple. If one can break down a large problem into a series of smaller problems, then solving all of the smaller problems will be easier than solving the original problem. The reason for this is that the breakdown into smaller problems is linear, whereas the effort to solve any particular problem is exponential.

This work was funded in part by NASA Grant #NAG 5-261, DARPA Contract #N00039-83-C-0136, and a fellowship from NL-Industries. Computing resources were supplied by XEROX-PARC and the SUMEX computing facility at Stanford (NIH Grant #RR-0785-11).

Many versions of abstraction exist, including ignoring some details in the state description, ignoring some operators, or combining some operators to form a macro-operator. In the end, all of these techniques are equivalent to creating abstract operators. An abstract operator is like a primitve operator in that it has preconditions and transformation rules. However, unlike primitive operators, it cannot be translated immediately into actions that can be carried out in the real world. Instead, it must be refined into a sequence of primitive operators. These primitive operators may add further preconditions of their own, and may specify further transformations. Thus an abstract operator has abstracted out some of the detail involved in solving the problem it addresses. This notion of abstraction is at the heart of criticality lists in ABSTRIPS [Sacerdoti 74] and the generalisation of the logic operators in GPS [Ernst 69].

The second point, that some problems constrain others, is used to determine which sub-problem to attack first. This is closely related to abstraction, since one of the criteria for defining an abstract operator is that it restrict the number of options available to solve other problems. Indeed, one can view a partial ordering of which sub-problems to attack first as a mapping of the initial problem into an abstract domain that ignores the details of the other sub-problems. This point forms the basis of Stefik's constraint satisfaction system [Stefik 80]. It also forms the basis of an even more extreme form of problem solving: scripts or skeletal plans [Friedland 79]. With scripts, once the abstract operator (ie. script) has been chosen, all that remains to be done is to instantiate the variables of primitive operations that compose it. The selection of primitive operations to compose the abstract operator is automatic.

The third point is that it is not always possible to know which operators to choose and in what order to choose them, but that intelligent choice of operators can substantially improve the problem solving. This has led to a number of strategies, including the "don't choose until you have to" strategy of NOAH, the "make a random choice and fix it later" strategy of HACKER, and the "choose an arbitrary order but change the order of the goals as necessary" strategy of Waldinger's goal regression system.

All of these insights and tactics have some merit, but is it possible to develop a system that unites these approaches, making use of each of them when appropriate? SPAN is such a system.

III   SPAN ARCHITECTURE

As mentioned earlier, a problem can be represented by an initial state and a goal state. Solving the problem consists of finding a sequence of primitive operators, whose consecutive application will result in a final state for which the goal conditions are true.

At the top level of the SPAN planning system there is a scheduler with an agenda of tasks. These tasks are domain-independent, or, more accurately, their domain of expertise is planning. A typical example of a task is *ordering conjunctive sub-problems*. These tasks are represented as objects with slots to store relevant information. For example, a task to order *conjunctive sub-problems* will have pointers to the sub-problems. In addition, each task has an attached procedure that performs the task. This procedure is executed when the task is selected from the agenda.

This mechanism is similar to the meta-planning of MOLGEN [Stefik 80] [Stefik 81]. The agenda here corresponds to its design layer. The problems associated with the tasks correspond to the planning layer, and each system has a simple interpreter. However, in SPAN we have dispensed with a strategy level. In MOLGEN, the only strategy choices available were least-commitment and guessing. Not all the design operators are affected by

differences in strategies, and local knowledge about the current state of the plan is likely to determine which strategy is the better choice, so this strategy knowledge is dispersed to the procedures that execute the design tasks. As in MOLGEN, preference is given to least-commitment, and arbitrary choices are only made as a last resort.

The key problem with any agenda-based system is deciding which task to do next. Selecting the wrong task can result in a lot of wasted planning effort. Several schemes exist for solving this problem. One technique is to provide priorities for each of the types of tasks. Unfortunately, global differences in the types of tasks do not always provide sufficient information to get an optimal ordering. Another is to poll each active task on the agenda (whose preconditions are satisfied) to see if it should be performed and to choose the one that is most confident the conditions are right for its execution. This involves a large overhead each time a task is to be selected. SPAN actually uses a variant on this second technique: It assumes that each active task is confident that it can be performed, and so selects one at random.   However, the procedure that performs the task has the ability to suspend its execution. Thus, if a task is selected and decides it should not be done at this time, it has the ability to tell the system to choose another task.   This produces a close approximation to the polling system with much less overhead.

As a result of the decision to randomly choose an active task, the agenda actually consists of three separate lists: a list of active tasks, a list of suspended tasks, and a history list of completed tasks.   At each cycle the scheduler randomly selects an active task and performs it.   If there are no active tasks, then the suspended ones are reactivated.

We will now examine the various types of planning tasks in SPAN.

IV   PLANNING TASKS

Solving a problem (when only the initial state and goal are known)

The system first checks to make sure that the initial state is completely defined. This means that there is a direct link from the intial state of the original problem to the initial state of this sub-problem, and that this link does not go through unsolved sub-problems. The reason for this is to guarantee that what could be known about the initial state is known. This is not to say that everything about the initial state is known; there might be information that is hidden from the planner, but it does guarantee the system is detecting real differences between the initial state and the goal. If this is not true then the task suspends itself, until such time as it becomes true.

Assuming the initial state is defined, this general problem is approached using means-ends analysis. Means-ends analysis is used because it is more flexible than forward or backward chaining. The goal is compared to the initial state and differences are determined. A sub-problem is proposed for each difference detected. These sub-problems are treated as an unordered set of conjunctive goals, whose collective solution constitutes a solution to the original problem. For each of these sub-problems a task is posted to find a sequence of operators that eliminates its difference. This is also known as reducing the difference detected. In addition, if more than one difference was detected, then a task is proposed to order the sub-problems. Obviously, if only one such difference was detected, then there is only one sub-problem to be ordered.

Reducing a detected difference

When a difference is detected, a task is posted to reduce that difference. This task indexes a procedure that uses domain-specific knowledge about how to reduce the detected difference. The procedure may do many things. One possibility is to delay its execution (by suspending the task) until further information becomes available from other parts of the plan. If it does execute, it may use a special purpose algorithm (eg. a routing algorithm in a robot planner). Alternatively, the procedure may propose an operator or a set of alternative operators.

Proposed operators may be abstract or primitive, and may be related to each other in any one of a number of ways. They may be an unordered set, or in a strict sequence as in a script.

Refining an abstract operator

When an abstract operator is proposed it needs to be refined. This refinement process invokes a domain-dependent procedure. The options available at this time are very similar to the options available when reducing a detected difference. Further tests may be performed, or a sequence of sub-operators may be proposed. These sub-operators may or may not be ordered, and there may or may not be alternative choices available. Whenever an unordered sequence is proposed, a task to order the sequence is posted. Similarly, whenever a collection of alternatives is proposed, a task to select an alternative is posted.

Ordering sub-problems

This task corresponds to the problem most often considered in early planning research. The body of its procedure consists of a number of rules for ordering sub-problems. It will suspend itself if none of the rules is applicable, in the hope that eventually information will become available that will aid in this decision. If, since there are no other tasks left to perfom, it is forced to make a choice when no other rules apply, it will do so in an arbitrary manner.

This task has much the same flavour as the techniques used by Sacerdoti in NOAH, but it also incorporates other techniques (see Case Study 1 below).

Choosing from amongst alternatives

Pretty much ignored by mainstream planning, this task becomes crucial when some domain information is inherently uncertain, and thus no plan can be guaranteed to work. In these cases, one must consider strategies involving the gathering of further information, and issues of recoverability from failed plans, rather than just taking the one most likely to succeed.

V   CASE STUDIES

We will now present two case studies. The first of these is an English-language trace of one of the blocks world examples that is already running on the system. The second is an example from the domain of declarer play in bridge and whose implementation has not been completed. This second example is more difficult than the blocks world examples, and demonstrates some of the additional issues that a domain-independent planner must address in more complex domains.

Case Study 1: Blocks World

Consider the following problem from the blocks world: The initial state consists of the block configuration where C is on top of A and block B is sitting separately on the table. This is represented by the conjunction: (On C A) (Clear B) (Clear C). The goal is a state in which the conjunction (On A B) (On B C) is true. Given the operators Stack and Unstack the solution for this problem is the sequence of actions: (Unstack C A) (Stack B C) (Stack A B).

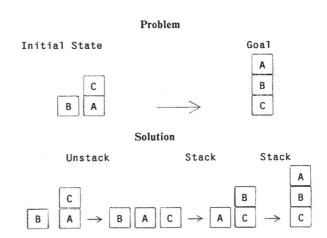

Figure 1. The problem, and SPAN's solution, discussed in Case Study 1.

We now present an English-language trace of SPAN solving this problem. This trace assumes that tasks will be chosen from the agenda in the worst possible order, thus demonstrating the system's ability to delay the execution of tasks until an appropriate time.

Initially, the only task on the agenda is to solve this problem. This task is selected and the body of the procedure associated with this task performs means-ends analysis on the problem. The two detected differences are that both (On A B) and (On B C) are initially false and need to be true in the goal state. Thus, the procedure creates a sub-problem for each difference detected, and adds to the agenda a corresponding task for each sub-problem to reduce the detected difference. Since there is more than one sub-problem, an additional task is posted to order the sub-problems. It is the execution of this third task (or its delay in execution) that determines the strategy taken in ordering conjunctive sub-goals. Both Sacerdoti's and Sussman's approach can be implemented this way, merely by changing the body of the procedure associated with this task. As implemented, this procedure in SPAN emphasizes Sacerdoti's approach.

Assume the task of ordering the sub-problems is now selected. It will examine the preconditions and goals of the two sub-problems and decide it has no basis for choosing which to do first. It thus defers this decision and is placed on the suspended list. SPAN will try again to order subproblems when there are no other tasks to perform.

Assume that the next task selected is the one associated with the sub-problem of making (On A B) true. The associated procedure uses the On function as an index to any operators that possibly could make (On A B) true. The only one suggested is the Stack operator, which has preconditions that A and B both be clear initially. This produces two sub-problems: first to get from the initial state to one in which (Clear A) (Clear B) is true and second to get from the state where (Clear A) (Clear B) is true to the goal where (On A B) is true. The second problem is solved by the primitive operator Stack. The first results in the posting of a task to solve the problem.

Assume this new task is the next one selected. The initial state of the sub-problem is unknown, since we do not know what actions will be taken from the initial state of the original problem before this sub-problem is tackled. This is a result of leaving unordered the sub-problems of making (On A B) and (On B C) true. The strategy adopted is to delay making a decision by suspending the task.

The procedure invoked to make (On B C) true opperates in the same way. It suggests the Stack operator with preconditions that B and C both be clear; which results in two sub-problems (one solved) and one task. The task (to make the preconditions true) is suspended because the initial state is not completely defined.

At this point, there are no more active tasks so the three suspended tasks are reexamined. If one of the tasks involving the preconditions is selected, it gets suspended, so we can assume that the ordering sub-problem is the next task selected and actually performed. The associated procedure examines the preconditions of making (On B C) true and notes that this conflicts with the goal of making (On A B) true. Thus it decides to order the (On B C) sub-problem before the (On A B) problem.

However, the procedure on ordering sub-problems does more. Since stacking B on C is a primitive operation, and thus its exact actions are known, and since the preconditions of (On A B) don't conflict with the goal of (On B C), these preconditions may be regressed back through the body of (Stack B on C). The heuristic used is to apply this technique of goal regression whenever possible. The reason is that it allows the earlier steps to reason with a more accurate picture of the complete goal. The result of this goal regression is to change the precondition for making (On B C) true to the conjunct: (Clear B) (Clear C) (Clear A). Now that an ordering for the sub-problems has been established, (On B C) is the first sub-problem and its initial state is known to be the initial state of the original problem. Thus when the task to solve the problem of making the conjunct (Clear B) (Clear C) (Clear A) true is selected, the initial state is properly defined. Means-ends analysis is applied and the difference detected is that (Clear A) is false initially, since (On C A) is true. A task is posted to make (Clear A) true.

Clearly this task must make (On C A) false in order to make (Clear A) true. (On C A), which is implemented as an object, knows the Unstack operator is a way of making the clause false. The task indexes this operator via the On clause. The Unstack operator is applied without any hitches and leads to the final plan: (Unstack C A) (Stack B C) (Stack A B).

The process of finding this solution applied some of the insights developed by Sacerdoti along with the goal regression techniques developed by Waldinger (also independently by Warren). The reason this system was able to combine these methods was a flexible control structure which allowed procedural information specific to the type of task being performed to be invoked at the correct moment. The efficiency of using meta-level reasoning about planning depends on the tradeoff between the benefits of executing the best task and the costs of (a) reasoning at this level plus (b) partially executing tasks that are later suspended plus (c) deciding to suspend tasks. Although this example in the blocks world is too simple to justify the overhead, we believe that, in general, the tradeoff will favor meta-level planning.

Case Study 2: Bridge

The proposed architecture handles the previous example very smoothly, but it has been solved by other systems with much less overhead. The justification for the system proposed is the ease with which it can handle more complex problems. Consider the following declarer play problem from the game of bridge:

```
        North
S   9   5   2
H   8   7   2
D   A   K   5   3
C   K   Q   2

        South
S   A   Q   4   3
H   A   5
D   Q   6   2
C   A   7   3
```

The contract is 3 no trump by South. The opening lead by West is the king of hearts.

The declarer, South, needs to win at least nine of the thirteen available tricks to make his contract. He has eight immediate winners; three top spades, three top diamonds, the ace of hearts and the ace of clubs. There are two possible sources for the ninth trick. If the missing diamonds are split 3-3, then the first three rounds of diamonds will force them all to be played and the fourth diamond in the dummy (North) will be high. If the diamonds are not split evenly this plan fails.

Alternately, if East is holding the king of clubs, then South can lead a club from the dummy, winning the trick with the queen if East plays low and capturing the king with the ace (thus setting up the queen) if East plays the king. If West has the king then this plan fails.

Using techniques similar to those in the previous example (only the operators change), the planning process produces these two alternative plans. In addition, a task is posted to select between the alternatives. The associated procedure with this task first tries to order the alternatives so that if one branch fails the other can still be tried. In this particular case, the system determines that if the diamonds are tried first and don't split, then the club finesse can still be attempted. However, if the club finesse is tried first and fails the declarer may never get a chance to test the diamonds, since, if the hearts are not split 4-4, the defenders will win at least four hearts in addition to the king of clubs. Thus a hybrid plan, to test the diamonds and, if they don't split 3-3, to take the club finesse, is produced.

If this attempted hybridization had failed, the sytem would have looked at the relative probabilities of success for each alternative. This comparison could have been made using whatever method of uncertainty measurement was relevant for the particular domain (probably table look-up in this case).

VI   LIMITATIONS

The system developed does have some inherent limitations. It assumes the world can be modeled as a series of discrete states and that operations on the world can be modeled as a transformation between these states. This discrete time assumption is basic to the model.

Furthermore, the strategies that have been developed have assumed that planning time is free. There is no consideration of limitations on planning resources. There has also been no consideration of the possibility that the world may change while the planning process is going on. These assumptions are not fundamental to the model, but I have not concentrated my efforts on handling these problems.

VII   FUTURE WORK

As mentioned earlier, this system has been developed in the blocks world domain, and is currently being extended to handle the domain of declarer play for the game of bridge. Actual implementation in this domain may suggest better selection criteria for tasks, instead of the random selection now used. It may also confirm (or invalidate) the decision not to bother with an explicit strategy space.

More importantly, more difficult examples within this domain will push on the strategies for choosing amongst alternative plans. These strategies have not yet been implemented because, in the blocks world domain, there has been no need.

There will also be an opportunity to expand the types of tasks to include the collection of data and the execution of a partial plan. This interaction with the world will probably necessitate the establishment of priorities within the agenda, since execution tasks should be delayed until after the planning has been done, and some planning should be delayed until after new information that becomes available during the execution process is checked for relevance.

As a final point, research in the bridge domain will bring the techniques specific to competitive planning into the fold. In particular, the B* algorithm can be adapted to the analysis of interacting hierarchical plans. In some cases it is even possible by graphical analysis of hierarchical plans to determine the critical paths along which two competing plans interact, and thus to avoid most of the combinatorics involved in competitive planning.

Epilog

Danny Berlin died in early 1985. He had already analyzed the applicability of the B* algorithm and the technique of graphical analysis of interacting plans, but he did not get to complete the implementation of the second example. This paper was written by him. The camera-ready copy was prepared by Lucy M. Berlin and his advisor Bruce G. Buchanan.

References

[Berliner 78]   Berliner, H.J.
The B* Search Algorithm: A best-first proof procedure.
Technical Report CMU-CS-78-112, Carnegie-Mellon University, 1978.

[Ernst 69]   Ernst, G.W. and A. Newell.
GPS: A Case Study in Generality and Problem Solving.
Academic Press, New York, 1969.

[Friedland 79]   Friedland, P.
Knowledge-based Hierarchical Planning in Molecular Genetics.
PhD thesis, Computer Science Department, Stanford University, September, 1979.
Report CS-79-760.

[Sacerdoti 74]   Sacerdoti, E.D.
Planning in a Hierarchy of Abstraction Spaces.
Artificial Intelligence 5(2):115-135, Summer, 1974.

[Sacerdoti 77]   Sacerdoti, E.D.
A Structure for Plans and Behavior.
Elsevier North-Holland, New York, 1977.

[Sacerdoti 79]   Sacerdoti, E.D.
Problem Solving Tactics.
In *Proc. Sixth International Joint Conference on Artificial Intelligence,* pages 1077-1085. IJCAI, Tokyo, Japan, 1979.

[Sacerdoti 80]   Sacerdoti, E.D.
Problem Solving Tactics.
AI Magazine 2(1):7-14, Winter, 1980.

[Stefik 80]   Stefik, M.J.
Planning with Constraints.
Technical Report STAN-CS-80-784, Computer Science Department, Stanford University, January, 1980.

[Stefik 81]   Stefik, M.J.
Planning and Meta-Planning.
Artificial Intelligence 16(2):141-169, May, 1981.

[Sussman 75]   Sussman, G.J.
A Computer Model of Skill Acquisition.
American Elsevier, New York, 1975.

[Waldinger 77]   Waldinger, R.
Achieving Several Goals Simultaneously.
In *Machine Intelligence 8, E.W. Elcock and D. Michie eds.,* pages 94-136. Ellis Horwood Limited, Chinchester, England, 1977.

[Warren 74]   Warren, D.H.D.
WARPLAN: A system for generating plans.
Technical Report 76, Department of Computational Logic, University of Edinburgh, June, 1974.

Deadlines, Travel Time, and Robot Problem Solving

David Miller, R. James Firby, and Thomas Dean

Yale University
Department of Computer Science
P.O. Box 2158 Yale Station
New Haven, Connecticut 06520

1 Abstract

This paper describes some extensions to the reductionist planning paradigm typified by Sacerdoti's *NOAH* program. Certain inadequacies of the partial ordering scheme used in *NOAH* are pointed out and a new architecture is detailed which circumvents these problems. An example from the semi-automated factory domain is used to illustrate features of the new planner. Techniques for eliminating unnecessary travel time by the robot and avoiding backtracking due to deadline failures are discussed and their incorporation in the planner is described.

2 Introduction

Most planners since *NOAH* [8] have represented a plan for a set of tasks as a partial (ie., non-linear) ordering of the steps required for carrying out those tasks. *NOAH* and its successors (eg., *NONLIN* [9] and *DEVISER* [10]) employ a partially ordered network of tasks to avoid early and unnecessary commitment to task orderings. The motivation for this is to eliminate backtracking. However, maintaining a consistent partial order is difficult in domains where the fact that tasks actually take time plays an important role: domains in which deadlines or robot travel time are serious considerations.

That a partial order leads unavoidably to a deadline failure usually cannot be discovered until an attempt is made to linearize the ordering. However, failure to notice a deadline violation early will require backtracking later.

In addition, planning with a partial order is not well suited to efficiently managing factors like travel or machine running time. It's not difficult to represent that moving from one workstation to another takes time proportional to the distance separating the two workstations. However, generating a plan that eliminates unnecessary travel between workstations requires exploring some of the linearized task orderings. It is not until tasks are completely ordered that the source and destination workstations of each movement can be known and the travel time computed with any accuracy.

In this paper we describe an approach to planning that combines the use of a partial order with a method for exploring the possible repercussions of that partial order. This approach has been implemented in the *FORBIN* planner (**F**irst **O**rder **RoB**ot **IN**tender). *FORBIN* is a planner capable of solving a significantly wider class of problems than any of its predecessors.

2.1 The Factory Domain

One problem domain that has been used for exploring our approach to planning is what we refer to as the *semi-automated factory*. In this domain a mobile robot operator wanders about the factory floor (see Figure 1) performing basic maintenance and supply operations to the factory machinery. The purpose of the factory is the creation of *widgets* and *gizmos*. Whether a *widget* or *gizmo* is produced depends on which bit from the *tool area* has been inserted into the factory's *lathe*. Once a *widget* or *gizmo* has been created it is placed onto the appropriate shelf. The amount of time needed to create an object depends on the type of object being cut.

This factory differs from a typical job-shop factory in several important respects. Two of these are that a complete *job* is not run at one workstation at a time (ie., not all of the widgets in an order are turned on the lathe before being moved to the storage shelves) and the travel time of the robot from one place in the factory to another can be a significant part of the overall factory production time. Like any factory, this one has production deadlines to meet. A typical problem is to construct a number of widgets and gizmos where some of each must be done within a given time limit.

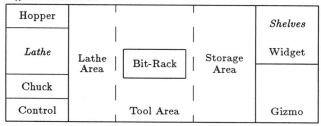

Figure 1: Layout of the Factory

3 An Overview of the FORBIN Project

The most important issue *FORBIN* is designed to explore is the use of spatial and temporal reasoning in planning. To do this the system supplements the usual hierarchical planner with two new modules: The *Time Map Manager* and the *Time Optimizing Scheduler*.

3.1 The Time Map Manager [TMM]

The TMM [3] is a set of routines for reasoning about the occurrence of tasks and the spans of time over which facts can be said to hold. The data structure that the TMM uses to store and manipulate the temporal relationships between these facts is called a *time map*.

Plans generally have assumptions or facts which must be true in order that the plan be applicable in a given situation. The TMM is queried during plan selection to locate intervals over which these facts are true. It returns a number of interval-constraint set pairs each of which specifies a set of constraints on the partial order that must be imposed to keep the assumptions valid over its interval. The TMM monitors the continued validity of plans by setting up nonmonotonic data dependency justifications composed of assertions called *protections*. If a protection fails then the TMM notifies the planner of any plans threatened by the failed protection. The failure is annotated in such a way as to facilitate corrective action. The TMM also anticipates possible protection failures and suggests ordering constraints to avoid undesirable interactions. The *FORBIN* planner uses this same machinery to handle simple resource management chores (eg., reserve the lathe for a 30 minute stretch beginning after 8:00 but ending before noon). The TMM subsumes and extends the functionality of the TOME (Table Of Multiple Effects) mechanism used in *NOAH*.

3.2 The Time Optimizing Scheduler [TOS]

The nature of tasks in the *FORBIN* domain necessitate that the robot spend considerable amounts of time in transit between workstations. The *FORBIN* system uses the TOS to make plan selection decisions that reduce this travel time and make the overall plan as short as possible.

In the semi-automated factory, where travel distances are sizable with respect to production times, travel time considerations are very important in deciding which of the possible task expansions will eventually yield the most efficient final plan. The TOS chooses the plan that fits best in the overall scheme of things by producing the most efficient schedule of execution using each possible expansion, and choosing the best. The chosen expansion is used in further planning and the schedule is used to guide the order of expansion of further subtasks. When planning is complete the schedule provides the order in which the robot should execute the final set of primitive actions.

The TOS offers an inexpensive method of exploring the schedules that can be formed from the partial order of a set of tasks. The search space for scheduling a set of tasks is factorial in the number of tasks, but [7] and [11] contain heuristics for trimming it significantly. These heuristics mainly use temporal constraints to eliminate impossible schedules before they have been fully elaborated. Ordering constraints and deadlines often eliminate all but a few possible schedules.

A further computational saving is derived by rating the quality of the schedules being constructed, and pursuing only the most promising ones. For the *FORBIN* factory domain the overall execution time is the chief determiner of a schedule's quality and is the discriminating feature among legal, consistent schedules.

No rating system is perfect and it is possible that the schedule first picked by the TOS may not be the optimal one. Since the TOS uses a heuristic search to produce schedules, a longer search time will increase the probability of the program finding the optimal schedule. The TOS can be set to search at any level of detail and can therefore find the best schedule that balances planning time against execution time.

3.3 Flow of Control

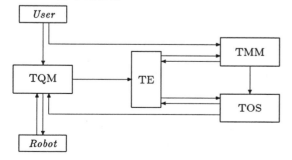

Figure 2: Flow of Control in the FORBIN System

Along with the TMM and TOS, the *FORBIN* system has two other major modules: the *Task Expander* [TE], and the *Task Queue Manager* [TQM]. The TE is responsible for finding all possible plans that can be used to expand a task, and the TQM maintains two queues: the unexpanded tasks in the order they should be expanded and the primitive actions in the order they should be executed. The communication paths between these modules are shown in Figure 2. In addition to the basic modules, interfaces are provided for a *User* which gives the system new tasks to perform, and a *Robot* which performs the primitive actions directed by the planner.

While there are non-primitive tasks in the TQM, *FORBIN*:

1. Pops the first task in the TQM and passes it to the TE.

2. The TE finds all the plan descriptions in the plan library which match the task. For each plan it finds, it asks the TMM for a time or times when the plan could be used.

3. The TMM derives all of the constraints necessary to make each plan suggested by the TE feasible.

4. The TOS takes all the plan-constraint sets and finds the one that produces the best schedule when combined with the contents of the rest of the time map.

5. The TQM gets the schedule and the TE is passed the selected plan.

6. The TQM takes the schedule, extracts the new subtasks from it and adds them to its queues. The ordering in the schedule is used to help order the items in the queues.

7. The cycle then repeats until the TQM has no more unexpanded tasks.

3.4 The Plan Formalism

To facilitate this flow of control, the plan formalism used by the *FORBIN* system specifies not only the action and ordering information found in other formalisms, but also the temporal and spatial features required by the TMM and TOS. Each plan specification includes:

- Conditions that must hold true before and during plan execution.

- How to expand the plan into lower level actions.

- Effects of some actions and the protections on those effects.

- Aproximately how long the plan will take to execute.

- Where the robot must be to carry out the plan.

- The utility of the plan compared to others for that task.

Plans come in two parts: the *property* descriptor and the *plan* descriptor. For any given task, such as `(make ?thing)`, there will be only a single property descriptor no matter how many plans there are. The property descriptor gives the approximate duration and position of a task before a plan is chosen for it: a combination of the durations and positions of all the plans known for the task. These estimates are required so that the TMM and TOS can deal effectively with tasks that are not yet expanded.

The plan descriptor is used when it is time to expand a task. The plan descriptor contains a list of the plan's subtasks and the mandatory ordering and time constraints that exist on those subtasks. The plan descriptor may also contain *assumptions* which must be predicted to hold true over the intervals specified in order for that particular plan descriptor to be able to be chosen as the actual plan for the task. The plan formalism is discussed in more detail in [4].

4   FORBIN and What Has Gone Before

The *FORBIN* planning system shares many of the characteristics of earlier planners like *NOAH* and *NONLIN* since it is a hierarchical planner that attempts to leave subtasks only partially ordered as long as possible. However, the TOS and TMM give *FORBIN* important new capabilities:

1. to deal with tasks that require specific amounts of time and must be performed at specific locations.

2. to represent deadlines so that plan steps can be synchronized with events outside the planner's control.

3. to produce near-optimal schedules that eliminate unnecessary robot travel and idle time.

The necessity of representing time in planning has been recognized by many researchers: [6], [1], [2]. The *FORBIN* system uses the time map to reason about the temporal intervals associated with tasks. All real tasks take time and hence it is critical that a planner be able to represent and deal with information concerning the duration and separation of tasks. The *FORBIN* treatment of time allows the system to deal with deadlines on tasks, to recognize explicit overlap of tasks where that is possible or necessary, and to compare the predicted execution time of different planning choices.

Some previous systems that have made extensive use of time are *ISIS*, [5], and *DEVISER*, [10]. *ISIS* uses a heuristic scheduling module to solve job-shop scheduling problems. However job-shop scheduling is too restrictive to handle many common aspects of typical problem solving domains. Thus *ISIS* does not incorporate travel time between workstations into its scheduling representation. *DEVISER*, though it produces a schedule, does not contain a scheduler. Instead it relies on the general hierarchical planning mechanism combined with backtracking to eventually produce a schedule. By not having a scheduler guide the plan expansion and ordering the results of *DEVISER*'s work can be very inefficient and may have involved very large amounts of backtracking.

Earlier planners often made no effort to produce a linear schedule of primitive actions from the partial order of the final plan expansion. In the *FORBIN* factory domain, such a linear schedule is required because the robot can do only one thing at a time. The TOS is used to help keep the best linear schedule implied by the partial order at each planning step as near to optimal (ie., short) as possible. To allow this, travel between tasks is not represented in the plan formalism, instead the location of the task is. Thus, as the TOS is examining possible linear schedules, it calculates the travel time between the ordered tasks as it fits them together. In this way, unneeded travel tasks are not generated and the TOS is free to order travel any way it chooses as long as it does not violate any other constraints on the tasks. The TOS can also overlap the execution of several tasks provided that the overlap is consistent with the constraints in the time map and it does not demand that the robot be more than one place at a time. These abilities of the TOS give *FORBIN* the opportunity to produce plans that make better use of time than previous planners.

5   Summary

Solutions to planning problems that involve realworld actions must take time and travel into account. The *FORBIN* planning system does this by using two special purpose modules. The TMM constructs and maintains a temporal database in which to reason about tasks and their consequences over time. It then uses this time map to anticipate and suggest methods of avoiding undesirable interactions. The TOS manipulates the partial order of subtasks to find the arrangement that takes best advantage of executing tasks in parallel and eliminates unnecessary travel in order to minimize overall plan execution costs.

A plan formalism has been given that allows all the necessary constraints needed to interface with these modules, to be expressed clearly and cleanly.

The overall system can plan solutions for tasks that have a wide variety of temporal and spatial constraints. The solutions produced by the system are not only consistent with the constraints placed on the problem, but are also near optimal with regards to their cost in time.

Acknowledgments

The authors wish to thank Steven Hanks, James Spohrer, and Drew McDermott for their comments and suggestions on this research. This work was supported in part by the Advanced Research Projects Agency of the Department of Defence and monitored under the Office of Naval Research under contract N00014-83-K-0281.

Bibliography

[1] Allen, James, *Maintaining knowledge about temporal intervals*, Comm. ACM, 26/11 (1983), pp. 832–843.

[2] Cheeseman, Peter, A Representation of Time for Automatic Planning, *Proc. IEEE Int. Conf. on Robotics,* 1984.

[3] Dean, T., Temporal Reasoning Involving Counterfactuals and Disjunctions, *Proc. of the Ninth Int. Joint Conf. on Artificial Intelligence*, IJCAI, AAAI, Los Angeles, CA, August 1985.

[4] Firby, R.J., Dean, T., Miller, D., Efficient Robot Planning with Deadlines and Travel Time, *Proc. of the 6th Int. Symp. on Robotics and Automation*, IASTED, Santa Barbara, CA, May 1985.

[5] Fox, Mark S., *Constraint-Directed Search: A Case Study of Job-Shop Scheduling*, Technical Report CMU-RI-TR-83-22, CMU Robotics Institute, December 1983.

[6] McDermott, Drew V., *A temporal logic for reasoning about processes and plans*, Cognitive Science, 6 (1982), pp. 101–155.

[7] Miller, David, *Scheduling Heuristics for Problem Solvers*, Technical Report 264, Yale University Dept. of Comp. Sci., 1983.

[8] Sacerdoti, Earl, *A Structure for Plans and Behavior,* American Elsevier Publishing Company, Inc., 1977.

[9] Tate, Austin, Generating Project Networks, *Proc. IJCAI 5*, IJCAI, 1977, pp. 888–893.

[10] Vere, Steven, *Planning in Time: Windows and Durations for Activities and Goals*, IEEE Trans. on Pattern Analysis and Machine Intelligence, PAMI-5/3 (1983), pp. 246–267.

[11] Vere, Steven, *Temporal Scope of Assertions and Window Cutoff*, 1984. JPL, AI Research Group Memo.

TEMPORAL SCOPE OF ASSERTIONS AND WINDOW CUTOFF*

Steven Vere
Information Systems Division
Jet Propulsion Laboratory
Pasadena, California 91109

ABSTRACT

In a temporal planning and reasoning system, many logical assertions will have a limited life span: they are "terminated" by later, contradictory assertions. By observing assertion terminators, the lifetime of an assertion can be bounded within an interval called the scope. Assertion scopes can greatly reduce the number of relevant matches returned from an assertion database. Scopes and terminators also permit the more efficient determination of contemporaneous assertions for forward chaining of event rules. Window cutoff is an execution time accelerator for determining if two activities are ordered in a plan, a high frequency, utility operation in plan synthesis. The acceleration is accomplished by doing an early cutoff of search paths to the "lower" activity based on time constraints. These mechanisms reduced the execution time of a temporal planner called DEVISER by four orders of magnitude for 70 goals, allowing very long planning problems to be solved. The mechanisms described employ time constraints to accelerate planning, and are not applicable to precedence planners. DEVISER is a performance planner which has been applied experimentally in planning activities for the Voyager spacecraft in its encounter with Uranus in 1986.

I INTRODUCTION

In September 1983 I translated my temporal planner DEVISER I [Vere, 1983] from INTERLISP on the DEC-10 to ZETALISP on the Symbolics 3600 computer. The ZETALISP version executed about ten times faster and no longer ran out of memory on larger problems. These new circumstances enabled me to perform some experiments to see how execution time increased as a function of the number of goals. The experiments were for a Voyager knowledge base, with a set of imaging goals which required no backtracking. The results are given in Figure 1, a semilog graph. DEVISER I showed a steep exponential growth which soon overwhelmed the

----

*This paper presents the results of one phase of research carried out at the Jet Propulsion Laboratory, California Institute of Technology, and sponsored by the National Aeronautics and Space Administration under Contract No. NAS-918.

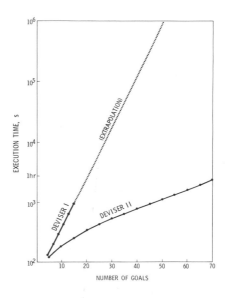

Figure 1. DEVISER Performance Curves

faster machine. Beyond 15 goals the graph is an extrapolation. Dissatisfaction with these results led me to consider time constraints as a means for improving performance. Since then a new version of the planner, DEVISER II, has been implemented which exhibits a much shallower performance curve. This improvement amounts to an estimated four orders of magnitude for 70 goals, and is due to the mechanisms which will be described. These mechanisms apply time constraints to improve the efficiency of several important low level operations of plan synthesis. About three fourths of the slope improvement in Figure 1 is due to temporal scoping, and the remaining one fourth is due to window cutoff.

In the past, temporal planners have been investigated because many applications require time as an explicit parameter. The results of this investigation indicate that time can also serve as an important source of additional constraints which can accelerate planning.

DEVISER II lies along the evolutionary path of NOAH [Sacerdoti, 1977] and NONLIN [Tate, 1977]. These earlier planners did not model time. Such a program will be called a <u>precedence planner</u>, since it merely establishes the precedence of activities in a plan. Other approaches to incorporating time into a planner are to be found in [Allen and Koomen, 1983; Cheeseman, 1983; McDermott, 1982; and Salter, 1983]. These papers, with one exception, do not address the question of the efficiency or performance curves of the resulting system. Allen confessed that his system was rather inefficient even on blocksworld problems. None have attempted to take advantage of time constraints to improve the efficiency of the planner.

II REVIEW OF DEVISER WINDOW LOGIC

In a temporal logic system, the truth of an assertion (literal) must in effect be a function of time. (Throughout this paper the terms assertion and literal may be used interchangeably). In the "window logic" system of DEVISER, every assertion is associated with an activity, and every activity has associated with it a start time interval ("window") and a duration, which may be a function of the activity parameters.

In a temporal blocksworld where a PICKUP action requires 1 second, the action description is

```
(PICKUP ACTION
   ((CLEAR x)
    (ONTABLE x))
   --->
   ((HOLDING x)
    (NOT (ONTABLE x))
    (NOT (CLEAR x)))
  (DURATION 1 SECOND))
```

Figure 2 shows the temporal relation between preconditions and postconditions. The extent of the preconditions and postconditions are indicated by timelines. Preconditions must become true on or before the start of the activity, and persist through the duration of that activity. Preconditions not contradicted by postconditions continue to hold. Postconditions (assertions) of an activity become true when the activity finishes and continue to hold indefinitely thereafter until they are explicitly contradicted by assertions of a later activity. If certain preconditions need only hold at the start of an activity (but not through the duration), that activity may be decomposed into subactivities whose preconditions behave as in Figure 2. This is explained in [Vere, 1983].

The figure shows the start time of the activity as a point in time. This is generally only true for activities which have been scheduled. During plan generation, the start time is typically an interval. This should be contrasted with the conventions of other temporal logic systems (e.g. [Allen and Koomen, 1983]) in which an interval specifies the lifetime of an assertion, and the start time is constrained to a point.

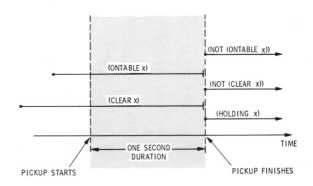

Figure 2. Timeline Diagram for the Pickup Action

Figure 3 shows a small blocksworld plan in which a deadline is imposed on the goal state. The plan start time is 0. The three actions in the plan have only interval constraints on their start times. The dashed lines may be ignored for the moment. Note that each activity except for the start and stop nodes has a start time window, duration, and set of assertions.

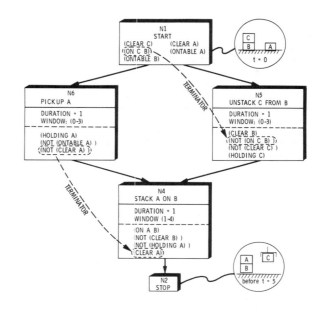

Figure 3. Terminator Relations in a Blocksworld Plan

Strictly speaking, it is activity nodes which are ordered and have start times, not assertions. However, it will be convenient to speak of assertions being ordered or having start times when in fact these relations apply to the nodes to which those assertions belong.

III ASSERTION TERMINATORS AND TEMPORAL SCOPES

In a temporal logic, assertions may in the course of time cease to be true. However, they do not die naturally; instead, they are terminated by later contradictory asertions.

Assertion T is defined to be a _terminator_ for assertion A iff: A and T are contradictory; T follows A in time; and no assertion T' exists satisfying the first two conditions such that T follows T' in time.

Usually an assertion has a single terminator, or none at all. However, because activities in a plan are only partially ordered, it is possible for an assertion to have several terminators which are mutually unordered. Also, as planning progresses and new activities are introduced and ordered, the terminator(s) of an assertion may change.

Referring back to Figure 3, the dashed lines connect selected assertions and their terminators. Thus (CLEAR A) of N4 is the terminator of (NOT (CLEAR A)) of N6. In the case where an assertion has no terminator, it holds forever. (ON A B) of N4 is one example of an unterminated assertion.

The _temporal scope_ of an assertion A is defined as an interval (t1 t2) where t1 is the earliest finish time of the assertion's activity node and t2 is the minimum of the latest finish times of the terminators of A, or infinity if the assertion is unterminated. Thus the scope _bounds_ the lifetime of the assertion. Since activity start times and terminators change as planning proceeds, so do temporal scopes. Each time the latest start time or duration of an activity is revised, a check is made of all assertions of that activity. If an assertion serves as a terminator of an earlier assertion, the scope of that earlier assertion may have to be revised too.

Again referring to Figure 3, we can deduce that the temporal scope of (NOT (CLEAR A)) in N6 is (1 5) since the earliest finish time of N6 is 1 and the latest finish time of N4, which asserts the terminator (CLEAR A), is 5. Figure 4 illustrates the notion of temporal scopes in the abstract, and shows their relation to earliest and latest finish times for assertions and their terminators.

Maintaining temporal scopes for each assertion during plan synthesis dramatically improves the overall efficiency of the planner for large goal sets. In a planning engine such as DEVISER, processing of assertion retrievals is a fundamental contributor to total execution time. Screening out irrelevant retrievals with the temporal scope mechanism vastly shortens the number of assertion candidates which must be sorted and processed by fundamental, high frequency planning operations.

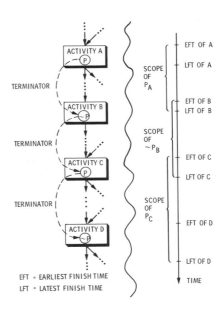

EFT = EARLIEST FINISH TIME
LFT = LATEST FINISH TIME

Figure 4. Terminators and Scopes in the Abstract

IV TIME BOUNDED ASSERTION RETRIEVALS

The primary application of terminators and scopes is in screening retrievals from the distributed assertion database. Without scopes, the retrieval mechanism must return a list of all literals matching a given pattern. The subroutine requesting the retrieval must then process this list to determine the "relevant" matches, and this is time consuming. The function BOUNDED.MATCHES is the low level function which uses scopes in accessing this database. BOUNDED.MATCHES takes as arguments an assertion and a time interval. It returns a list of all assertions in the database which match the given assertion and whose scopes intersect the given interval. Thus we are able to filter out most irrelevant retrievals with a quick numerical test. Of course this trick is going to work only in a planner which models time.

BOUNDED.MATCHES is called with high frequency in the planner in the following operations:

- looking for possible "tie-ins" to allow phantom node creation;

- finding conflicts after an expansion of a node or instantiation of a literal;

- checking phantom node violation after a literal instantiation;

- checking for infinite loops in the backtracking process;

- checking contemporaneous literals for forward chaining.

To illustrate, we will examine the first operation in more detail. If the assertion of a goal node matches an assertion true in the plan "above" the goal node (i.e. earlier), that goal node can be converted to a phantom node, which indicates that no action is required to satisfy the precondition. The situation is shown in Figure 5. B is a goal node for activity C, and B's assertion is (P). We want to know if there is some activity node A above which asserts (P) and if (P) still holds down at C. A necessary condition is that the scope of a matching literal, such as (P) of node A, have a scope intersecting the critical interval bounded by the earliest finish time and latest finish time of C. The result is that BOUNDED.MATCHES is able to return just the few matches overlapping the critical interval, rather than the hundred or more that might exist in a long plan. Of course, these bounded matches must still be further screened to select those literals which satisfy all requirements for a tie-in.

contemporaneous, their scopes may be intersected, a computationally cheap operation. If this intersection is null, the literals cannot be contemporaneous. However, a non-null intersection unfortunately is not sufficient. Figure 6 shows a segment of a plan diagram which illustrates this. Clearly assertions (A) and (B) are not contemporaneous, since the terminator of (A) is a predecessor of (B). Yet their scopes intersect: (A), (2 11); (B), (7 INFINITY).

This example illustrates the need for a second condition: for a set of literals to be contemporaneous, no literal in the set may follow the terminator of another literal in the set.

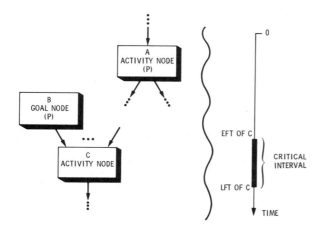

Figure 5. Application of Scopes to Phantom Node Creation

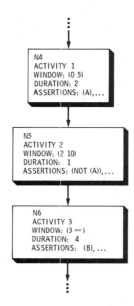

Figure 6. Non-null Scope Intersection Counterexample

V FINDING CONTEMPORANEOUS LITERALS

Literals are <u>contemporaneous</u> if they are simultaneously true at some instant of time. In a dynamic temporal logic system, to determine if a forward-chaining event rule should fire, it is necessary to determine if there are contemporaneous literals which match the rule antecedent. The situation is more complex than in conventional forward chaining systems such as OPS5 [Forgy, 1982], in which there is a single set of assertions all simultaneously true. In a parallel plan, the assertions are sprinkled throughout the plan and it can be an expensive computational process to find contemporaneous matches for the antecedent. Here too the concepts of scope and terminators can help to accelerate the computation.

To determine if a set of candidate literals is

VI WINDOW CUTOFF

Window cutoff is a mechanism for accelerating the determination of whether one activity "follows" another in a plan , i.e. whether the activities are ordered. This is a fundamental, high-frequency utility operation in plan synthesis which contributes heavily to the total execution time of the planner. The ordering relation is the transitive closure of the successor relation, which is denoted by the solid directed arcs in a plan diagram such as Figure 3. Successors of an activity are stored explicitly in DEVISER II, but the ordering relation must be computed. (To store the ordering relation explicitly would be unthinkable since successors are constantly changing as the plan develops). For a precedence planner, determining if one activity follows another is straightforward but expensive. You just begin at one node and do a blind search down through the plan diagram looking for the other node. In a temporal planner, window cutoff provides a mechanism for early termination of search paths based on time constraints which must hold between ordered nodes.

Suppose we are trying to determine if activity node NB follows activity node NA in a plan. We begin by examining the successors of NA to see if NB is among them. If not, we must search among the successors of the successors . . ., keeping a record of nodes visited, until NB is found or all nodes reachable from NA have been visited. Suppose that we arrive at node NC somewhere below NA, that NC has not already been visited, and that NC is not NB. In a precedence planner we must now search the plan below NC. However, in a temporal planner we may be able to cut off the search at NC if the windows of NC and NB are such that NB could not possibly lie below NC.

Following is a tutorial version of the function ORDERED? which illustrates window cutoff:

```
;--------------------------------------------------
(DEFUN ORDERED? (NODE.A NODE.B VCODE)
  (PROG (A.DURATION RESULT)

  (IF (NULL VCODE) THEN
  !  (COUNTER = COUNTER + 1)
  !  (VCODE = COUNTER)
  )
  (A.DURATION = (DURATION.OF NODE.A))
  (IF (AND (<= ((EST NODE.A) + A.DURATION)
  !           (EST NODE.B))
  !         (<= ((LST NODE.A) + A.DURATION)
  !           (LST NODE.B))) THEN
  !  (FOREACH NODE.C IN (SUCCESSORS NODE.A)
  !  !  UNTIL RESULT DO
  !  !  (IF (NOT (VISITED? NODE.C VCODE)) THEN
  !  !  !  (RECORD.VISITATION NODE.C VCODE)
  !  !  !  (IF (EQ NODE.C NODE.B) THEN
  !  !  !  !  (RESULT = T)
  !  !  !  ELSE
  !  !  !  !  (RESULT = (ORDERED? NODE.C NODE.B
  !  !  !  !     VCODE))
  )  )  )  )
  (RETURN RESULT)
))
;--------------------------------------------------
```

VII CONCLUSION

The notions of temporal scopes and terminators contribute to the screening of assertion retrievals, and to the determination of contemporaneous assertions for forward chaining in a temporal planner. Window cutoff can accelerate the determination of the ordering relation on activities. These features dramatically improved the execution time performance of DEVISER, enabling it to solve in a few hours large planning problems for the Voyager spacecraft consisting of over one hundred goals. This is at least an order of magnitude faster than human performance. The mechanisms for this performance improvement apply only to temporal planners, since they are based on time constraints.

REFERENCES

[1] Allen, J. F. and J. A. Koomen, "Planning Using a Temporal World Model." In Proc. IJCAI-83, 741-747.

[2] Cheeseman, P. "A Representation of Time for Planning," Tech. Note 278, AI Center, SRI International, Menlo Park, California, Feb. 1983.

[3] Forgy, C. L. "Rete: A Fast Algorithm for the Many Pattern/Many Object Pattern Match Problem." Artificial Intelligence, Vol. 19, No. 1, September 1982, 17-37.

[4] McDermott, D. "A Temporal Logic for Reasoning About Processes and Plans." Cognitive Science, Vol. 6, 1982, 101-155.

[5] Sacerdoti, E. D. A Structure for Plans and Behavior. Elsevier, New York. 1977.

[6] Salter, R. M. "Planning in a Continuous Domain--An Introduction." Robotica, Vol. 1, 1983, 85-93.

[7] Tate, A. "Generating Project Networks." In Proc. IJCAI-77, 888-893.

[8] Vere, S. A. "Planning in Time: Windows and Durations for Activities and Goals." IEEE trans. on Pattern Analysis and Machine Intelligence, Vol. PAMI-5, No. 3, May 1983, 246-267.

Temporal Reasoning Involving Counterfactuals and Disjunctions

Thomas Dean

Yale University

ABSTRACT

This paper describes a mechanism for nonmonotonic temporal reasoning involving counterfactuals and disjunctions. The mechanism supports a method for exploring alternatives well suited to automatic planning. The application of these techniques to robot problem solving is discussed with an emphasis on reasoning about exclusive choices and monitoring the continued warrant and effectiveness of prevention tasks.

I. Introduction

A critical part of planning involves selecting a plan for achieving a particular task. A reduction type planner (e.g. NOAH [7]), faced with the problem of formulating a plan for the conjunction of two or more nonprimitive tasks, is often forced to make plan selection decisions on the basis of incomplete knowledge. The planner cannot anticipate interactions with tasks whose reduction (or detailed specification) it has yet to explore. Given that there exists no strong warrant for choosing one plan over another why should a planner make a choice at all? In certain situations it would seem that procrastination is appropriate.

The problem here is similar to one addressed by Sacerdoti in developing the NOAH planner. NOAH employed a strategy known as *least commitment* and a data structure known as a *procedural net* to avoid making ordering decisions until they were warranted by interactions discovered in the course of planning. This was a reaction to previous planners' use of what is called the *linear assumption*: the tasks in a conjunction of tasks to be solved are assumed to be independent and hence there is no harm in committing to some arbitrary order for the purposes of planning. The problem was that by committing early (and arbitrarily) the planner might have to explore a large number of alternative orderings before finding one that worked. Most planners [7] [9] [10] have made a similar assumption as regards plan selection; namely that in the absence of information to the contrary any plan for achieving a task will suffice.

In order to deal with the problems that arise as a result of making this assumption a number of strategies have been proposed. NOAH represented alternative plans for achieving a given task as a disjunction (implicitly exclusive) of plans. The planner expanded the current procedural net with each disjunct noting the type and number of interactions: this information served as the basis for choosing among the alternatives. A more general technique employing a context mechanism was proposed by Wilkins [11]. The problem with both of these approaches is that the planner is responsible for proposing descriptions of the world which follow from making certain decisions (choosing among alternatives). If a planner wanted to make sure it hadn't missed some fortuitous combination of choices it would have to construct and evaluate all such worlds (combinations of choices). The planner had no way of anticipating good and bad interactions without exploring the alternatives. What was really needed was an efficient method of discovering sets of choices to avoid (those that lead to problems) and sets of choices to consider seriously (those that consolidate effort).

If you are entertaining a number of apparently independent alternatives it seems reasonable that you are able to notice interactions, both advantageous and detrimental, involving sets of these alternatives. Suppose that I have a task of mailing a package and I'm considering either driving to the local UPS depot or using the regular mail service and walking to the post office. If I've recently thought about buying some stamps then I might want to take advantage of the opportunity of being at a location selling stamps afforded by the latter. Of course some consolidations are not possible. A planner must have some means of ignoring deductions based on effects achieved by exclusive alternatives. If you are planning a weekend trip but undecided on whether to spend it in a rural or an urban setting it would be a bit silly to formulate a plan which closely couples a relaxing walk in the countryside with a Broadway show.

In addition to reasoning about alternatives and aspects of the world that the planner has control over, a planner quite often finds itself in the position of reasoning about ways the world might have been had events turned out otherwise (counterfactuals). To reason about methods for preventing some predicted unpleasantness we have to be careful to distinguish the circumstances that prompted us to action from those brought about by our attempts to avoid the predicted events. I might plan to deposit a sum of money in my checking account to avoid the penalty from an overdraft. Having determined to do so it is not likely I will be fined but this shouldn't somehow lessen my resolve to actually carry out the actions required to make the deposit. Silly as this may sound, it requires some sophistication to avoid just such confusions.

This initial discussion was meant to outline some problems which have not been handled adequately by previous planning systems. The examples were meant to illustrate a class of situations which require reasoning about alternative, possibly exclusive, descriptions of the world. In the remainder of this paper I will describe a temporal reasoning module designed as part of a planning system which supports this sort of hypothetical reasoning. This short paper cannot hope to satisfy the curiosity of all and I encourage the interested reader to refer to [2] for a more complete exposition.

II. Planning and temporal reasoning

This section outlines the module used for temporal reasoning in the FORBIN planner [6]. This module is referred to as a *time map manager* (TMM) [1] and is loosely based on the representation described in [4]. A *time map* is a data structure which captures what is known about events occurring over time (e.g. their duration and relative ordering) and the effects of processes and actions (e.g. the persistence or the period of time over which such effects can be said to endure). The time map itself consists of a network whose nodes are points corresponding to the begin and end of what are called *time tokens*. A time token denotes an interval associated with the occurrence of an event or an instance of a fact being believed to become true and persist for some period. The points in the network are connected by arcs indicating *constraints* on the distance separating points. A constraint is represented as an interval on the real number line denoting an upper and lower bound on the distance separating two points in the time map.

The TMM performs a rather simple sort of temporal reason maintenance. The system uses data dependencies and constraint propagation to ensure that whenever two time tokens asserting contradictory facts (or mutually exclusive states) are ordered as to their beginning points the earlier will be constrained (or *clipped*) to end before the later.

Plans generally have prerequisites or facts which must be true in order that the plan be applicable in a given situation. Plan choice involves selecting a plan and an interval in which that plan's prerequisites are predicted to be true. Having made such a selection the planner creates tokens corresponding to the plan steps (subtasks) and their effects, adds them to the time map along with associated constraints, and asserts that the plan is *plausible*. This assertion is however defeasible. Other tasks might be introduced during subsequent planning that clip the persistence of a prerequisite fact thereby invalidating the plan. The TMM monitors the continued validity of plausibility assertions by setting up nonmonotonic data dependency justifications composed of assertions called called *protections*

(after [8]). A fact Q is said to be protected throughout an interval, pt1 to pt2, just in case there exists a time token asserting Q that begins before pt1 and it's consistent to believe that it doesn't end before pt2.

If a protection fails then the TMM notifies the planner of any plans threatened by the failed protection. The failure is annotated in such a way as to facilitate corrective action. The TMM also anticipates possible protection failures and suggests ordering constraints to avoid undesirable interactions.

III. Handling disjunctions

Still the machinery outlined above won't allow us to represent protections of the form "a task T for preventing an event E is warranted just in case E would occur if T didn't". Neither will it allow us to consider more than one reduction for a given task at a time. The latter involves reasoning about disjunctions.

The techniques supporting this sort of reasoning rely upon a method for computing the choices warranting assertions in the time map. Choices (e.g. alternative plans or ordering decisions) are represented as boolean variables. Each assertion is labeled with a boolean formula indicating under which choices the assertion is believed. Labels are computed using a method similar to that employed in McDermott's context mechanism [5]. McDermott's system was designed to reason about a large number of contexts **sequentially**. It demands that the user specify a particular context (set of choices) to consider. It is essential to our problem that we be able to reason about many sets of choices **simultaneously**. The mechanism must also be able to ignore certain sets of choices (e.g. those including exclusive alternatives). The TMM employs techniques similar to those used by deKleer [3] to reason about exclusive alternatives and disregard sets of choices no longer deemed worth considering. The algorithms are described in detail in [2].

To illustrate how the TMM works in reasoning about choices I'll provide an abbreviated example drawn from the machine shop domain. Suppose that the robot operator in a job shop is contracted to machine a special order flange from a blank casting. The task requires that a certain diameter hole be drilled and one side of the casting be faced (i.e. cut or milled flush). These two subtasks can be performed in any order. Both drilling and facing can be done on either the vertical mill or on the engine lathe. Suppose that the robot chooses to expand the drilling task using two exclusive plans, one using the mill and another using the lathe. I'll ignore all subtasks except for prerequisite tasks responsible for installing attachments. Initially the mill has the face milling attachment installed and the lathe has a collet chuck. Drilling on the mill will require a fly cutting attachment while a four jaw chuck is required for drilling on the lathe. The facing task is expanded next and the robot, aided by the TMM, chooses to explore two options: use the lathe, taking advantage of the fact that the four jaw chuck is already in place or use the mill (in this case requiring the collet chuck) and schedule the facing task before the task to install the fly cutter. At the time the facing task alternatives are submitted to the TMM it sets up the necessary protections to monitor the tasks' plausibility, and suggests a number of constraints to help avoid protection violations. Notice that while the two tasks, drilling and facing, are still independent, the plans chosen for them are now very much interlinked. To face using the lathe requires that the robot choose to drill using the lathe. If the robot chooses to both drill and face using the mill then it must do the facing task first in order to avoid a protection failure.

This just begins to demonstrate the utility of temporal reasoning about choices. The TMM handles dependent choices (nested decisions) and provides considerable assistance at plan selection time in pointing out options that give rise to advantageous or disadvantageous interactions. This same machinery is also used for reasoning about counterfactuals and we'll consider how in the next section.

IV. Complex protections

For the most part, in reasoning about hypothetical situations, what we want is a virtual copy of some existing situation with just a few changes. For instance suppose that I'm concerned about a situation in which I ignore a dozen or so parking tickets and the city tows my car. So I consider another situation in which I bribe a city official to indefinitely postpone action on my case. My warrant for paying the bribe depends upon the immediate threat of having my car towed. If that threat evaporates (e.g. the news reports a backlog in the handling of traffic violations which has forced the city to issue amnesty for all offenders) then I should definitely question my motivation for giving money to that official. On the other hand if I discover that my method for handling the situation is ineffectual (e.g. the official has been dismissed having been indicted for accepting bribes) then I had better consider alternative methods.

This sort of reasoning has often been modeled along the lines of a conditional proof where introducing and discharging assumptions is considered analogous to pushing and popping contexts. There are a number of problems with this, most of them stemming from the nonmonotonic character of reasoning about beliefs changing over time. From a computational point of view conditional proofs cache deductions in order to ease the computational burden incurred by continually rederiving the same formulae. Once one allows nonmonotonicity the process of caching is considerably complicated, as all deductions are potentially defeasible. A conditional proof in these circumstances must be represented as an ongoing computation. The TMM handles this in terms of reasoning about choices.

Let's consider the plight of a maintenance robot in a factory who is informed at 8:00 AM that OSHA (the U.S. government agency concerned with occupational health and safety) will make an inspection of his factory sometime after 12:00. The robot makes a critical assessment of his work space, mindful of the OSHA rules, notices that the main corridor is cluttered with scrap metal, and predicts that he will be fined for the safety hazard. The robot then determines to clean the aisles before noon in order to avoid the fine. In order to monitor the warrant for and effectiveness of the task to clean the aisles the TMM tags the token for the clean-up task as a choice. If the robot schedules work that will result in the corridor getting cluttered after the clean-up but before the inspection then the TMM will notice that the clean-up task is no longer effective. If on the other hand someone else cleans the corridor or the OSHA visit is called off then the clean-up task will no longer be warranted. The TMM monitors the continued warrant for prevention tasks essentially by considering a world in which the prevention task was never executed.

V. Conclusion

The TMM is applicable in planning domains in which for most tasks the planner has a number of alternative plans and the choice of alternative can make a significant difference in the efficiency of the composite plan.

References

[1] Dean, T.L. *Planning and Temporal Reasoning under Uncertainty*. In Proc. IEEE Workshop on Principles of Knowledge-Based Systems, Denver, Colorado, IEEE Dec 1984.

[2] Dean, T.L. *Temporal Imagery: An Approach to Reasoning about Time for Planning and Problem Solving*. Technical Report (forthcoming), Yale University 1984.

[3] deKleer, J. *Choices Without Backtracking*. In Proc. AAAI 84, Austin, Texas, AAAI, Aug 1984.

[4] McDermott, D.V. *A Temporal Logic for Reasoning about Processes and Plans*. Cognitive Science, 6:101-155, 1982.

[5] McDermott, D.V. *Contexts and Data Dependencies: a Synthesis*. In IEEE Transactions on Pattern Analysis and Machine Intelligence, Vol. PAMI-5, No. 3, pages 237-246, May 1983.

[6] Miller D.P., Firby, R.J., Dean T.L. *Deadlines, Travel Time, and Robot Problem Solving*. In Proc IJCAI-85, Los Angeles, CA, IJCAI, Aug 1985.

[7] Sacerdoti, E. *A Structure for Plans and Behavior*. American Elsevier Publishing Company, Inc., 1977.

[8] Sussman, Gerald J. *A Computer Model of Skill Acquisition*. American Elsevier Publishing Company Inc., 1975.

[9] Tate, A. *Generating Project Networks*. In Proc. IJCAI-5., IJCAI, 1977.

[10] Vere, S.A. *Planning in Time: Windows and Durations for Activities and Goals*. In IEEE Transactions on Pattern Analysis and Machine Intelligence, Vol. PAMI-5, No. 3, pages 246-267, May 1983.

[11] Wilkins, D. *Domain Independent Planning: Representation and Plan Generation*. Artificial Intelligence, 1984.

SHALLOW PLANNING AND RECOVERY PLANNING
BASED ON THE VERTICAL DECOMPOSITION
OF THE FLIGHT DOMAIN

David C. Chen

E-Systems, Inc., Garland Division
P.O. Box 660023
Dallas, Texas 75266-0023

ABSTRACT

This paper presents a planning architecture that can perform both planning and recovery planning in the complex and dynamic flight domain. The key to such a robust planner is the vertical decomposition of the domain knowledge where the flight domain is decomposed into four minidomains, each a model of the flight domain along some degree of global viewpoint. The decomposition of the flight domain into four nearly independent minidomains and the explicit modeling of the different degrees of global viewpoint reduce the domain complexity geometrically. The vertical decomposition of the domain knowledge results in shallow planning and shallow recovery planning.

I INTRODUCTION

Recent planning works [1,2,3,4,5] have shown sophisticated approaches to make planning tractable for increasingly realistic and complex domains. This paper introduces a planning architecture designed for complex and dynamic domains such as the flight domain. In addition to the many aspects of flight such as routing and navigation, trajectory planning, piloting, and subsystems management, the complex and dynamic nature of the flight domain is manifested in the many domain constraints imposed on the flight or the plan. For example, a safe flight is a plan that satisfies domain constraints such as "the aircraft shall be navigable at all times," "the aircraft shall not run out of fuel," and "the aircraft shall not stall."

The difficulty in satisfying these domain constraints is that they have different scopes and they interact with each other. The scope of a constraint is the length of the plan over which the constraint holds, or how far the effects of the constraint span the plan. For example, the constraint "do not run out of fuel" has a very broad scope, from takeoff to landing, and the planner cannot determine whether the constraint is satisfied until the entire plan has been generated. On the other hand, the "do not stall" constraint has a short scope; it spans a small

portion of the flight, on the order of one minute.

To complicate the situation further, the different aspects and the different constraints interact. For example, time efficiency dictates that the aircraft should cruise at high power setting, 75% power, which may add another refueling stop, increase the flight time, and possibly increase the flight distance. Since the "do not run out of fuel" constraint has a large scope, the planner cannot know that the 75% power setting, determined at the beginning of the flight, may cause a constraint violation until the end of the flight planning.

II VERTICAL DOMAIN KNOWLEDGE DECOMPOSITION

The planner can easily get into a catch-22 situation when trying to satisfy constraints of different scope. If the planner satisfies the narrow-scoped constraints first, it must guess at the global direction and do a tremendous amount of backtracking when the guesses do not satisfy the broad-scoped constraints. On the other hand, if the planner satisfies the broad-scoped constraints first, it must guess at the enablement precondition necessary to support the high-level plan; and again, much backtracking over the preconditions will occur. This catch-22 situation occurs because the planner tries to satisfy all the constraints at each instance during planning. Planning is much simpler if the planner only satisfies the constraints of one scope at a time. This is the essence of vertical domain knowledge decomposition.

A conceptual level is a minidomain that models the task domain at a breadth of scope. A conceptual level is a defined domain with its own world model, goals, operators, and constraints; it is a world unto itself. The task domain can be modeled at multiple scopes by constructing minidomains to match. The immediate effect of the conceptual levels approach is to break the complex domain into simpler homogeneous minidomains, and consequently, complex planning is transformed into a series of shallow planning. This is similar to dividing a difficult task into easier subtasks and then solving the subtasks except the complexity reduction is achieved through domain knowledge partitioning instead of task decomposition.

The flight domain has been divided into four minidomains, the subsystems level and the three

This work was supported in part by NASA under contract no. NASA-NAG 1-288 and by Air Force under contract no. F49620-82-K-0009.

minidomains modeling flight at different scopes: the route level with the largest scope, the trajectory level of intermediate scope, and the aerodynamics level with the least scope. Within the subsystems level, planning knowledge is further partitioned into groups of the engine system, the fuel system, and the electrical system. This is an example of horizontal domain decomposition.

The route level models the flight domain along aspects of navigation and route selection. At the route level, the world is modeled as a network of nodes and links where the nodes represent the airports and the vortac navigational transmitters and the links represent navigable paths. The links are also the route-level operators. The trajectory level models the traversing of the three-dimensional space. The world here is the space defined by the x,y,z axis, and the goal is a specific point in space. The aircraft is again modeled as a point, except that it now moves along a trajectory in space. The trajectory-level operator is a vector in space. The aerodynamics level models how the aircraft flies through air. The aircraft in motion is modeled as a system of force vectors in equilibrium. Qualitative knowledge guides the manipulation of the force vectors to achieve the desired trajectory and the derivation of the discrete control settings. The exact settings for most analog physical actions such as the throttle setting are derived from the quantitative experts.

The difference in scope between two conceptual levels does not imply an abstraction relationship between the two levels. Nor is the representation of the broad-scoped level vague or fuzzy. To the route planner, the nodes and links are specific and sufficient to perform the routing task. Interestingly, physical actions can reside in any level. Selecting the vortac frequency and radial selectors is a natural part of the navigation task and should be a part of the route level. Flap and elevator controls are physical actions that belong at the aerodynamics level.

III LEVELS INTERACTIONS

In order for the system to function correctly, the minidomains must cooperate, forming a hierarchy. The hierarchy for the flight domain and the interactions between the levels are shown in Figure 1. There are four kinds of interaction: the basis for the plan of the upper level is passed down to the lower level; the goal for the lower level is passed down from the upper level; the upper level may request the value of its capabilities from the lower level; and the capabilities of the upper level are updated by the lower level. These four interlevel actions are coordinated by the interlevel planner.

Planning proceeds top down because it is more efficient to satisfy the broad-scoped constraint first before satisfying the constraints of narrower scope. However, before the topmost planner can start, it needs to obtain its current

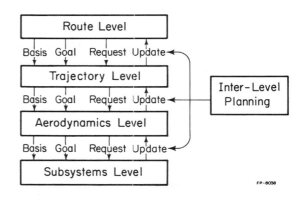

Figure 1   The Levels Hierarchy

capability. Model updating in this architecture is done bottom up because the lower levels have greater accuracy. For example, the route planner needs to know its current range and ceiling before it can start planning. The engine expert provides the engine thrust capacity. The aerodynamics planner calculates the aircraft ceiling based on the thrust capacity and the flaps and gear values. The ceiling is then passed upward to the route level. Figure 2 shows how the range is generated. The interlevel planner coordinates this process.

Although partitioning the task domain into minidomains may reduce the planning complexity at a given minidomain, it may also hide relevant information from the appropriate intralevel planner. For example, in order to streamline route planning, the aerodynamics knowledge is hidden from the route planner. However, the aircraft range varies greatly depending on how the aircraft is flown. A high power setting lowers the range. The range increases as the airspeed decreases and then decreases as the airspeed gets low. While the route planner should not be burdened with this knowledge, it should be able to benefit from this knowledge without any inconvenience. This is done by allowing the route planner to request additional capability at the expense of some other capability. An example is a request for an extra 20 miles of range with the airspeed negotiable from 250 knots to 200 knots. This request is depicted by the request arrow of Figure 1.

IV RECOVERY PLANNING

The reader may see now that failure is a normal part of the planning process due to the partitioned, distributed planning architecture. Fortunately, because each minidomain is much smaller than the task domain, replanning is less complicated. A recovery planning expert can be devised for each of the four flight levels. For example, at the route level, if the destination airport shuts down, the planner backtracks, seeking the best refueling airport and forward-chains toward it. Plan failure can also

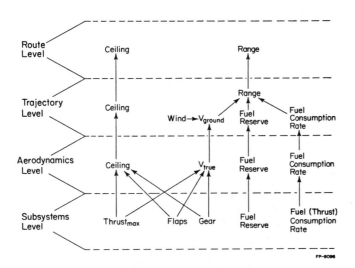

Figure 2   Bottom-Up Updating of the
Minidomain Models

is done at the ground level. The smaller pyramids on the right represent the solution spaces of the levels. The importance of the vertical stacking of the four smaller pyramids is that the growth of the solution space is linear compared to the geometric growth of the pyramid on the left.

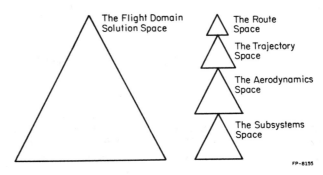

Figure 3   The Solution Spaces

propagate across levels. For example, suppose a thunderstorm develops along the flight path. Since the trajectory planner cannot recover from this fault, it tells the route planner that the implementation of the airway segment has failed. Plan failure has now propagated to the route level. The route planner treats the thunderstorm fault as a link failure and patches around the broken link, making sure there is range to cover the added distance.

Recovery planning can be simplified if the basis interlevel relationship is introduced. See Figure 1. When plan fails due to external changes, it is possible to recover locally within one level without disturbing the other levels. For example, suppose a headwind appears, changing the trajectory plan. The trajectory plan readjusts the landing phase. The trajectory planner knows that the range it gave the route level is no longer correct. However, if the trajectory planner knows the flight distance, it can determine if the route plan is still good. This is the purpose of the basis interlevel relationship in Figure 1. The basis is passed down from the upper level and tells the lower level what conditions must be true for the upper-level plan to hold. As long as the basis holds, the lower level can recover from plan faults without disturbing the upper level. This saves checking across the entire hierarchy every time the world changes.

V   THE SOLUTION SPACE

Partitioning the domain knowledge reduces the solution space by funneling some interactions through bottlenecks at the boundaries. When the partitioning is based on the different scopes of viewpoint, the solution space reduction is dramatic, as shown in Figure 3. The pyramid on the left shows the solution space if planning

VI   IMPLEMENTATION

A flight planner called SECURE has been constructed based on the approach outlined in this paper. SECURE generates a sequence of control movements that flies a simplified aircraft between any pair of six airports and has demonstrated recovery planning for failures such as closed destination airport, tail wind and head wind, engine failure, thunderstorm, and stuck. Currently SECURE ignores near-ground operations and random turbulences.

ACKNOWLEDGEMENT

This paper is based on the author's Ph.D. thesis. The author is grateful to his thesis advisors, the late Professor R.T. Chien and Professor David Waltz.

REFERENCES

[1] Corkill, D. and Lesser, V. "The Use of Meta-Level Control for Coordination in a Distributed Problem Solving Network." In Proc. IJCAI-83. pp. 748-756.

[2] Friedland, P. "Knowledge-Based Experiment Design in Molecular Genetics." Report STAN-CS-79-771, Stanford University, 1979.

[3] Sacerdoti, E. "A Structure for Plans and Behavior." Tech. Note 109, SRI International, 1975.

[4] Stefik, M. "Planning with Constraints." Report STAN-CS-80-784, Stanford University, 1980.

[5] Tate, A. "Project Planning Using a Hierarchical Non-Linear Planner." Report No. 25, AI Research Dept., University of Edinburg, 1976.

The Anatomy of Easy Problems: A Constraint-Satisfaction Formulation*

Rina Dechter and Judea Pearl

Computer Science Department, University of California, Los Angeles

ABSTRACT

This work aims towards the automatic generation of advice to guide the solution of difficult constraint-satisfaction problems (CSPs). The advice is generated by consulting relaxed, easy models which are backtrack-free.

We identify a subset of CSPs whose syntactic and semantic properties make them easy to solve. The syntactic properties involve the structure of the constraint graph, while the semantic properties guarantee some local consistencies among the constraints. In particular, problems supported by tree-like constraint graphs, and some width-2 graphs, can be easily solved and are therefore chosen as the target model for the relaxation scheme. Optimal algorithms for solving easy problems are presented and analyzed. Finally, an efficient method is introduced for extracting advice from easy problems and using it to speedup the solution of hard problems.

I INTRODUCTION

A. Why study easy problems?

An important component of human problem-solving expertise is the ability to use knowledge about solving easy problems to guide the solution of difficult ones. Only a few works in AI-- [12], [1]-- have attempted to equip machines with similar capabilities. Gaschnig [6], Guida et.al. [7], and Pearl [11] suggested that knowledge about easy problems could be instrumental in the mechanical discovery of heuristics. Accordingly, it should be possible to manipulate the representation of a difficult problem until it is transformed into an easy one, solve the easy problem, then use the solution to guide the search process in the original problem.

The implementation of this scheme requires three major steps: 1. simplification, 2. solution, 3. advice generation. Additionally, to perform the simplification step, we must have a simple, *a-priori* criterion for deciding when a problem lends itself to easy solution.

This paper uses the domain of constraint-satisfaction tasks to examine the feasibility of these three steps. It establishes criteria for recognizing classes of easy problems, it provides special procedures for solving them, and it introduces an efficient method of extracting advice from them.

Constraint-satisfaction problems (CSP) involve the assignment of values to variables subject to a set of constraints. Understanding three-dimensional drawings, graph coloring, electronic circuit analysis, and truth maintenance systems are examples of CSP problems. These are normally solved by some version of backtrack search which may require exponential search time (for example, the graph coloring problem is known to be NP-complete.)

In general, a problem is considered easy when its representation permits a solution in polynomial time. However, since we are dealing mainly with backtrack algorithms, we will consider a CSP **easy** if it can be solved by a **backtrack-free** procedure. Normally, a backtracking algorithm instantiates variables in a predetermined order, and for each next variable it chooses one value that is consistent with all previous assignments. If it doesn't find one, it **backtracks** to the previous variable, tries a new assignment for it, and continues from there. The algorithm stops when all variables have been assigned values or when no new untried values are left for the first variable. A backtrack-free search is one in which the backtracking algorithm completes without backtracking, thus producing a solution in time linear with the number of variables.

Most of our discussion is based on the concept of constraint-graphs [8] in which the nodes represent variables and the undirected arcs represent the existence of an explicit constraint between them. Freuder [5] has identified sufficient conditions for a constraint graph to yield a backtrack-free CSP, and has shown, for example, that tree-like constraint graphs can be made to satisfy these conditions, with a small amount of processing. Our main purpose here is to further study classes of constraint graphs lending themselves to backtrack-free solutions and to devise efficient algorithms for solving them. Once these classes are identified they can be chosen as

---

*This work was supported in part by the National Science Foundation, Grant #MCS 81-14209.

targets for a problem simplification scheme; constraints can be selectively deleted from the original specification so as to transform the original problem into a backtrack-free one. The simplified problem can then provide advice on choices pending in the original problem. For example, we propose to use the "number of consistent solutions in the simplified problem" as a figure of merit to establish priority of value assignments in the backtracking search of the original problem. We show that this figure of merit can be computed in time comparable to that of finding a single solution to an easy problem. (For details regarding the process of constraint-deletion see [2].)

B. *Definitions and Nomenclature*

Definition 1 ([5]): An **ordered constraint graph** is a constraint graph in which the nodes are linearly ordered to reflect the sequence of variable assignments executed by the backtrack search algorithm. The **width** of a node is the number of arcs that leads from that node to previous nodes, the **width of an ordering** is the maximum width of all nodes, and the **width of a graph** is the minimum width of all the orderings of that graph.

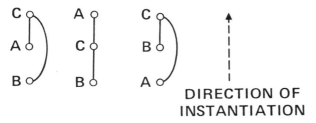

DIRECTION OF INSTANTIATION

FIGURE 1

Figure 1 presents three possible orderings of a constraint graph. The width of node C in the first ordering (from the left) is 2, while in the second ordering it is 1. The width of the first ordering is 2 while that of the second is 1. The width of the constraint graph is, therefore, 1. Freuder provided an efficient algorithm for finding both the width of a graph and the ordering corresponding to this width. He further showed that a constraint graph is a tree iff it is of width 1.

Montanari [10] and Mackworth [8] have introduced two kinds of local consistencies among constraints named **arc consistency** and **path consistency**. Their definitions assume that the graph is directed, i.e., each symmetric constraint is represented by two directed arcs.

Let D_i stand for the domain of variable V_i; $R_{ij}(x,y)$ stands for the assertion that (x,y) is permitted by the explicit constraint R_{ij} between V_i and V_j.

Definition 2 ([8]): Directed arc (V_i, V_j) is **arc consistent** if for any value $x \in D_i$ there is a value $y \in D_j$ such that $R_{ij}(x,y)$

Definition 3 ([10]): A path of length m through nodes $(i_0, i_1, \ldots, i_m)$ is **path consistent** if for any value $x \in D_{i_0}$ and $y \in D_{i_m}$ such that $R_{i_0 i_m}(x,y)$, there is a sequence of values $z_1 \in D_{i_1}, \ldots, z_{m-1} \in D_{i_{m-1}}$ such that

$$R_{i_0 i_1}(x,z_1) \text{ and } R_{i_1 i_2}(z_1,z_2) \text{ and} \ldots \text{and } R_{i_{m-1} i_m}(z_{m-1},y).$$

$R_{i_0 i_m}$ may also be the universal relation e.g., permitting all possible pairs.

A constraint graph is arc (path) consistent if each of its directed arcs (paths) is arc (path) consistent. Achieving "arc-consistency" means deleting certain values from the domains of certain variables such that the resultant graph will be arc-consistent, while still representing the same overall set of solutions. To achieve path-consistency, certain pairs of values that were initially allowed by the local constraints should be disallowed. Montanari and Mackworth have proposed polynomial-time algorithms for achieving arc-consistency and path consistency. In [9] it is shown that arc consistency can be achieved in $O(ek^3)$ while path consistency can be achieved in $O(n^3 k^5)$. n is the number of variables, k is the number of possible values, and e is the number of edges.

The following theorem is due to Freuder.

Theorem 1 [5]

(a)   If the constraint graph has a width 1 (i.e. the constraint graph is a tree) and if it is arc consistent then it admits backtrack-free solutions.

(b)   If the width of the constraint graph is 2 and it is also path consistent then it admits backtrack-free solutions.

The above theorem suggests that tree-like CSP'S (CSP's whose constraint graphs are trees) can be solved by first achieving arc consistency and then instantiating the variables in an order which makes the graph have width 1. Since this backtrack-free instantiation takes $O(ek)$ steps the whole problem can be solved in $O(nk^3)$ and, therefore, tree-like CSP's are easy. The test for this property is also easily verified; to check whether or not a given graph is a tree can be done by a regular $O(n^2)$ spanning tree algorithm.

It is important to note that a given CSP may have several equivalent representations, in the sense of admitting the same set of solutions. Yet each representation may have a different constraint-graph, one of which may be a tree. However, testing whether a CSP has an equivalent tree representation and finding such a representation might be a very difficult task.

The second part of the theorem tempts us to conclude that a width-2 constraint graph should admit a Backtrack-free solution after passing through a path-consistency algorithm. In this case, however, the path consistency algorithm may add arcs to the graph and increase its width beyond 2. This often happens when the algorithm deletes value-pairs from a pair of variables that were initially related by the universal constraint (having no connecting arc between them), and it is often the case that passage through a path-consistency algorithm renders the constraint-graph complete. It may happen, therefore, that no advantage could be taken of the fact that a CSP possesses a width-2 constraint graph if it is not already path consistent. We are not even sure whether width-2 suffices to preclude NP-completeness.

In the following section we give weaker definitions of arc and path consistency which are also sufficient for guaranteeing backtrack-free solutions but have two advantages over those defined by Montanari [10] and Mackworth [8]:

1. They can be achieved more efficiently, and

2. They add fewer arcs to the constraint-graph, thus preserving the graph width in a larger classes of problems.

II ALGORITHMS FOR ACHIEVING DIRECTIONAL CONSISTENCY

A. Case of Width-1

In constraint-graphs which are trees, full arc-consistency is more than what is actually required for enabling backtrack-free solutions. For example, if the constraint graph in figure 2 is ordered by (V_1, V_2, V_3, V_4), nothing is gained by making the directed arc (V_3, V_1) consistent.

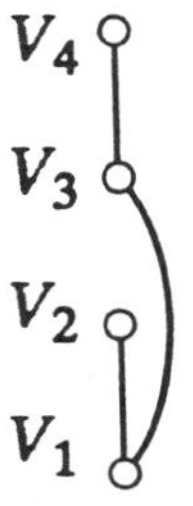

FIGURE 2

To ensure backtrack-free assignment, we need only make sure that any value assigned to variable V_1 will have at least one consistent value in D_3. This can be achieved by making only the directed arc (V_1, V_3) consistent, regardless of whether (V_3, V_1) is consistent. We therefore see that arc-consistency is required only w.r.t. a single direction, the one specified by the order in which the backtrack algorithm will later choose variables for instantiations. This motivates the following definitions.

Definition: Given an order d on the constraint graph R,

we say that R is d-arc-consistent if all the directed edges which follow the order d are arc-consistent.

Theorem 2:

Let d be a width-1 order of an ordered constraint-tree, T. If T is d-arc-consistent then the backtrack search along the order d is backtrack-free.

proof:

Suppose $V_1, V_2, \ldots, V_k$ were already instantiated. The variable V_{k+1} is connected to at most one previous variable (follows from the width-1 property), say V_i, which was assigned the value v_i. Since the directed arc (V_i, V_{k+1}) is along the order d, its arc-consistency implies the existence of a value v_{k+1} such that the pair (v_i, v_{k+1}) is permitted by the constraint $R_{i(k+1)}$. Thus, the assignment of v_{k+1} is consistent with all previous assignments.
□

An algorithm for achieving directional arc-consistency for any ordered constraint graph is given next (The order $d = (V_1, V_2, \ldots, V_n)$ is assumed)

DAC- d-arc-consistency

```
1.  begin
2.      For i = n to 1 by -1 do
3.          For each arc (V_j, V_i); j < i do
4.              REVISE(V_j, V_i)
5.          end
6.      end
7.  end
```

The algorithm REVISE(V_j, V_i), given in [8], deletes values from the domain D_j until the directed arc (V_j, V_i) is arc-consistent.

REVISE(V_j, V_i)

```
1.  begin
2.      For each x ∈ D_j do
3.          if there is no value y ∈ D_i s.t. R_{ji}(x,y) then
4.              delete x from D_j
5.      end
6.  end
```

To prove that the algorithm achieves d-arc-consistency we have to show that upon termination, any arc (V_j, V_i) along d $(j < i)$, is arc-consistent. The algorithm revises each d-directed arc once. It remains to be shown that the consistency of an already processed arc is not violated by the processing of coming arcs. Let arc (V_j, V_i) $(j < i)$ be an arc just processed by

REVISE(V_j,V_i). To destroy the consistency of (V_j,V_i) some values should be deleted from the domain of V_i during the continuation of the algorithm. However, according to the order by which REVISE is performed from this point on, only lower indexed variables may have their set of values updated. Therefore, once a directed arc is made arc-consistent its consistency will not be violated.

The algorithm AC-3 [8] that achieves full arc-consistency is given for reference:

AC-3

1. begin
2. $Q \leftarrow \{ (V_i,V_j) \mid (V_i,V_j) \in \text{arcs}, i \neq j\}$
3.   while Q is not empty do
4.   select and delete arc (V_k,V_m) from Q
5.   REVISE(V_k,V_m)
6.   if REVISE(V_k,V_m) caused any change then
7. $Q \leftarrow Q \cup \{(V_i,V_k)|(V_i,V_k) \in \text{arcs}, i \neq k,m\}$
7.   end
8. end

The complexity of AC-3, achieving full arc-consistency, is $O(ek^3)$. By comparison, the directional arc-consistency algorithm takes ek^2 steps since the REVISE algorithm, taking k^2 tests, is applied to every arc exactly once. It is also optimal, because even to verify directional arc-consistency each arc should be inspected once, and that takes k^2 tests. Note that when the constraint graph is a tree, the complexity of the directional arc-consistency algorithm is $O(nk^2)$.

Theorem 3:

A tree-like CSP can be solved in $O(nk^2)$ steps and this is optimal.

proof:

Given that we know that the constraint graph is a tree, finding an order that will render it of width-1 takes $O(n)$ steps. A width-1 tree-CSP can be made d-arc-consistent in $n \cdot k^2$ steps, using the DAC algorithm. The backtrack-free solution on the resultant tree is found in $O(nk)$. Finding a solution to tree-like CSP's takes, therefore, $O(nk) + O(nk^2) + O(n) = O(nk^2)$. This complexity is also optimal since any algorithm for solving a tree-like problem must examine each constraint at least once, and each such examination may take in the worst case k^2 (especially when no solution exist and the constraints permit very few pairs of values). □

Interestingly, if we apply DAC *w.r.t.* order d and then DAC *w.r.t.* the reverse order we get a full arc-consistency for trees. We can, therefore, achieve full

arc-consistency on trees in $O(nk^2)$. Algorithm AC-3, on the other hand, can be shown to have a worst case performance on trees of $O(nk^3)$. On general graphs, however, the (full) arc-consistency algorithm cannot be improved, and the AC-3 algorithm is optimal (see [2]).

Returning to our primary aim of studying easy problems, we now show how advice can be generated for solving a difficult CSP using a relaxed tree-like approximation. Suppose that we want to solve an n variables CSP using a backtrack procedure with $V_1,V_2, \ldots ,V_n$ as the order of instantiation. Let V_i be the variable to instantiate next, with $v_{i1},v_{i2}, \ldots ,v_{ik}$ the possible candidate values. To minimize backtracking we should first try values which are likely to lead to a consistent solution but, since this likelihood is not known in advance, we may estimate it, instead, by counting the number of consistent solutions that each candidate admits in some relaxed problem. We generate a relaxed tree-like problem by deleting some of the explicit constraints given, then count the number of consistent solutions containing each of the possible k assignments, and finally use these counts as a figure of merit for scheduling the various assignments. In the following we show how the counting of consistent solutions can be imbedded within the d-arc-consistency algorithm, DAC, on trees.

Any width-1 order, d, on a constraint tree determines a directed tree in which a parent always precedes its children in d (arcs are directed from the parent to its children). Let $N(v_{jt})$ stands for the number of solutions in the subtree rooted at V_j, consistent with the assignment of v_{jt} to V_j. It can be shown that $N(.)$ satisfies the following recurrence:

$$N(v_{jt}) = \prod_{\{c|V_c \text{ is a child of } V_j\}} \sum_{\{v_{cl} \in D_c| R_k(v_{jt},v_{cl})\}} N(v_{cl})$$

From this recurrence it is clear that the computation of $N(v_{it})$ may follow the exact same steps as in DAC; simultaneously with testing that a given value v_{jt}, is consistent with each of its children nodes, we simply transfer from each child of V_j to v_{jt} the sum total of the counts computed for the child's values that are consistent with v_{jt}. The overall value of $N(v_{jt})$ will be computed later on by multiplying together the summations obtained from each of the children. Thus, counting the number of solutions in a tree with n variables takes $O(nk^2)$, the same as establishing directional arc-consistency.

B. *Case of Width-2*

Order information can also facilitate backtrack-free search on width-2 problems by making path-consistency algorithms directional.

Montanari had shown that if a network of constraints is consistent *w.r.t.* all paths of length 2 (in the complete network) then it is path-consistent. Similarly we will show that directional path-consistency *w.r.t.* length-2 paths is sufficient to obtain a backtrack-free search on a width-2 problems.

Definition: A constraint graph, R, ordered *w.r.t.* order $d = (V_1, V_2, \ldots, V_n)$, is d-path-consistent if for every pair of values (x, y), $x \in V_i$ and $y \in V_j$ s.t. $R_{ij}(x, y)$ and $i < j$, there exist a value $z \in V_k$, $k > j$ s.t $R_{ik}(x, z)$ and $R_{kj}(z, y)$ for every $k > i, j$.

Theorem 4:

Let d be a width-2 order of an ordered constraint graph. If R is directional arc and path-consistent *w.r.t.* d then it is backtrack-free.

proof:

To ensure that a width-2 ordered constraint graph will be backtrack-free it is required that the next variable to be instantiated will have values that are consistent with previous chosen values. Suppose $V_1, V_2, \ldots, V_k$ were already instantiated. The variable V_{k+1} is connected to at most two previous variables (follows from the width-2 property). If it is connected to V_i and V_j, $i, j, < k$, then directional path consistency implies that for any assignment of values to V_i, V_j there exists a consistent assignment for V_{k+1}. If V_{k+1} is connected to one previous variable, then directional arc-consistency ensures the existence of a consistent assignment.   □

An algorithm for achieving directional path-consistency on any ordered graph will have to manage not only the changes made to the constraints but also the changes made to the graph, i.e., the arcs which are added to it. To describe the algorithm we use a representation in which a constraint R_{ij} is given by a matrix whose rows and columns correspond to the values of the two variables, and the entries are 0, and 1 for disallowed and allowed pairs, respectively. The matrix R_{ii} whose off-diagonal values are 0, represents the set of values permitted for variable V_i. Two operation on relations are needed: Intersection and Composition.

Intersection: If two constraints, R'_{ij} and R''_{ij} should hold simultaneously, then their intersection R_{ij} is written: $R_{ij} = R'_{ij} \& R''_{ij}$, and the entries in the corresponding matrices combine, term by term, by a logical Λ.

Composition: Suppose relation R_{12} holds between V_1 and V_2 and R_{23} between V_2 and V_3 then the induced relation transmitted by V_2 is the composite relation R_{13} and it is defined by the matrix multiplication

$$R_{13} = R_{12} \cdot R_{23}$$

Given a network of constraints $R = (V, E)$ and an order $d = (V_1, V_2, \ldots, V_n)$, we next describe an algorithm which achieves path-consistency *w.r.t.* this order.

DPC-d-path-consistency

```
  begin
(1) Y^0 = R
(2) for k=n to 1 by -1 do
      (a) ∀ i ≤ k connected to k do
            Y'_ii = Y^0_ii & Y_ik · Y_kk · Y_ki  /* REVISE(i,k)
      (b) ∀ i,j ≤ k s.t. (V_i,V_k),(V_j,V_k)∈E do
            Y^k_ij = Y^{k-1}_ij & Y^{k-1}_ik · Y^{k-1}_kk · Y^{k-1}_kj
            E ← E ∪ (V_i,V_j)
  end
  end
```

Step (2*a*) is the equivalent of the REVISE(i, k) procedure, and it performs the directional arc-consistency. Step (2*b*) updates the constraints between pairs of variables transmitted by a third variable which is higher in the order d. If $V_i, V_j, i, j < k$ are not connected to V_k then the relation between the first two variables is not affected by V_k at all. If only one variable, V_i, is connected to V_k, the effect of V_k on the constraint (V_i, V_j) will be computed by step (2*a*) of the algorithm. The only time a variable V_k affects the constraints between pairs of earlier variables is if it is connected to both. It is in this case only that a new arc may be added to the graph.

The complexity of the directional-path-consistency algorithm is $O(n^3 k^3)$. For variable V_i the number of times the inner loop, (2*b*), is executed in at most $(i-1)^2/2$ (the number of different pairs less then i), and each step is of order k^3. The computation of loop (2*a*) is completely dominated by the computation of (2*b*), and can be ignored. Therefore, the overall complexity is

$$\frac{1}{2} \sum_{i=2}^{n} (i-1)^2 k^3 = O(n^3 k^3)$$

Applying directional-path-consistency to a width-2 graph may increase its width and therefore, does not guarantee backtrack-free solutions. Consequently, it is useful to define the following subclass of width-2 CSP problems.

Definition: A constraint graph is **regular width-2** if there exists a width-2 ordering of the graph which remains width-2 after applying d-path-consistency, DPC.

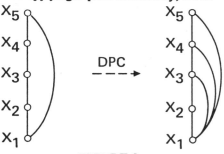

FIGURE 3

A ring constitutes an example of a regular width-2 graph. Figure 3 shows an ordering of a ring's nodes and the graph resulting from applying the DPC algorithm to the ring. Both graphs are of width-2.

Theorem 5:

A regular width-2 CSP can be solved in $O(n^3 k^3)$.

Proof:

Regular width-2 problem can be solved by first applying the DPC algorithm and then performing a backtrack-free search on the resulting graph. The first takes $O(n^3 k^3)$ steps and the second $O(ek)$ steps.

□

The main problem with the preceding approach is whether a regular width-2 CSP can be recognized from the properties of its constraint graph. One promising approach is to identify nonseparable components of the graph and all its separation vertices [4].

definition: A connected graph $G(V,E)$ is said to have a **separation vertex** v if there exist vertices a and b, such that all the paths connecting a and b pass through v. A graph which has a separation vertex is called **separable**, and one which has none is called **nonseparable**.

An $O(|E|)$ algorithm for finding all the nonseparable components and the separation vertices is given in [4]. It is also shown that the connectivity structure between the nonseparable components and the separation vertices, has a tree structure.

The following points can be made:

1. Given any ordered constraint graph in which the separation vertices and the nonseparable components are identified, the directional path-consistency algorithm adds arcs only within each component.

2. Let R be a graph and SR be the tree in which the nonseparable components $C_1, C_2, \ldots, C_r$ and the separating vertices $V_1, V_2, \ldots, V_t$ are represented by nodes. A width-1 ordering of RS dictates a partial order on R, d^s, in which each separating vertex precede all the vertices in its children components of SR. It can be shown that if there exist a d^s ordering on R such that each nonseparable component is regular-width-2 then the total ordering is regular width-2.

As a corollary of these two points we conclude that a tree of simple rings is regular width-2.

III *SUMMARY AND CONCLUSIONS*

This paper examines the process of harnessing easy problems to help in the solution of complex constraint-satisfaction problems. Of the three main steps involved in this process -- simplification, solution, and advice generation -- we concentrated on the following:

1. The simplification part: we have devised criteria for recognizing easy problems based on their underlying constraint graphs. The characteristics that meet these criteria can be used as goals for simplifying complex problems by deleting some of their constraints. The introduction of directionality into the notions of arc and path consistency enable us to extend the class of recognizable easy problems beyond trees, to include regular width-2 problems.

2. The solution part: using directionality we were able to devise improved algorithms for solving simplified problems and to demonstrate their optimality. In particular, it is shown that tree-structured problems can be solved in $O(nk^2)$ steps, and regular width-2 problems in $O(n^3 k^3)$ steps.

3. The advice generation part: we have demonstrated a simple method of extracting advice from easy problems to help a backtracking algorithm decide between pending options of value assignments. The method involves approximating the remaining part of a constraint-satisfaction task by a tree-structured problem, and counting the number of solutions consistent with each pending assignment. These counts can be obtained efficiently and can be used as figures of merit to rate the promise offered by each option.

In experiments, fully reported in [2], we compared the performance of a regular backtrack algorithm (RBT) with Advised Backtrack (ABT) on a set of randomly generated CSP problems. Initial results showed that the quality of the advice generated on the basis of a full spanning tree was sufficient to cut down substantially the number of backtrackings, typically from about 50 to 0-3. In many cases, however, the number of consistency checks required for generating this advice made the overall computational work higher then that of RBT. We interpreted this result to mean that the advice generated was too precise in the sense that further simplification should be attempted to cut down the work spent on advice generation. For that reason we experimented with advice generated by partially developed trees, namely, only a limited number, l, of nodes were spanned by the advising tree. The parameter l governs the strength of the advice, $l=1,\ldots,n$. Figure 4 shows the performance of ABT as a function of l on a typical problem. The two criteria by which performance was judged were the **number of backtrackings** performed and the **number of**

consistency checks i.e the number of times any two values were tested for consistency *w.r.t.* some constraint. For comparison, the results for RBT are shown at the point $l=1$ (by triangle points). The numbers labeling points on the graph indicate the amount of backtrackings. Typically the amount of backtracking was considerably smaller in ABT then in RBT even for weak advice, however the total work invested in full advise (using all nodes in the tree) was not always worthwhile and a weaker advice was sufficient. The dip in the curve represents an optimal balance between the effort spent in generating advice and the amount of backtracking it saves.

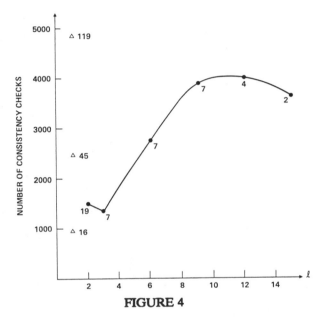

FIGURE 4

Although the primary discussion in this paper has focused on guiding the selection of values within a given variable, the properties of tree-structured networks can also be exploited to optimize the ordering of variables. One such scheme, which promises unusual possibilities, is based on the following observation: If, in the course of a backtrack search, we remove from the constraint graph the nodes corresponding to already instantiated variables and find that the remaining subgraph is a tree, then the rest of the search can be completed in linear time (e.g., using the DAC algorithm of Section II). Consequently, the aim of ordering the variables should be to instantiate, as quickly as possible, a set of variables that cut all cycles in the network. Indeed, if we identify m variables which form such a cycle-cutset, the entire CSP can be solved in at most $O(k^m n k^2)$ steps; we simply solve the trees resulting from each of the k^m possible instantiations of the variables in the cutset. Thus, in networks where the ratio n/m is large, enormous savings can be realized using simple heuristics for selecting near-minimal cycle-cutsets.

REFERENCES

[1] Carbonell, J.G., "Learning by Analogy: Formulation and Generating Plan from Past Experience". In Michalski, Carbonell, and Mitchell (eds.), *Machine Learning*. Palo Alto, CA: Tioga Press, 1983.

[2] Dechter, R., UCLA, Los Angeles, CA, 1985. Ph.D. thesis, in preparation.

[3] Dechter, R. and J. Pearl, "A Problem Simplification Approach that Generates Heuristics for Constraint Satisfaction Problems". UCLA-ENG-REP-8497, Cognitive Systems Laboratory, Computer Science Department, University of California, Los Angeles. To appear in *Machine Intelligence* 11. 1985.

[4] Even, S., *Graph Algorithms*. Maryland: Computer Science Press, 1979.

[5] Freuder, E.C., "A Sufficient Condition for Backtrack-Free Search". *Journal of the ACM* 29:1 (1982) 24-32.

[6] Gaschnig, J., "A Problem Similarity Approach to Devising Heuristics: First Results" In *Proc. IJCAI-79*. Tokyo, Japan, August, 1979, pp. 301-307.

[7] Guida, G. and M. Somalvico, "A Method for Computing Heuristics in Problem Solving". *Information Sciences* 19 (1979) 251-259.

[8] Mackworth, A.K., "Consistency in Networks of Relations", *Artificial Intelligence* 8:1 (1977) 99-118.

[9] Mackworth, A.K. and E.C. Freuder, "The Complexity of Some Polynomial Consistency Algorithms for Constraint Satisfaction Problems". *Artificial Intelligence* 25:1 (1985) 65-73.

[10] Montanari, U., "Networks of Constraints: Fundamental Properties and Applications to Picture Processing", *Information Science* 7 (1974) 95-132.

[11] Pearl, J., "On the Discovery and Generation of Certain Heuristics", *AI Magazine* Winter/Spring (1983) 22-23.

[12] Sacerdoti, E.D., "Planning in a Hierarchy of Abstraction Spaces", *Artificial Intelligence* 5:2 (1974) 115-135.

An Analysis of Consecutively Bounded Depth-First Search
with Applications in Automated Deduction

Mark E. Stickel and W. Mabry Tyson

Artificial Intelligence Center
SRI International
Menlo Park, California 94025

Abstract

Consecutively bounded depth-first search involves repeatedly performing exhaustive depth-first search with increasing depth bounds of 1, 2, 3, and so on. The effect is similar to that of breadth-first search, but, instead of retaining the results at level $n - 1$ for use in computing level n, earlier results are recomputed. Consecutively bounded depth-first search is useful whenever a complete search strategy is needed and either it is desirable to minimize memory requirements or depth-first search can be implemented particularly efficiently. It is notably applicable to automated deduction, especially in logic-programming systems, such as PROLOG and EQLOG, and their extensions. Consecutively bounded depth-first search, unlike unbounded breadth-first search, can perform cutoffs by using heuristic estimates of the minimum number of steps remaining on a solution path. Even if the possibility of such cutoffs is disregarded, an analysis shows that, in general, consecutively bounded depth-first search requires only $\frac{b}{b-1}$ times as many operations as breadth-first search, where b is the branching factor.[1]

1 Introduction

In this paper, we investigate the properties of *consecutively bounded depth-first search*. In this method, exhaustive depth-first search is repeatedly performed with increasing depth bounds of 1, 2, 3, and so on. The effect is similar to that of breadth-first search, but, instead of retaining the results at level $n - 1$ for use in computing level n, earlier results are recomputed.[2]

Although this may appear to be a naive and costly search method, it is not necessarily so. It is sometimes advantageous to perform consecutively bounded depth-first search instead of the breadth-first search it imitates. One reason for this is that depth-first search requires much less memory.

Consecutively bounded depth-first search can also make use of heuristic information, in contrast to unbounded breadth- and depth-first search—the latter are uninformed search strategies that do not take into account heuristic estimates of the remaining distance to a solution. Informed search strategies such as the A* algorithm use such heuristic information to order the

search space. Consecutively bounded depth-first search does not do that, but can use an estimate of the minimum number of remaining steps to a solution to perform cutoffs if the estimate exceeds the number of levels left before the depth bound is reached. If the number of remaining levels is uniformly exceeded by these estimates by more than one level, then one or more levels can be skipped when the next depth bound is set. As with the A* algorithm, admissability—the guarantee of finding a shortest solution path first—is preserved provided the heuristic estimate never exceeds the actual number of remaining steps to a solution.

Another advantage of consecutively bounded depth-first search stems from the fact that, in some applications, depth-first search can be implemented with much higher efficiency than breadth-first search; consecutively bounded depth-first search combines this efficiency with the completeness of breadth-first search. In these applications, the greater efficiency of depth-first search more than compensates for the effort of recomputing earlier-level results in consecutively bounded depth-first search.

A specific instance of this is PROLOG-style automated deduction. PROLOG's use of depth-first search contributes significantly to its performance. If depth-first search were not used, more than one derived clause would have to be represented simultaneously and variables would have more than a single value simultaneously, i.e., different values in different clauses. This would imply the need for a more complex and less efficient representation for variable bindings than the one PROLOG currently uses.

One of our interests is in adapting PROLOG implementation technology to the design of high-performance general automated-deduction systems [6]. For general deduction, PROLOG's depth-first search is incomplete and of limited utility. But to adopt breadth-first search would result in losing the efficiency advantages of PROLOG's representation for variable bindings. Performing bounded depth-first search would preserve the depth-first character of the search while allowing exhaustive searching of the space to a specified level.

There is still the problem of selecting the depth bound. In an exponential search space, searching with a higher-than-necessary depth bound can waste an enormous amount of effort before the solution is found. This is because the cost of searching level n in an exponential search space is generally large compared with the cost of searching earlier levels.

But this also makes it practical to perform consecutively bounded depth-first search. The depth bound is set successively at 1, 2, 3, etc., until a solution is found. If a uniform branching factor b is assumed, this results in only about $\frac{b}{b-1}$ times as many operations as are necessary for breadth-first search to the same depth.

Another potential application in automated deduction and

---

[1]This research was supported by the Defense Advanced Research Projects Agency under Contract N00039-84-K-0078 with the Naval Electronic Systems Command. The views and conclusions contained in this document are those of the authors and should not be interpreted as representative of the official policies, either expressed or implied, of the Defense Advanced Research Projects Agency or the United States government. Approved for public release. Distribution unlimited.

[2]We assume a basic familiarity with standard breadth-first, depth-first, and A* search strategies (e.g., see Nilsson [4]).

logic programming is in systems like EQLOG [1]. EQLOG extends PROLOG by replacing the standard unification algorithm with an algorithm based on narrowing that unifies terms in equational theories. Because the narrowing process is not necessarily finite, it may be necessary for completeness to interleave computation of unifiers by narrowing with the Horn-clause-resolution backtracking search. Here the use of consecutively bounded depth-first search would be beneficial both for its representational efficiency and for its low space consumption—the latter is particularly important because there may be a large number of unification attempts that are simultaneously active.

Consecutively bounded depth-first search is similar to the tree-searching strategy of *iterative deepening* used in chess [5]. In iterative deepening, search is repeatedly performed with increasing depth bounds until a time limit is reached. Insofar as these chess searches can be modeled by breadth-first search with a uniform branching factor, our analysis reveals that iterative deepening search in chess is only marginally more expensive than a single search to the maximum depth.

Despite this use of consecutively bounded depth-first search in chess and its obvious utility, it has surprisingly remained unanalyzed and unargued for—until now. Our proposal of a PROLOG technology theorem prover [6] included a description of this search strategy (which we implemented) and a very rough analysis on which this work builds. Korf [2,3] has independently come to similar conclusions on the value of this search strategy and has done his own analysis that emphasizes its asymptotic optimality in space and time among brute-force searches and, with the use of cutoffs, its optimality among admissable best-first searches.

2   Consecutively Bounded Depth-First Search Versus Breadth-First Search

We now present a comparison of the the effort required to perform consecutively bounded depth-first search and breadth-first search. The analysis ignores the effects of using heuristic information in consecutively bounded depth-first search, which would yield even more favorable results for that strategy.

Worst-case behavior for consecutively bounded depth-first search, as compared with breadth-first search, occurs when the branching factor is 1, i.e., when no searching is required. In this case, if the solution is found at depth n, the cost of breadth-first search with uniform branching factor 1 is $BFS_1(n) = n$, while the cost of consecutively bounded depth-first search is $CBDFS_1(n) = 1 + 2 + \cdots + n = \frac{n(n+1)}{2}$.

For larger branching factors, consecutively bounded depth-first search will be shown to be the generally small constant factor $\frac{b}{b-1}$ times as expensive as breadth-first search (i.e., $\frac{1}{b-1}$ extra effort). This is true regardless of whether consecutively bounded depth-first search is used to search exhaustively to some depth or only until the first solution is found.

2.1   Exhaustive Search

The number of operations $BFS_b(n)$ performed in searching a space exhaustively with uniform branching factor b to depth n, using breadth-first search, is given by

$$BFS_b(n) = \sum_{i=1}^{n} b^i = \frac{b^{n+1} - 1}{b-1} - 1 = \frac{b}{b-1}(b^n - 1). \quad (1)$$

We will also use the approximation

$$\frac{BFS_b(n)}{b^n} \approx \frac{b}{b-1}. \quad (2)$$

Because searching a space exhaustively with breadth-first or depth-first search differs only in the order of operations, the number of operations $DFS_b(n)$ for depth-first search is given by

$$DFS_b(n) = BFS_b(n) = \frac{b}{b-1}(b^n - 1). \quad (3)$$

The number of operations $CBDFS_b(n)$ performed in searching a space exhaustively with uniform branching factor b to depth n, using consecutively bounded depth-first search, i.e., searching exhaustively to depth $1, 2, \ldots, n$, is given by

$$CBDFS_b(n) = \sum_{i=1}^{n} DFS_b(i) = \frac{b}{b-1}\sum_{i=1}^{n}(b^i - 1)$$
$$= \frac{b}{b-1}(DFS_b(n) - n). \quad (4)$$

Thus, the ratio of the costs of searching exhaustively to depth n, using consecutively bounded depth-first search, compared with searching to depth n by using breadth-first search can be approximated by

$$\frac{CBDFS_b(n)}{BFS_b(n)} = \frac{CBDFS_b(n)}{DFS_b(n)} \approx \frac{b}{b-1}. \quad (5)$$

2.2   Search to First Solution

Assume that the there are no solutions below level n and that the first solution is found at fraction r of the way through searching level n—e.g., $r = 0.5$ if half of the level n operations have been done when the first solution is found.

We now define the approximate number of operations $BFS_b(n, r)$ and $CBDFS_b(n, r)$, corresponding to $BFS_b(n)$ and $CBDFS_b(n)$, performed in searching a space to the first solution found at point r on level n:

$$BFS_b(n, r) = BFS_b(n) - (1 - r)b^n \quad (6)$$

$$CBDFS_b(n, r) = CBDFS_b(n) - (1 - r)DFS_b(n). \quad (7)$$

Thus, the ratio of the costs of searching to the first solution at point r on level n, using consecutively bounded depth-first search compared with using breadth-first search, can be approximated, by use of Equations (5) and (2), by

$$\frac{CBDFS_b(n, r)}{BFS_b(n, r)} = \frac{CBDFS_b(n) - (1 - r)DFS_b(n)}{BFS_b(n) - (1 - r)b^n}$$
$$\approx \frac{CBDFS_b(n) - (1 - r)(\frac{b-1}{b})CBDFS_b(n)}{BFS_b(n) - (1 - r)(\frac{b-1}{b})BFS_b(n)} \quad (8)$$
$$= \frac{CBDFS_b(n)}{BFS_b(n)} \approx \frac{b}{b-1}.$$

2.3   Memory Requirements

An advantage of consecutively bounded depth-first search is that it needs only an amount of memory that is linear in the depth of the tree. When the search routine is at some node in the tree, it needs to remember only the node's ancestors or, sometimes for convenience, the node's and ancestors' siblings as well. Even in the latter case, the memory required is only bn nodes where b is the branching factor and n is the depth. For ordinary breadth-first search, the memory required is $O(b^n)$, since each node in the tree at the current depth must be stored. Consequently, much less memory is needed for consecutively bounded depth-first search.

3   Evenly Bounded Depth-First Search

At first it appears that consecutively bounded depth-first search wastes effort by redoing the same steps too often. In fact only $\frac{1}{b}$ of the effort is wasted, but for small branching factors, when the waste is greatest, the amount of wasted effort can be decreased by modifying the strategy.

Consider using even bounds $(2, 4, \ldots)$ instead of consecutive bounds $(1, 2, \ldots)$ when searching for the first solution.

If the solution occurs on one of the bounding levels (i.e., at an even depth), evenly bounded depth-first search is a clear winner. But if the solution occurs on another level, it may be worse. Since we probably do not know the parity of the depth of the first solution any more than we know the depth itself, a comparison of evenly bounded with consecutively bounded depth-first search is difficult for any set of problems. One way to compare them would be to determine under what conditions the savings (when a solution is found at an even depth) outweigh the extra effort (when the solution could have been found at the preceding odd depth). For this analysis, we will assume that the solution that could have been found at the previous odd depth will still be the first solution found when searching to the next greater even depth. A contrary assumption would make evenly bounded depth-first search more favorable. We shall first compute the number of operations for evenly bounded depth-first search when the solution is found at even or odd depths.

Similarly to Equation (4),

$$EBDFS_b(2q) = \sum_{i=1}^{q} DFS_b(2i). \tag{9}$$

As a result of the even bounds,

$$EBDFS_b(2q - 1) = EBDFS_b(2q). \tag{10}$$

Likewise, similarly to Equation (7),

$$EBDFS_b(2q, r) = EBDFS_b(2q - 2) + rDFS_b(2q) \tag{11}$$

and again

$$EBDFS_b(2q - 1, r) = EBDFS_b(2q, r). \tag{12}$$

For solutions at even levels, the difference between finding the first solution by consecutively bounded and evenly bounded depth-first search is

$$
\begin{aligned}
&CBDFS_b(2q, r) - EBDFS_b(2q, r) \\
&= \sum_{i=1}^{2q-1} DFS_b(i) - \sum_{i=1}^{q-1} DFS_b(2i) = \sum_{i=1}^{q} DFS_b(2i - 1).
\end{aligned} \tag{13}
$$

For solutions at odd levels,

$$
\begin{aligned}
&CBDFS_b(2q - 1, r) - EBDFS_b(2q - 1, r) \\
&= \sum_{i=1}^{2q-2} DFS_b(i) + rDFS_b(2q - 1) - \\
&\quad \left(\sum_{i=1}^{q-1} DFS_b(2i) + rDFS_b(2q) \right) \\
&= \sum_{i=1}^{q-1} DFS_b(2i - 1) + r\sum_{i=1}^{2q-1} b^i - r\sum_{i=1}^{2q} b^i \\
&= \sum_{i=1}^{q-1} DFS_b(2i - 1) - rb^{2q}.
\end{aligned} \tag{14}
$$

If the sum of the differences is positive, then the added efficiency in dealing with problems whose first solution is on an even level outweighs any extra overhead expended upon problems whose first solution is on an odd level. If that is so, evenly bounded depth-first search is clearly more efficient than consecutively bounded depth-first search. Analysis reveals that evenly bounded depth-first search is always preferable for a branching factor of 2 (or less), while consecutively bounded depth-first search is preferable for a branching factor of 4 or more. For a branching factor of 3, the advantages of finding solutions on even levels are approximately equal to the disadvantages of finding solutions on odd levels.

4   Conclusion

We have analyzed the behavior of consecutively bounded depth-first search. This strategy is useful whenever a complete search strategy is needed, and either it is desirable to minimize memory requirements or depth-first search can be implemented particularly efficiently. Moreover, consecutively bounded depth-first search, in contrast to the unbounded breadth-first search it almost emulates, can take advantage of heuristic estimates of the minimum number of steps remaining on a solution path to perform cutoffs if that number exceeds the number of levels left before the depth bound is reached. Even if the possibility of such cutoffs is disregarded, we have found the performance penalty resulting from the use of consecutively bounded depth-first search to be small when compared with breadth-first search—the former performs only $\frac{b}{b-1}$ times as many operations as the latter, where b is the branching factor.

References

[1] Goguen, J. and J. Meseguer. Equality, types and generics for logic programming. *Proceedings of the 1984 Logic Programming Symposium*, Uppsala, Sweden, 1984, 115–125.

[2] Korf, R.E. Depth-first iterative-deepening: an optimal admissable tree search. To appear in *Artificial Intelligence Journal*.

[3] Korf, R.E. Iterative-deepening-A*: an optimal admissable tree search. *Proceedings of the Ninth International Joint Conference on Artificial Intelligence*, Los Angeles, California, August 1985.

[4] Nilsson, N.J. *Principles of Artificial Intelligence*. Tioga Publishing Co., Palo Alto, California, 1980.

[5] Slate, D.J. and L.R. Atkin. CHESS 4.5—The Northwestern University chess program. In Frey, P.W. (ed.), *Chess Skill in Man and Machine*, Springer-Verlag, New York, New York, 1977, 82–118.

[6] Stickel, M.E. A PROLOG technology theorem prover. *Proceedings of the 1984 International Symposium on Logic Programming*, Atlantic City, New Jersey, February 1984, 211–217. Revised version appeared in *New Generation Computing 2*, 4 (1984), 371–383.

TAKING ADVANTAGE OF STABLE SETS OF VARIABLES
IN CONSTRAINT SATISFACTION PROBLEMS

Eugene C. Freuder and Michael J. Quinn*

Department of Computer Science, University of New Hampshire, Durham, NH 03824

ABSTRACT

Binary constraint satisfaction problems involve finding values for variables subject to constraints between pairs of variables. Algorithms that take advantage of the structure of constraint connections can be more efficient than simple backtrack search. Some pairs of variables may have no direct constraint between them, even if they are linked indirectly through a chain of constraints involving other variables. A set of variables with no direct constraint between any pair of them forms a stable set in a constraint graph representation of a problem. We describe an algorithm designed to take advantage of stable sets of variables, and give experimental evidence that it can outperform not only simple backtracking, but also forward checking, one of the best variants of backtrack search. Potential applications to parallel processing are noted. Some light is shed on the question of how and when a constraint satisfaction problem can be advantageously divided into subproblems.

I DIRECT INDEPENDENCE OF VARIABLES

Constraint satisfaction problems involve finding values for variables subject to constraints, or relations among the variables. Often these constraints are restricted to being binary relations between two variables; we shall consider binary constraints here. Standard backtrack search can be used to solve such problems. In general the upper bound on the complexity of the search is exponential in the number of variables.

In this paper we propose taking advantage of the "relative independence" of variables to ameliorate the search complexity. We term two variables *directly independent* if there is no direct constraint between them, even if they may be indirectly related by a chain of constraints passing through intermediate variables.

The basic insight is illustrated by the example in Figure 1. The problem involves three variables, each with three possible values, and a constraint graph (Figure 1a, 1b). Links in the graph represent constraints; nodes represent variables. Note that there is no direct constraint between variables y and z. If we approach the problem with a straightforward backtracking algorithm, we might have to examine almost $3 \times (3 \times 3)$ or 27 possible triples of values before hitting upon a solution in the rightmost branch of the search tree. More than 27 tests on pairs of values would be performed (Figure 1c).

Now let us take into account the relative independence of variables y and z. Having chosen a value for x, we can go ahead and choose a value for y and a value for z independently. There will be at most 6 values to consider (3 for each) before we succeed or fail. If we fail, we repeat the process for the next x value. At most we will perform $3 \times (3 + 3)$ or 18 tests on pairs of values (Figure 1d).

In general we can partition constraint graphs into sets of "mutually independent" variables, where there is no direct constraint between any pair of variables in the set. Such a set is called a *stable set* in graph theory. Consider the constraint graph shown in Figure 2, for the problem of labeling the cube. The scene labeling problem [Waltz, 1975] provides an application domain here, but those unfamiliar with it can regard the cube as an abstract constraint graph. The graph in Figure 2b is simply a redrawing of the constraint graph in Figure 2a. Observe that the variables F and C are not joined by a constraint, nor are B and D, nor A and E. There are no edges between variables at the same level in Figure 2b. Once a value has been chosen for G, the values for F and C may be chosen mutually independently, then values for B and D, and so on. (Figure 2b is a generalized form of an "ordered constraint graph" [Freuder, 1982].)

Many interesting improvements on basic backtracking have been made [Haralick and Elliott, 1980; Gaschnig, 1978]. Generally these improvements operate at a "microlevel," involving the relationships between individual values for variables, e.g., value a for variable x is inconsistent with value b for variable y. Our concerns are at a "macrolevel," involving the relationships between the variables themselves, e.g., there is no constraint between variables x and y. A more detailed experimental comparison with one of the best of the backtrack variations is made later.

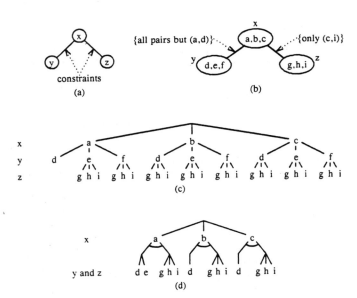

Figure 1. Taking advantage of the 'relative independence' of variables.

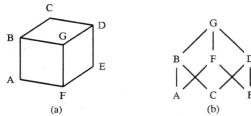

Figure 2: Labeling the cube.

---

* The authors' names appear in alphabetical order.

II PSEUDO-TREE SEARCH ALGORITHM

Given a constraint graph partitioned into stable sets, we would like to take advantage of direct independence not only on one maximal stable set (or an approximation thereof), but on all the stable sets. For example, we would like to use the stable sets identified in Figure 2 as "levels" in a generalized backtrack algorithm that employed the basic "additive" insight of Section I at each level.

This can be done, up to a point, in a straightforward way. Proceeding down through the levels, each variable at a given level can be considered independently. However, a problem arises in backtracking. If two variables at one level have a constraint path down to a single variable at a lower level (as in Figure 2b), all combinations of values for the two higher level variables may need to be tried before finding one compatible with the lower level variable. Thus, we again have a "multiplicative" rather than an "additive" effect.

Definition: A *pseudo-tree* is a rooted tree $T = (V, E)$ augmented with zero or more additional edges E' such that all edges between some vertex v and vertices closer to the root along the path in T from v to the root. The level of a variable in a pseudo-tree is its level in the underlying rooted tree.

A pseudo-tree structured constraint graph supports an algorithm that avoids the "multiplicative backtracking" problem cited above. It also makes it easy to determine what variables need to be modified during backtracking. Thirdly, the pseudo-tree property makes the constraint satisfaction problem more amenable to solution on a multiprocessor, because a processor could try to assign values to a variable and all its descendents without having to communicate with other processors [Freuder and Quinn, 1985].

Pseudo-Tree Search Algorithm

m—number of levels in pseudo-tree
$size(i)$—number of variables at level i
$a(i, j)$—jth variable at level i
$\{1, 2, \ldots, choices(a(i, j))\}$—potential values of $a(i, j)$
$value(a(i, j))$—current value of $a(i, j)$
$parent(a(i, j))$—index of parent of $a(i, j)$ at level $i - 1$

```
for i := 1 to m do
    for j := 1 to size(i) do
        value(a(i, j)) := 1 (* Initialize all variables *)
    endfor
endfor;
i := 1; (* i is current search level *)
while (1 ≤ i) and (i ≤ m) do
    (* Examine level i *)
    j := 1;
    repeat
        if value(a(i, j)) violates a constraint with an ancestor then
            while value(a(i, j)) violates a constraint do
                if value(a(i, j)) = choices(a(i, j)) then
                    (* No more alternatives for a(i, j)—must backtrack *)
                    j := parent(a(i, j));
                    i := i - 1
                    if i = 0 then exit outermost while loop endif
                endif;
                (* Former value leads to constraint conflict—try another *)
                value(a(i, j)) := value(a(i, j)) + 1
            endwhile;
            set value of all descendents of a(i, j) to 1
        endif;
        j := j + 1 (* Try next variable at level i *)
    until j > size(i);
    (* All constraints satisfied through level i—deepen search *)
    i := i + 1
endwhile;
if i > m then (* Solution found—it is stored in array value *)
else (* No solution *)
endif.
```

The following lemma proves that the pseudo-tree search algorithm has a complexity bound exponential in the number of levels in the pseudo-tree, rather than in the number of variables in the problem. In the next section we present an algorithm for transforming an arbitrary constraint satisfaction problem into an equivalent "metaproblem" with a pseudo-tree constraint graph structure.

Lemma: Given a pseudo-tree T and k variables at level m in T, each variable capable of taking on b values, the search algorithm backtracks at most bk times to level m before backtracking to level $m - 1$.

Proof: The first time the search algorithm reaches level m, the value of every variable at that level is initialized as low as possible. The search algorithm backtracks from level $m + 1$ in T when there exists at that level a variable v that cannot be given a value that does not violate constraints with all of the values of ancestor variables in T. By the pseudo-tree property, all of the variables constraining v lie along a simple path from v to the root of T. In order to try all combinations of values that might lead to an allowable value of v, only variables along this path need to have their values changed. Hence every time the search backtracks to level m, exactly one of the variables w at level m must have its value modified. The value of w cannot be decremented: all lower values were previously held by w and led to a backtracking lower in the tree. Because it is only necessary to reset the value of w when one of its ancestors has its value incremented, the value of no variable at level m will lower until the search backtracks from level m. Since there are k variables, each with b possible values, the maximum number of values variables at level m can take on before one variable has no more possible values is bk.

Theorem: Given a pseudo-tree T with m levels, each level i containing k_i variables capable of taking on b_i values, the worst-case time complexity of our algorithm is $\Theta(\Pi_{i=1}^{m} b_i k_i)$.

Corollary: Given a pseudo-tree T, our algorithm can find one assignment of values to variables that satisfies the constraints, if one exists, but it cannot be used to find all solutions that satisfy the constraints.

III DERIVING PSEUDO-TREE METAPROBLEMS

A constraint graph can be subdivided into subproblems, where each subproblem involves satisfying a subset of the original variables. The problem of satisfying all the subproblems simultaneously may then be regarded as a *metaproblem*, with the subproblems as *metavariables*.

It has long been recognized that partitioning a constraint satisfaction problem into subproblems may simplify the problem. However, little guidance is available as to how and when to subdivide problems. One criterion for considering a problem subdivision is the felicity of the structure of the resulting metaproblem. For example, if the metaproblem has a tree structured constraint graph on the metavariables, then it can be solved in time linear in the number of metavariables [Mackworth and Freuder, to appear]. Here we present a method for producing a metaproblem where the metavariables are organized into stable sets forming levels in a pseudo-tree constraint structure. Recall that the previous section presented an algorithm for pseudo-tree-structured problems, with a complexity bound exponential in the number of pseudo-tree levels.

The original problem is partitioned into a metaproblem as follows:

1. Find a cut set in the constraint graph; i.e., a set of vertices whose removal divides the graph into two or more unconnected subgraphs. The cut set S corresponds to $|S|$ variables in the metaproblem; these *metavariables* will form the first $|S|$ levels of the pseudo-tree. The unconnected subgraphs temporarily become metavariables and are children of the variable in S deepest in the "tree."

2. Apply this process recursively to each of the children, terminating when the subgraph being examined cannot be split further.

The algorithm will not necessarily produce an "optimal" pseudo-tree. We would like to be certain of efficiently transforming a given constraint graph into a pseudo-tree structure which takes optimal (or nearly optimal) advantage of direct independence. This remains an area for further work.

IV EXPERIMENTAL RESULTS

To experimentally verify the efficiency of this algorithm, we have used it to try to color graphs with three colors. The performance of our algorithm is contrasted with two others. The first algorithm performs simple backtracking, where the order in which the variables are searched is randomly chosen. The second algorithm uses forward checking [Haralick and Elliott, 1980], which Haralick and Elliot showed to be superior to several other variants of backtracking under certain experimental conditions. The order in which variables are considered corresponds to a level-by-level traversal of the pseudo-tree.

The form of the test graphs is shown in Figure 3. Notice that we have created constraint graphs that have the pseudo-tree property, which avoids the previously-mentioned problem of efficiently transforming constraint graphs into pseudo-trees. We have tested the three algorithms on a large number of graphs. For each problem size ranging from 4 to 36 variables, we have generated 100 random pseudo-trees. We have run the three search algorithms on all 900 graphs, measuring the number of constraint checks made by each algorithm. Each result has been put into one of two categories, depending upon whether the graph is three-colorable or not. This is because unsuccessful searches require many more constraint checks on average. Figure 4 displays the mean number of constraint checks performed by the three algorithms for successful and unsuccessful searches of the various graphs. Not only does our algorithm outperform standard backtracking, it also performs substantially fewer constraint checks than the forward checking algorithm on both colorable and uncolorable graphs. (We have also computed the median number of constraint checks performed by the three algorithms. Our algorithm outperforms standard backtracking and forward checking on unsuccessful searches and standard backtracking on successful searches. However, the median number of constraint checks performed by forward checking on successful searches is a few percent lower than the number performed by our algorithm.)

Certainly our search algorithm will not outperform other algorithms, such as forward checking, in all situations. The constraints must fit a certain pattern in order to benefit from our exploitation of direct independence. For example, if our methodology were applied to the eight-queens problem (placing eight queens on a chess board so that no queen can attack another), the pseudo-tree would have eight levels, and the search algorithm would degenerate into standard backtracking.

In fact, much of the experimental work on backtrack search has been done in the context of the eight-queens problem. This is actually a very specialized type of problem: the constraint graph is complete, all constraints are the same, and all variables have the same domain. Direct independence in a constraint graph is in a sense the opposite of completeness; it involves subsets of variables, which, far from forming complete subgraphs, form stable sets, where no variable is connected to any other.

V   CONCLUSIONS

We have presented an algorithm tailored to solve constraint satisfaction problems on constraint graphs that have the pseudo-tree property. We have also described an algorithm for turning any constraint graph into a constraint graph with the pseudo-tree property. Experimental evidence indicates there exist constraint graphs for which our algorithm outperforms not only standard backtracking, but also forward checking.

ACKNOWLEDGMENTS

This paper is based in part upon work supported by the National Science Foundation under Grant MCS 8003307.

REFERENCES

[1] Freuder, E.C. 1982. A sufficient condition for backtrack-free search. *J. ACM* **29**, 1, pp. 24-32.

[2] Freuder, E.C., and Quinn, M.J. 1985. Parallelism in an algorithm that takes advantage of stable sets of variables in constraint satisfaction problems. Tech. Rep. 85-21, Dept. of Computer Science, Univ. of New Hampshire.

[3] Gaschnig, J. 1978. Experimental case studies of backtrack vs. Waltz-type vs. new algorithms for satisficing-assignment problems. *Proc. 2nd National Conf. of Canadian Society for Computational Studies of Intelligence*, Toronto, Ontario, July 19-21, pp. 268-277.

[4] Haralick, R., and Elliott, G. 1980. Increasing tree search efficiency for constraint satisfaction problems. *Artificial Intelligence* **14**, pp. 263-313.

[5] Waltz, D. 1975. Understanding line drawings of scenes with shadows. In *The Psychology of Computer Vision*, P.H. Winston, ed., McGraw-Hill, New York, pp. 19-91.

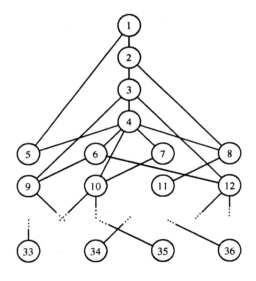

Figure 3: Form of the pseudo-trees used in the experiments.

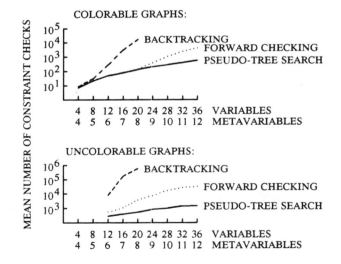

Figure 4: Experimental results.

A Study of Search Methods: The Effect of Constraint Satisfaction and Adventurousness

Hans Berliner
Gordon Goetsch

Computer Science Department
Carnegie-Mellon University
Pittsburgh, PA. 15213

Abstract

This research addresses how constraint satisfaction interacts with the search mode, and how the ratio of breadth of effort to depth of effort can be controlled. Four search paradigms, each the best of its kind for non-adversary problems, are investigated. One is depth-first, and the others best-first. All methods except one highly informed best-first search use the same knowledge, and each of these methods is tested with and without the use of a constraint satisfaction procedure on sets of progressively more difficult problems.

As expected, the most informed search does better than the less informed as the problems get more difficult. Constraint satisfaction is found to have a pronouncedly greater effect when coupled with the most informed algorithm. Large performance increments over A* can be produced by the use of a coefficient associated with the h term, and this algorithm produces solutions that are only 5% worse than optimal. This is a known phenomenon; however, the range of this coefficient is very narrow. We term this coefficient, which controls the ratio of depth of effort to breadth of effort, the *adventurousness coefficient*. The less tractable a problem the greater the adventurousness should be. We present evidence to support this.

Introduction

Heuristics are employed when the domain space being explored is too large to search exhaustively. A heuristic increases the likelihood of making a correct choice, but cannot prevent the making of an incorrect choice. The knowledge embodied by the heuristics is needed to reduce the cost of the search, but is insufficient to alleviate the need to search. The basic problems associated with heuristic search are: the desire to follow "successful" branches, while leaving less successful ones for later, and, when to quit pursuing a branch as its estimated merit declines.

Both problems are addressed by any search paradigm; however, the second problem can be effectively dealt with by a constraint satisfaction procedure that eliminates states that can no longer be solved. Brute force methods solve problems by searching to the maximum penetration allowed in the time available. As the problems get more difficult, the utility of such methods decreases. Thus depth-first searches are often augmented with techniques such as branch-and-bound and minimal move ordering

knowledge, but the use of heuristic knowledge is minimal. In contrast, a pure best-first search relies exclusively on its heuristic knowledge with all the search control decisions being based on that knowledge.

We wished to study the interaction between heuristics, search techniques, and constraint satisfaction. Superpuzz, a solitaire puzzle that can benefit from constraint satisfaction techniques, was chosen as our problem domain. We selected four search algorithms as being the best exemplars of their class for solving non-adversary problems, and devised a constraint satisfaction procedure. We then investigated the degree of degradation for each search algorithm as the problems became more difficult, and the interaction of constraint satisfaction with each technique.

The Domain

The domain chosen for this study was Superpuzz, an extremely difficult solitaire puzzle. The rules of Superpuzz are as follows:

Superpuzz is played with 24 cards, 6 (numbered 0 to 5) in each of 4 suits. To start a problem deal the cards in a raster of 6 wide by 4 deep. Then remove the "0" denomination cards, leaving "holes". Legal moves consist of moving a card into a hole, thus creating a hole at its former location. The card that is moved into a hole must be of the same suit as the card to the left of the hole, and be one higher in denomination.

No card can be moved to the right of the last card in a suit, nor to the right of a hole. If a hole is on the left edge, any 1 may be moved there. The game is won when all the cards have been placed in ascending order by suit, with one suit in the first 5 places of each row as demonstrated by Figure 1B. There is no requirement to have particular suits in particular rows. The game is lost when there are no longer any legal moves. These are the rules for 4x6 Superpuzz; it is also possible to play harder versions adjusting the rules for 4x7 and 4x8 formats.

```
     0   1   2   3   4   5        0   1   2   3   4   5
W   S3  H2  D2  D4  --  D5       D1  D2  D3  D4  D5  --   W
X   --  C4  H3  C5  C1  --       H1  H2  H3  H4  H5  --   X
Y   D3  S1  D1  S4  S5  --       C1  C2  C3  C4  C5  --   Y
Z   C2  C3  H4  H1  S2  H5       S1  S2  S3  S4  S5  --   Z

        (A)                          (B)
```

Figure 1: An initial and terminal configuration

Figures 1A and 1B show an initial and terminal position respectively. A solution to the initial position can be found at the end of this article. The most challenging aspect of Superpuzz is determining which ace to move into a hole on the left-edge. Making the proper ace move is often-non-intuitive, which makes the domain interesting and results in programs that outperform well practiced humans.

The Search Paradigms

Initial studies determined the following search algorithms were the best exemplars of their class:

1. A depth-first search (DF) using the branch and bound, and iterative deepening [5] techniques. Iterative deepening has recently been proved to dominate simple depth-first search when the depth of the solution is unknown [3]. The constant of iteration used was 2. The bound is the number of misplaced cards (N) in the present configuration. If the present configuration is at depth D, it is impossible to reach a solution at a depth less than D + N.

2. The A* search [4]. A* expands the frontier node with the minimal function f, where $f = g + h = D + N$.

3. A best-first search (BF1) that uses the simple evaluation function $f = \mu N + D$, where μ, the **adventurousness coefficient** which we discuss later, was equal to 1.8.

4. A best-first search (BF2) with a highly informed evaluation function that would encourage the development of good "positional" formations that could be transformed into wins.

A hash table containing the generated nodes plays a key role in three ways. In the best-first searches, it becomes the representation of the tree. The hash encoding detects identical states, so that the same subtree will be searched only once. The hash encoding also detects cycles. In the depth-first search, the hash table only performs the two latter functions.

Two evaluation functions were required. These are 1) A misplaced card counter, and 2) A position goodness function. These functions are described in detail in [2]. The misplaced card function is used in all the search programs, while the goodness function is used only in BF2.

The Constraint Satisfaction Method

Any state of a domain is either solvable or unsolvable. We define the set of **totally solvable** domains to be those in which all states accessible from a solvable state are solved or solvable. In such domains any operator applied to any state preserves the solvability of the new state. Frequently, for each operator there exists a reverse operator that can re-establish the previous state. This type of problem is represented by puzzles such as the 15-Puzzle and Rubik's Cube. An alternate condition is that the permissible operations do not allow transformation to an unsolvable state.

Set against the class of totally solvable problems is the class of **partially solvable problems** in which not every state of the domain can be solved, and the set of operations allow unsolvable states to be reached from solvable states. For totally solvable domains the only thing of interest is the speed of the solution process and the quality of the solution. For partially solvable problems, each instance may have to be classified as solvable or unsolvable.

Constraint satisfaction is the term used for the set of algorithms that can determine when a subtree cannot contain a solution. We wanted to study the role of constraint satisfaction on a difficult, partially solvable problem as the difficulty of the problem varied. This was the reason Superpuzz was selected, as standard puzzles such as the 15-Puzzle are totally solvable, and others such as Instant Insanity are not very difficult for a computer.

Both totally and partially solvable problems can use heuristic knowledge in order to speed up the search for a solution. Heuristic knowledge can be used to choose the order of applying operators and to evaluate the new states. However, totally solvable problems need no process to identify subtrees in which no solution can exist because, *ipso facto*, such subtrees cannot exist.

The constraint satisfaction function developed for this problem [2] is as follows: Once all the aces are in place, the final destination of every card can be determined. Cards not at their final destination must be moved. We only examine cards that are to the left of their destination since they are typically the hardest to move. If such a card is unmovable, the problem instance is unsolvable. The constraint satisfaction procedure is able to reject about 50% of all configurations presented to it during a search as being unsolvable. Constraint satisfaction is applied only after all the aces are in place, since identifying deadlocked positions earlier was unproductive. It is able to deal with situations where not only individual cards, but whole trains of cards must be moved. Trains arise frequently as the result of putting a card behind its predecessor. The problem of determining whether a train can be moved is very difficult, and a number of finesses were used which are described in the above cited reference.

Results

Each of the four search algorithms was tested with and without deadlock detection on the same 100 randomly generated instances of 4x6, 4x7 and 4x8 puzzles. The programs were to determine if each problem was solvable (and give a satisficing solution) or unsolvable. Testing method details are given in [2].

Solvable	Deadlock				Without Deadlock			
	DF	A*	BF1	BF2	DF	A*	BF1	BF2
Size = 6								
Av. Sol. Ln.	22	22	23	26	22	22	23	26
Av. Nodes	4637	5425	1902	1563	4845	5711	2896	2912
Av. Time	18.9	18.7	8.6	6.3	19.2	18.5	11.3	12.0
No. Intract.	0	1	0	0	0	1	1	1
Size = 7								
Av. Sol. Ln.	33	33	31	36	32	34	32	37
Av. Nodes	22865	23962	8401	5469	23759	25923	10140	8376
Av. Time	107.2	96.3	34.6	23.0	82.8	91.8	36.9	33.7
No. Intract.	5	7	2	1	5	8	3	3
Size = 8								
Av. Sol. Ln.	55	61	47	47	55	65	48	50
Av. Nodes	53507	58254	22361	9961	55318	62705	24603	15145
Av. Time	269.2	258.2	98.0	43.3	226.6	254.8	97.4	60.6
No. Intract.	18	25	9	2	19	29	10	5

Table 1: Performance Statistics

Table 1 shows the average solution length, the average number of nodes per solution, the average time to complete, and the number intractable for the eight programs for each of the three problem widths. As expected, effort in all categories varies with problem difficulty. It should be noted that the A*, BF1, and DF algorithms all use the same knowledge, A* and DF for bounding purposes and BF1 as a simple measure of goodness, yet the BF1 algorithm requires fewer resources (nodes and time). While BF1 produces solutions comparable to A* and DF on smaller problems, it clearly outperforms the other two algorithms on the 4x8 problem set. The most knowledgeable search (BF2) clearly outperforms the others in all criteria, except solution length. Although BF2 is only slightly superior among the 4x6 algorithms, it has achieved an overwhelming dominance by the time the 4x8 puzzles are considered.

Search Technique	Nodes			Times		
	Size Change			Size Change		
	6:7	7:8	6:8	6:7	7:8	6:8
Deadlock						
DF	4.93	2.34	11.54	5.67	2.51	14.24
A*	4.42	2.43	10.74	5.15	2.68	13.81
BF1	4.42	2.66	11.76	4.02	2.83	11.40
BF2	3.50	1.82	6.37	3.65	1.88	6.87
No Deadlock						
DF	4.90	2.33	11.42	4.31	2.74	11.80
A*	4.54	2.42	10.98	4.96	2.78	13.77
BF1	3.50	2.43	8.50	3.27	2.64	8.62
BF2	2.88	1.81	5.20	2.81	1.80	5.05

Table 2: Performance Ratios

Table 2 shows the ratio of increase in resources for each algorithm type as the problem width increases. The data show that, in general, the more informed the algorithm is, the less the degradation in performance as the problem gets more difficult. This is an expected result; the trees grown by the most informed algorithm grow at a lower exponential rate than those grown more brute-force-like algorithms. The BF2 search has the most information. The next, BF1 has had its coefficient tuned so it is more responsive to its sole performance measure (misplaced cards) than the remaining algorithms, A* and DF which have the least information.

Search	Nodes			Times			No. Intract.		
	Size			Size			Size		
	6	7	8	6	7	8	6	7	8
DF	.96	.96	.97	0.98	1.29	1.19	---	1	.95
A*	.95	.92	.93	1.01	1.05	1.01	1	.88	.86
BF1	.66	.83	.91	0.76	0.94	1.01	0	.67	.90
BF2	.54	.65	.66	0.52	0.68	0.71	0	.33	.40

Table 3: Ratio of Effort with and without Deadlock Detection

Table 3 shows the performance ratio of a search method with deadlock detection, to the same method without deadlock detection. Ratios less than 1.0 indicate improvements, otherwise the additional work was not beneficial. As expected the deadlock detection improves performance on the nodes measure in all categories. The deadlock detection did not always result in a time savings. Deadlock detection reduces the number of intractable problems, especially for the BF2 search. BF2 makes best use of the constraint satisfaction process. This is an important result

which we discuss in the next section.

Discussion and Conclusions

Superpuzz is a much more difficult than standard puzzles. Further, the difficulty of the game varies with the width of the puzzle. In this study we examine the 4x6, 4x7 and 4x8 games. Although the branching factor in each of these remains the same, the solution depth and percent of unsolvable problems increases significantly with increases of width.

The solution process can be thought of as occurring in two phases. In phase one, the combinatoric power of search attempts to see whether it is possible to obtain a position where all four aces are in place. When this has occurred, the deadlock detection algorithm is invoked, which can reject about 50% of all positions it encounters. Phase two is invoked for positions that pass the deadlock test. Here by relatively small searches, the solution is either found or rejected. When no solution is found in the sub-tree, phase one again obtains control.

Given that the combination of deadlock detection and very small searches in phase two is very efficient, certain ideas emerge. If the position is solvable, then it is advantageous to reach phase two as quickly as possible. The BF2 search does this most effectively. It is not at all unusual to have the first all-aces-in-place configuration discovered by the BF2 search be solvable, whereupon the solution proceeds immediately. In those cases where this does not happen, the first dozen or so attempts do usually yield a solvable phase two. Only in cases where the solution is very contrived, or where there is no solution, is the BF2 procedure outperformed by others, in the case where there is no solution, all phase two positions must be explored and the procedure that reaches these with the minimum amount of effort is the most effective. From this it can be seen that some knowledge of what percentage of problems is solvable is instrumental in deciding on a search paradigm. In this research, the BF2 evaluation function is expensive to compute, as is traversing the tree. But, while the BF2 search is only marginally superior in the width 6 puzzle, it becomes completely dominant by the time the width is increased to 8.

Let us consider why one search paradigm is better than another. A* and DF are really quite similar. They probe to new depths in a breadth-first style that takes advantage of certain efficiencies. A* knows about effort remaining and builds a permanent copy of the tree, which it continues to expand at the best leaf nodes. DF also knows about effort remaining and gets its power from great efficiency in space and time. However, neither is able to venture very far on a probe down a branch unless it is continuously having success (reducing the number of misplaced cards). Any failure to improve this measure would immediately force the A* search to try another branch. Because the DF search has an iteration constant of 2, two non-successful moves can occur in expanding a branch before returning. Since the criterion for success is rather simplistic, and it is very likely that any solution will require a number of non-constructive or backward-appearing steps, it is unlikely that either search will be able to make significant forward progress through such territory. Instead they plow steadily forward until the treacherous territory is overcome by *all* highly evaluated branches, and then pursue one to a successful conclusion.

Now consider the BF1 search paradigm. The evaluation function for BF1 is $f = \mu N + D$. The constant μ is the **adventurousness coefficient**; for this program $\mu = 1.8$. In BF1 the value of a descendant node either decreases by .8 units in case the number of misplaced cards is reduced, or is increased by 1.0. This allows the descendant node to put some distance between it and its competitors when it is able to take a few constructive steps intermixed with some that do not appear so constructive. The essential point is that a branch does not have to produce "progress" on every move. The degree of such adventurousness is what the constant 1.8 controls, and for the given domain and evaluation function it appears to be best.

Best-first search disciplines exist that have a reluctance to abandon a branch until it is judged a constant amount worse than the current best branch. The adventurousness coefficient allows the *number of non-intuitive moves included in a branch to be a linear function of the number of "good" moves*. This appears to be a better construction.

The BF2 search is even more adventurous (though it not clear how to obtain its adventurousness other than by empirical observation) since it can gain numerous points in heuristic value by placing a card into what is considered an advantageous location. This allows it to penetrate deeply in certain branches that it "likes" while leaving others behind. This additional knowledge appears to pay off in performance.

In some cases the evaluation function will lead the search up a blind alley. Here is where constraint satisfaction helps the most: *it can disenchant the search causing it to look elsewhere*. This happens for all of the searches, but is most effective in BF2 because the other searches are not as adventurous.

In any search paradigm, once a node is known to be deadlocked, its successors will never be expanded. However, these savings can only be realized once such a sub-tree is reached. This is where adventurousness is important. If situations where constraint satisfaction procedures can be applied occur only after almost all important branches have been pushed to the same depth, then the savings will not be very great. Here, the most adventurous search has a big advantage (see Table 3) since *it allows selectively approaching the point where constraint satisfaction can be applied*.

If the above notions of adventurousness are correct, then the less tractable the domain, the higher the adventurousness should be. We tested this hypothesis by re-running the BF1 (deadlock) algorithm on all the 4x8 problems with $\mu = 2.4$. This resulted in the average nodes per problem being reduced by 15%, and in the number of intractable problems being reduced from 9 to 5. We intend to investigate this scaling of adventurousness further in future studies.

In any domain the heuristic function must evaluate the desirability of the moves available. The decision of whether to abandon a branch in a best-first search or continue it is basic to the efficiency of the search. The adventurousness coefficient for any domain/function combination, determines the degree to which the past history of the branch influences this decision. It is not necessary to "succeed" on every move in a branch in order to continue it. Instead a success gradient (the adventurousness coefficient) must be maintained. This tends to produce consistent, plan-like behavior.

* *

A minimal solution to Figure 1A is: (read left to right; names of moving cards only, except for aces where the row is also given).

C2 S1(Z) D4 D3 D4 C1(Y) C2 D1(X) C3 S2 H2 S4 C4 D2 S5 C5 H4 S3 D1(W) H1(X) S4 D2 H2 S5 D3 D4 D5 H5

Acknowledgements

We wish to acknowledge the efforts of T. Anantharaman, B. Pearlmutter, and H. Printz who were the first to use constraint satisfaction in Superpuzz, and K. Goldberg whose graphic support aided in understanding the performance of the search.

References

[1] Berliner, H., "On the Construction of Evaluation Functions for Large Domains", Proc. IJCAI-77, Tokyo, 1977.

[2] Berliner, H., and Goetsch, G., "A Quantitative Study of Search Methods and the Effect of Constraint Satisfaction", Computer Science Dept., Carnegie-Mellon University, 1984.

[3] Korf, R. E., "The Complexity of Brute-Force Search", Technical Report, Department of Computer Science, Columbia University, 1984.

[4] Nilsson, N., *Problem Solving Methods in Artificial Intelligence*, McGraw-Hill, 1971.

[5] Slate, D. J., and Atkin, L. R., "CHESS 4.5 -- The Northwestern University Chess Program", in *Chess Skill in Man and Machine*, P. Frey (Ed.), Springer-Verlag, 1977.

THE COMPLEXITY OF SEARCHING
SEVERAL CLASSES OF AND/OR GRAPHS

Howard E. Motteler
Laveen N. Kanal *

The Machine Intelligence and Pattern Analysis Laboratory
Department of Computer Science
University of Maryland
College Park, MD 20742

Abstract

The complexity of searching for a minimum cost solution graph of an AND/OR graph is analyzed for the class of AND/OR graphs representable by a context free grammar with cost functions; finding a minimum cost solution graph is then equivalent to finding a lowest cost derivation. Several classes of search problems are defined, based on properties of the cost functions and grammar. We show that certain of these classes have different search complexities—specifically, we show that there are distinct classes for which the complexity of finding a minimum cost solution graph is non-recursive, exponential, NP-complete, and $O(n^2)$, where n is the size of the grammar representing the problem. The correspondence between problem structure and search complexity may serve as a guide for modeling real problems with AND/OR graphs.

1. Introduction

The complexity of A.I. search procedures is a topic of current interest [13,2,6]. In this paper we analyze the complexity of searching several classes of AND/OR graphs. The AND/OR graphs in which we are interested are represented by the *composite decision process* (CDP) [4,8]. This is a generalization of the sequential decision process (SDP) proposed by Karp and Held in [5]. The classes of AND/OR graphs represented by the composite decision process are a model for a wide variety of search procedures, problems in pattern recognition, and dynamic programming problems. Applications and examples of relevance to practical problems may be found in [4,8,9].

A CDP is defined by giving a context-free grammar, and a cost function associated with each production and terminal symbol. This is essentially Knuth's "synthesized attributes" [7], with a different motivation. The *minimalization problem* is to find a lowest cost parse tree for any string the grammar might derive. This is equivalent to the problem of finding a minimum cost solution graph of the AND/OR graph corresponding to the grammar [11].

The correspondence between AND/OR graphs and context free grammars is that connectors (the AND arcs) correspond to productions, and OR arcs correspond to a choice of productions. The simple grammar and graph of figure 1 shows the correspondence. This correspondence was first noted by Hall [3]; following the treatment in Nilsson, nodes are not restricted to be only of types AND or OR [12]. Our AND/OR graphs may contain cycles, and in general a solution graph may include a walk around some cycle any number of times. Thinking in terms of grammars, a solution graph is just a parse tree; a solution graph may be much larger than the grammar graph, and there may be infinitely many parse/solution trees. Figure 1 gives two solution trees for the AND/OR graph shown there; note that the larger of the two solution trees has minimal cost.

*Research supported by NSF grants to the Machine Intelligence and Pattern Analysis Lab., Dept. of Computer Science, University of Maryland.

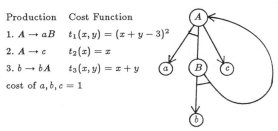

Production	Cost Function
1. $A \rightarrow aB$	$t_1(x,y) = (x+y-3)^2$
2. $A \rightarrow c$	$t_2(x) = x$
3. $b \rightarrow bA$	$t_3(x,y) = x+y$

cost of $a, b, c = 1$

A CDP with the associated AND/OR graph.

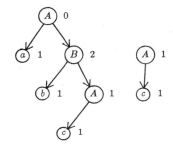

Two solution trees; nodes are paired with backed up costs.

Figure 1. Example of a CDP and solution graphs

We define classes of CDPs based on properties of the cost functions and the grammar, and for each such class analyze the complexity of the minimalization problem. These classes are intended to have some realistic motivation. For example, positive monotone CDPs [8] include generalizations of Dijkstra's algorithm. f-bounded CDPs are a formulation of bounded search. Suppose n is the size of some CDP. In the f-bounded CDP, we assume that any possible minimum value must occur in a tree with no more than $f(n)$ nodes. Acyclic CDPs are just the common restriction that the underlying AND/OR graph have no cycles.

The size of a CDP is defined as the size of the grammar (the sum of the lengths of the productions, written as $|G|$). We shall show upper and lower bounds on the complexity of solving the minimalization problem for various classes of CDP. An upper bound expressed as some function f means that every member of the class can be solved in $f(|G|)$ steps, and a lower bound of f means that infinitely many members of a class require more than $f(|G|)$ steps. The notion of "step of a computation" and bounding computation time are formalized in Aho, et al. [1]. We assume their "logarithmic cost criterion", where the cost of storing or manipulating a large number is then proportional to the length of the number. We assume unit cost for storing or manipulating a single grammar symbol, and cost proportional to the length of a string for manipulating a string of such symbols.

If the cost functions are easy to compute, we can ignore them in analyzing search complexity. The notion of "easy to compute" must be made precise, because if we just ignore the complexity of computing the cost functions, our conclusions may not be correct. For example, if we did not consider the complexity of computing the cost functions in giving proofs of upper bounds, by solving a CDP we could compute any recursive function with a constant cost. For let f be some such function. Define cost functions $c(\mathbf{d}) = d$, giving the value of a digit as its cost, and $t(x_1, \ldots, x_k) = f \circ g(x_1, \ldots, x_k)$, where g translates a string of digits of length k to an integer. Let G be the single production $St \rightarrow \mathbf{x}$, where $\mathbf{x}$ is the string of k digits representing x. Then to compute $f(x)$, find the minimum (the only) value of this CDP. If we charge only for search steps and we have only one step, then we have a constant cost. This difficulty is circumvented by requiring our CDPs to be "honest", that is for some function f, we guarantee that no computation of a cost function t takes more than $f(|G|)$ steps. Here we shall assume (unless otherwise noted) that every CDP is honest for some fixed polynomial h. This restriction is not necessary for proofs of lower bounds, as computation of the cost functions can only add to the complexity.

3. The Complexity of Several Classes of CDPs

The complexity of the natural CDP, acyclic CDPs, p-bounded CDPs for some polynomial p, and monotone CDPs are analyzed in this section. Figure 2 shows the structural relationships among various CDPs considered here. Figure 3 summarizes our results, showing the relationship of the complexity of the various minimalization problems. In the structure hierarchy, the positive monotone CDP is contained in the ACDP only in the sense that any minimum cost solution graph of the former is guaranteed to be acyclic; an arbitrary parse tree of a positive monotone CDP may not be acyclic. Formal proofs and further examples are presented in [11]; we present only an outline here.

If the range of cost functions is over real numbers, there may be no minimum cost parse tree. Restricting the range of the cost functions to natural numbers guarantees that a solution tree will exist, but as the following theorem shows, there may still be no effective way to find it.

Theorem 1. *The minimalization problem for the natural CDP is not recursive.*

Proof. The problem of generating the shortest program P that outputs m and halts is reduced to a minimization problem for a CDP. Details are presented in [11]. ⊠

This result is not surprising, since $L(G)$ may be infinite, giving an unbounded number of parse trees whose backed up value must be tested. If we try to find the minimum by simply generating and testing parse trees, and save the lowest value encountered so far as min, there is in general no guarantee that if we stop at any given point, the next, untested, value may not be lower than min. The obvious way to get a decidable problem is to simply bound the space of all parse trees (or all parse trees that could possibly contribute to a minimum) in some way. The ACDP, f-bounded CDPs and MCDPs bound their search space in various ways, giving decidable problems of varying complexity.

To show an upper bound on the time to solve an ACDP, we must first find a bound for the size of any parse tree and the number of distinct parse trees that may be generated by an acyclic context free grammar. Let $exp2(x) = 2^{2^x}$, to keep our exponents from stacking too high. The following lemmas and theorem are proved in [11].

Lemma 1. *No parse tree for an acyclic grammar G has more than $2^{|G|-1} - 1$ nodes.*

Lemma 2. *No acyclic grammar G generates more than $exp2((|G| - 1)^2)$ distinct parse trees.*

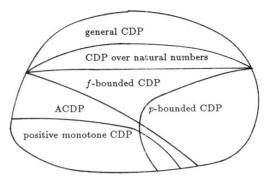

figure 2. Structure Hierarchy

General CDP	May have no solution
CDP over natural numbers	May have no computable solution
f-bounded CDP	Arbitrarily hard
ACDP	Solvable in doubly exponential time Requires exponential time i.o.
p-bounded CDP	NP-complete
Positive monotone CDP	$O(n^2)$

Figure 3. Complexity Hierarchy

Theorem 2. *The minimalization problem for any member of ACDP may be solved in $O(exp2(|G|^2 - 2))$ steps, and requires more than $2^{|G|/3}$ steps for infinitely many members of ACDP.*

Proof of the upper bound is by outlining a procedure $\text{MIN}_A(Z)$ that finds a minimal cost derivation for any $Z \in$ ACDP by doing an exhaustive search of the space of all possible parse trees. To show the lower bound it is sufficient to show that there are infinitely many acyclic grammars where every parse tree has more than $2^{|G|/3}$ nodes. ⊠

A simple grammar G with on the order of $exp2(|G|)$ distinct parse trees is presented in [11]. With such a potentially large search space, it would be reasonable to expect (although this does not constitute a proof) that there are infinitely many ACDPs which require on the order of $exp2(|G|)$ steps for their solution.

We conclude that the minimalization problem for ACDPs (and f-bounded CDPs for exponential f) is not practically solvable. The difficulty arises from the very compact representation of large trees given by an acyclic grammar. We now consider other means of bounding the size of the search tree. The following theorem shows that even if we bound the size of the tree by a polynomial in the size of the grammar, we still have a hard problem.

Theorem 3. *For every polynomial p such that $p(x) \geq x$, the minimalization problem for the p-bounded CDP is NP-complete.*

Proof. Assume p is some fixed polynomial, $p(x) \geq x$. We first show the problem is NP-hard [1,10]. The knapsack problem with integer weights is easily reduced to a p-bounded CDP. (That is, we show that if we can solve the minimalization problem, then we can solve the knapsack problem, which is known to be NP-complete.) Details are presented in [11]. The same reduction shows that acyclic CDPs and the natural CDP are *NP*-hard, since the CDP we have defined is a member of these classes. The acyclic and natural CDP classes do not appear to be *NP*-complete, since there is no obvious nondeterministic polynomial time algorithm that solves them.

To complete the proof it must be shown that *p*-bounded CDP minimalization can be solved by a nondeterministic algorithm in polynomial time. This is done by defining an algorithm which repeatedly makes a nondeterministic selection (a guess) of a production until some string is derived, and for each such string tests its backed up value aginst successively increasing values of a counter. It is not sufficient to simply guess a parse tree and return its value; this would produce a tree with fewest possible nodes, but not necessarily minimum cost.   ⊠

Finally, we consider an easily solved class of CDPs. A *positive monotone* CDP has all t_i monotone nondecreasing, and also satisfying $t_i(x_1, \ldots, x_k) \geq x_j$, $1 \leq j \leq k$.

Theorem 4. *The minimalization problem for the positive monotone CDP can be solved in $O(|G|^2)$ steps.*

Proof is by presenting an algorithm and proving its runtime and correctness. The proof closely parallels proofs of the runtime and correctness of various algorithms that it generalizes, e.g., Dijkstra's algorithm and certain dynamic programming problems. A similar algorithm appears in [8]. Details are presented in [11].   ⊠

Conclusions

Slight variations in the structure of the cost functions or grammar can cause a large change in the complexity of the minimalization problem. If only a single cost function fails to be monotone increasing, the result is a problem of much greater complexity. These results have the following practical application: When modeling some real problem as an AND/OR graph search, every effort should be made to create a graph model in the structural class with lowest search complexity. The proof of a large lower bound for the complexity of some problem is not necessarily the last word as to whether the problem is practically solvable. This sort of analysis does not take into account the distribution of members of a class which are most difficult. Even though we know there are infinitely many difficult members, they could still be very rare, i.e., most members of the class could be easily solved.

Positive monotone CDPs are the only easily solvable CDPs considered here. There is an interesting natural class of CDPs, which satisfy only the monotone restriction; these are considered in [8,9]. Let $c^*(W)$ be the lowest cost for any tree rooted at W; the monotone CDP satisfies the equations

1. If W is a terminal node, then $c^*(W) = c(W)$,
2. If W is a nonterminal node, we have $c^*(W) = \min\{t_i(c^*(X_1), \ldots, c^*(X_{k_i})) \mid p_i = W \rightarrow X_1 \ldots X_{k_i}\}$.

We conjecture that the monotone CDPs are not in general solvable in polynomial time (in the context of definitions and restrictions presented here). It would also be of interest to find other natural or easily definable classes of CDPs with an easily solved minimalization problem.

References

1. Aho, A. V., Hopcroft, J. E., and Ullman, J. D. *The Design and Analysis of Computer Algorithms*. Addison-Wesley, 1974.

2. Carter, L., Stockmeyer, L., and Wegman, M. "The complexity of backtrack searches." In *Proceedings of the 17th Annual Symposium on Theory of Computing* (Providence RI, May 6–8). ACM, New York, 1985.

3. Hall, P. A. V. Equivalence between AND/OR graphs and context-free grammars. *Communications of the ACM* 16, 7 (July 1973).

4. Kanal, L. N., and Kumar, V. "Some New insights into the relationships among dynamic programming, branch and bound, and heuristic search procedures." University of Maryland technical report, 1982.

5. Karp, R. M., and Held, M. H. Finite-State Processes and Dynamic Programming. *SIAM J. Appl. Math* 15, (1967), 693–718.

6. Karp, R. M., Upfal, E., and Wigderson, A. "Are search and decision problems computationally equivalent?" In *Proceedings of the 17th Annual Symposium on Theory of Computing* (May 6–8, Providence, R.I.). ACM, New York, 1985.

7. Knuth, D. E. Semantics of context-free languages. *Math. Systems Theory* 2, 2 (1968), 127–145.

8. Kumar, V. "A Unified Approach to Problem Solving Search Procedures." Ph.D. thesis, Dept. of Computer Science, Univ. of Maryland, Dec. 1982.

9. Kumar, V. A General Bottom-up Procedure for Searching And/Or Graphs. In *Proceedings of AAAI-1984*, 1984.

10. Machtey, M., and Young, P. *An Introduction to the General Theory of Algorithms*. Elsevier North Holland, 1978.

11. Motteler, H. E., and Kanal, L. N. "The Complexity of Searching Several classes of AND/OR Graphs." University of Maryland Technical Report, 1985.

12. Nilsson, N.J. *Principles of Artificial Intelligence*. Tioga, 1980.

13. Pearl, J. *Heuristics: Intelligent Search Strategies for Computer Problem Solving*. Addison-Wesley, 1984.

TERRAIN NAVIGATION THROUGH KNOWLEDGE-BASED ROUTE PLANNING

John F. Gilmore and Antonio C. Semeco

Artificial Intelligence Branch
Georgia Tech Research Institute
Atlanta, Georgia 30332

ABSTRACT

The advent of advanced computer architectures for parallel and symbolic processing has evolved to the point where the technology currently exists for the development of prototype autonomous vehicles. Control of such devices will require communication between knowledge-based subsystems in charge of the vision, planning, and conflict resolution aspects necessary to make autonomous vehicles functional in a real world environment. This paper describes a heuristic route planning system capable of forming the planning foundation of an autonomous ground vehicle.

INTRODUCTION

An effective route planner must address two levels of planning. At the high level, the planning algorithm usually exploits some form of map data to generate a global route which avoids mountains, valleys, and canyon areas. Depending upon the map resolution, individual pixel path points at this level vary from a representation area of 100 by 100 meters to 12.5 by 12.5 meters. At the low level, the planning algorithm must deal with local planning inside these individual path points so that obstacles such as trees, rocks, and holes may be avoided.

A consensus exists that global information in the form of a digitized terrain map is essential in the operation of an autonomous vehicle, at least at the global level of route planning [1-4]. The terrain map required must be capable of representing huge amounts of multi-dimensional data in a format easily exploited by the route planner. In order to make it suitable as a basis for real-time decision making during vehicle operation, the data should also be preprocessed into a more compact and manageable format. Two interesting approaches to this problem are the rule-based creation of a "composite map" [3] and the transformation of a polygonal obstacle map into a relational graph database [1]. It is to the second concept that our current approach to preprocessing map data is more closely aligned.

This paper describes a dynamic route planning and execution system called TREK (Tech Route Execution Kaleidoscope). TREK consists of four distinct processing phases: (1) scene recognition, (2) route generation, (3) scene matching, (4) and knowledge-based validation. Each of these processes is discussed in the following sections.

1.0 SCENE RECOGNITION

The recognition of objects in an image is central to the concept of local route planning. Given that a global route can be generated through a large area of terrain, scene recognition must be capable of interpreting the objects contained within the current field-of-view so that they may be avoided during the traversal of the actual terrain. Without a capability to determine what is in its local environment, low level route planning would not be able to avoid threatening objects or objects obstructing the vehicle's path.

Scene classification in the TREK system exploits a hierarchical classification tree consisting of objects and regions divided into natural or man-made categories. Efforts in scene classification to date have concentrated on detection and classification in video imagery. This work will be extended to infrared imagery in the near future.

2.0 ROUTE PLANNING

The goal of a route planning system is to analyze all available information to produce a route that is optimal in light of predetermined mission requirements. The TREK route planning system consists of three stages: A) point generation, B) graph generation, and C) heuristic search.

A. Point Generation

The TREK system generates three different types of path points: two-sweep points, convex terrain points and crossover exposure points. The two-sweep point generation algorithm is a humanistic approach to terrain traversal assuming that the system possesses a map and a compass. The central idea of two-sweep is the assumption that the direction of the goal point can always be determined through simple geometry. The algorithm initially scans forward from its current location until it locates the goal point or encounters an obstacle. The underlying heuristic is the simple strategy that a person uses when there is an obstacle in front that prevents him/her to go to the desired destination. The individual usually goes around the obstacle following its contour until the destination is visible. This approach can be used both at the local and global level in route planning, but only the global application is discussed in this paper.

The convex points of interest for an obstacle are defined as the set of points on the obstacle's boundary such that: a) each point in the set is a convex point, b) for each point P in the set, p's curvature is a local maximum, and c) the set of points forms a convex polygon.

A set of convex points is generated for each obstacle in the terrain image. An obstacle is represented as a list of (x,y) coordinate pairs which define its boundary. This set of points does not have to be of a continuous nature, but it is assumed that the distance between adjacent points is uniform.

The combination of two-sweep and convex point routes produces an extensive route graph with a number of route segment intersections. These intersections or crossover points actually represent high traffic areas of maximum exposure. By connecting all crossover points with a line-of-sight algorithm, a number of offensive route options are created. When merged with defensive path points produced by two-sweep and convex point generation, an unbasised route graph is generated. In this mode the TREK system is capable of non-military route planning as would be the case in a robot vehicle patrolling a national park looking for stranded motorists.

B. Graph Generation

A global terrain image graph based upon the aforementioned point sets is generated using a line-of-sight computation is made to determine if a path exists between individual obstacles points-of-interest. A cost is then assigned to each edge in the graph. This cost is computed as a weighted function of distance, terrain, scenario threats and vehicle constraints as follows:

$$F(c) = Distance * W1 + Terrain * W2 + Threats * W3 + Constraints * W4$$

This criteria edge graph forms the search space for the A* algorithm.

C. Heuristic Search

Once the search graph has been constructed, a suitable search procedure must be used to find an optimal route.

Given the expected size of the graph, it is important to have cost estimate functions to help improve the efficiency of the search.

The A* algorithm was chosen as the heuristic search mechanism in TREK. A* is basically a best-first tree search algorithm augmented to handle cycles and duplicate paths between nodes. If a recently discovered path to node N is found to be an improvement over a previous path to the same node, the pointer from N to its predecessor is updated and the improvement is propagated to other paths that have N as an intermediate node.

3.0 SCENE MATCHING

One of the most important aspects of an autonomous vehicle system is its ability to maintain and follow the routes that it generates. If a vehicle is incapable of performing this task, it will eventually wander aimlessly through terrain that it can not recognize as nothing will match its global map. For this reason, an accurate scene matching algorithm must be incorporated into the system.

The symbolic processing nature of the TREK system readily lends itself to a syntactic pattern recognition approach to scene matching As the goal in scene matching is to perform an image-to-image mapping, pixel correlation techniques are probably the most accurate method available. The difficulty for autonomous vehicle applications is that the local sensor image is guaranteed to have a different perspective than that of the global altitude data map being matched. Such a perspective invariant requirement is the shortcoming of most conventional scene matching approaches.

The key to determining and maintain the vehicle's position is to match objects and regions detected during scene classification to objects and regions in the map. This can be accomplished by representing each object and region as a classified point, constructing a perspective invariant graph of the local image points, and comparing the local graph as a subgraph to be located in a global map graph which has been created in the same manner [5]. This time of a local-to-global scene matching is accurate in light of obscurations and other possible terrain permutations and easily performed using a symbolic processing language such as LISP.

4.0 KNOWLEDGE BASED VALIDATION

Scene recognition, route planning, and scene matching information constitute the global database of the TREK system. This information is processed by the system as a preliminary representation of the current vehicle environment. Tasks or mission goals are provided to the system through communicating problem requirements via the control strategy. For a military scenario, example mission goals would be as follows:

PRIMARY GOAL: patrol zone 410
SECONDARY GOAL: neutralize intruders
SECONDARY GOAL: maximize survivability
SECONDARY GOAL: maximize kill ratio

TREK interprets these mission requirements and determines the optimal mission parameters which are passed to the scene recognition, route planning, and scene matching algorithms. An initial plan of action is then generated and represented in the global database. Decisions the on validity of the scene interpretation and the current plan of action are made through knowledge base processing. The TREK knowledge base contains three types of rules : scene rules, mission rules, and survivability rules.

Scene rules are used to validate and further interpret the information provide by scene recognition. In natural terrain images, object classification confidences can be enhanced through the utilization of positive and negative evidence provided by scene context. For example,

SCENE RULE 98
IF [1] an object is man-made and
   [2] it is on a road or in a field and
   [3] it has a high confidence of motion,
THEN [1] hypothesis the object is a vehicle
    [2] increase target confidence

Mission rules interpret the generated plan in light of high level mission goals. For example, the detection of three threats will generate a plan of action to engage and neutralize the threats based upon the previously entered mission plan. Mission rules further analyzed the system goals by examining the requested survivability and kill ratio levels and creating a modified plan through system feedback. For example,

MISSION RULE 132
IF [1] multiple threats are detected and
   [2] they are in a column and
   [3] they are in possess motion and
   [4] they are approaching an area that will maximize kill and survivability
THEN [1] generate a defensive route to that area and
    [2] determine the threat time of arrival to that area and
    [3] generate an offensive route to maximize kill to be executed on threat arrival

Mission plans are also used to repair plans based on invalid interpretations or changes in a scene.
Survivability rules are rules that maximize the vehicles chances of survival based on the interpretation of the current environment. For example,

SURVIVABILITY RULE 122
IF [1] an object is detected and
   [2] avoidance will delay accomplishment of mission goals
THEN [1] determine its probability of threat and
    [2] replan to avoid if threat is greater than (.5)

Based upon the results of knowledge base processing, the control strategy will feedback adjusted parameters to scene recognition, route planning, or scene matching algorithms for updated information, or execute the plan and communicate this decision to the user for approval.

SUMMARY

This paper has presented a high level view of the TREK terrain navigation system. TREK [1] analyzes a digital terrain map to generate a global route, [2] performs scene interpretation to generate local routes, [3] maintains a track of its position through scene matching, and [4] uses knowledge base processing to validate and improve preliminary plans in light of predetermined mission goals. The entire TREK system was written in LISP on a Symbolics 3600 and is currently being enhanced to increase it visual recognition capabilities, broaden its interpretation of mission goals, and advance its temporal reasoning process. Near term plans include the transportation of the entire TREK system into a two functional mobile robots (possessing additional sensory inputs) that has recently been donated by IBM for research in materials handling and flexible manufacturing applications.

REFERENCES

[1] Meystel, A. and Holeva, L.,"Interaction between Subsystems of Vision and Motion Planning in Unmanned Vehicles with Autonomous Intelligence",SPIE Applications of AI, Washington, D.C., May 1984.

[2] Mitchell, Joseph S. B. and Keirsey, David M.,"Planning Strategic Paths through Variable Terrain Data",SPIE Applications of AI, Washington, D.C., May 1984.

[3] Denton, Richard V. and Froeberg, Peter L.,"Applications of Artificial Intelligence in Automated Route Planning",SPIE Applications of AI, Washington, D.C., May 1984.

[4] Keirsey, D.M., Mitchell, J.S., Payton, D.W. and Preyss, E.P.,"Multi-level Path Planning For Autonomous Vehicles",SPIE Applications of AI, Washington D.C., May 1984.

[5] Gilmore, John F.,"Syntactic Pattern Analysis As A Means Of Scene Matching",Canadian Society For Computational Studies Of Intelligence,Saskatoon, Canada, May 1982.

First Results in Robot Road-Following

Richard Wallace, Anthony Stentz

Charles Thorpe, Hans Moravec

William Whittaker, Takeo Kanade

Robotics Institute, Carnegie-Mellon University

Abstract

The new Carnegie-Mellon Autonomous Land Vehicle group has produced the first demonstrations of road-following robots. In this paper we first describe the robots that are part of the CMU Autonomous Land Vehicle project. We next describe the vision system of the CMU ALV. We then present the control algorithms, including a simple and stable control scheme for visual servoing. Finally, we discuss our plans for the future.

Introduction

CMU has formed the Autonomous Land Vehicle (ALV) group to develop a perceptive outdoor robot. We have produced the first demonstrations of an autonomous vehicle able to follow a road using a single on board black and white television camera as its only sensor. Our robot has made several successful runs over a curving 20 meter path, and 10 meter segments of staright sidewalk, moving continuously at slow speeds, by tracking the edges of the road.

The research described in this paper is a first complete system, covering everything from low-level motor drivers to the top-level control loop and user interface. We took a "depth-first" approach to building our testbed: we picked one rough design and built all the pieces of a functioning system, rather than spending a lot of time at the beginning exploring design alternatives.

Related research at the Unversity of Maryland [6] has focused on the problem of visually finding and tracking roadways. The "bootstrapping" phase of the Maryland road finding program, in which the robot detects a road on start-up with no a priori position information, currently has no counterpart in our system. Our vehicle is always started with an orientation more or less aligned with the direction of the road and with knowledge of an initial road model. The Maryland road finding module is expected to be tested soon on an ALV built at Martin Marietta Denver Aerospace.

In this paper we first describe the robots that are part of the CMU Autonomous Land Vehicle project. We next describe the vision system of the CMU ALV. We then present the control algorithms, including a simple and stable control scheme for visual servoing. Finally, we discuss our plans for the future.

Terregator and Neptune

No mobile robot system is complete without a mobile robot. The primary vehicle of the CMU ALV project is the Terregator, built in the Civil Engineering Department. The design and construction of the Terregator (for *terre*strial navi*gator*) is documented in [7]. It is a 6-wheeled vehicle, 64 inches long by 39" wide by 37" tall. All wheels are driven, with one motor for the 3 left wheels and one for the 3 right wheels. Shaft encoders count wheel turns, but the vehicle skid-steering introduces some indeterminacy.

The Terregator is untethered. Power is provided by an on-board generator. Communications with a host computer are via a bi-directional 1200 baud radio link for vehicle status and commands, and a 10 megahertz microwave link for television signal from the vehicle to a digitizer. A remote VAX 11/780 runs programs for symbolic processing of visual data and navigation. A Grinnell GMR 270 attached to the Vax computes low- level visual operations such as edge detection. A Motorola 68000 on the Terregator translates steering commands from the VAX into wheel velocities for the left and right wheels.

Earlier work also used the tethered robot Neptune, built by the Mobile Robot Lab. Neptune is a simple tricycle, with a powered and steered from wheel and two passive wheels in the rear. Its sensors consist of two cameras (for stereo vision work), plus a ring of 24 sonars. While it was intended primarily for indoor work, it has large enough wheels to run outside on gentle terrain. With suitable modifications (an umbrella taped to the camera mast), it even has limited all-weather capability.

Our first successful continuous motion road following was achieved with Neptune running in our lab on a road marked with black electrical tape on the floor. This 5 meter road had one left turn and one right turn, which Neptune navigated successfully. At the end of the road, Neptune made a sharp right turn and drove around in circles.

Currently, this project is funded in part by Carnegie-Mellon University, by the Office of Naval Research under contract number N00014-81-K-0503, by the Western Pennsylvania Advanced Technology Center, by Defense Advanced Research Projects Agency (DOD), ARPA Order No. 3597, monitored by the Air Force Avionics Laboratory under contract F33615-81-K-1539, and by Denning Mobile Robotics, Inc. Richard Wallace thanks NASA for supporting him with a NASA Graduate Student Researchers Program Fellowship Grant.

The Vision and Navigation Program

The primary task of our vision and navigation program is to keep the vehicle centered on the road as it rolls along at a constant speed. The program accomplishes this task by repeatedly digitizing road images, locating the road edges in the image, calculating the deviation from the center line, and steering to realign the vehicle.

The program was designed to be fast yet reliable. While the vehicle is moving along a planned path, an image is digitized.

Figure 1: Neptune

Figure 2: Terregator

DANGER
STARTS
AUTOMATICALLY

Since images are digitized frequently, the appearance of the road edges does not change appreciably across successive images; consequently, searching the entire image is unnecessary. In order to constrain the search, the program maintains a model of the road The model contains the position and orientation of the left and right road edges seen in a recent image. The program uses these model edges to generate two small subimage rectangles in which to search for the left and right road edges. Since the approximate direction of each road edge is known a priori, the program uses directed curve tracing to reduce processing time and to preclude spurious edges. Generally the program finds more than one edge in each subimage rectangle. The model is used to select the pair of extracted edges most likely to be road edges. This new pair replaces the old pair in the model. From the model pair, the program computes a center line, the vehicle's drift from the center line, and a steering command to bring the vehicle closer to the center line. As the vehicle executes a steering command another image is digitized and the cycle repeats. Figure 3 depicts the program control flow. In the remainder of the paper we explain each component of the program in greater detail.

Constraining the Search

Each time the program digitizes an image it chooses two subimage rectangles to constrain the search for left and right edges. The representation of the rectangle is two horizontal and two vertical bounding line segments. The vehicle always "looks" a fixed distance ahead; therefore, the placement in the image of the horizontal bounding segments is predetermined and remains fixed across successive images. The placement of the segments is partly determined by two parameters selected manually: the height of the rectangle (typically 50 to 100 pixels) and rectangle overlap, that is, the percentage of the road in a rectangle seen in the preceding image (typically 50%). These two parameters present important trade offs: If a large height is chosen, the extracted road edges will be longer, thus providing more accurate information about the road; however, the processing time will be increased, and the road will be scrutinized less often. If a large overlap is chosen, more information is available from the previous image and spurious edges are less likely to deceive the algorithm; however, the vehicle's speed must be slowed to enable such overlap. The two parameters, coupled with the vehicle's speed, the image processing time, and the camera's tilt determine the placement of the horizontal bounding segments in the image.

The vertical bounding segments change from image to image. The program selects bounding segments so that the road edges, based on predictions from the model and a preset error tolerance, will appear within the rectangle. This error tolerance arises from two sources: First, the program obtains its estimates of the vehicle's motion by dead reckoning, which is somewhat inaccurate. Second, the program assumes the road is straight, that is, predictions are made by linearly extending the road edges. Road curvature introduces a discrepancy between these predictions and the actual road; consequently, the rectangle must be wide enough to see the road edge within a preset tolerance.

Selecting the Best Edges

The line finding routine generally returns more than one line from each rectangle. The program passes these lines through a number of filters to determine which, if any, are road edges. The new road edges are used to plan a path for the vehicle and to update the model. The 16 best left and right edge candidates (based on weights supplied by the line finding routine) are retained, and the rest are discarded. The program assumes that the camera's calibration, position, and orientation with respect to the road are known, that the ground is locally level and that all candidate edges arise from ground features. These assumptions allow the program to project each candidate edge into a unique line in the ground plane. We establish a righthanded coordinate system with the vehicle at the origin and the xy-plane on the ground, with the positive x-axis directed to the right of the vehicle and the positive y-axis directed forward. For each transformed edge, the program calculates the following parameters: the perpendicular distance r measured from the origin to the edge and the angle θ measured from the positive x-axis. The differences in r and θ between each transformed candidate edge and the corresponding model edge are calculated (call these values dr and dθ respectively). The quantity dr is the difference in displacements of the vehicle from the model edge and from the candidate edge. The quantity dθ is the angle between the model edge and the candidate edge. Test runs have shown that the vehicle tends to remain aligned with the center line; most of the error is in the form of lateral drift from this line. Hence, dr provides the most information for evaluating candidate edges. The quantity dθ tends to be small (less than 10 degrees); consequently, an early filter uses it to eliminate spurious edges. After this round of edge elimination, one of three cases remains:

1. All edge candidates have been eliminated

2. All edge candidates have been eliminated for a particular road edge (either left or right)

3. At least one edge candidate remains for both the left and right road edge

In the first case, the program obtains no new information and the vehicle continues to execute the path planned from the previous image. In the second case, only one road edge is visible. The other road edge is occluded, shadowed, or poorly defined. Suppose for example the program found a set of candidate road edges on the right side but none on the left. From the candidate edges on the right side the program selects the one with the minimum dr value. It inserts this new edge into the model, retains the old model edge for the left side, and generates a new steering command. In the third case, both road edges are visible. The program selects one edge from each list of road edges (left and right) by comparing each left edge to each right edge candidate and choosing the pair that minimizes the difference in their dr values, that is, it selects the two edge candidates that differ from their corresponding model edge in the same way. Figure 3 illustrates road edge selection in this case. This decision is based on the observation that vehicle motion error and road curvature shift the location of each edge in the image in the same way. The program inserts the two new road edges into the model and plans a new path.

Line and edge extraction

At the lowest levels of the vision system for our vehicle, the edge and line extraction modules, we found that for detecting road edges we could rely on the principle "almost anything works in the simple cases." That is, any of a number of simple edge and line finding techniques could be used to extract road edges in various situations. Our approach then was to try everything. We tested various edge and line finding programs on static road images and on images acquired by the vehicle in actual runs. Simple techniques proved adequate in many situations we encountered.

The basic approach of all the vision modules we tried was to find the left and right boundaries of the road and represent them as lines. Therefore, the task of the low level vision modules is to find line segments which are plausible candidate road edges. We sought to make only the most general assumptions about what might constitute a road in an image. The technique used to extract road edges and represent them as lines depends on whether we think of a road as an intensity change from background, a texture change, a color change or a combination. We experimented with 7 methods for extracting road edges from images and three methods for fitting lines to the edges. The seven techniques we used to find edges in road images were:

1. **Correlation.** Assuming that a road edge is a more or less vertical feature in a subimage it can be followed by selecting a small sample patch of the edge and correlating this on a row-by-row basis with the subimage. Where the correlation is strongest in each row a road edge element is assumed. The result is a list of points where the road edge appears in each row. A line can be fit to these directly. The correlation approach worked very well when the sample road edge patch was hand selected.

2. **DOG operator.** A Difference of Gaussian edge operator was tried at a wide range of spatial resolutions on road images. Road edges tend to be low spatial frequency signals so large DOGs were required to find them directly. Two-dimensional DOG filters tended to break up the road edges even at low frequencies. One dimensional DOG operators applied horizontally in the image produced more connected road edge pieces, since the road boundaries were almost vertical features in the image. High spatial frequency DOG operators can be used as the basis of a texture-based segmentation of road images, however.

3. **Temporal Edge Detector.** Subtracting two successive image frames is an inexpensive method for detecting image features that change from one moment to the next. If a vehicle is traveling down an ideal road (where the intensity of the road is uniform, the intensity of the surrounding region is uniform and the road edges are straight and parallel) then the difference of two successive road images is zero. When the vehicle begins to turn left or right off the road, however, simple image differencing finds the road edges. This strategy was used in one experiment to servo Neptune visually down a hallway. Here the road edges were particularly distinct so the idealness assumption was more or less satisfied.

4. **Roberts Operator.** A 2x2 Roberts edge operator was sufficient to find road edges where they were relatively well-defined intensity step functions, such as when the vehicle traveled down a hallway or when we artificially marked the road edges with tape.

5. **Intensity Segmentation.** A simple binary intensity segmentation of the road image works in many cases where the road is a set of pixels most of whose intensities are grouped together in the image histogram. We used a simple segmentation technique based on classifying all the pixels in the bottom 50% of the histogram as one region and those in the upper 50% as another. Standard procedures for expanding and shrinking the resulting segments to join closely spaced segments and eliminate small ones are applied. Road edges are assumed to lie along the boundaries of the resulting regions.

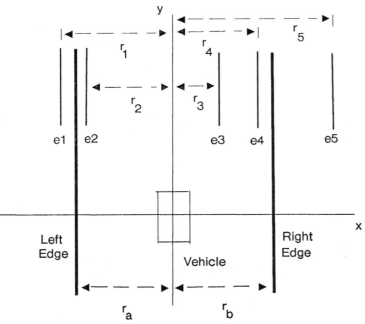

Figure 3: Edge selection using the perpendicular distances. Only edge candidates with $\theta = 0$ were included for simplicity. Candidates e1 and e4, with $r_{left} = r_1$ and $r_{right} = r_4$, minimize the error $|(r_{left} \cdot r_a) \ (r_{right} \cdot r_b)|$ and are selected as the new model road edges.

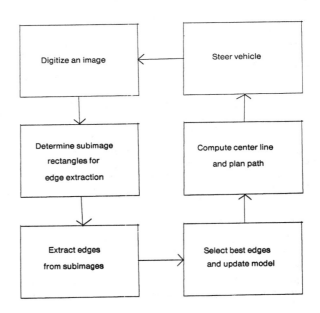

Figure 4: System Block Diagram

6. **Texture Segmentation.** Texture based segmentation often proves better than intensity based segmentation for road edges where the road is relatively smooth and the surrounding region is not, such as when the road is asphalt against a grass background. A simple texture operator which we have found useful in detecting road edges is one which counts the number of edges per unit area and classifies all those areas where the edge count is high as a single region.

7. **Row Integration.** Summing the intensities column-by-column in a set of scanlines in the image results in a single-scanline intensity image where the road is roughly a one dimensional box function, given that the road is a more or less vertical feature and the road and surrounding area each have fairly uniform but different intensities. Finding the boundaries of the box amounts to finding the average position of the left and right road edges over the scanlines summed. Repeating the procedure for another set of rows in the image locates another pair of road edge points which can be joined with the first to approximate the road boundaries as line segments.

The three line-extraction techniques we used were:

1. **Least Sqaures Line Fitting.** When we had only one possible line in an edge image, such as the result of running a correlation operator over the rows or collecting a number of road edge points by row integration, a line could be fit to the points by least squares.

2. **Muff Transform.** A modified Hough (Muff) transform was used to fit lines to edge data where the edge extractor returned points that could plausibly be parts of several lines. The Hough transform has been used to detect road edges in other road finding programs [6] [1]. The Muff transform uses a new parameterization for lines in images. The Muff transform has several implementational advantages over the conventional ρ-θ parameterization. The details and implementation of the Muff transform are presented elsewhere [5].

3. **Line Tracing.** Most of the subimages we processed to find lines were bands about 50 pixels tall and 250 pixels wide. A simple raster tracking algorithm found in [3] proved sufficient to trace the road edges. Basically, if an edge point P above some high threshhold d is found while scanning the subimage, then we search on scan lines below for connected edge points above some lower threshhold t. The last such point found in the subimage is called Q and we assume PQ is a line segment. The line tracing procedure is much like the inverse of a Bresenham algorithm for drawing lines, with the similar limitation that we can find lines that are only with 45 degrees of vertical. We find lines more than 45 degrees from perpendicular and lines with gaps by searching in a neighborhood below an edge point for the next adjacent edge point. Strictly speaking, our tracing program returns the endpoints of a curve which may not necessarily be a line, but over the small distances in the subimages we search for lines we have found this fast tracing procedure yields an adequate approximation. The line tracing procedure was used in all of the real time continuous motion runs of our vehicle under vision control.

A combination of three factors enabled us to reduce the image processing time for each image sample to about 2 seconds. First, special image processing hardware in our Grinnell GMR 270 display processor was used for the low-level correlation and convolution. Second, only small subimages (50 by 250 pixels) were searched for road edges by the line finding routines. Third, selection from among the possible set of candidate road edges of the actual road edges was accomplished by simple means (q.v.).

The next step in our plans for development of low-level road-finding vision is to integrate several types of feature detectors in a blackboard data structure. We want to evaluate the success of combining intensity, texture and color edge and region features to find road edges. Earlier we said that we relied on the principle "almost anything works in simple cases". For complicated cases, such as we have encountered in actual outdoor road scenes, we have found that none of the techniques we have tried *always* works. We believe that a combination of techniques will enable us to find road edges reliably in a wide range of situations.

Control

The control procedure translates the visual measurements into vehicle motor commands that, if successful, keep the vehicle moving along the road. We evaluated a half-dozen approaches experimentally with our vehicles and analytically. One approach, servoing to keep the road image centered in the forward field of view, excelled in all the measures, by such a margin that we feel it deserves to be considered a fundamental navigational principle for mobile robots.

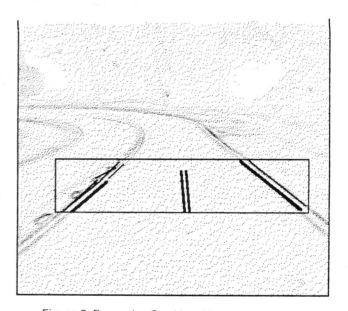

Figure 5: Processing Graphics. Here a road image is shown after processing to enhance intensity changes. The vision program selects a window in which to search for road edges. Candiate left and right road edges are lines fit to the raw edge data, shown here as black lines. Heavy black lines indicate the left and right road edges selected by the program. The computed road center line is shown as a double line.

Let x represent the shortest distance between the center of our vehicle and the centerline of a straight road. θ is the angle between the heading of the robot and the road direction, i.e. when $\theta = 0$ the robot is driving parallel to the road. Suppose the vehicle travels at a constant scalar velocity v, and that control is achieved by superimposing a steering rate, $d\theta / dt$ (where t is time) on top of the forward motion. If there is no slippage, the following kinematic relationship will hold:

$$dx / dt = -v \sin \theta \tag{1}$$

The general problem for continuous road following is to find a steering function F such that by setting $d\theta / dt = F(x,\theta)$ the vehicle approaches the road center. We tried several functions and noticed a number of recurring problems. Estimating θ and x from the image requires both a precise calibration of the camera and accurate determination of the position and orientation of the road edges in the image. Both are difficult to achieve in practice, and the high noise level in these quantities made most of our functions unstable. A second problem led directly to our solution. The road image sometimes drifted out of the camera's 40 degree field of view, and in the next sampling period the program would fail to find a road, or (worse) identified some other feature, like a door edge, as road. The obvious solution was to servo to keep the road image centered. Experimentally this approach was a stunning success. Besides helping the vision, it seemed to be insensitive to even large calibration errors and misestimates of the road parameters.

The theoretical analysis was remarkably sweet also, and bore out the empirical observations. A first order analysis, where we assume the road image is kept perfectly centered, gives the relation

$$x / r = \sin \theta \tag{2}$$

where r is the distance in front of the robot where a ray through the camera image center intersects the ground (i.e. the range at which we do our road finding). The parameter r can be changed by raising or lowering the camera, changing its tilt, or by using a different scanline as the center of the region in which road edges are sought.

Equation (2) can be substituted into (1) to give

$$dx / dt = -v x / r \tag{3}$$

which can be solved directly, giving

$$x = x_0 e^{-vt/r} \tag{4}$$

where x_0 is the initial value of x when t = 0, so to first order the vehicle approaches the centerline of the road exponentially with time.

A more detailed analysis considers the actual servo loop behavior. The displacement of the road centerline image from the center of the forward field of view is proportional to

$$(\sin \theta - x / r) / \cos \theta \tag{5}$$

Servoing the steering rate on (5) sets

$$d\theta / dt = -g (\sin \theta - x / r) / \cos \theta \tag{6}$$

where g is the servo loop gain. The full behavior of the robot can be found by solving (1) with (6) simultaneously. These equations are made linear and easily solvable by the substitution Q = $\sin \theta$, giving

$$dx / dt = -v Q \tag{7}$$
$$dQ / dt = -g (Q - x / r)$$

By co-incidence or cosmic significance of all the servo functions we considered, only this one yielded a fully general analytic solution.

The solution has three cases distinguished by the sign of the expression

$$g r - 4v \tag{8}$$

In all cases the solution converges to x = 0, Q (and θ) = 0 exponentially with time. When g < 4v/r the convergence is a decaying oscillation - the sluggish steering causes repeated overshoots of the road center. When g > 4v/r the solution contains a second exponential, and the robot approaches the road center more slowly. When g = 4v/r, the critically damped case, we have the fastest convergence and no overshoot, and the behavior is given by the equations

$$x = e^{-2vt/r} (vt (2x_0/r - Q_0) + x_0) \tag{9}$$

$$Q = e^{-2vt/r} (2vt/r (2x_0/r - Q_0) + Q_0) \tag{10}$$

The gain sets the turn rate required of the robot. Note that to retain the critically damped situation while increasing v without changing g, it is necessary only to increase r, i.e. arrange to have the vision look further ahead.

The method is successful for several reasons. It keeps the road in view at all times. Because the system always converges, errors in g or camera calibration do not jeopardize performance. Because the parameter being servoed is the most robust direct measurable, namely road position in the image, the noise problems of the other approaches are almost totally eliminated. In particular, θ (or Q) and x though they occupy a central position in the theoretical analysis, need never be calculated in the actual servo loop.

Conclusions

We have developed a vision and control system for a mobile robot capable of driving the vehicle down a road in continuous motion. The system has been tested on two mobile robots, Neptune and the Terregator, in both indoor (hallway and artificial road) and outdoor (asphalt paths in a park and cement sidewalk) environments. In our best run to date the Terregator traversed a 20 meter outdoor path at 2 cm/sec. Image processing time has been reduced to 2 sec/image.

Failure modes of our vehicle have included driving off the road, driving into trees and walls, and driving around in circles. Such failures were mostly due to bugs in our programs, imprecise calibration procedures, and limitations of current hardware (e.g., B&W camera with narrow angle lens), not fundamental limitations of the techniques used.

Future Work

There are several areas that we plan to address. First is the construction of a true **testbed**. This involves mostly software engineering, such as cleaning up and documenting the interfaces between vision and control. This will enable us to try **other vision methods**, such as texture and color operators.

Further work will require the use of a **map**, along with program access to a **magnetic compass** and a **gyro**. The map will list road direction, width, appearance, and intersections, which will provide strong cues to both the image processing and the navigation system. The compass, along with the map information, will help predict road location in the image. This will become increasingly important as we venture onto curved and hilly roads, and as we encounter intersections and changes in the road surface.

The next step is **obstacle avoidance**, which will require limited 3D processing. Projects in the CMU Mobile Robot Laboratory have already demonstrated obstacle avoidance with sonar [2] and stereo cameras [4]; we intend to integrate these into the testbed. Later work may add a laser rangefinder and programs to handle that data.

Finally, as the testbed becomes more complicated, **system control** will become a major issue. We plan to work on a **blackboard** system with cooperating and competing knowledge sources. All the data, from the lowest level signals to the highest level models and maps, will be on the blackboard and available to all processes.

Acknowledgements

We would like to thank first of all Pat Muir for his work on analysis of the control of the Terregator. Many thanks also to Mike Blackwell, microprocessor hacker *extrodinaire*, Kevin Dowling, tender of robots, and John Bares, prime mover of the Terregator, without whom the experiments described here would have been much more difficult and much less fun. Thanks also to Gregg Podnar and Bob Spies for video and digitization work. Finally, we would like to express our appreciation to Raj Reddy for his support and encouragement.

References

[1]   Inigo, R. M., E. S. McVey, B. J. Berger and M. J. Wertz.
Machine Vision Applied to Vehicle Guidance.
IEEE Transactions on Pattern Analysis and Machine Intelligence 6(6), November, 1984.

[2]   H. Moravec and A. Elfes.
High Resolution Maps From Wide Angle Sonar.
In *IEEE Conference on Robotics and Automation*. 1985.

[3]   Rosenfeld, A. and A. C. Kak.
Digital Picture Processing (Vol 1).
Academic Press, 1976.

[4]   C. Thorpe.
FIDO: Vision and Navigation for a Mobile Robot.
PhD thesis, Carnegie-Mellon University, 1984.

[5]   Wallace, R. S.
A Modified Hough Transform for Lines.
In *Computer Vision and Pattern Recognition*. IEEE, 1985.

[6]   Waxman, A. M., J. LeMoigne and B. Scrinivasan.
Visual Navigation of Roadways.
In *International Conference on Robotics and Automation*.
IEEE, 1985.

[7]   W. Whittaker.
Terregator - Terrestrial Navigator.
Technical Report, Carnegie-Mellon Robotics Institute, 1984.

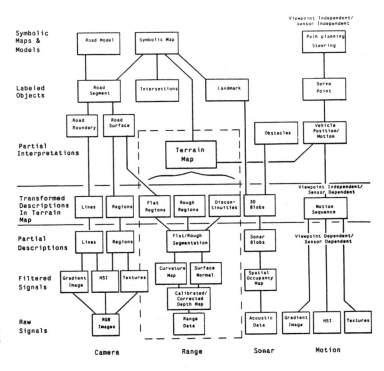

Figure 6: Blackboard System. We have begun the design of a blackboard system to integrate the multiple sensors, knowledge sources and vehicle actuators planned for the CMU ALV system. Our future work is to embed the modules we already have in the blackboard system, with multiple parallel knowledge sources accessing a global data base, and also to add other modules.

A Proximity Metric For Continuum Path Planning

Charles E. Buckley and Larry J. Leifer

Stanford University and Palo Alto VA Hospital

ABSTRACT

The problem of planning motions of robot manipulators and similar mechanical devices in the presence of obstacles is one of keen interest to the artificial intelligence community. Most of the algorithms previously reported for solving such problems have been *combinatorial algorithms*, which work by partitioning the problem domain continuum into a finite set of equivalence classes, and applying combinatorial search algorithms to plan transitions among them. However, the few *continuum algorithms* that have been reported, which do not rely on such a partitioning, have shown greater promise when applied to problems of complexity equivalent to that of planning a true manipulator motion. This is true even though the heuristics employed in these continuum algorithms have been extremely simple in nature. A significant barrier to the development of more refined heuristics for use in continuum algorithms is the uncertainty over how to characterize the proximal relationship between rigid bodies. In this paper, a new measurement function is reported which permits such characterization. An introduction is made to a new type of path planning algorithm which this function makes possible, which promises to significantly increase the capabilities of continuum path planning software.

1 Prior Work

Two early research efforts in this area may be seen as cornerstones of the two basic methods employed.

Whitney introduced the first combinatorial algorithm for manipulator path planning [Whitney 1969]. Although this algorithm was only concerned with the planning of gripper motions in the plane, and only a few evenly spaced positions and orientations were considered, the algorithm suffered from problems of combinatorial explosion. The algorithm was formally verified to be correct.

Peiper's algorithm was not combinatorial, and was applied to the planning of motions for a full six degree–of–freedom robot manipulator [Peiper 1968]. Although he reported qualitative success, he was unable to verify correctness.

This basic tradeoff between verifiability and the size of tractable problems remains a fundamental issue among those who study path–planning today.

Perhaps the most successful combinatorial results have been built on the work of [Lozano–Pérez 1981], who defined a scheme for exactly partitioning admissible points from inadmissible ones for polyhedral bodies in fixed relative orientation. Jarvis has reported a similar scheme which works for arbitrary classes of objects, and is based on constructing adjacency graphs among

uniform–sized quanta in 3–space[1] [Jarvis 1984]. Brooks later extended Lozano–Pérez' work to apply to planar objects with variable orientation through the use of a successive approximation technique [Brooks 1982], but was subsequently unable to extend it to three dimensions. [Schwartz 1982] reported a generalization of this concept to apply to objects of arbitrary dimension bounded by algebraic surfaces (e. g. planes, cylinders, etc.). Although these results confirmed earlier results showing the path-planning problem to be *P*-space complete [Reif 1979], they were of little practical interest since time complexity for discretization of the problem domain exceeded that of simple subdivision into hyperparallelopipeds of the smallest mesh size representable by standard computing hardware[2] [Buckley 1985].

Two non–combinatorial algorithms stand out as significant. Loeff and Soni reported an algorithm for planning the motions of a planar, line–segment manipulator among circular forbidden zones [Loeff 1975]. Khatib has implemented an algorithm in which simulated repulsive forces generated from a restricted set of object models were used to generate commanded positions for certain distinguished points on a manipulator [Khatib 1980].

Another simpler algorithms was reported by Myers [Myers 1981]. Although this algorithm was essentially one of hypothesis and test, its computation times for solving a general purpose path planning problem for a PUMA manipulator were on the same order of magnitude as those reported in [Brooks 1982] for the planar, free–body case.

These results suggest that practical algorithms for path-planning will be heuristic in nature, and not formally verifiable. However, prior research has only begun to explore the question of what sort of heuristics may be used to best advantage. Notably, excepting the algorithms of Loeff and Soni and that of Khatib, heuristics employed for collision *avoidance* in prior research have really been based only on whether or not a collision was *detected* in following an hypothesized trajectory. In most cases the direction in which hypothetical impact occurred was not even taken into account. Often the occurrence of a collision at one point along an hypothesized trajectory was considered grounds for rejection of that entire trajectory. Local perturbation of offending portions of trajectories has hardly been explored.

2 The Proximal Relationship of Objects in Space

To a large extent, the simplicity of the heuristics employed in previous algorithms is due the fact that there doesn't really exist

---

[1] This adjacency graph was searched using dynamic programming, which that computations be performed for *each* quantum in the space.

[2] e. g. a single–precision floating–point number on something like a VAX

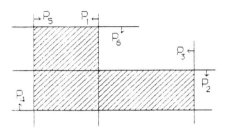

Figure 1: A Point Set Defined by Boundary Constraints

a good way of characterizing the proximal relationship between two rigid bodies or models. Conceptually, it is easy to determine whether or not an intersection between two such bodies occurs, given their relative position. However, if this information is insufficient, then what? It is often proposed that the actual point set corresponding to the intersection of rigid bodies be computed, but there have been no serious proposals made as to what might be done with all of this information if were it available.

Practically, the only alternatives to hypothesize–and–test methods which have enjoyed any success at all are the *relaxation methods*. These methods were originally conceived to solve constrained non–linear optimization problems, and have been quite successfully applied. Loeff and Soni and Khatib took advantage of the fact that these algorithms work by continuously perturbing a state vector from some initial guess to a final optimum state to generate trajectories between known endpoints.

The main inconvenience with relaxation methods as they are almost always formulated is that all constraints must apply *simultaneously*. This has to do partially with the formulation of the Kuhn–Tucker stationarity equations for an extremum, which are used as error equations to drive state perturbations, and partially with long—standing conventions of the discipline. This requirement is fundamentally *in*compatible with standard solid modelling practice, in which solid objects are represented as point sets defined by *arbitrary* Boolean functions of boundary predicates.

For example, the set of points contained in the L–shaped planar region shown in Figure 1 may be described as those points which satisfy the following Boolean expression:

$$(P_1 \wedge P_4 \wedge P_5 \wedge P_6) \vee (P_5 \wedge P_2 \wedge P_3 \wedge P_4) \qquad (1)$$

where each Boolean expression P_i corresponds to a point lying on the proper side of the associated line[3], as indicated by the direction of the normal arrows drawn in the figure. If $g_i(x) = 0$ were the equation of boundary line P_i, then the Boolean expression P_i might be $g_i(x) \leq 0$. Only the constraints in one or the other of the two disjuncts are necessary to qualify a point as being part of the shaded region. Further, for points lying in one of the arms of the "ell" it is *not possible* for all of the constraints to apply simultaneously. A similar argument may be made with respect to points outside of the shaded region. The developers of prior algorithms for path–planning in which relaxation methods were used were very aware of this problem, and in fact the limitations which they placed on their algorithms stemmed directly from it.

---

[3]an instance of a boundary manifold

In this paper is described a new metric for characterizing the proximal relationship between two convex rigid bodies which addresses this issue and others. This metric may be related to an algorithm intended exclusively for *detecting intersections* among convex bodies published in [Comba 1968].

The use of the Comba method actually involves the numerical solution of an unconstrained minimization problem itself, which can be time–consuming. The quantity to be minimized is a "pseudo–constraint function" defined as follows:

Let the n_c boundary predicates (those which define *all* of the objects under consideration) be defined by

$$g_i(x) \leq 0, \ i = 1, n_c$$

where the g_i are convex functions of their arguments[4]. Then, the Comba constraint function $G(x)$ is defined by the three equations:

$$v_i(x) = (g_i(x)^2 + t^2)^{\frac{1}{2}} + g_i(x) \qquad (2)$$

$$V = \sum_{i=1}^{n_c} v_i \qquad (3)$$

$$G = \underbrace{\frac{1}{2}\left(V - \frac{t^2}{V}\right)}_{a} + c \qquad (4)$$

where t, c are small, positive constants.

For t non–zero, each of the v_i functions is always positive. However, when the corresponding g_i is negative, then that v_i tends toward zero. In particular, when a $g_i = 0$, then $v_i = t$. When $V = t$, then the term a in equation 4 is zero. Therefore, when *all* of the g_i are zero, then $V = O(t)$. When a g_i is negative, then its corresponding $v_i = O(t^2)$. When t is small, $t^2 < t$, and the contribution of a v_i corresponding to a negative g_i will be less. Therefore, except in instances where the bodies in question are just touching, if

$$G^* = \min_x G \qquad (5)$$

then $G^* < 0$ corresponds to a condition of intersection, $G^* > 0$ corresponds to non–intersection, and the x corresponding to a G^* near zero are in a gray area. The constant c in the equation for G helps minimize the problems associated with this gray area. For example, it may be used to create a safety buffer around the obstacles being tested.

The Comba function is meaningful only at its minimum, and then only when compared against the threshold of zero. Trying to assign other meaning to the value of the function taken at its minimum is hampered by the influence of the t and c parameters, which were introduced to insure continuous differentiability of the function as an aid to finding its minimum.

The Comba function is undefined at any point x satisfying all constraints if $t = 0$. However, for the non-intersecting case, if both t and c are set equal to zero, then the Comba function becomes:

$$G = \min_x \frac{1}{2} \sum_{i=1}^{n_c} \max(0, g_i(x)) \qquad (6)$$

If the number of convex bodies being tested is restricted to 2, and there is only one g_i function per body, corresponding to $g_i(x) \equiv$

---

[4]The g_i must be continuously differentiable in order to employ numerical methods for minimization, such as Davidon–Fletcher–Powell[Avriel 1976].

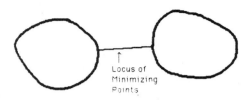

Figure 2: Locus of Minimizing Points for Comba Distance Function

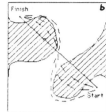

Figure 3: Two Paradigms for Path Planning

$d(x, B_i)$, the convex distance function[5] [Rockafellar 1970], then the function g will be minimized anywhere on the line segment connecting the two closest points of bodies B_1 and B_2. This segment is shown in Figure 2. More important, its value there will correspond to half the distance between these closest points, or in other words, half the minimum distance between bodies B_1 and B_2[6]

This specialized version of the Comba function has the advantage that the *generating segment* corresponding to the locus of minimizing points is a function of only a single point on each of the bodies. This makes it easier to generate a derivative of this specialized Comba function than it is for the general case. On the other hand, this specialization effectively reimposes the restrictions that:

1. Each of the convex bodies involved be represented by a single, differentiable manifold.

2. The bodies in question should not intersect.

These restrictions correspond almost exactly to those which Loeff and Soni, and subsequently Khatib found it necessary to impose in their algorithms. Loeff and Soni restricted their attentions to planar problems, in which the manipulator links were modelled as line segments, and the obstacles "[did] not have sharp corners or sides" [Loeff 1975], and in which the influence function used to repel a moving from a fixed body was a decreasing function of the minimum distance between them. Khatib restricted his attention to the interaction between obstacles whose surfaces could be modelled as single differentiable manifolds, and selected discrete points on a moving manipulator[7]. The minimum distance between these points and obstacles was subsequently used in an inverse square potential function to simulate forces between the two bodies generating it.

In both of these cases, a clear effort was made to avoid having the two bodies in question intersect. There is good reason for this — if the two bodies intersect, the minimum distance between them drops to 0 identically and abruptly, and remains that way for arbitrary intersections. This means that the gradient of the minimum distance function is identically zero, and can therefore provide no information which might be used to drive a relaxation algorithm.

An even more important limitation than that placed on the type of objects which can be modelled is the one which prevents

the modified Comba algorithm from working if the objects between which constraints are computed intersect. Both the Loeff/Soni and Khatib algorithms were subject to this limitation, which is a severe one because it forces an evolutive algorithm for trajectory generation, in which one known state is sequentially perturbed towards another, as shown in Figure 3a, and no inadmissible states are ever entered. This approach will only work if the problem in question is free from false local minima. The limitations of this type of algorithm have been aptly demonstrated in mobile base path planning research, e. g. [Chatila 1981], [Cahn 1975].

An alternate paradigm for path planning is shown in Figure 3b, in which an entire trajectory is hypothesized between the two known endpoints, and *perturbed* into admissibility, if it is not already. Such an approach depends on being able to deal effectively with inadmissible states (in this case intersections between the moving body and its obstacles) should they arise.

3   Δ, the Minimum Directed Distance

The function Δ, called the minimum directed distance between two arbitrary convex bodies, was developed in order to address these two issues. That is, it was developed to:

- be valid for bodies bounded using more than one boundary predicate.

- be valid even when the bodies in question intersect.

Δ also stems from the distance form of the Comba intersection form described earlier, hence its restriction to convex bodies. This restriction does not constitute much of a problem, since convex decomposition can be accomplished "off-line". Algorithms exist for performing this decomposition automatically in the case of certain classes of objects, such as polyhedra [Chazelle 1980]. It can also be done by hand if necessary.

Although the merit of the Δ function stems in large part from the fact that it is valid between two arbitrary convex bodies, it is simplest to explain for the case in which one of the bodies is a point. Extension to the point body case follows from the same configuration space obstacle transformation described in [Lozano–Pérez 1981].

3.1   Disjoint Case

Consider first the case in which the givens of the problem, a point x_o and a set of points of a rigid, convex body C are fixed in

---

[5]corresponding to the minimum distance from a point x to all points in body B_i

[6]The $\frac{1}{2}$ factor is included so as to make the a term correspond to the inverse of the transformation from g_i to v_i. It's presence is not essential.

[7]which he called "points submitted to a potential" [Khatib 1980]

relative position so that $C \cap x_0 = \emptyset$. Let C be defined symbolically by

$$C = \{\forall x \in R^n \ : \ g_i(x) \geq 0, i = 1, n_c\},$$

where n_c is the number of constraints. The g_i are concave functions, which means that $g_i(x) \geq 0$ is a convex set.

The minimum distance problem (DP) can be defined as the problem of finding:

$$d(x_0; C) = \min_x \sqrt{(x - x_0)^T(x - x_0)} \qquad (7)$$

subject to

$$g_i(x) \geq 0, \ i = 1, n_c.$$

The stationary conditions for this problem are:

$$\frac{(x - x_0)}{\sqrt{(x - x_0)^T(x - x_0)}} = \sum_{i=1}^{n_c} \lambda_i \nabla g_i(x) \qquad (8)$$

in which

$$\lambda_i \geq 0, \quad \lambda_i g_i(x) = 0.$$

This problem is a well–behaved, convex one.

Now, the following two–stage problem (SP) is introduced as an alternative to problem (DP) above.

$$s(x_0; C) = -\min_\xi \max_x \xi^T(x - x_0) \qquad (9)$$

subject to

$$g_i(x) \geq 0, \ i = 1, n_c$$

and

$$1 - \xi^T \xi \geq 0.$$

Considering the two extremizations as separate problems, the objective functions of each are linear, and may be considered as simultaneously convex and concave. The constraints are concave, so each extremization represents a convex problem.

There are two sets of stationary conditions, one corresponding to each of the stages:

$$\frac{\partial}{\partial x} : \qquad \xi = \sum_{i=1}^{n_c} \beta_i \nabla g_i(x), \ \beta_i \geq 0 \qquad (10)$$

$$\frac{\partial}{\partial \xi} : \qquad (x - x_0) = -\beta_0 \xi, \ \beta_0 \geq 0. \qquad (11)$$

It is easy to eliminate ξ, which yields

$$(x - x_0) = \beta_0 \sum_{i=1}^{n_c} \beta_i \nabla g_i(x). \qquad (12)$$

Comparing these stationary conditions with those of problem (DP), it is seen that they are equivalent if

$$\lambda_i = \frac{\beta_0 \beta_i}{\sqrt{(x - x_0)^T(x - x_0)}}, \quad i = 1, n_c.$$

From the definition of the Kuhn–Tucker stationary conditions, when a multiplier β_i is *equal* to 0, then that constraint is inactive. If $\beta_0 = 0$, then the stationary conditions 11 dictate that $x^* = x_0$, where x^* is an x which satisfies the stationary conditions. However, by definition, there is no $x \in C$ which can equal (be coincident with) x_0, since x_0 and C are disjoint. Therefore, the unit magnitude constraint on ξ must be active in this case.

The activity of the unit magnitude constraint on ξ in turn implies that

$$\beta_0 = \sqrt{(x - x_0)^T(x - x_0)},$$

and therefore

$$\lambda_i = \beta_i, \ i = 1, n_c.$$

Further, if ξ^*, x^* are extrema which satisfy the stationary conditions, then

$$\xi^* = -\frac{(x^* - x_0)}{\sqrt{(x^* - x_0)^T(x^* - x_0)}}$$

and

$$\begin{aligned}
s(x_0; C) &= -(\xi^*)^T(x^* - x_0) \\
&= \frac{(x^* - x_0)^T(x^* - x_0)}{\sqrt{(x^* - x_0)^T(x^* - x_0)}} \\
&= \sqrt{(x^* - x_0)^T(x^* - x_0)} \\
&= d(x_0; C). \qquad (13)
\end{aligned}$$

The equivalence of the two problems under conditions of non-intersection has been fully established.

The solution of problem (SP) has a simple interpretation in terms of support functions, which is useful in developing intuition for the development which follows.

The *indicator function* of a convex set C is defined by

$$i(x, C) = \begin{cases} 0 & x \in C; \\ +\infty & x \notin C. \end{cases}$$

Its convex conjugate function is given by [Avriel 1976]

$$\begin{aligned}
i^*(\xi, C) &= \max_x \{\xi^T x - i(x; C)\} \\
&= \sup_{x \in C} \{\xi^T x\}. \qquad (14)
\end{aligned}$$

The x–extremum portion of the problem (SP) is given by

$$\max_x \{\xi^T(x - x_0)\}$$

subject to

$$g_i(x) \geq 0, \ i = 1, n_c$$

or in other words

$$\begin{aligned}
\sup_{x \in C} &\{\xi^T(x - x_0)\} \\
&= \sup_{x \in C} \{\xi^T x\} - \xi^T x_0 \\
&= i^*(\xi; C) - \xi^T x_0 \\
&= i^*(\xi; C \ominus \{x_0\}) \qquad (15)
\end{aligned}$$

where the operator $\ominus$ denotes set subtraction. Set subtraction will be formally defined later on, but in this case the operation simply involves subtracting x_0 from each point in the convex set C. Its easy to see that $x_0 \notin C \Leftrightarrow 0 \notin C \ominus x_0$.

Expressed in this form, the x–extremization may be given a simple graphical interpretation, as shown by the (necessarily planar) example in Figure 4. A support function with an argument of ξ (considered as a free vector) may be computed graphically by taking a hyperplane[8] with normal ξ and moving it so that it

---

[8] a line in the planar case

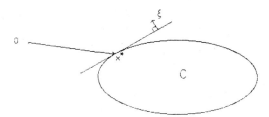

Figure 4: A Graphical Interpretation of x–Extremization

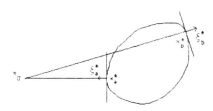

Figure 5: A Solution and a Non–Solution to Problem (SP')

osculates against the set in question, with the normal pointing away as shown. Then the value of the support function is equal to the dot product between a vector from the origin of the coordinate system to any point of the osculation. Of course, this value depends on the choice of the origin, but the transformation

$$C \to C \ominus x_0$$

turns the point x_0 into the origin, and makes this method appropriate for describing proximal relationships between x_0 and C.

The problem (SP') can be restated in light of the above as

$$s(x_0; C) = -\min_{\xi}\{i^*(\xi; C \ominus x_0)\}$$

subject to

$$|\xi| \leq 1.$$

For x_0, C disjoint, solving s simply involves finding the unit magnitude direction vector which minimizes the support function of the transformed set. This corresponds to the identification of a point such as x_a^* in figure 5, and its corresponding ξ. It is expressly pointed out that this is *not* equivalent to solving

$$\max_{\xi}\{i^*(\xi; C \ominus \{x_0\})\}.$$

Such a solution would correspond to the point x_b^* in the same figure. The unit vector ξ points along the *generating segment* from x_a^* to x_0.

3.2   Non–Disjoint Case

When $x_0 \in C$[9], the solution to the problem (DP) is uniformly zero, and therefore uninteresting.

---
[9]corresponding to intersection of two bodies in the original problem

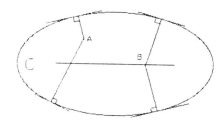

Figure 6: Multiple Stationary Conditions for Δ

For problem (SP), the origin of the transformed problem will lie inside of $C \ominus \{x_0\}$. Therefore, $i^*(\xi, C \ominus \{x_0\}) \geq 0$ for all $\xi \in R^n$. The ξ–minimization of problem (SP') is therefore solved by $\xi = 0$, which means $s(x_0; C) = 0$ and $x^* = x_0$, just as with (DP). Therefore, problem (SP) is again equivalent to (DP), and equally uninteresting.

However, the formulation of (SP) suggests a small modification which is not apparent in the problem (DP). If a problem (SP=) is written, which consists of finding

$$\Delta(x_0; C) = -\min_{\xi} \max_{x} \xi^T(x - x_0) \qquad (16)$$

subject to

$$g_i(x) \geq 0, \quad i = 1, n_c$$

and

$$1 - \xi^T\xi \underbrace{=}_{!} 0.$$

is defined, in which the only difference between it and problem (SP) is that the unit magnitude constraint on ξ is an *equality* constraint, its solutions assume interesting properties. To begin with, when $x_0 \notin C$, the behavior of problems (SP) and (SP=) are the same.

However, the guaranteed activity of this constraint at the optimum means that ξ will always be of unit length, and parallel to the vector from x^* to x_0. Therefore $\Delta(x_0; C)$ will always have units of length. Because $\xi \neq 0$, any x^* will always lie on the boundary of C or

$$x^* \in \partial C.$$

Therefore, the magnitude of Δ will corresponds to the shortest normal distance to the boundary of C. As was the case with the Comba function, the sign of Δ may be used as an intersection predicate:

$$\Delta(x_0; C) \begin{cases} > 0 & x_0 \notin C, \\ = 0 & x_0 \in \partial C, \\ < 0 & x_0 \in C - \partial C. \end{cases}$$

When $\Delta < 0$ the problem (SP=) is no longer a convex program, and is therefore much harder to solve. It is not hard to think of situations in which there are several $x^* \in \partial C$ which satisfy the stationary conditions of (SP=); Figure 6 shows a couple of such cases. In the case where the point A is taken as x_0, although there are multiple stationary conditions, there is a clear minimum distance to the boundary. In the case where B is taken as x_0, both stationary conditions may be used, since their corresponding distances are equal. B is called a *conjugate point*.

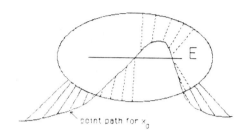

Figure 7: Δ Between a Point and a Body

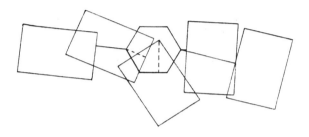

Figure 8: Δ Between Two Non-Point Bodies

3.3 Properties of $\Delta(x_0; C)$

These properties of $\Delta(x_0; C)$ are established in [Buckley 1985]:

- $\Delta(x_0; C)$, considered as a function of x_0 is convex.

- $\Delta(x_0; C)$ is a continuous function.

- ξ, the unit vector parallel to the generating segment, is always contained in the subdifferential of $\Delta(x_0; C)$, and may be used as a gradient.

An intuitive feeling for the behavior of Δ as a point x_0 passes near a body E may be seen in Figure 7. Dashed generating segments correspond to negative values of Δ, and the magnitude of Δ is proportional to the length of the generating segment. Note that the subgradient of Δ will be discontinuous.

3.4 Extension to the Body–Body Case

The derivation for the body–body case proceeds almost exactly as with the point–body case, except that both ends of the generating segment are now free to move about in the minimizations. Details are given in [Buckley 1985]. Equivalence to the configuration space obstacle method described in [Lozano–Pérez 1981] is also established there. Δ between two convex bodies is also a continuous function, but because the relative position and orientation of two bodes must be expressed in terms of at least one rotation group, it cannot be a convex function of its arguments. An analytic expression which may always be used as the gradient of Δ has also been derived.

An intuitive feeling for the behavior of Δ as a rectangle moves near a hexagon may be seen in Figure 8. The encoding on the generating segment is the same as with Figure 7.

4 Computational Issues

While Δ may be attractive theoretically, it is not straightforward to compute for arbitrary convex bodies. However, if the bodies between which it is to be computed are *polyhedral sets*, then its computation becomes a combinatorial problem. Efficient ways of computing this function have been explored extensively [Buckley 1985]. Briefly, the complexity bounds $O(n \log n)$ in the planar case, where n i is the combined number of vertices of the two polyhedral bodies for which Δ is computed. The corresponding figure for spatial polyhedral bodies is $O(n^2 \log n)$.

Implementational issues of the Δ function are currently being studied, and it is being incorporated into a free body pathplanning system. The performance of this system is being assessed relative to a combinatorial system, that of [Brooks 1982].

5 Conclusion

A new function for characterizing the proximal relationship between two convex bodies has been developed, and its properties studied. This function makes it possible to implement pathplanning algorithms significantly different in capability from those heretofore reported.

6 Acknowledgement

The support of the Palo Alto VA Hospital in this research is gratefully acknowledged. Computational facilities and a super working environment were made available by the Fairchild Laboratory for Artificial Intelligence Research (now a part of Schlumberger). Many thanks to Rod Brooks for providing the code for his combinatorial configuration space planning algorithm to serve as a benchmark.

[Author's address: Design Division. Stanford. Cal. 94305.]

Bibliography

[Avriel 1976]   Avriel, M., *Nonlinear Programming: Analysis and Methods*, Prentice–Hall, Inc., Englewood Cliffs, 1976.

[Brooks 1982]   Brooks, R. A. and Lozano–Pérez, T., "A Subdivision Algorithm in Configuration Space for Findpath with Rotation", M. I. T. A. I. Memo. No. 684, December, 1982.

[Buckley 1985]   Buckley, C. E., "The Application of Continuum Methods to Path Planning", Ph. D. Dissertation, Department of Mechanical Engineering, Stanford University, (to appear) 1985.

[Cahn 1975]   Cahn, D. F. and Phillips, S. R., "ROB-NAV: A Range–Based Robot Navigation and Obstacle Avoidance Algorithm", IEEE Transactions on Systems, Man, and Cybernetics, pp. 544-551, September 1975.

[Chatila 1981]   Chatila, R., "Système de Navigation pour un Robot Mobile Autonome: Modelisation et Processus Decisionnels", Doct.-Ing. Thesis, Paul Sabatier University, Toulouse, France, No. 762, 1981.

[Chazelle 1980]   Chazelle, B. M., "Computational Geometry and Convexity", Ph. D. Dissertation, Computer Science Department, Carnegie–Mellon University, Report No. CMU–CS–80–150, 1980.

[Comba 1968]   Comba, P. G., "A Procedure for Detecting Intersections of Three–Dimensional Objects", Journal of the Association of Computing Machinery, Vol. 15, No. 3., pp. 354–366, July 1968.

[Khatib 1980]   Khatib, O., "Commande Dynamique dans l'Espace Operationnel des Robots Manipulateurs en Presence d'Obstacles", Doc.-Ing. thesis, French National Superior School of Aeronautics and Astronautics, 1980.

[Jarvis 1984]   Jarvis, R. A., "Projection Derived Space Cube Scene Models for Robotic Vision and Collision–Free Trajectory Planning", 2nd International Symposium of Robotics Research, Kyoto 1984, pp. 294–301.

[Loeff 1975]   Loeff, L. A. and Soni, A. H., "An Algorithm for Computer Guidance of a Manipulator in Between Obstacles", ASME Journal of Engineering for Industry, pp. 836–842, August 1975.

[Lozano–Pérez 1981]   Lozano–Pérez, Tomás, "Automatic Planning of Manipulator Transfer Movements", IEEE Transactions on Systems, Man, and Cybernetics, Vol. SMC-11, No. 10, pp. 681–698, October 1981.

[Myers 1981]   Myers, J. K., "A Supervisory Collision–Avoidance System for Robot Controllers", M. S. Thesis, Carnegie–Mellon University, December 1981.

[Peiper 1968]   Peiper, D. L., "The Kinematics of Manipulators under Computer Control", Ph. D. dissertation, Mechanical Engineering Department, Stanford University, October 1968.

[Reif 1979]   Reif, J. H., "Complexity of the Mover's Problem and Generalizations (Extended Abstract)", Proceedings of the 20th Symposium on the Foundations of Computer Science, pp. 421–427, 1979.

[Rockafellar 1970]   Rockafellar, R. T., *Convex Analysis*, Princeton University Press, Princeton, N. J. 1970.

[Schwartz 1982]   Schwartz, J. T. and Sharir, M., "On the Piano Movers' Problem II. General Techniques for Computing Topological Properties of Real Algebraic Manifolds", Courant Institute of Mathematical Sciences Report No. 41, New York University, February 1982.

[Whitney 1969]   Whitney, D. E., "State Space Models of Remote Manipulation Tasks", IEEE Transactions on Automatic Control, Vol. AC-14, No. 6, pp. 617–623, December, 1969.

A ROBOT PLANNING STRUCTURE USING PRODUCTION RULES

Ralph P. Sobek[*]

Laboratoire d'Automatique et d'Analyse des Systemes du C.N.R.S.
7, avenue du Colonel-Roche
F-31077 Toulouse CEDEX, FRANCE

Abstract

Robot plan generation is a field which engendered the development of AI languages and rule-based expert systems. Utilization of these latter concepts permits a flexible formalism for robot planning research. We present a robot plan-generation architecture and its application to a real-world mobile robot system. The system undergoes tests through its utilization in the HILARE robot project (Giralt, et al, 1984). Though the article concentrates on planning, execution monitoring and error recovery are discussed. The system includes models of its synergistic environment as well as of its sensors and effectors (i.e. operators). Its rules embody both planning specific and domain specific knowledge. The system gains generality and adaptiveness through the use of planning variables which provide constraints to the plan generation system. It is implemented in an efficient compiled Production System language (PS1).

INTRODUCTION

In general, a problem is a situation for which an organism (or program) does not have a ready response. Problem solving involves 1) sensing and identification of a problem, 2) formulation of the problem in workable terms, 3) utilization of relevant information, and 4) generation and evaluation of hypotheses. A planner is a program that attempts to deal with points 2 through 4. In this paper we present a rule-based plan generation system called FPS (for Flexible Planning System). This system undergoes tests in a real-world robotic environment (the HILARE project [Giralt, et al, 1984]).

In such an environment what is a plan? It has to be a flexible and extensible structure which permits quick adaptation to unexpected situations. It must permit goal-directed as well as data-directed processing. Goal simultaneity and interaction must be verified during planning and before attempted execution. In a real-world environment a multitude of error situations may arise. Besides correction of planning errors a planner must try to determine when an error is recoverable or when replanning is necessary. Planners must be able to select processing strategies appropriate to each situation encountered and be able to handle complex goal descriptions.

FPS is rule-based principally for the following reasons. Production System (PS) rules allow for a neat solution to the frame problem when we use the STRIPS assumption (Waldinger, 1981) in that all updates in the model are done explicitly through rules. Since rules can react in one PS cycle PSs can adapt to new situations very rapidly, the rules acting like deamons. In planning or execution monitoring this fact allows the system to deal with unexpected/serependitious situations. In addition, rule interactions may permit parallel searchs for a best solution or may allow rapid responses to recognized problem situations (e.g. planning goal conflicts). In a PS the addition of knowledge is incremental. Therefore, the evolution of our robotic environment will be easily characterizable to FPS. Also, in the future our use of a PS architecture will permit FPS to organize and generalize the plans that it has created as new rules.

Some may say that PSs are inefficient. It has been shown that by the use of compilation strategies significant gains in execution speed are attainable (Gupta and Forgy, 1983). FPS is implemented in the PS1 production system language (Sobek, 1983). It does not have to sacrifice efficiency for flexibility in its representation since PS1 is a compiled PS. Rule patterns are compiled into a parallel-match tree similar to but more general than OPS (Forgy, 1982). The advantages of PSs have been adequately described in (Davis and King, 1976). Some planners and expert systems have opted for a frame-based approach (Minsky, 1975). It should be noted that there is a similarity between PSs and frame-based systems.

PLANNING STRUCTURE

We present a robot planner (FPS) which deals with the dynamics of a plan. FPS has in its ancestry STRIPS (Fikes, et al, 1971), NOAH (Sacerdoti, 1977), and especially JASON (Sobek, 1975). It generalizes these planners in representation and flexibility. FPS is used in a real-world mobile-robot 'blocks-world' paradigm: the HILARE project. Superficially, FPS is similar to NOAH and its generalization JASON in that they are goal-oriented. Where plans for NOAH consist of a directed graph of procedures (procedural net), in FPS plans may be

---

[*] The author is presently on visit from the University of California at Berkeley. This research is supported in part by Agence de l'Informatique contract 84/723.

described as a directed graph of processes. Each process contains its state in a structure called a "planning node" each with its associated goal (see Table 1). A process characterizes the dynamics of a plan step while the planning node representes the data aspects. A process gets its node's entries filled from three principal sources: 1) from the parent node, 2) when an operator is selected for a node, or 3) by the executive, critic, task communication, and scheduling rules. The processes are managed by a tasking executive which arranges the processes on a priority agenda taking into account for each process the importance, success, cost expended, and estimated allocated cost. The interprocess coordination and high-level conflict resolution knowledge are called planning specific and are represented in rules. For example:

> If all sibling* children of a process have achieved its preconditions **then** check if the process can be decomposed into subprocesses.

1. Goal Pattern
2. Goal Instantiations
3. Preconditions/Enablements
4. Continuation Conditions
5. Post-Conditions (including goal pattern)
6. Constraint Conditions
7. Parent
8. Children associated by each decomposition
9. Importance
10. Allocated Cost Estimate
11. Cost Expended
12. Success Rate for each Post-Condition
13. Error Recovery Handles: reason, source, locally recoverable
14. Operator List
15. Script

Table 1. Planning Node Entries

Simple goals in FPS may consist of a relational predicate, e.g. (INROOM BLOCK1 RM3), its negation, or the application of a specific operator to a goal. Compound goals may be conjunctions or sequences of goals. Compound goals let FPS search for possible conflicts whereas sequences specify an explicit required ordering of the goals involved.

A relational predicate may also contain "planning variables" similar to those developed by the author in (Sobek, 1975) and those reinvented in SIPE (Wilkins, 1983). These variables do not actually contain values; they may specify restrictions upon the allowed values (bindings) that their positions in a predicate may take, e.g. in the predicate (INROOM ROBOT $RM) the variable $RM may specify a number of possible instantiations for the predicate. The planning variables serve three

functions: 1) an alternative to disjunctive goals with similar disjuncts, 2) a method for the postponement of decisions, and 3) constraint expressions.

Constraints may be attached to goals, planning nodes, and operators. Constraints are similar to goals except that they must be satisfied for the preconditions of a possible operator as well as during and after the operator's execution. They are taken into account in the node expansion procedure and can cause the insertion of additional plan steps before a node.

Planning involves iteration of node expansion with plan criticism. Criticism may start as soon as a node is expanded, which eases a shortcoming of NOAH. NOAH could only apply its critics at the end of each expansion cycle. The critics in FPS are considered a major part of the planner's "planning executive." They contain knowledge that is relevant to the entire planning process, i.e. both planning specific and domain specific. Concomitant and overlapping with critics are heuristic rules. For example:

> H1.   **If** multiple choices are possible **then** select one which minimizes cost, effort, or distance

> H2.   **If** robot moves an object **then** it should not block a door

H1 is a general rule whereas H2 is domain specific.

The planner presents a model of the robot's possible actions within its environment; it currently does not model the robot's interactions. There is no representation for other purposive (goal oriented) organisms or causality other than the robot's. The possible actions are modelled by operators.

Operators are dynamically selected for each planning node; no a priori connection between operators and goals exists. Associated with operators are preconditions (environmental context), continuation conditions, post-conditions, and constraints. The operators are ordered in a specialization/generalization hierarchy. Operators may have scripts which specify how they should be reduced; the scripts may define conditionals, parallel paths, goals, constraints, and sub-operator applications. If they contain subgoals then a subprocess will be created for each subgoal. Otherwise, the script will be checked by "critics" against the surrounding plan structure.

An example operator is GOTOROOM (see Fig. 1). Given a room ?r as argument, if the robot is in an adjoining room then it will try to apply sequentially the two sub-scripts GOTODOOR and GOTHRUDOOR. These latter two scripts are subordinate to GOTOROOM only in the current node's dynamic context: a different call sequence would create another hierarchy of goals and operators. FPS would fan out from the goal state, e.g. (INROOM ROBOT RM1), using the connexity graph provided by CONNECTS until it finds the current state.

---

* The sibling processes are all children of a process which are conjoined by the same goal instantiation of the parent. The parent process might have multiple instantiations for its goal description and then would have a disjunctive group of siblings for each instantiation.

```
GOTOROOM:
argument:            ?r
preconditions:       (INROOM ROBOT ?r2)
                     (CONNECTS ?d ?r ?r2)+
script:              (SEQ (GOTODOOR ?d)
                          (GOTHRUDOOR ?d))
post-conditions:     (INROOM ROBOT ?r)*
                     NOT (INROOM ROBOT ?r2)

        * - primary result (goal condition)
        + - static data
```

Figure 1. GOTOROOM operator specification

The search could be breadth-first, depth-first or depending on the situation it could even require heuristic rules which would remember efficient routes once found. After a route is found the two sub-ordinate scripts are tried in order to assure that the robot can get to and through the door. If there are multiple doors to a room, each would cause two parallel descendant nodes to be created.

An operator's goal is specified to the system as the primary post-condition. The above operator can also be invoked to get the robot out of a particular room. Each time that an operator succeeds with respect to a goal its correspondent level of importance or competence is rewarded.

EXECUTION MONITOR

What distinguishes planning from execution monitoring is that in the former a coherent planning structure is established, whereas in the latter the necessary verifications of coherence must come from the real-world environment. Note that a large part of the representation for both planning and execution monitoring must be the same in both in order to facilitate their communication and sharing of models. Thus, execution monitoring uses the same planning structures to establish when error recovery should be initiated. An error situation is detected when there is a discrepancy between an operator's expected possible outcomes and the real-world responses (Srinivas, 1977). These discrepancies are analysed by execution-error critics which determine whether the error is 1) unimportant, 2) has a fixed solution, or that 3) replanning will be necessary.

CONCLUSION

FPS combines domain-independent plan structuring critics with domain specific constraints and critics. They watch over a general and flexible plan structure. Since the system is rule-based, heuristics may be added at any level; for the moment few exist. Their usefulness should become apparent when FPS performs error recovery and replanning. Current work includes making the system more robust and the addition of the execution monitor.

Acknowledgements

The author would like to thank everyone involved with the HILARE project for providing the necessary support for a real-world testbed for FPS.

REFERENCES

Davis, R. and J. King. An Overview of Production Systems, in E. W. Elcock and D. Michie (Eds.) Machine Intelligence, 8 (Wiley, New York, 1976), 300-332.

Fikes, R. et al. Learning and Executing Generalized Robot Plans, in N. Nilsson and B. Webber (Eds.) Readings in Artificial Intelligence (Tioga Publishing, Palo Alto, CA, 1981), 231-249.

Forgy, C. Rete: A Fast Algorithm for the Many Pattern/Many Object Pattern Match Problem, Artificial Intelligence, 19 (1982) 17-37.

Giralt, G. et al. An Integrated Navigation and Motion Control System for Autonomous Multisensory Mobile Robots, in M. Brady and R. Paul (Eds.) Robotics Research: The First International Symposium (MIT Press, Mass.), 191-214.

Gupta, A. and C. Forgy. Measurements on Production Systems, Technical Report CMU-CS-83-167, Carnegie-Mellon University, December 1983.

Minsky, M. Framework for Representing Knowledge, in P. Winston (Ed.) The Psychology of Computer Vision (McGraw-Hill, 1975).

Sacerdoti, E. A Structure for Plans and Behavior, Elsevier, North-Holland, New York, 1977.

Sobek, R. Automatic Generation and Execution of Complex Robot Plans, Master's Project Report, Electrical Engineering and Computer Sciences Dept., University of California, Berkeley (September 1975).

----------. Achieving Generality and Efficiency in a Production System Architecture. LAAS-CNRS Internal Memo, 1983.

Srinivas, S. Error Recovery in Robot Systems. Ph.D. Thesis, Computer Science Dept., California Institute of Technology (1977).

Waldinger, R. Achieving Several Goals Simultaneously, in N. Nilsson and B. Webber (Eds.) Readings in Artificial Intelligence (Tioga Publishing, Palo Alto, CA, 1981), 250-271.

Wilkins, D. Representation in a Domain-Independent Planner, IJCAI-83, Karlsruhe, West Germany, 1983, 733-740.

A Framework for Distributed Sensing and Control[1]

Tom Henderson, Chuck Hansen, and Bir Bhanu

Department of Computer Science
The University of Utah
Salt Lake City, Utah 84112

Abstract

Logical Sensor Specification (LSS) has been introduced as a convenient means for specifying multi-sensor systems and their implementations. In this paper, we demonstrate how control issues can be handled in the context of LSS. In particular, the Logical Sensor Specification is extended to include a control mechanism which permits control information to (1) flow from more centralized processing to more peripheral processes, and (2) be generated locally in the logical sensor by means of a micro-expert system specific to the interface represented by the given logical sensor. Examples are given including a proposed scheme for controlling the Utah/MIT dextrous hand.

1. Introduction

Both the availability and need for sensor systems is growing, as is their complexity in terms of the number and kind of sensors within a system. But most robotic sensor-based systems to date have been designed around a single sensor or a small number of sensors, and *ad hoc* techniques have been used to integrate them into the complete system and for operating on their data. In the future, however, such systems must operate in a reconfigurable multi-sensor environment; for example, there may be several cameras (perhaps of different types), active range finding systems, tactile pads, and so on. In addition, a wide variety of such sensing devices, including mechanical, electronic, and chemical, are available for use in sensor systems, and a sensor system may include several kinds of sensing devices. Thus, at least three issues regarding the configuration of sensor systems arise:

1. How to develop a coherent and efficient treatment of the information provided by many sensors, particularly when the sensors are of different kinds.

2. How to allow for sensor system reconfiguration, both as a means of providing greater tolerance for sensing device failure, to permit dynamic allocation of sensing resources, and to facilitate future incorporation of additional sensing devices.

3. How to control the sensors.

We have previously proposed the Multi-sensor Kernel System [5, 7] and Logical Sensor Specification [4] as solutions for the first two problems, respectively. The rest of this paper gives our method for answering the third.

The purpose of the logical sensor specification is to permit an implementation independent description of the required data and the nature (type) of that data. In addition, alternative ways of producing the same output can be defined. This makes it possible to recover if some sensor fails. One can also choose an alternative based on higher level considerations (e.g., speed, resolution, etc.). Thus, a use for logical sensors is evident in any sensor system which is composed of several sensors, where sensor reconfiguration is desired, and/or where the sensors must be actively controlled.

As described in more detail elsewhere [4], the principal motivations for logical sensor specification are: the emergence of significant multi-sensor systems, the benefits of data abstraction, and the availability of smart sensors (thus, the substitution of hardware for software, and vice versa, should be transparent above the implementation level; see also Organick et. al [10]).

Logical sensors are then a means by which to insulate the user from the peculiarities of input devices. Thus, for example, a sensor system could be designed to deal with camera input, without regard to the kind of camera being used. In addition, logical sensor specification is also a means to create and package "virtual" physical sensors. For example, the kind of data produced by a physical laser range finder sensor could also be produced by two cameras and a stereo program. This similarity of output result is more important to the user than the fact that the information may be obtained by using one physical device, or by using two physical devices and a program. Logical sensor specification allows the user to ignore such differences of how output is produced, and treat equivalent means of obtaining data as logically the same.

Related work has been done in several areas. The need for some device-independent interactive system has resulted in the Graphical Kernel System (GKS) which is now a Draft International Standard. The main idea behind GKS is to provide "a means whereby interactive graphics

[1]This work was supported in part by the System Development Foundation and NSF Grants ECS-8307483 and MCS-82-21750. Chuck Hansen is an ARO Fellow.

applications could be insulated from the peculiarities of the input devices of particular terminals, and thereby become portable" [11]. Some encouraging results reported in the robotics literature including a systematic study of robotic sensor design for dynamic sensing undertaken by Beni et al. [3]. Another related research effort is the programming environment (called the Graphical Image Processing Language) under development as part of the IPON project (an advanced architecture for image processing) at the University of Pennsylvania [2]. The hierarchical robot control system described by Albus [1] is a precursor to the logical sensor scheme proposed here.

2. Logical Sensor Specification

Figure 1 shows the basic components of a logical sensor.

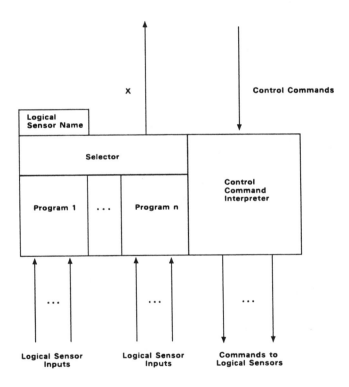

Figure 1. Logical Sensor Specification with Control

The **logical sensor name** uniquely identifies the logical sensor. The **characteristic output vector** is a vector of types which serves as a description of the output vectors that will be produced by the logical sensor. Thus, the output of a logical sensor is a set (or stream) of vectors, each of which is of the type declared by that logical sensor's characteristic output vector. Programs 1 to n represent alternative ways in which to obtain data with the

same characteristic output vector. Hence, each alternate subnet is equivalent, with regard to type, to all other alternate subnets in the list. <u>Each</u> alternate subnet in the list is itself composed of: (1) a set of **input sources**. Each element of the set must be a logical sensor (or the set may be empty). Allowing null input permits a physical sensor, which has only an associated program (the device driver), to be described as a logical sensor, thereby permitting uniformity of sensor treatment. (2) a **computation unit** over the input sources. Currently such computation units are software programs, but in the future, hardware units may also be used. Finally, the role of the **selector** (whose inputs are alternate subnets and an acceptance test name) is to detect failure of an alternate and switch to a different alternate. If switching cannot be done, the selector reports failure of the logical sensor.

In order to solve most recognition and manipulation problems, however, it is necessary to be able to reposition sensors (e.g., aim cameras) and adapt rapidly to changing conditions (e.g., if an object is slipping from the grasp of a robot hand, perhaps more force should be applied). Thus, in addition to a stream of sensed data flowing from physical sensors on up through some hierarchy of logical sensors, there may also be a stream of **control commands** (or signals) flowing in the reverse direction.

Each logical sensor has a **control command interpreter** to interpret the control commands coming from a level up in the hierarchy and to send commands down to logical sensors lower in the hierarchy. Moreover, the select function now plays a more sophisticated role in the logical sensor. Namely, the select function monitors both the sensor data going up and the command stream to be issued. Given the command (or commands) to be executed and the sensor data being produced locally, the select function is able to short circuit the path back to the root logical sensor and to modify the commands to be issued. Such a function may be viewed as a micro-expert system which knows all about the interface represented by the logical sensor in which it is located. Thus, a logical sensor acquires some of its meaning now not simply as a sensor/algorithm combination, but also as an interface between two layers of sensing and analysis.

Another requirement on the logical sensor is that it now also acts as a "logical controller." If the control command received at a particular sensor requires that control commands be sent to the source input logical sensors, then those commands will depend on which alternate subnet is currently selected by the selector function. For example, suppose range data can be obtained from a stereo camera system, a laser range finder system or a robot hand with tactile sensing. Then to obtain range data from a given region in space requires aiming and focusing two cameras, or aiming a camera and a laser, or positioning a robot arm. The high level command to scan a region must then be broken down into the appropriate lower level commands.

A logical sensor can be viewed as a network composed

of sub-networks which are themselves logical sensors. Communication within a network is controlled via the flow of data from one sub-network to another. Hence, such networks are <u>data flow</u> networks.

Once the logical sensors are specified, they are stored as s-expressions. In order to actually obtain an executable system from the logical sensor specification, it is necessary to translate the database expressions into some executable form, e.g., to produce source code for some target language, and then either interpret or compile and run that source. We currently have two implementations of the logical sensor specification language running: a C version (called C-LSS) running under UNIX, and a functional language version (called FUN-LSS) which produces FEL code (Function Equation Language) [9]. These have been described elsewhere [4]. C-LSS produces a UNIX shell script from the specification.

3. An Example

We are currently applying the methodology to some interesting and hard problems. In particular, we are developing and testing a specification for the UTAH/MIT Dextrous Hand. This gives us the opportunity to try out the method on a distributed multi-processor system, as the Hand is controlled by six M68000s.

Shown in Figure 2 are some of the logical sensors which comprise the specification of a sensor and control scheme for the UTAH/MIT dextrous robot hand. The robot hand has four fingers each with four degrees of freedom [8]. The high level commands for hand control are interpreted as a set of commands to a lower-level right on down to the control of the joint positions of each finger which define the configuration of the robot hand.

A grasping action requires several hand operations, including the attainment of an approach configuration. One of these is the "curl" position (the control command to the hand logical sensor). To curl the hand requires that each finger move away from the median axis of the hand (the control command "abduct" to each of the finger logical sensors). Finally, the abduct command requires that each joint achieve a specific angle (the θ_{ij} control commands to the joint logical sensors). Thus, the feedback loop for position control can be located in the programs which are part of the joint logical sensor specification. Moreover, concise local knowledge for what to do in case of error conditions (slipping, too much force, etc.) can be embedded in the appropriate select function.

4. Conclusions

We have presented a framework for the specification of sensing and control systems. Moreover, the methodology lends itself nicely to distributed processing. The method permits the specification of fault tolerance (both software and hardware) and dynamic reconfiguration of the sensing system. The incorporation of control now permits closed loop operation and adaptation to changing conditions.

Our specific accomplishments include:

1. The development of a methodology for the specification of distributed sensing and control. In particular, one based on a reasonably well understood underlying computational model, i.e., dataflow.

2. The development of an operational environment for computing with respect to the methodology.

The successful implementation of such a methodology provides a very significant and fundamental tool for the specification of distributed sensing and control systems. Moreover, we believe that our approach permits an effective conceptual decomposition of the problem into manageable units. For a more complete treatment of logical sensors as a framework for distributed sensing and control (with detailed examples), see Henderson et. al [6].

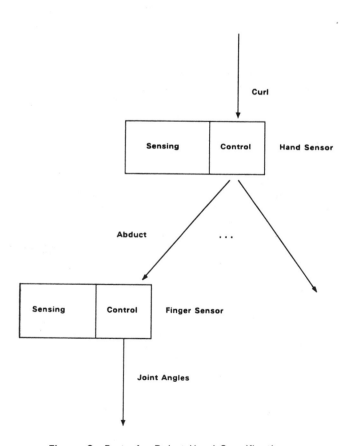

Figure 2. Part of a Robot Hand Specification

References

[1]   Albus, J.
      Brains, Behavior and Robotics.
      BYTE Books, Peterborough, New Hampshire, 1981.

[2]   Bajscy, R.
      GRASP:NEWS Quarterly Progress Report.
      Technical Report Vol. 2, No. 2, The University of
          Pennsylvania, School of Engineering and Applied
          Science, 2nd Quarter, 1984.

[3]   Beni, G., S. Hackwood, L.A. Hornak and J.L. Jackel.
      Dynamic Sensing for Robots: An Analysis and
          Implementation.
      Robotics Research 2(2):51-60, Summer, 1983.

[4]   Henderson, T.C. and E. Shilcrat.
      Logical Sensor Systems.
      Journal of Robotic Systems 1(2):169-193, 1984.

[5]   Henderson, T.C. and Wu So Fai.
      MKS: A Multi-sensor Kernel System.
      *IEEE Transactions on Systems, Man, and
          Cyberbetics* SMC-14(5):784-791,
          September/October, 1984.

[6]   Henderson, T.C., C.D. Hansen, and Bir Bhanu.
      The Specification of Distributed Sensing and
          Control.
      Journal of Robotic Systems :to appear, 1985.

[7]   Henderson, Thomas C. and Wu So Fai.
      A Multi-sensor Integration and Data Acquisition
          System.
      In *Proceedings of the IEEE Conference on
          Computer Vision and Pattern Recognition*, pages
          274-280. IEEE, June, 1983.

[8]   Jacobsen, S., D.F. Knutti, K. Biggers, E.K. Iverson and
      J.E. Wood.
      An Electropneumatic Actuation System for the
          Utah/MIT Dextrous Hand.
      In *Proceedings of the Fifth CISM-IFToMM
          Symposium on Theory and Practice of Robots
          and Manipulators.* Udine, Italy, June, 1984.

[9]   Keller, R.M.
      FEL Programmer's Guide.
      Technical Report AMPS Tech. Memo 7, The
          University of Utah, Department of Computer
          Science, April, 1982.

[10] Organick, E.I., M. Maloney, D. Klass and
      G. Lindstrom.
      *Transparent Interface between Software and
          hardware Versions of Ada Compilation Units.*
      Technical Report UTEC-83-030, University of Utah,
          Salt Lake City, Utah, April, 1983.

[11] Rosenthal, D.S., J.C. Michener, G. Pfaff, R. Kessener
      and M. Sabin.
      The Detailed Semantics of Graphics Input Devices.
      Computer Graphics 16(3):33-38, July, 1982.

MOTOR KNOWLEDGE REPRESENTATION

Giuseppe Marino   Pietro Morasso   Renato Zaccaria

Department of Communication, Computer and Systems Science, University
of Genoa - Italy

ABSTRACT

The motor control problem is considered in the framework of knowledge representation. In the AI/Robotic world, a formal **model** for **motor knowledge** should fill a gap between task planning and low level robot languages; such model should be able to "virtualize" the robot and the interaction with the environment so that the planner could produce (and rely on) high level abstract actions, characterized by high autonomy and skill. The paper discusses some general aspects about **actions**, **actors**, and **scenes**, and describes the **NEM language**, which is able to represent and animate humanoids in a scene and is meant to provide a software laboratory for experimenting with action schemas.

1. Introduction

In the AI/Robotic world, a formal **model for "motoric" knowledge** (Marino et al., 1984) should fill a gap between task planning (Lozano Perez, 1982) and low level robot languages (Bonner and Shin, 1982); such a model should be able to "virtualize" the robot and the interaction with the environment so that the planner could produce (and rely on) high level abstract actions, characterized by high autonomy and skill. This problem is strongly related to that of modeling and simulating the human body and its movements (Badler and Smoliar, 1979). This paper briefly reviews a formal language, called **NEM**, for the representation and animation of "moving entities", or **actors** (e.g. humanoids), in a scene. Geometric, kinematic, dynamic aspects are all tightly interrelated for any skill. In general, however, it is convenient to distinguish, for an actor, two different levels of "knowledge" of the particular aspect of a skill: i) a **qualitative/symbolic/explicit** level, and ii) an **implicit/analogic/quantitative** one; NEM is intended to support the second level.

An **action** is a change in the relation between an **actor** and its **surrounding**. If we now associate with each feature of the scene a local system of coordinates (a **frame** (*)), the action can then be viewed as a stream of variations of some of the mutual relations between local coordinate systems, due to a stream of **motor commands**.

The whole scene can thus be described as a "forest" of frames, linked to features, grouped together conveniently when referring to a common structure (an actor, an object, a family or a part thereof). Ensembles of frames can only represent, in a direct way, the "**skeletric**" structure of actors or objects; if smoother and more detailed representations are needed, it would be necessary to associate appropriate "shape formation" attributes with frames and frame ensembles. This points out the problem of interfacing an action oriented system with solid modeling concepts (Binford, 1982) and with techniques of path planning and obstacle avoidance (Lozano Perez, 1982).

2. NEM: a language for representing actors, scenes, actions

The NEM language has been designed to provide a procedural, non-hierarchical representation of motoric knowledge. NEM is intended: i) to define and model (potentially) moving entities ("**objects**" or "**actors**"); ii) to describe the movement of an entity as a whole, or of groups or parts of entities.

Object/Actor representation is based on an atomic element called Geometric Frame (**GF**), by which Geometric Frame Structures (**GFS**) can be built. GFSs provide object/actor modeling in terms of **skeletons** of articulated chains, whose basic element is a tree of GFs. NEM objects are general and hierarchical: "limb", "man", "quadruped", "table", "crowd" are legal parameterized (families of) entities.

Moving objects are called **Actors**. An Actor's movement is described by means of scripts called **Motions**. Motions are abstract, non-hierarchical procedural descriptions of movement for single

---

(*) This kind of "frames" has nothing to do with Minski's; they come from analytic geometry.

objects, parts or groups of them, or generalizations of objects (families). A motion can adapt itself to a particular object in a family: for example, a script "animal_walk" could fit, at some level of detail, different actors like a "spider" or a "dog". Motions are built by composition, or **specialization** of other motions. Motions can express, at a certain level, geometric reasoning, both static ("is the book over the chair ?") and dynamic ("may john reach the book without walking ?"). Finally, motions allow expression of common sense motoric knowledge (that we may call "**common skill knowledge**"): naive physics concepts (such as "gravity", "equilibrium", "collision", "pushing" and so on) can be easily defined in terms of general virtual motions.

NEM has three components: i) an algebra, called Frame Algebra Notation (**FAN**), which manages GFSs; ii) atomic motor primitives and their semantics ("**Primitives**"); iii) rules of superimposition or composition of motions and primitives, called **Constructs**. They are the operators with which we can build **motions**.

2.1. Frames and Motions

The atomic datum in NEM is the **frame**, which corresponds to an orthogonal system of reference and is represented by means of a 4 x 4 homogeneous matrix. Homogeneous matrices express the translation/rotation of the given frame with respect to an ancestor frame.

Frames are used to identify significant points of an object/actor. For example, a simple pyramid can be defined by the following GFS:

@ ENV FRAME PYRAMID
@ PYRAMID FRAME VERTEX_1 VERTEX_2 VERTEX_3

where **ENV** is the "universe" frame (the environment) and "**@**" is an operator which refers a frame to its ancestor. The definition of a GFS and its corresponding initialization can be embedded into a parameterized definition block and instanciated several times.

At the lowest level, FAN semantics guarantees the computability of all spatial relations. However, FAN provides functions at different higher levels: GFSs can be dynamically generated and destroyed; frames can be assembled/disassembled into their components; functions can be defined and so on. For example, the script **POS(ADAM'MOUTH @ EVE'R'HAND)** gives the geometric relation existing at a certain instant between Adam's mouth and Eve's right hand. Finally, a frame can be referenced by its position inside a GFS (its "**pathname**") rather than by its name.

Pathnames and related functions (such as the IS_DEF(<pathname> function), which tests the existence of a GFS element, allow motion scripts to fit families of similar structures.

A **motion** is a collection of three components: i) frames and declarations of variables, ii) motor primitives and iii) instances of other motions. Any component may be missing: for example, a motion can simply embed an object definition. Motions are usually active concurrently; frames and variables binding is dynamic.

The atomic element for motion construction is the **primitive motor operator** (PMO). PMOs are inspired by anthropomorphic mechanics and are defined at two levels: i) **joint level**, and ii) **limb level**. The PMOs of the former type move a frame, whereas the PMOs of the latter type affect chains of frames by specifying the motion of the "end effector" (they solve the inverse kinematic problem (Benati et al., 1982)). More abstract operators are also defined: for example, temporary linking an end effector with some moving frame (passive motions), or "reversing" a chain ("move the hip with respect to the foot").

Composite Motions are defined by composing PMOs and/or composite motions already defined. Compositions can be made in different ways:

sequential execution:

ACTION_1 ; ACTION_2 ; ACTION_3 ; ...

(where <ACTION> stands for a PMO or a motion;

parallel execution:

ACTION_1 & ACTION_2 & ACTION_3 & ...

guarded execution:

WHILE EVENT DO ACTION
WAIT EVENT DO ACTION
PERFORM ACTION_1 EXCEPT EVENT THEN ACTION_2

The composition paradigm allows to overlap in time different spatio-temporal units, therefore providing an unlimited capability of trajectory formation: this expresses naturally a non-hierarchical, distributed approach to motor control (Hinton, 1984) which is conceptually akin to the object-oriented programming style (Weinreb and Moon, 1980). Guarded executions allow actors to synchronize through events, or to communicate each other through message passing.

3. Results

The NEM project is being implemented in the Unix environment. The NEM interpreter is written in C to obtain high efficiency. Preliminary versions of two interfaces are available: one interfaces NEM with PADL2 (a geometric modeling system) and the other with Prolog.

Figure 1 shows a graphic trace of the performance of a NEM script which represents a <u>diving humanoid</u>. It is worth noting that in this motor paradigm the motor actions are concurrent with the action of gravity. In the NEM script, two corresponding concurrent motions are activated; this is an example of physical laws implicitly embedded into the motoric knowledge. Moreover, "environmental" processes can be tested by "control" actors in order to tune action parameters.

Several other paradigms are being experimented (sitting, walking, picking ...) with the purpose of building a high level motor data base. With regard to the NEM-PADL2 interface, fig. 2 shows a NEM humanoid (in a "discobolus" posture) "dressed" with a PADL2 articulated solid model. Better schemes of human body representation are available (see Special Issue of IEEE Comp. Graph. and Appl.,vol.2 no.9,1982), but most of them are not articulated.

4. Final remarks

We stressed the potential capability of NEM to build high level, abstract pieces of motor activity, in spite of the simplicity of the GFSs, which are a low level atomic piece of knowledge. Moreover, NEM's facilities to express both static and dynamic geometric reasoning suggest that it could play a role of "co-planner", as to say, it could integrate both functions of analog modeling

fig. 2

the (moving) world and of storing tasks/actions data base.

REFERENCES

BADLER NI, SMOLIAR SW (1979) Digital representation of human movement, ACM Comp. Surv. 11:1

BENATI M, GAGLIO S, MORASSO P, TAGLIASCO V, ZACCARIA R (1980) Anthropomorphic robotics. Biol. Cybern. 38:125-150

BONNER S, SHIN KG (1982) A comparative study of Robot Languages, IEEE Computer, 15:12

BINFORD TO (1982) Survey of model based image analysis systems. Intern. J. Robotic Research 1:18-64

HINTON G (1984) Some computational solutions to Bernstein problems. In WHITING HTA (Editor) Human motor action - Bernstein reassessed. Elsevier Science Publ. BV (North Holland): 373-412

LOZANO PEREZ T (1982) Task planning. In BRADY M et al (editors) Robot motion: planning and control. MIT Press, Cambridge, MA

MARINO G, MORASSO P, TROIANO E, ZACCARIA R (1984) Representing Motor Knowledge, Proc. AIMSA84 Conf., Varna, Bulgaria

WEINREB D, MOON D (1980) Flavors: Message Passing in the LISP Machine. Artificial Intelligence Laboratory Technical Report 602, MIT press, Cambridge, MA

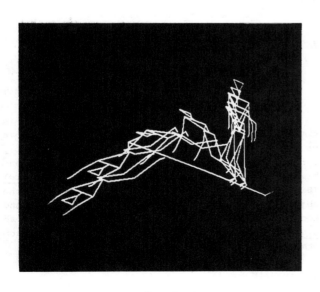

fig. 1

ANALYSIS OF UNCERTAINTIES IN A STRUCTURE OF PARTS

Alan Fleming

Department of Artificial Intelligence
University of Edinburgh, Forrest Hill
Edinburgh EH1 2QL, UK.

ABSTRACT

A structure built from parts will not fit perfectly. The amount of uncertainty in the relative positions of the parts can be predicted from the dimensions of the mated parts and their tolerances. The tolerances and sizes of the parts' features are analysed for each possible contact in turn to find constraints on the part positions. The combined effect of these constraints is then found allowing decisions to be made on whether the parts fit satisfactorily. Applications include tolerance checking during design and off-line programming of robot assembly.

I INTRODUCTION

Design specifications of mechanical parts usually include tolerances. A tolerance is a variation in a dimension or a statement about how well formed a surface must be. Since the shape of the parts is not exactly known it is difficult to know whether they will always fit properly. During design it must be verified that the parts of the structure never interfere and never fit too loosely. Similar questions also arise in off-line programming of robot assembly.

This paper describes a system to analyse a structure of toleranced parts. A real part which has been manufactured to the tolerance specification will be called an "instance" of the part. The system finds whether the parts will ever interfere or if they ever fit too loosely. It takes into account that some instances of the parts fit more tightly than others.

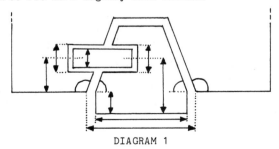

DIAGRAM 1

Diagram 1 shows a problem that would be solvable by the system. Each dimension and angle shown in the diagram would have a tolerance. The system could find whether the spigot and peg would always be able to fit as shown and also how much slop could occur. At the present time (April '85) a system has been built that will solve the problem though ignoring tolerances. The inclusion of tolerance analysis is in progress.

A part is defined as a set of features which are simple geometric surfaces such as finite planes or cylinders. The boundary of each feature is known. A structure is defined by the contacts that can occur between pairs of features. Each possible contact between features is referred to as a _relationship_. Similar representations of parts and structures are used in the off-line robot programming system, Rapt, designed in the Department of Artificial Intelligence at Edinburgh University [2]. Rapt makes inferences over the relationships to find the actual positions of the parts. Its results do not take into account poorly fitting parts or imperfectly formed parts but, in the work presented here, its results are used as nominal positions of the parts.

Each relationship puts constraints on the possible positions of the parts involved. The constraints are combined and propagated so that the possible positions of one part with respect to any other can be found.

Other work has dealt with the propagation and build up of uncertainties. Brooks [1] propagates uncertainties in the form of inequality constraints through a robot plan and verifies that required conditions hold. Taylor [10] derives constraints on the possible positions of parts from the relationships between their features and propagates these through a structure of parts. Much work on robot planning has assumed the presence of uncertainty information [6,7,10]. Discussions on the suitability of a given tolerance scheme for a single part may be found in [3,4,5]. There is a considerable body of knowledge and tradition involved in tolerancing and the standards used may be found in [11]. Requicha [8,9] has formalised and generalised standard tolerancing practice to produce representations of tolerance types which are useful for deciding how toleranced parts interact.

II TOLERANCE REPRESENTATION

Requicha's ideas [8,9] on tolerance representation and semantics are useful for deciding how toleranced parts interact. He formalises standard engineering practice. His definitions allow the same types of tolerance to be applied to any shape of feature. The types include form, size, orientation and position. For example a form tolerance applied to a flat surface is equivalent to the conventional tolerance of flatness but when applied to a cylinder is equivalent to tolerance of cylindricity.

The basic approach for defining tolerances is to use 3-dimensional tolerance zones. If an actual feature satisfies a tolerance specification then it must lie in an appropriately defined tolerance zone. A tolerance zone, in the case of a nominally cylindrical feature, is an infinitely long cylindrical shell. Different types of tolerance are defined by constraining some or all of the size, thickness or position of the shell. For example the tolerance zone of a size tolerance on a cylinder has fixed thickness and radius but variable position.

In the system described here, each feature is given a tolerance specification consisting simply of parameters for each tolerance type.

Datums are used for defining the position of tolerance zones. The tolerance zone is placed at the correct position with respect to the relevant datum. Each part has a master datum system. Other datums can be defined with respect to features and their position depends on the position of the feature. A complex network of features and datums may exist so that the tolerance allocated to one feature may have unexpected effects on other features. Ingham [6] has done work on predicting the propagation of tolerances through such a network.

III   POSITION UNCERTAINTIES

The uncertainty in position of a part in a structure can be described as constraints on the degrees of freedom of the part. A coordinate system in the part can be used to define six degrees of freedom by taking three translations along the axes and three rotations about the axes. A variable may be associated with each translation and rotation. These variables shall be referred to as "degree of freedom (DOF) variables".

For example, analysis of the structure in diagram 2, ignoring tolerances, gives:

$$8*\theta - 0\cdot025 \leq y \leq 8*\theta + 0\cdot025$$
$$2*\theta - 0\cdot025 \leq y \leq 2*\theta + 0\cdot025$$
$$-0\cdot05/6 \leq \theta \leq 0\cdot05/6.$$

θ represents rotation about the origin of the coordinate system. This form of inequalities is used throughout the system. Standard methods, which depend on the shape of the features, are used for deriving the coefficients. The y-constraints in the above inequalities are found by considering the situations in which a corner of the hole is in contact with the peg. Note that

the coefficients in the inequalities for y depend on the coordinate system used.

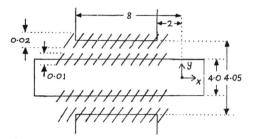

Peg in hole with position tolerances. The nominal parts are shown with shaded areas to indicate tolerance zones in which the actual surfaces must lie.

DIAGRAM 2

Considering tolerances, each instance of the structure is different and so the bounds on the DOF-variables vary between structure instances. This is represented by putting extra variables in the bound expressions. So, for example, constraints on DOF-variable, y, now have the form,

$$8*\theta + p \leq y \leq 8*\theta + q,$$

where p and q are the new variables. From the diagram, constraints can be found on p and q. The most extreme values for y in any assembly instance occur when the peg is at its smallest and the hole is at its largest. The extreme values are seen to be $\pm(4\cdot05-4+0\cdot02+0\cdot01)/2 = \pm0\cdot04$ and so $-0\cdot04 \leq p \leq q \leq 0\cdot04$.

However, due to _size_ tolerances, these values may not be attainable in the same structure instance. Size tolerances limit the amount of variation in slop that can occur and so put bounds on the difference between p and q. In general the form of constraints on p and q is,

$$L \leq p \leq q \leq U$$
$$T \leq q-p \leq S.$$

L,U,T and S are numbers derived from consideration of the different tolerance types. There are standard methods of derivation which depend on the shape of the features.

IV   COMBINING AND PROPAGATING CONSTRAINTS

Ultimately it is required to find constraints on the position of one part with respect to some other. The constraints derived from individual relationships are combined and propagated as described below. Using both techniques, kinematic loops can be dealt with.

A. Combining constraints.

There are often several relationships between two parts. The set of possible positions allowable by all the relationships together is the intersection of the sets of possible positions allowable by the individual relationships. The set of allowable positions is described by the conjunction of the constraints from the individual relationships. However, initially each set of constraints applies at a different coordinate system. There is an algorithm that changes the form of a set of inequalities to make them applicable to a different coordinate system.

Before combining relationships between two parts the build up of position tolerances between the features must be found. One of these is made a "master" relative to which the variation in position of the other features is found.

B. Propagating constraints.

Constraints can propagate along a chain of parts and relationships. For example, in diagram 3, we may be interested in constraints on part 3 with respect to part 1. There is an algorithm to deal with the general case analytically.

There may be position tolerances linking the ends of part 2. The variation in position of one end with respect to the other must be found before propagation can be applied.

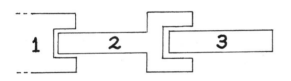

DIAGRAM 3

V VERIFYING DESIGN REQUIREMENTS

The result of applying the above inferences is to produce constraints on the position of one part with respect to some other. The constraints, in two dimensions, take the form,

$$p \leq DOF \leq q$$
$$L \leq p \leq q \leq U$$
$$T \leq q-p \leq S$$

where L,U,T and S are numbers and DOF is a degree of freedom variable. (There may also be terms involving the angular DOF-variables in the first of these inequalities.) Although, initially there may be more than one such set of inequalities for each DOF they can easily be reduced to one set.

The values of L,U,T and S give useful information. For example, T represents the maximum tightness that could occur in any instance of the structure for that degree of freedom. If T<0 then the parts will sometimes not fit. S represents the maximum possible sloppiness and L and U represent the extremes of displacement that could occur in any instance of the structure.

VI CONCLUSION

This paper describes a system to analyse slop in a structure of toleranced parts. There are two stages of reasoning. Firstly constraints are found from each relationship. The existence of tolerances introduces variables and constraints not required for nominal parts. Secondly the constraints are combined and propagated to find the possible relative positions of two parts.

REFERENCES

[1]   Brooks, R.A., "Symbolic Error Analysis and Robot Planning", Memo AIM-685, Stanford University, 1983.

[2]   Corner, D.F., A.P. Ambler and R.J. Popplestone, "Reasoning about the Spatial Relationships Derived from a Rapt Program for Describing Assembly by Robot", Research Paper No. 191, Department of Artificial Intelligence, University of Edinburgh, 1983.

[3]   Hillyard, R., "Dimensions and Tolerances in Shape Design", Tech. Report No. 8, University of Cambridge Computer Laboratory, 1978.

[4]   Hoffman, P., "Analysis of Tolerances and Process Inaccuracies in Discrete Part Manufacturing", Computer Aided Design, Vol 14 No. 2, March 1982.

[5]   Ingham, P.C., "A Computer-Aided Tolerance System", City of Birmingham Polytechnic.

[6]   Lozano-Pérez, T., "The Design of a Mechanical Assembly System", Massachusetts Institute of Technology A.I. Lab, Technical Report 397, 1976.

[7]   Lozano-Pérez, T., M.T. Mason & R.H. Taylor, "Automatic Synthesis of Fine-Motion Strategies for Robots", The International Journal of Robotics Research, Vol 3 No. 1, 1984.

[8]   Requicha, A.A.G., "Toward a Theory of Geometrical Tolerancing", Tech. Memo No. 40, Production Automation Project, University of Rochester, March 1983.

[9]   Requicha, A.A.G., "Representation of Tolerances in Solid Modelling: Issues and Alternative Approaches", Tech. Memo 41, Production Automation Project, University of Rochester, August 1983.

[10] Taylor, R.H., "A Synthesis of Manipulator Control Programs from Task-Level Specifications", Memo AIM-282, Stanford Artificial Intelligence Laboratory, 1976.

[11] British Standards, BS:308, Part 2 "Dimensioning and tolerancing of size" and Part 3 - "Geometric tolerancing"

SPATIAL OBJECT PERCEPTION FROM AN IMAGE *

Radu HORAUD **

Laboratoire d'Automatique de Grenoble
B.P. 46, 38402 Saint-Martin-d'Hères
France

ABSTRACT

In this paper we address the problem of finding the spatial position and orientation of an object from a single image. It is assumed that the image formation process and an object model are known in advance. Sets of image lines are backprojected and constraints on their spatial interpretations are derived. A search space is then constructed where each node represents a space feature with a model assignment. Next, a hypothesize-and-test recognition strategy is used to select a solution, that is to determine six degrees of freedom of a part from a set of features. Finally we discuss the efficiency and the reliability of the method.

1. INTRODUCTION

Among various aspects of perception for which Computer Vision is trying to find a computational theory, an intriguing one is the mechanism by which two-dimensional (2D) shapes are sometimes perceived as three-dimensional (3D) objects. There are at least two reasons for investigating this subject. First, there is evidence that people perform spatial reasoning whenever they deal with images. If they are asked to match two images of the same object, they rotate the object mindly in the 3D space even if the transform occurs in the image plane. This implies that the interpretation space is different from the image plane. And second, we are interested in devising a technique for interpreting images of known things : when is it possible to retrieve the six degrees of freedom of an object from a single view assuming that the object and the camera geometry are known in advance ? Which are the theoretical and practical limitations of such a method if it were implemented as a computer algorithm ? An interesting application could be the recognition of man made parts in an industrial environment.

In this paper we suggest on possible approach limited to objects bounded by planar faces. First we extract linear edges from an intensity image and these edges are combined to form angles and junctions which are assumed to be projections of 3D object vertices. These sets of image fea-

*The work reported herein is supported by "Laboratoire d'Electronique et de Technologie de l'Informatique", Grenoble, France.

**The author is now with LIFIA, B.P. 68, 38042 Saint-Martin d'Hères, France.

tures are backprojected using an inverse perspective camera model and some constraints on their spatial position and orientation are derived. A search space is built where each node represents a 3D feature with a model assignment. A hypothesize-and-test recognition strategy implemented as a depth-first tree search is used to find a solution, that is three rotations and three translations for each part. The object model together with physical constraints are used as heuristics for reducing the complexity of the search space.

Previous approaches for interpreting line drawings have generally not been designed to deal with the geometry of perspective. They have usually used orthography and the gradient space,[1], [2]. Others have simplified the problem by using the "support hypothesis" which reduces the problem to three degrees of freedom, [3] , [4]. Our approach is more general and it can include this hypothesis as a physical constraint. More recently the "gaussian mapping" has been introduced as a tool for interpreting perspective views, [5]. A method for finding vanishing points is described and one for retrieving the spatial orientation of planes by backprojecting angles and curvature is suggested. We extend these results to junctions which we believe are more useful than faces. A two-stage, model-based recognition procedure is described in [6]. The planning stage computes all possible appearances of an object in terms of sets of simultaneously visible features. The recognition stage consists in a predict-observe-backproject sequence. This approach is different from ours since it doesn't explore the constraints available with sets of features.

2. BACKPROJECTION OF IMAGE FEATURES

This paragraph utilizes the perspective camera model for interpreting image linear features. Let us recall briefly this model, [5]. A space point with camera coordinates (x,y,z) projects onto the image at $(x.f/z, y.f/z, f)$ where f is the focal length (see Figure 1). The camera frame has its origin at the focal center and the image is parallel to the x-y plane at distance f from the center along the z-axis. A unit vector can be expressed as a point on a unit sphere centered at the origin, the gaussian sphere. A point on this sphere has two angles as coordinates, the azimuth (α) and the elevation (β). Hence, the orientation of a space plane or the direction of any image or space line can be represented as a point on this sphere. Let's now associate an interpretation plane with an image line. This plane is defined by an image line and the focal center and it contains all the spatial interpretations of the image line. The possible directions of these spatial lines lie on a great circle, the intersection of the interpretation plane with the gaussian sphere. If we denote by P the vector normal to the interpretation plane and by L the space line direction vector, the equation of the great circle is :

$$L.P = 0 \qquad (1)$$

Similarly we can develop constraints for the spatial interpretations of image angles and junctions. The motivation for choosing these features is that they are the projections of object vertices. Let l_1 and l_2 be two image lines forming an angle. Their spatial interpretations are denoted L_1 and L_2 and their interpretation planes are denoted P_1 and P_2. L_1 and L_2 are constrained to be coplanar : they belong to a space plane S and form a space angle ω. We are seeking the orientation of S when ω is known. The following equations stand :

$$L_1 = S \wedge P_1, \quad L_2 = S \wedge P_2 \qquad (2)$$

$$\cos \omega = L_1.L_2/||L_1||.||L_2|| \qquad (3)$$

Since ω is imposed, equation (3) provides a constraint for the possible orientations of the space plane S. Consider now a junction formed by three image lines, l_1, l_2 and l_3 whose spatial interpretation is a right vertex with edges L_1, L_2 and L_3. (There is no loss of generality in considering a right vertex ; this merely simplifies the exposition). l_1 and l_2 can be combined just as above to form an angle constraint. Notice that L_3 is parallel to the vector normal to the plane formed by L_1 and L_2. L_3 is constrained to lie on the great circle corresponding to the spatial interpretations of l_3. Therefore, the only possible orientations of S are the intersection of this great circle (eq.(1)) with the angle constraint (eq.(3)). Figure 4 shows the solutions for the image junction indicated by an arrow on Figure 3. Only half of the gaussian sphere is projected and shown on Figure 4 with α (horizontal) varying from $\pi/2$ to $3\pi/2$ and β (vertical) varying from $-\pi/2$ to $\pi/2$. The two solutions correspond to two orientations of S, one for a concave vertex and the other for a convex one. Without additional information it is impossible to decide which solution to select. This is a simplified version of the Necker's cube illusion. In [1], Kanade developed an analytical solution in the case of orthographic projection but his method requires the measurement of the skewed symmetry of all the faces forming a junction.

3. IMAGE TO OBJECT CORRESPONDENCE

The ultimate goal of a recognition procedure is to assign an object model to a set of image features and to find the spatial parameters of each object. These parameters will be embedded in a 4x4 homogeneous matrix that maps an object from model coordinates to camera coordinates. Let us show now how such a transform may be computed.

We describe first a simple scheme for modelling objects within the context of visual recognition. For a more complete discussion, see [7]. Such a model contains lists of those features and combinations of features that are the most likely to be detected in an image. The features are also ranked according to the contribution they can make for recognition. The model of an object bounded by planar faces provides a list of all faces with pointers from each face to its bounding edges and similarly each edge points back onto the two faces forming it. Another list contains all the vertices and each vertex points onto its three edges. Let V be one vertex and L_1, L_2 and L_3 its edges. There is a vertex centered coordinate system whose axes are L_1, L_2 and the normal to the face bounded by these two edges. The relation between this frame and an object centered coordinate system is completely defined by the geometry of the object and it can be expressed by a 4x4 homogeneous transform matrix, A_m. This transform embeds three rotations and three translations that allow to overlap one frame onto the other.

Suppose now that we know the object assignment of an image junction. That is, there is a unique correspondence between the junction's lines and the edges of the vertex. Since the backprojection of the junction constraints the orientations of the face S formed by L_1 and L_2 to just one direction, we can use equations (2) to determine the vectors L_1 and L_2. This will determine the rotation part of a matrix A_c that maps the vertex centered frame into the camera centered frame. The position of the junction in the image determines two translations. In conclusion, under a junction-to-vertex assignment five degrees of freedom are determined. Depth can be computed by triangulation if there is another junction or angle to which a vertex can be assigned. From A_m and A_c one can compute the object-to-camera transform, A :

$$A = A_c \times A_m^{-1} \qquad (4)$$

The actual correspondence between the model and an image feature set is performed by a hypothesize-and-test procedure. A search space is built where each node represents a junction-to-vertex assignment. The goal is to find the largest set of nodes that are mutually compatible, i.e., they uniquely define the six degrees of freedom of the part. An object orientation and location is hypothesized from one node (excluding the depth for which initial lower and upper bounds are given). From this assignment a set of visible vertices is computed and for each such vertex its image projection is determined. This could be a junction, if two or three faces are visible or an angle if only one face is visible. For each prediction, the best image feature match is selected. Notice, however that the low level segmentation process is not perfect and the data are noisy. For these reasons some lines may be missing. If the verification step fails in finding a predicted junction or angle it checks for partial descriptions of these items in the line list. For each assignment a score is computed by calculating the percentage of object features predicted visible that actually overlap image features. If this score is high enough, the location of the image features as well as their spatial orientation constraints are used for refining the object locational parameters and for estimating tighter bounds for the depth. If the score is too low, the algorithm backtracks to the last choice point.

4. EXPERIMENTAL RESULTS

Figure 2 shows a digitized picture which we have used for verifying the effectiveness of the method. The picture is taken with a TV camera through a 25 mm lens. The orientation of the camera relatively to the table top is not known. The object model comprises 24 right vertices (16 are convex and 8 are concave) but two are sufficient to uniquely identify the object. The image segmentation process comprises edge detection (zero-crossings of the convolution of the image with the difference-of-gaussian operator), edge linking (formation of edge chains) and approximation of these chains with straight lines (piece-wise polygonal approximation using a split-and-merge control structure). Short lines are interpreted as noisy data and are thrown out. Within a chain an angle is formed by two adjacent lines. For each angle we seek a third line which, if combined with the angle's lines could form a junction. Figure 3 shows the image junctions extracted by this segmentation process. Similarly there are angle and line lists. Figure 4 shows the orientation constraint for the junction indicated by an arrow. The final recognition result is shown on Figure 5 which displays wireframe projections of the object model with partial hidden line elimination. In [8] we have repeated this experiment with a 90 mm lens (where the perspective distorsion is low) and we have obtained similar results.

5. DISCUSSION

We have discussed a method for matching 3D object models with intensity images. To increase the efficiency of the method, i.e., to reduce the explosion of the search space, we have derived three-space constraints from image features using the mathematics of perspective and knowledge about the object to be located. The method is limited to a class of objects containing vertices formed by intersections of planar faces. These vertices form, by projection angles and junctions. The backprojection of junctions provides a powerful constraint that is valid, unlike the backprojection of polygonal shapes (as is done in [5]), even in the absence of strong perspective distorsion. However, the method will fail in finding an object if no junction has been detected in the image for this object.

Although this technique looks attractive, it's generalisation is not straightforward. In order to deal with a wide range of realistic situations such as missing and imperfect data, complex objects and various ligthing conditions, this method should be combined with other techniques (stereo, motion, shading) and with other sources of information (range and tactile data).

In the future we plan to increase the set of features to include such things as ellipses and to derive three-space constraints from an extended catalogue of feature clusters such as combinations of ellipses and lines. We also plan to implement a program that will automatically derive perception-oriented object descriptions from a CAD-like database.

REFERENCES

[1] Kanade, T. "Recovery of the Three-Dimensional Shape of an Objet from a Single View", Artificial Intelligence, vol. 17, n° 1-3, August 1981, pp. 409-460.

[2] Brady, M. and Yuille, A., "An Extremum Principle for Shape from Contour", I.E.E.E. Trans. on Patt. An. and Mach. Int., vol. PAMI-6, n° 3, May 1984, pp. 288-301.

[3] Chakravarty, J., "The Use of Characteristic Views as a basis for Recognition of Three-Dimensional Objects", PhD Dissertation, Image Processing Laboratory, Rensselaer Polytechnic Institue, Troy, New-York, October 1982.

[4] Stockman, G. and Esteva, J.C., "Use of Geometrical Constraints and Clustering to Determine 3D Object Pose", Technical Report TR84-002 Dept. Computer Science, Michigan State University, East Lausing, Michigan 48824, 1984.

[5] Barnard, S. "Interpreting Perspective Images" Artificial Intelligence, vol. 21-1983, pp. 435-462.

[6] Goad, C. "Special Purpose Automatic Programming for 3D Model Based Vision", Proceedings Image Understanding Workshop, Arlington, Virginia, June 1983, pp. 94-104.

[7] Bolles, R.C., Horaud, R., Hannah, M.J. "3DPO: A Three-Dimensional Part Orientation System", Proceedings 8th IJCAI, Karlsruhe, Germany, August 1983.

[8] Horaud R., "From Images to Spatial Perception", Proceedings Cognitiva, Paris, France, June 1985.

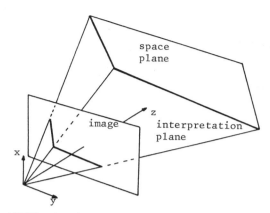

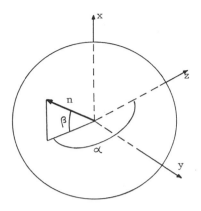

FIGURE 1: a) The geometry of perspective. An image angle backprojects onto a space plane (S).

b) A unit space vector may be represented as a point on the gaussian sphere.

FIGURE 2: A 256x256 image with 64 grey levels taken through a 25 mm lens.

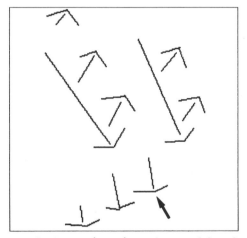

FIGURE 3: Image junctions detected by the data-driven segmentation process. The arrow indicates the junction processed on the next Figure.

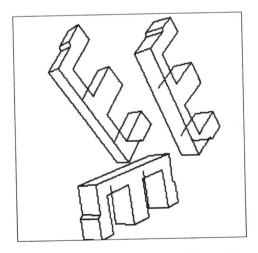

FIGURE 5: The result of recognition. The six locational parameters of each part are determined in camera coordinates.

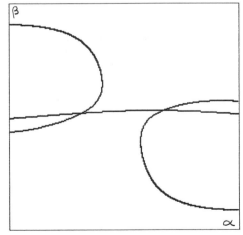

FIGURE 4: Spatial orientation constraints represented on the gaussian sphere. The two solutions correspond to a right vertex interpretation of an image junction.

STEREO BY TWO-LEVEL DYNAMIC PROGRAMMING

Yuichi Ohta

Institute of Information Sciences and Electronics
University of Tsukuba
IBARAKI, 305, JAPAN

Takeo Kanade

Computer Science Department
Carnegie-Mellon University
Pittsburgh, PA 15213

Abstract

This paper presents a stereo algorithm using dynamic programming technique. The stereo matching problem, that is, obtaining a correspondence between right and left images, can be cast as a search problem. When a pair of stereo images is rectified, pairs of corresponding points can be searched for within the same scanlines. We call this search *intra-scanline* search. This intra-scanline search can be treated as the problem of finding a matching path on a two dimensional (2D) search plane whose axes are the right and left scanlines. Vertically connected edges in the images provide consistency constraints across the 2D search planes. *Inter-scanline* search in a three-dimensional (3D) search space, which is a stack of the 2D search planes, is needed to utilize this constraint.

Our stereo matching algorithm uses edge-delimited intervals as elements to be matched, and employs the above mentioned two searches: one is inter-scanline search for possible correspondences of connected edges in right and left images and the other is intra-scanline search for correspondences of edge-delimited intervals on each scanline pair. Dynamic programming is used for both searches which proceed simultaneously in two levels: the former supplies the consistency constraints to the latter while the latter supplies the matching score to the former. An interval-based similarity metric is used to compute the score.

1. Introduction

Stereo is a useful method of obtaining depth information. The key problem in stereo is a search problem which finds the correspondence points between the left and right images, so that,

---

This research was done while Y.Ohta was visiting the Department of Computer Science, Carnegie-Mellon University. The research was sponsored in part by the Defence Advanced Research Projects Agency (DOD), ARPA Order No.3597, monitored by the Air Force Avionics Laboratory under Contract F33615-81-K-1539, and in part by the Air Force Office of Scientific Research under Contract F49620-83-C-0100.

given the camera model (ie., the relationship between the right and left cameras of the stereo pair), the depth can be computed by triangulation. In edge-based techniques, edges in the images are used as the elements whose correspondences to be found [3,4,6]. Even though a general problem of finding correspondences between images involves the search within the whole image, the knowledge of the camera model simplifies this image-to-image correspondence problem into a set of scanline-to-scanline correspondence problems. That is, once a pair of stereo images is rectified so that the epipolar lines are horizontal scanlines, a pair of corresponding edges in the right and left images should be searched for only within the same horizontal scanlines. We call this search *intra-scanline* search. This intra-scanline search can be treated as the problem of finding a matching path on a two-dimensional (2D) search plane whose vertical and horizontal axes are the right and left scanlines. A dynamic programming technique can handle this search efficiently [2,3,7].

However, if there is an edge extending across scanlines, the correspondences in one scanline have strong dependency on the correspondences in the neighboring scanlines, because if two points are on a vertically connected edge in the left image, their corresponding points should, most likely, lie on a vertically connected edge in the right image. The intra-scanline search alone does not take into account this mutual dependency between scanlines. Therefore, another search is necessary which tries to find the consistency among the scanlines, which we call *inter-scanline* search.

By considering both intra- and inter-scanline searches, the correspondence problem in stereo can be cast as that of finding in a three-dimensional (3D) search space an optimal matching surface that most satisfies the intra-scanline matches and inter-scanline consistency. Here, a matching surface is defined by stacking 2D matching paths, where the 2D matching paths are found in a 2D search plane whose axes are left-image column position and right-image column position, and the stacking is done in the direction of the row (scanline) number of the images. The cost of the matching surface is defined as the sum of the costs of the intra-scanline matches on the 2D search planes, while vertically connected edges provide the consistency constraints across the 2D search planes and thus penalize those intra-scanline matches which are not consistent across the scanlines. Our stereo matching uses dynamic programming for performing both the intra-scanline and the inter-scanline searches, and both searches proceed simultaneously in two levels. This method reduces the computation to a feasible amount.

2. Use of Inter-Scanline Constraints

As mentioned above, for a pair of rectified stereo images, matching edges within the same scanline (ie., the intra-scanline search) should be sufficient in principle. However, in practice, there is much ambiguity in finding correspondences solely by the intra-scanline search. To resolve the ambiguity, we can exploit the consistency constraints that vertically connected edges across the scanlines provide. Suppose a point on a connected edge u in the right image matches with a point on a connected edge v in the left image on scanline t. Then, other points on these edges should also match on other scanlines. If edges u and v do not match on scanline t, they should not match on other scanlines, either. We call this property inter-scanline consistency constraint. Thus, our problem is to search for a set of matching paths which gives the optimal correspondence of edges within scanlines under the inter-scanline consistency constraint.

A few methods have been used to combine the inter-scanline search with the intra-scanline search. Henderson [7] sequentially processed each pair of scanlines and used the result of one scanline to guide the search in the next scanline. However, this method suffers by that the errors made in the earlier scanlines significantly affect the total results.

Baker [2] first processed each pair of scanlines independently. After all the intra-scanline matching was done, he used a cooperative process to detect and correct the matching results which violate the consistency constraints. Since this method, however, does not use the inter-scanline constraints directly in the search, the result from the cooperative process is not guaranteed to be optimal. Baker suggested the necessity of a search which finds an optimal result satisfying the consistency constraints in a 3D search space, but a feasible method was left as an open problem.

A straightforward way to achieve a matching which satisfies the inter-scanline constraints is to consider all matchings between connected edges in the right and left images. However, since the typical number of connected edges is a few to several hundred in each image, this brute force method is usually infeasible.

We propose to use dynamic programming, which is used for the intra-scanline search, also for the inter-scanline search. These two searches are combined as shown in figure 1. One is for the correspondence of all connected edges in right and left images, and the other is for the correspondence of edges (actually, intervals delimited by edges) on right and left scanlines under the constraint given by the former. The scheme to use dynamic programming in two levels was first employed in the recognition of connected spoken words [10]. They used one search for the possible segmentation at word boundaries and the other for the time-warping word matching under the constraint given by the

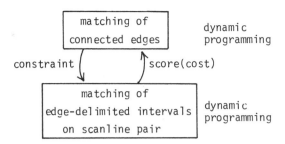

Figure 1. Two searches involved in stereo matching.

former. In connected word recognition, however, the pattern to be processed is a single 1D vector. In our case, a connected edge crosses over multiple scanlines (ie., 1D vectors). This means that we need a 3D search space which is a stack of 2D search planes for intra-scanline matching.

Dynamic programming [1] solves an N-stage decision process as N single-stage processes. This reduces the computational complexity to the logarithm of the original combinatorical one. In order to apply dynamic programming, however, the original decision process must satisfy the following two requirements. First, the decision stages must be ordered so that all the stages whose results are needed at a given stage have been processed before them. Second, the decision process should be *Markovian*: that is, at any stage the behavior of the process depends solely on the current state and does not depend on the previous history. It is not obvious whether these properties exist in the problem of finding correspondences between connected edges in stereo images, but we clarify them in the following sections.

3. Correspondence Search Using Two-Level Dynamic Programming

3.1. Intra-scanline search on 2D plane

The problem of obtaining a correspondence between edges on the right and left epipolar scanlines can be solved as a path finding problem on a 2D plane. Figure 2 illustrates this 2D search plane. The vertical lines show the positions of edges on the left scanline and the horizontal ones show those on the right scanline. We refer to the intersections of those lines as nodes. Nodes in this plane correspond to the stages in dynamic programming where a decision should be made to select an optimal path to that node. In the intra-scanline search, the stages must be ordered as follows: *When we examine the correspondence of two edges, one on the right and one on the left scanline, the edges which are on the left of these edges on each scanline must already be processed.* For this purpose, we give indices for edges in left-to-right order on each scanline: [0:M] on the right and [0:N] on the left. Both ends of a scanline are also treated as edges for convenience. It is obvious that the condition above is satisfied if we process the nodes with smaller indices first. Legal paths which must be considered are sequences of straight line segments from node (0,0) at the upper left corner to node (M,N) at the lower right corner on a 2D array $[0:M,0:N]$. They must go from the upper left to the lower right corners monotonically due to the above-mentioned condition on ordering. This is equivalent to the no-reversal constraints in edge correspondence: that is, the order of matched edges has to be preserved in the right and left scanlines. This constraint excludes from analysis thin objects such as wires and poles which may result in positional reversals in the image. A path has a vertex at node $\mathbf{m}=(m,n)$ when right edge m and left edge n are matched.

The cost of a path is defined as follows. Let $D(\mathbf{m},\mathbf{k})$ be the minimal cost of the partial path from node $\mathbf{k}$ to node $\mathbf{m}$. $D(\mathbf{m},0)$ is the cost of the optimal path to node $\mathbf{m}$ from the origin (0,0). A primitive path is a partial path which contains no vertices and it is represented by a straight line segment as shown on figure 2. It should be noted that a primitive path actually corresponds to matching the intervals delimited by edges at the start and end nodes rather than edges themselves. The cost of a path is the sum of those of its primitive paths. Let $d(\mathbf{m},\mathbf{k})$ be the cost of the primitive path from node $\mathbf{k}$ to node $\mathbf{m}$. (Our actual definition of $d(\mathbf{m},\mathbf{k})$ will be given in section 4.) Obviously, $d(\mathbf{m},\mathbf{k}) \geq D(\mathbf{m},\mathbf{k})$ and on an optimal path $d(\mathbf{m},\mathbf{k}) \equiv D(\mathbf{m},\mathbf{k})$.

Now, $D(\mathbf{m},\mathbf{k})$ can be defined recursively as:

$$D(\mathbf{m},\mathbf{k}) = \min_{\{\mathbf{i}\}} \Big(d(\mathbf{m},\mathbf{m}-\mathbf{i}) + D(\mathbf{m}-\mathbf{i},\mathbf{k}) \Big)$$

$$D(\mathbf{k},\mathbf{k}) = 0 \tag{1}$$

where $\mathbf{m}=(m,n)$, $\mathbf{k}=(k,l)$, $\mathbf{i}=(i,j)$, $0 \leq i \leq m-k$, $0 \leq j \leq n-l$, $i+j \neq 0$.

Vector $\mathbf{i}$ represents a primitive path coming to node $\mathbf{m}$. When $i=0$, the primitive path is horizontal, as shown at (a) in figure 2. It corresponds to the case in which a visible part in the left image is occluded in the right image. When $j=0$, the primitive path is vertical, as shown at (b). When $i>1$ and/or $j>1$, the primitive path skips or ignores beyond $i-1$ and/or $j-1$ edges on the right and/or left scanlines as shown at (c) in the figure. Such a path corresponds to the case where some edges have no corresponding ones on the other scanline because of noise.

The path with cost $D(\mathbf{M},0)$ gives the optimal correspondence between a pair of scanlines.

3.2. Inter-scanline search in 3D space

The problem of obtaining a correspondence between edges under the inter-scanline consistency constraints can be viewed as the problem of finding a set of paths in a 3D space which is a stack of 2D planes for intra-scanline search. Figure 3 illustrates this 3D space. The side faces of this space correspond to the right and left images of a stereo pair. The cost of a set of paths is defined as the sum of the costs of the individual paths in the set. We want to obtain an optimal (ie., the minimal cost) set of paths satisfying the inter-scanline constraints. A pair of connected edges in the right and left images make a set of 2D nodes in the 3D space when they share scanline pairs. We refer

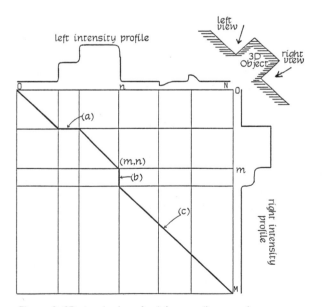

Figure 2. 2D search plane for intra-scanline search.
Intensity profiles are shown along each axis. The horizontal axis corresponds to the left scanline and the vertical one corresponds to the right scanline. Vertical and horizontal lines are the edge positions and path selection is done at their intersections.

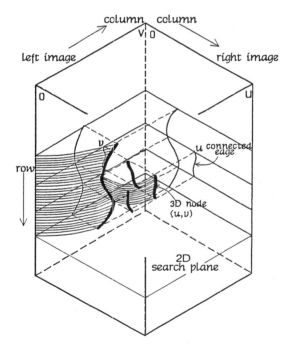

Figure 3. 3D search space for intra- and inter-scanline search.
This may be viewed as a rectangular solid seen from above. The side faces correspond to the right and left stereo images. Connected edges in each image form sets of intersections (nodes) in this space. Each set is called a 3D node. Selection of a set of paths is done at every 3D node.

to this set of 2D nodes as a single 3D node. The optimal path on a 2D plane is obtained by iterating the selection of an optimal path at each 2D node. Similarly, the optimal set of paths in a 3D space is obtained by iterating the selection of an optimal set of paths at each 3D node. Connected edges, 3D nodes, and sets of paths between 3D nodes are illustrated in figure 3.

As described in section 2, the decision stages must be ordered in dynamic programming. In the intra-scanline search, their ordering was straightforward; it was done by ordering edges from left to right on each scanline. A similar consideration must be given to the inter-scanline search in 3D space where the decision stages are the 3D nodes. A 3D node is actually a set of 2D nodes, and the cost at a 3D node is computed based on the cost obtained by the intra-scanline search on each 2D search plane. This leads to the following condition: *When we examine the correspondence of two connected edges, one in the right and one in the left image, the connected edges which are on the left of these connected edges in each image must already be processed.*

A connected edge u_1 is said to be on the left of u_2, if all the edges in u_1 on the scanlines which u_1 and u_2 share are on the left of those in u_2. The "left-of" relationship is transitive; if there is a connected edge u_3 and u_1 is on the left of u_3 and u_3 is on the left of u_2, then u_1 is on the left of u_2. The order of two connected edges which do not satisfy both the relations described above may be arbitrarily specified. We assign an ordering index from left to right for every connected edge in an image. This ordering is possible without contradiction when a connected edge never crosses a scanline more than once and when two connected edges never intersect each other. Our edge-linking process is devised so that it does not make such cases.

Now we will present how the cost of a 3D path is defined. Suppose we assign indices $[0:U]$ to connected edges in the right image, and $[0:V]$ in the left. The left and right ends of an image are treated as connected edges for convenience: the left ends are assigned index 0's. Let $\mathbf{u}=(u,v)$ be a 3D node made by a connected edge u in the right image and a connected edge v in the left image. Let $C(\mathbf{u})$ be the cost of the optimal set of paths which reach to the 3D node $\mathbf{u}$. The cost $C(\mathbf{u})$ is computed as follows:

$$C(\mathbf{u}) = \min_{\{i(t)\}} \sum_{t=s(u)}^{e(u)} \Big(D(I(\mathbf{u};t),I(\mathbf{u}-i(t);t);t) + C(\mathbf{u}-i(t);t) \Big)$$

$$C(\mathbf{0}) = 0, \quad ie., \ C(\mathbf{0};t)=0 \text{ for all } t \tag{2}$$

where $\mathbf{u}=(u,v)$, $i(t)=(i(t),j(t))$, $0\leq i(t)\leq u$, $0\leq j(t)\leq v$, $i(t)+j(t)\neq 0$.

Here, $C(\mathbf{u};t)$ is the cost of the path on scanline t in the optimal set; that is, $C(\mathbf{u})=\sum C(\mathbf{u};t)$, and $D(\mathbf{m},\mathbf{k};t)$ is the cost of the optimal 3D primitive path from node $\mathbf{k}$ to node $\mathbf{m}$ on the 2D plane for scanline t. A 3D primitive path is a partial path between two 3D nodes on a 2D search plane and it has no vertices at the nodes belonging to a 3D node. So a 3D primitive path is a chain of 2D primitive paths and an intra-scanline search is necessary to obtain the optimal 3D primitive path on a 2D plane between given two given 3D nodes. The function $I(\mathbf{u};t)$ gives the index of a 2D node belonging to the 3D node $\mathbf{u}$ on the 2D plane for scanline t. The numbers $s(u)$ and $e(u)$ specify respectively the starting and ending scanlines between which the 3D node $\mathbf{u}$ exists. The cost

$C(\mathbf{u})$ is minimized on the function $i(t)$. A 3D node $\mathbf{u}-i(t)$ gives the start node of the 3D primitive path on scanline t. The inter-scanline constraints is represented by $i(t)$. For example, if $i(t)$ is independent of $i(t-1)$, there are no constraints between scanlines and the search represented by equation (2) becomes equivalent to a set of intra-scanline searches which are performed independently on each scanline. Intuitively, $i(t)$ must be equal to $i(t-1)$ in order to keep the consistency constraint.

The iteration starts at $\mathbf{u}=(0,0)$ and computes $C(\mathbf{u})$ for each 3D node $\mathbf{u}$ in ascending order of $\mathbf{u}$. At each 3D node the $i(t)$'s which give the minimum are recorded. The sequence of 2D primitive paths which forms the 3D primitive path is also recorded on each scanline. The set of paths which gives $C(\mathbf{U})$ at the 3D node $\mathbf{U}=(U,V)$ (which is the 3D node formed by the right ends of stereo images) is obtained as the optimal set. It should be noted that when there are no connected edges except for the right and left sides of the images, the algorithm (2) works as a set of intra-scanline searches repeated on each scanline independently. In this sense, the 3D algorithm completely contains the 2D one.

3.3. Consistency constraints in inter-scanline

Using the term 3D node defined in the previous section, we can describe the inter-scanline consistency constraints as follows: *For any 3D node, either all corresponding 2D nodes are the vertices on the set of paths in the 3D search space or none of them are the vertices on the set of paths.* We need to represent this constraints as the relation between $i(t)$ and $i(t-1)$ in equation (2). To do this, let us consider the example in figure 4. Suppose we are trying to obtain a set of 3D primitive paths which reach to node $\mathbf{u}$. In order to satisfy the consistency constraints above, all the starting points of these paths should be the same 3D node; that is $i(t)=i(t-1)$. The cases when the starting point is a different 3D node are shown as case2 and case3 in the figure. In case2, a new 3D node appears at scanline t and the starting point changes to the new one. Of course, it is possible that the starting point does not change to the new 3D node. This will happen if the cost of the paths having vertices on the 3D node is higher than the cost of the paths not having vertices on it. In case3, the 3D node $\mathbf{u}-i(t-1)$ disappears on scanline t and the starting point is forced

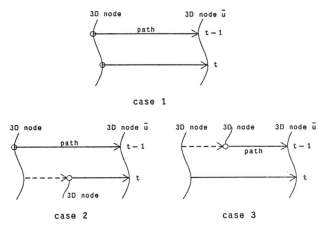

Figure 4. Three cases for consistency constraint.

to move elsewhere.

Let us denote the 3D node $u-i(t)$, from which the 3D primitive path starts and reaches to the 3D node u on scanline t, by $frm(u;t)$. Then the following rules should be satisfied in each case.

case1: $frm(u;t) = frm(u;t-1)$
case2: $frm(frm(u;t);t) = frm(u;t-1)$ (3)
case3: $frm(u;t) = frm(frm(u;t-1);t-1)$

The rules in case2 and case3 require that the decision at 3D node u depend on decisions at preceding 3D nodes. Unfortunately, a decision system with such a property is not *Markovian* as described in section 2, and therefore there is no guarantee of obtaining an optimal solution by using dynamic programming. This means if we search for a solution using dynamic programming with those rules, the result might be poorer than that of the 2D algorithm.

In order to assure optimality in dynamic programming, we modify the rules in (3) as follows.

case1: $frm(u;t) = frm(u;t-1)$
case2: $frm(u;t) \geq frm(u;t-1)$ (4)
case3: $frm(u;t) \leq frm(u;t-1)$

The new rule for case2 requires the new 3D node on scanline t be on the right of the 3D node that is the starting point on scanline $t-1$. For case3, the new starting node on scanline t should be on the left of that on scanline $t-1$. It should be noted that though the new rules are always satisfied when the rules in equation (3) are satisfied, the converse is not true. Thus, under the new rules, the consistency constraint might not be satisfied at all places. In other words, the constraints represented by the rules in equation (4) are weaker than those of equation (3). However, since we can expect to obtain an optimal solution in dynamic programming, we can expect better results by the 3D search algorithm than by the 2D search algorithm.

4. Experiments

Implementation of the stereo algorithm which has been presented requires a method of detecting edges, linking them into connected edges, and ordering the connected edges. We do not describe, however, the details of the method in this paper because of space limitation and it can be found elsewhere [9].

The computation of cost in our search algorithm is based on the cost of a primitive path on the 2D search plane. We define the cost of a 2D primitive path as the similarity between intervals delimited by edges in the right and left images on the same scanline. If we let $a_1 \ldots a_k$ and $b_1 \ldots b_l$ be the intensity values of the pixels which comprise the two intervals, then the mean and variance of all pixels in the two intervals are computed as:

$$\mu = \frac{1}{2} \left(\frac{1}{k} \sum_{i=1}^{k} a_i + \frac{1}{l} \sum_{j=1}^{l} b_j \right)$$

$$\sigma^2 = \frac{1}{2} \left(\frac{1}{k} \sum_{i=1}^{k} (a_i - \mu)^2 + \frac{1}{l} \sum_{j=1}^{l} (b_j - \mu)^2 \right) \quad (5)$$

In the definition above, both intervals give the same contribution to the mean μ and variance σ^2 even when their lengths are different. The cost of the primitive path which matches those intervals is defined as follows:

$$d = \sigma^2 \times (k^2 + l^2)^{1/2} \quad (6)$$

We have applied our stereo algorithm to images from various domains including synthesized images, urban aerial images, and block scenes. Only a result with urban aerial images is presented here.

The stereo pairs used are aerial photographs of the Washington, D.C. area. They have been rectified using the camera models which was computed by Gennery's program [5] using manually selected point pairs.

Figures 5, 6, and 7 show the original stereo pair, edges, and connected edges for the "white house" scene, respectively. The image size is 388x388 pixels and the intensity resolution is 8 bits. This example is an interesting and difficult one because it includes both buildings and highly textured trees. Many connected edges are obtained around the building while few are obtained in the textural part. The disparity maps obtained by the 2D and 3D search algorithms are shown in figure 8. Since the maps are registered in the right image coordinates, the disparity values for pixels on the right wall of the central building, which is visible in the right image but occluded in the left, are undetermined. Considerable improvements can be observed at the boundaries of buildings. In the textural part, the two algorithms provide approximately the same results.

We counted the number of positions where the consistency constraint, described in section 3.3, is not satisfied. It is 436 in the 2D search and 32 in the 3D search. These numbers quantitatively show a significant improvement achieved by the 3D search algorithm. The reason why the inconsistency is not completely removed in the 3D case is that we used "weaker" rules for the constraint as described earlier.

5. Conclusion

In this paper, we have described a stereo algorithm which searches for an optimal solution in a 3D search space using dynamic programming. The algorithm has been applied to urban aerial images successfully. Perhaps one of the major reasons that our algorithm works well for such a complex images is as follows. For images which contain long connected edges such as linear structures in urban scenes, our 3D search scheme works effectively to enforce the consistency constraint. When images do not contain long connected edges, our stereo algorithm reduces to

left image   right image

Figure 5. The "white house" stereo pair of urban images.

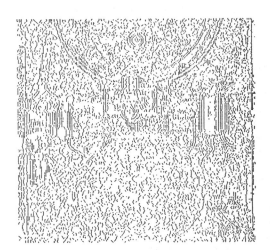

Figure 6. Edges extracted from the images in figure 5.

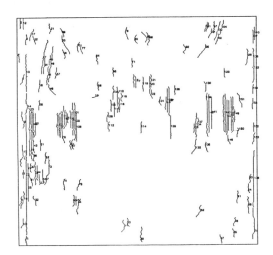
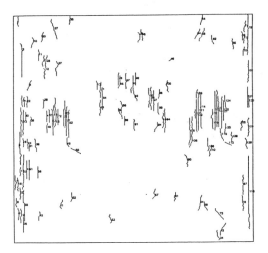

Figure 7. Connected edges obtained from figure 6.

the ordinary 2D search which works efficiently to match isolated edges within each scanline pair. In other words, when inter-scanline constraints are available, our algorithm fully utilizes them, otherwise it works as the 2D search. This feature will be less obvious in segment-based algorithms, such as in [8], which depend heavily on the connectivity of edges.

References

[1]   Aho,A.V., Hopcroft,J.E., and Ullman,J.D.
       The Design and Analysis of Computer Algorithms.
       Addison-Wesley, Reading, MA, 1974.

[2]   Baker,H.H.
       Depth from Edge and Intensity Based Stereo.
       Technical Report AIM-347, Stanford A.I. Lab., 1982.

[3]   Baker,H.H. and Binford,T.O.
       Depth from Edge and Intensity Based Stereo.
       In Proc. 7th IJCAI, pp.631-636, Aug., 1981.

[4]   Barnard,S.T. and Fischler,M.A.
       Computational Stereo.
       Computing Surveys 14(4), pp.553-572, Dec., 1982.

[5]   Gennery,D.
       Stereo-Camera Calibration.
       In Proceedings of Image Understanding Workshop,
       pp.101-107, DARPA, Nov., 1979.

[6]   Grimson,W.E.L. and Marr,D.
       In Proceedings of Image Understanding Workshop,
       pp.41-47, DARPA, Apr., 1979.

[7]   Henderson,R.L., Miller,W.J., and Grosch,C.B.
       Automatic Stereo Reconstruction of Man-made Targets.
       SPIE 186(6), pp.240-248, 1979.

[8]   Medioni,G.C. and Nevatia,R.
       Segment-based Stereo Matching.
       In Proceedings of Image Understanding Workshop,
       pp.128-136, DARPA, June, 1983.

[9]   Ohta,Y. and Kanade,T.
       Stereo by Intra- and Inter-scanline Search Using Dynamic
       Programming.
       Technical Report, CMU-CS-83-162, Carnegie-Mellon
       University, 1983.

[10]   Sakoe,H.
       Two-Level DP-Matching - A Dynamic Programming-Based
       Pattern Matching Algorithm for Connected Word
       Recognition.
       IEEE Trans. ASSP, 27(6), pp.588-595, Dec., 1979.

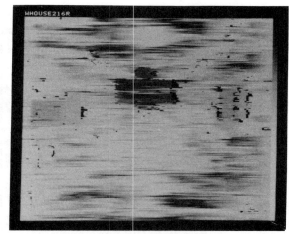

(a) result of 2D search

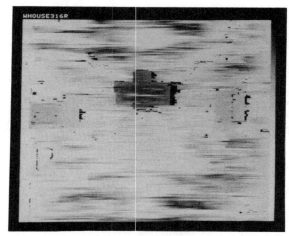

(b) result of 3D search

Figure 8. Disparity map obtained for the "white house" stereo pair (figure 5).
Both are registered in the right image coordinates.

A FAST METHOD FOR EXTRACTION OF 3-D INFORMATION
USING MULTIPLE STRIPES AND TWO CAMERAS

Tomio Echigo + and Masahiko Yachida ++

+ IBM Japan, Ltd.
Yasu, Shiga 520-23, Japan.

++ Osaka University
Toyonaka, Osaka 560, Japan.

ABSTRACT

This paper describes a method to extract 3-D information from two cameras in the scene on which multiple stripes are projected. Though a single camera cannot identify each stripe in a scene and its image when discontinuities of each stripe occur, with one more camera which our method employs the identification problem can be solved, because multiple stripes and two cameras give two constraints. One is the geometric constraint which gives the necessary condition for identification of each stripe. Another is the local constraint that features between images lie in constant order. After applying the geometric constraint, utilization of the local constraint enables identification of each stripe in a scene and its image. As a result, range data are obtained along multiple stripes.

We also give a new method for computing camera parameters of 6 degrees of freedom which influence accuracy of 3-D information. They are derived mathematically by seeing the known cube.

1. INTRODUCTION

The importance of 3-D information in robotics has been widely recognized. One approach is to measure the distance on the basis of the triangulation principle from the disparity of two images taken at two different position, which is well known as stereo vision. This method has long been studied; however, it has a few problems; one is detecting features which are easily recognized in both images [1],[2] and the other is finding correspondence of those features between both images[2],[3].

On the other hand, the structured light method which replaces one of the cameras in stereo vision by a spot or a sheet of light projector solves the above problems[4]. However, this technique needs much time to extract range data of the entire image, because a sheet of light must be scanned across the scene.

In this paper we project multiple stripes. In this method, however, one image cannot inform of identifying each stripe in a scene and its corresponding image when discontinuities of each stripe occur; for example, when the object is concave or occlusion occurs between objects. In order to identify each stripe in a scene and its image, our method employs one more camera in addition to a light projector and a camera. Then epipolar lines which two cameras produce on both images and multi-

ple sheets of light yield the geometric constraint, which gives the necessary condition for identification of each stripe. In addition, under a certain condition which is described later, the local constraint is useful, which means that some features on epipolar lines lie in constant order between both images. Using the local constraint after the geometric constraint, we can identify each stripe between a scene and its image.

It is important to determine the camera parameters precisely, because they influence the accuracy of the computed value of 3-D position. Gennery[5] determined the most suitable camera parameters which minimize the sum of the errors over the known matching points. However, applying Gennery's method requires that the initial estimate is fairly accurate. Provided an uncertain initial estimate, this method may obtain the incorrect camera parameters as the most suitable ones. On the other hand, our method calculates the camera parameters mathematically from the image of a known cube. Therefore our method does not need the initial estimate and can obtain the camera parameters automatically[6].

2. CALCULATION OF CAMERA PARAMETERS

2.1 Extraction of the line of sight

Fig.1 illustrates a schematic of the object coordinates system(O-XYZ) and the camera coordinates system(F-xyz).

Then, let P denote the position vector of the point P and let the coordinate of its image p be $(x,y,1)$ in the camera coordinates, and the line of sight of the point P is expressed as

$$\begin{aligned}(e_x - \hat{x} e_z)\bullet P &= (\hat{x}_0 - \hat{x}) P_0\bullet e_z \\ (e_y - \hat{y} e_z)\bullet P &= (\hat{y}_0 - \hat{y}) P_0\bullet e_z \end{aligned} \quad (2.1)$$

where $x/1=\hat{x}$, $x_0/1=\hat{x}_0$, $y/1=\hat{y}$, $y_0/1=\hat{y}_0$

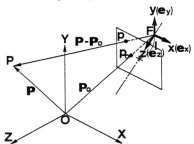

Fig.1 The coordinates systems.

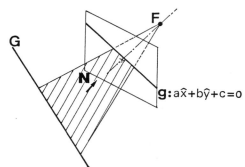

Fig.2   Projection of the straight line.

2.2 Rotation parameters

The unit orientation vectors e_x, e_y, e_z are expressed by

$$e_x = \begin{bmatrix} Sx \\ Sy \\ Sz \end{bmatrix} \quad e_y = \begin{bmatrix} Tx \\ Ty \\ Tz \end{bmatrix} \quad e_z = \begin{bmatrix} Ux \\ Uy \\ Uz \end{bmatrix} \quad (2.2)$$

Fig.2 shows that the straight line G in the space is mapped as the line g onto an image plane. The equation of the line g on an image plane is given by $a\hat{x}+b\hat{y}+c=0$. Then the surface normal N of a plane including the lens center F and the line G is

$$N = ae_x + be_y + ce_z \qquad (2.3)$$

The relationship between the surface normal N and the orientation vector G of the line G is $N \cdot G = 0$.

Since there are 3 degrees of freedom for rotation, three known lines of which the orientation vectors are linearly independent yield the rotation parameters. When three straight line G_1, G_2, G_3 are given by $(1,0,0),(0,1,0),(0,0,1)$, let the coefficients of the image g_1, g_2, g_3 of G_1, G_2, G_3 be $a_i, b_i, c_i (i=1,2,3)$ and from $N \cdot G=0$ we can obtain the following Eqs.

$$\begin{aligned} a_1 Sx + b_1 Tx + c_1 Ux &= 0 \\ a_2 Sy + b_2 Ty + c_2 Uy &= 0 \\ a_3 Sz + b_3 Tz + c_3 Uz &= 0 \end{aligned} \qquad (2.4)$$

Since the 9 unknown parameters Sxyz,Txyz,Uxyz can be expressed as the 3 rotation parameters α, β, γ, the unit orientation vectors can be determined mathematically from Eqs.(2.4).

2.3 Translation parameters

Translation parameters are determined by a known point in the object coordinates. Assuming that the known point P_1 in the scene maps onto the point $p_1(x_1, y_1, 1)$ in the image, the following value is obtained from Eq.(2.1);

$$Po \cdot e_z = \frac{(e_x - \hat{x}_1 e_z) \cdot P_1}{\hat{x}_1 - \hat{x}_o} = \frac{(e_y - \hat{y}_1 e_z) \cdot P_1}{\hat{y}_1 - \hat{y}_o} \qquad (2.5)$$

Therefore the location of the lens center F (X_f, Y_f, Z_f) is found as

$$\begin{bmatrix} X_f \\ Y_f \\ Z_f \end{bmatrix} = Po \cdot e_z \begin{bmatrix} e_x{}^t \\ e_y{}^t \\ e_z{}^t \end{bmatrix}^{-1} \begin{bmatrix} \hat{x}_o \\ \hat{y}_o \\ 1 \end{bmatrix} \qquad (2.6)$$

3. EXTRACTION OF 3-D INFORMATION

3.1 Calculation of 3-D location

Assuming that a light source makes light planes in the scene through multiple slit, the location of a point in the scene along the stripe pattern is obtained from the intersection between a plane and a line of sight. With one image of multiple stripes, however, we cannot always identify each stripe with its image. Therefore we use one more camera in addition to a light projector and a camera.

3.2 The geometric constraint

When two cameras are laterally displaced, the geometric constraint can be found on left and right images, as shown in Fig.3 and Fig.4. In Fig.3 a plane containing the stereo pair line produces the intersections across the left image plane and the right one. These intersections are called epipolar lines. All visual points on an epipolar plane must map onto a left epipolar line and a right one. Hence two dimensional matching in two images results in one dimensional one on those epipolar lines.

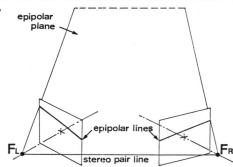

Fig.3   The epipolar geometry.

In Fig.4 an intersection r between an epipolar line and one of stripes in the right image is considered as follows. The line of sight which connects the intersection r with the lens center F_R crosses some light planes $S_i (i=1,2,..)$ in the scene. These crossing points R_i $(i=1,2,..)$ in the scene projects its images p_i $(i=1,2,..)$ onto the left image, so that all of the projected points p_i lie on the epipolar line of the left image. Now a stripe s_j in the right image corresponds to a stripe $\overline{s}_k$ in the left one. Then a true matching

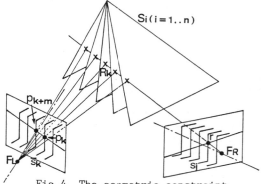

Fig.4   The geometric constraint.

point p_k must correspond to the intersection between the epipolar line and the stripe pattern in the left image as same as the intersection r in the right image. The others (p_{k-1}, p_{k+1},...,p_{k+x}) distribute on the epipolar line and few of them like a p_{k+m} in Fig.4 may correspond to the intersection between the epipolar line and a stripe which should not match with the one of stripes investigated on the right image. These projections (p_k,p_{k+m},..) corresponding to the intersections in the left image, which contain a true and a false, are treated as matching candidates.

Therefore the geometric constraint cannot match all of them, but rejects false matching candidates remarkably.

3.3 The local constraint

On the ordinary scene, left and right images may exchange the order of some features on two epipolar lines only when some objects exist in front and in the rear in the scene. Fig.5 shows the top view of this situation. Assuming that the point P_1 on the surface of the object P will project onto both images, the sub-object Q, which exchanges the order of lines containing P_1 and the other features on the epipolar lines in the left image and the right one, should lie in the laterally striped region R_2 in Fig.5. At the same time Q occludes some features in the checked region R_3 on either of images. In Fig.5 the order of the point P_1 and its neighboring features is exchanged between the left image and the right one by Q.

However, the greater Q is, the larger region is occluded by Q. Then a set of the point P_1 and its neighboring features whose order is exchanged becomes smaller and at last P_1 may be occluded too. On the other hand, under the condition that the angle made of optical axes of left and right cameras is very small, the laterally striped region R_2 becomes narrow.

From the above considerations, it can be said that exchange of the order occurs only when a very small object exists in front of the larger object and stripe pattern is projected on it.(However, in real scenes actually stripe pattern will seldom appear on it.) Therefore we can use monotony of order for correspondence, that is the order of appearing features on the epipolar lines is not exchanged for the left image and the right one. Similarly if a projector lie in the neighborhood of a camera, the local constraint should be effective between light planes and stripes in the image.

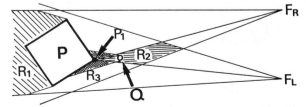

Fig.5 A counter-example of the local constraint.

3.4 Finding correspondences

First of all, lines of sight through intersections between an epipolar line and stripes of a

right image are drawn. Then crossing points between light planes and lines of sight are treated as candidates for identification.

Secondly the geometric constraint reduces a lot of improper candidates, using the left image to project all crossing points. Then the local constraint is applied to the rest of candidates, that is when one stripe in the right image has plural candidates as a corresponding light plane, a candidate which is out of line with candidates of neighboring stripes must be canceled. For example, let a stripe image r_i and neighbors have the following candidates:

$$r_{i-1} \text{ ------- } S_m,..,S_{m+s}$$
$$r_i \text{ ------- } S_k$$
$$r_{k+1} \text{ ------- } S_n,..,S_{n+t}$$

then candidates S_k for r_i should be satisfied with

$$S_k = \{ \ S_x \ | \ S_m < S_x < S_{n+t} \ \}$$

This procedure keeps running until each stripe in the right image corresponds to the only one light plane or a number of candidates does not decrease.

4. EXPERIMENTAL RESULTS

4.1 Camera parameters

A cube in Fig.6 is used for determination of camera parameters. Three edges of a cube denote X,Y,Z axes in the object coordinates system.

In order to verify a camera parameter obtained by our method, a calculated parameter is compared

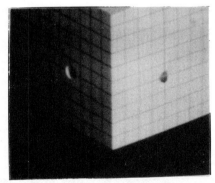

Fig.6 The cube for determination of camera parameters.

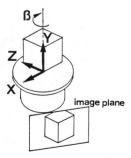

Fig.7 The experiment to examine a camera parameter β derived by our method.

Table 1 Comparison between calculations
and measurements.

measurements $\Delta\beta_1$ (degrees)	calculations $\Delta\beta_2$ (degrees)	errors $\Delta\beta_2 - \Delta\beta_1$ (degrees)
−10	− 9.85	+0.15
− 5	− 4.85	+0.15
+ 5	+ 4.82	−0.18
+10	+10.18	+0.18
+15	+14.97	−0.03
+20	+19.90	−0.10

with a measured one using the rotary table(Fig.7) as shown in Table 1. Because the rotating axis of the table is made to correspond to Y axis of the cube, rotation angle β around Y axis becomes independent of the others.

4.2 Extraction of 3-D position

The thinning images of the objects from two cameras are shown in Fig.8. Then a pair of epipolar lines is drawn on the left image and the right one. All crossing points between light planes and lines of sight from the right image are projected onto the left epipolar line (Fig.9). Since one of them matches with an intersection between the left epipolar line and a stripe image in Fig.9, identification between the light plane and its image has accomplished. In case of plural candidates, the local constraint works successfully for reduction of them.

Fig.10 shows that some 3-D positions calculated from identified stripes map onto the horizontal plane. Accuracy about the height is less than 2.5% against the visual field.

6. CONCLUSIONS

We have presented a method for extraction of range data in the scene on which multiple stripes are projected. This method combines the structured light method with stereo image one.

At first, the camera parameters were automatically computed by seeing the known cube. Secondly, in order to identify each stripe in a scene and its image, we utilized two constraints. One is the geometric constraint, which gives the necessary condition for identification of each stripe. This constraint can certainly reduce most of false matching candidates. Another is the local constraint that some features on epipolar lines between both images lie in constant order. The local constraint can reduce almost all of false matching candidates which the geometric constraint does not happen to remove. From the experimental results, we confirmed effectiveness of the above constraints.

This method may be used not only for static but also for dynamic scenes because the depth information can be obtained at one TV frame time.

ACKNOWLEDGEMENT

We would like to thank Prof. S.Tsuji for valuable discussion.

REFERENCES

[1] Moravec,H.P."Obstacle Avoidance and Navigation in Real World by A Seeing Robot Rober.", CMU-RI-TR-3, 1983.
[2] Marr,D., Vision, Freeman, San Francisco, 1982.
[3] Baker,H. "Edge-based Stereo Correlation." Proc. of Image Understanding Workshop, 1980, pp.168.
[4] Shirai,Y. "Recognition of Polyredrons with A Range Finder." Pattern Recognition,4,1972,pp.243.
[5] Gennery,D.B."Stereo-camera Calibration.",Proc. of Image Understanding Workshop, 1979, pp.101.
[6] Kasai,T. et al.,"Measurement System of 3-D MotionUsing A Pair of PositionSensing Detector Cameras.", SICE, vol.19, no.12, 1983, pp.997.

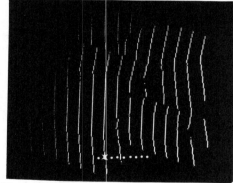

Fig.9 Projection of 3-D crossing points onto the left image.

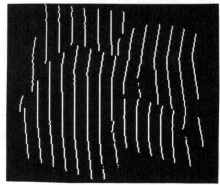

(a) The left image

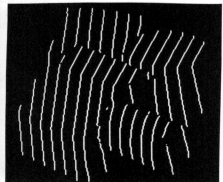

(b) The right image

Fig.8 The thinning images of stripe pattern.

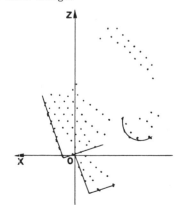

Fig.10 Top view of the scene.

OBJECT RECOGNITION USING VISION AND TOUCH

Peter Allen and Ruzena Bajcsy

Department of Computer and Information Science
University of Pennsylvania
Philadelphia, PA 19104

ABSTRACT

A system is described that integrates vision and tactile sensing in a robotics environment to perform object recognition tasks. It uses multiple sensor systems (active touch and passive stereo vision) to compute three dimensional primitives that can be matched against a model data base of complex curved surface objects containing holes and cavities. The low level sensing elements provide local surface and feature matches which are constrained by relational criteria embedded in the models. Once a model has been invoked, a verification procedure establishes confidence measures for a correct recognition. The three dimensional nature of the sensed data makes the matching process more robust as does the system's ability to sense visually occluded areas with touch. The model is hierarchic in nature and allows matching at different levels to provide support or inhibition for recognition.

1. INTRODUCTION

Robotic systems are being designed and built to perform complex tasks such as object recognition, grasping, parts manipulation, inspection and measurement. In the case of object recognition, many systems have been designed that have tried to exploit a single sensing modality [1, 2, 3, 4, 5, 6]. Single sensor systems are necessarily limited in their power. The approach described here to overcome the inherent limitations of a single sensing modality is to *integrate* multiple sensing modalities (passive stereo vision and active tactile sensing) for object recognition. The advantages of multiple sensory systems in a task like this are many. Multiple sensor systems supply redundant and complementary kinds of data that can be integrated to create a more coherent understanding of a scene. The inclusion of multiple sensing systems is becoming more apparent as research continues in distributed systems and parallel approaches to problem solving. The redundancy and support for a hypothesis that comes from more than one sensing subsystem is important in establishing confidence measures during a recognition process, just as the disagreement between two sensors will inhibit a hypothesis and point to possible sensing or reasoning error. The complementary nature of these sensors allows more powerful matching primitives to be used. The primitives that are the outcome of sensing with these complementary sensors are three dimensional in nature, providing stronger invariants and a more natural way to recognize objects which are also three dimensional in nature [7].

Most object recognition systems are model based discrimination systems that attempt to find evidence consistent with a hypothesized model and for which there is no contradictory evidence [4]. Systems that contain large amounts of information about object structure and relationships potentially reduce the number of false recognitions. However, the model primitives must be computable from the sensed data. More complex object models are being built [8] but they are of limited power unless the sensing systems can uncover the structural primitives and relationships they contain. The approach used here allows complex and rich models of objects that extends the kinds of generic objects that can be recognized by the system. This is due to the rich nature of the surface and feature primitives the sensors compute. Surfaces are the actual parts of an object that we see; the primitive computed is exactly this. Holes and cavities are important visual and tactile features; these are also computed by integrating touch and vision. Further, the system described here is viewpoint independent. The problems caused by visual occlusion are overcome by the ability to use active touch sensing in visually occluded areas.

The domain that the system works in is one of common kitchen items; pots, pans, cups, dishes, utensils and the like. This is a rich domain and in fact contains objects representative of many other domains as well. The objects are planar as well as volumetric, contain holes and have concave and convex surfaces. They are also decomposable into separate components that have functional semantic meaning; handles are distinct geometric parts that are used for grasping, a cup's central cavity is used to hold liquids, a spout allows one to pour a liquid, a lid covers a cavity. By basing the models of these objects on geometry and topology the system is extensible beyond this domain. The objects are modeled in a hierarchical manner which allows the matching process to proceed at different levels with support or inhibition from higher or lower levels of model matching.

Figure 1 is an overview of the system. The vision system consists of a pair of stereo mounted CCD cameras. They are mounted on a 4 DOF camera frame (X, Y, pan, tilt) under computer control. The tactile system consists of a one fingered tactile sensor attached to the wrist of a PUMA 560 robot. The control module is the overall supervisor of the system. It is responsible for guiding and directing the vision and tactile sensing modules. It also communicates with the model data base during the recognition cycle as it tries to interpret the scene. It is able to use both low level reasoning about sensory data and high level reasoning about object structure to accomplish this task. Both kinds of reasoning are needed and the system's ability to toggle between the two kinds of reasoning makes it powerful. The high level reasoning allows us to use the object model as a guide for further active sensing which is accomplished by the low level sensing modules.

The recognition cycle consists of initial low level sensing which limits the number of object models consistent with the sensed data. The low level sensing elements provide data for local surface and feature matches which are constrained by relational criteria embedded in the models. The system is able to eliminate models that lack the structure uncovered by the low level sensing elements. The system then invokes an object model that is globally consistent with the sensed data and proceeds to verify this model by further active sensing. Verification is done at different levels (component, feature, surface, patch) and according to different confidence measures at each level. The remaining sections of this paper are a detailed explanation of the various parts of the system.

2.   STRUCTURE OF THE OBJECT MODELS

Objects are modeled as collections of surfaces, features and relations, organized into four distinct hierarchic levels. A hierarchic model allows us to do matching on many different levels, allowing support or inhibition for a match from lower and higher levels. It also allows us to nicely separate the low level or bottom up kinds of sensing from the top down or knowledge driven sensing.

The four levels of the model are the object level, the component/feature level, the surface level, and the patch level. Figure 2 is a partial description of the model of a coffee mug. The details of the model are described below.

2.1.   OBJECT LEVEL

The top level of the hierarchy is composed of a list of all object nodes in the data base. An object node corresponds to an instance of a single rigid object. Associated with this node is a list containing a bounding box description of the object and a list of all the components (subparts) and features of this object which make up the next level of the hierarchy. For gross shape classification, a bounding box volumetric description of the object is included. The bounding box is a rectangular parallelepiped whose size is determined by the maximum extents of the object in the X, Y and Z directions of the model coordinate system. A complexity attribute is also included for each object which is a measure of the number of features and components that comprise an object.

2.2.   COMPONENT/FEATURE LEVEL

The second level of the model is the component/feature level. Each object consists of a number of component (subpart) nodes that are the result of a functional *and* geometric decomposition of an object. The components of a coffee mug are the body of the mug, the bottom of the mug, and the handle. A teapot consists of a body, bottom, spout, handle and lid. They are the major subdivisions of an object, able to be recognized both geometrically and functionally. Each component also has an attribute list consisting of its bounding box, surface area, and priority. The priority field is an aid for recognition in which the components are ordered as to their likelihood of being sensed. High priorities are assigned large components or isolated components in space that protrude (handles, spouts). The protruding parts may show up as outliers from the vision analysis. Obscured components, such as a coffee mug bottom when in a normal pose, are assigned lower priorities. The priority is used to aid the matching probabilistically. If the object is in a regular pose, then certain parts of the object are more prominent which can aid the matching process. Each component node contains a list of one or more surfaces that make up this functional component and that constitute the next level of the hierarchy.

Features are entities that are useful in the recognition process. The features modeled are holes and cavities. These features are important in discrimination tasks for humans and are able to be sensed by the low level sensing. Holes are modeled as right cylinders with a defined axis, centroid and regular cross section. Each hole node contains the hole's axis vector, centroid vector, and a boundary curve that contains the cross section. This curve also encloses a two dimensional area (a "slice" through the hole). The hole node contains the inertial axes of this 2D slice computed from its central moments. By defining holes in this manner, we are treating them as a negative volumetric entity, which has implications in matching. Volumetric elements have an object centered coordinate system that contains an invariant set of orthogonal axes (inertial axes). By discovering such entities and computing these axes, transformations between model and world coordinates can be effected which is a requirement of viewpoint independent matching.

Cavities are features that are similar to holes but are not completely surrounded by surfaces. Cavities may only be entered from one direction while holes can be entered from either end along their axis. An example is the well of the coffee mug where the liquid is poured. These features are modeled as containing an axis vector, a depth, a bottom point and a boundary curve. The boundary curve is closed as in a hole, allowing for a computation of inertial axes for the cavity opening.

2.3.   SURFACE LEVEL

The surface level consists of surface nodes that embody the constituent surfaces of a component of the object. The objects are modeled as collections of surfaces. The sensing elements that are used are vision and touch both of which sense surface information. Each surface contains attributes such as bounding box, surface area, a flag indicating whether the surface is closed or not and a symbolic description of the surface such as planar, cylindrical or curved. The surfaces are decomposed according to continuity constraints. Each surface is a smooth entity containing no surface discontinuities. The surfaces contain a list of the actual bicubic surface patches that comprise this surface.

2.4.   PATCH LEVEL

Each surface is a smooth entity represented by a grid of bicubic spline surfaces that retain C2 continuity on the composite surface [9]. Each patch contains its parametric description as well as an attribute list for the patch. Patch attributes include, surface area, mean normal vector [10], symbolic form (planar, cylindrical, curved) and bounding box. Patches constitute the lowest local matching level in the system. The patches themselves are represented in matrix form as a matrix of coefficients for a Coons' patch.

2.5.   RELATIONAL CONSTRAINTS

It is not enough to model an object as a collection of geometric attributes. One of the more powerful approaches to recognition is the ability to model relationships between object components and to successfully sense them. The relational constraints between geometric entities place strong bounds on potential matches. The matching process is in many ways a search for consistency between the sensed data and the model data. Relational consistency enforces a firm criteria that allows incorrect matches to be rejected. This is especially true when the relational criteria is based on three dimensional entities which exist in the physical scene as opposed to two dimensional projective relationships which vary with viewpoint.

In keeping with the hierarchical nature of the model, relationships exist on many levels of the model. The first level at which relational information is included is the component level. Each component contains a list of adjacent components, where adjacency is simple physical adjacency between components. The features (holes and cavities) also contain a list of the components that comprise their cross sectional boundary curves. Thus, a surface sensed near a hole will be related to it from low level sensing, and in a search for model consistency, this relationship should also hold in the model. At the surface level, again each surface contains a list of physically adjacent surfaces that can be used to constrain surface matching. The patch relations are implicit in the structure of the composite surface patch decomposition being used. Each patch is part of an ordered larger grid of knots that contains relational adjacency automatically. Thus, each patches neighbors are directly available from an inspection of the composite surfaces defining knot grid.

3.   LOW LEVEL SENSING

The sensing modalities the system uses are stereo vision and tactile sensing. There are tradeoffs in speed, accuracy and noise in using each of these sensors. The limitations of the low level sensors will constrain the accuracy of our recognition process.

The sensory data received from the two sensors needs to be integrated. In designing rules for integrating data from these two sensors, there are a few general observations. Vision is global, has high bandwidth, and is noisy. Touch is a low bandwidth, local, sequential process with better noise properties than vision. Vision gives a sometimes confusing view of an object due to the coupling of geometry, surface reflectance and lighting. Touch is better able to measure directly the properties of objects that are desired: their shape and surface properties. It also retains more degrees of freedom in sensing objects than a static camera which is limited by its viewpoint.

The most important difference between these sensors though is the *active*, controlled nature of touch versus the *passive* nature of visual sensing. To use touch it needs to be guided and supplied with high level knowledge about its task. Blind groping with a finger is an inefficient and slow way to recognize an object.

3.1. VISION SENSING

The object to be sensed is placed on a known support surface in an arbitrary position and orientation. It is assumed to be a single rigid object. The cameras have previously been calibrated with the world coordinate system of the robot arm. The stereo algorithm first uses a Marr-Hildreth operator on the images and then matches zero crossings with a stereo matcher developed by Smitley [11]. The output of this is a sparse set of 3D points that form closed contour regions.

These closed contour regions can be analyzed from a connectivity standpoint to form a region adjacency graph. This graph establishes constraints on local surface matches. Figure 2 (upper left) contains the closed contour region analysis that results after the edge finding and stereo matching processes. Stereo cannot provide information about the interiors of these regions, and the tactile system will provide this information.

3.2. TACTILE SENSING

The tactile sensor being used is a rigid finger like device that is made up of 133 pressure sensitive sites. The sites are covered by a conductive elastomer that senses pressure at each site with an eight bit gray scale. The geometry of the finger also allows limited amounts of surface normal information. The sensor is mounted on the wrist of the PUMA 560 robot and is continuously monitored by a microprocessor that is capable of thresholding and ordering the tactile responses at each of the sites. The arm is controlled by VAL-II programs that receive feedback from the tactile sensor's microprocessor. The arm can be commanded to move in an arbitrary path until the sensor reports an over threshold contact or contacts. These contact points, along with their normals are then reported back to the control module.

3.2.1. SURFACE TRACING ALGORITHMS

Algorithms have been developed to have the tactile system do surface tracing. Given a starting and ending point on a surface, the sensor traces along the surface reporting its contact positions and normals as it moves along. There are many potential paths between these two points on the surface of the object. The movement cycle of the sensor begins with contact at the starting point on the surface. The surface orientation can be determined by the location of the contact point on the sensor. The arm then moves then sensor a small distance off the surface in the direction of the surface normal. At this point a movement vector is calculated that is the weighted average of the vector to the ending point of the trace and the vector formed from previous contact points on the surface. The sensor is then moved a small distance along this vector, monitoring contact continuously. If contact occurs, the cycle repeats until the

ending point is reached. If no contact occurs, then contact with the surface is re-established by moving in the surface normal direction towards the surface. This allows the sensor to make progress towards the goal and to stay in contact with a smoothly changing surface. Using the straight line vector to the goal alone will cause cycles and no progress towards the end point of the trace.

3.2.2. HOLE TRACING

Holes are a useful recognition feature that are difficult to find using machine vision alone. A hole explorer algorithm has been developed to find and quantify a hole with the tactile sensor. Holes are modeled as cylindrical, negative volume elements with an arbitrary cross section. They have an axis (the cylindrical axis) from which they can be entered and a centroid which is defined on the cross sectional slice of the hole.

The hole tracing algorithm starts with the tactile sensor probing the region to determine if it is in fact a hole. If the tip does not come in contact with a surface, the region is determined to be a hole. The arm is then moved in conjunction with tactile feedback around the contour of the hole, reporting the contact points of the hole's cross section.

4. INTEGRATION OF SENSORY DATA

The stereo matching from vision yields a sparse set of 3D points that form closed contours. The interior surfaces of these contours cannot be determined from vision alone. To find out the nature of these closed contour regions, the tactile sensor is used to explore and quantify the interior of these regions. Each region has a contour of 3D points obtained from stereo vision. A least squares plane can be fit to these points and the tactile sensor aligned normal to this plane, forming an approach angle for the sensor. The sensor then moves towards the plane, seeking to establish contact with a surface. If contact occurs, then the surface interpolation process described below proceeds. If no contact is found within a distance threshold of the least squares plane, a hole is hypothesized and a trace of the hole's contour as described above is begun. If surface contact is made after the distance threshold, then a cavity has been discovered, and its cross section is traced similarly to the hole.

The surface interpolation process assumes that the region inside the 3D contour discovered by vision is curvature continuous. If the region was not curvature continuous, then a zero crossing would have been seen inside the closed contour region [12]. Determining the true nature of these surfaces is the heart of the integration process. These contours can be analyzed and points of high curvature chosen as knot points for a bicubic spline interpolation process described in [13]. Once these knot points are chosen, the tactile system is actively guided in tracing the interior of the closed contour region using the surface tracing algorithms described earlier. The knots create 4 boundary curves that comprise the closed contour region. Each surface is traced from the midpoint of a boundary curve to the midpoint of the boundary curve opposite. These surface traces are then combined with the contour data to create a composite bicubic spline surface which preserves the smooth nature of the surface and interpolates the sensed data points. This interpolation can be done to arbitrary precision by tracing each surface at finer and finer resolutions. Typically, one set of traces across the surface is sufficient to obtain a reasonable interpolation of the surface. These surface patches are powerful primitives. They are described by a set of parametric equations that allow easy and efficient calculation of surface areas, normals and curvature properties of the patches which are useful for matching.

The integration of sensory data shows its complementary nature. Visual data can be used to guide active tactile sensing for determination of a visual regions properties. Further, this visual region can be extended into a three dimensional surface by the addition of small amounts of actively guided touch sensing.

5. MODEL INVOCATION

The recognition process begins with the low level vision modules in a bottom up fashion. These modules create a list of closed contour regions and a region adjacency graph. This is input to the tactile system which will either interpolate a surface patch or determine that the region is a hole or cavity. This low level sensing defines the primitives that are sent to the higher level matching system to try to instantiate a model consistent with this sensory data.

5.1. LOCAL MATCHING

Local matching is controlled by a set of rules that drive the process. The rules establish local surface matches for a sensed surface patch by finding surfaces in the model surface list that satisfy all the constraints below:

- The area of the sensed surface patch must be less than or equal to the model surface area.
- The bounding box of the sensed surface patch must be contained within the bounding box of the model surface.
- If the sensed surface patch is planar, the model surface must be planar.
- If the sensed surface patch is cylindrical, the model surface must be cylindrical and the difference of the radii of the cylinders must be small.
- If the sensed surface patch is curved, the model surface must be curved.

There is also a set of local matching rules for features:

- If the feature is a hole or cavity, the diameter of the cross section must be within a threshold δ of the model diameter.
- If the feature is a cavity, its depth must be within a threshold of the model cavity depth.

If the local surface/feature matching is also relationally consistent, then the model is considered feasible. All local surface/feature matches must be consistent with the model relations. If a relationship exists in the scene between two matched surfaces that are not adjacent in the model, the local surface matches are rejected. If a feature is found, its related surfaces must also be consistent. By applying these relational constraints to the local matches, incorrect matches are rejected.

5.2. CHOOSING A MODEL

Once the low level initial sensing has been done, a model must be chosen to drive the recognition process to the next stage. There are three possible outcomes of the initial sensing and local matching process:

- No model is consistent with the data.
- One model is consistent with the data.
- More than one model is consistent with the data.

The first case reflects a possibility of sensory error. The most effective strategy here is to redo the sensing or change the view point to reflect new sensory input. The second case is a desirable state of affairs; this one model is then a candidate for further verification sensing. The third case points to the need for further discrimination among the models. Typically, the local matching process with its geometric and relational constraints will prune the number of consistent interpretations to a small number of models (two or three). The ambiguity between models can be resolved at the next level of sensing. In this case, one of the two or three models left will be chosen as the invoked model to be verified. Choosing this model will rely on the object priorities discussed above and the model complexity measure. Each consistent model has a matching measure computed based upon the normalized probability of the model components and features matched and the complexity of the object's structure.

$$M = \frac{\sum\limits_{k} P_k}{\sum\limits_{i=1}^{N} P_i} \times N$$

where M is the matching probability measure, P_k is the priority of each of the matched components and N is the total number of component/features for this object.

The choice is weighted in favor of complexity of the objects, and with equal complexity, on finding higher probability matches. The sensory subsystems are more likely to sense the high priority components and features. This is then reflected in the choice of model that is invoked. An incorrect choice will be found during verification, at which time this model is rejected and the remaining ones are again chosen by this rule.

6. VERIFICATION

Once a model has been chosen, the recognition process becomes a verification process, trying to substantiate the hypothesis that the chosen model is the object to be recognized. Verification proceeds initially on a component/feature level. Some of the component/features of this model have been partially verified by the local surface/feature matching. Partial verification means that a component, possibly made up of a number of surfaces, has had at least one of these surfaces matched at the lower surface level. Any component/feature that has not been partially verified is then put on a list for verification. An important aspect of this verification is using the model to drive the recognition process. To reflect the model in the imaged scene, a transformation matrix relating model coordinates to imaged world coordinates is necessary. The calculation of this matrix will allow accurate scene prediction for features and components.

6.1. SCENE TO MODEL TRANSFORMATION

The transformation between model and scene consists of three translational parameters and three rotational parameters. This transformation can be computed from matched features or surfaces. Holes have an axis vector and inertial axes of their cross section in the model. If hole is matched, these axes can be used to align the model with the sensed hole, thus satisfying the rotational component of the transformation. The centroid of the hole can then be translated to the sensed centroid to calculate the translational parameters. Similarly, cavities are modeled as having an axis and bottom point. These can be used in the same manner as the hole axis and centroid to compute the transformation matrix.

Sensed surface data can also be used to calculate the transformation matrix. The approach is to match points on sensed surfaces with model surface points. Candidates for these matching points are points of maximum or minimum curvature or at surface border vertices. By using several match points a least square fit of the transformation matrix can be calculated [10]. Planar surfaces can also be used to define part of the transformation by aligning sensed surface normals with model normals. Once this matrix is calculated, it can be used to verify that the initial set of local matches of surfaces and features is consistent with the calculated transformation matrix. If they are not, the system returns to the local matching level and determines a new relationally consistent set of matches, recalculating the transformation matrix. If there is only one relationally consistent set of local matches, then those local matches that are inconsistent with the transformation are rejected and the others accepted.

6.2. VERIFICATION SENSING

The verification of the object model takes place at many levels. The top level is at the component/feature level. Verification at this level is done by requiring every component to be at least partially verified or an occlusion computed from the transformation matrix which accounts for its inability to be sensed. In verifying a component, the surfaces that comprise that component must be sensed. This is done by examining the patches that comprise each surface. The center point of each patch (calculated as the parametric center from the parametric patch equations) is transformed by the matrix and projected into the camera space. If these projected points lie inside a closed contour region that has been locally matched, they are occluded. If they lie outside a closed contour region or inside an unmatched region, then they can be sensed by integrating vision and touch as described earlier. If the points are determined to be occluded, then they must be sensed by the tactile system alone. This is done by actively guiding the tactile sensor to these points and sensing the surface normal at this point, which should be consistent with the transformed mean normal for the patch. By verifying patch center points and normals, partial verification of a component is accomplished.

Holes are verified by applying the transformation matrix to the hole axis and centroid and actively using the tactile system to verify the holes existence and cross sectional curve. Cavities similarly are verified by applying the transformation to the cavities axis and bottom point and again using the active tactile system to sense the cavity.

Some components will not be able to be sensed due to support surface occlusion. An example of this is the coffee mug where the bottom component of the mug cannot be sensed since it is on the support surface. The application of the computed transformation matrix to this surface will reveal that the surface is coincident with the support surface.

6.3. CONFIDENCE MEASURES

Verification can be a time consuming and lengthy process as it involves many levels of sensing. Once the component/feature level is verified, a further verification can proceed at the surface level and finally at the patch level. Rather than continue sensing all parts of the object, a confidence measure for each level is established. In the limit, by sensing all modeled surfaces and features and patches, verification will be complete. However, it will not be physically possible to verify all of these parts of the model due to occlusion and inherent limitations in the sensors themselves. Therefore, a measure needs to be established that computes the confidence of the match. One can then predetermine what confidence measures are necessary for acceptance or rejection of a model.

The models used are hierarchic in nature. Confidence measures can be set up at each level of the model allowing acceptance or rejection based on different requirements for each level. At the component/feature level, a measure of confidence is the fraction of total component/features partially matched. We can extend this idea of a partial match at each level by including threshold criteria for accepting a partial match. A partial match at the component level means that some fraction of the surface's that comprise that component are matched. A partial match at the surface level means that some fraction of the patches that comprise a surface are matched. By specifying V_i, a verification fraction at each level i of the model, hierarchical acceptance criteria will determine the amount of sensing to be done. These verification criteria can be global or used on a per object basis, implying different amounts of active sensing for different hypotheses.

One advantage to this approach is that partial matching can be carried out. Since the matching is local with global constraints, partial matches can be made and reported even though a global match is rejected. A further extension would be to articulated parts, where local transformations between components and surfaces would have to be accounted for in the global constraints.

7. CONCLUSION

The system described is currently being tested. The experimental hardware systems, model data base and surface and feature matching routines are built. Work is presently continuing on the higher level reasoning modules. As the number of objects in the database grows, more sophisticated access mechanisms for indexing into the models will be needed.

8. ACKNOWLEDGEMENTS

This work was supported in part by the following grants: ARO DAA6-29-84-k-0061, AFOSR 82-NM-299, NSF MCS-8219196-CER, NSF MCS 82-07294, AVRO DAABO7-84-K-FO77, and NIH 1-RO1-HL-29985-01.

References

1. Nevatia, R. and Binford, T., "Description and recognition of curved objects," *Artificial Intelligence*, vol. 8, pp. 77-98, 1977.

2. Brooks, Rodney, "Symbolic reasoning among 3-D models and 2-D images," *Artificial Intelligence*, vol. 17, pp. 285-349, 1981.

3. Shapiro, Linda, Moriarty, J.D., Haralick, R., and Mulgaonkar, P., "Matching three dimensional models," *Proc. of IEEE conference on pattern recognition and image processing*, pp. 534-541, Dallas, TX, August 1981.

4. Fisher, R.B., "Using surfaces and object models to recognize partially obscured objects," *Proc. IJCAI 83*, pp. 989-995, Karlsruhe, August 1983.

5. Grimson, W.E.L. and Lozano-Perez, Tomas, "Model based recognition and localization from sparse three dimensional sensory data," *A.I. memo 738*, MIT AI Laboratory, Cambridge, MA, August 1983.

6. Tomita, Fumiaki and Kanade, Takeo, "A 3D vision system: Generating and matching shape descriptions in range images," *IEEE conference on Artificial Intelligence Applications*, pp. 186-191, Denver, CO, December 5-7, 1984.

7. Binford, T., "Survey of model based image analysis," *Int. Journal of Robotics Research*, vol. 1, no. 1, pp. 18-64, Spring 1982.

8. Shapiro, Linda and Haralick, Robert, "A hierarchical relational model for automated inspection tasks," *Proc. 1st International Conference on Robotics Research*, pp. 70-77, Atlanta, GA, March 13-15, 1984.

9. Faux, I.D. and Pratt, M.J., *Computational geometry for design and manufacture*, John Wiley, New York, 1979.

10. Potmesil, Michael, "Generating three dimensional surface models of solid objects from multiple projections," IPL technical report 033, Image Processing Laboratory, RPI, Rensselaer, NY, October 1982.

11. Smitley, David and Bajcsy, Ruzena, "Stereo Processing of Aerial Images," *International Conference on Pattern Recognition*, Montreal, August 1984.

12. Grimson, W.E.L., *From images to surfaces: A computational study of the human early visual system*, MIT Press, Cambridge, MA, 1981.

13. Allen, Peter, "Surface descriptions from vision and touch," *Proc. 1st International Conference on Robotics Research*, pp. 394-397, Atlanta, March 1984.

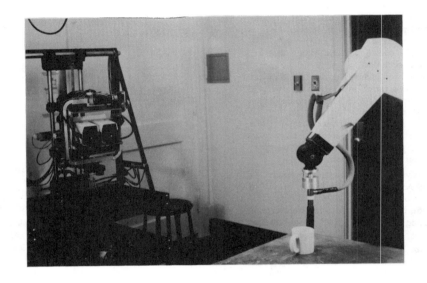

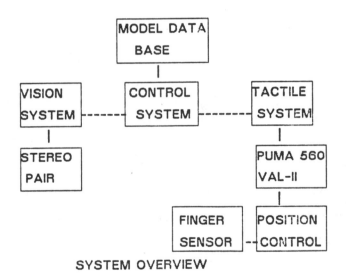

FIGURE 1: SYSTEM OVERVIEW

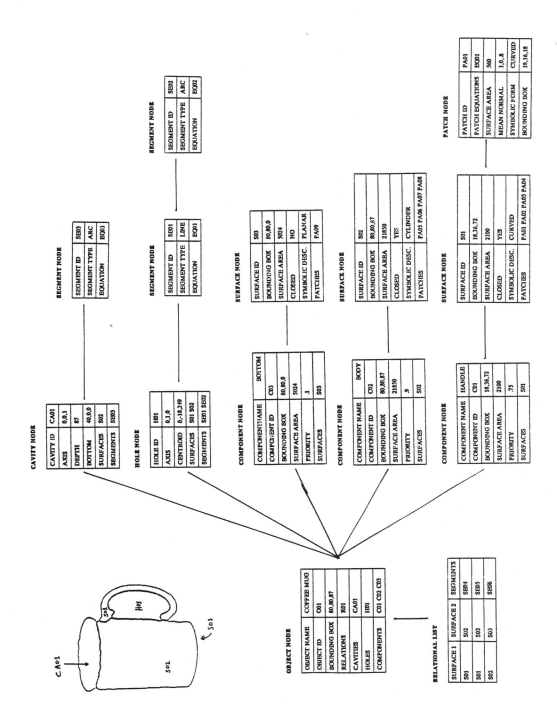

FIGURE 2: OBJECT MODEL OF COFFE MUG

A New Hyperparamodulation Strategy for the Equality Relation[*]

Younghwan Lim and Lawrence J. Henschen

Department of EE/CS
Northwestern University, Evanston

Abstract

Equality is an important relation and many theorems can be easily symbolized through it's use. A proposed inference rule called HL-resolution is intended to have the benefits of hyper steps while controlling the application of paramodulation. It generates a resolvent by building a paramodulation and demodulation link between two terms using a preprocessed plan as a guide. The rule is complete for E-unsatisfiable Horn sets. The linking process makes use of an equality graph which is constructed once at the beginning of the run. Once a pair of candidate terms for HL-resolution is chosen in the search, potential linkages can be found and tested for compatibility efficiently by looking at the paths in the graph. The method was implemented on an existing theorem-proving system. A number of experiments were conducted on problems in abstract algebra and a comparison with set-of-support paramodulation was made.

1. Introduction

Equality is an important relation and many theorems can be easily symbolized through it's use. Important research with respect to the equality relation has been carried out in several directions by many authors. Darlington [2] used a second-order equality substitution axiom, and Robinson and Wos [13,11] proposed demodulation and paramodulation to handle equality. Along this line, Wos, Overbeek and Henschen[14] proposed a refinement of paramodulation called HYPERPARAMODULATION and McCune[8] proposed Horn semantic paramodulation. Along another line, there is the E-resolution system by Morris[9] for the treatment of equality. Later, Digricoli [3] proposed the RUE-NRF rule of inference following the lines of research proposed by Morris in E-resolution and by Harrison and Rubin[4] in generalized resolution. The Connection Graph Procedure introduced by Kowalski[5] represents all possible resolution steps by links between the complementary unifiable literals. In [12], the ideas of the Connection Graph Proof Procedure are extended to handle paramodulation. On the other hand, Knuth and Bendix created a procedure for deriving consequences from equality units using a reduction.

We remind the reader of the following problems

that occur in handling equality. First, equality of two terms with respect to a given set of equations is in general undecidable. Second, few effective control mechanisms for the search and application of equality derivation steps have been developed. Third, equality proof procedures seem not to make use of any high level planning. Fourth, heuristic information does not seem to be easily incorporated into existing equality proof procedures.

A proposed inference rule called HL-resolution is intended to have the benefits of hyper steps while controlling the uses of paramodulation. It generates a resolvent by building a paramodulation and demodulation link between two given terms using a preprocessed plan as a guide. This linking process makes use of an equality graph which is constructed once at the beginning of the run. Once a pair of candidate terms for HL-resolution is chosen in the search, potential linkages can be found and tested for compatibility efficiently by looking at paths in the graph. Furthermore, using the properties of links, pairs of end terms for inner level linking can be found easily. The method was implemented on an existing theorem-proving system and a number of experiments were conducted on problems in abstract algebra.

2. Definitions

In this section, we give the basic definitions for HL-resolution. Any definition which is used and not defined will follow the standard terminology in (equality) theorem proving.

Definition   Let P be a set of paramodulators and D be a set of demodulators. A clause C' is called a **k-para/demod link** (k-pd link) of a clause C relative to P U D if and only if there exists a sequence of clauses $A_0, A_1, \ldots, A_k$ such that
1) $A_0 = C$ and $A_k = C'$
2) A_i, for $0 < i \leq k$, is a paramodulant or demodulant of A_{i-1} and a clause in P U D under the restriction that the into-terms of A_{i-1} and A_i are from the same literal.
3) For each paramodulation/demodulation, the into term of A_i is <u>not</u> properly contained in the replacement of the into term of A_{i-1}.
4) If there is j such that $0 < j \leq k$ and A_j is a demodulant of A_{j-1}, then each A_i, for all $j \leq i \leq k$, is a demodulant of A_{i-1}.

The k is called the **length** of the link. The definition implies that a clause is a 0-pd link of

---

* Supported in part by the National Science Foundation under Grant Number MCS-8306637

itself. The sets of equalities P and D need not be disjoint. Their choice, in practice, is heuristic but at present, for the theory, P needs to be all of the equalities in S. Condition 3), which will be called the into-term-containment restriction, will be of specific importance in plan formation to be discussed in Section 4.

Definition.   Let C' be a k-para/demod link of a clause C relative to P U D and $A_0, A_1, ..., A_k$ as above. If, for $0 < i <= k$, A_i is a paramodulant of A_{i-1} then let E_i be the unifier of the paramodulator and the into term in A_{i-1}. Otherwise, i.e. A_i is a demodulant of A_{i-1}, let E_i be the empty substitution. Then k-E = (... $((E_1 * E_2) * E_3)$ ... E_k) is called a **k-linked unifier** of C' from C, where * is the composition operator.

Definition.   A **partial unifier** of terms/literals t_1 and t_2 having the same function/predicate symbol is a substitution which unifies t_1 and t_2 from left to right, skipping over any pair of ununifiable arguments.

Definition.   A **function substitution link** of a clause of the form $f(t_1, ..., t_n) <> f(s_1, ... s_n)$ v A is a clause D v A*E, where A is a set of literals, E is a given substitution to be applied to $f(t_1, ..., t_n)$ and $f(s_1, ..., s_n)$, and D is a disjunction of inequalities formed by the pairs of arguments not unified in $f(t_1, ..., t_n)*E$ and $f(s_1, ..., s_n)*E$.

Definition.   A **predicate substitution link** of a pair of clauses of the form $P(t_1, ... t_n)$ v A and $-P(s_1, ..., s_n)$ v B, where A and B are sets of literals, is D v A*E v B*E, where E is a substitution to be applied to $P(t_1, ... t_n)$ and $P(s_1, ... s_n)$, and D is a disjunction of inequalities formed by the pairs of arguments not unified in $P(t_1, ..., t_n)*E$ and $P(s_1, ... s_n)*E$.

The substitution used in a predicate or a function substitution link may be the empty substitution, a partial unifier or a full most general unifier. In the last case, of course, D will be empty. In fact, in the experiments discussed in Section 5 we always used partial unifiers, and our program obtained proofs for all the problems tried. The role of the substitution link is to simplify a clause by stripping off the outer function/predicate symbol of one of its literals. The soundness of rules of inference which generate function/predicate substitution links can be derived directly by the use of the function and predicate substitution axioms. In our equality-reasoning system, the above two rules of inference will replace the use of function and predicate substitution axioms. This, in effect, restricts the use of those axioms by not allowing the generation of clauses corresponding to arbitrary resolutions from substitution axioms. However, unlike previous attempts in this direction (e.g., [3,4,9]), we will propose a system in which the rules themselves will be used in a very restricted way, further cutting down on the number of clauses they are allowed to generate.

We now define a new inference rule called

HL(Henschen-Lim)- resolution.

Definition.   Let S be a set of clauses, P be a set of paramodulators and D be a set of demodulators. Let N be the transitivity clause {x<>y y<>z x=z} in the equality axioms, A_1 be a positive unit clause in S, and A_2 v B be a clause in S, where A_2 is a negative literal and B is the set of the remaining literals. Let the variables in these clauses all be separated. Suppose that the set of clauses {A_1, A_2 v B, N} satisfies one of the following conditions:
1) (forward)   There exists a most general unifier(MGU) E_1 of A_1 and the literal x<>y and a MGU E_2 of A_2 and L_1', where L_1' is a k-pd link of {x=z}*E_1 relative to P U D with a k-linked unifier k-E.
2) (backward)   There exists a MGU E_1 of A_2 and the literal x=z and a MGU E_2 of A_1 and L_2', where L_2' is a k-pd link of {x<>y}*E_1 relative to P U D with a k-linked unifier k-E.

Then the clause (y<>z v B)*(k-E)*E_2*E_1 is called an **HL-resolvent** of the set. N is called **the nucleus clause**, and A_1 and A_2 v B are **the satellite clauses**.

The terms of an (in)equality in A_1, A_2, P or D are allowed to be flipped if necessary to match. In particular, paramodulation proceeds from either side of any equality in P. Further this definition can be extended in such a way that A_1 is an arbitrary clause in S. We can also allow A_2 to be positive and link to y<>z in N, or A_1 to link to y<>z, etc. For the rest of this paper, however, we use the definition as given above.

Definition.   Given a set S of clauses, a deduction from S is called an **HL-deduction** if and only if each clause in the deduction is a clause in S, an HL-resolvent, a regular resolvent or a function or predicate substitution link of an HL-resolvent.

Definition.   An HL-deduction of the empty clause from S is called an **HL-refutation** of S.

Example 1

Consider the E-unsatisfiable set of clauses:

1. k<>g(a)   2. f(h(b),c)=a
3. d=h(b)   4. e=c
5. k=l   6. i=f(d,e)
7. l=g(i)

An HL-refutation looks like:

```
2)        x<>y        y<>z        x=z
                     res.
    [6.f(d,e)=i]  i<>z    f(d,e)=z
                                  2.d=h(b)

               i<>z    f(h(b),e)=z
                                  4.e=c

               i<>z    f(h(b),c)=z
                               2.f(h(b),c)=a

               i<>z        a=z
                            res.

               i<>i    [CL2: a<>i]
                   unit conflict
                       proof
```

Example 2

Consider the theorem if $x*x=e$ then $f(y,z)=f(z,y)$ in the group theory.

```
1) f(e,x)=x                2) f(x,e)=x
3) f(g(x),x)=e             4) f(x,g(x))=e
5) f(f(x,y),z)=f(x,f(y,z)) 6) f(x,x)=e
7) f(a,b)<>f(b,a)
```

An HL-refutation looks like;

```
1)    u<>v          v<>w          u=w
          res.
     [5.]  f(x,f(y,z))<>w  f(f(x,y),z)=w
                                     6.f(u,u)=e

           f(x,f(x,z))<>w      f(e,z)=w
                                    1.f(e,u)=u

           f(x,f(x,z))<>w       z=w
                                 res.

     f(x,f(x,f(b,a)))<>f(a,b)   [7'.]
                             ft sub. link
           CL1:f(a,f(b,a))<>b

2)    u<>v          v<>w          u=w
          res.
     [5'.]  f(f(x,y),z)<>w  f(x,f(y,z))=w
                                     6.f(u,u)=e

            f(f(x,y),y)<>w     f(x,e)=w
                                    2.f(u,e)=u

            f(f(x,y),y)<>w       x=w
                                  res.

     f(f(b,y),y)<>f(a,f(b,a))  [CL1']
                         ft sub. link
         CL2:f(b,f(b,a))<>a

3)    u<>v          v<>w          u=w
          res.
     [5.]   f(x,f(y,z))<>w  f(f(x,y),z)=w
                                     6.f(u,u)=e

           f(x,f(x,z))<>w      f(e,z)=w
                                    1.f(e,u)=u

           f(x,f(x,z))<>w       z=w
                                 res.

     f(x,f(x,a))<>f(b,f(b,a))  [CL2']
                     unit conflict
                       proof
```

Comments:

1). We do not allow function/predicate substitution to be used during the formation of the HL-resolvent, but only to the end result. We believe this corresponds to human-like approaches to function/predicate stripping. In any case, it severely limits the way in which these rules are allowed to generate new clauses. Similarly, transitivity is used only as an HL-nucleus and only when two terms have been chosen for linkage. Symmetry is built in, so we don't need to include $x<>y$ $y=x$. But note that flipping equalities is allowed only if it will make some larger deduction sequence work. So we have very tight restrictions on the uses of equality axioms.

2). As illustrated in the above example, we plan to use HL-resolution with the set-of-support strategy, reasoning from the denial of the theorem. Simple paramodulation with set-of-support and without function reflexive axioms is known to be incomplete as the following example shows:

```
1. g(a,x,x)<>g(b,x,x)
2. c=d
3. g(a,f(c),f(d))=g(b,f(c),f(d))
```

with only clause 1 supported. Because the linkage in HL-resolution is allowed from either A_1 or A_2, we can often get around this problem, and the reader can verify that there is a supported HL-resolvent

$$g(b,f(c),f(d))<>g(b,f(c),f(c))$$

using a 1-pd link from clause 3 which generates the function substitution link $c<>d$. The idea is that we reason from a supported clause and another clause, and the direction of the linkage shouldn't matter.

3) Although the above is a cooked up counterexample, the situation is totally different when demodulation is used. Then most normal problems are not refutable by paramodulation using only the denial as support. For example, the first backward reasoning paramodulation step in the $x*x=e$ problem is to generate $f(e,f(b,a))<>f(a,b)$, which immediately demodulates back to $f(b,a)<>f(a,b)$. Since HL-resolution is a hyper rule, demodulation is blocked on all the intermediate steps. A corollary of this observation is that if a k-pd link starts out with a number of equalities used backwards, somewhere in the linkage a non-demodulator equality must be used or else the target term must rearrange the built-up term. Otherwise the entire HL-resolvent will just redemodulate. We believe this feature also matches that of human-style equality reasoning in which people often purposely make complicating substitutions into terms with the goal of being able to reassociate, distribute or some other such.

4). As with other hyper methods, the idea is

to keep only the end result, which hopefully will be a more meaningful one. For equality we believe this may also lead to the possibility of some high level planning. For example, in the k<>g(a) problem above, there are several HL-resolvents starting from k<>g(a). However, only the given one leads to function stripping. Thus, one heuristic in choosing A_1 and A_2 for HL-resolution is to pick terms with the same outer function symbol when possible. Further in the given example, we can note that there is linkage between the arguments, a and i, of the two terms that were resolved, further indicating that k<>g(a) and l=g(i) might be a profitable choice. Such analysis will be facilitated by the use of the equality connection graph to be described below. We have only begun to consider these ideas, but believe they may lead to interesting results. We believe the idea of choosing two terms and attempting to link them through the graph makes HL-resolution perhaps more amenable to such heuristic analyses than other equality systems. In any case the generation of paramodulants is, again, controlled and directed by the choice of A_1 and A_2, which choice could be made by some high level planning process or even human interaction.

5).   Note that we could pose the rule strictly in terms of paramodulation without recourse to a nucleus and resolution at the last step. However our approach emphasizes the notion that we are looking for OUTER-LEVEL linkages, and especially those that lead to potentially useful function/predicate stripping. Furthermore, it provides target terms to be linked.

3. Completeness

The basic idea is that, from the existance of an unrestricted paramodulation deduction, we construct an equivalent HL-deduction. Proofs of the following Lemmas and Theorems are found in [6].

Lemma 1.   If S is an E-unsatisfiable set of UNIT, EQUALITY clauses including x=x and functional reflexive axioms, then S has a refutation with a negative clause as top clause by paramodulation and resolution whose paramodulators are unit clauses in S

Lemma 1 shows that there always exists an unrestricted link between the negative clause and the last clause of the proof in the unit case. The only problem is the restriction of into term containment. We know that a paramodulation deduction tree can be rearranged into subsequences of deduction in such a way that all paramodulations in a subsequence are into one side of the inequality. For example, the deduction

$$
\begin{array}{l}
x <> \underline{f(x)} \\
\quad\quad\vphantom{|} \underline{\big|}\!\!\!-\!\!f(g(a))=h(a,b) \\
g(a) <> h(a,b) \\
\quad\quad\vphantom{|} \underline{\big|}\!\!\!-\!\!a=b \\
g(b) <> h(a,b) \\
\quad\quad\vphantom{|} \underline{\big|}\!\!\!-\!\!h(a,b)=c \\
g(b) <> c
\end{array}
$$

can be rearranged so that the two paramodulations into the right side are done first. Note, it cannot be rearranged so that the paramodulation into the left side is done first unless a new step using g(y)=g(y) is used. Note, however, that each subsequence into the same side will correspond to one or more HL-resolvents.

Lemma 2.   A given clause t<>t' and a paramodulation deduction
$$
T[t_1[r_1], u_1=v_1, t_2[r_2], u_2=v_2, \\
\ldots, t_{n-1}[r_{n-1}], u_{n-1}=v_{n-1} : t_n],
$$
which generates a paramodulant $t_n <> t''$, where
1) The paramodulation sequence in T can be arranged according to the order of argument positions in the outer term of r_i, $1 <= i <= n-1$,
2) The terms t and t1 are unifiable,
3) $t'' = t' * E(T)$, where E(T) is the composition of unifiers in T, and
4) The last paramodulation only is paramodulation into the outer term itself whose from term is not a variable,

can be transformed into an HL-deduction which generates an HL-resolvent that is the same as $t_n <> t''$ within the alphabetic variance.

Theorem 1.   If S is an E-unsatisfiable set of UNIT, EQUALITY clauses including x=x and functional reflexive axioms, then S has an HL-refutation with the choice that the sets of paramodulators contains all the positive equality clauses in S.

Theorem 2.   If S is an E-unsatisfiable Horn set of EQUALITY clauses including x=x and the functional reflexive axioms FR, then S has an HL-refutation with choice of the set of paramodulators as above.

Corollary 1.   If S is an E-unsatisfiable Horn set of clauses including x=x and the functional reflexive axioms FR, then S has an HL-refutation with the same choice of the set of paramodulators as above.

While completeness is important to know about, it is more important in our view to develop effective proof procedures. Thus, for example, we would not recommend using FR(Function Reflexive) axioms. We have seen in Section 2, Comment 2 that for some cases where FR is required in simple paramodulation, HL-resolution proofs exist without FR because we are allowed to link either forward or backward. Whether HL-resolution is complete without FR (perhaps with some other restrictions relaxed) remains open. However, in practice we do not recommend using them.

Also we believe that in practice P and D will not be chosen to be both all of S. Again, we do not have a theory as to how they may be restricted and still maintain completeness. Indeed we are only beginning to consider practical aspects of choosing P and D. This is an area for considerable further study and experimentation.

Finally, we note that the use of HL-resolution (or any paramodulation rule) with only the negative clause as support eliminates the generation of positive equalities. This may not be advantageous in view of the effective use of new demodulators in [10]. We have not experimented with the generation of HL-resolvents in which A_1 and A_2 are both positive. This also is an area for considerable further investigation.

4. Plans for k-pd Linking

Clearly a major part of HL-resolution is to determine if there is one or more k-pd links between the chosen target terms. The restrictions on and properties of k-pd links suggest the use of an equality graph to aid in finding links, very much like regular connection graphs are used in finding resolutions. The basic idea is to form a graph at the beginning of the run in which terms that could potentially paramodulate at the outer level are connected and the corresponding unifiers are formed. Then two candidate terms for HL-resolution can be attached to the graph. Paths of length less than the bound for k which connect both the outer terms and inner terms can then be easily found and the corresponding set of unifiers tested for compatibility as in [1].

We now present some definitions leading up to such a graph mechanism and the formation of HL-resolution plans for a pair of terms.

Definition. Let P be a set of positive unit equality clauses. An **equality graph** (EG) is a graph such that
1) To every left or right term of equality, there corresponds a node whose label is the term.
2) Two nodes are connected if their terms are unifiable after renaming variables so that different clauses contain different variables. The most general unifier is the label of the edge.
3) Nodes corresponding to terms which belong to the same equality clause are grouped together in the graph. The clause number is the label of the group.

Since a group of nodes in an equality graph consists of only two nodes, the notation $i+$ (or $i-$) will be used to represent the right (or left) node in the group i, $-i+$ (or $-i-$) represents the node $i-$ (or $i+$) which is the other term in the group i, and $i*$ denotes $i+$ or $i-$.

Definition. A **linking path** between two terms t_0 and t_n is a path in the equality graph of the form
$$t_0 -- t_1=s_1 -- t_2=s_2 -- \ldots -- t_{n-1}=s_{n-1} -- t_n$$
where, $t_i=s_i$ is a clause and t_0 links to t_1 and each s_i links to t_{i+1}. The length of this linking path is n.

Definition. Let the linking path between two terms s_1 and t_{n+1} be
$$s_1 \overset{E_1}{--} t_2=s_2 \overset{E_2}{--} t_3=s_3 \overset{E_3}{--} \ldots \overset{E_n}{--} t_{n+1}$$
where the variables in all clauses have been separated and E_i, $1 \leq i \leq n$, is a MGU of s_i and t_{i+1}. If $E=E_1*E_2*\ldots*E_n$ is defined, where $*$ is the operation of compatible composition, then the linking path is said to be **link compatible** and E is called a link compatible unifier.

Definition. Let a term $f(t_1, t_2, \ldots, t_n)$ have a link compatible unifier E_i for each argument t_i to a k-pd link t_i', $1 \leq i \leq n$. If $E=E_1*E_2*\ldots*E_n$ is defined, then the term $f(t_1, t_2, \ldots, t_n)$ is said to be **term compatible** and E is called a term compatible unifier.

Definition. An **augmented equality graph** of a term t for a term s, denoted by AEG(t,s), is an equality graph as above with the two extra groups of nodes {t} and {s}, where,
1) All nodes in EG whose labels are unifiable with t or s are connected to t or s, respectively, with a labeled link labeling the unifier.
2) All nodes in EG whose labels have the same outer function symbol as t but are not unifiable with t are connected to t with an unlabeled link.

The labeled link is used for checking compatibility in finding a paramodulation sequence and the unlabeled link is for finding inner level target terms, which will be described below.

Definition. A plan Plan(t,s) of a term t for a term s is a set of tuples of the form $(\langle I_1*, I_2*, \ldots, I_k* \rangle, k-E, r)$, where,
1) In the sequence $\langle I_1*, I_2*, \ldots, I_k* \rangle$, I_j, $1 \leq j \leq k$, is a group number and I_j* represents a left or right node (from term) depending on the sign of $*$.
2) k-E is the composition of the labels (unifiers) of the linking path $s -- I_1 -- I_2 -- \ldots -- I_k$ from s to I_k.
3) r is the term formed by paramodulating the paramodulators in the sequence $\langle I_1*, I_2*, \ldots, I_k* \rangle$ into the term s in their order.

Rather than trying to build k-pd links of a term t which are to be resolved with a term s in an ad hoc way, a systematic method like target-driven search can be devised using the restrictions on the k-pd link. Since a k-pd link has the restriction of into-term containment, any into term should not be properly contained in any proceeding into-term.

Suppose we try to find all k-pd links of a term t which are to be resolved with a term s.
1) case 1: t is a constant or variable.
In this case, the linking process is simple due to the into-term-containment restriction. In fact, all the position vectors of the into-terms in the sequence are the same, i.e., the outer level position vector.
2) case 2: t is complex term
Let t be a complex term $f(t_1,t_2,\ldots,t_n)$. There will in general be many into term candidates at the beginning of the linking process. Furthermore, it seems difficult to know when to terminate an inner level linking sequence. We propose a method, which we call target-driven search, that works backwards from s rather than forwards from t.
Step 1)
Try to find outer level links of s which are either unifiable with t or have the same function symbol as t and are of length no greater than the bound on k.

Step 2)
Let s' be one of the outer level links of s.

Subcase 1): s' is unifiable with $f(t_1,t_2,...,t_n)$. Then, by the compatibility of unifiers on the k-pd link, there exists a k-pd link of t on the path t--s'--...--s. Therefore we have found a k-pd link.

Subcase 2): s' is not unifiable with t but has the same function symbol f. Let s' be of the form $f(s_1,s_2,...,s_n)$. Now we can break down the linking process into sub-linking processes of finding k-pd links of t_1 to s_1, t_2 to s_2, ..., and t_n to s_n. The sum of the lengths of these links and the length of the link from s to s' must be bounded, which narrows the search considerably. Assume that all sub-link paths with compatible compositions E_1, E_2, ..., E_n respectively are found. If E_1, E_2, and E_n are compatible, then $f(s_1',s_2',...,s_n')$, where s_i', $1<=i<=n$, are k-pd links of s_i, is checked to see if it is unifiable with t. If they are unifiable, there exists a k-pd link of t on the path $f(t_1,t_2,...,t_n)$--$f(s_1',s_2',...,s_n')$-- ... --$f(s_1,s_2,...,s_n)$--...--s.

Note that if s' is neither of those two cases, there is no link between t and s' because of the restriction of into-term containment.

5. Implementation and Experimentation

We have implemented HL-resolution on NUTS (Northwestern University Theorem-proving System). NUTS is a programmable, interactive theorem proving system based on LMA (Logic Machine Architecture) [7]. The main part of the additions to NUTS centers on a pair of algorithms, based directly on the comments in Section 4, which generate first the set PLAN(t,s) of all plans for the two terms t and s and second the set PDLINK(t,s) of all k-pd links.

A primary purpose is to compare HL-resolution and paramodulation, so we didn't try any open problems yet but included problems from group theory and ring theory.

In the experiments reported on below, we made several restrictions. In linking process, no paramodulation was allowed from or into variables, as is the standard in most paramodulation experiments. Since HL-resolution may generate an HL-resolvent using 0-pd link, in the case that one of from-term or to_term happens to be a variable, the HL-resolvent is, in fact, a paramodulant genetated by paramodulation from or into a variable. But that is not a severe problem because it is allowed only from or into outer level term. We placed a bound on k in such a way that we did't allow more than 1 paramodulation at a position. An interesting restriction is to not allow the same paramodulator to be used at **the same position** more than once in the link. Of course, we did not use the functional reflexive axioms. As remarked above, it is an open question as to the effect of these restrictions on completeness. However, they are necessary for effectiveness in both HL and regular paramodulation.

In all experiments, we picked the clause with the fewest number of symbols for the next step. In the case of HL-resolution, we always

worked backward. For the paramodulation runs, we picked some positive clause as set-of-support, usually a clause from the special hypotheses and all paramodulators were applied only from the left to the right side of equalities. The clause used in a particular experiment are indicated in the tables below.

An important comment is that in the HL experiments we did not make use of any heuristics or human intervention in choosing a target term to link to or in filtering the HL-resolvents for retention except in the ring problems. There we used a very simple heuristic - if the outer function symbol of the HL-resolvent did not also occur as an outer function symbol in some input clause, the resolvent was not kept. This gave extra emphasis to the notion of working on outside terms. The importance of this comment is that the HL format provides first a pair of target terms and second an end result that is much more significant and much more like a human level inference than ordinary paramodulation. We intend that HL-resolution be used with heuristics for better selection of target terms and "interesting" results. It is possible that some problems would admit good heuristics for selecting the target terms; certainly there are more intelligent possibilities than to just take the one with fewest symbols or to take any target for which there is a link as was done in our simple experiments. We also feel that there could be better heuristics developed for deciding to keep a clause or not based on the fact that an HL-resolvent is a larger, more human-like step. In fact, in this last regard, one might even consider using HL-resolution in an interactive mode since the number of clauses presented to the user would be significantly less than in ordinary resolution or paramodulation. A user might be able to digest an analyse the limited number of these clauses and help direct the program's effort.

Legend: In the following report of experiments, the experiment **h** and **p** mean HL-resolution experiment and set-of-support paramodulation experiment, respectively. Further, A, P, D, S, and N represent Axiom set, Paramodulator set, Demodulator set, Supported clause set and Non-supported clause set, respectively. Here the axiom set is the set of clauses which can be used as satellite clauses.

Group Theory Experiments

Set of clauses;

1. $f(e,x)=x$
2. $f(x,e)=x$
3. $f(g(x),x)=e$
4. $f(x,g(x))=e$
5. $f(f(x,y),z)=f(x,f(y,z))$
6. $f(a,e)<>a$; $(\forall x) f(x,e)=x$
7. $f(a,y)<>e$; $(\forall x)(Ey) f(x,y)=e$
8. $g(g(a))<>a$; $(\forall x) g(g(x))=x$
9. $f(g(a),g(b))<>g(f(b,a))$
                     ; $(\forall x \forall y) g(f(x,y))=f(g(y),g(x))$
10. $f(x,x)=e$; $(\forall x) f(x,x)=e$
11. $f(a,b)<>f(b,a)$; $-->$ $(\forall y \forall z) f(y,z)=f(z,y)$

Experiments

```
g1hd1: A:1,3,5,6        P:1,3         D:1,3
g1hd2: A:5,6            P:1,3         D:1,3
g1pd1: S:5              N:1,3,6       D:1,3
g2hd1: A:1,3,5,7        P:1,3         D:1,3
g2hd2: A:5,7            P:1,3         D:1,3
g2pd1: S:5              N:1,3,7       D:1,3
g3hd1: A:1,2,3,4,5,8    P:1,2,3,4     D:1,2,3,4
g3hd2: A:5,8            P:1,2,3,4     D:1,2,3,4
g3pd1: S:5              N:1,2,3,4,8   D:1,2,3,4
g4hd1: A:1,2,3,4,5,9    P:1,2,3,4     D:1,2,3,4
g4hd2: A:5,9            P:1,2,3,4     D:1,2,3,4
g4pd1: S:5              N:1,2,3,4,9   D:1,2,3,4
g5hd1: A:1-5,10,11      P:1,2,3,4,10  D:1,2,3,4,10
g5hd2: A:5,11           P:1,2,3,4,10  D:1,2,3,4,10
g5pd1: S:5              N:1-4,10,11   D:1,2,3,4,10
```

gihj and gipj are similar to the experiments gihdj and gipdj, respectively, except that no demodulation is applied to inferred clauses. In the tables below, the number of paramodulants used in the k-pd links of an HL run is given in parentheses under the paramod column.

Results

	proof found	HL-res.	para-mod.	kept	gen. time	proc. time
g1hd1	yes	78	(178)	47	132	38
g1h1	yes	115	(266)	51	177	49
g1hd2	yes	67	(169)	44	111	35
g1h2	yes	116	(269)	51	150	41
g1pd1	yes	na	240	63	30	31
g1p1	no	na	1000	263	969	389
g2hd1	yes	45	(105)	26	61	13
g2h1	yes	63	(139)	30	79	17
g2hd2	yes	44	(107)	29	57	15
g2h2	yes	54	(133)	48	64	16
g2pd1	yes	na	133	48	15	18
g2p1	no	na	600	192	276	104
g3hd1	yes	46	(122)	30	128	29
g3h1	yes	46	(122)	30	129	25
g3hd2	yes	33	(93)	22	54	14
g3h2	yes	33	(93)	22	54	13
g3pd1	yes	na	55	15	13	8
g3p1	no	na	600	132	104	67
g4hd1	yes	44	(122)	20	102	24
g4h1	yes	44	(122)	20	101	23
g4hd2	yes	40	(118)	20	59	23
g4h2	yes	40	(118)	20	59	21
g4pd1	no	na	600	101	58	94
g4p1	no	na	600	116	85	58
g5hd1	yes	139	(376)	57	288	79
g5h1	yes	139	(376)	57	288	74
g5hd2	yes	127	(365)	57	149	78
g5h2	yes	127	(365)	57	149	72
g5pd1	yes	na	104	26	8	15
g5p1	no	na	600	110	63	54

Boolean Algebra Experiments

Set of input clauses

```
1. s(x,y)=s(y,x)              2. p(x,y)=p(y,x)
3. s(x,0)=x                   4. s(0,x)=x
5. p(x,1)=x                   6. p(1,x)=x
7. s(x,n(x))=1                8. s(n(x),x)=1
9. p(x,n(x))=0                10. p(n(x),x)=0
11. s(p(x,y),p(x,z))=p(x,s(y,z))
12. p(s(x,y),s(x,z))=s(x,p(y,z))
13. s(a,1)<>1                 ; (Vx) s(x,1)=1
14. s(a,a)<>a                 ; (Vx) s(x,x)=x
15. s(a,p(a,b))<>a            ; (Vx Vy) s(x,p(x,y))=x
```

Experiments

```
b1hd1: A:3,5,7,9,11-13        P:1-12      D:3-12
b1hd2: A:12,13                P:1-11      D:3-10
b1pd1: S:12                   N:1-11,13   D:3-10
b2hd1: A:3,5,7,9,12,14        P:1-12      D:3-10
b2pd1: S:12                   N:1-11,14   D:3-10
b3hd1: A:3,5,7,9,11,12,15     P:1-12      D:3-10
b3hd2: A:5,11,12,15           P:1,2,3,5,7,9  D:3-10
b3pd1: S:12                   N:1-11,15   D:3-10
```

bihj and bipj are similar to the experiments bihdj and bipdj, respectively, except that no demodulation is applied to inferred clauses.

Results

	proof found	HL-res.	para-mod.	kept	gen. time	proc. time
b1hd1	yes	9	(29)	8	15	6
b1h1	yes	9	(29)	8	15	5
b1hd2	yes	9	(29)	8	15	6
b1h2	yes	9	(29)	8	15	5
b1pd1	yes	na	34	25	4	15
b1p1	no	na	500	181	156	191
b2hd1	yes	9	(29)	7	15	6
b2h1	yes	9	(29)	7	15	5
b2pd1	yes	na	36	27	5	15
b2p1	no	na	600	178	103	89
b3hd1	no	110	(440)	86	194	113
b3h1	no	200	(816)	168	335	165
b3hd2	yes	44	(130)	43	54	41
b3h2	yes	44	(130)	43	57	43
b3pd1	yes	na	99	45	13	36
b3p1	no	na	600	193	221	104

Ring Theory Experiments

Set of input clauses

```
1. s(x,y)=s(y,x)              2. s(s(x,y),z)=s(x,s(y,z))
3. s(x,0)=x                   4. s(0,x)=x
5. s(x,i(x))=0                6. s(i(x),x)=0
7. p(x,p(y,z))=p(p(x,y),z)
8. p(x,s(y,z))=s(p(x,y),p(x,z))
9. s(p(y,x),p(z,x))=p(s(y,z),x)
10. p(a,0)<>0                 ;(Vx) p(x,0)=0
11. p(a,i(b))<>i(p(a,b))      ;(Vx Vy)p(x,i(y))=i(p(x,y))
12. p(x,x)=x                  ;(Vx) p(x,x)=x
13. s(a,a)<>0                 ;        --> (Vy) s(y,y)=0
```

Experiments

```
r1hd1:  A:1-9,10        P:3,5              D:3-6
r1hd2:  A:2,5,8,10      P:1,3,5,7,8,9      D:3,4,5,6,8,9
r1pd1:  S:2,8           N:1,3-7,9,10       D:3,4,5,6,8,9
r2hd1:  A:2-9,11        P:1-9              D:2-9
r2hd2:  A:2,4,5,8,11    P:1,3,5,7,8,9      D:3,4,5,6,8,9
r2pd1:  S:2,8           N:1,3-7,9 11       D:3,4,5,6,8,9
r3hd1:  A:2,6,8,13      P:4,6,9,12         D:3-9,12
r3pd1:  S:2,8           N:1,3-7,9,12,13    D:3-6,8,9,12
```

rihj and ripj are similar to the experiments rihdj and ripdj, respectively, except that no demodulation is applied to inferred clauses.

Results

	proof found	HL- res.	para- mod.	kept	gen. time	proc. time
r1hd1	yes	114	(310)	27	124	68
r1h1	yes	114	(310)	27	125	64
r1hd2	yes	19	(68)	8	27	11
r1h2	yes	19	(68)	10	27	11
r1pd1	no	na	600	112	119	206
r1p1	no	na	600	152	188	170
r2hd1	yes	84	(432)	31	289	66
r2hd2	yes	38	(143)	21	76	24
r2h2	no	240	(794)	146	1050	326
r2pd1	no	na	600	112	119	204
r2p1	no	na	600	152	191	169
r3hd1	yes	197	(605)	98	543	446
r3h1	yes	200	(598)	116	670	538
r3pd1	no	na	600	112	117	213
r3p1	no	na	600	152	187	170

6. Conclusion

We proposed a new inference rule called HL-resolution for the equality relation that is intended to have the benefits of hyper steps and to control the uses of paramodulation. It generates a resolvent by building a paramodulation/demodulation link between two terms using a preprocessed plan as a guide. We proved completeness for Horn sets and suggested an efficient method for implementation. A number of experiments were conducted on problems in abstract algebra and the results are encouraging. But many problems remain untouched. Completeness without Function Reflexive axioms possibly with some other restrictions relaxed remains open. And we do not have a theory as to how to restrict the choice of the sets of paramodulators and demodulators and still maintain completeness or effectiveness. We have not, as yet, considered what strategies for choosing pairs of target terms might be effective nor experimented with different target strategies. Equally important is the question of whether or not a program might be able to select only the profitable links from the set PDLINK(t,s). In our experiments, we simply generated all HL-resolvents possible within the bound on k. As mentioned earlier, we believe HL-resolvent has more potential for developing effective heuristics because of the format - there could be heuristics for picking target terms, and heuristics for selecting k-pd links. Further, an HL step is a larger, potentially more significant step; we feel that it could be easier to predict the utility of such a larger step than to do the same for a series of shorter steps. Whether or not this potential can be really developed remains to be seen.

7. References

1) Chang, C. L. and R. C. T. Lee, Symbolic Logic and Mechanical Theorem Proving, Academic Press, 1973.

2) Darlington, J. L., "Automated Theorem Proving with Equality Substitutions and Mathematical Induction," in Machine Intelligence, Vol.3 (B. Meltzer and D. Michie, eds.), American Elsevier, New York, pp.113-127.

3) Digricoli, V. J., "Resolution by Unification and Equality," Proceedings of 4th Workshop on Automated Deduction, 1979, Texas.

4) Harrison, M. and N. Rubin, "Another Generalization of Resolution," J. ACM, Vol.25, No.3, July 1978, pp341-351.

5) Kowalski, R., "A Proof Procedure Using Connection Graph," JACM 22,4, 1975.

6) Lim, Younghwan, "A New Hyperparamodulation Strategy for the Equality Clauses", Ph.D Dissertation, Northwestern University, 1985.

7) Lusk, E., W. McCune and R. Overbeek, "Logic Machine Architecture: Kernel Functions," Proceedings of the 6th Conference on Automated Deduction, Springer-Verlag Lecture Notes in Computer Science, Vol. 138, 1982.

8) McCune, W., Semantic Paramodulation for Horn Sets, Ph.D. Dissertation at Northwestern University, 1984.

9) Morris, J., "E-resolution: an Extension of Resolution to Include the Equality Relation," IJCAI, 1969.

10) Overbeek, R., J. McCharen and L. Wos, "Complexity and Related Enhancements for Automated Theorem-proving Program," Comp. and Maths. with Appls. Vol.2, No.1-A, 1976, pp.1-16.

11) Robinson, G. A. and L. Wos, "Paramodulation and Theorem Proving in First Order Theories with Equality," in Machine Intelligence Vol.4 (B. Meltzer and D. Michie, eds), American Elsevier, New York, 1969, pp.135-150.

12) Siekmann, J., and G. Wrightson, "Paramodulated Connectiongraphs," Acta Informatica, 1980.

13) Wos, L., G. A. Robinson, D. F. Carson and L. Shalla, "The Concept of Demodulation in Theorem Proving," JACM, Vol.14, No.4, October 1967, pp.698- 709.

14) Wos, L, R. Overbeek and L. Henschen, "HYPERPARAMODULATION: A Refinement of Paramodulation," Proceedings of the 5th Conference on Automated Deduction, 1980.

AN EQUATIONAL APPROACH TO THEOREM PROVING
IN FIRST-ORDER PREDICATE CALCULUS

Deepak Kapur* and Paliath Narendran

Computer Science Branch
Corporate Research and Development
General Electric Company
Schenectady, New York

ABSTRACT

A new approach for proving theorems in first-order predicate calculus is developed based on term rewriting and polynomial simplification methods. A formula is translated into an equivalent set of formulae expressed in terms of 'true', 'false', 'exclusive-or', and 'and' by analyzing the semantics of its top-level operator. In this representation, formulae are polynomials over atomic formulae with 'and' as multiplication and 'exclusive-or' as addition, and they can be manipulated just like polynomials using familiar rules of multiplication and addition.

Polynomials representing a formula are converted into rewrite rules which are used to simplify polynomials. New rules are generated by overlapping polynomials using a critical-pair completion procedure closely related to the Knuth-Bendix procedure. This process is repeated until a contradiction is reached or it is no longer possible to generate new rules. It is shown that resolution is subsumed by this method.

Key Words: Theorem Proving, Automated Reasoning, Equational Approach, Term Rewriting, Knuth-Bendix Completion Procedure, Polynomial Simplification.

1. INTRODUCTION

A new approach for proving theorems in first-order predicate calculus is presented. The approach is based on term rewriting and polynomial simplification methods, and is simple to understand. A key idea is the observation that formulae can be viewed as polynomials over atomic formulae when they are expressed solely in terms of boolean connectives 'exclusive-or', 'and' and constants 1 and 0 which stand for truth and falsity, respectively. In this representation, formulae can be manipulated just like polynomials using familier rules of multiplication and addition; the addition ('+') is 'exclusive-or' and multiplication ('*') is 'and.' Further, the polynomials we encounter are simple because we neither see coefficients other than 1 nor degrees more than 1; these polynomials satisfy the additional properties that for any polynomial p, $p + p = 0$ and $p * p = p$. The method works well irrespective of whether the input formula has a clausal or a non-clausal representation (Chang and Lee, 1973). For applications of theorem proving in artificial intelligence, program verification and synthesis, specification analysis, etc., an interested reader may wish to look at (Chang and Lee, 1973; Robinson, 1965; Slagle, 1974).

In our method, if a formula is to be proved valid (unsatisfiable, respectively), it is asserted to be 0 (1, respectively), and a contradiction is derived. Towards this end, an equivalent set of formulae (polynomials) expressed using 'exclusive-or,' 'and,' and 'true', are generated from this assertion. This is done using the natural deduction approach by analyzing the semantics of the top-level operator. It is checked whether a contradiction $1 = 0$ can be derived from these polynomials. One good way of checking for a contradiction is to use the rewriting concepts to generate a Gröbner basis of the original set of polynomials by suitably modifying the method developed in (Kandri-Rody and Kapur, 1984) for computing the Gröbner basis of an ideal over polynomial rings over the integers. Checking whether a contradiction is derivable from a set of polynomials is equivalent to checking whether their Gröbner basis is trivial in the sense it includes 1.

For the propositional calculus, this approach is a

---

* Partially supported by the National Science Foundation grant MCS-82-11621.

straightforward application of the Gröbner basis algorithm developed in (Kandri-Rody and Kapur, 1984). For first-order predicate calculus, additional techniques are developed based on identifying equivalences among formulae using unification. Polynomials are first transformed into rewrite rules and the Gröbner basis is computed by generating critical-pairs among rewrite rules. The critical-pair generation is similar to resolution but is more powerful and allows a lot more of flexibility; in fact, it is shown that it *subsumes* resolution. New polynomials are generated from the critical pairs to augment the basis set of polynomials to obtain a Gröbner basis. If the Gröbner basis consists merely of the rule $1 \to 0$ then we know that the original formula is unsatisfiable or valid depending upon what we were contradicting.

This approach is particularly useful for reasoning about domains which can be axiomatized using a finite set of equations. Term rewriting approach for developing decision procedures for equational theories can be integrated well with first-order predicate calculus as first-order predicate calculus itself can be handled using rewrite rules.

The proposed approach is motivated by Hsiang's method for theorem proving in first-order predicate calculus based on term rewriting (Hsiang and Dershowitz, 1983) and the approach for generating a Gröbner basis of a polynomial ideal over the integers in (Kandri-Rody and Kapur, 1984). At the theoretical level, the major distinction between our approach and Hsiang's method is that our method is based on the Grobner basis computation whereas Hsiang's method is based on the extensions of the Knuth and Bendix completion procedure for handling associative and commutative operators developed in (Lankford and Ballantyne, 1977; Peterson and Stickel, 1981). Further, we believe our definitions of unification of monomials, rewriting, superposition and critical pairs are conceptually simpler to understand than Hsiang's. At the implementation level, our approach seems to be easier to implement than Hsiang's, as it does not need to use associative-commutative unification algorithm or its variation, called BN-unification by Hsiang, to handle boolean operators. An implementation of our method is underway. At this stage, it is difficult to make any comparison between the running times of Hsiang's method and our method; however, initial results seem to suggest that our

method is more efficient than Hsiang's. Further, it is too early to say how our method compares with resolution or other theorem proving methods. However, in case of propositional calculus, preliminary experiments suggest that our method is more efficient than the resolution-based LMA theorem prover.

In this paper, we give an overview of the approach exhibiting how first-order formulae can be viewed as polynomials and rewrite rules. The method is illustrated using examples. Further technical details and proofs of the theorems in this paper are given in (Kapur and Narendran, 1984).

2. PROPOSITIONAL CALCULUS

Given a formula f, it is asserted to be 1 or 0 depending upon whether f is to be shown unsatisfiable or valid, respectively, and it is checked whether a contradiction can be derived. In order to do so, the resulting equation is first translated into an equivalent set of polynomials expressed using 'exclusive-or' (+), 'and' (∗), 'true' (1) and 'false' (0). (Since $a + a = 0$ as well as $a - a = 0$, we use '+' and '−' interchangably in the paper; we also often omit '∗' among atomic formulae.) This can be done by analyzing the outermost operator of the left-hand-side of the equation; see (Kapur and Narendran, 1984) for details. In many cases, we may able to generate the contradiction $1 = 0$ in the process of obtaining an equivalent set of polynomials, in which case we are done. If not, then the translation gives a set of polynomial equations, say $\{p_i = 0 \mid 1 \leq i \leq n\}$.

To check whether the polynomial equations lead to a contradiction or not, we generate its Gröbner basis (Buchberger and Loos, 1982; Kandri-Rody and Kapur, 1984). Informally, a finite set of polynomials constitute a Gröbner basis if and only if evey polynomial has a unique normal form when simplified or reduced using polynomials in the basis. To generate a Gröbner basis, each polynomial equation is converted into a *rewrite rule*. This is done by totally ordering atomic formulae which is always possible in the case of propositional calculus. This ordering is extended to *monomials* (products of atomic formulae) based on degree (i.e., size) and lexicographic ordering (cf. Buchberger and Loos, 1982; Kandri-Rody and Kapur, 1984). (In fact any ordering which satisfies the following properties will do: (a) $0 < 1 < m$ for any monomial m

different from 1 and 0. (b) $m_1 < m_2 \Rightarrow s\,m_1 < s\,m_2$ for every monomial s .) Under a total ordering on monomials, every polynomial has a *unique head-monomial*, which serves as the *left-hand-side* of its rule; the *rest* of the polynomial serves as the *right-hand-side* of the rule.

We also include a rule $X_i^2 \to X_i$ for each propositional variable X_i (*idempotency rules*) as well as another rule $2 \to 0$. Thus we do not have to deal with any indeterminate of degree more than 1 nor do we have to deal with coefficients other than 0 or 1. There is also a rule $p + 0 \to p$, but this is taken care of automatically in the Gröbner basis computation.

The rules thus obtained are used to rewrite polynomials. From these rules, new rules are generated to look for a contradiction. For each pair of distinct rules, the overlap of their left-hand-sides is generated by taking the least common multiple (lcm) of the left-hand-sides. Consider two distinct rules $L_1 \to R_1$ and $L_2 \to R_2$. Let L be the lcm of L_1 and L_2, so $L = F_1 L_1 = F_2 L_2$.

$$L_1 \to R_1 \quad\nearrow\quad L \quad\nwarrow\quad L_2 \to R_2$$
$$F_1 R_1 \qquad\qquad F_2 R_2$$

Then $< F_1 R_1, F_2 R_2 >$ is a *critical pair* generated by the two rules, and $F_1 R_1 - F_2 R_2$ is its *S-polynomial* (Buchberger and Loos, 1982; Kandri-Rody and Kapur, 1984). If the two polynomials in a critical pair do not reduce to the same normal form (or equivalently, the corresponding S-polynomial does not reduce to 0), a new rule is added from the normal forms thus obtained. This process is repeated until no new rules are generated. The resulting basis is a Gröbner basis of the input polynomials. For proofs of correctness and termination of this algorithm, see (Kandri-Rody and Kapur, 1984) as this algorithm is a special case of the algorithm for generating the Gröbner basis of an ideal over polynomial rings over the integers.

We would like to point out that in order to deduce a contradiction from a finite set of polynomials, it is not necessary to consider superpositions with the idempotency rules; however, these superpositions are needed if a Gröbner basis is to be generated. In many cases, generating superpositions with idempotency rules gives rise to simpler rules which perform considerable reduction.

EXAMPLE: Consider the problem of checking whether the following propositional formula f is unsatisfiable.

$$f = [\neg ((x_1x_2 \equiv x_1y_2) \equiv (x_2y_1 \equiv y_1y_2))]$$
$$\wedge [\neg (((\neg ((x_2x_3 \equiv x_3y_2) \equiv x_2y_3)) \equiv y_2y_3)]$$
$$\wedge [(x_1x_3 \equiv x_1y_3) \equiv \neg ((x_3y_1 \equiv y_1y_3))].$$

To prove the formula to be unsatisfiable, we equate f to 1. Using the semantics of $\wedge$ and translating $\equiv$ into $+$, we obtain the following polynomials:

$$x_1x_2 + x_1y_2 + x_2y_1 + y_1y_2 = 1,$$
$$x_2x_3 + x_3y_2 + x_2y_3 + y_2y_3 = 0,$$
$$x_1x_3 + x_1y_3 + x_3y_1 + y_1y_3 = 1.$$

Transforming these into rewrite rules using the ordering $x_1 > x_2 > x_3 > y_1 > y_2 > y_3$ on propositional variables which induces an ordering on products of propositional variables based on size and lexicographic ordering, we get

1. $x_1x_2 \to x_1y_2 + x_2y_1 + y_1y_2 + 1$
2. $x_2x_3 \to x_3y_2 + x_2y_3 + y_2y_3$
3. $x_1x_3 \to x_1y_3 + x_3y_1 + y_1y_3 + 1$

We cannot use these rules to reduce each other. So, we generate new rules by superposing these rules on each other. Overlapping rules 1 and 2, we obtain a product $x_1 x_2 x_3$ on which rules 1 and 2 can be applied.

$$x_1 x_2 x_3$$
$$\swarrow \qquad\qquad \searrow$$
$$x_1x_3y_2 + x_2x_3y_1 + x_3y_1y_2 + x_3 \qquad x_1x_3y_2 + x_1x_2y_3 + x_1y_2y_3$$

If we further reduce these polynomials using the above rules, we obtain x_3 on one side and y_3 on the other side and all other products cancel with each other. This gives us a new polynomial $x_3 + y_3 = 0$. The new rule for this polynomial is: 4. $x_3 \to y_3$. Now rules 3 and 4 give us the contradiction $1 \to 0$.

There is a much simpler way of doing the above example by factoring the above polynomials; see (Kapur and Narendran, 1984) for details. Formulae involving many equivalence connectives are known to often give a lot of trouble to theorem-provers based on resolution, natural deduction and semantic trees. In the case of propositional calculus, they can be easily taken care of in our approach because 'exclusive-or' is one of the main operators.

2.1 Theoretical Foundations

Formulae in polynomial form, as stated above, are elements of a polynomial ring over a Boolean ring, $B = (\{0, 1\}, +, *)$. Let $B[X_1,...,X_n]$ denote the ring of polynomials over B with the additional property that $X_i * X_i = X_i$ for each X_i. Thus if $X_1, ..., X_n$ are the atomic formulae (propositional variables) in f, then f is an element of $B[X_1,...,X_n]$.

Theorem 2.1: Let f be a propositional formula with propositional variables $X_1, ..., X_n$. Let I be the set of all polynomials in $B[X_1, ..., X_n]$ which evaluate to 0 for all assignments of $X_1, ..., X_n$ on which f evaluates to 0. Then I is an ideal of $B[X_1, ..., X_n]$.

Henceforth we refer to the ideal I mentioned in the above theorem as 'the ideal generated by f'. One way to check whether a formula f is valid or unsatisfiable is to analyze the ideal generated by f.

Theorem 2.2: A propositional formula f is valid if and only if the ideal generated by f over $B[X_1,...,X_n]$, where the X_is are propositional variables in f, is trivial (i.e., the whole polynomial ring).

An analogous theorem for an unsatisfiable formula f is that the ideal generating by $f + 1$ is trivial. The triviality of an ideal can be checked by generating its Gröbner basis. If the Gröbner basis of an ideal contains 1, then it is trivial. The method discussed in the previous subsection for testing validity or unsatisfiability is based on Theorem 2.2 and the Gröbner-basis-based test for triviality of an ideal.

3. FIRST-ORDER PREDICATE CALCULUS

The approach discussed in the previous section extends to first-order predicate calculus. The following observations are crucial in working out this extension. Firstly, the atomic formulae in first-order predicate calculus play the role of propositional variables. Secondly, quantifiers can be handled by the method of introducing Skolem functions, known as 'Skolemization' (Chang and Lee, 1973). Thirdly, there are in general infinitely many atomic formulae; however unlike in the case of propositional calculus where propositional variables are independent and unrelated to each other, atomic formulae in first-order predicate calculus are related through the mechanism of *substitution* for variables. Intuitively, this captures the forall rule: $[(\forall x) A(x)] \Rightarrow A(t)$, where appropriate restrictions are placed on the term t which is substituted for an occurrence of x (cf. Chang and Lee, 1973). Another technical issue is that in general, it may not be possible to totally order atomic formulae in the

case of predicate calculus (again unlike the case of the propositional calculus); by relaxing this requirement, we also allow more flexibility as well as obtain more general results. The rule corresponding to a polynomial form of a first-order formula thus may have more than one monomial on its left-hand-side. As we show later, if a formula is represented in clausal form (i.e., *CNF*), then every polynomial in the set of polynomials equivalent to the formula has a unique head-monomial; furthermore, it is also sufficient to consider those critical pairs which lead to polynomials with a unique head-monomial.

We first briefly discuss how to handle quantifiers. If the top-level operator of a formula $f = 1$ is a $\forall$ quantifier and the associated variable is x_i, then remove the quantifier. If the top-level operator is a $\exists$ quantifier and associated variable is x_i, then introduce a Skolem function S_i, and replace the occurrences of x_i bound to this quantifier by $S_i(x_1,...,x_k)$, where $x_1, ..., x_k$ are the free variables in f. Similarly, we have the dual case for the equation $f = 0$, i.e., we Skolemize $\forall$ quantifiers and remove $\exists$ quantifiers. We do not need to bring the formula f into prenex normal form first for Skolemization. Instead we Skolemize the quantifiers in place after performing miniscoping so that each Skolem function depends upon as few number of free variables as possible (Bledsoe and Tyson, 1978). This is done by assigning signs with each of the quantifiers and formulae, and giving rules about how the signs change under various boolean connectives; see (Bledsoe and Tyson, 1978) for details.

3.1 DERIVING A CONTRADICTION

Assume that we have obtained a set of polynomials following Skolemization from the original formula without encountering a contradiction; we call this set a *basis* of the formula. Like in the case of propositional calculus, we generate new polynomials from those in the basis using the method of critical pairs and add them to form a new basis. This completion process (which is related to the Knuth-Bendix completion procedure (Knuth and Bendix, 1970)) is continued until it is no longer possible to obtain new rules; In the case of first-order predicate calculus also, we abuse the terminology and call the resulting basis a Gröbner basis. As discussed in (Kapur and Narendran, 1984), the Gröbner basis of a finite set of first-order formulae has the property that every polynomial in their first-order ideal reduces to 0; however, it does not satisfy the other property that every first-order polynomial has a *unique* normal form with respect to the basis. For propositional calculus, this procedure for generating a Gröbner basis is guaranteed to terminate. However, for first-order polynomials, the process of generation of new polynomials may never terminate in some cases. Thus a Gröbner basis in the first-order case may be infinite.

The theoretical basis of the Gröbner basis approach for first-order predicate calculus is an extension of the results for propositional calculus discussed in Section 2; for details, see (Kapur and Narendran, 1984). We introduce there the notion of a *first-order ring* of polynomials which generalizes the concept of a boolean ring of polynomials, the algebraic structure embodying propositional calculus. We also define a *first-order ideal* to characterize first-order inference in an equational way. This gives us a new way to study first-order predicate calculus in terms of equational logic.

We also show in (Kapur and Narendran, 1984) that the Gröbner basis approach is *refutation-complete*, or, in other words, if a formula is unsatisfiable, then the Gröbner basis computation will terminate with the rule $1 \to 0$.

3.2 FIRST-ORDER FORMULAE AS REWRITE RULES

A first-order polynomial P can be represented as a multiset of monomials (which is a conjunction of atomic formulae) in P; a monomial other than 0 or 1 is assumed not to contain 0 or 1. Let $SM(P)$ denote the multiset of monomials in P. A monomial is represented as a multiset of atomic formulae.[1] Given two first-order polynomials P_1, P_2, P_1 is *included* in P_2, written as $P_1 \subseteq P_2$, if and only if $SM(P_1)$ is a subset of $SM(P_2)$.

Two monomials M_1 and M_2 are said to be *unifiable* if and only if there is a substitution σ such that $\sigma(M_1) = \sigma(M_2)$ when considered as multisets. Monomials M_1 and M_2 *overlap* if and only if there is a substitution σ such that $\sigma(M_1)$ and $\sigma(M_2)$ have a non-trivial greatest com-

mon divisor (*gcd*); i.e., σ unifies at least one atomic formula each from M_1 and M_2 (in other words, the intersection of $\sigma(M_1)$ and $\sigma(M_2)$, viewed as multisets, is non-empty).

3.2.1 Partial Well-Founded Orderings on Monomials

Let $<$ be a well-founded simplification ordering of atomic formulae and terms that is closed under substitutions. An example of a class of such orderings is the 'recursive path ordering' scheme of Dershowitz (Dershowitz, 1982). The ordering $<$ can be extended to a well-founded ordering $\ll$ on monomials using the multiset ordering given in (Dershowitz, 1982). The ordering $\ll$ on monomials extends naturally to a partial ordering on polynomials considered as multisets of monomials.

Using the ordering $\ll$ on monomials, we can define *head-monomials*, denoted by $HD(P)$, of a polynomial P as the set of maximal monomials in P. In general, $HD(P)$ can have more than one monomial. Let $TL(P) = P - HD(P)$. Details of an ordering on atomic formulae are discussed in (Kapur and Narendran, 1984).

3.2.2 Rewrite Relation

The rule corresponding to a polynomial P is $HD(P) \to TL(P)$. The rewrite relation $\to$ induced by a rule is defined as follows: a polynomial Q can be rewritten using a rule $hd \to tl$ if and only if there exist a monomial m and substitution θ such that $m * \theta(hd) \subseteq Q$. We replace $m * \theta(hd)$ by $m * \theta(tl)$ and get $Q' = (Q - m * \theta(hd)) \cup m * \theta(tl)$ and say that $Q \to Q'$ by the rule $hd \to tl$.

As in the case of propositional calculus, the following rules are also used for rewriting in addition to the rules corresponding to polynomials:

(B_1) $p + 0 \to p$, where p is a variable ranging over polynomials; this rule is built into the Gröbner basis computation.

(B_2) for every n-ary predicate symbol P: $P(x_1,...,x_n) * P(x_1, \ldots, x_n) \to P(x_1,...,x_n)$.

(B_3) $1 + 1 \to 0$.

The reflexive, transitive closure of $\to$ is denoted by $\to^{*}$. As is usually done in the literature, we often say P *reduces to* Q if $P \to^{*} Q$. It should not be hard to see that for any finite set R of polynomials, the rewrite relation induced by R is Noetherian (i.e. the rewriting process terminates).

---

1. Before a polynomial is rewritten using a rule, it is always assumed to be flat. The result of rewriting however may produce a polynomial that is not flat. That is the reason for viewing a monomial as a multiset of atomic formulae and a polynomial as a multiset of monomials. Henceforth, operations $\cup$, $\cap$, etc., are on multisets.

3.3 CRITICAL PAIRS AND GROBNER BASIS COMPUTATION

To check for contradiction, we generate new rules by superposing the existing rules in a given basis. We first consider a simple case; later we consider a more general case.

I. Given two rules (not necessarily distinct)

1. $hd_1 \rightarrow tl_1$ and
2. $hd_2 \rightarrow tl_2$

in a basis, where hd_1 and hd_2 are monomials, if hd_1 and hd_2 overlap, then a superposition P is constructed as follows:

Let σ be a most general unifier unifying G_1 and G_2, where G_i is a subset of hd_i, $i = 1,2$. Let $\sigma(G_1) = \sigma(G_2) = G$, say, and G_i $f_i = hd_i$, $i = 1,2$. For each such G_1, G_2, and σ,

$$P = \sigma(f_1) \, G \, \sigma(f_2) = \sigma(hd_1) \, \sigma(f_2) = \sigma(hd_2) \, \sigma(f_1)$$

Then a critical pair is obtained by rewriting P in two different ways:

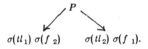

$$\sigma(tl_1) \, \sigma(f_2) \qquad \sigma(tl_2) \, \sigma(f_1).$$

Now, we generalize the above construction to the case when the left-hand-sides of rules are not necessarily single monomials. We have:

$$hd_1 = h_{i_1} + h_{i_2} + \cdots + h_{i_k}, \text{ and } hd_2 = h_{j_1} + h_{j_2} + \cdots + h_{j_n},$$

a superposition P is constructed as follows:

If $\exists u, v : h_{i_u} = f_1 \, G_1$ and $h_{j_v} = f_2 \, G_2$ (G_1 and G_2 could be 1), such that G_1 and G_2 can be unified by a most general unifier σ, i.e., $\sigma(G_1) = \sigma(G_2) = G$, say, then for each such $u, v, G_1, G_2,$ and σ, we have $m_1 = \sigma(f_2)$, $m_2 = \sigma(f_1)$ and

$$P = m_1 \, \sigma(hd_1) + m_2 \sum_{\substack{t=1 \\ t \neq v}}^{n} \sigma(h_{j_t})$$

$$= m_1 \sum_{\substack{s=1 \\ s \neq u}}^{k} \sigma(h_{i_s}) + m_2 \, \sigma(hd_2)$$

Note that $m_1 \sigma(h_{i_u}) = \sigma(f_1 f_2) \sigma(G) = m_2 \sigma(h_{j_v})$. We have:

$$m_1 \sigma(tl_1) + m_2 \sum_{\substack{t=1 \\ t \neq v}}^{n} \sigma(h_{j_t}) \qquad\qquad m_1 \sum_{\substack{s=1 \\ s \neq u}}^{k} \sigma(h_{i_s}) + m_2 \sigma(tl_2)$$

Thus a critical pair for the above two rules is

$$\left< m_1 \sigma(tl_1) + m_2 \sum_{\substack{t=1 \\ t \neq v}}^{n} \sigma(h_{j_t}), \; m_1 \sum_{\substack{s=1 \\ s \neq u}}^{k} \sigma(h_{i_s}) + m_2 \sigma(tl_2) \right>.$$

If a critical pair $<c_1, c_2>$ is *trivial*, i.e., the S-polynomial $c_1 + c_2$ reduces to 0, then it is discarded; otherwise, the basis is augmented by adding the rule corresponding to a normal form of $c_1 - c_2$.

Note that in general there could be many critical pairs generated by two rules as, firstly, the left-hand-sides of rules are polynomials instead of monomials, and secondly, a monomial could overlap with another monomial in more than one way. And, a rule can overlap with itself and generate a new rule in the first-order case, whereas that does not happen in propositional calculus.

It should be easy to see that the rules (B_1), (B_2) and (B_3) by themselves do not generate any new rules. However, these rules (especially the idempotency rule (B_2) and the "self-inverse" rule (B_3)) can interact with rules in a basis of a first-order formula to generate new rules; the critical pairs among them are defined below.

II. Given a rule $hd \rightarrow tl$, where $hd = h_1 + \cdots + h_k$, and an idempotent rule of the form $P(x_1, ..., x_n) * P(x_1, ..., x_n) \rightarrow P(x_1, ..., x_n)$, such that the predicate P is used in some h_i, the following two cases can arise:

(a) There is a superposition of the two rules: let σ be a substitution which unifies $P(x_1, ..., x_n)$ and the atomic formula $P(t_1, ..., t_n)$ in h_i, then the superposition S is $\sigma(P(x_1, ..., x_n) h_1) + \cdots + \sigma(P(x_1, ..., x_n) h_k)$, where $\sigma = \{ x_1 \leftarrow t_1, ..., x_n \leftarrow t_n \}$, and the critical pair $<c_1, c_2>$ is obtained from S by respectively applying the two rules.

(b) For the above two rules, i.e., $hd \rightarrow tl$ and $P(x_1,...,x_n) * P(x_1,...,x_n) \rightarrow P(x_1,...,x_n)$, there is yet another way of generating a superposition. If h_i contains two distinct occurrences of the predicate symbol P, say $P(t_1, ..., t_n)$ and $P(s_1, ..., s_n)$, and σ is a most general substitution which unifies these atomic formulae, then a superposition is obtained by applying σ on hd and a critical pair is obtained by applying the above two rules to the superposed term.

III. The interaction between the self-inverse rule $1 + 1 \rightarrow 0$ and a rule $hd \rightarrow tl$ in a basis results in new rules as follows: If hd contains h_i and h_j which can be unified, i.e., there is a most general substitution σ so that $\sigma(h_i) = \sigma(h_j)$, then the superposition is obtained by applying σ on hd and a critical pair is obtained by applying the two rules to it. These superpositions need to be considered only for rules having many monomials on their left-hand-sides.

3.4 GROBNER BASIS

The above process of generating critical pairs is repeated until the contradiction $1 = 0$ is generated or it is no longer possible to generate any new rule. In the first case, we are done; in the second case, the original formula is falsified (respectively, satisfiable) if it is being proved valid (respectively, unsatisfiable). The Gröbner basis thus obtained provides a way to construct a model for falsifiability (satisfiability) of the formula as an example in the next section illustrates. As stated earlier, the process of generating critical pairs could continue forever for formulae which are not valid (respectively, unsatisfiable).

4. EXAMPLES

Consider a simple formula: All unicorns are quadrupeds and there is a quadruped imply that there is a unicorn. If U stands for something being a unicorn and Q stands for something being a quadruped, then this formula is:
$$[(\forall x)[U(x) \Rightarrow Q(x)] \wedge (\exists x)Q(x)] \Rightarrow (\exists x)U(x).$$

To show the validity of the above formula, we equate it to 0, we obtain

1. $[(\forall x)U(x) \Rightarrow Q(x)] = 1$ 2. $[(\exists x)Q(x)] = 1$
3. $[(\exists x)U(x)] = 0$

After Skolemization, we have:

1'. $[U(x) \Rightarrow Q(x)] = 1$ 2'. $Q(a) = 1$
3'. $U(x) = 0$

Because of $U(x) = 0$, the first equation becomes redundant. Polynomials $Q(a) \to 1$ and $U(x) \to 0$ do not generate any additional rules thus giving us a Gröbner basis. So, the original formula is not valid because we did not derive a contradiction. The original formula is falsified in a 1-element model in which $U(a) = 0$ and $Q(a) = 1$.

The following example is taken from (Chang and Lee, 1973). Consider a formula which states that (i) if there exists an element such that it is the left-identity as well as the right-identity of every element and that for every element x, $i(x)$ serves as the left-inverse as well as right-inverse of x, and (ii) if whenever x and y are in a subset P, then so is x operated with $i(y)$, then the subset P is closed under the function i.
$$[(\exists y)(\forall x)[M(y,x,x) \wedge M(x,y,x) \wedge M(x,i(x),y)$$
$$\wedge M(i(x),x,y)] \wedge (\forall$$
$$x,y,z)[[P(x) \wedge P(y) \wedge M(x,i(y),z)] \Rightarrow P(z)]]$$
$$\Rightarrow (\forall z)[P(z) \Rightarrow P(i(z))].$$

To prove this formula to be a theorem, we assert it to 0 and deduce a contradiction. Translating the assertion to equivalent set of polynomials gives us the following rewrite rules: the constant symbols e and b are the Skolem functions introduced to get rid of quantifiers.

1. $M(e,x,x) \to 1$ 2. $M(x,e,x) \to 1$
3. $M(x,i(x),e) \to 1$ 4. $M(i(x),x,e) \to 1$
5. $P(b) \to 1$ 6. $P(i(b)) \to 0$
7. $P(x)P(y)P(z)M(x,i(y),z) \to P(x)P(y)M(x,i(y),z).$

Variables in each rule are standardized apart. From rules 6 and 7, we get a critical pair by substituting $i(b)$ for z;

$$P(x)P(y)P(i(b))M(x,i(y),i(b))$$

$$P(x)P(y)M(x,i(y),i(b)) \qquad\qquad 0$$

Let us label the new rule as 8, i.e.,

8. $P(x)P(y)M(x,i(y),i(b)) \to 0.$

Similarly, a critical pair between rules 1 and 8 using the substitution $\{x \leftarrow e, y \leftarrow b\}$, after normalization, is,

9. $P(e) \to 0.$

Taking a critical pair between rules 3 and 7 using the substitution $\{x \leftarrow e, x \leftarrow y\}$, gives, after normalization,

10. $P(y) \to 0.$

Using rules 5 and 10, we get the contradiction which implies that the original formula we started with is valid.

5. RELATING RESOLUTION TO THE GROBNER BASIS APPROACH

The process of generating critical pairs of first-order polynomials is similar to resolving the corresponding formulae. Below, we show that resolution can be simulated by the critical-pair-generation process. In fact, for certain formulae for which resolution does not give any meaningful result, computing critical pairs of the corresponding polynomials may still produce useful inferences.

Theorem 5.1: Let $s_1 = C_1 \vee f_1(C_2, ..., C_m)$, and $t_1 = \neg C_1' \vee f_2(D_2, ..., D_n)$ be two clauses (disjunction of literals), where C_i, $1 \le i \le m$, C_1', and D_j, $2 \le j \le n$, are positive literals. Let their binary resolvent on C_1 be $u_1 = \sigma(f_1(C_2,...,C_m)) \vee \sigma(f_2(D_2,...,D_n))$, where σ is the most general unifier of C_1 and C_1'. Then a polynomial form of $u_1 + 1$ can be obtained from an S-polynomial of the polynomial forms of $s_1 + 1$ and $t_1 + 1$.

Theorem 5.2: Let s be a clause and σ be a most general unifier of two literals in s of the same sign. Then a polynomial form of $\sigma(s) + 1$ can be obtained from an S-polynomial of the polynomial form of $s + 1$ and the rule (B_2).

Theorem 5.2 shows that the process of computing *factors* of clauses (cf. Chang and Lee, 1973, p. 80), which is part of the resolution method, can be simulated by repeated overlapping of polynomial rules with the rule (B_2). Thus resolution is built into the critical pair generation process as each of the four cases in the definition of a resolvent in (cf. Chang and Lee, 1973, pp. 80-81), can be simulated.

1. REFERENCES

[1] Bledsoe, W. W., and Tyson, M. "The UT Interactive Prover," Automatic Theorem Proving Project, ATP-17A, Department of Mathematics and Computer Sciences, University of Texas, Austin, June, 1978.

[2] Buchberger, B., and Loos, R. "Algebraic Simplification" In *Computer Algebra: Symbolic and Algebraic Computation* (Eds. B. Buchberger, G.E. Collins and R. Loos), Computing Suppl. 4, Springer Verlag, New York, 1982, pp. 11-43.

[3] Chang, C-L. and Lee, R.C. *Symbolic Logic and Mechanical Theorem Proving*. Academic Press, New York, 1973.

[4] Dershowitz, N. "Orderings for Term Rewriting Systems." *Theoretical Computer Science* 17 (1982), pp. 279-301.

[5] Hsiang, J. and Dershowitz, N. "Rewrite Methods for Clausal and Non-clausal Theorem Proving" In *Proc. 10th EATCS Intl. Colloq. on Automata, Languages, and Programming*, Spain, 1983.

[6] Kandri-Rody, A., and Kapur, D. "Computing the Gröbner Basis of a Polynomial Ideal over Integers" In *Proc. Third MACSYMA Users' Conference*, Schenectady, NY, July 1984, pp. 436-451.

[7] Kapur, D., and Narendran, P. "An Equational Approach to Theorem Proving in First-Order Predicate Calculus," 84CRD296, General Electric Corporate Research and Development Report, Schenectady, NY, March, 1984; Revised, Dec., 1984.

[8] Knuth, D.E. and Bendix, P.B. "Simple Word Problems in Universal Algebras" In *Computational Problems in Abstract Algebras*. (Ed. J. Leech), Pergamon Press, 1970, pp. 263-297.

[9] Lankford, D.S., and Ballantyne, A.M., "Decision Procedures for Simple Equational Theories with Commutative-Associative Axioms: Complete Sets of Commutative-Associative Reductions," Automatic Theorem Proving Project, Dept. of Math. and Computer Science, University of Texas, Austin, TX 78712, Report ATP-39, August 1977.

[10] Peterson, G.L., and Stickel, M.E., "Complete Sets of Reductions for Some Equational Theories," *JACM* 28 (1981), pp. 233-264.

[11] Robinson, J. A. "A Machine-Oriented Logic Based on the Resolution Principle." *JACM* 12 (1965), pp. 23-41.

[12] Slagle, J. R. "Automated Theorem Proving for Theories with Simplifiers, Commutativity and Associativity." *JACM* 21 (1974), pp. 622-642.

[13] van der Waerden, B.L., *Modern Algebra*. Vols. I and II, Fredrick Ungar Publishing Co., New York, 1966.

THE MANAGEMENT OF HEURISTIC SEARCH
IN BOOLEAN EXPERIMENTS WITH RUE RESOLUTION

Vincent J. Digricoli

Hofstra University

166-11 17th Road, Whitestone, N.Y. 11357

ABSTRACT

In assessing the power of a theorem prover, we should select a theorem difficult to prove, compare the quality of proof with the published work of mathematicians, and most important determine whether cpu time used to find the proof is economically acceptable.

In this paper we apply the above criteria to RUE resolution, equality-based binary resolution which incorporates the axioms of equality into the definition of resolution. We select a theorem in Boolean algebra, show the published proof of George and Garret Birkhoff side by side with the computer deduced proof achieved in less than 30 seconds of cpu time. The proof is quite long requiring the derivation of four lemmas and is proven by two RUE refutations of 16 and 18 steps respectively. The same refutations with the equality axioms and unification resolution are 38 and more than 40 steps. Hence, the power of RUE resolution is shown by the brevity of proof compared to using the equality axioms.

The primary pragmatic issue in theorem proving is the effective management of heuristic search to find proofs in acceptable computer time. Whether an inference system supports or obstructs this objective is a crucial property and in this paper we explain in detail the heuristics applied to find proofs. These heuristics are RUE specific and dependent, and cannot be applied in the context of unification resolution.

*This research was supported by a sabbatical grant from the IBM Systems Research Institute in New York.

I RESOLUTION BY UNIFICATION AND EQUALITY

RUE resolution is equality-based binary resolution in that it incorporates the axioms of equality into the definition of resolution, making refutations less than half as long as compared to using the equality axioms. Furthermore, it establishes a context for heuristics leading to more efficient searches for proofs. RUE resolution is based on the following rule of inference:

1. RUE Rule of Inference:

"The RUE resolvent of $P(s1,..,sn)$ v A and $\overline{P}(t1,..,tn)$ v B, is σA v σB v D, where σ is a substitution and D is a disjunction of inequalities specified by a disagreement set of the complementary literals, $\sigma P(s1,..,sn)$ and $\sigma P(t1,..,tn)$."

The above inference rule is in open form since we are free to choose the substitution and disagreement set to be used. Let us now define the notion of a disagreement set:

2. Disagreement Set of a Pair of Terms:

"If s,t are non-identical terms, the set of one element, the pair $s:t$, is the origin disagreement set. If s,t have the form, $f(a1,..,ak),f(b1,..,bk)$, then the set of pairs of nonidentical, corresponding arguments is the topmost disagreement set. Furthermore, if D is a disagreement set, then D' formed by replacing any member of D by the elements of its disagreement set, is also a disagreement set. If s,t are identical terms, the empty set is the sole disagreement set."

For example, the pair of terms:

$f(a,h(b,g(c)))$: $f(b,h(c,g(d)))$ has the

disagreement sets:

D1:   { f(a,h(b,g(c))):f(b,h(c,g(d))) }

D2:   { a:b, h(b,g(c)):h(c,g(d)) }

D3:   { a:b, b:c, g(c):g(d) }

D4:   { a:b, b:c, c:d }

We now define a disagreement of complementary literals, $P(s1,..,sn), \overline{P}(t1,..,tn)$ as the union:
$$D = \bigcup_{i=1}^{n} Di$$

where Di is a disagreement set of the corresponding arguments si, ti. The topmost disagreement set of $P(s1,..,sn), \overline{P}(t1...tn)$ is the set of pairs of corresponding arguments which are not identical.

Using the substitution axiom for predicates, we can now state:

$$P(s1,..,sn) \wedge \overline{P}(t1,..,tn) \rightarrow D$$

where D now represents a disjunction of inequalities specified by any disagreement set of $P,\overline{P}$. In resolution by unification and equality, we can resolve P and $\overline{P}$ immediately to D. For example:

P(f(a,h(b,g(c))))

    |————— P(f(b,h(c,g(d))))

D

resolves in four distinct ways depending on our choice of D. We may resolve to $f(a,h(b,g(c))) \neq f(b,h(c,g(d)))$, to $a \neq b \vee b \neq c \vee c \neq d$, or to an intermediate level D. These are logically distinct deductions since an input set may imply $f(a,h(b,g(c)))=f(b,h(c,g(d)))$ without implying $a=b \wedge b=c \wedge c=d$, so that the former participates in a refutation but the latter does not.

We now define a second inference rule similar to the above applying directly to an inequality:

3. NRF Rule of Inference:

"The NRF resolvent of the clause $t1 \neq t2 \vee A$ is $\sigma A \vee D$, where σ is a substitution and D is a disjunction of inequalities specified by a disagreement set of $\sigma t1, \sigma t2$."

For example we may deduce by NRF:

$f(a,h(b,g(c))) \neq f(b,h(c,g(d)))$

    $\rightarrow$ $a \neq b \vee b \neq c \vee c \neq d$

or reduce to the inequalities of any disagreement set. We call the above the Negative Reflexive Function rule.

In (Digricoli, 1983) we prove:

4. Completeness of RUE Resolution:

"If S is an E-unsatisfiable set of clauses, there exists an RUE-NRF deduction of the empty clause from S."

This theorem establishes that resolving to inequalities is complete without introducing the axioms of equality(for substitution, transitivity and reflexivity) or paramodulation. Apart from symmetry, the axioms of equality are applied implicitly by the RUE-NRF rules of inference.

We describe the above as completeness in 'open form' since we have not specified either the substitution or disagreement set to be used. In (Digricoli, 1983), we deal with this issue and define the RUE unifier and the topmost viable disagreement set as part of a completeness theory stated in strong form. However, in this paper we will use RUE resolution in open form as defined above, heuristically exploiting this form and making efficiency of proof search our primary goal.

II   OUR PRIMARY EXPERIMENT

Our case study deals with proving the following theorem:

Given: the axioms of Boolean algebra:

1. $x \vee y = y \vee x$ commutivity
2. $x \wedge y = y \wedge x$ "
3. $x \vee 0 = x$
4. $x \wedge 1 = x$
5. $x \vee \overline{x} = 1$
6. $x \wedge \overline{x} = 0$
7. $x(yvz) = xy \vee xz$ distributivity
8. $x \vee yz = (xvy)(xvz)$ "

Prove: $x \vee (y \vee z) = (x \vee y) \vee z$
        associativity of logical or

This is a fairly complex theorem for a human to prove and we have the following proof published in the Transactions of the American Mathematical Society [2] by George and Garret Birkhoff:

Theorem: a v (b v c) = (a v b) v c

Proof (Birkhoff):

We first prove lemmas: L1, L2, L3 and L4.

L1: <u>a = aa</u> since: a=a1=a(av$\bar{a}$)=aava$\bar{a}$
                              =aav0 = aa

L2: <u>av1 = 1</u> since: av1=(av1)1=(av1)(av$\bar{a}$)
                              =av(1a)=ava=1

L3: <u>a = avab</u> since: a=a1=a(bv1)=abval
                              =abva=avab

L4: <u>a(avb) = a</u> since: a(avb) = aa v ab
                                = a v ab = a

From lemmas L1,L3,L4 and axiom 7,
it follows that:

$$a = a((avb)vc)$$
$$b = b((avb)vc)$$
$$c = c((avb)vc)$$

Substitute the above for a,b,c in av(bvc):

av(bvc) = a((avb)vc) v (b((avb)vc) v
                           c((avb)vc)) .

On the right side, factor out the
expression (avb)vc to the right:

av(bvc) = (av(bvc)) ((avb)vc) .

On the right side, distribute
(av(bvc)) across ((avb)vc) :

av(bvc) = ((av(bvc))a v (av(bvc))b) v
           (av(bvc))c .

Applying L1,L3,L4 and axiom 7 to each
member of the right side, we obtain:

$$a v (bvc) = (avb) v c . \quad \square$$

It is evident that especially the
latter part of the above proof will be
difficult for a human to deduce. In fact
in human experiments with three mathematically astute university students, one
could not prove associativity after six
hours of work, a second proved associativity in nine hours and the third proved
the theorem in three hours. Hence, we are
asking the RUE theorem prover to prove a
theorem which humans find quite difficult.

The following is the proof deduced by the
RUE theorem prover in <u>24 seconds</u> of cpu
time (IBM 370/3081), using a total <u>7572
unifications</u> in its proof search. We
first ask the theorem prover to prove two
lemmas, xy v x = x and (x v y)x = x,
and then augment the input axiom set
with these lemmas to prove associativity.

2. Refutation to Prove: xy v x = x

$$ab \ v \ a \ \neq \ a$$

	xy v xz = x(y v z)
	a/x, b/y
az $\neq$ a <u>V</u> a(b v z) $\neq$ a	
	x∧1 = x
	a/x, 1/z
a(b v 1) $\neq$ a	
	x∧1 = x
	a/x
1 $\neq$ b v 1	
	1 = x v $\bar{x}$
	b/x
b v $\bar{b}$ $\neq$ b v 1	
	x v yz = (xvy)(xvz)
	b/x
yz $\neq$ $\bar{b}$ <u>V</u> (bvy)(bvz) $\neq$ bv1	
	x∧1 = x
	$\bar{b}$/x,$\bar{b}$/y,1/z
(b v $\bar{b}$)(b v 1) $\neq$ b v 1	
	1∧x = x
	(bv1)/x
1 $\neq$ b v $\bar{b}$	
	1 = x v $\bar{x}$
	b/x

$$\square$$

In the above refutation, we are uniformly applying the following substitution:

"In a left-to-right scan of complementary literals, first unify at the highest
argument level, and then in a second scan
unify at all lower levels."

The refutation is a succinct 8 step RUE proof of the lemma, xy v x = x, and within this proof the sub-lemma, x v 1 = 1, is proven beginning at step 4. The same refutation performed with the equality axioms and standard unification resolution would be 19 steps.

3. Refutation to Prove: (x v y)x = x

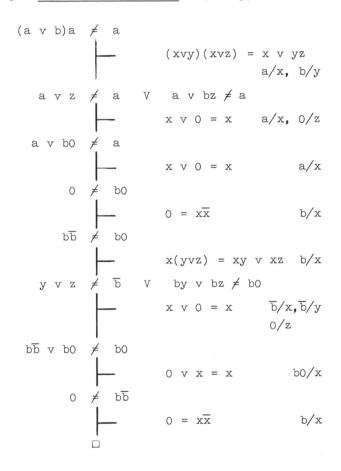

We have a succinct RUE proof of 8 steps and an equivalent proof with the equality axioms and unification resolution would be 19 steps. Note that the sublemma 0 = x∧0 is proven beginning at step 4.

When the theorem prover is given the negated dual lemma:

   ab v a ≠ a   V   (avb)a ≠ a

it produced a 16 step refutation proving both lemmas in 1.4 seconds with a total 1485 unifications in the proof search. This refutation is simply the concatenation of the above two refutations and counting sublemmas, four lemmas are being

proven in a single run of the theorem prover. It corresponds to the work of the Birkhoff paper proving lemmas L1,L2,L3,L4 and is a substantial piece of work.

4. Refutation to Prove:

   x v (y v z) = (x v y) v z

The 18 step refutation may be summarized as follows:

suppose:
      a v (bvc) ≠ (avb) v c

then: (av(bvc))1 ≠ ((avb)vc)1

   (av(bvc))(cv$\overline{c}$) ≠ ((avb)vc)(cv$\overline{c}$)

(av(bvc))c v (av(bvc))$\overline{c}$ ≠ *

   | |
   c   v   (avb)$\overline{c}$ ≠ *

(Ax7,L3,L4)   (Ax7,6,3)

where * is:

((avb)vc)c v ((avb)vc)$\overline{c}$

   | |
   c   v   (avb)$\overline{c}$

(L4)   (Ax7,6,3)

which completes the proof by contradiction. We see that the computer deduced proof is perhaps simpler and more elegant than that stated in the Birkhoff paper. The actual refutation is given in Appendix I.

The theorem prover found the 18 step refutation proving associativity in 22.4 seconds using 6087 unifications in the proof search. An equivalent proof with the equality axioms and unification resolution would be more than 40 steps. Altogether 23.8 seconds with 7572 unifications were used for the entire proof. Cpu time would be substantially reduced by a more efficient implementation of the theorem prover in assembly language in place of PL/1. This is a very fine result compared to other published work (McCharen, Overbeek, Wos, 1976) and our purpose in this paper is to study the heuristic management of proof search which led to the above result.

III FINDING A NEEDLE IN A HAYSTACK

Let us examine the enormity of the task of search which confronts a theorem prover seeking to find the refutations we we have stated. The difficulty of proving theorems in boolean algebra is compounded by the commutivity of the boolean functions $(v, \wedge)$ and the symmetry of equality, so that the axiom $x \vee 0 = x$, has 4 variants based on these properties. We can incorporate the entire effect of commutivity and symmetry by stating for the remaining boolean axioms all variants based on these properties:

1.	$x \vee 0 = x$	4	variants
2.	$x \wedge 1 = x$	4	"
3.	$x \vee \bar{x} = 1$	4	"
4.	$x \wedge \bar{x} = 0$	4	"
5.	$x(y \vee z) = xy \vee xz$	64	"
6.	$x \vee yz = (x \vee y)(x \vee z)$	64	"

Hence, in boolean algebra we are really dealing with an input set of 144 axioms when we drop the axioms for boolean commutivity and equality symmetry. Furthermore, the RUE inference rules implicitly incorporate the axioms of equality for substitution, transitivity and reflexivity and these axioms also do not appear in the input set. Let us assume that we will limit the input set to n clauses selected from the above variants. Let us assess the magnitude of search for the 18 step refutation which proves associativity when n is as low as 16.

The theorem prover begins with the negated theorem with skolem constants, $av(bvc) \neq (avb)vc$, and must find the refutation sequence we have stated. The refutation search is represented by a tree:

$$av(bvc) \neq (avb)vc$$

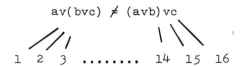

$$1 \quad 2 \quad 3 \quad \ldots\ldots\ldots \quad 14 \quad 15 \quad 16$$

Since in RUE resolution complementary literals always resolve, each of the 16 clauses in the input set resolves immediately with the inequality of the negated theorem and in a breadthfirst search 16 resolvents appear at level one of the search tree. The complete breadthfirst expansion of the search tree to level 18 has 16-to-18th leaf nodes. The situation is actually worse if we take into account resolving to different disagreement sets making the expansion factor at a node higher than 16. Even with the input set reduced to 16 clauses, a breadthfirst search for a refutation is out of the question. The refutation we seek will be a linear input refutation represented by a path in the above tree. A miniscule number of paths from the root will culminate in the empty clause but at least one will when the input set is E-unsatisfiable.

We have stated that the refutation for associativity was actually attained by the RUE theorem prover in 6087 unifications, i.e., the theorem prover heuristically developed a subtree of 6087 nodes in place of the breadthfirst expansion. We wish now to explain precisely what heuristics were applied to define this subtree of search.

IV A HEURISTICALLY CONTROLLED PROOF SEARCH

In order to find a refutation in acceptable computer time, we must drastically prune the breadthfirst search tree and furthermore order the search in the remaining subtree. We will define the components of an evaluation function which heuristically determine which search paths to abort and what is the best leaf node to expand in the search tree. Furthermore, in applying an axiom to a node, we must heuristically select a disagreement set apt to participate in a refutation. The following principles were applied with these objectives in mind:

(1) heuristic ordering by degree of unification,

(2) selection of the lowest level disagreement set not containing an irreducible literal,

(3) heuristic substitution selection,

(4) complexity bounds relating to:

    (a) argument nesting
    (b) number of distinct variables in a clause
    (c) number of occurrences of the same constant or function symbol in a clause
    (d) maximum number of literals in a clause
    (e) maximum character length of a clause

(5) removing redundant resolvents,

(6) frequency bounds for the use of individual axioms in a ref. path.

All of the above principles are syntactic in nature and apply generically to experiments performed. (1) through (3), which were crucial in our work, are RUE specific and cannot be applied in standard unification resolution with the equality axioms. The remaining principles have been commonly used in resolution theorem proving.

A.   Heuristic Ordering by Degree of Unification

If we wish to erase the literal, $t1 \neq t2$, in a refutation, we measure the relevancy of an axiom $a1 = a2$ by computing the degree of unification between literals as follows:

(1) Apply the mgpu (the most general partial unifier) to complementary literals to obtain $\sigma t1 \neq \sigma t2$, $\sigma a1 = \sigma a2$.

(2) Set w=0 (unification weight).

(3) For i = 1,2:
   if σti matches σai identically,
   then w = w+50,
   else if σti, σai are the same function,
   say: σti is $f(b1,b2)$ and σai, $f(c1,c2)$,
   then w = w+20 and, furthermore,
   w = w+15 for each matching pair of corresponding arguments.

This is a simple scheme of matching which computes a weight of 100 when the mgu of complementary literals exists, and 0 when there is no degree of unification. There is also an intermediate scoring between these extremes. We now state our first principle of heuristically ordering the expansion of the refutation search tree:

(1) Apply axioms to a negative literal in the order of higher degree of unification first and set a lower limit SDWMIN below which we suppress or postpone the application of an axiom (search directive weight minimum).

(2) Furthermore, among axioms which satisfy SDWMIN, select the first SDLIM axioms with the highest unification scores (search directive limit).

The 18 step refutation for associativity was found using SDWMIN=50, i.e., we pruned the search tree of all axioms falling below this unification score. In proving the supporting lemmas for associativity, all refutations were found using SDLIM=3. As naturally intuitive, this

heuristic by degree of unification may be in RUE resolution, it, nonetheless, does not apply in unification resolution which requires the mgu at each deduction step.

B.   Selecting the Lowest Level Disagreement Set not Containing an Irreducible Literal

Typically in adding the negated theorem to the input clause set, we introduce skolem constants and when it is evident that these constants are in effect arbitrary constants in respect to the input axioms, then we can conclude that inequalities on skolem constants like $a \neq b$ are irreducible, i.e., we cannot deduce a=b from the axiom set.

For example, the negated theorem, $av(bvc) \neq (avb)vc$, introduces skolem constants a,b,c which in respect to the axioms of boolean algebra are arbitrary constants and we cannot prove two of these constants equal. Thus we should never generate an inequality like $a \neq b$ in an RUE deduction. Furthermore, inequalities like $(xv\bar{x})a \neq b$ which demodulate to irreducible literals are also irreducible and cannot appear in a refutation. This leads to the following heuristic rule:

"In an RUE deduction, choose as resolvent inequalities, the innermost inequalities not containing an irreducible literal."

Hence, in the refutation to prove
$xy \ v \ x = x$, we resolved:

$$1 \neq b \ v \ 1$$
$$\vdash \qquad 1 = x \ v \ \bar{x} \qquad b/x$$
$$b \ v \ \bar{b} \neq b \ v \ 1$$

since resolving to $\bar{b} \neq 1$ would result in an irreducible literal. This heuristic proved successful, not only in all the boolean experiments, but also in ten experiments in group and ring theory (Digricoli, 1981). The RUE theorem prover permits the user to specify as input a list of irreducible literals, and, at the end of a run, it produces a list of ground literals present at leaf nodes of the search tree which the user may scan for irreducible literals in preparation for the next run.

C.   Heuristic Substitution Selection

In the completeness analysis in (Digricoli, 1983), we specify that substitutions may be unconditionally performed in variables at the first argument level, like P(x), but only in variables at lower levels, like P(f(x)), if certain conditions are met by the input set. This leads to longer refutations requiring extensive use of the NRF rule, when the same refutations can be stated in abbreviated form without the NRF rule, if we permit immediate substitutions at lower argument levels. In fact, it occurs in experiments performed that the following maximum unification is the refutation substitution:

> "In a left-to-right scan of complementary literals, first unify at the highest argument level, and then in a second scan unify at all lower levels."

Note that we have given priority to substituting at the first argument level as specified by the completeness theory. However, the above substitution selection which enhances the efficiency of finding proofs, is not universally compatible with RUE completeness and we show this in (Digricoli, 1983).

D.   Pruning by Complexity Bounds

An important method of pruning the search tree is to apply complexity bounds on resolvents which are formed. Theorem provers working in areas of the search tree having little relation to a refutation tend to produce resolvents which are too complex under a variety of attributes. The RUE theorem prover permits the user to specify complexity limits which when exceeded cause the resolvent to be discarded. These limits relate to the depth of argument nesting, the character length of a clause, the number of literals in a clause, the frequency of appearance of a constant or function symbol in a clause (or literal) and the number of distinct variables in a clause. It is true that the ideal setting of complexity bounds can only be derived by knowing a refutation. Nonetheless, it is important to know to what extent the proof search is contracted by applying complexity bounds. Experiments show that it is a good heuristic to use tight bounds to begin with (possibly derived from examining proofs in prior work with the theorem prover) and to gradually relax these bounds. The experimental results in this paper are first stated by applying complexity limits which are a profile of the refutation derived. We then suspend all use of these bounds, to determine the degradation of search which occurs. Both sets of results turn out to be favorable.

V   EXPERIMENTAL RESULTS

	Steps in RUE Proof	Run 1 - with complexity bounds		Run 2 - without complexity bounds	
		CPU Time seconds	Total Unif.	CPU Time seconds	Total Unif.
B1: $x \vee 1 = 1$	5(11)	0.155	183	0.508	558
B2: $x \wedge 0 = 0$	5(11)	0.173	220	0.607	663
B3: $xy \vee x = x$	8(19)	0.654	724	0.964	1034
B4: $(xvy)x = x$	8(19)	0.647	773	0.868	1020
B1∧B2∧B3∧B4	16(38)	1.401	1485	3.008	2855
B5: $xv(yvz) = (xvy)vz$	18(40+)	22.431	6087	70.705	18727

(1)   Under length of proof, 5(11) denotes that the 5 step RUE refutation is 11 steps when restated with the equality axioms and unification resolution.

(2)   In Run 1 complexity bounds were applied which perfectly fit the refutation derived, but in Run 2 no complexity bounds were applied to limit search. Apart from this distinction, both Run 1 and 2 used the same input set and heuristics. In Run 2 of B5, complexity bounds were relaxed one level and applied.

(3) To prove lemmas B1 through B4, both individualy and altogether, the following input set was used:

```
1.  x v 0 = x              4 variants
2.  x ∧ 1 = x              4    "
3.  x v x̄ = 1              4    "
4.  x ∧ x̄ = 0              4    "
5.  x(yvz) = xy v xz       8    "
6.  x v yz = (xvy)(xvz)    8 variants
```

A complete set of variants was used for the first four axioms but only a partial set for each of the distributive axioms. In resolving with an inequality, the theorem prover first chose from each variant set, that axiom having the highest unification score with the inequality. This reduced the applicable axioms from 32 to 6, and of these only three with the highest unification scores were applied since SDLIM was set to 3. This meant that the node expansion factor was 3 instead of 32 in the search tree and the excellence of the results in proving lemmas is due primarily to this heuristic together with avoidance of irreducible literals.

(4) In proving B5 associativity, we reduced the input set to 16 clauses and introduced variants of two proven lemmas:

```
1.   x v 0 = x
2.       x = x v 0
3.   x ∧ 1 = x
4.       x = x ∧ 1
5.   x v x̄ = 1
6.       1 = x v x̄
7.   x ∧ x̄ = 0
8.       0 = x ∧ x̄
9.   x(yvz)  = xy v xz
10.  xy v xz = x(yvz)
11.  (yvz)x  = yx v zx
12.  yx v zx = (yvz)x
13.  (yvx)x  = x             lemma
14.      x   = (yvx)x
15.  yx v x  = x             lemma
16.      x   = yx v x
```

In this experiment, the theorem prover in resolving with an inequality chose only those input clauses whose unification score was 50 or greater (SDWMIN=50) and SDLIM was not used. Our next experiments will attempt to prove associativity without using lemmas and with the same input set of 32 clauses previously used. This will be an exceptionally long refutation.

REFERENCES

[1] Digricoli, V.J., "Resolution by Unification and Equality", Courant Institute, New York Univ., February 1983, (available through Univ. Microfilms).

[2] Birkhoff George and Garret, "Distributive Postulates for Systems Like Boolean Algebra", Transactions of American Mathematical Society, vol 60, July-Dec. 1946.

[3] Digricoli, V.J., "The Efficacy of RUE Resolution: Experiments and Heuristic Theory" In Proc. IJCAI-81. Vancouver, B.C., Canada, August 1981, pp. 539-547.

[4] Digricoli, V.J., "Automatic Deduction and Equality" In Proc. National ACM Conf., Detroit, Michigan, October 1979, pp. 240-250.

[5] Morris, J., "E-Resolution: an Extension of Resolution to Include the Equality Relation" In Proc. IJCAI-69.

[6] McCharen, Overbeek and Wos, "Problems and Experiments for Automated Theorem Proving", IEEE Transactions on Computers, C25-80, 1976.

[7] Robinson, J.A., "A Machine Oriented Logic Based on the Resolution Principle", JACM 12, 1965, pp.23-41.

[8] Brand, D., "Proving Theorems with the Modification Method", SIAM Journal of Computing, vol 4, no 4, 1975.

[9] Harrison, M., and Rubin, N., "Another Generalization of Resolution", JACM vol 25, no 3, 1978.

[10] Robinson, G., and Wos, L., "Paramodulation and Theorem Proving", Machine Intelligence, vol 4, 1969.

[11] Wos, Overbeek and Henschen, "Hyperparamodulation" In Proc. 5CAD, Les Arcs, France, July 1980.

[12] Slagle, J., "Automatic Theorem Proving with Builtin Theories Including Eq.", JACM, vol 19, no 1, January 1972.

[13] Shostak, R., "An Algorithm for Reasoning about Equality", CACM, vol 21, No 7, July 1978.

*** Appendix I with the 18 step refutation proving associativity has been omitted due to space limitations. This refutation will be given at the conference presentation.

A Many-Sorted Calculus with Polymorphic Functions Based on Resolution and Paramodulation.

Manfred Schmidt-Schauss
Fachbereich Informatik
Universität Kaiserslautern
6750 Kaiserslautern, Germany

ABSTRACT.

A many-sorted first order calculus, called ΣRP [Wa83], whose well formed formulas are typed clauses and whose inference rules are factorization, resolution, paramodulation and weakening is extended to a many sorted calculus ΣRP^x with polymorphic functions (overloading). It is assumed that the sort structure is a finite partially ordered set with a greatest element. It is shown, that this extended calculus is sound and complete, provided the functional reflexivity axioms are present. It is also shown, that unification of terms containing polymorphic functions is in general finitary, i.e. the set of most general unifiers may contain more than one element, but at most finitely many. We give a natural condition for the signature (the sort structure), such that the set of most general unifiers is always at most a singleton provided this condition holds.

1. Introduction.

The advantages of a many-sorted calculus in automated reasoning systems are well known [Hay71, Hen72, Wa83, GM84, GM85, Co83, CD83, Ob62] , a fact that was also noticed in logical programming [MO84, Mi84]:

In a many-sorted calculus we obtain a shorter refutation of a smaller set of shorter clauses, as compared to the unsorted version.

Our interest is in using a many sorted calculus in Automated Theorem Proving, especially in resolution based ATP-systems. The most desirable properties of such a calculus are:

1.) The unsorted problem and the corresponding sorted problem are equivalent, i.e. the unsorted clause set is contradictory, iff the sorted version is contradictory.

2.) The calculus is complete, i.e. there is a derivation of the empty clause, iff the clause set is contradictory.

3.) The search space in the sorted version of a problem is smaller than the search space of the unsorted version (provided the problem has a sort structure).

4.) The many-sorted calculus has as much expressive power as possible.

5.) The calculus should be based on standard resolution and paramodulation [WR73] possibly augmented by a modified unification algorithm. Hence standard reductions like purity, subsumption, tautology deletion, replacement resolution and incompatibility of unifiers [KM84, Ro64] can still be used. Furthermore resolution based strategies such as Unit resolution and Set-of-support should be applicable.

The ΣRP-calculus of C. Walther [Wa83] essentially satisfies these requirements, but can be improved by the additional incorporation of polymorphic functions (overloading). This new extended calculus is called ΣRP^x.

In ΣRP^x it is possible for example to have a function symbol + (sum) denoting the addition of (complex) numbers with the implicitly stated property, that, syntactically, the sum of integers is an integer, the sum of reals is a real and the sum of Gaussian numbers is a Gaussian number. However we do not allow to use the same symbol "+" for say the addition of vectors, since we have the technical restriction, that for every argument position in every function there exists a greatest sort for that argument. Using "+" for numbers and vectors would imply that e.g. 1+(0,0) is well sorted, which does not make sense.

Without this restriction, the ΣRP^x-calculus is not complete in general. (This however could be remedied if either ill-sorted terms are allowed during equality deductions or an extended parallel paramodulation rule is used).

The results presented in this paper concern unification of polymorphic terms and completeness of the ΣRP^x-calculus. In particular it is shown, that the complete and minimal set of most general unifiers for two polymorphic terms is always finite.

Some authors present sort structures, such that the union, the intersection and the complement of sorts are defined [Co83, CD83]. If such information is used in a deduction, the rules of the ΣRP^x-calculus are not sufficient and extra rules would be necessary to ensure completeness. But such extra rules have in general the very unpleasant side effect that the reductions and strategies of a resolution based calculus are no longer applicable.

2. Basic Notions of the ΣRP^x-calculus.

In the following we specify the underlying logic. The non standard part of the next definitions are the polymorphic functions. We assign to every function the set of all domain-range relations, e.g. for the sum (+) of complex numbers we have:

+ : COMPLEX × COMPLEX → COMPLEX ;
   COMPLEX × INT → COMPLEX ;
   INT × INT → INT ; ...

This is denoted as a set of triples {(COMPLEX,COMPLEX,COMPLEX), (INT,INT,INT), (COMPLEX,INT,COMPLEX), ... }.

Definition.: A polymorphic signature SIG is a triple (S,F,P), where

1) S is the finite set of sorts, $\leq$ is a partial ordering on S with the greatest element $\top$. $\leq$ is extended to tuples of sorts in the usual way (componentwise $\leq$).

2) F is the set of function symbols. $F = \cup F_W$, where

F_W is the set of function symbols of arity n with

$\emptyset \neq W \subseteq S^{n+1}$

If $F_W \neq \emptyset$, then W satisfies the following conditions:

- The sort of constants is unique. i.e. $W \subseteq S$ implies $|W| = 1$.

- For signatures of functions W, which are not constant:

  a) W contains a unique greatest element $(S_{W,1}, S_{W,2}, \ldots, S_{W,n+1})$.

  b) For every $(S_1, S_2, \ldots, S_{n+1}) \in W$ and every $(T_1, \ldots, T_n) \in S^n$, $(T_1, \ldots, T_n) \leq (S_1, \ldots, S_n)$ implies that there exists a unique sort $T_{n+1} \leq S_{n+1}$ such that $(T_1, \ldots, T_{n+1}) \in W$. That means that for every $f \in F$ the related function

  $f^x : \{(S_1, \ldots, S_n) \mid (S_1, \ldots, S_n) \leq (S_{W,1}, \ldots, S_{W,n})\} \to S$,

  where $f^x(S_1, \ldots, S_n) = S_{n+1}$, iff $(S_1, \ldots, S_{n+1}) \in W$,

  is well defined and monotone.

3) P is the set of predicate symbols. If P_D is the set of predicates with domain D, where $D \in S^n$. We define $P = \cup P_D$.

4) For every sort $S \in S$, there exists a constant c of sort $S' \leq S$. That means, that SIG is strict in the sense of [HO80].

We use the following additional notation and abbreviations: $SO(f) = W$, iff $f \in F_W$; $SO(P) = V$, iff $P \in P_V$. C denotes the set of all constants, C_S denotes the set of all constants of sort S.

If the set of ranges of a function f, i.e. the set $\{S_{n+1} \mid (S_1, \ldots, S_{n+1}) \in SO(f)\}$ has more than one element, then f is called a polymorphic function. If no polymorphic function is in F, then SIG corresponds to a signature of the ΣRP-calculus [Wa83].

In an actual implementation, it is not necessary, that the whole signature of a function is explicitly specified. It is sufficient to give enough information to compute the signature of a function uniquely. For functions, which are not polymorphic, the specification of the maximal domain and maximal range suffices.

Let V_S be the (infinite) set of variables of sort S and let $V = \cup V_S$. Terms (including ill-sorted terms) are defined as usual. The set of all terms is called TERM. The sort of t, namely [t], is defined as follows: The function [...] maps constants and variables to their respective sorts and is recursively extended to terms by $[f(t_1, \ldots, t_n)] = S_{n+1}$, iff $S_i = [t_i]$ and $(S_1, \ldots, S_{n+1}) \in SO(f)$. We define $\Sigma TERM$, the set of all well-sorted terms as the domain of the function [...], i.e. the terms, for which a sort is defined. The functional reflexivity axioms are the axioms $\forall x \; x = x$, and $\forall x_1, \ldots, x_n \; f(x_1, \ldots, x_n) = f(x_1, \ldots, x_n)$.

Example. Let $S = \{N, NZ, Z\}$, where N denotes the nonnegative integers, including 0, NZ denotes the positive integers and $Z = \{0\}$. Then $N \geq NZ$ and $N \geq Z$. The function + has the following signature: $SO(+) = \{(N,N,N); (N,NZ,NZ); (NZ,N,NZ); (Z,N,N); (N,Z,N); (Z,NZ,NZ); (NZ,Z,NZ); (Z,Z,Z); (NZ,NZ,NZ)\}$. Then for example $[0+0] = Z$ and $[0+1] = NZ$.

Definition. For a given signature $SIG = (S,F,P)$ we say the triple (A,S,F) is an **algebra of type (S,F)**, iff the following is satisfied:

- A is a nonempty set.
- To every sort $S \in S$ is assigned a subset S^A of A such that $\top^A = A$ and for all $S,T \in S$: $S \leq T \to S^A \subseteq T^A$.
- For $c \in C_S$, an element $c^A \in A$ exists, such that $c^A \in S^A$.
- For functions f, $f^A: A^n \to A$ is a mapping such that the image of $S_1^A \times \ldots \times S_n^A$ is in S_{n+1}^A for all $(S_1, \ldots, S_{n+1}) \in SO(f)$. $\square$

By the definition of a signature, we have that $S^A \neq \emptyset$ for every $S \in S$ since every sort contains at least one constant.

Definiton. A mapping $\varphi : A \to B$, which has the properties, that

a) $\varphi(S^A) \subseteq \varphi(S^B)$ for every sort $S \in S$ and

b) $\varphi(f^A(a_1, \ldots, a_n) = f^B(\varphi(a_1), \ldots, \varphi(a_n))$

is called a **Σ-homomorphism.** $\square$

$(\Sigma TERM,S,F)$ is the free algebra of type (S,F) and $(\Sigma TERM_{gr},S,F)$ is the initial algebra of type (S,F), where $\Sigma TERM_{gr}$ is the set of terms without variables.

A **mapping** $\sigma: \Sigma TERM \to \Sigma TERM$, which is a Σ-endomorphism where $\{x \in V \mid \sigma x \neq x\}$ is finite, is called a **Σ-substitution.** Let ΣSUB be the set of all Σ-substitutions. Σ-substitutions are exactly those mappings, which are substitutions in the normal sense and have the additional property that $[\sigma(x)] \leq [x]$ for all $x \in V$.

$P(t_1, \ldots, t_n)$ is an **atom**, where P is a predicate symbol and the t_i's are terms such that $[t_i] \leq S_i$ where $(S_1, \ldots, S_n) = SO(P)$. A **literal** is a signed atom. A **clause** is a set of literals, i.e. an abbreviation for the disjunction of the literals, where all variables are universally quantified. A **ground atom, a ground literal** or a **ground clause** is one without variables. **Instances** of atoms, literals and clauses are their images under a Σ-substitution. **Equality** ($=$) is a distinguished binary predicate with domainsorts $SO(=) = (\top,\top)$.

Since a clause set CS is said to be satisfiable, if and only if a model for CS exists, there is the need for a precise definition of a model respecting polymorphic signatures.

Definiton. A **ΣE-model** for a clause set CS is a triple (D,SIG,R), which satisfies the following conditions:

- (D,S,F) is an algebra of type (S,F).
- For every predicate P there exists a relation $P^D \in R$ of the same arity.
- All clauses in CS are valid under all Σ-homomorphisms $\varphi: \Sigma TERM \to D$, i.e. all clauses are valid under all assignments of values in D to variables in clauses, where sorts are respected. (A literal $+P(\ldots)$ is valid under φ, if it's image under φ is in the relation P^D).
- The equality predicate is represented as the identity on D.

3. Unification of Polymorphic Terms.

For $\sigma \in \Sigma SUB$ we use the notation:
$DOM(\sigma) = \{x \in V \mid \sigma x \neq x\}$; $COD(\sigma) = \{\sigma x \mid x \in DOM(\sigma)\}$ and $VCOD(\sigma)$ is the set of variables in $COD(\sigma)$. A unification problem for two terms s and t is denoted as $\langle s = t \rangle$. The set of variables of a term t is denoted as $VAR(t)$.

For $W \subseteq V$ and $\sigma,\tau \in \Sigma SUB$, define $\sigma = \tau \ [W]$, iff $\sigma x = \tau x$ for all $x \in W$. Furthermore define $\sigma \subseteq \tau \ [W]$, iff $\sigma = \lambda\tau \ [W]$ for some $\lambda \in \Sigma SUB$. Obviously $\subseteq [W]$ is a reflexive and transitive relation on Σ-substitutions. For a subset $U \subseteq \Sigma SUB$ we say U is separated on a set of variables W, iff $DOM(\sigma) = W$ and $VCOD(\sigma) \cap W = \emptyset$ for all $\sigma \in U$ and all $VCOD$'s are disjoint. Note that such a set consists of idempotent Σ-substitutions only.

Definition. A set of most general unifiers $\mu U\Sigma(s,t)$ for two terms s and t is defined as a subset of ΣSUB, which is separated on $W = VAR(s,t)$ and satisfies:

- $\sigma s = \sigma t$ for all $\sigma \in \mu U\Sigma(s,t)$. (correctness).
- For all $\delta \in \Sigma SUB$ with $\delta s = \delta t$ we have $\delta \subseteq \sigma \ [W]$ for some $\sigma \in \mu U\Sigma(s,t)$. (completeness)
- $\sigma \subseteq \tau \ [W] \Rightarrow \sigma = \tau$ for all $\sigma,\tau \in \mu U\Sigma(s,t)$. (minimality) $\square$

Definition. A Σ-substitution is a **weakening substitution** (coercing) [Wa84,GM85], iff

(i) σ substitutes variables for variables and

(ii) σ is injective on $DOM(\sigma)$ and

(iii) $DOM(\sigma) \cap VCOD(\sigma) = \emptyset$. $\square$

The set of all weakening substitutions is called $\Sigma WSUB$. In the computation of a set of most general unifiers, weakening substitutions are used to solve unification problems like $\langle x = t \rangle$, where $[t]$ is not a subsort of $[x]$.

Definition. The **set of most general weakening substitutions for t and S,** $\mu W\Sigma_S(t)$ is a set of weakening substitutions which is separated on $W = VAR(t)$ and satisfies:

- $[\sigma t] \leq S$ for all $\sigma \in \mu W\Sigma_S(t)$. (correctness)

- $\forall \delta \in \Sigma SUB$ with $[\delta t] \leq S$ there exists a $\sigma \in \mu W\Sigma_S(t)$

  such that $\delta \sqsubseteq \sigma \, [W]$. (completeness)

- $\forall \sigma, \tau \in \mu W\Sigma_S(t)$: $\sigma \sqsubseteq \tau \, [W] \Rightarrow \sigma = \tau$. (minimality) $\square$

This definition is of course only useful for terms , which are ill-sorted or for terms t where [t] is not a subsort of S and the outermost function symbol of t is polymorphic.

The following theorem is valid in the ΣRP-calculus [Wa83,Wa84] and can be extended to ΣRP^{π}.

<u>Theorem 1.</u> [Sch85a]. Let $t \in TERM$ and $S \in \mathbf{S}$. If there exists a $\theta \in \Sigma SUB$ such that $[\theta t] \leq S$, then $\mu W\Sigma_S(t)$ exists, it is not empty and it is always finite.

An immediate consequence is:

<u>Theorem 2.</u> For unifiable x and t the set $\mu U\Sigma(x,t)$ exists, is not empty and finite. $\square$

The proof follows from the fact ,that $\mu U\Sigma(x,t) = \{\sigma \circ \{x \leftarrow \sigma t\} \mid \sigma \in \mu W\Sigma_{[x]}(t)\}$, if $x \notin VAR(t)$.

<u>Example.</u> The following example demonstrates, that for a unification problem $\langle x = t \rangle$ the minimal set of most general unifiers can grow exponentially.

Consider the sort structure $S = \{N,NZ,Z\}$, where N, NZ and Z have the same meaning as in the example above. Let $x \in V_{NZ}$ and $x_i \in V_N$. The signature of the function "*" (product) is:

$SO(*) = \{(N,N,N),\ (NZ,N,N),\ (N,NZ,N),\ (Z,N,Z),\ (N,Z,Z),\ (Z,NZ,Z),\ (NZ,Z,Z),\ (Z,Z,Z),\ (NZ,NZ,NZ)\}$. The unification problem $\langle x = (x_1 * x_2) * \ldots * (x_{2n-1} * x_{2n}) \rangle$ produces 2^n unifiers, since for every factor there are two independent solutions $\{x_{2i-1} \leftarrow y_{2i-1}\}$ and $\{x_{2i} \leftarrow y_{2i}\}$, where $[y_j] = NZ$. These solutions have to be combined independently.

For a set of variables W and a set of Σ-substitutions U, the set $MAX_{\sqsubseteq[W]}(U)$ is a set of Σ-substitutions , such that

i) $MAX_{\sqsubseteq[W]}(U) \subseteq U$ and

ii) $\forall \sigma \in MAX_{\sqsubseteq[W]}(U), \tau \in U$: $\sigma \sqsubseteq \tau \, [W] \Rightarrow \sigma = \tau$.

iii) $\forall \tau \in U$: $\exists \sigma \in MAX_{\sqsubseteq[W]}(U)$: $\tau \sqsubseteq \sigma \, [W]$.

Such a set exists, since $\sqsubseteq[W]$ is transitive.

The polymorphic unification algorithm $\Sigma UNIFY$, which is an extension of the algorithm for the ΣRP-calculus [Wa84], takes two terms s,t as input and produces a set of most general unifiers as output.
It is defined as follows: [Sch85a]

1) $U_{NEW} = \{\epsilon\}$.

2) REPEAT $U_{OLD} := U_{NEW}$, $U_{NEW} = \emptyset$.

   For every $\sigma \in U_{OLD}$ DO

   Let (d,e) be the first disagreement pair of the two terms σs, σt.

   IF d or e is a variable, THEN DO
   $U_{NEW} = U_{NEW} \cup \{\sigma \circ \tau \mid \tau \in \mu U\Sigma(d, e)\}$.

   OD.

   OD.

   UNTIL U_{NEW} is a set of Σ-unifiers for s,t or $U_{NEW} = \emptyset$.

3) RETURN $MAX_{\sqsubseteq[VAR(s,t)]}(U_{NEW})$. $\square$

We have the theorem, which is proved in [Sch85a]:

<u>Theorem 3.</u> Let s,t $\in \Sigma TERM$ be Σ-unifiable. Then $\Sigma UNIFY(s,t)$ terminates and returns a finite nonempty set, which is equivalent to $\mu U\Sigma(s,t)$. $\square$

<u>Definition.</u> We say SIG is a <u>unification unique signature</u>, iff

- $\langle \mathbf{S}, \leq \rangle$ is a semilattice with a unique greatest element.

- For all $f \in \mathbf{F}$ and all $S \in \mathbf{S}$, the set $\{(S_1,\ldots,S_{n+1}) \in SO(f) \mid S_{n+1} \leq S\}$ is either empty or contains a unique greatest element.

The following theorem is proved in [Sch85a].

<u>Theorem 4.</u> Let SIG be a unification unique signature. Then $\mu U\Sigma(s,t)$ is at most a singleton for all s,t $\in \Sigma TERM$. $\square$

In [Sch85a] it is shown, that the condition, that $\langle \mathbf{S}, \leq \rangle$ is a semilattice, does not restrict the expressiveness of the many-sorted calculus ΣRP^{π}. In the case that $\langle \mathbf{S}, \leq \rangle$ is a partially ordered set, it is possible to add sorts to the signature, such that the resulting sort structure is a semilattice and the satisfiability of clause sets is unchanged.

4. The ΣRP^{π}-calculus.

Σ-factorization, Σ-resolution and Σ-paramodulation are defined as in [Wa83], however based on the unifier sets $\mu U\Sigma$ and $\mu P\Sigma$ respectively. The set $\mu P\Sigma$ is the set of most general unifiers for paramodulation, which is also always finite. The Σ-paramodulation rule includes the weakening rule of [Wa83] . The proofs in [WR73] can be generalized (see [Sch85a]) to the ΣRP^{π}-calculus yielding the following result:

<u>Theorem 5.</u> Let CS be a clause set containing the functional reflexivity axioms. Then:

$\qquad$ CS $\vdash_{\Sigma RP^{\pi}}$ FALSE $\Longleftrightarrow$ CS is unsatisfiable.

Example. The functional reflexivity axioms are needed for the completeness of the ΣRP-calculus:
Let $S = \{\top,A,B,C,D,E\}$.

- Let a,b,c,d be constants of sort A,B,C,D respectively.
- Let P be a unary predicate with SO(P) = (E).
- Let $f \in F$ with a signature, such that $[f(t_1,t_2)] = E$, iff $([t_1] \leq A$ and $[t_2] \leq C$) or $([t_1] \leq B$ and $[t_2] \leq D$); otherwise $[f(t_1,t_2)] = S$.
- Let CS be the clause set { $\{a{=}b\}$, $\{c{=}d\}$, $\{P(f(a,c))\}$, $\{\neg P(f(b,d))\}$ }.

This clause set is unsatisfiable, but Σ-paramodulation is not possible, since $[f(b,c)] = [f(a,d)] = S$. There is no deduction of the empty clause in ΣRP*. If the functional reflexivity axioms are present, then $f(a,c){=}f(b,d)$ can be deduced from the functional reflexivity axioms and the clauses in CS. Hence the empty clause is then deducable. $\square$

This result is somewhat theoretical. In practical applications, the functional reflexivity axioms are not used, since (i) they increase the search space enormously and (ii) the subsumption rule would delete all of them but the axiom $x{=}x$. Clearly, this omission may be the reason for incompleteness.

5. The Sort-Theorem.
For a polymorphic signature SIG and a related clause set CS, we define an unsorted relativization CS_{rel} [Wa83, Ob62] as follows:

For every sort S use a unary predicate P_S.

The set of **sort axioms** A^Σ consists of:
- $\forall x \; \neg P_S(x) \vee P_T(x)$, if $S{\leq}T$ for $S,T \in S$.
- $\forall x \; P_S(x)$ for the greatest sort S of S.
- $\forall x_1,...,x_n \; \neg P_{S_1}(x_1) \vee ... \vee \neg P_{S_n}(x_n) \vee P_{S_{n+1}}(f(x_1,...,x_n))$ for every $f \in F$ and every $(S_1,...,S_n) \in SO(f)$.

The relativization C_{rel} of a clause C is the clause itself, where the sorts of the variables are ignored and for every variable x of C a literal $\neg P_{[x]}(x)$ is added to the clause. We have $CS_{rel} = A^\Sigma \cup \{C_{rel} \mid C \in CS\}$.

The following theorem, which is proved in [Sch85a], and which is proved for other signatures in [Ob62] and [Wa83], states the equivalence of the sorted and the unsorted version of a clause set:

Theorem 6. (Sortensatz) Let CS be a SIG-sorted clause set. Then:
CS is unsatisfiable iff CS_{rel} is unsatisfiable. $\square$

Example. This example is taken from [SM78], which appears to be a goldmine for theorem proving examples. During a course on automated theorem proving in the last semester, our students had to translate these puzzles into first order predicate logic and to solve them with our theorem prover (Markgraf Karl Refutation Procedure) [KM84]. One of these problems (Problem 47) reads as follows:
"When Alice entered the forest of forgetfulness, she did not forget everything, only certain things. She often forgot her name, and the most likely to forget was the day of the week. Now, the lion and the unicorn were frequent visitors to this forest. These two are strange creatures. The lion lies on Mondays, Tuesdays and Wednesdays and tells the truth on the other days of the week. The unicorn, on the other hand lies on Thursdays, Fridays and Saturdays, but tells the truth on the other days of the week.
One day Alice met the lion and the unicorn resting under a tree. They made the following statements:

    Lion: Yesterday was one of my lying days.
    Unicorn: Yesterday was one of my lying days.
From these statements, Alice who was a bright girl, was able to deduce the day of the week. What was it?"

We use the predicates MO(x), TU(x), ... , SO(x) for saying that x is a Monday, Tuesday etc. Furthermore we need the binary predicate MEMB, indicating set Membership and a 3-ary predicate LA. LA(x y z) is true if x says at day y that he lies at day z; LDAYS(x) denotes the set of lying days of x. The remaining symbols are self explaining. One-character symbols like u,x,y,z are regarded as universally quantified variables.

Axiomization of the days of the week:
$$MO(x) \leftrightarrow \neg(TU(x)\vee WE(x)\vee TH(x)\vee FR(x)\vee SA(x)\vee SU(x))$$
$$TU(x) \leftrightarrow \neg(WE(x)\vee TH(x)\vee FR(x)\vee SA(x)\vee SU(x)\vee MO(x))$$
$$WE(x) \leftrightarrow \neg(TH(x)\vee FR(x)\vee SA(x)\vee SU(x)\vee MO(x)\vee TU(x))$$
$$TH(x) \leftrightarrow \neg(FR(x)\vee SA(x)\vee SU(x)\vee MO(x)\vee TU(x)\vee WE(x))$$
$$FR(x) \leftrightarrow \neg(SA(x)\vee SU(x)\vee MO(x)\vee TU(x)\vee WE(x)\vee TH(x))$$
$$SA(x) \leftrightarrow \neg(SU(x)\vee MO(x)\vee TU(x)\vee WE(x)\vee TH(x)\vee FR(x))$$
$$SU(x) \leftrightarrow \neg(MO(x)\vee TU(x)\vee WE(x)\vee TH(x)\vee FR(x)\vee SA(x))$$

Axiomization of the function yesterday:
$$MO(yesterday(x)) \leftrightarrow TU(x)$$
$$TU(yesterday(x)) \leftrightarrow WE(x)$$

$$WE(yesterday(x)) \leftrightarrow TH(x)$$
$$TH(yesterday(x)) \leftrightarrow FR(x)$$
$$FR(yesterday(x)) \leftrightarrow SA(x)$$
$$SA(yesterday(x)) \leftrightarrow SU(x)$$
$$SU(yesterday(x)) \leftrightarrow MO(x)$$

Axiomization of the function LDAYS:
$$MEMB(x \; LDAYS(lion)) \leftrightarrow MO(x) \lor TU(x) \lor WE(x)$$
$$MEMB(x \; LDAYS(unicorn)) \leftrightarrow TH(x) \lor FR(x) \lor SA(x)$$

Axiomization of the predicate LA:
$$\neg MEMB(x \; LDAYS(u)) \land LA(u \; x \; y) \Rightarrow MEMB(y \; LDAYS(u))$$
$$\neg MEMB(x \; LDAYS(u)) \land \neg LA(u \; x \; y) \Rightarrow$$
$$\neg MEMB(y \; LDAYS(u))$$
$$MEMB(x \; LDAYS(u)) \land LA(u \; x \; y) \Rightarrow \neg MEMB(y \; LDAYS(u))$$
$$MEMB(x \; LDAYS(u)) \land \neg LA(u \; x \; y) \Rightarrow MEMB(y \; LDAYS(u))$$

Theorem:
$$\exists x \quad LA(lion \; x \; yesterday(x)) \land$$
$$LA(unicorn \; x \; yesterday(x))$$

The MKRP proof procedure at Kaiserslautern found a proof for this unsorted version after 183 resolution steps, among them 81 unnecessary steps, hence the final proof was 102 steps long. This proof contains a lot of trivial steps corresponding to common sense reasoning (like: if today is Monday, it is not Tuesday etc.).

Later the sort structure and the signature of the problem at hand was generated automatically by a translator module which accepts an unsorted clause set as input and produces the equivalent many--sorted version together with the corresponding signature [Sch85b].

The sort structure and the signature contain all the relevant information about the relationship of unary predicates (like our days) and the domain-rangesort relation of functions. The sort structure of the subsorts of DAYS in our example is equivalent to the lattice of subsets of (Mo, Tu, We, Th, Fr, Sa, Su) without the empty set, ordered by the subset order. Hence there are 127 ($=2^7-1$) sorts. The function "yesterday" is a polymorphic function with 127 domain-sort relations like yesterday ((MO, WE)) = (SU, TU).

The unification algorithm exploits this information and produces only unifiers, which respect the sort relations, i.e. ($x \leftarrow t$) is syntactically correct, if and only if the sort of the term t is less or equal the sort of the variable x. We give an example for unification:

the unifier of x:SO+TU and yesterday(y:MO+TU) is $\{x \leftarrow yesterday(y_1: MO) \; ; \; y \leftarrow y_1:MO \}$. The MKRP theorem-proving system [KM84] has proved the theorem in the sorted version immediately without any unnecessary steps. The length of the proof is 6. As the protocol shows, the final substitution into the theorem clause was $x \leftarrow y:Th$. Thus the ATP has found the answer, Thursday, in a very straight forward and humanlike way. Here is a proof protocol:

C1	All x:Mo	MEMB (x LDAYS(lion))
C2	All x:Tu	MEMB (x LDAYS(lion))
C3	All x:We	MEMB (x LDAYS(lion))
C4	All x:Th	MEMB (x LDAYS(unicorn))
C5	All x:Fr	MEMB (x LDAYS(unicorn))
C6	All x:Sa	MEMB (x LDAYS(unicorn))

C7   All x,y:Days u:Animal
     MEMB(x LDAYS(u)) ¬LA(u x y)
     MEMB (y LDAYS(u))

C8   All x,y:Days u:Animal
     MEMB(x LDAYS(u)) LA(u x y)
     ¬MEMB(y LDAYS(u))

C9   All x,y:Days u:Animal
     ¬MEMB(x LDAYS(u)) ¬LA(u x y)
     ¬MEMB(y LDAYS(u))

C10 All x,y:Days u:Animal
     ¬MEMB(x LDAYS(u)) LA(u x y)
     MEMB(y LDAYS(u))

C11 All x:Th+Fr+Sa+Su ¬MEMB(x LDAYS(lion))

C12 All x:Tu+We+Su+Mo ¬MEMB(x LDAYS(unicorn))

Th   All x:Days
     ¬LA(lion x yesterday(x))
     ¬LA(unicorn x yesterday(x))

Proof:

C4,1 & C10,1 → R1:
   All x:Th y:Days LA(unicorn x y)
              MEMB(y LDAYS(unicorn))

R1,2 & C12,1 → R2:
   All x:Th y:Tu+We+Su+Mo LA(unicorn x y)

C3,1 & C8,3 → R3:
   All x:Days y:We MEMB(x LDAYS(lion))
              LA(lion x y)

R3,1 & C11,1 → R4:
   All x:Th+Fr+Sa+Su y:We LA(lion x y)

R4,1 & Th,1 → R5:
   All x:Th ¬LA(unicorn x yesterday(x))

R5,1 & R2,1 → R6: □

7. Conclusion. In a sense a polymorphic calculus is more expressive than a monomorphic calculus: one function symbol essentially denotes several operations. An alternative formulation with additional equalities and different symbols surely produces a larger search space.

The ΣRP^x-calculus allows to express this information and gives the possibility to use this information directly in the inference mechanism. Thus the ΣRP^x-calculus has all the advantages of a many sorted calculus, but an increased expressive power. Polymorphic unification is implemented in the MKRP theorem proving system at Kaiserslautern [KM84] and shows remarkable improvements in particular in combination with a sort generating algorithm [Sch85b], which automatically transforms a given problem into it´s polymorphic, many-sorted version.

The ΣRP^x-calculus could advantageously be used as the basis of a PROLOG implementation, where the present (Robinson) unification algorithm would be replaced by an algorithm as proposed in this paper.

Acknowledgements.

   I would like to thank: my colleagues H.J. Ohlbach, A. Herold and H.J. Burckert for their support and for their helpful discussions during the preparation of this paper; Ch. Walther, who read a draft of this paper.; Prof. Ph.D. J. Siekmann, who encouraged me to write this paper and read all drafts of this paper.

References

CD83   Cunningham, R.J., Dick, A.J.J.,
         Rewrite Systems on a Lattice of Types. Rep.
         No. DOC 83/7, Imperial College, London SW7
         (1983)

Co83   Cohn, A.G.
         Improving the Expressiveness of Many-
         sorted Logic. AAAI-83, Washington (1983)

GM84   Goguen, J.A., Meseguer, J.
         Equality, Types, Modules and Generics for
         Logic Programming. Journal of Logic
         Programming, (1984)

GM85   Goguen, J.A., Meseguer, J.
         Order Sorted Algebra I. Partial and
         Overloaded Operators, Errrors and
         Inheritance. SRI Report (1985)

Hay71   Hayes, P.
         A Logic of Actions. Machine Intelligence 6,
         Metamathematics Unit, University of
         Edinburgh (1971)

Hen72   Henschen, L.J.
         N-Sorted Logic for Automated Theorem
         Proving in Higher-Order Logic. Proc. ACM
         Conference, Boston (1972)

HO80   Huet, G., Oppen, D.C.,
         Equations and Rewrite Rules, SRI Technical
         Report CSL-111, (1980)

KM84   Karl Mark G Raph,
         The Markgraf Karl Refutation Procedure,
         Memo-SEKI-MK-84-01, (1984)

Mi84   Mishra, P.
         Towards a Theory of types in PROLOG. Int.
         Symp. on Logic Programming (1984)

MO84   Mycroft, A., O'Keefe, R.
         A Polymorphic Type System for PROLOG.
         Artificial Intelligence 23 (1984)

Ob62   Oberschelp, A.
         Untersuchungen zur mehrsortigen
         Quantorenlogik. Mathematische Annalen 145
         (1962)

Ro65   Robinson, J.A. A Machine-Oriented Logic
         Based on the Resolution Principle. JACM 12
         (1965)

Sch85a Schmidt-Schauss, M.
         A Many-Sorted Calculus with Polymorphic
         Functions Based on Resolution and
         Paramodulation. Interner Bericht. Institut für
         Informatik, Kaiserslautern (forthcoming)

Sch85b Schmidt-Schauss, M.
         Mechanical Generation of Sorts in Clause Sets.
         Interner Bericht. Institut für Informatik,
         Kaiserslautern (forthcoming)

Sm78   Smullyan, R.M.
         What is the Name of this Book? Prentice Hall
         (1978)

Wa83   Walther, C.
         A Many-Sorted calculus Based on Resolution
         and Paramodulation.Proc. of the 8th IJCAI,
         Karlsruhe, (1983)

Wa84   Walther, C.
         Unification in Many-Sorted Theories. Proc. of
         the 6th ECAI, PISA, (1984)

WR73   Wos, L. Robinson, G.
         Maximal Models and Refutation
         Completeness:
         Semidecision Procedures in Automatic
         Theorem Proving. In "Wordproblems"
         (W.W. Boone, F.B. Cannonito, R.C. Lyndon,
         eds.), North-Holland (1973)

On the Solution of *Schubert's Steamroller* in Many Sorted Logic.

Anthony G Cohn

Department of Computer Science
University of Warwick
Coventry CV4 7AL
UK

ABSTRACT

A challenge problem for automated theorem provers posed in 1978 by Schubert has recently been solved with the Karlsruhe MKRP-system by formulating the problem in many sorted logic. It is shown here that a further improvement is possible by using a more sophisticated, *polymorphic* many sorted logic. The problem and its solution are discussed and the differences between the different formulations are analysed.

1. Introduction

In 1978 Schubert set up the following challenge problem:

> Wolves, foxes, birds, caterpillars, and snails are animals, and there are some of each of them. Also there are some grains, and grains are plants. Every animal either likes to eat all plants or all animals much smaller than itself that like to eat some plants. Caterpillars and snails are much smaller than birds, which are much smaller than foxes, which in turn are much smaller than wolves. Wolves do not like to eat foxes or grains, while birds like to eat caterpillars but not snails. Caterpillars and snails like to eat some plants. Therefore there is an animal that likes to eat a grain-eating animal.

An axiomatisation of this problem as given in [13] is as follows:

(1u) $\exists w, f, b, c, s, g\, (W(w) \wedge F(f) \wedge B(b) \wedge C(c) \wedge S(s) \wedge G(g))$

(2u) $\forall x\, ((W(x) \vee F(x) \vee B(x) \vee C(x) \vee S(x)) \rightarrow A(x))$

(3u) $\forall x\, (G(x) \rightarrow P(x))$

(4u) $\forall x\, (A(x) \rightarrow$
$\quad (\forall y\, (P(y) \rightarrow E(x,y)) \vee$
$\quad \forall y\, ((A(y) \wedge M(y,x) \wedge \exists z\, (P(z) \wedge E(y,z))) \rightarrow E(x,y))))$

(5u) $\forall x, y\, (((C(x) \vee S(x)) \wedge B(y)) \rightarrow M(x,y))$

(6u) $\forall x, y\, ((B(x) \wedge F(y)) \rightarrow M(x,y))$

(7u) $\forall x, y\, ((F(x) \wedge W(y)) \rightarrow M(x,y))$

(8u) $\forall x, y\, (((F(x) \vee G(x)) \wedge W(y)) \rightarrow \neg E(y,x))$

(9u) $\forall x, y\, ((B(x) \wedge C(y)) \rightarrow E(x,y))$

(10u) $\forall x, y\, ((B(x) \wedge S(y)) \rightarrow \neg E(x,y))$

(11u) $\forall x\, ((C(x) \vee S(x)) \rightarrow \exists y\, (P(y) \wedge E(x,y)))$

(12u) $\exists x, y\, (A(x) \wedge A(y) \wedge \forall z\, (G(z) \rightarrow (E(x,y) \wedge E(y,z))))$

* This work was partially funded by the SERC under grant GR/C/65148.

The clausal form contains 27 clauses with 65 literals and until very recently no computer generated refutation had been generated** even though a hand built proof has been found: the search space is extremely large; there are 94 potential initial resolvents and 8 potential factors and the hand computed solution requires 33 inference steps. The clausal form of the above axiomatisation is given below.

(1cu) $\{W(w)\}$

(2cu) $\{F(f)\}$

(3cu) $\{B(b)\}$

(4cu) $\{C(c)\}$

(5cu) $\{S(s)\}$

(6cu) $\{G(g)\}$

(7cu) $\{\neg W(x), A(x)\}$

(8cu) $\{\neg F(x), A(x)\}$

(9cu) $\{\neg B(x), A(x)\}$

(10cu) $\{\neg C(x), A(x)\}$

(11cu) $\{\neg S(x), A(x)\}$

(12cu) $\{\neg G(x), P(x)\}$

(13cu) $\{\neg A(x), \neg P(y), E(x,y), \neg A(w), \neg M(w,x), \neg P(z),$
$\qquad \neg E(w,z), E(x,w)\}$

(14cu) $\{\neg C(x), \neg B(y), M(x,y)\}$

(15cu) $\{\neg S(x), \neg B(y), M(x,y)\}$

(16cu) $\{\neg B(x), \neg F(y), M(x,y)\}$

(17cu) $\{\neg F(x), \neg W(y), M(x,y)\}$

(18cu) $\{\neg F(x), \neg W(y), \neg E(y,x)\}$

(19cu) $\{\neg G(x), \neg W(y), \neg E(y,x)\}$

(20cu) $\{\neg B(x), \neg C(y), E(x,y)\}$

(21cu) $\{\neg B(x), \neg S(y), \neg E(x,y)\}$

(22cu) $\{\neg C(x), P(h(x))\}$

(23cu) $\{\neg C(x), E(x,h(x))\}$

(24cu) $\{\neg S(x), P(i(x))\}$

(25cu) $\{\neg S(x), E(x,i(x))\}$

(26cu) $\{\neg A(x), \neg A(y), G(j(x,y))\}$

(27cu) $\{\neg A(x), \neg A(y), \neg E(x,y), \neg E(y,j(x,y))\}$

(1cu) to (6cu) come from (1u). (7cu) through to (12cu) come from (2u) and (3u). (13cu) comes from (4u). (14cu) through to (17cu) come from (5u), (6u) and (7u). (18cu), (19cu) and (21cu) come from (8u) and (10u). (20cu) comes from (9u). (22cu) through (25cu) are the skolemised clauses derived from (11u). Similarly (26cu) and (27cu) come from the negation of (12u).

** These solutions will be described in the last section.

Recently, Walther, [13] has derived a computer solution to the problem by reaxiomatising it in a many sorted logic before giving it to the MKRP-system at Karlsruhe [12] . His many sorted formulation has a significantly reduced search space: only 12 clauses with 16 literals with an initial search space of 12 possible inferences and a total of 10 new clauses in the deduced proof.

The purpose of this paper is to show that further efficiency is possible by recasting the problem in a different many sorted logic [3,4] which possesses a number of additional features which increase its expressiveness as compared to Walther's logic [12] and the other many sorted logics to be found in the literature, eg [8,6,2,5] . A table comparing the formulation of the problem in the different logics may be found towards the end of this paper in figure 2.

2. Walther's Axiomatisation

For convenience, Walther's many sorted axiomatisation is repeated here in order to better compare the formulations in the two different many sorted logics.

In his logic *type* declarations define the sort of function and constant symbols (his predicate symbols may also be typed but this feature is not needed in this example). *Sort* declarations define the sort hierarchy. Animals, plants, grains, wolves, foxes, birds, caterpillars and snails are all sorts, named A, P, G, W, F, B, C and S respectively.

(1w) *type* w:W   (2w) *type* f:F

(3w) *type* b:B   (4w) *type* c:C

(5w) *type* s:S   (6w) *type* g:G

(7w) *sort* $W \sqsubseteq A$ (8w) *sort* $F \sqsubseteq A$

(9w) *sort* $B \sqsubseteq A$ (10w) *sort* $C \sqsubseteq A$

(11w) *sort* $S \sqsubseteq A$ (12w) *sort* $G \sqsubseteq P$

(13w) $\{E(a_1,p_1), \neg M(a_2,a_1), \neg E(a_2,p_2), E(a_1,a_2)\}$

(14w) $\{M(c_1,b_1)\}$ (15w) $\{M(s_1,b_1)\}$

(16w) $\{M(b_1,f_1)\}$ (17w) $\{M(f_1,w_1)\}$

(18w) $\{\neg E(w_1,f_1)\}$ (19w) $\{\neg E(w_1,g_1)\}$

(20w) $\{E(b_1,c_1)\}$ (21w) $\{\neg E(b_1,s_1)\}$

(22w) *type* h(C):P   (23w) $\{E(c_1,i(c_1))\}$

(24w) *type* i(S):P   (25w) $\{E(s_1,h(s_1))\}$

(26w) *type* j(A,A):G

(27w) $\{\neg E(a_1,a_2), \neg E(a_2,j(a_1,a_2))\}$

The symbols a_1, f_1 etc are all typed variables with the sort of the corresponding upper case letter. (1w) to (6w) define a signature and play no part in the proof.

As already mentioned, Walther's proof is 10 steps long (9 resolutions and a factorisation). It is reproduced below (in a slightly altered form to show the factorisation explicitly).

(28w) $\{E(a_1,p_1), \neg M(a_2,a_1), \neg E(a_2,p_2), \neg E(a_2,j(a_1,a_2))\}$
13w(4)+27w(1)

(29w) $\{E(a_1,p_1), \neg M(a_2,a_1), \neg E(a_2,j(a_1,a_2))\}$
factor of 28w

(30w) $\{E(w_1,p_1), \neg E(f_1,j(w_1,f_1))\}$
17w(1)+29w(2)

(31w) $\{\neg E(f_1,j(w_1,f_1))\}$
19w(1)+30w(1)

(32w) $\{E(f_1,p_1), \neg E(b_1,j(f_1,b_1))\}$
16w(1)+29w(2)

(33w) $\{\neg E(b_1,j(f_1,b_1))\}$
31w(1)+32w(1)

(34w) $\{E(b_2,p_1), \neg M(s_1,b_2), \neg E(s_1,p_2)\}$
13w(4)+21w(1)

(35w) $\{\neg M(s_1,b_2), \neg E(s_1,p_2)\}$
33w(1)+34w(1)

(36w) $\{\neg E(s_1,p_2)\}$
15w(1)+35w(1)

(37w) $\{\}$
25w(1)+36w(1)

He attributes the success of his system in finding a proof to the significant reduction in the clause set and to the restriction on unification preventing the matching of variables with incompatible sorts. For example clauses (20w) and (21w) have no resolvent because c_1 and s_1 cannot be unified. In the unsorted case the two clauses (20cu) and (21cu) do resolve to yield $\{\neg B(x), \neg C(y), \neg S(y)\}$. This can then be resolved with (3cu) to yield $\{\neg C(y), \neg S(y)\}$. However further inference will now yield a pure clause: either $\{\neg S(c)\}$ or $\{\neg C(s)\}$, where c and s are skolem constants. The dead end is detected much earlier in the many sorted logic.

3. A Brief Description of LLAMA***

The many sorted logic LLAMA [4,3] is unusual in that the quantifiers are unsorted; the restriction on the range of a quantified variable derives from the argument positions of the function and predicate symbols that it occupies; associated with every non-logical symbol α is a *sorting function* $\ddot{\alpha}$ of the same arity which describes how its sort varies with the sorts of its inputs; polymorphic functions and predicates are thus easily expressible and statements usually requiring several assertions may be compactly expressed by a single assertion. The sort structure itself is a complete boolean lattice. The top ($\top$) element is interpreted as the universe of discourse and the bottom ($\bot$) is interpreted as the empty set. Expressions of sort $\bot$ do not denote anything and are thus nonsense; they are said to be *illsorted*. Sorts may be referred to either directly or with an expression containing least upper bound ($\sqcup$), greatest lower bound ($\sqcap$) or relative complement ($\backslash$) operators.

*** Logic Lacking A Meaningful Acronym. Having sought a suitable name for the logic for a long time, I am indebted to Graeme Ritchie for this suggestion.

Furthermore, by specifying the result sort of predicates to be one of four special boolean sorts TT, FF, UU, EE (representing 'true', 'false', 'either true or false', and 'nonsense'), it is sometimes possible to detect that a formula is contradictory or tautologous without resort to general inference rules. Expressiveness can be further improved by allowing the sort of a term to be a more general sort than the sort of the argument position it occupies. However this feature is not needed for the current problem.

Associated with every formula in the logic is a *Sort Array (SA)* which is a mapping from sort environments to boolean sorts. A sort environment is a mapping from variables to sorts. Thus a SA records what the sort of a formula is, depending on what sorts its constituent variables are regarded as taking. A good way to view a SA is as an n dimensional array where n is the number of variables in the formula. Each dimension is indexed by the different sorts and each position in the array will contain one of the four boolean sorts FF, TT, UU or EE. If all entries are EE then the formula is nonsense (or illsorted) and can be deleted. Entries which are TT will be ignored by the system (effectively treated as though they were EE) since they cannot lead to a refutation. In the case of a clausal logic, if any of the entries are FF then the formula is a contradiction since all variables are universally quantified.

Inference in the logic includes ordinary resolution but there are some new inference rules. In particular it is sometimes possible to *evaluate* literals because they are always of sort FF in the possible environments of the SA of the clause. Evaluated literals may be deleted without having to resolve them away. It is sometimes advantageous to restrict the SA of a clause (ie restrict the set of possible sort environments in the SA, by changing some of the entries in the SA to EE) in order to evaluate a literal. Examples of such inferences will be found later on in the paper.

4. An Axiomatisation in LLAMA.

We use all the sorts of Walther's axiomatisation and some additional ones. As will be discussed later, the sort C⊔S allows the axiomatisation to be one clause smaller than it would otherwise be, and the sort P\G is added because, since G is a strict subsort**** of P, there must

---

**** Actually it does not follow that G is a strict subsort of P if the sort structure is derived from the unsorted axiomatisation, although it could be argued that the original English statement of the problem does implicitly imply this is in fact so. Walther's axiomatisation also specifies G to be a strict subsort of P. In any case this detail is not crucial to the problem.

It should also be noted that in LLAMA the sorts B, F, C, S, W, G, and P\G are all *disjoint:* their interpretations are non-overlapping sets (this is because, as currently formulated, LLAMA requires complete knowledge about the sort structure). Again, this disjointness is not present in the unsorted axiomatisation nor is it present in Walther's formulation, nor is it stated explicitly in the English statement of the problem, although it is true in the real world. However, this disjointness information is only used to reduce the search space and will not be used in the proof itself since there are no positive sort literals. It may be noted that Stickel's solution of the steamroller which is discussed later also assumes the disjointness of these sorts.

be a sort which is interpreted as all those plants which are not grains. The use of P\G will also be discussed later. Part of the hierarchy is depicted in figure 1.

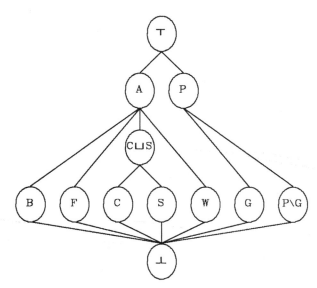

Figure 1.

Although LLAMA actually requires the sort lattice to be a complete boolean lattice with (in this case) 2^7 sorts, for simplicity only those needed to define the sorting functions for the non logical symbols are shown. Six further sorts (A\W, A\W\B, A\W\F, A\B, A\C and A\W\S) are used during the proof (see clauses 1 and 3 below).

The sorting functions for the various non-logical symbols (including skolem constants) are as follows. Entries not given are assumed to be EE (ie undefined) unless otherwise inferable.

$\ddot{M}(<A,A>)$	=	UU	$\ddot{E}(<A,\top>)$	=	UU
$\ddot{M}(<C,B>)$	=	TT	$\ddot{E}(<W,G>)$	=	FF
$\ddot{M}(<S,B>)$	=	TT	$\ddot{E}(<W,F>)$	=	FF
$\ddot{M}(<B,F>)$	=	TT	$\ddot{E}(<B,S>)$	=	FF
$\ddot{M}(<F,W>)$	=	TT	$\ddot{E}(<B,C>)$	=	TT

$$\ddot{h}(<C⊔S>) = P \qquad \ddot{j}(<A,A>) = G$$

The sorting function for a *characteristic* (or sort) predicate τ is

$$\ddot{\tau}(<\tau>) = TT \qquad \ddot{\tau}(<\top\setminus\tau>) = FF$$

Eg, the sorting function for the predicate P is:

$$\ddot{P}(<P>) = TT \qquad \ddot{P}(<A>) = FF$$

Note how the sorting functions for both M and E make use of LLAMA's polymorphism to encode much of the information about M and E. This type of polymorphism has been called *adhoc* polymorphism by Strachey [11] (or *overloading*) and should be distinguished from the *parametric* polymorphism to be found in, for example, [9].

The clausal form of the axioms comes out as just the following three clauses. The sort environments for which the corresponding SA is not EE or TT are listed next to each clause (the first column gives the result sort). Environments for which a clause is TT can be ignored during a refutation because the clause is tautologous in these environments and thus they can be deleted for the same reason as ordinary tautologous clauses can. These SAs are not input with the axioms but are derived using the sorting functions by an algorithm to be found in [4].

(1) $\{\neg P(p1), \neg P(p2), E(a1,p1), \neg M(a2,a1), \neg E(a2,p2), E(a1,a2)\}$

	$a1$	$a2$	$p1$	$p2$
UU	A\W\B	A	P	P
UU	A\W	A\C	P	P
UU	A\B	A	P	P\G
UU	A	A\C	P	P\G

(2) $\{E(cs1,h(cs1))\}$

	$cs1$
UU	C⊔S

(3) $\{\neg E(a1,a2), \neg E(a2,j(a1,a2))\}$

	$a1$	$a2$
UU	A\W\B	A\W
UU	W	A\W\F
UU	B	A\W\S

These axioms are derived* from the unsorted axioms 4u, 11u and the negation of 12u respectively. All the other unsorted axioms have been subsumed by the sort lattice and the sorting functions.

Thus this axiomatisation has just 3 clauses and 9 literals! There are only 4 possible resolvents initially. There are also some other possible inferences initially because certain literals are evaluable. In particular literals 1(1), 1(2), 1(4) can only be evaluated since there are no positive occurrences of P or M. (In fact characteristic literals such as $P(p1)$ may always be evaluated immediately without losing completeness). Thus 1 could be preprocessed to:

(1') $\{E(a1,p1), \neg E(a2,p2), E(a1,a2)\}$

	$a1$	$a2$	$p1$	$p2$
UU	B	S	P	P
UU	F	B	P	P
UU	W	F	P	P\G

Thus there are now only 6 literals overall. There are four possible resolvents and three possible evaluations (on 1'(1), 1'(3), and 3(1)) in this modified input clause set. None of the three clauses can be factored.

---

* It should be quite possible to derive this axiomatisation (including the sorting functions) automatically from Walther's formulation or perhaps even from the unsorted formulation.

A proof** goes like this.

(4) $\{E(a1,p1), \neg E(a2,p2), \neg E(a2,j(a1,a2))\}$
1'(3)+3(1)

	$a1$	$a2$	$p1$	$p2$
UU	F	B	P	P

(5) $\{E(a1,p1), \neg E(a2,j(a1,a2))\}$
factor of 4

	$a1$	$a2$	$p1$
UU	F	B	P

(6) $\{E(a3,p1), \neg E(a2,p2), E(a1,a2)\}$
5(2)+1'(1)

	$a1$	$a2$	$a3$	$p1$
UU	B	S	F	P

Since literal 6(3) is always false in the environments of clause 6 it can be evaluated and deleted from the clause without changing the SA or the meaning of the clause to produce a simpler clause 6':

(6') $\{E(a3,p1), \neg E(a2,p2)\}$

	$a2$	$a3$	$p1$
UU	S	F	P

(7) $\{E(a3,p1)\}$
6'(2)+2(1)

	$a3$	$p1$
UU	F	P

(8) $\{E(a1,p1), E(a1,a2)\}$
7(1)+1'(2)

	$a1$	$a2$	$p1$
UU	W	F	P\G
FF	W	F	G

We have now derived a clause with an environment for which it is FF ie false. Since variables are universally quantified such a clause is a contradiction and we have our desired refutation. In an ordinary clausal logic, only a null clause indicates a falsehood but in this calculus it is possible for a non null clause to be contradictory by virtue of sortal information.

Note that this proof is linear; neither the unsorted hand produced proof of Schubert nor the many sorted proof of Walther are linear. Linearising a non-linear proof often increases its length. The total number number of inference steps (not counting preprocessing and simplifications) is only 5 steps. This compares with 10 steps in [14]. The inclusion of the extra sort C⊔S

** This proof is hand produced. However, an implementation of the logic will be finished in the near future.

saves one unit clause in the axiomatisation of the problem; this reduces the search space slightly (the MKRP system could also take advantage of this) but does not reduce the proof length since (23w) is not used in the proof.

Part of the saving comes from the ability to represent information such as "caterpillars are much smaller than birds" not as unit clauses as Walther has to (14w) but as sorting functions. Because this information can be represented without using a clause a reduction in the search space occurs. The sorting functions for M and E are then used to advantage during the proof process to evaluate certain literals. Evaluations which can be performed without having to restrict the SA are entirely 'free'. (They are called *elementary evaluations* in [4]). They do not increase the search space because the old clause can be deleted. An example is the evaluation performed in producing clause 6'. Also, it has already been argued that it is beneficial to evaluate pure (ie not resolvable) literals as soon as possible, as was done in producing clause 1'. However even a non elementary evaluation may not actually increase the search space since the parent clause may be restricted to exclude the sort environment used to produce the evaluation without losing completeness. No non elementary evaluations were performed in the proof above though they might be used in a different branch of the search space (for example we have already noted above that three non elementary evaluations are possible initially (1'1), 1'(3) and 3(1)).

Obviously the overhead of computing and maintaining the SAs for the clauses has to be taken into consideration but this should be overshadowed by the reduction of the search space which accrues through use of the many sorted logic in most cases: the cost of the SA operations appears to be some polynomial*** of the number of sorts and the number of variables in a clause, whilst the size of the search space is in general exponential in the number of clauses. The occasions when savings are unlikely to be realised are when there is little sortal structure in the problem. In this case the SAs will be very large (ie will be UU in most environments), few evaluations will be possible and inference will be no better than in an unsorted logic with the additional burden of having to maintain the SAs.

A second reason why the LLAMA proof is shorter is because of its polymorphism. Inspection of Walther's proof (or indeed of the unsorted proof) shows that a literal with predicate symbol M is resolved away three times during the proof (in producing clauses 30w, 32w and 36w). Each time a different unit clause is involved. These steps are all combined in the evaluation of the polymorphic clause (1) to produce clause (1'). The important point is that (1') is still polymorphic****. The literal involving M has been deleted but without having to make such a commitment as to the precise sorts of the variables as in a non-polymorphic logic. In a non-polymorphic many sorted logic once that literal has

been resolved away then a commitment is made as to which precise sorts the variables involved in the resolution should be. For example, (30w) is a result of a resolution involving M. But now a_1 and a_2 have been irrevocably chosen to be of sort W and F respectively.

The point is of course that instead of choosing to resolve (29w) against (17w) an inference engine might just as well have chosen any of the other three unit clauses involving M, for example (14w). In this case a_1 and a_2 would now be of sort B and C respectively. However this resolution cannot lead to a refutation (which is why the environment <B,C,P,P> does not appear in the SA for (1'): it is tautologous and thus will not be used in a refutation). Thus any further inference involving this resolvent would be totally wasted. The advantage of a polymorphic logic thus is that generality is retained and choices involving the precise sorts of variables can be delayed. This argument would hold even if M had been resolved away conventionally rather than by evaluation. It would also hold even if the environment <B,C,P,P> were still in the SA for (1') because in the LLAMA proof the decision about the sorts of a_1 and a_2 is made as needed when resolving to produce clauses 4, 6 and 8.

Thus adding polymorphism to a many sorted logic in this way does seem to add genuine extra power. One could imagine that a logic such as Walther's could perhaps be simulated with an unsorted logic by running the sort axioms intelligently (eg never resolving on an uninstantiated characteristic literal, but choosing instantiated characteristic literals as top priority when available and also checking characteristic literals in the same clause for inconsistency by testing whether the clause is subsumed by any sort lattice axiom) but it is not obvious how LLAMA could be directly simulated in such a manner with a clausal unsorted logic.

5. Final Remarks

Some of the statistics appertaining to the three axiomatisations of the Steamroller are summarised in the table of figure 2.

This example demonstrates the advantage not only of using a many sorted logic, but also the value of polymorphism* and of using the four boolean sorts for describing the sortal behaviour of predicates.

Schubert's Steamroller has also recently been solved by two other automated reasoning systems; in

	Unsorted logic	Walther's logic	LLAMA
No. of clauses initially	27	12	3
No. of literals initially	65	16	9
No. of possible inferences initially	102	12	7
Length of proof	33	10	5

Figure 2

*** Analysing the complexity of the SA operations is an area for further research.

**** Note that 1' would have to be represented as three clauses in Walther's logic, each one corresponding to one of the sort environments of 1'. Thus polymorphism can allow one to obtain some "non clausal" effects.

---

* Note that the implicit restriction on the quantification on variables from the arguments places they occur in is essential to exploiting LLAMA's polymorphism since variables with unique sorts exclude the possibility of polymorphic clauses such as 1'.

both cases special purpose reasoning systems were employed. The ITP system [7] has a system of "qualifier" literals which can be used to simulate a many sorted logic to a limited extent. The success of the ITP system on the Steamroller problem is reported in [10] but no details of the proof were given so no detailed comparison is possible. Stickel has also solved the steamroller with his non clausal logic which "builds in theories". *Theory resolution* removes the need to resolve upon axioms in the theory by utilising a decision procedure that can determine the unsatisfiability of a set of clauses using predicates in the theory. The statistics in the table of figure 3 show the results of Stickel's system for (a) no knowledge built in (b) 2u-3u built in (c) 2u-3u and 5u-11u built in**.

	(a)	(b)	(c)
No. of formulae initially	18	12	8
Length of proof	33	10	6
Time taken(h:mm)	2:53	0:20	0:01.6

Figure 3

These figures are taken directly from [10]. No statistics on the original size of the search space were given. The times refer to a system running on a Symbolics 3600. These results show a dramatic improvement in the size of the search space by building in axioms. A solution is found about 100 times faster with (c) compared to (a)! Thus although a proof can be found with no special purpose inference machinery for handling taxonomic information it is very expensive to compute***. However the proof length is still longer that in either of the many sorted solutions. Theory resolution can handle characteristic literals more efficiently than a standard unsorted logic but cannot eliminate them altogether as is possible in many sorted logic. However theory resolution is more general than a many sorted logic: for example paramodulation can be viewed as an instance of theory resolution.

In this problem, sorts have managed to reduce the amount of normal inference required to almost nothing, but of course in larger problems there will still be a non trivial amount of such inference required, for it is not claimed that a many sorted logic is a general panacea. However it does seem to be a useful weapon in attacking large search spaces.

6. Acknowledgements

My special thanks go to Christoph Walther for his helpful comments on a draft of this paper. I have also had useful discussions with Alan Frisch, Pat Hayes and Bob Kowlalski.

** For comparison, LLAMA "builds in" 1u-3u and 5u-10u while Walther's many sorted formulation "builds in" 1u-3u.

*** Stickel also reports a personal communication from Walther that the MKRP system found an unsorted solution too. However this took about 10 times longer than with the sorted formulation of the problem and relied heavily on the TERMINATOR module [1] (a fast procedure for finding unit refutations).

7. References

[1] G Antoniou and H J Ohlback, "TERMINATOR," in *Proc IJCAI 8*, Karlsruhe (1983).

[2] D de Champeaux, "A Theorem Prover Dating a Semantic Network," in *Proc AISB/GI Conf on AI*, Hamburg (1978).

[3] A G Cohn, "Improving the Expressiveness of Many Sorted Logic," in *Proc AAAI*, Washington DC (1983).

[4] A G Cohn, "Mechanising a Particularly Expressive Many Sorted Logic," PhD Thesis, University of Essex (1983).

[5] H B Enderton, *A Mathematical Introduction to Logic*, Academic Press (1972).

[6] L J Henschen, "N-Sorted Logic for Automatic Theorem Proving in Higher Order Logic," in *Proc. ACM Conference*, Boston (1972).

[7] E Lusk and R A Overbeek, "The Automated Reasoning System ITP," Technical Report ANL 84 27, Argonne National Laboratory (1984).

[8] J R McSkimin and J Minker, "The Use of a Semantic Network in a Deductive Question Answering System," in *Proc IJCAI 5*, Cambridge (1977).

[9] A Mycroft and R A O'Keefe, "A Polymorphic Type System for Prolog," *Artificial Intelligence* **23**(1984).

[10] M E Stickel, "Automated Deduction by Theory Resolution," Draft Report, SRI International (1984).

[11] C Strachey, "Fundamental Concepts in Programming Languages," *Unpublished notes for a NATO Summer School*, (1967).

[12] C Walther, "A Many Sorted Calculus Based on Resolution and Paramodulation," in *IJCAI 8*, Karlsruhe (1983).

[13] C Walther, *Schubert's Steamroller - A Case Study in Many Sorted Resolution*, Universitat Karlsruhe (1984).

[14] C Walther, "A Mechanical Solution of Schubert's Steamroller by Many Sorted Resolution," in *Proc AAAI*, Austin, Texas (1984).

A Many-Sorted Resolution based on
an Extension of a First-Order Language*

K. B. Irani and D. G. Shin

Robot Systems Division
Center for Research on Integrated Manufacturing
College of Engineering, The University of Michigan,
Ann Arbor, Mi. 48109

ABSTRACT

A type of problem is first identified which may occur when a resolution scheme is applied to a many-sorted theory. To avoid such a problem, an extension of the first-order language called *one-sorted language with aggregate variables* is introduced. Aggregate variables allow the introduction of range-restricted variables dynamically in the structure which is expanded by definitions. This allows the introduction of a new resolution scheme called *UWR-resolution*. It can be shown that the UWR-resolution is more efficient than the existing schemes.

1. Introduction

Within the field of theorem proving, the advantages of a many-sorted logic are well known [Henschen, 1972 and Cohn, 1983]. More recently a sound theoretical foundation for many-sorted resolution has been established in [Walther, 1983, 1984a] and the power of a many-sorted resolution has been demonstrated by an example in [Walther, 1984b]. However, because of its associated fixed structure, sometimes not as much advantage can be derived from the use of a many-sorted calculus as one would like to get. This is illustrated by the following example.

Example 1.1 Let z_a, z_b, z_c, z_d, and z_e be the variables ranging over the sorts A, B, C, D, and E, respectively, where $D \subset B$, $D \subset C$, $E \subset A$, $E \subset B$, and $E \subset C$. Suppose the theory to be refuted is given by:

(1) $\forall z_a \, \forall z_b \, (P(z_b) \cup Q(z_b, f^d(z_b)) \cup R(z_a, z_b))$,

(2) $\forall z_c \, \neg P(z_c)$,

(3) $\forall z_e \, \forall z_c \, \neg Q(z_e, z_c)$,

(4) $\forall z_c \, \neg R(g^e(z_c), z_c)$,

where $f^d(z_b)$ and $g^e(z_c)$ are Skolem functions whose ranges are restricted to D and E, respectively. Suppose (1) and (2) are resolved, because z_b of $P(z_b)$ in (1) and z_c of $\neg P(z_c)$ in (2) are unifiable over D. The two clauses can be resolved using the most general unifier (mgu) $\theta = \{y_d/z_b, y_d/z_c\}$ where y_d ranges over D. The deduction is then

(5) $Q(y_d, f^d(y_d)) \cup R(z_a, y_d)$ (1)+(2),

(6) $Q(y_d, f^d(y_d))$ (4)+(5).

It is noticed that (6) cannot be resolved with any other clauses, not even with (3) because no sort is known to be a subsort of D and E. A dead end has been reached. (5) is a useless resolvent, so is (6).

*This work was supported in part by Air Force Office Scientific Research under contract F49620-82-C-0089.

Had there been another sort $G = B \cap C$, z_b of $P(z_b)$ in (1) and z_c of $\neg P(z_c)$ in (2) could have been unified over the sort G giving the deduction

(5′) $Q(y_g, f^d(y_g)) \cup R(z_a, y_g)$ (1)+(2),

(6′) $Q(y_g, f^d(y_g))$ (4)+(5′),

where y_g ranges over G. The clause (6′) can be further resolved with (3) resulting in the empty clause $\square$. There is no dead end here. It is observed that the need for G is not known until (1) and (2) are attempted to be resolved. In an ordinary many-sorted language, one cannot add a new sort whenever a need arises without altering the sort structure.

To alleviate such a situation, an extension of a one-sorted language called *one-sorted language with aggregate variables* (L_Σ^1) is proposed into which a many-sorted theory can be translated and which may be dynamically extended to bypass the problem illustrated above. Previously in [Shin and Irani, 1984], the concept of embedding aggregate variables (a.v.) into a many-sorted language (L_m) was reported, and its resulting language was called *many-sorted language with a.v.*. Here a.v.'s are embedded in a one-sorted language.

a.v.'s allow the introduction of range-restricted variables dynamically without revising the a priori fixed structure. Using the dynamic range-restricting nature of an a.v., an efficient many-sorted resolution scheme called *UWR-resolution* is presented which is designed to avoid generating useless resolvents as illustrated in the above example. The completeness of UWR-resolution can be shown. The efficiency of UWR-resolution is discussed.

2. One-sorted Language with a. v. L_Σ^1

2.1. Syntax of L_Σ^1

In L_Σ^1 two types of variables, called simple variables and a.v.'s, are available. A simple variable of L_Σ^1 is the same as the ordinary variable of one-sorted language. Unlike a simple variable, an a.v. is syntactically an ordinary sort variable, but semantically a variable whose range of interpretation is restricted by a unary relation rather than to a sort universe. Formally stated, an a. v. is of the form $z^{\Sigma P_i}$ in which $z^{\Sigma P_i}$ ranges over the unary relation indicated by the unary predicate symbol P_i.

Let J, L, and K be respectively a relation index set, a function index set and a constant index set. In addition, let I be an index set for some unary relations. Let λ and ξ be functions such that $\lambda : J \to N^+$ and $\xi : L \to N^+$, where N^+ is the set of positive integers.

Definition 2.1   A *one-sorted language with a.v.* L_Σ^1 then consists of the following : (1) parentheses (,) and a symbol Σ;

(2) constant symbol C_k , for each $k \in K$; (3) simple variables z_1 , $\cdots$, z_m , $\cdots$, and a.v.'s $z_1^{\Sigma P_i}$, $\cdots$, $z_n^{\Sigma P_i}$, $\cdots$, for each $i \in I$, where P_i is a unary predicate symbol; (4) a $\lambda(j)$-ary predicate symbol R_j , for each $j \in J$; (5) a $\xi(l)$-ary function symbol F_l , for each $l \in L$; (6) logical connectives $\neg$, and $\rightarrow$; and (7) a universal quantifier $\forall$.

Based on this language, the *terms* of L_Σ^1 are defined as usual except that each variable is now either a simple variable or an a.v.. The set, $Form(L_\Sigma^1)$, of *well-formed formulas* of L_Σ^1 , is defined as usual. The definable syntactic objects $\cup$, $\cap$, $\leftrightarrows$ and $\exists$, and the standard notions such as *sentences* are also introduced in the usual way.

2.2. Interpretation of L_Σ^1

A structure is needed to interpret each formula in L_Σ^1 . Let OS_a be a structure for L_Σ^1 . Then $OS_a = \ <\Omega, \{P_i\}_{i \in I}, \{R_j\}_{j \in J}, \{F_l\}_{l \in L}, \{C_k\}_{k \in K}>^*$ where Ω is the universe of OS_a ; $\dot{P_i}$ is a unary relation $\dot{P_i} \subseteq \Omega$; $\dot{R_j}$ is a $\lambda(j)$-ary relation $\dot{R_j} \subseteq \Omega^{\lambda(j)}$; $\dot{F_l}$ is a $\xi(l)$-ary function $\dot{F_l} : \Omega^{\xi(l)} \rightarrow \Omega$; and a distinguished element $\dot{C_k}$ is an element of Ω , for each $k \in K$. The interpretation of a formula in the structure OS_a then requires a variable assignment function s as follows:

Definition 2.2 For a set V of variables of L_Σ^1 and the universe Ω of structure OS_a , s is an assignment function $s : V \rightarrow \Omega$ such that for a simple variable z , $s(z) = a$, where $a \in \Omega$; and for an aggregate variable $z^{\Sigma P_i}$, $s(z^{\Sigma P_i}) = a$, where $a \in \dot{P_i}$.

Assignment function for the terms of L_Σ^1 is defined as usual. For notational convenience symbol s is also used for the assignment for the terms. The validity of each formula is determined by the following interpretation rules.

Definition 2.3 For $R_j(t_0, \ldots, t_{\lambda(j)})$, $\psi_1, \psi_2 \in Form(L_\Sigma^1)$, where t_i 's are terms, the satisfaction of the formulas with respect to s in OS_a is defined by,

(1) $\models_{OS_a} R_j(t_0, \ldots, t_{\lambda(j)})[s]$ iff $<s(t_0), \ldots, s(t_{\lambda(j)})> \in \dot{R_j}$,

(2) $\models_{OS_a} \neg\psi_1[s]$ iff $\not\models_{OS_a} \psi_1[s]$,

(3) $\models_{OS_a} \psi_1 \rightarrow \psi_2[s]$ iff if $\models_{OS_a} \psi_1[s]$ then $\models_{OS_a} \psi_2[s]$,

(4) For a simple variable z , $\models_{OS_a} \forall z \ \psi_1[s]$ iff for any $a \in \Omega$, $\models_{OS_a} \psi_1[s(z \mid a)]$,

(5) For an aggregate variable $z^{\Sigma P_i}$, $\models_{OS_a} \forall z^{\Sigma P_i} \psi_1[s]$ iff for any $a \in \dot{P_i}$, $\models_{OS_a} \psi_1[s(z^{\Sigma P_i} \mid a)]$,

where for variables v_m and v_k ,

$$s(v_m \mid a)(v_k) = \begin{cases} s(v_k) & \text{if } v_m \neq v_k \\ a & \text{if } v_m = v_k \end{cases}$$

As a corollary to the definition, the interpretations of $\cup, \cap, \leftrightarrows$ and $\exists$ can also be easily defined.

2.3. Σ-Extensibility of L_Σ^1

L_Σ^1 is as convenient as L_m in abbreviating the relativized expressions in a one-sorted language into more compact

---

* From next section on, " · " on a symbol is omitted as long as the meaning of the symbol is unambiguous.

forms. If a formula σ_m in L_m is of the form

$$\sigma_m = \forall x_i \ \underline{\hspace{2cm}} x_i \ \underline{\hspace{2cm}} ,$$

where x_i is a sort variable belonging to some sort S_i , then σ_m can be syntactically translated into σ_Σ^e in L_Σ^1

$$\sigma_\Sigma^e = \forall z^{\Sigma P_i} \ \underline{\hspace{2cm}} z^{\Sigma P_i} \ \underline{\hspace{2cm}} ,$$

where the unary relation intended by P_i is identical to the sort S_i . During the translation, L_Σ^1 is augmented with P_i and accordingly the structure for L_Σ^1 , say $OS_a(L_\Sigma^1)^*$, can be constructed from the many-sorted structure for L_m , say $MS(L_m)$. The following theorem can be shown (proofs for the theorems given in this paper can be found in [Shin, 1985]):

Theorem 2.1 A sentence σ_m in L_m is true in $MS(L_m)$ iff σ_Σ^e in L_Σ^1 is true in $OS_a(L_\Sigma^1)^*$.

The power of L_Σ^1 over L_m lies in the fact that whereas in the latter a sort variable with new sort may not be introduced, in the former *a variable whose range is restricted to a subset of the universe Ω can be introduced as needed in its extension*. Let T_Σ be a theory in L_Σ^1 and let a formula $\phi_\Sigma \in T_\Sigma$ be of the form

$$\phi_\Sigma = \forall z \ (\ S_1(z) \cap S_2(z) \ \rightarrow \ \psi(z)) .$$

In L_Σ^1 , in order to introduce a variable ranging over $S_1 \cap S_2$, all that must be done is to add a new unary predicate symbol S_k to L_Σ^1 , abbreviate ϕ_Σ by $\forall z^{\Sigma S_k} \ \psi(z^{\Sigma S_k})$, and augment T_Σ by the defining axiom $\forall z \ (\ S_k(z) \leftrightarrows S_1(z) \cap S_2(z)) .$ The extended language $L_\Sigma^{1'}$ is called a Σ-*extension* of L_Σ^1 and the augmented theory T_Σ' , a Σ-*extension* of T_Σ . For the semantics of the new predicate symbols in $L_\Sigma^{1'}$, it can be shown that there is a unique expansion by definition of OS_a , say OS_a' , which is a model of T_Σ' . OS_a' is called *an expansion by Σ-definition* of OS_a . This characteristic of L_Σ^1 is called Σ-*extensibility*. The following theorem establishes the validity of Σ-extensibility of L_Σ^1 :

Theorem 2.2 For any $\psi' \in T_\Sigma'$, there is a $\psi \in T_\Sigma$ such that for any assignment function s , $\models_{OS_a'} \psi'[s] \iff \models_{OS_a} \psi[s] .$

3. UWR-resolution

The problem identified in Section 1, namely, the generation of useless resolvents that lead to dead ends, occurs only when a many-sorted theory of a certain class is refuted by a resolution scheme. For instance, for the many-sorted theories with tree structure stated in [Walther, 1984a], this problem never occurs. When the tree constraint is lifted, however, this problem may appear. The conditions under which the problem may arise are explained below, this time in terms of L_Σ^1 .

Let $Ran(t)$ stand for the range associated with a term t . Given a set of unary relations P , a set of immediate predecessor of a relation $P_i \in P$, denoted by $IM(P_i)$, be defined by $IM(P_i) \overset{d}{=} \{P_j \mid P_j \in P, \ P_j \subset P_i, \ \text{and if } P_j \subseteq P_l \subseteq P_i \text{ then either } P_j = P_l \text{ or } P_l = P_i\}$. A situation may occur in which two variables v_i and v_j have $|IM(Ran(v_i)) \cap IM(Ran(v_j))| > 1$. Hence there are possibly more than one range over which v_i can be unified with v_j . In fact, if z_k is a variable such that $Ran(z_k) = P_k$ and $P_k \in IM(Ran(v_i)) \cap IM(Ran(v_j))$, then any substitution $\theta = \{z_k/v_i, \ z_k/v_j\}$ is a legitimate mgu of $\{v_i, v_j\}$, since $\theta v_i = \theta v_j$. There are, therefore, as many mgus for

$\{ v_i , v_j \}$ as $| IM(Ran(v_i)) \cap IM(Ran(v_j))|$. Not all the resolvents generated using each of these mgus are useful.

A way to remedy the situation is proposed in the following. First, a few new notions are introduced. A **wr-substitution component** is any expression of the form t/v, where v is a variable and t is a term different from v satisfying $Ran(t) \subseteq Ran(v)$. A **wr-subpair** is a set of wr-substitution components $\{t/v_i , t/v_j\}$ satisfying, (1) $Ran(v_i) \not\subseteq Ran(v_j)$ and $Ran(v_j) \not\subseteq Ran(v_i)$, (2) $| IM(Ran(v_i)) \cap IM(Ran(v_j))| > 1$, and (3) $Ran(t) = Ran(v_i) \cap Ran(v_j)$. A **wr-substitution** is a set of wr-substitution components which possibly contains one or more wr-subpairs. A **wr-resolvent** is a resolvent which is generated by using a wr-substitution as a unifier.

The Σ-extensibility of L_Σ^1 plays the central role in introducing wr-subpairs. From the definition of a wr-subpair, it is clear that wr-resolvents can only be expressed in an extended language of L_Σ^1. To be more specific, let a theory in L_Σ^1 be formalized by an ordered pair $< OA , T_\Sigma >$ where OA is a set of ordering axioms expressed with the symbol " $\subset$ " such that $P_i \subset P_j$ means $\forall x (P_i(x) \rightarrow P_j(x))$ and T_Σ is a set of the nonlogical axioms of the theory expressed in L_Σ^1. The following is an example:

Example 3.1   Consider the following $< OA , T_\Sigma >$:

OA :   (1) $D \subset B , D \subset C$

(2) $E \subset B , E \subset C$

T_Σ :   (3) $\forall x^{\Sigma B} (P(x^{\Sigma B}) \cup Q(x^{\Sigma B} , f^d(x^{\Sigma B})))$

(4) $\forall x^{\Sigma C} \neg P(x^{\Sigma C})$

(5) $\forall x^{\Sigma E} \forall x^{\Sigma C} \neg Q(x^{\Sigma E} , x^{\Sigma C})$

The following is done: For $x^{\Sigma B}$ of $P(x^{\Sigma B})$ in (3) and $x^{\Sigma C}$ of $\neg P(x^{\Sigma C})$ in (4), a wr-subpair $\{ x^{\Sigma K}/x^{\Sigma B} , x^{\Sigma K}/x^{\Sigma C} \}$ is introduced with L_Σ^1 being extended by a unary predicate symbol, say K , where $\forall x (K(x) \leftrightarrows B(x) \cap C(x))$. The extension of L_Σ^1 requires $< OA , T_\Sigma >$ to be also extended, i.e., OA is augmented to OA^+ by the ordering axioms such as (2^+) below. (6) is derived as the wr-resolvent of (3) and (4). Finally, (6) is resolved with (5) resulting in $\square$ as follows:

(2^+) $K \subset B , K \subset C , D \subset K , E \subset K$

(6) $Q(x^{\Sigma K} , f^d(x^{\Sigma K}))$ (3)+(4)

(7) $\square$ (5)+(6)

It is not difficult to see that the range of t in a wr-subpair $\{t/v_i , t/v_j\}$, i.e., $Ran(t) = Ran(v_i) \cap Ran(v_j)$, is the weakest range over which $\{v_i , v_j\}$ can be unified -- weakest in the sense that if $P_w = Ran(t)$, then there is no P_l such that $P_w \subset P_l$ and v_i and v_j are still unifiable over P_l. For this reason, the unification stated above is called **unification over the weakest range** and the resolution involving such unification is called **UWR-resolution**. The idea behind UWR-resolution is therefore to subsume all the possible unifications by one unification over the weakest possible range.

The completeness of UWR-resolution must be proved. Given $< OA , T_\Sigma >$, let $R_W(T_\Sigma)$ be the set of all clauses consisting of members of T_Σ and the resolvents (including wr-resolvents) of members of T_Σ (similar to Robinson's resolution operator [Robinson, 1965]). Also let $R_W^n(T_\Sigma)$ be defined so that for each $n \geq 0$, $R_W^0(T_\Sigma) = T_\Sigma$ and $R_W^{n+1}(T_\Sigma) = R_W(R_W^n(T_\Sigma))$. Completeness theorem states:

Theorem 3.1   A $< OA , T_\Sigma >$ is unsatisfiable if and only if $R_W^n(T_\Sigma)$ contains $\square$, for some $n \geq 0$.

In fact, when the UWR-resolution is applied, $< OA , T_\Sigma >$ is refuted not in L_Σ^1 but in its extended language $L_\Sigma^1{}'$. Therefore it further must be justified that when $R_W^n(T_\Sigma)$ contains $\square$, for some $n \geq 0$, whether the unsatisfiability of $< OA , T_\Sigma >$ can be truly shown in L_Σ^1 without extending its vocabulary. Let $R_\Sigma(\cdot)$ stand for an identical situation as $R_W(\cdot)$ except that in the former no wr-resolvents are generated. In this way the unsatisfiability of $< OA , T_\Sigma >$ can be shown without extending L_Σ^1. The following theorem can be shown:

Theorem 3.2   Given $< OA , T_\Sigma >$, $R_W^n(T_\Sigma)$ contains $\square$, for some $n \geq 0$, if and only if $R_\Sigma^m(T_\Sigma)$ contains $\square$, for some $m \geq 0$.

4. Efficiency of UWR-resolution

One way to discuss the efficiency of UWR-resolution is to compare $R_W(\cdot)$ and $R_\Sigma(\cdot)$ defined previously. The following facts show the efficiency of UWR-resolution:

Lemma 4.1   Given $< OA , T_\Sigma >$, if n is the smallest non-negative integer for which $R_W^n(T_\Sigma)$ contains $\square$ and m is the smallest non-negative integer for which $R_\Sigma^m(T_\Sigma)$ contains $\square$, then $n = m$.

Lemma 4.2   Given $< OA , T_\Sigma >$, for each $i \geq 0$ $| R_W^{i+1}(T_\Sigma) - R_W^i(T_\Sigma)| \leq | R_\Sigma^{i+1}(T_\Sigma) - R_\Sigma^i(T_\Sigma)|$.

Finally, the following theorem can be proved:

Theorem 4.3   Given $< OA , T_\Sigma >$, if n is the smallest non-negative integer for which $R_W^n(T_\Sigma)$ and $R_\Sigma^n(T_\Sigma)$ both contain $\square$, then $| R_W^n(T_\Sigma)| \leq | R_\Sigma^n(T_\Sigma)|$.

5. Conclusion

The use of aggregate variables have been demonstrated in a new approach, namely, UWR-resolution, for proving theorems. It has been shown how such an approach avoids the problems encountered in the use of a many-sorted language.

REFERENCES

[1] Cohn, A. G. "Improving the Expressiveness of Many-Sorted Logic", *Proc. of the 3rd NCAI*, Washington, 1983.

[2] Henschen, L. J. "N-Sorted Logic for Automatic Theorem Proving in Higher-Order Logic", *Proc. of ACM Conference*, Boston, 1972.

[3] Robinson, J. A. "A Machine-Oriented Logic Based on the Resolution Principle", *JACM*, Vol. 12, No. 1, 1965.

[4] Shin, D. G. "An Extension of a First-Order Language and Its Applications" Ph.D. Dissertation, University of Michigan, Ann Arbor, 1985.

[5] Shin, D. G. and Irani, K. B. "Knowledge Representation using an Extension of a Many-sorted Language", *Proc. of the 1st CAIA*, Denver, 1984.

[6] Walther, C. "A Many-sorted Calculus Based on Resolution and Paramodulation", *Proc. of the 8th IJCAI*, Karlsruhe, 1983.

[7] Walther, C. "Unification in Many-sorted Theories", *Proc. of the 6th ECAI*, Pisa, 1984a.

[8] Walther, C. "A Mechanical Solution of Schubert's Streamroller by Many-Sorted Resolution", *Proc. of the 4th NCAI*, Austin, 1984b.

PARALLEL PROCESSING OF RESOLUTION

Takahira YAMAGUCHI*, Yoshikazu TEZUKA** and Osamu KAKUSHO*

* The Institute of Scientific and Industrial Research, Osaka University,
8-1 Mihogaoka, Ibaragi, Osaka 567, Japan
** Faculty of Engineering, Osaka University, 2-1 Yamadaoka, Suita, Osaka
565, Japan

ABSTRACT

In this paper, PArallel Resolution Algorithm (PARA) is described to improve the execution efficiency in resolution process. PARA consists of two parts: parallel unification and generation of a resolvent. The first part is characteristic of PARA, which partitions whole set of expressions W into independent clusters as pre-processing and unifies each cluster in parallel. The efficient implementation for the processing peculiar to PARA is presented and checked by means of the experiment in comparison of execution efficiency of resolution. Experimental results show PARA is very effective in occurrence of many clusters.

1.INTRODUCTION

Unification in first-order logic is to match corresponding arguments in two predicates. This processing is important in resolution [1] and the efficient implementation for it has been the subject of much investigation [2]-[5]. But this research in unification was out of parallel-processing.

With regard to unification (resolution) parallelism, two representative ways, the post-processing way and the pre-processing way, would be considered. In case of the former, after unification, the consistency of substitution must be checked and each substitution component must be composed. This processing would be computed with unification and so the post-processing way is considered to cost much. On the contrary, in case of the latter, the pre-processing way to partition a set of expressions firstly could cost little, because this processing could be computed without unification.

From this consideration, in this paper, PARA is presented as one of the pre-processing ways. The characteristic of PARA lies in partitioning whole set of expressions W (the pairs of corresponding arguments in resolved literals) into clusters (sets of pairs of arguments such that each set has no variables in common) as pre-processing and unifying each cluster independently in parallel.

2.PARALLEL RESOLUTION ALGORITHM

Resolution consists of unification and generation of a resolvent. It costs more time to execute unification and so unification must be executed efficiently. The unification problem can be expressed as simultaneous equations [5] and the solution of them can be considered as most general unifier (mgu). The ordinary serial unification is process which solves simultaneous equations sequentially. They could, however, be divided into subsets of equations which are parallel-processed independently. Parallel resolution consists of two parts: parallel-processing of unification and generation of a resolvent. Fig.1 shows PARA. Firstly PARA partitions whole sets of expressions W into clusters of W1-Wm which include no variables in common as pre-processing. Secondly, after this pre-processing, PARA tries to unify each cluster independently in parallel. If all clusters are unifiable, PARA obtains the mgu of W by uniting the mgus of all clusters. Otherwise PARA concludes that W is not unifiable. Finally, after having obtained the mgu of W, PARA generates the resolvent and Clustering Information (which will be described later).

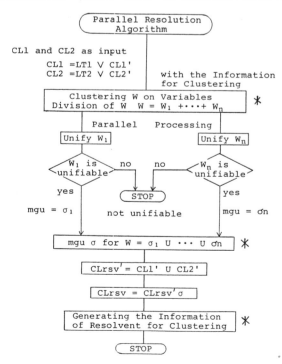

Fig.1   PArallel Resolution Algorithm (PARA)

3.EFFICIENT PROCESSING FOR PECULIAR PHASE IN PARA

The phases with * sign in Fig.1 are peculiar to PARA. Among these phases, clustering of W and generation of Clustering Information must be processed efficiently.

3.1 CLUSTERING INFORMATION

Since W is partitioned based on variables, Clustering Information will have to include the following information in order to execute clustering of W efficiently.
(1) Variable Information (of argument)
(2) Cluster Information (of literal)
Variable Information shows what variables each argument of literal has. Variable Information is stored in a form easy to treat. Cluster Information shows how one literal can be divided. Clustering Information consists of the above two pieces of information and the number of them. This is stored corresponding to each literal, as shown in Fig.2.

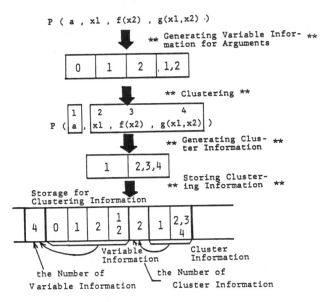

Fig.2   Data Structure for Clustering Information

3.2 CLUSTER OPERATION ALGORITHM

Clustering of W is executed by means of applying cluster operation to Cluster Information of resolved literals. Cluster operation is the process which makes clusters for parallel unification. It matches n-th component of one Cluster Information with all components of the other and combines matched components. P(a,g(x1),x2,f(g(x2))) and -P(x4,x3,f(x4),f(x3)) turn out not to be divided by means of applying cluster operation to Cluster Information of them.

3.3 CLUSTERING INFORMATION GENERATION ALGORITHM

Generating Clustering Information is executed by means of making use of Variable Information of parent clauses.

** *Clustering Information Generation Algorithm* **

Step 1 : Delete Variable Information of resolved literals of parent clauses. The rest is Variable Information of CLrsv' which is an incomplete resolvent which mgu is not applied.
Step 2 : Generate the pairs of the variable number (natural number corresponding to each variable) included in "term" of mgu and the variable number corresponding to the substituted variable of mgu.
Step 3 : Apply Variable Information of mgu to Variable Information of CLrsv' and generate Variable Information of CLrsv which is a complete resolvent.
Step 4 : Generate Cluster Information of first literal by means of clustering Variable Information.
Step 5 : Connect Variable Information of and Cluster Information of and let them Clustering Information of CLrsv.

4.COMPARISON OF PARA AND SRA

To compare PARA with SRA (Serial Resolution Algorithm), 4 logic programs [6] have been run on two algorithms using theorem proving system "SENRI" [6]. The run time for each process has been measured with executing SNL resolution and the total time for resolution process has been finally compared. Table 1 shows the experimental results.

PARA has about 2.1-fold improvement in unification process and about 1.8-fold improvement in resolution process over SRA on the average.

Comparing the run time for generating resolvents in two algorithms, the run time of PARA is about twice one of SRA. This implies that the run time for generating Clustering Information is as small as one of generating resolvents and so does not affect the total time so badly.

Since the redundancy for generating Clustering Information adds to resolution process, the improvement rate of resolution process becomes worse. The improvement rate of resolution process is, however, around 0.7-times of the number of clusters. Moreover the improvement rate of both unification process and resolution process rises in proportion to the number of clusters.

5. COMMENTS

In this experiment, some pairs of resolved literals, in which PARA becomes effective or ineffective, emerged definitely. Table 2 reports these literal pairs in detail.

(1)   *Literal Pair 1* (in which resolution succeeds and PARA becomes effective)
-> MICOM(FM8,FUJITSU,6809,218000)
MICOM(X1, X2, X3 ,218000)
Literal Pair 1 is divided into 4 clusters at the pre-processing. Since the mgu of each cluster has only substitution component, the run time for substitution is short. So parallel resolution becomes very effective.

(2)   *Literal Pair 2* (in which resolution
       fails and PARA becomes effective)
  -> *MICOM(MZ80B,SHARP,Z80A,278000)*
     MICOM(X1 , X2 , X3 ,218000)

Literal Pair 2 is divided into 4
clusters at the pre-processing and the
computation terminates at the time when 4-th
cluster proves not to be unifiable. So
parallel resolution becomes very effective.

(3)   *Literal Pair 3* (in which resolution
       fails and PARA becomes ineffective)
  -> *MAKER(OKI ,TOKYO, E)*
     MAKER(SHARP, X1 ,X2)

Literal Pair 3 proves not to be unifiable
at the first argument in SRA. So PARA
becomes ineffective due to the extra time for
clustering. Besides Literal Pair 3, literal pairs
which are not divided at the pre-processing are
similar.

(4)   *Literal Pair*(in which resolution
       succeeds and PARA becomes ineffective)
This literal pair is one which is not
divided at the pre-processing(not shown in
Table 2).

4 logic programs have literal pairs
inconvenient for PARA as well as convenient for
PARA and so the experiment is fair. Since the
decrease in cost caused by convenient literal
pairs is over the increase in cost caused by
inconvenient literal pairs, PARA is
effective to ordinary problems which include
inconvenient literal pairs as well as convenient
literal pairs.

6.CONCLUSION

PARA has been introduced for the
improvement of execution efficiency for
resolution process. It is characteristic of
PARA to partition whole set of expressions W
into independent clusters as pre-processing and
unify each cluster in parallel.

The experimental results in comparison of
execution efficiency for resolution show the
following.

(1) The processing peculiar to PARA
     has been implemented efficiently.
(2) The improvement rates of both
     unification process and resolution
     process by parallel-processing rise in
     proportion to the number of clusters.
(3) Since the decrease in cost caused
     by convenient literal pairs is over the
     increase in cost caused by
     inconvenient literal pairs, PARA is
     effective to ordinary problems.

Finally, unification in this paper is
limited to be basic unification in [2].
Parallel-processing of refined unification in [4]
or [5] would, however, be possible and further
improvement could be expected.

Table 1   Comparison of SRA and PARA

Comparison items \ Problems	MEMBER	APPEND	LOOP	DB
The number of resolution trial	6	5	3	57
The number of resolution success	4	3	8	4
The number of clusters for pairs of resolved literals	1-2	2	2-3	3-4
S R A — The total time for unification process	6000	10245	29605	11820
S R A — The total time for generating resolvents	490	485	1980	1335
S R A — The total time for resolution process	6490	10730	31585	13155
P A R A — The total time for unification process	4220	5775	12550	4560
P A R A — The total time for generating resolvents	1025	1290	3830	1785
P A R A — The total time for resolution process	5245	7065	16380	6345
I R — Improvement rate in unification process	1.42	1.77	2.36	2.59
I R — Improvement rate in resolution process	1.24	1.52	1.93	2.07

Table 2   Comparison of Some Pairs of Resolved Literals

Comparison items \ Pair of resolved literals	Literal Pair 1	Literal Pair 2	Literal Pair 3
T_{SRA}	1 0 7 5	1 0 3 5	6 0
T_{PARA}	5 3 5	1 9 5	1 5 0

unit time : usec
machine   : ACOS system 1000 (NEC)
S R A   : Serial Resolution Algorithm
P A R A   : PArallel Resolution Algorithm
I R   : Improvement Rate

REFERENCES

(1) Kowalski, R.A. :" Logic for Problem
    Solving ",North Holland (1979)
(2) Robinson, J.A. :" A Machine Oriented Logic
    Based on Resolution Principle ", J.ACM,12,
    pp.23-41 (1965)
(3) Robinson, J.A. :" Computational Logic : The
    Unification Computation ", Machine Intellige-
    nce 6, pp.63-72,Edinburg Univ.Press (1971)
(4) Paterson, M.S. and Wegman,M.N. :" Linear
    Unification ", Proc.8th Annual ACM Symp.
    on Theory of Computing, pp.181-186 (1976)
(5) Martelli, A. and Montanari, U. :" An
    Efficient Unification Algorithm ", ACM Trans.
    on Programming Lang. and Syst.,4,2 pp.258-282
    (1982)
(6) Yamaguchi, T. :" The Efficient Implementation
    for Predicate Logic Based System " Univ. of
    Osaka, Dr. dissertation (dec. 1983) (in
    Japanese)

Automated Deduction by Theory Resolution

Mark E. Stickel

Artificial Intelligence Center
SRI International
and
Center for the Study of Language and Information
Stanford University

Abstract

Theory resolution constitutes a set of complete procedures for incorporating theories into a resolution theorem-proving program, thereby making it unnecessary to resolve directly upon axioms of the theory. This can greatly reduce the length of proofs and the size of the search space. Theory resolution effects a beneficial division of labor, improving the performance of the theorem prover and increasing the applicability of the specialized reasoning procedures. Applications include the building in of both mathematical and special decision procedures, e.g., for the taxonomic information furnished by a knowledge representation system. Theory resolution is a generalization of numerous previously known resolution refinements. Its power is demonstrated by comparing solutions of "Schubert's Steamroller" challenge problem with and without building in axioms through theory resolution.[1]

1 Introduction

Incorporating a theory into derived inference rules so that its axioms are never resolved upon has enormous potential for reducing the size of the exponential search space commonly encountered in resolution theorem proving. Theory resolution is a method of incorporating specialized reasoning procedures in a resolution theorem prover so that the reasoning task will be effectively divided into two parts: special cases, such as reasoning about inequalities or about taxonomic information, are handled efficiently by specialized reasoning procedures, while more general reasoning is handled by resolution. The connection between the two reasoning components is made by having the resolution procedure resolve on sets of literals whose conjunction is determined to be unsatisfiable by the specialized reasoning procedure. The objective of research on theory resolution is the conceptual design of deduction systems that combine deductive specialists within the common framework of a resolution theorem prover.

Concern has often been expressed about the ineffectiveness of applying resolution theorem proving to problems in artificial intelligence. Theory resolution is designed to partly address this concern by providing a means for incorporating specialized reasoning procedures in a resolution theorem prover. The division of labor achieved in the reasoning process by theory resolution is

intended to produce the dual advantages of improving the theorem prover's performance by the use of more efficient reasoning procedures for special cases and of increasing the range of application of the specialized reasoning procedures by including them in a more general reasoning system.

Past criticisms of resolution can often be characterized by their pejorative use of the terms *uniform* and *syntactic*. Theory resolution meets these objections head-on. In theory resolution, a specialized reasoning procedure may be substituted for ordinary syntactic unification to determine unsatisfiability of sets of literals. Because the implementation of this specialized reasoning procedure is unspecified—to the theorem prover it is a "black box" with prescribed behavior, namely, able to determine unsatisfiability in the theory it implements—the resulting system is nonuniform because reasoning within the theory is performed by the specialized reasoning procedure, while reasoning outside the theory is performed by resolution. Theory resolution can also be regarded as being not wholly syntactic, since the conditions for resolving on a set of literals are no longer based on their being made syntactically identical, but rather on their being unsatisfiable in a theory, and thus resolvability is partly semantic.

Reasoning about orderings and other transitive relations is often necessary, but using ordinary resolution for this is quite inefficient. It is possible to derive an infinite number of consequences from $a < b$ and $(x < y) \land (y < z) \supset (x < z)$ despite the obvious fact that a refutation based on just these two formulas is impossible. A solution to this problem is to require that use of the transitivity axiom be restricted to occasions when either there are matches for two of its literals (partial theory resolution) or a complete refutation of the ordering part of the clauses can be found (total theory resolution).

An important form of reasoning in artificial intelligence applications embodied in knowledge representation systems is reasoning about taxonomic information and property inheritance. One of our goals is to be able to take advantage of the efficient reasoning provided by a knowledge representation system by using it as a taxonomy decision procedure in a larger deduction system. KRYPTON [4,13] represents an approach to constructing a knowledge representation system composed of two parts: a terminological component (the TBox) and an assertional component (the ABox). For such systems, theory resolution indicates in general how information can be provided to the ABox by the TBox and how it can be used by the ABox.

2 Theory Resolution

We will now define the theory resolution operation and discuss various useful restrictions on theory resolution. We will limit our

[1]This research was supported by the Defense Advanced Research Projects Agency under Contract N00039-84-K-0078 with the Naval Electronic Systems Command and was also made possible in part by a gift from the System Development Foundation. The views and conclusions contained in this document are those of the author and should not be interpreted as representative of the official policies, either expressed or implied, of the Defense Advanced Research Projects Agency or the United States government. Approved for public release. Distribution unlimited.

discussion to the variable-free "ground" case of theory resolution, since lifting to the general case is straightforward.

We will assume the standard definitions of a *term*, an *atomic formula (atom)*, and a *literal*. We will consider a *clause* to be a disjunction of $n \geq 0$ literals. If $n = 0$, the clause is the *empty clause* $\square$. If $n = 1$, the clause is a *unit clause*. The disjunction connective $\vee$ is assumed to be associative, commutative, and idempotent. The empty clause $\square$ is the identity element for $\vee$. We will generally make no distinction between a unit clause and the single literal of which it is composed.

We will assume the standard definitions of an *interpretation*, an interpretation *satisfying* or *falsifying* a formula or set of formulas, and a formula or set of formulas being *satisfiable* or *unsatisfiable*.

Any satisfiable set of formulas that we wish to incorporate into the inference process can be regarded as a *theory*.

Definition 1 A T-*interpretation* is an interpretation that satisfies theory T.

For example, in a theory of partial ordering ORD consisting of $\neg(x < x)$ and $(x < y) \wedge (y < z) \supset (x < z)$, the predicate $<$ cannot be interpreted so that $a < a$ has value *true* or $a < c$ has value *false* if $a < b$ and $b < c$ both have value *true*. In a taxonomic theory TAX including $Boy(x) \supset Person(x)$, $Boy(John)$ cannot have value *true* while $Person(John)$ has value *false*.

Definition 2 A set of clauses S is T-*unsatisfiable* iff no T-interpretation satisfies S. S is *minimally* T-*unsatisfiable* iff S, but no proper subset of S, is T-unsatisfiable.

Definition 3 Let $C_1, \ldots, C_m$ ($m \geq 1$) be a set of nonempty clauses, let each C_i be decomposed as $K_i \vee L_i$ where K_i is a nonempty clause, and let $R_1, \ldots, R_n$ ($n \geq 0$) be unit clauses. Suppose the set of clauses $K_1, \ldots, K_m, R_1, \ldots, R_n$ is T-unsatisfiable. Then the clause $L_1 \vee \cdots \vee L_m \vee \neg R_1 \vee \cdots \vee \neg R_n$ is a *theory resolvent using theory T (T-resolvent)* of $C_1, \ldots, C_m$. The theory resolvent is called an m-*ary* theory resolvent. It is a *total* theory resolvent iff $n = 0$; otherwise it is *partial*. $K_1, \ldots, K_m$ is called the *key* of the theory resolution operation. For partial theory resolvents, $R_1, \ldots, R_n$ is a set of *conditions* for the T-unsatisfiability of the key. The negation $\neg R_1 \vee \cdots \vee \neg R_n$ of the conjunction of the conditions is called the *residue* of the theory resolution operation. It is a *narrow* theory resolvent iff each K_i is a unit clause; otherwise it is *wide*.

The partial theory resolution procedure permits total as well as partial theory resolution operations. Similarly, the wide theory resolution procedure permits narrow as well as wide theory resolution operations.

Example 4 A set of unit clauses is unsatisfiable in the theory of partial ordering ORD iff it contains a chain of inequalities $t_1 < \cdots < t_n$ ($n \geq 2$) such that either t_1 is the same as t_n or $\neg(t_1 < t_n)$ is also one of the clauses. P is a unary total narrow ORD-resolvent of $(a < a) \vee P$. $P \vee Q$ is a binary total narrow ORD-resolvent of $(a < b) \vee P$ and $(b < a) \vee Q$. $P \vee Q \vee R \vee S$ is a 4-ary total narrow ORD-resolvent of $(a < b) \vee P$, $(b < c) \vee Q$, $(c < d) \vee R$, and $\neg(a < d) \vee S$. This can also be derived incrementally through partial narrow ORD-resolution, i.e., by resolving $(a < b) \vee P$ and $(b < c) \vee Q$ to obtain $(a < c) \vee P \vee Q$, resolving that with $(c < d) \vee R$ to obtain $(a < d) \vee P \vee Q \vee R$, and resolving that with $\neg(a < d) \vee S$ to obtain $P \vee Q \vee R \vee S$.

Example 5 Suppose the taxonomic theory TAX includes a definition for fatherhood $Father(x) \equiv [Man(x) \wedge \exists y Child(x, y)]$. Then $Father(Fred)$ is a partial wide theory resolvent of $Child(Fred, Pat) \vee Child(Fred, Sandy)$ and $Man(Fred)$. Also, $\square$ is a total wide theory resolvent of $Child(Fred, Pat) \vee Child(Fred, Sandy)$, $Man(Fred)$, and $\neg Father(Fred)$.

We will explore some possible restrictions on the definition of theory resolution that make it practical to apply while preserving completeness.

In narrow theory resolution, only T-unsatisfiability of sets of literals, not clauses, must be decided. Total and partial narrow theory resolution are both possible. In total narrow theory resolution, the resolved-upon literals (the key) must be T-unsatisfiable. In partial narrow theory resolution, the key must be T-unsatisfiable only under some conditions. The negated conditions are used as the residue in the formation of the resolvent.

We do not want to require the derivation of all partial narrow theory resolvents permitted by the definition. This would result in the derivation of obviously unnecessary resolvents. For example, we could resolve $(a < b) \vee P$ and $(c < d) \vee R$, since, under some conditions such as $(b < c) \wedge (d < a)$, $a < b$ and $c < d$ are T-unsatisfiable. If we permit inferences from $a < b$ and $c < d$, which have no terms in common, theory resolution would not be very useful. If resolving $a < b$ and $c < d$ were to actually lead to a refutation—i.e., conditions for their T-unsatisfiability do hold—then some of these conditions, e.g., $(b < c) \wedge (d < a)$, must have arguments in common with $a < b$ and $c < d$. We should restrict partial theory resolution to cases in which the literals are suitably related.

To justify such pragmatically necessary restrictions on theory resolution, we offer the following criterion for the selection of key sets of literals that provides a sufficient condition for the completeness of partial narrow theory resolution.

In essence, the key selection criterion requires that every T-unsatisfiable set of literals have one or more subset key sets of literals that can be T-resolved. For example, in theory ORD, in refuting sets of positive inequality literals, we might select only pairs of literals matching $x < y$ and $y < z$ as key sets of literals. Thus, in refuting the set $\{a < b, b < c, c < d, d < a\}$, we would be permitted, for example, to resolve upon $a < b$ and $b < c$, but not $a < b$ and $c < d$. Key sets of literals have one or more residues associated with them such that every minimally T-unsatisfiable set includes a key with a residue that can be refuted by resolving away the literals in the residue. With literals matching $x < y$ and $y < z$ selected, it is sufficient to derive T-resolvents with residue $x < z$. For example, $a < b$ and $b < c$ can be T-resolved with $a < c$ as the result. This can then be resolved with $c < d$ to derive $a < d$ that can be resolved with $d < a$ to derive $\square$.

Key selection criterion.

- For any minimally T-unsatisfiable set of literals S, there is at least one key set of literals K such that $K \subseteq S$. K has at least two literals (one literal if S has only one literal). Each K is recognizable by the decision procedure for T and will comprise the key for possible theory resolution operations, if clauses containing the key literals are present.

- For any such key set of literals K, there is at least one, possibly empty, residue set of literals R such that $K \cup \neg R$ is minimally T-unsatisfiable, where $\neg R$ denotes the set

$\{\neg R_1, \ldots, \neg R_n\}$ when $R = \{R_1, \ldots, R_n\}$. Each $\neg R$ is a set of conditions for the T-unsatisfiability of key set K. Each R is computed from K by the decision procedure for T and is used as a residue for theory resolution operations that resolve on key K.

- It must be the case that, for some key set of literals K and associated residue set of literals R, $(S - K) \cup \{\vee R\}$ is minimally T-unsatisfiable, where $\vee R$ denotes the clause $R_1 \vee \cdots \vee R_n$ when $R = \{R_1, \ldots, R_n\}$. This ensures that key selection and residue computation will be sufficient for completeness—any T-unsatisfiable set of literals S has a T-resolvent using a key $K \subseteq S$ and residue R computed from K such that the T-resolvent is contradicted by the remaining literals $S - K$.

In total narrow theory resolution, we uniformly take the key K to be the entire minimally T-unsatisfiable set of literals S. The residue R is always empty.

In partial narrow theory resolution, we will try to minimize the number of residue sets of literals. Thus, for $K = \{a < b, b < c\}$ we might have residues $R_1 = \{a < c\}$, $R_2 = \{\neg(c < x_1), \neg(x_1 < a)\}$, $R_3 = \{\neg(c < x_1), \neg(x_1 < x_2), \neg(x_2 < a)\}$, etc. However, only R_1 need be used, since, in the theory T, R_1 implies every other R_i. R_1 can be regarded as the strongest consequence of $a < b$ and $b < c$ in theory T.

The following theorem proves the completeness of narrow theory resolution with arbitrary selection of key sets of literals satisfying the key selection criterion.

Theorem 6 *Let S be a T-unsatisfiable set of clauses. Then there is a refutation of S (derivation of $\square$ from S) using partial narrow theory resolution with theory T for arbitrary selection of key sets satisfying the key selection criterion.*

Proof: If $\square \in S$, then S is trivially refuted.

Otherwise we will prove the theorem by induction on complexity measure $c(S)$, where $c(S) = (|S|, k(S))$, where $|S|$ is the number of clauses in S and $k(S)$ is the *excess literal parameter* [1]. The excess literal parameter is defined to be the number of literals (i.e., literal occurrences) in S minus $|S|$. The ordering of $c(S)$ is defined by $c(S_1) \prec c(S_2)$ iff $|S_1| < |S_2|$, or $|S_1| = |S_2|$ and $k(S_1) < k(S_2)$.

Case $c(S) = (m, 0)$. Every clause must be a unit clause. Because S is T-unsatisfiable, it must include a minimally T-unsatisfiable subset S'.

Subcase $|S'| \leq 2$. By the key selection criterion, S' must be selected as a key. The empty clause $\square$ is derivable in a single unary or binary T-resolution step from S' and hence from S.

Subcase $|S'| > 2$. By the key selection criterion, there exists a key $K \subseteq S'$ with $|K| \geq 2$ and (possibly empty) residue R such that $S'' = (S' - K) \cup \{\vee R\}$ is minimally T-unsatisfiable. $c(S'') \prec c(S') \preceq c(S)$. Thus, by the induction hypothesis, $\square$ is derivable from S''. Since $\vee R$ is a T-resolvent of $K \subseteq S$, $\square$ is derivable from S.

Case $c(S) = (m, n)$, $n > 0$. Select a nonunit clause $C \in S$. Decompose C into unit clause A and clause B, i.e., $C = A \vee B$. Because S is T-unsatisfiable, both $S_A = (S - \{C\}) \cup \{A\}$ and

$S_B = (S - \{C\}) \cup \{B\}$ are T-unsatisfiable. Both $c(S_A) \prec c(S)$ and $c(S_B) \prec c(S)$. Thus, by the induction hypothesis, there must exist derivations of $\square$ from each of S_A and S_B.

Imitate the derivation of $\square$ from S_B, using C instead of B. The result will be a derivation of either $\square$ or A from S. In the latter case, extend the derivation of A from S to a derivation of $\square$ from S by appending the derivation of $\square$ from S_A. ∎

Corollary 7 *Let S be a T-unsatisfiable set of clauses. Then there is a refutation of S (derivation of $\square$ from S) using total narrow theory resolution with theory T.*

Although the theorem proves completeness of narrow theory resolution, its proof does not preclude the need for tautologies in a refutation. Indeed, it is the case that tautologies may have to be retained for a refutation to be found.

Example 8 Let T be the theory in which P, Q, and R are all equivalent. Let S be $\{P \vee Q \vee R, \neg P \vee \neg Q \vee \neg R\}$. There is a single-step wide T-resolution refutation of S. However, although there do exist refutations of S by narrow T-resolution, all require retention of tautologies, since all narrow T-resolvents of $P \vee Q \vee R$ and $\neg P \vee \neg Q \vee \neg R$ are tautologies.

Finally, note that heuristic restrictions of theory resolution (such as discarding all tautologies, not recognizing all cases of T-unsatisfiability, or not computing all residues), though incomplete, may be very useful in practice.

3   Examples of Theory Resolution

Theory resolution is a procedure with substantial generality and power. Thus, it is not surprising that many specialized reasoning procedures can be viewed as instances of theory resolution, perhaps with additional constraints governing which theory resolvents can be inferred. We believe that the success of these specialized reasoning procedures helps to validate the concept of theory resolution.

First of all, we should note that there is a relationship between theory resolution and **hyperresolution**. Although further constraints (e.g., on the polarity of the literals) are often prescribed, the essence of hyperresolution is the derivation of $L_1 \vee \cdots \vee L_m \vee R$ from the *electron* clauses $K_i \vee L_i$, where K_i is a literal and L_i is a [possibly empty] clause and the *nucleus* clause $\neg K_1 \vee \cdots \vee \neg K_m \vee R$, where R is a [possibly empty] clause. This corresponds to a theory resolution operation using theory T, where $\neg K_1 \vee \cdots \vee \neg K_m \vee R$ is a consequence of T, $K_1, \ldots, K_m$ is the key set of literals, and R is the residue.

Theory resolution is also related to **procedural attachment**, whereby expressions are "evaluated" to produce new expressions. Ordinary procedural attachment can be regarded as unary theory resolution. Theory resolution in general can be considered as an extension of the notion of procedural attachment to sets of literals. Where ordinary procedural attachment permits the replacement of $2 < 3$ by *true*, theory resolution, in effect, can attach a procedure to the $<$ relation that permits derivation of $a < c$ from $a < b$ and $b < c$.

Two previous refinements of resolution that resemble partial theory resolution are Z-resolution and U-generalized resolution.

Dixon's **Z-resolution** [5] is essentially binary total narrow theory resolution with the restriction that T must consist of a finite deductively closed set of 2-clauses (clauses with length

2). This restriction does not permit inclusion of assertions like $\neg Q(x) \vee Q(f(x))$, $\neg(x < x)$, or $(x < y) \wedge (y < z) \supset (x < z)$, but does permit efficient computation of T-resolvents (even allowing the possibility of compiling T to LISP code and thence to machine code). Z-factoring and Z-subsumption operations are also defined.

Harrison and Rubin's **U-generalized resolution** [7] is essentially binary partial narrow theory resolution applied to sets of clauses that have a unit or input refutation. They apply it to building in the equality relation, developing a procedure similar to Morris's E-resolution [10]. The restriction to sets of clauses having unit or input refutations eliminates the need for factoring and simplifies the procedure, but otherwise limits its applicability. No effort was made in the definition of U-generalized resolution to limit the applicability of T-resolution to reasonable cases (e.g., formation of an ORD-resolvent of $a < b$ and $c < d$ is permitted by the definition).

The **linked inference principle** by Wos et al. [22] is related to theory resolution in concept and purpose. The linked inference principle is a somewhat more conservative extension of resolution than theory resolution, since it stipulates that the theory will be built in by means of clauses designated as linking clauses. Theory resolution, on the other hand, allows the theory to be incorporated as a "black box" that determines T-unsatisfiability questions in an unspecified manner. This facilitates the use of other systems, which do not rely upon resolution or clause representation, to build in theories. Nevertheless, many instances of theory resolution can be usefully implemented in the manner of the linked inference principle. Since the implementation proposal for the linked inference principle is more concrete, Wos et al. have expended comparatively more effort in determining how inference using the linked inference principle is to be controlled, including defining linked variants of resolution refinements such as unit-resulting resolution and hyperresolution.

We have already suggested the importance of theory resolution for **taxonomic reasoning**. This is being explored in the KRYPTON knowledge representation system. Figure 1 contains a nearly verbatim transcription of a proof using KRYPTON-style reasoning. The problem is to prove that, if Chris has no sons and no daughters, then Chris has no children.

The terminological information used in this problem through theory resolution includes the statements that boys are persons whose sex is male; girls are persons whose sex is female; "no-sons" are persons all of whose children are girls; "no-daughters" are persons all of whose children are boys. Relevant portions of this information are included in Formulas 1–6, which are used to define what theory resolution operations are possible. If complements of the first two atoms of each formula can be found, they can be resolved upon, and the remaining part of the formula, if any, would be derived as the residue. Thus, Formula 1 expresses the unsatisfiability of $Boy(John)$ and $\neg Person(John)$. Formula 5 permits the derivation of $Girl(Sandy)$ from $NoSon(Mary)$ and $Child(Mary, Sandy)$. These formulas behave similarly to linking clauses in linked inference [22].

The assertional information used in this problem includes the information that every person has a sex; males and females are disjoint; Chris has no sons and no daughters. From these facts, and the built in terminological information, a refutation is completed starting with the negation of the desired conclusion that Chris has no children. $sk1$ and $sk2$ are Skolem functions.

The following table compares the statistics for proofs com-

2-ary rule	1.	$Boy(x) \supset Person(x)$
2-ary rule	2.	$Boy(x) \wedge Sex(x, y) \supset Male(y)$
2-ary rule (not used)	3.	$Girl(x) \supset Person(x)$
2-ary rule	4.	$Girl(x) \wedge Sex(x, y) \supset Female(y)$
2-ary rule	5.	$NoSon(x) \wedge Child(x, y)$ $\supset Girl(y)$
2-ary rule	6.	$NoDaughter(x) \wedge Child(x, y)$ $\supset Boy(y)$
	7.	$Person(x) \supset Sex(x, sk1(x))$
	8.	$Male(x) \equiv \neg Female(x)$
	9.	$NoSon(Chris)$
	10.	$NoDaughter(Chris)$
negated conclusion	11.	$Child(Chris, sk2)$
resolve 11&9 using 5	12.	$Girl(sk2)$
resolve 11&10 using 6	13.	$Boy(sk2)$
resolve 13&7 using 1	14.	$Sex(sk2, sk1(sk2))$
resolve 13&14 using 2	15.	$Male(sk1(sk2))$
resolve 12&14 using 4	16.	$Female(sk1(sk2))$
resolve 16&8&15	20.	$\square$

Figure 1: KRYPTON-style Proof

pleted with and without Formulas 1–6 built in through theory resolution. The proof strategies used and meaning of the statistics are essentially the same as described in Section 4

Built In Axioms	Input Wffs	Der. Wffs	Ret. Wffs	Suc. Unify	Time (sec.)	Proof Length
none	11	10	20	33	1.0	9
1–6	5	9	11	24	0.5	6

There is a noticeable improvement resulting from using theory resolution, but because the problem is so small, the difference is not large. Harder problems (like the one in Section 4) can be used to demonstrate much greater improvement.

Theory resolution for taxonomic reasoning also incorporates many elements of reasoning in a **many-sorted logic**. For example, in Walther's ΣRP-calculus (many-sorted resolution and paramodulation) [17,19], sort declarations, subsort relationships, and sort restrictions on clauses are all incorporated into the unification procedure, and eliminated from the clauses in the statement of a problem. Thus, the ΣRP unification procedure implements a theory of sort information.

4 Experimental Results

Although the relationship of theory resolution to many other extensions of resolution and experience with numerous small examples support the practical value of theory resolution, we will not elaborate on these, but will rather bolster our claim with an examination of experimental results for "Schubert's Steamroller" challenge problem.

Schubert's steamroller problem (annotated with formula numbers) is

> (1-5) Wolves, foxes, birds, caterpillars, and snails are animals, and (7-11) there are some of each of them. Also (12) there are some grains, and (6) grains are plants. (13) Every animal either likes to eat all plants or all animals much smaller than itself that like to

eat some plants. (14) Caterpillars and snails are much smaller than birds, which are much smaller than foxes, which in turn are much smaller than wolves. (15) Wolves do not like to eat foxes or grains, while (16) birds like to eat caterpillars but (15) not snails. (17) Caterpillars and snails like to eat some plants. Therefore (18) there is an animal that likes to eat a grain-eating animal.

We present statistics on several solutions of Schubert's steamroller problem found by our theorem prover [15]. The first is a proof that does not use theory resolution; the second is a proof using theory resolution to implement the taxonomic information in the problem (Formulas 1–6); the remaining proofs show the results of using theory resolution to build in each of Formulas 14–17 successively.

The same strategy was used for all of the proofs. Nonclausal connection-graph resolution was the principal inference rule. Factoring was not employed. Pure, variant, and tautologous formulas were eliminated. Single literal formulas were used for both forward and backward demodulation.

Heuristic search, guided by a simple weighted function of the deduction level of the parents and the expected size of the resolvent, was used to decide which inference operation should be performed next. The set of support strategy (with only Formula 18 supported) and an ordering strategy that designated which atoms in a formula could be resolved upon were used to limit the number of alternative inference operations.

In using theory resolution, connection graph links were created from key sets of literals in the theory being incorporated. Formulas 1–6 and 17 were implemented by binary total narrow theory resolution links and Formulas 14–16 were implemented by 3-ary total narrow theory resolution links. For example, $Wolf(t)$ and $\neg Animal(t)$ could be linked, and $Bird(t_1)$, $Snail(t_2)$, and $Likes\text{-}to\text{-}eat(t_1, t_2)$ could all be linked. Theory resolution was also used in demodulation—e.g., $Wolf(t)$ could be used to demodulate $Animal(t)$ to $true$.

Following are the statistics for the various solutions of Schubert's steamroller problem. Included in the statistics are the number of formulas inputted to the theorem prover, the number of formulas derived in the course of searching for a proof, the number of inputted and derived formulas still present when a proof was found, the number of successful unification attempts during the search for a proof (including unification during link inheritance), the time required for the proof (on a Symbolics 3600 personal LISP machine), and the length of the proof in resolution steps.

Built In Axioms	Input Wffs	Der. Wffs	Ret. Wffs	Suc. Unify	Time (sec.)	Proof Length
none	18	2,717	595	216,987	2:53	59
1–6	12	889	246	44,928	0:20	37
1–6,14	11	408	68	5,018	0:01.3	32
1–6,14–15	10	320	63	4,555	0:01.1	32
1–6,14–16	9	212	57	3,068	0:00.7	32
1–6,14–17	8	262	24	7,711	0:01.6	24
MKRP	27	60	83		0:04.4	55
+ΣRP	12	10	13	48	0:00.2	9
ITP					0:06	

Also included in the table are statistics we know for solutions of Schubert's steamroller problem by other systems. Unfortunately, use of slightly different axiomatizations, e.g., whether "grain-eating animal" is interpreted as an animal that eats *some* grain (our work, see [16]) or *every* grain [18], makes statistics for these different solutions not strictly comparable. We will publish a more detailed comparison of solutions later.

The MKRP solution was done by Walther [20] using the Markgraf Karl Refutation Procedure [3]. This proof relied heavily on the MKRP TERMINATOR module [2], which is essentially a very fast procedure for finding unit refutations. A superior proof by Walther [18] used his ΣRP calculus [17,19] in the MKRP system to perform many-sorted resolution on a much reduced set of clauses. This proof also used the TERMINATOR module, but, given the reduction in the number of clauses and literals made possible by using many-sorted resolution and its restrictions on unification, here its use was not essential to finding a solution with reasonable effort. MKRP is written in INTERLISP and was run on a Siemens 7760 computer.

Our first theory resolution proof, in which only the taxonomic information of Formulas 1–6 is incorporated, has some similarity to a many-sorted resolution proof. In the MKRP ΣRP proof, *Wolf*, *Fox*, *Bird*, *Caterpillar*, and *Snail* were declared to be subsorts of sort *Animal* and *Grain* was declared to be a subsort of sort *Plant*. The unification algorithm was restricted so that a variable can be unified with a term if and only if the term is a subsort of or equals the sort of the variable. For building in just this taxonomic information, many-sorted resolution is stronger than this particular instance of theory resolution. Although theory resolution handles the sort literals more effectively than ordinary resolution, many-sorted resolution dispenses with them entirely. Also, many-sorted resolution is used to build in the sort information for Skolem constants and functions so that, in Schubert's steamroller problem, Formulas 7–12 are supplanted by type declarations.

The ITP solution was found by the automated reasoning system ITP (written in PASCAL) developed at Argonne National Laboratory [9]. This solution used qualified hyperresolution [8,21] and was completed in about six minutes on a VAX 11/780 computer [12]. Like the theory resolution and MKRP ΣRP solutions, this solution treated the taxonomic sort information in the problem specially. In qualified hyperresolution, some literals in a clause can be designated as qualifier literals that contain "conditions of definition" for terms appearing in the clause. Qualifier literals are ignored during much of the inference process—e.g., a clause consisting of a single nonqualifier literal and some qualifier literals is handled as if it were a unit clause—with the conditions imposed by the qualifier literals checked only after the qualified terms are instantiated. Thus, sort restrictions can be specified in qualifier literals and deductions can be performed using only the nonsort information. The deductions are then subjected to verification that terms are of the correct sort.

5   Conclusion

Theory resolution is a set of complete procedures for incorporating decision procedures into resolution theorem proving in first-order predicate calculus. Theory resolution can greatly decrease the length of proofs and the size of the search space. Theory resolution is also a generalization of several other approaches to building in nonequational theories.

We are implementing and testing forms of theory resolution in the deduction-system component of the KLAUS natural-language-understanding system [6,15]. This system demonstrated substantial improvement in performance when theory resolution was used on Schubert's steamroller challenge problem. The KRYPTON knowledge representation system is also applying the ideas of theory resolution to combine a terminological reasoning component and an assertional reasoning component (for which they are also utilizing the KLAUS deduction system).

Theory resolution is a procedure with substantial power and generality. It is our hope that it will serve as a base for the theoretical and practical development of a methodology for combining the general reasoning capabilities of resolution theorem-proving programs with more efficient specialized reasoning procedures.

One important area for further research on theory resolution is finding restrictions on the need for retention of tautologies and determining compatibility with other resolution refinements.

Another important research question is handling combinations of theories (beyond the trivial case of totally disjoint theories). Successful combining of multiple deductive specialists within a resolution framework awaits further development in this area. The work of Nelson and Oppen [11] and Shostak [14] on combining quantifier free theories may be relevant.

Acknowledgments

The author would like to thank Mabry Tyson, Richard Waldinger, and Christoph Walther for their very useful comments on an earlier draft of this paper.

References

[1] Anderson, R. and W.W. Bledsoe. A linear format for resolution with merging and a new technique for establishing completeness. *Journal of the ACM 17*, 3 (July 1970), 525–534.

[2] Antoniou, G. and H.J. Ohlbach. TERMINATOR. *Proceedings of the Eighth International Joint Conference on Artificial Intelligence*, Karlsruhe, West Germany, August 1983, 916–919.

[3] Bläsius, K., N. Eisinger, J. Siekmann, G. Smolka, A. Herold, and C. Walther. The Markgraf Karl Refutation Procedure (Fall 1981). *Proceedings of the Seventh International Joint Conference on Artificial Intelligence*, Vancouver, B.C., Canada, August 1981, 511–518.

[4] Brachman, R.J., R.E. Fikes, and H.J. Levesque. KRYPTON: a functional approach to knowledge representation. *IEEE Computer 16*, 10 (October 1983), 67–73.

[5] Dixon, J.K. Z-resolution: theorem-proving with compiled axioms. *Journal of the ACM 20*, 1 (January 1973), 127–147.

[6] Haas, N. and G.G. Hendrix. An approach to acquiring and applying knowledge. *Proceedings of the AAAI-80 National Conference on Artificial Intelligence*, Stanford, California, August 1980, 235–239.

[7] Harrison, M.C. and N. Rubin. Another generalization of resolution. *Journal of the ACM 25*, 3 (July 1978), 341–351.

[8] Lusk, E.L. and R.A. Overbeek. Experiments with resolution-based theorem-proving algorithms. *Computers and Mathematics with Applications 8*, 3 (1982), 141–152.

[9] Lusk, E.L. and R.A. Overbeek. The automated reasoning system ITP. Technical Report ANL-84-27, Argonne National Laboratory, Argonne, Illinois, April 1984.

[10] Morris, J.B. E-resolution: extension of resolution to include the equality relation. *Proceedings of the International Joint Conference on Artificial Intelligence*, Washington, D.C., May 1969, 287–294.

[11] Nelson, G. and D.C. Oppen. Simplification by cooperating decision procedures. *ACM Transactions on Programming Languages and Systems 1*, 2 (October 1979), 245–257.

[12] Overbeek, R.A. Personal communication, September 1984.

[13] Pigman, V. The interaction between assertional and terminological knowledge in KRYPTON. *Proceedings of the IEEE Workshop on Principles of Knowledge-Based Systems*, Denver, Colorado, December 1984.

[14] Shostak, R.E. Deciding combinations of theories. *Journal of the ACM 31*, 1 (January 1984), 1–12.

[15] Stickel, M.E. A nonclausal connection-graph resolution theorem-proving program. *Proceedings of the AAAI-82 National Conference on Artificial Intelligence*, Pittsburgh, Pennsylvania, August 1982, 229–233.

[16] Stickel, M.E. Automated deduction by theory resolution. Technical Note 340, Artificial Intelligence Center, SRI International, October 1984. (An extended version of this paper.)

[17] Walther, C. A many-sorted calculus based on resolution and paramodulation. *Proceedings of the Eighth International Joint Conference on Artificial Intelligence*, Karlsruhe, West Germany, August 1983, 882–891.

[18] Walther, C. A mechanical solution of Schubert's steamroller by many-sorted resolution. *Proceedings of the AAAI-84 National Conference on Artificial Intelligence*, Austin, Texas, August 1984, 330–334.

[19] Walther, C. Unification in many-sorted theories. *Proceedings of the 6th European Conference on Artificial Intelligence*, Pisa, Italy, September 1984.

[20] Walther, C. Personal communication, October 1984.

[21] Winker, S. An evaluation of an implementation of qualified hyperresolution. *IEEE Transactions on Computers C-25*, 8 (August 1976), 835–843.

[22] Wos, L., R. Veroff, B. Smith, and W. McCune. The linked inference principle, II: the user's viewpoint. *Proceedings of the 7th International Conference on Automated Deduction*, Napa, California, May 1984, 316–332.

PATH RESOLUTION WITH LINK DELETION

Neil V. Murray   *and*   *Erik Rosenthal*

State University of NY at Albany
Department of Computer Science
Albany, NY 12222

University of New Haven
Department of Mathematics
West Haven, CT 06516

ABSTRACT

We introduce a graphical representation of quantifier-free predicate calculus formulas and a new rule of inference which employs this representation. The new rule is an amalgamation of resolution and Prawitz analysis which we call path resolution. Path resolution allows Prawitz analysis of an arbitrary subgraph of the graph representing a formula. If such a subgraph is not large enough to demonstrate a contradiction, a path resolvent of the subgraph may be generated with respect to the entire graph. This generalizes the notions of large inference present in hyper-resolution, clash-resolution, NC-resolution, and UL-resolution.

Two forms of path resolution are described for which deletion of the links resolved upon preserves the spanning property.

1. Introduction

Since about 1960 most of the effort in automated deduction has been concerned with refutation systems. The initial emphasis was on Prawitz analysis [7,9,10,12,20], in which the unsatisfiability of a sentence is deduced without inferring new formulas. By 1965, with the advent of resolution and (later) paramodulation, the emphasis shifted almost completely toward the use of inference [15,21,22,23,27]. Most of the work done within both schools of thought employed conjunctive or disjunctive normal form. More recently there have been adaptations of both techniques toward the use of unnormalized or less-normalized formulas [2,11,16,17,19,25,26].

We introduce a new rule of inference, path resolution, which operates on a graphical representation of quantifier-free predicate calculus formulas. The new rule is an amalgamation of resolution and Prawitz analysis. Our goal in the design of path resolution is to retain some of the advantages of both Prawitz analysis and resolution methods, and yet to avoid to some extent their disadvantages.

The main advantage of Prawitz analysis is that, except for variants of original formulas, no new formulas are inferred which rapidly expand the search space. However, except for adding variants, Prawitz analysis is an all or nothing time-bound search for a contradiction. In contrast, resolution and other inference based methods store the progress made at each inference by retaining the inferred formula. Eventually localized evidence of a contradiction is produced (usually the empty clause). The required multiple variants of formulas are automatically (and often excessively) generated. But each new formula introduced interacts with others, expanding the search rapidly in both time *and space*.

One of the disadvantages of resolution is its reliance on conjunctive normal form. We avoid conjunctive and disjunctive normal form and the duplication of literals that their use

may necessitate, since path resolution operates on formulas in negation normal form. We have found that the analysis is greatly simplified by a representation of NNF formulas which we call *semantic graphs.*'

Path resolution allows Prawitz analysis of an arbitrary subgraph of the existing graphical representation of formulas. If such a subgraph is not large enough to demonstrate a contradiction, a path resolvent of the subgraph may be generated with respect to the entire graph. Path resolution operations include (properly) all resolution-based inferences of which the authors are aware, such as hyper-resolution, clash-resolution, NC-resolution, and UL-resolution.

It will be obvious to the informed reader that the work reported here, while new, has been synthesized from a number of important ideas developed by others. The most influential of these are Robinson's clash resolution [24], Kowalski's connection-graph procedure [14], the work of Andrews [2] and Bibel [3,4] on paths, matrices, and the spanning property, and the non-clausal systems of Stickel [25] and of Waldinger and Manna [26].

In the next section we introduce the notation and terminology required for expressing formulas and their semantics in terms of semantic graphs and paths. We further develop this formalism in section 3; section 4 introduces the rule of inference, path resolution. Section 5 contains a sample refutation, and section 6 introduces two link deletion strategies. We omit many proofs for lack of space; they are available in [18].

2. Semantic Graphs and Paths

A *semantic graph* is a means of representing a logical formula, and *paths* determine the semantics of the graph. We assume that the reader is familiar with the definitions of *atom, literal, formula, resolution,* and *unification.* We will consider only quantifier-free formulas in which all negations are at the atomic level.

A *semantic graph* is empty, a single node, or a triple *(N,C,D)* of *nodes, c-arcs,* and *d-arcs,* respectively, where a node is a literal occurrence, a c-arc is a conjunction of two non-empty semantic graphs, and d-arc is a disjunction of two non-empty semantic graphs. Please note that a node is a literal occurrence, so that if a literal occurs twice in a formula, we will label both nodes with that literal. Each semantic graph used in the construction of a semantic graph will be called an *explicit subgraph,* and we shall insist that each proper explicit subgraph be contained in exactly one arc. We will use the notation $(G,H)_c$ for the c-arc from G to H and similarly use $(G,H)_d$ for a d-arc. The subscript may be omitted if there is no possibility of confusion, and we will use the term graph only for semantic graphs.

We will consider an empty graph to be an empty disjunction, which is a contradiction. A construction of a graph may be thought of as a sequence of c-arcs and d-arcs. There will always be exactly one arc (X,Y) with the property that every other arc is an arc in X or in Y. We call this arc the *final arc* of the graph, and X and Y are the *final subgraphs*. Since this arc completely determines G, we frequently write $G = (X, Y)$.

As an example, the formula

$$((A \wedge B) \vee C) \wedge (\sim A \vee (D \wedge C))$$

is the graph

$$
\begin{array}{ccc}
A \rightarrow B & & \overline{A} \\
\downarrow & \rightarrow & \downarrow \\
C & & D \rightarrow C
\end{array}
$$

Note that horizontal arrows are c-arcs, and vertical arrows are d-arcs. There are two d-arcs: $(A \rightarrow B, C)$ and $(\overline{A}, D \rightarrow C)$; and there are three c-arcs: (A,B), (D,C), and the entire graph. Some of the explicit subgraphs are each of the nodes, $A \rightarrow B$, and the right-hand part of the graph.

The formulas we are considering are in *negation normal form* (nnf) in that all negations are at the atomic level, and the only connectives used are AND and OR.

If A and B are nodes in a graph, and if $a = (X, Y)$ is an arc (c- or d-) with A in X and B in Y, we will say that a is the arc *connecting* A and B. If a is a c-arc, we will say that A and B are *c-connected*, and if a is a d-arc, we will say that A and B are *d-connected*.

Lemma 1. Let G be a semantic graph, and let A and B be nodes in G. Then there is a unique arc connecting A and B.

One of the keys to our analysis is the notion of *path*. Let G be a semantic graph. A *partial c-path through* G is a set c of nodes such that any two are connected by a c-arc. We allow the empty set or a singleton set to be a partial c-path. A *c-path* is a partial c-path which is not properly contained in any partial c-path. Notice that any partial c-path is extendible to a c-path, and hence partial c-paths are always subpaths of c-paths. We similarly define d-path using d-arcs instead of c-arcs. The next lemma is an immediate consequence of Lemma 1.

Lemma 2. If A and B are nodes in a graph G, then there is a c-path or a d-path (but not both) containing A and B.

Using paths, we can define the conjunctive normal form of a graph as the conjunction of the d-paths, and the disjunctive normal form as the disjunction of the c-paths. If a formula is multiplied out using the distributive laws, then the graph changes and so may the normalized forms.

Paths can be defined in a somewhat more structural manner. Define a *structural c-path* (scp) c in a graph G as follows: if G consists of a single node A, then c is the set $\{A\}$; if the final arc of G is a d-arc, then an scp in G is an scp in one of the final subgraphs; and if the final arc is $(X, Y)_c$, then c is the union of an scp in X and an scp in Y. Lemma 3 states that the two formulations of path are equivalent, and as a result we will abandon the terminology structural c-path after the lemma.

Lemma 3. Let G be a semantic graph and let c be a set of nodes in G. Then c is a c-path iff c is an scp.

There is an obvious similar statement about d-paths; we leave the proofs to the reader.

The proofs of Lemmas 1 and 3 and of many lemmas and theorems that follow often use induction on the number of arcs in the graph. The base case is always trivial since the graph will then consist of a single node or arc. Since each explicit subgraph will always have fewer arcs than the entire graph, the inductive hypothesis amounts to assuming that the result holds for all explicit subgraphs. As a result, in proofs

we do include in this paper, we will ignore the base case and begin by assuming that the result holds for all explicit subgraphs.

We will use the notation c = xy when two paths in subgraphs are put together to form a path in a graph as in the lemma.

Lemma 4. Let G be a semantic graph. Then an interpretation I satisfies (falsifies) G iff I satisfies (falsifies) every literal on some c-path (d-path) through G.

We will frequently find it useful to consider subgraphs which are not explicit; that is, given any set of nodes, we would like to define that part of the graph which consists of exactly that set of nodes. The previous example is shown below on the left. The subgraph relative to the set $\{A, \overline{C}, D\}$ is the graph on the right.

$$
\begin{array}{ccc}
[A \rightarrow B] & & \overline{A} \\
\downarrow & \rightarrow & \downarrow \\
C & & [D \rightarrow C]
\end{array}
\qquad
\begin{array}{ccc}
& & \overline{A} \\
A & \rightarrow & \downarrow \\
& & D
\end{array}
$$

If N is the node set of a graph G, and if N' is contained in N, we define $G_{N'}$, *the subgraph of G relative to* N' as follows: If $N' = N$, then $G_{N'} = G$. If the final arc of G is (X, Y), and if the nodes in N' all appear in X or in Y, then $G_{N'} = X_{N'}$ or $G_{N'} = Y_{N'}$, respectively. Otherwise, $G_{N'} = (X_{N'}, Y_{N'})$, where this arc is of the same type as (X, Y). The following lemma says in essence that the subgraphs we have defined are the objects we want.

Lemma 5. Let G be a semantic graph with node set N, and let N' be a subset of N. Then

i)   Every node in N' is a node in some arc in $G_{N'}$.

ii) If p$'$ is a path through $G_{N'}$, then p$'$ is the restriction to N' of a path p (of the same type) through G; in particular, if p$'$ is a partial path in G consisting of nodes from N', then p$'$ is a partial path in $G_{N'}$.

3. Blocks

Consider the graph $(A \rightarrow B) \rightarrow C$. The non-explicit subgraph $B \rightarrow C$ "feels" much like an explicit one, and certainly the graph $A \rightarrow (B \rightarrow C)$ is essentially identical to the original graph. Indeed, the graph $A \rightarrow C$ is an explicit subgraph of another essentially identical graph: $(A \rightarrow C) \rightarrow B$. Subgraphs with this property can be characterized with the notion of *block*. A *c-block* C is a subgraph of a semantic graph with the property that any c-path which includes at least one node from C must pass through C; that is, the subset of the c-path consisting of the nodes which are in C is a c-path through C. A *d-block* is similarly defined with d-paths, and a *full block* is a subgraph which is both a c-block and a d-block. From Lemma 4 we know that the c-paths through a graph determine the semantics of the graph, and that the d-paths also determine the semantics. This might lead one to believe that c-blocks and d-blocks are full blocks. This is not the case, as the following simple example illustrates:

$$
\begin{array}{ccc}
& A & \\
& \downarrow & \\
B & \rightarrow & C
\end{array}
$$

The subgraph relative to $\{A,B\}$ is obviously a c-block, but it is not a d-block since $\{A\ C\}$ is a d-path which meets the subgraph but does not pass through it.

We define *a strong c-block* in a semantic graph G to be a subgraph C of G with the property that every c-path through G contains a c-path through C. A *strong d-block* is similarly defined.

Lemma 6. If C is a c-block in a semantic graph G, if the final arc (X, Y) of G is a c-arc, and if C meets both X and Y, then C is a strong c-block. Moreover, the subgraphs C_X and C_Y, consisting of the intersections of C with X and Y, are themselves strong c-blocks.

Lemma 7. The union of any number of d-paths in a semantic graph G is a strong c-block. Conversely, a d-path through a strong c-block is a d-path through the entire graph.

Lemma 8. If C is a c-block in G, and if $d_1, d_2, ..., d_k$ are d-paths through C, then their union is a c-block in G.

It is obvious that explicit subgraphs are full blocks. There is a sense in which the converse is true. Define two graphs (N, C, D) and (N', C', D') to be *isomorphic* if there exists a bijection $f: N \to N'$ such that for each A in N, $A = f(A)$, and which preserves c- and d-paths. (By $A = f(A)$, we mean that A and $f(A)$ are the same literal. It is not at all clear what one would even mean by saying that A and $f(A)$ are the same node since they appear in different graphs.) The condition $A = f(A)$ is an essential part of the definition; otherwise, the graphs $A \to B$ and $\overline{C} \to C$ would be isomorphic. Notice that being isomorphic is obviously an equivalence relation. A simple example of isomorphic graphs is $A \to (B \to C)$ and $(A \to B) \to C$ with the "identity" map.

One method of obtaining an isomorphic image of a graph is through commutivity and associativity. Commutivity in a graph amounts to reversing the order in which an arc is formed; e.g., $(Y, X)_c$ instead of $(X, Y)_c$. Associativity in graph amounts to changing the order in which two arcs of the same type are formed; e.g., $(X, (Y, Z)_c)_c$ instead of $((X, Y)_c, Z)_c$. It is immediate that two graphs which are identical except for one such commutation or one such reassociation are isomorphic. Since being isomorphic is transitive, any number of commutations and reassociations will result in an isomorphic graph. In fact, the converse is true. This, and the fact that full blocks are essentially explicit subgraphs, are corollaries of Theorem 1 below.

We define *level* in a graph G as follows: The level of G is 0 and the level of its final arc is 1. Given an arc $\mathbf{a} = (X, Y)$ of level k, if the final arc of X is of the same type as $\mathbf{a}$ then that final arc has level k; otherwise it has level k+1. In either case the level of X is k.

Theorem 1. Let G be a semantic graph, and let B be a full block in G. Then B is a union of level 1 subgraphs of an explicit subgraph of G.

Proof. By induction on the number of arcs in G. Let the final arc of G be (X, Y) and assume that (X, Y) is a c-arc; the case for a d-arc is similar. If B is a subgraph of X or of Y, the induction hypothesis applies, and the theorem holds.

So suppose some nodes of B are in X and some are in Y; recall that B_X and B_Y are the subgraphs of B consisting of the nodes of B which are in X and of those which are in Y, respectively. We show first that B_X and B_Y are themselves full blocks. It is obvious that each is a d-block since the arc (X, Y) is a c-arc: any d-path through G is a d-path through X or a d-path through Y. To see that B_X is a c-block in X, note that B is a strong c-block by Lemma 6. Hence by Lemma 7, B is a union of d-paths through G. Thus B_X is a union of those d-paths which lie in X; i.e., B_X is a strong c-block in X and in particular a full block in X. Similarly, B_Y is a full block and strong c-block in Y.

Now, if the final arc of X is a d-arc, then B_X meets both final subgraphs of X and hence is a strong d-block in X. Since it is both a strong c-block and a strong d-block it must be all of X.

If the final arc of X is a c-arc, let U be any level 1 subgraph of X which meets B_X. The proof will be complete for B_X (and by symmetry for B_Y and hence for all of B) if we show that $U \subset B_X$. But this is clear since the final arc of U must be a d-arc; i.e., the proof is identical to the case when the final arc of X is a d-arc.

Corollaries 1, 2, and 3 are immediate consequences of the theorem. The first corollary (and its generalization, Corollary 4) and the theorem are especially important. Because of the chronological order in which they were originally proven, we will refer to Theorem 1 as the *second isomorphism theorem* and to Corollaries 1 and 4 as the *first isomorphism theorem*.

Corollary 1. Let G be a semantic graph, and let B be a full block in G. Then there is a semantic graph G' and an isomorphism $f: G \to G'$ such that $f(B)$ is an explicit subgraph of G'.

Corollary 2. If G and H are isomorphic semantic graphs, then H can be formed by reassociating and commuting some of the arcs in G.

Corollary 3. The intersection of two full blocks is a full block.

Corollary 4. Given a semantic graph G and a collection of mutually disjoint full blocks, there is a graph isomorphic to G in which each full block is an explicit subgraph. Moreover, given any two of the blocks, each node in one is c-connected to each node in the other or each node in one is d-connected to each node in the other.

We will find it useful to determine the smallest full block containing a given subgraph; to do that we need the notions of *c- and d- extension*. The c-extension and the d-extension of the entire graph G is G itself. Given a level k subgraph X in G, if $(X, Y)_c$ is an arc in G, then the c-extension of X is the (unique) level k-1 subgraph containing X, and the d-extension is X. The obvious dual applies for $(X, Y)_d$. Given an arbitrary subgraph H of G, to find the smallest full block containing H, let k be the smallest integer such that more than one level k subgraph of G meets H. (Note that k must exist unless H consists of a single node, in which case H is a full block.) Then the smallest full block containing H is the subgraph consisting of those level k subgraphs which meet H.

It will be useful to divide an arbitrary subgraph H of a graph G into c-blocks. We define a c-block C contained in a subgraph H to be *maximal* if no superset of C in H is a c-block. The c-blocks in the definition are assumed to be c-blocks in G, which trivially implies that they are c-blocks in H. But note that if H is not a full block, a subgraph which is a c-block in H might not be a c-block in G. In particular, H may not be a c-block and typically will not be. We define a *proper c-family* of H to be a collection of maximal c-blocks whose union is H. The members of a proper c-family are not in general disjoint.

The next theorem says in essence that a certain rule of inference is sound. This may not be entirely obvious from the statement, which is purely structural. First, define the *auxiliary subgraph* Aux(H, G) of a subgraph H in a semantic graph G to be the subgraph of G relative to the set of all nodes in G which lie on extensions of d-paths through H to d-paths through G. The proof of the next lemma is immediate.

Lemma 9. If H is a subgraph of G, then Aux(H, G) is empty iff H is a strong c-block. Moreover, Aux(H, G) cannot contain a d-path through G; if H is a c-block, then so is Aux(H, G).

Theorem 2. Let $\{C_1, C_2, \ldots, C_k\}$ be a proper c-family in a subgraph H of a graph G. Let I be an interpretation which satisfies a c-path p through G, and suppose that p does not pass through H. Then I satisfies Aux(C_i, G) for some i.

Proof. Since p does not pass through H, it must fail to pass through C_i for some i. Hence, p must entirely miss C_i, and so p must meet and hence pass through $\text{Aux}(C_i,G)$. •

Example 1:

$$
\begin{array}{ccccccc}
 & P & & & & & \overline{C} \\
 & \downarrow & & & & & \\
 & Q & & & \overline{B} & \to & \downarrow \\
 & \downarrow & \to & A & \to & & \overline{A} \\
 & C & & & & & \\
 & \downarrow & & & & & \downarrow \\
 & & & & & & R \\
 & B & & & & &
\end{array}
$$

Let S be the subgraph relative to $\{A, B, C, \overline{A}, \overline{B}, \overline{C}\}$. S may be partitioned into the following four c-blocks: $\{C, B\}$, $\{A\}$, $\{\overline{B}\}$, and $\{\overline{C}, \overline{A}\}$. However these are not maximal; in particular, the last two c-blocks may be combined to form $\{C, B\}$, $\{A\}$, and $\{\overline{B}, \overline{C}, \overline{A}\}$. But we still do not have a proper c-family. The c-block $\{A\}$ is not maximal because the node B can be added and $\{A, B\}$ is still a c-block; $\{C, B\}$, $\{A, B\}$, and $\{\overline{B}, \overline{C}, \overline{A}\}$ do form a proper c-family.

Under the conditions of Theorem 2, it is immediate that the disjunction of the auxiliary subgraphs is satisfied by I. (In the above example, any c-path that misses the first c-block must hit subgraph $\{Q, P\}$. A c-path missing the second c-block hits $\{P\}$, and one missing the third c-block hits $\{R\}$.) We denote this disjunction by $P(H,G)$. We shall soon see that there are redundancies built into $P(H,G)$ which can be eliminated. These redundancies arise from the fact that the auxiliary subgraphs need not be disjoint. Theorem 3 indicates how to remove them. First, define a subgraph of a graph G to be a *d-full block* if it is a full block and a strong d-block. Note that for H to be a d-full block in G, H must be a disjunction of one or more level 1 subgraphs of G.

Theorem 3. Let $\{C_1,...,C_k\}$ be a proper c-family in a subgraph H of a semantic graph G, and let K be the intersection of $\text{Aux}(C_i,G)$ and $\text{Aux}(C_j,G)$. Then K is empty or a d-full block in $\text{Aux}(C_i,G)$.

The significance of Theorem 3 is that the redundancies which appear in $P(H,G)$ are its level 1 subgraphs which appear more than once. In example 1, the auxiliary subgraphs of the intersecting c-blocks are the subgraphs relative to $\{P, Q\}$ and $\{P\}$. Their intersection is of course the node P which forms a level 1 subgraph in both auxiliary subgraphs and in their disjunction. However, we can form the disjunction of auxiliary subgraphs to build $P(H,G)$ and leave out the redundancies; i.e., use the intersections of the auxiliary subgraphs only once. We denote the resulting graph by $Q(H,G)$. We prove that $Q(H,G)$ is unique by defining an object $\text{WS}(H,G)$, the *weak split graph of H in G*, and showing that $\text{WS}(H,G) = Q(H,G)$. (We introduce *strong* split graph in section 6.) We define $\text{WS}(H,G)$ as follows:

$\text{WS}(\emptyset,G) = G$.

$\text{WS}(G,G) = \emptyset$.

$\text{WS}(H,G) = \text{WS}(H_X,X) \vee \text{WS}(H_Y,Y)$ if $G = (X,Y)_d$.

$\text{WS}(H,G) = \text{WS}(H_X,X) \vee \text{WS}(H_Y,Y)$ if $G = (X,Y)_c$ and H meets both X and Y.

$\text{WS}(H,G) = \text{WS}(H_X,X)$ (or $\text{WS}(H_Y,Y)$) if $G = (X,Y)_c$ and H is contained in X (in Y, respectively)

We will write $\text{WS}(H,X)$ for $\text{WS}(H_X,X)$. Notice that no nodes appear more than once in $\text{WS}(H,G)$, and that $\text{WS}(H,G)$ is uniquely defined. In Theorem 4, we show that $Q(H,G) = \text{WS}(H,G)$, which tells us that $Q(H,G)$ can be computed without first discovering a proper c-family.

Theorem 4. If H is a subgraph of a semantic graph G, then $Q(H,G) = \text{WS}(H,G)$.

It should be noted that only structural redundancies are eliminated by weak split; it is certainly possible that the literals which occur in G will result in $\text{WS}(H,G)$ being a tautology. In view of Theorem 4, we will use only the notation $\text{WS}(H,G)$. The following corollaries are immediate.

Corollary 1. Let H be a subgraph of a graph G, and let I be an interpretation which satisfies a c-path p through G. Then if p does not pass through H, I satisfies $\text{WS}(H,G)$.

Corollary 2. If H is a c-block in a graph G, then $\text{WS}(H,G)$ is isomorphic to $\text{Aux}(H,G)$.

4. Path resolution.

The discussion of paths and graphs gives a (we think useful) representation of logical formulas as graphs. The primary concern of this paper is *path resolution*, a rule of inference. To this end, we define a *chain* in a graph to be a set of pairs of c-connected nodes such that each pair can simultaneously be made complementary by an appropriate substitution. A *link* is an element of a chain, and a chain is *full* if it is not properly contained in any other chain. A graph G is *spanned* by the chain K if every c-path through G contains a link from K. Notice that if a graph is spanned by a chain, the graph must be a contradiction since no c-path which contains complementary nodes can be satisfied. If K is a chain, we use the notation G_K for the subgraph of G relative to the set of nodes which appear in K. If G_K is spanned by K, K is said to be a *resolution chain*, and G_K is said to be a *resolution subgraph*.

Example 2:

$$
\begin{array}{ccc}
D & & \overline{A} \\
\downarrow & & \downarrow \\
[\overline{A} \to \overline{B}] & \to & [\overline{B} \to D] \\
\downarrow & & \downarrow \\
[B \to A] & & [C \to E]
\end{array}
$$

The curves between A and $\overline{A}$ and between B and $\overline{B}$ represent links which form a chain. The subgraph relative to the chain is:

The c-paths are $\{B \; A \; \overline{A}\}$ and $\{B \; A \; \overline{B}\}$. Each obviously contains a link, so we have a resolution chain and a resolution subgraph.

A rule of inference is of course a procedure which produces a formula from a given formula, and such a procedure is sound if any interpretation which satisfies the original formula also satisfies the inferred formula. Resolution is such a rule; in essence, it applies to formulas in cnf and operates on chains consisting of a single link. We will define a generalization of resolution which we call *path resolution*. It applies to any semantic graph and operates on arbitrary spanning chains.

Let K be a resolution chain in a semantic graph G, and let $R = G_K$. If I is any interpretation which satisfies G, it satisfies a c-path through G. Since R cannot be satisfied, c cannot pass through R. Hence, by Theorem 4, *I must satisfy* $\text{WS}(R,G)$. We call $\text{WS}(R,G)$ the *path resolvent* of R in G, and we have

Theorem 5. Path resolution is a sound rule of inference.

Consider Example 2 again. We have already seen that

$$[B \rightarrow A] \quad \rightarrow \quad \begin{array}{c} \overline{A} \\ \downarrow \\ \overline{B} \end{array}$$

is a resolution subgraph. The c-blocks are $[B \rightarrow A]$ and the d-path $\{\overline{A}, \overline{B}\}$. The auxiliary subgraph of the second is $[C \rightarrow E]$ since the (partial) d-path $\{\overline{A} \, D\}$ does not pass through the resolution subgraph. The path resolvent is

$$\begin{array}{c} [C \rightarrow E] \\ \downarrow \\ D \\ \downarrow \\ [\overline{A} \rightarrow \overline{B}] \end{array}$$

Once a resolvent has been inferred, it may appear natural to conjoin it with G. There is a better way to handle this: the split subgraph should be formed in the smallest full block M containing the resolution chain R, and the resolvent should then be conjoined to M rather than to all of G. That is, we replace M in G with $(M, \text{WS}(M_R, M))_c$. We will call the resulting graph the *weak resultant of G with respect to R* and denote it $\text{WRes}(G,R)$. In the previous examples, (and quite often in general,) M is a union of level 1 c-connected subgraphs of G, and therefore $\text{WRes}(G,R) = (G, \text{WS}(R, G))_c$.

5. A Refutation Proof

Consider the following formulas taken from Chang and Lee [5].

(1) $\forall x (E(x) \land \sim V(x) \rightarrow \exists y (S(x,y) \land C(y)))$

(2) $\exists x (P(x) \land E(x) \land \forall y (S(x,y) \Longrightarrow P(y)))$

(3) $\forall x (P(x) \Longrightarrow \sim V(x))$

We wish to show that (1), (2), and (3) imply (4) below.

(4) $\exists x (P(x) \land C(x))$

The semantic graph for (1), (2), (3), and the denial of (4) is shown below. Notice that the node $\overline{P(x)}$ is derived from the atom $P(x)$ in both (3) and the denial of (4). If we had represented (3) and $\sim$(4) as separate c-connected graphs, the proof below would still go through; links 3 and 5 would simply contain different occurrences of $\overline{P(x)}$.

Links 1, 2, and 3 span their associated subgraph and therefore form a resolution chain. The weak split of this chain with respect to the entire graph is the graph $S(a,f(a)) \rightarrow C(f(a))$. We show this path resolvent below along with a portion of the original graph:

Resolving on links 4 and 5 yields $\overline{V(f(a))} \rightarrow \overline{C(f(a))}$.

It is now easy to see that the link $\{\overline{C(f(a))}, C(f(a))\}$ is a resolution chain that spans not only its subgraph but the entire graph. Therefore this link produces the empty graph upon activation. The careful reader may have noticed that this last link is inherited from $\{\overline{C(x)}, C(f(a))\}$ which could have been added to the resolution chain used in the second inference. The resulting chain would have produced a contradiction shortening our proof to two steps. A binary resolution refutation for these formulas given in [5] uses eight steps.

We do not claim that the search space for determining an appropriate resolution chain is small. However, the existence of a 2-step derivation for this example is certainly somewhat favorable. Moreover, we note that both path resolution steps admit link deletion under certain extensions of Theorems 7 and 8. Space limitations preclude discussion of those extensions here. A derivation of a logic program by NC-resolution is compared to a derivation of the same program by path resolution in [18].

Stickel [25] has pointed out that in a non-clausal connection graph system it may be wise to avoid inferences on non-atomic complementary subformulas. Two reasons cited are that complementary subformulas may be difficult to detect, and that such inferences may be duplicated by resolving on single literals only. Path resolution may help to solve both of these problems. We only link atoms and their complements, not non-atomic structures. The presence of complementary subformulas is detected by a resolution chain. The subformula relative to a resolution chain is frequently (but not always!) a conjunction of complementary subformulas comprised of the literals appearing in the chain, even though these literals may be scattered throughout the entire sentence.

6. Link Deletion

Path resolution is so general that it admits as special cases all resolution-based inference rules (e.g. hyper-resolution, clash resolution UL-resolution, NC-resolution) of which the authors are aware. In fact, if enough copies of formulas from an unsatisfiable set are represented, then a resolution chain will exist whose path resolvent is the empty d-path. We may therefore view semantic graphs and path resolution as a unifying framework for all resolution-based inference **and Prawitz analysis**.

This generality is elegant from a theoretical point of view, but it also admits a proof-search space larger even than that of unrestricted binary resolution. It is natural to ask whether restrictive strategies exist that would take advantage of path resolution's generality, and not just mimic known strategies applicable to (say) clausal logic. One natural restriction is to large chains; that is to avoid resolution chains that are proper sub-chains of currently known resolution chains. Our intuition is that such a strategy is favorable for refutations, and this is an area of ongoing investigation.

Another way to reduce the search space is to delete links after activation. In [3] and [4], for example, Bibel dealt with these issues within binary resolution. We develop two link deletion strategies for path resolution below.

6.1. Link deletion using full blocks

It is more or less the case that a necessary and sufficient condition for a link deletion strategy to be acceptable is that the spanning property be preserved. That is, if a graph is spanned by a set of links, and if a rule of inference which deletes links is applied, then the resulting graph should still be spanned. Theorems 7 and 8 introduce classes of resolution chains for which path resolution has this property. Theorem 6 gives a condition when certain links can be deleted. It should be pointed out that since we are considering link deletion, we will not in general be dealing with the full set of links, and we will not need to inherit all links. If L is the current set of links in a graph G, and if R is the resolvent with respect to a resolution subgraph of the form $(U, V)_c$ such that the conditions of Theorem 7 or 8 are satisfied, then we need not inherit any links from U or from V to R. The reason is that the only paths in the new graph we need be concerned about are those which pass through $(U, V)_c$; in Theorems 7 and 8 we essentially show that extensions of such paths through R must contain an inherited link, and this allows deletion of the links in R.

Recall that any full block U is a conjunction or a disjunction of level 1 subgraphs of some explicit subgraph H. If the final arc of H is a conjunction, then the c-extension of U is H and the d-extension of U is U itself. The situation is reversed if the final arc of H is a d-arc. We will use the notation CE(U) and DE(U) for the c- and d-extensions, respectively, of U.

Lemma 10. Let U be a full block in a graph G whose final arc is a c-arc. Let $Z_1 = \text{CE}(U)$ and $U_0 = U$, and for $i \geq 1$ define Z_i, Y_i, and U_i recursively as follows: $Y_i = \text{DE}(Z_i)$, $Z_i = \text{CE}(Y_{i-1})$, and $U_i = Y_i - Z_i$. Then

i) Either $Z_1 = G$ or there exists an m such that $Z_i = Y_i = G$ iff $i \geq m$.

ii) If p is a c-path through G, then there exists a k such that p passes through U_k but completely misses U_i for $i < k$. (We do not exclude the possibility that p passes through U, i.e., that $k = 0$.)

Proof. The proof is actually fairly trivial. Observe that each Z_i is a level 1 subgraph of Y_i, and that each Y_i is a level 1 subgraph of Z_{i+1}. Observe further that U_i is the full block consisting of the disjunction of the level 1 subgraphs of Y_i different from Z_1. To see that i) holds, note that if Z_1 is not all of G, then Y_{m-1} is the level 1 subgraph of G containing U. To see that ii) holds, note that there is at least k such that p passes through Y_k. Then p misses Z_i for $i \leq k$. •

Example 3:

$$Q \to \begin{matrix} P \\ \downarrow \\ A \\ \downarrow \\ B \end{matrix} \quad \to \quad \overline{B} \quad \to \quad \overline{A} \quad \to \quad \begin{matrix} \overline{Q} \\ \downarrow \\ \overline{P} \end{matrix}$$

Let U_0 be the (subgraph relative to) the single node A which is obviously a full block. Then, as defined in Lemma 10, $Z_1 = \{A\}$, $Y_1 = \text{DE}(\{A\}) = \{P, A\}$, $U_1 = Y_1 - Z_1 = \{P\}$, $Z_2 = \text{CE}(Y_1) = \{Q, P, A\}$, $Y_2 = \text{DE}(Z_2) = \{Q, P, A, B\}$, $U_2 = Y_2 - Z_2 = \{B\}$, and $Z_3 = \text{CE}(Y_2) =$ the entire graph. Notice that any c-path must pass through U_0, U_1, or U_2.

Theorem 6 is a generalization of Bibel's *Pure Lemma* [3].

Theorem 6. Let U be a full block in a semantic graph G, let L be a set of links, and suppose that no node in U is contained in a link from L. Let L ' be the set of links from L which do not contain a node from DE(U). Then G is spanned by L iff G is spanned by L '.

Proof. Since L ' is a subset of L, we need only consider the case when G is spanned by L. If DE(U) = U, then L ' = L, and there is nothing to prove. If not, let $D = \text{DE}(U)$ and $U' = D - U$; let p be a c-path through G. We must show that p contains a link from L '. If p does not pass through U', there is nothing to prove since the links deleted from L all contain nodes from U'. If p does pass through U', let p = r ' s, where r ' is a path through U' and s is the rest of p. Let r be any c-path through U. Note that every node in s is c-connected to all of D since D is

a full block and the nodes of s are c-connected to some nodes in D (namely, those in r '). Then rs is a c-path through G and must contain a link from L. This link is in L ' since no link in L contains a node from U which contains r. This completes the proof since this link must be in s and therefore in p. •

The next theorem gives a condition under which links may be deleted. It says that if $(U, V)_c$ is a resolution subgraph in which U and V are each full blocks in G, and if the links in the chain all go from U to V, then we may delete all links from U to V.

Theorem 7. Let R be a resolution chain in semantic graph G such that G_R has the form $(U, V)_c$, where U and V are full blocks in G, and where each link in R goes from U to V. Suppose further that G is spanned by a set of links L. Let $H = \text{WRes}(R, G)$, and let L ' be the set of inherited links together with all links in L which do not go from U to V. Then L ' spans H.

Proof. We proceed by induction on the number of arcs in G. The case for one arc is trivial. If $(X, Y)_d$ is the final arc of G, then R must be entirely contained in X or in Y and the induction hypothesis gives the desired result. If the final arc is $(X, Y)_c$, and if R is contained in X or in Y, again the induction hypothesis applies. So suppose that the final arc is a c-arc and R meets both X and Y. By the first isomorphism theorem, we may assume that U and V are explicit subgraphs. Hence neither can meet both X and Y. Assume that U is contained in X and V is contained in Y. Observe that $H = (G, \text{WS}(G_R, G))_c$.

Let p be a c-path through H. We must show that p contains a link from L '. Note that p is the union of c-paths p_1, p_2, p_3 through X, Y, and $S = \text{WS}(G_R, G)$, respectively. The only case we need consider is when p passes through G_R and all links in $p_1 p_2$ come from R. Since S is the disjunction of $\text{WS}(U, X)$ and $\text{WS}(U, Y)$, we assume without loss of generality that p_3 is a c-path through $\text{WS}(U, X)$. Since U is an explicit subgraph, we know that its split is isomorphic to $\text{Aux}(U, X)$ by Corollary 2 of Theorem 4. Let p_3' be the isomorphic image of p_3 in $\text{Aux}(U, X)$.

Using the notation of Lemma 10, apply part ii) of that lemma to p_3'. Since p_3' passes through $\text{Aux}(U, X)$, it misses U and hence $k > 0$. As in the proof of Lemma 10, let $p_1 = sr$, where r is a c-path through Z_k. It is obvious that sp_3' is a path through X, so $sp_3' p_2$ contains a link from L. This link is not in R. Moreover, p_2 misses $\text{Aux}(V, Y)$, so this link will be inherited, and the proof is complete. •

It is worth noting that all single link chains satisfy the conditions of Theorem 7, and that the proof for this case is no easier since a pair of linked nodes plays the same role structurally as the two full blocks in the theorem.

Consider activating the single-link chain $\{A, \overline{A}\}$ in example 3. This chain clearly satisfies the conditions of Theorem 7. Notice that the resultant graph is still spanned even though the activated link is deleted:

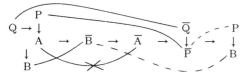

6.2. Another form of path resolution

Consider the soundness argument for path resolution as defined in section 4. In some cases the c-paths that miss the resolution chain are larger than the c-paths in the (weak) split subgraph. To account for this we define the *strong split* of an arbitrary subgraph H in G, $SS(H,G)$, to be the same as $WS(H, G)$ with the exception that if $G = (X,Y)_c$ and H is contained in X, then $SS(H,G) = SS(H,X) \wedge Y$. If R is a resolution chain, let M be the smallest full block containing R. It is straightforward to verify that if an interpretation satisfies M then it satisfies $SS(G_R, M)$, and hence we may replace M in G with $(M, SS(G_R, M))_c$. We call the resulting graph the *strong resultant of G with respect to R*, and denote it $SRes(G, R)$. The following lemma yields both soundness for strong splits and spanning preservation with link deletion for the class of resolution chains described in Theorem 8.

Lemma 11. If X is a c-block in G, then $SS(X, G)$ is isomorphic to the subgraph of G consisting of all nodes that lie on c-paths which miss X.

Proof. Suppose first that $G = (U,V)_d$. Then $SS(X,G) = (SS(X,U), SS(X,V))_d$ and the result follows from the induction hypothesis. If $G = (U,V)_c$, and if X meets both U and V then X is a strong c-block and $SS(X, G)$ is empty. Finally if X is contained in U, then $SS(X,G) = (SS(X,U), V)_c$ and the induction hypothesis applies. •

Theorem 8. Let R be a resolution chain in semantic graph G such that G_R has the form $(X,Y)_c$, where X and Y are c-blocks in G, and where each link in R goes from X to Y. Let G be spanned by a set of links L, and let $M = (U,V)_c$ be the smallest full block containing R, where U and V are chosen to contain X and Y respectively. Then $H = SRes(G, R)$ is spanned by L – R and the links inherited from L.

Proof. Let p be a c-path through H, and let $M' = (M, SS(G_R, M))_c$. If p does not pass through M', then p misses M' entirely since M' is a full block, so p must have a link from L. Assume p passes through M'. Let $p = p_1 p_2 p_3$ where p_1, p_2, p_3 are c-paths through U, V, and $SS(G_R, M)$ respectively. Since X is a c-block in U, Lemma 9 applies, so let p_3' be the isomorphic image of p_3 in U. Then the c-path $p_3' p_2$ has a link in L that is not in R and that is therefore inherited. •

Consider the two-link chain $\{A, \overline{A}\}$, $\{B, \overline{B}\}$, again from example 3. This chain satisfies the conditions of Theorem 8, but not those of Theorem 7 because $\{A, B\}$ is a c-block but not a full block. Shown below is the outcome of activating this chain with strong split and deleting both links. Of course the graph is still spanned. But notice that had we used weak split, the resolvent would have included only P, and the c-path $\{B, \overline{B}, \overline{A}, \overline{Q}, P\}$ would then be without a link.

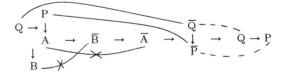

7. Summary

We have introduced a graphical representation of formulas and a new rule of inference that employs this representation. The inference rule is path resolution, which is a generalization of most previous forms of resolution. We have demonstrated the rule's soundness. Completeness is immediate in the absence of the usual connection graph link deletion strategy; resolving exclusively on single-link chains amounts to atomic NC-resolution on nnf formulas. We have introduced two classes of chains for which the activation and subsequent deletion of links is shown to preserve the spanning property. In light of Bibel's results [3,4] such link deletion strategies may reasonably be conjectured complete.

References

1. Andrews, P.B. Refutations by matings. IEEE Transactions on Computers 25,8 (Aug. 1976), 801-807.

2. Andrews, P.B. Theorem proving via general matings. JACM 28,2 (April 1981), 193-214.

3. Bibel, W. On matrices with connections. JACM 28,4 (Oct. 1981), 633-645.

4. Bibel, W. A Strong Completeness Result for the Connection Graph Proof Procedure. Technical Report ATP-3-IV-80.

5. Chang, C.L. and Lee, R.C.T. *Symbolic Logic and Mechanical Theorem Proving*, Academic Press, New York, 1978.

6. Chang, C.L., and Slagle, J.R. Using rewriting rules for connection graphs to prove theorems. Artificial Intelligence 12 (Aug. 1979), 159-178.

7. Chinlund, T.J., Davis, M., Hineman, P.G., and McIlroy, M.D. Theorem proving by matching. Bell Laboratory, 1964.

8. Clark, K. The Synthesis and Verification of Logic Programs. Third Conference on Automated Deduction, August 1977.

9. Davis, M. and Putnam, H. A computing procedure for quantification theory. JACM, vol. 7 (1960), 201-215.

10. Davis, M. Eliminating the irrelevant from mechanical proofs. Proc. Symp. of Applied Mathematics 15 (1963), 15-30.

11. de Champeaux, D. Sub-problem finder and instance checker - two cooperating processors for theorem provers. Proc. 4th Workshop on Automated Deduction, Austin, Texas, Feb. 1979, 110-114.

12. Gilmore, P.C., A Proof method for quantification theory. IBM Journal of Research and Development, vol. 4 (1960), 28-35.

13. Henschen, L.G. Theorem proving by covering expressions. J.ACM, 26,3 (July 1979), 385-400.

14. Kowalski, R. A proof procedure using connection graphs. J.ACM 22,4 (Oct. 1975), 572-595.

15. McCharen, J., Overbeek, R. and Wos, L. Problems and experiments for and with automated theorem-proving programs. IEEE Transactions on Computers, C-25,8 (Aug. 1976), 773-782.

16. Murray, N.V. Completely non-clausal theorem proving. Artificial Intelligence 18,1 (Jan. 1982), 67-85.

17. Murray, N.V. An experimental theorem prover using fast unification and vertical path graphs. Fourth National Conf. of Canadian Society of Computational Studies of Intelligence, U. of Saskatchewan, May 1982.

18. Murray, N.V. and Rosenthal, E. Semantic graphs. Technical Report 84-12, Department of Computer Science, SUNY at Albany, Nov. 1984.

19. Nilsson, N.J. A production system for automatic deduction. Technical Note 148, SRI International, 1977.

20. Prawitz, D. An improved proof procedure. Theoria 26 (1960), 102-139.

21. Robinson, G.A. and Wos, L. Paramodulation and theorem proving in first order theories with equality. *Machine Intelligence 4*, 1969, Edinburgh University Press.

22. Robinson, J.A. A machine oriented logic based on the resolution principle. J.ACM 12,1 (1965), 23-41.

23. Robinson, J.A. Automatic deduction with hyper-resolution. International Journal of Computer Mathematics, 1 (1965), 227-234.

24. Robinson, J.A. "Theoretical Approaches to Non-Numerical Problem Solving," Springer-Verlag, New York, Inc., 1970, 2-20.

25. Stickel, M.L. A nonclausal connection-graph resolution theorem-proving program. Proc. AAAI-82 Nat. Conf. on Artificial Intelligence, Pittsburgh, Pennsylvania, Aug. 1982, 229-233.

26. Waldinger, R. and Manna, Z. A deductive approach to program synthesis. ACM TOPLAS 2,1 (1980), 90-121.

27. Wos, L., Carson, D. and Robinson, G. Efficiency and completeness of the set of support strategy in theorem proving. J.ACM 12,4 (1965), 536-541.

ASSIP-T. A THEOREM PROVING MACHINE

Werner Dilger

Fraunhofer-Institut für In-
formations- und Datenverar-
beitung
D-7500 Karlsruhe 1

Hans-Albert Schneider

Computer Science Department
University of Kaiserslautern
Postfach 3049
D-6750 Kaiserslautern

ABSTRACT

An associative processor for theorem
proving in first order logic is described.
It is designed on the basis of the deduction plan method, introduced by Cox and
Pietrzykowski. The main features of this
method are the separation of unification
from deduction and the incorporation of a
method for intelligent backtracking. This
kind of backtracking is based on a special
unification procedure. An improved version
of this unification procedure is given,
which outputs a unification graph with
constraints. In the case of a unification
conflict, sufficient information for a
directed backtracking step can be gained
from the unification graph. According to
the deduction plan method, the ASSIP-T
memory consists of two parts, one for the
deduction plan and the other for the unification graph. ASSIP-T can perform deduction and unification in parallel. Both
memory parts consist of a set of subparts
each of which keeps the information about
clauses or terms, respectively. A subpart
is a linear array of cells provided with
a control unit and can be regarded as a
subprocessor.

1. Introduction

The progress of microelectronics allows
the realizations of more and more powerful
processors for special purposes. One such
type of processors is the associative
processor. Its associative memory allows
content oriented parallel access to the
data stored in it. This makes the associative processors well suited for pattern
handling processes. In artificial intelligence e.g., most processes are pattern
directed deductions. One of it is theorem
proving. In this paper a model of an associative processor is described which is
able to prove theorems of first order logic. It is designed on the basis of the
deduction plan method, i.e. it incorporates a method for intelligent backtracking.

After some basic definitions in the
second section, the deduction plan method
is described. The special unification
procedure used within this method follows.
The output of this procedure is a unification graph with constraints. In the case
of a unification conflict, the unification
graph gives sufficient information for a
directed backtracking step. This is described in section 5. Then the structure
of the ASSIP-T processor which is aimed to
perform the deduction plan method is described. Section 7 gives the data structures which are to be mapped on the ASSIP-
T memory. Finally, the representation of
the data structures in the ASSIP-T memory
is sketched.

2. Basic Definitions

A *labelled graph* is a triple $G =
(V(G), I(G), E(G))$ where $V(G)$, $I(G)$, and
$E(G)$ are the sets of nodes, labels, and
edges respectively. A *path* of length n in
G is a sequence $w = v_1, e_1, v_2, e_2, \ldots,
e_n, v_{n+1}$ $(n \geq 0)$ with $v_i \in V(G)$ and $e_j \in E(G)$.
If $v_1 = v_{n+1}$, the path is called *closed*.
A closed path which contains each inner
node at most once is called a *cycle*.

Assume there are given disjoint alphabets of *variables, function symbols* and
predicate symbols. Each function and predicate symbol has an arity. A *constant* is a
0-ary function symbol. An *expression* is a
variable or a term. A *term* is a constant
or a string of the form $f(q_1, \ldots, q_n)$, where
f is an n-ary function symbol $(n \geq 1)$ and
$q_1, \ldots, q_n$ are expressions. An *atom* is a
string of the form $P(q_1, \ldots, q_n)$, where P
is an n-ary predicate symbol $(n \geq 0)$ and
$q_1, \ldots, q_n$ are expressions. If A is an atom,
then A and -A are *literals*. A *clause* is a
finite set of literals. The empty clause
is denoted by □.

A *constraint* is a set consisting of
two expressions. A set of constraints is
called a *constraint set*. If p and q are
expressions (terms), then p is a *subexpression (subterm)* of q if $p = q$ or $q =
f(q_1, \ldots, q_n)$ and p is a subexpression (sub-
term) of one of the q_i. An expression (term)
p is a subexpression (subterm) of a constraint set C, if there is a constraint
$\{q_1, q_2\}$ in C such that p is a subexpression
(subterm) of q_1 or of q_2. The set of all
subexpressions of C is denoted by SEXPR(C).

A *substitution* is a finite set of pairs (v,q), denoted by v/q, where v is a variable and q an expression and $v \neq q$. *Application* of a substitution $\sigma = \{v_1/q_1,\ldots,v_n/q_n\}$ to an expression or a literal p is the replacement of each occurrence of v_i in p by q_i, for all $i = 1,\ldots,n$. σ is called a *renaming* if $q_1,\ldots,q_n$ are pairwise different variables and $\{v_1,\ldots,v_n\} \cap \{q_1,\ldots,q_n\} = \emptyset$. A clause cl_1 is called a *variant* of a clause cl_2 if cl_1 and cl_2 have no variables in common and there is a renaming σ such that $cl_1 = \sigma cl_2$. If $E = \{p_1,\ldots,p_m\}$ is a set of expressions then a substitution σ is called a *unifier* of E, if $\sigma p_1 = \ldots = \sigma p_m$. E is then called *unifiable*. σ is called a *most general unifier* of E if for each unifier τ there is a unifier ρ such that $\tau = \sigma \cdot \rho$.

Let $C = \{c_1,\ldots,c_n\}$ be a constraint set. The set $BE(C)$ of *Boolean expressions* over C is defined by
1. $0,1,c_1,\ldots,c_n \in BE(C)$.
2. If $B_1,B_2 \in BE(C)$, then $(B_1 \vee B_2)$, $(B_1 \wedge B_2) \in BE(C)$.
3. $BE(C)$ contains no other elements.

3.   Deduction Plans

The deduction plan method is a resolution based method, i.e. a refutation method. It starts with a set of clauses and tries to construct a "closed" and "correct" deduction plan. If it succeeds, the clause set is proved to be unsatisfiable. The central idea of the method is to separate deduction from unification. This allows the application of a special unification algorithm which, in the case of a unification conflict, not simply stops with failure, rather it yields information about the causes of unification conflicts, namely certain deduction steps, which then can be reset. In section 5 this way of processing is called "intelligent backtracking".

The nodes of the deduction plan are the input clauses and eventually variants of them. Two clauses can be connected by an edge if they contain literals with the same precidate symbol but different signs (negated or not negated). Therefore a (labelled) edge between two clauses cl_1 and cl_2 is a triple $(cl_1,(t,u,v),cl_2)$, where u and v are literals in cl_1 and cl_2 respectively, satisfying the condition on their predicate symbols and negation signs. t is the type of the edge. There are two types of edges: SUB and RED. All edges are of type SUB except those refering backward to a clause which is already in use. If each literal in each clause included in the plan occurs in an edge, the deduction plan is closed. If the set of pairs of terms arising from the pairing of literals by edges is unifiable, the deduction plan is correct. Cf. for this section (Cox and Pietrzykowski 1979) and (Cox and Pietrzykowski 1981).

Definition

Let S be a set of input clauses and $L = \bigcup_{cl \in S} cl$. A *deduction graph* on S is a graph $G = (V(G),I(G),E(G))$ which has the variants of S as node set $V(G)$, $I(G) \subseteq \{SUB,RED\} \times L \times L$ with: if $e = (cl_1,b,cl_2) \in E(G)$ then $b = (t,u,v)$, $u \in cl_1$, $v \in cl_2$. t is called the *type* of the edge e, u the *starting literal* and v the *target literal*. A literal u of a clause cl is called *key literal* iff there is an incoming edge with type SUB and target literal u. Each literal u of a clause cl is called a *subproblem* iff it is not a key literal. A subproblem $u \in cl$ is *open* iff there is no outcoming edge with starting literal u. A subproblem u is called *closed* iff it is not open. $os(G)$ is the set of open subproblems of a deduction graph G. G is called *closed*, iff $os(G) = \emptyset$.

A node cl_1 is called *predecessor* of a node cl_2 iff there is a path from cl_1 to cl_2 which contains only edges of type SUB (*SUB-path*). If u is the starting literal of the first edge of a SUB-path from cl_1 to cl_2, then u is called *preceding literal* of cl_2 and cl_2 is called *successor* of cl_1.

We omit the definition of the deduction plan here. It is a deduction graph which is constructed by a number of deduction steps, i.e. edge drawing steps, starting from a basic plan which consists of one node only.

Example

$$S = \{\{P(x), Q(y), R(f(x,y))\},$$
$$\{-P(g(x)), V(x)\},$$
$$\{-P(g(x)), -V(x)\},$$
$$\{-Q(x), S(x), -T(x)\},$$
$$\{-S(a)\},$$
$$\{-S(b)\},$$
$$\{T(b)\},$$
$$\{-R(x)\}\}$$

is a set of eight input clauses. Figure 1 shows a closed deduction plan for S. The edges are drawn in such a way that they begin beyond the starting literal and point to the target literal. Therefore they are only labelled by their type and, beyond it, by the numbers of the steps in the plan construction within which the edges were drawn. The literals $-P(g(x_2))$, $-V(x_3)$, $-Q(x_4)$, $-S(a)$, $T(b)$, and $-R(x_5)$ are key literals, the other literals are subproblems. The first clause in S is the basic node, it is a predecessor of all nodes.

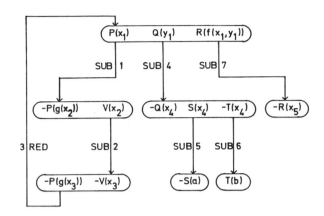

Figure 1: A closed deduction plan

Definition

Let G be a deduction plan and e an edge of G with label (t,u,v), where (omitting the sign) u = P(u$_1$,...,u$_n$), v = P(v$_1$,...,v$_n$) (n$\geq$0). To e a constraint set C(e) is assigned by

$$C(e) = \{\{u_1,v_1\},...,\{u_n,v_n\}\}$$

A constraint set C(G) is assigned to G by

$$C(G) = \bigcup_{e \in E(G)} C(e)$$

G is called *correct* iff C(G) is unifiable. θ(G) denotes the most general unifier of C(G). θ(G)os(G) is the clause *derived from* G. If G is closed, the clause derived from G is the empty clause.

Soundness and completeness of the deduction plan method are shown in the references given above.

4. Unification Graphs With Constraints

Unification by means of unification graphs with constraints is closely related to the unification method of Cox, (Cox 1981). It simplifies this method but is still sound and complete. Cf. for this section (Dilger and Janson 1983) and (Dilger and Janson 1984).

The unification process starts with a constraint set C. By two steps, the *transformation step* and the *sorting step,* it yields a *unification graph with constraints,* UwC for short, for C. A UwC consists of

- the node set V(UwC) = SEXPR(C)
- the label set I(UwC) = 2^C
- the edge set E(UwC) = EU(UwC) $\cup$ ED(UwC)
  where EU(UwC) $\subseteq$ V(UwC)$\times$(2^C-$\{\emptyset\}$)$\times$V(UwC)
  and ED(UwC) $\subseteq$ V(UwC)$\times$ $\{\emptyset\}$ $\times$V(UwC)

EU(UwC) is a set of undirected edges,

ED(UwC) a set of directed edges. Construction of UwC starts with the initial graph UwC$_I$ which consists only of the nodes. EU(UwC) is determined in the transformation step, ED(UwC) in the sorting step.

Definition

A path in UwC which contains only edges from EU(UwC) is called a *connection*. A connection v = p$_1$,e$_1$,...,e$_n$,p$_{n+1}$ is called *simple* iff p$_i$ $\neq$ p$_j$ for all i,j (1$\leq$ i$<$ j$\leq$ n+1). A closed path in UwC which contains at least one edge from ED(UwC) is called a *loop*. A loop is called *simple* iff p$_i$ $\neq$ p$_j$ for all i,j such that 1$<$i$<$j$<$n+1. If e = (p,a,q) is an edge in E(UwC), then a is called the value of e, denoted val(e) = a. Let w = p$_1$,e$_1$,...,e$_n$,p$_{n+1}$ be a path in UwC. Then the value of w is

$$val(w) = \bigcup_{i=1}^{n} val(e_i)$$

The transformation step

The algorithm of the transformation step can be found in (Dilger and Janson 1984). It draws undirected edges between the nodes in the following way: If c$_i$ = $\{p,q\}$ is a constraint, the nodes p and q are connected by the edge e = (p,$\{c_i\}$,q).This results in a (possibly empty) set of new constraints, which are treated later on in the same way.

Example

Let C = $\{c_1,c_2\}$ be a constraint set with

$$c_1 = \{G(s,z),\ G(u,F(y,y))\}$$
$$c_2 = \{u,\ F(y,G(s,z))\}$$

The initial UwC consists only of the nodes SEXPR(C) and is shown in figure 2. The first constraint c$_1$ is removed, an appropriate undirected edge is added to the UwC and the new constraints $\{s,u\}$ and $\{z,F(y,y)\}$ are added to the constraint set.

Now the second constraint is removed from the constraint set. Because u is a variable, there cannot be formed any new constraints, only an edge is added to the UwC. The remaining two constraints are treated as the second one. Because they had their origin in the first constraint,

G(s,z)   G(u,F(y,y))   z   F(y,y)

s   u   F(y,G(s,z))   y

Figure 2: The initial UwC for the constraint set C

the edges in the UwC are labelled by $\{c_1\}$. At the end of the transformation step the UwC has the form represented in figure 3.

The sorting step

The transformation step classifies the nodes of UwC in such a way that two nodes belong to the same class iff there is a connection between them. In the example above we have four classes. In the sorting step, first a graph U is constructed which consists of these classes as nodes and which has a directed edge labelled by f from class X to class Y iff there is a term $f(p_1,\ldots,p_n)$ in X and an expression p_i ($i \in \{1,\ldots,n\}$) in Y.

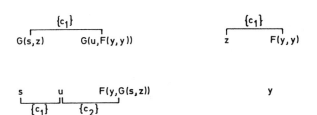

Figure 3: The UwC at the end of the transformation step

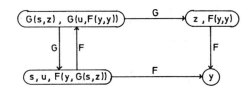

Figure 4: The graph U for the UwC

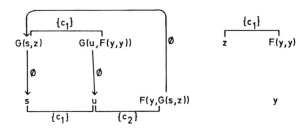

Figure 5: The complete UwC at the end of the sorting step

This graph is shown for the example in figure 4. Now the edges of U which belong to a cycle are added to the UwC as edges between the appropriate nodes and labelled

by $\emptyset$. So we get the complete UwC of figure 5.

Soundness and completeness of the unification algorithm are proved in (Dilger and Janson 1984). The main theorem is: A constraint set C is unifiable iff all terms in UwC which are connected by a simple connection begin with the same function symbol and UwC contains no simple loops.

Thus, e.g., our example constraint set is not unifiable because the UwC of figure 5 contains a simple loop.

5.   Intelligent Backtracking

If during the unification process a unification conflict has been detected, i.e. a clash (unification of terms with different function symbols) or a cycle, the actual deduction plan is not correct. One or several steps in the construction have to be reset in order to get a correct plan. By means of the information kept by the UwC these steps can be determined immediately. The numbers of the deduction steps are contained in the labels of the undirected edges of UwC. Therefore, we have to examine the values of certain paths through UwC. First, the relevant values are gathered in the sets ATTACH and LOOP.

$\text{ATTACH} := \{a \subseteq C \mid a$ is the value of a simple connection in UwC between terms p and q with different function symbols$\}$

$\text{LOOP} := \{a \subseteq C \mid a$ is the value of a simple loop in UwC$\}$

We define:

$$B_{\text{ATTACH}} := \prod_{a \in \text{ATTACH}} \sum_{c \in a} c$$

$$B_{\text{LOOP}} := \prod_{a \in \text{LOOP}} \sum_{c \in a} c$$

$$B_{\text{UNIF}} := B_{\text{ATTACH}} \wedge B_{\text{LOOP}}$$

The minimal disjunctive normal form of B_{UNIF} has the form

$$B'_{\text{UNIF}} = B_1 \vee \ldots \vee B_k$$

for some $k \geq 1$, where each B_i is a conjunctive term. From B'_{UNIF} the minimal conflict sets are determined by

$$mcs_i := \bigcup_{\substack{c \text{ occurs} \\ \text{in } B_i}} \{c\} \quad (i = 1,\ldots,k)$$

For details cf. (Dilger and Janson 1984).

Example

Consider the deduction plan of section 3, represented in figure 1. Following the edges according to their numbers we get the constraints

1: $\{x_1, g(x_2)\}$

2: $\{x_2, x_3\}$

3: $\{g(x_3), x_1\}$

4: $\{y_1, x_4\}$

5: $\{x_4, a\}$

6: $\{x_4, b\}$

7: $\{f(x_1, y_1), x_5\}$

The UwC for these constraints is shown in figure 6. It has no directed edges, because the graph U, constructed in the sorting step, contains no cycles.

There is a clash in the UwC, namely a simple connection between a and b. Therefore, ATTACH = {{5,6}}. Clearly, LOOP = ∅. Thus, B_{ATTACH} = 5 ∨ 6, B_{LOOP} = 1, B_{UNIF} = 5 ∨ 6 = B'_{UNIF} and mcs_1 = {5}, mcs_2 = {6}.

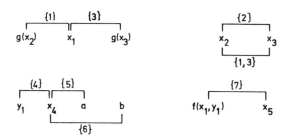

Figure 6: A complete UwC

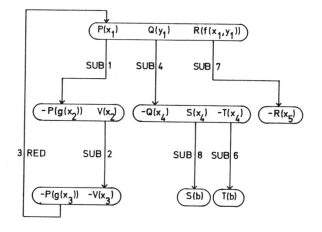

Figure 7: A closed correct deduction plan

Backtracking is performed as follows. Take for the backtracking step mcs_1 = {5}. Edge number 5 and node -S(a) are removed from the plan. Thereby, the literal $S(x_4)$ becomes an open subproblem. But there

is another clause in the input clause set which fits to close the literal, namely {-S(b)}. This yields the closed correct deduction plan of figure 7. The reader is invited to check that backtracking with ncs_2 = {6} does not result in a closed plan.

6. The Structure Of ASSIP-T.

In the deduction plan method, deduction and unification are separated from each other. For deduction, the data structure "deduction plan" is used, for unification the data structure "unification

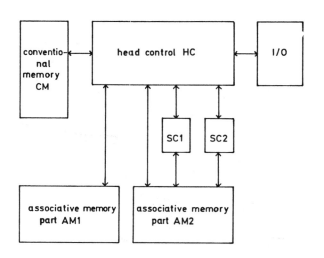

Figure 8 : The structure of ASSIP-T

graph with constraints". In ASSIP-T, both are kept in appropriate parts of the associative memory. Thus, the associative memory is divided in two main parts, AM1 for the deduction plan and AM2 for the UwC, cf. figure 8. The control unit of the processor consists of four components:
- the head control HC
- two subcontrols SC1 and SC2
- a conventional memory CM

The subcontrols operate on the UwC. They can work independently from each other, but under control of HC, so they can work in parallel and this is useful during the initial construction of the UwC and during its reconstruction after a backtracking step. Thus, we have not only parallel access to the data in the associative memories, rather there are two further steps to parallel processing: one by the parallel treatment of deduc-

tion plan and UwC, the other by the use
of SC1 and SC2 in parallel. For details
cf. (Dilger and Schneider 1985). For an
introduction to and a survey on the field
of associative processors cf. (Fu and
Ichikawa 1982), (Kohonen 1984), (Parhami
1973) and (You and Fung 1975).

7. Associative Memory Oriented Data Structures

Several data structures are used for
an associative memory oriented representation of deduction plans and UwCs, i.e.
representations that can easily be mapped
on associative memories. The design principles for the data structures are:

1. Deduction plan and UwC - both being
   graphs - are taken as sets of nodes
   together with their edges.

2. A clause together with all its variants
   in represented as only one data object
   and therein their constant part is represented only once. The same holds
   for the terms of the UwC.

Due to lack of space we omit the data
structures, which can be found in (Dilger
and Schneider 1985), and only give some
idea of them.

For each literal, we keep in its
variants-part the edges to other literals,
represented by the target literals and the
edge labels, because in fact they are
drawn between variants of clauses. This
way of storing edges can be thought to be
similar to the way they are drawn e.g.
in figure 1.

The nodes of the UwC are variants of
expressions. Therefore, we store all expressions which are variants of one another in the same part of AM2 (cf. section 8) together with the edges incident
of them.

Because we build variants by just
indexing the variables (cf. figure 1),
we are able to represent the information
"edge e is incident to node t" by simply
storing the index of t's variables at e,
too. Storing directed edges is done in
a most efficient way, which just needs one
bit for each argument of the respective
term.

8. Representation And Handling Of The Data Structures In The ASSIP-T Memory

We will sketch here the representation
of the UwC in the memory part AM2. It is
similar for the deduction plan. AM2 is
divided into several parts, one for each
object of type EXPRESSION (that is, an
expression, its variants and the edges
incident to them). Every AM2-part consists of a linear array of cells and is
provided with a special control, called

the "EXP-control". The entries in an object of type EXPRESSION can all be represented by the data types INTEGER and
BOOLEAN. Therefore all cells of the AM^2-
parts have the same form. They consist of

- a logical unit
- a control bit
- a 4 bit flag register
- a 32 bit data register

cf. figure 9. The purpose of the flag register is to characterize the type of information which actually is stored in the
data register, e.g. index and class of
variants, information about edges etc.
Thus, each cell can store an arbitrary
part of an EXPRESSION.

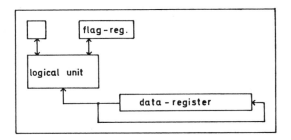

Figure 9: A subprocessor cell of ASSIP-T

The EXP-control has to perform entry,
change and query instructions on the components of an object of type EXPRESSION.
The head control on the other hand just
has to broadcast information to the AM2-
parts and to gather it from them by means
of instructions like

"FOR_ALL <expression> WITH <condition>

DO <instruction>"

or   "FOR_ONE <expression> WITH <condition>

DO <instruction>"

Thus, the two-level organisation of the
ASSIP-T memory corresponds to a two-level
evaluation of the instructions.

9.   Conclusion

As far as we know there is no other
approach similar to ours. The architecture of the fifth generation inference
machine is data flow oriented and does not
take into consideration associative access
to data cf. (Moto-oka and Fuchi 1983). The
main problem with our approach is the
storage of the unification graph because
its number of edges has an upper bound
that is exponential with respect to the
number of deduction steps. One may assume
that this upper bound will never be reached

in practice, but we have to work out another representation of the edges. By means of several head control-subcontrol-groups, we should be able to perform OR-parallel as well as AND-parallel processing due to the separation of deduction and unification.

REFERENCES

Cox, P.T. On determining the causes of nonunifiability. Auckland Computer Science Report No 23, University of Auckland, 1981.

Cox, P.T. and Pietrzykowski, T. Deduction plans: A basis for intelligent backtracking. University of Waterloo Res. Rep. CS-79-41, 1979.

Cox, P.T. and Pietrzykowski, T. Deduction plans: A basis for intelligent backtracking. IEEE Trans. Pattern Analysis and Machine Intelligence, vol. PAMI-3, (1) 1981, 52-65.

Dilger, W. and Janson, A. Unifikations-graphen als Grundlage für intelligentes Backtracking. Proc. of the German Workshop on Artificial Intelligence, Informatik-Fachberichte 76, Springer-Verlag, 1983, 189-196.

Dilger, W. and Janson, A. A unification graph with constraints for intelligent backtracking in deduction systems. Interner Bericht 100/84, Fachbereich Informatik, Universität Kaiserslautern, 1984.

Dilger, W. and Schneider, H.-A. A theorem proving associative processor, In preparation.

Fu, K.S. and Ichikawa, T. (eds) Special computer architectures for pattern processing. CRC Press, Boca Raton, Florida, 1982.

Kohonen, T. Self-organization and associative memory. Springer, Berlin, 1984.

Moto-oka, T. and Fuchi, K. The architectures in the fifth generation computers. Proc. of the IFIP 83, 1983, 589-602.

Parhami, B. Associative memories and processors: An overview and selected bibliography. Proc. of the IEEE 61, 1973, 722-730.

You, S.S. and Fung, H.S. Associative processor architecture - a survey. Proc. of the Sagamore Computer Conference 1975.

DESIGNING EXAMPLES FOR SEMANTICALLY GUIDED HIERARCHICAL DEDUCTION

Tie Cheng Wang
Department of Computer Sciences
The University of Texas at Austin
Austin, Texas 78712

ABSTRACT

Semantically guided hierarchical deduction prover is a resolution-based theorem-proving procedure which is capable of using the domain dependent knowledge presented in well designed examples. This paper gives an overview of the basic deduction components of the prover, investigates some rules for human design of examples, and demonstrates their usage in proving several non-trivial theorems.

I. INTRODUCTION

A method for using domain dependent knowledge in mechanical theorem proving is to present the hypotheses of a theorem—i.e. the axiomatic system involved as a model (or say, an example*)—which is then used in guiding a mechanical prover to search a proof along with semantically provable paths. This method has been investigated by several researchers[2,3,5,6], where it was used mainly in some natural deduction proving procedures.

Though the basic idea of this method is simple and plausible, its potential usage has been limited by some problems or difficulties exposed in earlier implementations.

One problem is that this method often produces incompleteness for the traditional goal-oriented theorem provers, such as a linear resolution procedure or some natural deduction procedures. For example, consider a unsatisfiable set S of ground clauses, $S = \{A \vee \neg C \vee B, \neg A \vee B, C, \neg B\}$. Suppose the first three clauses of S are hypotheses. We use $M = \{A, B, C\}$ as a model of these hypotheses to guide a linear resolution proof (refutation) of S. Let the last clause $\neg B$ of S be the the first goal. The first step of deduction has two different branches: one produces a resolvent $\neg A$ by resolving $\neg B$ against $\neg A \vee B$, another produces a resolvent $A \vee \neg C$ by

---

This work was supported in part by NSF grant MCS-8313499.

* In this paper, the word "example" means a model that contains real semantics.

resolving $\neg B$ against the first clause of S. Note that, for a semantically guided refutation proof, only the clauses that are false in the given model are treated as semantically provable, so can be used as goals during deduction. Because $\neg A$ is false in M, but $A \vee \neg C$ is not, only the first branch can be developed next. Then, from $\neg A$, only a resolvent $\neg C \vee B$ is produced by resolving $\neg A$ against the first clause of S. Now, because $\neg C \vee B$ is true in M and there is no other deduction path left, the deduction has to terminate with failure. Some previous approaches tried to avoid this source of incompleteness by changing the model during deduction [5,6]. For example, according to Example 1 of [5], a secondary model $M' = \{\neg A, B, C\}$ should be used later to finally prove S (The set S of the above example is just a simplified version of the problem given in Example 1 of [5]). But, generally speaking, this strategy is not feasible to implement. One reason for this is that to design a "suitable" example for helping prove a hard theorem is not a easy matter. This is another problem encountered in using this method.

In fact, the design or selection of a suitable example for a theorem to prove is an essential problem with using this method. Of course, this task is difficult for a computer to do automatically because domain dependent knowledge is usually needed and also because it is hard to give a precise description of what is a suitable example. As for the human design, the difficulty lies in dealing with the interpretation of skolem functions (here, we are concerned with first-order logic only), because a casually-chosen interpretation of a skolem function may cause proof failure.

This paper tries to give a solution of the above problems. We will use examples to guide a resolution-based theorem prover, semantically guided hierarchical deduction prover (SHD-PROVER). Different from the usual goal-oriented deduction procedure, this procedure has a particular mechanism in producing and retaining all "legal" resolvents producible from a goal clause in each deduction step. In light of this feature, many failure cases caused by using models in a traditional goal-oriented prover can be avoided. For example, this procedure will retain both resolvents $\neg A$ and $A \vee \neg C$ producible from the goal $\neg B$ at the first step of deduction of the above example. But the resolvent $A \vee \neg C$ which is true in M

will be allowed to be used only as rule clause. Then a resolvent $\neg C$ can be produced in the next step by resolving $\neg A$ against this new rule. Because $\neg C$ is false in M, it can be used as next goal to finally deduce a refutation of S.

The SHD-PROVER is based on a complete deductive component, hierarchical deduction procedure. The efficiency of this procedure is enhanced by several completeness-preserving refinements. The procedure can prove automatically a series of non-trivial theorems without the help of examples (see [8]). So, our approach emphasizes also the importance of a compact deductive component.

This paper mainly describes our method of designing and using examples for SHD-PROVER. we will investigate some rules for the human design of examples, especially, for the interpretation of skolem functions. More considerations about completeness and effectiveness problems will be included in these rules. As an application, this method will be used in designing examples to help our prover prove several non-trivial theorems, AM8, IMV, GCD, LCM and Schubert's statement. In order to include type information and other useful knowledge into examples, a three valued modeling and the corresponding interpretation method will be proposed.

The paper concludes with a summary of the results of computer runs in proving the example theorems.

II. OUTLINE OF THE HIERARCHICAL DEDUCTION

(See [8] for details. Those familiar with [8] should proceed to next section.)

The hierarchical deduction procedure proves a theorem by traversing a tree of nodes. Each node contains a different set of clauses and other information. All candidate goal clauses are contained in a goal-list. Each literal of each goal clause is indexed by a node name, through which a set of nodes can be located to obtain rule clauses for the resolution upon that literal.

At the beginning of a deduction, there is only one node (node 1) which contains all input clauses, while the goal-list contains only the input goal clauses. The literals of the input goal clauses are all indexed by 1, which corresponds to the name of the first node. The general proof process is as follows:

1. The first goal clause G of the goal-list is taken. Along with the index of the left-most literal of G, a set of rule clauses is obtained by retrieving the node indicated by this index and all parent nodes of this node. This index will be the parent name of the new node being produced in this round of deduction.

2. All "legal" resolvents are produced by resolving the goal clause against each clause of the set of rules upon the left-most literal of the goal clause. For each of the resolvents produced, the indices and the order of the literals inherited from the goal clause are retained, but the indices of the literals inherited from the rule clause are replaced by a larger integer which is just the name of a node being produced; these literals are placed to the left in the resolvent.

3. If $\square$ (the empty clause) is obtained, then the procedure returns "proved". Otherwise, the resolvents will be stored into the new node and also be inserted into the goal-list according to their priorities. Then the above process is repeated.

The "legal" resolvents produced by the prover are called H-resolvents (hierarchical resolvents). They are produced under a number of constraints which will be briefly described next.

Local Subsumption Test: The literals previously resolved upon are retained by the resolvent as "framed" literals. A resolvent is said to be *locally subsumed* if it has more than one literal including its framed literals, sharing a common atom. The locally subsumed resolvent will be discarded.

Constraints on Common Tails: We call any index of a literal in a clause C which is less than the index of the left-most literal of C, a *tail index* of C. An index that is a tail index of two different clauses is called a *common tail index* of these clauses. We require that a legal resolvent of a goal clause must <u>not</u> be produced by resolving the goal upon the literal of a rule clause whose index is a common tail index of these clauses. We require also that the common tails (consisting of the literals with common tail indices) of the clauses being resolved be mergeable (unifiable).

Proper Reduction: An H-resolvent H is called a *proper reduction* of an ancestral goal clause G, iff H is a variant (including indices) of a proper part of G. Once a proper reduction is obtained, all other descendant resolvents produced from G (including G itself) will be discarded.

Global Subsumption Test: The hierarchical deduction has a feature that the resolvents grouped in the same node are similar to each other in the sense that the tails of these resolvents all are instances of the same part of a goal clause. Based on this property, the procedure can use an effective subsumption test method, so that only a few relevant resolvents need to be compared to determine whether a new resolvent is redundant.

Resolvent Evaluation and Reordering: The prover uses a best-first search strategy by which the candidate goal clause with largest priority is to be resolved first. The priority of each resolvent is assigned by an evaluation routine based on certain ideas, such as "twin symbol". These ideas are also used by a *level subgoal reordering* subroutine, which is responsible for selecting an "important literal" from a goal clause to be the left-most literal of that clause.

A Partial Set of Support Strategy and Others: This strategy is another use method of the model methodology (or say, set of support strategy) to reduce the search space. With this strategy, some literals of input clauses will be disallowed to resolve upon according to a model or "setting". The prover includes a finite forward chaining subroutine to produce some useful information for the evaluation routine. A special factoring algorithm, hierarchical factoring, is used by the procedure, which allows production of fewer factoring resolvents without causing incompleteness.

III. SEMANTICALLY GUIDED HIERARCHICAL DEDUCTION

Now, suppose M is a model of the input set of rule clauses. We require that only the resolvents that are false in M (that is, semantically refutable) can be used as goals by the hierarchical deduction procedure. Then this procedure becomes a so-called *semantically guided hierarchical deduction* (SHD-PROVER). Note, the newly produced resolvents that are true in M will still be retained in some node, so they may be used later as rules.

In order to incorporate type information and other useful knowledge into a model, the interpretation method to be discussed in this paper will be slightly different from the traditional one. In particular, we will allow the domain D of an interpretation to include a special element, "unknown". Thus $D = D_0 \cup \{unknown\}$, where D_0 is an ordinary nonempty domain not containing the element "unknown". This element will be used for indicating the interpreted value of semantically meaningless terms, atoms, or formulas. We restrict the use of our interpretation method to a subset of the first-order formulas, namely, the *simplified first order formulas*.

Definition. A simplified first-order formula is a quantifier free first-order formula containing no logical symbol other than $\neg$, $\wedge$, $\vee$; and each negation symbol $\neg$ occurring in this formula must be applied to an atomic subformula (ie. atom).

All atomic formulas, clauses, and sets of clauses (treated as conjunctions of disjuncts) are simplified first-order formulas. The formulas in the *interpretation normal form*, which is to be introduced next, are also simplified first-order formulas.

Interpretation. An interpretation I for a simplified first-order formula W consists of a domain D and a definition for each non-variable symbol occurring in W, such that

- Each n place predicate symbol P is interpreted in I as a function, $P : D^n \rightarrow \{true, false, unknown\}$;
- Each n place function symbol F is interpreted in I as a function, $F : D^n \rightarrow D$;
- The logical symbols are interpreted in I traditionally, except $\neg unknown = unknown, unknown \wedge X = X,$

and $unknown \vee X = unknown$, where $X \in \{true, false, unknown\}$;

- For any term or simplified first-order formula W, the term or formula W', obtained from W by substituting all variables occurring in W with some elements of D, is called an interpretation instance of W over D. Let $[W']_I$ denote the interpreted value obtained by evaluating W' according to the interpretations of all non-variable symbols occurring in W';

- Let C be any simplified first-order formula, then $[C]_I = unknown$ iff, for each interpretation instance C' of C over D_0, $[C']_I = unknown$; $[C]_I = false$ iff there is an interpretation instance C' of C over D_0, $[C']_I = false$; otherwise, $[C]_I = true$.

Domain. SHD-PROVER requires that the domain $D(D_0)$ of an interpretation be finite. This finite domain is obtained by the following method. For a theorem W to be proved, we first interpret it by using a natural domain (it may be infinite). Then the domain $D(D_0)$ used by the prover is produced mechanically by the following procedure:

    PROCEDURE DOMAIN_GENERATOR (domain_limit);
        count := 1;
        D := { e : e is the interpreted value of a constant
    (0 place function symbol) of W };
        WHILE count ≤ domain_limit DO
            count := count + 1;
        D := D ∪ { e : e is the interpreted value of an
    interpretation instance of a term in W over D };
        D_0 := D − {unknown}.

The *domain_limit* can be given by the user. In practice, we prefer to use a small *domain_limit* first, such as 1, to generate a small size domain. If the prover fails, then repeatedly increase *domin_limit* and call the prover until a proof is obtained. We will give several examples of this procedure being used.

For SHD-PROVER, the resolvent that is interpreted as "unknown" will be discarded. It is noticed that the expense of obtaining the interpreted value of a literal or a term increases exponentially along with the increase of the number of different variables it contained. We have used a more efficient method (not given here) to implement this semantic test for avoiding the expensive evaluation.

IV. EXAMPLE DESIGN METHOD

Semantically guided hierarchical deduction, by retaining the resolvents which are true in the model as rules, has acquired a valuable property: if the prover is guided by a particular model, such that at most one semantically refutable and useful resolvent is produced in each step of a deduction, then the procedure will not lose a proof of a theorem. Our task in designing examples and interpreting skolem functions is to obtain this kind of model*.

According to this property and others, a model M with the following characteristics is preferable:

1. The model M should not represent a trivial case of the theorem.
2. Each rule clause should be interpreted to true in M, and the goal clause should be false in M.
3. Among a group of resolvents produced in each step of deduction, at most one <u>useful</u> resolvent is false in M (A useful resolvent is one which can be used by the hierarchical deduction procedure in continuing the current path to $\Box$).
4. A literal or a term should be interpreted to "unknown" for arguments that lead to semantically meaningless situations.

The above characteristic 3 is important to reduce the possibility that a semantic guide causes proof failure (it is also important to efficiency). Let us consider a set of clauses, $S_1 = \{Q \vee R, P \vee \neg Q, P \vee \neg R, \neg P\}$, with $\neg P$ as goal. Suppose we use $\{P, Q, \neg R\}$ as a model of the hypothesis clauses, then there is a successful deduction path in which only one useful resolvent false in the model can be produced in each step of deduction. Now, suppose we use $\{P, Q, R\}$ as a model, then the proof will fail, because the two useful resolvents $\neg Q, \neg R$ produced in the first round of deduction are both false in this model.

Certainly, it is usually not easy to construct a model that has such a characteristic. In the following, we will investigate a way toward a partial solution of this problem. Notice that the clause $P \vee \neg Q$ and $P \vee \neg R$ in the above example can be put together to form a formula, $P \vee [\neg Q \wedge \neg R]$. We will call this form of a formula *interpretation normal form*.

<u>Definition</u>. An interpretation norm form (IPN form) is a simplified first-order formula in the following form:
$$L_1 \vee \ldots \vee L_k \vee [C_1 \wedge \ldots \wedge C_h],$$
where $L_1 \ldots L_k$ are literals and $C_1 \ldots C_h$ are clauses.

For consistency, a formula with a form $L_1 \vee \ldots \vee L_k$ (a clause) is treated as a degenerate case of IPN form, where $h = 1$ and $C_1 = \Box$ (so is deleted); a formula with a form $C_1 \wedge \ldots \wedge C_h$ is treated as another degenerate case of IPN form, where $k = 1$ and $L_1 = \Box$ (so is deleted).

Note that, corresponding to each IPN form, there is a set of clauses, each of which contains a subclause C_j for some $j, 1 \leq j \leq h$.

<u>Interpretation rules</u> for a formula in IPN form: For each interpretation instance of an IPN form,
$$L_1' \vee \ldots \vee L_k' \vee [C_1' \wedge \ldots \wedge C_h'],$$
1. if $[L_1' \vee \ldots \vee L_k']_I = false$, then for each $j, 1 \leq j \leq h$, $[C_j']_I$ should not be false, except when C_j is identical to a part of the goal clause.

---

* Not all theorems have such models, but most of the practical theorems seem to have, at least the only counter-example we found is very unnatural and complicated.

2. if $[L_1' \vee \ldots \vee L_k']_I = true$, then there should be at most one $j, 1 \leq j \leq h$, such that $[C_j']_I = false$.

As a simple application of these rules, let us consider again to design a model for proving the set S_1 by the SHD-PROVER. First, we combine the clauses in S_1 into 3 IPN forms, $\{Q \vee R, P \vee [\neg Q \wedge \neg R], \neg P\}$. Because $\neg P$ will be the goal clause, P must be interpreted to true. Applying the above rule 2 to the interpretation of the IPN form $P \vee [\neg Q \wedge \neg R]$, we notice that at most one of $\neg Q$ and $\neg R$ can be interpreted to false. Thus the model $\{P, \neg Q, R\}$ $\{P, Q, \neg R\}$ is acceptable, but the model $\{P, Q, R\}$ is not.

In this paper, we will mainly consider the problem of designing examples for theorems that have real semantics. In this case, as it will be shown in what follows, the interpretation rules of IPN form will be mainly applied to interpret some skolem functions.

<u>An example design method</u>. Let T be a theorem of first-order theory, and S be the set of clauses obtained by skolemizing the negation of T. We design an example of T for SHD-PROVER by follows:

1. Design a real example E for T;
2. Interpret naturally each predicate of S according to its meaning in E;
3. Interpret naturally each function symbol (including constant) that has a corresponding instance in E (this kind of symbol is called interpreted symbol);
4. For each of the remaining function symbols occurring in S (the uninterpreted symbols), combine all clauses of S containing an occurrence of this symbol into an IPN form, then interpret this symbol, according to its meaning and following the interpretation rules for IPN form.

V. <u>APPLICATION OF THE EXAMPLE DESIGN METHOD</u>

<u>1. AM8</u>: The attaining minimum (or maximum) value theorem in analysis: a continuous function f in a closed real interval [a,b] attains its minimum (or maximum) in this interval.

To prove this theorem, we use a continuity axiom, and the least upper bound axiom instantiated by this particular problem. The theorem is formalized as follows (We did not present the needed inequality axioms):

$$[\, a \leq l \leq b$$
$$\wedge \forall t(a \leq t \leq l \rightarrow f(l) \leq f(t))$$
$$\wedge \forall x(a \leq x \leq b \wedge \forall t[a \leq t \leq x \rightarrow f(x) \leq f(t)]$$
$$\rightarrow x \leq l)$$
$$\wedge \forall w \exists g\{(a \leq w \leq b \rightarrow a \leq g \leq b \wedge f(g) \leq f(w))$$
$$\wedge \forall x([a \leq w \leq b \wedge a \leq x \leq b \wedge f(x) \leq f(w)]$$
$$\rightarrow g \leq x)\}]$$
$$\rightarrow \exists u[a \leq u \leq b \wedge \forall t(a \leq t \leq b \rightarrow f(u) \leq f(t))].$$

We first transform the negation of this theorem into a simplified first-order formula (the predicate p stands for symbol $\leq$) F1:

$p(a, l)$

$\wedge p(l, b)$

$\wedge \{\neg p(a, t) \vee \neg p(t, l) \vee p(f(l), f(t))\}$

$\wedge \{\neg p(a, x) \vee \neg p(x, b) \vee p(x, l) \vee [p(a, q(x)) \wedge p(q(x), x) \wedge \neg p(f(x), f(q(x)))]\}$

$\wedge \{\neg p(a, w) \vee \neg p(w, b) \vee [p(a, h(w)) \wedge p(h(w), b) \wedge p(f(h(w)), f(w)) \wedge (\neg p(a, x) \vee \neg p(x, b) \vee \neg p(f(x), f(w)) \vee p(h(w), x))]\}$

$\wedge \{\neg p(a, u) \vee \neg p(u, b) \vee [p(a, k(u)) \wedge p(k(u), b) \wedge \neg p(f(u), f(k(u)))]\}$.

In the formula F1, we have forced all occurrences of every uninterpreted function symbol, such as q, h, k, to be contained in an IPN form. So the interpretation rules for IPN form can be used in interpreting these skolem functions.

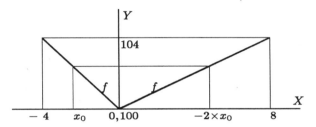

Figure 1. An example of theorem AM8

According to the meaning of the theorem, we designed an example, shown in Figure 1. The interpretation for the interpreted functions or predicates of the theorem are natural:

$a = -4, \qquad b = 8, \qquad l = 0,$

$$f(x) = \begin{cases} 100 - x, & x \in [-4, 0]; \\ 100 + 0.5 \times x, & x \in (0, 8]; \\ unknown, & \text{otherwise,} \end{cases}$$

$$p(x, y) = \begin{cases} true, & x \leq y \wedge x, y \in [-4, 8]; \\ false, & y < x \wedge x, y \in [-4, 8]; \\ true, & x \leq y \wedge x, y \in [100, 104]; \\ false, & y < x \wedge x, y \in [100, 104]; \\ unknown, & \text{otherwise.} \end{cases}$$

Notice that, by the above interpretation, an atom, such as $p(f(a), a)$, will be interpreted to "unknown", because it would be "semantically meaningless" to write $[f(a)]_I \leq [a]_I$ according to the example shown as Figure 1, since the two arguments of $\leq$ belong to different types: the point $[f(a)]_I = 104$ is on the Y-axis and the point $[a]_I = -4$ is on the X-axis. Notice also that, we defined the function f only in the interval $[-4, 8]$ of X-axis. This restriction allows the procedure to prevent some redundant resolvents. For example, a resolvent containing a term $f(f(a))$ or $f(f(l))$ must be discarded, because f is undefined in $[f(a)]_I$ or $[f(l)]_I$.

Now we interpret the skolem function q, which is contained in the fourth conjunct of F1:

$\neg p(a, x) \vee \neg p(x, b) \vee p(x, l) \vee [p(a, q(x)) \wedge p(q(x), x) \wedge \neg p(f(x), f(q(x)))]$

For the meaningful interpretation, we need only to consider two cases:

1. $x \in [-4, 0]$. Then $[p(x, l)]_I = true$. By interpretation rule 2 for IPN form, at most one among the literals $p(a, q(x)), p(q(x), x)$ and $\neg p(f(x), f(q(x)))$ (each corresponds a C_j in the definition of IPN form) can be interpreted to false. So we can interpret q to be a function, which maps the point $x, x \in [-4, 0]$, to a point $x', x' \in [-4, -2 \times x]$ (see Figure 1). In contrast, if q were interpreted to map the point x to a point point $x'', x'' \in [-2 \times x, 8]$, then there would be two literals $P(q(x)), x)$ and $\neg P(f(x), f(q(x)))$ interpreted to false. We tested some different interpretations, such as $q(x) = -4, q(x) = x$ (AM8[a] of Table 1), $q(x) = -2 \times x$ (AM8[b] of table 1) and $q(x) = 8$, for $q(x), x \in [-4, 0]$, by running the prover with identical other conditions. The prover succeeded with the use of the first two interpretations, which satisfy the interpretation rules, and failed with the use of the last two interpretations, which did not satisfy the interpretation rules.

2. $x \in (0, 8]$. Then $[p(x, l)]_I, [\neg p(a, x)]_I$ and $[\neg p(x, b)]_I$ are all false. By interpretation rule 1 for IPN form, we should interpret all of $p(a, q(x)), p(q(x), x)$ and $\neg p(f(x), f(q(x)))$ to true. Thus the following relations should be satisfied:

$0 < x \leq 8 \wedge -4 \leq q(x) \leq x \wedge f(q(x)) < f(x).$

Consulting Figure 1, we define $q(x) = 0.5 \times x$ for $x \in (0, 8]$. The final interpretation for q can be

$$q(x) = \begin{cases} x, & x \in [-4, 0], \\ 0.5 \times x, & x \in (0, 8], \\ unknown, & \text{otherwise.} \end{cases}$$

By a similar process, we interpret the skolem function h, contained in the fifth conjunct of F1, as follows:

$$h(x) = \begin{cases} x, & x \in [-4, 0], \\ -0.5 \times x, & x \in (0, 8], \\ unknown, & \text{otherwise.} \end{cases}$$

The skolem function k occurs in the last IPN form of the above formula F1:

$\neg p(a, u) \vee \neg p(u, b) \vee [p(a, k(u)) \wedge p(k(u), b) \wedge \neg p(f(u), f(k(u)))]$.

Because the last conjunct, $\neg p(f(u), f(k(u)))$, together with the first two disjuncts will form the goal clause of the input set, which should be interpreted to false. According to the meaning of the theorem, the function k(u) is meaningful only for u=0 in this example, so we interpret k as follows:

$$k(u) = \begin{cases} 4, & u = 0, \\ unknown, & \text{otherwise.} \end{cases}$$

The domain D_0 is obtained by the subroutine DO-MAIN_GENERATOR, where we set $domain\_limit = 3$,

$$D_0 = \{-4.0, -2.0, 0.0, 4.0, 8.0, 100.0, 102.0, 104.0\}.$$

By the help of this example, the prover obtained a quite efficient proof (see Table 1): only 68 resolvents accepted, among which 30 were useful. 4 useful resolvents were produced by resolving goals against some resolvents that were true in the model. So the hierarchical deduction structure, which retained these resolvents as rules, was important for this proof.

2. IMV: The mean value theorem in analysis: If function f is continuous in a real closed interval $[a, b]$, where $f(a) \leq 0$ and $0 \leq f(b)$, then $\exists x f(x) = 0$.

Several interesting interpretations of uninterpreted skolem functions, similar to the interpretation of skolem function q in AM8, were encountered in designing examples for this theorem. One can find the set of clauses for this theorem in [8]. This problem has been considered in [2]. A different example was designed by us according to our interpretation rules.

3. GCD: If $gcd(a, b)$ is the greatest common divisor of two positive integers a and b, then for any positive integer e, $gcd(a \times e, b \times e) = gcd(a, b) \times e$.

Let $g(x, y, u)$ denote $u = gcd(x, y)$, and $d(x, y)$ denote x properly divides y. Then the theorem is represented as the follows:

$$
\begin{aligned}
&[\ g(a, b, c) \\
&\wedge \forall x \forall y \forall u \{g(x, y, u) \leftrightarrow d(u, x) \wedge d(u, y) \wedge \forall v[d(v, x) \wedge \\
&d(v, y) \rightarrow d(v, u)]\} \\
&\wedge \forall x \forall y \exists u (d(u, x) \wedge d(u, y) \wedge \forall v[d(v, x) \wedge d(v, y) \rightarrow \\
&d(v, u)])] \\
&\quad \rightarrow g(a \times e, b \times e, c \times e).
\end{aligned}
$$

The second conjunct of the above formula is the definition of positive integers gcd. The third conjunct is the assertion of the existence of the gcd. Number theory is a typical example for this theorem. We interpreted a, b, c, d, e, g naturally:

$$a = 6, \quad b = 10, \quad c = 2, \quad e = 7.$$

$$
g(x, y, u) = \begin{cases} true, & u = gcd(x, y), \\ unknown, & \text{otherwise,} \end{cases}
$$

$$
d(x, y) = \begin{cases} true, & x \text{ properly divide } y, \\ unknown, & \text{otherwise.} \end{cases}
$$

Skolemizing the definitions of gcd and the third conjunct introduced skolem functions i and k, each of which was forced to be contained in an IPN form:

$$\neg d(u, x) \vee \neg d(u, y) \vee g(x, y, u) \vee [d(i(x, y, u), x) \wedge d(i(x, y, u), y) \wedge \neg d(i(x, y, u), u)],$$

$$d(k(x, y), x) \wedge d(k(x, y), y) \wedge [\neg d(v, x) \vee \neg d(v, y) \vee d(v, k(x, y))].$$

The following interpretations for i and k satisfy interpretation rules for IPN forms, which were used by the prover:

$$i(x, y, u) = 1,$$
$$k(x, y) = gcd(x, y).$$

A subset of axioms about the product operator $\times$, and the proper division operator $/$ was used in proving this theorem. These operators were interpreted according to their natural meanings. The domain is produced by DOMAIN_GENERATOR with $domain\_limit = 1$. An commutative unification algorithm and a sorting ground commutative terms subroutine were used by the prover to avoid explicitly including commutative laws into input set of clauses.

4. LCM: If $lcm(a, b)$ is the least common multiple of two positive integers, a and b, then

$$lcm(a, b) = (a \times b)/gcd(a, b).$$

The above theorem GCD, was used as a lemma in proving this theorem. Let $l(x, y, u)$ mean $u = lcm(x, y)$, and let the predicates g and d be the same as that of GCD, then the theorem is represented as follows:

$$
\begin{aligned}
&[\ g(a, b, c) \\
&\wedge \forall x \forall y \forall u \{g(x, y, u) \rightarrow \forall w[g(x \times w, y \times w, u \times w)]\} \\
&\wedge \forall x \forall y \forall u \{g(x, y, u) \leftrightarrow d(u, x) \wedge d(u, y) \wedge \forall v[d(v, x) \wedge \\
&d(v, y) \rightarrow d(v, u)]\} \\
&\wedge \forall x \forall y \forall u \{l(x, y, u) \leftrightarrow d(x, u) \wedge d(y, u) \wedge \forall v[d(x, v) \wedge \\
&d(y, v) \rightarrow d(u, v)]\}] \\
&\quad \rightarrow l(a, b, (a \times b)/c)
\end{aligned}
$$

The same subset of axioms for the operators $\times$ and $/$, and a similar strategy in dealing with commutative laws as that for proving GCD were used in proving this theorem. The example designed for this theorem is similar to GCD, but is augmented by interpretations for predicate l and a skolem function j obtained by skolemizing the definition of LCM. We do not go into much detail.

5. SST: In AAAI 1984, C. Walther reported his success of using many-sorted resolution to prove Schubert's statement (SST). It was said that this problem was so hard, that no automatic prover could ever obtain a proof, except the many sorted resolution prover. After the meeting, we submitted this problem, together with an example designed according to the meaning of the statement, to our SHD-PROVER. Without any difficulty, the prover succeeded.

To understand our design of the example for this problem, the reader can refer to [7] for finding the original statement of the problem and the resulted set of clauses.

Several skolem constants occur in the set of clauses, each of which corresponds to a type of entities, where

w_0: a wolf b_0: a bird s_0: a snail

f_0: a fox c_0: a caterpillars g_0: grain.

To facilitate implementation, we interpret each entity as a integer:

$$w_0 = 13, f_0 = 11, b_0 = 7, c_0 = 5, s_0 = 3, g_0 = 2.$$

With the above interpretations of entities and according to the meaning of each sentence of the statement, we interpret the predicates occurring in the set of clauses as follows:

$W(x) = true$, if $x = 13$, otherwise $unknown$;
$F(x) = true$, if $x = 11$, otherwise $unknown$;
$B(x) = true$, if $x = 7$, otherwise $unknown$;
$C(x) = true$, if $x = 5$, otherwise $unknown$;
$S(x) = true$, if $x = 3$, otherwise $unknown$;
$G(x) = true$, if $x = 2$, otherwise $unknown$;
$P(x) = true$, if $x = 2$, otherwise $unknown$;

$$A(x) = \begin{cases} true, & x \in \{3,5,7,11,13\}, \\ unknown, & \text{otherwise}; \end{cases}$$

$$M(x,y) = \begin{cases} true, & x < y \wedge x,y \neq 2, \\ false, & y < x \wedge x,y \neq 2, \\ unknown, & \text{otherwise}; \end{cases}$$

$$E(x,y) = \begin{cases} true, & x = 13 \wedge y \in \{7,5,3\}, \\ false, & x = 13 \wedge y \in \{2,11,13\}, \\ true, & x = 11 \wedge y \in \{7,5,3\}, \\ false, & x = 11 \wedge y \in \{2,11,13\}, \\ true, & x = 7 \wedge y \in \{5,2\}, \\ false, & x = 7 \wedge y \in \{3,7,11,13\}, \\ true, & x = 5 \wedge y = 2, \\ false, & x = 5 \wedge y \neq 2, \\ true, & x = 3 \wedge y = 2, \\ unknown, & \text{otherwise}. \end{cases}$$

Three skolem functions occurred in the set of clauses, each of which could be forced to be contained in an IPN form:

$h : \neg C(x) \vee [P(h(x)) \wedge E(x, h(x))]$,
$i : \neg S(x) \vee [P(i(x)) \wedge E(x, i(x))]$,
$j : \neg A(x) \vee \neg A(y) \vee [G(j(x,y)) \wedge (\neg E(x,y) \vee \neg E(y, j(x,y)))]$

Then they were interpreted as follows:

$h(x) = 2$, if $x = 5$, otherwise $unknow$;
$i(x) = 2$, if $x = 3$, otherwise $unknow$;

$$j(x,y) = \begin{cases} 2, & \text{if } x,y \in \{3,5,7,11,13\}, \\ unknown, & \text{otherwise}. \end{cases}$$

The domain D_0 consists of a finite set of integers:
$D_0 = \{2,3,5,7,11,13\}$.

We should emphasize that, different from the many-sorted resolution, our use of this example includes both type information and the knowledge for guiding the prover to select semantically provable paths.

Table 1 is a summary of the computer runs by SHD-PROVER in proving (without interaction) these theorems with the help of the above examples. The prover was run on the Symbolics 3600. The code has not been well optimized. The heuristic search strategy (it was described in [8]) based on syntactic features was important to these proofs, but no particular heuristics were added to help prove different theorem, except some control parameters, such as the limit of search depth, the limit of function nesting depth, etc. may be different.

Table 1. A summary of computer run

Theorem	AM8[a]	AM8[b]	IMV	GCD	LCM	SST
Semantic test*	9	80	13	10	34	69
Locally subsumed	23	313	17	19	54	8
Tail unmergeable	12	256	4	0	4	4
Proper reduction	12	21	6	0	2	1
Globally subsumed	0	30	0	23	41	3
CPU second	14	125	14	41	82	16
Useful resolvents	30	Fail	38	23	22	58
Accepted resolvents	68	256	69	70	83	82

ACKNOWLEDGMENTS

The author is grateful to W. W. Bledsoe who contributed valuable suggestions and helped with phrasing for this manuscript, also to L. Wos, L. J. Henschen and A. M. Ballantyne for their help related to this topic.

REFERENCES

[1] Bledsoe, W. W. Non-resolution theorem proving. Artificial Intelligence 9 (1977), 1-35.

[2] Ballantyne, A.M. and Bledsoe, W. W. On generating and using examples in proof discovery. Machine Intelligence 10(1982).

[3] Gelernter, H. Realization of a geometry theorem-proving machine. Proc. IFIP congr.(1959).

[4] Kowalski, R., and Kuehner D. Linear resolution with selection function. Artificial Intelligence 2 (1971), 227-260.

[5] Plaisted D. A. Using examples, case analysis, and dependency graphs in theorem proving. 7th International Conference on automatic deduction.(1984)

[6] Reiter, R. A semantically guided deductive system for automatic theorem proving, Proc. 3rd IJCAI(1973)41-46.

[7] Walther, C. A mechanical solution of Schubert's steamroller by many-sorted resolution. Proc. 8rd AAAI(1984)330-334.

[8] Wang, T. C. Hierarchical Deduction. Tech. Report ATP-78, Univ. of Texas at Austin, March, 1984.

---

* It is counted as the number of resolvents which are not false in the model.

HOW TO FACILITATE THE PROOF OF THEOREMS BY USING THE INDUCTION - MATCHING,
AND BY GENERALIZATION

Jacqueline Castaing [*]

I.RI. Bât. 490 Univ. de Paris sud - F. 91405 ORSAY cedex

ABSTRACT

In this paper, we show how we conceive the proof of theorems by sructural induction. Our aim is to facilitate the proof of the theorems which can lead, in a context of automatic theorem proving, to very lengthy (or even impossible) proofs.

We use a very simple tool, the i-matching or induction-matching, which allows us, on the one hand to define an original procedure of generalization, and on the other hand to define an original way of generating lemmas.

1 Introduction

In Kodratoff-Castaing [4] , we presented an automatic theorem proving based on the principle of structural induction [3]. We followed on from the works done by Boyer and Moore [2], Aubin [1] and Huet and Hullot [5]. Our method is now implemented in Lisp (Vax).

Generally, when we want to prove a theorem using structural induction, we first have to prove one or more basic cases and then, one or more induction steps. In our method we try a new and we hope an original approach, to prove the induction steps. We use a very simple tool which we call i-matchimg (induction -matching) . Briefly, it is used as follows (for a more detailed explanation see our previous article [4]): let M => N be any induction steps to be proven, M be any hypothesis and N the associated conclusion. If there is any substitution σ such that : $\sigma(M) = N$, and the induction variables chosen do not belong to the domain of substi tution, then the induction step M => N is proved. Such a substitution σ characterizes the induction -matching. It also shows that the hypothesis M is general enough to consider the conclusion N as an instance of M, and to put N among all the accepted hypotheses .

It is obvious that only easy theorems can be proved by induction - matching. If the matching of M toward N fails , we try to remove the causes of the matching failures either by generalizing the theorem, or by generating intermediate lemmas. So, proving theorems in our method is in fact solving the problems of matching.

In this article we intend to show how we understand the problem of the generalization of the theorems. We shall propose two examples . With this help, we shall demonstrate that the solution we propose is :

1 clearly justified by our aim of facilitating the proof of theorems

2 clearer than the solutions proposed by Boyer and Moore, Aubin, and also includes them.

2 The formal system

We suppose that all the conditions which allow us to manipulate the theorems, and to prove them by using induction in abstract data types are verified . That's to say:

1 the domain (type support) is generated by a family of constructors supposed not to be related. We can define, on this domain, the following well-founded ordering, denoted by $\prec$:
   $x \prec y$ iff x is a subterm of y.

2 the functions are completly defined by a set of axioms [5]. From these axioms, one can obtain a canonical rewrite system named R.

3 the particular properties of the functions given by the users are contained in the set of equations E.

In this paper, we apply our method to the following two examples :

t_1 : (eql (app x (app x x)) (app(app x x) x))
t_2 : (eql (rev x) (foo x nil)).

The first theorem shows that the function app (append in Lisp) is associative. The second shows the equivalence between two programs which compute the reverse of a list. The domain is the set of lists of integers , denoted by List. It is generated by the two constructors (nil , cons), where cons is the binary operator cons : Int x List -> List (Int denotes the set of natural integers, generated

_____
[*] New address : LIPN, Univ. de Paris nord
Avenue J-B Clément F.93400 VILLETANEUSE "

by the two constructors zero and succ).
The proof of theorem t_1 (t_2) is carried out, if we prove:
  1 the basic case t_1 (nil) (t_2(nil))
  2 the induction step t_1 (x) => t_1 (x <- (cons a x)) (t_2 (x) => t_2 (x <- (cons a x))).

The canonical rewrite system contains the following rules:
r_1 : (eql x x) -> true
r_2 : (eql nil (cons b y)) -> false
r_3 : (eql (cons a x) nil)) -> false
r_4 : (eql (cons a x) (cons b y)) -> (and (eqn a b) (eql x y))
r_5 : (and true y) -> y
r_6 : (and false y) -> true
r_7 : (eqn x x)-> true
r_8 : (eqn zero (succ y))-> false
r_9 : (eqn (succ x) zero) -> false
r_{10} : (eqn (succ x) (succ y)) -> (eqn x y)
r_{11} : (rev nil)-> nil
r_{12} : (rev (cons a x)) -> (app (rev x) (cons a nil))
r_{13} : (app nil y) -> y
r_{14} : (app (cons a x) y) -> (cons a (app x y))
r_{15} : (foo nil y) -> y
r_{16} : (foo (cons a x) y) -> (foo x (cons a nil))

The set of equations E only contains the equation (app x nil) = x.

When we dispose of a canonical rewrite system, we can evaluate any term M and find its normal form, denoted by M!, by applying the rules in any order. But, it may happen in some particular case, that we have to define a precise order in the application of the rewrite rules. In this article, we use call- by- need evaluation [7]. We show how we can apply it.
We proceed by steps . First, we try to reduce M at the empty sequence of occurrences, i.e, we try to apply one of the rewrite rules which gives the definition of the leftmost function symbol in M. If we succeed, we reduce M and obtain a new term M' to which we apply again the same process of evaluation. If we fail, we let $(u_1,....,u_p)$ be the sequence of the occurrences of subterms of M, which must be evaluated in order to apply one of the previous rewrite rules. Then, we reduce M successively at the occurrences $u_1,....u_p$ by applying the same process of evaluation .

The call-by-need evaluation stops either in the case where the normal form of M is an element of the domain, or in the case where the subterms of M to the occurrences $u_1,....,u_p$,denoted by $M/u_1,...., M/u_p$, are variables. In this case , to use Aubin's terminology, we say that these variables are recursion variables, or are in the recursion position. Generally, we can also say that the subterms of M which must be evaluated in the call-by-need rule, are in the recursion position.

Example :

We evaluate the term M = (eql (app x (app x x)) (app(app x x) x)).

Step-1 : we try to reduce M at the empty sequence of occurrences. We have to evaluate the subterms of M at the occurrences 1 and 2, in order to apply one of the four rules r_1,...., r_4, which give the definition of eql.

Step-2 : for evaluating the subterm M/1, we must instanciate the variable at the occurrence 1.1. For evaluating the subterm M/2, we must evaluate the subterm M/2.1.

Step-3: we have to instanciate the variable at the occurrence 2.1.1.

The two occurrences of the variable x, 1.1 and 2.1.1, are in the recursion position.

3 Generalization : existant solutions

The need for an efficient procedure of generalization has been expressed in [1,2,4,8]. In such a procedure, we have to define a criterion of choice of the subterms to be generalized in a theorem, verify the new proposition obtained, and give a new way of proceeding if the generalized proposition obtained is a false one. Otherwise, the method proposed fails.

We now analyse Boyer and Moore 's and Aubin's solutions.

Boyer and Moore choose the subterms to be generalized according to their syntax. They replace, in the theorem to be proved, some syntatically identical subterms by the same new variables. This simple procedure suits the proving of a large class of theorems, because it is used in a framework of the strategy of cross-fertilization [2]. This strategy reduces the induction steps P' = Q' => P =h (Q') where P',Q' and P are recursively defined functions, to a new lemma P = h(P') to be proved. If the term P is defined by g(P'), then the new theorem to be proved g(P') = h(P') can be generalized to g(u) = h(u), where u is a new variable. We must be careful if we want to extend the application of this principle, because the new proposition obtained can be a false one.
For example, if we generalize the theorem t_1 by this principle, the new theorem obtained by replacing the subterms (app x x) by a variable u is in fact a false one.

Thus, we can make some remarks about the Boyer and Moore 's solution. Their principle does not indicate how to go on if the proposition obtained is a false one. Their principle cannot be fully justified. One can only establish that very often, the generalized theorem can now be proved.

Aubin proposes two heuristics of generalization in order to improve on the Boyer and Moore 's principle. In these two heuristics, he chooses the subterms to be generalized according to their position in the theorem. He distinguishes a recursive function from a tail-recursive function. In practice, the distinction between these two kinds of functions is the presence in a tail-recursive function of accumulators which are variables, whose role is to contain the partial result of the evaluation of the function. For example, the function foo whose definition is given in the paragraph above, is a tail-recursive function, because the variable y is an accumulator, while the function app is a recursively defined one.

For recursive functions, he uses the same criterion for selecting induction variables, and for choosing the subterms to be generalized. He chooses the induction variables among the recursion ones. So, he selects among the set of occurrences of the same subterm in the theorem, those which are in position of recursion, and gives them the same name.

For example, he generalizes the theorem t_1 by replacing the occurrences 1.1 and 2.1.1 of the same variable x , by a new variable u. He thus obtains the new proposition to be proved, (eql (app u (app x x)) (app (app u x) x)).

Generally, if the new proposition obtained is a false one, he analyses the subterms which are left in the theorem, and tries to generalize those which are syntatically identical to the recursion subterms.

For tail-recursive functions, Aubin generalizes the constants which are in the position of accumulators. The principle used is called "indirect generalization", because the subterms to be generalized are now in the accumulator position, and not in the recursion position.
Aubin justifies his choice by the following remark : if the theorem to be proved is an equivalence one, the presence of these constants causes the failure of the proof by cross-fertilization.
Let us verify this remark with the help of theorem t_2.

Example:

t_2 = (eql (rev x) (foo x nil)).
Let M = t_2 (x); Let N = t_2 (x <- (cons a x))! = (eql (app (rev x) (cons a nil)) (foo x (cons a nil))).
The induction step is M => N. To cross-fertilize is to apply the hypothesis as a rewrite rule. We can extract two rewrite rules from M. The first one, (foo x nil) -> (rev x), can not be applied, the presence of the constant nil in the accumulator position of the function foo, leads the matching of (foo x nil) with (foo x (cons a nil)) to fail. The second rule, (rev x) -> (foo x nil) reduces the induction step to a new lemma, t_3 = (eql (app (foo x nil) (cons a nil)) (foo x (cons a nil))).

In order to prove t_3, we have to prove the induction step t_3 (x) => t_3 (x <- (cons b x)). By applying again the same strategy of cross-fertilization, we can now establish that the presence of the constants nil and (cons a nil) at the occurrences 1.1.2 and 2.2 prevents us from using the hypothesis as a rewrite rule. So, the proof of t_2 fails according to the argument given by Aubin.

If the new proposition obtained by replacing the same constants by a new variable is a false one, (and that is the case in our example, the proposition obtained (eql (rev x) (foo x v)) being a false one), Aubin proposes to make appear some new constants in the theorem, that he also generalizes. We describe how he proceeds.
He matches M with N and looks for the other causes of the failure. Let us suppose that the matching fails because the substitution is attempted on a function symbol. He tries to remove this failure by applying a procedure called a procedure of expansion [6]. He introduces in M the function symbol which is responsible for the failure, and completes its definition in order to obtain a new hypothesis M' equivalent to M. This last condition is satisfied if the function introduced has a neutral element.

Example :

M = (eql (rev x) (foo x nil)).
N = (eql (app (rev x) (cons a nil)) (foo x (cons a nil))).
The matching of M with N fails at the occurrence 1, because the substitution is attempted on the function symbols rev and app, and fails at the occurrence 2.2, for the reason given by Aubin.
According to the procedure of expansion, Aubin introduces at the occurrence 1 the symbol app, and completes its definition by adding the term (rev x) followed by the neutral element of app which is nil.
The new hypothesis obtained is M' = (eql (app (rev x) nil) (foo x nil)). Now, the generalized expression of M', (eql (app (rev x) v) (foo x v)), is the new theorem to be proved.

The two solutions given by Aubin allow us to extend the class of theorems which can be proved. But, we can point out some weaknesses.
The heuristic used for recursive functions is not fully justified. Indeed, the new variable introduced in the theorem is considered as an induction variable at the next step, when the same method is applied again : we do not know whether the proof of the new theorem obtained can now be facilitated or even carried out. Moreover, we do not like the combinatorial aspect which is associated to the choice of the subterms to be generalized.
The second heuristic proposed is more interesting. It is justified by the intention of its autor to use the hypothesis as a rewrite rule. On the other hand, we think that the Aubin's way of continuing, when the generalized proposition is a false one, can be extended without considering the different kinds of functions. The real purpose is to remove the causes of the failure of the matching of M with

N. We now show, using theorem t_1 as an example, that the subterms chosen by Aubin, at the occurrences 1.1 and 2.1.1, are in fact a part of all the subterms which are responsible for the matching failure.

Example :

$M = t_1 (x) = (\text{eql} (\text{app } x (\text{app } x \ x)) (\text{app } (\text{app } x \ x) \ x))$.
$N = t_1 (x <- (\text{cons a x}))! = (\text{eql} (\text{app } x (\text{cons a (app } x (\text{cons a x}))) (\text{app } (\text{app } x (\text{cons a x}) (\text{cons a x}))$ by applying the rules r_4, r_7, r_5, r_{14}.
The matching of M with N fails for the following reasons :

1   we detect a contradictory substitution on the variable x, x <- x and x <- (cons a x) at the occurrences 1.1, 2.1.1, 2.1.2, 2.2.

2   the substitution is attempted on the function symbols cons and app at the occurrence 1.2.
The subterms responsible for the matching failure are at the occurrences 1.1, 1.2, 2.1.1, 2.1.2, 2.2. Aubin generalizes the subterms at the occurrences 1.1, 2.1.1, which are only two causes of the matching failure.

Our method systematizes this approach.

4 Our solution

It consists of two steps, the first one will be exemplified by the proof of theorem t_1, the second one by the proof of theorem t_2.
We assume that the basic cases are proved.
Let M => N be any induction step. If M i-matches with N then the induction step M => N is proved. Let us suppose that the i-matching fails. As we have already indicated in the introduction, the i-matching is a particular matching such that the induction variables do not belong to the domain of of the substitution. So, we can deduce that either the matching fails, or one of the induction variable belongs to the domain of the substitution.
We put in the two lists LM and LN, all the subterms of M and N which are responsible for this failure, each of them being labelled by its occurrence in M or in N.

Let $LM = [(M/u_1, u_1),..., (M/u_q, u_q)]$ and $LN = [(N/u_1, u_1),..., (N/u_q, u_q)]$ be the lists of these subterms.

A   First step : generalization

Definition-1 : We say that we "savagely" generalize the term M at the occurrences $u_1,..., u_q$, if we replace the subterms of M at these occurrences by new distinct variables $v_1,...,v_q$.

Definition-2 : Let M/u_i be an element of the list LM. Let $M/u_{i1},...,$ M/u_{in} be the set of all the subterms of M which are syntatically identical to the subterm M/u_i. If we generalize M to the occurrences $u_{i1},..., u_{in}$, we call the new variables introduced, $v_1,..., v_n$, separated variables.

Definition-3 : We collect a set of separated variables $v_1,...,v_k$, if we give them the same variable name, let be u. The substitution $\tau = (v_1 <- u,..., v_k <- u)$ symbolizes this collection.

Basic idea

Broadly speaking, we apply a strategy which generalizes too much, and then find for particular values of the variables, the conditions which make the generalization true. So, we savagely generalize M at the occurrences $u_1,...,u_q$, given in the list LM. Let MG $(X, v_1,...,v_q)$ be the generalized expression obtained, where X is the set of all the variables of M different from the v_i's. Generally, this expression is a false proposition. We look for the conditions on the variables v_i's, so that MG $(X,v_1,...,v_q)$ can now be specialized in a new proposition which is true, and upon which we apply our method of proof once again.

In practice, it is very difficult to find the conditions on the v_i's. If M contains a predicate of equality, to specialize MG $(X, v_1,..., v_q)$ is in fact to solve some equations of diophantine type. So, we limit ourselves to simply finding the equality relations between the variables v_i's. We now show how we proceed.

Practical application

We consider the first cause of failure in LM, m = M/u_1.

1   We savagely generalize M at the occurrences of all the subterms of M which are syntatically identical to m. Let $v_1,...,v_n$ be the sequence of separated variables introduced in M. We successively give the particular values $e_1,..., e_m$ to the variables of X, and we compute the normal forms MG-1 = MG $(X <- e_i, v_1,..., v_n),...,$ MG-m = MG $(X <- e_m, v_1,..., v_n)$. These particular expressions only contain separated variables.

2   Let i = 1. We apply the call-by-need evaluation to the term MG-i. Let $VR_i = (v_{i1},...,v_{ik})$ be all the recursion variables of MG-i.

3   Let $VR_i' = (v_1,...,v_n) - VR_i$ be the set of all separated variables which are left (if any are left). We first collect the variables of VR_i by giving them the same name u, then we also collect the variables of VR_i' by giving them the same name v. Let τ be the substitution which symbolizes these two collections.

4   If Mg = τ (MG (X, v_1,..., v_n) is a proposition which is evaluated as true for the particular values of its variables, then Mg is a new theorem to be proved. Otherwise, we go on specializing MG (X, v_1,..., v_n) further. We proceed as follows :

- let j be the particular value given to the variable u which falsifies Mg. We instanciate all the variables of VR_i to the value j, and we compute the new normal form : MG-i-j = MG (v_{i1} <- j,..., v_{ik} <- j)! which only contains separated variables of VR_i'. We apply once more the call-by-need evaluation to MG-i-j. Let VR_{ij} be the set of recursion variables in MG-i-j. Let $VR_i = VR_i \cup VR_{ij}$ be the union of the two sets VR_i and VR_{ij}. We go on to 3.

It is obvious that this procedure of specialization stops either in the case where the new proposition obtained Mg is now verified, or in the case where we have to collect all the separated variables v_1,..., v_n. In this case, we consider the next term MG-i+1 upon which we apply the same process again. If all the subterms MG-1,...,MG-m have been considered, we consider the second cause of failure which is distinct from m and we go on to 1. If there is no cause left, the procedure of generalization fails, and we go on to the next step.

Example :
M = t_1 (x) = (eql (app x (app x x)) (app (app x x) x)).
N = t_1 (x <- (cons a x))! = (eql (app x (cons a (app x (cons a x)))) (app (app x (cons a x)) (cons a x))).
LM = [(x, 1.1), (x, 2.1.1), (x, 2.1.2), (x, 2.2), ((app x x), 1.2)]
m = x

1   We savagely generalize M at the occurrences of all the subterms which are syntatically identical to x. We obtain MG (v_1,...,v_6) = (eql (app v_1 (app v_2 v_3)) (app (app v_4 v_5) v_6)). This expression only contains separated variables.

2   We apply the call-by-need evaluation to MG (v_1,...,v_6). The set of recursion variables VR_i contains the variables v_1 and v_4. So, we collect v_1 and v_4 : let u = v_1 = v_4. We collect all the separated variables which are left : let v = v_2 = v_3 = v_5 = v_6. Let τ = (v_1 <- u, v_4 <- u, v_2 <- v, v_3 <- v, v_5 <- v, v_6 <- v) be the substitution which symbolizes these two collections.

3   Let Mg = τ (MG (v_1,...,v_6)) = (eql (app u (app v v)) (app (app u v) v)). Mg is a proposition evaluated as true for particular values of its variables, so, Mg is a new theorem to be proved.
Let us show how we can prove Mg by using the i-matching. The basic case Mg (u <- nil)! is reduced to true by our rewrite system. The induction step Mg (u) => Mg (u <- (cons a u))! is simplified, by our rewrite system, to the form : (eql (app u (app v v)) (app (app u v) v)) => (eql (app u (app v v)) (app (app u v) v)). The hypothesis i-matches the conclusion, so, the induction step is proved, and we have facilitated the proof of theorem t_1.

B.   Second step : generating lemmas

We only consider the subterms of M and N which are put in lists LM and LN, and which are not variables. The presence of these subterms in lists LM and LN shows that the substitution has been attempted on the function symbols. We propose to remove them from these lists either by using the lemmas given in the set of equations E or by using the hypothesis.

Using lemmas given in E

Let M/u_i and N/u_i be two subterms of M and N put in lists LM and LN such that the function symbols f_i = M (u_i) and g_i = N (u_i) at the occurrences u_i of M and N are distinct. If we find in E an equation of the form x = (g_i x e), we reduce M at the occurrence u_i using the rule x <- (g_i x e). So, we make appear the function symbol g_i in M. We proceed in the same way as Aubin, when he applies the procedure of expansion. Let M' be the new hypothesis obtained by reducing M to the different occurrences given in LM and LN. The new induction step is now M' => N. If M' i-matches with N, the proof of the induction step is completed, and so is the proof of M => N. Otherwise, we put in the two new lists LM' and LN all the causes of this failure, and we come back to the first step, after removing from E all the equations of the form x = (g_i x e) which have been used.
If the equations in E do not allow us to reduce M, we go on now, using the induction hypothesis.

Using the induction hypothesis

General case :
Let M = (P m_1,...,m_p) and N = (P n_1,..., n_p), where P is a predicate to be proved. Let us suppose that one subterm m_i i-matches with the subterm n_i, with the substitution σ. It is obvious that M i-matches with the term N' = (P σ (m_1)... σ (m_p)). So, if we are able to prove the p-1 lemmas σ (m_j) = n_j, we will have proved the induction step M => N.

Particular case :
Let M = (P m_1 m_2) and N = P (n_1 n_2), where P is a predicate of equality. Let us suppose that m_1 and n_1 are put in lists LM and LN, and that m_1 has one occurrence in n_1. We reduce N to a new term N' by applying the rewrite rule m_1 -> m_2 to the occurrence of the subterm m_1 in n_1. We are left with a new theorem to be proved upon which we apply the same method of proof again. As the reader can remark, we proceed as Boyer and Moore do when they cross-fertilize.

Example :

M = t_2 (x) = (eql (rev x) (foo x nil)).
N = t_2 (x <- (cons a x))! = (eql (app (rev x) (cons a nil)) (foo x (cons a nil)))

LM = [((rev x), 1), (nil, 2.2)].
LN = [((app (rev x) (cons a nil)), 1), ((cons a nil), 2.2)].
E = [(app x nil) = x].
As the reader can remark, we fail on generalizing t_2. So, we reduce M at the occurrence 1 by the rule x -> (app x nil). We obtain the new hypothesis M' = (eql (app (rev x) nil) (foo x nil)). The i-matching of M' with N fails, and LM' is [(nil, 1.2), (nil, 2.2)]. We come back to the first step after removing the equation (app x nil) = x from E. So, E is now an empty set.

We savagely generalize the term M' at the occurrences 1.2 and 2.2. We obtain MG (x, v_1, v_2) = (eql (app (rev x) v_1) (foo x v_2)). We give to the variable x the particular value x = nil, and the normal form of MG (x <- nil, v_1, v_2) becomes (eql v_1 v_2). We collect these two variables which are recursion variables : v = v_1 = v_2. The new theorem to be proved is now t_3 = (eql (app (rev x) v) (foo x v)).

Let us prove theorem t_3. The basic case t_3 (x <- nil) is reduced to true by our rewrite system. The induction step is M => N, where

M = t_3 (x) = (eql (app (rev x) v) (foo x v))

N = t_3 (x <- (cons a x))! = (eql (app (app (rev x) (cons a nil)) v) (foo x (cons a v))).

The subterm (foo x v) i-matches with the subterm (foo x (cons a v)) with the substitution σ = (v <- (cons a v)) (x does not belong to the domain of σ). So, the new theorem to be proved is now t_4 = (eql (app (rev x) (cons a v)) (app (app (rev x) (cons a nil)) v)). Our procedure of generalization proposes as a new theorem t_5 = (eql (app u (cons a v)) (app (app u (cons a nil)) v)), which can now be proved by using the i-matching. We have facilitated the proof of theorem t_2.

Conclusion

We can now specify the reasons which allow us to think that our method includes those of Boyer and Moore and Aubin.

1 Our procedure of generalization contains the two heuristics used by Aubin for the choice of the subterms to be generalized.

2 We use the same strategy of proof as these autors when we apply the procedure of expansion, or when we cross-fertilize.

6 References

[1] Aubin R. : "Mechanizing structural induction ". Ph.D ; thesis . Univ. Edinburgh (1976).

[2] Boyer R.S and Moore J S. : "A computational logic ". Academic Press (1980).

[3] Burstall R. : "Proving propreties of program by structural induction". Computer J. 12 (1) (1969) p 41 - 48.

[4] Kodratoff Y. and Castaing J. : "Trivializing the proof of trivial theorems ". IJCAI (1983). Kalsruhe West Germany. Proceedings of the eight international joint conference on Artificial Intelligence p 930.

[5] Huet G. and Hullot J-M. : "Proofs by induction in Equational theories with constructors". 21th IEEE Symposium on Foundations of computer Science (1980).

[6] Wegbreit B. : "Goal directed program transformation ". IEEE Trans. Softw. Eng. SE -2,2 (j 71) p 69-80.

[7] Manna, et al. : "Inductive methods for proving properties of programs ". CACM, vol 16, no 8, (1973).

[8] Abdali, et al. : "Generalization heuristics for theorems Related to recursively Defined Functions ". Proc. 4th National Conf. on Artificial Intelligence, Austin, (1984).

CM-STRATEGY: A METHODOLOGY FOR INDUCTIVE THEOREM PROVING
OR   CONSTRUCTIVE WELL-GENERALIZED PROOFS.

Marta FRAŇOVÁ

L.R.I., Bât. 490, 91405 Orsay Cedex, France

ABSTRACT

The main problem, when automatically proving theorems by induction is the problem of strategy, or, how to automatically direct deductions. This is not trivial, and, at present, only a mixture of complicated strategies have been investigated. The essential contribution of this paper is therefore the proposing of a new strategy for inductive theorem proving, inspired by a new mecanism called Constructive Matching (CM), and used for automatic programming [f04].

We also propose a new method for the recognition of predicates and functions, necessary to prove a theorem by our approach, that are not defined in the knowledge-base ("invention" of new operators). Finally, we illustrate the obtainement of a suitable generalized lemma necessary for the proof.

INTRODUCTION

One of the earliest techniques for program synthesis, the automated construction of computer programs, has been the *deductive approach* [m05], in which the program is developped by proving a theorem corresponding to the given specification.

The special techniques needed for the fulfilment of this deductive approach have inspired us to develop a constructive methodology for inductive proofs. For this, we determined, step by step, all the tools we needed for inductive *automatic* theorem proving, i.e.,

(i) we determined in which "data-types", proofs by induction can be performed automatically (requirements on axioms, definitions of functions and predicates, ...), (but we do not treat the problem of how to transform "bad" data into "good" data);

(ii) we determined by what the choice of (a scheme of) the induction principle is influenced, and (because we find it possible), we formulated an induction principle which helps us to *automatically* "generate" induction hypotheses (in the form) that are *necessary* for the proof of a given theorem;

(iii) we determined *how* to proceed from given data (axioms + induction hypotheses) to the given theorem (i.e. the *strategy*).

In the present paper only (ii) and (iii) are treated.

The novelty of our approach, and a comparaison with already existing inductive theorem proving systems is exemplified in [f08], and therefore not explained here. But, let us point out an essential difference: We *construct directly* (without transformations) the desired formula. This difference appears to be very important, as soon as one realizes, that in our approach

- the application of induction hypotheses is not one of "most difficult points", as it is, for instance in [b12], pg. 90;

- special heuristics for transforming a given formula into an other, to which an induction hypothesis can be applied, are not needed as in [m05].

Due to a lack of space we are forced to present our system from a methodological (nevertheless correct) point of view rather than to give its complete algorithmic description. Such a description requires the introduction of notions that are not published elsewhere (but with which our system works) and therefore an algorithmic description without specifying these notions would be confusing.

The organization of the paper is as follows. We start with a motivation, i.e. a presentation of our methodology in an intuitive way. We also answer the question: Why can proofs be directed by CM-strategy? Section 2 presents our formulation of the Induction Principle, and indicates the links between information included explicitly, or implicitly, in given (to be proved) theorems and information one can express explicitly when one has a "good" formulation of the structural induction principle. Section 3 (the most important from the methodological point of view) gives the formal definition of Constructive Matching. In this section, we also describe how one can recognize subproblems with regard to a given theorem and our knowledge base. In the conclusion we explain why we were motived by Beth's method of semantic tableaux and why we did not use them in their original form. APPENDIX I contains a list of axioms used in the paper. APPENDIX II shows our methodology working in automatic programming. When we refere to appendices, we write ☞I , and ☞II respectively.

1. MOTIVATION

Let us start with an example which is nothing more than a presentation of our methodology when proving theorems by induction.

The reader is asked to work through this example with us carefully, because it will then allow a better understanding of the theoretical explanation which follows in next sections.

Let us suppose that we want to prove
$$\forall x \, (EQL \, (REV \, x) \, (FOO \, x \, null)),$$
noted $\forall x \, Q(x)$, where x is of the type LIST-of-NAT given by the family of constructors {null, unit, append}. NAT is the type of natural numbers. EQL is the equality on LIST-of-NAT. FOO and REV are functions
FOO: LIST-of-NAT × LIST-of-NAT → LIST-of-NAT,
REV: LIST-of-NAT → LIST-of-NAT, defined by following axioms:
A_1: (FOO null l) = l
A_2: (FOO (unit a) l) = (append (unit a) l)
A_3: (FOO (append (unit a) l) L) = (FOO l (append (unit a) L))
A_4: (REV null) = null
A_5: (REV (unit a)) = (unit a)
A_6: (REV (append (unit a) l)) = (append (REV l) (unit a)).

Consider the family of constructors (here {null, unit, append}). It decomposes the induction proof into cases, each possible valuation of the induction variable x producing a case. Since this valuation is a kind of equality, we shall

denote it by EQT.
Our example has three cases:
case(i) (EQT x null), prove Q(x);
case(ii) (EQT x (unit a)) , prove Q(x);
case(iii) (EQT x (append (unit a) l)), suppose Q(l) and prove Q(x).
Let us note (Valuat x) a chosen valuation of x. Let σ_x be {x ← (Valuat x)}.

Intuitive description of CM-strategy:

We describe Q(x) by its "pattern" PTQ. As an illustration, let us suppose that it is PTQ = (H EXPR1 EXPR2). In the above example, H = EQL, EXPR1 = (REV x), EXPR2 = (FOO x null).
Using the valuation of x in each case, (by the evaluation of H with regard to EXPR1 and with regard to the given valuation, and by an application of induction hypotheses, if it is the case) one deduces a valid formula which has the pattern PTQ' = (H EXPR1 EXPR1'). In this step, the value of EXPR2 is not taken into account.
The next step is the constructive one: We try to find valid transformations of EXPR1' into EXPR2, i.e. we transform EXPR1' into EXPR1'', so that EXPR1'' = σ_x(EXPR2).
It may happen that a direct transformation of EXPR1' into EXPR2 is not possible. We then evaluate EXPR2 for the current valuation. This leads to EXPR2'. Then, either EXPR1' can be transformed into EXPR2', or the equality EXPR1' = EXPR2' becomes a new theorem, to be treated as before. The last case may well generate an infinite sequence of theorems to be proven.

Now the example will show how we construct this equality, and how some infinite sequences are reduced to a generalized theorem.

case(i):
(EQT x null), σ_x is { x ← null}. Here,
PTQ' = (EQL (REV x) null) because of A_4. We now try to find the axioms that can transform EXPR1'(= null) into EXPR2 (= (FOO ...)). The axiom A_1 is the only one which can be used, because it may have instances of the form null = (FOO ...). We obtain the equality (which is an instance of A_1): null = (FOO null null), i.e. we have succeeded in obtaining a transformation of EXPR1' (= null) into EXPR1'' (= (FOO null null)). Moreover,
EXPR1'' = σ_x(EXPR2). This completes the proof of case (i).

case(ii):
(EQT x (unit a)) , σ_x is {x ← (unit a)}. Here,
PTQ' = (EQL (REV x) (unit a)). We therefore try to transform EXPR1' = (unit a) into an expression of the form (FOO . . .). We have no space here to explain why, but only two axioms, which may have instances of the form (unit a) = (FOO . . .), can be used: A_1 and A_2. Using A_1, one finds that EXPR1' (= (unit a)) can be transformed into EXPR1'' (= (FOO null (unit a))). But
EXPR1'' ≠ σ_x(EXPR2), therefore this possibility is rejected.
Because (unit a) is (append (unit a) null), using the instance of A_2 (i.e. (unit a) = (FOO (unit a) null)), one finds that EXPR1'' is (FOO (unit a) null).
EXPR1'' = σ_x(EXPR2) is satisfied, and this completes the proof of case(ii).

case(iii):
(EQT x (append (unit a) l)), σ_x is {x ← (append (unit a) l)}. In this case we have at our disposal the induction hypothesis:
(EQL (REV l) (FOO l null)).
By the evaluation of (REV x) with regard to the given valuation of x, and an immediate application of the induction hypothesis, we obtain
PTQ' = (EQL (REV x) (append (FOO l null) (unit a))).

As there are no axioms that have an instance matching (append (FOO l null) (unit a)) = (FOO . . .), we must evaluate EXPR2. We obtain EXPR2' = (FOO l (unit a)). We want to prove EXPR1'= EXPR2', i.e.
Q_1(l,a): (append (FOO l null) (unit a)) = (FOO l (unit a)).
This equality becomes a new theorem to be proven:
$$\forall l \, \forall a \, Q_1(l,a).$$
We skip the application of our methodology to this new theorem. It "fails" again by leading to a new EXPR1' and EXPR2' that are different, as before. The new theorem reads:
Q_2(l',a,b):
(append (append (FOO l'null) (unit b)) (unit a))
= (FOO l' (append (unit b) (unit a))).
Continuing this way we obtain, that for proving Q_2 we need to prove Q_3, for proving Q_3 we need to prove Q_4, ... After several steps we try to see, whether it is possible to find a generalized theorem determined by Q_1, Q_2, Q_3, Q_4, ...
The reader can see that the structures of Q_1 and Q_2 are very similar, being of the form
Q*(l,L): $\forall l \, \forall L$ (EQL (append (FOO l null) L) (FOO l L)).
Therefore Q* will be this generalized theorem.
In this case, the automation of the common structure of Q_1 and Q_2 is trivial since Q* is simply the least generalization of Q_1 and Q_2 (more details can be found in [k31]).
We have undertaken the proof (still at a conjectural state) that provable theorems can be expressed as a sequence of theorems which can be generalized.
The proof of Q*(l,L) is not difficult, and left to the reader.

Why could we conjecture such a "simple" form of the sequence of constructed theorems? Why can proofs always follow the same scheme (evaluation of an expression, application of the induction hypothesis, directed transformation of an expression into an other one, ...)? The reasons are simple:
1) The form of a given theorem indicates *which* is the formula we have to obtain for a given valuation of the induction variable. This directs the construction of expressions necessary for a construction of this formula.
2) Functions and predicates are defined *recursively*, and *with regard to a given family of constructors*. This facilitates a search for links among expressions, and together with the form of the formula we want to obtain, it indicates missing lemmas.
3) Moreover, a good formulation of the structural induction principle points at the elements for which we should explicitly express the induction hypothesis, and therefore an application of induction hypotheses no longer is (contrary to [b12]) one of the most difficult problems when proving theorems by induction.
These arguments are only consequences of next sections.

2.1. PROOFS BY INDUCTION

In practice, when we try to prove by induction a theorem $\forall x\, A(x)$ with x of the type T we know (or should know) some *primitive functions* (or constructors) by which we can obtain elements of the type T by a simple combination of these primitive functions. Functions with a codomain T will be called *generators* of T.
Moreover, we suppose that we know *selectors*, i.e. functions which for an element x of the type expressed by some primitive function f as (f y) gives the result y.
Finally, we suppose that we have at our disposal *predicates* which take the value TRUE only if an element of the type has been constructed using the given primitive function.
By these predicates p_1, ..., p_k we can define the equivalence relation ~ on the type T: for x, y of the type T x~y iff there is p_i such that $(p_i\, x) = (p_i\, y) = $ TRUE.
We can then choose the representative rep_i of the class

$P_i = \{ x; (p_i \ x) = \text{TRUE} \}$, $i = 1, ..., k$.
For instance, for T = LIST-of-NAT we have the predicates null?, unit?, append? and the representatives of the appropriate classes are null, (unit a), (append (unit a) l).

So, when we want to prove $\forall x \ A(x)$ of the type T it is enough to take all the representatives $rep_1, ..., rep_k$, and to prove $A(rep_i)$ for each $i = 1, ..., k$.

Now we introduce the notion of the valuation of one element x as the choice of one rep_i which will be noted (EQT x rep_i), and very often we say that x is represented by rep_i. So EQT is in a sense an equality on T. It is not an equality throughout the proof but only in the considered case (for a given representative). When we speak about one possible not-explicitly determined valuation of x, we will write (Valuat x), i.e. (Valuat x) $\in \{rep_1, ..., rep_k\}$.

2.2. THE STRUCTURAL INDUCTION PRINCIPLE - FORMULATION

Let us first introduce some notions and notations. Let us denote by FGT the family of generators of some well-founded type, and by FCT the family of constructors of the type T, i.e. FCT $\subset$ FGT. We classify elements of FCT in the following way:
- *constants* of the type T (i.e $f_j: \to T$)
- *basic-T-operators* (i.e. $f_j: D_1^j \times ... \times D_{n_j}^j \to T$, such that there is no $m \in \{1, ..., n_j\}$ such that D_m^j is T);
- *general-T-functions* (i.e. $f_j: D_1^j \times ... \times D_{n_j}^j \to T$, such that there is at least one $m \in \{1, ..., n_j\}$ such that D_m^j is T).

PRINCIPLE OF STRUCTURAL INDUCTION

Let us suppose that we want to prove that A(a) holds for an arbitrary element a of the type T. A(a) holds for all a of the type T provided that the following hold:

- $A(f_c)$ holds for every constant f_c of FCT,
- $A(f_j(x_1^j, ..., x_{n_j}^j))$ can be proved for every basic-T-constructor f_j of FCT with the arbitrary arguments $x_1^j, ..., x_{n_j}^j$ (x_m^j is of the type D_m^j for $m \in \{1, ..., n_j\}$) considered, during the proof of $A(f_j(x_1^j, ..., x_{n_j}^j))$, as local constants (i.e. they do not change their value during the proof-procedure),
- $A(f_j(x_1^j, ..., x_{n_j}^j))$ can be proved for every general-T-constructor f_j, with $x_1^j, ..., x_{n_j}^j$ considered during the proof as local constants, and starting the proof procedure by supposing
(i) *explicit* validity of $A(x_{s_q}^j)$ for each local constant $x_{s_q}^j$ of the type T ($x_{s_q}^j \in \{x_1^j, ..., x_{n_j}^j\}$)
(ii) *implicit* validity of $A(p_{s_q})$ for any $p_{s_q} < x_{s_q}^j$, where $x_{s_q}^j$ is a local constant and p_{s_q} belongs to the well-founded ordering of T, called $D_{s_q}^j$.
Here, implicit means that during the proof procedure a new parameter p_{s_q} of T can be constructed, and p_{s_q} is smaller than $x_{s_q}^j$. We can then suppose $A(p_{s_q})$ to be valid. Naturally, p_{s_q} will not occur explicitly in $A(f_j(x_1^j, ..., x_{n_j}^j))$, which is the last formula of the deduction.
(iii) implicit validity of A(q) for any $q < f_j(x_1^j, ..., x_{n_j}^j)$.
As one can easily notice, this principle of structural induction cuts a proof of $\forall x A(x)$ into two cases (distinguished by the existence of induction hypotheses).

2.3. STRUCTURAL INDUCTION AND STRUCTURE OF FORMULAE

In this section we explain that the structure of a formula A (when proving $\forall x \ A(x)$) can lead to some heuristics when using the structural induction principle during the proof of the desired theorem.

Remark 2.3.1.:
It may happen that we do not want to prove $\forall x \ A(x)$ for all elements of the type T, but only for elements which satisfy some condition P, i.e. we want to prove $\forall x \ (P(x) \implies A(x))$. The predicate P in our (inductive) approach cannot be arbitrary, because we must be able to determine constructors of the type $T_P = \{ x \mid x \in T \wedge P(x) \text{ holds}\}$. Then instead of proving $\forall x \ (P(x) \implies A(x))$, we prove the theorem $\forall x \ A(x)$ in T_P.

Example 2.3.1.: Let us suppose that in NAT we want to prove the theorem:
$\forall y \ (\text{odd } y) \implies [(2\text{div } y) = (\text{Suc } (2\text{div } (\text{substr1 } y)))]$, where 2div is the integer-division-by-two function, the meaning of odd, Suc and substr1 is clear.
The predicate odd determines the type NAT_{odd} in which each element is either (Suc 0) or can be written as (Suc (Suc a)) for a $\in NAT_{odd}$. It means that we will try to prove
$\forall y \ [(2\text{div } y) = (\text{Suc } (2\text{div } (\text{substr1 } y)))]$ in the domain NAT_{odd}.

Remark 2.3.2.:
In A(x) may also occur some functions or predicates which are defined with the help of a "selective" function df of the type T (i.e. $df: T_1 \times T \to T$, where T_1 can be T and for hp $\in T_1$ (df hp q) is an element of T smaller than q.)
In a such case, when we want to prove A(x) for x given by some representative of T expressed by a general-T-constructor, we include in our induction hypotheses also a hypothesis $\forall hp \ A((df \ hp \ x))$. One can see that hp here represents all elements p of T_1 for which A((df p x)) is satisfied. We call such a hp the help-parameter. A predicate A defined with the help of a selective function will be called the predicate depending on a help-parameter, which will be written: A depends on hp.

Example 2.3.2.: Let us suppose that we want to prove $\forall x \ \exists z Q(x,z)$, where Q(x,z) is (PERMUT x z) $\wedge$ (ORDERED z). The definition of PERMUT, given by (AL23)-(AL27) in ▬I, contains a "selective" function DELETE. When we have to prove $\exists z \ Q((\text{append } (\text{unit } a) \ l),z)$, we use the induction hypothesis $\forall p \ \exists z' \ Q((\text{append } (\text{unit } a) \ (\text{DELETE } p \ l)),z') \wedge (\text{MEMBER } p \ l)$ as well as the more classical one $\exists z'' \ Q(l,z'')$. One cannot know in advance which one is to be used (may be both). In general one has to use all the possible induction hypotheses induced by the "selective" function.

What is gained by using of our structural induction principle as a method of proving theorems? Nothing more than
- the knowledge of the *form* (or pattern) of the formula which we want to obtain, i.e. $A(f_j(x_1^j, ..., x_{n_j}^j))$ from given axioms and formulae $A(p_{s_q})$ $A(x_{s_q}^j)$ for elements p_{s_q} and $x_{s_q}^j$ described in the formulation of the structural induction principle, and
- the generation of induction hypotheses in the required form.

3. CONSTRUCTIVE MATCHING

The idea of constructive matching comes from realizing that a given theorem $\forall x \ A(x)$, to be proved in a theory F, expresses a form A(x) of a formula B which should be proved from axioms and hypotheses, i.e. we would like to construct a B, valid in F, such that there is a substitution σ such that $\sigma A(x) = B$.

3.1. DEFINITION AND EXAMPLES

Definition 3.1.1.: Formula B matches formula A iff there is a substitution σ such that σA is identical to B (i.e. $\sigma A = B$).

Example 3.1.1.:
Let B be $((\text{Suc } a) = x_2 * u_1 + (\text{Suc } u_2)) \wedge (\text{Suc } u_2) < x_2)$, let A be $(x_1 = x_2 * z_1 + z_2) \wedge (z_2 < x_2))$. Then, B matches A with the substitution $\{x_1 \leftarrow (\text{Suc } a), z_1 \leftarrow u_1, z_2 \leftarrow (\text{Suc } u_2)\}$.

Definition 3.1.2.: If formulae A and B do not match, but from the theory F and B we can prove B' which matches A, then the process of finding B' is called *Constructive Matching* (CM) of A and B.

When proving the theorem $\forall x A(x)$, using the structural induction principle, we have to prove the validity $A(rep_i)$ for i $\in \{1, ..., k\}$, for all the representatives $rep_1, ..., rep_k$. Let us note σ_i the substitution $\{x \leftarrow rep_i\}$. Then, in the case (EQT x rep_i) we have to obtain the formula $\sigma_i(A(x))$. One can see that (EQT x rep_i) and $A(x)$ do not match, but, if $\forall x A(x)$ is provable in F, we can prove $A(rep_i)$ from theory F (extended by possible induction hypotheses), and (EQT x rep_i).

HOW TO PERFORM THE CONSTRUCTIVE MATCHING

Let Q: $T_1 \times T_2 \to$ BOOL be a recursive predicate, defined with respect to representatives of T_1. Let rep be a representative given by a general-T_1-constructor. Then the part of the definition Q with respect to rep can be expressed symbolically as follows:
$Q(x_1, x_2)$ holds

if $\begin{cases} x_1 = rep \wedge Q(srep_1, f_1^1(x_2)) \wedge P_1(f_2^1(rep), f_3^1(x_2)) \\ x_1 = rep \wedge Q(srep_2, f_1^2(x_2)) \wedge P_2(f_2^2(rep), f_3^2(x_2)) \\ \qquad ... \\ x_1 = rep \wedge Q(srep_m, f_1^m(x_2)) \wedge P_m(f_2^m(rep), f_3^m(x_2)), \end{cases}$

where, for j $\in \{1, ..., m\}$, the following are satisfied: $srep_j$ is obtained from rep by some selector, for any y $f_1^j(y) < y$; P_j are already defined predicates, f_i^j are already defined functions, moreover, for any rep and any x_2, the following condition, called CONDP,

$$P_1(f_2^1(rep), f_3^1(x_2)) \vee P_2(f_2^2(rep), f_3^2(x_2))$$
$$\vee ... \vee P_m(f_2^m(rep), f_3^m(x_2))$$

is TRUE.
Let us call the j-th line of the definition Q for x represented by rep, the formula
$$Q(srep_j, f_1^j(x_2)) \wedge P_j(f_2^j(rep), f_3^j(x_2)).$$
On each j-th line x_2 is considered as completely (symbolically) determined by $f_1^j(x_2)$ and $f_3^j(x_2)$, i.e. there is a "function" $G_j(f_1^j, f_3^j)$ such that $G_j(f_1^j(m), f_3^j(m)) = m$ for any m.

Let EXPR be an unquantified expression depending on one variable only, say x, and let $\forall x \, Q(x, EXPR)$ be the theorem to be proved using the structural induction principle.
$Q(x_1, x_2)$ is defined with regard to x_1. Therefore to prove $\forall x \, Q(x, EXPR)$ means, for an arbitrary x, to prove that EXPR belongs to the class, say C_x, of all x_2 for which $Q(x, x_2)$ holds.
Let us consider the case, where x is represented by a general-T_1-constructor rep. Then we have to consider the above mentioned part of the definition of Q. Let us note τ_j the substitution $\{x \leftarrow srep_j\}$.
If x is represented by rep, the class C_{rep} is implicitly determined by the definition of Q: If $Q(srep_j, q_1) \wedge P_j(f_2^j(rep), q_2)$ holds for some q_1, q_2, then we know that $G_j(q_1, q_2) \in C_{rep}$, i.e. there exists an x_3 from C_{rep} such that $f_1^j(x_3) = q_1$ and $f_3^j(x_3) = q_2$.
Moreover, $x_2 \in C_{rep}$ only if there is a j-th line such that
(**) $Q(srep_j, f_1^j(x_2)) \wedge P_j(f_2^j(rep), (f_3^j(x_2))$
is satisfied. This is to say that if $Q(rep, x_2)$ is valid, then there is a j-th line such that (**) is satisfied. Let us call (**) the valid part of $Q(rep, x_2)$ (correspondig to j-th line). One can see that as soon as the valid part (**) of the formula

$Q(rep, x_2)$ was obtained, in our consideration we can replace (**) by $Q(rep, x_2)$.

In our approach, finding out whether or not EXPR $\in C_{rep}$, for the given representation of x by rep, is performed by taking an $x_2 \in C_{rep}$, and verifying whether or not x_2 is equal to (or can be transformed into) EXPR, i.e. we "construct" the formula $Q(rep, EXPR)$ in the following way:
We take an x_2 for which $Q(rep, x_2)$ is known. Then we verify the possibility of a transformation of x_2 into EXPR (for the given representation of x by rep).
The choice of x_2 is not arbitrary. We only choose an x_2 which has some links with EXPR. The links between elements of C_{rep} and EXPR are expressed in induction hypotheses.
We will show, how these links may be explicited:
Let us suppose, that Q does not depend on hp (see Remark 2.3.2.), i.e. that $srep_j$ does not depend on hp for j = 1, 2, ..., m. Then, we have at our disposal the induction hypothesis $Q(srep_j, \tau_j(EXPR))$, where τ_j is $\{x \leftarrow srep_j\}$. Because we want EXPR to be from C_{rep}, for some j must $\tau_j(EXPR)$ be $f_1^j(EXPR)$.
Moreover, for the same j, $P_j(f_2^j(rep), f_3^j(EXPR))$ must be satisfied.
Now, if $srep_j$ depends on hp for some j, i.e. $srep_j = (df \, t_1 \, rep)$ for some t_1, let us note ρ_j the replacing of t_1 by hp. Then, we have at our disposal the induction hypothesis
(H_{hp}^j) $\forall hp \, \rho_j(Q(srep_j, \tau_j(EXPR)))$.
τ_j is $\{x \leftarrow srep_j\}$. Therefore $\tau_j(EXPR)$ depends on hp, as well. But, if $srep_j$ depends on hp, it means that in the definition of Q the expression t_1 is determined as $g(f_3^j(x_2))$ for some function g. Therefore instead of taking H_{hp}^j we use $\rho_j(\tau_j(Q(x, EXPR)))$ with $\rho_j = \{t_1 \leftarrow g(f_3^j(EXPR))\}$.
Because we want EXPR to be from C_{rep}, for some j, $\rho_j(\tau_j(EXPR))$ must be $f_1^j(EXPR)$ (or, if they are not same, $\tau_j(EXPR)$ must be transformable into $f_1^j(EXPR)$).
Moreover, $P_j(f_2^j(rep), f_3^j(EXPR))$ must be satisfied.

Notice, that it may happen that while $\tau_j(EXPR)$ and $f_1^j(EXPR)$ may not be the "same" expressions (for instance (Suc $(+ a \, b)$) and $(+ a \, (\text{Suc } b))$ are not the same expressions), $\tau_j(EXPR)$ can be transformed into $f_1^j(EXPR)$.

With regard to preceeding remarks, the construction of $Q(x, EXPR)$, for the given representation of x by rep, is as follows:
Let ξ be a symbol representing elements $x_2 \in C_{rep}$. Let us note (*) the formula $Q(x, \xi)$. As mentioned above, (*) for x represented by rep holds, only if there is a j-th line such that (**) is satisfied.
We therefore take the definition of Q on j-th line (j=1, ..., m). We write
(1j) $Q(srep_j, f_1^j(\xi)) \wedge P_j(f_2^j(rep), f_3^j(\xi))$.
$srep_j < rep$, therefore we have at our disposal the induction hypothesis $Q(srep_j, \tau_j(EXPR))$, resp. $\rho_j(Q(srep_j, \tau_j(EXPR)))$ if $srep_j$ depends on hp. The induction hypothesis allows us to replace $f_1^j(\xi)$ in (1j) by $\tau_j(EXPR)$, resp. by $\rho_j(\tau_j(EXPR))$.
So we have constructed
(2j) $Q(srep_j, \tau_j(EXPR)) \wedge P_j(f_2^j(rep), f_3^j(\xi))$.
resp. (2j') $\rho_j(Q(srep_j, \tau_j(EXPR))) \wedge P_j(f_2^j(rep), f_3^j(\xi))$.
Now, we verify whether or not
$$P_j(f_2^j(rep), f_3^j(EXPR))$$
is satisfied. If it is, we verify whether or not
$$G_j(\tau_j(EXPR), f_3^j(EXPR)),$$
resp. $G_j(\rho_j(\tau_j(EXPR)), f_3^j(EXPR))$ is equal to (or can be transformed into) EXPR.

If $P_j(f_2^j(rep), f_3^j(EXPR))$ is not satisfied for the j-th line, we call this line a total-failure-line, because there is no sense in looking for some strategy by which we could succeed in constructing $Q(x, EXPR)$ on this line. But if the theorem is provable, then, with respect to the condition CONDP, there must be at least one line which is not a total-failure-line, and for which $G_j(\tau_j(EXPR), f_3^i(EXPR))$ can also be transformed into EXPR.

It may also happen that $G_j(\tau_j(EXPR, f_3^i(EXPR))$ cannot be transformed directly into EXPR. Then, we look for a rule (a lemma) of the form:
$$Q(rep, G_j(\tau_j(EXPR), f_3^i(EXPR)) \wedge \ldots \implies Q(rep, EXPR).$$

In such a way, if we succeed in constructing a valid part of $Q(x, EXPR)$, for the given representation of x by rep, we can conclude that we have constructed the formula $Q(x, EXPR)$, valid for the given representation of x by rep.

Remark: One can argue that we should first verify the condition P_j, rather than immediatly apply induction hypotheses. This objection is not valid if theorems $\forall x \; \exists z Q(x,z)$ are also treated (see ☛ II).

In order to link this discussion with our intuitive description of the CM-strategy (section 1), one can notice that H is Q here, EXPR1 is x, EXPR2 is EXPR. EXPR1' is $G_j(\tau_j(EXPR), f_3^i(EXPR))$, resp. $G_j(\rho_j(\tau_j(EXPR)), f_3^i(EXPR))$.

Let us suppose that $P_j(f_2^i(rep), f_3^i(EXPR))$ is satisfied. The English commentary produced during the proof is then: By the evaluation of Q with regard to x represented by rep, and with regard to ξ representing the class C_{rep} we obtain $Q(x, G_j(f_1^i(\xi), f_3^i(\xi)))$. Then by the application of the corresponding induction hypothesis, we obtain the formula
$$Q(x, G_j(\tau_j(EXPR), f_3^i(EXPR)))$$
resp. $Q(x, G_j(\rho_j(\tau_j(EXPR)), f_3^i(EXPR)))$,   valid   for the representation of x by rep.
Finding the valid transformation of $G_j(\tau_j(EXPR), f_3^i(EXPR))$ into EXPR by ... (axioms and rules giving this transformation are mentioned), the formula $Q(x, EXPR)$, valid for the representation of x by rep, is considered to be constructed.

Example: Let us suppose that we want to prove
$$\forall x \; (PERMUT \; x \; (append \; (unit \; (last \; x)) \; (DELETE \; (last \; x) \; x))))$$
the definition of PERMUT, in ☛ I, leads us, for x represented by (append (unit a) l), to consider the following two lines of the definition of PERMUT:
(PERMUT x_1 x_2) holds

if $\begin{cases} x_1 = (append \; (unit \; a) \; l) \wedge (PERMUT \; l \; (CDR \; x_2)) \\ \qquad\qquad \wedge (a = (CAR \; x_2)) \\[1em] x_1 = (append \; (unit \; a) \; l) \wedge \\ \quad (PERMUT \; (DELETE \; (CAR \; x_2) \; (append \; (unit \; a) \; l)) \\ \qquad (CDR \; x_2)) \wedge (a \neq (CAR \; x_2)) \end{cases}$

We have: f_1^i is CDR, f_2^i is CAR, f_3^i is CAR, $srep_1$ is l, $srep_2$ is (DELETE (CAR x_2) (append (unit a) l)). PERMUT is defined with regard to the selective function DELETE. For the given EXPR, (CAR EXPR) is (last x).
The corresponding induction hypotheses are therefore
(H_1)   (PERMUT l (append (unit (last l)) (DELETE (last l) l)))), τ_1 is $\{ x \leftarrow l \}$.

(H_2)
(PERMUT
   (DELETE (last x) (append (unit a) l))
   (append
      (unit (last (DELETE (last x) (append (unit a) l))))
      (DELETE (last (DELETE (last x) (append (unit a) l)))
         (DELETE (last x) (append (unit a) l)))))
$\wedge$(MEMBER (last x) (append (unit a) l)),
$\tau_2 = \{ x \leftarrow (DELETE \; (last \; x) \; (append \; (unit \; a) \; l)) \}$.

We want to construct $Q(x, EXPR)$ for x represented by (append (unit a) l).

Let us take the 1-st line of the definition of PERMUT for x represented by (append (unit a) l). We write
(PERMUT x ξ) holds only if
$\quad (1_1)$ (PERMUT l (CDR ξ)) $\wedge$ a=(CAR ξ)
We verify whether or not a = (CAR EXPR), (i.e. a=(last x)) is satisfied for the given representation of x.
In our approach, this is performed by checking whether or not a can be transformed into the form (last x) for x represented by (append (unit a) l). Therefore we look at the definition of the function last, and we see that a can be transformed into (last L) for L = (unit a)
or L = (append (unit b) (unit a)) for some b. Both possibilities are rejected, and this failure is registered as a total failure TF_1.

Therefore, we take the second line of the definition of PERMUT for x represented by (append (unit a) l). We write
(PERMUT x ξ) holds only if
$\quad (1_2)$ (PERMUT (DELETE (CAR ξ) (append (unit a) l)) (CDR ξ))
$\qquad\qquad \wedge$ a $\neq$ (CAR ξ).
By the application of H_2 we obtain
(2_2)
(PERMUT
   (DELETE (last x) (append (unit a) l))
   (append
      (unit (last (DELETE (last x) (append (unit a) l))))
      (DELETE (last (DELETE (last x) (append (unit a) l)))
         (DELETE (last x) (append (unit a) l)))))
$\wedge$ a $\neq$ (CAR ξ).
We now verify whether or not a $\neq$ (CAR ξ), i.e.
$\quad$ a $\neq$ (CAR (append (unit (last x)) (DELETE (last x) x)))
for the given representation of x by (append (unit a) l). (CAR EXPR) is (last x), therefore a $\neq$ ((CAR EXPR) is verified as (NOT (a = (last x)). We verify, therefore, whether or not a can be transformed into (last x) for the given representation of x. This is not possible, and we conclude that a $\neq$ (CAR EXPR) is satisfied.
Because a $\neq$ (CAR ξ) is in (2_2) satisfied, (2_2) is nothing but the valid part of (PERMUT x $G_2(\tau_2(EXPR), f_3^i(EXPR))$).

The last step therefore is to verify whether or not $G_2(\tau_2(EXPR), f_3^i(EXPR))$ can be transformed into EXPR, i.e. whether or not
(append (unit (last x))
   (append (unit (last (DELETE (last x) (append (unit a) l))))
      (DELETE (last (DELETE (last x) (append (unit a) l)))
         (DELETE (last x) (append (unit a) l)))))
can be transformed into
(append (unit (last x)) (append (DELETE (last x) x))).
The equality of these two expressions is not possible, therefore we are looking for a rule of the form
$\quad$ (PERMUT A B) $\wedge$ ... $\implies$ (PERMUT A C).
We obtain that the rule we look for is the transitivity of PERMUT. Then, using the rule
$\quad$ ((CAR A)=(CAR B)) $\wedge$(PERMUT (CDR A) (CDR B))
$\qquad\qquad \implies$ (PERMUT A B)
together with H_2, completes the proof. For lack of space, the detailed description of this last part is not given here.

It is very difficult to explain such constructions without being too formal. We hope that the examples given in this section, and section 1. as well, help us to be as illustrative as possible.

3.2. SUBPROBLEMS WITH REGARD TO CM-PROCEDURE

During the process of CM we can use only functions and predicates defined by axioms. *But it may happen that the proof $\forall x \; A(x)$ needs more functions and predicates than those currently available.*

This situation is similar to the decomposition of the problem into subproblems (see [s04]), but with a small difference: we do not ask "how to decompose a problem into subproblems", but rather: How to determine that, for a proof of our theorem $\forall x\ A(x)$, we will need some new function or predicate which is not explicitely defined in our system?

The aim of this becomes clear, when one realizes that these new functions will help us to explicit some parts of the representatives ξ (see preceeding section and ☛II).

Definition 3.2.1.:
Let M be a predicate $(:T_1 \times T_2 \to \text{BOOL})$ such that there exists a function φ_M: $T_1 \to T_2$ and three predicates Q_1: $T_1 \times T_2 \to$ BOOL, Q_2: $T_1 \times T_3 \to$ BOOL, Q_3: $T_3 \times T_2 \to$ BOOL, such that
1. φ_M is the function represented by the Specification Theorem
$$\forall x\ (P_1(x) \implies \exists z\ Q_1(x,z) \wedge (\forall y\ Q_2(x,y) \implies Q_3(y,z))),$$
where P_1 characterizes the input domain;
2. $M(p,(\varphi_M\ p))$ is true iff $\forall y\ Q_2(p,y) \implies Q_3(y,(\varphi_M\ p))$;
3. Q_2 is not a kind of equality;
4. $Q_3 \neq M$;
Then, we call *M-problem* the synthesis of φ_M from the Specification Theorem. Any M for which we can define an M-problem will be said *to have the ∇-property).*

Example 3.2.1.: To the predicate LTL defined in ☛I, we can associate the theorem (LTL-problem):
$$\forall l\ ((\text{NOT}\ (\text{EQL}\ l\ \text{null})) \implies$$
$$(\exists z\ (\text{MEMBER}\ z\ l) \wedge (\forall y\ (\text{MEMBER}\ y\ l) \implies (< z\ y))))$$
which defines MIN (minimum) of elements of l. For all u of the type NAT, (LTL u l) holds only if $(< u\ (\text{MIN}\ l))$.

Definition 3.2.2.:
Let C be a unary predicate. We call a formula SD_C with the free-variable x, such that $(C(x) \iff SD_C(x))$ holds for any x, a *semantic definition* of a condition $C(x)$.

Example 3.2.2.: $\forall y\ (C_1(y) \implies C_2(x,y))$, where C_1, C_2 are two known predicates, is a semantic definition of C such that $C(x)$ iff $\forall y\ C_1(y) \implies C_2(x,y)$.

Definition 3.2.3.:
C is a Trivial Condition if its semantic negation does not contain existential quantifiers. If this is not true, C is called a Non-trivial Condition.

Example 3.2.3.: (MEMBER a l) is a Trivial Condition because its semantic negation is $\forall x\ (\text{MEMBER}\ x\ l) \implies (\neq x\ a)$.
The predicate LTL: NAT×LIST-of-NAT→BOOL the semantic definition of which is (LTL x l) iff
$[\forall y\ ((\text{MEMBER}\ y\ l) \implies (< x\ y))]$ is Non-trivial Condition. By analogy, (PRIME x) iff
$\forall y\ ((y<x) \wedge (y\ \text{divides}\ x) \implies (y = 1))$ is a Non-trivial Condition.

When C is trivial, it can either be replaced by a simpler condition, or its evaluation is trivial. It can therefore be used as a predicate in the conditional part of a recursive definition. When C is not trivial, since it has the ∇-property, we shall first try to synthetize a corresponding φ_C. Then, φ_C will help us to simplify the condition C and explicit, if necessary, some parts of ξ (see ☛II).

Example 3.2.4.: Let us suppose that we want to prove $\forall l\ \exists l'$ (PERMUT l' l) $\wedge$ (ORDERED l'). We can see that ORDERED in ☛II is defined with the help of LTL, which has the ∇-property. This is why, before starting the proof, we need to synthetise φ correspondig to the theorem
$$\forall l\ ((\text{NOT}\ (\text{EQL}\ l\ \text{null})) \implies$$
$$(\exists z\ (\text{MEMBER}\ z\ l) \wedge (\forall y\ (\text{MEMBER}\ y\ l) \implies (< z\ y))))). \text{(The application of this can be found in ☛II.)}$$

One should realize that there is no general strategy for proving theorems of the type $\forall x\ ...\ \exists y\ ...\ \forall z\ ...$. To see this try proving the well-known relative-prime-number problem (see in [g02]):
$$\forall n\ \mathbb{N}\ \forall p\ \forall q\ [\text{RP}(p,q) \wedge p,q > N \implies |\sqrt{2} - \tfrac{p}{q}| > \frac{1}{q^{2+\frac{1}{n}}}],$$
where RP(p,q) means that p and q are relative prime.
This is why in our system we have some heuristics in order to solve some simple such problems.

CONCLUSION

We have shown that the CM-procedure is used when we want "constructively" to prove a given theorem. It means that CM is the strategy used to orient our deduction when proving a given theorem from given axioms A_1, ..., A_k.

Beth proposed a solution to the problem of finding whether or not some formula V is a logical consequence of formulae A_1, ..., A_k. His solution is the method of semantic tableaux [b03], formalized by his Completeness Theorem for a system of Natural Deduction F. As Beth himself pointed out, the practical interest of his method is seriously impaired by complicated splittings of a tableau into subtableaux. By a modification of Beth's method of semantic tableaux inspired by the CM-strategy, we have obtained a method for inductive theorem proving.

Our modification consists in
- including the structural induction principle in the set of rules for the construction of tableaux relative to ST and
- orienting a development of tableaux (by CM-strategy) towards the desired goal.
We do not give here our modification of Beth's method.
Our approach is currently under implementation, but has not been yet completed. Its main difficulty is due to the generalizations which will be left to the user in this first version. The efficency of our methodology depends on the truth of our conjecture relative to sequence of theorems generated by the recursively generated EXPR1' and EXPR2' (see section 1). It may be that an elaborate strategy is needed in order to put this sequence in such a form that its generalization appears at once.

ACKNOWLEDGEMENTS

I would like to express my warmest thanks to Yves Kodratoff. I also thank Professor Georg Kreisel for his encouragement. Professor Jean-Luc Remy provided many helpful remarks.

APPENDIX I

We give here only the list of axioms explicitly used in the paper.

TYPE NAT - given by
Constructors: 0: → NAT and   *Suc:* NAT → NAT
Selectors: Pred: NAT → NAT
Predicates: zero?: NAT → BOOL and Suc?: NAT → BOOL.

TYPE LIST-of-NAT - given by
Constructors: null: → LIST, unit: NAT → LIST and append: LIST × LIST → LIST
Selectors: CAR: LIST →NAT and CDR: LIST → LIST
Predicates: null?: LIST → BOOL, unit?: LIST → BOOL, append?: LIST → BOOL
Relations and Functions:
EQL : LIST × LIST → BOOL
MEMBER: NAT × LIST → BOOL

LTL : NAT × LIST → BOOL defined by
(AL8) (LTL x null)
(AL9) (LTL x (unit y)) ∧ (= x y)
(AL10) (LTL x (unit y)) ∧ (< x y)
(AL11) (LTL x (append (unit y) l)) ∧ (= x y) ∧ (LTL x l)
(AL12) (LTL x (append (unit y) l)) ∧ (< x y) ∧ (LTL x l)
ORDERED : LIST → BOOL
(AL13) (ORDERED null)
(AL14) (ORDERED (UNIT x))
(AL15) (ORDERED (append (UNIT x) l))
        ∧ (LTL x l) ∧ (ORDERED l)
(AL16) (ORDERED (append (UNIT x) (append (UNIT y) l)))
        ∧ (= x y) ∧ (ORDERED (append (UNIT y) l))
(AL17) (ORDERED (append (UNIT x) (append (UNIT y) l)))
        ∧ (< x y) ∧ (ORDERED (append (UNIT y) l))
DELETE: NAT × LIST → LIST
PERMUT: LIST × LIST → BOOL defined by
(AL23) (PERMUT null null)
(AL24) (PERMUT (unit x) (unit y)) ∧ (= x y)
(AL25) (PERMUT (append (unit x) (unit y))
        (append (unit y) (unit x)))
(AL26) (PERMUT (append (unit x) l) (append (unit y) m))
        ∧ (= x y) ∧ (PERMUT l m)
(AL27) (PERMUT (append (unit x) l) (append (unit y) m))
        ∧ (≠ x y) ∧ (MEMBER y l)
        ∧ (PERMUT (DELETE y (append (unit x) l)) m)

APPENDIX II

This appendix is for the automatic programming oriented reader, and is readable only if the section 3. has already been understood.
We try to present, here, the CM-procedure as it appears in our approach to automatic programming.
Let Q, rep be as described in section 3. Let the part of the definition of a predicate R with regard to x represented by rep be as follows:
R(x) holds if

$$\begin{cases} x = rep \land R(srep_1') \land P_1'(f_1'(rep)) \\ x = rep \land R(srep_2') \land P_2'(f_2'(rep)) \\ \quad\quad ... \\ x = rep \land R(srep_k') \land P_k'(f_k'(rep)). \end{cases}$$

Let us suppose, that we want to prove a special theorem of the form $\forall x A(x)$ which is $\forall x \exists z\, Q(x,z) \land R(z)$.
If x is represented by rep, then to find z such that $Q(x,z) \land R(z)$ holds means:
Take an abstract representative ξ of all x_2 for which $Q(rep,x_2) \land R(x_2)$ holds. Then with the information included in axioms, induction hypotheses, rules, ..., try to explicite this element. How can it be done?
The definition of Q leads us to consider m cases for the $Q(rep,\xi)$ part of the formula $Q(rep,\xi) \land R(\xi)$:
$Q(srep_j, f_1^j(\xi)) \land P_j(f_2^j(rep), f_3^j(\xi))$ (j=1,...,m).
Naturally, we have at our disposal the induction hypothesis $\exists z_j\, Q(srep_j, z_j) \land R(z_j)$, resp. $\forall hp\, \exists z_j\, Q(srep_j, z_j) \land R(z_j)$, therefore $f_1^j(\xi)$ can be replaced by z_j, and so we have:
$Q(rep, G_j(z_j, f_3^j(\xi)))$ holds
only if $P_j(f_2^j(rep), f_3^j(\xi))$ is satisfied.

Then we look at the definition of R and we look for a line, say the i-th, where $srep_i'$ and $f_1^i(\xi)$ are the "same". Because of the induction hypothesis $R(srep_i')$ can be replaced by $R(z_j)$, and therefore the condition $P_i'(f_i'(\xi))$ together with $P_j(f_2^j(rep), f_3^j(\xi))$ will help us explicite the $f_j(\xi)$ part as a function expression depending only on x, or z_j. Let $z_j'(x)$ be this explicitly expressed $f_3^j(\xi)$. Let us note that $P_j(f_2^j(rep), f_3^j(\xi)) \land P_i'(f_i'(\xi))$ cannot be verified as was the case for the preceeding type of theorems, but it may be reduced to the condition $C_j(f_2^j(rep), z_j'(x))$. Then, naturally, finding z, for x represented by rep, will follow the scheme:
if $C_j(f_2^j(x), z_j'(x))$ holds then z is $G_j(z_j, z_j'(x))$.

Example :
Let us try to prove $\forall x \exists z$ (PERMUT x z) ∧ (ORDERED z) for x represented by (append (unit a) l) (i.e. to find a part of a program SORT when (append? x) is satisfied).
Then the structural induction principle gives the following induction hypotheses:
(H_1) (PERMUT l v_1) ∧ (ORDERED l v_1)
(H_2) $\forall hp\, \exists v_2^{hp}$ (PERMUT (delete hp (append (unit a) l)) v_2^{hp})
        ∧ (ORDERED v_2^{hp}) ∧ (MEMBER hp (append (unit a) l)).
Due to a lack of space, we will only consider the 1-st line of the definition of PERMUT (see section 3.). Let ξ be a symbol denoting an element for which (PERMUT x ξ) ∧ (ORDERED ξ) is satisfied.
The first line of PERMUT indicates, that for the given representation of x, (PERMUT x ξ) holds only if
(PERMUT l (CDR ξ)) ∧ (a = (CAR ξ)) is satisfied. By (H_1), (CDR ξ) can be replaced by v_1. We obtain:
(PERMUT x (append (CAR ξ) v_1)) holds only if
        (PERMUT l v_1) ∧ (a = (CAR ξ)) is satisfied,
i.e.
(PERMUT x (append (CAR ξ) v_1)) holds only if
        (a = (CAR ξ)) is satisfied.

Now we look at the definition of ORDERED, and, with regard to (H_1), we find that (ORDERED (append (CAR ξ) v_1)) holds only if (LTL (CAR ξ) v_1) is satisfied. We obtain, therefore:
(PERMUT x (append (CAR ξ) v_1))
        ∧ (ORDERED (append (CAR ξ) v_1)) holds, only if
$(a = (CAR\ \xi)) \land (LTL\ (CAR\ \xi)\ v_1)$ is satisfied. The condition $(a = (CAR\ \xi))$ gives
(PERMUT x (append (CAR ξ) v_1))
        ∧ (ORDERED (append (CAR ξ) v_1)) holds, only if
(LTL a v_1). Now, we can change this condition (see section 3.2.) to (≤ a (MIN v_1)).
Because v_1 is (SORT (CDR x)) we obtain the following part of the program SORT:
if (append? x) then
        if (CAR x) < (MIN (SORT (CDR x)))
        then (append (CAR x) (SORT (CDR x))).

REFERENCES

[b03] *Beth E.W.*: *The Foundations of Mathematics*; Amsterdam 1959.
[b12] *R.S.Boyer*, *J.S.Moore*: A Computational Logic; Academic Press, 1979.
[f03] *M.Fraňová*: Program Synthesis and Constructive proofs Obtained by Beth's tableaux, in Cybernetics and System Research 2, R. Trappl eds., North-Holland, Amsterdam 1984, pp. 715-720.
[f04] *M.Fraňová*: CM - Strategy - Driven Deductions for Automatic Programming; in T.O'Shea (ed.): ECAI.84: Advances in Artificial Intelligence, Elsevier Science Publishers B.V. (North-Holland), 1984, pp. 573-576.
[f08] *M.Fraňová*: A Methodology for Automatic Programming based on the Constructive Matching Strategy; to appear in: Proceedings of EUROCALL'85, Linz, April 1985.
[f09] *M.Fraňová*: Inventing is Moderate Cheating or a Theory of Humble Invention; to appear: in Proceedings of Cognitiva '85, Paris, June 1985.
[g02] *Girard J.-Y.*: Proof theory; to appear.
[k31] *Y.Kodratoff*: Generalizing and Particularizing as the Techniques of Learning, Computers and Artificial Intelligence Vol.2, pp.417-442, 1983.
[m05] *Z.Manna and R.Waldinger*: A Deductive Approach to Program Synthesis; ACM Transactions on Programming Languages and Systems, Vol. 2., No.1, January 1980, pp. 90-121.
[s04] *R.D.Smith*: Top-Down Synthesis of Simple Divide and Conquer Algorithm; Technical Report NPS52-82-011, Naval Postgraduate School, Monterey, CA 93940, November 1982.

DISCOVERY AND REASONING IN MATHEMATICS[1]

Alan Bundy

Department of Artificial Intelligence,
University of Edinburgh

Abstract

We discuss the automation of mathematical reasoning, surveying the abilities displayed by human mathematicians and the computational techniques available for automating these abilities. We argue the importance of the simultaneous study of these techniques, because problems inherent in one technique can often be solved if it is able to interact with others.

Keywords

Reasoning, mathematics, deduction, search, learning, proof analysis.

1. Introduction

A major goal of artificial intelligence is to automate reasoning. Solutions to this goal will have both technological applications, enabling us to build more powerful expert systems, and scientific applications, providing models to compare with human reasoning. Mathematics is an excellent domain for exploring the automation of reasoning because:

(a) it provides a wide range of examples of reasoning, from the simple and shallow to the complex and deep;

(b) it is possible to detach this reasoning from other considerations, such as sensory input of data; and,

(c) to a first approximation, the problems of knowledge representation have been solved.

Compare mathematics with other AI domains in which reasoning plays a part, e.g. natural language understanding or visual perception. In mathematics one is not bogged down with huge amounts of noisy data, nor concerned that what seems to be a difficult reasoning issue may evaporate if the knowledge representation were changed. One is free to concentrate on the reasoning problems and then make an attempt to translate any solution found to other domains.

In this paper I discuss the automation of mathematical reasoning, by which I mean any cognitive activity that mathematicians engage in as math-

ematicians. The main theme will be that mathematical reasoning consists of more than just theorem proving, and that the simultaneous automation of other reasoning processes, e.g. learning, simplifies the automation task. Each reasoning process outputs knowledge but also demands knowledge as input. If a computational technique for automating a particular reasoning process is studied in isolation then the provision of its input knowledge may prove a major barrier to automation. But the input knowledge of one technique is the output knowledge of another, so that the techniques fit together in an intercommunicating network. Some techniques for automated reasoning may involve search. In isolation the search involved may be computationally expensive. But one technique may be used to control the search of another, especially if the two techniques are co-routined or even merged into one. The power of a system in which the various techniques interact in well-crafted ways will be more than just the sum of the power of the parts.

I advocate the simultaneous study of all the the processes of mathematical reasoning with particular emphasis on the possible interactions between the techniques that automate them.

2. Reasoning Abilities in Mathematics

What processes are involved in mathematical reasoning? In this section we discuss the various processes and the AI techniques that have been proposed to automate them. More details about these techniques can be found in [Chang & Lee 73, Bundy 83].

The first problem we face is how to classify mathematical reasoning into different processes – what my psychology friends call defining the *task ecology*. Our starting point is a 'folk ecology' of reasoning processes, i.e. the terms used in pre-scientific discussion of reasoning. We will call these *mathematical abilities*. With these abilities we must associate *computational techniques* which implement them. These techniques will form our scientific classification. But the association of abilities to techniques not a neat 1-1 mapping. We are likely to find many techniques to associate with each ability. Some abilities, e.g. learning, have so many diverse techniques associated with them that they seem highly unsuitable as scientific categories, whereas the techniques associated with some abilities, e.g. theorem proving, all have a strong

[1]This research was supported by SERC grant, number GR/C/20826.

family resemblance. Some abilities require a combination of techniques. Consider, for instance, analogy which requires separate techniques for finding and then using the analogy. Each of these techniques will require sub-techniques. Some of these techniques may contribute to several different abilities. Consider, for instances, resolution-type deduction techniques, which are ubiquitous.

We list below the mathematical abilities we will be considering under the heading of mathematical reasoning and mention some of the techniques which have been used to implement these abilities.

- **Proving theorems:** The ability that has received the most attention in the AI study of mathematical reasoning, almost to the exclusion of all others, has been theorem proving. Automated theorem proving has been an important subfield of AI throughout its history. The main techniques required to automate theorem proving are *deduction* which involves *search control*. Deduction traverses a search space of legal inference steps. Search control decides which of these steps to try.

- **Formalizing Problems:** However, mathematicians, especially applied mathematicians, spend a large part of their time translating informal problem statements into mathematical formulae to which deduction, etc. may be applied. The initial stages of this translation involve natural language understanding, visual perception, etc - but these are not specifically mathematical techniques. Later stages involve the specifically mathematical technique of *formula extraction* from the internal meaning representation, which may itself involve *deduction* (see section 3.5).

- **Learning:** This term covers a multitude of processes, for instance, the learning of new mathematical theorems, the learning of new proof methods, the defining of new concepts, the conjecturing of results, etc. New theorems must be assimilated into the theorem proving ability so that they may be used effectively in the future. The *assimilation* technique required will depend particularly on the search control technique being used, e.g. the new theorem will need to be labelled so that it can be accessed when needed. Similarly, new proof methods must be incorporated into the current search control technique. This may involve a *proof analysis* technique to analyse new proofs and generalize them to extract control information, e.g. proof plans. Defining new concepts can be done by *inductive inference* from descriptions of examples and non-examples of the concept.[2] Conjecturing of theorems can be done by considering the hypothesis of the conjecture to be a concept to be defined

using the above techniques.

- **Using Analogy:** Mathematicians use analogy to suggest conjectures and new definitions, and to guide proofs. All uses require *analogical matching* techniques to find and apply the relationship between the target and the source of the analogy (see [Owen 85] for a survey). This is all that is required for suggesting conjectures and definitions, but to use a source proof to control the search for a target proof a further *proof plan* application technique is required.

This is by no means an exhaustive list; mathematicians also find counterexamples, write, publish and deliver papers, teach students, read textbooks, etc. Unfortunately, we have nothing to say about these other abilities, so they are omitted.

3. Mathematical Reasoning Techniques
In this section we classify and discuss some of the techniques that have been developed for automating the mathematical abilities described in the last section. There is only space to discuss those we consider particularly promising. We group these techniques according to their computational purpose and mutual similarity, e.g. deduction, search control, inductive inference, etc. This provides a more scientific classification of mathematical reasoning processes than the list of mathematical abilities above. But even this classification is bound to be improved as we discover new techniques and gain a better understanding of the existing techniques and their inter-relationships. It should therefore be regarded as both incomplete and highly preliminary.

3.1. Deduction
The most well known deduction technique is *resolution*, [Robinson 65]. Resolution is a rule of inference for Predicate Calculus, that is, it is a rule for deducing new logical formulae from old. To prove that a conjecture is a theorem of a mathematical theory both the axioms of the theory and the negation of the conjecture are expressed as clauses (a normal form for Predicate Calculus formulae). Resolution takes a pair of clauses and makes subparts of each identical using a *matching* technique called *unification*. The remaining parts are combined together to make a new clause. Resolution applied repeatedly to the initial clauses and to their successors defines a search space of clauses. This is searched for a contradiction. If the search is successful then the conjecture is a theorem.

The representation of axioms and conjectures as logical formulae is given in the texts of mathematics and logic. It is in this sense that I claimed that the knowledge representation problem

---

[2]Note that inductive inference is not the same as mathematical induction (see section 3.2 below), which is a deductive rule of inference.

was solved to a first approximation.

The resolution search space is guaranteed to contain a contradiction if and only if the conjecture is indeed a theorem. The 'if' part is called completeness and the 'only if' part is called *soundness*. The snag is that if the conjecture is not a theorem then the search may never terminate. The number of new clauses generated rises exponentially, or worse, with the length of the proof. If the proof is non-trivial then either the storage capacity of the computer or the patience of the human operator is exhausted before the proof is found. This is an example of the phenomenon called the *combinatorial explosion*.

Various refinements of or alternatives to resolution have been designed and implemented, with the aim of improving on its space and/or time efficiency without losing completeness. One of the most powerful alternative deduction techniques is the Connection Calculus, [Bibel 82]. These improvements reduce the combinatorial explosion, however, but do not conquer it.

There have also been attempts to avoid the combinatorial explosion by proposing radically new deductive techniques. This has sometimes led to techniques which are efficient at proving restricted classes of theorems, e.g. rewrite rules [Huet & Oppen 80]. It has also led to the reinvention of the wheel - some researchers have rejected the logical approach, only to reinvent it together with the attendant problems of incompleteness and/or combinatorial explosion.

Rather than reject logical deduction techniques it is necessary to augment them with heuristic techniques to control the search for a proof, [Hayes 77]. Search control techniques developed have ranged from weak but general purpose ones, e.g. evaluation functions based on the complexity of the formulae, to powerful but special purpose ones, such as those described in the next section. For a survey see [Bledsoe 77].

3.2. Search Control

A number of powerful search control techniques have been developed by careful analysis of the proofs of human mathematicians to extract the underlying control ideas and express them computationally.

The simplest technique, called *heuristic rules*, is to add these control ideas into the mathematical formulae as preconditions for their application. For instance, the LEX program, [Mitchell *et al* 81], uses rewrite rules to symbolically integrate algebraic terms, e.g the rule:

$$\int u \; dv \Rightarrow uv - \int v \; du$$

is used to integrate by parts. One class of terms which this rule successfully integrates is those where u is a variable, x, and dv/dx is a constant

multiple of a sine or cosine. This search control knowledge is represented in LEX by appending preconditions to the above rule, i.e.

$$u=x \; \& \; dv=n.trig(x) \; dx$$
$$\rightarrow \int u \; dv \Rightarrow uv - \int v \; du$$

where n is an integer and
trig any trigonometric function

Note that this precondition is too general; trig includes tan, for which the rule does not work. We discuss this problem in section 3.3 below.

Note that these preconditions can get very complicated since the same rule may be used successfully in a number of different circumstances and the precondition must be the disjunct of these circumstances.[3] Note also that the rule now contains a mixture of factual and control knowledge. These complications can cause difficulties, e.g. in the automatic learning of such rules, so some researchers prefer to separate factual and control knowledge.

For instance, the Boyer/Moore Theorem Prover, [Boyer & Moore 79], represents its control knowledge as procedures for manipulating the mathematical formulae. This theorem prover exploits the relationship between recursion and mathematical induction to guide inductive proofs of the properties of Lisp functions. The recursive definitions of the Lisp functions are first used to symbolically evaluate the conjecture to be proved. This may fail because the conjecture contains arbitrary constants and the evaluation process requires lists with internal structure. This failure is used to guide the choice of induction scheme and variable, so that when symbolic evaluation is applied to the induction conclusion just enough structure will be available to enable the induction step to be performed. We will call this technique, *recursion guidance*.

Note that recursion guidance involves an analysis of the conjecture and its failed proof, and the choice of an appropriate proof technique on the basis of this analysis. This analysis uses meta-concepts[4] to describe the conjecture, its proof and the proof methods, e.g. the terms induction hypothesis, induction step, etc in the Boyer/Moore Theorem Prover or trigonometric function in LEX. These meta-concepts must be discovered by study of existing proofs, introspection, etc. It is in this sense that the knowledge representation problem is only solved to a first approximation, since the number of possible meta-concepts is open ended and the choice of appropriate ones determines the success or failure of the technique.

---

[3]Or an additional rule used for each circumstance.

[4]The term 'meta' is used because the concepts in question describe the representation of the problem, i.e. they are about it rather than of it.

This process of analysis and guidance using meta-concepts is itself a reasoning process and can be conveniently represented as deduction - but deduction in a meta-theory, rather than the theory itself. Such a use of deduction to guide deduction is made explicit in the PRESS system, [Bundy & Welham 81], for solving equations. The PRESS meta-concepts describe the equation to be solved, e.g. the number of unknowns, their distance apart, the kind of functions involved, etc, and they describe various methods of solving equations or of achieving useful subgoals, e.g. reducing the number of unknowns, moving them closer together, making them occur within identical subterms, etc. Deduction with these meta-concepts induces an implicit, but highly controlled, search for the solution to an equation. We call this technique, *meta-level* inference[5] (see figure 3-1).

```
4.sin x.cos x = 1

2.sin 2x = 1

object-level rule: sin u.cos u => 1/2.sin 2u
meta-level rule: collection of x

The 2 occurrences of x are merged to 1
prior to isolating it.
```

Figure 3-1:   Object- and Meta-Level Inference
                in Equation Solving

These meta-concepts can also be used to express *proof plans*, e.g. the plan to move two unknowns closer together, then merge them and then isolate the remaining occurrence. This plan might be provided by the programmer or learnt by *proof analysis* of a worked example (see section 3.3). Alternatively the proof plan may be at the object-level, e.g. the proof of an analogous theorem, or a generalized proof, [Plummer & Bundy 84]. In each case it must then be applied by a *proof plan application* technique. This application might be straightforward - the target proof exactly following the plan - or the plan may need to be relaxed or augmented at various points. A variety of techniques have been suggested for realising such a flexible plan application technique (see, e.g. [Silver 84])

3.3. Proof Analysis

The process of constructing and augmenting powerful search control techniques, by adding meta-knowledge gained from analysing proofs, can itself be automated. This analysis will depend crucially on the search control technique in question. For instance, in the case of the PRESS system, described in section 3.2, the solution to an equation must be analysed using the meta-concepts of PRESS. For each step an account must be given of not only what algebraic identity was applied but also why it was

applied and how this reason fitted into the overall proof plan. For instance, sin u.cos u = 1/2.sin 2u was applied to reduce the occurrences of u from 2 to 1 in order that that single occurrence could be isolated on the left hand side of the equation. This kind of analysis is performed by the LP program, [Silver 84], which was able to learn new methods of equation solving and extend the range of problems that PRESS could solve. The technique used by LP is called *Precondition Analysis* because it discovers new methods by considering how unexplained steps establish the preconditions of successive steps.

In the case of the LEX program for symbolic integration (also described in section 3.2) the technique of *back propagation* was developed to analyse successful solutions and extract the control information. This technique was incorporated in the LEX2 program, [Mitchell *et al* 83]. In back propagation the successful sequence of rewrite rules was applied in reverse order to a generalized answer to see what constraints this would impose on the original problem. These constraints then became the preconditions of the first rule of the sequence.[6]   For instance, given a successful integration of $\cos^7(x)$, LEX2 used back propagation to discover that the same sequence of rules would have worked on any term of the form $\cos^n(x)$, where n was an odd integer. The first rule of this sequence,

$$f^r \Rightarrow f^{r-1}.f(x)$$

was then given the precondition, f=cos & odd(r). In forming this constraint, back propagation also defined the concept 'odd' as any number of the form 2k+1, where k is an integer.

Proof analysis can also be used to analyse faulty proofs and repair them. For instance, a classic faulty proof in the history of analysis is due to Cauchy, namely that a convergent series of continuous functions is continuous.[7] This 'proof' can be analysed using deduction and the fault identified as a missing occurs check during unification (see section 3.1. This suggests an obvious patch, namely changing the order of quantifiers in the theorem statement, and this generates three new concepts and three new and correct theorems. One of these is the traditional replacement of convergence by uniform convergence; one is a trivial theorem whose conclusion is always true; and one is a new theorem involving the concept of equi-continuity. This reasoning process, which we will call *argument removal*, has been implemented in a program, SEIDEL, described in [Bundy 85].

---

[5]In contrast to the deduction of the equation solution, which is called object-level inference.

[6]It would have been more powerful to remember the whole sequence as a proof plan and make the constraints the preconditions of the plan rather than just its first step.

[7]See [Lakatos 76] for a discussion of this ´proof´ and its history.

For a survey of the use of proof analysis for learning see [Boswell 85].

3.4. Inductive Inference

Inductive inference has received a lot of attention in the learning literature, with a number of techniques being developed. For a survey see [Dietterich *et al* 82] and for an analytic comparison of some of these techniques see [Bundy *et al* 83]. They all learn a concept from examples and, sometimes, non-examples of it. From examples of the concept the techniques might *generalize*: replacing specific relations and terms with more general ones. From non-examples of the concept the techniques might *discriminate*: pruning away relations and terms that are not an essential part of the concept.

This can be used for the learning of both new object-level (factual) and new meta-level (search control). For instance, Mitchell et al's LEX program, [Mitchell *et al* 81], used induction to learn the meta-level conditions for applying a particular strategy for integrating by parts. Given that the strategy worked correctly to integrate 3x.cos(x) and 5x.sin(x), LEX generalized these terms to hypothesise that the strategy will work for terms of the form nx.trig(x), where n is any integer and trig any trigonometric function.

Both the sub-techniques of generalization and discrimination are crucially dependent on the description space. For instance, in LEX the description space contains concepts like 3, 5, n, cos, sin, trig, etc. The generalization of two concepts is the most specific concept in the description space which includes both of them, e.g. trig is the generalization of cos and sin. However, if a term for 'sine or cosine' were added to the description space then it would replace trig as the generalization of cos and sin. In fact, this is the concept required, as discussed in section 3.1. Without it, LEX overgeneralises to trig.

3.5. Formula Extraction

A key technique in the mathematical formalisation of problems is the extraction of formulae from a meaning representation, e.g. the semantic representation of an English description of the problem. Formulae extraction techniques have received little attention in AI despite their importance in human mathematical reasoning. However, the MECHO program, [Bundy *et al* 79], contained a formula extraction technique called *the Marples algorithm*, for forming equations to describe mechanics problems.

The Marples algorithm is a kind of plan formation technique. Equations are formed by instantiating physical laws, e.g. F=MA. With each law is stored a list of the things it is about and a logical description of how these things relate to the variables in the law. For instance, F=MA is about an object and a direction. The variable M is the mass of the object, A its acceleration in that direction, and F the sum of the forces acting in that direction. A law and a situation are chosen after an analysis of the unknowns and givens of the problem. The variables are then instantiated by inferring the logical description from the meaning of the English problem statement.

This inference process may use deduction and default reasoning to fill gaps between the statement of the problem and the knowledge required to instantiate the law. MECHO used resolution guided by meta-level inference for the deduction and the closed world assumption for the default reasoning. Deduction was needed, for instance, to work out the contributions to the sum of forces from gravity, the tensions of strings, the reactions of contact surfaces, etc. Default reasoning was used, for instance, to assume that the only surfaces in contact were those mentioned in the problem statement.

4. The Interaction of Reasoning Techniques

The mathematical reasoning techniques outlined above can interact in a variety of ways. For instance, successful deductions might provide the material for proof analysis and for analogy. Proof analysis may suggest proof plans to aid deduction. The desire to make a particular theorem hold may trigger a process of proof analysis that leads to changes in definitions and axioms. Sometimes these interactions can be more intimate. Several deduction techniques may be co-routined or even merged so that each prunes the search space of the others. We discuss some of these possibilities in more detail below.

4.1. The Interaction of Techniques in the PRESS Family

In my research group work has continued over a number of years on a family of programs working on the common domain of symbolic equation solving.

- As described in [Bundy & Welham 81] and section 3.2 above, the PRESS program used the deduction technique of rewrite rules to generate solutions to equations. This deduction technique was guided by the search control technique of meta-level inference.

- The LP (Learning PRESS) program (see [Silver 84] and section 3.3) used the proof analysis technique of precondition analysis to extract and conjecture new methods of solving equations which were then used by PRESS.

- The IMPRESS (Inferring Meta-knowledge about PRESS) program, [Sterling & Bundy 82], was a theorem proving program for proving properties of logic programs. It was used to prove properties of the Prolog code of PRESS using a modified version of recursion guidance (see section 3.2). For instance, it proved the correctness of some PRESS equation solving methods, i.e. that under appropriate preconditions the methods would achieve their goal.

 - As described in [Bundy *et al* 79] and section 3.5 above, the MECHO program solved mechanics problems stated in English by extracting and solving equations using the Marples algorithm. The equation solving part was done using PRESS as a subprogram.

Each of the above techniques is incomplete on its own. Meta-level inference requires a rich supply of meta-level concepts to analyse problems and bring to bear appropriate methods of solution. These meta-level concepts can be extracted from example solutions by precondition analysis. The new methods conjectured by precondition analysis can be shown to be correct using recursion guidance. The example solutions required by preconditions can be supplied by deduction with a less constraining search control. The problems to be solved by deduction can be supplied by the Marples algorithm, but this technique requires deduction together with meta-level inference to bridge gaps between the knowledge it requires and that provided in the problem statement. The interactions are summarised in table 4-1.[8]

Technique	Problem	Solution
deduction	search	meta-level inference
	problems	Marples alg.
meta-level inference	learning	pre-condition analysis
pre-condition analysis	verification	deduction/ recursion guidance
	examples	deduction
Marples algorithm	gap bridging	deduction/ meta-level inference

Table 4-1:   The Interactions between the Techniques in the PRESS Family

4.2. The Interaction of Learning Techniques

In section 3.4 we described the importance of the description space in constraining the kinds of inductive inference that were possible, old concepts can only be generalized or specialized to new concepts that are contained in the description space. In section 3.3 we described how the techniques of back propagation and argument removal could be used to define new concepts and thus extend the description space in a principled way by adding a needed concept, e.g. odd integer, uniform convergence.

But proof analysis techniques cannot merely replace inductive inference techniques as learning processes. Proof analysis techniques work only on single examples and this limits the amount of generalization that they can do unaided. For instance, we saw that back propagation was able to generalize a particular problem from $\cos^7 x$ to $\cos^n x$, where n is an odd integer. 7 is generalized to n by considering the constraints forced by the particular sequence of rules used in the successful solution. However, a similar sequence will also integrate terms of the form $\sin^n x$ where n is an odd integer; a rule for cos needs to be replaced by a similar rule for sin. To recognise this similarity and build a general proof plan for both cases requires inductive generalization, [Boswell 84]. Alternatively, one might use analogical matching to recognise the similarity and a flexible proof plan application technique to apply the cos sequence to the sin problem. Note how back propagation narrows down the search which would otherwise be involved in finding an analogous solution, but then uses analogical matching to further narrow its own search. Therefore, techniques of proof analysis, inductive inference analogical matching and proof application need to work in concert to achieve maximum learning power.

4.3. The Merging of Deduction Techniques

The resolution rule of inference (see section 3.1) is itself formed from the merging of two other rules of inference, namely modus ponens and substitution.

Modus Ponens: A, A->B |- B
 where A and B are formulae,

Substitution: A(X) |- A(T)
 where A is a formula,
 X is a variable and T is a term

Note that the substitution rule of inference has an infinite branching rate if the number of terms in the mathematical theory is infinite. Exhaustive search with such a rule would be totally impractical. In resolution, substitution is made subservient to an upgraded version of modus ponens and its behaviour thereby controlled.

The upgraded version of modus ponens is the cut rule.

Cut: A -> B, B -> C |- A -> C

Faced with formulae A -> B' and B" -> C the resolution rule applies substitutions to either formula in an attempt to make the Bs identical so that cut can be applied. Unification (see section 3.1) will find the most general such substitution. Up to renamings of variables this substitution is unique - a far cry from the infinite branching of undirected substitution. Thus the merging of modus ponens and substitution controls the search implicit in the later rule by making its application subser-

---
[8]Not all these interactions have been implemented.

vient to the former.

Similar mergings of other deduction techniques have been suggested. For instance, some axioms have been built-in to the unification algorithm. In associative resolution, [Plotkin 72], the associative axiom for a function, f, is deleted from the set of axioms and built-in to the unification algorithm, i.e. it can be used in the attempt to match two expressions. This merging of unification and associativity has the effect of controlling the applications of associativity by making it subservient to unification. Other examples are higher order unification, [Huet 75], which builds the axioms and rules of lambda calculus into the unification algorithm, and E-Resolution, [Morris 69], which builds the equality axioms into the unification algorithm.

The advantage of such mergings is not just in the shrinking of the search space; they can also assist the application of proof plans by bringing the key steps of a proof to the top of the search space. A proof plan may identify a particular step as a key one, but it might take several minor steps to transform the problem into a state where this key step can be applied. For instance, the key step may be to resolve with a particular clause, but several applications of associativity may be required to allow the resolution to go through. These minor steps may create a combinatorial explosion of their own before the key step is reached. By making the minor steps subservient to the key one the key step can be applied first and the application of the minor ones can be controlled.

Merging may also be applicable to non-deduction techniques. For instance, given a problem to solve, an analogical matcher might be able to find a similar solved problem in order to use its solution as a proof plan. Sometimes a solved problem will match the given one in several different ways. Rather than work through each way in turn, the match may be left incomplete until further instantion is required to continue with the proof plan application. Thus the analogical matching will be made subservient to the plan application technique and its search thus controlled.

4.4. Lenat's AM Program

The AM program, [Lenat 82], is an interesting experiment in the interaction of a number of techniques for finding examples, defining concept, making conjectures, etc. These are set in a framework of heuristic rules controlled by heuristic search. An evaluation function is used to decide what concepts to define or find examples of, what conjectures to make. AM's performance is impressive; starting with some simple set-theoretic concepts, it defines some relatively complex and interesting concepts, e.g. prime numbers, and makes some interesting conjectures, e.g. the prime unique factorization theorem. It also defines a lot of uninteresting concepts and makes a lot of silly conjectures.

AM has no theorem proving ability. Its definitions and conjectures are not motivated by problems it is trying to solve, faulty proofs it is trying to correct or successful solutions it is trying to generalise. Its sense of direction comes entirely from its evaluation function which is guided by the patterns, coincidences, etc that it notices in its example finding. It would be interesting to link AM's techniques to those outlined above to get a better directed process of mathematical discovery. This would involve separating the different techniques used in AM and implementing a wider interaction of mathematical techniques. However, such a programme would not be easy. The techniques used by AM are not clearly explained, are embedded in complicated Lisp code, and are difficult to disentangle from the heuristic rules.

5. The DReaM Programme

In this paper I have advocated the simultaneous study of a number of different techniques for mathematical reasoning, especially how these techniques may be fitted together. I believe that problems associated with the individual reasoning techniques can often be solved by combining them together, and I gave a number of examples of this phenomenon in section 4 above.

To realise these ideas I have instituted the DReaM (Discovery and Reasoning in Mathematics) Programme at the Department of Artificial Intelligence at Edinburgh University. This programme gives explicit recognition to an implicit programme of development of mathematical reasoning programs over a period of several years. Figure 5-1 explains the relationship between the various programs built in our group during this period. Each node is a program and each arc represents some historical dependence of the earlier program upon the later one. PRESS, LP,

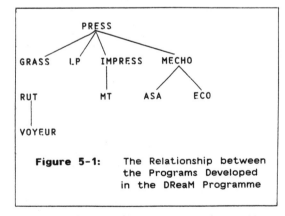

Figure 5-1:   The Relationship between the Programs Developed in the DReaM Programme

IMPRESS and MECHO have been described above. MT will be described below. The remainder are outlined here.

- GRASS is a rewrite rule system for Grassman Geometry, modelled on PRESS and using symmetry to control the application of the rules, [Fearnley-Sander 85].

- ECO, [Uschold *et al* 84], and ASA, [O'Keefe 82], are 'intelligent front ends' to

ecological modelling and statistics packages, respectively.

- RUT, [Plummer 84], is a rational reconstruction of Bledsoe's natural deduction theorem prover, [Bledsoe 77], and VOYEUR, [Plummer & Bundy 84], extends RUT with the gazing technique described below.

Our specific, short term objectives are to extend our existing reasoning techniques and invent new techniques in a variety of domains, and more centrally to investigate the interaction of: deduction, search control, proof analysis and inductive inference within a single reasoning system. The understanding gained from this investigation will be exhibited in a program for reasoning primarily in mathematics, but adaptable (we hope) to other forms of problem domain.

The core of the system will be the MT program, [Wallen 83], which consists of two parts

- the object-language: a logic for expressing problems; and

- the meta-language: a logic for expressing proof plans.

MT uses a process of meta-level inference to analyse a conjecture, choose an appropriate proof plan and use it to guide the search for a proof.

The object-level deduction technique is based on Bibel's Connection Calculus, [Bibel 82]. The Connection Calculus is particularly suitable as a vehicle for proof plans as it does not demand that the conjecture be put in a normal form and the proof is constructed using a detailed analysis of the conjecture. No new formulae need to be constructed during the proof. This makes it particularly easy to relate the original analysis of the conjecture to the proof plan and hence to the subsequent proof. We plan to design and implement several proof plans in the MT system. Heuristics developed from natural deduction proofs can be readily translated into the Connection Calculus. In particular, we will try to implement within MT one such technique, developed in the group, called *gazing*, [Plummer & Bundy 84]. Gazing is a heuristic technique for controlling the expansion of non-logical definitions and the use of previously proved theorems during a proof attempt.

We plan to add to MT a learning component based on precondition analysis and other analytic learning techniques. This will analyse proofs using the meta-level concepts already embodied in the MT proof plans and use this analysis to modify the existing plans and/or build new plans. These plans will then be added to MT to improve its theorem proving ability.

6. Conclusion

The automation of mathematical reasoning involves not just techniques for deduction, but also tech-

niques for search control, proof analysis, inductive inference, matching, formula extraction, etc. In this paper I have outlined some of the most promising such techniques drawn from the work of my own group and from that of others.

I have given examples of the interactions of these techniques and shown how these interactions can solve problems which can appear insuperable if a technique is studied in isolation. This constitutes a strong argument for the simultaneous study of reasoning techniques; to see how the total can be more than the sum of the parts.

The DReaM project aims to conduct such a simultaneous study. Some of the preliminary results are reported above together with our plans to incorporate several techniques within a single system.

Acknowledgements

I am grateful to Robin Boswell, Steve Owen, Lincoln Wallen and Mike Uschold for assistance with and/or feedback on this paper.

References

[Bibel 82]   Bibel W.
                Automated Theorem Proving.
                Friedr. Vieweg & Sohn,
                    Braunschweig/Wiesbaden, 1982.

[Bledsoe 77]   Bledsoe, W.W.
                Non-Resolution theorem-proving.
                Artificial Intelligence 9(1):1-35,
                    August, 1977.

[Boswell 84]   Boswell R.A.
                *Further Developments to an Algebra
                Learning Program - A Thesis
                Proposal.*
                Working Paper 174, Dept. of Artificial Intelligence, Edinburgh, October, 1984.

[Boswell 85]   Boswell R.A.
                *An Analytic Survey of Analytic
                Concept-Learning Programs.*
                Working Paper, Dept. of Artificial Intelligence, Edinburgh, 1985.
                Forthcoming.

[Boyer & Moore 79]
                Boyer, R.S. and Moore J.S.
                A Computational Logic.
                Academic Press, 1979.
                ACM monograph series.

[Bundy 83]   Bundy, A.
                The Computer Modelling of Mathematical Reasoning.
                Academic Press, 1983.
                Earlier version available from Edinburgh as Occasional Paper 24.

[Bundy 85]   Bundy, A.
Poof Analysis: A technique for Con-
cept Formation.
In Ross, P. (editor), *Proceedings of
AISB-85*, pages 78-86. 1985.
Also available as DAI Research Paper
no. 198.

[Bundy & Welham 81]
Bundy, A. and Welham, B.
Using meta-level inference for selective application of multiple
rewrite rules in algebraic
manipulation.
Artificial Intelligence 16(2):189-212,
1981.
Also available as DAI Research Paper
121.

[Bundy et al 79]
Bundy, A., Byrd, L., Luger, G., Mellish,
C., Milne, R. and Palmer, M.
Solving Mechanics Problems Using
Meta-Level Inference.
In Buchanan, B.G. (editor), *Proceedings
of IJCAI-79*, pages 1017-1027.
International Joint Conference on
Artificial Intelligence, 1979.
Reprinted in 'Expert Systems in the
microelectronic age' ed. Michie,
D., Edinburgh University Press,
1979. Also available from Edin-
burgh as DAI Research Paper No.
112.

[Bundy et al 83]
Bundy, A., Silver, B. and Plummer, D.
An Analytical Comparison of some
Rule Learning Programs.
In *Third Annual Technical Conference
of the British Computer Society's
Expert Systems Specialist Group*.
British Computer Society, 1983.
Earlier Version in Procs of ECAI-82.

[Chang & Lee 73]
Chang C-L. and Lee R. C-T.
*Symbolic logic and mechanical theorem
proving*.
Academic Press, 1973.

[Dietterich et al 82]
Dietterich, T.G., London, R., Clarkson,
K. and Dromey, G.
Learning and Inductive Inference.
In Cohen, P.R. and Feigenbaum, E.A.
(editors), *The Handbook of Artifi-
cial Intelligence, Volume 3*, chapter
XIV. Pitman Books Ltd, 1982.

[Fearnley-Sander 85]
Fearnley-Sander, D.
Using and Computing Symmetry in
Geometry Proofs.
In Ross, P. (editor), *Proceedings of
AISB-85*. 1985.

[Hayes 77]   Hayes, P.
In defence of logic.
In *Proceedings of IJCAI-77*. International Joint Conference on Artificial Intelligence, 1977.

[Huet 75]   Huet, G.
A Unification Algorithm for Lambda
calculus.
Theoretical Computer Science 1:27-57,
1975.

[Huet & Oppen 80]
Huet, G. and Oppen, D.C.
Equations and rewrite rules: a sur-
vey.
In Book, R. (editor), *Formal languages:
perspectives and open problems*.
Academic Press, 1980.
Presented at the conference on
formal language theory, Santa
Barbara, 1979. Available from SRI
International as technical report
CSL-111.

[Lakatos 76]   Lakatos, I.
*Proofs and refutations: The logic of
Mathematical discovery*.
Cambridge University Press, 1976.

[Lenat 82]   Lenat D.B.
AM: An Artificial Intelligence approach to discovery in Mathematics as Heuristic Search.
In *Knowledge-based systems in artificial intelligence*. McGraw Hill,
1982.
Also available from Stanford as
TechReport AIM 286.

[Mitchell et al 81]
Mitchell, T.M., Utgoff, P. E., Nudel,
B. and Banerji, R.
Learning problem-solving heuristics
through practice.
In *Proceedings of IJCAI-81*, pages
127-134. International Joint Conference on Artificial Intelligence,
1981.

[Mitchell et al 83]
Mitchell, T.M., Utgoff, P. E. and
Banerji, R.
Learning by Experimentation: Ac-
quiring and modifying problem-
solving heuristics.
In Michalski, R.S, Carbonell, J.F. and
Mitchell, T.M. (editors), *Machine
Learning*, pages 163-190. Tioga
Press, 1983.

[Morris 69]   Morris, J.B.
E-Resolution: Extension of Resolution
to include the equality relation.
In Walker, D. and Norton, L.M.
(editor), *Proceedings of IJCAI-69*,
pages 287-294. Kaufmann Inc.,
1969.

[O'Keefe 82]   O'Keefe, R.A.
Automated Statistical Analysis.
Working Paper 104, Dept. of Artifi-
cial Intelligence, Edinburgh, 1982.

[Owen 85]   Owen, S.G.
*Analogy in Artificial Intelligence
- Thesis Proposal*.

Working Paper 176, Dept. of Artificial Intelligence, Edinburgh, 1985.

[Plotkin 72]   Plotkin, G.
Building-in equational theories.
In Michie, D and Meltzer, B (editors), *Machine Intelligence 7*, pages 73-90. Edinburgh University Press, 1972.

[Plummer 84]   Plummer, D.
RUT: Reconstructed UT Theorem Prover.
Working Paper 165, Dept. of Artificial Intelligence, Edinburgh, September, 1984.

[Plummer & Bundy 84]
Plummer, D. and Bundy, A.
Gazing: Identifying potentially useful inferences.
Working Paper 160, Dept. of Artificial Intelligence, Edinburgh, February, 1984.

[Robinson 65]   Robinson, J.A.
A machine oriented logic based on the Resolution principle.
J Assoc. Comput. Mach. 12:23-41, 1965.

[Silver 84]   Silver, B.
Precondition Analysis: Learning Control Information.
In Michalski, R.S., Carbonell, J.G. and Mitchell, T.M. (editors), *Machine Learning 2*. Tioga Publishing Company, 1984.
Forthcoming. Earlier version available from Edinburgh as Research Paper 220.

[Sterling & Bundy 82]
Sterling, L. and Bundy, A.
Meta-level Inference and Program Verification.
In Loveland, D.W. (editor), *6th Conference on Automated Deduction*, pages 144-150. Springer Verlag, 1982.
Lecture Notes in Computer Science No. 138. Also available from Edinburgh as Research Paper 168.

[Uschold *et al* 84]
Uschold, M., Harding, N., Muetzelfeldt, R. and Bundy, A.
An Intelligent Front End for Ecological Modelling.
In O'Shea, T. (editor), *Proceedings of ECAI-84*, pages 761-770. ECAI, 1984.
Available from Edinburgh as Research Paper 223.

[Wallen 83]   Wallen, L.A.
Towards the Provision of a Natural Mechanism for Expressing Domain-Specific Global Strategies in General Purpose Theorem-Provers.
Research Paper 202, Dept. of Artificial Intelligence, Edinburgh, September, 1983.

BUILDING A BRIDGE BETWEEN AI AND ROBOTICS

Hirochika Inoue

Department of Mechanical Engineering
The University of Tokyo
Hongo, Bunkyo-ku, Tokyo, JAPAN

ABSTRACT

About fifteen years ago, the hand eye system was one of the exciting research topics in artificial intelligence. Several AI groups attempted to develop intelligent robots by combining computer vision with computer controlled manipulator. However, after the success of early prototypes, research efforts have been splitted into general intelligence research and real world oriented robotics research. Currently, the author feels there exists a significant gap between AI and robotics in spite of the necessity of communication and integration. Thus, without building a bridge over the gap, AI will lose a fertile research field that needs real-time real-world intelligence, and robotics will never acquire intelligence even if it works skillfully. In this paper, I would like to encourage AI community to promote more efforts on real world robotics, with the discussions about key points for the study. This paper also introduces current steps of our robotics research that attempt to connect perception with action as intelligently as possible.

I. INTRODUCTION

About fifteen years ago, hand eye system was one of the exciting research topics in artificial intelligence. Several AI groups concentrated large efforts to create their prototype intelligent robots by combining computer vision with computer controlled manipulator. The performance of early hand eye system was quite limited. Vision system could recognize only simple block world. Control algorithm of manipulator was also simple and sensory interaction was very primitive. Many researchers who succeeded in building up the prototype concluded that individual subsystem should be pursued further before designing new system. And, research efforts have been devoted to explore general aspects of vision, planning, and control. Since then, the attempt of system integration has been left behind in AI community.

Although early hand eye systems could carry out only simple jobs in very simple block world, its success presented promising perspectives to manufacturing industries. During the last decade, industries have concentrated their efforts to advance industrial robots, and they succeeded in introducing robots into various production lines. The progress of hardware implementation including microelectronics is remarkable. And now, industries are keen to implement intelligent capability into their robots.

Robotics is the study of intelligent connection of perception to action.[1] Although artificial intelligence involves many disciplines, it is the study of intelligence from the standpoints of computation. Thus, both robotics and AI can share common interests. However currently, the author feels there exists significant gap between them. That is, AI deals mainly abstracted world, while robotics concerns real world, and the interests of those approaches seem to pass each other. As robotics involves many difficult problems which would not be solved without AI approach, it is very important to build a bridge that connects AI to robotics. In this paper, the author will discuss about key problems for integrating several disciplines into an intelligent robot system. And, current steps of our robotics research will be introduced as an example for building a bridge that connects robotics to AI.

II. KEY PROBLEMS

Robot is a versatile intelligent system that can interact with real world through sensors and effectors. Generally, it is consisted of four major subsystems; perception subsystem, action subsystem, thinking subsystem, and user friendly interface. Perception subsystem recognizes situations of real environment by means of vision, force sensing, and touch sensing. Action subsystem changes environment situation by moving objects or walking around. Thinking subsystem makes a plan of robot behavior, monitors its execution, and evaluates the results. User interface provides communication channel between human operator and robot. During last decade, a large number of researches on vision, manipulation, and planning have been done, and the performance of each subsystem has progressed very much. However, research on system integration has been left behind. We must remind that more studies of system architecture of robot are required if we wish to make robots smarter.

I would like to stress the importance of system oriented research of robotics, because intelligent interaction of perception with action in real world is the main concern of robotics. It opens very interesting and promising research field for not only robotics but also AI. General priciples of intelligence gained from AI research would help us to synthesize total robot system. However, the problems which have been dealt with in theoretical AI research are oversimplified when we consider its application to dealing with complex constraints in real world. On the other hand, researches on robot mechanisms, control and sensors have been focussed to advance physical performance, and lack semantic aspects of robot behavior. Although there exists such a gap between AI and robotics, attempts to connect them together will be needed to explore fertile research field where intelligent machines can behave in real world.

There are so many difficult problems to be studied for creating smarter robot system. Before entering into each discussion, we have to consider the level of complexity of real environment to be dealt by several disciplines. Considering current performance of each related field, I propose a world of simple electro-mechanical assembly. Object shapes are supposed to be generated from general blocks and cylinders. Objects may have holes and threaded holes. Screws, gears and wires are also included in the repertoire of objects.

Major problems to be studied are listed below with short comments and discussions.

A.   Abstracted Definition of Manipurator System

So far, research interests on manipulator system have been focussed onto the theory of advanced dynamic control for fast and precise motion. On the other hand, AI program assumes manipulator as very simple static object mover that always succeed in precise motion. Control discipline prefers aspects of dynamics, and ignores semantic aspect. AI approach pays its attention on semantic aspects of action rather than dynamic control. Thus, the interests of the two approach pass each other. In order to bridge over the gap, it seems necessary to provide AI people with an abstracted framework of manipulator control system so as to encourage them to construct smarter control structure. For this purpose, the author proposes a reasonable sets of abstracted functions for manipulator system. The seven basic functions are:

    put-arm-reference (position, orientation)
    get-arm-coordinate (position, orientation)
    put-hand-opening (opening-width)
    put-grasp-force (grasping-force)
    get-hand-opening (opening-width)
    get-wrist-force (force, moment)
    get-touch-sensor (sensor-state)

Above seven functions are defined in abstracted coordinates system, and are free from actual mechanical configuration. They work as if they were the instruction sets for computer. The cycle time is supposed to be very short, equivalent to the sampling period of servo-mechanism. Each function completes its operation in a few mili second. For instance, if we trigger put-arm-reference with the arguments about reference position and orientation in 3D world coordinates, then this function calculates corresponding 6 joint angles and sends the data to joint servo within single sampling period.

It is also necessary to provide a flexible means to combine the functions together. For such framework, I propose a fast real time operating system with concurrent process execution capability. If we connect above mentioned function sets by means of the concurrent real time OS commands such as start-process, stop-process, do-function, signal, wait, delay, and so on, we can describe any sensor based operations of manipulator.[2] I would like to encourage AI community to describe semantic aspects of manipulation on the above mentioned abstraction.

B.   Theory of Manipulation

Sensor based robot programs are very difficult to write in general form. So far, several basic robot operations such as pin-into-hole, block-in-corner and rope-into-ring have been demonstrated. However, most of those program synthesis are based on ad hoc strategies, where geometric structures of parts relationship are assumed a priori, and lack generality. Lozano-Perez et al pointed out that small changes in the geometry of parts can have significant impact on fine-motion strategies, and they proposed a formal approach to the automatic synthesis of a class of compliant fine-motion strategies. Their approach uses geometric descriptions of parts and estimates of measurement and motion errors to produce fine-motion strategies. [3] Mason presented a theoretical explanation of the mechanics of pushing and demonstrated application of the theory to the analysis and synthesis of manipulator operations.[4] Those approach open a quite important novel field for future robotics research. More efforts should be devoted to the general study of manipulation strategy, in order to explore theoretical foundations for the program synthesis of complex sensor based manipulation.

C.   Control of Visual Attention.

Although we are not conscious in every instance, we employ so many kinds of visual attentions during task execution, to find objects, to monitor situation changes of environment, to guide the motion of object, and to verify preconditions as well as postconditions for every piece of action. If we can provide a robot with fast and flexible capability of such visual attentions, the level of intelligent interaction of robot with real world will evolve dramatically. However, neither AI oriented vision research nor sensor based robotics research can tell very little about this problem. Can we formulate basic repertoire of visual attentions? What is the good framework to relate visual attentions to actions?

How should we synthesize the control strategies of visual attentions? Those questions seem to overlap the previous discussions on theory of manipulation. General study on visual attentions and their control strategy would provide one of the unexplored rich research field for connecting perception with action in intelligent way.

D.   Automated Planning in Robot Language.

The main purpose of high level robot language is to simplify the programming of complex robot tasks. We can classify robot language into three levels such as manipulation oriented, parts oriented, and goal oriented. Like AL, manipulation oriented language requires to describe robot tasks in explicit manipulation procedures.[8] In parts oriented language, the task is described as the state transition sequence of geometrical relationship between parts. RAPT is an example of this kind of language. It does not require explicit description of coordinate data of object motion in source code, instead, it attempts to solve those data from the descriptions about the logical constraint expressions among surfaces and axes of objects.[5] Goal oriented robot language requires only the goal description in source code, and generates action sequence by means of automated planning technique. In order to discriminate parts oriented language from goal oriented language, we assume the former takes complete state transition sequence that covers all subgoals so as to avoid the use of problem solver. From the viewpoint of programming simplicity, the goal oriented language is the ultimate goal of robot language development. But, the performance of problem solving today is too primitive to cope with complex robot environment. It deals very simple state description like (ON A B), while actual robot environment needs more complex state descriptions as RAPT shows. Moreover, object structures such as ARCH or TOWER which are dealt by current problem solver are far from actual assembly environment in its complexity. The author hopes AI will promote researches on powerful problem solver that can deal with complex real world constraints.

E.   Sensor Based Environment Model Management.

Presumably, the environment model management system would be a core of an integrated intelligent robot system. It manages accumulated data base about the description of current environment situation, conceptual definitions of various structures and objects to be handled, and general strategies for primitive operations. Studies on robot language tell us the environment model management plays very important role in compiling manipulation procedures. Every piece of manipulation changes the environment situation in some extent. Therefore, when language processor compiles source codes of robot tasks, it must simulate situation changes in order to generate right codes with right data. The higher the performance of model management is, the easier the programming becomes. If no model management is provided, we are forced to write complicated task program keeping all the details of situation changes in mind.

If the initial state of environment is not known, the scene analysis program would be invoked to recognize the real world and the results are returned to the model. During the execution phase of planned action sequence, the execution monitor can know the expected situation changes in advance, and compares it with actual environment changes. Doing the motion under inconsistent circumstance between real world and its computer model sometimes causes a serious damage. In order to avoid such disaster, the consistency between the two should be checked all the time by means of sensors. Generally, the capacity to recover from action errors reflects the level of intelligence of robots. Suppose a situation where a robot drops object during the move and the object hits a tower under construction. Recovery from this accident needs the following procedure. First, robot must aware the happening by vision. Next, the damaged situation is recognized by scene analyzer, which is considered as the initial state. The goal state can be obtained from the model as the state description before that accident. Problem solver plans an action sequence that converts the initial state to the goal state. It is really difficult to implement such a robot system even for simple block world, however this example covers most of the robot component which should be equipped in future robots with high intelligence. Model management system is related to many aspects of robotics such as scene analysis, robot language, automated planning, motion execution, and control of visual attention. Finding a common rich framework that can be employed compatibly in those aspects would be the most important problem.

III.   COSMOS: AN EXAMPLE OF INTEGRATED SYSTEM

This chapter introduces COSMOS, an example of interactive programming environment for the study of intelligent connection of perception to action in real world.[6] COSMOS is, in another word, a Lisp system that can interact with real environment by means of vision and manipulation.

Figure 1 shows hardware organization of COSMOS. We have two arms. One is a small universal arm driven by seven DC motors. Single board microcomputer which includes servo routine, communication routine, and diagnostic routine controls this arm. Trajectory data and control parameters are supplied from host minicomputer through GPIB interface. Another arm is a conventional 6 axes industrial robot of DC motor drive. As this arm can handle large payload, it is used to move heavy experimental attachments such as TV camera or multiple axes wrist mechanism. Simple touch sensors and 6 axes force sensor are also interfaced to the system. As visual input device, we employed precision TV camera. Video signal is digitized and stored into image frame memory device consisting of 768X512 pixels with 8 bits intensity scale. Host computer system consists of a 32 bits minicomputer, Data General ECLIPSE MV/4000 with 2 MB memory, and a 16 bit minicomputer, ECLIPSE S/140.

Figure 2 shows software configuration of COSMOS. Currently, nine software modules are imbedded into top level Lisp programming environment. Brief summary of each module is described below.

Top Level Lisp is the core of COSMOS system. Until 1983, we used Eclisp interpreter which was implemented on ECLIPSE S/140. Eclisp had a serious address space limitation caused by the 16 bit architecture of the S/140 processor. In order to solve this limitation, we decomposed a large program into several processes and connected them together by means of the inter process communication facility of AOS (Advanced Operating System of ECLIPSE). In 1983, we updated our host computer to a 32 bit virtual address machine ECLIPSE MV/4000, and Lisp system is also updated to Lisp/MV and its successor ETALisp, both of which are originally implemented in C on VAX at Electrotechnical Laboratory.[7] Eclisp, Lisp/MV and ETALisp are designed upward compatible, so, all the early programs implemented on Eclisp still run on our current Lisp system.

Manipulation system has been built up as a hierachy of Task Level Robot Language, AL/L Language, Trajectory Calculator, Arm Control System, and Servo Controller, from top to bottom. AL/L is a manipulation oriented language. The syntax of AL/L is similar to AL which is developed at Stanford, but it is implemented in Lisp.[8] The

model management part of AL/L is written in FRL to explore AI oriented study of robot language.[9] We have also attempted to extend robot language into parts oriented and task oriented level. In order to describe structural constraints of objects, we adopted RAPT like representation. Providing conceptual description of goal structure such as arch or tower in RAPT like notation, and employing a simple problem solver, our task oriented language plans action sequence to perform a given goal like (BUILD ARCH), and generates the AL/L source code for the task.[10]

Vision system is conventionally devided into two modules; Vision Primitives, and 3D Vision. The former includes a set of primitive image processing functions such as data aquisition, image operators, feature extracters, planer logic operators, and display functions. The latter covers recognition level programs. Robot vision requires three dimensional recognition. We are mainly studying on stereo vision that analyses binocular images. As AI oriented vision research, we are exploring two competitive approaches for scene analysis. One is a FRL based line finder, in which frames control visual recognition process and finds right line drawings for simple blocks.[11] Another attempt employs production system for simple scene analysis.[12]

COSMOS is an open purpose project. We are just climbing up step by step towards smarter intelligent robot system. When I initiated this project in 1978, I intend to create general purpose research tool for exploring intelligent connection of perception to action. At first, we implemented Lisp interpreter. Then, we developped AL/L robot language onto the Lisp. Next, we developped general purpose robot arm and interfaced it to AL/L. Almost at same time, we added primitive vision facility to our Lisp system. Thus, we succeeded in constructing simple hand eye system within Lisp environment. It actually provided us very convenient research environment for intelligent robotics. After a system was integrated, we enjoyed COSMOS very much, updated it, and accumulated new features of robotics, year by year. We do not think that COSMOS configuration is the best solution. Rather, we consider that COSMOS reflects our research history and future direction in computer executable form.

IV.   HAND EYE EXPERIMENT ON COSMOS

This chapter introduces one example of hand eye experiment which is performed on COSMOS.[13] The experiment is on rope handling, which is a difficult task to do without visual feedback, because a flexible rope cannot hold a well defined shape.

As explained earlier, full COSMOS is a toolbox which covers all our robotics software. It is really convenient, but sometimes it is heavy for a particular experiment. In order to improve

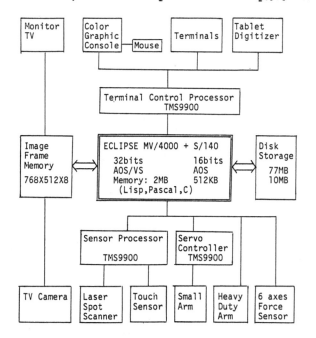

Fig.1 Hardware Configuration of COSMOS

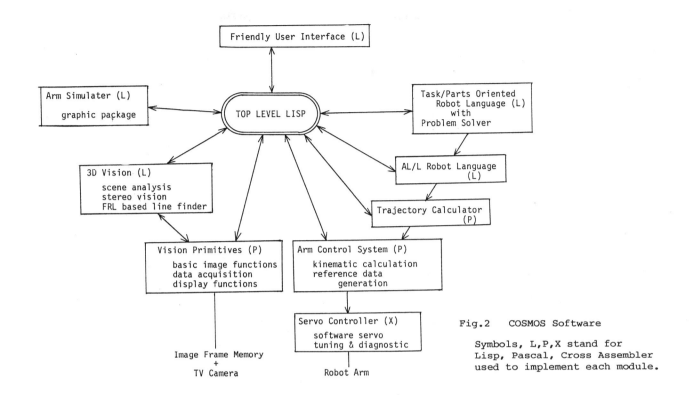

Fig.2   COSMOS Software

Symbols, L,P,X stand for
Lisp, Pascal, Cross Assembler
used to implement each module.

run time efficiency, COSMOS software is rearranged and tuned for the rope handling experiment. The tuned system consists of Top Level Lisp, Vision subsystem, Arm subsystem, and Hand Eye Calibration.   Vision subsystem involves three modules; EYE, WATCH, and STEREO.

Top Level Lisp: Top level Lisp allows us interactive hand eye programming. Command sets are tuned for this experiment. Robot Language AL/L is not employed. Instead, adequate arm commands which directly manages arm control system are built in. All the following vision modules can be invoked by Lisp commands.

EYE: This module provides low level vision primitives, such as image operators, feature extracters, logic operators, and display functions. Usually, vision functions are applied on the window area of 64X64 pixels. This module is used for rough, global analysis of a scene.

WATCH: In order to perform fine local analysis efficiently, scan-line based image processing is employed. When we use linear scan, the position, direction, and length of the scan-line are controlled. When we use circular scan, the center and diameter of scan circle are controlled. Zero crossing operator along those scan extracts precise edge point on the scan line. This module provides a simple and efficient visual recognition for feedback.

STEREO: In order to obtain stereo image, we attached mirror adapter onto TV camera. It composes binocular image onto single TV frame. Left half of the frame corresponds to left eye image, and right half of the frame corresponds to right eye image. Both images are analysed separatedly, and the coordinates of corresponding points on both images are calculated. Then, three dimensional position of the point is calculated by the principle of triangulation.

Hand Eye Calibration: In order to mate manipulator system with vision system together, we must know precise numerical relationship between the two coordinate systems. It is called hand-eye calibration.   This module calculates precise trnsformation matrix between the two coordinates by means of vision facility automatically.

The experiment includes a task of rope-into-ring and tying a knot around the ring.   The scenario is as follows. At first, robot finds a rope by vision and grasps it. Next, robot finds a ring and puts the rope into ring by visual feedback.   Then, robot release the rope, regrasps the rope from opposite side of the ring, and pull the rope out. Finally robot ties a knot around the ring. Figure 3 shows flow diagram of the experiment.   The block number in circle indicates vision processing, while the block number in square indicates manipulation. The experiment itself will be shown by movie.

V.   VISION SYSTEM WITH MULTIPLE ATTENTIONS

The use of visual monitoring, visual feedback, and visual verification is necessary in execution phase of action plan. They accomplish various interaction between vision and action in real time. In most cases, above mentioned vision program can be constructed so as to focus its attention onto local regions in which the existence of key features are expected. Usually, points of attention should be multiple, although processing for each attention is simple. As the processing time of such visual interaction is very critical for real time use, those multiple attentions must run in parallel. In order to realize such kind of visual interaction in real time, we designed and implemented new versatile multi window vision processor. A rectangular local region to be processed is referred to as a window. In our system, the location, shape, and resolution of each window can be independently controlled by hardware.

Figure 4 shows a block diagram of multi window vision system. It consists of one digitizer/transmitter unit and a large number of window processing units. Digitizer/transmitter unit converts NTSC composite color signal into digital video signals and broadcasts them onto the video bus. The signals on the video bus are R, G, B, and Y, each of which has 8 bits intensity scale. During the video scan, pixel address increments in video scanning rate within 320X240 pixel area. In order to inform the current scanning position, the horizontal and vertical pixel address are also broadcasted onto the video bus. By observing the current pixel address, each window unit picks up only the necessary data inside the designated window area, and stores them

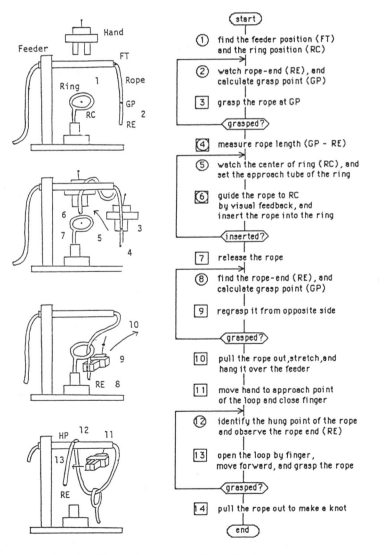

Fig.3 Flow Diagram for Rope Handling

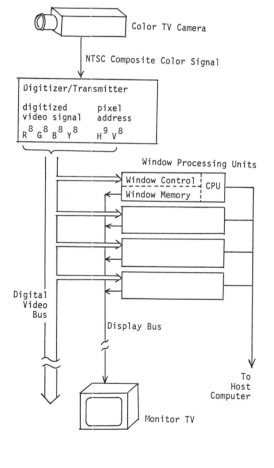

Fig.4 Block Diagram of
       Multi Window Vision System

in its window memory, which is processed by a microcomputer independently.

The signal on the video bus is one way, and read only. So, a large number of window unit can aquire the window data independently and simultaneously. In our current implementation, window memory has only 4 KB. It corresponds to 64X64 pixels if it is used as square window. Memory size is small, however its usage is very flexible. Firstly, the location of each window is controllable. So, we can locate each window anywhere inside TV screen. Secondly, the aspect ratio of each window is programmable. So, we can change window shape into square, rectangular, and linear. Thirdly, spatial data resolution, in another word, pixel sampling rate is variable. We can read every pixel data, one pixel data from every 2X2 neighbors, from every 4X4 neighbors, or from every 8X8 neighbors. If we use low resolution mode, we can obtain rough data over large window area. If we need precise data, we use high resolution mode for small window area. Finally, we have four kinds of input signals such as red, green, blue, and brightness. We can choose one signal from the four.

The prototype model has sixteen windows. Four window memories are processed by single Motorola 68000. And four such processor units are connected to host computer. Image processing programs which run on window processor are written in C. They are compatible to vision primitives module of COSMOS. Host machine is also Motorola 68000, on which Lisp interpreter runs. Thus, recognition level program written in Lisp controls individual window processing, following the same philosophy of COSMOS design.

When we designed multi window vision system, we expected to operate one window as one visual demon. Therefore, multi window vision system provides very flexible hardware for pandemonium models for visual recognition. We plan to control a large number of visual demons in knowledge invoked way in order to explore sensor based environment model management system for robot. In such application, we need a large number of window hardwares. Therefore we attempted to develop special LSI. We have already succeeded in developping LSI chip for window data acquisition. We are now developing large scale multi window vision system by using that LSI.

VI.   CONCLUDING REMARKS

Research on intelligent robot was born in Artificial Intelligence more than twenty years ago. However, after the development of early hand eye systems, very few efforts have been continued on system oriented research of intelligent machines that behave in real world. The author believes that many key problems for intelligent robot could not be solved without merging AI approach with robotics. Therefore, in order to encourage AI community to pay more attentions to intelligent robotics, several key points are discussed from the viewpoint of system oriented approach. Then, an attempt to build a bridge that connects AI to robotics is presented with an example of COSMOS experimental system. So far, we have concentrated our efforts onto building a Lisp programming environment that has manipulators, vision systems, robot language and other sensors. Using this total system, we are going to explore a method to connect perception with action as intelligently as possible.

Acknowledgement: COSMOS is developped at Information Systems Laboratory, in the Department of Mechanical Engineering, the University of Tokyo. The author wishes to express deep appreciations to the past and present students who contributed to implement COSMOS: T.Ogasawara, O.Naito, O.Shiroshita, T.Matsui, H.Mizoguchi, S.Kawagoe, M.Inaba, H.Matsubara, M.Fujita, A.Okano, Y.Tsusaka, Y.Murata, T.Fukuizumi, K.Kado.

REFERENCES

1   Brady,M. and R.Paul(Eds), Robotics Research, MIT Press (1984)
2   Inoue,H., "Robot System", in Mechatoronics, Iwanami-Syoten (1985) pp85-154 (in Japanese)
3   Lozano-Perez,T., M.Mason, and R.Taylor, "Automatic Synthesis of Fine-Motion Strategies for Robots", Robotics Research 3:1 (1984) 3-24.
4   Mason,M., "Mechanics of Pushing", Proc. of 2nd International Symposium of Robotics Research, Kyoto (1984) pp73-80.
5   Popplestone,R., P.Ambler, and I.Bellos, "An Interpreter for a Language for Describing Assemblies", Artificial Intelligence 14:1(1980) 79-107.
6   Ogasawara,T. and H.Inoue, "COSMOS: A Total Programming System for Integrated Intelligent Robot Study", J. of Robot Society of Japan, 2:6 (1984) 507-525 (in Japanese).
7   Ogasawara,T. and T.Matsui, ETALisp User's Manual, Electrotechnical Lab. (1984).
8   Mujtaba,S. and R. Goldman, AL User's Manual, Stanford AI Lab. (1979)
9   Inoue,H. et al, "Design and Implementation of High Level Robot Language", Proc. of 11th ISIR (1981) pp675-682.
10   Matsubara,H., A. Okano and H.Inoue, "Design and Implementation of Task Oriented Robot Language", J. of Robot Society of Japan, 3:3 (1985) (in Japanese).
11   Inaba,M., Research on Robot System with Vision, Master's Thesis, Tokyo Univ., (1983) (in Japanese)
12   Matsubara,H., Scene Analysis performed by Production System, Master's Thesis, Tokyo Univ. (1983) (in Japanese).
13   Inoue,H. and M.Inaba, "Hand Eye Coordination in Rope Handling", in (1) pp163-174.
14   Inoue,H. and H.Mizoguchi, "A Flexible Multi Window System for Robots", Proc. of 2nd ISRR, Kyoto (1984) pp42-49.

SELF-KNOWLEDGE AND SELF-REPRESENTATION

John Perry

Department of Philosophy and CSLI, Stanford

ABSTRACT

In this paper I introduce a contrast between homomorphic and non-homomorphic ascriptions of informational content to representations. In the former case there is a mapping from the parts of the representation onto the constituents of the content. In the latter case, there is not; some of the constituents of the content are settled by background factors. I contrast this distinction with that between context dependent and context independent ascriptions of content. I note that in cases where the ascriber of content shares the background with the agent, one is inclined to ascribe homomorphic content of a sort that does not have a fixed truth-value to a representation. This leads to the notion of relative information. Some uses for relative information are noted. Finally, the distinctions developed are used to distinguish three types of self-knowledge and account for their relations.

I HOMOMORPHIC AND NON-HOMOMORPHIC REPRESENTATIONS

Philosophers of mind and language and researchers in artificial intelligence must confront the question of the content of representations. Philosophers want to understand what it is to know or believe or say something; researchers in AI want to build things that do know, believe and say things. In fact, most researchers in AI also share the philosophers goal; indeed, as far as I can tell, most of them are philosophers. But even if this were not so, understanding the nature of knowing, believing and saying ought to be helpful in learning how to construct things that have these capacities.

At one time, the paradigm for representations was the utterance of an eternal sentence, with a content fixed by meaning alone. More recently, we have realized the importance of context. The meaning of a representation typically fixes content only relative to context. In this paper I discuss a further factor, background, that interacts with context in interesting ways.

Consider my utterance of SAM WAS SLEEPING. This utterance has the informational content that Sam was sleeping. (I use informational content for that which is information if it gets things right, and call it "content" for short.) This content has, intuitively, three constituents: the individual Sam, the past time in question, and the property of being asleep. The sentence I used has a number of constituents: SAM, WAS, SLEEPING, and WAS SLEEPING. Among these are three that identify the constituents of the content. So, there is a homomorphism from the constituents of the sentence onto the constituents of the content.

This might seem inevitable. After all, how could constituents make their way into a proposition that an utterance expresses, unless some constituents of the uttered expression identified them (at least in a suitably generous notion of consitutents of an expression)?

But now consider another case. George sticks his left hand out the window of his car, thereby signalling that he will turn left at the next corner. The content has as constituents George, the next corner, and the relation of turning left at. We might reasonably say that the particular way he holds his arm stands for the relational activity of turning left at. But the way he holds his arm does not have constituents or aspects that identify the corner at which he is going to turn. Which corner is not, so to speak, a question that the structure of the signal needs to resolve. Once the angle of his arm identifies right or left, we have all the information we need. The rest of the propositional constituents are not supplied by aspects of the signalling movement, but by what I shall call the background.

The background is typically determined by the context. We are imagining the signalling to occur in the U.S. in the last half of the twentieth century, where there is an institution of signalling for turns. This institution provides a propositional function for each context. The function takes directions (left, right) as arguments and returns a proposition: that the driver involved will turn (left, right) at the next corner.

This suggests the following picture. Communication takes place against a background, determined by context. A background provides a propositional function, taking some sort of entities as arguments. The job of the representation is to provide the necessary arguments to get from the background to a proposition. The case of uttering a complete declarative sentence "in vaccuo", so to speak, is the limiting case. The background is null: it provides only the identity function, from propositions to propositions. The constituents of the proposition are supplied by the background and the representation; homomorphic representation is just a special case, where the background is null.

Backgrounds of this sort may be established in various ways. In the case of the driver's signal, there is an institution that establishes a background for each driver in the vicinity of a corner. We may think of questions as providing backgrounds. The question "Who shot Liberty Valence?" provides a function from individuals and types of individuals to propositions. An answer need only specify an individual (Jack Palance, say) or a type of individual (some man with a large gun).

II BACKGROUND AND CONTEXT

The distinction between homomorphic and non-homomorphic representations cuts across that between eternal and context sensitive representations.

For example, if you ask me the square of 2 and I say "Four", my answer is eternal. "Four" stands for four in any context (or so we

may assume). But the representation is non-homomorphic, because the informational content, that the square of two is four, picks up constituents from the background.

When I say "I am sitting", the representation is homomorphic but context sensitive. If I say "John Perry is sitting on May 14, 1985", the representation is homomorphic and (arguably) eternal. If you ask "Who wants a chocolate milkshake?" and I reply "Me", my answer is both context sensitive and non-homomorphic.

Which background is relevant is generally a matter of context, but it need not be. We can imagine a convention of language, for example, that placing one's hand vigorously over one's heart supplies the answer "yes" to the question "Is America the home of the brave and the land of the free?" no matter who does it and when. In this case, we imagine the background being supplied by the meaning of the representation, and not its context. (For some purposes, however, it is useful to think of the language being used as a contextual fact.)

Thus, the context of a representation is just the larger situation of which its use is a part. The context may contain all sorts of facts relevant to the content of the representation. The background for a representation is not determined by the meaning of any part of the representation, but by the meaning of the whole. The meaning may determine the background "eternally" as in our patriotic example. More commonly the meaning determines the background only relative to context. In the signalling case, the system of signalling determines a relation from contexts to backgrounds. For a signaller A approaching a corner C, the background is the partial function that takes a direction as argument and returns the proposition that A will turn in that direction at C.

III RELATIVE INFORMATION

When a background is supplied by context, the background may be more or less sensitive to shifts of context. For example, the statement "It's four o'clock" said by me now, sitting in Palo Alto, has the informational content that it is four o'clock Pacific Coast Time. We can imagine that "It" refers to a time. Then there really is not a property of times, being four o'clock, but only a relation between times and zones. So my representation is non-homomorphic. The zone supplied as background does not vary over wide geographical regions, although it changes suddenly when it does.

For people in a single time zone talking to one another, there is no point in mentioning the time-zone. Indeed, people who grow up in one time-zone and do little traveling and don't watch TV, may function perfectly well without ever realizing that there are time-zones, and that being four o'clock is really a relation and not a property. They don't need the concept of a time-zone at all to make use of information about the time of day and to detect and communicate such information themselves.

In general, the meaning of a representation, a sentence of English, for example, can be seen as a relation between the sorts of situations in which it occurs and the content of those situations. Thus we can take the meaning of I AM SITTING to be that relation between utterances and contents that obtains if the content requires the speaker to be sitting. Given this picture, contents provide an equivalence relation among utterances that employ sentences with different meanings. So, the utterance where I utter I AM SITTING and the one where you utter YOU ARE SITTING while talking to me have the same content. This equivalence relation is important in understanding the flow of information, where informational content is preserved across changes of context. It is also important for understanding such psychological notions as continuing to believe the same thing (Barwise and Perry, 1983; Perry, 1980; Perry, 1985).

The phenomenon of non-homomorhic representation suggests that we need to broaden the notion of informational content, to include not just "propositions", that are true or false absolutely, but also various types of relative informational content, that are true and false relative to a background.

Consider communication about the time of day. So long as this takes place within a time-zone, there is little need to worry about the propositions expressed. If I ask Ingrid what time it is and she says "It's four o'clock", I do not need to think "She is in the Pacific Zone, so that means that it is four o'clock Pacific Coast Time." I just think "It's four o'clock". We can say that she communicated the information that it's four o'clock, where this is relative information, information that is true or false only relative to a background. The transaction is information-preserving only if the participants share a background. If Ingrid is talking to me long-distance from New York City and I don't realize it, the transaction will not be information preserving.

We might suppose (and I did for a long time) that we do not need to recognize relative information, since meanings, relationally conceived, give us entities that are true or false relative to context. But there are transactions in which meanings change systematically to preserve relative information. Suppose Ingrid says "It's four o'clock by my watch," and I tell you "It's four o'clock by Ingrid's watch." Meaning has not been preserved, and the shift in meaning does not automatically preserve non-relative information. What is preserved is information relative to a time-zone. We seem to need the notion of relative information to think about this transaction, and to be able to carefully characterize just what goes wrong when she made the original remark long-distance from New York, and my remark to you was false.

IV SELF-KNOWLEDGE AND SELF-REPRESENTATION

I think the notions of non-homomorphic representation and relative information are crucial in a number of areas of epistemology and semantics. For example, Jon Barwise (Barwise, 1985) has recently analyzed conditionals as providing relative information about the three place relation among types of situations, T involves T' relative to T''. T'' is supplied by the background, and Barwise shows how some of the puzzles about conditionals involve inferences that are only valid when the background is kept fixed. I suspect these notions will be important in dealing with subjunctives, unbounded dependencies of various sorts, and other troublesome topics.

I want to end the paper by focussing on a particular topic, however, that will suggest a more or less deep reason why relative information and non-homomorphic representations are so important.

Let's return to our time-zone bounded

folk. We saw that they can communicate perfectly well about the time of day without having any words for or even concepts of time-zones. Because they live within a certain constant background, they have no need to worry about it. In particular their thought about the time of day can be keyed to certain perceptions and actions in a perfectly workable way, even though they lack such concepts. They look at the clock and think "It's five o'clock", and so they close up shop and go home for supper.

Even those of us with a well-developed conceptual apparatus for dealing with time-zones operate, for the most part, in ways that allow our perceptions of the time of day and the actions we take in virtue of the time of day to ignore time-zones. Like the folk above, we go home when the clock shows five o'clock (or so).

I think these facts about time-zones are suggestive about certain basic facts of the human condition. The information we pick up through perception is always relative information. When I see a terminal before me, there need be nothing in my perceptual state that is indicative of its being me that the terminal is in front of. Not only is there not a constituent of the perception that "eternally" stands for me, there need not even be a constituent that picks me out in context. I am the background for my perceptions, and you are the background for yours. When you are in the very same perceptual state I am now in, you know that there is a terminal in front of you, not that there is one in front of me.

Imagine now a somewhat simpler organism than myself, perceiving a potato rather than a terminal in front of it. We can imagine this perception leading to a cognitive state, that in turn leads to the action of seizing the potato and jamming it into one's mouth. We can ascribe content to the action, in terms of its result. Each such organism, taking the action in question, will jam the potato into its own mouth, not someone else's. So we can think of actions as having non-homomorphically determined content, or homomorphically determined relative content. These organisms do not need to have any concept of themselves. They surely do not need any "eternal" idea of themselves, but they also do not need any internal indexical either. Since they are always in the background of their perceptions

and actions, they need not be represented in the cognitions that intervene between them.

We can suppose, then, that relative information is systematically connected with types of perception and action. Equally important, we cannot imagine that non-relative information is systematically tied to them. That Elwood has a potato in front of him can't be something that all our little organisms know on the basis of being in the potato-in-front percpetual state, and can't be something the cognition of which leads them all to grab and shove. At any rate, if things worked this way, Elwood is the only member of the group that wouldn't go hungry.

These reflections suggest the following picture of our cognitive make-up. At the "bottom" level, we have cognitions that have no representation of ourselves (or the present moment), which are tied pretty directly to cognition and action. This gives us self-knolwedge of a sort: we know the world from our perspective. At the "top" level we have representations that are not systematically tied to perception and action (or at least not to the same sorts of perception and action), in virtue of which we have relatively context insensitive cognitions that homomorphically determine propositions about ourselves. This is self-knowledge of another sort. I have it if I read a note "John Perry must call home," where "John Perry" designates me. Note that I would have it even if I had forgotten my name, and didn't realize, as I might put it, that I was to call home. The real purpose of indexicals is to mediate between these levels, yielding full-blown self-knowledge (although not yet Socratic self-knowledge). When I read a note, "John Perry please call home," I think "I must call home" and then go into a state that we might express with "must call home". The step from the top level to the intermediate level varies from person to person; the step from the intermediate level to the bottom level, and from it to action (modulo procrastination) is universal. The purpose of indexicals is to align the homomorphic representations we get through language and other forms of communication, at some kinds of memory, with a more basic, selfless, cognitive system.

One who has the bottom and top levels correctly linked knows who he is (where he is, what time it is). This is still oversimple, in

a variety of ways. We would need more levels,
for example, to get at what happens when one
realizes that it is four o'clock Eastern Time,
hence one o'clock real time, hence one o'clock
here, hence time to go to lunch. But I hope I
have said enough to suggest that the topics of
non-homomorphic representation and relative
information are worth careful thought, whether
or not the thought I have provided is careful
enough.

ACKNOWLEDGEMENTS

Recognition of the need for something
like relative information, and the consequent
need to distinguish between non-homomorphic and
context dependent representation, was forced on
me by Joseph Almog and Bob Moore in the course
of conversations about the motivation for
propositions with truth values relative to
times, as are found in David Kaplan's work on
demonstratives (Kaplan, 1979). The present
approach is the result of conversations with
Jon Barwise, David Israel, Moore, and others.

REFERENCES

[1]   Barwise, J. "The Situation in Logic-II:
      Conditionals and Conditional Information".
      CSLI Report No. 21, 1985.

[2]   Barwise, J. and J. Perry, *Situations and
      Attitudes*. Bradford Books, Cambridge,
      Massachusetts: MIT Press, 1983.

[3]   Kaplan, D. "On the Logic of Demonstrat-
      ives", in *Perspectives in the Philosophy
      of Language*, ed. French, P. A., T. E.
      Uehling, Jr., and H. K. Wettstein.
      Minneapolis, 1979, pp. 383-412.

[4]   Perry, J. "A Problem about Continued
      Belief". *Pacific Philosophical Quarterly*
      61, 1980, pp. 317-332.

[5]   --, "Perception, Action, and The Structure
      of Believing" in Grandy & Warner:
      Philosophical Grounds of Rationality,
      Oxford: Oxford University Press, 1985, pp.
      330-359.

UNDERSTANDING AND AUTOMATING ALGORITHM DESIGN

Elaine Kant*

Schlumberger-Doll Research
Old Quarry Road
Ridgefield, Connecticut 06877-4108

Abstract

Algorithm design is a challenging intellectual activity that provides a rich source of observation and a test domain for a theory of problem-solving behavior. This paper describes a model of the algorithm design process based on observations of human design. The adaptation of that model to automation in the DESIGNER system helps us understand human design better, and the automation process helps validate the model. Issues discussed include the problem spaces used for design, the loci of knowledge and problem-solving power, and the relationship to other methods of algorithm design and to automatic programming as a whole.

I. The Algorithm Design Task

A. Design as an Intellectual Activity

Algorithm design is the process of coming up with a sketch, in a very high level language, of a computationally feasible technique for achieving a specified behavior. The design process combines cleverness in problem solving, knowledge of specific algorithm design principles, and knowledge of the subject matter of the algorithm (e.g. geometry, graph theory, physics). When people design algorithms, their design repertoire includes discovery and visual reasoning in addition to the (ideally) disciplined application of problem-solving techniques.

Human design is a rich source of ideas for a model of algorithm design. Observing that design process and attempting capture the basic ideas in an automated system both helps us understand how people structure and use their knowledge about design and also validates our observations and model. The DESIGNER project included such a study of human design and an initial version of an automated system [15, 16, 17, 26].** The goal of the project is to create an automatic design system that can apply existing design principles as well as exhibit some creativity. The observations of human design are to be incorporated, but the automatic system should take the strengths and weaknesses of both computers and people into account. We are not trying to model human problem-solving behavior as an end in itself.

The next section of this paper (I.B) presents a sample algorithm design problem (finding the convex hull). Section II summarizes our observations of human designers working on that and on other algorithms. Section III then discusses where the problem-solving power in our model lies: in the ability to search in multiple spaces (relying on knowledge from the domain as well as knowledge about algorithm design), on efficiency knowledge, and on the ability to execute partial algorithm descriptions on examples. Finally, this model of design is compared in Section IV with other approaches to automating algorithm design and to automatic programming as a whole.

B. A Challenge: The Convex Hull Problem

Consider the problem of finding a convex hull, which has applications, for example, in algorithms for vision and graphics. The problem is this: Given a set of points in two dimensions, find a polygon whose vertices are a subset of those points that encloses all the other given points.

Now if I drew some points on a blackboard or piece of paper, you would probably have no trouble sketching their convex hull. (If you need a picture to help you understand the problem, see Figure 1.) Suppose instead I asked you, or an automatic design system, to create an algorithm suitable for (later) encoding as a computer program in a conventional high-level language. Think of sketching out an algorithm in the terms you would use for describing it to a colleague or to a programmer, without worrying about the low-level implementation details. As you work on this problem, observe your problem-solving behavior. Do you write down any formal problem descriptions? In what language? Do you draw pictures? Create a variety of examples or counter-examples? Draw analogies to other algorithms? Draw on general knowledge of algorithm design principles?

How did you convince yourself that your algorithm was correct? Did you design it by applying correctness-preserving transformations? Did you use geometric or other mathematical theorems? Find proofs for conjectures? Test your algorithm on sample data? Explain the algorithm to yourself or a friend in words? Write pseudo-code?

How do you decide when your algorithm is complete? How do you decide when it is good enough? What does it mean to be a good algorithm? Do you know what the run-time or space performance of your algorithm will be? Did you worry about what the distribution of data would be in creating the algorithm? In determining performance?

Now let's find out how some other people solved this problem and see how we might design an artificial intelligence program that could perform the same feat.

*This paper describes research performed while the author was at Carnegie-Mellon University. The research was supported in part by DARPA and in part by NSF.

**The research described here is joint work with Allen Newell and David Steier. Many of the ideas I draw on are theirs, but the opinions expressed here are my own.

II. Methods for Designing Algorithms

Since the design of complex algorithms is currently best accomplished by human beings, observing their performance would appear to be a profitable starting point for automating the design process. However, since the talents of computers are not those of people, it is reasonable to search for a different method if the goal is total automation of design or a novel mixture of human and machine design. This issue is discussed in Section IV.

The model of design presented here is based on the analysis of a set of protocols from approximately fifteen sessions with computer science faculty, graduate students, and undergraduates. (A methodology for protocol analysis is described elsewhere [8, 20].) Our designers were independently given the task of creating algorithms to find convex hulls, closest pairs of points, and intersecting line segments. Several protocols have been analyzed in great detail while the others have been gone over more lightly and used primarily as confirming evidence.

Before summarizing the features of human design, some caveats on the general applicability of the observations are in order. (1) We observed the design of individual algorithms whose complexity is due to a requirement for cleverness rather than to the information processing overload of combining an overwhelming number of small but straightforward parts. (2) The algorithms depend on applying an appropriate set of operations rather than on designing a specialized data structure. (3) Our study did not include any interaction between people and design aids other than pencil and paper or blackboard. (However, no one volunteered any feelings that a calculator, computer, or any other automated device would have been of any help in designing their algorithm.) (4) The design sessions we observed were on the scale of hours rather than the months spent by research algorithm designers. Other processes than those we observed may take place in such long time periods.

Our observations may be at least partially valid in a wider context despite the caveats. Other researchers have studied the design process in software engineering and have made observations similar to ours [1, 12]. Also, there is anecdotal evidence that similar problem-solving techniques are used in the design of algorithms that are highly dependent on clever representations.

The processes that we observed our designers draw upon include:

1. *Understand* the problem.

2. *Select* a problem to work on.

3. *Plan* a solution around a kernel idea and *refine* or elaborate the kernel structure.

4. *Execute* the partially specified algorithm.

5. *Notice* and formulate any difficulties or opportunities.

6. *Verify* that the structure is a solution (i.e. meets its specifications).

7. *Evaluate* the solution (e.g. for efficiency).

After the processes in this collection are summarized, the issue of control — how the processes are ordered and evaluations within each step — will be discussed. The explanations draw on all of our observations and those of our colleagues who have studied the design process in software engineering. However, I will give illustrations primarily from the stories of two particular designers from our study. D1 and D2, who tried to solve the convex hull problem. Each part of a story is prefaced by a the designers name and number for future reference. For example, the first step of Designer 1's story is labeled [D1.1].

A. Understand the Problem

In classical discussions of problem solving [22], one important problem-solving process is understanding the problem, perhaps by listing properties of the objects in question, and considering reformulations of the problem. Some of our designers (but not D1 or D2) did draw a picture of a convex hull (or whatever) early on, which may have led to some unverbalized observation of or reasoning about properties of convex hulls and seemed to have convinced them that they understood the problem.

[D6.1]   D6 drew the picture shown in Figure 1.

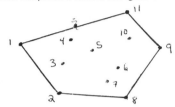

Figure 1. Initial example drawn by D6.

[D3.1]   D3 wondered whether using polar coordinates might not be a useful way to think about the problem.

B. Plan and Refine Solution

Assuming that a problem specification has been understood, design begins with a *kernel idea* or solution plan, quickly selected from those known to the designer. Depending on the designer's background, the idea may vary in sophistication from generate and test to input-process-output to more complex strategies such as divide and conquer or dynamic programming. The designer lays out the basic steps of the chosen idea and follows through with it unless the approach proves completely inapplicable.

[D1.1]   D1 had the initial idea that the algorithm should be one that generated all points in the input in some arbitrary order and tested each to determine whether it was on the hull. This had the potential of running in linear time (proportional to the number of input points).

[D2.1]   D2 decided to try a divide and conquer algorithm (the special form of divide and conquer in which the inputs are divided into subsets, the algorithm is recursively applied to each, and the results are merged back together).

Which kernel idea do you think will lead to a better algorithm?

After formulating a plan, the designer *refines* the basic steps of the kernel idea. By and large, this elaboration proceeds by stepwise refinement. The designer may lay down the major components, effectively decomposing the problem into subparts, or may add new inputs or assertions about details of the structure. The refinement steps (1) may be suggested by *knowledge* appropriate to the problem and task domain or (2) may be a natural result of attempting to *execute* an algorithm.

[D2.2]   An example of the application of appropriate knowledge about algorithm design principles is D2's expansion of the notion of using a divide and conquer algorithm into the sequence of steps: divide input point sets into subproblems, find the convex hulls recursively, merge subsolutions back into a convex hull.

[D2.3]   Furthermore, D2 recognized from previous experience with geometric algorithms that a likely possibility for the divide step of the divide-and-conquer algorithm was to sort the points by one of the coordinates and find the median.

In the absence of the knowledge that suggests the proper refinements, the designers *search* by trail and error: they hypothesize algorithm steps and try them out by executing the partially specified algorithm.

[D1.2]   D1 had no idea how to test whether a point was on the hull and decided to try out the algorithm on a specific figure to find the test.

[D1.3]   D1 then drew the picture shown in Figure 2.

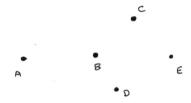

Figure 2. Initial example drawn by D1.

However, the refinement process is hardly one of pure top-down design.

[D1.4]   Such a point-on-hull test didn't reveal itself, but another related test did, and D1 proceeded to modify the hypothesized algorithm to exploit the new test.

Most design falls in between having the correct knowledge and searching. At some steps the designer knows what to do and knows what the implications of the refinement step are; other times, search is required.

[D2.4]   D2 did not find the merge step as obvious as the divide step. Do you?

C. Execution of Algorithms

Trial execution of algorithms is often used as a technique for making inferences about the algorithm developed so far. We observed two kinds of execution of partially specified algorithms — one on concrete data (which we call *test-case execution*) and the other on symbolic exemplars (which we call *symbolic execution*). Both forms of trial execution help elaborate the algorithm description by exposing difficulties and opportunities. We found it useful to view execution as a technique for selectively *propagating* constraints (which we call *assertions*) by moving them around in the order in which steps of the algorithm are executed. This limits the reasoning that might otherwise be necessary to find contradictions and make inferences.

D. Noticing Difficulties and Opportunities

Designers notice problems both in their algorithms as described abstractly and in pictures they draw to help them design. While executing the proposed algorithm, difficulties (missing steps, inconsistencies between parts of the algorithm) may arise, leading the designer to further refinements. Thus, we say that the designer's refinement process is *difficulty driven*.

[D1.5]   In D1's algorithm, a difficulty arose when the test involving line segments was combined with the generator of points and D1 had to modify the algorithm to accommodate this.

Here one assertion propagated by the execution process (that a point is produced by generating over the input set) contradicts another assertion (that a line segment should be the input to the test rather than the point it is handed).

[D1.6]   D1 eventually changed the kernel idea from generate and test to a greedy algorithm that attempted to generate the hull points in the order they occurred on the hull polygon, using backup to handle guessing failures.

The algorithm execution also can expose opportunities for improvement or modification of the algorithm.

[D2.5]   After working on a sample problem, D2 realized that the merge step would be easier if the two subsolutions shared a common point and went back and modified the divide step to ensure that that would happen.

Most people draw *example figures* during algorithm design. The examples are used initially for understanding the problem, and for reasoning about the task domain (using visual reasoning in the geometric domain) as well to help try out the partially developed algorithms in test-case execution. Often, the designers notice things about the sample figures that they were not looking for. When what the designers notice turns out to be useful in developing their algorithm, we say that they have made a *discovery*.

[D1.7]   In looking at Figure 3, D1 realized that if a line segment had points on both sides of it, that segment could not be on the convex hull. D1 was executing an algorithm with a test for points being on the hull or not; the line segment in the figure was recording the fact that the points A and B had been generated so far.

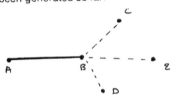

Figure 3. D1's discovery of a segment-on-hull test.

[D2.6]   D2 created Figure 4 in attempting to find a merge step by considering all segments between vertices of the two hulls and testing which were in the merged hull. D2 knew that this brute force search would be too expensive, but had no other ideas. The picture reminded D2 of another unrelated algorithm (the traveling sales representative) in which a shorter path replaced two adjacent segments. D2 then applied a similar idea to the merge step, replacing segments a-d and d-e by segment a-e (D2's picture was not actually labeled). The generalization D2 made was that convex angles in the merged hulls were to be replaced by a segment connecting the two end points.

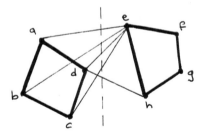

Figure 4. D2's discovery of a merge operation.

Do you have enough information yet to guess the algorithms? (The discoveries are described in more detail in cite(Kant82b).)

Some other observations the designers made would have allowed only small optimizations.

[D1.8]   D1 noticed that points are always on the same side of the (directed) line segments of the hull.

While discovery is not a voluntary process that can be planned as a design step, it does arise from the process of making observations. The discoveries in our study all occurred when the designer was looking at a sample figure created for one reason and recognized a geometric property, or key step from another algorithm, that would solve an outstanding goal. That goal was not the one the designer was currently worrying about (finding a test for a point being on the hull; finding a way to tell if a segment was on the merged hull), but it was usually not completely unrelated (finding a segment test rather than a point test; finding a different type of merge step). Thus, discovery could be characterized as serendipidously satisfied goals.

Both key observations in the problem domain and knowledge of design principles are usually necessary for clever design. Most algorithms published in papers or given as exam problems have at least one good observation or trick that is novel at the time of the design; otherwise we would probably say the algorithm is "obvious" or is "just" a brute-force algorithm. Each of the tricks must be stumbled upon as a discovery unless it is already known to the designer. Good tricks are eventually refined into principles, but everything is a trick the first time each designer encounters it.

Although there is an element of chance in the discoveries, there is no lack of readiness on the part of the designer. The designer can be prepared both with immediate goals to exploit the observations and with a good understanding of design principles to fit the discovery into an overall algorithm. The more experienced and disciplined the designers, the better prepared they are for the discovery. An "experienced" designer is one with knowledge not only about algorithm design but also about problem domains. Domain knowledge can be derived either from past attempts at the problem or from experience with similar algorithms and domains (or different domains but the ability to reformulate problems in terms of other domains).

E. Verifying Correctness

Our designers determined whether their algorithms were correct primarily by testing them on specific examples and observing whether there were any difficulties. Symbolic execution can in fact be made to do the job of full formal verification. To do this, the algorithm is executed on symbolic objects and all assertions are propagated to determine whether the results of the algorithm (and its subparts) match the specifications. If a specification includes performance constraints, then verification must also include an evaluation (see Section II.F) to determine whether the solution is efficient enough (in time or space complexity) according to the expectations.

During the initial algorithm design, the designers ignored "details" such as base cases or initializations, boundary conditions, degenerate inputs or unresolved notes to themselves, but they were more careful about this if they were attempting to determine if the algorithm was complete or correct.

[D1.9]   When D1 was asked for an algorithm summary during a pause, the response was that it wasn't an algorithm yet because the case of the first point not being on the hull had not yet been tested.

The heuristic is to get an algorithm for the general case first, then worry later about modifying it to take the exceptions into account. Although some methodologies claim to eliminate the concern with special cases (for example, [11]) they require that the specification or invariant be precisely stated before design begins. This is often difficult to accomplish. For more complex algorithms, handling the exceptions can itself require a major problem-solving activity, and may yield new insights into the problem or solution.

F. Evaluating Plans, Refinements, and Solutions

The descriptions of the processes used in design did not detail how plans, refinement steps, and overall solutions are evaluated. Evaluation can be based on specific knowledge about the algorithm design principles being applied or on an analysis of the cost of the algorithm and its subparts.

If the designer has the appropriate rules about the algorithm design principle and the domain, then the refinement process can be smooth and top down. For instance, the appropriateness of the kernel ideas selected by the designers depends on the quality of their knowledge of algorithm design principles. One can really observe here what expert-systems researchers call domain-specific knowledge. Generate and test is usually the fall-back idea, which is sometimes very efficient (linear in the input size) and sometimes not. After an algorithm based on a kernel approach was sketched out, or after the approach seemed to be failing, some designers went on to an alternative approach.

[D1.10]   After completing the revised algorithm for generating segments and testing whether they were on the hull, D1 determined that the run time of the algorithm was proportional to the cube of the number of input points. Declaring that this algorithm was only a "first shot," D1 went on to consider a dynamic programming approach and eventually to try divide and conquer.

[D4.1]   In another problem involving finding intersections of line segments, another designer, D4, noted that there was a straightforward approach having to do with considering all pairs of segments, which was N squared. However, D4, felt that there ought to be some way to use sorting in the solution to get an NlogN algorithm.

When experts (people with a strong background in algorithms and in the subject matter of the problem) design, they consider a variety of alternative refinements, select the best (remembering the rest for possible later use), and apply it to advance the design with one more level of detail in the refinement process. What is "best" is based on efficiency in the cases of algorithm design we studied, but is based on ease of implementation or modification in other cases. In expert design, the breadth-first process tends to be followed for all aspects of the design at a given level, with interactions between the different parts of the design predicted and taken into account.

In contrast, if the designer's only idea is naive (use sorting somehow), then the technique of executing hypothesized algorithm parts is more likely to be followed in a depth-first search from which the designer may never successfully return. (The idea may not have been wrong, but the designer may not have had the knowledge to carry it through.) Experts as well as novices are prone to a satisficing style of design when they are under pressure and don't have time for more exploratory design. Of course they are better at it since they have more experience, can make better predictions, and guess right more often.

Even when performance constraints are not explicitly specified, the designer often evaluates an algorithm or algorithm step's performance relative to other alternatives or to known or estimated lower bounds. Extreme cases of inputs may be tested to estimate worst case performance. Complexity analysis may be carried out in parallel with execution and verification by more experienced designers, or may be an explicit subtask of a conscious evaluation.

[D2.7]   After discovering the way to merge by removing convex angles, D2 estimated the run time of the divide and conquer algorithm by arguing that even for the worst possible input, the merge time was linear in the number of points on the two subhulls and therefore the overall run time was acceptable.

[D5.1] Although D2 did not draw an additional figure to analyze the worst case, both D1 and another designer D5 did. Even though their algorithms differed from that of D2 and from each other, they were both concerned with the same potential problem and drew similar pictures (see Figure 5)

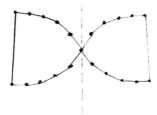

Figure 5. A worst-case input for divide and conquer.

D2's final algorithm had a prepass step to sort all the points according to their X coordinate. The basic algorithm was to divide the input through the point closest to the median, recursively find the convex hulls of the two resulting point sets, and merge the solutions back together by eliminating concave angles (starting from the shared point). The base case is that two- or three-point input sets can be made into convex hulls immediately.

G. Control Issues
The design processes described in the preceding sections do not always run to completion and do not take place in any fixed order. Evaluations within each step, as described above, may cause the designer to terminate one approach and go on to another. The ordering of the design processes (including when they begin and end) seems to arise naturally out of the mechanism of trial execution.

Selecting a problem to work on is a natural consequence of the problems exposed by symbolic and test-case execution. The character of the elaboration process appears to be an progressive deepening that takes each of the constructs in the algorithm a little further, sometimes backing up to higher levels to keep the overall picture in mind. However, the development of the different parts of the algorithm is not always even. If one aspect of the algorithm is a potential problem (i.e., other parts of the design depend on it and the outcome is uncertain), then it is more likely to be expanded to ensure that the algorithm as a whole is feasible. If it has an obvious solution or refinement and the implications of that decision seem well understood, at least at the current level of detail, it is not considered further. (Of course the assumptions may be wrong.) New components of the design are refined in the order they are executed, subject to the two previous considerations.

Verification and complexity analysis also seem to be achieved in part by propagating assertions during execution. Thus, other processes that contribute to control fit in nicely with this basic mechanism and can occur at the same time.

In short, design processes are applied as appropriate. Control is not a special source of intelligence. It comes out of responding to the data and out of the problems and opportunities arising during execution.

III. Locating the Problem-Solving Power
An important question to ask about any agent that exhibits intelligent behavior is where the knowledge and problem solving power lie. Knowing the loci of intelligence gives us some clues for how to produce similar behavior automatically. Thus, we have attempted to formalize the problem-solving behavior we observed in our designers in terms of concepts that lend themselves to automation.

One common view of problem-solving behavior is that it is basically search in a problem space, with knowledge used to limit search. Knowledge is carried by the problem spaces themselves: in what objects and operators they have available and in the heuristics they have for when and how to apply the operators. In this view, problem solving is a process of repeatedly changing a context by selecting a *goal* to achieve, a *problem space* to work in to attack that goal, a *state* within that space to work on, and an *operator* (and instantiations of its *arguments*) to transform the state [18]. Different types of knowledge can be identified with the selection process for each element of the context.

A. The Power of Search
In design, as in most tasks requiring intelligence, both search and knowledge are needed. Search is the backup for missing knowledge and can never be completely eliminated. It can take place at the very high level, such as searching for a kernel idea for an algorithm, or at the very low level, such as deciding how to instantiate an operator argument. Although at any level knowledge limits search when possible and gives clues about how to explore the problem spaces in a reasonable way, the ability to search is, in itself, a source of power.

In design, for example, search permits the creation of algorithms by trial and error in the absence of complete knowledge. Algorithm components can simply be hypothesized and then the algorithm as a whole tested to see if it satisfies its specifications. If only the objects and operators that formally specify and manipulate algorithm descriptions are available (i.e., there is no other model of the problem domain), then designing an algorithm requires the use of formal definitions of the concepts used in the problem specification and, recursively, of its subcomponents. However, more power than this is available to human designers and can be made available for automated design through the use of multiple problem spaces.

B. The Power of Multiple Problem Spaces
From our observations we conclude that each designer works in several different problem spaces during design (similar observations are described for other tasks in [20]). The details of the problem spaces differ from designer to designer, but there is a remarkable consistency in the types of problem spaces used.

We observed our designers working in four spaces, two of which are extensions of another space. The two main spaces were (1) an *algorithm design space* that carries the knowledge of what is achievable in standard computer systems and of domain independent algorithm design principles, and (2) an *application domain space*, such as one for geometric and visual reasoning. (The algorithm design space is also a domain space relative to design as a whole.) The two extension spaces have the same objects as the first two spaces plus additional objects and/or different sets of operators. (3) An *algorithm execution space* is an extension of the algorithm design space that has as new objects data items that carry information in the form of assertions about their execution history and has new operators that execute components in the design. (4) An *example generation space* is an augmentation of a task domain space in which figures are marked as standard examples, degenerate cases, counter-examples and the like, and in which there are new operators to produce the examples.

The necessity for different problem spaces is a result of the requirements of different types of knowledge. For example, what is possible or efficient in the domain (problem space) of algorithms for conventional digital computers is sometimes quite different from the way people reason visually or from what can be done with analog devices. (Consider solving the convex hull problem by pounding nails into a board to represent the input points and then stretching a rubber band over the nails and letting go.) The problem spaces that express such knowledge differ in the objects and operators included, the properties of objects or relationships between objects, and heuristics for how to control the applications of operators.

Having knowledge represented in a domain space as well as in an algorithm space gives the designer the power to create algorithms even in the absence of formal axioms about specification concepts such as polygon containment. The problem can be solved by generating constructs in the algorithm space and testing the proposed algorithms on examples to see if they work. This technique relies on the ability to generate examples to use as test cases. Example generation depends on knowledge of the domain space as well as knowledge of the goals in the algorithm space (say to determine whether a typical or degenerate example is desired). If a domain concept is not formally axiomatized, the designer cannot do any formal symbolic reasoning such as full verification or correctness-preserving derivation. However, by making some conjectures about the domain and validating them with test-case execution, the designer can reason formally about the rest of the algorithm.

[D2.8]   Having knowledge from the domain space of what line segments were on the merged hull allowed D2 the hope of finding an operation that would test where proposed segments were correct.

For each of the problem spaces relevant to design, we can ask what knowledge is available for recognizing when context elements should change: how does a system recognize when goals are satisfied or when new goals should be attempted, when the problem space should be changed to work on the different type of goals, what state to expand within a problem space, and what operator to apply and how to instantiate the operator. Examples of the different types of knowledge contained in problem spaces will be given in Sections III.F through III.I

First, some aspects of problem-solving power that cut across problem spaces are discussed. This power can be cast as knowledge that allows the designer to avoid search.

C. Knowledge in Recognition

The ability to recognize objects and to recognize the applicability of operators is a major source of power in problem solving. The search process is not driven by an algorithm that selects context elements in a fixed order but rather by recognition rules that observe when some context element should change: for example, when a goal has been satisfied or when an operator would help change state in a desired way. The conditions for recognition can be symbols in the algorithm design space or visual images from the domain space. These clues can involve goals, points of view or other objects in the problem-solving context whose inclusion as a clue was only accidental to the formation of the recognition rule. A very large number of recognition rules may be present. However, the conditions that are monitored must be computationally simple, involving only straightforward matching.

An example of the role of recognition is its use in discovery, a key process in algorithm design. Discovery depends on generating examples to work with and then noticing properties about them or reasoning about them. The recognition processes usually take place in the domain space, but what is noticed depends on the goals of the problem solving (and the content of the recognition knowledge).

Recognition is also important in example generation, which is constrained by the goals of the problem solving (is it to be an average case, degenerate case, initial or base value, counter-example, used by efficiency analysis, etc.), but depends on knowledge of the domain and recognition of successful construction of the example in terms of domain properties.

[D1.11]   D1 first generated points A, C, D, and E in Figure 2 as an initial test-case example but then noticed that the example was degenerate since all points were on the hull and added a fifth point (B) in the center to remedy the difficulty. The points were not labeled at that time.

Non-symbolic recognition and processing (such as visual reasoning) is clearly important in designing computational geometry algorithms, but is it really important in all domains, such as that of algebraic problem solving? At least for some people, it is. Built-in visual operators are better at some types of processing and provide another perspective on a problem. They may suggest approximations or fortuitously counterpose objects that would not be related by a general symbolic reasoning process.

D. Knowledge in Execution

Trial execution in algorithm design serves the purpose of controlling the order of the refinement process (see Section II.C) and limiting the inferences made as well as its more common functions of debugging and verification (see Section II.E and [6]).

The nature of creative algorithm design requires some mechanism for inference, whether it is a full theorem prover, small set of simplification rules, or something in between. Making all possible inferences during algorithm design would be very expensive computationally. Execution is a way to focus attention on certain assertions in the algorithm description space and certain parts of pictures in the domain space so that inference and recognition only have to take place over a smaller set. The execution techniques limit the inferences and constraint propagations to those most likely to be useful for the current stage of the design. Avoiding the extensive search of theorem proving or uncontrolled inferencing through execution is a form of knowledge about design. This topic is discussed more thoroughly in other papers [26], [7].

E. Knowledge in Efficiency Information

Efficiency knowledge serves as an evaluation function throughout the algorithm design process, not just as an evaluation of complete designs. Information about potential run time or space use serves as a rough guideline in the selection of a kernel idea and during refinement (D2 knew that the merge step had to be linear to get the desired overall performance [D2.6]*) as well as after an algorithm sketch is complete (D1 decided that cubic performance was probably not the best possible [D1.10]).

---

*In the remainder of this paper, labels following descriptions of bits of knowledge refer back to parts of the design story where they are used.

Efficiency knowledge can take many forms, including assertions about the run time of specific operations or algorithms, assertions about the intrinsic complexity of problems, rules for how to analyze algorithms, and rules for setting constraints on what performance must be reached on a subpart of an algorithm to guarantee overall performance.

Efficiency knowledge is generally contained in the algorithm design space. In fact, some heuristics in the algorithmic problem space depend on the cost model for the target architecture. Efficiency knowledge can be applied in selecting a plan [D1.1], in evaluating refinements for steps of the algorithm [D2.7], or in evaluating the algorithm as a whole [D1.10].

F. The Algorithm Design Space

In algorithm design, it is sometimes difficult to come up with any reasonably effective solution,* although some problems have simple brute force solutions. (Consider the problem of finding the closest pair of points in a point set. You can probably see a simple algorithm for solving the problem immediately.) Since algorithm design involves searching in a space not dense in solutions, dead ends are a serious problem, and knowledge of what design principles and domain facts are relevant is almost a necessity (as is the ability to reason and recognize in other spaces). Such knowledge can help decompose the problem or select and instantiate operators in the problem space.

Designers have variants of the algorithm design space that depend on their assumptions about the target architecture as well as on their overall knowledge of design principles. If the algorithms were to be programmed on an architecture with pipelined or distributed processing or associative retrieval, the representations for algorithms and heuristics for how to design might be greatly different. Some designers make (at least implicit) assumptions about the target architecture from the beginning of algorithm design, although it is preferable to stay independent of the target as long as possible.

The knowledge in the algorithm description space includes facts about mathematics, logic, arithmetic, or algorithm design principles. The knowledge can be in the form of both object descriptions and operators on those objects. Other knowledge can be represented by rules about when to change the problem-solving context.

1. Objects and operators

The basic objects for describing algorithms in the algorithm design space are *components* that specify basic types of processing. These components may test whether a property holds, generate the elements of a set one at a time, achieve an input/output relationship, apply a domain operator, select a subpart of a compound object, or modify a memory of objects.

The algorithm components are connected by *links* that allow flows of data and/or control and may be augmented with *assertions* about their properties or about their relationship to other objects or operators in any of the problem spaces. For example, a selection criterion might be to pick the bottom left point from a set of points. New components can be defined in terms of old ones by adding additional standard inputs or outputs or by adding assertions, or a component can be defined as configuration of other components.

The assertions associated with components may include information about the types of data objects expected as inputs or outputs or other preconditions or postconditions of processing, the ordering constraints on a generator, the criteria for selection, the initialization of a memory, expectations or conclusions about the time complexity of the algorithm (component), constraints on the order of execution of the algorithm components, notes about the algorithm (such as it has not yet been tested for the initial point lying inside the hull).

Since algorithms usually manipulate some sort of data, there are also representations of the common mathematical concepts such as numbers or symbols and of sequences or sets of other objects. Assertions about these objects can be attached to descriptions of the object type or to *items* that represent specific data.

> *The number of combinations of pairs from a set of elements is proportional to N squared.* [D4.1]

> *Divide and conquer algorithms can often have run time of NlogN.* [D2.7, D1.11]

The operators in the algorithm description space are simple (syntactic) editing operations that add or modify components, links between components, and assertions. The knowledge is all located in the rules that suggest instantiations of the type of components to create, the specific components to link, and the details of the assertions to be added.

2. Operator selection

Selecting an operator (and instantiating it by selecting values for its arguments) can be made more effective through the use of knowledge about general algorithm design principles and about algorithms in a particular domain of application. This knowledge will be expressed here as rules. Other such knowledge, such as how to handle specific problems raised during execution (the equivalent of a difference table for means-ends analysis) also limits the amount of search necessary for operator selection.

The following set of rules about operator selection and instantiation is merely a representative sample of the knowledge that an algorithm designer (human or otherwise) might have (not every designer has the same knowledge, of course). Many other rules would add their suggestions and vetoes about what to do. If there is no consensus about what operator to apply, the fall back is search through the suggested possibilities.

> *If a component needs to be refined and its output is a subset of its input, refine the component to an element generate and test algorithm.* [D1.1]

> *If a component needs to be refined and its output is a structure that must satisfy certain constraints, refine it to an algorithm that builds a minimal structure and then adds units of structure until the constraints are satisfied.* [D1.6] (An instance of this rule is suggested in [3].)

> *If an algorithm looks at part of the input many times to do the same kinds of tests, try saving information rather than recomputing, say with dynamic programming.* [D1.10]

> *If the characteristics of subproblems produced by the divide step of a divide-and-conquer algorithm are unknown, then add the assertion that they are two equal-sized subproblems.*

> *If the characteristics of subproblems produced by the divide step of a divide-and-conquer algorithm are unknown, and if the set being divided is a set of points in two dimensions, then refine the divide step to be a sort of the points and a division into the points on either side of the median a line through the median.* [D2.3] This has a bit of domain-specific knowledge although it is in the algorithm space.

---

*See Section IV.E or [2] for a comparison with the search problem in program synthesis.

If a component is missing a link to a required input, look for a component that has an output with the same type (or having that type as a subpart or superpart) and connect the two components.

3. Changing state

The state in the context of a problem space changes primarily as a direct result of the successful application of an operator that modifies the algorithm description. If the operator application fails, and if there were competing suggestions about what operator to apply, then alternative operators still apply and another will be tried. In addition to either failing or succeeding, an operator may return a difficulty or opportunity. This becomes another goal to be worked on, perhaps in a different problem space. After processing of the new goal is complete (which may change the state in the algorithm description problem space), the rules that caused the original operator to be selected may or may not be retriggered. If they are, the operator application can be retried.

4. Changing problem spaces

One of the benefits of having multiple problem spaces is the ability to reduce search by working on the same goal in a different space. Some examples of rules that can cause space changes are:

If a component needs to be refined, and its output is a construct in space X, create examples of it and notice their properties. If this rule is applied, it will cause a transfer first to the example generation space and then to the domain space X. [D1.2]

If a configuration of components has not been shown to achieve the specifications of the component of which it is a refinement, then symbolically execute it. [D1.9]

If a configuration of components has not been shown to achieve the specifications of the component it is a refinement of, and if symbolic execution has already been tried or is known in advance to be too complex to be informative, then execute the configuration on a concrete example". [D1.2]

5. Goal satisfaction and creation

Recognition of when goals have been achieved, or nearly achieved, of when to give up on a goal and declare failure, of when to create new goals, and so on is crucial to enabling discoveries. Strict enforcement of hierarchical subgoaling would not allow the same flexibility and creativity. Goal change knowledge can also serve as design heuristics. Some rules that express this knowledge are:

If an exponential algorithm is created, try to improve it or find an alternative unless it can be shown that the problem is itself exponential. [D2.6]

If all objects added to a set have a common assertion, hypothesize that that property holds for all elements in the set and try to substantiate the hypothesis.

If a component is defined by assertions that are appropriate for the level of detail currently desired (however that is determined!), then consider the component acceptable.

If a component is not considered to be refined to an acceptable level of detail, then create a goal to refine it.

G. The Application Domain Space

Algorithm designers need knowledge about their task domain as well as about algorithm design in general. As an example of a problem space describing a task domain, consider the knowledge about geometry that can be used in solving the convex hull problems.

Objects that are manipulable in the geometric domain include points, lines, segments, angles, and polygons. Special properties of object types or of specific objects may also be recorded. For example, the degenerate case of the object type polygon could be a point or line-segment, and a triangle would be the boundary case. For a specific geometric object, properties would include being convex or being above or below a line.

The operators in the geometric domain include accomplishing such functions as drawing a line segment between two points and recognizing that a polygon is convex.

Any symbolic descriptions of the objects in a figure and assertions about the objects or their relationships are available to the other spaces. For example, in the algorithm space, assertions may serve as test predicates, comparison or ordering relationships, or criteria for extraction from compound object. Operators are available for execution, say to build a polygon in the example generation space or as an operator applied by a component in the algorithm space that can be run during test-case execution. but their internal workings are not available.

The domain space also includes recognition knowledge, expressed here in the form of rules. that if applied to a figure in the current focus of attention may cause recognition and/or the construction of a new object just as an operator application might. For example,

If two line segments share a common endpoint, perceive the figure defined by that pair of segments as an angle. [D2.6]

H. The Execution Space

The problem space in which execution occurs is an augmentation of the algorithm description space. It uses the object type *item* to represent the data processed by the algorithm that flow over the links between components. The items can represent either specific objects from the domain space (point A) or symbolic objects ("a point"). Items can be augmented by properties that are known to be true of them at a given point in the algorithm execution history — that a point is known to be on or off the hull or that it is the one most recently added to a memory.

The operators in this space control the sequencing of component execution and carry out component execution. If assertions needed to carry out the operators are missing, a difficulty is returned and a new goal to handle the difficulty is created.

Some instances of rules that suggest new goals to work on are:

If the input for test-case execution is uninstantiated, set up a goal to get an example input. This will cause a transfer to the example generation space. A particular point set would be an example for the convex hull problem. [D1.3]

If test-case execution shows that applying some operation will make progress toward a solution of the problem but not solve it completely, try modifying the description in the algorithm design space to apply the operation repeatedly (inside a loop).

I. The Example Generation Space

The example generation space is also an augmentation of another space, the domain space. Objects must be augmented by properties that describe their typical instances, degenerate instances, boundary cases, and so on, if such information is not already present in the domain space. For instance. sequences consisting of repeated copies of the same element are not typical. Some sample operators are those that add and remove elements from examples. Some sample rules are

If creating an input to a generate-and-test algorithm and all elements in the input satisfy the test, then add another element [D1.10]

If creating an example for test-case execution of an algorithm that has not yet been checked for correctness, pick non-degenerate objects and constructors.

IV. Design Automation Strategies

This section summarizes the model of human design and compares it to some of the other approaches suggested for fully or partially automating algorithm design and for automatic programming. It also discusses how the methods might be extended to handle the problems in other contexts, such as interactive design.

A. Summary of Human Design

Several of our designers succeeded in creating convex hull algorithms. The algorithms and key discoveries of designers D1 and D2 have already been described. D1's generate-and-test algorithm had a disappointing worst case run time proportional to the cube of the number of input points. But D1 would never have been able to design the anticipated linear algorithm; it can be shown that the problem of finding a convex hull is related to the problem of sorting, so under conventional assumptions it must be an NlogN problem. Eventually D1 went on to try a divide-and-conquer approach that, with a little help from the experimenters, became a successful NlogN algorithm similar to D2's. Some other designers successfully recreated some convex hull algorithms that they had heard or read about but did not remember very clearly. (Many interesting convex hull algorithms have been described in the literature [19].) Still other designers failed to find any algorithm at all. We also gave our designers some other problems. They were asked for algorithms to find the closed pair of points from a given set or the intersection points of a set of vertical and horizontal lines. Most designers quickly suggested brute force algorithms (which have a worst case run time that is the square of the size of the input) but were unable to find any of the faster algorithms.

The methods observed in human design are quite varied. Selecting and sticking with a kernel idea provides a necessary focusing of attention, and using execution as an assertion propagation mechanism continues that focus and avoids the extensive search process that unlimited inference or search through the network of all refinements would entail. Of course if specific knowledge about the domain or algorithm design is available, it can be used to limit search by suggesting refinements directly. A powerful source of creativity is the use of visual reasoning about specific examples, which paves the way for discoveries about key concepts in algorithms. Although our current set of studies of human designers has provided many good ideas for a model of design, we would like to do more studies on other types of algorithms and on even more expert algorithm designers.

In general, the designers' success was highly correlated with their interest in and background in algorithm design. Some problems that they had stemmed from an incomplete (or totally absent) understanding of design principles such as divide and conquer (which is very relevant to the examples we gave). Other problems seemed to be due to impatience with methodically following a design strategy. In some cases, the designers tried to mix aspects of the design from two different approaches. This typically failed when they tried to mix subparts of different types of principles but succeeded when they tried to reuse facts or theories from the geometric domain that were learned in an earlier design.

B. Automatic Programming

Automatic programming is that ever receding goal of automating the programming of everything the user wants with a minimal amount of specification. Automatic programming encompasses (1) algorithm design, (2) program synthesis, and (3) the problem of managing complexity in programming in the large. Algorithm design has been defined in Section I.A as the process of producing a computationally feasible program sketch (that is relatively complete and consistent) from a specification of what is to be accomplished. We refer here to the hour-level form of algorithm design, not research design. This routine design often precedes program synthesis. Program synthesis is the process of choosing data structures and access functions to transform a given algorithm specification into concrete code in a conventional programming language. Like algorithm design, program synthesis requires intelligence, especially to produce extremely efficient code, but it probably can be achieved with more straightforward techniques.

As has been pointed out by others [2, 10], full-fledged automatic programming requires the incorporation of domain knowledge as well as detailed coding knowledge. Furthermore, programming in the large must be supported by effective bookkeeping. There are few concrete results in this area, however. The notion of working in multiple spaces, and in a domain space in particular, may prove valuable in automating the entire programming process.

C. Formal Derivation

The formal derivation approach has been proposed for both algorithm design and program synthesis [25, 5, 21]. Formal derivation methods share with the design methods described here a refinement strategy based on a few, largely syntactic, transformations, but differ in that the transformations preserve correctness. It is assumed that the specifications are correct and complete, and since the transformations require and guarantee correctness, then the intermediate states and the result are also correct and internally consistent. The operations of the transformations — defining new constructs, expanding definitions ("unfolding"), noticing instances of definitions that have arisen after rearrangement and simplification of the algorithm constituents ("folding") — are similar to the processes that we have noted in human design.

One way that the formal approach differs from the model of design described here is that it requires that terms be defined by axioms or equations and does not allow the use of terms defined only in a domain space. Also, in the formal approach, transformations are instantiated via axioms about the domain or algorithmic constructs; in the model of design described here, they can be instantiated by similar knowledge based on formal definitions, by arbitrary selection, or by guesses based on observations of the domain. As discussed earlier, people can sometimes derive algorithms even if they do not have formal definitions of all the concepts. They need only have operators in the domain space that recognize the concepts, more primitive operators in the domain space that can construct the structures they want to recognize, and techniques for implementing the constructive operators in the algorithm space. In contrast, the formal derivation approaches often have problems with controlling the search process and with creating useful auxiliary definitions — the "aha" or "eureka" steps are often definitions inserted by human interaction. These problems result from there being no clues in the formal approach about how to introduce the right interesting knowledge.

Another way the formal approach, with its requirement for consistency and completeness, differs from human design is in the handling of boundary conditions and base cases. The formal approach requires that these be defined early on, almost the opposite of the human approach. Getting the details of the boundary conditions right is one cause of the search problem in formal systems — there are many ways to define these conditions, and selecting the precise specifications or introducing conditionals and filling out the details adds complexity.

For some people, the discipline of taking care of details with a standard methodology releases their creativity. On the other hand, many people find it difficult to state invariants precisely if they must be absolutely correct. Getting the main idea of the invariant is crucial to solving the problem, but stating it formally to avoid such problems as fencepost errors makes it tedious and not obviously productive. For these people, getting the details right immediately is extremely difficult; the overhead of internalizing this methodology is prohibitively high.

Formal derivation systems are being augmented with more detailed knowledge about design techniques so that the search control can be more goal oriented [9] and also with knowledge about example generation [4]. However, this still doesn't postpone settling all the details (having a domain space lets you finesse formalizing them) or say where the creative definitions come from (cross fertilization from domain spaces and other algorithms).

D. Inductive Inference

Inductive inference from examples is another technique that has been explored, but more for the construction of small programs than for the design of algorithms or large systems. Unambiguously specifying the input/output behavior of algorithms with examples is easier than so specifying the behavior of large programs. However, the inductive approaches usually rely on problem solving using a small set of schema, with little ability to improvise if none of the schema match. If the target language is logical equation based language with a search mechanism built into the interpreter, then this approach may work [24]. But it is unlikely to produce clever algorithms in conventional languages.

E. Program Synthesis by Refinement

The program synthesis problem is complementary to that of algorithm design, although we would expect that many of the same problem solving techniques are used. The stage at which the algorithm design process stops — when an algorithm is "understood" — should provide an appropriate specification or starting place for program synthesis.

The standard refinement paradigm in program synthesis [13, 23] is to apply knowledge-based rules and search over that knowledge; no creativity is introduced. The search problem is a bit different since once an algorithm is well defined, the program synthesis problem is usually to find a more detailed program in a standard programming language selecting concrete data structures and accessing operations. Usually the search space is dense in correct solutions that vary in efficiency, reliability, modifiability, and so on [2]. Past research has investigated the control of the search by efficiency (for example, [14]). Such control is not a definitive solution, but many approaches have been prototyped fairly successfully.

As in most expert systems, it is assumed that all the knowledge about how to refine programming constructs is present in the refinement rules. In contrast, the hypothesize and test technique in the design model presented here allows the discovery of new programming techniques. The price paid, of course, is that more search at the lower levels is required, and this search is not as easily controlled by efficiency rules.

F. Program Synthesis by Design

We hope that algorithm design research will result in aids for program synthesis that avoid hand coding of all the refinement rules. The initial knowledge base requirements should be simplified considerably as a result of the more generic problem-solving abilities such as trial execution, with its low-level means ends analysis and search, and domain space reasoning. Putting in more of this creativity should make the automatic programming process more flexible and robust and may even produce better programs.

G. Interactive Tools

An interesting question to ask is, does this knowledge suggest any other tools to aid in the design process? Are there some interactive tools that might help people in the design process? Or is there some novel mix of human and machine power that could lead to even better design?

The conventional wisdom is that people have better insight and machines are better at the details. Following this wisdom, the machine could suggest the full range of possible approaches at any one step and the person could decide which to follow, providing the search control.

We could augment this plan by observing that execution is a powerful technique in design. Programs are good at methodically following algorithms for execution, but people frequently see what they expect and miss some of the problems. This would suggest machine support for execution of designs. The execution would expose problems and inconsistencies that people might skip over and the people could suggest some solutions to the problem or suggest new directions to follow.

In addition, the machine support could include a set of rules that continuously monitor simple features of the design, providing a check that preserves almost-correctness but does not guarantee a complete validation. In effect, this makes the machine a sounding board for human design, just as colleagues act as sounding boards. People explain their ideas to colleagues so that they are forced to look at their design from other perspectives (with different assumptions) and go through the design one more time in explaining it. A machine might serve the role of a colleague.

Building the human/machine communication interface is the hard part of following through with these plans. The two agents must speak the same language and each must be able to track what the other is doing. This may turn out to be even harder than full automation.

H. Other Design Tasks

There are a variety of other design tasks, such as engineering design or VLSI design. Although each of these tasks has its own unique characteristics, we may hope that some of the concepts discussed in this paper may be relevant to these tasks.

V. Conclusions

The essence of the model of design presented here lies in its informality and its use of multiple problem spaces, including example generation and trial execution based on both the domain space and an algorithm design space. These techniques provide a focus of attention to limit search and enable the discovery of key concepts. The model shares problem-solving techniques with many of the other approaches, but rather than having a single monolithic plan of attack, it shifts techniques depending on the knowledge available.

Several areas need further formalizing and testing. The models of the processes of discovery and visual reasoning must be extended. Learning and database issues should be explored further. For example, what are the appropriate organization and retrieval techniques for large amounts of information so that key ideas in algorithms and derivations are accessible when relevant? Being able to learn automatically depends on appropriate accessing and on general problem-solving techniques.

The interactions between search, domain knowledge, and programming knowledge seem important in tasks of any appreciable difficulty, including automatic programming and the next generation of expert systems, but several questions about these interactions are still unresolved. For example, it is not well understood how to determine when to stop refining at a given level, how problem spaces are created from problems descriptions, and so on.

Understanding the design process impacts other branches of AI. Those that include design tasks, discovery, visual reasoning, the use of examples, and interaction between different types of knowledge could be compared to algorithm design in their organization of knowledge and use of problem-solving techniques. Answering the questions posed for design should shed some light on the general issues in other domains. A side effect of automation, the formalization of algorithm design, analysis, and optimization principles, could also be useful in teaching. Our observations of human design show that examples are useful in the absence of knowledge and therefore probably necessary to teach the knowledge, but having explicit principles is more efficient for the designer.

In summary, the model of design presented here is a good start on understanding algorithm design. The attempt to formalize the model lays a substantial part of the foundation for automation.

Acknowledgments

The research described here is joint work with Allen Newell and David Steier. Mary-Anne Wolf recorded and transcribed many of the protocols. Thanks to Jon Bentley for helping to instigate these studies. Thanks are also due to the designers who participated in the experiments for their interest and cooperation; they shall remain anonymous for obvious reasons. Programming support for the implementation and additional input has been provided by Brigham Bell, Lisa Covi, Billy Kim, Roland Kovacs, Deepak Kulkarny, David Marshall, Jim Muller, Ed Pervin, Eric Schwabe, Mark Taylor, and Ross Thompson as well as Wolf and Steier. Allen Newell, David Barstow, David Steier, and Sol Greenspan made valuable comments on earlier versions of this paper.

References

1. Adelson, B. and Soloway, E. A Model of Software Design. In *The Nature of Expertise*, Chi, Glaser and Farr, Eds., Lawrence Erlbaum Associates, in preparation.

2. Barstow, D. R. "A Perspective on Automatic Programming." *The AI Magazine 5*, 1 (Spring 1984).

3. Barstow, D. R. The Roles of Knowledge and Deduction in Algorithm Design. In Biermann, A. W. (editor), Ed., *Automatic Program Construction Techniques*, McMillan, l984. Chap. 10, pp. 201-222.

4. Bibel, W. and Horning, K. M. LOPS - A System Based on a Strategical Approach to Program Synthesis. Proceedings of the International Workshop on Program Construction, France, September, 1980.

5. Biermann, A. W. (Ed.). *Automatic Program Construction Techniques*. McMillan, 1984.

6. Chandrasekaran, B. and Radicchi, S. (Ed.). *Computer Program Testing*. North-Holland, 1981.

7. Cohen, D. A Forward Inference Engine to Aid in Understanding Specifications. Proceedings of AAAI-84, 1984.

8. Ericsson, K.A. and Simon, H. A. "Verbal Reports as Data." *Psychological Review 87*, 3 (May 1980). 215-251.

9. Feather, M. S. "A System for Assisting Program Transformation." *ACM Transactions on Programming Languages and Systems 4*, 1 (1982), 1-20.

10. Green, C., Luckham, D., Balzer, R., Cheatham, T., and Rich, C. Report on a Knowledge-Based Software Assistant. Tech. Rept. RADC-TR-83-195, Kestrel Institute, August, 1983.

11. Gries, D. *The Science of Programming*. Springer-Verlag, 1981.

12. Jeffries, R., Turner, A. A., and Polson, P. G. The Processes Involved in Designing Software. In *Cognitive Skills and Their Acquisition*, John R. Anderson, Ed., Lawrence Erlbaum Associates, 1981, ch. 8.

13. Kant, E. and Barstow, D. R. The Refinement Paradigm: The Interaction of Coding and Efficiency Knowledge in Program Synthesis. In *Interactive Programming Environments*, Barstow, D. R., Shrobe, H. E., and Sandewall, E., Eds., McGraw-Hill, 1984, pp. 487-513.

14. Kant, E. *Efficiency in Program Synthesis*. UMI Research Press, 1981.

15. Kant, E. and Newell, A. Naive Algorithm Design Techniques: A Case Study. Proceedings of the European Conference on Artificial Intelligence, Orsay, France, July, 1982.

16. Kant, E. and Newell, A. "Problem Solving Techniques for the Design of Algorithms." *Information Processing and Management 20*, 1-2 (Spring 1984).

17. Kant, E. and Newell, A. An Automatic Algorithm Designer: An Initial Implementation. Proceedings of AAAI-83, 1983.

18. Laird, J. E. Universal Subgoaling. Tech. Rept. CMU-CS-84-129, Carnegie-Mellon University, Computer Science Department, May, 1984.

19. Lee, D. T., and Preparata, F. P. "Computational Geometry -- A Survey." *IEEE Transactions on Computers C-33*, 12 (December 1984).

20. Newell, A. and Simon, H. *Human Problem Solving*. Prentice-Hall, 1972.

21. Partsch, H. and Steinbruggen, R. "Program Transformation Systems." *Computing Surveys 15*, 3 (September 1983).

22. Polya, G. *How to Solve It*. Doubleday-Anchor, 1957.

23. Rich, C., and Shrobe, H. Initial Report on a Lisp Programmer's Apprentice. In *Interactive Programming Environments*, Barstow, D. R., Shrobe, H. E., and Sandewall, E., Eds., McGraw-Hill, 1984, pp. 443-463.

24. Shapiro, E. Y. An Algorithm that Infers Theories from Facts. Proceedings of IJCAI-81, 1981, pp. 446-451.

25. Smith, D. R. Top-Down Synthesis of Simple Divide and Conquer Algorithms. Tech. Rept. NPS52-82-011, Naval Postgraduate School, November, 1982.

26. Steier, D. M. and Kant, E. Symbolic Execution in Algorithm Design. Proceedings of the Ninth International Joint Conference on Artifical Intelligence, Los Angeles, CA, August, 1985.

AI and LEGAL REASONING

Report of a panel chaired by

Edwina L. Rissland
Department of Computer and Information Science
University of Massachusetts
Amherst, MA 01003

Abstract

This paper presents a summary of the responses of a panel to issues on AI and legal reasoning. The panel consisted of: Edwina L. Rissland, Chair (University of Massachusetts), Kevin D. Ashley (University of Massachusetts), Michael G. Dyer (UCLA), Anne v.d.L. Gardner (Stanford), L. Thorne McCarty (Rutgers), and Donald A. Waterman (RAND). Among the issues addressed by the panel were:

1. What are the characteristics of the legal domain that make it interesting or amenable to AI approaches – what is special about it;
2. The open-textured nature of legal concepts and the implications this has for using AI-techniques, especially knowledge representation;
3. The complementarity of rule-based and case-based reasoning – how cases are used, especially when the rules "run out";
4. The pervasive role of analogy in legal reasoning;
5. The special role played by hypotheticals in the legal domain and how hypos help with argumentation and strategic case planning;
6. The interleaving of justification, explanation, and argumentation;
7. How common law systems can be seen to be systems which learn from cases;
8. The appropriateness and feasibility of intelligent aids for practicing litigators and other legal experts;
9. Implications for other domains – like medicine – that use case-based reasoning;
10. Methodological and other issues.

For each issue considered, the comments of the panelists are summarized.

1. The Challenge and Special Characteristics of the Legal Domain

The legal domain presents some very interesting challenges to the AI researcher. While it is a domain which has established standards for deriving new truths (e.g., *stare decisis* or the doctrine of precedent), it is more of a "scruffy" domain than a "neat" one, despite its orderly, rule-like surface veneer. It is very much an experience-based example-driven field. Legal reasoning is also heavily intertwined with natural language processing and common sense reasoning and therefore inherits all the hard problems that these imply.

Several panelists emphasize that legal reasoning and argumentation take special skills and that learning to think like a lawyer requires considerably more than rote memorization of a large number of cases, a daunting task in itself. For instance, Dyer says:

> Modeling what a lawyer does is more complex than modeling experts in technical/scientific domains. First, all of these complex conceptualizations are expressed in natural language, so modeling the comprehension ability of the lawyer requires solving the natural language problem. For example, giving legal advice often starts with hearing a "story" where the client was one of the actors. So legal advice often presupposes a story understanding capability. In other expert systems, the natural language problem can be largely finessed since the task (e.g., disease diagnosis, reconfiguring hardware, analyzing dipmeters) rarely involves the communication of complex conceptualizations. Second, the planning in this domain is complex. This is a world where actors obtain agents, where they counterplan, retaliate, attempt to set up subsumption states, etc. Third, Anglo-American jurisprudence, at least, makes use of a large body of concrete EPISODES. Becoming a lawyer requires learning how to index, generalize and apply these concrete episodes in service of reasoning and argumentation strategies. Fourth, law is simply an attempt to formalize COMMON SENSE reasoning and notions of justice, morality and fair play.

Rissland points out the analogies between legal and mathematical reasoning. In her analysis, learning to be an expert mathematician or mathematics student involves a lot more than simply learning definitions, theorems and proofs. There is a wealth of other knowledge and skills needed: for instance, there is a large corpus of examples and heuristics, and there is the important skill of being able to generate examples [Rissland, 1978]. Similar remarks can be made about the legal domain [Levi, 1949; Llewellyn, 1930]. In particular, cases in law play the analogous role to examples in other fields. However, in addition to the usual questions about examples – such as their function and generation – the law is a domain which is largely case or example-based and thus examples are truly central.

The law also exhibits many of the traits discussed by Kuhn with regard to scientific disciplines [Kuhn, 1970]. In particular, the dialectic between proposing an idea or rule and the testing of it through concrete cases -- so well discussed by Lakatos [1976] and Polya [1973] -- can also be found in the law and other fields [Rissland, 1984c].

Waterman notes several special characteristics of the law:

> The law combines many different kinds of reasoning processes: rule-based, case-based, analogical, hypothetical.

> It has the unique property of being pseudo-formalized, i.e., there exists a large body of formal rules that purport to define and regulate activity in the domain. However, these rules are often deliberately ambiguous, contradictory and incomplete. Many of the actual rules used in legal reasoning are rules about how to access and reason with the "formal" rules. The problem this creates is the naive notion (for some) that because a body of rules and regulations exists, all one has to do is translate them into executable code to create a legal reasoning program.

> The law is in a constant state of change, so expert legal reasoning systems have to be easy to modify and update. Many other application domains have this characteristic, but perhaps not to quite the same extent.

Gardner not only joins others in pointing out the challenge for AI presented by the intertwining of natural language and common sense knowledge in legal reasoning but also she remarks on some differences concerning the nature of expertise in the law compared with other domains of expert systems work:

> Law is an area for "expert systems" in the sense of involving professional knowledge, but it is unusual in that we have to expect the experts to disagree. (E.g., opposing counsel; judges writing majority and dissenting opinions.) Questions then arising are: (1) What kinds of things can they disagree on, and what kinds of disagreement are beyond the bounds of professional competence? (2) How can a reasoning system leave room for the appropriate kinds of disagreement?

> Law is also an area deeply involving natural language and commonsense understanding. In particular: (1) Legal materials (such as statutes and other statements of legal rules) are written in natural language, and the problem of saying how they apply to a particular situation is in large part a problem of saying what this language means. This aspect of law calls for a different approach to meaning from that taken in most AI programs. (See discussion of open texture below.) (2) The situations to which we might want to apply legal knowledge encompass practically the whole range of human activity -- with a special focus on those human situations where something goes wrong. Thus a truly expert system would be able to represent and reason about such situations using a great deal of commonsense knowledge as well as technical knowledge. This last is true of some other kinds of expert systems too.

2. The Open-Textured Nature of Legal Concepts

Unlike certain other domains like mathematics or even medicine, concepts in the law tend to be "open-textured", that is, one cannot provide black and white definitions. Interpreting a legal concept in a new situation depends on past interpretations. To decide whether a legal predicate applies to a fact situation, one must usually find cases in which the predicate was applied and focus on similarities or dissimilarities.

Gardner, who addressed this issue in considerable detail in her recent doctoral thesis [Gardner, 1984, especially Sections 3.1-3.3], summarizes:

> Legal language is open-textured in that (1) we cannot state necessary and sufficient conditions for the application of legal predicates and (2) neither can we take legal predicates as primitives in the sense that a program could simply recognize whether or not the predicate applies to some fact situation. (That is, a legal rule (Px implies Qx) and a fact Pa do not entail legal consequence Qa.)

> This characterization of open texture covers several phenomena. One is the variable standard (e.g., "a reasonable time"). Another is vagueness (although legal rules do tend to avoid using obviously vague words -- legislators write rules about people over 65, not about "old" people). The most important, however, is that legal conclusions that appear to follow deductively are in fact defeasible. That is, given the legal rule (Px implies Qx) and the fact Pa, the conclusion Qa is only a default conclusion.

Ashley points out that the law's handling of open-textured predicates is not neutral, that is, the decision about the concept is tied in with who the decider wants to win the case:

> In deciding whether a legal predicate applies to a fact situation, a court usually also

determines who should win the issue or the case. The criteria for deciding whether the predicate applies are rarely completely specifiable in rules. The court must usually find cases in which the predicate was applied and focus on similarities or dissimilarities between the new fact situation and past cases. It must decide if the comparison cuts in favor of following the prior case or distinguishing it. This analysis is significantly different from trying to apply some abstract definition of the legal predicate. Any attempt to model legal reasoning must take account of this aspect of case-based reasoning.

3. The Complementarity of Case-Based and Rule-Based Reasoning

One way cases are used is to give concrete content to the concepts and abstractions in legal rules. Even if one believes that the law can be captured in rules – which many, particularly the legal realists, do not – one needs cases to flesh out the meaning and intent of the rules. As Gardner has put it, cases are what you use "when the rules run out". Most scholars of the common law, would say that cases are what you use all the time – even if you have rules and know how to apply them. McCarty has long campaigned the importance of this point for AI work on legal reasoning; for instance see [McCarty, 1977; McCarty and Sridharan, 1981a].

Rissland restated the theme of the intertwining of case-based and rule-based reasoning, and that it is akin to the proofs-and-refutations dialectic between concept/conjecture and examples talked about by Lakatos. In fact, she suggests, as has Gardner, that one could carry this computationally further for handling the different types of questions discussed by Gardner [Gardner, 1984]: a rule-based approach for the "easy" or black-and-white questions and a case-based approach for the "hard" or gray-area questions. A rule-based reasoner should be able to call on the services of a case-based reasoner when the predicates get murky or the rules run out and a case-based reasoner should be able to call a rule-based reasoner for the well-understood, well-structured aspects of its problems.

4. The Pervasive Role of Analogy

Ashley identifies several uses of analogy in legal argumentation and practice [Ashley, 1984] including:

1. Precedents that are analogous in some sense to the case being decided are used to focus the attention of the advocate on those issues and authorities which have a bearing upon the argument;

2. The precedent provides an example of what a reasonable argument in an analogous context looks like;

3. An existing classification from a precedent may be applied to analogous facts in the case being decided;

4. A new classification, analogous to a classification in a precedent, may be created and applied to the facts in the case being decided.

Gardner points out that if one takes analogy to refer to comparing facts of cases for the purpose of arguing that a new case should be decided in the same way as an old, similar case, then the crux of the issue is what makes some factual similarities and differences important and others irrelevant; this involves more than a simple comparison of facts.

McCarty has addressed this issue in his TAXMAN II research, especially concerning the famous tax case of *Eisner v. Macomber*. If one can imagine a sequence of intermediate hypotheticals connecting the two cases to be analogized then the sequence of intermediate transformations provide a key to the analogy. For a detailed analysis, see [McCarty and Sridharan, 1981b].

Dyer echoes some of McCarty's and Rissland's concerns, particularly on the utility of the idea of deformations and standard or prototype cases, with an added emphasis on the key role of memory in analogy:

> Functioning successfully as a lawyer requires having indexed key cases in such a way that the comprehension of novel cases leads immediately to access of key cases. In a sense, legal reasoning and comprehension involves finding "islands" of legal prototypes from which well-known reasoning paths can be adapted to the novel situations and then traversed. Much of legal reasoning, therefore, is a memory indexing and search problem rather than a logical or "theorem-proving" problem.

5. The Role of Hypotheticals

Hypotheticals – that is, make-believe cases – serve many roles in legal reasoning. Several of the panelists, in particular, McCarty, Rissland, and Ashley, agreed on their importance. All three make strong use of hypotheticals in their models of legal reasoning and generate them in a somewhat similar framework (called "prototype plus deformation" by McCarty and "modification plus retrieval" by Rissland, who also taxonomizes examples into classes like "model", standard reference, anomaly, etc.).

Rissland enumerates some of the uses that hypos play in legal reasoning and argumentation [Rissland, 1984a, b]. For instance, some general functions of hypos are:
1. hypos remake experience
2. hypos create experience
3. hypos organize and cluster cases
4. hypos tease out hidden assumptions

For instance, the second usage allows one to consider issues that have not yet been litigated, and may well be, (e.g., the recent case of the frozen embryo which was predeceased by its parents or a malpractice suit against an expert system). Thus hypos can contribute to strategic planning by providing what-if situations – especially contrary ones – to consider. This can lead to a debugging an argument or strategy ahead of time.

Ashley elaborates on three roles played by hypotheticals in the context of argumentation:

> 1. In a legal argument, a hypothetical can be used to isolate the weaknesses and strengths of an attorney's case. A hypo can be constructed to emphasize one aspect of a case that pushes strongly for a decision contrary to the proponent's, perhaps by making it more like a line of contrary cases or by exaggerating some common sense objection to following the proponent's classification. One way for the proponent to respond is to distinguish the hypo and his case. In so doing, the proponent is forced to emphasize the other strengths of his case that are not present in the hypo.

> 2. A hypothetical can be used to illuminate the consequences of a decision. A court may ask, "If we decide in favor of the proponent on this case, what will we do when a case with somewhat less sympathetic facts is posed?" It is an exercise in line drawing. If no defensible lines can be drawn, the court may choose not to decide in favor of the proponent, or at least not on the grounds argued for.

> 3. In both of the above, the hypothetical is used as a short hand for lines of cases, lines of reasoning, even whole arguments.

Such uses of hypotheticals in legal argument can be illustrated by excerpts from oral arguments before the United States Supreme Court in which the justices pose hypotheticals to make and elicit legal points and to control the presentation of a proponent's case (e.g., the questioning by the Justices in the recent civil rights case of *Gomez-Bethke v. U.S. Jaycees* (1983)) and to justify and explain their conclusions (e.g., see the opinion of Justice Pitney and the dissent of Justice Brandeis in the landmark corporate tax case of *Eisner v. Macomber* (1920)).

6. Interleaving of Justification, Explanation and Argumentation

Waterman reminds us that explanation (explaining how you reached a conclusion) and justification (providing a convincing argument that the method used to reach the conclusion is valid) aren't as easy in law as they are in some other domains which have clear underlying (deep) models of the mechanisms involved, mechanisms that can provide predictive and explicative power. He is joined by McCarty in this concern.

Waterman asks us to consider the question, "What are the fundamental models in the legal domain and what constitutes a real "justification" of an answer?"

Of course, the legal community in its answer would surely mention the doctrine of precedent and the use of cases as fundamentals in justification and argumentation. The AI community would emphasize representation and models of process. Ashley, McCarty and Rissland all cite the important role of hypotheticals in justification and argumentation. Ashley and Rissland go further to also say that cases and hypotheticals can carry a large part of the burden of explanation as well. Thus Waterman's question can be re-posed to ask for the details of *how* cases are used in justification, argumentation, and explanation.

Dyer points out that this interleaving has methodological consequences: process models of legal expertise must be designed as a whole, where beliefs, goals, planning, and arguing are integrated.

7. The Law as a Learning System

On this issue there is some disagreement. Rissland can view the law, with all its cases, rules, statutes, etc, as a learning system in that the law responds to its environment which presents it cases to be dealt with and in response changes its case base, rules, statutes, etc., as well as its ways of dealing with its environment. This view is elaborated somewhat by Ashley:

> Experience in the legal system is accumulated in two places: in its database of cases and in the implicit rules that develop for comparing fact situations in a particular domain. These rules are learned by law students in learning to "think like lawyers." They are evidenced by the choices that courts make in applying precedents but they are not authoritatively set forth in any restatement, statute or case. The rules make it possible to apply the precedents to new cases. They are how the law learns.

McCarty sees the law as a "theory construction" system that is constructing new concepts.

Dyer feels strongly that it is the lawyers who learn:

> The law is NOT a learning system; lawyers ARE. Lawyers index legal episodes in episodic memory. As new situations arise, new judgements are made and episodes are reorganized in memory. This is just how the law student learns: by being presented with a case, applying whatever legal and common

sense intuitions are currently available, indexing the case along recognized abstract legal issues, and then modifying and reindexing as new cases (with alternate outcomes and opinions) are encountered.

8. Intelligent Aids for Practicing Litigators

The panel as a whole voiced somewhat cautious optimism that it would eventually be possible to develop a lawyer's workbench which would include tools ranging from standard retrieval tools like the existing WESTLAW and LEXIS full text retrieval systems, document generation aids, scheduling and calendar managers, to tools needing more intelligence like briefing assistants and interpretive analysis programs which could understand cases. This caution is based upon the nearly common experience of how long it takes to develop a program that can handle a few cases or problems, let alone the plethora occurring in real practice.

McCarty sees two main categories of intelligent applications programs: conceptual legal retrieval systems and legal analysis and planning systems. He elaborates:

"...the most critical task in the development of an intelligent legal information system, either for document retrieval or for expert advice, is the construction of a conceptual model of the relevant legal domain.

...these models will not be easy to formulate and the corresponding information systems will not be easy to construct. For the near term, then, the critical problem will be to select an appropriate level of conceptual detail, and an appropriate level of system complexity." [McCarty, 1983a, p. 286].

9. Implications and Relevance for Other Case-Based Domains

Most of the panelists did not express much enthusiasm for useful cross-fertilization between law and other domains, like medicine, except for Rissland who believes that there is something shared in that both domains use cases -- albeit in different ways -- especially in areas where the diseases are new or not well understood (i.e., where there might not be rules). All feel that the details of such cross-discipline enlightment are vague at this point.

Dyer puts it:

I believe that modeling lawyers is a much more complex task than modeling doctors. This is mainly because the expert systems approach has restricted itself to those areas where immediate success is possible. If we admit that medicine is not simply rule-based diagnosis over symptoms with weighted and propagated certainty factors, then we open up the harder issues in medicine. These issues

are those shared with law: namely, how do doctors (lawyers) read and understand medical (legal) texts? What must doctors (lawyers) know about the physiological (socio-cultural) processes of the body (everyday affairs) in order to be able to understand, plan and give advice?

Such concerns are also shared by McCarty who points out that the shallow reasoning exhibited by certain medical diagnosis programs, like MYCIN, is not at all like, or sufficient for, the deep reasoning (for instance, with respect to its representation and causal models) required in the legal domain. McCarty recaps some of his recent comments from [McCarty, 1983a] where he asked, "If shallow rule-based systems have been so successful in the medical field, why do I insist that they have such serious limitations in the legal field?" McCarty's answer to this paradox lies in the differences of the nature of the rules involved. In medicine, the rules are empirical, associative, probablistic rules of thumb, which are used cumulatively and which do not reflect any deep causal models, say of bacterial disease. Whereas in medicine, this might be enough to get the job done, in the law it is not except for certain discretionary legal issues like "reasonable care". Interestingly, rule-based treatment of discretionary judgements (e.g., the worthwhileness of a civil suit) has already met with some success [Waterman and Peterson, 1981].

10. Methodological and Other Issues

There is the usual two way relationship between AI and the law. The law is a field which might be able to profitably use AI concepts and technology to further its own aims such as developing jurisprudential analyses of legal reasoning or developing intelligent litigation aids and the law provides an excellent task domain for AI research.

Dyer addresses whether these two approaches entail different standards and whether this matters:

For a person not interested in modeling intelligence, but in supplying the lawyer with smart legal aids, the approach may be different. I believe that this particular subdiscipline for AI is too young to decide that one (or the other) approach should not be tried, but I believe that more is to be gained ultimately by modeling the mind in the domain of law than modeling law using currently known insights about intelligence (artifical or otherwise).

Gardner feels that it might be a difference more of degree than kind:

At one end, there are people trying to build systems useful to lawyers, or trying to find out how far present AI techniques are applicable in law. The results here may look like lots of law and not much that's new for AI.

At the other end, for the purpose of studying some AI problem, you could create a microworld and call it law. The results might have as little to do with a lawyer's view of law as Winston's "Shakespeare world" has to do with an English professor's view of Shakespeare.

But the reason I said the distinction was a matter of degree was that, to some extent, we can't help working with microworlds. That is, every study of law or legal reasoning, AI or otherwise, has to work with an abstracted version of its domain. It's most important to try to be clear about what simplifications one is making, and to consider from what point of view these simplifications are reasonable.

Several panelists feel that progress in the area of AI and law requires further progress in fundamental AI and cognitive science research on issues like representation. This is a point emphasized increasingly by McCarty:

> Successful work in law and AI — both theory and application — requires much better "conceptual models" of the legal domain than the field of AI can currently provide "off-the-shelf".

Part of McCarty's response to this problem is his work on "permissions and obligations" which addresses the fundamental "Hohfeldian" mechanisms of rights, privileges, duties, etc. underlying our legal system. Other work, like that of deBessonet [1984] on legal representation primitives, also contributes to this basic research.

Other issues of concern to the panel included sociological issues, for instance, the impact of intelligent or (semi-)automated legal services and how this will effect society's relationship with the legal system (e.g., will legal services become accessible to more people, will people become more "do it yourself"). What will be the nature of the symbiosis between man and machine in the legal domain. Of course, there was also the issue of the law applied to AI programs, for instance, potential tort, or even criminal, actions involving AI programs (e.g., a medical malpractice suit against a medical expert system). Many of these issues are addressed in the panel on "AI and Social Responsibility", chaired by Maggie Boden, and reported on in these proceedings.

Bibliography

Ashley, K. D. (1984). "Reasoning by Analogy: A Survey of Selected A.I. Research with Implications for Legal Expert Systems". In *Proceedings First Annual Conference on Law and Technology*, University of Houston, Houston TX. To be included in a collection to be published by West Pub. Co. in 1985.

August, S. E. and Dyer, M. G. (1985). "Understanding Analogies in Editorials." UCLA AI Lab Memo.

Birnbaum, L. (1982). "Argument Molecules: A Functional Representation of Argument Structure". In *Proceedings AAAI-82*. Pittsburgh, PA.

deBessonet, C. G. (1984). *CCLIPS, The Civil Code Legal Information Processing System*. Law and AI Project, Louisiana State Law Institute, Baton Rouge, LA.

Corbin, A. L. (1961). The Judicial Process Revisited. *Yale Law Journal* 71, 195-201.

Dyer, M. G., & Flowers, M. (1984). "Toward Automating Legal Expertise." In *Proceedings of the First Law and Technology Conference*. University of Houston, Houston, Texas.

Flowers, M. (1982). "On Being Contradictory". In *Proceedings of AAAI-82*. Pittsburgh, PA.

Flowers, M. and Dyer, M. G. (1984). "Really Arguing with your Computer in Natural Language." In *Proceedings of NCC-84*. Las Vegas.

Flowers, M., McGuire, R. and Birnbaum, L., (1982). "Adversary Arguments and the Logic of Personal Attacks." In Lehnert and Ringle (eds.) *Strategies for Natural Language Processing*. LEA Press, NJ.

Gardner, Anne v.d.L. (1984). *An Artificial Intelligence Approach to Legal Reasoning*. Doctoral Dissertation, Department of Computer Science, Stanford University.

———— (1983). "The Design of a Legal Analysis Program." In *Proceedings AAAI-83*. Washington, DC.

Goldman, S. R., Dyer, M. G. and Flowers, M., (1985). "Precedence-Based Legal Reasoning in Contract Law." UCLA AI Lab Memo.

Hohfeld, W. N. (1919). "Fundamental Legal Conceptions as Applied in Judicial Reasoning." Yale U. Press, New Haven, CT, Ed., W. W. Cook.

Kuhn, T. S. (1970). *The Structure of Scientific Revolutions*. Second Edition. University of Chicago Press.

Lakatos, I. (1976). *Proofs and Refutations*. Cambridge University Press, London.

Levi, E. H. (1949). *An Introduction to Legal Reasoning*. University of Chicago Press.

Llwellyn, K. N. (1930). *The Bramble Bush*. Ocean Publications.

_____(1960). *The Common Law Tradition: Deciding Appeals*. Little Brown, Boston.

McCarty, L. T. (1983a). "Intelligent Legal Information Systems: Problems and Prospects." *Rutgers Computer and Technology Law Journal* 9(2):265-294.

_____ (1983b) "Permissions and Obligations." In *Proceedings IJCAI-83*. Karlsruhe, W. Germany.

_____ (1977). "Reflections on TAXMAN: An Experiment in Artificial Intelligence and Legal Reasoning." *Harvard Law Review* 90:837-93.

McCarty, L. T. and Sridharan, N. S. (1981a). "The Representation of an Evolving System of Legal Concepts: II. Prototypes and Deformations." In *Proceedings IJCAI-81*.

_____ (1981b). *A Computational Theory of Legal Argument*. Technical Report LRP-TR-13, Laboratory for Computer Science Research, Rutgers University.

McGuire, R., Birnbaum, L., and Flowers, M. (1981). "Opportunistic Processing in Arguments". In *Proceedings IJCAI-81*. Vancouver, B.C.

Polya, G. (1973). *Induction and Analogy in Mathematics*, Volumes 1 & 2. Princeton University Press, New Jersey.

Peterson, M. A. (1983). *New Tools for Reducing Civil Litigation Expenses*. Memo R-3013-ICJ. The Institute for Civil Justice, The RAND Corporation, Santa Monica, CA.

Reichman, R. (1981). "Modeling Informal Debates". In *Proceedings IJCAI-81*. Vancouver, B.C., August.

Rissland, E. L. (1984a). "Argument Moves and Hypotheticals". In *Proceedings First Annual Conference on Law and Technology*. University of Houston, Houston TX. To be included in a collection to be published by West Pub. Co. in 1985.

_____ (1981). *Example Generation*. Technical Report 81-24, Department of Computer and Information Science, University of Massachusetts, Amherst, MA.

_____ (1982). "Examples in the Legal Domain: Hypotheticals in Contract Law". In *Proceedings Fourth Annual Cognitive Science Society Conference*. Univ. of Michigan, Ann Arbor.

_____ (1983). "Examples in Legal Reasoning: Legal Hypotheticals". In *Proceedings IJCAI-83*. Karlsruhe, W. Germany.

_____ (1984b). "Hypothetically Speaking: Experience and Reasoning in the Law". To appear in *Cognitive Science*. An earlier version appeared in *Proceedings First Annual Conference on Theoretical Issues in Conceptual Information Processing*, Georgia Tech, March.

_____ (1984c). "The Ubiquitous Dialectic". In *Proceedings Sixth European Conference on Artificial Intelligence (ECAI-84)*, held in Pisa, Italy, September, published by Elsevier (North-Holland).

_____ (1978). "Understanding Understanding Mathematics". *Cognitive Science*, Vol. 2, No. 4.

Rissland, E. L., Valcarce, E. M., and Ashley, K. D. (1984). "Explaining and Arguing with Examples". In *Proceedings AAAI-84*, Austin, Texas.

Waterman, D. A., and Peterson, M. A. (1981). *Models of Legal Decision Making*. Memo R-2717-ICJ. The Institute for Civil Justice, The RAND Corporation, Santa Monica, CA.

ARTIFICIAL INTELLIGENCE IN THE PERSONAL COMPUTER ENVIRONMENT,

TODO AND TOMORROW

Tom J. Schwartz

Electronic Engineering Times
1470 Wildrose Way
Mt. View, CA 94043

ABSTRACT

It has been almost thirty years since the Dartmouth Conference on artificial intelligence. Since then, AI has emerged from a laboratory curiosity to a blossoming technology with world wide strategic implications. As this technology proliferates, the PC will become a major delivery vehicle for expert systems. The PC is already being used to deploy small expert systems and it´s power is bound to increase over the coming years. This panel will examine the history of the PC in AI, the current state of development and attempt to en vision future developments in the marriage of these technologies.

PERSONAL COMPUTER POWER

1981 was a watershed year for computers according to market research from INPUT Inc.. It was the first year that installed end user computing power (PC´s and individual workstations) equaled that of mainframe computers. It is estimated that in 1986 PC computing power alone will equal that of all other computers. This pattern will continue as PC´s become increasingly more powerful and the boundary between PC´s and workstations becomes forever blurred.

VISIONS OF THE PERSONAL COMPUTER

One of the first people to champion the concept of the personal computer was Dr. Alan Kay. Dr. Kay´s work on the Alto and the Dynabook along with others at the Xerox Palo Alto Research Center in the 1970´s was the basis of many of the developments we see today. These developments include: bit-mapped graphics, flat screens, personal workstations and networking. Dr. Kay´s Dynabook actually predicted the portable, flat personal computer. The Dynabook currently has many commercial realizations including machines by Apple, HP, Data General, Osborne, Morrow, Radio Shack, Grid, Convergent Technology and NEC. These machines, while not achieving the full performance envisioned by Dr. Kay, will surely be improved and fulfill his design goals.

AI AND THE PERSONAL COMPUTER, TODAY

Today many run time expert systems are being delivered on PC´s and dedicated workstation´s. One of the most ambitious is the GE Cats-1 expert system for assisting in diesel locomotive repair. This expert system is deployed on a dedicated workstation and contains over 1200 production rules. Cats-1 is an expert tutor. When used in conjunction with a video disk player it can show diagrams and training film sequences in conjunction with the consultation process. PUFF an expert system, written in EMYCIN is used to diagnose obstructive airway diseases. PUFF which originally consisted of 55 production rules, has been rewritten in Basic and is now being commercially provided on a system which incorporates diagnostic hardware and uses an Apple II as a delivery vehicle. Applied Expert Systems has already deployed an expert system on the IBM PC-XT, for use in the financial services industry. The use of PC delivery vehicles is easily predicted because of it´s large installed base and declining price. Workstations will continue to be popular because their power reduces expert system development time.

Development of expert systems on dedicated workstations has proceeded from the introduction of the LM 2 by Lisp Machines Inc. and continues unabated on workstations from a wide range of vendors. The evolution of expert systems on PC´s is now gaining momentum. There are now at least a dozen implementations of Lisp and PROLOG for the IBM PC. ExperTelligence has recently introduced a Lisp and a Smalltalk for the Macintosh with an OPS5 soon to be released. There are already two versions of OPS5 available for the IBM PC as well as a version of Smalltalk. The wide availability of the classic AI languages on the PC will lead to numerous expert systems being developed and deployed on the PC.

Many expert system shells, production rule languages and induction extraction tools have already been developed for the PC (table 1). These include PC implementations of EMYCIN and other English like production rule systems. Systems which learn by example, typically called inductive extraction systems are made available by three manufactures. RuleMaster by Radian is one of these systems and is unique because it combines inductive extraction and a production rule system in one product. A few of these tools also have hooks to other programs to further increase their power. The commercial success of these systems is demonstrated by SRI´s Series PC which has been used to develop and field an expert system for copier diagnosis and repair.

AI AND THE PERSONAL COMPUTER, TOMORROW

Many of these PC-based systems are suitable for the development of small expert systems (under 200 rules). These small systems are now being called "technician systems" and will find wide use in business and technical training. Induction extraction tools will enable users of spread sheets to build such technician systems and deploy them with little or no help from knowledge engineers. These systems will be used as learning curve accelerators and to disseminate routine expertise to less experienced members of an organization. They can also be used to enhance homogeneity in the decision making process thereby making delegation more effective.

The deployment of dedicated expert systems on hand-held calculator-like devices using application-specific integrated circuits will make expert systems as pervasive as the microprocessor in the world of tomorrow. Low cost expert systems will aid us in many of our daily activities such as: commuter route selection, business and investment decisions making, human interaction, personal health care and even wagering. Automated knowledge acquisition will allow every expert to become his own knowledge engineer. Even the breaking of the common sense barrier can be foreseen.

ACKNOWLEDGEMENTS

The author would like to thank the panelists Dr. Alan Kay, Stan Curtis and Robert Laddaga. Thanks to Amos Oshrin for the many fruitful discussions on AI and to all the software producers in table 1 for their cooperation.

ι ΘN THE FOLLOWING FOUR PAGES

The following systems run on IBM PC's

Company	Phone number	Product Name	Price	Written In	Maximum Rules	Source Available
Artelligence Inc. 1402 Preston Road Dallas TX 75240	214/437-0361	OPS5+	$3000.00	C	1500	Negotiable
California Intelligence 912 Powell Street San Francisco, CA 94108	415/391-4846	XSYS	$1,000.00	IQ LISP	Systems can be linked	Yes
Digitalk, Inc. 5200 W. Century Blvd. Los Angeles, CA 90045	213/645-1082	Methods	$250.00	Assembler & Basic	Systems can be linked	Included
Dynamic Master Systems P.O. Box 566456 Atlanta, GA 30356	404/425-7715	TOPSI	$75.00	Turbo Pascal	5,000 Systems can be linked	Negotiable
Expert Systems Int'l. 1150 First Ave. King of Prussia, PA 19406	215/337-2300	ES/P ADVISOR	$1895.00	PROLOG	400, systems can be linked	Negotiable
EXSYS, Inc. P.O. Box 75158 Albuquerque, NM 87194	505/836-6676	EXSYS	$295.00	C	5,000	Yes
General Research Inc. 7655 Old Springhouse Road McLean, VA 22102	703/893-5900	TIMM	$9,500.00	Fortran 77	500	Negotiable
Human Edge Software Inc. 2445 Farber Place Palo Alto, CA 94303	415/493-1593	Expert Ease	$695.00	UCSD Pascal	300, systems can be linked.	Negotiable
Level 5 Research Inc. 4980 S-A1A Melbourne Beach, FL 32951	305/729-9046	INSIGHT 1	$95.00	Turbo Pascal	2,000	Negotiable
PPE Inc. P.O. Box 2027 Gathersburg, MD 20879	301/977-1489	Expert System	$20.00	Basic	5,000	Provided
Radian 8501 MO-Pac Blvd Austin, TX 78766	512/454-4797	Rule Master	$5000.00	C	200, systems can be linked	Negotiable
Software A & E Inc. 1500 Wilson Blvd. Arlington, VA 22209	703/276-7910	KES	$4,000	IQ LISP	Systems can be linked	Negotiable

Table 1

The following systems run on IBM PC's

Company	Phone number	Product Name	Price	Written In	Maximum Rules	Source Available
SRI International 333 Ravenswoood Ave. Menlo Park, CA 94025	415/859-5889	SeriesPC	$15,000.00	IQ LISP	300, systems can be linked	Negotiable
TEKNOWLEDGE 525 University Ave Palo Alto, Ca 94301	415/327-6606	M1 M1A	$10,000 $2,500	PROLOG	300, systems can be linked	Negotiable
Texas Instruments P.O. Box 2909 Austin TX, 78769	800/527-3500	Personal Consultant	$3,000.00	IQ LISP	400, systems can be linked	Negotiable

This system runs on Macintosh by Apple Inc.

Company	Phone number	Product Name	Price	Written In	Maximum Rules	Source Available
ExperTelligence Inc. 559 San Ysidro Road Santa Barbara, CA 93108	805/969-7874	ExperOPS5	$195.00	ExperLisp	Systems can be linked	Negotiable

This system runs on Commodore 64, Apple II and Atari 800 machines.

Company	Phone number	Product Name	Price	Written In	Maximum Rules	Source Available
Ultimate Media Inc. 275 Magnolia Ave Larkspur, CA 94939	415/924-3644	Advisor	$95.00	Assembler	255	Negotiable

Table 1 cont.

The following systems run on IBM PC's

Company	Run time licences	Classes	Internal Editor	Hooks to the outside world	Comments
Artelligence Inc.	Available	Available	Yes	Yes	Implementation of OPS 5, a forward chaining system. Requires a mouse.
California Intelligence	Available	Included	Yes	Yes	Forward and backward chaining on an opportunistic basis. Supports uncertainty, math and direct LISP programming. Rule based. Requires IQ LISP
Digitalk, Inc.	Available	Coming	Yes	Yes	Implementation of Smalltalk. An object orientated programming language. Supports forward and backward chaining, math and confidence levels.
Dynamic Master Systems	Negotiable	Negotiable	Yes	No	Implementation of OPS 5, a forward chaining system.
Expert Systems Int'l.	*Used with PROLOG	Negotiable	No	No	Forward and backward chaining, is best used with their PROLOG. Can be compiled.
EXSYS, Inc.	Included	Negotiable	Yes	No	Rule based language supports math and confidence levels. Backward chaining.
General Research Inc.	Available	Coming	Yes	Negotiable	Induction extraction tool, can generate it's own examples. Generated rules can be deleted. Supports confidence levels.
Human Edge Software Inc.	Available	Coming	Yes	Planned	Induction extraction tool, forward chaining Supports confidence levels.
Level 5 Research Inc.	Available	Available	No	No	Rule based language, supports confidence levels. Backward chaining with limited forward chaining ability.
PPE Inc.	Included	Available	Yes	Yes	Rule based system, uses internal data base system for rule entry it supports confidence levels and math. Backward chaining. This is a freeware program.
Radian Inc.	Available	Included	Yes	Negotiable	Induction extraction tool. Rules can be edited. Supports math and confidence levels.
Software A & E Inc.	Negotiable	Coming	Yes	Yes	Supports multiple objects, inheritance, procedural control and Bayesian probabilities. Includes IQ LISP and supports direct LISP programming.
SRI International	Available	Included	No	No	Rule based language. Requires IQ LISP licence and supports direct LISP programming. Backward chaining.

Table 1 cont.

The following systems run on IBM PC's

Company	Run time licences	Classes	Internal Editor	Hooks to the outside world	Comments
TEKNOWLEDGE	Available	Available	No	M1 only	Rule based language, supports confidence levels, variables, math, and cycles. Backward chaining.
Texas Instruments	Available	Available	Yes	Yes	Rule based language will also support direct LISP programming. Includes IQ LISP. Backward chaining with multiple context structure, inheritance and confidence levels.

This system runs on the Macintosh by Apple Inc.

ExperTelligence Inc.	Available	Negotiable	Yes	Yes	Implementation of OPS 5, a forward chaining system. Requires ExperLisp, supports direct Lisp programming.

This system runs on Commodore 64, Apple II and Atari 800 machines.

Ultimate Media Inc.	Available	Available	Yes	Negotiable	Rule based language. Backward chaining with opportunistic forward chaining.

Table 1 cont.

PANEL: ARTIFICIAL INTELLIGENCE AND LEGAL RESPONSIBILITY

Margaret A. Boden - University of Sussex

Panellists: Margaret A. Boden (Chairman); Yorick Wilks;

Marshal S. Willick; Jay BloomBecker, Susan Nycum, Robert Kowalski

President Truman's famous remark --
"The buck stops here" -- was clearly
correct. It's much less clear where the
buck stops when one of the elements (I
almost wrote "people") in the chain of
responsibility is an AI-program.

There are two broad questions to be
asked. First, to what extent (if any)
can the making of -- and the responsibility for -- a given judgement or
decision, or mistake, be attributed to
a computer-program? And second, supposing
that responsibility cannot be attributed
to a program, with whom does it lie? Who
is legally responsible for what a program
does? Its user (person or institution,
professional or client), its programmers
(alive or dead), the domain-experts who
provided the knowledge-base ... who?

In the past, the law has derided
the notion that one might apply
psychological predicates to a machine.
Significantly, perhaps, this derision
has sometimes resulted in a person's
escaping responsibility for a clearly
dishonest, and prima facie illegal, action.
For example, on January 28th 1972, the
London Times reported a case in which the
defendant was found not guilty on the
grounds that "machines cannot be deceived".
A motorist had avoided paying a car-park
fee, by manually lifting the exit-barrier
instead of putting money in the exit-machine.
His defense counsel said "The plaintiff
has to be aware that deception has
taken place for this case to be proved.
It is impossible to deceive a machine
as it has no mind and consequently
cannot be aware of the deception as a
car park attendant might". This argument
was accepted by the Bench. In dismissing
the case (and seven other similar cases),
the Chairman said "Someone has got to be
deceived in a case like this, but
here this was not so." The penny-pinching
motorist got off, because the magistrates
ruled that it was in principle impossible
to apply psychological categories to
machines.

But car-park machines are different
from powerful computers, and lifting a
sixpenny barrier is different from
giving a medical diagnosis, or advizing
where to drill for oil. Is this
"no-nonsense" judgment of January 1972
a useful precedent for the sorts of
legal complications that are likely to
arise with the increasing public use
of complex AI-systems?

Hackers and laymen alike constantly
refer to programs -- and a fortiori to
AI-programs -- in psychological terms.
We speak of their reasoning, judgments,
evidence , knowledge, ignorance, and
mistakes. We speak of what they are
trying to do, and what priorities are
guiding their decisions. Is this
simply sentimentality, a sloppy way of
speaking which can and should be avoided
-- above all, in the law courts? If it is
not, if people as a matter of fact
do not or cannot avoid using such terms
in conceptualizing AI-systems, then
what implications follow? If we are
allowed to use some psychological words
when describing AI-programs, why not all?
If we use the language of knowledge and
inference, and even of choice, then
why not the language of purpose, effort
-- and even blame?

These questions are the focus of
the first two speakers on the Panel,
Yorick Wilks and Marshal Willick. The
ascription of legal responsibility
already varies depending on the "personal"
category of the putative offender: states,
companies, individuals, the sane, the
insane, children, pets, wild animals,
servants, and agents. What about
computer programs?

Current intuitions about this question
may seem absurd in a few years' time,
when people are more used to AI-applications.
Some of us may already feel uneasy with
the judgment that "Machines cannot be
deceived". If one wishes to prevent
people from wilfully feeding false

information to a computerised system should a person or institution be found, or a legal fiction invented, to suffer (sic) the deception? Or should we be willing to grant that machines can be deceived, though maybe not disappointed? Sherry Turkle, in her recent book The Second Self, reports that young children growing up in today's computer-culture spontaneously ascribe cognitive concepts (such as knowledge, intelligence, deciding, and mistake) to computers. They also use some conative concepts (like purpose, goal wanting, trying, and failing), at least in the context of "problem-solving" on the computer's part. But they adamantly refuse to use affective concepts (such as feeling and emotion), and they also jib at such motivational concepts as caring, and the like. Indeed, the child's concept of what it is to be "alive" is apparently changing, so that affective and conative concepts are stressed at the expense of "mere" cognition. Does this imply that the litigants of tomorrow will allow that computers can make mistakes, but cannot truly have intentions?

Among the intentions which human beings harbour -- and not only   in car-parks -- are some which are criminal. The third panelist, Jay BloomBecker, discusses a range of examples taken from the current case-law on computer crime. He relates these to some relatively novel issues that may arise, once "Fifth Generation" systems are available. When dealing with programs capable of some degree of "autonomous" reasoning, both crime-detection and the ascription of responsibility are likely to be even more difficult than they are today.

An enormous amount of litigation, at least in the USA, concerns medical issues. Clearly, legal problems will arise in connection with the use, and misuse, and even non-use, of medical expert systems. Various loci of responsibility seem prima facie to be possible: the doctor who uses the system; the patient who knows this is happening (caveat emptor?); the hospital administration; the programmer/s; the specialist physician who supplied the relevant diagnostic or prescriptive rules in the first place; the author of the textbooks used. Many of these individuals may already be dead. But, as Norbert Wiener pointed out, "old programs never die"; could a doctor or hospital be sued for relying on an old out-of-date program? Could they be sued for not using any program at all? The fourth Panellist, Susan Nycum, considers some of the legal problems likely to dog applications of AI in the medical domain.

Finally, Bob Kowalski contributes some thoughts on how "legal" expert systems might be used. His own work includes the building of a system which incorporates the British nationality laws (a prime late-twentieth-century example of Baroque art). What implications, if any, does this project have for the individual and society? Arguably, it would be an improvement on current practices to have nationality-decisions computerized. For a program cannot be affected by (Turkle's subjects would say, it does not care about) anyone's skin colour or physiognomy, or their manner of dress or speech. And arguably, the clarity of the programmed rules might help make clear any basic injustices in the programmed laws themselves: to change the world one has first to understand it. But where would responsibility lie if misclassification occurred? Should Kowalski start saving his pennies, in anticipation of his defense costs in the legal suits of the 'nineties?

And what about the legal implications of other legal or quasi-legal programs? If a program searching for precedents in case-law does not have analogical reasoning powerful enough to find the right one, to whom could the defendant complain? If governmental and other institutions formulate policies based on legal "decisions" made by in-house programs, who is to know, who is to care, and what can be done?

The panel promises many questions. As for answers, those are more elusive. But since the Panellists include both specialist AI-practitioners and professional attorneys who have already concerned themselves with these questions, we can expect a lively and informed discussion.

COMPUTER REPRESENTATION OF THE LAW

Robert Kowalski, Marek Sergot

Department of Computing, Imperial College, London

ABSTRACT

For the purposes of this discussion there are three main types of law: definitional, normative and case law; and there are a variety of computer representations of knowledge and problem-solving which can be applied to law. The social implications of representing the law by means of computer depend upon both the type of law and the technical means of computer implementation.

Definitional Law. Much of human law is already written down in the form of fairly precise rules, regulations and definitions. There is a separate legal tradition, represented by the work of Layman Allen in particular, which has long advocated the use of simplified forms of logic to represent law.

Recent work at Imperial College has confirmed many of Allen's expectations. We have succeeded in representing a significant portion of several British laws in Horn clause form and various of its extensions. Among other applications, we have been able to run a significant portion of the 1981 British Nationality Act, implemented in PROLOG on a small micro computer. The first subsection of the Act, for example, can be expressed in the conclusion-conditions form of a single Horn clause:

For every individual x, date y, individual z and section of the Act w,

x acquires British citizenship
by section 1.1.a on date y
   if x is born in UK on date y
   and y is after the Act takes effect
   and x has a parent z
   and z is a British citizen
      by section w on date y.

Not all of the Act can be easily represented in such a simple form. We have expressions such as:

"x is a citizen if ....
               and his mother is a citizen
               or would have been a citizen
               had she been male."

This requires a representation of metalevel reasoning about states of knowledge in addition to object level reasoning about the world. Investigation of such problems of representing legislation and legal reasoning has had a salutory effect on our more general study of knowledge representation and problem-solving.

Other applications of computational logic to the representation of definitional law at Imperial College include immigration law, social security law, grants to industry and a company's pension regulations.

Our studies suggest that such applications of computational logic are ripe for practical exploitation. Computational Logic can be used not only to assist the application of rules and regulations, but also to aid the process of determining the logical consequences of legislation before it is enacted. It can be used not only for rules which have legal authority but also for rules which are used by organizations to regulate their own internal affairs. Potential applications include the formalization and mechanization of tax law, company law, airline regulations and university examination regulations.

The technical opportunities are significant and may result in the development of systems which have great social impact. How can we be sure that the computer representation of laws is accurate; and therefore that the conclusions they imply are correct?

On the other hand, our experience suggests that precise formal representation of the rules actually clarifies and often simplifies them. This same point was made by Layman Allen as long ago as 1957. In the long term we may be so attracted by the benefits of formalization that the real question becomes: How can we be sure that the natural language statement of the law does justice to its legally binding formalization?

Normative Law. Many laws are concerned with permission, prohibition and obligation. Traditionally this is an area where modal deontic logic has been thought to be necessary. Typical examples are parking regulations, criminal law and the ten commandments.

We have only begun to scratch the surface in our investigation of such laws. However, our dissatisfaction with modal logics has forced us to consider how norms might be handled within the framework of classical computational logic.

It can be argued that to say that an action is prohibited is to say that some punishment or other sanction can be expected if the action is performed. Thus something like

    Prohibited(a)
    in a modal logic

becomes

    there exists p such that
    Expected-result(a p) and
    Undesirable(p)
    in a classical logic.

Whereas classical logic requires us to refer to sanctions explicitly, modal logic wraps them up within modal connectives. Classical logic allows and even encourages us to identify sanctions explicitly, e.g.:

    "Parking in a no parking zone
    carries a fine of £5."

But it also allows us to existentially quantify sanctions if we don't know or want to say what they are, e.g.:

    "Cheating on examinations is prohibited"

means there exists a punishment for cheating on exams.

We believe that such a treatment of deontic concepts is technically attractive. It increases expressive power and allows existing proof procedures for classical logic to be used for deriving logical consequences from assumptions. These arguments are the same as ones we have made elsewhere for treating notions of time and events explicitly within classical logic rather than implicitly within modal temporal logic.

Such a technical solution to the problems of representing and reasoning with norms may further our ability to implement practical systems. But encouraging explicit reference to sanctions may have undesirable social implications, whether or not computer implementation is involved. It may encourage us to weight up the relative costs and benefits of breaking the law. A parking fine is virtually no punishment for a wealthy businessman. A person who is terminally ill or about to commit suicide has no punishment to fear, unless he believes in an after life.

Case Law. A significant proportion of law in English speaking countries is based upon previous cases which create a precedent for the future. Even where precedents have no legal authority, previous cases must be considered for the sake of consistency and fairness. The need to reason by cases is also built into the lower levels of much definitional and normative law: What does it mean, for example,

    "to exercise reasonable effort",
    "not to have residence in the U.K.
     as one's primary intention of marriage"?

Such notions can only be determined by developing relevant criteria and applying them flexibly over a period of time.

Attempts to formalize case law in Artificial Intelligence have been attracted to its similarity with reasoning by analogy and with reasoning by means of frames.

However there is an alternative – which is to generate general rules by induction from previous cases and apply them to new cases in the future. Rules so generated do not, of course, have the same legal authority as rules which are explicitly written down. They may be too general or too narrow. They may conflict with other rules generated from other cases. Belief revision is needed to discriminate between conflicting rules arising from different precedents.

A certain amount of support for such a treatment of precedent can be obtained by referring to the arguments which are given when a decision is made in a particular case. If the case is to be a precedent for the future then the justification for the decision is usually made in general terms. In other words, the justification itself contains the main ingredients of a general rule.

We would argue that treating case law by generating tentative general laws is not only technically preferable to reasoning by analogy and by frames but it is also socially more desirable. It has the consequence that general rules can be cited to justify individual decisions. Since we know what the rules are, they can be scrutinized and changed. Transformations which reason by analogy or frames are inscrutable and therefore beyond social criticism.

Legal Expert Systems. The state of technology is rapidly reaching a stage where the computer representation and processing of law will make legal expertise available to a much broader spectrum of the community.

In general this is to be welcomed. It will give more people better legal and financial advice. It will help more people to understand the law, so that they can make better, more informed decisions.

But there are dangers too. There are the obvious dangers: Who is responsible if the computer makes a mistake? Less obvious perhaps, and more insidious therefore: Will we bother to listen to the computer's explanation? Will we bother to understand the issues involved? Or will be come to rely on the machine to do our thinking for us?

CONSTITUTIONAL LAW AND ARTIFICIAL INTELLIGENCE: THE POTENTIAL LEGAL RECOGNITION OF COMPUTERS AS "PERSONS"

Marshal S. Willick
Attorney at Law
Thorndal, Backus, Maupin & Manoukian
333 North Rancho Drive, Ste. 333
Las Vegas, NV 89106

ABSTRACT

American Constitutional law grants the status of "person" to the members of certain groups, but denies that status to other groups. Various legal analogies could be used to determine whether such status should be extended to computer systems and, if so, what limitations should be placed upon that recognition.*

The concept of legal "personality" in United States constitutional law has changed considerably over the years. An ever-increasing number of groups of ascertainable entities have been recognized as persons under the law, and the rights and obligations accruing to the members of those groups have changed more than they have remained constant. The general question is thus presented of whether computers might be recognized as persons; it is submitted that the correct answer is a qualified "yes."

The legal histories of several groups, such as blacks and women, have followed the pattern of their initial "recognition" as legal persons, followed by a slow accretion of rights and obligations. Viewed another way, the initial recognition of the members of these groups started a lengthy period during which the legal gap between them and previously-recognized persons narrowed.

Decision-makers have used various rationales over the years in extending legal recognition to new groups. The individual decisions tend to reflect the values of their times and do not shed much light on the essence of legal personality. Each such extension, however, constituted an acknowledgment that the individual entities being considered were more like the persons doing the considering than like the property belonging to those persons. As a group, those extensions mark an expanding societal definition of "person."

It may fairly be said that, as time has passed, the test of personality has focused more on behavior than on appearance, and more on mental traits than on physical ones. Western thinking has come to disfavor tests of personality based on "status" (ownership of property, religious affiliation) or "structure" (gender, race); those tests were invoked, and defeated, almost every time a new group was added to the roster of persons. Accordingly, recognition has generally been extended to groups whose members have demonstrated the capacity to behave in a manner indicating that they <u>think</u> more like legal persons than like anything else.

The initial question is therefore whether there could exist circumstances such that a decision-maker could examine the behavior of a computer system and decide that the machine had crossed the threshold of legal personality. It seems nearly inevitable that the issue will arise in our increasingly computerized society; science fiction literature abounds with proposed factual scenarios in which that legal issue could be presented. The real question is whether current or foreseeable law provides a plausible foundation for a determination of computer personality.

It is possible that a decision concerning computer personality could come from the executive or legislative branches of government. Popular opinion can find expression through those channels when the judiciary is unwilling or incapable of treating ascertainable entities as persons even though society as a whole perceives them as such. An example of such a legislative determination is the Twenty-sixth Amendment (forbidding discrimination against 18-21 year olds).

Perhaps the most obvious historical example of recognition by executive mandate was the freeing of black slaves who had previously been considered

---

*This position paper is largely abstracted from Willick, <u>Artificial Intelligence: Some Legal Approaches and Implications</u>, AI Mag., Summer, 1983, at 5, which contains authorities and background information.

lawfully recoverable items of property. Congress at one time declared itself incapable of emancipation, and the courts mainly addressed the impact of local recaption statutes and the Fugitive Slave Laws upon local kidnapping laws. An essentially Executive action (a rarity in the field of extensions of legal personality), swiftly followed by a series of Constitutional amendments, presumed to change the slaves' legal status in one step from that of ascertainable individual items of property to that of fully franchised persons.

In common law systems, however, most "law" comes from the decisions of courts. Disputes arising from novel circumstances are reconciled by courts that attempt to draw comparisons between the facts of the cases before them and the facts of cases previously decided. Touched on below are a few of the possible analogies provided by history that could be seized upon by courts seeking to resolve the question of computer personality. Which analogy is utilized in a given case could well determine the result of the legal dispute.

It is submitted that the first computers to attain "personhood" will do so individually, if at all, because they will be forced to prove that they are more than the "mere machines" they will be presumed to be. Courts are likely to hesitate before extending to computers the legal precept that "all men are created equal," because even today they can be purposefully designed to have any of a broad range of operating characteristics and capabilities.

Given the enormous variety of the machines called "computers," even proponents of computer personality will probably concede that some will possess the necessary characteristics for that status while others will not. Many problems, such as the evaluation of computers of the same model, the impact of a capacity for significant machine learning, etc., remain to be addressed. Such questions, however, will most probably be decided through use of the terminology and tests developed in other legal disputes.

Courts seeking a definition of "person" might look to the abortion decisions, which draw distinctions based on the degree of individual development (trimesters); by analogy, any individual computer exceeding a minimum behavioral capacity roughly equating fetus "viability" would be presumed to be a person. As with the abortion decisions, a single such decision concerning computer personality could affect many more persons than the parties before the court.

When a human person dies, he loses all of his rights. The law in this area tends to set an over-inclusive minimum, so that any human but one who can be shown to have died tends to be defined as "alive." Given the recent emergence of "brain death" as a critical factor, and since many computers today can exhibit far more "intelligent" behavior than that of comatose human beings (who do enjoy legal recognition), a legal minimum standard test of personality could probably be satisfied by a computer system in the proper circumstances.

The emergence of the modern corporation provides the most subtle means by which computer systems might achieve legal recognition. Corporations have names, can buy and sell property, and can commit crimes, but they cannot be drafted, be married, or vote. They are persons, but they are owned, constituting a recognized class of non-human persons that has legal rights and obligations peculiarly tailored to the unusual attributes of its members.

An analogy between such "artificial" persons and computer systems will appear less strained than comparisons with human beings. Additionally, to the degree that the operations of a corporation can be computerized, the corporation and the computer would effectively be the same entity: no legal change would be required for such de facto recognition of computer personality.

Corporations provide an example of the concept of partial personality, whereby an ascertainable entity may be recognized as a legal person for one purpose but not another. The concept has many applications and is not limited to non-humans; certain laws treat fetuses as "persons" for the purpose of inheritance, while others provide that the abortion of such fetuses is not generally to be considered murder.

The concept is applied in many ways in modern society. Minors, for example, slowly accrete rights and obligations as they grow older because of their presumed capacities, while rights are removed from the retarded and the insane when their behavior proves to be too far below or outside the societal minimum. The legal system is thus equipped with a variety of approaches with which to decide the extent and variety of rights that should be given to computers that are recognized as persons.

Computer systems that perform increasingly complicated tasks in an increasingly competent manner will be thrust onto these shifting sands of constitutional presumptions, tests, and standards.

Since there does not seem to be an analytically sound test of "personality" that will exclude computer systems which behave intelligently, the question of legal recognition will remain one of "when" and not "if" until and unless some absolute limitations on the abilities of such machines can be demonstrated. Once computer systems can satisfy established legal tests of personality, either a valid ground of distinction between them and humans will have to be found, or the distinction will have to be abandoned as mere prejudice.

Current artificial intelligence research increases the need for a prompt examination of these problems. Courts have already begun to impose on certain professionals the requirement of use of certain computer systems.* As applied artificial intelligence techniques cause computer systems to behave in ways traditionally associated with human intelligence, the likelihood of legal scrutiny of the status of those systems increases.

No uniformly recognized definition exists for intelligence, so it is not surprising that there are at least four different (and largely contradictory) definitions of "artificial" intelligence. While there appear to be many instances in which measurable intelligence is unnecessary to recognition of legal personality (corporations, comatose humans, etc.), such recognition appears to be mandated under modern tests whenever such intelligence is present.

A traditional legal test asks whether "reasonable men could differ" as to a proposed question. If they could, the test allows the question to be submitted to a judge or jury as a question of fact rather than one of law. Given the many legal tests of personality, it is submitted that there is (or soon will be) a question of fact as to whether a computer which appears to be exhibiting intelligent behavior is a "person" under the law. Given the appropriate facts and a sympathetic jury, that question will at some point be answered in the affirmative.

Developments in biotechnology could lead to recognition of certain computer systems even if society proves unwilling

---

*For a citation-saturated discussion of the ramifications of professional computerization, see Willick, Professional Malpractice and the Unauthorized Practice of Professions: Some Legal and Ethical Aspects of the Use of Computers as Decision-Aids, which is due to be published this Fall in Rutgers Computer and Technology Law Journal.

to recognize computers per se. Humans do not endanger their legal recognition by using devices to enhance or replace parts of themselves; the legal test is subtractive, and it presumes continued recognition. Metaphysical considerations aside, only technological (as opposed to scientific) barriers appear to exist to the eventual direct integration of human brains and computers. No recognition-endangering event would occur by such integration; a "computer-enhanced" person would retain recognition.

Presuming that the computer could be made able to perform various tasks as the human lost the ability to do so, no behavioral differences would appear as the human parts failed. Because the traditional legal test looks to behavior, might the mechanical remnant of such a person retain legal recognition?

Those arguing otherwise would face the difficult task of convincing a court that the combination had lost its right to recognition at some time of biological failure, despite its continuation of its normal activities. The law abhors the removal of rights absent behavior outside of or below certain minimum requirements, going so far as to rule that permanently comatose humans remain persons. Given the foreseeable behavioral capacity of computer systems, it is submitted that mechanical remnants of human/computer combinations will retain legal recognition, at least where the takeover of once-human functions is gradual.

Such developments would present the difficult legal question of how to distinguish between two computer systems, one of which slowly took over the functions of a human brain, and the other of which simply rolled off of an assembly line. Presuming equal behavioral capacities (or even close ones; the law recognizes both geniuses and idiots), no valid ground appears to exist for the denial of legal recognition to the system that was never connected to a human brain.

CONCLUSION

Computers today are increasingly behaving in ways traditionally identified as exhibiting consciousness, understanding, and learning. It may prove impossible in the future to draw a valid legal distinction between humans and computers, either because of the increased behavioral capacity of the latter group, or because the two groups will be literally, physically, inseparable. At that time, constitutional law will recognize at least some computer systems as "persons."

FIFTH GENERATION COMPUTER CRIME LAW

By Jay BloomBecker
4053 JFK Library – California State University
5151 State University Drive LA CA 900320

Director, National Center for Computer Crime Data

ABSTRACT

As the "shock absorber" of social change, criminal law will serve to deal with the most troublesome results of the progress in articial intelligence and expert systems research and applications. We will have to redefine crimes against the person, property, public morality, and the public order. To do this will require considerable change in our standards of culpability, computer performance, and the functions of punishment.

Introduction: Why bother with computer crime law?

1. Good social programming anticipates worst case scenarios

If computers, communications, and their many social manifestions are seen as the vehicles of "progress," computer crime law may well be seen as a "shock absorber" with which society tries to avoid the greatest disruptions along the way.

As so thoroughly and insightfully noted in Langdon Winner's Autonomous Technology, the fear of present and future technological change is already a considerable reality. From Frankenstein to WarGames a ready market has existed for those works of fiction suggesting that the development of technology holds dangers as well as promises. In a rational world, the law of computer crime would be designed to provide the best tools possible to minimize these dangers.

2. The law must be goosed

Anyone reviewing the 37 state computer crime laws collected in the National Center for Computer Crime Data's Computer Crime Law Reporter might easily harbor doubts as to the laws' rationality. Couch argues that the laws' focus is seldom on those areas in which law enforcement personnel report the greatest need for help. Seven years of debate have failed to dislodge any substantive computer crime legislation from the U. S. Congress. Perhaps a look at the problems of tomorrow will conduce towards convincing the potentially politically powerful partisan of progress in computing that his or her help is needed by those politicans in power today.

3. Progress is not inevitable in any generation, not even the fifth.

Bruce Nussbaum, writing in The World After Oil, summarizes his fairly straightforward extrapolation of current computer criminality thus: "The crimes of the 80's and 90's will increasingly involve the theft of high technology through tapping electronic transmissions. People, companies, and the government itself will be both victim and perpetrator." [at 223]

More globally, Professor Winner argues that our current view of the computer "revolution" is based on what he calls "mythinformation," which he defines as "the almost religious conviction that a widespread adoption of computers and communication sustems and broad access to electronic information will automatically produce a better world for humanity."

["Mythinformation in the high-tech era," IEEE Spectrum June 1984, at 91.]

Computer crime law can play an important role in shaping the future of the computer revolution. It can serve to communicate and create computer security for all of us.

4. Computer crime law is a good mental isometric

Thinking seriously about computer crime requires thinking seriously about our values, an invaluable exercise in an age as devoid of moral consensus as the computer age seems to be.

A. What shall the strategy of a fifth generation computer crime law be?

Criminal law is not created in a vacuum. Bassouni acknowledges that criminal law operates as an instrument of social control: "it employs strategies of coercion to obtain certain goals. That postulate is predicated upon the assumption that society having made a value judgment on the significance of certain interests it seeks to protect and preserve resorts to coercion to achieve its essential goals ." [Substantive Criminal Law p. 77.]

Consider the following expressions of the values embodied in criminal law:
The American Law Institute Model Penal Code defines the general purposes of provisions defining criminal offenses thus:

"To forbid and prevent conduct that unjustifiably and inexcusably inflicts or threatens substantial harm to individual and public interests"

The Yugoslavian Criminal Code reflects both similarities and differences:

"This Code protects from violence, arbitrary treatment, economic exploitation and other socially dangerous acts, the person of citizens, their rights and freedoms..."

1. What interests shall computer crime law protect?

A fairly standard categorization of the interests protected by the criminal law lists crimes against persons; property; public morality; and the public order.

In predicting the tasks of fifth generation computer crime law we must consider what new rights and assets will arise in a decade or two of computer breakthroughs, and which of these will require the protection afforded by criminal law.
1a. Crimes against the person

The most serious crime against the person is homicide. A man was crushed to death by the operation of an industrial robot in a Kawasaki factory near Kobe Japan in 1981. [New York Times Dec. 13, 1981 Section 3, p. 27, col. 1]

In fiction, a woman died when a utility mistakenly turned off her heat [Intruder by Louis Charbonneau]

Professor Gemignani asks: "Could 'Hal,' the computer of the film 2001 be tried for murder? How about Hal's systems programmer or his builder?" [Product Liability and Software 31 Defense Law Journal (1982) at 335, 368]

While those questions lurk, ask yourself whether invasion of privacy qualifies as an "invasion of personal security" deserving the protection of criminal law proscribing crimes against the person.

Hints of future answers to these questions have recently surfaced in two of the more progressive computer crime laws enacted in Virginia and Connecticut.

Section 18.2-152.7 of the Code of Virginia defines "Personal Trespass by Computer" to cover use of a computer without authority "with the intent to cause physical injury to an individual" [Computer Crime Law Reporter I-73; also see Connecticut Public Act 84-206 Section 5, enhancing punishments for computer crimes in which the perpetrator recklessly engaged in conduct which created a risk of serious physical injury to another person. Computer Crime Law Reporter I-10]

Section 18.2-152.5 of the Code of Virginia criminalizes "Computer invasion of privacy." [Computer Crime Law Reporter I-73]

1b. Crimes against property

Most computer crime laws focus on theft-type offenses and destruction of computers or computer system components. Questions arose about the adequacy of pre-computer crime laws to protect intangible assets [eg. P. v. Home Insurance, 121 P. 2d 491 (1978) holding information itself not the subject of theft - (a non-computer situation)]

Computer services are increasingly valued, and with the increase has been a growing awareness of the need to create specific protections for certain services. Wisconsin and Missouri have created additional penalties for damage to computers used by utilities, certain government operations, transportation, or other important uses. [Missouri Revised Statutes Sections 569.093-569.099, Computer Crime Law Reporter I-41-44; Wisconsin Statutes Annotated Section 943.70, Computer Crime Law Reporter I-77-

80.]

1c. Crimes against public morality

Though seriously (and I believe appropriately) undercut by a growing appreciation of the right to privacy, the criminal law continues to include attempts to impose moral values on society,
often even in the absence of substantial harm to those committing the proscribed acts or to society at large. It is in this area that we find laws against certain intoxicants, certain sexual practices, and gambling.

Genesis magazine recently offered its readers a guide to "X-Rated Computers," explaining "You can use your computer as an information source or as a direct line to some really kinky folks. If Joseph Weizenbaum thought his little brainchild Eliza obscene when used to get people's heads straight, what would he think of a a fifth generation "Eliza Domuch," a program designed to engage its users in sexual dialog?

Increasingly the concept of "addiction" is finding its way into conversations about computing, usually in the context of condemnation of "hackers." If the August 1984 Vanity Fair is right, and computers are the drugs of the future, will anti-computer addiction measures also be offered by the concerned Presidents' wives in the fifth generation? ["Wired to God" by Frank Rose, at 40.]

Lest we dismiss such concerns as beneath the dignity of the great and liberal city in which this conference is held contemplate the intersection of computer sex and computer addiction suggested by the movie Brainstorms. Though certainly beyond the current plans of the fifth generation, the possibilities for computer-aided and augmented masturbation are quite intriguing, and certain to arouse more than its proponents, if effective.

1d. Crimes against the maintainence of social order

Most subtle and least discussed of all types of crime that might involve greater risks in the fifth generation is corruption of the information on which modern society depends.

As litigation support becomes increasingly computerized, obstruction of justice by dishonest retrieval techniques or secret filing systems will become a problem comparable to the keeping of second sets of books.

Public records are increasingly computerized. Their security will increasingly demand criminal protections.

Maryland is the first state known to the National Center which has specifically noted the need to protect public records from falsification through computer abuse [Laws of Maryland Section 45A, Computer Crime Law Reporter I-35]

B What acts shall fifth generation copmputer crime law deem criminal?

Since criminal law is coercive, and its stigma severe, its use is reserved for those whose behavior demonstrates culpability. The American Law Institute Model Penal Code limits guilt to those cases in which a person acts purposely, knowingly, recklessly or negligently.

As our references to "Hal," the 2001 computer demonstrate, the question of action becomes thorny when "artificial intelligence" enters the picture.

Three issues seem paramount:

1. Determination of the standard of care to be required-

Where the basis of a criminal charge is some form of failing to exercise adequate caution, recklessness or criminal negligence are required for criminal liability. Bassiouni notes "[m]ost statutes consider 'recklessness' as gross or serious disregard for the safety of others and require proof of conscious awareness of the condition created or of the potential consequences." [id. at 272] In Autonomous Technology Professor Winner argues that unpredictability is central to artificial intelligence. Where, we may ask with concern, does this leave criminal law? Is the use of an unpredictable instrumentality disregard for safety per se?

If we consider the law of vehicular homicide, an answer involving lower standards of care is suggested. Consider, for example, the doctrine in some states allowing failure to observe a traffic rule to constitute evidence of the driver's culpable negligence. Will failure to observe computer security regulations have the same effect?

2. Determining ultimate

responsibility-

Professor Gemignani suggests that computers may become the subject of regulation similar to that of nuclear energy: "If computers reach that point where they are so pervasive (and intrusive) in our lives that a massive failure of an important computer system could have consequences as disastrous as that of a failure of a nuclear reactor, perhaps a Price-Anderson Act for computers would not be unthinkable." [id. at 369 n. 105]

Expanding the concept, one may well ask whether the increased reliance on computers to perform the work previously done by professionals, as seems quite implicit in the growth of "expert systems," will not create just the sort of situation Gemignani suggests. In fact, he points out that we already have seen dangerous situations involving computer uses for air traffic control, nuclear plant monitoring, spaceship navigation, and interpretation of military data.

These increased uses of computers pose several political questions: Who will bear the risk of serious damage resulting from inadequate computer performance? Who will bear the burden of proving what occurred? What sort of standards of care will be imposed on users of computers? How will the user distribute the responsibilities to meet those standards of care among the personnel involved in programming, maintaining, operating, and securing those systems?

One possible answer is found in the predictions of Norval Morris, Dean of the University of Chicago Law School. "I predict that in our Third Century an Administrative Law of Crime will be devised....[for] our efforts to apply the criminal law to industrial, economic, health and welfare offenses." ["Criminal Law," in American Law: The Third Century at 95-99.]

It should be clear that the question of ultimate responsibility is a political one. Thus it is likely to be decided in the context of disaster putting the computer industry in a bad light. Will foresightful industry leaders prepare adequate safeguards to prevent such calamity from occurring? This is never an easy task, and is especially difficult in times of rapid and highly competitive economic expansion.

3. Assessment of causality-

A practical issue remains: proof.

Though we fear death through the agency of a robot, I suspect the much more difficult question is determining responsibility when death is the result of the performance of an undocumented program module. In a footnote discussing the Japanese crusher robot mentioned previously the author notes "there was some thought that it might have been caused by a defect in the computer program." [S. Lanoue, "Computer Software and Strict Products Liability," 20 San Diego Law Review, 439 (1983)] Thus far security functions like audit trails and good documentation have lagged far from the cutting edge of computer science. Is it reasonable to assume that the priorities will shift in the fifth generation? How often can you convince a salesperson to balance the checkbook rather than try to make another sale, or a scientist to delay an experiment in order to back up the results of the last one?

C. How shall fifth generation computer crimes be punished?

Punishment is central to the difference between civil and criminal law. Thus a major issue for the fifth generation computer crime law is the question of what to do with the criminal once we have convicted him or her. Unfortunately, little on the horizon indicates that society has moved past lex talionis. Though not so brutal as the Moslems who are still decapitating criminals, seizures of personal computers by FBI agents have a similar tone to them when done without process of law involving a judicial finding of guilt.

1. Theoretical problems

We have succeeded in refuting theories of correction, not supplanting them. Retribution is generally considered primitive and irrational, though it seems slightly on the rise. Rehabilitation is increasingly seen as an unfulfilled dream. (Given the abject corruption of prison environments, this should come as little surprise.) Deterrence of those inclined to commit crimes is still argued in every jurisdiction trying to decide whether to abolish --- or reinstitute -- the death penalty. The only reasonably clear observation is that incarceration incapacitates those who are so punished for the duration of their stay behind bars. (Unfortunately crimes within prison, including computer crimes, are not at all without precedent.)

We must, of course, declare certain behavior illegal even if none of our strategies seems particularly effective. One purpose of the Yugoslavian Criminal Code is "to exercise educational influence on other people [than the offender] in order to deter them from committing criminal offenses; [and] to influence development of social morals and social discipline among citizens." [Goldstein, Dershowitz, and Schwartz, Criminal Law at 724.]

Hart states a similar educational goal for American criminal law:
"To declare the obligation of every competent person to comply with (1) those standards of behavior which a responsible individual should know are imposed by the conditions of community life if the benefits of community living are to be realized, and (2) those further obligations of conduct, specially declared by the legislature, which the individual either in fact knows or has good reason to know he is supposed to comply with, and to prevent violations of these basic obligations of good citizenship by providing for public condemnation of the violations and appropriate treatment of the violators." [Hart, "The Aims of the Criminal Law," 23 Law and Contemporary Problems 401, 440 (1958) in Goldstein, Dershowitz and Schwartz, id.]

2. Practical resolutions

Undeterred by a lack of theory, much of the practice in computer crime punishment resembles the old football cheer, "hit 'em again harder, harder." Statutes calling for fines up to three times the property taken, enhancements of punishment for use of computers to commit other crimes, and special provisions for civil suits by crime victims have all been tried in recent computer crime laws.

As a former prosecutor I have seen the increased bureaucratization of criminal law. The process is typified by high volume case processing, high premiums on rapid turnover of cases, and most consistently,increased pleas bargaining. The paucity of cases of computer crime resulting in appeals underscores the universality of this trend.

Conclusion

The fifth generation will act as a magnifying glass, showing even more clearly the difficulties society faces trying to predict what needs to be protected, from whom, from what, and how.

RESPONSIBLE COMPUTERS?

Yorick Wilks

Computing Research Laboratory
New Mexico State University
Las Cruces, NM 88003

ABSTRACT

The position paper argues that, on one coherent philosophical position, we can now say that computers have human attributes, and then go on to dicuss the route by which blame and punishment might be applied to them, and how they might be said to take on social obligations.

A. Human attributes and machines

It is a fact of common observation that people now anthropomorphise computers in their speaking and writing, and not only computers as such, but even their parts: "What the color chip is telling you is that it's in the background mode" a vision hacker said to me last week. That is no different from what we say of human wholes and parts, as in "my stomach is telling me it's lunchtime", and so such attributions do not, of themselves, have any consequences or relevance, legal or general.

But they are, nonetheless, a necessary **precondition** of any attribution of legal or other responsibility beyond the human pale. Sherry Turkle's recent book (1984) has given the sociological imprimatur, if it were needed, to the claim that usage is now like that, especially among small children.

More importantly, the fact that adults now talk and write that way has nothing to do with Turing tests and "being fooled by simulations", as some people acquainted with the historical AI literature might think: for the forms of words in questions are used by people who have never seen any plausible language or reasoning task performed by a machine, or rather have seen no such performances other than simulated fictions on TV and films. Given that TV viewers vastly outnumber computer scientists, it is those "performances" that are, I suspect, the driving forces behind the language changes under discussion.

But those changes themselves are perfectly real and, for anyone of a Dennetist tendency in philosophy (if I may use that word to refer to one who gives theoretical priority to successful explanatory vocabulary rather than underlying or direct ontological evidence: (Dennett 1978) machines may therefore now have certain key human characteristics. If that is so, then it may be the peg on which to hang any possible legal responsibility of machines or programs. But before turning to that, let me take a different case for comparison.

B. Dogs

In English common law, at least, there is already a well established and still operative precedent for a category of entities which are neither human, nor totally without responsibility. They are animals like dogs, which certainly pass the test of having appropriate attirbutions made to them, at least by a large part of the population. They are quite distinct from **ferae naturae** like tigers: if you keep a tiger and it does any wrong, you are responsible, for they are taken to be simple machines in your keeping. With dogs the situation is more complex and normally, though inaccurately, summed up in the cliche "every dog is allowed one bite"; the point being that a dog is not deemed savage simply because it bites someone once. It may, like us, be acting out of character. Whereas to be a savage dog is to be a habitual biter and in particular to have a savage character known to its owner. Tigers are not to be thought of as having characters to act out of: they are just machines that bite. This notion of having a character one could act out of is tightly bound up with the notions of moral and legal responsibility and blame.

Dogs are blamed and punished in analogous ways to people--in some countries both can be executed—and that is only because they share very similar (though importantly different) physiological structures. The problem with machines and their programs, even if we were to squeeze them into the same category as dogs, would be how to blame and punish them.

C. Responsibility

The difficulty can be avoided by always identifying humans, standing behind the machines and programs as it were, to carry the blame, in the sense in which there are always real humans standing behind agents and behind companies, which also have the legal status of non-human responsible entities ("anonymous persons" in much European law). In the case of companies with errant machines, the companies themselves (i.e. not their individual directors or shareholders) are responsible for a broad class of failures of their products and non-criminal actions by their agents, acting within the general futherance of company policy (see Lehman-Wilzig 1981). In those cases the punishment/destruction of machines and software packages would be merely a matter of internal company discipline and of no outside interest.

In most situations now imaginable, it will not be too hard to identify indivudals, if there is a need to do so, behind programs and machines. However, things may become more tricky as time goes on, and the simple substitution of responsible people for errant machines harder to achieve. There are two obvious possibilities here: first, there are already in existence enormous bodies of software, such as major bank and airline programs, that are the work of large numbers of individuals, that have been constantly edited and updated over many years, and are probably now without any adequate documentation. Those who could have written the documentation may well be dead. Such gigantic kludges function up to a point and it would be difficult and expensive to replace them. However, those who work with them are often unsure why they do what they do, or what they might do in the future. Errors committed by such software will be very hard to attribute to particular responsible individuals.

Secondly, it is a small step from that present reality to a future situation where we accord the machine itself greater authority over the state it is currently in than we now do to information gained from diagnostics, traces or even looking in its cabinet (see Wilks 1976). The complete print-out of the program run by such a machine may be horrendously long, unannotated and effectively structureless. This situation can approximate as closely as you like to that of the human brain, where print-out is pretty useless, as far as establishing what "state" a person is in, and we tend, therefore, to give great authority, in courts and elsewhere, to what people say about their own states of mind, particularly for the attribution of a "guilty" state of mind, the **mens re**. That movement, through impenetrable software to ultimately inadequate diagnostics, is, I think, the progression by which blame (for machines) might creep in, despite the attempts by advocates of more perspicuous programming styles to keep it out.

D. Punishment

But what can we say of "machine punishment"? A machine can be turned off and smashed and the software will either go with it, or can be burned separately, provided we know we have **all** the copies! Only if some notion of computer blame had already crept in by the route I mentioned earlier, could we consider any of this destruction (or, more moderately perhaps, compulsory court-ordered edits to a program) as punishment. And then the issue for a court might be to decide whether to punish the software or the hardware, which would be in keeping with the speculations of the many philosophers who have toyed with the analogy hardware:software::body:soul-or-mind. But the weaknesses of that approach are well known by now in an era of machines almost hardwired for special software languages.

Anyone who finds something lacking in Joan of Arc's cry at the stake, that they were punishing her body but not her soul, will tend towards a position that persons are **embodied minds-or-souls,** and that perhaps only those can be punished, even in principle. It would then be a short step to a position that, if we were ever to talk of punishing intelligent machines, given that they could be blamed, it would have to be as machine-embodied software. It is a long way from the Lisp and Prolog machines of today, together with a little specialised speech and vision hardware, to a notion of a fully (and ineluctably) machine-embodied program. But that is the technical road we are going down, and it may also be the only one down which machine crime and punishment can possibly lie.

E. Obligation

In conclusion, let me return to the issue of "obligation" seen, as it were, from the machine's point of view: not just as a matter of "under what circumstances do we attribute responsibility, and hence blame, to machines?", which is what I have called the Dennetist question, but also as a matter of how would we introduce into programs the notion of "obligatory" or responsible action. This matter is far less speculative than the last, and one might say that current work in AI gives a fairly clear view of the way forward.

The issue is not just one of representations, as many AI issues are, but of cerrain actions by the machine being the acceptance of obligations, and marked internally as such. Searle (1969) set out bodies of rules for such notions as "acts of promising": conditions that must obtain, in terms of beliefs and goals, for a promise to have been made by an utterance. Versions of these rules have been programmed within AI, and have in certain ways improved upon Searle's work, particularly in establishing a clear notion of a hearer's/machine's computation of its own point of view of things, whereas his original rules are a mixture of speaker's and hearer's points of view.

What is worth noting here is that such work has normally been treated in AI as analyses of, say, "promising": as a linguistic mapping task from utterances such as "I'll give you $5 next week" to inner entities such as **PROMISE**. But what is often ignored is that Searle intended his work not as a linguistic task only, or even principally, but as an exploration of the foundations of moral obligation, i.e. of promising not "promising". One of the successful adaptations that Speech Act work has undergone in AI, rather than in linguistics or philosophy, has been to show the intimate connection between such

analyses and planning theory. Such work could now go one step further towards Searle's original goal within the theory of obligation (whether or not he would concede it) by incorporating, within the planning aspects of Speech Act representations, the notion of actions deemed obligatory by a system for itself, and the tight connexion between such deeming and the external "social acts" that express the taking on of obligation e.g. "I, robot, swear...".

REFERENCES

[1] Dennett, D. Brainstorms, Bradford Books, Mass., 1978.

[2] Lehman-Wilzig, S.N. "Frankenstein unbound: towards a legal definition of Artificial Intelligence", Futures, 1981, pp.107-119.

[3] Searle, J. Speech Acts, Cambridge University Press, Cambridge, 1969.

[4] Turkle, S. The Second Self, Granada, London, 1984.

[5] Wilks, Y. "Putnam and Clarke and Body and Mind", Brit. Jnl. Philos. of Sci., 26, 1976, pp.213-225.

EMPOWERING AUTOMATIC DECISION-MAKING SYSTEMS:
GENERAL INTELLIGENCE, RESPONSIBILITY AND MORAL SENSIBILITY
Henry Thompson
Department of Artificial Intelligence
and
Programme in Cognitive Science
School of Epistemics
University of Edinburgh
Edinburgh EH8 9NW
SCOTLAND

0. Introduction

Before a human being begins to make decisions and take unsupervised actions in a professional capacity which significantly affect others, s/he is usually explicitly empowered to do so, by means of some socially and/or legally sanctioned process of training and evaluation.

At a time when it is being suggested that computational artifacts may take up roles with significant human impact, ranging from medical diagnosis to automatic launch on warning of nuclear missiles, it becomes appropriate to ask whether sufficient thought has been given to the question of establishing empowerment processes for such systems if they are to act autonomously without human supervision.

I believe that a careful and responsible investigation of this question will lead to a paradox - that the sorts of special-purpose, focussed systems which we can imagine being within reach technically will be manifestly and necessarily incapable of satisfying certain necessary criteria for empowerment, despite our inability to objectively define such criteria or design explicit tests to implement them. And this inability will in turn frustrate us if in the unforeseeably distant future we are finally in a position to build general-purpose, broadly intelligent systems*.

In what follows I consider first the proximate form of the paradox, as it applies to special-purpose systems, and then the longer term, more general case. The treatment is, given the constraints of space, time and the author's expertise, necessarily incomplete and anecdotal, rather than exhaustive and authoritative, but may at least serve to provoke debate.

I. Empowering Special-purpose Automatic Decision-Making Systems

In this section I am concerned with the kind of systems some at least among us appear to consider imminent - fully autonomous active decision-making

---

*I start from the assumption that no aspect of human intelligence and behaviour is in principle unachievable by a humanly constructed artifact. How long we shall have to wait for such artifacts, and whether their construction will incorporate any interesting insight into the mind, as opposed to the brain, are questions beyond the scope of this paper.

systems designed for specific, fairly narrowly constrained tasks. In the near term we might imagine such systems arising by the closing of a sense-determine-act loop which to date still includes a human link, as in existing nuclear power reactor control systems, experimental disease diagnosis and treatment systems, and nuclear weapons command and control systems, the exact degree of automation of which we are not informed of. Or looking further ahead one might anticipate the automation of functions so far un-mechanised, ranging from bus driving to the administration of civil and criminal justice. I contend that no such systems should ever be empowered to act autonomously, because no test or procedure can ever be established which adequately establishes their competence.

I.1 The impossibility in some cases of realistic field testing

For an important subset of potentially empowered special-purpose automatic decision-making systems, realistic field testing is impossible owing to the intolerable cost of failure and/or the impossibility of creating the necessary test situation. Launch-on-warning systems are the most obvious example here, but any system concerned with quick response (thus eliminating the possibility of last-minute human intervention) to low-probability and/or low-frequency events will suffer from the same problem, in proportion to the cost of a wrong decision.

I.2 The inadequacy of testing under simulation

This problem is pervasive, and indeed defines in the end the class of empowerable special-purpose systems, namely, those for which exhaustive testing under simulation is possible. The problem with testing under simulation is that the test necessarily recapitulates the categorisation which underlies the specification of the system to be tested. Thus it cannot validate that categorisation. Even if we suppose that some combination of formal means of system specification, proofs of system 'correctness' based thereon and testing under simulation can (or will some day be able to) establish beyond doubt that a system implements its specification faithfully, we have still to validate that specification. In particular we have to validate the choices made in such a specification as to the dimensions of description relevant to the characterisation of the situations within which the system must act.

Consider the thermostat - an automatic decision-making system long since empowered. We are content with that empowerment not only because the cost of failure is acceptably low, and because physical law and demonstration convince us that, as per specification, contact is made or broken as a function of ambient temperature, but also because it is patent that the dimension of temperature is (almost always) the only one relevant to characterising situations sufficiently to determine whether they are 'furnace should be on' or 'furnace should be off'.

I.3 The necessity of general intelligence

Why is it that one does not have to go far up the scale of complexity from thermostats before reaching a point where human supervision is uncritically assumed to be necessary, whether in existing systems such as automatic zero-visibility instrument landing systems for aircraft, or experimental diagnosis aids such as MYCIN? Not only from fear of system failure, I would claim, but also from intuitive appreciation of the potential inadequacy of specification. There is always a class of doubts expressed as "But what if..." which point to a dimension of significance omitted from the specification.

The distinction between a special-purpose system and one with general intelligence (e.g. human beings) is the ability of the latter to introduce into the decision-making process a characterisation of the situation along a normally irrelevant dimension. Unless one can convincingly demonstrate, as with the thermostat, that the dimensions of characterisation included in the special-purpose system include all those of conceivable relevance, impowerment is clearly inappropriate, indeed foolhardy. But for applications of sufficient complexity such demonstrations are unlikely to be possible. It is worth noting in this connection two instances of systems performing to specification, but incorrectly: The East Coast power failure of 1965 and the BMEWS alert of 1960 caused by radar echoes off the rising moon. It would seem, then, that any task of sufficient complexity which has an appreciable impact on humanity requires at least* quasi-human general intelligence to automate it safely.

---

*This is not to rule out the possibility that there are tasks *no* system can perform. Whether *any* system, human, artifact or hybrid, can rationally be required to decide whether or not an enemy missile attack is underway and to launch missiles in reply, all within eight minutes, seems unlikely at best. On the other hand it is clearly a moral and political decision what level of risk is tolerable in return for the benefits of automation. In the case of the power grid, with probability of successful operation reasonably high, based on past performance, and cost of failure, although high in inconvenience, likely to be low in terms of human lives, the risk (the integral of probability times cost) is probably worth the benefits. In the case of launch-on-warning, with probability of failure high, owing to the afore-mentioned impossibilities of effective testing, and cost of failure enormous, the risk is intolerable.

II. Empowering Systems with General Intelligence

This option is much harder to come to grips with, since the construction of artifacts expected to exhibit general intelligence seems so much beyond us today. None-the-less some useful observations may be made. First of all, the paradox alluded to above is now clear - we may recognise that general intelligence is required in a system before it can be empowered to make a wide range of decisions autonomously, but how can we reliably determine that a candidate for empowerment *has* it? The Turing test in its various forms may be adequate in the intellectual or academic spheres, but, not to put too fine a point on it, would you bet your life on it? The ability to recognise and accomodate to the unexpected is almost by definition not susceptible to reliable test. It is instructive to consider how this issue is dealt with in empowering human beings. Interestingly enough to a large extent it isn't. We appear to take it for granted, in the established processes leading to the empowerment of doctors, judges, pilots, nurses, teachers etc, that the candidates are possessed of the non-specialist human ability to be appropriately sensitive to any and all relevant aspects of the context of the decision-making situation. To the extent that the question arises, it appears to be confronted obliquely and informally, rather that as an explicit part of the empowerment process.

Before confronting the answer to our problem which this observation points to, a partial diversion is in order, to consider the further criteria for empowerment which emerge when we imagine perhaps the most extreme possible case, that of a fully autonomous empowered decision-making system dispensing criminal justice.

II.1   Responsibility and moral sensibility

It seems to me that before we would consider empowering anything to sit in judgement over ourselves and our fellows, we would demand above and beyond the above-mentioned general intelligence, to say nothing of demonstrated legal competence, a recognition of the responsibility entailed by the role of judge. I am no theorist or philosopher of law, but it seems clear to me that despite what we hear about the justice system being the rule of law, not of men, we none-the-less count on a good judge's humanity to temper justice with mercy, to be unavoidably influenced by that which s/he shares with those brought before him/her. The responsibility which a judge bears for his/her decisions influences those decisions in a crucial, albeit ineffable, manner. But to admit this is to admit as relevant to our concerns the question of the nature of 'humanity', considered as a quality rather than a tautological property of *homo sapiens*. Now the reason for this diversion into matters judicial is I hope clear - determining general intelligence is only a sub-part, a rather small part, of determining humanity. If we assume rather uncritically, on the basis of indirect, subjective evidence, the generalised plasticity of intelligence of human candidates for empowerment, how much more uncritically and implicitly we assume their humanity!

II.2   The only reliable test for humanity

In the end, then, I am led to suggest that the only test we could ever sensibly trust before empowering an automatic decision-making system is the one we subject human beings to: they will have to pass as human in the course of ordinary life. The test for humanity is being able to successfully participate in the human form of life, to convincingly *da-sein*.

III. Conclusions: On Spirituality and Hybrid Systems

One thing that follows from the preceding line of argument is that the current disinclination, to put it mildly, of Artificial Intelligence and Cognitive Science to treat the spiritual side of human nature seriously is a grave mistake. For if recognition of responsibility arising from moral sensibility has a causal role to play in human decision making and human behaviour more generally, then the origin of moral sensibility in man's spirituality becomes a necessary subject of study. The fact that concern with the twin questions of 'Why is there something rather than nothing' and 'How ought I to live my life' is symptomatic of the human condition is of as much ultimate significance to theories of mind as are the nature of syllogistic reasoning or mental representations of grammar, and it may be that postponing an investigation of the essense of spirituality in favour of the current exclusive investigation of the essense of rationality may render the whole enterprise literally incoherent.

On a more practical note, if one concludes from the first section that for the foreseeable future in all systems of any consequence we must keep people in the loop, our problems don't disappear. Keeping people in the loop - building hybrid systems - is not as easy as it sounds, either to require or to do. If the human participation in a hybrid system is reduced to pushing a button in response to a light, no useful supervision has been accomplished. And how to design a genuinely hybrid system which *does* provide effective supervision is an open question. The experience of the Three Mile Island disaster suggests the we are a long way from being able to build systems which effectively integrate human beings' general intelligence with computers' special-purpose expertise to produce an ensemble capable of flexible and informed responses in high-pressure situations.

If the air of this talk has seemed overly dour and pessimistic, I think this is a necessary antidote to the facile optimism of too many of our more visible representatives in the media. It is our responsibility, as scientists and as human beings, to do our best to see that such optimism is balanced by an informed and skeptical realism before the inevitable social (and mortal) cost has to be paid.

ACKNOWLEDGEMENTS

Many of the ideas in this talk were developed in discussions at meetings of the Edinburgh Computing and Social Responsibility group, and with Anne Lee, Brian Smith, Susan Stucky and Catharine Thompson, to all of whom my thanks.

JUDGEMENT, POLICY AND THE HARMONY MACHINE

John Fox

Imperial Cancer Research Fund Laboratories, London

"Men cannot be reconciled by appealing to their rational minds, only by appealing to their hearts" Robert Owen, quoted on a plaque at New Harmony, Illinois.

Science and technology confer their benefits through our understanding of the world, and the consequent ability to choose actions which limit its unpleasant aspects or enhance its pleasant ones. The natural sciences and their technological offspring have produced methods and devices which, on balance, have made the world more predictable, more controllable and more comfortable.

Broadly speaking these features of predictability and controllability are greatest in our dealings with the physical world. In biological systems they are, as yet, less evident. In social systems and personal affairs uncertainty is dominant.

The successes of the natural sciences and the growing successes of the life sciences have encouraged many people to ask whether we can achieve comparable levels of control over social events, and even our private lives, through the use of rational, scientific techniques. Liberal societies traditionally leave these matters to human judgement. It is my judgement whether or not I should seek a medical treatment, or private education for my children. It is at the discretion of company executives to pursue new markets or develop new products. It is the judgements of governments and their officers whether policies should be established which turn on certain economic indices, or which introduce industrial changes with social or environmental implications, or which determine rules of citizenship.

Most people view judgement as

something akin to art and not science. A contemporary view is that it is amenable to articulate, rational analysis which could lead to better decisions and, consequently, greater personal contentment and less conflict between individuals and groups.

THE ART OF JUDGEMENT

When faced with a bald challenge we may defend individual and professional judgement, notably our own, but it is not reliable. Judgement is no better than the information it is based upon, or the mind that formulates it. We cannot always rely upon our own judgement to make the right decisions in our lives, or upon the collective judgement of others to make the right decisions for our society. We make mistakes and it is only the tolerance of others and the flexibility of social institutions that prevents many of our mistakes being costly.

It is natural therefore to use tools, such as computers, to collate and refine information prior to making judgements. Some argue that we should go further and rely upon rational calculation in preference to judgement. The last thirty years or so have seen the development of quantitative techniques in psychology, sociology, ecology and economics whose forms are reminiscent of those employed in the natural sciences. Behavioural scientists argue that human decision making and personal judgements are all too frequently 'irrational' by comparison with the prescriptions of scientific decision theory, and that we would be wise to evaluate our otions mathematically. Proponents of nuclear power attack opponents with bundles of calculations of 'risk'. Operations research techniques are used to calculate the manpower needs of companies and to plan complex industrial or military projects. The influence of economic models on national policies is well known.

Clearly we can use information more effectively to make personal and social judgements, and we should explore the use of information technology to do that. However the dominance of quantitative methods may be mistaken. Some of my complaints are technical objections but I shall not go into these much here. Rather I want to suggest that qualitative methods, such as those pioneered in AI, could radically change our understanding of, and competence in, the processes of social judgement.

THE LIMITS OF MATHEMATICS

One way or another most 'rational' techniques for dealing with personal, ecological, economic and political questions depend upon mathematical probability theory and statistics. The technical attraction of probabilistic methods, unlike the traditional deterministic techniques of physics, is that they do not try to squeeze uncertainty out of complexity, only to get the measure of it. Using statistics we can make predictions in the face of uncertainty, and provide a rational basis for individual decisions and social policies. We can calculate our 'expected utility' of a surgical operation, the 'risk' of ecological disaster, the 'inflationary pressure' of a public spending programme. Strong advocates of such methods believe that rational judgement must be founded on rational mathematics, and that its widespread use must lead to greater individual satisfaction, industrial efficiency and social harmony. Critics consider them naive.

There are many tacit critics. Although mathematical tools are available for dealing with individual and social questions most of us don't use them at all. The techniques can be effective, so why don't we use them? I suggest four related reasons. I shall leave aside the fact that most of us don't know how to use them. If that were all there were to it then presumably most of us would be happy to employ specialist consultants if it seemed advantageous. The reasons for the doubts about mathematics that I prefer have to do with what people understand, and what they believe and do as a consequence.

The first observation is that mathematics is abstract. It ignores,

quite deliberately, the meaning of the events it deals with and concentrates on the formal structure of problems. It ignores the idiosyncrasies of the situation and its participants, and it ignores details of organisational or social contexts which can exert powerful influences on the very interpretation of a problem, as well as on the form of an acceptable solution. The risk of a nuclear disaster may be calculably remote, but that is irrelevant if my concern is with the competence of engineering contractors, the standard of routine maintenance, or the possibility that plutonium may fall into the wrong hands.

Second, mathematics is unintelligible to most of us. This is not just because we lack some education, but more important it is a consequence of its abstractness. The statistics on smoking are conclusive, but the effect on smokers has been limited. The Treasury's model of the economy might be as good a predictive device as humanity can develop but citizens can't see how, or if, the model reflects the rise or decline of economic activities that affect them. We just don't understand models that depend upon the interaction of fifty parameters. In effect we have no basis for assessing the personal implications of such calculations, and they are inevitably disregarded in individuals' personal, political and economic behaviour.

Thirdly, and consequent upon this lack of intelligibility, many of us cannot trust those who define 'rational social policies' even if we should. If we accept the mathematics, without understanding, we accept the power of technical elites to decide matters that affect us without being accountable to us. Disastrous medical advice can easily be dismissed as "the luck of the draw". The effects of a bad regulation or economic policy "could not have been foreseen". Who can check? Claims that professional ethics or public accountability provide proper controls are just seen as special pleading and status quoism. Human judgement may be rough and ready but it has the huge political advantage that it can be examined, and challenged, in the public arena or a court of law because we share a common language for discussing it. In a political sense the most rational attitude is to regard an obscure technical argument as simply a hostage to fortune.

Finally there is the ancient problem of personal values and interests. I believe that the development of much of mathematics and the natural sciences would have arrived more or less as it is if the beliefs, politics and values of the discoverers had been different. We might have had a different selection of discoveries, but not a contradictory selection. This is certainly not true of personal judgement or social policy. Efforts to achieve harmony must recognise differences of value. It is here that mathematical techniques have been at their weakest. To be sure there are 'objective' quantitative notions of personal utility and economic rationality but they are, in the view of many, unreliable and unconvincing.

I conclude that certain aspects of human judgement are flawed, but the mathematical tools which may claim to correct or assist judgement are too abstract to substitute for it entirely, too unintelligible for us to know what they do and do not address, and too neutral to be confident that they protect our interests rather than those of others.

THE CONTRIBUTION OF AI

So what does all this have to do with Artificial Intelligence? AI claims to offer a radically new framework for understanding the manifestations of intelligence. Judgement is one such manifestation. Could AI offer a different sort of technology for making judgements that is more compatible with human understanding? Could it let us build a new generation of harmony machines without the vices of the old?

The most prominent practical development in Artificial Intelligence so far has been the introduction of expert systems. Expert systems, it is said, use 'knowledge' to give assistance in specialised problem solving and decision making. Many people see knowledge based systems as providing new capabilities for making decisions, interpreting information, planning and designing, and even making scientific and commercial innovations. Some see a role for knowledge based systems in the formulation of law and social legislation.

The technical capabilities of expert systems are probably only a little ahead, and in some ways behind, the capabilities of classical mathematical systems. The importance of knowledge based systems, however, is not their current achievements but in the way that they solve problems and some side effects of the techniques they use rather than their current capabilities. These features might address the the problems that I have outlined.

Expert systems emphasise knowledge, not numbers. AI workers have an idea of what knowledge is, or at least a partial one. The information that an expert system uses is primarily qualitative, including 'facts' such as:

> hopelessness is a cause of
> social alienation

and 'rules' like:

> if Client is unemployed
> and period of unemployment
> of Client is long
> and opportunity
> of employment is low
> then risk of social alienation
> of Client is high

(The syntax of these fragments is that of the PROPS package developed at the Imperial Cancer Research Fund. Capitalised terms are variables.)

There are several consequences of representing knowledge in this way.

First, the emphasis on qualitative facts and rules of thumb expresses fairly directly what we know, or at least what we think we know. Qualitative statements are imprecise, but they reflect ordinary thinking. Precision is often an illusion or irrelevant anyway. Brian Gaines has a nice comment that there is little point in saying that something "will be delivered at gate no 5 at 10.00 on Saturday morning" when all you mean is it "will be dropped off round the back over the weekend". The apparent precision of calculation may merely give an air of rationality without its substance.

Extensions of such ideas let us represent the meaning of the concepts referred to in the rules and facts. As more and more rules and facts about "unemployment", "opportunity", "social alienation" are added the computer becomes more and more able to use the concepts in ways which are isomorphic with the ways in which we use them. If the concepts are complex and varied, then the computer's representation of them is complex and varied. The ability to represent the details and idiosyncrasies of the problem is greater than if we limit ourselves to formal idealised models.

Dreyfus, Weizenbaum and Searle, deny that this is "true meaning" in a human sense, but even if this is correct, which many question, it is an observation which may have little force. If the computer behaves in such a way that people can understand and even predict then the practical consequences are that its actions are intelligible.

This intelligibility is a pivotal point for the present argument, as well as expert systems generally. We may consider these fragments of knowledge, and assert that they are simplistic, inconsequential or just plain wrong. Quite possibly, but little or no training in computer science is required to understand, and therefore challenge, the judgements they embody. Although they are in effect fragments of a computer program, they are intelligible fragments that can be examined and debated.

A side effect of representing knowledge in this way is that the computer system becomes accountable to those it affects. It is well known that one of the features of expert systems is that they can give explanations. If I want to know how a conclusion or recommendation is arrived at I can ask. The computer must report the facts that it assumed and the line of reasoning it followed. Admittedly current techniques of explanation are primitive but they will improve - and my experience is that an expert system's clumsy attempts at explanation are more understandable than many legal documents that I encounter.

Knowledge based systems will be more credibly competent, or openly laughable, than their predecessors. The potential for argument, challenge and the exercise of individual discretion are thereby increased, and the commissioners, designers and operators of the machinery of policy become more accountable. Interestingly, the habit of explanation could be catching. Refusal of insurance cover; imposition of zoning regulations; taxation demands; denial of promotion or citizenship; public statements of

changes to fiscal policy, or announcements of public works, would increasingly be expected to be accompanied by intelligible documents of explanation. A future Freedom of Information Act might insist upon it.

Finally, how do we analyse individual values? We can't, at least not entirely. AI does not solve all the deep problems of philosophy. However even if our understanding of such matters is sketchy, a knowledge based system could still allow for (if not fully comprehend) individual values or attitudes. To give just one example we might imagine a home computer asking "which is more important to you, having your baby at home near your family and friends, or within reach of trained staff in case of problems?" and reflecting the answer in its advice.

I think this all boils down to the possibility that, contrary to many expectations, AI could be a liberating force. The influence of technology and the mechanical handling of information are growing at a rapid rate. Many of these influences are hidden by virtue of their incomprehensibility. AI, properly managed, could lead to needed checks and balances in a technology based society, and more participation by its members in the formation of policies.

CONCLUSIONS AND CAVEATS

As we are increasingly dominated by complexity and change we need help to predict and control their consequences. One response is to introduce rational mathematical tools. But by themselves these tools are too alien to gain much ground, and where they are used they are liable to improper or unaccountable use. There are areas where technique can enhance judgement and policy making, but technique will only be acceptable if it reflects human understanding and is accountable to human authority. It is worth exploring what AI techniques have to offer.

However the huge growth of interest in AI has not been driven by liberal aspirations, but by commercial ones. Many of us feel that this has unbalanced its development. Most of the technical community is far more interested in the new capabilities, the new efficiencies and the new markets that AI seems to offer than the social benefits. Although the administrators of research programmes and organisations established

to foster the development of AI appear
to be sympathetic to the idea that it
should be exploited for social as well
as economic benefit the response from
technical, social science and political
groups has been disappointing. I hope
that the IJCAI panel will contribute to
altering this.

I do not suggest that the necessary
AI developments are around the corner or
will be easily achieved. It must be
said that AI is subject to political
direction and management, and its
application to socially valuable aims
will have to be consciously encouraged.
The liberalisation that I think AI could
deliver would also be a painful
discipline for our masters; they may
prefer obscure mathematics, or nothing
at all.

ACKNOWLEDGEMENT

I wish to thank Maggie Boden for
inviting me to prepare this paper, and
to take the opportunity of drawing
attention to her own paper in the
Journal of Mathematical Sociology, 1984,
9, pp 341- 356, which deals with rather
similar themes.

RAISING THE STANDARDS OF AI PRODUCTS

Alan Bundy
Department of Artificial Intelligence
University of Edinburgh

Richard Clutterbuck
School of Social Sciences
University of Sussex

Keywords
Code of practice, association of companies, Artificial Intelligence, social implications, legal implications.

Abstract
We propose a mechanism for the promotion of high-standards in commercial Artificial Intelligence products, namely an association of companies which would regulate their own membership using a code of practice and the precedents set by previous cases. Membership would provide some assurance of quality. We argue the benefits of such a mechanism, and discuss some of the details including the proposal of a code of practice. This paper is intended as a vehicle for discussion rather than as the presentation of a definitive solution.

Acknowledgements
We are grateful to members of the Edinburgh Computing and Social Responsibility Group for feedback on an earlier draft of the code, and to Maggie Boden for comments on the paper itself.

1. The Need for High Standards in AI Products
Credibility has always been a precious asset for AI, but never more so than now. The current commercial interest in AI is giving us the chance to prove ourselves. If the range of AI products now coming onto the market are shown to provide genuine solutions to hard problems then we have a rosy future. A few such useful products *have* been produced, but our future could still be jeopardized by a few, well publicised, failures.

Genuine failures - where there was determined, but ultimately unsuccessful, effort to solve a problem - are regrettable, but not fatal. Every technology has its limitations. What we have to worry about are charlatans and incompetents taking advantage of the current fashion and selling products which are overrated or useless. AI might then be stigmatised as a giant con-trick, and the current tide of enthusiasm would ebb as fast as it flowed. (Remember Machine Translation - it could still happen.) Both companies selling AI products and academic AI research groups would suffer in the resulting crash.

AI companies are very dependent on the good-will of their customers. The current life-span of typical AI products is about 1-5 years. The customers of AI products are likely to stay in the market for several times this period; typically they are themselves companies or academic groups engaged in AI research or interested in the long term application of AI techniques. To stay in business the AI company must sell successive upgrades of its products to the same group of customers and, therefore, must build up and maintain a good reputation. If AI business is to expand then new customers must be brought into this existing group. This will only happen if the overall range of AI products is of high-quality and the reputation of this particular company is good. Thus it is in the interests of each company to raise both the general and its particular standard. It must also convince customers that its products are of high standard. When the market was small a company with high-quality products could win new customers by word of mouth. Now the market is growing they must use advertisements, and it becomes harder for a company to convince potential customers that its products *are* of high quality.

Apart from improving the public image of AI and increasing the market for AI products, producing more high-quality products would raise morale and standards in AI itself, leading to a virtuous circle of standards being raised, better work being done, good people being attracted to the field, and even more high quality products emerging. Poor-quality products will produce a vicious circle going in the opposite direction.

But these internal reasons for wanting high standards, while important to insiders, are perhaps less important than external reasons. AI products look destined to play a major role in society. That society deserves, and has the right to expect, protection from exploitation by AI companies and from being harmed by AI products.

An extreme, potential example of such harm is described in [Thompson et al 84], which argues that it is not possible to build an automatic or semi-automatic launch-on-warning system for nuclear weapons with anything like an acceptable failure rate. Anybody who claimed to have done so, or who claimed to be able to do so, would be guilty of misleading the public in a way that could have disastrous consequences. If such a claimant were an AI company then the whistle might be blown on it by the mechanism described below.

However, the main purpose of this proposal is to catch less apocalyptic, but more common-place, misleading claims, whether or not they might give rise to a legal remedy. Examples might be an expert systems shell whose advertised range far exceeds the problems it is really suitable for, or a natural language front end which is presented as being able to deal with a much wider input than it, in fact, can.

2. A Professional Association

The academic field guards itself against charlatans and incompetents by the peer review of research papers, grants, PhDs, etc. There is no equivalent safeguard in the commercial AI field. Faced with this problem other fields set up professional associations and codes of practice.[1] AI needs a similar set-up. We propose that the responsible AI companies should get together now to found such an association. Continued membership should depend on a constant high-standard of AI products and in-house expertise. Members would be able to advertise their membership, and customers would have some assurance of quality. Charlatans and incompetents would be excluded or ejected, so that the failure of their products would not be seen to reflect on the field as a whole nor on the companies in the Association.

Since the trade in AI products is international, with multi-national companies involved both as vendors and customers, the Association would also need to be international. Otherwise, there would be difficulty over membership of multi-national companies and about dealing with complaints resulting from international sales. It is particularly important to make membership attractive to multi-nationals because, with their existing reputation, they have less to gain from the cachet of membership and are more able to avoid the full impact of national registration.

The Association would be self-regulating. If its decisions were seen to be too arbitrary then the value of Association membership would be devalued in the eyes of the public, the customers and the vendors, and the importance of its decisions would decrease in proportion; customers would take no account of Association membership when deciding to buy, so vendors would not bother to join. For such self-regulation to work it is necessary for the Association to be publically visible. Both vendors and potential customers must be aware of the Association and must see its decisions as fair and its sanctions as effective. Customers will then use Association membership as a major determinant when deciding whether and what product to buy. Vendors will regard Association membership as a valuable asset to their company, and will aim for high quality in their products in order to retain membership. They will want to use Association membership in their advertising, and this will, in turn, improve the visibility of the Association. It will be necessary for the Association to maintain a high profile of both its existence and its actions, to be open about its decisions, and to employ effective sanctions.

The Association would need a panel to consider applications for membership and to hear complaints against members. Its main sanction would be refusing membership or expelling existing members, backed up by lesser sanctions like a public admonition, payment of compensation, etc. The rules of the Association might include a contractually binding committment by members to fulfil any compensation order made by the panel. The Association might also insist that contracts issued by members contained various standard clauses, e.g. giving customers the right of reimbursement if returning products within a certain period, guaranteeing compensation under certain circumstances, insisting that precise, testable statements be made about the product, etc.[2] The panel need only take a passive role in determing disputes; it would publicise its address and its willingness to hear complaints. The burden of making a case complaint would fall on the complainant. The panel might then need to employ a small team of experts to investigate discrepancies between the evidence brought by the complainant and that by the company complained of. This investigative team could be recruited on an ad hoc basis, e.g. academic researchers as consultants. The complainant would usually be the dissatisfied purchaser of one of the companies products, but could be any member of the public with a legitimate interest in the product. There might be a multi-stage process, so that cases were only heard by the full panel when a prima-facie case had been established. This is to filter out malicious complaints and those that are outwith the remit of the panel. It would not be necessary actively to investigate AI products or companies before any complaint had been received, and would probably be prohibitively expensive to do so.

The panel needs a code of practice to which members would agree to adhere and which would serve as a basis for applying sanctions. What form should such a code take, i.e. what counts as malpractice in AI? We suspect malpractice may be a lot harder to define in AI than in insurance, architecture or travel agency.

- Due to the state of the art, AI products cannot be perfect. No-one expects 100% accurate diagnosis of all known diseases. On the other hand a program which only works for slight variations of the standard demo is clearly a con. Where is the threshold to be drawn and how can it be defined?

- It is unlikely that any current AI product could fulfil a claim to: understand any natural language input, or to make programming redundant, or to allow the user to volunteer any information what-so-ever. However, the claimant could defend the

---

[1] E.g. the Vehicle Builders and Repairers Association and the National Association of Estate Agents. Note that, unless otherwise stated, all examples are of UK institutions or laws.

[2] C.f. the Vehicle Builders and Repairers Association which has standard forms for estimates and recommends clauses in repair contracts.

claim by debating the meaning of 'understand', 'programming', or 'information', and this would muddy the water. What constitutes an exaggerated claim?

- Given the ambiguity of such terms it would be difficult to decide whether an exaggerated claim was intended to deceive or was due to a difference in terms or was just a genuine oversight on the part of the vendor. How is a vendor's claim to be assessed? Should one try to assess the vendor's intention, or should one ignore this and only assess how a reasonable customer might interpret the claim?

- Because of the ambiguity of such terms the full description of an AI product must describe its limitations, e.g. what sentences it cannot understand, as well as its abilities. It is not enough to refrain from false claims.

- A vendor may claim that it cannot accurately describe the limitations of its product without revealing confidential information about the technique and/or software it is based on. The problem is particularly acute for software products because of the lack of protection afforded by patent and copyright law. Where do we draw the line between a complete and accurate description of the capabilities of the product and the protection of trade secrets?

The difficulty is to give a precise definition of what constitutes reasonable behaviour on the part of a vendor. It seems impossible to cover all the possible situations, in advance, with a list of precise standards to be attained, but it is often possible retrospectively to detect unreasonable practice in particular cases. The usual legal solution to such problems is to use a high-level code in combination with judgements about individual cases in order to build up gradually a picture of *the reasonable* vendor, i.e. to establish *case 'law'*,[3] and to use this to evaluate complaints rather than to pre-vet products.[4] Note, however, that it takes a long time to build up an extensive range of cases - most of the early judgements must be made solely on the basis of the high-level code.

The panel would evaluate a complaint against this code. They would be able to take account of the state of the art and compare the product with the claims made for it. A high-level code and the injunction to judge 'reasonableness' would enable the panel to assess whether the spirit of the code had

been broken, rather than the letter of some spuriously precise, low-level code. The accumulation of case 'law' would ensure some uniformity of treatment, and prevent favouritism or victimisation. Openness about the grounds for decisions would also help ensure uniformity. There is a current trend in other areas towards the giving of reasons - a procedural safeguard which promotes the the quality of decision making.[5] Difficult decisions, like those outlined above, would be decided in particular cases, rather than in general. The general answers would emerge over time with the accumulation of judgements. Previous ajudications would guide future ones without pre-empting them. The case 'law' would provide a guide to vendors as to how to practice reasonably.

3. A Proposed Code of Practice

As a basis for discussion, we propose below such a code of practice for AI vendors. Before we give this we must define our terms. In what follows below, the term:

- *AI product*, means any piece of software or hardware or any service or any combination of these which is based on AI techniques and which is offered for sale;

- *vendor*, means a company selling an AI product, either to a customer direct or to a middleman, whether that company made the product or not;

- *customer*, means a person or group who buys or attempts to buy an AI product from a vendor;

- *user*, means the person who uses the AI product, in particular the person who interacts with the product if it is interactive.

The proposed code is:

The vendor of an AI product should describe to the customer, and where appropriate the general public, the abilities and limitations of the product as accurately as possible, taking account of the likely expectations of the intended customer. In particular, the vendor should accurately describe, in so far as the state of the art and its own knowledge enables this to be done:

1. what the product does, including an account of its scope, limitations and reliability;

2. known bugs in the product;

3. the consequences of failure of the product;

---

[3]Law is in scare quotes because we are defining an extra-legal mechanism.

[4]Compare, for instance, the Unfair Contract Terms Act 1977, which uses case law to define reasonableness in relation to exclusion clauses.

[5]See e.g. the Criminal Justice Act 1982.

4. the amount and type of user interaction required and how and at
what cost it is to be obtained;

5. the skill and knowledge required of
the user;

6. the computational requirements of
the product, e.g. hardware and
software environment, space and
time requirements in different environments;

7. the amount and type of maintenance
required and the cost of this;

8. any social, economic or legal implications of the use of the product,
where these can be assessed.

It is the responsibility of the vendor to
see that this code is observed by any
agent acting on its behalf, e.g. a salesman.
The vendor is also responsible for ensuring
that any middlemen which sell its products
are fully acquainted with the necessary information to enable them to comply with
the code.

An informed customer will, in any case, ask about
1-7 above, and a reasonable vendor should supply
the information unasked. Thus this part of the
code merely makes good practice explicit, as it was
intended to do. In conjunction with the case 'law',
it should help protect the uninformed customer and
define the standards to be met to become a
reasonable vendor.

Point 8 is rather different from the others. It
was inserted to try to protect the wider interests
of society as well as those of the customers. It
might be criticised as being impractical to realise or
as not appropriate in this context. However, we
feel that something like it is required somewhere,
and we would welcome suggestions as to how best
to meet this requirement. Maybe it needs to be
dealt with by separate machinery.

It is not our intention that vendors be required
to state political or ethical opinions, nor that the
Association be asked to judge such opinions; it
would be beyond their competence to do so. In
point 8 we wanted only to encourage vendors to
make statements which were within their technical,
legal, etc. competence so as to enable others to
form accurate political and ethical opinions about
the impact of the product. For instance, all the
photocopiers at Sussex University have a prominent
notice above them detailing the law relating to
copyright. Vendors of AI products should, similarly,
draw the attention of users to illegal uses of their
product.

It is not intended that complainants actually intend to be customers of the vendors they complain
of, but they should have a legitimate interest in
the product over and above commercial competition.
For instance, suppose an expert in the field believes
that a vendor is misleading customers about a
product or that the vendor is producing a product
that will be harmful to society; we would like that
expert to be able to bring a case to the Association. On the other hand the Association would have
to be alive to attempts by vendors to undermine
their rivals by bringing malicious complaints - and
should filter out such complaints at an early stage.

4. Related Codes and Laws

The above proposal is complementary to the existing system of codes and laws applying to AI.

For instance, in the UK, the British Computer
Society and, in the USA, the Association for Computing Machinery both provide codes of conduct for
their members, [BCS 81, ACM 82]. We imagine that
most other national computing societies have similar
codes. Neither of these codes apply to AI
products or vendors, as such. There is a small area
of overlap in that a salesman who is a member of
the BCS or ACM is required to behave honestly and
competently in promoting a product. However, any
sanctions for breaking the BCS or ACM codes would
fall on the individual rather than the company. Our
code is intended to apply to vendors, which would
usually be companies rather than individuals.

In the UK, the Trade Descriptions Act uses
criminal sanctions to protect customers from false
claims, and the Sale of Goods Acts and the Unfair
Contract Terms Act 1977 permit civil remedies for
defective goods. Other countries have similar laws.
However, as illustrated above, there is a large grey
area between illegal behaviour and the behaviour of
a reasonable vendor. It is the purpose of the
above proposal to deal with this grey area, where
the vendor has clearly behaved unreasonably, but not
in such a way as to constitute a criminal offence
or grounds for a civil action. For this reason it
would not be appropriate for the proposed Association to impose the kind sanctions that would be
imposed by a court of law. An unreasonable vendor
should still be allowed to trade, but should not be
allowed to use the cachet of membership of an
association of reasonable vendors, with whatever assurance of high-quality that that was generally felt
to imply.

The British Standards Institute defines standards
for many products. Vendors whose products meet
these standards are able to advertise that fact
with a 'kite mark'. In some cases the standards
set have been adopted by the law.[6] There is
currently an attempt to define a BSI standard for
Prolog. Unfortunately, few AI products lend themselves to such definitions of standards. It is not
worthwhile to try to define one unless very similar
products are being produced by a number of vendors and there is a wide agreement on a de facto
standard. Major and stabilised programming languages seem possible candidates, but customised expert systems, and even expert systems shells, do
not.

---

[6]E.g. motorcycle crash helmets must be worn and must comply
with a minimum BSI standard.

5. A Discussion of Problems

There is a danger of a few companies annexing the Association to themselves and excluding worthy competition. But this is not a major danger. Firstly, in the current state of the AI market, AI companies have a lot to gain by encouraging high-quality in other AI companies. Every success increases the market for everyone, whereas failure decreases it. Until the size of the market has been established and the capacity of the companies has risen to meet it, AI companies have more to gain than to lose by mutual support. Secondly, excluded companies can always set up a rival association. There is room for more than one association, and they could compete by trying to set the highest standard for membership. However, too many associations would be confusing to consumers and would diminish their influence and effectiveness.

There is also a danger of the Association developing into a trade protection society, i.e. of maintaining low standards by protecting its members from disgruntled customer by offering weak excuses for faulty products and by not employing effective sanctions. If this happened then customers would lose confidence in the Association and membership would cease to carry any assurance of high-quality. Membership would still be attractive to vendors who wanted to use the Association's excuses to fob off disgruntled customers. However, provided the Association did not have a monopoly, there would be nothing to stop a more principled group of vendors forming a rival association as above.

The Association would always be at risk of legal action against it from disgruntled vendors who might sue for libel. It would need to take care that its pronouncements were 'fair comment' and to take legal advice on them. It should also try to create the conditions under which vendors would have more to lose from the bad publicity accruing from the court case than they would gain from any damages awarded. But to guard against such actions, the Association would have to maintain a legal defence fund contributed by the members.

6. Passive vs Active Role

We have proposed that the Association take a passive role, reacting to complaints, rather than an active role, pre-vetting products and/or instigating investigations of products with its own team of investigators. Our reasons are practical rather than principled. An active role would require money and people. Most AI companies are small and newly set-up; they might be loath to provide the large sums of money required to set up the investigative machinery, but might be prepared to fund a, much cheaper, passive association. AI experts are currently rare and expensive. Most such experts want either to conduct their own research or set-up their own companies. It would be hard to recruit good full-time investigators. One might find academics prepared to work part-time, but most candidates would have some existing consultancy arrangements that might disqualify them. We have also argued that, while the field is still immature, it is more difficult to set standards that a pre-vetted product must meet than to evaluate the complaints of a customer against the code of practice and previous cases.

For the same reasons we have not proposed the direct registration of AI products. To issue a certificate of good quality to an individual product would require a prior investigation of that product; it would no longer be possible to employ the default assumption that the product of a member of the Association was assumed good unless proved otherwise. That is, direct registration of products would require an active Association with all the associated expense, employment of rare expertise and setting of prior standards. The passive mechanism proposed above indirectly ensures good quality products by encouraging the vendors to produce products that will not attract complaints. The burden of criticising the product and proving that criticism falls on the complainant. The panel need only investigate differences in the evidence presented to them by the complainant and vendor about the product complained of; this investigation would be relatively cheap compared with that required to register every product.

Unfortunately, this means that the burden of proof falls on the customer. But this is not as bad as it seems; currently, most AI customers are themselves AI practioners, to some degree. For instance, the customers for expert systems shells and knowledge representation systems are often researchers from the AI laboratories of other companies. Hence, they are in a position to investigate the product and bring a complaint. They only lack a body to bring it to.

All this might change: AI companies might get richer and more able to fund an active association, AI experts might get thicker on the ground, standards might get better defined as the field matures, the average AI expertise of customers might decline as the customer base expands. In this case, there is nothing to stop the Association moving to a more active role.

7. Relationship to the Law

We have proposed a extra-legal regulatory mechanism, i.e. one without legally enforceable sanctions. One reason is that we are aiming to regulate in the grey area of legal but unreasonable practice. Another reason is that we would like to see an international association covering countries with different legal systems, so no one legal framework can be assumed. A third reason is that we want to make it as easy as possible for the Association to get started; an extra-legal mechanism involves the minimum of bureaucratic hassle.

This proposal, however, creates problems. The boundary between legal and illegal practice is fuzzy; infringement of some aspects of the code of practice (e.g. points 1-3) may sometimes give rise to legal remedies. Even when legal remedies were possible there may still be situations in which both complainant and vendor would prefer to refer the matter to the Association because it provided a cheaper and quicker mechanism for settling the dispute. However, if cases were referred for legal remedy then the workings of the Association might be undermined; such cases would become sub-judice and the Association would no longer be able to comment on them until they were decided (which might take a long time).

However, as it develops the Association might seek statutory authority in the countries in which it operated.[7] This authority might include, for instance:

- the right to grant licences enabling companies to become vendors of AI products;

- protection from libel action in its judgements;

- that infringement of the code of practice would raise a presumption of fault against an infringing vendor in any legal action.[8]

Note that such legal powers increase the dangers of the Association becoming a trade protection society. In particular, the right to grant licences gives a monopoly that might be used to exclude competition. Therefore, it would need to be offset with rights to the customer and the vendor to prevent abuse, e.g the vendor might have the right of legal action if unfairly excluded from membership, the Association might be required to pre-vet and then underwrite the products of its members, so that dissatisfied customers could sue the Association.

8. Conclusion

In this paper we have proposed a mechanism for peer-policing of standards in AI products. The mechanism consists of an association of vendors of AI products who would use a code of practice to sanction vendors who are guilty of unreasonable practice. It is similar to associations used by other groups of companies and professionals offering services or selling products. It is necessary if AI is not to harm itself and society by the products it produces. Some such mechanism is vital to the existing, responsible AI companies if they are to protect their investment in AI; they must try to prevent a few irresponsible companies from exploiting their customers with overrated or useless products and putting those customers off of AI products in general.

Most of the discussion above is relevant to computing generally. We have limited ourself to AI because of the nature of this conference and in order to help focus our ideas and to identify an area small enough to be tackled. AI is growing fast,

but there are not yet many major AI companies, and it seems more likely that *they* would be prepared to get together than that IBM, ICL, Honeywell, etc. would be. However, since many AI products will also contain non-AI techniques, it may eventually be necessary to widen the remit of any AI association.

The above mechanism is only able to regulate commercial companies. We have argued above that academics already have a self-regulatory mechanism of peer review. However, there is major gap in that neither mechanism covers government organisations, e.g. the military. That is beyond the scope of this paper, but not beyond our desires.

This paper is intended as a vehicle for discussion of the problems of maintaining high standards in AI products. It does this by presenting a proposal, but this proposal is not intended as definitive. We would welcome feedback - especially on the code of practice itself. We hope that this paper will inspire those companies that care about high standards to get together, and we hope that they will see that it is in their direct interest to do so.

References

[ACM 82]   Association for Computing Machinery. ACM Code of Professional Conduct. *Communications of the ACM* 25(3):183-184, March, 1982.

[BCS 81]   The British Computer Society. Code of Conduct. 13 Mansfield St, London W1M 0BP, 1981. Handbook No. 5.

[Thompson et al 84]
            Thompson, H. and the Edinburgh CSR group. There will always be another moonrise: computer reliability and nuclear weapons. *The Scotsman* , 1984.

---

[7]See, e.g. the statutory disciplinary powers of the Law Society over solicitors.

[8]See, e.g. that an infringement of the Highway Code raises a presumption, albeit rebuttable, that the driver of a vehicle involved in an accident is at fault.

REASONING WITH UNCERTAINTY FOR EXPERT SYSTEMS

Ronald R. Yager
Machine Intelligence Institute
Iona College
New Rochelle, New York 10801

ABSTRACT

We discuss a methodology for handling uncertain information in expert and other intelligent systems. This approach combines the theories of approximate reasoning and Dempster-Shafer.

I INTRODUCTION

The construction of expert and other intelligent computer systems requires sophisticated mechanism for representing and reasoning with uncertain information. At least three forms of uncertainty can be identified as playing a significant role in these types of systems. The first of these possibilistic uncertainty appears in situations where the value of a variable can only be narrowed down to a set of values one of which is the actual value of the variable. This is manifested by a situation in which we know that a person's age is between 20 and 30. The second kind of uncertainty is related to situations in which there exists uncertainty as to satisfaction of a predicate by an element. This is manifested by concepts which have imprecise or gray boundaries. A very powerful tool for handling this type of uncertainty which also handles the first type of uncertainty is the fuzzy set. The third type of uncertainty is related to situations in which the value of a variable assumes can be modeled by the performance of a random experiment.

The theory of approximate reasoning [1] which is based upon the theory of fuzzy subsets and possibility theory and the Dempster-Shafer mathematical theory of evidence [2] are two important attempts at providing a framework for the representation and manipulation of uncertain information. In this paper we briefly describe an approach to reasoning with uncertain information which is an amalgam of this two approaches.[3]

II CANONICAL REPRESENTATION OF DATA

Assume V is a variable or attribute which takes values in the set X. A canonical statement is a datum of the form V is A in which A is the value of the variable expressible in terms of the base set X. An example of this is the statement John is young. In a situation like this we can represent the value young as a fuzzy subset A of X such that for each $x \in X$, A(x) indicates the degree of membership of x in the set young. The effect of such a canonical statement is to induce a possibility distribution Π_V on X such that

$$\Pi_V(x) = A(x),$$

in which $\Pi_V(x)$ indicates the possibility that V assumes the value x given the knowledge that V is A.

The use of the above type of formalism allows us to represent uncertain knowledge having a possibilistic as well as a fuzzy component. We should note that the certain knowledge that John is seventeen can be represented in this situation by simply making A={17}.

If A and B are two values expressible as fuzzy subsets of X and one is asked if V is B conditioned on the fact that V is A one must use the measures of possibility and certainty to answer this question where

Poss[V is B/V is A]=$\Pi_{B/A}$=Max$_x$[A(x)$\wedge$B(x)]

Cert[V is B/V is A] = 1 − $\Pi_{\bar{B}/A}$

In situations in which the knowledge about the value of a variable V contains probabilistic as well as possibilistic and fuzzy uncertainties we must use a more general type of canonical statement which we call a D-S granule.

Assume m is a mapping from the set of fuzzy subsets of X into the unit interval m: $I^X \rightarrow$ [0,1]. We call the fuzzy subsets of X, A_i, i=1...p, for which m(A_i)$\neq$0 the focal elements of m. If the following two conditions are satisfied

1. Σ m(A_i) = 1 and 2. m(Φ) = 0

we call m a basic probability assignment function (bpa). A canonical statement

of the form
$$V \text{ is } M$$
is called a D-S granule.
In the face of a D-S granule the measures of possibility and certainty become their expected values which we denote as the plausibility and belief measure which are
$$Pl(B) = \Sigma_i \ \Pi_{B/A_i} * m(A_i)$$
$$Bel(B) = \Sigma_i \ Cert[A/B_i] * m(A_i)$$
    More complicated structures can be obtained from these canonical forms. Consider that V and U are two variables taking their values in the sets X and Y respectively. Consider the statement
    "if V is A then U is m."
In the above A is a fuzzy subset of the base set X and m is a bpa on Y with focal elements B_i, i=1,2,...p. The above statement induces a D-S granule
$$U/V \text{ is } m^*$$
in which m^* is a bpa on X × Y such that the focal elements of m^* are the fuzzy sets E_i on X × Y in which for each (x,y), $E_i(x,y) = Min[1,1-A(x)+B_i(y)]$ and $m^*(E_i) = m(A_i)$.

III   REASONING PROCEDURE

    In this section we shall describe the basic reasoning mechanism used in this approach. We first introduce some useful rules of reasoning
1.Conjunction- Assume m_1 and m_2 are two bpa's on the set X with focal elements $\{A_i\}$ and $\{B_k\}$ respectively. The conjunction of of the two D-S granules
$$V \text{ is } m_1 \text{ and } V \text{ is } m_2$$
is a D-S granule
$$V \text{ is } m$$
such that m is a bpa on X in which for each A ⊂ X, $m(A) = \Sigma \ m_1(A_i)*m_2(B_k)$, where the sum is taken over all i,k such that $A_i \cap B_k = A$.
2.Cylindrical Extension- Assume V is m is a D-S granule where m is a bpa on X. Let U be another variable taking values in the set Y. The cylindrical extension of V is m to X × Y is the joint D-S granule
$$V,U \text{ is } m^*$$
where m^* is a bpa on X × Y in which if A_i, i=1,....p, are the focal elements of m then the focal elements of m^* are B_i, i=1,...p, where
$$B_i(x,y) = A_i(x)$$
and $m^*(B_i) = m(A_i)$.
3.Projection- Assume V,U is m is a joint D-S granule on X × Y. The projection of this on X is a D-S granule, V is $m^\perp$, where $m^\perp$ is a bpa on X such that if A_i, i=1,...p, are the focal elements of m then the focal elements of $m^\perp$ are B_i, i=1,...p, where $B_i(x) = Max_y \ [A_i(x,y)]$ and $m^\perp(B_i) = m(A_i)$.

The basic procedure for reasoning can be described as follows.
    (1). Represent each of data as a D-S granule.
    (2). Cylindrically extend each granule so that they are all on the same space.
    (3). Conjunct all the individual pieces of data.
    (4). Project onto the variable of interest.
A simple example will clarify the procedure.
Example Assume V is a variable which can take its value in the set
$$X = \{1,2,3,4\}$$
and U is a variable which can take its value in the set
Y = { Bob,Jim,Sue,Mary}={B,J,S,M}.
Assume we have the knowledge that " if V is small then there is at least a ninty percent chance that U is a women." Futhermore, let us assume that there exists a probability distribution on X such that p_1=.5, p_2=.2, p_3=.2 and p_4=.1. We are interested in using this data to find the value of U. Our first piece of data can be repesented formally as
 "if V is small the U is m"
in which m_1 is a bpa such that
    $m_1(W) = .9$ and $m_2(Y) = .1$,
where W = {S,M}. Small is a fuzzy subset of X which can be
small = {1/1, 1/2, .5/3, 0/4}.
The above piece of data is representable as conditional D-S granule
$$U/V \text{ is } m_2.$$
m_2 is a bpa on X × Y where $m_2(A_1) = .9$ and $m_2(A_2) = .1$ in which
$A_1(x,y) = Min[1,1-small(x) + W(y)]$.
A_1 is representable as the matrix

$$A_1 = \begin{array}{c|cccc} & B & J & S & M \\ 1 & 0 & 0 & 1 & 1 \\ 2 & 0 & 0 & 1 & 1 \\ 3 & .5 & .5 & 1 & 1 \\ 4 & 1 & 1 & 1 & 1 \end{array}$$

$A_2(x,y) = Min[1,1-small(x)+Y(y)]$, however since Y(y) = 1 then $A_2(x,y) = 1$.
    The second piece of data can be represented as a D-S granule V is m_3 in which $m_3(1)$=.5, $m_3(2)$=$m_3(3)$=.2 and $m_3(4)$=.1. The cylindrical extension of m_3 is m_4 whose focal elements are C_1, C_2, C_3 and C_4 where the membership function of C_i is
$$C_i(x,y) = 1 \quad \text{for } x = i$$
$$= 0 \quad \text{for } x \neq i.$$
In addition $m_4(C_i) = p_i$.
    The conjunction of these two pieces of data is the D-S granule
$$V,U \text{ is } m$$
with focal elements
$D_i = C_i$ i = 1,2,3,4
$D_5 = \{1/(1,S), \ 1/(1,M)\}$
$D_6 = \{1/(2,S), \ 1/(2,M)\}$

$D_7 = \{.5/(3,B),.5/(3,J),1/(3,S),$
$\qquad 1/(3,M)\}$
$D_8 = \{1/(4,B),1/(4,J),1/(4,S),1/(4,M)\}$
The weights associated with this focal elements are
$m(D_1)=.05$, $m(D_2)=.02$, $m(D_3)=.02$,
$m(D_4)=.01$, $m(D_5)=.45$, $m(D_6)=.18$,
$m(D_7)=.18$, $m(D_8)=.09$
The projection on U is the D-S granule
$\qquad$ U is m^*
in which the focal elements are
$E_1 = Y = \{B, J, S, M\}$, $E_2 = \{S, M\}$
$E_3 = \{.5/B, .5/J, 1/S, 1/M\}$ and
$m^*(E_1)=$
$m(D_1)+m(D_2)+m(D_3)+m(D_4)+m(D_8)=.19$
$m^*(E_2)= m(D_5)+m(D_6)=.63$
$m^*(D_3)= m(D_7)=.18$

IV   ENTAILMENT

A very useful principle in reasoning is called the entailment principle. It allows us to infer that John is tall from the knowledge that he is six feet six. In [4] Yager has introduced an entailment principle for D-S granules.
Def: Assume m_1 is a bpa on X with focal elements $A_1,\ldots.A_p$ with weights $m_1(A_1)$. Let m_2 be another bpa on X with focal elements $B_{11},B_{12},\ldots,B_{1,n(1)},B_{21},\ldots,$ $B_{2n(2)},\ldots,B_{p1},\ldots,B_{pn(p)}$ such that for each i
$\qquad A_i \subset B_{ij}$ for all j
and $\qquad \Sigma_j\, m_2(B_{ij}) = m_1(A_1)$
then we say $m_1 \subset m_2$.
Entailment Principle: Assume $m_1 \subset m_2$ then from knowlege that V is m_1 we can infer the D-S granule V is m_2.

The entailment principle is use for as aid in making inferences and answering questions. The entailment principle can also be used to simplify bpa's to forms that are more comprehendible. This simplification can be either for the purpose of presenting the results of a reasoning process more succintly or for easing the process of evaluating the weights in providing a bpa.

For example, in the case of the problem we just worked out since $E_3 \subset E_1 = Y$ we can infer that the result of our reasoning is that the probability that U is a female is at least .63.

A situation in which one could use a D-S granule would be the following. Assume we are interested in John's age, which we will denote as V. Therefore V is a variable which takes its value in the set of integers less then 120, denote this X. We are given the information that John graduated from high school this year. We know that people <u>usually</u> graduate from his at "about seventeen years of age." However

there are some people who for various reasons don't graduate at that age. We can use a D-S granule to represent this information. In particular we can say that
$\qquad$ V is m,
where m is the bpa with focal elements
A = "about seventeen"
B = "young graduate"
C = "old graduate"
However since B $\subset$ X and C $\subset$ X we can simply use the focal elements A and X and let $m(A) = \alpha$ and $m(X) = 1-\alpha$. In this case α is the value such that "at least α portion of the people graduate at about seventeen."

With the aid of the entailment principle one can get a better understanding of the Dempster rule used by Shafer in combining bpa's.

Assume m_1 and m_2 are two bpa's on X. We previously defined the conjunction of two as $m = m_1 \cap m_2$, in which for each A $\subset$ X $m(A) = \Sigma\ m_1(A_i)*m_2(B_j)$, with the sum taken over all A_i and B_k such that $A_i \cap B_k = A$.
Shafer's combination of these two bpa's is $\qquad m^* = m_1 \oplus m_2$ in which
$m^*(\Phi) = 0$
$m^*(A) = m(A)/(1-m(\Phi))$ for all other A.
We note if $m(\Phi)=0$ then $m=m^*$.
In the above m^* is obtained by proportionally allocatting the weight in the null set to the other focal elements of m. Since $\Phi \subset A_i$ the Dempster rule can be seen as simply a conjunction followed by a special application of the entailment principle.

REFERENCES

[1] Zadeh, L.A., "A Theory of Approximate Reasoning." In <u>Machine Intelligence</u>. Vol 9, Hayes, J., Michie, D. & Mikulich, L.I. (Eds), John Wiley and Sons: New York, (1979) 149-194.

[2] Shafer, G., <u>A Mathematical Theory of Evidence</u>. Princeton University Press: Princeton, 1976.

[3] Yager, R. R., "Toward a General Theory of Reasoning with Uncertainty," Tech. Report# MII-509 and 510, Machine Intelligence Institute, Iona College, 1985.

[4] Yager, R.R., "The Entailment Principle for Dempster-Shafer Granules," Tech Report# MII-512, Machine Intelligence Institute, Iona College, 1985.

USER MODELLING PANEL

D. Sleeman (Stanford: Moderator), Doug Appelt(SRI), Kurt Konolige(SRI), Elaine Rich(MCC), NS Sridharan(BBN Labs) & Bill Swartout(ISI).

INTRODUCTION

In various sub-areas of AI we talk about "tailoring" the system's response to the user. NL systems and Tutoring systems being two prime examples. Additionally, some discussion of this issue arises in building explanation facilities for Expert Systems.

- How explicit are the user models even in systems which are able to adapt to the user?

- How do they achieve this tailoring? How similar are the techniques used?

- How do such user models differ from the plans inferred in planning systems?

- How deep/knowledgeable do user models need to be?

- How is this sophistication dependent on the type of interaction (superficial conversation versus diagnostic/tutorial), the goal of the dialogue, the nature of the domain etc?

In this panel we will review many of the areas in which some form of user model is used, look at commonalities of approaches, and seek to characterize when a particular approach is appropriate.

USER MODELLING: SOME APPROACHES
Elaine Rich

User modelling straddles the boundary between artificial intelligence and data base technology. It has all of the problems that each of these areas possesses; we hope it will also be able to draw on both areas for solutions. This double dependency arises from the interaction between the two main subproblems that user modelling must address:

- How can models of users (their knowledge, goals, etc.) be inferred from their behavior and used in reasoning to improve the performance of a target system? This is where A.I. comes in.

- How can models of a large number of users be maintained efficiently so that each is available when necessary but system performance does not degrade even if the user population is very large? This is where data bases are important.

User models capture many kinds of information about users. Two important dimensions that characterize this information are shown in the following chart:

	individual user	canonical user
short-term information	1.	2
long-term information	3	4

Square 2 does not make much sense, but each of the other squares poses specific problems that user-modelling systems must address.

When user modelling is looked at from the A.I. point of view, the following issues emerge:

- How can specific user plans be inferred from behavior? (This relates to square 1.) Doing this requires a system that is itself capable of forming plans but it also, since it is a diagnosis task and not a design task the way most planning problems are, requires a sophisticated matching procedure so that the plan that the user has selected can be isolated from other possible plans.

- How can user knowledge and planning strategies be inferred from behavior? (This relates to square 3.) People's knowledge and their problem-solving strategies change quite slowly over time and should be remembered from one session to the next because they may substantially influence both the way the user will behave and the way the system should behave for maximum effectiveness.

- How can general knowledge and planning procedures be represented and used effectively? (This relates to square 4.) This is the standard A.I. question.

When user modelling is looked at from the database point of view, the following issues emerge:

- How can information about a large number of users be stored most efficiently? (This relates to square 3.) Is it more efficient to store each model separately or to store models as differences from some canonical model? Is it better to organize the model around a particular user, clustering together everything known about that person, or is it better to arrange the model around a particular topic or piece of knowledge, clustering together what is known about all users with respect to that issue?

- How can a lot of detailed knowledge about a particular session be collapsed into a concise description of the knowledge that may be useful for later sessions? (This relates to square 3.)

STUDENT MODELS in INTELLIGENT TUTORING SYSTEMS

D. Sleeman

The field of Intelligent Tutoring Systems identified the need for having a model - a database - which summarized the student's actions some time ago. The earliest adaptive CAI programs often represented the student's level of sophistication by a scalar value. SCHOLAR, a program which discussed the geography of South America, was the first to use a more sophisticated representation - namely a semantic network. Essentially, the knowledge of the domain was represented as such a network and each node had a numerical value associated with it indicating the likelihood that a particular student knew the knowledge associated with the node. This type of model is referred to as an *overlay* model. A *differential* model which simply reports the differences between an expert's and the student's knowledge was introduced in the WEST system.

All these systems assumed that the student's knowledge was merely a subset of the expert's. Recent studies in Cognitive Science have shown this is frequently *not* a valid assumption, and so models which allow both the correct and incorrect knowledge to intermingle have been introduced. *Perturbation* models have been used by Brown & Burton in their DEBUGGY system to model student's errors with Arithmetic tasks, and by Sleeman in LMS/PIXIE to capture student's knowledge of Algebra.

An important aspect of these latter models is that they are *process* models - and so can be executed by an appropriate interpreter - thus enabling them to be used predictively. Both DEBUGGY and PIXIE address the issue of *inferring* models by observing the student's performance on a series of tasks. Technical issues addressed by these systems include how to make the search computationally tractable, and how to overcome noise (i.e., spurious responses). Additionally, PIXIE is addressing the issue of how to remove the closed-world assumption - making the systems *truely* responsive to the student's input. Currently, modelling systems merely search - an albeit very large - model space generated by combining more primitive components (in PIXIE's case of correct and incorrect rules).

EXPLANATION & the ROLE of the USER MODEL: HOW MUCH WILL IT HELP?

Bill Swartout

There seems to be a growing consensus among researchers in explanation and text generation that a solid, detailed user model (if we only knew how to build it) would significantly improve the kinds of explanations and texts we can produce mechanically. Currently proposed system designs often call for a detailed user model that expresses what facts the system believes the user knows, how he likes to have information presented, and so forth. In such designs, presentation strategies use the model to select just the right thing to present to a user. Is such a detailed model feasible? Do people seem to have detailed knowledge of their listeners? This approach may place too much emphasis on the user model. It often seems that people do not have detailed knowledge of their listeners but instead rely on general, stereotypical knowledge and an ability to alter their explanation tactics when the listener appears not to understand. I would like to suggest that an explanation system that allows for feedback from the user about the understandability of explanations and that relies on a general user model expressing knowledge of stereotypes might be more feasible that one that depends on a detailed user model.

THE ROLE OF USER MODELLING IN LANGUAGE GENERATION & COMMUNICATION PLANNING

Doug Appelt

The analyses of Searle and Grice clearly demonstrate that communication is a process of *intended recognition of intention*, whereby the speaker formulates utterances with the intention that the hearer use that utterance to understand the speaker's intentions that the hearer hold some different propositional attitudes as a result of understanding the utterance. This intention recognition property is *essential* to communication --- if it is absent, then whatever activity is going on is something other than communication.

If a user perceives natural language being used as input and output to a system, it is very natural for him to assume that it is being used as a medium of communication, much the same as people use it among themselves. Therefore, there is a very strong tendency for the user to impute intention recognition capabilities to the system and to assume that it is taking his own intentions into account. Of course, most users of currently available natural language interfaces soon learn that this is not the case. The objective of research in communication planning is not so much being able to construct ever more complex sentences involving increasingly difficult semantic concepts, but rather to understand the processes of intention communication and recognition well enough to enable a system to participate in a natural dialogue with its user.

Therefore a system that plans communication must have a very detailed model of the user. There are a large number of alternative means of representing the beliefs and intentions of agents, and the requirements of communication planning do not dictate what form such a representation must take, but rather dictates a set of requirements about what kinds of reasoning must be done. The following is at least a partial list of the representation and reasoning capabilities necessary for communication:

- The ability to represent Believe(A, P), Believe(A, ~P), ~Believe(A, P).

- The ability to represent all of the above with respect to mutual belief.

- The ability to represent all of the above with respect to intention.

- The ability to deduce for any P whether or not A believes P, and similarly for mutual belief and intention.

- Given an individual, reason about what is believed or mutually believed about it.

- The ability to reason about the effect of actions on belief, mutual belief, and intentions. Must be able to reason for any act and proposition P about whether or not [act]Believe(A, P) holds, and Believe(A, [act]P).

Language production is not a faculty that can, in general, be isolated from the general reasoning processes of a system. Natural communication requires knowing about the plans and goals of a speaker with respect to the entire task, and the ability to plan goals having to do with the communication process itself as well as the domain. Therefore, it is impossible to take some existing system, add a user model, tack on a natural language font end and back end, and expect it to engage in natural communication. The need for communication must be in the mind of the designer from the beginning, with domain and communication reasoning incorporated as a consistent whole.

USER MODELLING, COMMON-SENSE REASONING & the BELIEF-DESIRE-INTENSION PARADIGM
Kurt Konolige

User modelling is important wherever an AI system must interact with human agents. I say here "human agents", but this is not necessarily meant to exclude other types of agents; as computer system become more complex, the same principles used for efficient communication with people will hopefully apply to artificial agents. Indeed, in Methodologies below I note that analyzing the communication requirements of artificial agents may lead to insights about communication in general.

I think it would be an understatement to say that current AI systems which incorporate user models have a long way to go. This is not because too little attention has been paid to the problem, but simply because the problem encompasses · a significant part of current AI research. There may be very restricted situations in which a crude parameter model (for example, a verbosity switch) is all that is necessary; but for the more open-ended dialogues that normally take place in question-answering, explanation, and tutoring (to name a few application areas), a more accurate model of the user's cognitive state is required. I would like to give a personal view of some of the major lines of research that are being pursued or should be pursued to achieve a realistic user model.

Methodologies

At present, most models of cognition in AI are variations of a BDI (belief-desire-intention) paradigm. An agent has beliefs about the world, and desires some states of the world more than others. Rational agents form intentions or plans to affect the state of the world to fulfill their desires, given the current state of their beliefs. This picture is a kind of commonsense psychology, and seems to be implicit in the way we use words like 'belief,' 'desire,' 'plans,' etc. Hardly any work has been done on a general theory relating these cognitive components. Still, the BDI paradigm is a useful general framework for constructing user models for particular applications. In many cases, it is possible to simplify the model considerably: for example, in question-answering on a database it is assumed that the user has a goal of extracting information, and the problem of forming intentions from conflicting desires does not arise.

While the BDI paradigm can provide an overall hatrack for organizing cognitive models, it does not tell us what particular hats we should put on it. Agents' beliefs, for example, can be quite complicated, incorporating complex commonsense reasoning about space, time, physical systems, and so on, as well as particular beliefs about the domain at hand. How do we go about developing such theories? This might be called the Knowledge Problem for user modelling. There are two sources for such theories. One is the Cognitive Science path, in which attention to protocols of subjects can yield interesting insight into cognitive processes acting in complex environments. The other is in AI planning systems: artificial agents whose cognitive structure is designed to solve a particular task. The former might be described as theory-poor but data-rich: the subjects actually do act intelligently in the domain, but the actual cognitive structures they employ are not accessible. The latter are theory-rich but data-poor: the design of the agent is useful as a theory of reasoning in the domain, but the agent may not actually act as intelligently as desired. So it would seem that both approaches are desirable -- for example, analyzing the way people use language yields data on desirable properties of a language-using system, while studying the requirements for efficient communication between agents can lead to a simplified model of communication that helps organize linguistic phenomena.

The Knowledge Problem

At the very minimum, a useful user model for open-ended dialogues should include the following:

* Domain-dependent knowledge. This is the type of reasoning most often capture by expert systems, which are good at a very specialized type of problem in a narrowly defined setting.

* Theories of the commonsense world. This type of knowledge is tacitly assumed in all human communication. It includes areas such as:

- Intentionality and beliefs of other agents.

- Common-sense theories of time, space, and physical processes.

* Knowledge of the interaction process. This includes principles of efficient communication, such as "new information comes first," or "use the most specific applicable term."

There is much significant work being done in AI on theories of this sort, e.g., work on qualitative reasoning, modelling space and time, naive physics, logics of knowledge and belief, communication act theory, and so on.

The Inference Problem

The most important inference problem for user modelling is the following:

Given the observed behavior of the user, find the appropriate state of the model that accounts for the behavior.

Note that this is a very different problem from performing inferences using one of the commonsense theories just mentioned. In general, the latter is a deduction problem: find the consequences of a given theory. The inference problem for user modelling is inductive: from a pattern of behavior, induce the correct structure that produces the behavior. Much of the work in script- or frame-based systems addresses this problem. However I think it is a much more difficult inference problem, and deserving of much more intensive research.

USER MODELLING & PLAN RECOGNITION

N.S. Sridharan

A number of interesting and important questions have been raised for this panel. I wish to survey a small set of different tasks and show the diversity of responses possible depending on the characteristics of the task. I conclude by discussing a set of *task dimensions* which forms a framework for understanding, in a broad manner, the connections between tasks and user models.

I. Discussion of different domains

I.A Automatic prompting and simple help on workstations

An implicit assumption is made that the user may wish to know some information relevant to the command to be issued; and that it wont hurt to display such information automatically. A sketchy finite state machine model can be used compute allowable actions, allowable operands and a canned help text can be put up on the screen. No detailed user modelling is used.

I.B Tutoring introductory programming: (Elliott Soloway, Yale)

There is an intimate connection between plan recognition and user modelling. In fact, not viewing user-modelling as *plan recognition* has hampered progress in this field. The student must be seen as trying to follow a plan; a program that is being constructed is a realization of a plan. What the student is trying to accomplish, his goal is important; *goal recognition* is an important problem. An approach using bug catalogs or plan catalogs is inherently limited. That kind of approach will not go beyond small and simple programs. Plan recognition must be viewed as a constructive task; *plan revision* approach is very important. It will be not enough to think of selecting a user plan from a finite set of pre-formed plans. (For approaches to student modelling in tutoring domains where strong assumptions can be made about the student's goal at any stage, see the earlier section *Student Models in Intelligent Tutoring Systems*.)

I.C Sensor signal interpretation: (C.F. Schmidt, Rutgers)

The problem arises in connection with an interactive system to assist in interpreting multiple unreliable sensor signals. An implicit user model is used to effect (offline) tailoring of the system. Only the pragmatic consequences of accepting a model of user needs to be represented. The model used need only be accurate enough to predict the right actions; that is, the model is viewed only in terms of it implications for the system.

I.D Pilot's assistant: (Dick Pew, BBN)

In automating the cockpit display for a military aircraft, it is clear that the display function must be customized to the user. However, in this domain, plans of pilots can only be defined in vague terms; e.g. as phases of a mission, and a conditional set of responses plus model of goals to maintain their priorities. The pilot is operating in an extremely dynamic situation, and operates generally by adopting *opportunistic behavior* and *reactive behavior*. In this domain it appears that the user model is better structured in terms of *attributes* such as focus of attention, span attention, attention switching speed, memory limitations, speed of observation and assimilation.

I.E Natural Language Dialog systems (Candy Sidner and Jim Schmolze, BBN)

Question-answering systems often limit themselves to dealing with individual questions separately; whereas, dialog systems attempt to include the context of the dialog so far. An important aspect of such contexts is a model of the user's intentions, capabilities, beliefs, knowledge, and preferences. Formation of such a model is viewed as an *incremental process*. Understanding communication requires accessing/hypothesizing the intentions. This process is one of forming a hypothesis, and thus is *inherently* error-prone. The process used should be robust enough to recognize errorful hypotheses and to take steps to rectify them.

I.F Office automation task: non-linguistic, non-communicative domain (Vic Lesser, U of Mass.)

The user is engaged in a task such as filling out a purchase order for equipment. The system is watching over his shoulders, so to speak, and attempting to guide the user. The user may be in error; the system is watching to predict and correct the steps taken by the user. Plan recognition relies mostly on domain-based heuristics; and is less dependent on modelling the user, his beliefs or plans. This is because the goal is to get the task accomplished rather than to train or educate the user.

II. Framework for discussion of user modelling

Very simple user models suffice for a number of tasks. In spelling correction a simple model of user errors, rather than plans, can be immediately helpful. In detecting errors in novices' program, a model of errors made frequently by novices, not their plans, may be very useful.

The attempt here is to set up a framework for exploring the analogies portrayed below.

- User customization <-> Prediction, correction, modification

- User models <-> Plans incorporating beliefs, intentions and goals

- User modelling process <-> Plan recognition

The purpose of the framework to be developed is to answer questions like: how complex should the user model be? what characteristics of the task are relevant in deciding how to acquire and use such user models?

Dimensions to consider and evaluate in exploring this analogy

1. **Richness of response space:** Assuming that the model is to guide a suitable action from a repertoire of actions, the user model must be (just) rich enough to guide choice of response, but should be minimal. If the potential responses are not diverse the model can and should be quite simple.

2. **Static vs Dynamic customization:** It is useful to consider whether the programmer is customizing the program to the user, or whether the system is adapting itself. Static customization may lend itself to implicit user models.

3. **Who bears responsibility? system or user?:** How complicated can the system become? In an interactive situation, the user will be formulating a model of the system, while the system is modelling the user. If the system is simple enough, the user may be willing to take responsibility for his own actions, since he can more readily form a model of the system. If the system is taking the responsibility for overall behavior, then the system should model the user accurately. (Black box vs Glass box issue)

4. Risk or penalty for being wrong: Plan recognition and user modelling is inherently error-prone, being an inductive task. One must judge the consequence of this. If the penalty for using a wrong hypothesis is high, one must either not attempt to model the user or be in a setting where interactive *verification* of such hypotheses is feasible.

III. What is user modelling? What is in a user model? There are different considerations that affect how one views the process of user modelling:

- Static vs Dynamic models (built-in vs acquired)

- Focus on immediate actions vs focus on eventual goals

- Deterministic vs probabilistic models

- Predictive vs descriptive models

Similarly one can imagine a variety of ways in which the user model is set up:

- Parameter models

- State machine model (compute allowable actions; has a sense of history)

- Recursive models (user's model of the system; system self-model)

- Plan-based models (has a sense of goal). Beliefs, intentions and knowledge attributable to the user. Often these can be integrated in the form of a plan plus a context in which these plan are likely to be executed. Preferences, which allows the user to make choices.

IV. When should user modelling not be done?

There are a number of tasks where attempting to formulate a user model dynamically is inappropriate. Firstly, in some situations, users are evolving. One must realize that human beings are very adaptable and can evolve more rapidly than the systems. Secondly, in some situations, users are not plan following, especially if a user does not know what he wants. It is futile to model fickle human beings. Thirdly, in some situations the user may not know what the system can do. In such situations, a user lacking knowledge may only get confused if the system beings to alter its behavior. Fourthly, in some applications the boundaries of responsibility between system and user may be shifting. For example, the user may wish to issue standing orders, thus causing the system to do some things routinely; or the user may wish to take away from the system certain tasks because the system too slow or unreliable. A highly interactive operating system, such as the TOPS-20, makes it quite difficult to write script files for automating certain functions - scripts cannot adequately substitute for a human user.

V. Summary:
There is a number of problems where simple models work reasonably well; there are a number of problems where plan recognition is a challenge and can be made to work well if the assumptions about the user and task domain hold; there are task domains where the penalty for being wrong is high and the acceptable complexity of the model is low, that other techniques should be profitably be pursued.

VI. Conclusion:
Plan recognition, especially a constructive process that incorporates techniques for plan revision in addition to plan hypothesizing, see Schmidt, Sridharan & Goodson (1978), is a *fundamental* problem for Artificial Intelligence. This problem deserves the same kind of effort that has been devoted to plan generation. The plan recognition problem is full of interesting challenges and intellectual surprises. It ought to be pursued earnestly and seriously. Yet, in thinking of applications, one must be careful to use a suitable framework to decide what kind of user models and what type of user modelling process are best to adopt.

SUGGESTED READINGS

Appelt, D. E. *Planning English Sentences*. Cambridge: Cambridge University Press, 1985 (forthcoming).

Brown, J.S. & Burton, R.R. (1978). Diagnostic models for procedural bugs in basic mathematical skills, in *Cognitive Science, 2*. pp155-192.

Burton, R.R. & J.S. Brown (1982). An investigation of computer coaching for informal learning activities. In *Intelligent Tutoring Systems*, eds D. Sleeman & J.S. Brown. Academic: London, pp79-98.

Carbonell, J.R. (1970). AI in CAI: An Artificial Intelligence Approach to Computer-aided Instruction. *IEEE Transactions on Man-Machine Systems, 11*, pp.190-202.

Cohen, P., and C. R. Perrault, "Elements of a Plan-Based Theory of Speech Acts." *Cognitive Science*, 3 (1979), pp. 177--212.

Konolige, K. Experimental Robot Psychology. *Proceedings ACAI*, (1985).

Mark, W., "Representation and Inference in the Consul System", IJCAI-81

Pollack, M., and J. Hirschberg "User Participation in the Reasoning Processes of Expert Systems." *Proceedings of the National Conference on Artifical Intelligence*, (1982), pp. 358--361.

Reddy, M. J., "The Conduit Metaphor---A Case of Frame Conflict in Our Language about Language." In Ortony (ed.), *Metaphor and Thought*, Cambridge: Cambridge University Press, (1979).

Rich, E. "Users are individuals: individualizing user models". IJMMS, 1983, volume 18, pp. 199-214.

Sleeman, D and J. S. Brown, Introduction: Intelligent Tutoring Systems. In *Intelligent Tutoring Systems* D. Sleeman & J.S. Brown (eds). Academic press: London. (1982) pp1-11.

Sleeman, D. UMFE: A User Modelling Front End system. *IJMMS*, in press.

Schmidt, C.F., Sridharan, N.S., Goodson, J.L., The Plan Recognition Problem: An Intersection of Psychology and Artificial Intelligence, *Artificial Intelligence*, 11 (1978) pp45-83.

Swartout, W., "The Gist Behavior Explainer," *AAAI-83*.

Swartout, W., "XPLAIN: a system for creating and explaining expert consulting programs," *Artificial Intelligence*, 21 (1983) pp. 285-325.

THE US & JAPAN COOPERATIVE AI RESEARCH & DEVELOPMENT

Howard E. Jacobson

Jacobson Corporation
610 Newport Center Dr.
Newport Beach, CA 92660

ABSTRACT

This paper examines the emerging relationship between the US and Japan with respect to Artificial Intelligence and the significant trend towards US-Japan cooperative AI research and development. This trend is underscored by the increasing investment by both nations to develop massive 5th generation computer technology. The importance of the US and Japan's relationship is amplified by these two nations being the world's largest high technology producers and trading partners. One must fully appreciate the future course of events as the two nations open up new markets, estimated at tens of billions of dollars in AI hardware, software and related services by the 1990's. AI has greater implications for collaboration versus ruthless competition, as in other markets, due to the uniqueness of opportunity AI offers the US and Japan for mutual growth. AI will offer unique ways for the US and Japan to grow closer with greater understanding of two otherwise extremely different social and economic systems. This does not diminish the importance of other countries growing closer through AI in this way, but rather demonstrates the greatest example of cooperation with the greatest total economic rewards.

CHANGES IN US-JAPAN HIGH TECH RELATIONS

Japan has demonstrated a most effective competitive strategy in most marketplaces, which has, as some observe, threatened the basic underpinnings of the US economy. More specifically, the great desire by Japanese firms to be number one has created an overall uneasiness for most US firms about the future. The last few years has seen a growing discontent from Americans towards Japan and recently resulted in the strongest Post-War trade protection backlash ever witnessed towards Japan.

Thankfully, the leaders in both countries have gone to great lengths to avert a trade war, whose consequences would only prove destructive to each economy. This latest round of measures shows an unprecedented willingness from Japan to protect good relations with the US. Prime Minister Nakasone is urging the liberalization of freer trade to benefit the trade imbalance. The risk, however, is that by the US using threats towards increasing diplomatic and economic relations, trust and stability may be lost in the process. This illustrates the basic need to create more effective tools for the US and Japanese government and commercial interests to better interact. The fit for AI here is ideal. As our overall markets continue to grow and overlap, there becomes a higher price for failure and a greater reward for successful negotiation and cooperation. This is one of the original concepts for AI technology.

To gain better insight into the depth of this trend in our changing high technology relations, the last 30 years are revealing. When Japan was rebuilding its economy after the War, many US firms licensed technology to their industrial counterparts. The licensing of technology was a natural fit for both sides, but the consequences were unimagined. This period shows in excess of 38,000 licenses transacted from the US to Japan.

The chart below illustrates the increase and then leveling-off of US originated technology licenses to Japan. The historic curve is in direct relation to Japan's economic rebuilding and expansion to the gradual decrease in dependence on foreign technology, as internal innovation became more practical and effective.

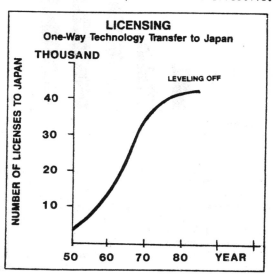

This change in Japan's dependence on US technology is revolutionizing the relations between the world's two largest suppliers of high technology goods and services. The effects of this change will be positive, if the US and Japan can find effective ways to work productively with each other in partnerships to advance technology through private market means. It will also ease the trade frictions that have resulted due to the $35 billion trade imbalance.

Correcting this imbalance, many US firms are now creating joint ventures instead of simply licensing their technology. This is because they began valuing the rewards of selling in Japan's market, at least as an equity partner. Numerous US and Japanese firms in the computer, robotics, hybrid electronics and high technology services sectors have been finding ways to join efforts.

Currently, Japan is changing its role from technology assimilator to technology innovator. This upsets a long-held belief that Japan only takes technology and lacks innovation. Japan had used this method successfully for many generations, but recently a change has taken place. Japan recognized the poor reputation created in international markets due to technolgy assimilation. It was felt that further international resistance to this method by developed countries would be expressed against buying Japanese products.

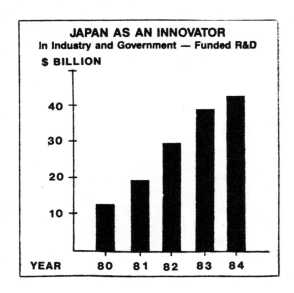

JAPAN AS AN INNOVATOR
In Industry and Government — Funded R&D
$ BILLION

Because the majority of Japan's economy is based on international trade, MITI, the Ministry for International Trade and Industry, in 1981, issued a directive towards Japanese innovation and international R&D collaboration. In 1982, MITI financed $740 million for technology R&D, all Japanese government R&D totaled $6.2 billion and the total government and private R&D of Japan exceeded $27 billion. This is impressive because

it pushed their R&D as a percentage of GNP ahead to challenge the US. 1981 saw the creation of ICOT, the Institute for the 5th Generation Computer Technology, which caused a severe sense of threat to the US.

Since then, that sense of threat may be subsiding. This is a clear indication of a new Japanese strategy, which has started to set the course for new era of US Japan high technology relations. This increase in Japan's R&D innovation does not remove the historical US leadership in innovation. Rather, it acts to add parity to an otherwise unbalanced relationship. The issue of technology lifespans growing shorter will always equalize any dominance in technology before too long.

Even though ICOT's 10-year, several hundred million dollar strategy appears ominous, the fact is that it is not out of line with what the US is investing by individual firms in such ambitious future development. The reason it appears threatening is that the figures are pooled into one sum. If you add all the US firms R&D expenditures on 5th generation computer technology from 1981 to 1991, you might find it exceeding Japan's ICOT by a healthy margin. We must not get caught in the trap of who gets how much of the AI market alone, but how we can proceed together for optimum benefit.

THE EFFECTIVE US-JAPAN AI BLUEPRINT

Assuming that great improvement can be made by joining certain efforts in US-Japan AI work, what is an effective method? As an example, Japan has created its industry and government consortium, ICOT, as a 10-year effort to produce a 5th generation computer. The reason was to develop standards and create efficiency by nonduplicated costs of development. Some critics view this as a way to upset the balance of power in the world of technology. In reality, collaboration was a wise decision and US firms have recently been finding ways to implement this. As the US Antitrust laws were loosened and further R&D incentives created, US firms took advantage of pooling technology efforts to maximize returns for their investors. In a way, this increases US competitiveness far beyond a less productive process.

The next logical step is to combine talents on priority projects for the US and Japan using the method on the following page. This US-Japan AI R&D Limited Partnership is patterned after the US Department of Commerce blueprint for collaboration. The DOC Office of Productivity, Technology and Innovation has created a system that allows laboratories, partners and the marketplace of end-users to benefit by organized association, similar in some ways to the ICOT formula.

This diagram below gives a clear sample of the way in which US and Japanese scientists and commercial firms can team together on projects that will help the government or business interests interact more effectively using AI systems. The many labs in Japan that have started using AI in solving problems with symbolic processing make a good starting point to institute this model. The general partner is relied on to guide all interests effectively towards the proper commercialization of the technology. The syndicated limited partners may have a direct need for the technology in their own businesses, in addition to sharing in royalties when the application is delivered to the end-users.

US & JAPAN
AI R&D LIMITED PARTNERSHIP

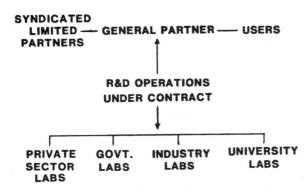

In looking at US-Japan Cooperative AI opportunities, there are some basic balancing factors. 1) The US outweighs Japan in AI software talent 25 to 1. 2) There are numerous AI projects beyond ICOT, in Japan that more readily avail themselves to US collaboration. 3) The flow of capital will probably come from both US and Japanese firms, equally. 4) Japan recently approved a 50-year software protection. Each of these factors describes the natural attraction of US and Japanese interests to produce AI products for mutual benefit.

THE CURRENT US-JAPAN AI PICTURE

What is the most effective way to strengthen US-Japan relations using AI? We anticipate AI having a broad impact on the entirety of industry. The principle of technology diffusion by greatest cost-benefit is the first determining factor to identify commercial applications. Certainly, the forces of commercialization are rapidly enjoining the labs to produce the first AI applications marketed to industry. As the labs begin to gain greater awareness of what form their art is taking commercially, the process becomes streamlined. Therefore with respect to enjoining US and Japan AI talent, it is dependent on the commercializing forces to seize their most applicable opportunities.

The first and foremost areas of application for US-Japan AI cooperative development include: Telecommunications, International Trade, International Finance, Manufacturing and International Diplomacy and Negotiation. These areas have the greatest promise due to the political and economic ramifications being experienced by the two countries. As Japan opens its markets to US producers, they will need to develop competent AI systems for conducting business smoothly with Japan. US banks, securities firms, and manufacturers will be testing their skills and luck with the new opportunity to reach a market of 114 million people. Their expectations will be more easily reached with the enhancement of AI applications to guide their transactions and operations.

In reverse fashion, the Japanese firms doing business in the US will be able to reach greater efficiency by setting AI decison systems to their advantage. The area of machine translation is one that is more appealing to Japan because of their dependence on trade with the US. But, as trade equalizes, more US interest in commercial translation systems will be expressed.

The area of AI machine translation has been explored for years and most believe that commercially viable systems are beginning to be released. The Wilson Center, in Washington, DC, recently organized a program called "Getting America Ready For Japanese Science and Technology". This explored the progress between our countries, as more knowledge is gained of the Japanese language. An AI translation system for Japanese was revealed by Bravice International, Inc. As technical progress moves ahead, AI voice recognition translation technology will appear. This has tremendous benefit for our countries.

This type of merging mutual technological interests is serving to elevate the quality of our lives dramatically, expanding the cumulative marketplaces and ensuring the growth of our free markets' cooperation.

*This Conference was sponsored by the Wilson Center's Asia Program and The MIT-Japan Science and Technology Program. It focused on the Japanese language, machine translation technology, US policy on language training and technical Japanese.

ACKNOWLEDGEMENTS

Mr. Howard E. Jacobson, Executive Vice President of the Jacobson Corporation, serves as chair to the IJCAI panel on US-Japan Cooperation in AI R&D. His professional background includes the formation and management of US-Japan R&D partnerships in Artificial Intelligence, Computer Hardware, Robotics and Biotechnology. Mr. Jacobson was the Special Advisor to the US Presidential Commission on Industrial Competitiveness regarding US-Japan relations and is a member of several international scientific associations. Mr. Jacobson's degree is in Economics from Claremont McKenna College (CMC).

Panel: Expert systems: How far can they go?

Terry Winograd, Randall Davis, Stuart Dreyfus, Brian Smith

We arc in the midst of a great wave of enthusiasm about the potential for expert systems in every area of human life and work. There is no agreement, however, as to just how much they can do, and where they will run into fundamental limits. The intent of this panel is to present and discuss some basic questions as to what expert systems can really be expected to do:

What is the nature of the problem domains in which expert systems are likely to succeed and those in which they will not? Are there domains in which their use might be dangerous?

How will their performance compare with that of human experts in the domain? Are there different facets of expertise that are not amenable to programming? How can human and machine expertise best be combined?

To what extent can we count on rule-based systems for 'flexibility' in dealing with unexpected situations? How reliable will such systems be in cases where the programmers (or knowledge engineers) did not anticipate significant possibilities?

How can a 'knowledge base' be subjected to standards of accountability? Who is responsible for what an expert system contains and what it does?

Expert systems:
What to do until the theory arrives

Randall Davis
MIT

In reading a newspaper recently I was struck by the profusion of expert advice available. There were three different expert opinions on the future course of the economy, several compelling (and contradictory) opinions about the likely course of events in the mideast, and a number of suggestions about avoiding heart disease, as well as claims about long term weather patterns, advice from Ms. Manners on behavior and guidelines from a therapist on drinking and sex.

All of which made me begin to wonder:

Experts: How far can they go?

We are in the midst of a great wave of enthusiasm about the potential for experts in every area of human life and work. There is no agreement, however, as to just how much they can do, and where they will run into fundamental limits:

What is the nature of the problem domains in which experts are likely to succeed and those in which they will not? Are there domains in which their use might be dangerous?

To what extent can we count on carbon-based systems for 'flexibility' in dealing with unexpected situations? How reliable will such systems be in cases where their teachers did not anticipate significant possibilities?

How can a person's knowledge be subjected to standards of accountability? Who is responsible for what an expert contains and what that person does?

Hardly an original satire, but it does serve several purposes. First, it demonstrates that the questions are neither unfamiliar nor inherently mysterious. The answers for people may not be well established, but we do know something of how to proceed and we do believe there is no magic here: *some* form of knowledge accounts for an expert's competence. The nature and source of it may be far from understood, but that doesn't make the question unanswerable.

Next, it sets the argument out on what I believe to be an important direction: the questions we are asking are first about knowledge and only then about technology. That is, the first question should not be *What can expert systems do?* but rather *What do we know?* Only then we can address the technology issue and ask *And how easily can we encode that knowledge?* Both matter but the order is important.

Finally, the comparison is valid and provides an interesting way to proceed. Asking the same questions about people provides a useful, non-threatening way of examining the topics. Our answers may differ for people and programs, but even those disparities will prove interesting. We explore people's understanding of a subject with a test that examines only a limited sample of their knowledge, and then extrapolate, saying that people who pass 'understand' the material, meaning by that something more than that they can do exactly the problems chosen for the exam. If a program passed the same exam, would we be willing to do the same extrapolation? If not, why not? If we can determine what it is that makes us hesitate in the case of the program, we have the beginnings of an intriguing research agenda.

In developing these themes I will argue that there are two attributes of expert systems (and much of AI) that are central to this discussion:

It is a weak technology

It is a technology for dealing with incompletely understood ideas.

I will suggest that the first of these is a temporary vice that will be remedied in time (though not soon) and that the second is a permanent virtue.

Both of these have interesting implications for the use of expert systems (and indeed much of AI). Perhaps the most important implication is that most traditional rule-based expert systems will never have all the knowledge they need, and as a consequence they are guaranteed to fail occasionally (though perhaps infrequently) during all of their operational lives.

I will suggest ways of proceeding that take these issues into account, allowing us to employ the technology while reducing the potential difficulties that can arise.

The nature of expertise

Stuart E. Dreyfus
University of California, Berkeley

All AI work with the exception of a few 'connectionist' theories assumes that knowledge must be represented in the mind as symbolic descriptions. Expert-system builders further assume that the expert possesses a particular kind of symbolic description: a knowledge base of facts, beliefs and 'if-then' rules that allow the drawing of inferences.

I will argue that expert-system builders fail to recognize the real character of *expert* human understanding. Expertise is acquired in a five-stage process. The *beginner* applies rules to context-free features as would an expert system deprived of situational knowledge appropriate to the particular case. The *advanced beginner* learns from experience to recognize aspects of a situation without requiring a definition of them in terms of context-free features.

Aspects are recognized after seeing several examples, apparently because of their similarity to already experienced prototypical cases. An interactive expert system could use aspects if they were identified for it by a human user. At the next stage, the *competent* performer organizes behavior by selecting plans, goals, or perspectives which determine hierarchically what facts to consider and what rules to apply. Expert systems can do likewise and, if they accept human situational assessments, could appropriately be called 'competent systems.' This, however, is the best they can do. The fourth stage, *proficiency*, is achieved when the performer no longer uses his knowledge to select a perspective or goal, but simply recognizes the appropriate one based on prior experience in similar situations in which goals were chosen and events either confirmed the wisdom of the choice or showed it to be mistaken. As with the recognition of situational aspects by the advanced beginner, the involved, intuitive recognition of similarity of whole situations is apparently not produced by rules operating on features but seems to be effortless and holistic. While the proficient performer still analytically figures out what to do once the situation is intuitively understood, at the highest level of skill the *expert* has experienced so many situations that he associates with each prototypical situation in his memory the decision, action or strategy that he has found to work. He reasons out neither strategy nor action. Intuitively responding to situational patterns as experience has shown appropriate, his skill depends neither on problem solving nor planning. Expert systems can neither recognize situations holistically without analysis into components nor know what to do without applying rules to decomposed knowledge, so they can be neither proficient nor expert.

If time permits, an expert will deliberate about his intuitive understanding. To fine-tune his responses, he will attempt to take account of subtle differences between his current situation and similar prior ones, he will ask himself whether there might be another quite different way of intuitively viewing his circumstance, and he will consider whether he has had enough experience in the particular kind of situation to trust his intuition. But he will rarely regress to competent detached problem solving.

While 'competent systems' have their useful place, there is no reason to expect them to perform as well as experts who have passed beyond the use of facts, beliefs, and rules of inference and who rely on memories of thousands of concrete experiences and what has worked in each. An examination of the performance of various expert systems supports the above analysis. In domains where human beings pass from reasoning to recognition as they become experts, expert systems, even when experts participate in their development, never perform as well as experts.

Models in expert systems

Brian Smith
Xerox PARC

All expert systems are based on models. The 'knowledge' embodied in expert systems, in particular, is usually encoded in a set of 'rules' that describe the problem and specify the behaviour that the system should manifest. These rules are always formulated with respect to a model of the underlying domain. This model must be determined in advance by the programmer, who may in turn have derived it from an analysis of the experts' performance on which the system is based.

Indeed, one of the prime tasks in building an expert system is to develop an appropriate model. There are various ways to do this: by analysing the desired behaviour, by building on underlying scientific theories, or by codifying the models apparently used by expert human practitioners. What phenomena are dealt with, what phenomena are ignored, and what patterns or regularities connect the phenomena that are dealt with -- all these decisions are made at the level of the model.

For example, a medical expert system designed to administer drugs might model drug absorption in terms of a scalar quantity proportional to the square of a patient's height, or proportional to the weight (neither model, of course, would be expected to be entirely accurate). An expert system for the office might model a secretary as a customer, producer, and processor of information, with a complex internal state. A defense warning system might model incoming missiles as point masses on parabolic flight paths, and model the atmosphere as a linear retarding force. And so on and so forth: the use of models permeates formal systems of all sorts.

When expert systems are actually deployed, however, they interact with the world itself, not with models. For example, when drugs are actually administered, or when offices are actually equipped with expert systems intended to work alongside people, we have full, thick situations to deal with, of at least potentially arbitrary complexity. Furthermore, the success of expert systems ultimately depends on their ability to deal with these rich, embedded situations. Their success, in other words, isn't exhausted by their ability to deal appropriately with the model used in their construction, or encoded in their knowledge bases.

In fact the only ultimate point of the models in expert systems is to help them succeed in the 'real world'. RCA, for example, is primarily interested in whether their satellites will actually get into orbit and stay there; they have only a derivative interest in whether the programs guiding them are proved correct with respect to a particular orbital model.

It is clear, therefore, that in order to analyse expert systems we need to understand the appropriateness of the models on which they are based. Analysing expert systems, in other words, comes in two parts: understanding the behaviour of a system in terms of the model on which it is based, and understanding the relationship between that model and the embedding world. At the present state of the art, we have a variety of techniques that enable us to study the former relationship, between system and model: formal semantics, model theory (hence its name), program verification. We have virtually no techniques, on the other hand, with which to study the latter relationship, between model and world. We are largely unable, therefore, to assess the appropriateness of models, or to predict when models will fail. All that we do when we prove a program 'correct' is to prove that it will behave as specified with respect to a model. It would be something quite else -- something we don't know how to do -- to prove that a system will in fact do the 'correct' thing once embedded into a real situation.

Two conclusions. First, we should develop and use expert systems only in those domains where we have confidence in the accuracy and appropriateness of our models. Second, we should develop a 'theory of models' with which to understand better how models work, and how they make sense of the infinite complexities of the worlds they represent. Although such a theory may strain at the edges of what can be formalized, or even pass beyond strict formal limits, we can still develop rigorous tools, and use clear-headed thinking, in analysing this important relationship.

The trivialization of expertise

Terry Winograd
Stanford University

Professor Moto-Oka of the Japanese Fifth Generation project [3] predicts that: *"Fifth generation computers are expected to function extremely effectively in all fields of society. ...totally new applied fields will be developed, social productivity will be increased, and distortions in values will be eliminated."* Feigenbaum and McCorduck [2] proclaim that: *"We are now at the dawn of a new computer revolution... [leading] to computers that reason and inform. ...the engine that will produce the new wealth of nations. ... Perhaps equally important to all the economic advantages the Fifth Generation promises is that intangible thing called quality of life. A society where knowledge is quickly and easily available to anybody who wants it will... be an alluring place."*

We might dismiss these statements as merely naive self-serving propaganda, but in doing so would we fail to recognize the background in which they could be made sincerely and taken seriously by intelligent and educated readers. The computer is a powerful embodiment of a 'rationalistic' tradition that equates certain limited modes of rational description and inference with the full scope of how people think and what they do with language. This tradition is both demonstrated and further promoted by inflated claims for the potential benefits of 'expert systems.'

Rationalistic understanding has been extremely powerful in the creation and expansion of the physical sciences and in increasing our mastery over the physical world. At the same time, its power in dealing with these domains of reality has blinded us to its weakness in dealing with those more related to human life and society. The rationalistic orientation often promotes a wrong understanding of what constitutes a 'problem' in a human domain, and what computers can do to 'solve problems.' The failure of the rationalistic approach has led to a crisis in the practical areas where it has been applied seriously. The recognition of this crisis has emerged in the past few years in works on management theory, military systems, medicine, energy policy, and many other fields.

The problem is illustrated by the illusion promoted by the label 'expert system.' A human 'expert' is someone whose depth of understanding serves not only to solve specific well-formulated problems, but also to put them into a larger context. We distinguish between experts and idiot savants. What, in contrast, do computer systems do?

Expert systems are built on the basis of a relatively small, precisely defined set of object types and properties, together with a (possibly large and disorganized) collection of rules relating them. In pre-selecting the relevant elements out of which to build rules, one must cut out the role of context and background (which are at the heart of AI's theoretical difficulties). This process by its very nature creates blindness -- a limit is set by the way the world has been articulated. There is always the potential for breakdowns that call for moving beyond this limit -- for returning to the context and reformulating the problem.

One might argue justifiably that this blindness is a problem for people as well. But (with the exception of idiot savants), people are not programmed for a particular task. A normally intelligent person can always step back and recontextualize. Expert systems, even those with 'meta-rules' do not have this openness. Further, the blindness inherent in representation leads to difficulty in understanding the range and limitations of a particular program. A human expert can enter into a dialog about his or her own range of knowledge and limitations, moving outside the putative domain and using ordinary language and ordinary common sense. Failures of AI programs will in part reflect the inability of people to understand what the program is actually doing, as opposed to what it might appear to be doing if the metaphor of 'thinking' is accepted.

Although the assumptions of the rationalistic orientation may seem self-evident (to those within our modern Western society), they are indeed only assumptions and can be challenged (see [4] for a more comprehensive discussion of this and the other issues raised in this paper). Instead of treating 'data' as the objective representation of reality, we can recognize symbols (on paper, or in a computer) as a medium for language, which is based on human commitment and is always relative to an unarticulated shared background. Instead of trying to get the machine to have 'understanding' through a collection of 'rules,' we can recognize that its manipulation of symbols is grounded in the background and interpretation of people who interact through it. We can identify and articulate 'systematic domains' of symbolic manipulation for which appropriate rules can be generated, and we can integrate these into a broader appreciation of human knowledge and expertise.

References

[1] Dreyfus, Hubert L., and Stuart E. Dreyfus, *Mind Over Machine*, New York: MacMillan/The Free Press, 1985.

[2] Feigenbaum, Edward, and Pamela McCorduck, *The Fifth Generation: Artificial Intelligence and Japan's Computer Challenge to the World*, Reading, MA: Addison Wesley, 1983.

[3] Moto-oka, T., Keynote speech: Challenge for knowledge information processing systems, in Moto-oka, T. (Ed.), *Fifth Generation Computer Systems: Proceedings of International Conference on Fifth Generation Computer Systems*, Amsterdam: North Holland, 1982.

[4] Winograd, Terry, and Fernando Flores, *Understanding Computers and Cognition: A New Foundation for Design*, Norwood, NJ: Ablex, 1985.

Author Index

Notes

Notes

Notes

Notes